STUDENT SOLUTIONS MANUAL

KEVIN BODDEN ▪ RANDY GALLAHER

Lewis & Clark Community College

INTRODUCTORY & INTERMEDIATE ALGEBRA

for college students

SECOND EDITION

Blitzer

PEARSON

Prentice Hall

Upper Saddle River, NJ 07458

Editor-in-Chief, Developmental Math: Christine Hoag
Executive Editor: Paul Murphy
Assistant Editor: Christina Simoneau
Executive Managing Editor: Kathleen Schiaparelli
Assistant Managing Editor: Becca Richter
Production Editor: Gina M. Cheselka
Supplement Cover Manager: Paul Gourhan
Supplement Cover Designer: Joanne Alexandris
Manufacturing Buyer: Ilene Kahn

© 2006 Pearson Education, Inc.
Pearson Prentice Hall
Pearson Education, Inc.
Upper Saddle River, NJ 07458

The author and publisher of this book have used their best efforts in preparing this book. These efforts include the development, research, and testing of the theories and programs to determine their effectiveness. The author and publisher make no warranty of any kind, expressed or implied, with regard to these programs or the documentation contained in this book. The author and publisher shall not be liable in any event for incidental or consequential damages in connection with, or arising out of, the furnishing, performance, or use of these programs.

Printed in the United States of America

10   9   8   7   6   5   4   3   2   1

ISBN   0-13-192179-7   Standalone
       0-13-185793-2   Student Study Pack Component

Pearson Education Ltd., *London*
Pearson Education Australia Pty. Ltd., *Sydney*
Pearson Education Singapore, Pte. Ltd.
Pearson Education North Asia Ltd., *Hong Kong*
Pearson Education Canada, Inc., *Toronto*
Pearson Educación de Mexico, S.A. de C.V.
Pearson Education—Japan, *Tokyo*
Pearson Education Malaysia, Pte. Ltd.

TABLE OF CONTENTS for STUDENT SOLUTIONS

INTRODUCTORY & INTERMEDIATE ALGEBRA FOR COLLEGE STUDENTS, 2E

ESSENTIALS OF INTRODUCTORY & INTERMEDIATE ALGEBRA FOR COLLEGE STUDENTS

Chapter 1
The Real Number System

1.1 Exercise Set

1. $2\dfrac{3}{8} = \dfrac{2 \cdot 8 + 3}{8} = \dfrac{16 + 3}{8} = \dfrac{19}{8}$

3. $7\dfrac{3}{5} = \dfrac{7 \cdot 5 + 3}{5} = \dfrac{35 + 3}{5} = \dfrac{38}{5}$

5. $8\dfrac{7}{16} = \dfrac{8 \cdot 16 + 7}{16} = \dfrac{128 + 7}{16} = \dfrac{135}{16}$

7. 23 divided by 5 is 4 with a remainder of 3, so $\dfrac{23}{5} = 4\dfrac{3}{5}$.

9. 76 divided by 9 is 8 with a remainder of 4, so $\dfrac{76}{9} = 8\dfrac{4}{9}$.

11. 711 divided by 20 is 35 with a remainder of 11, so $\dfrac{711}{20} = 35\dfrac{11}{20}$.

13. $22 = 2 \cdot 11$

15. $20 = 4 \cdot 5 = 2 \cdot 2 \cdot 5$

17. 37 has no factors other than 1 and 37, so 37 is prime.

19. $36 = 4 \cdot 9 = 2 \cdot 2 \cdot 3 \cdot 3$

21. $140 = 10 \cdot 14 = 2 \cdot 5 \cdot 2 \cdot 7$
$ = 2 \cdot 2 \cdot 5 \cdot 7$

23. 79 has no factors other than 1 and 79, so 79 is prime.

25. $81 = 9 \cdot 9 = 3 \cdot 3 \cdot 3 \cdot 3$

27. $240 = 10 \cdot 24$
$ = 2 \cdot 5 \cdot 2 \cdot 12$
$ = 2 \cdot 5 \cdot 2 \cdot 3 \cdot 4$
$ = 2 \cdot 5 \cdot 2 \cdot 3 \cdot 2 \cdot 2$
$ = 2 \cdot 2 \cdot 2 \cdot 3 \cdot 5$

29. $\dfrac{10}{16} = \dfrac{\cancel{2} \cdot 5}{\cancel{2} \cdot 8} = \dfrac{5}{8}$

31. $\dfrac{15}{18} = \dfrac{\cancel{3} \cdot 5}{\cancel{3} \cdot 6} = \dfrac{5}{6}$

33. $\dfrac{35}{50} = \dfrac{\cancel{5} \cdot 7}{\cancel{5} \cdot 10} = \dfrac{7}{10}$

35. $\dfrac{32}{80} = \dfrac{\cancel{16} \cdot 2}{\cancel{16} \cdot 5} = \dfrac{2}{5}$

37. $\dfrac{44}{50} = \dfrac{\cancel{2} \cdot 22}{\cancel{2} \cdot 25} = \dfrac{22}{25}$

39. $\dfrac{120}{86} = \dfrac{\cancel{2} \cdot 60}{\cancel{2} \cdot 43} = \dfrac{60}{43}$

41. $\dfrac{2}{5} \cdot \dfrac{1}{3} = \dfrac{2 \cdot 1}{5 \cdot 3} = \dfrac{2}{15}$

43. $\dfrac{3}{8} \cdot \dfrac{7}{11} = \dfrac{3 \cdot 7}{8 \cdot 11} = \dfrac{21}{88}$

45. $9 \cdot \dfrac{4}{7} = \dfrac{9}{1} \cdot \dfrac{4}{7} = \dfrac{9 \cdot 4}{1 \cdot 7} = \dfrac{36}{7}$ or $5\dfrac{1}{7}$

47. $\dfrac{1}{10} \cdot \dfrac{5}{6} = \dfrac{1 \cdot 5}{10 \cdot 6} = \dfrac{5}{60} = \dfrac{5 \cdot 1}{5 \cdot 12} = \dfrac{1}{12}$

49. $\dfrac{5}{4} \cdot \dfrac{6}{7} = \dfrac{5 \cdot 6}{4 \cdot 7} = \dfrac{30}{28} = \dfrac{2 \cdot 15}{2 \cdot 14} = \dfrac{15}{14}$ or $1\dfrac{1}{14}$

51. $\left(3\dfrac{3}{4}\right)\left(1\dfrac{3}{5}\right) = \dfrac{15}{4} \cdot \dfrac{8}{5} = \dfrac{120}{20} = \dfrac{\cancel{20} \cdot 6}{\cancel{20} \cdot 1} = 6$

53. $\dfrac{5}{4} \div \dfrac{4}{3} = \dfrac{5}{4} \cdot \dfrac{3}{4} = \dfrac{5 \cdot 3}{4 \cdot 4} = \dfrac{15}{16}$

55. $\dfrac{18}{5} \div 2 = \dfrac{18}{5} \cdot \dfrac{1}{2}$

$= \dfrac{18 \cdot 1}{5 \cdot 2} = \dfrac{18}{10} = \dfrac{\cancel{2} \cdot 9}{\cancel{2} \cdot 5} = \dfrac{9}{5} \text{ or } 1\dfrac{4}{5}$

57. $2 \div \dfrac{18}{5} = \dfrac{2}{1} \cdot \dfrac{5}{18} = \dfrac{10}{18} = \dfrac{\cancel{2} \cdot 5}{\cancel{2} \cdot 9} = \dfrac{5}{9}$

59. $\dfrac{3}{4} \div \dfrac{1}{4} = \dfrac{3}{4} \cdot \dfrac{4}{1} = \dfrac{3 \cdot 4}{4 \cdot 1} = \dfrac{12}{4} = 3$

61. $\dfrac{7}{6} \div \dfrac{5}{3} = \dfrac{7}{6} \cdot \dfrac{3}{5} = \dfrac{7 \cdot 3}{6 \cdot 5} = \dfrac{21}{30} = \dfrac{\cancel{3} \cdot 7}{\cancel{3} \cdot 10} = \dfrac{7}{10}$

63. $\dfrac{1}{14} \div \dfrac{1}{7} = \dfrac{1}{14} \cdot \dfrac{7}{1} = \dfrac{7}{14} = \dfrac{\cancel{7} \cdot 1}{\cancel{7} \cdot 2} = \dfrac{1}{2}$

65. $6\dfrac{3}{5} \div 1\dfrac{1}{10} = \dfrac{33}{5} \div \dfrac{11}{10}$

$= \dfrac{33}{5} \cdot \dfrac{10}{11} = \dfrac{33}{55} = \dfrac{\cancel{11} \cdot 3}{\cancel{11} \cdot 5} = \dfrac{3}{5}$

67. $\dfrac{2}{11} + \dfrac{4}{11} = \dfrac{2+4}{11} = \dfrac{6}{11}$

69. $\dfrac{7}{12} + \dfrac{1}{12} = \dfrac{8}{12} = \dfrac{\cancel{4} \cdot 2}{\cancel{4} \cdot 3} = \dfrac{2}{3}$

71. $\dfrac{5}{8} + \dfrac{5}{8} = \dfrac{10}{8} = \dfrac{\cancel{2} \cdot 5}{\cancel{2} \cdot 4} = \dfrac{5}{4} \text{ or } 1\dfrac{1}{4}$

73. $\dfrac{7}{12} - \dfrac{5}{12} = \dfrac{2}{12} = \dfrac{\cancel{2} \cdot 1}{\cancel{2} \cdot 6} = \dfrac{1}{6}$

75. $\dfrac{16}{7} - \dfrac{2}{7} = \dfrac{14}{7} = \dfrac{\cancel{7} \cdot 2}{\cancel{7} \cdot 1} = 2$

77. $\dfrac{1}{2} + \dfrac{1}{5} = \dfrac{1}{2} \cdot \dfrac{5}{5} + \dfrac{1}{5} \cdot \dfrac{2}{2}$

$= \dfrac{5}{10} + \dfrac{2}{10} = \dfrac{5+2}{10} = \dfrac{7}{10}$

79. $\dfrac{3}{4} + \dfrac{3}{20} = \dfrac{3}{4} \cdot \dfrac{5}{5} + \dfrac{3}{20}$

$= \dfrac{15}{20} + \dfrac{3}{20}$

$= \dfrac{18}{20} = \dfrac{\cancel{2} \cdot 9}{\cancel{2} \cdot 10} = \dfrac{9}{10}$

81. $\dfrac{3}{8} + \dfrac{5}{12} = \dfrac{3}{8} \cdot \dfrac{3}{3} + \dfrac{5}{12} \cdot \dfrac{2}{2}$

$= \dfrac{9}{24} + \dfrac{10}{24} = \dfrac{19}{24}$

83. $\dfrac{11}{18} - \dfrac{2}{9} = \dfrac{11}{18} - \dfrac{2}{9} \cdot \dfrac{2}{2} = \dfrac{11}{18} - \dfrac{4}{18} = \dfrac{7}{18}$

85. $\dfrac{4}{3} - \dfrac{3}{4} = \dfrac{4}{3} \cdot \dfrac{4}{4} - \dfrac{3}{4} \cdot \dfrac{3}{3}$

$= \dfrac{16}{12} - \dfrac{9}{12} = \dfrac{7}{12}$

87. $\dfrac{7}{10} - \dfrac{3}{16} = \dfrac{7}{10} \cdot \dfrac{8}{8} - \dfrac{3}{16} \cdot \dfrac{5}{5}$

$= \dfrac{56}{80} - \dfrac{15}{80} = \dfrac{41}{80}$

89. $3\dfrac{3}{4} - 2\dfrac{1}{3} = \dfrac{15}{4} - \dfrac{7}{3}$

$= \dfrac{15}{4} \cdot \dfrac{3}{3} - \dfrac{7}{3} \cdot \dfrac{4}{4}$

$= \dfrac{45}{12} - \dfrac{28}{12} = \dfrac{17}{12} \text{ or } 1\dfrac{5}{12}$

2

91. $\dfrac{3}{4} \cdot \dfrac{a}{5} = \dfrac{3 \cdot a}{4 \cdot 5} = \dfrac{3a}{20}$

92. $\dfrac{2}{3} \div \dfrac{a}{7} = \dfrac{2}{3} \cdot \dfrac{7}{a} = \dfrac{2 \cdot 7}{3 \cdot a} = \dfrac{14}{3a}$

93. $\dfrac{11}{x} + \dfrac{9}{x} = \dfrac{11+9}{x} = \dfrac{20}{x}$

94. $\dfrac{10}{y} - \dfrac{6}{y} = \dfrac{10-6}{y} = \dfrac{4}{y}$

95. $\left(\dfrac{1}{2} - \dfrac{1}{3}\right) \div \dfrac{5}{8} = \left(\dfrac{3}{6} - \dfrac{2}{6}\right) \div \dfrac{5}{8}$

$= \dfrac{1}{6} \div \dfrac{5}{8}$

$= \dfrac{1}{6} \cdot \dfrac{8}{5} = \dfrac{8}{30} = \dfrac{\cancel{2} \cdot 4}{\cancel{2} \cdot 15} = \dfrac{4}{15}$

96. $\left(\dfrac{1}{2} + \dfrac{1}{4}\right) \div \left(\dfrac{1}{2} + \dfrac{1}{3}\right) = \left(\dfrac{2}{4} + \dfrac{1}{4}\right) \div \left(\dfrac{3}{6} + \dfrac{2}{6}\right)$

$= \dfrac{3}{4} \div \dfrac{5}{6}$

$= \dfrac{3}{4} \cdot \dfrac{6}{5}$

$= \dfrac{18}{20} = \dfrac{\cancel{2} \cdot 9}{\cancel{2} \cdot 10} = \dfrac{9}{10}$

97. **a.** The number of adults that do not find television the most believable news source is

$\dfrac{1}{4} + \dfrac{3}{25} + \dfrac{2}{25}$

$= \dfrac{25}{100} + \dfrac{12}{100} + \dfrac{8}{100} = \dfrac{45}{100}$

The number of adults that do find television the most believable news source is

$1 - \dfrac{45}{100} = \dfrac{100}{100} - \dfrac{45}{100} = \dfrac{55}{100} = \dfrac{11}{20}$.

b. $2000 \cdot \dfrac{3}{25} = \dfrac{2000}{1} \cdot \dfrac{3}{25} = 240$

240 people found radio the most believable news source.

99. $\dfrac{\text{Hispanic}}{\text{female}} = \dfrac{16}{40} = \dfrac{2}{5}$

The ratio of Hispanic judges to female judges appointed by Carter was $\dfrac{2}{5}$.

101. $\dfrac{\text{desired}}{\text{recipe}} \times \text{amount in recipe}$

$= \dfrac{8}{5} \times \dfrac{3}{4} = \dfrac{24}{20} = \dfrac{6}{5} = 1\dfrac{1}{5} \text{cups}$

103. Total distance covered is

$\dfrac{3}{4} + \dfrac{2}{5} = \dfrac{15}{20} + \dfrac{8}{20} = \dfrac{23}{20} = 1\dfrac{3}{20} \text{ miles}$.

Subtract to find out how much further you walked.

$\dfrac{3}{4} - \dfrac{2}{5} = \dfrac{15}{20} - \dfrac{8}{20} = \dfrac{7}{20} \text{ miles farther}$.

105. $2\dfrac{3}{8} \cdot 16 = \dfrac{19}{8} \cdot \dfrac{16}{1} = \dfrac{304}{8} = 38 \text{ miles}$

107. – 115. Answers will vary.

117. Statements a, b, and c are false. The methods illustrated are incorrect. The only true statement is d.

1.2 Exercise Set

1. -20

3. 8

5. -3000

7. −4 billion

9. 2

11. −5

13. $3\dfrac{1}{2}$

15. $\dfrac{11}{3}$

17. −1.8

19. $-\dfrac{16}{5}$

21.
$$\begin{array}{r} 0.75 \\ 4\overline{)3.00} \\ \underline{28} \\ 20 \\ \underline{20} \\ 0 \end{array}$$

$\dfrac{3}{4} = 0.75$

23.
$$\begin{array}{r} 0.35 \\ 20\overline{)7.00} \\ \underline{60} \\ 100 \\ \underline{100} \\ 0 \end{array}$$

$\dfrac{7}{20} = 0.35$

25.
$$\begin{array}{r} 0.875 \\ 8\overline{)7.000} \\ \underline{64} \\ 60 \\ \underline{56} \\ 40 \\ \underline{40} \\ 0 \end{array}$$

$\dfrac{7}{8} = 0.875$

27.
$$\begin{array}{r} 0.818... \\ 11\overline{)9.000...} \\ \underline{88} \\ 20 \\ \underline{11} \\ 90 \\ \underline{88} \\ 20 \end{array}$$

$\dfrac{9}{11} = 0.\overline{81}$

29.
$$\begin{array}{r} 0.5 \\ 2\overline{)1.0} \\ \underline{1.0} \\ 0 \end{array}$$

$-\dfrac{1}{2} = -0.5$

31.
$$\begin{array}{r} 0.833... \\ 6\overline{)5.000...} \\ \underline{48} \\ 20 \\ \underline{18} \\ 20 \\ \underline{18} \\ 20 \end{array}$$

$\dfrac{5}{6} = 0.8\overline{3}$

33. **a.** $\sqrt{100}$ $(=10)$

b. $0, \sqrt{100}$

c. $-9, 0, \sqrt{100}$

d. $-9, -\dfrac{4}{5}, 0, 0.25, 9.2, \sqrt{100}$

e. $\sqrt{3}$

f. $-9, -\dfrac{4}{5}, 0, 0.25, \sqrt{3}, 9.2, \sqrt{100}$

35. **a.** $\sqrt{64}$ $(=8)$

b. $0, \sqrt{64}$

c. $-11, 0, \sqrt{64}$

d. $-11, -\dfrac{5}{6}, 0, 0.75, \sqrt{64}$

e. $\sqrt{5}, \pi$

f. $-11, -\dfrac{5}{6}, 0, 0.75, \sqrt{5}, \pi, \sqrt{64}$

37. The only whole number that is not a natural number is 0.

39. Answers will vary. As an example, one rational number that is not an integer is $\dfrac{1}{2}$.

41. Answers will vary. As an example, 6 is a number that is an integer, a whole number, and a natural number.

43. Answers will vary. As an example, one number that is an irrational number and a real number is π.

45. $\dfrac{1}{2} < 2$ since $\dfrac{1}{2}$ is to the left of 2 on the number line.

47. $3 > -\dfrac{5}{2}$ since 3 is to the right of $-\dfrac{5}{2} = -2\dfrac{1}{2}$.

49. $-4 > -6$ since -4 is to the right of -6

51. $-2.5 < 1.5$ since -2.5 is to the left of 1.5

53. $-\dfrac{3}{4} > -\dfrac{5}{4}$ since $-\dfrac{3}{4}$ is to the right of $-\dfrac{5}{4}$

55. $-4.5 < 3$ since -4.5 is to the left of 3

57. $\sqrt{2} < 1.5$ since $\sqrt{2} \approx 1.414$ is to the left of 1.5.

59. $0.\overline{3} > 0.3$ since $0.\overline{3} = 0.333...$ is to the right of 0.3

61. $-\pi > -3.5$ since $-\pi \approx -3.14$ is to the right of -3.5

63. $-5 \geq -13$ is true because $-5 > -13$ is true.

65. $-9 \geq -9$ is true because $-9 = -9$ is true.

67. $0 \geq -6$ is true because $0 > -6$ is true.

69. $-17 \geq 6$ is false because neither $-17 > 6$ nor $-17 = 6$ is true.

71. $|6| = 6$ because the distance between 6 and 0 on the number line is 6 units.

73. $|-7| = 7$ because the distance between -7 and 0 on the number line is 7 units.

75. $\left|\dfrac{5}{6}\right| = \dfrac{5}{6}$ because the distance between $\dfrac{5}{6}$ and 0 on the number line is $\dfrac{5}{6}$ units.

77. $\left|-\sqrt{11}\right| = \sqrt{11}$ because the distance between $-\sqrt{11}$ and 0 on the number line is $\sqrt{11}$ units.

79. $|-6| \; \square \; |-3|$

$6 \; \square \; 3$

$6 > 3$

Since $6 > 3$, $|-6| > |-3|$.

80. $|-20| \; \square \; |-50|$

$20 \; \square \; 50$

$20 < 50$

Since $20 < 50$, $|-20| < |-50|$.

81. $\left|\dfrac{3}{5}\right| \; \square \; |-0.6|$

$|0.6| \; \square \; |-0.6|$

$0.6 \; \square \; 0.6$

$0.6 = 0.6$

Since $0.6 = 0.6$, $\left|\dfrac{3}{5}\right| = |-0.6|$.

82. $\left|\dfrac{5}{2}\right| \; \square \; |-2.5|$

$|2.5| \; \square \; |-2.5|$

$2.5 \; \square \; 2.5$

$2.5 = 2.5$

Since $2.5 = 2.5$, $\left|\dfrac{5}{2}\right| = |-2.5|$.

83. $\dfrac{30}{40} - \dfrac{3}{4} \; \square \; \dfrac{14}{15} \cdot \dfrac{15}{14}$

$\dfrac{30}{40} - \dfrac{30}{40} \; \square \; \dfrac{\cancel{14}}{\cancel{15}} \cdot \dfrac{\cancel{15}}{\cancel{14}}$

$0 \; \square \; 1$

$0 < 1$

Since $0 < 1$, $\dfrac{30}{40} - \dfrac{3}{4} < \dfrac{14}{15} \cdot \dfrac{15}{14}$.

84. $\dfrac{17}{18} \cdot \dfrac{18}{17} \; \square \; \dfrac{50}{60} - \dfrac{5}{6}$

$\dfrac{\cancel{17}}{\cancel{18}} \cdot \dfrac{\cancel{18}}{\cancel{17}} \; \square \; \dfrac{50}{60} - \dfrac{50}{60}$

$1 \; \square \; 0$

$1 > 0$

Since $1 > 0$, $\dfrac{17}{18} \cdot \dfrac{18}{17} > \dfrac{50}{60} - \dfrac{5}{6}$.

85. $\dfrac{8}{13} \div \dfrac{8}{13} \; \square \; |-1|$

$\dfrac{8}{13} \cdot \dfrac{13}{8} \; \square \; 1$

$1 \; \square \; 1$

$1 = 1$

Since $1 = 1$, $\dfrac{8}{13} \div \dfrac{8}{13} = |-1|$.

86. $|-2| \; \square \; \dfrac{4}{17} \div \dfrac{4}{17}$

$2 \; \square \; \dfrac{4}{17} \cdot \dfrac{17}{4}$

$2 \; \square \; 1$

$2 > 1$

Since $2 > 1$, $|-2| > \dfrac{4}{17} \div \dfrac{4}{17}$.

87. -2

89. The years for which money collected < money spent are 1997 and 2002. There was a budget deficit in these years.

91. – 101. Answers will vary

103. Statement c is true since there are an infinite number of rational numbers that are not positive. -5 is one example.

105. Since $\sqrt{36} = 6$ and $\sqrt{49} = 7$, $-\sqrt{47}$ is between -7 and -6.

107. $\sqrt{3} \approx 1.732$ and should be graphed between 1 and 2.

109. $1 - \sqrt{2} \approx -0.414$ and should be graphed between -1 and 0.

1.3 Exercise Set

1. Quadrant I

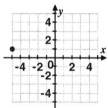

3. Quadrant II

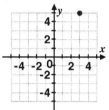

5. Quadrant III

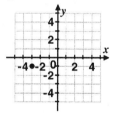

7. Quadrant IV

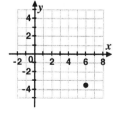

9-23. All points for Exercises 9 through 23 are graphed on the same set of axes and labeled accordingly.

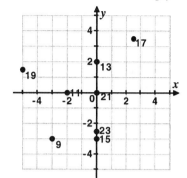

25. $A\,(5,2)$

27. $C\,(-6,5)$

29. $E(-2,-3)$

31. $G(5,-3)$

33. The y-coordinates are positive in Quadrants I and II.

35. The x- and y-coordinates have the same sign in Quadrants I and III.

37. Answers will vary. Some examples are $(-2, 2)$ and $(2, 2)$, and $(-1, 1)$ and $(1, 1)$.

7

38. Answers will vary. Some examples are (2, −2) and (2, 2), and (1, −1) and (1, 1).

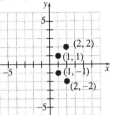

39.

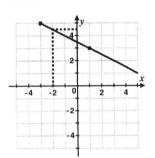

It appears that the point $\left(-2, 4\frac{1}{2}\right)$ is on the line, so y is approximately $4\frac{1}{2}$ or $\frac{9}{2}$.

41. The coordinates of point A are (2,7). When the football is 2 yards from the quarterback, its height is 7 feet.

43. The coordinates of point C are approximately (3, 9.25).

45. The football's maximum height is 12 feet. It reaches this height when it is 15 yards from the quarterback.

47. Point A is (91, 125). This means that in 1991, 125,000 acres were used to cultivate opium crops.

49. Opium cultivation was at a minimum in 2001 when approximately 25,000 acres were used.

51. Opium cultivation did not change between 1991 and 1992.

53. In 1985, oil consumption was approximately 7.1 million barrels per day.

55. In 1990, oil consumption and domestic production were the same. During that year approximately 7.2 million barrels were produced and consumed per day.

57. Domestic oil production was at an all time high in 1970 when about 9.8 million barrels per day were produced.

59. The difference between production and consumption is 1980 was about $8.7 - 7 = 1.7$ million barrels per day.

61. *The Bodyguard* grossed about $120 million.

63. *No Way Out, The Postman,* and *Dragonfly* have a box-office gross of less than $50 million.

65. Life expectancy for men born in 1900 was approximately 48 years.

67. Women born in 1996 can expect to live approximately $(80 - 65 = 15)$ more years than men born in 1950.

69. The median income for African-American men is $22 thousand.

71. The difference in median income between Hispanic men and women is $20 - 13 = \$7$ thousand.

73. The average number of days before the convention that candidates declared in 1992 was approximately 270. Clinton's declaration exceeded this by $284 - 270 = 14$ days.

75. The United States obtained more than $\dfrac{1}{2} = \dfrac{5}{10}$ of its oil from other countries in 2002.

77. The fraction of imported oil exceeded $\dfrac{1}{5} = \dfrac{2}{10}$ but was at most $\dfrac{1}{2} = \dfrac{5}{10}$ in 1972, 1982, and 1992.

79. In 2002, $\dfrac{5}{10}$ of oil was imported from other countries. Of this, $\dfrac{1}{10}$ was imported from Saudi Arabia. This means that $\dfrac{5}{10} \cdot \dfrac{1}{10} = \dfrac{1}{2} \cdot \dfrac{1}{10} = \dfrac{1}{20}$ of oil used in the U.S. in 2002 was from Saudi Arabia.

81. – 87. Answers will vary.

89. a. A

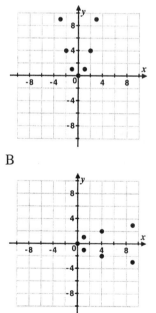

B

b. In set A, each x-coordinate with exactly one y-coordinate. In set B, x-coordinates are associated

with more than one y-coordinate. Points line up vertically when x-coordinates are associated with more than one point.

91. $\dfrac{3}{4} + \dfrac{2}{5} = \dfrac{3}{4} \cdot \dfrac{5}{5} + \dfrac{2}{5} \cdot \dfrac{4}{4} = \dfrac{15}{20} + \dfrac{8}{20} = \dfrac{23}{20}$

92. $-\dfrac{1}{4} < 0$ since $-\dfrac{1}{4}$ is to the left of 0 on the number line.

93. $\left| -5.83 \right| = 5.83$ because the distance between -5.83 and 0 on the number line is 5.83 units.

1.4 Exercise Set

1. When $x = 4$, $x + 11 = 4 + 11 = 15$.

3. When $x = 10$, $8x = 8 \cdot 10 = 80$.

5. When $x = 8$,
$5x + 6 = 5 \cdot 8 + 6 = 40 + 6 = 46$.

7. When $x = 2$,
$7(x+3) = 7(2+3) = 7(5) = 35$.

9. When $F = 77$,
$\dfrac{5}{9}(F - 32) = \dfrac{5}{9}(77 - 32) = \dfrac{5}{9}(45) = 25$

11. $3x + 5$
   a. 2 terms
   b. 3
   c. 5
   d. No like terms

13. $x + 2 + 5x$
   a. 3 terms
   b. 1
   c. 2
   d. x and $5x$ are like terms.

15. $4y + 1 + 3$
   a. 3 terms
   b. 4
   c. 1
   d. No like terms

17. $y + 4 = 4 + y$

19. $5 + 3x = 3x + 5$

21. $4x + 5y = 5y + 4x$

23. $5(x + 3) = 5(3 + x)$

25. $9x = x \cdot 9 \text{ or } x9$

27. $x + y6 = x + 6y$

29. $7x + 23 = x7 + 23$

31. $5(x + 3) = (x + 3)5$

33. $7 + (5 + x) = (7 + 5) + x = 12 + x$

35. $7(4x) = (7 \cdot 4)x = 28x$

37. $3(x + 5) = 3(x) + 3(5) = 3x + 15$

39. $8(2x + 3) = 8(2x) + 8(3) = 16x + 24$

41. $\dfrac{1}{3}(12 + 6r) = \dfrac{1}{3}(12) + \dfrac{1}{3}(12) + \dfrac{1}{3}(6r)$
$$= 4 + 2r$$

43. $5(x + y) = 5x + 5y$

45. $3(x - 2) = 3(x) - 3(2) = 3x - 6$

47. $2(4x - 5) = 2(4x) - 2(5) = 8x - 10$

49. $\dfrac{1}{2}(5x - 12) = \dfrac{1}{2}(5x) + \dfrac{1}{2}(-12)$
$$= \dfrac{5}{2}x - 6$$

51. $(2x + 7)4 = 2x(4) + 7(4) = 8x + 28$

53. $6(x + 3 + 2y) = 6(x) + 6(3) + 6(2y)$
$$= 6x + 18 + 12y$$

55. $5(3x - 2 + 4y) = 5(3x) - 5(2) + 5(4y)$
$$= 15x - 10 + 20y$$

57. $7x + 10x = (7 + 10)x = 17x$

59. $11a - 3a = (11 - 3)a = 8a$

61. $3 + (x + 11) = (3 + 11) + x = 14 + x$

63. $5y - 3 + 6y = (5y + 6y) - 3 = 11y - 3$

65. $2x + 5 + 7x - 4 = (2x + 7x) + (5 - 4)$
$$= 9x + 1$$

67. $11a + 12 - 3a - 2 = (11a - 3a) + (12 - 2)$
$$= 8a + 10$$

69. $5(3x + 2) - 4 = 15x + 10 - 4 = 15x + 6$

71. $12 + 5(3x - 2) = 12 + 15x - 10$
$$= 15x + 12 - 10 = 15x + 2$$

73. $7(3a + 2b) + 5(4a + 2b)$
$$= 21a + 14b + 20a + 10b$$
$$= 21a + 20a + 14b + 10b$$
$$= 41a + 24b$$

75. Commutative Property of Addition

76. Commutative Property of Addition

77. Associative Property of Addition

78. Commutative Property of Multiplication

79. False

80. True

81. True

82. False

83. When $x = 20$, $15x = 15(20) = 300$.

This means that you can stay in the sun for 300 minutes (or 5 hours) without burning with a number 15 lotion.

85. When $x = 8$,
$$405x + 5565 = 405(8) + 5565$$
$$= 3240 + 5565 = 8805$$
According to the graph in the year $1994 + 8 = 2002$, credit card debt per U.S. household was $8940. The model fits the data fairly well.

87. a. $2(0.18x + 0.01) + 0.02x$
$$= 0.36x + 0.03 + 0.02x$$
$$= 0.38x + 0.03$$

b. $2002 - 1997 = 5$, so evaluate the expression for $x = 5$.
$$0.38x + 0.03 = 0.38(5) + 0.03$$
$$= 1.9 + 0.03 = 1.93$$
According to the graph, the number of testosterone prescriptions in 2002 was approximately 1.9 million. The model is fairly accurate.

89. – 99. Answers will vary.

101. The only correct statement is *c*, which is an example of the distributive property.

103. a. When $x = 100$,
$$\frac{0.5x + 5000}{x} = \frac{0.5(100) + 5000}{100}$$
$$= \frac{50 + 5000}{100}$$
$$= \frac{5050}{100} = 50.5$$

The average cost per clock for 100 clocks is $50.50.

When $x = 1000$,
$$\frac{0.5x + 5000}{x} = \frac{0.5(1000) + 5000}{1000}$$
$$= \frac{500 + 5000}{1000}$$
$$= \frac{5500}{1000} = 5.5$$
The average cost per clock for 1000 clocks is $5.50.

When $x = 10,000$,
$$\frac{0.5x + 5000}{x} = \frac{0.5(10,000) + 5000}{10,000}$$
$$= \frac{5000 + 5000}{10,000}$$
$$= \frac{10,000}{10,000} = 1$$
The average cost per clock for 10,000 clocks is $1.

b. When $x = 2000$,
$$\frac{0.5x + 5000}{x} = \frac{0.5(2000) + 5000}{2000}$$
$$= \frac{1000 + 5000}{2000}$$
$$= \frac{6000}{2000} = 3$$

The average cost per clock to manufacture 2000 clocks is $3.

Since the clocks cannot be sold for more than $1.50, the business cannot make a profit so it doesn't have a promising future.

11

104.

$$9\overline{)4.00...} = 0.44...$$

$$\underline{36}$$
$$40$$
$$\underline{36}$$
$$40$$
$$\vdots$$

$$\frac{4}{9} = 0.\overline{4}$$

105.

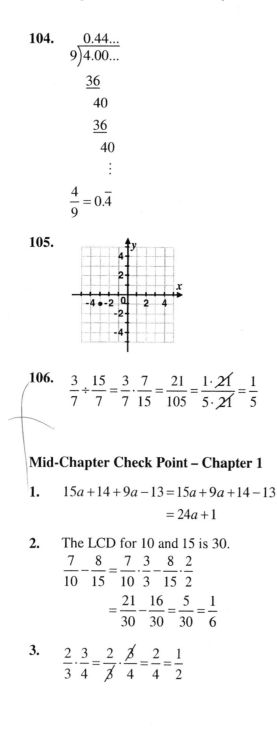

106. $\dfrac{3}{7} \div \dfrac{15}{7} = \dfrac{3}{7} \cdot \dfrac{7}{15} = \dfrac{21}{105} = \dfrac{1 \cdot \cancel{21}}{5 \cdot \cancel{21}} = \dfrac{1}{5}$

Mid-Chapter Check Point – Chapter 1

1. $15a + 14 + 9a - 13 = 15a + 9a + 14 - 13$
$$= 24a + 1$$

2. The LCD for 10 and 15 is 30.
$$\frac{7}{10} - \frac{8}{15} = \frac{7}{10} \cdot \frac{3}{3} - \frac{8}{15} \cdot \frac{2}{2}$$
$$= \frac{21}{30} - \frac{16}{30} = \frac{5}{30} = \frac{1}{6}$$

3. $\dfrac{2}{3} \cdot \dfrac{3}{4} = \dfrac{2}{\cancel{3}} \cdot \dfrac{\cancel{3}}{4} = \dfrac{2}{4} = \dfrac{1}{2}$

4. $7(9x + 3) + \dfrac{1}{3}(6x - 15)$

$$7(9x) + 7(3) + \frac{1}{3}(6x) - \frac{1}{3}(15)$$

$$= 63x + 21 + 2x - 5$$

$$= 63x + 2x + 21 - 5 = 65x + 16$$

5. $\dfrac{5}{22} + \dfrac{5}{33} = \dfrac{5}{22} \cdot \dfrac{3}{3} + \dfrac{5}{33} \cdot \dfrac{2}{2} = \dfrac{15}{66} + \dfrac{10}{66} = \dfrac{25}{66}$

6. $\dfrac{3}{5} \div \dfrac{9}{10} = \dfrac{3}{5} \cdot \dfrac{10}{9} = \dfrac{3}{5} \cdot \dfrac{2 \cdot 5}{3 \cdot 3} = \dfrac{\cancel{3}}{\cancel{5}} \cdot \dfrac{2 \cdot \cancel{5}}{\cancel{3} \cdot 3} = \dfrac{2}{3}$

7. $\dfrac{23}{105} - \dfrac{2}{105} = \dfrac{21}{105} = \dfrac{\cancel{3} \cdot \cancel{7}}{\cancel{3} \cdot 5 \cdot \cancel{7}} = \dfrac{1}{5}$

8. $2\dfrac{7}{9} \div 3 = \dfrac{25}{9} \div \dfrac{3}{1} = \dfrac{25}{9} \cdot \dfrac{1}{3} = \dfrac{25}{27}$

9. $5\dfrac{2}{9} - 3\dfrac{1}{6} = \dfrac{47}{9} - \dfrac{19}{6}$

$$= \frac{47}{9} \cdot \frac{2}{2} - \frac{19}{6} \cdot \frac{3}{3}$$

$$= \frac{94}{18} - \frac{57}{18} = \frac{37}{18} \text{ or } 2\frac{1}{18}$$

10.

The point lies in Quadrant IV.

11. $5(x + 3) = (x + 3)5$

12. $5(x + 3) = 5(3 + x)$

13. $5(x + 3) = 5 \cdot x + 5 \cdot 3 = 5x + 15$

14. $13\% - 6\% = 7\%$
There was about a 7% increase in the number of people listening to internet radio between 2001 and 2004.

15. The percentage exceeded 7% in 2002, 2003, and 2004.

16. $-8000 < -8\dfrac{1}{4}$

17. $-11,\ -\dfrac{3}{7},\ 0,\ 0.45,$ and $\sqrt{25}$ are rational numbers.

18. When $x = \dfrac{3}{5}$,

$10x + 7 = 10\left(\dfrac{3}{5}\right) + 7 = 6 + 7 = 13$.

19. When $x = \dfrac{5}{2}$,

$8(x-2) = 8\left(\dfrac{5}{2} - 2\right)$

$= 8\left(\dfrac{5}{2} - \dfrac{4}{2}\right) = 8\left(\dfrac{1}{2}\right) = 4$

20. (67, 20); In 1967, 20% of grades earned by undergraduates were A's.

21. The percentage of grades of C or below reached a maximum in 1970. Approximately 23% of grades were C or below.

22. The difference between the percentage of A's and the percentage of C's or below in 2003 was about $45 - 5 = 40\%$.

23. $|-19.3| = 19.3$

24. $\dfrac{1}{11} = 0.\overline{09}$

25. $8(7x - 10 + 3y) = 8 \cdot 7x - 8 \cdot 10 + 8 \cdot 3y$

$= 56x - 80 + 24y$

1.5 Exercise Set

1. $7 + (-3) = 4$

3. $-2 + (-5) = -7$

5. $-6 + 2 = -4$

7. $3 + (-3) = 0$

9. $-7 + 0 = -7$

11. $30 + (-30) = 0$

13. $-30 + (-30) = -60$

15. $-8 + (-10) = -18$

17. $-0.4 + (-0.9) = -1.3$

19. $-\dfrac{7}{10} + \left(-\dfrac{3}{10}\right) = -\dfrac{10}{10} = -1$

21. $-9 + 4 = -5$

23. $12 + (-8) = 4$

25. $6 + (-9) = -3$

27. $-3.6 + 2.1 = -1.5$

29. $-3.6 + (-2.1) = -5.7$

31. $\dfrac{9}{10} + \left(-\dfrac{3}{5}\right) = \dfrac{9}{10} + \left(-\dfrac{6}{10}\right) = \dfrac{3}{10}$

33. $-\dfrac{5}{8} + \dfrac{3}{4} = -\dfrac{5}{8} + \dfrac{6}{8} = \dfrac{1}{8}$

35. $-\dfrac{3}{7} + \left(-\dfrac{4}{5}\right) = -\dfrac{15}{35} + \left(-\dfrac{28}{35}\right) = -\dfrac{43}{35}$

13

37.
$$4+(-7)+(-5)=\left[4+(-7)\right]+(-5)$$
$$=-3+(-5)$$
$$=-8$$

39.
$$85+(-15)+(-20)+12$$
$$=\left[85+(-15)\right]+(-20)+12$$
$$=70+(-20)+12$$
$$=\left[70+(-20)\right]+12$$
$$=50+12$$
$$=62$$

41.
$$17+(-4)+2+3+(-10)$$
$$=13+2+3+(-10)$$
$$=15+3+(-10)$$
$$=18+(-10)$$
$$=8$$

43.
$$-45+\left(-\frac{3}{7}\right)+25+\left(-\frac{4}{7}\right)$$
$$=(-45+25)+\left[-\frac{3}{7}+\left(-\frac{4}{7}\right)\right]$$
$$=-20+\left(-\frac{7}{7}\right)$$
$$=-20+(-1)$$
$$=-21$$

45.
$$3.5+(-45)+(-8.4)+72$$
$$=\left[3.5+(-8.4)\right]+(-45+72)$$
$$=-4.9+27$$
$$=22.1$$

47.
$$-10x+2x=(-10+2)x=-8x$$

49.
$$25y+(-12y)=\left[25+(-12)\right]y=13y$$

51.
$$-8a+(-15a)=\left[-8+(-15)\right]a$$
$$=-23a$$

53.
$$-4+7x+5+(-13x)$$
$$=-4+5+7x+(-13x)$$
$$=(-4+5)+\left[7+(-13)\right]x$$
$$=1-6x$$

55.
$$7b+2+(-b)+(-6)$$
$$=7b+(-b)+2+(-6)$$
$$=\left[7+(-1)\right]b+\left[2+(-6)\right]$$
$$=6b-4 \text{ or } -4+6b$$

57.
$$7x+(-5y)+(-9x)+2y$$
$$=7x+(-9x)+(-5y)+2y$$
$$=\left[7+(-9)\right]x+(-5+2)y$$
$$=-2x-3y$$

59.
$$4(5x-3)+6=4\cdot5x+4(-3)+6$$
$$=20x-12+6$$
$$=20x-6$$

61.
$$8(3-4y)+35y=8\cdot3+8(-4y)+35y$$
$$=24-32y+35y$$
$$=24+(-32+35)y$$
$$=24+3y$$

63.
$$6(2-9a)+7(3a+5)$$
$$=6\cdot2+6(-9a)+7\cdot3a+7\cdot5$$
$$=12-54a+21a+35$$
$$=(12+35)+(-54+21a)$$
$$=47-33a$$

65.
$$\left|-3+(-5)\right|+\left|2+(-6)\right|=\left|-8\right|+\left|-4\right|$$
$$=8+4$$
$$=12$$

66. $\left|4+(-11)\right|+\left|-3+(-4)\right|=\left|-7\right|+\left|-7\right|$

$= 7+7$

$= 14$

67. $-20+\left[-\left|15+(-25)\right|\right]$

$= -20+\left[-\left|-10\right|\right]$

$= -20+\left[-10\right]$

$= -30$

68. $-25+\left[-\left|18+(-26)\right|\right]$

$= -25+\left[-\left|-8\right|\right]$

$= -25+\left[-8\right]$

$= -33$

69. $6+\left[2+(-13)\right]\square-3+\left[4+(-8)\right]$

$6+\left[-11\right]\square-3+\left[-4\right]$

$-5\square-7$

$-5>-7$

70. $\left[(-8)+(-6)\right]+10\;\square\;-8+\left[9+(-2)\right]$

$-14+10\;\square\;-8+7$

$-4\;\square\;-1$

$-4<-1$

71. $-56+100=44$

The high temperature was 44°F.

73. $-1312+712=-600$

The elevation of the person is 600 feet below sea level.

75. $-7+15-5=3$

The temperature at 4:00 P.M. was 3°F.

77. $27+4-2+8-12$

$= (27+4+8)+(-2-12)$

$= 34-14$

$= 25$

The location of the football at the end of the fourth play is at the 25-yard line.

79. $126+110-109-233-349$

$= (126+110)+(-109-233-349)$

$= 236+(-691)$

$= -455$

There was a \$455 billion deficit in 2003.

81. – 87. Answers will vary.

89. Statement d is true. (Statement a is sometimes true, but not considered true because it is not always true.)

91. $\underline{}+11x+(-3y)+3x=7(2x-3y)$

$11x+3x+\underline{}+(-3y)=7\cdot2x-7\cdot3y$

$14x+\underline{}+(-3y)+=14x-21y$

Since the x terms are the same, the y terms must match. This means that $\underline{}+(-3y)+=-21y$ and the missing term must be $-18y$.

93. Answers will vary according to the exercises chosen. For example,

$3\sqrt{5}-2\sqrt{7}-\sqrt{11}+4\sqrt{3}\approx5.0283$.

94. $-19\geq-18$ is true because $-19>-18$ is true.

95.
  a. $\sqrt{4}\,(=2)$

  b. $0,\sqrt{4}$

  c. $-6,0,\sqrt{4}$

  d. $-6,0,0.\overline{7},\sqrt{4}$

  e. $-\pi,\sqrt{3}$

  f. $-6,-\pi,0,0.\overline{7},\sqrt{3},\sqrt{4}$

96. Quadrant IV

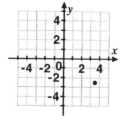

15

Exercise Set 1.6

1.   **a.** -12
      b. $5-12 = 5+(-12)$

3.   **a.** 7
      b. $5-(-7) = 5+7$

5. $14-8 = 14+(-8) = 6$

7. $8-14 = 8+(-14) = -6$

9. $3-(-20) = 3+20 = 23$

11. $-7-(-18) = -7+18 = 11$

13. $-13-(-2) = -13+2 = -11$

15. $-21-17 = -21+(-17) = -38$

17. $-45-(-45) = -45+45 = 0$

19. $23-23 = 23+(-23) = 0$

21. $13-(-13) = 13+13 = 26$

23. $0-13 = 0+(-13) = -13$

25. $0-(-13) = 0+13 = 13$

27. $\dfrac{3}{7}-\dfrac{5}{7} = \dfrac{3}{7}+\left(-\dfrac{5}{7}\right) = -\dfrac{2}{7}$

29. $\dfrac{1}{5}-\left(-\dfrac{3}{5}\right) = \dfrac{1}{5}+\dfrac{3}{5} = \dfrac{4}{5}$

31. $-\dfrac{4}{5}-\dfrac{1}{5} = -\dfrac{4}{5}+\left(-\dfrac{1}{5}\right) = -\dfrac{5}{5} = -1$

33. $-\dfrac{4}{5}-\left(-\dfrac{1}{5}\right) = -\dfrac{4}{5}+\dfrac{1}{5} = -\dfrac{3}{5}$

35. $\dfrac{1}{2}-\left(-\dfrac{1}{4}\right) = \dfrac{1}{2}+\dfrac{1}{4} = \dfrac{2}{4}+\dfrac{1}{4} = \dfrac{3}{4}$

37. $\dfrac{1}{2}-\dfrac{1}{4} = \dfrac{1}{2}+\left(-\dfrac{1}{4}\right) = \dfrac{2}{4}+\left(-\dfrac{1}{4}\right) = \dfrac{1}{4}$

39. $9.8-2.2 = 9.8+(-2.2) = 7.6$

41. $-3.1-(-1.1) = -3.1+1.1 = -2$

43. $1.3-(-1.3) = 1.3+1.3 = 2.6$

45. $-2.06-(-2.06) = -2.06+2.06 = 0$

47. $5\pi - 2\pi = 5\pi +(-2\pi) = 3\pi$

49. $3\pi -(-10\pi) = 3\pi +10\pi = 13\pi$

51. $13-2-(-8) = 13+(-2)+8$
      $= (13+8)+(-2)$
      $= 21+(-2)$
      $= 19$

53. $9-8+3-7 = 9+(-8)+3+(-7)$
      $= (9+3)+[(-8)+(-7)]$
      $= 12+(-15)$
      $= -3$

55. $-6-2+3-10$
      $= -6+(-2)+3+(-10)$
      $= [(-6)+(-2)+(-10)]+3$
      $= -18+3$
      $= -15$

57. $-10-(-5)+7-2$
      $= -10+5+7+(-2)$
      $= [(-10)+(-2)]+(5+7)$
      $= -12+12$
      $= 0$

59.
$$-23-11-(-7)+(-25)$$
$$=(-23)+(-11)+7+(-25)$$
$$=\left[(-23)+(-11)+(-25)\right]+7$$
$$=-59+7$$
$$=-52$$

61.
$$-823-146-50-(-832)$$
$$=-823+(-146)+(-50)+832$$
$$=\left[(-823)+(-146)+(-50)\right]+832$$
$$=-1019+832$$
$$=-187$$

63.
$$1-\frac{2}{3}-\left(-\frac{5}{6}\right)=1+\left(-\frac{2}{3}\right)+\frac{5}{6}$$
$$=\left(1+\frac{5}{6}\right)+\left(-\frac{2}{3}\right)$$
$$=\left(\frac{6}{6}+\frac{5}{6}\right)+\left(-\frac{2}{3}\right)$$
$$=\frac{11}{6}+\left(-\frac{2}{3}\cdot\frac{2}{2}\right)$$
$$=\frac{11}{6}+\left(-\frac{4}{6}\right)$$
$$=\frac{7}{6}\text{ or }1\frac{1}{6}$$

65.
$$-0.16-5.2-(-0.87)$$
$$=-0.16+(-5.2)+0.87$$
$$=\left[(-0.16)+(-5.2)\right]+0.87$$
$$=-5.36+0.87$$
$$=-4.49$$

67.
$$-\frac{3}{4}-\frac{1}{4}-\left(-\frac{5}{8}\right)=-\frac{3}{4}+\left(-\frac{1}{4}\right)+\frac{5}{8}$$
$$=-\frac{4}{4}+\frac{5}{8}$$
$$=-\frac{8}{8}+\frac{5}{8}=-\frac{3}{8}$$

69.
$$-3x-8y=-3x+(-8y)$$
The terms are $-3x$ and $-8y$.

71.
$$12x-5xy-4=12x+(-5xy)+(-4)$$
The terms are $12x$, $-5xy$, and -4.

73.
$$3x-9x=3x+(-9x)$$
$$=\left[3+(-9)\right]x=-6x$$

75.
$$4+7y-17y=4+7y+(-17y)$$
$$=4+\left[7+(-17)\right]y$$
$$=4-10y$$

77.
$$2a+5-9a=2a+5+(-9a)$$
$$=2a+(-9a)+5$$
$$=\left[2+(-9)\right]a+5$$
$$=-7a+5a\text{ or }5-7a$$

79.
$$4-6b-8-3b$$
$$=4+(-6b)+(-8)+(-3b)$$
$$=4+(-8)+(-6b)+(-3b)$$
$$=4+(-8)+\left[-6+(-3)\right]b$$
$$=-4-9b$$

81.
$$13-(-7x)+4x-(-11)$$
$$=13+7x+4x+11$$
$$=13+11+7x+4x$$
$$=24+11x$$

83.
$$-5x-10y-3x+13y$$
$$=-5x+(-10y)+(-3x)+13y$$
$$=-5x+(-3x)+(-10y)+13y$$
$$=\left[-5+(-3)\right]x+(-10+13)y$$
$$=-8x+3y\text{ or }3y-8x$$

85.
$$-\left|-9-(-6)\right|-(-12)=-\left|-9+6\right|+12$$
$$=-\left|-3\right|+12$$
$$=-3+12$$
$$=9$$

17

86.

$$-\left|-8-(-2)\right|-(-6) = -\left|-8+2\right|+6$$
$$= -\left|-6\right|+6$$
$$= -6+6$$
$$= 0$$

87.

$$\frac{5}{8}-\left(\frac{1}{2}-\frac{3}{4}\right) = \frac{5}{8}-\left(\frac{1}{2}\cdot\frac{2}{2}-\frac{3}{4}\right)$$
$$= \frac{5}{8}-\left(\frac{2}{4}+\left(-\frac{3}{4}\right)\right)$$
$$= \frac{5}{8}-\left(-\frac{1}{4}\right)$$
$$= \frac{5}{8}+\frac{1}{4}$$
$$= \frac{5}{8}+\frac{1}{4}\cdot\frac{2}{2}$$
$$= \frac{5}{8}+\frac{2}{8}$$
$$= \frac{7}{8}$$

88.

$$\frac{9}{10}-\left(\frac{1}{4}-\frac{7}{10}\right) = \frac{9}{10}-\left(\frac{1}{4}\cdot\frac{5}{5}-\frac{7}{10}\cdot\frac{2}{2}\right)$$
$$= \frac{9}{10}-\left(\frac{5}{20}-\frac{14}{20}\right)$$
$$= \frac{9}{10}-\left[\frac{5}{20}+\left(-\frac{14}{20}\right)\right]$$
$$= \frac{9}{10}-\left(-\frac{9}{20}\right)$$
$$= \frac{9}{10}\cdot\frac{2}{2}+\frac{9}{20}$$
$$= \frac{18}{20}+\frac{9}{20}$$
$$= \frac{27}{20} \text{ or } 1\frac{7}{20}$$

89.

$$\left|-9-(-3+7)\right|-\left|-17-(-2)\right|$$
$$= \left|-9-4\right|-\left|-17+2\right|$$
$$= \left|-9+(-4)\right|-\left|-17+2\right|$$
$$= \left|-13\right|-\left|-15\right|$$
$$= 13+(-15)$$
$$= -2$$

90.

$$\left|24-(-16)\right|-\left|-51-(-31+2)\right|$$
$$= \left|24+16\right|-\left|-51-(-29)\right|$$
$$= \left|24+16\right|-\left|-51+29\right|$$
$$= \left|40\right|-\left|-22\right|$$
$$= 40-22$$
$$= 18$$

91. Elevation of Mount Kilimanjaro – elevation of Qattara Depression
$$= 19{,}321-(-436) = 19{,}757$$
The difference in elevation between the two geographic locations is 19,757 feet.

93. Increase teachers – decrease farmers
$$= 711-(-328) = 711+328 = 1039$$
The difference is 1039 thousand jobs.

95.
$$\text{phone} - \text{farmers} = -60-(-328)$$
$$= -60+328$$
$$= 268$$
The decline for phone workers exceeds the decline for farmers by 268 thousand jobs.

97. $2-(-19) = 2+19 = 21$
The difference between the average daily low temperature for March and February is 21°F.

99. $-19-(-22) = -19+22 = 3$
February's average low temperature is 3°F warmer than January's.

101. The maximum point on the graph is $(3, 0.05)$. This means that the drug's maximum concentration is 0.05 milligrams per 100 milliliters and this occurs 3 hours after the injection.

18

103. $0.045 - 0.03 = 0.045 + (-0.03) = 0.015$
The difference in concentrations between 4 hours and 1 hour after injection is about 0.015 milligrams.

105. The drug's concentration is increasing between 0 and 3 hours after the injection (from the time of the injection to three hours later).

107. – 111. Answers will vary.

113. Consider dates B.C. as negative numbers and dates A.D. as positive numbers:
$500 - (-212) = 500 + 212 = 712$.
Because there was no year 0, the number of elapsed time is 712 – 1 = 711 years.

115. Student answers will vary according to the exercises chosen.

117.

118. $10(a+4) = 10(4+a)$

119. Examples will vary. One integer that is not a natural number is –7.

1.7 Exercises Set

1. $5(-9) = -(5 \cdot 9) = -45$

3. $(-8)(-3) = +(8 \cdot 3) = 24$

5. $(-3)(7) = -21$

7. $(-19)(-1) = 19$

9. $0(-19) = 0$

11. $\frac{1}{2}(-24) = -12$

13. $\left(-\frac{3}{4}\right)(-12) = \frac{3 \cdot 12}{4 \cdot 1} = 9$

15. $-\frac{3}{5} \cdot \left(-\frac{4}{7}\right) = \frac{3 \cdot 4}{5 \cdot 7} = \frac{12}{35}$

17. $-\frac{7}{9} \cdot \frac{2}{3} = -\frac{7 \cdot 2}{9 \cdot 3} = -\frac{14}{27}$

19. $3(-1.2) = -3.6$

21. $-0.2(-0.6) = 0.12$

23. $(-5)(-2)(3) = 30$

25. $(-4)(-3)(-1)(6) = -72$

27. $-2(-3)(-4)(-1) = 24$

29. $(-3)(-3)(-3) = 9(-3) = -27$

31. $5(-3)(-1)(2)(3) = 90$

33. $(-8)(-4)(0)(-17)(-6) = 0$

35. The multiplicative inverse of 4 is $\frac{1}{4}$.

37. The multiplicative inverse of $\frac{1}{5}$ is 5.

39. The multiplicative inverse of –10 is $-\frac{1}{10}$.

41. The multiplicative inverse of $-\frac{2}{5}$ is $-\frac{5}{2}$.

19

43.

a. $-32 \div 4 = -32 \cdot \dfrac{1}{4}$

b. $-32 \cdot \dfrac{1}{4} = -8$

45.

a. $\dfrac{-60}{-5} = -60 \cdot \left(-\dfrac{1}{5}\right)$

b. $-60 \cdot \left(-\dfrac{1}{5}\right) = 12$

47. $\dfrac{12}{-4} = 12 \cdot \left(-\dfrac{1}{4}\right) = -3$

49. $\dfrac{-21}{3} = -21 \cdot \dfrac{1}{3} = -7$

51. $\dfrac{-90}{-3} = -90 \cdot \left(-\dfrac{1}{3}\right) = 30$

53. $\dfrac{0}{-7} = 0$

55. $\dfrac{-7}{0}$ is undefined.

57. $-15 \div 3 = -15 \cdot \dfrac{1}{3} = -5$

59. $12 \div (-10) = 120 \cdot \left(-\dfrac{1}{10}\right) = -12$

61. $(-180) \div (-30) = -180 \cdot \left(-\dfrac{1}{30}\right) = 6$

63. $0 \div (-4) = 0$

65. $-4 \div 0$ is undefined.

67. $\dfrac{-12.9}{3} = -12.9 \cdot \dfrac{1}{3} = -4.3$

69. $-\dfrac{1}{2} \div \left(-\dfrac{3}{5}\right) = -\dfrac{1}{2} \cdot \left(-\dfrac{5}{3}\right) = \dfrac{5}{6}$

71. $-\dfrac{14}{9} \div \dfrac{7}{8} = -\dfrac{14}{9} \cdot \dfrac{8}{7}$

$= -\dfrac{112}{63} = -\dfrac{\cancel{7} \cdot 16}{\cancel{7} \cdot 9} = -\dfrac{16}{9}$

73. $\dfrac{1}{3} \div \left(-\dfrac{1}{3}\right) = \dfrac{1}{3} \cdot (-3) = -1$

75. $6 \div \left(-\dfrac{2}{5}\right) = 6 \cdot \left(-\dfrac{5}{2}\right) = -\dfrac{30}{2} = -15$

77. $-5(2x) = (-5 \cdot 2)x = -10x$

79. $-4\left(-\dfrac{3}{4}y\right) = \left[-4 \cdot \left(-\dfrac{3}{4}\right)\right]y = 3y$

81. $8x + x = 8x + 1x = (8+1)x = 9x$

83. $-5x + x = -5x + 1x = (-5+1)x = -4x$

85. $6b - 7b = (6-7)b = -1b = -b$

87. $-y + 4y = -1y + 4y = (-1+4)y = 3y$

89. $-4(2x-3) = -4(2x) - 4(-3) = -8x + 12$

91. $-3(-2x+4) = -3(-2x) - 3(4) = 6x - 12$

93. $-(2y-5) = -2y + 5$

95. $4(2y-3) - (7y+2)$
$= 4(2y) + 4(-3) - 7y - 2$
$= 8y - 12 + 7y - 2$
$= 8y - 7y - 12 - 2$
$= y - 14$

97. $4(-10) + 8 = -40 + 8 = -32$

98. $3(-15) + 14 = -45 + 14 = -31$

99. $(-9)(-3) - (-2) = 27 + 2 = 29$

20

100. $(-6)(-4)-(-5)=24+5=29$

101. $\dfrac{-18}{-15+12}=\dfrac{-18}{-3}=6$

102. $\dfrac{-25}{-21+16}=\dfrac{-25}{-5}=5$

103. $-6-\left(\dfrac{12}{-4}\right)=-6-(-3)=-6+3=-3$

104. $-11-\left(\dfrac{20}{-5}\right)=-11-(-4)$
$$=-11+4=-7$$

105. Since $2000-1994=6$, let $t=6$:
$$-1.4t+14.7=-1.4(6)+14.7$$
$$=-8.4+14.7=6.3$$
The model predicts that there were 6.3 million welfare recipients in 2000. The graph shows approximately 6 million so the model gives a slight overestimation.

107. a. From the graph, a reasonable estimate is 11 words.

    b. $\dfrac{5x+30}{x};x=5$
$$\dfrac{5x+30}{x}=\dfrac{5(5)+30}{5}$$
$$=\dfrac{25+30}{5}=\dfrac{55}{5}=11$$
According to the model, 11 Latin words will be remembered after 5 days. This is the same as the estimate from part (a).

109. a. $\dfrac{200x}{100-x};x=50$
$$\dfrac{200x}{100-x}=\dfrac{200(50)}{100-50}$$
$$=\dfrac{10,000}{50}=200$$
The cost for removing 50% of the containments is
$200(\$10,000)=\$2,000,000$.

    b. $\dfrac{200x}{100-x};x=80$
$$\dfrac{200x}{100-x}=\dfrac{200(80)}{100-80}$$
$$=\dfrac{16,000}{20}=800$$
The cost for removing 80% of the containments is $80(\$10,000)=\$8,000,000$.

    c. As the percentage of contaminant removed increases, the cost of the cleanup rises very rapidly.

111. – 117. Answers will vary.

119. Statement b is true.

121. $5x$

123. $\dfrac{x}{12}$

125. Student solutions will vary according to the exercises chosen.

127. $0.3(4.7x-5.9)-0.07(3.8x-61)$
$$=0.3(4.7x)+0.3(-5.9)-(0.07)(3.8x)$$
$$-(0.07)(-61)$$
$$=1.41x-1.77-0.266x+4.27$$
$$=\left[1.41x+(-0.266x)\right]+(-1.77+4.27)$$
$$=1.144x+2.5$$

129. $-6 + (-3) = -9$

130. $-6 - (-3) = -6 + 3 = -3$

131.
$$-6 \div (-3) = -6 \left(-\frac{1}{3} \right) = 2$$

1.8 Exercise Set

1. $9^2 = 9 \cdot 9 = 81$

3. $4^3 = 4 \cdot 4 \cdot 4 = 64$

5. $(-4)^2 = (-4)(-4) = 16$

7. $(-4)^3 = (-4)(-4)(-4) = -64$

9. $(-5)^4 = (-5)(-5)(-5)(-5) = 625$

11. $-5^4 = -5 \cdot 5 \cdot 5 \cdot 5 = -625$

13. $-10^2 = -10 \cdot 10 = -100$

15. $7x^2 + 12x^2 = (7 + 12)x^2 = 19x^2$

17. $10x^3 + 5x^3 = (10 + 5)x^3 = 15x^3$

19. $8x^4 + x^4 = 8x^4 + 1x^4 = (8 + 1)x^4 = 9x^4$

21.
$$26x^2 - 27x^2 = 26x^2 + (-27x^2)$$
$$= [26 + (-27)]x^2$$
$$= -1x^2 = -x^2$$

23.
$$27x^3 - 26x^3 = 27x^3 + (-26x^2)$$
$$= 1x^3 = x^3$$

25. $5x^2 + 5x^3$ cannot be simplified. The terms $5x^2$ and $5x^3$ are not like terms because they have different variable factors, namely, x^2 and x^3.

27.
$$16x^2 - 16x^2 = 16x^2 + (-16x^2)$$
$$= [16 + (-16)]x^2$$
$$= 0x^2 = 0$$

29. $7 + 6 \cdot 3 = 7 + 18 = 25$

31. $45 \div 5 \cdot 3 = 9 + 18 = 27$

33. $6 \cdot 8 \div 4 = 48 \div 4 = 12$

35. $14 - 2 \cdot 6 + 3 = 14 - 12 + 3 = 2 + 3 = 5$

37.
$$8^2 - 16 \div 2^2 \cdot 4 - 3 = 64 - 16 \div 4 \cdot 4 - 3$$
$$= 64 - 4 \cdot 4 - 3$$
$$= 64 - 16 - 3$$
$$= 48 - 3$$
$$= 45$$

39.
$$3(-2)^2 - 4(-3)^2 = 3 \cdot 4 - 4 \cdot 9$$
$$= 12 - 36$$
$$= 12 + (-36)$$
$$= -24$$

41.
$$(4 \cdot 5)^2 - 4 \cdot 5^2 = 20^2 - 4 \cdot 25$$
$$= 400 - 100$$
$$= 300$$

43.
$$(2 - 6)^2 - (3 - 7)^2 = (-4)^2 - (-4)^2$$
$$= 16 - 16$$
$$= 0$$

45.
$$6(3 - 5)^3 - 2(1 - 3)^3$$
$$= 6(-2)^3 - 2(-2)^3$$
$$= 6(-8) - 2(-8)$$
$$= -48 + 16$$
$$= -32$$

47. $[2(6 - 2)]^2 = (2 \cdot 4)^2 = 8^2 = 64$

49. $2[5+2(9-4)] = 2[5+2(5)]$
$$= 2(5+10)$$
$$= 2 \cdot 15 = 30$$

51. $[7+3(2^3-1)] \div 21$
$$= [7+3(8-1)] \div 21$$
$$= (7+3 \cdot 7) \div 21$$
$$= (7+21) \div 21$$
$$= 28 \div 21 = \frac{28}{21} = \frac{7 \cdot 4}{7 \cdot 3} = \frac{4}{3}$$

53. $\dfrac{10+8}{5^2-4^2} = \dfrac{18}{25-16} = \dfrac{18}{9} = 2$

55. $\dfrac{37+15 \div (-3)}{2^4} = \dfrac{37+(-5)}{16} = \dfrac{32}{16} = 2$

57. $\dfrac{(-11)(-4)+2(-7)}{7-(-3)} = \dfrac{44+(-14)}{7+3}$
$$= \frac{30}{10} = 3$$

59. $4|10-(8-20)| = 4|10-(-12)|$
$$= 4|10+12|$$
$$= 4|22| = 4 \cdot 22 = 88$$

61. $8(-10)+|4(-5)| = -80+|-20|$
$$= -80+20 = -60$$

63. $-2^2+4[16 \div (3-5)]$
$$= -4 + 4[16 \div (-2)]$$
$$= -4+4(-8) = -4-32 = -36$$

65. $24 \div \dfrac{3^2}{8-5} - (-6) = 24 \div \dfrac{9}{3} - (-6)$
$$= 24 \div 3 - (-6)$$
$$= 8+6 = 14$$

67. $\dfrac{\frac{1}{4}-\frac{1}{2}}{\frac{1}{3}} = \dfrac{\frac{1}{4}-\frac{2}{4}}{\frac{1}{3}} = \dfrac{-\frac{1}{4}}{\frac{1}{3}} = -\frac{1}{4} \cdot \frac{3}{1} = -\frac{3}{4}$

69. $-\dfrac{9}{4}\left(\dfrac{1}{2}\right)+\dfrac{3}{4} \div \dfrac{5}{6} = -\dfrac{9}{4}\left(\dfrac{1}{2}\right)+\dfrac{3}{4} \cdot \dfrac{6}{5}$
$$= -\frac{9}{8}+\frac{18}{20}$$
$$= -\frac{45}{40}+\frac{36}{40} = -\frac{9}{40}$$

71. $\dfrac{\frac{7}{9}-3}{\frac{5}{6}} \div \dfrac{3}{2}+\dfrac{3}{4} = \dfrac{\frac{7}{9}-\frac{27}{9}}{\frac{5}{6}} \cdot \dfrac{3}{2}+\dfrac{3}{4}$
$$= \frac{-\frac{20}{9}}{\frac{5}{6}} \cdot \frac{3}{2}+\frac{3}{4}$$
$$= -\frac{20}{9} \cdot \frac{6}{5} \cdot \frac{2}{3}+\frac{3}{4}$$
$$= -\frac{240}{135}+\frac{3}{4}$$
$$= -\frac{15 \cdot 16}{15 \cdot 9}+\frac{3}{4}$$
$$= -\frac{16}{9}+\frac{3}{4}$$
$$= -\frac{64}{36}+\frac{27}{36}$$
$$= -\frac{37}{36} \text{ or } -1\frac{1}{36}$$

73. $x^2+5x; \ x=3$
$$x^2+5x = 3^2+5 \cdot 3$$
$$= 9+5 \cdot 3 = 9+15 = 24$$

23

75. $3x^2 - 8x; \ x = -2$

$3x^2 - 8x = 3(-2)^2 - 9(-2)$

$\qquad = 3 \cdot 4 - 8(-2) = 12 + 16 = 28$

77. $-x^2 - 10x; \ x = -1$

$-x^2 - 10x = -(-1)^2 - 10(-1)$

$\qquad = -1 + 10 = 9$

79. $\dfrac{6y - 4y^2}{y^2 - 15}; \ y = 5$

$\dfrac{6y - 4y^2}{y^2 - 15} = \dfrac{6(5) - 4(5^2)}{5^2 - 15}$

$\qquad = \dfrac{6(5) - 4(25)}{25 - 15}$

$\qquad = \dfrac{30 - 100}{25 - 15} = \dfrac{-70}{10} = -7$

81. $3[5(x - 2) + 1] = 3(5x - 10 + 1)$

$\qquad = 3(5x - 9)$

$\qquad = 15x - 27$

83. $3[6 - (y + 1)] = 3(6 - y - 1)$

$\qquad = 3(5 - y)$

$\qquad = 15 - 3y$

85. $7 - 4[3 - (4y - 5)]$

$= 7 - 4(3 - 4y + 5)$

$= 7 - 12 + 16y - 20$

$= -25 + 16y \ \text{ or } \ 16y - 25$

87. $2(3x^2 - 5) - [4(2x^2 - 1) + 3]$

$= 6x^2 - 10 - (8x^2 - 4 + 3)$

$= 6x^2 - 10 - (8x^2 - 1)$

$= 6x^2 - 10 - 8x^2 - 1$

$= -2x^2 - 9$

89. $-10 - (-2)^3 = -10 - (-8) = -10 + 8 = -2$

90. $-100 - (-5)^3 = -100 - (-125)$

$\qquad = -100 + 125$

$\qquad = 25$

91. $[2(7 - 10)]^2 = [2(-3)]^2 = [-6]^2 = 36$

92. $[2(9 - 11)]^4 = [2(-2)]^4 = [-4]^4 = 256$

93. $x - (5x + 8) = x - 5x - 8 = -4x - 8$

94. $x - (3x + 9) = x - 3x - 9 = -2x - 9$

95. $5(x^3 - 4) = 5x^3 - 20$

96. $4(x^3 - 6) = 4x^3 - 24$

97. $R = 165 - 0.75A; \ A = 40$

$R - 165 - 0.75A = 165 - 0.75(40)$

$\qquad = 165 - 30 = 135$

The desirable heart rate during exercise for a 40-year old man is 135 beats per minute. This corresponds to the point (40, 135) on the graph.

99. Since 2000 − 1995 = 5, the year 2005 corresponds to $x = 5$.

$N = 1.2x^2 + 15.2x + 181.4; \ x = 5$

$N = 1.2x^2 + 15.2x + 181.4$

$\qquad = 1.2(5^2) + 152.5(5) + 181.4$

$\qquad = 1.2(25) + 15.2(5) + 181.4$

$\qquad = 30 + 76 + 181.4$

$\qquad = 287.4$

According to the formula, the cost of Medicare in 2000 was $287.4 billion. This is a very good estimate for the cost shown by the bar graph.

24

101. Since $2002 - 1992 = 10$, let $x = 10$

$N = 0.12x^3 - x^2 + 3x + 15$

$\quad = 0.12(10)^3 - 10^2 + 3(10) + 15$

$\quad = 0.12(1000) - 100 + 3(10) + 15$

$\quad = 120 - 100 + 30 + 15 = 65$

According to the formula, approximately 65 thousand bariatric surgeries were performs in 2002. The graph shows approximately 63 thousand so this is a slight overestimation.

103. $C = \dfrac{5}{9}(F - 32); \quad F = 68$

$C = \dfrac{5}{9}(F - 32)$

$\quad = \dfrac{5}{9}(68 - 32)$

$\quad = \dfrac{5}{9}(36) = \dfrac{5}{9} \cdot \dfrac{36}{1} = \dfrac{180}{9} = 20$

Thus, $68°F = 20°V$.

105. $C = \dfrac{5}{9}(F - 32); \quad F = -22$

$C = \dfrac{5}{9}(F - 32)$

$\quad = \dfrac{5}{9}(-22 - 32)$

$\quad = \dfrac{5}{9}(-54) = \dfrac{5}{9} \cdot \dfrac{54}{1} = -\dfrac{270}{9} = -30$

Thus, $-22°F = -30°C$.

107. – 111. Answers will vary.

113.

$\dfrac{1}{4} - 6(2 + 8) \div \left(-\dfrac{1}{3}\right)\left(-\dfrac{1}{9}\right)$

$= \dfrac{1}{4} - 6(10) \div \left(-\dfrac{1}{3}\right)\left(-\dfrac{1}{9}\right)$

$= \dfrac{1}{4} - 60 \div \left(-\dfrac{1}{3}\right)\left(-\dfrac{1}{9}\right)$

$= \dfrac{1}{4} - 60 \div (-3)\left(-\dfrac{1}{9}\right)$

$= \dfrac{1}{4} + 180\left(-\dfrac{1}{9}\right)$

$= \dfrac{1}{4} - 20 = \dfrac{1}{4} - \dfrac{80}{4} = \dfrac{79}{4}$

115.

$\left(2 \cdot 5 - \dfrac{1}{2} \cdot 10\right) \cdot 9 = (10 - 5) \cdot 9$

$\qquad\qquad\qquad = 5 \cdot 9 = 45$

117. Answers will vary.

119. $-8 - 2 - (-5) + 11$

$= -8 + (-2) + 5 + 11$

$= \left[(-8) + (-2)\right] + (5 + 11)$

$= -10 + 16 = 6$

120. $-4(-1)(-3)(2) = -24$

121. Any rational number is a real number that is not an irrational number. One example is $-\dfrac{3}{4}$.

Chapter 1 Review Exercises

1. $3\dfrac{2}{7} = \dfrac{3 \cdot 7 + 2}{7} = \dfrac{21 + 2}{7} = \dfrac{23}{7}$

2. $5\dfrac{9}{11} = \dfrac{5 \cdot 11 + 9}{11} = \dfrac{55 + 9}{11} = \dfrac{64}{11}$

3. 17 divided by 9 is 1 with a remainder of 8, so $\dfrac{17}{9} = 1\dfrac{8}{9}$.

4. 27 divided by 5 is 5 with a remainder of 2, so $\dfrac{27}{5} = 5\dfrac{2}{5}$.

5. Composite
$60 = 6 \cdot 10 = 2 \cdot 3 \cdot 2 \cdot 5 = 2 \cdot 2 \cdot 3 \cdot 5$

6. Composite
$63 = 7 \cdot 9 = 7 \cdot 3 \cdot 3 = 3 \cdot 3 \cdot 7$

7. 67 is a prime number.

8. $\dfrac{15}{33} = \dfrac{\cancel{3} \cdot 5}{\cancel{3} \cdot 11} = \dfrac{5}{11}$

9. $\dfrac{40}{75} = \dfrac{\cancel{5} \cdot 8}{\cancel{5} \cdot 15} = \dfrac{8}{15}$

10. $\dfrac{3}{5} \cdot \dfrac{7}{10} = \dfrac{3 \cdot 7}{5 \cdot 10} = \dfrac{21}{50}$

11. $\dfrac{4}{5} \div \dfrac{3}{10} = \dfrac{4}{5} \cdot \dfrac{10}{3} = \dfrac{40}{15} = \dfrac{\cancel{5} \cdot 8}{\cancel{5} \cdot 3} = \dfrac{8}{3}$

12. $1\dfrac{2}{3} \div 6\dfrac{2}{3} = \dfrac{5}{3} \div \dfrac{20}{3}$

$= \dfrac{5}{\cancel{3}} \cdot \dfrac{\cancel{3}}{20} = \dfrac{5}{20} = \dfrac{1 \cdot \cancel{5}}{4 \cdot \cancel{5}} = \dfrac{1}{4}$

13. $\dfrac{2}{9} + \dfrac{4}{9} = \dfrac{2+4}{9} = \dfrac{6}{9} = \dfrac{2 \cdot \cancel{3}}{3 \cdot \cancel{3}} = \dfrac{2}{3}$

14. $\dfrac{5}{6} + \dfrac{7}{9} = \dfrac{5}{6} \cdot \dfrac{3}{3} + \dfrac{7}{9} \cdot \dfrac{2}{2}$

$= \dfrac{15}{18} + \dfrac{14}{18} = \dfrac{29}{18}$ or $1\dfrac{11}{18}$

15. $\dfrac{3}{4} - \dfrac{2}{15} = \dfrac{3}{4} \cdot \dfrac{15}{15} - \dfrac{2}{15} \cdot \dfrac{4}{4} = \dfrac{45}{60} - \dfrac{8}{60} = \dfrac{37}{60}$

16. $1 - \dfrac{1}{4} - \dfrac{1}{3} = \dfrac{12}{12} - \dfrac{3}{12} - \dfrac{4}{12} = \dfrac{5}{12}$

At the end of the second day, $\dfrac{5}{12}$ of the tank is filled.

17. -2.5

18. $4\dfrac{3}{4}$

19.
$$\begin{array}{r} 0.625 \\ 8\overline{)5.000} \\ \underline{48} \\ 20 \\ \underline{16} \\ 40 \\ \underline{40} \\ 0 \end{array}$$

$\dfrac{5}{8} = 0.625$

20.
$$\begin{array}{r} 0.2727... \\ 11\overline{)3.0000...} \\ \underline{22} \\ 80 \\ \underline{77} \\ 30 \\ \underline{27} \\ 30 \\ \underline{22} \\ 8 \\ \vdots \end{array}$$

$\dfrac{3}{11} = 0.\overline{27}$

26

21.

   a. $\sqrt{81}\ \left(=9\right)$

   b. $0,\sqrt{81}$

   c. $-17,0,\sqrt{81}$

   d. $-17,-\dfrac{9}{13},0,0.75,\sqrt{81}$

   e. $\sqrt{2},\pi$

   f. $-17,-\dfrac{9}{13},0,0.75,\sqrt{2},\pi,\sqrt{81}$

22. Answers will vary. One example of an integer that is not a natural number is -7.

23. Answers will vary. One example of a rational number that is not an integer is $\dfrac{3}{4}$.

24. Answers will vary. One example of a real number that is not a rational number is π.

25. $-93 < 17$; -93 is to the left of 17, so $-93 < 17$.

26. $-2 > -200$; -2 is to the right of -200, so $-2 > -200$.

27. $0 > -\dfrac{1}{3}$; 0 is to the right of $-\dfrac{1}{3}$, so $0 > -\dfrac{1}{3}$.

28. $-\dfrac{1}{4} < -\dfrac{1}{5}$; $-\dfrac{1}{4} = -0.25$ is to the left of $-\dfrac{1}{5} = -0.2$, so $-\dfrac{1}{4} < -\dfrac{1}{5}$.

29. $-13 \geq -11$ is false because neither $-13 > -11$ nor $-13 = -11$ is true.

30. $-126 \leq -126$ is true because $-126 = -126$.

31. $|-58| = 58$ because the distance between -58 and 0 on the number line is 58.

32. $|2.75| = 2.75$ because the distance between 2.75 and 0 on the number line is 2.75.

33.

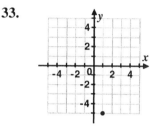

Quadrant IV

34.

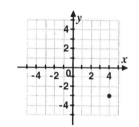

Quadrant IV

35.

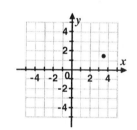

Quadrant I

36.

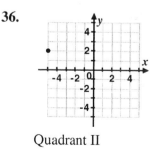

Quadrant II

27

37. $A(5,6)$, $B(-3,0)$, $C(-5,2)$, $D(-4,-2)$, $E(0,-5)$, $F(3,-1)$

38. There were approximately 65 democracies in 1989.

39. There were $120 - 40 = 80$ more democracies in 2002 than in 1973.

40. The number of democracies increased at the greatest rate between 1989 and 1993.

41. The number of democracies increased at the slowest rate between 1981 and 1985.

42. There were 49 democracies in 1977.

43. There are approximately 85 televisions per 100 people in the U.S.

44. Finland, Germany, and Austria have more than 50 but fewer than 70 televisions per 100 people.

45. $7x + 3$; $x = 10$
$$7x + 3 = 7(10) + 3 = 70 + 3 = 73$$

46. $5(x - 4)$; $x = 12$
$$5(x - 4) = 5(12 - 4) = 5 \cdot 8 = 40$$

47. $7 + 13y = 13y + 7$

48. $9(x + 7) = (x + 7)9$

49. $6 + (4 + y) = (6 + 4) + y = 10 + y$

50. $7(10x) = (7 \cdot 10)x = 70x$

51. $6(4x - 2 + 5y) = 6(4x) + 6(-2) + 6(5y)$
$$= 24x - 12 + 30y$$

52. $4a + 9 + 3a - 7 = 4a + 3a + 9 - 7$
$$= (4 + 3)a + (9 - 7)$$
$$= 7a + 2$$

53. $6(3x + 4) + 5(2x - 1)$
$$= 6(3x) + 6(4) + 5(2x) + 5(-1)$$
$$= 18x + 24 + 10x - 5$$
$$= 18x + 10x + 24 - 5$$
$$= (18 + 10)x + [24 + (-5)]$$
$$= 28x + 19$$

54. $x - 0.25x$; $x = 2400$
$$x - 0.25x = 2400 - 0.25(2400)$$
$$= 2400 - 600$$
$$= 1800$$

This means that a computer with a regular price of $2400 will have a sale price of $1800.

55. Start at -6. Move 8 units to the right because 8 is positive. Finish at 2.

56. $8 + (-11) = -3$

57. $-\dfrac{3}{4} + \dfrac{1}{5} = -\dfrac{3}{4} \cdot \dfrac{5}{5} + \dfrac{1}{5} \cdot \dfrac{4}{4}$
$$= -\dfrac{15}{20} + \dfrac{4}{20} = -\dfrac{11}{20}$$

58. $7 + (-5) + (-13) + 4$
$$= [7 + (-5)] + (-13) + 4$$
$$= 2 + (-13) + 4$$
$$= [2 + (-13)] + 4 = -11 + 4 = -7$$

59. $8x + (-6y) + (-12x) + 11y$
$$= 8x + (-12x) + (-6y) + 11y$$
$$= [8 + (-12)]x + (-6 + 11)y$$
$$= -4x + 5y \text{ or } 5y - 4x$$

60. $10(4-3y)+28y$

$=10(4)+10(-3y)+28y$

$=40-30y+28y$

$=40+(-30+28)y$

$=40-2y$

61. $-1312+512=-800$

The person's elevation is 800 feet below sea level.

62. $25-3+2+1-4+2$

$=25+(-3)+2+1+(-4)+2$

$=23$

The reservoir's water level at the end of five months is 23 feet.

63. $9-13=9+(-13)$

64. $-9-(-13)=-9+13=4$

65. $-\dfrac{7}{10}-\dfrac{1}{2}=-\dfrac{7}{10}-\dfrac{1}{2}\cdot\dfrac{5}{5}$

$=-\dfrac{7}{10}-\dfrac{5}{10}=-\dfrac{12}{10}=-\dfrac{6}{5}$

66. $-3.6-(-2.1)=-3.6+2.1=-1.5$

67. $-7-(-5)+11-16$

$=-7+5+11+(-16)$

$=\left[(-7)+(-16)\right]+(5+11)$

$=-23+16$

$=-7$

68. $-25-4-(-10)+16$

$=-25+(-4)+10+16$

$=\left[(-25)+(-4)\right]+(10+16)$

$=-29+26$

$=-3$

69. $3-6a-8-2a=3-8-6a-2a$

$=\left[3+(-8)\right]+\left[-6a-2a\right]$

$=-5+(-6-2)a$

$=-5-8a$

70. $26,000-(-650)=26,500+650$

$=27,150$

The difference in elevation is 27,150 feet.

71. $(-7)(-12)=84$

72. $\dfrac{3}{5}\left(-\dfrac{5}{11}\right)=-\dfrac{3\cdot\cancel{5}}{\cancel{5}\cdot 11}=-\dfrac{3}{11}$

73. $5(-3)(-2)(-4)=-120$

74. $\dfrac{45}{-5}=45\left(-\dfrac{1}{5}\right)=-9$

75. $-17\div 0$ is undefined.

76. $-\dfrac{4}{5}\div\left(-\dfrac{2}{5}\right)=-\dfrac{4}{5}\left(-\dfrac{5}{2}\right)=\dfrac{20}{10}=2$

77. $-4\left(-\dfrac{3}{4}x\right)=\left[-4\left(-\dfrac{3}{4}\right)\right]x=3x$

78. $-3(2x-1)-(4-5x)$

$=-3(2x)+(-3)(-1)-4+5x$

$=-6x+3-4+5x$

$=-6x+5x+3-4$

$=(-6+5)x+\left[3+(-4)\right]$

$=-1x-1=-x-1$

79. $(-6)^2=(-6)(-6)=36$

80. $-6^2=-6\cdot 6=-36$

81. $(-2)^5=(-2)(-2)(-2)(-2)(-2)=-32$

29

82. $4x^3 + 2x^3 = (4+2)x^3 = 6x^3$

83. $4x^3 + 4x^2$ cannot be simplified. The terms $4x^3$ and $4x^2$ are not like terms because they have different variable factors, x^3 and x^2.

84. $-40 \div 5 \cdot 2 = -8 \cdot 2 = -16$

85. $-6 + (-2) \cdot 5 = -6 + (-10) = -16$

86. $6 - 5(-3+2) = 6 - 4(-1) = 6 + 4 = 10$

87. $28 \div (2 - 4^2) = 28 \div (2-16)$
$$= 28 \div [2 + (-16)]$$
$$= 28 \div (-14)$$
$$= -2$$

88. $36 - 24 \div 4 \cdot 3 - 1 = 36 - 6 \cdot 3 - 1$
$$= 36 - 18 - 1$$
$$= 18 - 1$$
$$= 17$$

89. $-8[-4 - 5(-3)] = -8(-4+15)$
$$= -8(11) = -88$$

90. $\dfrac{6(-10+3)}{2(-15) - 9(-3)} = \dfrac{6(-7)}{-30+27}$
$$= \dfrac{-42}{-3} = 14$$

91. $\left(\dfrac{1}{2} + \dfrac{1}{3}\right) \div \left(\dfrac{1}{4} - \dfrac{3}{8}\right)$
$$= \left(\dfrac{3}{6} + \dfrac{2}{6}\right) \div \left(\dfrac{2}{8} - \dfrac{3}{8}\right)$$
$$= \dfrac{5}{6} \div \left(-\dfrac{1}{8}\right) = \dfrac{5}{6} \cdot \left(-\dfrac{8}{1}\right) = -\dfrac{40}{6} = -\dfrac{20}{3}$$

92. $\dfrac{1}{2} - \dfrac{2}{3} \div \dfrac{5}{9} + \dfrac{3}{10}$
$$= \dfrac{1}{2} - \dfrac{2}{\cancel{3}_1} \cdot \dfrac{\cancel{9}^3}{5} + \dfrac{3}{10}$$
$$= \dfrac{1}{2} - \dfrac{6}{5} + \dfrac{3}{10}$$
$$= \dfrac{5}{10} - \dfrac{12}{10} + \dfrac{3}{10} = -\dfrac{4}{10} = -\dfrac{2}{5}$$

93. $x^2 - 2x + 3;\ x = -1$
$$x^2 - 2x + 3 = (-1)^2 - 2(-1) + 3$$
$$= 1 + 2 + 3$$
$$= 6$$

94. $-x^2 - 7x;\ x = -2$
$$-x^2 - 7x = -(-2)^2 - 7(-2)$$
$$= -4 + 14$$
$$= 10$$

95. $4[7(a-1) + 2] = 4(7a - 7 + 2)$
$$= 4(7a - 5)$$
$$= 4(7a) + 4(-5)$$
$$= 28a - 20$$

96. $-6[4 - (y+2)] = -6(4 - y - 2)$
$$= -6(2 - y)$$
$$= -6(2) + (-6)(-y)$$
$$= -12 + 6y \text{ or } 6y - 12$$

97. $W = 1.5x + 7 = 1.5(4) + 7 = 6 + 7 = 13$

After 4 months, she weighs 13 pounds. This is shown on the graph as the point (4, 13).

98. $W = 1.5x + 7 = 1.5(6) + 7 = 9 + 7 = 16$

After 6 months, she weighs 16 pounds. This is shown on the graph as the point (6, 16).

30

99. Since $2002 - 1997 = 5$, let $x = 5$.

$$N = -26x^2 + 143x + 740$$

$$= -26(5)^2 + 143(5) + 740$$

$$= -26(25) + 143(5) + 740$$

$$= -650 + 715 + 740$$

$$= 805$$

805 million CDs were sold in 2002. According to the model, CD sales were 800 million. The model fits the data fairly well, but there is a slight overestimation.

100. Sales increase from 1998 to 2000, and decrease from 2000 to 2002.

Chapter 1 Test

1. $1.4 - (-2.6) = 1.4 + 2.6 = 4$

2. $-9 + 3 + (-11) + 6$

$$= [-9 + (-11)] + (3 + 6)$$

$$= -20 + 9 = -11$$

3. $3(-17) = -51$

4. $\left(-\dfrac{3}{7}\right) \div \left(-\dfrac{15}{7}\right) = \left(-\dfrac{3}{7}\right)\left(-\dfrac{7}{15}\right)$

$$= \dfrac{21}{105} = \dfrac{\cancel{21} \cdot 1}{\cancel{21} \cdot 5} = \dfrac{1}{5}$$

5. $\left(3\dfrac{1}{3}\right)\left(-1\dfrac{3}{4}\right) = \left(\dfrac{10}{3}\right)\left(-\dfrac{7}{4}\right)$

$$= -\dfrac{10 \cdot 7}{3 \cdot 4} = -\dfrac{70}{12}$$

$$= -\dfrac{\cancel{2} \cdot 35}{\cancel{2} \cdot 6}$$

$$= -\dfrac{35}{6} \text{ or } -5\dfrac{5}{6}$$

6. $-50 \div 10 = -50\left(\dfrac{1}{10}\right) = -5$

7. $-6 - (5 - 12) = -6 - (-7) = -6 + 7 = 1$

8. $(-3)(-4) \div (7 - 10)$

$$= (-3)(-4) \div [7 + (-10)]$$

$$= (-3)(-4) \div (-3)$$

$$= 12 \div (-3)$$

$$= -4$$

9. $(6 - 8)^2 (5 - 7)^3 = (-2)^2 (-2)^3$

$$= 4(-8) = -32$$

10. $\dfrac{3(-2) - 2(2)}{-2(8 - 3)} = \dfrac{-6 - 4}{-2(5)}$

$$= \dfrac{-6 + (-4)}{-2(5)} = \dfrac{-10}{-10} = 1$$

11. $11x - (7x - 4) = 11x - 7x + 4$

$$= 11x + (-7x) + 4$$

$$= [11 + (-7)]x + 4$$

$$= 4x + 4$$

12. $5(3x - 4y) - (2x - y)$

$$= 5(3x) - 5(4y) - 2x + y$$

$$= 15x - 20y - 2x + y$$

$$= 15x - 2x - 20y + y$$

$$= 13x - 19y$$

13. $6 - 2[3(x + 1) - 5] = 6 - 2[3x + 3 - 5]$

$$= 6 - 2(3x - 2)$$

$$= 6 - 6x + 4$$

$$= 10 - 6x$$

31

14. Rational numbers can be written as the quotient of two integers.

$$-7 = -\frac{7}{1}, -\frac{4}{5} = \frac{-4}{5}, 0 = \frac{0}{1}, 0.25 = \frac{1}{4},$$

$$\sqrt{4} = 2 = \frac{2}{1}, \text{ and } \frac{22}{7} = \frac{22}{7}.$$

Thus, -7, $-\frac{4}{5}$, 0, 0.25, $\sqrt{4}$, and $\frac{22}{7}$ are the rational numbers of the set.

15. $-1 > -100$; -1 is to the right of -100 on the number line, so -1 is greater than -100.

16. $|-12.8| = 12.8$ because the distance between 12.8 and 0 on the number line is 12.8

17. Quadrant II

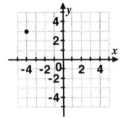

18. The coordinates of point A are $(-5, -2)$.

19. $5(x-7)$; $x = 4$

$$5(x-7) = 5(4-7) = 5(-3) = -15$$

20. $x^2 - 5x$; $x = -10$

$$x^2 - 5x = (-10)^2 - 5(-10)$$
$$= 100 + 50 = 150$$

21. $2(x+3) = 2(3+x)$

22. $-6(4x) = (-6 \cdot 4)x = -24x$

23. $7(5x - 1 + 2y) = 7(5x) - 7(1) + 7(2y)$
$$= 35x - 7 + 14y$$

24. The coordinates of point A are $(30, 200)$. This means that 30 years after the elk were introduced into the habitat, the elk population was 200.

25. The point $(0, 50)$ indicates that 50 elk were introduced into the habitat.

26. According to the bar graph, about 725 million DVD's were sold in 2002.

27. $T = 3(A - 20)^2 \div 50 + 10$; $A = 30$

$$T = 3(A - 20)^2 \div 50 + 10$$
$$= 3(30 - 20)^2 \div 50 + 10$$
$$= 3(10^2) \div 50 + 10$$
$$= 300 \div 50 + 10$$
$$= 6 + 10 = 16$$

According to the formula, it takes a 30-year-old runner 16 seconds to run the 100-yard dash.

28. $16,200 - (-830) = 17,030$

The difference in elevations is 17,030 feet.

29. According to the graph, the average price of an existing single family home in 1999 was about \$135,000.

30. Since x is years after 1989, find N when $x = 1999 - 1989 = 10$

$$N = 0.3(10)^2 + 1.2(10) + 92.7$$
$$= 0.3(100) + 12 + 92.7$$
$$= 30 + 12 + 92.7$$
$$= 134.7$$

Thus, the price in 1999 was \$134,700.

Chapter 2
Linear Equations and Inequalities in One Variable

2.1 Exercise Set

1.
$$x - 4 = 19$$
$$x - 4 + 4 = 19 + 4$$
$$x + 0 = 23$$
$$x = 23$$
Check:
$$x - 4 = 19$$
$$23 - 4 = 19$$
$$19 = 19$$
The solution is 23, or the solution set is $\{23\}$.

3.
$$z + 8 = -12$$
$$z + 8 - 8 = -12 - 8$$
$$z + 0 = -20$$
$$z = -20$$
Check:
$$z + 8 = -12$$
$$-20 + 8 = -12$$
$$-12 = -12$$
The solution is -20, or the solution set is $\{-20\}$

5.
$$-2 = x + 14$$
$$-2 - 14 = x + 14 - 14$$
$$-16 = x$$
Check:
$$-2 = -16 + 14$$
$$-2 = -2$$
The solution is -16, or the solution set is $\{-16\}$.

7.
$$-17 = y - 5$$
$$-17 + 5 = y - 5 + 5$$
$$-12 = y$$
Check:
$$-17 = -12 - 5$$
$$-17 = -17$$
The solution is -12, or the solution set is $\{-12\}$.

9.
$$7 + z = 11$$
$$z = 11 - 7$$
$$z = 4$$
Check:
$$7 + 4 = 11$$
$$11 = 11$$
The solution is 4, or the solution set is $\{4\}$.

11.
$$-6 + y = -17$$
$$y = -17 + 6$$
$$y = -11$$
Check:
$$-6 - 11 = -17$$
$$-17 = -17$$
The solution is -11, or the solution set is $\{-11\}$.

33

13.
$$x + \frac{1}{3} = \frac{7}{3}$$
$$x = \frac{7}{3} - \frac{1}{3}$$
$$x = 2$$

Check:
$$2 + \frac{1}{3} = \frac{7}{3}$$
$$\frac{6}{3} + \frac{1}{3} = \frac{7}{3}$$
$$\frac{7}{3} = \frac{7}{3}$$

The solution is 2, or the solution set is $\{2\}$.

15.
$$t + \frac{5}{6} = -\frac{7}{12}$$
$$t = -\frac{7}{12} - \frac{5}{6}$$
$$t = -\frac{7}{12} - \frac{10}{12} = -\frac{17}{12}$$

Check:
$$-\frac{17}{15} + \frac{5}{6} = -\frac{7}{12}$$
$$-\frac{17}{12} + \frac{10}{12} = -\frac{7}{12}$$
$$-\frac{7}{12} = -\frac{7}{12}$$

The solution is $-\frac{17}{12}$, or the solution

set is $\left\{ -\frac{17}{12} \right\}$.

17.
$$x - \frac{3}{4} = \frac{9}{2}$$
$$x - \frac{3}{4} + \frac{3}{4} = \frac{9}{2} + \frac{3}{4}$$
$$x = \frac{21}{4}$$

Check:
$$\frac{21}{4} - \frac{3}{4} = \frac{9}{2}$$
$$\frac{18}{4} = \frac{9}{2}$$
$$\frac{9}{2} = \frac{9}{2}$$

The solution is $\frac{21}{4}$, or the solution set

is $\left\{ \frac{21}{4} \right\}$.

19.
$$-\frac{1}{5} + y = -\frac{3}{4}$$
$$y = -\frac{3}{4} + \frac{1}{5}$$
$$y = -\frac{15}{20} + \frac{4}{20} = -\frac{11}{20}$$

Check:
$$-\frac{1}{5} + \left(-\frac{11}{20} \right) = -\frac{3}{4}$$
$$-\frac{4}{20} - \frac{11}{20} = -\frac{3}{4}$$
$$-\frac{15}{20} = -\frac{3}{4}$$
$$-\frac{3}{4} = -\frac{3}{4} \quad \text{true}$$

The solution is $-\frac{11}{20}$.

21.
$$3.2 + x = 7.5$$
$$3.2 + x - 3.2 = 7.5 - 3.2$$
$$x = 4.3$$

Check:
$$3.2 + 4.3 = 7.5$$
$$7.5 = 7.5$$

The solution is 4.3, or the solution set is $\{4.3\}$.

34

23.

$$x + \frac{3}{4} = -\frac{9}{2}$$

$$x + \frac{3}{4} - \frac{3}{4} = -\frac{9}{2} - \frac{3}{4}$$

$$x = -\frac{21}{4}$$

Check:

$$-\frac{21}{4} + \frac{3}{4} = -\frac{9}{2}$$

$$-\frac{18}{4} = -\frac{9}{2}$$

$$-\frac{9}{2} = -\frac{9}{2}$$

The solution is $-\frac{21}{4}$, or the solution

set is $\left\{ -\frac{21}{4} \right\}$.

25.

$$5 = -13 + y$$

$$5 + 13 = y$$

$$18 = y$$

Check:

$$5 = -13 + 18$$

$$5 = 5$$

The solution is 18, or the solution set is $\{18\}$

27.

$$-\frac{3}{5} = -\frac{3}{2} + s$$

$$-\frac{3}{5} + \frac{3}{2} = s$$

$$-\frac{6}{10} + \frac{15}{10} = s$$

$$\frac{9}{10} = s$$

Check:

$$-\frac{3}{5} = -\frac{3}{2} + \frac{9}{10}$$

$$-\frac{6}{10} = -\frac{15}{10} + \frac{9}{10}$$

$$-\frac{6}{10} = -\frac{6}{10}$$

The solution is $\frac{9}{10}$, or the solution set

is $\left\{ \frac{9}{10} \right\}$.

29.

$$830 + y = 520$$

$$y = 520 - 830$$

$$y = -310$$

Check:

$$830 - 310 = 520$$

$$520 = 520$$

The solution is -310, or the solution

set is $\{-310\}$.

31.

$$r + 3.7 = 8$$

$$r = 8 - 3.7$$

$$r = 4.3$$

Check:

$$4.3 + 3.7 = 8$$

$$8 = 8$$

The solution is 4.3, or the solution set

is $\{4.3\}$.

33.

$$-3.7 + m = -3.7$$

$$m = -3.7 + 3.7$$

$$m = 0$$

Check:

$$-3.7 + 0 = -3.7$$

$$-3.7 = -3.7$$

The solution is 0, or the solution set is $\{0\}$.

35

35.
$$6y + 3 - 5y = 14$$
$$y + 3 = 14$$
$$y = 14 - 3$$
$$y = 11$$

Check:
$$6(11) + 3 - 5(11) = 14$$
$$66 + 3 - 55 = 14$$
$$14 = 14$$

The solution is 11, or the solution set is $\{11\}$.

37.
$$7 - 5x + 8 + 2x + 4x - 3 = 2 + 3 \cdot 5$$
$$x + 12 = 2 + 15$$
$$x = 17 - 12$$
$$x = 5$$

Check:
$$7 - 5(5) + 8 + 2(5) + 4(5) - 3 = 2 + 3 \cdot 5$$
$$7 - 25 + 8 + 10 + 20 - 3 = 2 + 15$$
$$45 - 28 = 17$$
$$17 = 17$$

The solution is 5, or the solution set is $\{5\}$.

39.
$$7y + 4 = 6y - 9$$
$$7y - 6y + 4 = -9$$
$$y = -9 - 4$$
$$y = -13$$

Check:
$$7(-13) + 4 = 6(-13) - 9$$
$$-91 + 4 = -78 - 9$$
$$-87 = -87$$

The solution is -13, or the solution set is $\{-13\}$.

41.
$$12 - 6x = 18 - 7x$$
$$12 + x = 18$$
$$x = 6$$

Check:
$$12 - 6(6) = 18 - 7(6)$$
$$12 - 36 = 18 - 42$$
$$-24 = -24$$

The solution is 6, or the solution set is $\{6\}$.

43.
$$4x + 2 = 3(x - 6) + 8$$
$$4x + 2 = 3x - 18 + 8$$
$$4x + 2 = 3x - 10$$
$$4x - 3x + 2 = -10$$
$$x + 2 = -10$$
$$x = -10 - 2$$
$$x = -12$$

Check:
$$4(-12) + 2 = 3(-12 - 6) + 8$$
$$-48 + 2 = 3(-18) + 8$$
$$-46 = -54 + 8$$
$$-46 = -46$$

The solution is −12, or the solution set is $\{-12\}$.

45.
$$x - \square = \triangle$$
$$x - \square + \square = \triangle + \square$$
$$x = \triangle + \square$$

46.
$$x + \square = \triangle$$
$$x + \square - \square = \triangle - \square$$
$$x = \triangle - \square$$

47. $2x + \triangle = 3x + \square$

$\triangle = 3x - 2x + \square$

$\triangle = x + \square$

$\triangle - \square = x + \square - \square$

$\triangle - \square = x$

48. $6x - \triangle = 7x - \square$

$6x - \triangle - 6x = 7x - \square - 6x$

$-\triangle = x - \square$

$-\triangle + \square = x - \square + \square$

$\square - \triangle = x$

49. $x - 12 = -2$

$x = -2 + 12$

$x = 10$

The number is 10.

50. $x - 23 = -8$

$x - 23 + 23 = -8 + 23$

$x = 15$

The number is 15.

51. $\dfrac{2}{5}x - 8 = \dfrac{7}{5}x$

$-8 = \dfrac{7}{5}x - \dfrac{2}{5}x$

$-8 = \dfrac{5}{5}x$

$-8 = x$

The number is -8.

52. $3 - \dfrac{2}{7}x = \dfrac{5}{7}x$

$3 - \dfrac{2}{7}x + \dfrac{2}{7}x = \dfrac{5}{7}x + \dfrac{2}{7}x$

$3 = \dfrac{7}{7}x$

$3 = x$

The number is 3.

53. $C + M = S;\ S = 1850,\ M = 150$

$C + M = S$

$C + 150 = 1850$

$C = 1850 - 150$

$C = 1700$

The cost of the computer is $1700.

55. $d + 525{,}000 = 5000c;\ c = 210$

$d + 525{,}000 = 5000c$

$d + 525{,}000 = 1{,}050{,}000$

$d = 1{,}050{,}000 - 525{,}000$

$d = 525{,}000$

According to the formula, 525,000 deaths per year from heart disease can be expected at this cholesterol level.

57. $S - 1.6x = 5.8$

$S - 1.6(7) = 5.8$

$S - 11.2 = 5.8$

$S = 5.8 + 11.2$

$S = 17$

According to the model, Americans will spend $17 billion of statins in 2005.

For Exercises 59-63, answers will vary.

65. Answers will vary. Any equation with $x - 100$ on one side and a number ≥ -101 on the other side.

One example is as follows.
$x - 100 = -101$

67.
$$6.9825 = 4.2296 + y$$
$$6.9825 - 4.2296 = y$$
$$2.7529 = y$$
The solution set is $\{2.7529\}$.

68.

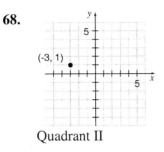

Quadrant II

69. $-16 - 8 \div 4 \cdot (-2) = -16 - 2(-2)$
$$= -16 + 4$$
$$= -12$$

70. $3[7x - 2(5x - 1)]$
$$= 3(7x - 10x + 2)$$
$$= 3(-3x + 2)$$
$$= -9x + 6 \text{ or } 6 - 9x$$

2.2 Exercise Set

1.
$$\frac{x}{6} = 5$$
$$6 \cdot \frac{x}{6} = 6 \cdot 5$$
$$1x = 30$$
$$x = 30$$
Check:
$$\frac{30}{6} = 5$$
$$5 = 5$$
The solution is 30, or the solution set is $\{30\}$.

3.
$$\frac{x}{-3} = 11$$
$$-3 \cdot \frac{x}{-3} = -3(11)$$
$$1x = -33$$
$$x = -33$$
Check:
$$\frac{-33}{-3} = 11$$
$$11 = 11$$
The solution is -33, or the solution set is $\{-33\}$.

5.
$$5y = 35$$
$$\frac{5y}{5} = \frac{35}{5}$$
$$y = 7$$
Check:
$$5(7) = 35$$
$$35 = 35$$
The solution is 7, or the solution set is $\{7\}$.

7.
$$-7y = 63$$
$$\frac{-7y}{-7} = \frac{63}{-7}$$
$$y = -9$$
Check:
$$-7(-9) = 63$$
$$63 = 63$$
The solution is -9, or the solution set is $\{-9\}$.

9. $-28 = 8z$

$$\frac{-28}{8} = \frac{8z}{8}$$

$$-\frac{7}{2} = z$$

Check:

$$-28 = 8\left(-\frac{7}{2}\right)$$

$$-28 = -28$$

The solution is $-\frac{7}{2}$ or $-3\frac{1}{2}$, or the

solution set is $\left\{-\frac{7}{2}\right\}$.

11. $-18 = -3z$

$$\frac{-18}{-3} = \frac{-3z}{-3}$$

$$6 = z$$

Check:

$$-18 = -3(6)$$

$$-18 = -18$$

The solution is 6, or the solution set is

$\{6\}$.

13. $-8x = 6$

$$\frac{-8x}{-8} = \frac{6}{-8}$$

$$x = -\frac{6}{8} = -\frac{3}{4}$$

Check:

$$-8\left(-\frac{3}{4}\right) = 6$$

$$\frac{24}{4} = 6$$

$$6 = 6$$

The solution is $-\frac{3}{4}$, or the solution set

is $\left\{-\frac{3}{4}\right\}$.

15. $17y = 0$

$$\frac{17y}{17} = \frac{0}{17}$$

$$y = 0$$

Check:

$$17(0) = 0$$

$$0 = 0$$

The solution is 0, or the solution set is

$\{0\}$.

17. $\frac{2}{3}y = 12$

$$\frac{3}{2}\left(\frac{2}{3}y\right) = \frac{3}{2}(12)$$

$$1y = \frac{3}{2} \cdot \frac{12}{1} = \frac{36}{2}$$

$$y = 18$$

Check:

$$\frac{2}{3}(18) = 12$$

$$\frac{2}{3} \cdot \frac{18}{1} = 12$$

$$\frac{36}{3} = 12$$

$$12 = 12$$

The solution is 18, or the solution set is

$\{18\}$.

39

19.
$$28 = -\frac{7}{2}x$$
$$-\frac{2}{7}(28) = -\frac{2}{7}\left(-\frac{7}{2}x\right)$$
$$-\frac{56}{7} = 1x$$
$$-8 = x$$

Check:
$$28 = -\frac{7}{2}(-8)$$
$$28 = \frac{56}{2}$$
$$28 = 28$$

The solution is -8, or the solution set is $\{-8\}$.

21.
$$-x = 17$$
$$-1x = 17$$
$$-1(-1x) = -1(17)$$
$$x = -17$$

Check:
$$-(-17) = 17$$
$$17 = 17$$

The solution is -17, or the solution set is $\{-17\}$.

23.
$$-47 = -y$$
$$47 = y$$

Check:
$$-47 = -47$$

The solution is 47, or the solution set is $\{47\}$.

25.
$$-\frac{x}{5} = -9$$
$$5\left(-\frac{x}{5}\right) = 5(-9)$$
$$-x = -45$$
$$x = 45$$

Check:

$$-\frac{45}{5} = -9$$
$$-9 = -9$$

The solution is 45, or the solution set is $\{45\}$.

27.
$$2x - 12x = 50$$
$$(2 - 12)x = 50$$
$$-10x = 50$$
$$\frac{-10x}{-10} = \frac{50}{-10}$$
$$x = -5$$

Check:
$$2(-5) - 12(-5) = 50$$
$$-10 + 60 = 50$$
$$50 = 50$$

The solution is -5, or the solution set is $\{-5\}$.

29.
$$2x + 1 = 11$$
$$2x + 1 - 1 = 11 - 1$$
$$2x = 10$$
$$\frac{2x}{2} = \frac{10}{2}$$
$$x = 5$$

Check:
$$2(5) + 1 = 11$$
$$10 + 1 = 11$$
$$11 = 11$$

The solution is 5, or the solution set is $\{5\}$.

31.

$$2x - 3 = 9$$
$$2x - 3 + 3 = 9 + 3$$
$$2x = 12$$
$$\frac{2x}{2} = \frac{12}{2}$$
$$x = 6$$

Check:
$$2(6) - 3 = 9$$
$$12 - 3 = 9$$
$$9 = 9$$

The solution is 6, or the solution set is $\{6\}$.

33.

$$-2y + 5 = 7$$
$$-2y + 5 - 5 = 7 - 5$$
$$-2y = 2$$
$$\frac{-2y}{2} = \frac{2}{-2}$$
$$y = -1$$

Check:
$$-2(-1) + 5 = 7$$
$$2 + 5 = 7$$
$$7 = 7$$

The solution is -1, or the solution set is $\{-1\}$.

35.

$$-3y - 7 = -1$$
$$-3y - 7 + 7 = -1 + 7$$
$$-3y = 6$$
$$\frac{-3y}{-3} = \frac{6}{-3}$$
$$y = -2$$

Check:
$$-3(-2) - 7 = -1$$
$$6 - 7 = -1$$
$$-1 = -1$$

The solution is -2, or the solution set is $\{-2\}$.

37.

$$12 = 4z + 3$$
$$12 - 3 = 4z + 3 - 3$$
$$9 = 4z$$
$$\frac{9}{4} = \frac{4z}{4}$$
$$\frac{9}{4} = z$$

Check:
$$12 = 4\left(\frac{9}{4}\right) + 3$$
$$12 = 9 + 3$$
$$12 = 12$$

The solution is $\frac{9}{4}$, or the solution set is $\left\{\frac{9}{4}\right\}$.

39.

$$-x - 3 = 3$$
$$-x - 3 + 3 = 3 + 3$$
$$-x = 6$$
$$x = -6$$

Check:
$$-(-6) - 3 = 3$$
$$6 - 3 = 3$$
$$3 = 3$$

The solution is -6, or the solution set is $\{-6\}$.

41

41.
$$6y = 2y - 12$$
$$6y + 12 = 2y - 12 + 12$$
$$6y + 12 = 2y$$
$$6y + 12 - 6y = 2y - 6y$$
$$12 = -4y$$
$$\frac{12}{-4} = \frac{-4y}{-4}$$
$$-3 = y$$

Check:
$$6(-3) = 2(-3) - 12$$
$$-18 = -6 - 12$$
$$-18 = -18$$

The solution is -3, or the solution set is $\{-3\}$.

43.
$$3z = -2z - 15$$
$$3z + 2z = -2z - 15 + 2z$$
$$5z = -15$$
$$\frac{5z}{5} = \frac{-15}{3}$$
$$z = -3$$

Check:
$$3(-3) = -2(-3) - 15$$
$$-9 = 6 - 15$$
$$-9 = -9$$

The solution is -3, or the solution set is $\{-3\}$.

45.
$$-5x = -2x - 12$$
$$-5x + 2x = -2x - 12 + 2x$$
$$-3x = -12$$
$$\frac{-3x}{3} = \frac{-12}{-3}$$
$$x = 4$$

Check:
$$-5(4) = 2(4) - 12$$
$$-20 = -8 - 12$$
$$-20 = -20$$

The solution is 4, or the solution set is $\{4\}$.

47.
$$8y + 4 = 2y - 5$$
$$8y + 4 - 2y = 2y - 5 - 2y$$
$$6y + 4 = -5$$
$$6y + 4 - 4 = -5 - 4$$
$$6y = -9$$
$$\frac{6y}{6} = \frac{-9}{6}$$
$$y = -\frac{3}{2}$$

Check:
$$8\left(-\frac{3}{2}\right) + 4 = 2\left(-\frac{3}{2}\right) - 5$$
$$-12 + 4 = -3 - 5$$
$$-8 = -8$$

The solution is $-\frac{3}{2}$, or the solution set is $\left\{-\frac{3}{2}\right\}$.

49.

$$6z - 5 = z + 5$$
$$6z - 5 - z = z + 5 - z$$
$$5z - 5 = 5$$
$$5z - 5 + 5 = 5 + 5$$
$$5z = 10$$
$$\frac{5z}{5} = \frac{10}{5}$$
$$z = 2$$

Check:
$$6(2) - 5 = 2 + 5$$
$$12 - 5 = 2 + 5$$
$$7 = 7$$

The solution is 2, or the solution set is $\{2\}$.

51.

$$6x + 14 = 2x - 2$$
$$6x - 2x + 14 = -2$$
$$4x = -2 - 14$$
$$4x = -16$$
$$x = -4$$

Check:
$$6(-4) + 14 = 2(-4) - 2$$
$$-24 + 14 = -8 - 2$$
$$-10 = -10$$

The solution is −4, or the solution set is $\{-4\}$.

53.

$$-3y - 1 = 5 - 2y$$
$$-3y + 2y - 1 = 5$$
$$-y = 5 + 1$$
$$-y = 6$$
$$y = -6$$

Check:
$$-3(-6) - 1 = 5 - 2(-6)$$
$$18 - 1 = 5 + 12$$
$$17 = 17$$

The solution is −6, or the solution set is $\{-6\}$.

55.

$$\frac{x}{\square} = \triangle$$
$$\square \cdot \frac{x}{\square} = \triangle \cdot \square$$
$$x = \triangle \square$$

56.

$$\triangle = \square x$$
$$\frac{\triangle}{\square} = \frac{\square x}{\square}$$
$$\frac{\triangle}{\square} = x$$

57.

$$\triangle = -x$$
$$\triangle(-1) = -x(-1)$$
$$-\triangle = x$$

58.

$$\frac{-x}{\square} = \triangle$$
$$-\square \cdot \frac{-x}{\square} = -\square \cdot \triangle$$
$$x = -\square \cdot \triangle$$

59.

$$6x = 10$$
$$\frac{6x}{6} = \frac{10}{6}$$
$$x = \frac{10}{6} = \frac{5}{3}$$

The number is $\frac{5}{3}$.

60.

$$-6x = 20$$
$$\frac{-6x}{-6} = \frac{20}{-6}$$
$$x = \frac{20}{-6} = -\frac{10}{3}$$

The number is $-\frac{10}{3}$.

61.

$$\frac{x}{-9} = 5$$
$$\frac{x}{-9}(-9) = 5(-9)$$
$$x = -45$$

The number is −45.

43

62.
$$\frac{x}{-7} = 8$$

$$-7 \cdot \frac{x}{-7} = -7 \cdot 8$$

$$x = -56$$

The number is -56.

63.
$$M = \frac{n}{5}; M = 2$$

$$M = \frac{n}{5}$$

$$2 = \frac{n}{5}$$

$$5(2) = 5\left(\frac{n}{5}\right)$$

$$10 = n$$

If you are 2 miles away from the lightening flash, it will take 10 seconds for the sound of thunder to reach you.

65.
$$M = \frac{A}{740}; M = 2.03$$

$$M = \frac{A}{740}$$

$$2.03 = \frac{A}{740}$$

$$740(2.03) = 740\left(\frac{A}{740}\right)$$

$$1502.2 = A$$

The speed is 1502.2 miles per hour.

67.
$$P = -0.5d + 100; P = 70$$

$$P = -0.5d + 100$$

$$70 = -0.5d + 100$$

$$70 - 100 = -0.5d + 100 - 100$$

$$-30 = -0.5d$$

$$\frac{-30}{-0.5} = \frac{-0.5d}{-0.5}$$

$$60 = d$$

The parallel distance of separation is 60 yards.

For Exercises 69-71, answers will vary.

73. Statement d is true since the solution to $6x = 0$ is 0, which is not a natural number.

75. Answers will vary. As an example, start with an integer solution, such as 10, and set it equal to x. That is, we have $x = 10$. The solution was obtained by multiplying both sides by $\frac{4}{5}$. To undo this, we multiply both sides of our equation by the reciprocal, $\frac{5}{4}$. This give,

$$\frac{5}{4}x = \frac{5}{4}(10)$$

$$\frac{5}{4}x = \frac{25}{2}$$

Therefore, an example equation would be $\frac{5}{4}x = \frac{25}{2}$.

77.
$$-72.8y - 14.6 = -455.43 - 4.98y$$

$$-72.8y - 14.6 + 4.98y =$$
$$-455.43 - 4.98y + 4.98y$$

$$-67.82y - 14.6 = -455.43$$

$$-67.82y - 14.6 + 14.6 = -455.43 + 14.6$$

$$-67.82y = -440.83$$

$$\frac{-67.82y}{-67.82} = \frac{-440.83}{-67.82}$$

$$y = 6.5$$

The solution is 6.5, or the solution set is $\{6.5\}$.

78. $(-10)^2 = (-10)(-10) = 100$

79. $-10^2 = -10 \cdot 10 = -100$

80. $x^3 - 4x; x = -1$

$$x^3 - 4x = (-1)^3 - 4(-1) = -1 + 4 = 3$$

2.3 Exercise Set

For exercises 1-45, students should check the proposed solutions. The checks will not be shown here.

1.
$$5x + 3x - 4x = 10 + 2$$
$$8x - 4x = 12$$
$$4x = 12$$
$$\frac{4x}{4} = \frac{12}{4}$$
$$x = 3$$
The solution set is $\{3\}$.

3.
$$4x - 9x + 22 = 3x + 30$$
$$-5x + 22 = 3x + 30$$
$$-5x - 3x + 22 = 30$$
$$-8x + 22 = 30$$
$$-8x = 30 - 22$$
$$-8x = 8$$
$$\frac{-8x}{-8} = \frac{8}{-8}$$
$$x = -1$$
The solution set is $\{-1\}$.

5.
$$3x + 6 - x = 8 + 3x - 6$$
$$2x + 6 = 2 + 3x$$
$$2x + 6 - 2 = 2 + 3x - 2$$
$$2x + 4 = 3x$$
$$2x + 4 - 2x = 3x - 2x$$
$$4 = x$$
The solution set is $\{4\}$.

7.
$$4(x + 1) = 20$$
$$4x + 4 = 20$$
$$4x = 20 - 4$$
$$4x = 16$$
$$\frac{4x}{4} = \frac{16}{4}$$
$$x = 4$$
The solution set is $\{4\}$.

9.
$$7(2x - 1) = 42$$
$$14x - 7 = 42$$
$$14x - 7 + 7 = 42 + 7$$
$$14x = 49$$
$$\frac{14x}{14} = \frac{49}{14}$$
$$x = \frac{7}{2}$$
The solution set is $\left\{\frac{7}{2}\right\}$.

11.
$$38 = 30 - 2(x - 1)$$
$$38 = 30 - 2x + 2$$
$$38 = 32 - 2x$$
$$38 - 32 = -2x$$
$$6 = -2x$$
$$\frac{6}{-2} = \frac{-2x}{-2}$$
$$-3 = x$$
The solution set is $\{-3\}$.

13.
$$2(4z + 3) - 8 = 46$$
$$8z + 6 - 8 = 46$$
$$8z - 2 = 46$$
$$8z - 2 + 2 = 46 + 2$$
$$8z = 48$$
$$\frac{8z}{3} = \frac{48}{8}$$
$$z = 6$$
The solution set is $\{6\}$.

15.
$$6x - (3x + 10) = 14$$
$$6x - 3x - 10 = 14$$
$$3x - 10 = 14$$
$$3x - 10 + 10 = 14 + 10$$
$$3x = 24$$
$$\frac{3x}{3} = \frac{24}{3}$$
$$x = 8$$
The solution set is $\{8\}$.

45

17.
$$5(2x+1)=12x-3$$
$$10x+5=12x-3$$
$$10x-10x+5=12x-10x-3$$
$$5=2x-3$$
$$5+3=2x-3+3$$
$$8=2x$$
$$\frac{8}{2}=\frac{2x}{2}$$
$$x=4$$
The solution set is {4}

19.
$$3(5-x)=4(2x+1)$$
$$15-3x=8x+4$$
$$15-3x-8x=8x+4-8x$$
$$15-11x=4$$
$$15-11x-15=4-15$$
$$-11x=-11$$
$$\frac{-11x}{-11}=\frac{-11}{-11}$$
$$x=1$$
The solution set is {1}.

21.
$$8(y+2)=2(3y+4)$$
$$8y+16=6y+8$$
$$8y+16-16=6y+8-16$$
$$8y=6y-8$$
$$8y-6y=6y-8-6y$$
$$2y=-8$$
$$y=-4$$
The solution set is {−4}.

23.
$$3(x+1)=7(x-2)-3$$
$$3x+3=7x-14-3$$
$$3x+3=7x-17$$
$$3x+3-3=7x-17-3$$
$$3x=7x-20$$
$$3x-7x=7x-20-7x$$
$$-4x=-20$$
$$\frac{-4x}{-4}=\frac{-20}{-4}$$
$$x=5$$
The solution set is {5}.

25.
$$5(2x-8)-2=5(x-3)+3$$
$$10x-40-2=5x-15+3$$
$$10x-42=5x-12$$
$$10x-42+42=5x-12+42$$
$$10x=5x+30$$
$$10x=5x+30-5x$$
$$5x=30$$
$$\frac{5x}{5}=\frac{30}{5}$$
$$x=6$$
The solution set is {6}.

27.
$$6=-4(1-x)+3(x+1)$$
$$6=-4+4x+3x+3$$
$$6=-1+7x$$
$$6+1=-1+7x+1$$
$$7=7x$$
$$\frac{7}{7}=\frac{7x}{7}$$
$$1=x$$
The solution set is {1}.

29. $10(z+4)-4(z-2)=3(z-1)+2(z-3)$

$10z+40-4z+8=3z-3+2z-6$

$6z+48=5z-9$

$6z+48-48=5z-9-48$

$6z-5z=5z-57-5z$

$z=-57$

The solution set is $\{-57\}$.

31. $\dfrac{x}{5}-4=-6$

To clear the equation of fractions, multiply both sides by the least common denominator (LCD), which is 5.

$5\left(\dfrac{x}{5}-4\right)=5(-6)$

$5\cdot\dfrac{x}{5}-5\cdot 4=-30$

$x-20=-30$

$x-20+20=-30+20$

$x=-10$

The solution set is $\{-10\}$.

33. $\dfrac{2x}{3}-5=7$

LCD = 3

$3\left(\dfrac{2}{3}x-5\right)=3(7)$

$3\cdot\dfrac{2}{3}x-3\cdot 5=21$

$2x-15=21$

$2x-15+15=21+15$

$2x=36$

$\dfrac{2x}{2}=\dfrac{36}{2}$

$x=18$

The solution set is $\{18\}$.

35. $\dfrac{2y}{3}-\dfrac{3}{4}=\dfrac{5}{12}$

LCD = 12

$12\left(\dfrac{2y}{3}-\dfrac{3}{4}\right)=12\left(\dfrac{5}{12}\right)$

$12\left(\dfrac{2y}{3}\right)-12\left(\dfrac{3}{4}\right)=5$

$8y-9=5$

$8y-9+9=5+9$

$8y=14$

$\dfrac{8y}{8}=\dfrac{14}{8}$

$y=\dfrac{14}{8}=\dfrac{7}{4}$

The solution set is $\left\{\dfrac{7}{4}\right\}$.

37. $\dfrac{x}{3}+\dfrac{x}{2}=\dfrac{5}{6}$, LCD = 6

$6\left(\dfrac{x}{3}+\dfrac{x}{2}\right)=6\left(\dfrac{5}{6}\right)$

$2x+3x=5$

$5x=5$

$\dfrac{5x}{5}=\dfrac{5}{5}$

$x=1$

The solution set is $\{1\}$.

39. $20-\dfrac{z}{3}=\dfrac{z}{2}$, LCD = 6

$6\left(20-\dfrac{z}{3}\right)=6\left(\dfrac{z}{2}\right)$

$120-2z=3z$

$120-2z+2z=3z+2z$

$120=5z$

$\dfrac{120}{5}=\dfrac{5z}{5}$

$24=z$

The solution set is $\{24\}$.

41.

$$\frac{y}{3} + \frac{2}{5} = \frac{y}{5} - \frac{2}{5}$$

LCD = 15

$$15\left(\frac{y}{3} + \frac{2}{5}\right) = 15\left(\frac{y}{5} + \frac{2}{5}\right)$$

$$15\left(\frac{y}{3}\right) + 15\left(\frac{2}{5}\right) = 15\left(\frac{y}{5}\right) + 15\left(-\frac{2}{5}\right)$$

$$5y + 6 = 3y - 6$$

$$5y + 6 - 3y = 3y - 6 - 3y$$

$$2y + 6 = -6$$

$$2y + 6 - 6 = -6 - 6$$

$$2y = -12$$

$$\frac{2y}{2} = \frac{-12}{2}$$

$$y = -6$$

The solution set is $\{-6\}$.

43.

$$\frac{3x}{4} - 3 = \frac{x}{2} + 2$$

LCD = 8

$$8\left(\frac{3x}{4} - 3\right) = 8\left(\frac{x}{2} + 2\right)$$

$$8\left(\frac{3x}{4}\right) - 8 \cdot 3 = 8\left(\frac{x}{2}\right) + 8 \cdot 2$$

$$6x - 24 = 4x + 16$$

$$6x - 24 - 4x = 4x + 16 - 4x$$

$$2x - 24 = 16$$

$$2x - 24 + 24 = 16 + 24$$

$$2x = 40$$

$$\frac{2x}{2} = \frac{40}{2}$$

$$x = 20$$

The solution set is $\{20\}$.

45.

$$\frac{x-3}{5} - 1 = \frac{x-5}{4}$$

LCD = $4 \cdot 5 = 20$

$$(20)\left(\frac{x-3}{5} - 1\right) = 20\left(\frac{x-5}{4}\right)$$

$$4(x-3) - 20 = 5(x-5)$$

$$4x - 12 - 20 = 5x - 25$$

$$4x - 5x - 32 = 5x - 5x - 25$$

$$-x - 32 = -25$$

$$-x - 32 + 32 = -25 + 32$$

$$-x = 7$$

$$-1(-x) = -1(7)$$

$$x = -7$$

The solution set is $\{-7\}$.

47.

$$3x - 7 = 3(x+1)$$

$$3x - 7 = 3x + 3$$

$$3x - 7 - 3x = 3x + 3 - 3x$$

$$-7 = 3$$

The original equation is equivalent to the false statement $-7 = 3$, so the equation is inconsistent and has no solution. The solution set is $\{\ \}$ or $\varnothing$.

49.

$$2(x+4) = 4x + 5 - 2x + 3$$

$$2x + 8 = 2x + 8$$

$$2x - 8 - 2x = 2x + 8 - 2x$$

$$8 = 8$$

The original equation is equivalent to the true statement $8 = 8$, so the equation is an identity and all real numbers are solutions. The solution set is $\mathbb{R}$.

51.
$$7+2(3x-5)=8-3(2x+1)$$
$$7+6x-10=8-6x-3$$
$$6x-3=5-6x$$
$$6x+6x-3=5-6x+6x$$
$$12x-3=5$$
$$12x-3+3=5+3$$
$$12x=8$$
$$\frac{12x}{12}=\frac{8}{12}$$
$$x=\frac{2}{3}$$
The solution set is $\left\{\frac{2}{3}\right\}$.

53.
$$4x+1-5x=5-(x+4)$$
$$-x+1=5-x-4$$
$$-x+1=1-x$$
$$-x+1+x=1-x+x$$
$$1=1$$
Since $1=1$ is a true statement, the original equation is an identity and all real numbers are solutions. The solution set is $\mathbb{R}$.

55.
$$4(x+2)+1=7x-3(x-2)$$
$$4x+8+1=7x-3x+6$$
$$4x+9=4x+6$$
$$4x-4x+9=4x-4x+6$$
$$9=6$$
Since $9=6$ is a false statement, the original equation is inconsistent and has no solution. The solution set is $\{\ \}$ or $\varnothing$.

57.
$$3-x=2x+3$$
$$3-x+x=2x+x+3$$
$$3=3x+3$$
$$3-3=3x+3-3$$
$$0=3x$$
$$\frac{0}{3}=\frac{3x}{3}$$
$$0=x$$
The solution set is $\{0\}$.

59.
$$\frac{x}{3}+2=\frac{x}{3}$$
Multiply by the LCD, which is 6.
$$6\left(\frac{x}{3}+2\right)=6\left(\frac{x}{3}\right)$$
$$2x+12=2x$$
$$2x+12-2x=2x-2x$$
$$12=0$$
Since $12=0$ is a false statement, the original equation has no solution. The solution set is $\{\ \}$ or $\varnothing$.

61.
$$\frac{x}{2}-\frac{x}{4}+4=x+4$$
$$\text{LCD}=4$$
$$4\left(\frac{x}{2}-\frac{x}{4}+4\right)=4(x+4)$$
$$4\left(\frac{x}{2}\right)-4\left(\frac{x}{4}\right)+16=4x+16$$
$$2x-x+16=4x+16$$
$$x+16=4x+16$$
$$x-x+16=4x-x+16$$
$$16=3x+16$$
$$16-16=3x+16-16$$
$$0=3x$$
$$\frac{0}{3}=\frac{3x}{3}$$
$$0=x$$
The solution set is $\{0\}$.

49

63.

$$\frac{2}{3}x = 2 - \frac{5}{6}x$$

LCD = 6

$$6\left(\frac{2}{3}x\right) = 6(2) - 6\left(\frac{5}{6}x\right)$$

$$2(2x) = 12 - 5x$$

$$4x = 12 - 5x$$

$$4x + 5x = 12 - 5x + 5x$$

$$9x = 12$$

$$\frac{9x}{9} = \frac{12}{9}$$

$$x = \frac{12}{9} = \frac{4}{3}$$

The solution set is $\left\{\frac{4}{3}\right\}$.

65.

$$\frac{x}{\square} + \triangle = \$$$

$$\frac{x}{\square} + \triangle - \triangle = \$ - \triangle$$

$$\frac{x}{\square} = \$ - \triangle$$

$$\square\left(\frac{x}{\square}\right) = \square(\$ - \triangle)$$

$$x = \square\$ - \square\triangle$$

66.

$$\frac{x}{\square} - \triangle = -\$$$

$$\frac{x}{\square} - \triangle + \triangle = -\$ + \triangle$$

$$\frac{x}{\square} = -\$ + \triangle$$

$$\square \cdot \frac{x}{\square} = \square(-\$ + \triangle)$$

$$x = -\square\$ + \square\triangle$$

67.

$$\frac{x}{5} - 2 = \frac{x}{3}$$

$$\frac{x}{5} - \frac{x}{5} - 2 = \frac{x}{3} - \frac{x}{5}$$

$$-2 = \frac{5x}{15} - \frac{3x}{15}$$

$$-2 = \frac{2x}{15}$$

$$15(-2) = 15\left(\frac{2x}{15}\right)$$

$$-30 = 2x$$

$$\frac{-30}{2} = \frac{2x}{2}$$

$$-15 = x$$

If $x = -15$, evaluate $x^2 - x$.

$$(-15)^2 - (-15) = 225 + 15 = 240$$

68.

$$\frac{3x}{2} + \frac{3x}{4} = \frac{x}{4} - 4$$

LCD = 4

$$4\left(\frac{3x}{2} + \frac{3x}{4}\right) = 4\left(\frac{x}{4} - 4\right)$$

$$6x + 3x = x - 16$$

$$9x = x - 16$$

$$9x - x = x - 16 - x$$

$$8x = -16$$

$$\frac{8x}{8} = \frac{-16}{8}$$

$$x = -2$$

If $x = -2$, evaluate $x^2 - x$.

$$(-2)^2 - (-2) = 4 + 2 = 6$$

69.

$$\frac{1}{3}x + \frac{1}{5}x = 16$$
$$\text{LCD} = 15$$
$$15\left(\frac{1}{3}x\right) + 15\left(\frac{1}{5}x\right) = 15(16)$$
$$5x + 3x = 240$$
$$8x = 240$$
$$\frac{8x}{8} = \frac{240}{8}$$
$$x = 30$$

The number is 30.

70.

$$\frac{2}{5}x + \frac{1}{4}x = 13$$
$$\text{LCD} = 20$$
$$20\left(\frac{2}{5}x + \frac{1}{4}x\right) = 20(13)$$
$$8x + 5x = 260$$
$$13x = 260$$
$$\frac{13x}{13} = \frac{260}{13}$$
$$x = 20$$

The number is 20.

71.

$$\frac{3}{4}x - 3 = \frac{1}{2}x$$
$$\text{LCD} = 4$$
$$4\left(\frac{3}{4}x\right) - 4(3) = 4\left(\frac{1}{2}x\right)$$
$$3x - 12 = 2x$$
$$3x - 2x - 12 = 2x - 2x$$
$$x - 12 = 0$$
$$x - 12 + 12 = 0 + 12$$
$$x = 12$$

The number is 12.

72.

$$\frac{7}{8}x - 30 = \frac{1}{2}x, \quad \text{LCD} = 8$$
$$8\left(\frac{7}{8}x - 30\right) = 8\left(\frac{1}{2}x\right)$$
$$7x - 240 = 4x$$
$$7x - 240 - 7x = 4x - 7x$$
$$-240 = -3x$$
$$\frac{-240}{-3} = \frac{-3x}{-3}$$
$$80 = x$$

The number is 80.

73.

$$F = 10(x - 65) + 50; \ F = 250$$
$$F = 10(x - 65) + 50$$
$$250 = 10(x - 65) + 50$$
$$250 - 50 = 10(x - 65) + 50 - 50$$
$$200 = 10x - 650$$
$$200 + 650 = 10x - 650 + 650$$
$$850 = 10x$$
$$\frac{850}{10} = \frac{10x}{10}$$
$$85 = x$$

A person receiving a $250 fine was driving 85 miles per hour.

75. Substitute 10 for D in the low humor formula. The LCD is 9.

$$10 = \frac{10}{9}N + \frac{53}{9}$$
$$9(10) = 9\left(\frac{10}{9}N\right) + 9\left(\frac{53}{9}\right)$$
$$90 = 10N + 53$$
$$90 - 53 = 10N + 53 - 53$$
$$37 = 10N$$
$$\frac{37}{10} = \frac{10N}{10}$$
$$3.7 = N$$

The intensity of the event was 3.7. This is shown as the point (3.7, 10) on the graph.

77. $p = 15 + \frac{5d}{11}$; $p = 201$

$$201 = 15 + \frac{5d}{11}$$

$$201 - 15 = 15 + \frac{5d}{11} - 15$$

$$186 = \frac{5d}{11}$$

$$11(186) = 11\left(\frac{5d}{11}\right)$$

$$2046 = 5d$$

$$\frac{2046}{5} = d \text{ or } 409.2 = d$$

He descended to a depth of 409.2 feet below the surface.

For Exercises 79-81, answers will vary.

83. Statement c is true. The solution to the linear equation is -3. When -3 is substituted into $y^2 + 2y - 3$, the result is 0.

85. $\dfrac{2x-3}{9} + \dfrac{x-3}{2} = \dfrac{x+5}{6} - 1$

LCD = 18

$$18\left(\frac{2x-3}{9} + \frac{x-3}{2}\right) = 18\left(\frac{x+5}{6} - 1\right)$$

$$18\left(\frac{2x-3}{9}\right) + 18\left(\frac{x-3}{2}\right) = 18\left(\frac{x+5}{6}\right) - 18 \cdot 1$$

$$2(2x-3) + 9(x-3) = 3(x+5) - 18$$

$$4x - 6 + 9x - 27 = 3x + 15 - 18$$

$$13x - 33 = 3x - 3$$

$$13x - 33 - 3x = 3x - 3 - 3x$$

$$10x - 33 = -3$$

$$10x - 33 + 33 = -3 + 33$$

$$10x = 30$$

$$\frac{10x}{10} = \frac{30}{10}$$

$$x = 3$$

Check:

$$\frac{2(3)-3}{9} + \frac{3-3}{2} = \frac{3+5}{6} - 1$$

$$\frac{6-4}{9} + \frac{0}{2} = \frac{8}{6} - 1$$

$$\frac{3}{9} + 0 = \frac{4}{3} - 1$$

$$\frac{1}{3} = \frac{1}{3}$$

The solution set is $\{3\}$.

87. $2.24y - 9.28 = 5.74y + 5.42$

$$2.24y - 9.28 - 5.74y = 5.74y + 5.42 - 5.74y$$

$$-3.5y - 9.25 = 5.42$$

$$-3.5y - 9.28 + 9.28 = 5.42 + 9.28$$

$$-3.5y = 14.7$$

$$\frac{-3.5y}{-3.5} = \frac{14.7}{-3.5}$$

$$y = -4.2$$

The solution set is $\{-4.2\}$

89. $-24 < -20$; -24 is to the left of -20 on the number line, so -24 is less than -20.

90. $-\frac{1}{3} < -\frac{1}{5}$; $-\frac{1}{3}$ is to the left of $-\frac{1}{5}$ on the number line, so $-\frac{1}{3}$ is less than $-\frac{1}{5}$.

To compare these numbers, write them with a common denominator:

$$-\frac{1}{3} = -\frac{5}{15}, -\frac{1}{5} = -\frac{3}{15}.$$

91. $-9 - 11 + 7 - (-3)$

$$= (-9) + (-11) + 7 + 3$$

$$= (7+3) + \left[(-9) + (-11)\right]$$

$$= 10 + (-20)$$

$$= -10$$

2.4 Exercise Set

1. $d = rt$ for r

$$\frac{d}{t} = \frac{rt}{t}$$

$$\frac{d}{t} = r \text{ or } r = \frac{d}{t}$$

This is the distance traveled formula:
distance = rate · time.

3. $I = Prt$ for P

$$\frac{I}{rt} = \frac{Prt}{rt}$$

$$\frac{I}{rt} = P \text{ or } P = \frac{I}{rt}$$

This is the formula for simple interest:
interest = principal · rate · time.

5. $C = 2\pi r$ for r

$$\frac{C}{2\pi} = \frac{2\pi r}{2\pi}$$

$$\frac{C}{2\pi} = r \text{ or } r = \frac{C}{2\pi}$$

This is the formula for finding the
circumference of a circle if you know
its radius.

7. $E = mc^2$

$$\frac{E}{c^2} = \frac{mc^2}{c^2}$$

$$\frac{E}{c^2} = m \text{ or } m = \frac{E}{c^2}$$

This is Einstein's formula relating
energy, mass, and the speed of light.

9. $y = mx + b$ for m

$$y - b = mx$$

$$\frac{y-b}{x} = \frac{mx}{x}$$

$$\frac{y-b}{x} = m \text{ or } m = \frac{y-b}{x}$$

This is the slope-intercept formula for
the equation of a line. (This formula
will be discussed later in the textbook.)

11. $T = D + pm$ for p

$$T - D = D + pm - D$$

$$T - D = pm$$

$$\frac{T-D}{m} = \frac{pm}{m}$$

$$\frac{T-D}{m} = p \text{ or } p = \frac{T-D}{m}$$

13.

$$A = \frac{1}{2}bh \text{ for } b$$

$$2A = 2\left(\frac{1}{2}bh\right)$$

$$2A = bh$$

$$\frac{2A}{h} = \frac{bh}{h}$$

$$\frac{2A}{h} = b \text{ or } b = \frac{2A}{h}$$

This is the formula for the area of a
triangle: area = $\frac{1}{2}$ · base · height.

15.

$$M = \frac{n}{5} \text{ for } n$$

$$5M = 5\left(\frac{n}{5}\right)$$

$$5M = n \text{ or } n = 5M$$

53

17. $\dfrac{c}{2} + 80 = 2F$ for c

$$\dfrac{c}{2} + 80 - 80 = 2F - 80$$

$$\dfrac{c}{2} = 2F - 80$$

$$2\left(\dfrac{c}{2}\right) = 2(2F - 80)$$

$$c = 4F - 160$$

19. $A = \dfrac{1}{2}(a + b)$ for a

$$2A = 2\left[\dfrac{1}{2}(a + b)\right]$$

$$2A = a + b$$

$$2A - b = a + b - b$$

$$2A - b = a \text{ or } a = 2A - b$$

This is the formula for finding the average of two numbers.

21. $S = P + Prt$ for r

$$S - P = P + Prt - P$$

$$S - P = Prt$$

$$\dfrac{S - P}{Pt} = \dfrac{Prt}{Pt}$$

$$\dfrac{S - P}{Pt} = r \text{ or } r = \dfrac{S - P}{Pt}$$

This is the formula for finding the total amount owed (or earned) using simple interest.

Total = Principle + Interest

23. $A = \dfrac{1}{2}h(a + b)$ for b

$$2A = 2\left[\dfrac{1}{2}h(a + b)\right]$$

$$2A = h(a + b)$$

$$2A = ha + hb$$

$$2A - ha = ha + hb - ha$$

$$2A - ha = hb$$

$$\dfrac{2A - ha}{h} = \dfrac{hb}{h}$$

$$\dfrac{2A - ha}{h} = b \text{ or } b = \dfrac{2A}{h} - a$$

This is the formula for the area of a trapezoid.

25. $Ax + By = C$ for x

$$Ax + By - By = C - By$$

$$Ax = C - By$$

$$\dfrac{Ax}{A} = \dfrac{C - By}{A}$$

$$x = \dfrac{C - By}{A}$$

This is the standard form of the equation of a line.

27. To change a decimal number to a percent, move the decimal point two places to the right and add a percent sign. $0.89 = 89\%$

29. $0.002 = 0.2\%$

31. $4.78 = 478\%$

33. $100 = 10,000\%$

35. To change a percent to a decimal number, move the decimal point two places to the left and remove the percent sign. $27\% = 0.27$

37. $63.4\% = 0.634$

39. $170\% = 1.7$

41. $3\% = 0.03$

43. $\dfrac{1}{2}\% = 0.5\% = 0.005$

45. $A = PB;\ P = 3\% = 0.03, B = 200$

$A = PB$

$A = 0.03 \cdot 200$

$A = 6$

3% of 200 is 6.

47. $A = PB;\ P = 18\% = 0.18,\ B = 40$

$A = PB$

$A = 0.18 \cdot 40$

$A = 7.2$

18% of 40 is 7.2.

49. $A = PB;\ A = 3, P = 60\% = 0.6$

$A = PB$

$3 = 0.6 \cdot B$

$\dfrac{3}{0.6} = \dfrac{0.6B}{0.6}$

$5 = B$

3 is 60% of 5.

51. $A = PB;\ A = 40.8, P = 24\% = 0.24$

$A = PB$

$40.8 = 0.24 \cdot B$

$\dfrac{40.8}{0.24} = \dfrac{0.24B}{0.24}$

$170 = B$

24% of 170 is 40.8.

53. $A = PB;\ A = 3,\ B = 15$

$A = PB$

$3 = P \cdot 15$

$\dfrac{3}{15} = \dfrac{P \cdot 15}{15}$

$0.2 = P$

$0.2 = 20\%$

3 is 20% of 15.

55. $A = PB;\ A = 0.3,\ B = 2.5$

$A = PB$

$0.3 = P \cdot 2.5$

$\dfrac{0.3}{2.5} = \dfrac{P - 2.5}{2.5}$

$0.12 = P$

$0.12 = 12\%$

0.3 is 12% of 2.5.

57. Use the formula,

increase = percent · original.

The increase is $8 - 5 = 3$.

$3 = P \cdot 5$

$\dfrac{3}{5} = \dfrac{P \cdot 5}{5}$

$0.60 = P$

This is a 60% increase.

59. Use the formula, decrease = percent · original. The decrease is $4 - 1 = 3$.

$3 = P \cdot 4$

$\dfrac{3}{4} = \dfrac{P \cdot 4}{4}$

$0.75 = P$

This is a 75% decrease.

61.

$y = (a + b)x$

$\dfrac{y}{(a + b)} = \dfrac{(a + b)x}{(a + b)}$

$\dfrac{y}{a + b} = x$ or $x = \dfrac{y}{a + b}$

62.

$y = (a - b)x$

$\dfrac{y}{(a - b)} = \dfrac{(a - b)x}{(a - b)}$

$\dfrac{y}{a - b} = x$ or $x = \dfrac{y}{a - b}$

63.
$$y = (a-b)x + 5$$
$$y - 5 = (a-b)x + 5 - 5$$
$$y - 5 = (a-b)x$$
$$\frac{y-5}{a-b} = \frac{(a-b)x}{a-b}$$
$$\frac{y-5}{a-b} = x \quad \text{or} \quad x = \frac{y-5}{a-b}$$

64.
$$y = (a+b)x - 8$$
$$y + 8 = (a+b)x - 8 + 8$$
$$y + 8 = (a+b)x$$
$$\frac{y+8}{(a+b)} = \frac{(a+b)x}{(a+b)}$$
$$\frac{y+8}{a+b} = x \quad \text{or} \quad x = \frac{y+8}{a+b}$$

65.
$$y = cx + dx$$
$$y = (c+d)x$$
$$\frac{y}{c+d} = \frac{(c+d)x}{c+d}$$
$$\frac{y}{c+d} = x \quad \text{or} \quad x = \frac{y}{c+d}$$

66.
$$y = cx - dx$$
$$y = (c-d)x$$
$$\frac{y}{(c-d)} = \frac{(c-d)x}{(c-d)}$$
$$\frac{y}{c-d} = x \quad \text{or} \quad x = \frac{y}{c-d}$$

67.
$$y = Ax - Bx - C$$
$$y = (A-B)x - C$$
$$y + C = (A-B)x - C + C$$
$$y + C = (A-B)x$$
$$\frac{y+C}{A-B} = \frac{(A-B)x}{A-B}$$
$$\frac{y+C}{A-B} = x \quad \text{or} \quad x = \frac{y+C}{A-B}$$

68.
$$y = Ax + Bx + C$$
$$y - C = Ax + Bx + C - C$$
$$y - C = Ax + Bx$$
$$y - C = (A+B)x$$
$$\frac{y-C}{(A+B)} = \frac{(A+B)x}{(A+B)}$$
$$\frac{y-C}{A+B} = x \quad \text{or} \quad x = \frac{y-C}{A+B}$$

69. a.
$$A = \frac{x+y+z}{3} \text{ for } z$$
$$3A = 3\left(\frac{x+y+z}{3}\right)$$
$$3A = x + y + z$$
$$3A - x - y = x + y + z - x - y$$
$$3A - x - y = z$$

b. $A = 90, x = 86, y = 88$
$$z = 3A - x - y$$
$$z = 3(90) - 86 - 88 = 96$$

You need to get 96% on the third exam to have an average of 90%

71. a. $d = rt$ for t
$$\frac{d}{r} = \frac{rt}{r}$$
$$\frac{d}{r} = t$$

56

b.
$$t = \frac{d}{r}; \ d = 100, r = 40$$
$$t = \frac{100}{40} = 2.5$$

You would travel for 2.5 $\left(\text{or } 2\frac{1}{2}\right)$ hours.

73. $0.34 \cdot 1200 = 408$
408 single women would marry someone other than the perfect mate.

75.
$$A = P \cdot B$$
$$710,760 = 0.30B$$
$$\frac{710,760}{0.30} = \frac{0.30B}{0.30}$$
$$2,369,200 = B$$
The total number of deaths in 2002 was 2,369,200.

77.
$$A = P \cdot B$$
$$7080 = P \cdot 12,000$$
$$\frac{7080}{12,000} = \frac{P \cdot 12,000}{12,000}$$
$$0.59 = P$$
$0.59 = 59\%$ of hate crimes were motivated by race.

79. $A = PB; \ A = 7500, B = 60,000$
$$A = PB$$
$$7500 = P \cdot 60,000$$
$$\frac{7500}{60,000} = \frac{P \cdot 60,000}{60,000}$$
$$0.125 = P$$
The charity has raised $0.125 = 12.5\%$ of its goal.

81. $A = PB; \ p = 15\% = 0.15, B = 60$
$$A = PB$$
$$A = 0.15 \cdot 60 = 09$$
The tip was $9.

83. **a.** The sales tax is 6% of $16,800.
$$0.06(16,800) = 1008$$
The sales tax due on the car is $1008.

b. The total cost is the sum of the price of the car and the sales tax.
$$\$16,800 + \$1008 = \$17,808$$
The car's total cost is $17,808.

85. **a.** The discount is 12% of $860.
$$0.12(860) = 103.20$$
The discount amount is $103.20.

b. The sale price is the regular price minus the discount amount:
$$\$860 - \$103.20 = \$756.80.$$

87. Use the formula, decrease = percent · original. The decrease is $840 − $714 = $126.
$$126 = P \cdot 840$$
$$\frac{126}{840} = \frac{P \cdot 840}{840}$$
$$0.15 = P$$
This is a $0.15 = 15\%$ decrease.

89. Investment dollars decreased in year 1 are $0.30 \cdot \$10,000 = \$3000$. This means that $10,000 − $3000 = $7000 remains. Investment dollars increased in year 2 are $0.40 \cdot \$7000 = \$2800$. This means that $7000 + $2800 = $9800 of the original investment remains. This is an overall loss of $200 over the two years.
decrease = percent · original
$$200 = P \cdot 10,000$$
$$\frac{200}{10,000} = \frac{P \cdot 10,000}{10,000}$$
$$0.02 = P$$
The financial advisor is not using percentages properly. Instead of a 10% increase, this is a $0.02 = 2\%$ decrease.

For Exercises 91-95, answers will vary.

97. Statement d is true.

99. $v = -32t + 64; \; v = 16$

$16 = -32t + 64$

$-48 = -32t$

$\dfrac{-48}{-32} = \dfrac{-32t}{-32}$

$1.5 = t$

$h = -16t^2 + 64t; t = 1.5$

$h = -16(1.5^2) + 64(1.5) = 60$

When the velocity is 16 feet per second, the time is 1.5 seconds and the height is 60 feet.

100. $5x + 20 = 8x - 16$

$5x + 20 - 8x = 8x - 16 - 8x$

$-3x + 20 = -16$

$-3x + 20 - 20 = -16 - 20$

$-3x = -36$

$\dfrac{-3x}{-3} = \dfrac{-36}{-3}$

$x = 12$

Check:

$5(12) + 20 = 9(12) - 16$

$60 + 20 = 96 - 16$

$80 = 80$

The solution set is $\{12\}$.

101. $5(2y - 3) - 1 = 4(6 + 2y)$

$10y - 15 - 1 = 24 + 8y$

$10y - 16 = 24 + 8y$

$10y - 16 - 8y = 24 + 8y - 8y$

$2y - 16 = 24y$

$2y - 16 + 16 = 24 + 16$

$2y = 40$

$\dfrac{2y}{2} = \dfrac{40}{2}$

$y = 20$

Check:

$5(2 \cdot 20 - 3) - 1 = 4(6 + 2 \cdot 20)$

$5(40 - 3) - 1 = 4(6 + 40)$

$5(37) - 1 = 4(46)$

$185 - 1 = 184$

$184 = 184$

The solution set is $\{20\}$.

102. $x - 0.3x = 1x - 0.3x = (1 - 0.3)x = 0.7x$

Chapter 2 Mid-Chapter Check Points

1. $\dfrac{x}{2} = 12 - \dfrac{x}{4}$

The LCD is 4, so multiply both sides by 4.

$\dfrac{x}{2} = 12 - \dfrac{x}{4}$

$4\left(\dfrac{x}{2}\right) = 4(12) - 4\left(\dfrac{x}{4}\right)$

$2x = 48 - x$

$2x + x = 48 - x + x$

$3x = 48$

$\dfrac{3x}{3} = \dfrac{48}{3}$

$x = 16$

The solution set is $\{16\}$.

2.
$$5x - 42 = -57$$
$$5x - 42 + 42 = -57 + 42$$
$$5x = -15$$
$$\frac{5x}{5} = \frac{-15}{5}$$
$$x = -3$$
The solution set is $\{-3\}$.

3.
$$H = \frac{EC}{825}$$
$$H \cdot 825 = \frac{EC}{825} \cdot 825$$
$$825H = EC$$
$$\frac{825H}{E} = \frac{EC}{E}$$
$$\frac{825H}{E} = C$$

4.
$$A = P \cdot B$$
$$A = 0.06 \cdot 140$$
$$A = 8.4$$
8.4 is 6% of 140.

5.
$$\frac{-x}{10} = -3$$
$$10\left(\frac{-x}{10}\right) = 10(-3)$$
$$-x = -30$$
$$-1(-x) = -1(-30)$$
$$x = 30$$
The solution set is $\{30\}$.

6.
$$1 - 3(y - 5) = 4(2 - 3y)$$
$$1 - 3y + 15 = 8 - 12y$$
$$-3y + 16 = 8 - 12y$$
$$-3y + 12y + 16 = 8 - 12y + 12y$$
$$9y + 16 = 8$$
$$9y + 16 - 16 = 8 - 16$$
$$9y = -8$$
$$\frac{9y}{9} = \frac{-8}{9}$$
$$y = -\frac{8}{9}$$
The solution set is $\left\{-\frac{8}{9}\right\}$.

7.
$$S = 2\pi r h$$
$$\frac{S}{2\pi h} = \frac{2\pi r h}{2\pi h}$$
$$\frac{S}{2\pi h} = r$$

8.
$$A = P \cdot B$$
$$12 = 0.30 \cdot B$$
$$\frac{12}{0.30} = \frac{0.30 \cdot B}{0.30}$$
$$40 = B$$
12 is 30% of 40.

9.
$$\frac{3y}{5} + \frac{y}{2} = \frac{5y}{4} - 3$$
To clear fractions, multiply both sides by the LCD, 20.
$$20\left(\frac{3y}{5}\right) + 20\left(\frac{y}{2}\right) = 20\left(\frac{5y}{4}\right) - 20(3)$$
$$4(3y) + 10y = 5(5y) - 60$$
$$12y + 10y = 25y - 60$$
$$22y = 25y - 60$$
$$22y - 25y = 25y - 25y - 60$$
$$-3y = -60$$
$$\frac{-3y}{-3} = \frac{-60}{-3}$$
$$y = 20$$
The solution set is $\{20\}$.

10.
$$5z+7=6(z-2)-4(2z-3)$$
$$5z+7=6z-12-8z+12$$
$$5z+7=-2z$$
$$5z-5z+7=-2z-5z$$
$$7=-7z$$
$$\frac{7}{-7}=\frac{-7z}{-7}$$
$$-1=z$$
The solution set is $\{-1\}$.

11.
$$Ax-By=C$$
$$Ax-By+By=C+By$$
$$Ax=C+By$$
$$\frac{Ax}{A}=\frac{C+By}{A}$$
$$x=\frac{C+By}{A} \text{ or } \frac{By+C}{A}$$

12.
$$6y+7+3y=3(3y-1)$$
$$9y+7=9y-3$$
$$9y-9y+7=9y-9y-3$$
$$7=-3$$
Since this is a false statement, there is no solution. The solution set is $\{\ \}$ or $\varnothing$.

13.
$$D=0.12x+5.44$$
$$6.4=0.12x+5.44$$
$$6.4-5.44=0.12x+5.44-5.44$$
$$0.96=0.12x$$
$$\frac{0.96}{0.12}=\frac{0.12x}{0.12}$$
$$8=x$$
In the year 2000 + 8 = 2008, there will be 6.4 million children with disabilities.

14.
$$10\left(\frac{1}{2}x+3\right)=10\left(\frac{3}{5}x-1\right)$$
$$10\left(\frac{1}{2}x\right)+10(3)=10\left(\frac{3}{5}x\right)-10(1)$$
$$5x+30=6x-10$$
$$5x-5x+30=6x-5x-10$$
$$30=x-10$$
$$30+10=x-10+10$$
$$40=x$$
The solution set is $\{40\}$.

15.
$$A=P\cdot B$$
$$50=P\cdot 400$$
$$\frac{50}{400}=\frac{P\cdot 400}{400}$$
$$0.125=P$$
50 is 0.125 = 12.5% of 400.

16.
$$\frac{3(m+2)}{4}=2m+3$$
$$4\cdot\frac{3(m+2)}{4}=4(2m+3)$$
$$3(m+2)=4(2m+3)$$
$$3m+6=8m+12$$
$$3m-3m+6=8m-3m+12$$
$$6=5m+12$$
$$6-12=5m+12-12$$
$$-6=5m$$
$$\frac{-6}{5}=\frac{5m}{5}$$
$$-\frac{6}{5}=m$$
The solution set is $\left\{-\frac{6}{5}\right\}$.

17. Use the formula, increase = percent ·
original. The increase is
$50 - 40 = 10$.
$$10 = P \cdot 40$$
$$\frac{10}{40} = \frac{P \cdot 40}{40}$$
$$0.25 = P$$
This is a $0.25 = 25\%$ increase.

18. $12w - 4 + 8w - 4 = 4(5w - 2)$
$$20w - 8 = 20w - 8$$
$$20w - 20w - 8 = 20w - 20w - 8$$
$$-8 = -8$$
Since $-8 = -8$ is a true statement, the
solution is all real numbers. The
solution set is $\mathbb{R}$.

2.5 Exercise Set

1. $x + 7$

3. $25 - x$

5. $9 - 4x$

7. $\dfrac{83}{x}$

9. $2x + 40$

11. $9x - 93$

13. $8(x + 14)$

15. $x + 60 = 410$
$$x + 60 - 60 = 410 - 60$$
$$x = 350$$
The number is 350.

17. $x - 23 = 214$
$$x - 23 + 23 = 214 + 23$$
$$x = 237$$
The number is 237.

19. $7x = 126$
$$\frac{7x}{7} = \frac{126}{7}$$
$$x = 18$$
The number is 18.

21. $\dfrac{x}{19} = 5$
$$19\left(\frac{x}{19}\right) = 19(5)$$
$$x = 95$$
The number is 95.

23. $4 + 2x = 56$
$$4 - 4 + 2x = 56 - 4$$
$$2x = 52$$
$$\frac{2x}{2} = \frac{52}{2}$$
$$x = 26$$
The number is 26.

25. $5x - 7 = 178$
$$5x - 7 + 7 = 178 + 7$$
$$5x = 185$$
$$\frac{5x}{5} = \frac{185}{5}$$
$$x = 37$$
The number is 37.

27. $x + 5 = 2x$
$$x + 5 - x = 2x - x$$
$$5 = x$$
The number is 5.

29.
$$2(x+4)=36$$
$$2x+8=36$$
$$2x=28$$
$$x=14$$
The number is 14.

31.
$$9x=30+3x$$
$$6x=30$$
$$x=5$$
The number is 5.

33.
$$\frac{3x}{5}+4=34$$
$$\frac{3x}{5}=30$$
$$3x=150$$
$$x=50$$
The number is 50.

35. *Step 1* Let x = the cost to make *Waterworld* (in millions of dollars).
Step 2 $x + 25$ = the cost to make *Titanic*.
Step 3 The combined cost was $375 million, so the equation is
$$x+(x+25)=375$$
Step 4
$$x+x+25=375$$
$$2x+25=375$$
$$2x=350$$
$$x=175$$
It would cost $175 million to make *Waterworld* and $175 million + $25 million = $200 million to make *Titanic*.

37. Let x = the percentage of Conservatives. Then $2x + 4.4$ = the percentage of Liberals.
$$x+(2x+4.4)=57.2$$
$$x+2x+4.4=57.2$$
$$3x+4.4=57.2$$
$$3x+4.4-4.4=57.2-4.4$$
$$3x=52.8$$
$$\frac{3x}{3}=\frac{52.8}{3}$$
$$x=17.6$$
The percentage of Conservatives is 17.6% and the percentage of Liberals is
$$2x+4.4=2(17.6)+4.4=39.6\,\%.$$

39. Let x = the number of the left-hand page. Let $x + 1$ = the number of the right-hand page.
$$x+(x+1)=629$$
$$x+x+1=629$$
$$2x+1=629$$
$$2x+1-1=629-1$$
$$2x=628$$
$$\frac{2x}{2}=\frac{628}{2}$$
$$x=314$$
The pages are 314 and 315.

41. Let x = the amount grossed by Springsteen. Let $x + 1$ = the amount grossed by the Stones.
$$x+(x+1)=241$$
$$x+x+1=241$$
$$2x+1=241$$
$$2x+1-1=241-1$$
$$2x=240$$
$$\frac{2x}{2}=\frac{240}{2}$$
$$x=120$$
Springsteen grossed $120 million and the Rolling Stones grossed 120 + 1 = $121 million.

43. Let x = the smaller integer.
Then $x + 2$ = the larger integer.
$$x + (x + 2) = 66$$
$$2x + 2 = 66$$
$$2x = 34$$
$$x = 32$$
The smaller integer is 32. The larger integer is 32 + 2 = 34. Their sum is 32 + 34 = 66.

45. Let x = the number of miles you can travel in one week for $320.
$$200 + 0.15x = 320$$
$$200 + 0.15x - 200 = 320 - 200$$
$$0.15x = 120$$
$$\frac{0.15x}{0.15} = \frac{120}{0.15}$$
$$x = 800$$
You can travel 800 miles in one week for $320. This checks because $200 + 0.15($800) = $320.

47. Let x = the number of months it will take for a baby girl to weigh 16 pounds.
$$7 + 1.5x = 16$$
$$7 + 1.5x - 4 = 16 - 7$$
$$1.5x = 9$$
$$\frac{1.5x}{1.5} = \frac{9}{1.5}$$
$$x = 6$$
The average baby girl weighs 16 pounds after 6 months.

49. Let w = the width of the field (in yards).
Let $4w$ = the length.
The perimeter of a rectangle is twice the width plus twice the length, so
$$2w + 2(4w) = 500.$$
Solve this equation.

$$2w + 8w = 500$$
$$10w = 500$$
$$w = 50$$
The width is 50 yards and the length is $4(50) = 200$ yards. This checks because $2(50) + 2(200) = 500$.

51. Let w = the width of a football field (in feet).
Let $w + 200$ = the length.
$$2w + 2(w + 200) = 1040$$
$$2w + 2w + 400 = 1040$$
$$4w + 400 = 1040$$
$$4w = 640$$
$$w = 160$$
The width 160 feet and the length is $160 + 200 = 360$ feet. This checks because $2(160) + 2(200) = 720$.

53. As shown in the diagram, let x = the height and $3x$ = the length. To construct the bookcase, 3 heights and 4 lengths are needed. Since 60 feet of lumber is available,
$$3x + 4(3x) = 60.$$
Solve this equation.
$$3x + 12x = 60$$
$$15x = 60$$
$$x = 4$$
If $x = 4$, $3x = 3 \cdot 4 = 12$.
The bookcase is 12 feet long and 4 feet high.

55. Let x = the price before the reduction.
$$x - 0.20x = 320$$
$$1x - 0.20x = 320$$
$$0.80x = 320$$
$$\frac{0.80x}{0.80} = \frac{320}{0.80}$$
$$x = 400$$
The price before the reduction was $400.

63

57. Let x = the average salary in 2001
$$x + 0.30x = 87,100$$
$$1.30x = 87,100$$
$$\frac{1.30x}{1.30} = \frac{87,100}{1.30}$$
$$x = 67,000$$
The average salary in 2001 was $67,000.

59. Let x = the price of the car without tax.
$$x + 0.06x = 15,370$$
$$1x + 0.06x = 15,370$$
$$1.06x = 15,370$$
$$\frac{1.06x}{1.06} = \frac{15,370}{1.06}$$
$$x = 14,500$$
The price of the car without sales tax was $14,500.

61. Let x = the number of hours of labor.
$$63 + 35x = 448$$
$$63 + 35x - 63 = 448 - 63$$
$$35x = 385$$
$$\frac{35x}{35} = \frac{385}{35}$$
$$x = 11$$
It took 11 hours of labor to repair the car.

For Exercises 63-65, answers will vary.

67. Statement **a.** should be translated as $x - 10 = 160$ and statement **b.** should be translated as $5x + 4 = 6x - 1$.
Statement **c.** should be translated as $7 = x + 3$. Since none of these statements was translated correctly, the correct response is **d.**

69. Let x = the number of inches over 5 feet
$$W = 100 + 5x$$
$$135 = 100 + 5x$$
$$135 - 100 = 100 - 100 + 5x$$
$$35 = 5x$$
$$\frac{35}{5} = \frac{5x}{5}$$
$$7 = x$$
The height 5' 7" corresponds to 135 pounds.

71. Let x = the woman's age.
Let $3x$ = the "uncle's" age.
$$3x + 20 = 2(x + 20)$$
$$3x + 20 = 2x + 40$$
$$3x - 2x + 20 = 2x - 2x + 40$$
$$x + 20 = 40$$
$$x + 20 - 20 = 40 - 20$$
$$x = 20$$
The woman is 20 years old and the "uncle" is $3x = 3(20) = 60$ years old.

73.
$$\frac{4}{5}x = -16$$
$$\frac{5}{4}\left(\frac{4}{5}x\right) = \frac{5}{4}(-16)$$
$$x = -20$$
Check:
$$\frac{4}{5}(-20) = -16$$
$$\frac{4}{5} \cdot \frac{-20}{1} = -16$$
$$\frac{-80}{5} = -16$$
$$-16 = -16$$
The solution set is $\{-20\}$.

74.
$$6(y-1)+7=9y-y+1$$
$$6y-6+7=9y-y+1$$
$$6y+1=8y+1$$
$$6y+1-1=8y+1-1$$
$$6y=8y$$
$$6y-8y=8y-8y$$
$$-2y=0$$
$$\frac{-2y}{-2}=\frac{0}{-2}$$
$$y=0$$

Check:
$$6(0-1)+7=9(0)-0+1$$
$$6-10+7=0-0+1$$
$$-6+7=1$$
$$1=1$$

The solution set is $\{0\}$.

75.
$$V=\frac{1}{3}lwh \text{ for } w$$
$$V=\frac{1}{3}lwh$$
$$3V=3\left(\frac{1}{3}lwh\right)$$
$$3v=lwh$$
$$\frac{3V}{lh}=\frac{lwh}{lh}$$
$$\frac{3V}{lh}=w \quad \text{or} \quad w=\frac{3V}{lh}$$

2.6 Exercise Set

1. Use the formulas for the perimeter and area of a rectangle. The length is 6 m and the width is 3 m.
$$P=2l+2w$$
$$=2(6)+2(3)=12+6=18$$
$$A=lw=6\cdot3=18$$
The perimeter is 18 meters, and the area is 18 square meters.

3. Use the formula for the area of a triangle. The base is 14 in and the height is 8 in. The lengths of the other two sides are not used in calculating the area:
$$A=\frac{1}{2}bh=\frac{1}{2}(14)(8)=56$$
The area is 56 square inches.

5. Use the formula for the area of a trapezoid. The bases are 16 m and 10 m and the height is 7 m. The lengths of the other two sides of the trapezoid are not used in calculating the area.
$$A=\frac{1}{2}h(a+b)$$
$$=\frac{1}{2}(7)(16+10)=\frac{1}{2}\cdot7\cdot26=91$$
The area is 91 square meters.

7. $A=lw;\ A=1250,\ w=25$
$$A=lw$$
$$1250=l\cdot25$$
$$50=l$$
The length of the swimming pool is 50 feet.

9.

$$A = \frac{1}{2}bh; A = 20, b = 5$$

$$A = \frac{1}{2}bh$$

$$20 = \frac{1}{2} \cdot 5 \cdot h$$

$$20 = \frac{5}{2}h$$

$$\frac{2}{5}(20) = \frac{2}{5}\left(\frac{5}{2}h\right)$$

$$8 = h$$

The height of the triangle is 8 feet.

11.

$$P = 2l + 2w; \ P = 188, \ w = 44$$

$$188 = 2l + 2(44)$$

$$188 = 2l + 88$$

$$100 = 2l$$

$$50 = l$$

The length of the rectangle is 50 cm.

13. Use the formulas for the area and circumference of a circle. The radius is 4 cm.

$$A = \pi r^2 = \pi(4)^2 = 16\pi \approx 50$$

$$C = 2\pi r = 2\pi(4) = 8\pi \approx 25$$

The area is 16π cm^2 or approximately 50 cm^2, and the circumference is 8π cm or approximately 25 cm.

15. Since the diameter is 12 yd, the radius is $\frac{12}{2} = 6$ yd.

$$A = \pi r^2 = \pi(6)^2 = 36\pi \approx 113$$

$$C = 2\pi r = 2\pi \cdot 6 = 12\pi \approx 38$$

The area is 36π yd^2 or approximately 113 yd^2, and the circumference is 12π yd or approximately 38 yd.

17.

$$C = 2\pi r; \ C = 14\pi$$

$$C = 2\pi r$$

$$14\pi = 2\pi r$$

$$\frac{14\pi}{2\pi} = \frac{2\pi r}{2\pi}$$

$$7 = r$$

The radius is 7 in and the diameter is 2(7 in) = 14 in.

19. Use the formula for the volume of a rectangular solid. The length and width are each 3 inches and the height is 4 inches.

$$V = lwh = 3 \cdot 3 \cdot 4 = 36$$

The volume is 36 in^3.

21. Use the formula for the volume of a cylinder. The radius is 5 cm and the height is 6 cm.

$$V = \pi r^2 h$$

$$= \pi(5)^2 6 = \pi(25)6 = 150\pi \approx 471$$

The volume of the cylinder is 150π cm^3 or approximately 471 cm^3.

23. Use the formula for the volume of a sphere. The diameter is 18 cm, so the radius is 9 cm.

$$V = \frac{4}{3}\pi r^3 = \frac{4}{3}\pi(9)^3 = 972\pi \approx 3054$$

The volume is 972π cm^3 or approximately 3054 cm^3.

25. Use the formula for the volume of a cone. The radius is 4 m and the height is 9 m.

$$V = \frac{1}{3}\pi r^2 h = \frac{1}{3}\pi(4)^2 \cdot 9 = 48\pi \approx 151$$

The volume is 48π m^3 or approximately 151 m^3.

27. Solve $V = \pi r^2 h$ for h

$$\frac{V}{\pi r^2} = \frac{\pi r^2 h}{\pi r^2}$$

$$\frac{V}{\pi r^2} = h$$

29. Smaller cylinder: $r = 3$ in, $h = 4$ in.
$V = \pi r^2 h = \pi(3)^2 \cdot 4 = 36\pi$
The volume of the smaller cylinder is
$36\pi \, in^3$.

Larger cylinder: $r = 3(3) = 9$ in,
$h = 4$ in. $V = \pi r^2 h = \pi(9)^2 \cdot 4 = 324\pi$

The volume of the larger cylinder is
324π. The ratio of the volumes of the
two cylinders is $\dfrac{V_{larger}}{V_{smaller}} = \dfrac{324\pi}{36\pi} = \dfrac{9}{1}$.
So, the volume of the larger cylinder is
9 times the volume of the smaller
cylinder.

31. The sum of the measures of the three
angles of any triangle is $180°$, so
$x + x + (x + 30) = 180$.
Solve for x.
$3x + 30 = 180$

$3x = 150$

$x = 50$
If $x = 50$, $x + 30 = 80$, so the three
angle measures are $50°, 50°,$ and $80°$.
This solution checks because
$50° + 50° + 80° = 180°$.

33. $4x + (3x + 4) + (2x + 5) = 180$

$9x + 9 = 180$

$9x = 171$

$x = 19$
If $x = 19$, then $4x = 76$, $3x + 4 = 61$, and
$2x + 5 = 43$. Therefore, the angle
measures are $76°$, $61°$, and $43°$. This
solution checks because
$76° + 61° + 43° = 180°$.

35. Let $x =$ the measure of the smallest
angle.
Let $2x =$ the measure of the second
angle.
Let $x + 20 =$ the measure of the third
angle.
$x + 2x + (x + 20) = 180$

$4x + 20 = 180$

$4x = 160$

$x = 40$
Measure of smallest angle is $40°$.
Measure of second angle is $2x = 80°$.
Measure of third angle is $x + 20 = 60°$.

37. If the measure of an angle is $58°$, the
measure of its complement is
$90° - 58° = 32°$.

39. If the measure of an angle is $88°$, the
measure of its complement is $2°$.

41. If the measure of an angle is $132°$, the
measure of its supplement is
$180° - 132° = 48°$.

43. If the measure of an angle is $90°$, the
measure of its supplement is
$180° - 90° = 90°$.

45. Let $x =$ the measure of the angle.
Let $90 - x =$ the measure of its
complement.
The angle's measure is $60°$ more than
that of its complement, so the equation
is $x = (90 - x) + 60$.
Solve for x.
$x = 90 - x + 60$
$x = 150 - x$
$2x = 150$
$x = 75$
The measure of the angle is $75°$.
The complement of the angle is
$90° - 75° = 15°$, and $75°$ is $60°$ more
than $15°$.

47. Let x = the measure of the angle.
Let $180 - x$ = the measure of its supplement.
$$x = 3(180 - x)$$
$$x = 540 - 3x$$
$$4x = 540$$
$$x = 135$$
The measure of the angle is $135°$. The measure of its supplement is $180° - 135° = 45°$, and $135° = 3(45°)$, so the proposed solution checks.

49. Let x = the measure of the angle.
Let $180 - x$ = the measure of its supplement, and, $90 - x$ = the measure of its complement.
$$180 - x = 3(90 - x) + 10$$
$$180 - x = 270 - 3x + 10$$
$$180 - x = 280 - 3x$$
$$2x = 100$$
$$x = 50$$
The measure of the angle is $50°$. The measure of its supplement is $130°$ and the measure of its complement is $40°$. Since $130° = 3(40°) + 10$, the proposed solution checks.

51.

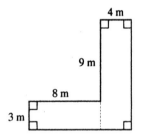

Divide the shape into two rectangles.
$$A_{\text{entire figure}} = A_{\text{bottom rectangle}} + A_{\text{side rectangle}}$$
$$A_{\text{entire figure}} = 3 \cdot 8 + 4(9 + 3)$$
$$= 24 + 4(12)$$
$$= 24 + 48$$
$$= 72$$
The area of the figure is 72 square meters.

52.

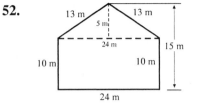

Divide the shape into a triangle and a rectangle.
$$A_{\text{entire figure}} = A_{\text{rectangle}} + A_{\text{triangle}}$$
$$A_{\text{entire figure}} = lw + \frac{1}{2}bh$$
$$= 10(24) + \frac{1}{2}(24)(15 - 10)$$
$$= 240 + \frac{1}{2}(24)(5)$$
$$= 240 + 60 = 300$$
The area of the figure is 300 m^2.

53.

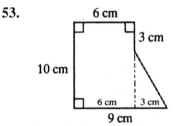

Divide the shape into a rectangle and a triangle.
$$A_{\text{entire figure}} = A_{\text{rectangle}} + A_{\text{triangle}}$$
$$A_{\text{entire figure}} = lw + \frac{1}{2}bh$$
$$= 10(6) + \frac{1}{2}(3)(10 - 3)$$
$$= 60 + \frac{1}{2}(3)(7)$$
$$= 60 + 10.5 = 70.5$$
The area of the figure is 70.5 cm^2.

54.

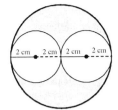

Subtract the area of the two smaller circles from the area of the larger circle. Note that the two smaller circles are the same size.

$A_{\text{shaded}} = A_{\text{larger circle}} - 2 \cdot A_{\text{smaller circle}}$

$\quad = \pi R^2 - 2 \cdot \pi r^2$

$\quad = \pi(2+2)^2 - 2 \cdot \pi(2)^2$

$\quad = \pi(4)^2 - 2 \cdot \pi(4)$

$\quad = 16\pi - 8\pi$

$\quad = 8\pi$

The shaded area is 8π cm^2.

55. Subtract the volume of the pyramid from the volume of the rectangular solid.

$V_{\text{shaded}} = V_{\text{rectangular solid}} - V_{\text{pyramid}}$

$\quad = lwh - \dfrac{1}{3}lwh$

$\quad = (6)(6)(7) - \dfrac{1}{3}(6)(6)(7)$

$\quad = 252 - 84$

$\quad = 168$

The volume of the shaded region is 168 cubic centimeters.

56. Subtract the volume of the smaller cylinder from the volume of the larger cylinder.

$V_{\text{shaded}} = V_{\text{larger cylinder}} - V_{\text{smaller cylinder}}$

$\quad = \pi R^2 h - \pi r^2 h$

$\quad = \pi \left(\dfrac{6}{2}\right)^2 \cdot 10 - \pi \left(\dfrac{2}{2}\right)^2 \cdot 10$

$\quad = \pi(3)^2 \cdot 10 - \pi(1)^2 \cdot 10$

$\quad = 90\pi - 10\pi$

$\quad = 80\pi$

The volume of the shaded region is 80π cubic inches.

57. The area of the office is

$(20\text{ ft})(16\text{ ft}) = 320\text{ ft}^2$. Use a proportion to determine how much of the yearly electric bill is deductible.

Let x = the amount of the electric bill that is deductible.

$\dfrac{320}{2200} = \dfrac{x}{4800}$

$2200x = (320)(4800)$

$2200x = 1,536,000$

$\dfrac{2200x}{2200} = \dfrac{1,546,000}{2200}$

$x \approx 698.18$

$698.18 of the yearly electric bill is deductible.

59. The radius of the large pizza is $\dfrac{1}{2} \cdot 14 =$ 7 inches, and the radius of the medium pizza is $\dfrac{1}{2} \cdot 7$ inches $= 3.5$ inches.

large pizza:

$A = \pi r^2 = \pi(7\,in.)^2$

$\quad = 49\pi$ in$^2 \approx 154$ in^2

medium pizza:

$A = \pi r^2 = \pi(3.5\,in)^2$

$\quad = 12.25$ in$^2 \approx 38.465$ in^2

For each pizza, find the price per inch by dividing the price by the area.
Price per square inch for the large pizza

$= \dfrac{\$12.00}{154\text{ in}^2} \approx \dfrac{\$0.08}{\text{in}^2}$ and the price per

square inch for the medium pizza

$= \dfrac{\$5.00}{28.465\text{ in}^2} \approx \dfrac{\$0.13}{\text{in}^2}$.

The large pizza is the better buy.

61. The area of the larger circle is
$A = \pi r^2 = \pi \cdot 50^2 = 2500\pi$ ft^2.
The area of the smaller circle is
$A = \pi r^2 = \pi \cdot 40^2 = 1600\pi$ ft^2.
The area of the circular road is the difference between the area of the larger circle and the area of the smaller circle.
$A = 2500\pi$ ft$^2 - 1600\pi$ ft$^2 = 900\pi$ ft^2
The cost to pave the circular road is
$\$0.80(900\pi) \approx \$2262$.

63. To find the perimeter of the entire window, first find the perimeter of the lower rectangular portion. This is the bottom and two sides of the window, which is 3 ft + 6 ft + 6 ft = 15 ft. Next, find the perimeter or circumference of the semicircular portion of the window. The radius of the semicircle is
$\frac{1}{2} \cdot 3\,\text{ft} = 1.5\,\text{ft},$ so the circumference is
$\frac{1}{2} \cdot 2\pi r \approx 3.14(1.5) = 4.7\,\text{ft}.$ So,
approximately 15 ft + 4.7 ft = 19.7 ft of stripping would be needed to frame the window.

65. First, find the volume of water when the reservoir was full.
$V = lwh = 50 \cdot 0 \cdot 20 = 30,000$
The volume was 30,000 yd^3. Next, find the volume when the height of the water was 6 yards.
$V = 50 \cdot 30 \cdot 6 = 9000$
The volume was 9000 yd^3. The amount of water used in the three-month period was 30,000 yd^3 – 9000 yd^3 = 21,000 yd^3.

67. For the first can, the diameter is 6 in so the radius is 3 in and
$V = \pi r^2 h = \pi(3)^2 \cdot 5 = 45\pi \approx 141.3$.
The volume of the first can is 141.3 in^3. For the second can, the diameter is 5 in, so the radius is 2.5 in and
$V = \pi r^2 h = \pi(2.5)^2 \cdot 6 = 37.5\pi \approx 117.75$.
The volume of the second can is 117.75 in^2. Since the cans are the same price, the can with the greater volume is the better buy. Choose the can with the diameter of 6 inches and height of 5 inches.

69. Find the volume of a cylinder with radius 3 feet and height 2 feet 4 inches.
$2 \text{ ft } 4 \text{ in} = 2\frac{1}{3} \text{ feet} = \frac{7}{3} \text{ feet}$
$V = \pi r^2 h$
$= \pi(3)^2 \left(\frac{7}{3}\right) = \pi \cdot 9 \cdot \frac{7}{3} = 21\pi \approx 65.94$
The volume of the tank is approximately 65.94 ft^3. This is a little over 1 ft^3 smaller than 67 ft^3 so it is too small to hold 500 gallons of water. Yes, you should be able to win your case.

71. – 79. Answers will vary

81. Area of smaller deck = (8 ft)(10 ft)
$\qquad\qquad\qquad\quad = 80 \text{ ft}^2$
Area of larger deck = (12 ft)(15 ft)
$\qquad\qquad\qquad\quad = 180 \text{ ft}^2$
Find the ratio of the areas.
$\frac{A_{larger}}{A_{smaller}} = \frac{180 \, ft^2}{80 \, ft^2} = \frac{2.25}{1} \text{ or } 2.25:1$
The cost will increase 2.25 times.

83. Let x = the radius of the original sphere.
Let $2x$ = the radius of the larger sphere. Find the ratio of the volumes of the two spheres.

$$\frac{A_{\text{larger}}}{A_{\text{original}}} = \frac{\frac{4}{3}\pi(2x)^3}{\frac{4}{3}\pi x^3} = \frac{8x^3}{x^3} = \frac{8}{1} \text{ or } 8:1$$

If the radius of a sphere is doubled, the volume increases 8 times.

85. The angles marked $(2x)^\circ$ and $(2x+40)^\circ$ in the figure are supplementary, so their sum is 180°.
$2x + (2x+40) = 180$.

$$2x + 2x + 40 = 180$$
$$4x + 40 = 180$$
$$4x = 10$$
$$x = 35$$

The angle of inclination is 35°.

86.
$$P = 2s + b \text{ for } s$$
$$P - b = 2s$$
$$\frac{P-b}{2} = \frac{2s}{2}$$
$$\frac{P-b}{2} = s \text{ or } s = \frac{P-b}{2}$$

87.
$$\frac{x}{2} + 7 = 13 - \frac{x}{4}$$
Multiply both sides by the LCD, 4.

$$4\left(\frac{x}{2} + 7\right) = 4\left(13 - \frac{x}{4}\right)$$
$$2x + 28 = 52 - x$$
$$2x + 28 + x = 52 - x + x$$
$$3x + 28 = 52$$
$$3x + 28 - 28 = 52 - 28$$
$$3x = 24$$
$$\frac{3x}{3} = \frac{24}{3}$$
$$x = 8$$

88.
$$\left[3\left(12 \div 2^2 - 3\right)^2\right]^2$$
$$= \left[3\left(12 \div 4 - 3\right)^2\right]^2$$
$$= \left[3(3-3)^2\right]^2 = \left(3 \cdot 0^2\right)^2 = 0^2 = 0$$

2.7 Exercise Set

1. $x > 5$

3. $x < -2$

5. $x \geq -4$

7. $x \leq 4.5$

9. $-2 < x \leq 6$

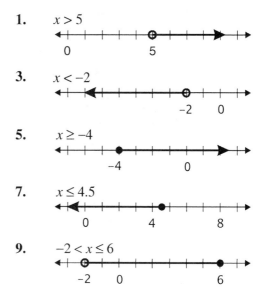

71

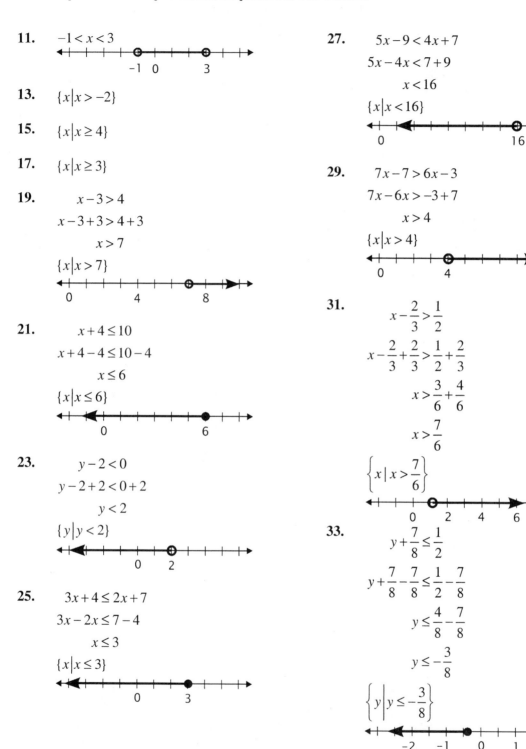

11. $-1 < x < 3$

13. $\{x | x > -2\}$

15. $\{x | x \geq 4\}$

17. $\{x | x \geq 3\}$

19. $x - 3 > 4$

$x - 3 + 3 > 4 + 3$

$x > 7$

$\{x | x > 7\}$

21. $x + 4 \leq 10$

$x + 4 - 4 \leq 10 - 4$

$x \leq 6$

$\{x | x \leq 6\}$

23. $y - 2 < 0$

$y - 2 + 2 < 0 + 2$

$y < 2$

$\{y | y < 2\}$

25. $3x + 4 \leq 2x + 7$

$3x - 2x \leq 7 - 4$

$x \leq 3$

$\{x | x \leq 3\}$

27. $5x - 9 < 4x + 7$

$5x - 4x < 7 + 9$

$x < 16$

$\{x | x < 16\}$

29. $7x - 7 > 6x - 3$

$7x - 6x > -3 + 7$

$x > 4$

$\{x | x > 4\}$

31. $x - \dfrac{2}{3} > \dfrac{1}{2}$

$x - \dfrac{2}{3} + \dfrac{2}{3} > \dfrac{1}{2} + \dfrac{2}{3}$

$x > \dfrac{3}{6} + \dfrac{4}{6}$

$x > \dfrac{7}{6}$

$\left\{ x \mid x > \dfrac{7}{6} \right\}$

33. $y + \dfrac{7}{8} \leq \dfrac{1}{2}$

$y + \dfrac{7}{8} - \dfrac{7}{8} \leq \dfrac{1}{2} - \dfrac{7}{8}$

$y \leq \dfrac{4}{8} - \dfrac{7}{8}$

$y \leq -\dfrac{3}{8}$

$\left\{ y \mid y \leq -\dfrac{3}{8} \right\}$

72

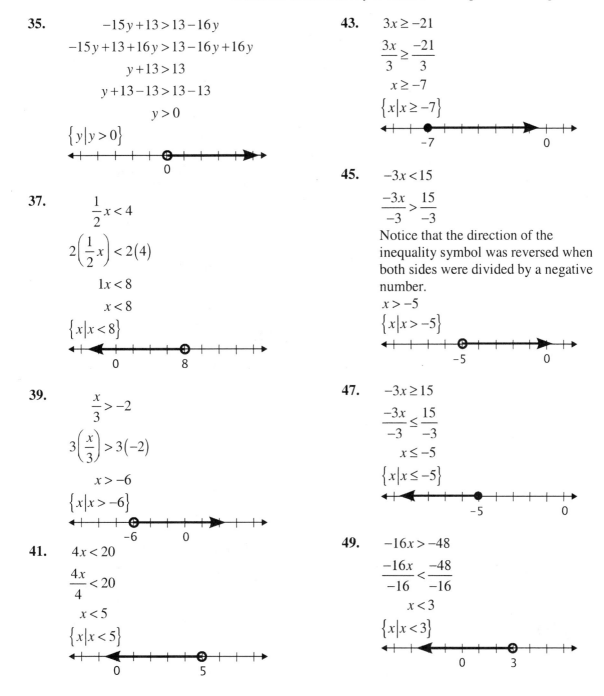

35.

$$-15y+13>13-16y$$
$$-15y+13+16y>13-16y+16y$$
$$y+13>13$$
$$y+13-13>13-13$$
$$y>0$$
$$\{y|y>0\}$$

37.

$$\frac{1}{2}x<4$$
$$2\left(\frac{1}{2}x\right)<2(4)$$
$$1x<8$$
$$x<8$$
$$\{x|x<8\}$$

39.

$$\frac{x}{3}>-2$$
$$3\left(\frac{x}{3}\right)>3(-2)$$
$$x>-6$$
$$\{x|x>-6\}$$

41.

$$4x<20$$
$$\frac{4x}{4}<20$$
$$x<5$$
$$\{x|x<5\}$$

43.

$$3x\ge-21$$
$$\frac{3x}{3}\ge\frac{-21}{3}$$
$$x\ge-7$$
$$\{x|x\ge-7\}$$

45.

$$-3x<15$$
$$\frac{-3x}{-3}>\frac{15}{-3}$$

Notice that the direction of the inequality symbol was reversed when both sides were divided by a negative number.

$$x>-5$$
$$\{x|x>-5\}$$

47.

$$-3x\ge15$$
$$\frac{-3x}{-3}\le\frac{15}{-3}$$
$$x\le-5$$
$$\{x|x\le-5\}$$

49.

$$-16x>-48$$
$$\frac{-16x}{-16}<\frac{-48}{-16}$$
$$x<3$$
$$\{x|x<3\}$$

51.

$$-4y \leq \frac{1}{2}$$

$$2(-4y) \leq 2\left(\frac{1}{2}\right)$$

$$-8y \leq 1$$

$$\frac{-8y}{-8} \geq \frac{1}{-8}$$

$$y \geq -\frac{1}{8}$$

$$\left\{ y \,\middle|\, y \geq -\frac{1}{8} \right\}$$

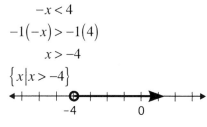

53.

$$-x < 4$$

$$-1(-x) > -1(4)$$

$$x > -4$$

$$\{x \mid x > -4\}$$

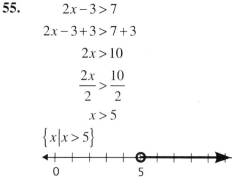

55.

$$2x - 3 > 7$$

$$2x - 3 + 3 > 7 + 3$$

$$2x > 10$$

$$\frac{2x}{2} > \frac{10}{2}$$

$$x > 5$$

$$\{x \mid x > 5\}$$

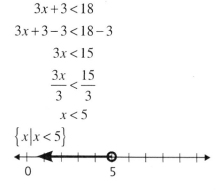

57.

$$3x + 3 < 18$$

$$3x + 3 - 3 < 18 - 3$$

$$3x < 15$$

$$\frac{3x}{3} < \frac{15}{3}$$

$$x < 5$$

$$\{x \mid x < 5\}$$

59.

$$3 - 7x \leq 17$$

$$3 - 7x - 3 \leq 17 - 3$$

$$-7x \leq 14$$

$$\frac{-7x}{-7} \geq \frac{14}{-7}$$

$$x \geq -2$$

$$\{x \mid x \geq -2\}$$

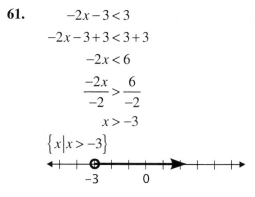

61.

$$-2x - 3 < 3$$

$$-2x - 3 + 3 < 3 + 3$$

$$-2x < 6$$

$$\frac{-2x}{-2} > \frac{6}{-2}$$

$$x > -3$$

$$\{x \mid x > -3\}$$

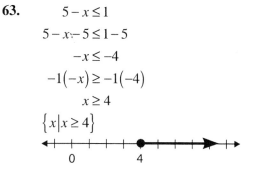

63.

$$5 - x \leq 1$$

$$5 - x - 5 \leq 1 - 5$$

$$-x \leq -4$$

$$-1(-x) \geq -1(-4)$$

$$x \geq 4$$

$$\{x \mid x \geq 4\}$$

74

65.

$$2x - 5 > -x + 6$$

$$2x - 5 + x > -x + 6 + x$$

$$3x - 5 > 6$$

$$3x - 5 + 5 > 6 + 5$$

$$3x > 11$$

$$\frac{3x}{3} > \frac{11}{3}$$

$$x > \frac{11}{3}$$

$$\left\{ x \middle| x > \frac{11}{3} \right\}$$

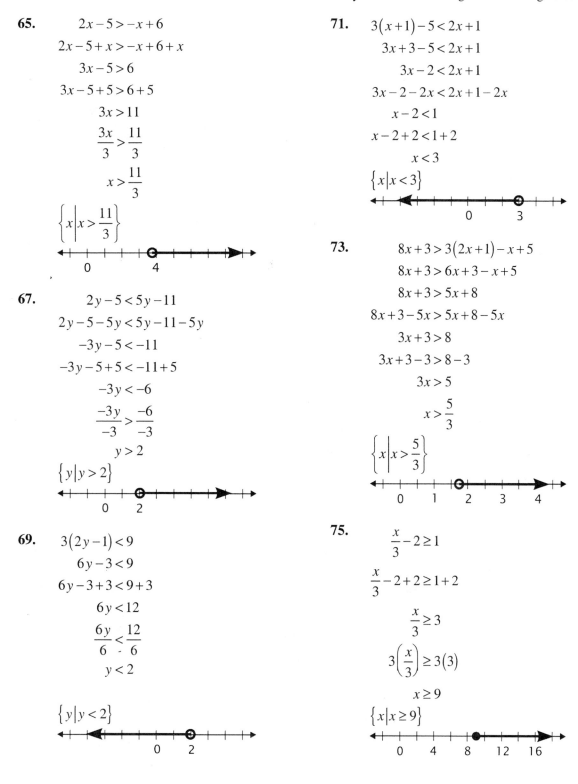

67.

$$2y - 5 < 5y - 11$$

$$2y - 5 - 5y < 5y - 11 - 5y$$

$$-3y - 5 < -11$$

$$-3y - 5 + 5 < -11 + 5$$

$$-3y < -6$$

$$\frac{-3y}{-3} > \frac{-6}{-3}$$

$$y > 2$$

$$\{ y | y > 2 \}$$

69.

$$3(2y - 1) < 9$$

$$6y - 3 < 9$$

$$6y - 3 + 3 < 9 + 3$$

$$6y < 12$$

$$\frac{6y}{6} < \frac{12}{6}$$

$$y < 2$$

$$\{ y | y < 2 \}$$

71.

$$3(x + 1) - 5 < 2x + 1$$

$$3x + 3 - 5 < 2x + 1$$

$$3x - 2 < 2x + 1$$

$$3x - 2 - 2x < 2x + 1 - 2x$$

$$x - 2 < 1$$

$$x - 2 + 2 < 1 + 2$$

$$x < 3$$

$$\{ x | x < 3 \}$$

73.

$$8x + 3 > 3(2x + 1) - x + 5$$

$$8x + 3 > 6x + 3 - x + 5$$

$$8x + 3 > 5x + 8$$

$$8x + 3 - 5x > 5x + 8 - 5x$$

$$3x + 3 > 8$$

$$3x + 3 - 3 > 8 - 3$$

$$3x > 5$$

$$x > \frac{5}{3}$$

$$\left\{ x \middle| x > \frac{5}{3} \right\}$$

75.

$$\frac{x}{3} - 2 \geq 1$$

$$\frac{x}{3} - 2 + 2 \geq 1 + 2$$

$$\frac{x}{3} \geq 3$$

$$3\left(\frac{x}{3} \right) \geq 3(3)$$

$$x \geq 9$$

$$\{ x | x \geq 9 \}$$

75

77.

$$1 - \frac{x}{2} > 4$$

$$1 - \frac{x}{2} - 1 > 4 - 1$$

$$-\frac{x}{2} > 3$$

$$2\left(-\frac{x}{2}\right) > 2(3)$$

$$-x > 6$$

$$-1(-x) < -1(6)$$

$$x < -6$$

$$\{x | x < -6\}$$

79.

$$4x - 4 < 4(x - 5)$$

$$4x - 4 < 4x - 20$$

$$4x - 4 + 4 < 4x - 20 + 4$$

$$4x < 4x - 16$$

$$4x - 4x < 4x - 16 - 4x$$

$$0 < -16$$

The original inequality is equivalent to the false statement $0 < -16$, so the inequality has no solution. The solution set is $\{ \ \}$ or $\emptyset$.

81.

$$x + 3 < x + 7$$

$$x + 3 - x < x + 7 - x$$

$$3 < 7$$

The original inequality is equivalent to the true statement $3 < 7$, so the solution is the set of all real numbers, written $\{x | x \text{ is a real number}\}$ or $\mathbb{R}$.

83.

$$7x \leq 7(x - 2)$$

$$7x \leq 7x - 14$$

$$7x - 7x \leq 7x - 14 - 7x$$

$$0 \leq -14$$

Since $0 \leq -14$ is a false statement, the original inequality has no solution. The solution set is $\emptyset$ or $\{ \ \}$.

85.

$$2(x + 3) > 2x + 1$$

$$2x + 6 > 2x + 1$$

$$2x + 6 - 2x > 2x + 1 - 2x$$

$$6 > 1$$

Since $6 > 1$ is a true statement, the original inequality is true for all real numbers the solution set is $\{x | x \text{ is a real number}\}$ or $\mathbb{R}$.

87.

$$5x - 4 \leq 4(x - 1)$$

$$5x - 4 \leq 4x - 4$$

$$5x - 4 + 4 \leq 4x - 4 + 4$$

$$5x \leq 4x$$

$$5x - 4x \leq 4x - 4x$$

$$x \leq 0$$

$$\{x | x \leq 0\}$$

88.

$$6x - 3 \leq 3(x - 1)$$

$$6x - 3 \leq 3x - 3$$

$$6x - 3 + 3 \leq 3x - 3 + 3$$

$$6x \leq 3x$$

$$6x - 3x \leq 3x - 3x$$

$$x \leq 0$$

The solution set is $\{x | x \leq 0\}$.

89.

$$3x + a > b$$

$$3x > b - a$$

$$\frac{3x}{3} > \frac{b - a}{3}$$

$$x > \frac{b - a}{3}$$

90.
$$-2x - a \leq b$$
$$-2x - a + a \leq b + a$$
$$-2x \leq b + a$$
$$\frac{-2x}{-2} \geq \frac{b+a}{-2}$$

Note that the direction of the inequality has switched because we divided both sides by a negative.

$$x \geq \frac{b+a}{-2}$$

91.
$$y \leq mx + b$$
$$y - b \leq mx$$

Reverse the inequality since $m < 0$.

$$\frac{y-b}{m} \geq \frac{mx}{m}$$
$$\frac{y-b}{m} \geq x$$

92.
$$y > mx + b$$
$$y - b > mx + b - b$$
$$y - b > mx$$
$$\frac{y-b}{m} > \frac{mx}{m}$$
$$\frac{y-b}{m} > x \quad \text{or} \quad x < \frac{y-b}{m}$$

Note that we did not switch the direction of the inequality because the problem stated that $m > 0$.

93. x is between -2 and 2, so $|x| < 2$.

94. x is between -3 and 3, so $|x| < 3$.

95. x is less than -2 and greater than 2, so $|x| > 2$

96. x is greater than 3 or less than -3, so $|x| > 3$.

97. Denmark, Netherlands, and Norway

99. Japan and Mexico

101. Netherlands, Norway, Canada, and U.S.

103.
$$N = 550 - 9x; \; N < 370$$
$$550 - 9x < 370$$
$$550 - 9x - 550 < 370 - 550$$
$$-9x < -180$$
$$\frac{-9x}{-9} > \frac{-180}{-9}$$
$$x > 20$$

According to the model, there will be 370 billion cigarettes consumed in $1988 + 20 = 2008$ and less than 370 billion after 2008 (from 2009 onward).

105. a. Let x = your grade on the final exam.

$$\frac{86 + 88 + x}{3} \geq 90$$
$$3\left(\frac{86 + 88 + x}{3}\right) \geq 3(90)$$
$$86 + 88 + x \geq 270$$
$$174 + x \geq 270$$
$$174 + x - 174 \geq 270 - 174$$
$$x \geq 96$$

You must get at least a 96% on the final exam to earn an A in the course.

b.

$$\frac{86+88+x}{3} < 80$$

$$3\left(\frac{86+88+x}{3}\right) < 3(80)$$

$$86+88+x < 240$$

$$174+x < 240$$

$$174+x-174 < 240-174$$

$$x < 66$$

If you get less than a 66 on the final exam, your grade will be below a B.

107. Let x = number of miles driven.

$$80+0.25x \le 400$$

$$80+0.25x-80 \le 400-80$$

$$0.25x \le 320$$

$$\frac{0.25x}{0.25} \le \frac{320}{0.25}$$

$$x \le 1280$$

You can drive up to 1280 miles.

109. Let x = number of cement bags.

$$245+95x \le 3000$$

$$245+95x-245 \le 3000-245$$

$$95x \le 2755$$

$$\frac{95x}{95} \le \frac{2755}{95}$$

$$x \le 29$$

Up to 29 bags of cement can safely be listed on the elevator in one trip.

For Exercises 111.-115., answers will vary.

117. Let x = number of miles driven.
Weekly cost for Basic Rental: $260.
Weekly cost for Continental: $80 + 0.25x$
The cost for Basic Rental is a better deal if $80+0.25x > 260$.
Solve this inequality.

$$80+0.25x-80 > 260-80$$

$$0.25x > 180$$

$$\frac{0.25x}{0.25} > \frac{180}{0.25}$$

$$x > 720$$

Basic Car Rental is a better deal if you drive more than 720 miles in a week.

119.

$$1.45-7.23x > -1.442$$

$$1.45-7.23x-1.45 > -1.442-1.45$$

$$-7.23x > -2.892$$

$$\frac{-7.23x}{-7.23} < \frac{-2.892}{-7.23}$$

$$x < 0.4$$

$$\{x|x<0.4\}$$

121. $A = PB$, $A = 8$, $P = 40\% = 0.4$

$$A = PB$$

$$8 = 0.4B$$

$$\frac{8}{0.4} = \frac{0.4B}{0.4}$$

$$20 = B$$

8 is 40% of 20.

122. Let w = the width of the rectangle.
Let $w + 5$ = the length.
The perimeter is 34 inches.

$$2(\text{width})+2(\text{length}) = \text{perimeter}$$

$$2w+2(w+5) = 34$$

$$2w+2w+10 = 34$$

$$4w+10 = 34$$

$$4w = 24$$

$$w = 6$$

The width is 6 inches and the length is $6 + 5 = 11$ inches.

123.
$$5x+16 = 3(x+8)$$
$$5x+16 = 3x+24$$
$$5x+16-3x = 3x+24-3x$$
$$2x+16 = 24$$
$$2x+16-16 = 24-16$$
$$2x = 8$$
$$\frac{2x}{2} = \frac{8}{2}$$
$$x = 4$$

Check: $5(4)+16\overset{?}{=}3(4+8)$

$$20+16\overset{?}{=}3(12)$$
$$36 = 36 \text{ true}$$
The solution set is $\{4\}$.

Chapter 2 Review Exercises

For Exercises 1-18 and 20-28, students should check all proposed solutions by substituting in the original equations. Checks will not be shown here.

1.
$$x-10 = 22$$
$$x-10+10 = 22+10$$
$$x = 32$$
The solution set is $\{32\}$.

2.
$$-14 = y+8$$
$$-14-8 = y+8-8$$
$$-22 = y$$
The solution set is $\{-22\}$

3.
$$7z-3 = 6z+9$$
$$7z-3-6z = 6z+9-6z$$
$$z-3 = 9$$
$$z-3+3 = 9+3$$
$$z = 12$$
The solution set is $\{12\}$.

4.
$$4(x+3) = 3x-10$$
$$4x+12 = 3x-10$$
$$4x+2-3x = 3x-10-3x$$
$$x+12 = -10$$
$$x+12-12 = -10-12$$
$$x = -22$$
The solution set is $\{-22\}$.

5.
$$6x-3x-9+1 = -5x+7x-3$$
$$3x-8 = 2x-3$$
$$3x-8-2x = 2x-3-2x$$
$$x-8 = -3$$
$$x-8+8 = -3+8$$
$$x = 5$$
The solution set is $\{5\}$.

6.
$$\frac{x}{8} = 10$$
$$8\left(\frac{x}{8}\right) = 8(10)$$
$$x = 80$$
The solution set is $\{80\}$.

7.
$$\frac{y}{-8} = 7$$
$$-8\left(\frac{y}{-8}\right) = -8(7)$$
$$y = -56$$
The solution set is $\{-56\}$.

8.
$$7z = 77$$
$$\frac{7z}{7} = \frac{77}{7}$$
$$z = 11$$
The solution set is $\{11\}$.

9.
$$-36 = -9y$$
$$\frac{-36}{-9} = \frac{-9y}{-9}$$
$$4 = y$$
The solution set is $\{4\}$.

10.
$$\frac{3}{5}x = -9$$
$$\frac{5}{3}\left(\frac{3}{5}x\right) = \frac{5}{3}(-9)$$
$$1x = -15$$
$$x = -15$$
The solution set is $\{-15\}$.

11.
$$30 = -\frac{5}{2}y$$
$$-\frac{2}{5}(30) = -\frac{2}{5}\left(-\frac{5}{2}y\right)$$
$$-12 = y$$
The solution set is $\{-12\}$.

12.
$$-x = 25$$
$$-1(-x) = -1(25)$$
$$x = -25$$
The solution set is $\{-25\}$.

13.
$$\frac{-x}{10} = -1$$
$$10\left(\frac{-x}{10}\right) = 10(-1)$$
$$-x = -10$$
$$-1(-x) = -1(-10)$$
$$x = 10$$
The solution set is $\{10\}$.

14.
$$4x + 9 = 33$$
$$4x + 9 - 9 = 33 - 9$$
$$4x = 24$$
$$\frac{4x}{4} = \frac{24}{4}$$
$$x = 6$$
The solution set is $\{6\}$.

15.
$$-3y - 2 = 13$$
$$-3y - 2 + 2 = 13 + 2$$
$$-3y = 15$$
$$\frac{-3y}{-3} = \frac{15}{-3}$$
$$y = -5$$
The solution set is $\{-5\}$.

16.
$$5z + 20 = 3z$$
$$5z + 20 - 3z = 3z - 3z$$
$$2z + 20 = 0$$
$$2z + 20 - 20 = 0 - 20$$
$$2z = -20$$
$$\frac{2z}{2} = \frac{-20}{2}$$
$$z = -10$$
The solution set is $\{-10\}$.

17.
$$5x - 3 = x + 5$$
$$5x - 3 - x = x + 5 - x$$
$$4x - 3 = 5$$
$$4x - 3 + 3 = 5 + 3$$
$$4x = 8$$
$$\frac{4x}{4} = \frac{8}{4}$$
$$x = 2$$
The solution set is $\{2\}$.

18.
$$3 - 2x = 9 - 8x$$
$$3 - 2x + 8x = 9 - 8x + 8x$$
$$3 + 6x = 9$$
$$3 + 6x - 3 = 9 - 3$$
$$6x = 6$$
$$\frac{6x}{6} = \frac{6}{6}$$
$$x = 1$$
The solution set is $\{1\}$.

19.
$$F = 1.2x + 21.6$$
$$40.8 = 1.2x + 21.6$$
$$40.8 - 21.6 = 1.2x + 21.6 - 21.6$$
$$19.2 = 1.2x$$
$$\frac{19.2}{1.2} = \frac{1.2x}{1.2}$$
$$16 = x$$
In the year, 1990 + 16 = 2006, the average income for a Puerto Rican family will be \$40,800.

20.
$$5x + 9 - 7x + 6 = x + 18$$
$$-2x + 15 = x + 18$$
$$-2x + 15 - x = x + 18 - x$$
$$-3x + 15 = 18$$
$$-3x + 15 - 15 = 18 - 15$$
$$-3x = 3$$
$$\frac{-3x}{-3} = \frac{3}{-3}$$
$$x = -1$$
The solution set is $\{-1\}$.

21.
$$3(x + 4) = 5x - 12$$
$$3x + 12 = 5x - 12$$
$$3x + 12 - 5x = 5x - 12 - 5x$$
$$-2x + 12 = -12$$
$$-2x + 12 - 12 = -12 - 12$$
$$-2x = -24$$
$$\frac{-2x}{-2} = \frac{-24}{-2}$$
$$x = 12$$
The solution set is $\{12\}$.

22.
$$1 - 2(6 - y) = 3y + 2$$
$$1 - 12 + 2y = 3y + 2$$
$$2y - 11 = 3y + 2$$
$$2y - 11 - 3y = 3y + 2 - 3y$$
$$-y - 11 = 2$$
$$-y - 11 + 11 = 2 + 11$$
$$-y = 13$$
$$-1(-y) = -1(13)$$
$$y = -13$$
The solution set is $\{-13\}$.

23.
$$2(x-4)+3(x+5)=2x-2$$
$$2x-8+3x+15=2x-2$$
$$5x+7=2x-2$$
$$5x+7-2x=2x-2-2x$$
$$3x+7=-2$$
$$3x+7-7=-2-7$$
$$3x=-9$$
$$\frac{3x}{3}=\frac{-9}{3}$$
$$x=-3$$
The solution set is $\{-3\}$.

24.
$$-2(y-4)-(3y-2)=-2-(6y-2)$$
$$-2y+8-3y+2=-2-6y-2$$
$$-5y+10=-6y$$
$$-5y+10+6y=-6y+6y$$
$$10+y=0$$
$$10+y-10=0-10$$
$$y=-10$$
The solution set is $\{-10\}$.

25.
$$\frac{2x}{3}=\frac{x}{6}+1$$
To clear fractions, multiply both sides by the LCD, which is 6.
$$6\left(\frac{2x}{3}\right)=6\left(\frac{x}{6}+1\right)$$
$$6\left(\frac{2x}{3}\right)=6\left(\frac{x}{6}\right)+6(1)$$
$$4x=x+6$$
$$4x-x=x+6-x$$
$$3x=6$$
$$\frac{3x}{3}=\frac{6}{3}$$
$$x=2$$
The solution set is $\{2\}$.

26.
$$\frac{x}{2}-\frac{1}{10}=\frac{x}{5}+\frac{1}{2}$$
Multiply both sides by the LCD, which is 10.
$$10\left(\frac{x}{2}-\frac{1}{10}\right)=10\left(\frac{x}{5}+\frac{1}{2}\right)$$
$$10\left(\frac{x}{2}\right)-10\left(\frac{1}{10}\right)=10\left(\frac{x}{5}\right)+10\left(\frac{1}{2}\right)$$
$$5x-1=2x+5$$
$$5x-1-2x=2x+5-2x$$
$$3x-1=5$$
$$3x-1+1=5+1$$
$$3x=6$$
$$\frac{3x}{3}=\frac{6}{3}$$
$$x=2$$
The solution set is $\{2\}$.

27.
$$3(8x-1)=6(5+4x)$$
$$24x-3=30+24x$$
$$24x-3-24x=30+24x-24x$$
$$-3=30$$
Since $-3=30$ is a false statement, the original equation is inconsistent and has no solution. The solution set is $\{\ \}$ or $\varnothing$.

28.
$$4(2x-3)+4=8x-8$$
$$8x-12+4=8x-8$$
$$8x-8=8x-8$$
$$8x-8-8x=8x-8-8x$$
$$-8=-8$$
Since $-8=-8$ is a true statement, the original equation is an identity and all real numbers are solutions. The solution set is $\mathbb{R}$.

Introductory & Intermediate Algebra for College Students, 2e
Essentials of Introductory & Intermediate Algebra for College Students

29. $r = 0.06(220 - a); \quad r = 120$

$$r = 0.6(220 - a)$$
$$120 = 0.6(220 - a)$$
$$120 = 132 - 0.6a$$
$$120 - 132 = -.06a$$
$$-12 = -0.6a$$
$$\frac{-12}{-0.6} = \frac{-0.6a}{-0.6}$$
$$20 = a$$

If the optimal heart rate is 120 beats per minute, the person is 20 years old.

30. $I = Pr$ for r

$$\frac{I}{P} = \frac{Pr}{P}$$
$$\frac{I}{P} = r \text{ or } r = \frac{I}{P}$$

31. $V = \frac{1}{3}Bh$ for h

$$3V = 3\left(\frac{1}{3}Bh\right)$$
$$3V = Bh$$
$$\frac{3V}{B} = \frac{Bh}{B}$$
$$\frac{3V}{B} = h \text{ or } h = \frac{3V}{B}$$

32. $P = 2l + 2w$ for w

$$P - 2l = 2l + 2w - 2l$$
$$P - 2l = 2w$$
$$\frac{P - 2l}{2} = \frac{2w}{2}$$
$$\frac{P - 2l}{2} = w \text{ or } w = \frac{P - 2l}{2}$$

33. $A = \frac{B + C}{2}$ for B

$$2A = 2\left(\frac{B + C}{2}\right)$$
$$2A = B + C$$
$$2A - C = B + C - C$$
$$2A - c = b \text{ or } B = 2A - C$$

34. $T = D + pm$ for m

$$T - D = D + pm - D$$
$$T - D = pm$$
$$\frac{T - D}{p} = \frac{pm}{p}$$
$$\frac{T - D}{p} = m \text{ or } m = \frac{T - D}{p}$$

35. $0.72 = 72\%$

36. $0.0035 = 0.35\%$

37. $65\% = 0.65$

38. $150\% = 1.50$

39. $3\% = 0.03$

40. $A = PB; \quad P = 8\% = 0.08, \ B = 120$

$$A = PB$$
$$A = 0.08 \cdot 120$$
$$A = 9.6$$
8% of 120 is 9.6

41. $A = PB; \quad A = 90, \ P = 45\% = 0.45$

$$A = PB$$
$$90 = 0.45B$$
$$\frac{90}{0.45} = \frac{0.45B}{0.45}$$
$$200 = B$$
90 is 45% of 200.

42. $A = PB$; $A = 36$, $B = 75$

$$A = PB$$
$$36 = P \cdot 75$$
$$\frac{36}{75} = \frac{P \cdot 75}{75}$$
$$0.48 = P$$

36 is 48% of 75.

43. Increase = Percent · Original
First, find the increase: $12 - 6 = 6$
$$6 = P \cdot 6$$
$$\frac{6}{6} = \frac{P \cdot 6}{6}$$
$$1 = P$$
The percent increase is $1 = 100\%$.

44. Decrease = Percent · Original
First, find the decrease: $5 - 3 = 2$
$$2 = P \cdot 5$$
$$\frac{2}{5} = \frac{P \cdot 5}{5}$$
$$0.4 = P$$
The percent decrease is $0.4 = 40\%$.

45. Increase = Percent · Original
First, find the increase: $45 - 40 = 5$
$$5 = P \cdot 40$$
$$\frac{5}{40} = \frac{P \cdot 40}{40}$$
$$0.125 = P$$
The percent increase is $0.125 = 12.5\%$.

46. Investment dollars lost last year were
$0.10 \cdot \$10,000 = \$1000$. This means
that $\$10,000 - \$1000 = \$9000$ remains.
Investment dollars gained this year are
$0.10 \cdot \$9000 = \$900$. This means that
$\$9000 + \$900 = \$9900$ of the original
investment remains. This is an overall
loss of $100.
decrease = percent · original

$$100 = P \cdot 10,000$$
$$\frac{100}{10,000} = \frac{P \cdot 10,000}{10,000}$$
$$0.01 = P$$

The statement is not true. Instead of
recouping losses, there is an overall 1%
decrease in the portfolio.

47. a. $$r = \frac{h}{7}$$
$$7r = 7\left(\frac{h}{7}\right)$$
$$7r = h \text{ or } h = 7r$$

b. $h = 7r$; $r = 9$
$$h = 7(9) = 63$$
The woman's height is 63 inches
or 5 feet, 3 inches.

48. $$A = P \cdot B$$
$$91 = 0.26 \cdot B$$
$$\frac{91}{0.26} = \frac{0.26 \cdot B}{0.26}$$
$$350 = B$$
The average U.S. household uses 350
gallons of water per day.

49. Let $x =$ the unknown number.
$$6x - 20 = 4x$$
$$6x - 20 - 4x = 4x - 4x$$
$$2x - 20 = 0$$
$$2x - 20 + 20 = 0 + 20$$
$$2x = 20$$
$$x = 10$$
The number is 10.

50. Let x = the number of unhealthy air days in New York.
Then $3x + 48$ = the number of unhealthy air days in Los Angeles.

$$x + (3x + 48) = 268$$
$$4x + 48 = 268$$
$$4x = 200$$
$$x = 55$$

New York has 55 unhealthy air days and Los Angeles has $3(55) + 48 = 213$ unhealthy air days.

51. Let x = the smaller page number.
Then $x + 1$ = the larger page number.

$$x + (x + 1) = 93$$
$$2x + 1 = 93$$
$$2x = 92$$
$$x = 46$$

The page numbers are 46 and 47. This solution checks because $46 + 47 = 93$.

52. Let x = the number of Madonna's platinum records.
Then $x + 2$ = the number of Barbra Streisand's platinum records.

$$x + (x + 2) = 96$$
$$2x + 2 = 96$$
$$2x = 94$$
$$x = 47$$

Madonna has 47 platinum records and Barbra Streisand has $47 + 2 = 49$ platinum records. This solution checks because $47 + 49 = 96$.

53. Let x = number of years after 2003.

$$612 + 15x = 747$$
$$612 + 15x - 612 = 747 - 612$$
$$15x = 135$$
$$\frac{15x}{15} = \frac{135}{15}$$
$$x = 9$$

According to this model, the average weekly salary will reach \$747 in 9 years after 2003 (in 2012).

54. Let x = the number of checks written.

$$6 + 0.05x = 6.90$$
$$6 + 0.05x - 6 = 6.90 - 6$$
$$0.05x = 0.90$$
$$\frac{0.05x}{0.05} = \frac{0.90}{0.05}$$
$$x = 18$$

You wrote 18 checks that month.

55. Let w = the width of the field.
Then $3w$ = the length.
The perimeter of a rectangle is twice the length plus twice the width, so the perimeter equation is
$2(3w) + 2w = 400$.
Solve the equation.

$$6w + 2w = 400$$
$$8w = 400$$
$$w = 50$$

The width is 50 yards and the length is $3(50) = 150$ yards.

56. Let x = the original price of the table.

$$x - 0.25x = 180$$
$$0.75x = 180$$
$$\frac{0.75x}{0.75} = \frac{180}{0.75}$$
$$x = 240$$

The table's price before the reduction was \$240.

57. Find the area of a rectangle with length 6.5 ft and width 5 ft.
$$A = lw = (6.5)(5) = 32.5$$
The area is 32.5 ft^2.

58. Find the area of a triangle with base 20 cm and height 5 cm.
$$A = \frac{1}{2}bh = \frac{1}{2}(20)(5) = 50$$
The area is 50 cm^2.

59. Find the area of a trapezoid with bases 22 yd and 5 yd and height 10 yd.
$$A = \frac{1}{2}h(a+b)$$
$$= \frac{1}{2}(10)(22+5)$$
$$= \frac{1}{2} \cdot 10 \cdot 27 = 135$$
The area is 135 yd^2.

60. Since the diameter is 20 m, the radius is $\frac{20}{2} = 10$ m.
$$C = 2\pi = 2\pi(10) = 20\pi \approx 63$$
$$A = \pi r^2 = \pi(10)^2 = 100 \approx 314$$
The circumference is 20π m or approximately 63 m; the area is 100π m^2 or approximately 314 m^2.

61.
$$A = \frac{1}{2}bh; A = 42, b = 14$$
$$A = \frac{1}{2}bh$$
$$42 = \frac{1}{2} \cdot 14 \cdot h$$
$$42 = 7h$$
$$6 = h$$
The height of the sail is 6 ft.

62. Area of floor:
$$A = bh = (12\,\text{ft})(15\,\text{ft}) = 180\,\text{ft}^2$$
Area of base of stove:
$$A = bh = (3\,\text{ft})(4\,\text{ft}) = 12\,\text{ft}^2$$
Area of bottom of refrigerator:
$$A = bh = (3\,\text{ft})(14\,\text{ft}) = 12\,\text{ft}^2$$
The area to be covered with floor tile is
$$180\,\text{ft}^2 - 12\,\text{ft}^2 - 12\,\text{ft}^2 = 156\,\text{ft}^2.$$

63. First, find the area of a trapezoid with bases 80 ft and 100 ft and height 60 ft.
$$A = \frac{1}{2}h(a+b)$$
$$= \frac{1}{2}(60)(80+100) = 5400$$
The area of the yard is 5400 ft^2. The cost is $0.35(5400) = \$1890$.

64. The radius of the medium pizza is $\frac{1}{2} \cdot 14$ inches $= 7$ inches, and the radius of each small pizza is $\frac{1}{2} \cdot 8$ inches $= 4$ inches.
Medium pizza:
$$A = \pi r^2 = \pi(7 \text{ in.})^2$$
$$= 49\pi \,\text{in}^2 \approx 154 \,\text{in}^2$$
Small pizza:
$$A = \pi r^2 = \pi(4 \text{ in.})^2$$
$$= 16\pi \,\text{in}^2 \approx 50.24 \,\text{in}^2$$
The area of one medium pizza is approximately 154 in^2 and the area of two small pizzas is approximately $2(50.24) = 100.48$ in^2. Since the price of one medium pizza is the same as the price of two small pizzas and the medium pizza has the greater area, the medium pizza is the better buy. (Because the prices are the same, it is not necessary to find price per square inch in this case.)

65. Find the volume of a rectangular solid with length 5 cm, width 3 cm, and height 4 cm.
$A = lwh = 5 \cdot 3 \cdot 4 = 60$
The volume is 60 cm^3.

66. Find the volume of a cylinder with radius 4 yd and height 8 yd.
$V = \pi r^2 h$
$\quad = \pi(4)^2 \cdot 8 = 128\pi \approx 402$
The volume is 138π yd$^3 \approx 402$ yd^3.

67. Find the volume of a sphere with radius 6 m.
$V = \dfrac{4}{3}\pi r^3$
$\quad = \dfrac{4}{3}\pi(6)^3 = \dfrac{4}{3} \cdot \pi \cdot 216$
$\quad = 288\pi \approx 905$
The volume is 288π m$^3 \approx 905$ m^3.

68. Find the volume of each box.
$V = lwh = (8\text{m})(4\text{m})(3\text{m}) = 96\text{m}^3$
The space required for 50 containers is
$50(96 \text{ m}^3) = 4800 \text{ m}^3$.

69. Since the diameter of the fish tank 6 ft, the radius is 3 ft.
$V = \pi r^2 h = \pi(3)^2 \cdot 3 = 27\pi \approx 84.78$
The volume of the tank is approximately 85 ft^3. Divide by 5 to determine how many fish can be put in the tank.
$\dfrac{84.78}{5} \approx 16.96$
There is enough water in the tank for 16 fish. Round down to 16, since 0.96 of a fish cannot be purchased.

70. The sum of the measures of the angles of any triangle is $180°$, so
$x + 3x + 2x = 180$.
Solve the equation for x.
$6x = 180$
$x = 30$
If $x = 30$, then $3x = 90$ and $2x = 60$, so the angles measure $30°$, $60°$, and $90°$.

71. Let $x =$ the measure of the second angle.
Let $2x + 15 =$ the measure of the first angle.
Let $x + 25 =$ the measure of the third angle.
$x + (2x + 15) + (x + 25) = 180$
$4x + 40 = 180$
$4x = 140$
$x = 35$
If $x = 35$, then $2x + 15 = 2(35) + 15 = 85$ and $x + 25 = 35 + 25 = 60$. The angles measure $35°$, $85°$, and $60°$.

72. If the measure of an angle is $57°$, the measure of its complement is
$90° - 57° = 33°$

73. If the measure of an angle is $75°$, the measure of its supplement is
$180° - 75° = 105°$.

74. Let $x =$ the measure of the angle.
Let $90 - x =$ the measure of its complement.
angle = 25 more than complement
angle = complement + 25
$x = (90 - x) + 25$
$x = 115 - x$
$2x = 115$
$x = 57.5$
The measure of the angle is $57.5°$.

75. Let x = the measure of the angle.
Let $180 - x$ = the measure of its supplement.
supplement = 45 less than 4 times angle

supplement = 4 times angle $- 45$

$$180 - x = 4x - 45$$
$$180 - 5x = -45$$
$$-5x = -225$$
$$x = 45$$

If $x = 45$, then $180 - x = 135$. The measure of the angle is $45°$ and the measure of its supplement is $135°$.

76. $x < -1$

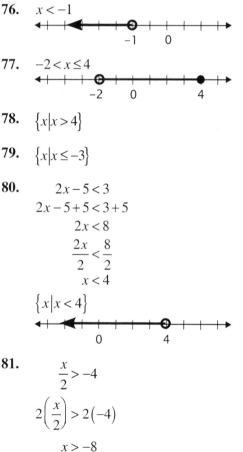

77. $-2 < x \le 4$

78. $\{x \mid x > 4\}$

79. $\{x \mid x \le -3\}$

80. $2x - 5 < 3$
$$2x - 5 + 5 < 3 + 5$$
$$2x < 8$$
$$\frac{2x}{2} < \frac{8}{2}$$
$$x < 4$$
$$\{x \mid x < 4\}$$

81. $\dfrac{x}{2} > -4$

$$2\left(\frac{x}{2}\right) > 2(-4)$$
$$x > -8$$
$$\{x \mid x > -8\}$$

82.
$$3 - 5x \le 18$$
$$3 - 5x - 3 \le 18 - 3$$
$$-5x \le 15$$
$$\frac{-5x}{-5} \ge \frac{15}{-5}$$
$$x \ge -3$$
$$\{x \mid x \ge -3\}$$

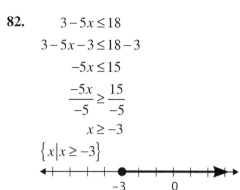

83.
$$4x + 6 < 5x$$
$$4x + 6 - 5x < 5x - 5x$$
$$-x + 6 < 0$$
$$-x + 6 - 6 < 0 - 6$$
$$-x < -6$$
$$-1(-x) > -1(-6)$$
$$x > 6$$
$$\{x \mid x > 6\}$$

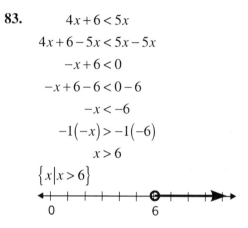

84.
$$6x - 10 \ge 2(x + 3)$$
$$6x - 10 \ge 2x + 6$$
$$6x - 10 - 2x \ge 2x + 6 - 2x$$
$$4x - 10 \ge 6$$
$$4x - 10 + 10 \ge 6 + 10$$
$$4x \ge 16$$
$$\frac{4x}{4} \ge \frac{16}{4}$$
$$x \ge 4$$
$$\{x \mid x \ge 4\}$$

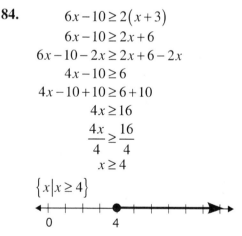

88

85.
$$4x + 3(2x - 7) \le x - 3$$
$$4x + 6x - 21 \le x - 3$$
$$10x - 21 \le x - 3$$
$$10x - 21 - x \le x - 3 - x$$
$$9x - 21 \le -3$$
$$9x - 21 + 21 \le -3 + 21$$
$$9x \le 18$$
$$\frac{9x}{9} \le \frac{18}{9}$$
$$x \le 2$$
$$\{x \mid x \le 2\}$$

86.
$$2(2x + 4) > 4(x + 2) - 6$$
$$4x + 8 > 4x + 8 - 6$$
$$4x + 8 > 4x + 2$$
$$4x + 8 - 4x > 4x + 2 - 4x$$
$$8 > 2$$

Since $8 > 2$ is a true statement, the original inequality is true for all real numbers, and the solution set is $\{x \mid x$ is a real number$\}$ or $\mathbb{R}$.

87.
$$-2(x - 4) \le 3x + 1 - 5x$$
$$-2x + 8 \le -2x + 1$$
$$-2x + 8 + 2x \le 2x + 1 + 2x$$
$$8 \le 1$$

Since $8 \le 1$ is a false statement, the original inequality has no solution. The solution set is $\emptyset$.

88. Let x = the student's score on the third test.
$$\frac{42 + 74 + x}{3} \ge 60$$
$$3\left(\frac{42 + 74 + x}{3}\right) \ge 3(60)$$
$$42 + 74 + x \ge 180$$
$$116 + x \ge 180$$
$$116 + x - 116 \ge 180 - 116$$
$$x \ge 64$$

The student must score at least 64 on the third test to pass the course.

89. $C = 10 + 5(x - 1); \; C \le 500$
$$10 + 5(x - 1) \le 500$$
$$10 + 5x - 5 \le 500$$
$$5x + 5 \le 500$$
$$5x + 5 - 5 \le 500 - 5$$
$$5x \le 495$$
$$\frac{5x}{5} \le \frac{495}{5}$$
$$x \le 99$$

You can talk no more than 99 minutes.

Chapter 2 Test

1.
$$4x - 5 = 13$$
$$4x + 5 + 5 = 13 + 5$$
$$4x = 18$$
$$\frac{4x}{4} = \frac{18}{4} = \frac{9}{2}$$
$$x = \frac{9}{2}$$

The solution set is $\left\{\frac{9}{2}\right\}$.

2.
$$12x + 4 = 7x - 21$$
$$12x + 4 - 7x = 7x - 21 - 7x$$
$$5x + 4 = -21$$
$$5x + 4 - 4 = -21 - 4$$
$$5x = -25$$
$$\frac{5x}{5} = \frac{-25}{5}$$
$$x = -5$$
The solution set is $\{-5\}$.

3.
$$8 - 5(x - 2) = x + 26$$
$$8 - 5x + 10 = x + 26$$
$$18 - 5x = x + 26$$
$$18 - 5x - x = x + 26 - x$$
$$18 - 6x = 26$$
$$18 - 6x - 18 = 26 - 18$$
$$-6x = 8$$
$$\frac{-6x}{-6} = \frac{8}{-6}$$
$$x = -\frac{8}{6} = -\frac{4}{3}$$
The solution set is $\left\{-\frac{4}{3}\right\}$.

4.
$$3(2y - 4) = 9 - 3(y + 1)$$
$$6y - 12 = 9 - 3y - 3$$
$$6y - 12 = 6 - 3y$$
$$6y - 12 + 3y = 6 - 3y + 3y$$
$$9y - 12 = 6$$
$$9y - 12 + 12 = 6 + 12$$
$$9y = 18$$
$$\frac{9y}{9} = \frac{18}{9}$$
$$y = 2$$
The solution set is $\{2\}$.

5.
$$\frac{3}{4}x = -15$$
$$\frac{4}{3}\left(\frac{3}{4}x\right) = \frac{4}{3}(-15)$$
$$x = -20$$
The solution set is $\{-20\}$.

6.
$$\frac{x}{10} + \frac{1}{3} = \frac{x}{5} + \frac{1}{2}$$
Multiply both sides by the LCD, 30.
$$30\left(\frac{x}{10} + \frac{1}{3}\right) = 30\left(\frac{x}{5} + \frac{1}{2}\right)$$
$$30\left(\frac{x}{10}\right) + 30\left(\frac{1}{3}\right) = 30\left(\frac{x}{5}\right) + 30\left(\frac{1}{2}\right)$$
$$3x + 10 = 6x + 15$$
$$3x + 10 - 6x = 6x + 15 - 6x$$
$$-3x + 10 = 15$$
$$-3x + 10 - 10 = 15 - 10$$
$$-3x = 5$$
$$\frac{-3x}{-3} = \frac{5}{-3}$$
$$x = -\frac{5}{3}$$
The solution set is $\left\{-\frac{5}{3}\right\}$.

7.
$$N = 2.4x + 180; \ N = 324$$
$$2.4x + 180 = 324$$
$$2.4x + 180 - 180 = 324 - 180$$
$$2.4 = 144$$
$$\frac{2.4x}{2.4} = \frac{144}{2.4}$$
$$x = 60$$
The US population is expected to reach 324 million 60 years after 1960, in the year 2020.

8. $V = \pi r^2 h$ for h

$$\frac{V}{\pi r^2} = \frac{\pi r^2 h}{\pi r^2}$$

$$\frac{V}{\pi r^2} = h \text{ or } h = \frac{V}{\pi r^2}$$

9. $l = \dfrac{P - 2w}{2}$ for w

$$2l = 2\left(\frac{P - 2w}{2}\right)$$

$$2l = P - 2w$$

$$2l - P = P - 2w - P$$

$$2l - P = -2w$$

$$\frac{2l - P}{-2} = \frac{-2w}{-2}$$

$$\frac{2l - P}{-2} = w \text{ or } w = \frac{P - 2l}{2}$$

10. $A = PB$; $P = 6\% = 0.06$, $B = 140$

$A = PB$

$A = 0.06(140)$

$A = 8.4$

6% of 140 is 8.4

11. $A = PB$; $A = 120$, $P = 80\% = 0.80$

$A = PB$

$120 = 0.80B$

$$\frac{120}{0.80} = \frac{0.80B}{0.80}$$

$150 = B$

120 is 80% of 150.

12. $A = PB$; $A = 12$, $B = 240$

$A = PB$

$12 = P \cdot 240$

$$\frac{12}{240} = \frac{P \cdot 240}{240}$$

$0.05 = P$

12 is 5% of 240.

13. Let x = the unknown number.

$$5x - 9 = 306$$

$$5x - 9 + 9 = 306 + 9$$

$$5x = 315$$

$$\frac{5x}{5} = \frac{315}{5}$$

$$x = 63$$

The number is 63.

14. Let x = the amount earned by a preschool teacher
Let $x + 22{,}870$ = the amount earned by a fitness instructor

$$x + (x + 22{,}870) = 79{,}030$$

$$x + x + 22{,}870 = 79{,}030$$

$$2x + 22{,}870 = 79{,}030$$

$$2x + 22{,}870 - 22{,}870 = 79{,}030 - 22{,}870$$

$$2x = 79{,}030 - 22{,}870$$

$$2x = 56{,}160$$

$$\frac{2x}{2} = \frac{56{,}160}{2}$$

$$x = 28{,}080$$

A preschool teacher makes $28,080 and a fitness trainer makes $28,080 + $22,870 = $50,950

15. Let x = number of minutes of long distance calls.

$$15 + 0.05x = 45$$

$$0.05x = 30$$

$$x = \frac{30}{0.05}$$

$$x = 600$$

You can talk long distance for 600 minutes.

16. Let w = width of field (in yards).
Then $2w$ = length of field.

$$2(2w) + 2w = 450$$
$$4w + 2w = 450$$
$$6w = 450$$
$$w = 75$$

The width is 75 yards and the length is $2(75) = 150$ yards.

17. Let x = the book's original price.

$$x - 0.20x = 28$$
$$0.80x = 28$$
$$x = \frac{28}{0.80}$$
$$x = 35$$

The price of the book before the reduction was $35.

18. Find the area of a triangle with base 47 m and height 22 m.

$$A = \frac{1}{2}bh = \frac{1}{2}(47)(22) = 517$$

The area of the triangle is 517 m^2.

19. Find the area of a trapezoid with height 15 in, lower base 40 in and upper base 30 in.

$$A = \frac{1}{2}h(a + b)$$
$$= \frac{1}{2}(15)(40 + 30)$$
$$= \frac{1}{2} \cdot 15 \cdot 70 = 525$$

The area is 525 in^2.

20. Find the volume of a rectangular solid with length 3 in, width 2 in, and height 3 in.

$$V = lwh = 3 \cdot 2 \cdot 3 = 18$$

The volume is 18 in^3.

21. Find the volume of a cylinder with radius 5 cm and height 7 cm.

$$V = \pi r^2 h$$
$$= \pi(5)^2 \cdot 7 = \pi \cdot 25 \cdot 7$$
$$= 175\pi \approx 550$$

The volume is 175π cm^3 or approximately 550 cm^3.

22. The area of the floor is
$$A = (40\,\text{ft})(50\,\text{ft}) = 2000\,\text{ft}^2.$$
The area of each tile is
$$A = (2\,\text{ft})(2\,\text{ft}) = 4\,\text{ft}^2.$$
The number of tiles needed is
$$\frac{2000\,\text{ft}^2}{4\,\text{ft}^2} = 500.$$
Since there are 10 tiles in a package, the number of packages needed is
$$\frac{500}{10} = 50.$$
Since each package costs $13, the cost for enough tiles to cover the floor is $50(\$13) = \$650$.

23.

$$A = \frac{1}{2}bh; A = 56, b = 8$$
$$A = \frac{1}{2}bh$$
$$56 = \frac{1}{2} \cdot 8 \cdot h$$
$$56 = 4h$$
$$14 = h$$

The height of the sail is 14 feet.

24. Let x = the measure of the second angle.
Let $3x$ = the measure of the first angle.
Let $x - 30$ = the measure of the third angle.

$$x + 3x + (x - 30) = 180$$
$$5x - 30 = 180$$
$$5x = 210$$
$$x = 42$$

The measure of the first angle = $3x$ = $3(42°) = 126°$.
The measure of the second angle = x = $42°$.
The measure of the third angle = $x - 30$ = $42° - 30° = 12°$.

25. Let x = the measure of the angle.
Let $90 - x$ = the measure of its complement.

$$x = (90 - x) + 16$$
$$x = 106 - x$$
$$2x = 106$$
$$x = 53$$

The measure of the angle is $53°$.

26. $x > -2$

27. $-4 \le x < 1$

28. $\{x | x \le -1\}$

29.
$$\frac{x}{2} < -3$$
$$2\left(\frac{x}{2}\right) < 2(-3)$$
$$x < -6$$
$$\{x | x < -6\}$$

30.
$$6 - 9x \ge 33$$
$$6 - 9x - 6 \ge 33 - 6$$
$$-9x \ge 27$$
$$\frac{-9x}{-9} \le \frac{27}{-9}$$
$$x \le -3$$
$$\{x | x \le -3\}$$

31.
$$4x - 2 > 2(x + 6)$$
$$4x - 2 > 2x + 12$$
$$4x - 2 - 2x > 2x + 12 - 2x$$
$$2x - 2 > 12$$
$$2x > 14$$
$$x > 7$$
$$\{x | x > 7\}$$

32. Let x = the student's score on the fourth exam.
$$\frac{76 + 80 + 72 + x}{4} \ge 80$$
$$4\left(\frac{76 + 80 + 72 + x}{4}\right) \ge 4(80)$$
$$76 + 80 + 72 + x \ge 320$$
$$228 + x \ge 320$$
$$x \ge 92$$

The student must score at least 92 on the fourth exam to have an average of at least 80.

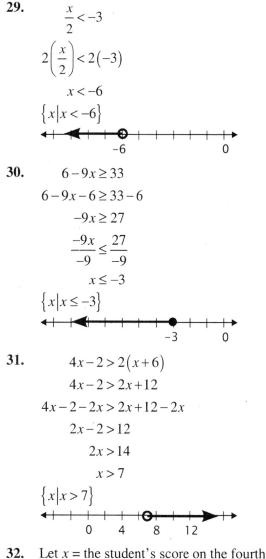

33. Let w = the width of rectangle.

$$2(20) + 2w > 56$$
$$40 + 2w > 56$$
$$2w > 16$$
$$w > 8$$

The width must be greater than 8 inches.

Cumulative Review Exercises (Chapters 1-2)

1. $-8 - (12 - 16) = -8 - (-4) = -8 + 4 = -4$

2. $(-3)(-2) + (-2)(4) = 6 + (-8) = -2$

3. $(8 - 10)^3 (7 - 11)^2 = (-2)^3 (-4)^2$
$$= -8(16) = -128$$

4. $2 - 5\left[x + 3(x + 7)\right]$
$$= 2 - 5(x + 3x + 21)$$
$$= 2 - 5(4x + 21)$$
$$= 2 - 20x - 105$$
$$= -103 - 20x$$

5. The rational numbers are
$$-4, -\frac{1}{3}, 0, \sqrt{4} \, (= 2), \text{ and } 1063.$$

6.

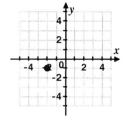

Quadrant III

7. $-10,000 < -2$ since $-10,000$ is to the left of -2 on the number line.

8. $6(4x - 1 - 5y) = 6(4x) - 6(1) - 6(5y)$
$$= 24x - 6 - 30y$$

9. Unemployment was a minimum of 2000, with about 4% unemployed.

10. The unemployment rate reached a maximum during 1992 of about 7.8%.

11. $5 - 6(x + 2) = x - 14$
$$5 - 6x - 12 = x - 14$$
$$-7 - 6x = x - 14$$
$$-7 - 6x - x = x - 14 - x$$
$$-7 - 7x = -14$$
$$-7 - 7x + 7 = -14 + 7$$
$$-7x = -7$$
$$\frac{-7x}{-7} = \frac{-7}{-7}$$
$$x = 1$$

The solution set is $\{1\}$.

12. $\dfrac{x}{5} - 2 = \dfrac{x}{3}$

Multiply both sides by the LCD, 15.

$$15\left(\frac{x}{5} - 2\right) = 15\left(\frac{x}{3}\right)$$
$$15\left(\frac{x}{5}\right) - 15(2) = 15\left(\frac{x}{3}\right)$$
$$3x - 30 = 5x$$
$$3x - 30 - 3x = 5x - 3x$$
$$-30 = 2x$$
$$\frac{-30}{2} = \frac{2x}{2}$$
$$-15 = x$$

The solution set is $\{-15\}$.

13. $V = \frac{1}{3} Ah$ for A

$$V = \frac{1}{3} Ah$$

$$3V = 3\left(\frac{1}{3} Ah\right)$$

$$3V = Ah$$

$$\frac{3V}{h} = \frac{Ah}{h}$$

$$\frac{3V}{h} = A \ \text{ or } \ A = \frac{3V}{h}$$

14. $A = PB; \ A = 48, \ P = 30\% = 0.30$

$$A = PB$$

$$48 = 0.30B$$

$$\frac{48}{0.30} = \frac{0.30B}{0.30}$$

$$160 = B$$

48 is 30% of 160.

15. Let w = width of parking lot (in yards).
Let $2w - 10$ = length of parking lot.

$$2(2w - 10) + 2w = 400$$

$$4w - 20 + 2w = 400$$

$$6w - 20 = 400$$

$$6w = 420$$

$$w = 70$$

The width is 70 yards and the length is $2(70) - 10 = 130$ yards.

16. Let x = number of gallons of gasoline.

$$0.40x = 30,000$$

$$\frac{0.40x}{0.40} = \frac{30,000}{0.40}$$

$$x = 75,000$$

75,000 gallons of gasoline must be sold.

17. $-2 < x \le 3$

18. $3 - 3x > 12$

$$3 - 3x - 3 > 12 - 3$$

$$-3x > 9$$

$$\frac{-3x}{-3} < \frac{9}{-3}$$

$$x < -3$$

$$\{x \mid x < -3\}$$

19. $5 - 2(3 - x) \le 2(2x + 5) + 1$

$$5 - 6 + 2x \le 4x + 10 + 1$$

$$2x - 1 \le 4x + 11$$

$$2x - 1 - 4x \le 4x + 11 - 4x$$

$$-2x - 1 \le 11$$

$$-2x - 1 + 1 \le 11 + 1$$

$$-2x \le 12$$

$$\frac{-2x}{-2} \ge \frac{12}{-2}$$

$$x \ge -6$$

$$\{x \mid x \ge -6\}$$

20. Let x = value of medical supplies sold.

$$600 + 0.04x > 2500$$

$$600 + 0.04x - 600 > 2500 - 600$$

$$0.04x > 1900$$

$$\frac{0.04x}{0.04} > \frac{1900}{0.04}$$

$$x > 47,500$$

You must sell more than \$47,500 worth of medical supplies.

95

Chapter 3
Linear Equations in Two Variables

1. $y = 3x$

$(2,3)$:

$3 = 3(2)$

$3 = 6$ false

$(2,3)$ is not a solution.

$(3,2)$:

$2 = 3(3)$

$2 = 9$ false

$(3,2)$ is not a solution.

$(-4,-12)$:

$-12 = 3(-4)$

$-12 = -12$ true

$(-4,-12)$ is a solution.

3. $y = -4x$

$(-5,-20)$:

$-20 = -4(-5)$

$-20 = 20$ false

$(-5,-20)$ is not a solution.

$(0,0)$:

$0 = -4(0)$

$0 = 0$ true

$(0,0)$ is a solution.

$(9,-36)$:

$-36 = -4(9)$

$-36 = -36$ true

$(9,-36)$ is a solution.

5. $y = 2x + 6$

$(0,6)$:

$6 = 2(0) + 6$

$6 = 6$ true

$(0,6)$ is a solution.

$(-3,0)$:

$0 = 2(-3) + 6$

$0 = 0$ true

$(-3,0)$ is a solution.

$(2,-2)$:

$-2 = 2(2) + 6$

$-2 = 10$ false

$(2,-2)$ is not a solution.

7. $3x + 5y = 15$

$(-5,6)$:

$3(-5) + 5(6) = 15$

$-15 + 30 = 15$

$15 = 15$ true

$(-5,6)$ is a solution.

$(0,5)$:

$3(0) + 5(5) = 15$

$0 + 25 = 15$

$25 = 15$ false

$(0,5)$ is not a solution.

$(10,-3)$:

$3(10) + 5(-3) = 15$

$30 - 15 = 15$

$15 = 15$ true

$(10,-3)$ is a solution.

9. $x + 3y = 0$

$(0,0)$:

$0 + 3(0) = 0$

$\qquad 0 = 0$ true

$(0,0)$ is a solution.

$\left(1, \dfrac{1}{3}\right)$:

$1 + 3\left(\dfrac{1}{3}\right) = 0$

$\qquad 1 + 1 = 0$

$\qquad\quad 2 = 0$ false

$\left(1, \dfrac{1}{3}\right)$ is not a solution.

$\left(2, -\dfrac{2}{3}\right)$:

$2 + 3\left(-\dfrac{2}{3}\right) = 0$

$\qquad 2 - 2 = 0$

$\qquad\qquad 0 = 0$ true

$\left(2, -\dfrac{2}{3}\right)$ is a solution.

11. $x - 4 = 0$

$(4,7)$:

$4 - 4 = 0$

$\qquad 0 = 0$ true

$(4,7)$ is a solution.

$(3,4)$:

$3 - 4 = 0$

$\quad -1 = 0$ false

$(3,4)$ is not a solution.

$(0,-4)$:

$0 - 4 = 0$

$\quad -4 = 0$ false

$(0,-4)$ is not a solution.

13.

x	$y = 12x$	(x, y)
-2	$y = 12(-2) = -24$	$(-2, -24)$
-1	$y = 12(-1) = -12$	$(-1, -12)$
0	$y = 12(0) = 0$	$(0, 0)$
1	$y = 12(1) = 12$	$(1, 12)$
2	$y = 12(2) = 24$	$(2, 24)$

15.

x	$y = -10x$	(x, y)
-2	$y = -10(-2) = 20$	$(-2, 20)$
-1	$y = -10(-1) = 10$	$(-1, 10)$
0	$y = -10(0) = 0$	$(0, 0)$
1	$y = -10(1) = -10$	$(1, -10)$
2	$y = -10(2) = -20$	$(2, -20)$

17.

x	$y = 8x - 5$	(x, y)
-2	$y = 8(-2) - 5 = -21$	$(-2, -21)$
-1	$y = 8(-1) - 5 = -13$	$(-1, -13)$
0	$y = 8(0) - 5 = -5$	$(0, -5)$
1	$y = 8(1) - 5 = 3$	$(1, 3)$
2	$y = 8(2) - 5 = 11$	$(2, 11)$

19.

x	$y = -3x + 7$	(x, y)
-2	$y = -3(-2) + 7 = 13$	$(-2, 13)$
-1	$y = -3(-1) + 7 = 10$	$(-1, 10)$
0	$y = -3(0) + 7 = 7$	$(0, 7)$
1	$y = -3(1) + 7 = 4$	$(1, 4)$
2	$y = -3(2) + 7 = 1$	$(2, 1)$

21.

x	$y = x$	(x, y)
-2	$y = -2$	$(-2, -2)$
-1	$y = -1$	$(-1, -1)$
0	$y = 0$	$(0, 0)$
1	$y = 1$	$(1, 1)$
2	$y = 2$	$(2, 2)$

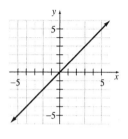

23.

x	$y = x - 1$	(x, y)
-2	$y = -2 - 1 = -3$	$(-2, -3)$
-1	$y = -1 - 1 = -2$	$(-1, -2)$
0	$y = 0 - 1 = -1$	$(0, -1)$
1	$y = 1 - 1 = 0$	$(1, 0)$
2	$y = 2 - 1 = 1$	$(2, 1)$

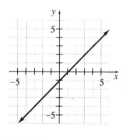

25.

x	$y = 2x + 1$	(x, y)
-2	$y = 2(-2) + 1 = -3$	$(-2, -3)$
-1	$y = 2(-1) + 1 = -1$	$(-1, -1)$
0	$y = 2(0) + 1 = 1$	$(0, 1)$
1	$y = 2(1) + 1 = 3$	$(1, 3)$
2	$y = 2(2) + 1 = 5$	$(2, 5)$

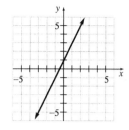

27.

x	$y = -x + 2$	(x, y)
-2	$y = -(-2) + 2 = 4$	$(-2, 4)$
-1	$y = -(-1) + 2 = 3$	$(-1, 3)$
0	$y = -0 + 2 = 2$	$(0, 2)$
1	$y = -1 + 2 = 1$	$(1, 1)$
2	$y = -2 + 2 = 0$	$(2, 0)$

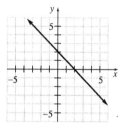

29.

x	$y = -3x - 1$	(x, y)
-2	$y = -3(-2) - 1 = 5$	$(-2, 5)$
-1	$y = -3(-1) - 1 = 2$	$(-1, 2)$
0	$y = -3(0) - 1 = -1$	$(0, -1)$
1	$y = -3(1) - 1 = -4$	$(1, -4)$
2	$y = -3(2) - 1 = -7$	$(2, -7)$

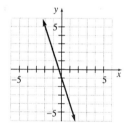

31.

x	$y = \dfrac{1}{2}x$	(x, y)
-4	$y = \dfrac{1}{2}(-4) = -2$	$(-4, -2)$
-2	$y = \dfrac{1}{2}(-2) = -1$	$(-2, -1)$
0	$y = \dfrac{1}{2}(0) = 0$	$(0, 0)$
2	$y = \dfrac{1}{2}(2) = 1$	$(2, 1)$
4	$y = \dfrac{1}{2}(4) = 2$	$(4, 2)$

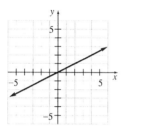

35.

x	$y = \dfrac{1}{3}x + 1$	(x, y)
-6	$y = \dfrac{1}{3}(-6) + 1 = -1$	$(-6, -1)$
-3	$y = \dfrac{1}{3}(-3) + 1 = 0$	$(-3, 0)$
0	$y = \dfrac{1}{3}(0) + 1 = 1$	$(0, -1)$
3	$y = \dfrac{1}{3}(3) + 1 = 2$	$(3, 2)$
6	$y = \dfrac{1}{3}(6) + 1 = 3$	$(6, 3)$

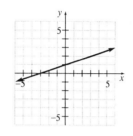

33.

x	$y = -\dfrac{1}{4}x$	(x, y)
-8	$y = -\dfrac{1}{4}(-8) = 2$	$(-8, 2)$
-4	$y = -\dfrac{1}{4}(-4) = 1$	$(-4, 1)$
-0	$y = -\dfrac{1}{4}(0) = 0$	$(0, 0)$
4	$y = -\dfrac{1}{4}(4) = -1$	$(4, -1)$
8	$y = -\dfrac{1}{4}(8) = -2$	$(8, -2)$

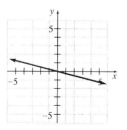

37.

x	$y = -\dfrac{3}{2}x + 1$	(x, y)
-4	$y = -\dfrac{3}{2}(-4) + 1 = 7$	$(-4, 7)$
-2	$y = -\dfrac{3}{2}(-2) + 1 = 4$	$(-2, 4)$
0	$y = -\dfrac{3}{2}(0) + 1 = 1$	$(0, 1)$
2	$y = -\dfrac{3}{2}(2) + 1 = -2$	$(2, -2)$
4	$y = -\dfrac{3}{2}(4) + 1 = -5$	$(4, -5)$

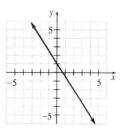

39.

x	$y = -\dfrac{5}{2}x - 1$	(x, y)
-4	$y = -\dfrac{5}{2}(-4) - 1 = 9$	$(-4, 9)$
-2	$y = -\dfrac{5}{2}(-2) - 1 = 4$	$(-2, 4)$
0	$y = -\dfrac{5}{2}(0) - 1 = -1$	$(0, -1)$
2	$y = -\dfrac{5}{2}(2) - 1 = -6$	$(2, -6)$
4	$y = -\dfrac{5}{2}(4) - 1 = -11$	$(4, -11)$

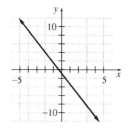

41.

x	$y = x + \dfrac{1}{2}$	(x, y)
-4	$y = -4 + \dfrac{1}{2} = -3.5$	$(-4, -3.5)$
-2	$y = -2 + \dfrac{1}{2} = -1.5$	$(-2, -1.5)$
0	$y = 0 + \dfrac{1}{2} = 0.5$	$(0, 0.5)$
2	$y = 2 + \dfrac{1}{2} = 2.5$	$(2, 2.5)$
4	$y = 4 + \dfrac{1}{2} = 4.5$	$(4, 4.5)$

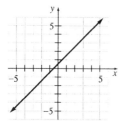

43.

x	$y = 0x + 4$	(x, y)
-6	$y = 0(-6) + 4 = 4$	$(-6, 4)$
-3	$y = 0(-3) + 4 = 4$	$(-3, 4)$
0	$y = 0(0) + 4 = 4$	$(0, 4)$
3	$y = 0(3) + 4 = 4$	$(3, 4)$
6	$y = 0(6) + 4 = 4$	$(6, 4)$

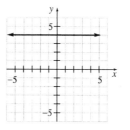

45.

x	$y = x^2$	(x, y)
-3	$y = (-3)^2 = 9$	$(-3, 9)$
-2	$y = (-2)^2 = 4$	$(-2, 4)$
-1	$y = (-1)^2 = 1$	$(-1, 1)$
0	$y = 0^2 = 0$	$(0, 0)$
1	$y = 1^2 = 1$	$(1, 1)$
2	$y = 2^2 = 4$	$(2, 4)$
3	$y = 3^2 = 9$	$(3, 9)$

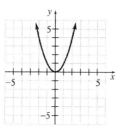

47.

x	$y = x^2 + 1$	(x, y)
-3	$y = (-3)^2 + 1 = 10$	$(-3, 10)$
-2	$y = (-2)^2 + 1 = 5$	$(-2, 5)$
-1	$y = (-1)^2 + 1 = 2$	$(-1, 2)$
0	$y = 0^2 + 1 = 1$	$(0, 1)$
1	$y = 1^2 + 1 = 2$	$(1, 2)$
2	$y = 2^2 + 1 = 5$	$(2, 5)$
3	$y = 3^2 + 1 = 10$	$(3, 10)$

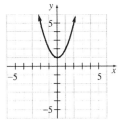

49.

x	$y = 4 - x^2$	(x, y)
-3	$y = 4 - (-3)^2 = -5$	$(-3, -5)$
-2	$y = 4 - (-2)^2 = 0$	$(-2, 0)$
-1	$y = 4 - (-1)^2 = 3$	$(-1, 3)$
0	$y = 4 - 0^2 = 4$	$(0, 4)$
1	$y = 4 - 1^2 = 3$	$(1, 3)$
2	$y = 4 - 2^2 = 0$	$(2, 0)$
3	$y = 4 - 3^2 = -5$	$(3, -5)$

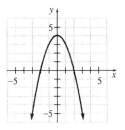

51. $y = x + 3$

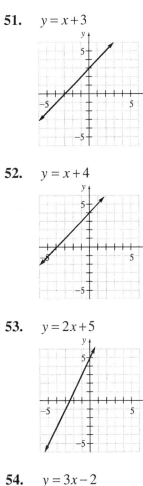

52. $y = x + 4$

53. $y = 2x + 5$

54. $y = 3x - 2$

55. **a.** $8x + 6y = 14.50$

 b. $8x + 6(0.75) = 14.50$
$$8x + 4.50 = 14.50$$
$$8x = 10.00$$
$$x = 1.25$$

Pens cost $1.25.

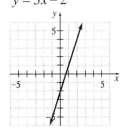

101

56. **a.** $3x + 4y = 22.00$

b. $3x + 4(2.50) = 22.00$

$3x + 10.00 = 22.00$

$3x = 12.00$

$x = 4.00$

Orange trees cost \$4.00.

57. **a.**

x	$y = 0.24x + 5.2$	(x, y)
0	$y = 0.24(0) + 5.2 = 5.2$	$(0, 5.2)$
10	$y = 0.24(10) + 5.2 = 7.6$	$(10, 7.6)$
20	$y = 0.24(20) + 5.2 = 10$	$(20, 10)$
30	$y = 0.24(30) + 5.2 = 12.4$	$(30, 12.4)$

The model does not fit the data very well. Some years are underestimated while others are overestimated.

b.

x	$y = 0.22x + 3.4$	(x, y)
0	$y = 0.22(0) + 3.4 = 3.4$	$(0, 3.4)$
10	$y = 0.22(10) + 3.4 = 5.6$	$(10, 5.6)$
20	$y = 0.22(20) + 3.4 = 7.8$	$(20, 7.8)$
30	$y = 0.22(30) + 3.4 = 9.0$	$(30, 9.0)$

The model fits the data moderately well.

c.

x	$y = 0.13x + 4.2$	(x, y)
0	$y = 0.13(0) + 4.2 = 4.2$	$(0, 4.2)$
10	$y = 0.13(10) + 4.2 = 5.5$	$(10, 5.5)$
20	$y = 0.13(20) + 4.2 = 6.8$	$(20, 6.8)$
30	$y = 0.13(30) + 4.2 = 8.1$	$(30, 8.1)$

The model fits the data fairly well.

58. **a.**

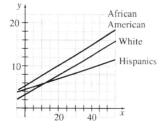

b. From the graph we obtain the following predictions for percent divorced in 2010:
African American: 14.8%
Whites: 10%
Hispanics: 9.4%

59. **a.** The x-coordinate of the intersection point is 40. This means that if you drive the moving truck 40 miles, the rental charge will be the same with both companies.

b. A reasonable estimate of the y-coordinate of the intersection point is 55.

c. $y = 40 + 35;\ x = 40$

$y = 40 + 0.35(40)$

$y = 40 + 14 = 54$

$y = 36 + 0.45x;\ x = 40$

$y = 36 + 0.45(40)$

$y = 36 + 18 = 54$

This value indicates that if you drive the moving truck 40 miles, the rental charge with either company will be \$54. This is almost the same as the estimate in part (b).]

60. **a.**

x	$y = 166x + 1781$	(x, y)
0	$y = 166(0) + 1781$ $= 1781$	$(0, 1781)$
5	$y = 166(5) + 1781$ $= 2611$	$(0, 2611)$
10	$y = 166(10) + 1781$ $= 3441$	$(10, 3441)$
15	$y = 166(15) + 1781$ $= 4271$	$(15, 4271)$
20	$y = 166(20) + 1781$ $= 5101$	$(20, 5101)$

b.

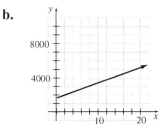

The cost of a four-year college has been increasing and will continue to increase at the same rate.

61. **a.**

x	$y = 50x + 30,000$	(x, y)
0	$y = 30,000$	$(0, 30,000)$
10	$y = 30,500$	$(10, 30,500)$
20	$y = 31,000$	$(20, 31,000)$
30	$y = 31,500$	$(30, 31,500)$
40	$y = 32,000$	$(40, 32,000)$

b.

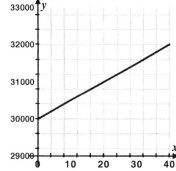

For Exercises 63-65, answers will vary.

67.

x	$y = |x|$	(x, y)
-3	$y = |-3| = 3$	$(-3, 3)$
-2	$y = |-2| = 2$	$(-2, 2)$
-1	$y = |-1| = 1$	$(-1, 1)$
0	$y = |0| = 0$	$(0, 0)$
1	$y = |1| = 1$	$(1, 1)$
2	$y = |2| = 2$	$(2, 2)$
3	$y = |3| = 3$	$(3, 3)$

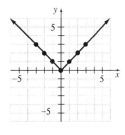

69. **a.** Set $x = 0$, and simplify.
$$y = 0.1x^2 - 0.4x + 0.6$$
$$= 0.1(0)^2 - 0.4(0) + 0.6$$
$$= 0.6$$
This solution is the pair, $(0, 0.6)$.
Set $x = 1$, and simplify.
$$y = 0.1x^2 - 0.4x + 0.6$$
$$= 0.1(1)^2 - 0.4(1) + 0.6$$
$$= 0.1(1) - 0.4 + 0.6$$
$$= 0.1 - 0.4 + 0.6$$
$$= 0.3$$
This solution is the pair, $(1, 0.3)$. Using similar calculations, we have $(2, 0.2)$, $(3, 0.3)$, $(4, 0.6)$, and $(5, 1.1)$.

b. Runners should run between 10:00 A.M. and noon in order to avoid unsafe air.

71. Answers will vary depending upon the points chosen. One example is shown here.

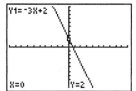

103

73. Answers will vary depending upon the points chosen. One example is shown here.

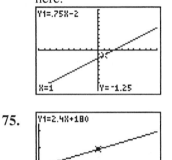

75.

U.S. population is increasing over time.

76.
$$3x + 5 = 4(2x - 3) + 7$$
$$3x + 5 = 8x - 12 + 7$$
$$3x + 5 = 8x - 5$$
$$3x + 5 - 8x = 8x - 5 - 8x$$
$$-5x + 5 = -5$$
$$-5x + 5 - 5 = -5 - 5$$
$$-5x = -10$$
$$\frac{-5x}{-5} = \frac{-10}{-5}$$
$$x = 2$$

The solution set is $\{2\}$.

77. $3(1 - 2 \cdot 5) - (-28) = 3(1 - 10) + 28$
$$= 3(-9) + 28$$
$$= -27 + 28 = 1$$

78. $V = \frac{1}{3}Ah$ for h

$$V = \frac{1}{3}Ah$$

$$3V = 3\left(\frac{1}{3}Ah\right)$$

$$3V = Ah$$

$$\frac{3V}{A} = \frac{Ah}{A}$$

$$\frac{3V}{A} = h \text{ or } h = \frac{3V}{A}$$

3.2 Exercise Set

1. **a.** The graph crosses the x-axis at $(3,0)$. Thus, the x-intercept is 3.

    b. The graph crosses the y-axis at $(0,4)$. Thus, the y-intercept is 4.

3. **a.** The graph crosses the x-axis at $(-4,0)$. Thus, the x-intercept is -4.

    b. The graph crosses the y-axis at $(0,-2)$. Thus, the y-intercept is -2.

5. **a.** The graph crosses the x-axis at $(0,0)$ (the origin). Thus, the x-intercept is 0.

    b. The graph also crosses the y-axis at $(0,0)$. Thus, the y-intercept is 0.

7. **a.** The graph does not cross the x-axis. Thus, there is no x-intercept.

    b. The graph crosses the y-axis at $(0,-2)$. Thus the y-intercept is -2.

9. To find the x-intercept, let $y = 0$ and solve for x.

$$2x + 5y = 20$$
$$2x + 5(0) = 20$$
$$2x = 20$$
$$x = 10$$

The x-intercept is 10.

To find the y-intercept, let $x = 0$ and solve for y.

$$2x + 5y = 20$$
$$2(0) + 5y = 20$$
$$5y = 20$$
$$y = 4$$

The y-intercept is 4.

11. To find the x-intercept, let $y = 0$ and solve for x.

$$2x - 3y = 15$$
$$2x - 3(0) = 15$$
$$2x = 15$$
$$x = \frac{15}{2}$$

The x-intercept is $\frac{15}{2}$.

To find the y-intercept, let $x = 0$ and solve for y.

$$2x - 3y = 15$$
$$2(0) - 3y = 15$$
$$-3y = 15$$
$$y = -5$$

The y-intercept is -5.

13.
x-intercept:

$$-x + 3(0) = -8$$
$$-x = -8$$
$$x = 8$$

y-intercept:

$$-0 + 3y = -8$$
$$3y = -8$$
$$y = -\frac{8}{3}$$

x-intercept: 8; y-intercept: $-\frac{8}{3}$

15.
x-intercept:

$$7x - 9(0) = 0$$
$$7x = 0$$
$$x = 0$$

y-intercept:

$$7(0) - 9y = 0$$
$$-9y = 0$$
$$y = 0$$

x-intercept: 0; y-intercept: 0

17.
x-intercept:

$$2x = 3(0) - 11$$
$$2x = -11$$
$$x = -\frac{11}{2}$$

y-intercept:

$$2(0) = 3y - 11$$
$$0 = 3y - 11$$
$$11 = 3y$$
$$\frac{11}{3} = y$$

x-intercept: $-\frac{11}{2}$; y-intercept: $\frac{11}{3}$

19. $x + y = 5$

x-intercept: 5
y-intercept: 5
checkpoint: $(2,3)$
Draw a line through $(5,0)$, $(0,5)$, and $(2,3)$.

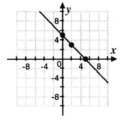

105

21. $x + 3y = 6$

x-intercept: 6

y-intercept: 2

checkpoint: $(3,1)$

Draw a line through $(6,0)$, $(0,2)$, and $(3,1)$.

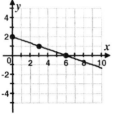

23. $6x - 9y = 18$

x-intercept: 3

y-intercept: -2

checkpoint: $\left(1, -\dfrac{4}{3}\right)$

Draw a line through $(3,0)$, $(0,-2)$, and $\left(1, -\dfrac{4}{3}\right)$.

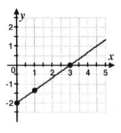

25. $-x + 4y = 6$

x-intercept: -6

y-intercept: $\dfrac{3}{2}$

checkpoint: $(2,2)$

Draw a line through $(-6,0)$, $\left(0, \dfrac{3}{2}\right)$, and $(2,2)$.

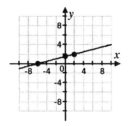

27. $2x - y = 7$

x-intercept: $\dfrac{7}{2}$

y-intercept: -7

checkpoint: $(1,-5)$

Draw a line through $\left(\dfrac{7}{2},0\right)$, $(0,7)$, and $(1,-5)$.

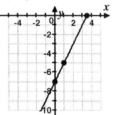

29. $3x = 5y - 15$

x-intercept: -5

y-intercept: 3

checkpoint: $\left(-\dfrac{10}{3}, 1\right)$

Draw a line through $(-5,0)$, $(0,3)$, and $\left(-\dfrac{10}{3}, 1\right)$.

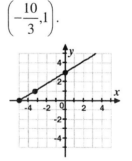

106

31. $25y = 100 - 50x$

x-intercept: 2
y-intercept: 4
checkpoint: $(1, 2)$
Draw a line through $(2,0)$, $(0,4)$, and $(1, 2)$.

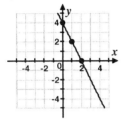

33. $2x - 8y = 12$

x-intercept: 6
y-intercept: $-\dfrac{3}{2}$
checkpoint: $(2, -1)$

Draw a line through $(6,0)$, $\left(0, -\dfrac{3}{2}\right)$, and

$(2, -1)$.

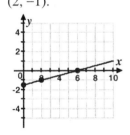

35. $x + 2y = 0$

x-intercept: 0
y-intercept: 0
Since the line goes through the origin, find two additional points.
checkpoint: $(2, -1)$
checkpoint: $(4, -2)$
Draw a line through $(0,0)$, $(2, -1)$, and $(4, -2)$.

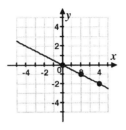

37. $y - 3x = 0$

x-intercept: 0
y-intercept: 0
Since the line goes through the origin, find two additional points.
checkpoint: $(1, 3)$
checkpoint: $(2, 6)$
Draw a line through $(0,0)$, $(1, 3)$, and $(2, 6)$.

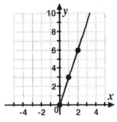

39. $2x - 3y = -11$

x-intercept: $-\dfrac{11}{2}$
y-intercept: $\dfrac{11}{3}$
checkpoint: $(-1, 3)$

Draw a line through $\left(-\dfrac{11}{2}, 0\right)$, $\left(0, \dfrac{11}{3}\right)$

and $(-1, 3)$.

107

41. The equation for this horizontal line is
$y = 3$.

43. The equation for this vertical line is
$x = -3$.

45. The equation for this horizontal line,
which is the x-axis is $y = 0$.

47. $y = 4$
All ordered pairs that are solutions will
have a value of y that is 4. Any value
can be used for x. Three ordered pairs
that are solutions are
$(-2,4)$, $(0,4)$, and $(3,4)$.
Plot these points and draw the line
through them. The graph is a horizontal
line.

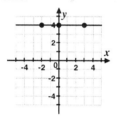

49. $y = -2$
Three ordered pairs are $(-3,-2)$, $(0,-2)$,
and $(4,-2)$. The graph is a horizontal
line.

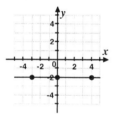

51. $x = 2$
All ordered pairs that are solutions will
have a value of x that is 2. Any value
can be used for y. Three ordered pairs
that are solutions are $(2, -3)$, $(2,0)$, and
$(2,2)$.
The graph is a vertical line.

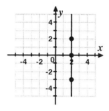

53. $x + 1 = 0$
$x = -1$
Three ordered pairs are $(-1,-3)$, $(-1,0)$,
and $(-1,3)$. The graph is a vertical line.

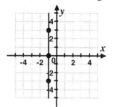

55. $y - 3.5 = 0$
$y = 3.5$
Three ordered pairs are $(-2, 3.5)$,
$(0, 3.5)$, and $(3.5, 3.5)$. The graph is a
horizontal line.

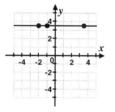

57. $x = 0$
Three ordered pairs are $(0,-2)$, $(0,0)$,
and $(0,4)$. The graph is a vertical line,
the y-axis.

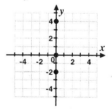

108

59. $3y = 9$

$y = 3$

Three ordered pairs are $(-3,3)$, $(0,3)$, and $(3,3)$. The graph is a horizontal line.

61. $12 - 3x = 0$

$-3x = -12$

$x = 4$

Three ordered pairs are $(4,-2)$, $(4,1)$, and $(4,3)$. The graph is a vertical line.

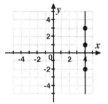

63. Using the x- and y-intercepts, we see that $3x + 2y = -6$ corresponds to Exercise 4.

64. $x + 2y = -4$

x-intercept: y-intercept:

$x + 2(0) = -4$ $0 + 2y = -4$

$\qquad x = -4$ $2y = -4$

$\qquad\qquad\qquad\qquad\quad y = -2$

Using the x- and y-intercepts, we see that $x + 2y = -4$ corresponds to Exercise 3.

65. Since $y = -2$ is a horizontal line at -2, it corresponds to Exercise 7.

66. Since $x = -3$ is a vertical line at -3, it corresponds to Exercise 8.

67. Using the x- and y-intercepts, we see that $4x + 3y = 12$ corresponds to Exercise 1.

68. $2x + 5y = 10$

x-intercept: y-intercept:

$2x + 5(0) = 10$ $2(0) + 5y = 10$

$\qquad 2x = 10$ $5y = 10$

$\qquad\quad x = 5$ $y = 2$

Using the x- and y-intercepts, we see that $2x + 5y = 10$ corresponds to Exercise 2.

69. a. Let $x + 5 + 5 = x + 10 = $ the width. Let $y + 8 = $ length. Using the formula for the perimeter of a rectangle, we have

$2(x+10) + 2(y+8) = 58$

$2x + 20 + 2y + 16 = 58$

$2x + 2y + 36 = 58$

$2x + 2y = 22$

$x + y = 11$

b.

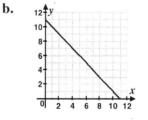

70. a. The base of the trapezoid has length x and the top has length $x - 2y$. The two sides each have length 25, so the perimeter equation for the trapezoid is given by:

$x + (x - 2y) + 2(25) = 84$

$x + x - 2y + 50 = 84$

$2x - 2y = 34$

$x - y = 17$

109

b.

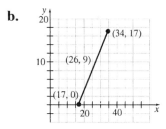

The total perimeter is 84 feet and two sides are each 25 feet. This leaves 34 feet for the remaining two sides. Thus, the largest value possible for x is 34, which is when we have an isosceles triangle.

71. The vulture's height is decreasing from 3 seconds to 12 seconds.

73. The y-intercept is 45. This means that the vulture's height was 45 meters at the beginning of the observation.

75. Five x-intercepts of the graph are 12, 13, 14, 15, and 16. During these times (12-16 minutes), the vulture was on the ground.

77. Your temperature is decreasing from 8 A.M. to 11 A.M.

79. Your temperature is increasing from 11 A.M. to 1 P.M.

81. a.
$$0.57x + y = 80$$
$$0.57(0) + y = 80$$
$$y = 80$$
The y-intercept is 80. This means that in 1994, carbonated beverages had 80% of the market share.

b. The model approximates the data very well for 1994.

c.
$$0.57x + y = 80$$
$$0.57x + 0 = 80$$
$$0.57x = 80$$
$$x \approx 140$$
The x-intercept is 140. This means that in $1994 + 140 = 2134$, carbonated beverages will have 0% of the market share. This means that there will be no consumption of carbonated beverages. Since this is extremely unlikely, model breakdown has occurred.

For Exercises 83-91, answers will vary.

93. $y = -1$ is a horizontal line. A line parallel to a horizontal line is also horizontal. The equation of a horizontal line passing through (5,6) is $y = 6$.

95. Since the x-intercept is -2, $y = 0$ when $x = -2$.
$$\square x + \square y = 12$$
$$\square(-2) + \square(0) = 12$$
$$\square(-2) = 12$$
$$\square = -6$$
So, the coefficient of x is -6. Similarly, since the y-intercept is 4, $x = 0$ when $y = 4$.
$$\square x + \square y = 12$$
$$\square(0) + \square(4) = 12$$
$$\square(4) = 12$$
$$\square = 3$$
So, the coefficient of y is 3. The equation of the line is $-6x + 3y = 12$.

97. $2x + y = 4$

$y = -2x + 4$

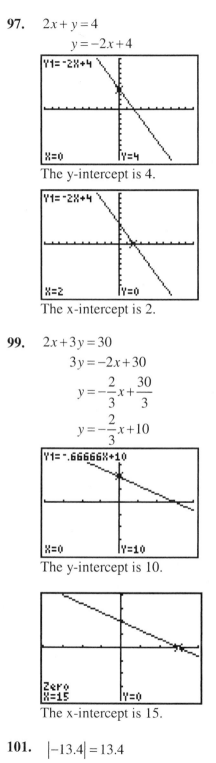

The y-intercept is 4.

The x-intercept is 2.

99. $2x + 3y = 30$

$3y = -2x + 30$

$y = -\dfrac{2}{3}x + \dfrac{30}{3}$

$y = -\dfrac{2}{3}x + 10$

The y-intercept is 10.

The x-intercept is 15.

101. $\left| -13.4 \right| = 13.4$

102. $7x - (3x - 5) = 7x - 3x + 5 = 4x + 5$

103. $-2 \le x < 4$

3.3 Exercise Set

1. Let $(x_1, y_1) = (4, 7)$ and $(x_2, y_2) = (8, 10)$.

$m = \dfrac{\text{Change in } y}{\text{Change in } x} = \dfrac{y_2 - y_1}{x_2 - x_1}$

$= \dfrac{10 - 7}{8 - 4} = \dfrac{3}{4}$

The slope is $\dfrac{3}{4}$. Since the slope is positive, the line rises.

3. $(-2, 1)$ and $(2, 2)$

$m = \dfrac{2 - 1}{2 - (-2)} = \dfrac{1}{4}$

Since the slope is positive, the line rises.

5. $(4, -2)$ and $(3, -2)$

$m = \dfrac{-2 - (-2)}{3 - 4} = \dfrac{0}{-1} = 0$

Since the slope is zero, the line is horizontal.

7. $(-2, 4)$ and $(-1, -1)$

$m = \dfrac{-1 - 4}{-1 - (-2)} = \dfrac{-5}{1} = -5$

Since the slope is negative, the line falls.

9. $(5, 3)$ and $(5, -2)$

$m = \dfrac{-2 - 3}{5 - 5} = \dfrac{-5}{0}$

Since the slope is undefined, the line is vertical.

111

11. Line through $(-2,2)$ and $(2,4)$:
$$m = \frac{4-2}{2-(-2)} = \frac{2}{4} = \frac{1}{2}$$

13. Line through $(-3,4)$ and $(3,2)$:
$$m = \frac{2-4}{3-(-3)} = \frac{-2}{6} = -\frac{1}{3}$$

15. Line through $(-2,1)$, $(0,0)$, and $(2,-1)$
Use any two of these points to find the slope.
$$m = \frac{0-1}{0-(-2)} = \frac{-1}{2} = -\frac{1}{2}$$

17. Line through $(0,2)$ and $(3,0)$:
$$m = \frac{0-2}{3-0} = -\frac{2}{3}$$

19. Line through $(-2,1)$ and $(4,1)$:
$$m = \frac{1-1}{4-(-2)} = \frac{0}{6} = 0$$
(Since the line is horizontal, it is not necessary to do this computation. The slope of every horizontal line is 0.)

21. Line through $(-3,4)$ and $(-3,-2)$:
$$m = \frac{-2-4}{-3-(-3)} = \frac{-6}{0}; \text{ undefined}$$
(Since the line is vertical, it is not necessary to do this computation. The slope of every vertical line is undefined.)

23. Line through $(-2,0)$ and $(0,6)$:
$$m = \frac{6-0}{0-(-2)} = 3$$
Line through $(1,8)$ and $(0,5)$:
$$m = \frac{5-8}{0-1} = \frac{-3}{-1} = 3$$
Since their slopes are equal, the lines are parallel.

25. Line through $(0,3)$ and $(1,5)$:
$$m = \frac{5-3}{1-0} = \frac{2}{1} = 2$$
Line through $(-1,7)$ and $(1,10)$:
$$m = \frac{10-7}{1-(-1)} = \frac{3}{2}$$
Since their slopes are not equal, the lines are not parallel.

27.

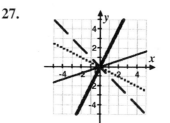

28.

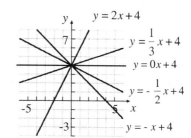

29.

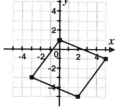

$$m = \frac{y_2 - y_1}{x_2 - x_1} = \frac{-3-1}{-3-0} = \frac{-4}{-3} = \frac{4}{3}$$

$$m = \frac{y_2 - y_1}{x_2 - x_1} = \frac{-1-1}{5-0} = \frac{-2}{5} = -\frac{2}{5}$$

$$m = \frac{y_2 - y_1}{x_2 - x_1} = \frac{-5-(-1)}{2-5} = \frac{-4}{-3} = \frac{4}{3}$$

$$m = \frac{y_2 - y_1}{x_2 - x_1} = \frac{-3-(-5)}{-3-2} = \frac{2}{-5} = -\frac{2}{5}$$

Slopes of opposite sides are equal, so the figure is a parallelogram.

112

30.

$$m_1 = \frac{y_2 - y_1}{x_2 - x_1} = \frac{-3 - 6}{2 - (-3)} = -\frac{9}{5}$$

$$m_2 = \frac{y_2 - y_1}{x_2 - x_1} = \frac{2 - (-3)}{11 - 2} = \frac{5}{9}$$

$$m_3 = \frac{y_2 - y_1}{x_2 - x_1} = \frac{11 - 2}{6 - 11} = -\frac{9}{5}$$

$$m_4 = \frac{y_2 - y_1}{x_2 - x_1} = \frac{6 - 11}{-3 - 6} = \frac{5}{9}$$

Since m_1 and m_3 are the same, the line connecting $(-3, 6)$ and $(2, -3)$ is parallel to the line connecting $(11, 2)$ and $(6, 11)$. Since m_2 and m_4 are the same, the line connecting $(-3, 6)$ and $(6, 11)$ is parallel to the line connecting $(2, -3)$ and $(11, 2)$.

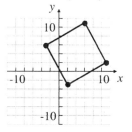

31. First find the slope of the line passing through (2, 3) and (−2, 1).

$$m = \frac{y_2 - y_1}{x_2 - x_1} = \frac{3 - 1}{2 - (-2)} = \frac{2}{4} = \frac{1}{2}$$

Now, use the slope formula, the slope and the points $(5, y)$ and $(1, 0)$ to find y.

$$\frac{1}{2} = \frac{y - 0}{5 - 1}$$

$$\frac{1}{2} = \frac{y}{4}$$

$$4\left(\frac{1}{2}\right) = 4\left(\frac{y}{4}\right)$$

$$2 = y$$

32. First find the slope of the line passing through $(-3, 4)$ and $(-5, -2)$.

$$m = \frac{-2 - 4}{-5 - (-3)} = \frac{-6}{-2} = 3$$

Now, use the slope formula, the slope and the points $(1, y)$ and $(7, 12)$ to find y.

$$3 = \frac{12 - y}{7 - 1}$$

$$3 = \frac{12 - y}{6}$$

$$18 = 12 - y$$

$$6 = -y$$

$$y = -6$$

33. $(1, 2)$ and $(3, 12)$

$$m = \frac{y_2 - y_1}{x_2 - x_1} = \frac{12 - 2}{3 - 1} = \frac{10}{2} = 5$$

$(3, 12)$ and $(6, 27)$

$$m = \frac{y_2 - y_1}{x_2 - x_1} = \frac{27 - 12}{6 - 3} = \frac{15}{3} = 5$$

$(6, 27)$ and $(1, 2)$

$$m = \frac{y_2 - y_1}{x_2 - x_1} = \frac{2 - 27}{1 - 6} = \frac{-25}{-5} = 5$$

The slope from $(1, 2)$ to $(3, 12)$ is the same as the slope from $(3, 12)$ to $(6, 27)$. Therefore, the three points are collinear.

34. $(1, 3)$ and $(3, 11)$

$$m = \frac{11 - 3}{3 - 1} = \frac{8}{2} = 4$$

$(3, 11)$ and $(6, 22)$

$$m = \frac{22 - 11}{6 - 3} = \frac{11}{3}$$

These two slopes are different, so the three points are not collinear.

113

35. Line through (1999,1000) and (2001,1500):

$$m = \frac{1500 - 1000}{2001 - 1999} = \frac{500}{2} = 250$$

The amount spent online per U.S. online household was projected to increase by $250 each year from 1999 to 2001.

37. Two points on the line segment representing men are (1972, 98) and (2002, 86).

$$m = \frac{98 - 86}{1972 - 2002} = \frac{12}{-30} = -0.4$$

The percentage of fill-time police officers who are men is decreasing at a rate of 0.4% per year.

39. Two points on the line segment representing highest-income are (2002, 161,800) and (1980, 98,000).

$$m = \frac{161,800 - 98,000}{2002 - 1980} = \frac{63,800}{22} = 2900$$

Mean income is increasing by $2900 per year.

41. Two points on the line are (20,000, 8000) and (40,000, 16,000).

$$m = \frac{16,000 - 8,000}{40,000 - 20,000} = \frac{8,000}{20,000} = 0.4$$

The cost increases $0.40 per mile driven.

43. $$m = \frac{\text{Change in } y}{\text{Change in } x} = \frac{6}{18} = \frac{1}{3}$$

The pitch of the roof is $\frac{1}{3}$.

45. The grade an access ramp is

$$\frac{1 \text{ foot}}{12 \text{ feet}} = \frac{1}{12} \approx 0.083 = 8.3\%.$$

For Exercises 47-51, answers will vary.

53. Statement b is true.

55. Use the graph to observe where each line crosses the y-axis. In order of decreasing size, the y-intercepts are b_2, b_1, b_4, b_3.

57.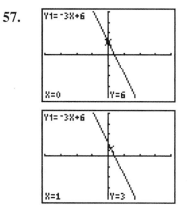

Find the slope using the points (0, 6) and (1, 3). Other points can be used, but the slope should be the same.

$$m = \frac{6 - 3}{0 - 1} = \frac{3}{-1} = -3$$

59.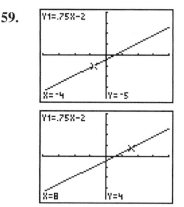

Two points on the graph are (−4,−5) and (8,4).

$$m = \frac{4 - (-5)}{8 - (-4)} = \frac{9}{12} = \frac{3}{4}$$

61. Let x = length of shorter piece (in inches).
Let $2x$ = length of longer piece.
$$x + 2x = 36$$
$$3x = 36$$
$$x = 12$$
The pieces are 12 inches and 24 inches.

62. $-10 + 16 \div 2(-4) = -10 + 8(-4)$
$$= -10 - 32$$
$$= -10 + (-32) = -42$$

63. $2x - 3 \le 5$
$$2x \le 8$$
$$x \le 4$$
$$\{x | x \le 4\}$$

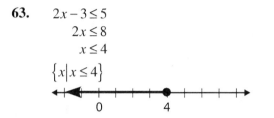

3.4 Exercise Set

1. $y = 3x + 2$
The slope is the x-coefficient, which is 3. The y-intercept is the constant term, which is 2.

3. $y = 3x - 5$
$$y = 3x + (-5)$$
$$m = 3; \ y-\text{intercept} = -5$$

5. $y = -\frac{1}{2}x + 5$
$$m = -\frac{1}{2}; \ y\text{-intercept} = 5$$

7. $y = 7x$
$$y = 7x + 0$$
$$m = 7; \ y\text{-intercept} = 0$$

9. $y = 10$
$$y = 0x + 10$$
$$m = 0; \ y\text{-intercept} = 10$$

11. $y = 4 - x$
$$y = -x + 4 = -1x + 4$$
$$m = -1; \ y\text{-intercept} = 4$$

13. $-5x + y = 7$
$$-5x + y + 5x = 5x + 7$$
$$y = 5x + 7$$
$$m = 5; \ y\text{-intercept} = 7$$

15. $x + y = 6$
$$y = -x + 6 = -1x + 6$$
$$m = -1; \ y\text{-intercept} = 6$$

17. $6x + y = 0$
$$y = -6x = -6x + 0$$
$$m = -6; \ y\text{-intercept} = 0$$

19. $3y = 6x$
$$y = 2x$$
$$m = 2; \ y\text{-intercept} = 0$$

21. $2x + 7y = 0$
$$7y = -2x$$
$$y = -\frac{2}{7}x$$
$$m = -\frac{2}{7}; \ y\text{-intercept} = 0$$

23. $3x + 2y = 3$
$$2y = -3x + 3$$
$$y = -\frac{3}{2}x + \frac{3}{2}$$
$$m = -\frac{3}{2}; \ y\text{-intercept} = \frac{3}{2}$$

25. $3x - 4y = 12$

$-4y = -3x + 12$

$y = \dfrac{3}{4}x - 3$

$m = \dfrac{3}{4}$; y-intercept $= -3$

27. $y = 2x + 4$

Step 1. Plot $(0,4)$ on the y-axis.

Step 2. $m = \dfrac{2}{1} = \dfrac{\text{rise}}{\text{run}}$

Start at $(0,4)$. Using the slope, move 2 units *up* (the rise) and 1 unit to the *right* (the run) to reach the point $(1,6)$.

Step 3. Draw a line through $(0,4)$ and $(1,6)$.

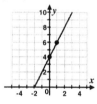

29. $y = -3x + 5$

Slope $= -3 = \dfrac{-3}{1}$; y-intercept $= 5$.

Plot $(0,5)$ on the y-axis. From this point, move 3 units *down* (because -3 is negative) and 1 unit to the *right* to reach the point $(1,2)$. Draw a line through $(0,5)$ and $(1,2)$.

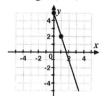

31. $y = \dfrac{1}{2}x + 1$

Slope $= \dfrac{1}{2}$; y-intercept $= 1$

Plot $(0,1)$. From this point, move 1 unit *up* and 2 units to the *right* to reach the point $(2,2)$. Draw a line through $(0,1)$ and $(2,2)$.

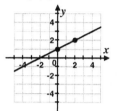

33. $y = \dfrac{2}{3}x - 5$

Slope $= \dfrac{2}{3}$; y-intercept $= -5$

Plot $(0,-5)$. From this point move 2 units *up* and 3 units to the *right* to reach the point $(3,-3)$. Draw a line through $(0,-5)$ and $(3,-3)$.

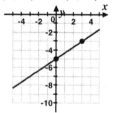

35. $y = -\dfrac{3}{4}x + 2$

Slope $= -\dfrac{3}{4} = \dfrac{-3}{4}$; y-intercept $= 2$

Plot $(0,2)$. From this point move 3 units *down* and 4 units to the *right* to reach the point $(4,-1)$.

Draw a line through $(0,2)$ and $(4,-1)$

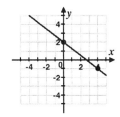

37.

$$y = -\frac{5}{3}x$$

Slope $= -\dfrac{5}{3} = \dfrac{-5}{3}$; y-intercept $= 0$

Plot (0,0). From this point, move 5 units *down* and 3 units to the *right* to reach the point (3,−5). Draw a line through (0,0) and (3,−5).

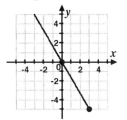

39. a. $3x + y = 0$

$$y = -3x$$

b. $m = -3$; y-intercept $= 0$

c.   Plot (0,0). Since $m = -3 = -\dfrac{3}{1}$, move 3 units *down* and 1 units to the *right* to reach the point (1,−3). Draw a line through (0,0) and (1,−3).

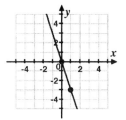

41. a. $3y = 4x$

$$y = \frac{4}{3}x$$

b. $m = \dfrac{4}{3}$; y-intercept $= 0$

c.   Plot (0,0). Move 4 units *up* and 3 units to the *right* to reach the point (3,4).
Draw a line through (0,0) and (3,4).

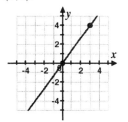

43. a. $2x + y = 3$

$$y = -2x + 3$$

b. $m = -2$; y-intercept $= 3$

c.   Plot (0,3). Since $m = -2 = -\dfrac{2}{1}$, move 2 units *down* and 1 units to the *right* to reach the point (1,1). Draw a line through (0,3) and (1,1).

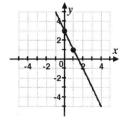

45. a. $7x + 2y = 14$

$$2y = -7x + 14$$

$$\frac{2y}{2} = \frac{-7x + 14}{2}$$

$$y = -\frac{7}{2}x + 7$$

117

b. $m = -\dfrac{7}{2}$; y-intercept $= 7$

c. Plot $(0,7)$. Since $m = -\dfrac{7}{2} = -\dfrac{7}{2}$, move 7 units *down* and 2 units to the *right* to reach the point $(2,0)$. Draw a line through $(0,7)$ and $(2,0)$.

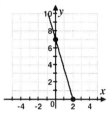

47. $y = 3x + 1$:

$m = 3$; y-intercept $= 1$

$y = 3x - 3$:

$m = 3$; y-intercept $= -3$

The lines are parallel because their slopes are equal.

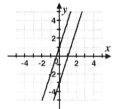

49. $y = -3x + 2$:

$m = -3$; y-intercept $= 2$

$y = 3x + 2$:

$m = 3$; y-intercept $= 2$

The lines are not parallel because their slopes are not equal.

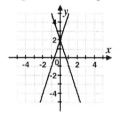

51.

$x - 2y = 2 \;\rightarrow\; y = \dfrac{1}{2}x - 1$

$2x - 4y = 3 \;\rightarrow\; y = \dfrac{1}{2}x - \dfrac{3}{4}$

The lines are parallel because their slopes are equal.

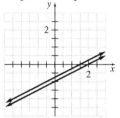

53. Find the slope of the parallel line.

$3x + y = 6$

$\qquad y = -3x + 6$

The slope is -3. We are given that the y-intercept is 5, so using slope-intercept form, we have $y = -3x + 5$.

54. Find the slope of the parallel line.

$2x + y = 8$

$\qquad y = -2x + 8$

The slope is -2. We are given that the y-intercept is -4, so using the slope-intercept form, we have $y = -2x - 4$.

55. Find the y-intercept of the line.

$16y = 8x + 32$

$\dfrac{16}{16}y = \dfrac{8}{16}x + \dfrac{32}{16}$

$\qquad y = \dfrac{1}{2}x + 2$

The y-intercept is 2.
Find the slope of the parallel line.

$3x + 3y = 9$

$\qquad 3y = -3x + 9$

$\qquad\quad y = -x + 3$

The slope is -1. Using slope-intercept form, we have $y = -x + 2$.

118

56. Find the y-intercept of the line.

$$2y = 6x + 8$$

$$\frac{2y}{2} = \frac{6x}{2} + \frac{8}{2}$$

$$y = 3x + 4$$

The y-intercept is 4.
Now, find the slope of the parallel line.

$$4x + 4y = 20$$

$$4y = -4x + 20$$

$$\frac{4y}{4} = \frac{-4x}{4} + \frac{20}{4}$$

$$y = -x + 5$$

The slope is -1. Using the slope-intercept form, we have $y = -x + 4$.

57. If the line rises from left to right, it has a positive slope. It passes through the origin, (0, 0) and a second point with equal x- and y-coordinates. The point (2, 2) is one example.
Use the two points to find the slope.

$$m = \frac{0-2}{0-2} = \frac{-2}{-2} = 1$$

The slope is 1. The y-intercept is 0.
Using slope-intercept form, we have $y = 1x + 0$ or $y = x$.

58. If the line falls from left to right, the slope must be negative. It passes through the origin, $(0,0)$, and has a second point with opposite x- and y-coordinates. The point $(2,-2)$ is one example.
Use the two points to find the slope.

$$m = \frac{-2-0}{2-0} = -\frac{2}{2} = -1$$

The slope is -1. The y-intercept is 0.
Using the slope-intercept form, we have $y = -x + 0$ or $y = -x$.

59. **a.** The slope of this model is 10. This indicates that the number of endangered animal species in the United States has been increasing at a rate of 10 species per year.

b. The y-intercept is 166. This indicates that in 1980 (the initial year for the model), there were 166 endangered animal species in the United States.

c. $E = 10x + 166$
$1980; x = 0$
$$E = 10(0) + 166 = 166$$
$1985; x = 5$
$$E = 10(5) + 166 = 216$$
$1990; x = 10$
$$E = 10(10) + 166 = 266$$
$1995; x = 15$
$$E = 10(15) + 166 = 316$$
$2000; x = 20$
$$E = 10(20) + 166 = 366$$
$2003; x = 23$
$$E = 10(23) + 166 = 396$$

According to the formula, the number of endangered animal species in the U.S. was 166 in 1980, 216 in 1985, 266 in 1990, 316 in 1995, 366 in 2000, and 396 in 2003. The model appears to describe the actual data quite well.

61. **a.** The y-intercept is 21. This means that 21 million people were living with AIDS in sub-Saharan Africa in 1997.

b. $$m = \frac{29-21}{5-0} = \frac{8}{5} = 1.6$$
The number of people living with AIDS in sub-Saharan Africa is increasing by 1.6 million each year.

c. $y = mx + b$

$y = 1.6x + 21$

d. Since $2006 - 1997 = 9$, find y when $x = 9$.

$y = 1.6(9) + 21 = 14.4 + 21 = 35.4$

35.4 million people will be living with the virus in 2006.

For Exercises 63-65, answers will vary.

67. First, find the slope using the points $(0, 32)$ and $(100, 212)$.

$$m = \frac{212 - 32}{100 - 0} = \frac{180}{100} = \frac{9}{5}$$

The slope is $\frac{9}{5}$. We also know that the y-intercept is 32. Using slope-intercept form, we have $F = \frac{9}{5}C + 32$.

69. $\frac{x}{2} + 7 = 13 - \frac{x}{4}$

Multiply by the LCD, which is 4.

$$4\left(\frac{x}{2} + 7\right) = 4\left(13 - \frac{x}{4}\right)$$

$2x + 28 = 52 - x$

$3x + 28 = 52$

$3x = 24$

$x = 8$

The solution set is $\{8\}$.

70. $3(12 \div 2^2 - 3)^2$

$= 3(12 \div 4 - 3)^2$

$= 3(3 - 3)^2$

$= 3 \cdot 0^2 = 3 \cdot 0 = 0$

71. $A = PB$; $A = 14$, $P = 25\% = 0.25$

$A = PB$

$14 = 0.25 \cdot B$

$$\frac{14}{0.25} = \frac{0.25B}{0.25}$$

$56 = B$

14 is 25% of 56.

Chapter 3 Mid-Chapter Check Points

1. **a.** The x-intercept is 4.

b. The y-intercept is 2.

c. The points $(4, 0)$ and $(0, 2)$ lie on the line.

$$m = \frac{2 - 0}{0 - 4} = \frac{2}{-4} = -\frac{1}{2}$$

2. **a.** The x-intercept is -5.

b. There is no y-intercept.

c. It is a vertical line, so the slope is undefined.

3. **a.** The x-intercept is 0.

b. The y-intercept is 0.

c. The points $(0, 0)$ and $(5, 3)$ lie on the line.

$$m = \frac{3 - 0}{5 - 0} = \frac{3}{5}$$

4. $y = -2x$

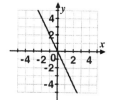

5. $y = -2$

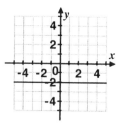

120

6. $x + y = -2$

$y = -x - 2$

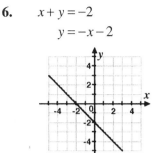

7. $y = \dfrac{1}{3}x - 2$

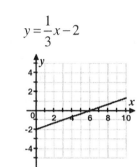

8. $x = 3.5$

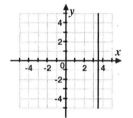

9. $4x - 2y = 8$

$-2y = -4x + 8$

$\dfrac{-2y}{-2} = \dfrac{-4x}{-2} + \dfrac{8}{-2}$

$y = 2x - 4$

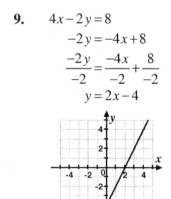

10. $y = 3x + 2$

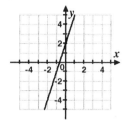

11. $3x + y = 0$

$y = -3x$

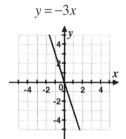

12. $y = x^2 - 4$

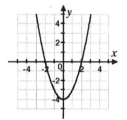

13. $y = x - 4$

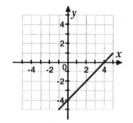

121

14. $5y = -3x$

$$y = -\frac{3}{5}x$$

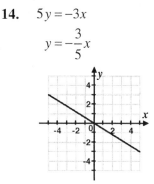

15. $5y = 20$

$$y = 4$$

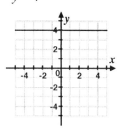

16. $5x - 2y = 10$

$$-2y = -5x + 10$$

$$y = \frac{5}{2}x - 5$$

The slope is $\frac{5}{2}$ and the y-intercept is

-5.

17.

$(2, -4)$ and $(7, 0)$: $m = \dfrac{0 - (-4)}{7 - 2} = \dfrac{4}{5}$

$(-4, 2)$ and $(1, 6)$: $m = \dfrac{6 - 2}{1 - (-4)} = \dfrac{4}{5}$

Since the slopes are the same, the lines are parallel.

18. **a.** The line is in slope-intercept form, so the y-intercept is 33.

b. In 1995, 33% of U.S. colleges offered distance learning by computer.

c. The line is in slope intercept form, so the coefficient of the x-term, 7.8, is the slope.

d. For the years 1995 through 2002, the percentage of colleges that offered distance learning by computer increased by 7.8% each year.

3.5 Exercise Set

1. Line with a slope 3 that passes through the point $(2, 5)$.

Begin with the point-slope equation of a line with $m = 3$, $x_1 = 2$, and $y_1 = 5$.

$$y - y_1 = m(x - x_1)$$
$$y - 5 = 3(x - 2)$$

Now solve this equation for y and write an equivalent equation in slope-intercept form.

$$y - 5 = 3x - 6$$
$$y = 3x - 1$$

3. Line with a slope 5 that passes through the point $(-2, 6)$.

Begin with the point-slope equation of a line with $m = 5$, $x_1 = -2$, and $y_1 = 6$.

$$y - y_1 = m(x - x_1)$$
$$y - 6 = 5(x - (-2))$$
$$y - 6 = 5(x + 2)$$

Now solve this equation for y and write an equivalent equation in slope-intercept form.

$$y - 6 = 5(x + 2)$$
$$y - 6 = 5x + 10$$
$$y = 5x + 16$$

122

5. Line with a slope -8 that passes through the point $(-3, -2)$.

Begin with the point-slope equation of a line with $m = -8$, $x_1 = -3$, and $y_1 = -2$.

$$y - y_1 = m(x - x_1)$$
$$y - (-2) = -8(x - (-3))$$
$$y + 2 = -8(x + 3)$$

Now solve this equation for y and write an equivalent equation in slope-intercept form.

$$y + 2 = -8(x + 3)$$
$$y + 2 = -8x - 24$$
$$y = -8x - 26$$

7. Line with a slope -12 that passes through the point $(-8, 0)$.

Begin with the point-slope equation of a line with $m = -12$, $x_1 = -8$, and $y_1 = 0$.

$$y - y_1 = m(x - x_1)$$
$$y - 0 = -12(x - (-8))$$
$$y = -12(x + 8)$$
$$y = -12x - 96$$

Now solve this equation for y and write an equivalent equation in slope-intercept form.

$$y = -12(x + 8)$$
$$y = -12x - 96$$

9. Slope $= -1$, passing through $\left(-\dfrac{1}{2}, -2\right)$

point-slope form:

$$y + 2 = -1\left(x + \dfrac{1}{2}\right)$$

$$y + 2 = -x - \dfrac{1}{2}$$

slope-intercept form: $y = -x - \dfrac{5}{2}$

11. Slope $= \dfrac{1}{2}$, passes through the origin: $(0,0)$

point-slope form: $y - 0 = \dfrac{1}{2}(x - 0)$

slope-intercept form: $y = \dfrac{1}{2}x$

13. Slope $= -\dfrac{2}{3}$, passing through $(6, -2)$

point-slope form:

$$y + 2 = -\dfrac{2}{3}(x - 6)$$

$$y + 2 = -\dfrac{2}{3}x + 4$$

slope-intercept form: $y = -\dfrac{2}{3}x + 2$

15. Passing through $(1,2)$ and $(5,10)$

slope $= \dfrac{10 - 2}{5 - 1} = \dfrac{8}{4} = 2$

point-slope form: $y - 2 = 2(x - 1)$

or $y - 10 = 2(x - 5)$

slope-intercept form:

$$y - 2 = 2x - 2$$
$$y = 2x$$

17. Passing through $(-3,0)$ and $(0,3)$

slope $= \dfrac{3 - 0}{0 + 3} = \dfrac{3}{3} = 1$

point-slope form: $y - 0 = 1(x + 3)$ or

$$y - 3 = 1(x - 0)$$

slope-intercept form: $y = x + 3$

19. Passing through $(-3, -1)$ and $(2,4)$

slope $= \dfrac{4 + 1}{2 + 3} = \dfrac{5}{5} = 1$

point-slope form: $y + 1 = 1(x + 3)$

or $y - 4 = 1(x - 2)$

slope-intercept form: $y = x + 2$

21. Passing through $(-4, -1)$ and $(3, 4)$

slope $= \dfrac{4-(-1)}{3-(-4)} = \dfrac{5}{7}$

point-slope form: $y - 4 = \dfrac{5}{7}(x-3)$

or $y + 1 = \dfrac{5}{7}(x+4)$

slope-intercept form: $y = \dfrac{5}{7}x + \dfrac{13}{7}$

23. Passing through $(-3, -1)$ and $(4, -1)$

slope $= \dfrac{-1+1}{4+3} = \dfrac{0}{7} = 0$

point-slope form: $y + 1 = 0(x+3)$

or $y + 1 = 0(x-4)$

slope-intercept form: $y = -1$

25. Passing through $(2,4)$ with x-intercept $= -2$

Use the points $(2,4)$ and $(-2,0)$ to find the slope.

slope $= \dfrac{0+4}{-2-2} = \dfrac{-4}{-4} = 1$

point-slope form: $y - 4 = 1(x-2)$

slope-intercept form: $y = x + 2$

27.

x-intercept $= -\dfrac{1}{2}$ and y-intercept $= 4$

Use the points $\left(-\dfrac{1}{2}, 0\right)$ and $(0,4)$.

slope $= \dfrac{4-0}{0+\dfrac{1}{2}} = \dfrac{4}{\dfrac{1}{2}} = 8$

point-slope form: $y - 0 = 8\left(x + \dfrac{1}{2}\right)$ or

$y - 4 = 8(x - 0)$

slope-intercept form: $y = 8x + 4$

29. a. For $y = 5x$, $m = 5$. A line parallel to this line would have the same slope, $m = 5$.

b. A line perpendicular to it would have a negative reciprocal slope. That is, slope $m = -\dfrac{1}{5}$.

31. a. For $y = -7x$, $m = -7$. A line parallel to this line would have the same slope, $m = -7$.

b. A line perpendicular to it would have a negative reciprocal slope. That is, slope $m = \dfrac{1}{7}$.

33. a. For $y = \dfrac{1}{2}x + 3$, $m = \dfrac{1}{2}$. A line parallel to this line would have the same slope, $m = \dfrac{1}{2}$.

b. A line perpendicular to it would have a negative reciprocal slope. That is, slope $m = -2$.

35. a. For $y = -\dfrac{2}{5}x - 1$, $m = -\dfrac{2}{5}$. A line parallel to this line would have the same slope, $m = -\dfrac{2}{5}$.

b. A line perpendicular to it would have a negative reciprocal slope. That is, slope $m = \dfrac{5}{2}$.

37. a. To find the slope, we rewrite the equation in slope-intercept form.
$4x + y = 7$

$\qquad y = -4x + 7$

So, $m = -4$. A line parallel to this line would have the same

slope, $m = -4$.

124

b. A line perpendicular to it would have a negative reciprocal slope. That is, slope $m = \dfrac{1}{4}$.

39. a. To find the slope, we rewrite the equation in slope-intercept form.

$$2x + 4y - 8 = 0$$
$$4y = -2x + 8$$
$$y = -\dfrac{1}{2}x + 2$$

So, $m = -\dfrac{1}{2}$. A line parallel to this line would have the same slope, $m = -\dfrac{1}{2}$.

b. A line perpendicular to it would have a negative reciprocal slope. That is, slope $m = 2$.

41. a. To find the slope, we rewrite the equation in slope-intercept form.

$$2x - 3y - 5 = 0$$
$$-3y = -2x + 5$$
$$y = \dfrac{2}{3}x - \dfrac{5}{3}$$

So, $m = \dfrac{2}{3}$. A line parallel to this line would have the same slope, $m = \dfrac{2}{3}$.

b. A line perpendicular to it would have a negative reciprocal slope. That is, slope $m = -\dfrac{3}{2}$.

43. a. We know that $x = 6$ is a vertical line with undefined slope. A line parallel to it would also be vertical with undefined slope.

b. A line perpendicular to it would be horizontal with slope $m = 0$.

45. Since L is parallel to $y = 2x$, we know it will have slope $m = 2$. We are given that it passes through $(4, 2)$. We use the slope and point to write the equation in point-slope form.

$$y - y_1 = m(x - x_1)$$
$$y - 2 = 2(x - 4)$$

Solve for y to obtain slope-intercept form.

$$y - 2 = 2(x - 4)$$
$$y - 2 = 2x - 8$$
$$y = 2x - 6$$

47. Since L is perpendicular to $y = 2x$, we know it will have slope $m = -\dfrac{1}{2}$. We are given that it passes through $(2, 4)$. We use the slope and point to write the equation in point-slope form.

$$y - y_1 = m(x - x_1)$$
$$y - 4 = -\dfrac{1}{2}(x - 2)$$

Solve for y to obtain slope-intercept form.

$$y - 4 = -\dfrac{1}{2}(x - 2)$$
$$y - 4 = -\dfrac{1}{2}x + 1$$
$$y = -\dfrac{1}{2}x + 5$$

49. Since L is parallel to $y = -4x + 3$, we know it will have slope $m = -4$. We are given that it passes through $(-8, -10)$. We use the slope and point to write the equation in point-slope form.

$$y - y_1 = m(x - x_1)$$
$$y - (-10) = -4(x - (-8))$$
$$y + 10 = -4(x + 8)$$

Solve for y to obtain slope-intercept form.

$$y + 10 = -4(x + 8)$$
$$y + 10 = -4x - 32$$
$$y = -4x - 42$$

51.

Since L is perpendicular to $y = \frac{1}{5}x + 6$, we know it will have slope $m = -5$. We are given that it passes through $(2, -3)$. We use the slope and point to write the equation in point-slope form.

$$y - y_1 = m(x - x_1)$$
$$y - (-3) = -5(x - 2)$$
$$y + 3 = -5(x - 2)$$

Solve for y to obtain slope-intercept form.

$$y + 3 = -5(x - 2)$$
$$y + 3 = -5x + 10$$
$$y = -5x + 7$$

53. To find the slope, we rewrite the equation in slope-intercept form.
$$2x - 3y - 7 = 0$$
$$-3y = -2x + 7$$
$$y = \frac{2}{3}x - \frac{7}{3}$$

Since the line is parallel to $y = \frac{2}{3}x - \frac{7}{3}$, we know it will have

slope $m = \frac{2}{3}$. We are given that it passes through $(-2, 2)$. We use the slope and point to write the equation in point-slope form.

$$y - y_1 = m(x - x_1)$$
$$y - 2 = \frac{2}{3}(x - (-2))$$
$$y - 2 = \frac{2}{3}(x + 2)$$

Solve for y to obtain slope-intercept form.

$$y - 2 = \frac{2}{3}(x + 2)$$
$$y - 2 = \frac{2}{3}x + \frac{4}{3}$$
$$y = \frac{2}{3}x + \frac{10}{3}$$

55. To find the slope, we rewrite the equation in slope-intercept form.
$$x - 2y - 3 = 0$$
$$-2y = -x + 3$$
$$y = \frac{1}{2}x - \frac{3}{2}$$

Since the line is perpendicular to $y = \frac{1}{2}x - \frac{3}{2}$, we know it will have slope $m = -2$. We are given that it passes through $(4, -7)$. We use the slope and point to write the equation in point-slope form.

$$y - y_1 = m(x - x_1)$$
$$y - (-7) = -2(x - 4)$$
$$y + 7 = -2(x - 4)$$

Solve for y to obtain slope-intercept form.

$$y + 7 = -2(x - 4)$$
$$y + 7 = -2x + 8$$
$$y = -2x + 1$$

57. Through (2, 4) and same y-intercept as $x - 4y = 8$. Solve the equation to obtain the y-intercept.

$x - 4y = 8$

$-4y = -x + 8$

$y = \dfrac{1}{4}x - 2$

Now, use the two points to find the slope.

$m = \dfrac{4 - (-2)}{2 - 0} = \dfrac{6}{2} = 3$

Now use the slope and one of the points to find the equation of the line.

$y - 4 = 3(x - 2)$

$y - 4 = 3x - 6$

$y = 3x - 2$

58. Through $(2, 6)$ with the same y-intercept as the graph of $x - 3y = 18$. Find the y-intercept:

$0 - 3y = 18$

$-3y = 18$

$\dfrac{-3y}{-3} = \dfrac{18}{-3}$

$y = -6$

The y-intercept is -6 so the point $(0, -6)$ is on the graph. Use the two points to obtain the slope of the line.

$m = \dfrac{-6 - 6}{0 - 2} = \dfrac{-12}{-2} = 6$

Using the slope-intercept form, the equation of the line is $y = 6x - 6$.

59. x-intercept at -4 and parallel to the line containing (3, 1) and (2, 6)
First, find the slope of the line going through the points (3, 1) and (2, 6).

$m = \dfrac{6 - 1}{2 - 3} = \dfrac{5}{-1} = -5$

The slope of the line is -5. Since this line is parallel to the line we are writing

the equation for, its slope is also -5. Since the x-intercept is -4, the line goes through the point $(-4, 0)$. Use the point and the slope to find the equation of the line.

$y - 0 = -5\big(x - (-4)\big)$

$y = -5(x + 4)$

$y = -5x - 20$

60. x-intercept at -6 and parallel to the line containing $(4, -3)$ and $(2, 2)$. Find the slope of the line.

$m = \dfrac{2 - (-3)}{2 - 4} = \dfrac{5}{-2} = -\dfrac{5}{2}$

The slope of the line is $-\dfrac{5}{2}$. Since this line is parallel to the new line, the slope of our line is also $-\dfrac{5}{2}$. Since the x-intercept is -6, the line goes through the point $(-6, 0)$. Use the point and the slope to find the equation of the new loan.

$y - 0 = -\dfrac{5}{2}\big(x - (-6)\big)$

$y = -\dfrac{5}{2}x - 15$

61. Since the line is perpendicular to $x = 6$ which is a vertical line, we know the graph is a horizontal line with 0 slope. The graph passes through $(-1, 5)$, so the equation is $y = 5$.

62. Since the line is perpendicular to $x = -4$ which is a vertical line, we know the graph is a horizontal line with 0 slope. The graph passes through $(-2, 6)$, so the equation is $y = 6$.

127

63. First we need to find the equation of the line with $x-$ intercept of 2 and $y-$ intercept of -4. This line will pass through $(2,0)$ and $(0,-4)$. We use these points to find the slope.

$$m = \frac{-4-0}{0-2} = \frac{-4}{-2} = 2$$

Since the graph is perpendicular to this line, it will have slope $m = -\frac{1}{2}$.

Use the point $(-6,4)$ and the slope $-\frac{1}{2}$ to find the equation of the line.

$$y - y_1 = m(x - x_1)$$

$$y - 4 = -\frac{1}{2}(x - (-6))$$

$$y - 4 = -\frac{1}{2}(x + 6)$$

$$y - 4 = -\frac{1}{2}x - 3$$

$$y = -\frac{1}{2}x + 1$$

64. First we need to find the equation of the line with $x-$ intercept of 3 and $y-$ intercept of -9. This line will pass through $(3,0)$ and $(0,-9)$. We use these points to find the slope.

$$m = \frac{-9-0}{0-3} = \frac{-9}{-3} = 3$$

Since the graph is perpendicular to this line, it will have slope $m = -\frac{1}{3}$.

Use the point $(-5,6)$ and the slope $-\frac{1}{3}$ to find the equation of the line.

$$y - y_1 = m(x - x_1)$$

$$y - 6 = -\frac{1}{3}(x - (-5))$$

$$y - 6 = -\frac{1}{3}(x + 5)$$

$$y - 6 = -\frac{1}{3}x - \frac{5}{3}$$

$$y = -\frac{1}{3}x + \frac{13}{3}$$

65. First put the equation $3x - 2y = 4$ in slope-intercept form.

$$3x - 2y = 4$$

$$-2y = -3x + 4$$

$$y = \frac{3}{2}x - 2$$

The equation will have slope $-\frac{2}{3}$ since it is perpendicular to the line above and has the same $y-$ intercept, -2.

So the equation is $y = -\frac{2}{3}x - 2$.

66. First put the equation $4x - y = 6$ in slope-intercept form.

$$4x - y = 6$$

$$-y = -4x + 6$$

$$y = 4x - 6$$

The equation will have slope $-\frac{1}{4}$ since it is perpendicular to the line above and has the same $y-$ intercept, -6.

So the equation is $y = -\frac{1}{4}x - 6$.

67. To find the slope of the line whose equation is $Ax + By = C$, put this equation in slope-intercept form by solving for y.

$$Ax + By = C$$
$$By = -Ax + C$$
$$y = -\frac{A}{B}x + \frac{C}{B}$$

The slope of this line is $m = -\frac{A}{B}$ so the slope of the line that is parallel to it is the same, $-\frac{A}{B}$.

68. From exercise 67, we know the slope of the line is $-\frac{A}{B}$. So the slope of the line that is perpendicular would be $\frac{B}{A}$.

69. **a.** Line through $(2,162)$ and $(8,168)$

$$m = \frac{168 - 162}{8 - 2} = \frac{6}{6} = 1$$

Using the point $(2,162)$ as (x_1, y_1), the point-slope equation is

$$y - 162 = 1(x - 2).$$

b. $y - 162 = x - 2$
$$y = x + 160$$

c. The year 2010 corresponds to $x = 20$.
$$y = 20 + 160 = 180$$
According to the equation, the average American adult will weigh 180 pounds in 2010.

71. Two points on the line are $(12,3)$ and $(15,1)$.

$$m = \frac{1 - 3}{15 - 12} = \frac{-2}{3} = -\frac{2}{3}$$

point-slope form using $(12,3)$:

$$y - 3 = -\frac{2}{3}(x - 12)$$

Use this equation to find the point-slope equation.

$$y - 3 = -\frac{2}{3}x + 8$$

$$y = -\frac{2}{3}x + 11$$

If $x = 7$, $y = -\frac{2}{3}(7) + 11 = -\frac{14}{3} + 11 \approx 6.3$.

The model predicts that a person with 7 years of education will score about 6.3 on the prejudice test.

73. **a.** Answers will vary.

b. Two points on the line are $(50,6)$ and $(80,5)$.

The slope is $m = \frac{5 - 6}{80 - 50} = -\frac{1}{30}$.

Using the point $(50,6)$, the point-slope form is

$$y - 6 = -\frac{1}{30}(x - 50).$$

Use this equation to find the slope-intercept equation.

$$y - 6 = -\frac{1}{30}x + \frac{5}{3}$$

$$y = -\frac{1}{30}x + \frac{23}{3}$$

$$y \approx -0.03x + 7.67$$

c. If $x = 130$, $y = -0.03(130) + 7.67$
$= 3.77$. This model predicts that a person exercising 130 minutes per week will have 3.77 or about 4 headaches per week.

129

d. As minutes per week spent exercising increases, the number of headaches per month decreases.

75. Answers will vary.

77. Statement *c* is true.
The line through $(2, -5)$ and $(2, 6)$ is vertical, so its slope is undefined.

79. Answers will vary.

81. a.

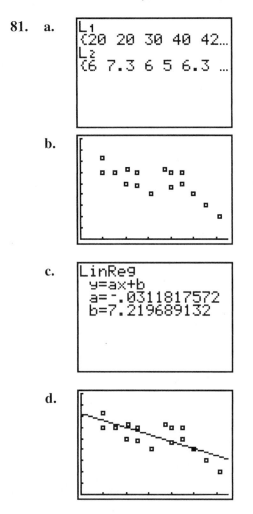

b.

c.

d.

82. Let x = the number of sheets of paper.
$$4 + 2x \le 29$$
$$2x \le 25$$
$$x \le \frac{25}{2} \text{ or } 12\frac{1}{2}$$
Since the number of sheets of paper must be a whole number, at most 12 sheets of paper can be put in the envelope.

83. The only natural numbers in the given set are 1 and $\sqrt{4}\,(=2)$

84. $3x - 5y = 15$

x-intercept: y-intercept:
$$3x - 5(0) = 15 \qquad 3(0) - 5y = 15$$
$$3x = 15 \qquad\qquad -5y = 15$$
$$x = 5 \qquad\qquad\quad y = -3$$

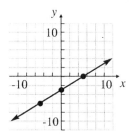

Chapter 3 Review Exercises

1. $(-3,3)$:

$3 = 3(-3)+6$

$3 = -6+9$

$3 = -3$ false

$(-3,3)$ is not a solution.

$(0,6)$:

$6 = 3(0)+6$

$6 = 6$ true

$(0,6)$ is a solution.

$(1,9)$:

$9 = 3(1)+6$

$9 = 9$ true

$(1,9)$ is a solution.

2. $(0,4)$:

$3(0)-4 = 12$

$-4 = 12$ false

$(0,4)$ is not a solution.

$(4,0)$:

$3(4)-0 = 12$

$12 = 12$ true

$(4,0)$ is a solution.

$(-1,15)$:

$3(-1)-15 = 12$

$-3-15 = 12$

$-18 = 12$ false

$(-1,15)$ is not a solution.

3. **a.**

x	$y = 2x-3$	(x,y)
-2	$y = 2(-2)-3 = -7$	$(-2,-7)$
-1	$y = 2(-1)-3 = -5$	$(-1,-5)$
0	$y = 2(0)-3 = -5$	$(0,-3)$
1	$y = 2(1)-3 = -1$	$(1,-1)$
2	$y = 2(2)-3 = 1$	$(2,1)$

b.

4. **a.**

x	$y = \frac{1}{2}x+1$	(x,y)
-4	$y = \frac{1}{2}(-4)+1 = -1$	$(-4,-1)$
-2	$y = \frac{1}{2}(-2)+1 = 0$	$(-2,0)$
0	$y = \frac{1}{2}(0)+1 = 1$	$(0,1)$
2	$y = \frac{1}{2}(2)+1 = 2$	$(2,2)$
4	$y = \frac{1}{2}(4)+1 = 3$	$(4,3)$

b.

131

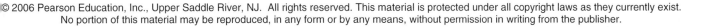

5.

x	$y = x^2 - 3$	(x, y)
-3	$y = (-3)^2 - 3 = 6$	$(-3, 6)$
-2	$y = (-2)^2 - 3 = 1$	$(-2, 1)$
-1	$y = (-1)^2 - 3 = -2$	$(-1, -2)$
0	$y = 0^2 - 3 = -3$	$(0, -3)$
1	$y = 1^2 - 3 = -2$	$(1, -2)$
2	$y = 2^2 - 3 = 1$	$(2, 1)$
3	$y = 3^2 - 1 = 6$	$(3, 6)$

6.

a.

x	$y = 5x - 41$	(x, y)
10	$y = 5(10) - 41 = 9$	$(10, 9)$
12	$y = 5(12) - 41 = 19$	$(12, 19)$
14	$y = 5(14) - 41 = 29$	$(14, 29)$
16	$y = 5(16) - 41 = 39$	$(16, 39)$

b. Answers will vary.

7. a. The graph crosses the x-axis at $(-2, 0)$, so the x-intercept is -2.

b. The graph crosses the y-axis at $(0, -4)$, so the y-intercept is -4.

8. a. The graph does not cross the x-axis, so there is no x-intercept.

b. The graph crosses the y-axis at $(0, 2)$, so the y-intercept is 2.

9. a. The graph crosses the x-axis at $(0, 0)$ (the origin), so the x-intercept is 0.

b. The graph also crosses the y-axis at $(0, 0)$, so the y-intercept is 0.

10. $2x + y = 4$

x-intercept:

$2x + 0 = 4$

$2x = 4$

$x = 2$

y-intercept:

$2(0) + y = 4$

$y = 4$

x-intercept: $(2, 0)$; y-intercept: $(0, 4)$

Find one other point as a checkpoint. For example, substitute 1 for x.

$2(1) + y = 4$

$2 + y = 4$

$y = 2$

checkpoint: $(1, 2)$

Draw a line through $(2, 0)$, $(0, 4)$, and $(1, 2)$.

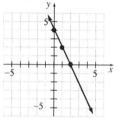

11. $3x - 2y = 12$

x-intercept: $(4, 0)$

y-intercept: $(0, -6)$

checkpoint: $(2, -3)$

Draw a line through $(4, 0)$, $(0, -6)$ and $(2, -3)$

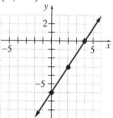

132

12. $3x = 6 - 2y$

x-intercept: $(2,0)$
y-intercept: $(0,3)$
checkpoint: $(4, -3)$
Draw a line through $(2,0)$, $(0,3)$ and
$(4, -3)$

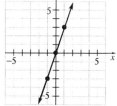

13. $3x - y = 0$

x-intercept: 0
y-intercept: 0
second point: $(1,3)$
checkpoint: $(-1, -3)$
Draw a line through $(0,0)$, $(1,3)$ and
$(-1, -3)$

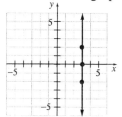

14. $x = 3$

Three ordered pairs are $(3, -2)$, $(3,0)$,
and $(3,2)$. The graph is a vertical line.

15. $y = -5$

Three ordered pairs are $(-2, -5)$,
$(0, -5)$, and $(2, -5)$. The graph is a
horizontal line.

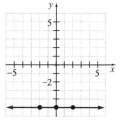

16. $y + 3 = 5$

$y = 2$

Three ordered pairs are $(-2,2)$, $(0,2)$,
and $(2,2)$. The graph is a horizontal
line.

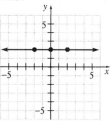

17. $2x = -8$

$x = -4$

Three ordered pairs $(-4, -2)$, $(-4,0)$,
and $(-4,2)$. The graph is a vertical line.

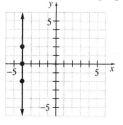

18. a. The minimum temperature
occurred at 5 P.M. and was $-4°F$.

b. The maximum temperature
occurred at 8 P.M. and was at
$16°F$.

133

c. The *x*-intercepts are 4 and 6. This indicates that 4 P.M. and 6 P.M., the temperature was 0°F.

d. The *y*-intercept is 12. This indicates that at noon the temperature was 12°F.

e. This indicates that the temperature stayed the same, at 12°F, from 9 P.M. until midnight.

19. Let $(x_1, y_1) = (3,2)$ and $(x_2, y_2) = (5,1)$.

$$m = \frac{y_2 - y_1}{x_2 - x_1} = \frac{1-2}{5-3} = -\frac{1}{2}$$

The slope is $-\frac{1}{2}$. Since the slope is negative, the line falls.

20. $(-1,2)$ and $(-3,-4)$

$$m = \frac{-4-2}{-3-(-1)} = \frac{-6}{-2} = 3$$

Since the slope is positive, the line rises.

21. $(-3,4)$ and $(6,4)$

$$m = \frac{4-4}{6-(-3)} = \frac{0}{9} = 0$$

Since the slope is 0, the line is horizontal.

22. $(5,3)$ and $(5,-3)$

$$m = \frac{-3-3}{5-5} = \frac{-6}{0}; \text{ undefined}$$

Since the slope is undefined, the line is vertical.

23. Line through $(-3,-2)$ and $(2,1)$:

$$m = \frac{1-(-2)}{2-(-3)} = \frac{3}{5}$$

24. Line through $(-2,3)$ and $(-2,-3)$:
The line is vertical, so its slope is undefined.

25. Line through $(-4,-1)$ and $(2,-3)$:

$$m = \frac{-3-(-1)}{2-(-4)} = \frac{-2}{6} = -\frac{1}{3}$$

26. Line through $(-2,2)$ and $(3,2)$:
The line is horizontal, so its slope is 0.

27. Line through $(-1,-3)$ and $(2,-8)$:

$$m = \frac{-8-(-3)}{2-(-1)} = \frac{-5}{3} = -\frac{5}{3}$$

Line through $(8,-7)$ and $(9,10)$:

$$m = \frac{10-(-7)}{9-8} = \frac{17}{1} = 17$$

Since their slopes are not equal, the lines are not parallel.

28. Line through $(5,4)$ and $(9,7)$:

$$m = \frac{7-4}{9-5} = \frac{3}{4}$$

Line through $(-6,0)$ and $(-2,3)$:

$$m = \frac{3-0}{-2-(-6)} = \frac{3}{4}$$

Since their slopes are equal, the lines are parallel.

29. a. $(1999,41315)$ and $(2001,41227)$

$$m = \frac{41227-41315}{2001-1999} = \frac{-88}{2} = -44$$

The number of new AIDS diagnoses decreased at a rate of 44 each year from 1999 to 2001.

b. $(2001,41227)$ and $(2003,43045)$

$$m = \frac{43045-41227}{2003-2001} = \frac{1818}{2} = 909$$

The number of new AIDS diagnoses increased at a rate of 909 each year from 2001 to 2003.

134

c. $(1999, 41315)$ and $(2003, 43045)$

$$m = \frac{43045 - 41315}{2003 - 1999} = \frac{1730}{4} = 432.5$$

$$\frac{-44 + 909}{2} = \frac{865}{2} = 432.5$$

Yes, the slope equals the average of the two values. Explanations will vary.

30. $y = 5x - 7$

$y = 5x + (-7)$

The slope is the x-coefficient, which is 5. The y-intercept is the constant term, which is -7.

31. $y = 6 - 4x$

$y = -4x + 6$

$m = -4$; y-intercept $= 6$

32. $y = 3$

$m = 0$; y-intercept $= 3$

33. $2x + 3y = 6$

$3y = -2x + 6$

$$y = \frac{-2x + 6}{3}$$

$$y = -\frac{2}{3}x + 2$$

$m = -\frac{2}{3}$; y-intercept $= 2$

34. $y = 2x - 4$

slope $= 2 = \frac{2}{1}$; y-intercept $= -4$

Plot $(0, -4)$ on the y-axis. From this point, move 2 units *up* (because 2 is positive) and 1 unit to the *right* to reach the point $(1, -2)$. Draw a line through $(0, -4)$ and $(1, -2)$.

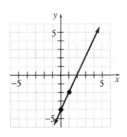

35. $y = \frac{1}{2}x - 1$

slope $= \frac{1}{2}$; y-intercept $= -1$

Plot $(0, -1)$. From the point, move 1 unit *up* and 2 units to the *right* to reach the point $(2, 0)$. Draw a line through $(0, -1)$ and $(2, 0)$.

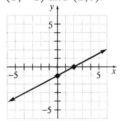

36. $y = -\frac{2}{3}x + 5$

slope $= -\frac{2}{3} = \frac{-2}{3}$; y-intercept $= 5$

Plot $(0, 5)$. Move 2 units *down* (because -2 is negative) and 3 units to the *right* to reach the point $(3, 3)$. Draw a line through $(0, 5)$ and $(3, 3)$.

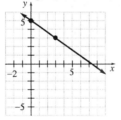

135

37. $y - 2x = 0$

$\qquad y = 2x$

slope $= 2 = \dfrac{2}{1}$; y-intercept $= 0$

Plot (0,0) (the origin). Move 2 units *up* and 1 unit to the *right* to reach the point (1,2). Draw a line through (0,0) and (1,2).

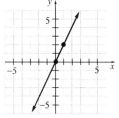

38. $\dfrac{1}{3}x + y = 2$

$\qquad y = -\dfrac{1}{3}x + 2$

slope $= -\dfrac{1}{3} = \dfrac{-1}{3}$; y-intercept $= 2$

Plot (0,2). Move 1 unit *down* and 3 units to the *right* to reach the point (3,1). Draw line through (0,2) and (3,1).

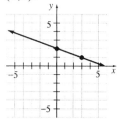

39. $y = -\dfrac{1}{2}x + 4 \qquad\qquad y = -\dfrac{1}{2}x - 1$

slope $= -\dfrac{1}{2} = \dfrac{-1}{2} \qquad$ slope $= -\dfrac{1}{2} = \dfrac{-1}{2}$

y-intercept $= 4 \qquad\qquad y$-intercept $= -1$

Graph each line using its slope and y-intercept.

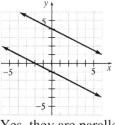

Yes, they are parallel since both lines have a slope of $-\dfrac{1}{2}$ and different y-intercepts

40. a. The smallest y-intercept is 25. This indicates that in 1990 the average age of U.S. Hispanics was 25.

b. Line through (0,35) and (10,38):

$$m = \frac{38 - 35}{10 - 0} = \frac{3}{10} = 0.3$$

This means that the average age for U.S. whites increased at a rate of about 0.3 each year from 1990 to 2000.

c. $y = 0.3x + 35$

d. The year 2010 corresponds to $x = 20$. If $x = 20$,

$y = 0.3(20) + 35 = 41$.

According to the model, the average age for U.S. whites in 2010 will be 41 years old.

41. Slope $= 6$, passing through $(-4,7)$ point-slope form:

$$y - 7 = 6\left[x - (-4)\right]$$

$$y - 7 = 6(x + 4)$$

slope-intercept form:

$$y - 7 = 6x + 24$$

$$y = 6x + 31$$

42. Passing through $(3,4)$ and $(2,1)$

First, find the slope.

$$m = \frac{1-4}{2-3} = \frac{-3}{-1} = 3$$

Next, use the slope and one of the points to write the equation of the line in point-slope form.

$$y - y_1 = m(x - x_1)$$

$$y - 4 = 3(x - 3)$$

Solve for y to obtain slope-intercept form.

$$y - 4 = 3x - 9$$

$$y = 3x - 5$$

43. Rewrite $3x + y - 9 = 0$ in slope-intercept form.

$$3x + y - 9 = 0$$

$$y = -3x + 9$$

Since the line we are concerned with is parallel to this line, we know it will have slope $m = -3$. We are given that it passes through $(4, -7)$. We use the slope and point to write the equation in point-slope form.

$$y - y_1 = m(x - x_1)$$

$$y - (-7) = -3(x - 4)$$

$$y + 7 = -3(x - 4)$$

Solve for y to obtain slope-intercept form.

$$y + 7 = -3(x - 4)$$

$$y + 7 = -3x + 12$$

$$y = -3x + 5$$

44. The line is perpendicular to $y = \frac{1}{3}x + 4$, so the slope is -3. We are given that it passes through $(-2, 6)$. We use the slope and point to write the equation in point-slope form.

$$y - y_1 = m(x - x_1)$$

$$y - 6 = -3(x - (-2))$$

$$y - 6 = -3(x + 2)$$

Solve for y to obtain slope-intercept form.

$$y - 6 = -3(x + 2)$$

$$y - 6 = -3x - 6$$

$$y = -3x$$

45. a. First, find the slope. $(1, 1.5)$ and $(3, 3.4)$.

$$m = \frac{3.4 - 1.5}{3 - 1} = \frac{1.9}{2} = 0.95$$

Next, use the slope and one of the points to write the point-slope equation of the line.

$$y - 1.5 = 0.95(x - 1) \text{ or}$$

$$y - 3.4 = 0.95(x - 3)$$

b.

$$y - 1.5 = 0.95(x - 1)$$

$$y - 1.5 = 0.95x - 0.95$$

$$y = 0.95x + .55$$

c. Since 2009 is 2009-1999 = 10, let $x = 10$.

$$y = 0.95(10) + .55$$

$$= 9.5 + .55 = 10.05$$

$10.05 billion in revenue was earned from online gambling in 2009.

Chapter 3 Test

1. $4x - 2y = 10$

$(0, -5)$:

$4(0) - 2(-5) = 10$

$0 + 10 = 10$

$10 = 10$ true

$(0, -5)$ is a solution

$(-2, 1)$:

$4(-2) - 2(1) = 10$

$-8 - 2 = 10$

$-10 = 10$ false

$(-2, 1)$ is not a solution.

$(4, 3)$:

$4(4) - 2(3) = 10$

$16 - 6 = 10$

$10 = 10$ true

$(4, 3)$ is a solution.

2. $y = 3x + 1$

x	$y = 3x + 1$	(x, y)
-2	$y = 3(-2) + 1 = -5$	$(-2, -5)$
-1	$y = 3(-1) + 1 = -2$	$(-1, -2)$
0	$y = 3(0) + 1 = 1$	$(0, 1)$
1	$y = 3(1) + 1 = 4$	$(1, 4)$
2	$y = 3(2) + 1 = 7$	$(2, 7)$

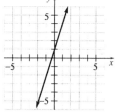

3. $y = x^2 - 1$

x	$y = x^2 - 1$	(x, y)
-3	$y = (-3)^2 - 1 = 8$	$(-3, 8)$
-2	$y = (-2)^2 - 1 = 3$	$(-2, 3)$
-1	$y = (-1)^2 - 1 = 0$	$(-1, 0)$
0	$y = 0^2 - 1 = -1$	$(0, -1)$
1	$y = 1^2 - 1 = 0$	$(1, 0)$
2	$y = 2^2 - 1 = 3$	$(2, 3)$
3	$y = 3^2 - 1 = 8$	$(3, 8)$

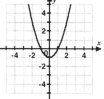

4. **a.** The graph crosses the x-axis at $(2, 0)$, so the x-intercept is 2.

b. The graph crosses the y-axis at $(0, -3)$, so the y-intercept is -3.

5. $4x - 2y = -8$

x-intercept: y-intercept:

$4x - 2(0) = -8$ $4(0) - 2y = -8$

$4x = -8$ $-2y = -8$

$x = -2$ $y = 4$

Find one other point as a checkpoint. For example, substitute -4 for x.

$4(-4) - 2y = -8$

$-16 - 2y = -8$

$-2y = -8$

$y = -4$

checkpoint: $(-4, -4)$

Draw a line through $(-2, 0)$, $(0, 4)$ and $(-4, -4)$.

138

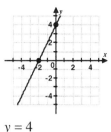

6. $y = 4$

Three ordered pairs are $(-2,4)$, $(0,4)$, and $(2,4)$. The graph is a horizontal line.

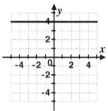

7. $(-3,4)$ and $(-5, -2)$

$$m = \frac{-2-4}{-5(-3)} = \frac{-6}{-2} = 3$$

The slope is 3. Since the slope is positive, the line rises.

8. $(6, -1)$ and $(6,3)$

$$m = \frac{3-(-1)}{6-6} = \frac{4}{0}; \text{ undefined}$$

Since the slope is undefined, the line is vertical.

9. Line through $(-1, -2)$ and $(1,1)$:

$$m = \frac{1-(-2)}{1-(-1)} = \frac{3}{2}$$

10. Line through $(2,4)$ and $(6,1)$:

$$m = \frac{1-4}{6-2} = \frac{-3}{4} = -\frac{3}{4}$$

Line through $(-3,1)$ and $(1, -2)$:

$$m = \frac{-2-1}{1-(-3)} = \frac{-3}{4} = -\frac{3}{4}$$

Since the slopes are equal, the lines are parallel.

11. $y = -x + 10$

$y = -1x + 10$

The slope is the coefficient of x, which is -1. The y-intercept is the constant term, which is 10.

12. $2x + y = 6$

$y = -2x + 6$

$m = -2$; y-intercept $= 6$

13. $y = \frac{2}{3}x - 1$

slope $= \frac{2}{3}$; y-intercept $= -1$

Plot $(0, -1)$. From this point, move 2 units *up* and 3 units to the *right* to reach the point $(3,1)$. Draw a line through $(0, -1)$ and $(3,1)$.

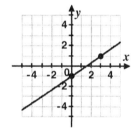

14. $y = -2x + 3$

slope $= -2 = \frac{-2}{1}$; y-intercept $= 3$

Plot $(0,3)$. Move 2 units *down* and 1 unit to the right to reach the point $(1,1)$. Draw a line through $(0,3)$ and $(1,1)$.

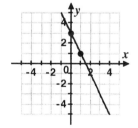

139

15. Slope $= -2$; passing through $(-1,4)$
point-slope form:
$$y - 4 = -2\left[x - (-1)\right]$$
$$y - 4 = -2(x + 1)$$
slope-intercept form:
$$y - 4 = -2x - 2$$
$$y = -2x + 2$$

16. Passing through $(2,1)$ and $(-1, -8)$
$$m = \frac{-8 - 1}{-1 - 2} = \frac{-9}{-3} = 3$$
Using the point $(2,1)$, the point-slope
equation is
$$y - 1 = 3(x - 2).$$
Rewrite this equation in slope-intercept
form
$$y - 1 = 3x - 6$$
$$y = 3x - 5$$

17. The line is perpendicular to
$y = -\frac{1}{2}x - 4$, so the slope is 2. We
are given that it passes through $(-2,3)$.
We use the slope and point to write the
equation in point-slope form.
$$y - y_1 = m(x - x_1)$$
$$y - 3 = 2(x - (-2))$$
$$y - 3 = 2(x + 2)$$
Solve for y to obtain slope-intercept
form.
$$y - 3 = 2(x + 2)$$
$$y - 3 = 2x + 4$$
$$y = 2x + 7$$

18. The line is parallel to $x + 2y = 5$.
Put this equation in slope-intercept
form by solving for y.
$$x + 2y = 5$$
$$2y = -x + 5$$
$$y = -\frac{1}{2}x + \frac{5}{2}$$
Therefore the slopes are the same;
$$m = -\frac{1}{2}.$$
We are given that it passes through
$(6, -4)$. We use the slope and point to
write the equation in point-slope form.
$$y - y_1 = m(x - x_1)$$
$$y - (-4) = -\frac{1}{2}(x - 6)$$
$$y + 4 = -\frac{1}{2}(x - 6)$$
Solve for y to obtain slope-intercept
form.
$$y + 4 = -\frac{1}{2}(x - 6)$$
$$y + 4 = -\frac{1}{2}x + 3$$
$$y = -\frac{1}{2}x - 1$$

19. Line through $(1970,2100)$ and
$(2000,5280)$:
$$m = \frac{5280 - 2100}{2000 - 1970} = \frac{3180}{30} = 106$$
This slope indicates that per-pupil
spending increases by about $106 each
year.

140

20. a. First, find the slope using the points $(1, 2.3)$ and $(4, 3.2)$.

$$m = \frac{3.2 - 2.3}{4 - 1} = \frac{0.9}{3} = 0.3$$

Then use the slope and a point to write the equation in point-slope form.

$$y - y_1 = m(x - x_1)$$
$$y - 3.2 = 0.3(x - 4)$$

or

$$y - 2.3 = 0.3(x - 1)$$

b. Solve for y to obtain slope-intercept form.

$$y - 3.2 = 0.3(x - 4)$$
$$y - 3.2 = 0.3x - 1.2$$
$$y = 0.3x + 2$$

c. To predict the number of worldwide death due to AIDS in 2007, let $x = 2007 - 1999 = 8$.

$$y = 0.3(8) + 2 = 2.4 + 2 = 4.4$$

If the current trend continues, the number of worldwide deaths due to AIDS in 2007 will be 4.4 million.

Cumulative Review Exercises (Chapters 1-3)

1. $\dfrac{10 - (-6)}{3^2 - (4 - 3)} = \dfrac{10 + 6}{9 - 1} = \dfrac{16}{8} = 2$

2. $6 - 2\left[3(x - 1) + 4\right]$
$= 6 - 2(3x - 3 + 4) = 6 - 2(3x + 1)$
$= 6 - 6x - 2 = 4 - 6x$

3. The only irrational number in the given set is $\sqrt{5}$.

4. $6(2x - 1) - 6 = 11x + 7$
$12x - 6 - 6 = 11x + 7$
$12x - 12 = 11x + 7$
$x - 12 = 7$
$x = 19$
The solution set is $\{19\}$.

5.
$$x - \frac{3}{4} = \frac{1}{2}$$
$$x - \frac{3}{4} + \frac{3}{4} = \frac{1}{2} + \frac{3}{4}$$
$$x = \frac{2}{4} + \frac{3}{4} = \frac{5}{4}$$

The solution set is $\left\{\dfrac{5}{4}\right\}$.

6. $y = mx + b$ for x.
$$y = mx + b$$
$$y - b = mx + b - b$$
$$y - b = mx$$
$$\frac{y - b}{m} = \frac{mx}{m}$$
$$\frac{y - b}{m} = x \text{ or } x = \frac{y - b}{m}$$

7. $A = PB;\ A = 120;\ P = 15\% = 0.15$
$$A = PB$$
$$120 = 0.15 \cdot B$$
$$\frac{120}{0.15} = \frac{0.15B}{0.15}$$
$$800 = B$$
120 is 15% of 800.

8. $y = 4.5x - 46.7;\ y = 133.3$
$$133.3 = 4.5x - 46.7$$
$$133.3 + 46.7 = 4.5x - 46.7 + 46.7$$
$$180 = 4.5x$$
$$\frac{180}{4.5} = \frac{4.5x}{4.5}$$
$$40 = x$$
The car is traveling 40 miles per hour.

141

9.
$$2 - 6x \geq 2(5 - x)$$
$$2 - 5x \geq 10 - 2x$$
$$2 - 6x + 2x \geq 10 - 2x + 2x$$
$$2 - 4x \geq 10$$
$$2 - 4x - 2 \geq 10 - 2$$
$$-4x \geq 8$$
$$\frac{-4x}{4} \leq \frac{8}{-4}$$
$$x \leq -2$$
$$\{x \mid x \leq -2\}$$

10.
$$6(2 - x) > 12$$
$$12 - 6x > 12$$
$$12 - 6x - 12 > 12 - 12$$
$$-6x > 0$$
$$\frac{-6x}{-6} < \frac{0}{-6}$$
$$x < 0$$
$$\{x \mid x < 0\}$$

11. $x^2 - 10x$
For $x = -3$, we get:
$$x^2 - 10x = (-3)^2 - 10(-3)$$
$$= 9 + 30$$
$$= 39$$

12. Since -2000 is further to the left on a real number line, we would write $-2000 < -3$.

13. $-4 - 11 + 21 = -15 + 21$
$$= 6$$
The temperature at noon was $6°F$.

14. $D = 4x + 30$
For a debt of $150 thousand, we have $D = 150$. Therefore, we get
$$150 = 4x + 30$$
$$150 - 30 = 4x + 30 - 30$$
$$120 = 4x$$
$$\frac{120}{4} = \frac{4x}{4}$$
$$30 = x$$
This debt will reach $150 thousand after 30 years. That is, in the year $1985 + 30 = 2015$.

15. Let w = the width of the field. Then the length is given by $14 + 2w$.
Using the formula for the perimeter of a rectangle, we get
$$P = 2L + 2W$$
$$346 = 2(14 + 2w) + 2w$$
$$346 = 28 + 4w + 2w$$
$$346 = 28 + 6w$$
$$346 - 28 = 28 + 6w - 28$$
$$318 = 6w$$
$$\frac{318}{6} = \frac{6w}{6}$$
$$53 = w$$
The field is 53 meters wide and 120 meters long (14+2(53)=14+106=120).

16. Let x = weight before the loss. Then $0.10x$ represents the amount of the loss.
$$x - 0.10x = 180$$
$$0.90x = 180$$
$$\frac{0.90x}{0.90} = \frac{180}{0.90}$$
$$x = 200$$
The person weighed 200 pounds before the loss.

17. Let x = the number of hours the plumber worked.

$18 + 35x = 228$

$35x = 210$

$x = 6$

The plumber worked 6 hours.

18. Let x = the measure of the first angle.
Let $x + 20$ = the measure of the second angle.
Let $2x$ = the measure of third angle.

$x + (x + 20) + 2x = 180$

$4x + 20 = 180$

$4x = 160$

$x = 40$

The angles measure $x = 40°$, $x + 20 = 60°$, and $2x = 80°$.

19. $2x - y = 4$

x-intercept: 2 and y-intercept : -4
checkpoint: (4,4)
Draw a line through (2,0), (0, −4), and (4,4)

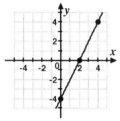

20. $y = -4x + 3$

slope $= -4 = \dfrac{-4}{1}$; y-intercept = 3.

Plot (0,3). Move 4 units *down* and 1 unit to the *right* to reach the point $(1, -1)$. Draw a line through (0,3) and $(1, -1)$.

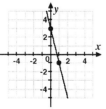

143

Chapter 4
Systems of Linear Equations

4.1 Exercise Set

1. $(2, -3)$

To determine if $(2, -3)$ is a solution to the system, replace x with 2 and y with -3 in both equations.

$$2x + 3y = -5$$
$$2(2) + 3(-3) = -5$$
$$4 + (-9) = -5$$
$$-5 = -5 \quad \text{true}$$
$$7x - 3y = 23$$
$$7(2) - 3(-3) = 23$$
$$14 + 9 = 23$$
$$23 = 23 \quad \text{true}$$

The ordered pair satisfies both equations, so it is a solution to the system.

3. $\left(\dfrac{2}{3}, \dfrac{1}{9}\right)$

$$x + 3y = 1$$
$$\frac{2}{3} + 3\left(\frac{1}{9}\right) = 1$$
$$\frac{2}{3} + \frac{1}{3} = 1$$
$$1 = 1 \quad \text{true}$$

$$4x + 3y = 3$$
$$4\left(\frac{2}{3}\right) + 3\left(\frac{1}{9}\right) = 3$$
$$\frac{8}{3} + \frac{1}{3} = 3$$
$$\frac{9}{3} = 3$$
$$3 = 3 \quad \text{true}$$

Since the ordered pair satisfies both equations, the pair is a solution to the system.

5. $(-5, 9)$

$$5x + 3y = 2$$
$$5(-5) + 3(9) = 2$$
$$-25 + 27 = 2$$
$$2 = 2 \quad \text{true}$$

$$x + 4y = 14$$
$$-5 + 4(9) = 14$$
$$-5 + 36 = 14$$
$$31 = 14 \quad \text{false}$$

The ordered pair does not satisfy both equations, so it is not a solution to the system.

7. $(1400, 450)$

$$x - 2y = 500$$
$$1400 - 2(450) = 500$$
$$1400 - 900 = 500$$
$$500 = 500 \quad \text{true}$$

$$0.03x + 0.02y = 51$$
$$0.03(1400) + 0.02(450) = 51$$
$$42 + 9 = 51$$
$$51 = 51 \quad \text{true}$$

The ordered pair satisfies both equations, so the ordered pair is a solution to the system.

9. $(8, 5)$

$$5x - 4y = 20$$
$$5(8) - 4(5) = 20$$
$$40 - 20 = 20$$
$$20 = 20 \quad \text{true}$$

144

$$3y = 2x + 1$$
$$3(5) = 2(8) + 1$$
$$15 = 16 + 1$$
$$15 = 17 \quad \text{false}$$

The ordered pair does not satisfy both equations, so it is not a solution to the system.

11. Graph both equations on the same axes.
$x + y = 6$:
x-intercept = 6; y-intercept = 6
$x - y = 2$:
x-intercept = 2; y-intercept = -2

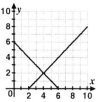

The lines intersect at (4, 2), so it is the solution to the system.
Solution set: $\{(4,2)\}$

13. Graph both equations on the same axes.
$x + y = 1$:
x-intercept = 1; y-intercept = 1
$y - x = 3$
x-intercept = -3; y-intercept = 3

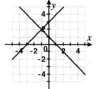

The lines intersect at (-1, 2), so it is the solution to the system.
Solution set: $\{(-1,2)\}$

15. Graph both equations.
$2x - 3y = 6$:
x-intercept = 3: y-intercept = -2
$4x + 3y = 12$:
x-intercept = 3: y-intercept = 4

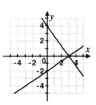

Solution: (3, 0)
Solution set: $\{(3,0)\}$

17. Graph both equations.
$4x + y = 4$:
x-intercept = 1: y-intercept = 4
$3x - y = 3$:
x-intercept = 1: y-intercept = -3

Solution: (1, 0)
Solution set: $\{(1,0)\}$

19. Graph both equations.
$y = x + 5$:
Slope = 1; y-intercept = 5
$y = -x + 3$:
Slope = -1; y-intercept = 3

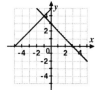

Solution: (-1, 4)
Solution set: $\{(-1,4)\}$

21. Graph both equations.
$y = 2x$:
slope = 2; y-intercept = 0
$y = -x + 6$:
slope = -1; y-intercept = 6

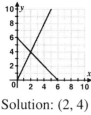

Solution: (2, 4)

Solution set: $\{(2,4)\}$

23. Graph both equations.

$y = -2x + 3$:

slope $= -2$; y-intercept $= 3$

$y = -x + 1$:

slope $= -1$; y-intercept $= 1$

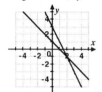

Solution: (2, −1)

Solution set: $\{(2,-1)\}$

25. Graph both equations.

$y = 2x - 1$:

Slope $= 2$; y-intercept $= -1$

$y = 2x + 1$:

Slope $= 2$; y-intercept $= 1$

The two lines are parallel. (Note that the lines have the same slope, but different y-intercepts.) The system has no solution.

Solution set: $\{ \ \}$ or $\varnothing$

27. Graph each equation.

$x + y = 4$:

x-intercept $= 4$; y-intercept $= 4$

$x = -2$:

vertical line with x-intercept -2

Solution: (−2, 6)

Solution set: $\{(-2,6)\}$

29. Graph each equation.

$x - 2y = 4$:

x-intercept $= 4$; y-intercept $= -2$

$2x - 4y = 8$:

x-intercept $= 4$; y-intercept $= -2$

Since the lines have the same slope and y-intercept, the two equations are the same line. The lines coincide, and the system has infinitely many solutions.

Solution set: $\{(x, y) \mid x - 2y = 4\}$ or

$\{(x, y) \mid 2x - 4y = 8\}$

31. Graph both lines.

$y = 2x - 1$:

slope $= 2$; y-intercept $= -1$

$x - 2y = -4$:

x-intercept $= -4$; y-intercept $= 2$

Solution: (2, 3)

Solution set: $\{(2,3)\}$

146

33. Graph both lines.
$x + y = 5$:
x-intercept = 5; y-intercept = 5
$2x + 2y = 12$:
x-intercept = 6; y-intercept = 6

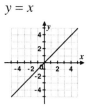

The lines are parallel, so the system has no solution.
Solution set: $\{\ \}$ or $\varnothing$

35. $x - y = 0$
$y = x$

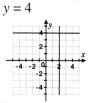

Because the lines coincide, the system has an infinite number of solutions.
Solution set: $\{(x, y) \mid x - y = 0\}$ or $\{(x, y) \mid y = x\}$

37. $x = 2$
$y = 4$

The vertical and horizontal line intersect at (2, 4), so the solution is (2, 4).
Solution set: $\{(2, 4)\}$

39. $x = 2$
$x = -1$

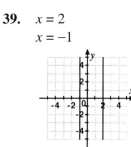

The two vertical lines are parallel, so the system has no solution.
Solution set: $\{\ \}$ or $\varnothing$

41. $y = 0$
$y = 4$

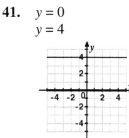

The two horizontal lines are parallel, so the system has no solution.
Solution set: $\{\ \}$ or $\varnothing$

43.
$y = \dfrac{1}{2}x - 3$:

slope = $\dfrac{1}{2}$, y-intercept = -3

$y = \dfrac{1}{2}x - 5$:

slope = $\dfrac{1}{2}$, y-intercept = -5

Since the slopes are the same, but the y-intercepts are different, the lines are parallel and there is no solution.

147

44.

$$y = \frac{3}{4}x - 2:$$

slope $= \frac{3}{4}$, y-intercept $= -2$

$$y = \frac{3}{4}x + 1:$$

slope $= \frac{3}{4}$, y-intercept $= 1$

Since the slopes are the same, but the y-intercepts are different, the lines are parallel and there is no solution.

45.

$$y = -\frac{1}{2}x + 4$$

slope $= -\frac{1}{2}$, y-intercept $= 4$

$$3x - y = -4$$
$$-y = -3x - 4$$
$$y = 3x + 4$$

slope $= 3$, y-intercept $= 4$
Since the lines have different slopes, there will be one solution.

46.

$$y = -\frac{1}{4}x + 3$$

slope $= -1/4$, y-intercept $= 3$

$$4x - y = -3$$
$$-y = -4x - 3$$
$$y = 4x + 3$$

slope $= 4$, y-intercept $= 3$
Since the lines have different slopes, there will be one solution.

47.

$$3x - y = 6$$
$$-y = -3x + 6$$
$$y = 3x - 6$$

slope $= 3$, y-intercept $= -6$

$$x = \frac{y}{3} + 2$$
$$3x = y + 6$$
$$3x - 6 = y$$
$$y = 3x - 6$$

slope $= 3$, y-intercept $= -6$
Since the lines have the same slopes and y-intercepts, the graphs will coincide and there are an infinite number of solutions.

48.

$$2x - y = 4$$
$$-y = -2x + 4$$
$$y = 2x - 4$$

slope $= 2$, y-intercept $= -4$

$$x = \frac{y}{2} + 2$$
$$2x = y + 4$$
$$2x - 4 = y$$
$$y = 2x - 4$$

slope $= 2$, y-intercept $= -4$
Since the lines have the same slopes and y-intercepts, the graphs will coincide and there are an infinite number of solutions.

49.

$$3x + y = 0$$
$$y = -3x$$

slope $= -3$, y-intercept $= 0$
$$y = -3x + 1$$

slope $= -3$, y-intercept $= 1$
Since the slopes are the same, but the y-intercepts are different, the lines are parallel and there is no solution.

50. $2x + y = 0$

$\qquad y = -2x$

slope = -2, y-intercept = 0
$y = -2x + 1$
slope = -2, y-intercept = 1
Since the slopes are the same, but the y-intercepts are different, the lines are parallel and there is no solution.

51. **a.** The intersection point is approximately $(1996, 41)$. This means that mothers 30 years old and older in Massachusetts had about 41 thousand (41,000) births in 1996.

    b. Since 1996, there have been more births in Massachusetts to mothers 30 years old and older than to those under 30 years old.

53.-59. Answers will vary.

61. Statement c is true.
If two lines have two points in common, they must coincide (be on the same line), so they will have equal slopes and equal y-intercepts.

63. Answers will vary.

65. Answers will vary depending on exercises chosen.

67. $y = -x + 5$

$\qquad y = x - 7$

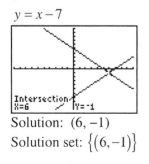

Solution: $(6, -1)$
Solution set: $\{(6, -1)\}$

69. $2x - 3y = 6$

$\qquad -3y = -2x + 6$

$\qquad y = \dfrac{2}{3}x - 2$

$4x + 3y = 12$

$\qquad 3y = -4x + 12$

$\qquad y = -\dfrac{4}{3}x + 4$

Solution: $(3, 0)$
Solution set: $\{(3, 0)\}$

71. $2x - 3y = 7$

$\qquad -3y = -2x + 7$

$\qquad y = \dfrac{2}{3}x - \dfrac{7}{3}$

$3x + 5y = 1$

$\qquad 5y = -3x + 1$

$\qquad y = -\dfrac{3}{5}x + \dfrac{1}{5}$

Solution: $(2, -1)$
Solution set: $\{(2, -1)\}$

73.

$$y = -\frac{1}{2}x + 2$$

$$y = \frac{3}{4}x + 7$$

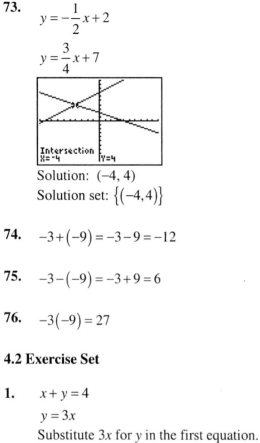

Solution: $(-4, 4)$

Solution set: $\{(-4, 4)\}$

74. $-3 + (-9) = -3 - 9 = -12$

75. $-3 - (-9) = -3 + 9 = 6$

76. $-3(-9) = 27$

4.2 Exercise Set

1. $x + y = 4$

$y = 3x$

Substitute $3x$ for y in the first equation.

$$x + y = 4$$

$$x + (3x) = 4$$

Solve this equation for x.

$$4x = 4$$

$$x = 1$$

Back substitute 1 for x into the second equation.

$$y = 3x$$

$$y = 3(1) = 3$$

The solution is $(1, 3)$.

Solution set: $\{(1, 3)\}$

3. $x + 3y = 8$

$y = 2x - 9$

Substitute $2x - 9$ for y in the first equation and solve for x.

$$x + 3y = 8$$

$$x + 3(2x - 9) = 8$$

$$x + 6x - 27 = 8$$

$$7x - 27 = 8$$

$$7x = 35$$

$$x = 5$$

Back-substitute 5 for x into the second equation and solve for y.

$$y = 2x - 9$$

$$y = 2(5) - 9 = 1$$

Solution: $(5, 1)$

Solution set: $\{(5, 1)\}$

5. $x + 3y = 5$

$4x + 5y = 13$

Solve the first equation for x.

$$x + 3y = 5$$

$$x = 5 - 3y$$

Substitute $5 - 3y$ for x in the second equation and solve for y.

$$4x + 5y = 13$$

$$4(5 - 3y) + 5y = 13$$

$$20 - 12y + 5y = 13$$

$$20 - 7y = 13$$

$$-7y = -7$$

$$y = 1$$

Back-substitute 1 for y in the equation $x = 5 - 3y$ and solve for x.

$$x = 5 - 3y$$

$$x = 5 - 3(1) = 2$$

Solution: $(2, 1)$

Solution set: $\{(2, 1)\}$

7. $2x - y = -5$

$x + 5y = 14$

Solve the second equation for x.

$x + 5y = 14$

$x = 14 - 5y$

Substitute $14 - 5y$ for x in the first equation.

$2(14 - 5y) - y = -5$

$28 - 10y - y = -5$

$28 - 11y = -5$

$-11y = -33$

$y = 3$

Back-substitute.

$x = 14 - 5y$

$x = 14 - 5(3) = 14 - 15 = -1$

Solution: $(-1, 3)$

Solution set: $\{(-1, 3)\}$

9. $2x - y = 3$

$5x - 2y = 10$

Solve the first equation for y.

$2x - y = 3$

$-y = -2x + 3$

$y = 2x - 3$

Substitute $2x - 3$ for y in the second equation.

$5x - 2(2x - 3) = 10$

$5x - 4x + 6 = 10$

$x + 6 = 10$

$x = 4$

Back-substitute.

$y = 2x - 3$

$y = 2(4) - 3 = 8 - 3 = 5$

Solution: $(4, 5)$

Solution set: $\{(4, 5)\}$

11. $-3x + y = -1$

$x - 2y = 4$

Solve the second equation for x.

$x - 2y = 4$

$x = 2y + 4$

Substitute $2y + 4$ for x in the first equation.

$-3x + y = -1$

$-3(2y + 4) + y = -1$

$-6y - 12 + y = -1$

$-5y - 12 = -1$

$-5y = 11$

$y = -\dfrac{11}{5}$

Back-substitute

$x = 2y + 4$

$x = 2\left(-\dfrac{11}{5}\right) + 4$

$x = -\dfrac{22}{5} + 4$

$x = -\dfrac{22}{5} + \dfrac{20}{5}$

$x = -\dfrac{2}{5}$

Solution: $\left(-\dfrac{2}{5}, -\dfrac{11}{5}\right)$

Solution set: $\left\{\left(-\dfrac{2}{5}, -\dfrac{11}{5}\right)\right\}$

13. $x = 9 - 2y$

$x + 2y = 13$

The first equation is already solved for x.

Substitute $9 - 2y$ for x in the second equation.

$$x + 2y = 13$$
$$(9 - 2y) + 2y = 13$$
$$9 = 13 \text{ false}$$

The false statement 9=13 indicates that the system is inconsistent and has no solution.

Solution set: $\{\ \}$ or $\varnothing$

15. $y = 3x - 5$

$21x - 35 = 7y$

Substitute $3x - 5$ for y in the second equation.

$$21x - 35 = 7y$$
$$21x - 35 = 7(3x - 5)$$
$$21x - 35 = 21x - 35$$
$$-35 = -35 \text{ true}$$

The true statement $-35 = -35$ indicates that the system contains dependent equations and has infinitely many solutions.

Solution set: $\{(x, y) \mid y = 3x - 5\}$ or $\{(x, y) \mid 21x - 35 = 7y\}$

17. $5x + 2y = 0$

$x - 3y = 0$

Solve the second equation for x.

$$x - 3y = 0$$
$$x = 3y$$

Substitute $3y$ for x in the first equation.

$$5x + 2y = 0$$
$$5(3y) + 2y = 0$$
$$15y + 2y = 0$$
$$17y = 0$$
$$y = 0$$

Back-substitute.

$$x = 3y$$
$$x = 3(0) = 0$$

Solution: $(0,0)$

Solution set: $\{(0,0)\}$

19. $2x - y = 6$

$3x + 2y = 5$

Solve the first equation for y.

$$2x - y = 6$$
$$-y = -2x + 6$$
$$y = 2x - 6$$

Substitute $2x - 6$ for y in the second equation.

$$3x + 2y = 5$$
$$3x + 2(2x - 6) = 5$$
$$3x + 4x - 12 = 5$$
$$7x - 12 = 5$$
$$7x = 17$$
$$x = \frac{17}{7}$$

Back-substitute.

$$y = 2x - 6 = 2\left(\frac{17}{7}\right) - 6$$
$$= \frac{34}{7} - 6 = \frac{34}{7} - \frac{42}{7} = -\frac{8}{7}$$

Solution: $\left(\frac{17}{7}, -\frac{8}{7}\right)$

Solution set: $\left\{\left(\frac{17}{7}, -\frac{8}{7}\right)\right\}$

152

21. $2(x-1)-y=-3$

$y=2x+3$

Substitute $2x+3$ for y in the first equation.

$2(x-1)-(2x+3)=-3$

$2x-2-2x-3=-3$

$-5=-3$ false

The false statement $-5=-5$ indicates that the system has no solution.

Solution set: $\{\ \}$ or $\varnothing$

23. $x=2y+9$

$x=7y+10$

Substitute $7y + 10$ for x in the first equation.

$x=2y+9$

$7y+10=2y+9$

$5y+10=9$

$5y=-1$

$y=-\dfrac{1}{5}$

Back-substitute.

$x=2y+9=2\left(-\dfrac{1}{5}\right)+9$

$=-\dfrac{2}{5}+9=-\dfrac{2}{5}+\dfrac{45}{5}=\dfrac{43}{5}$

Solution: $\left(\dfrac{43}{5},-\dfrac{1}{5}\right)$

Solution set: $\left\{\left(\dfrac{43}{5},-\dfrac{1}{5}\right)\right\}$

25. $4x-y=100$

$0.05x-0.06y=-32$

Solve the first equation for y.

$4x-y=100$

$-y=-4x+100$

$y=4x-100$

Substitute $4x-100$ for y in the

second equation.

$0.05x-0.06y=-32$

$0.05x-0.06(4x-100)=-32$

$0.05x-0.24x+6=-32$

$-0.19x+6=-32$

$-0.19x=-38$

$x=200$

Back-substitute.

$y=4x-100$

$=4(200)-100$

$=800-100=700$

Solution: $(200,700)$

Solution set: $\{(200,700)\}$

27. $y=\dfrac{1}{3}x+\dfrac{2}{3}$

$y=\dfrac{5}{7}x-2$

First, clear both equations of fractions. Multiply the first equation by the LCD, 3.

$3y=3\left(\dfrac{1}{3}x+\dfrac{2}{3}\right)$

$3y=3x+2$

Multiply the second equation by the LCD, 7.

$7y=7\left(\dfrac{5}{7}x-2\right)$

$7y=5x-14$

Now solve the new system

$3y=x+2$

$7y=5x-14$

Solve the first equation for x.

$3y=x+2$

$3y-2=x$

Substitute $3y-2$ for x in the second equation of the new system.

153

$$7y = 5x - 14$$
$$7y = 5(3y - 2) - 14$$
$$7y = 15y - 10 - 14$$
$$7y = 15y - 24$$
$$-8y = -24$$
$$y = 3$$

Back-substitute.
$$x = 3y - 2$$
$$x = 3(3) - 2 = 9 - 2 = 7$$
Solution: (7, 3)
Solution set: $\{(7,3)\}$

29. $$\frac{x}{6} - \frac{y}{2} = \frac{1}{3}$$
$$x + 2y = -3$$

Clear the first equation of fractions by multiplying 6.
$$6\left(\frac{x}{6} - \frac{y}{2}\right) = 6\left(\frac{1}{3}\right)$$
$$x - 3y = 2$$
Solve this equation for x.
$$x = 3y + 2$$
Substitute $3y + 2$ for x in the second equation of the system.
$$(3y + 2) + 2y = -3$$
$$5y + 2 = -3$$
$$5y = -5$$
$$y = -1$$
Back-substitute.
$$x = 3y + 2 = 3(-1) + 2 = -1$$
Solution: (−1, −1)
Solution set: $\{(-1,-1)\}$

31. $$2x - 3y = 8 - 2x$$
$$3x + 4y = x + 3y + 14$$
Simplify the first equation.
$$2x - 3y = 8 - 2x$$
$$2x - 3y + 2x = 8 - 2x + 2x$$
$$4x - 3y = 8$$
Simplify the second equation.
$$3x + 4y = x + 3y + 14$$
$$3x + 4y - x - 3y = x + 3y + 14 - x - 3y$$
$$2x + y = 14$$
Solve the last equation for y.
$$y = 14 - 2x$$
Substitute $14 - 2x$ for y in the equation $4x - 3y = 8$.
$$4x - 3y = 8$$
$$4x - 3(14 - 2x) = 8$$
$$4x - 42 + 6x = 8$$
$$10x - 42 = 8$$
$$10x = 50$$
$$x = 5$$
$$y = 14 - 2x = 14 - 2(5) = 14 - 10 = 4$$
Solution: (5, 4)
Solution set: $\{(5,4)\}$

33. $$x + y = 81$$
$$x = y + 41$$
Substitute $y + 41$ for x in the first equation.
$$x + y = 81$$
$$(y + 41) + y = 81$$
$$2y + 41 = 81$$
$$2y = 40$$
$$y = 20$$
Back-substitute.
$$x = y + 41 = 20 + 41 = 61$$
The numbers are 20 and 61.

34. $x + y = 62$

$\qquad x = y + 12$

Substitute $y + 12$ for x in the first equation.

$\qquad x + y = 62$

$\qquad (y + 12) + y = 62$

$\qquad y + 12 + y = 62$

$\qquad 2y + 12 = 62$

$\qquad 2y = 50$

$\qquad y = 25$

Back-substitute.

$x = y + 12 = 25 + 12 = 37$

The numbers are 25 and 37.

35. $x - y = 5$

$\qquad 4x = 6y$

Solve the first equation for x.

$x - y = 5$

$\qquad x = y + 5$

Substitute $y + 5$ for x in the second equation.

$\qquad 4x = 6y$

$4(y + 5) = 6y$

$\qquad 4y + 20 = 6y$

$\qquad 20 = 2y$

$\qquad 10 = y$

Back-substitute.

$x = y + 5 = 10 + 5 = 15$

The numbers are 10 and 15.

36. $x - y = 25$

$\qquad 2x = 12y$

Solve the first equation for x.

$x - y = 25$

$\qquad x = y + 25$

Substitute $y + 25$ for x in the second equation.

$\qquad 2x = 12y$

$2(y + 25) = 12y$

$\qquad 2y + 50 = 12y$

$\qquad 50 = 10y$

$\qquad 5 = y$

Back-substitute.

$x = y + 25 = 5 + 25 = 30$

The numbers are 5 and 30.

37. $x - y = 1$

$\qquad x + 2y = 7$

Solve the first equation for x.

$x - y = 1$

$\qquad x = y + 1$

Substitute $y + 1$ for x in the second equation.

$\qquad x + 2y = 7$

$(y + 1) + 2y = 7$

$\qquad y + 1 + 2y = 7$

$\qquad 3y + 1 = 7$

$\qquad 3y = 6$

$\qquad y = 2$

Back-substitute.

$x = y + 1 = 2 + 1 = 3$

The numbers are 2 and 3.

38. $x - y = 5$

$x + 2y = 14$

Solve the first equation for x.

$x - y = 5$

$x = y + 5$

Substitute $y + 5$ for x in the second equation.

$x + 2y = 14$

$(y + 5) + 2y = 14$

$y + 5 + 2y = 14$

$3y + 5 = 14$

$3y = 9$

$y = 3$

Back-substitute.

$x = y + 5 = 3 + 5 = 8$

The numbers are 3 and 8.

39. $0.7x - 0.1y = 0.6$

$0.8x - 0.3y = -0.8$

Multiply both sides of both equations by 10.

$7x - y = 6$

$8x - 3y = -8$

Solve the first equation for y.

$7x - y = 6$

$7x = 6 + y$

$7x - 6 = y$

Substitute $7x - 6$ for y in the second equation.

$8x - 3y = -8$

$8x - 3(7x - 6) = -8$

$8x - 21x + 18 = -8$

$-13x + 18 = -8$

$-13x = -26$

$x = 2$

Back-substitute.

$y = 7x - 6 = 7(2) - 6 = 14 - 6 = 8$

Solution: (2, 8)

Solution set: $\{(2,8)\}$

40. $1.25x - 0.01y = 4.5$

$0.5x - 0.02y = 1$

Multiply both sides of both equations by 100.

$125x - 1y = 450$

$50x - 2y = 100$

Solve the first equation for y.

$125x - 1y = 450$

$125x - y = 450$

$125x = y + 450$

$125x - 450 = y$

Substitute $125x - 450$ for y in the second equation.

$50x - 2y = 100$

$50x - 2(125x - 450) = 100$

$50x - 250x + 900 = 100$

$-200x + 900 = 100$

$-200x = -800$

$x = 4$

Back-substitute.

$y = 125x - 450 = 125(4) - 450$

$= 500 - 450 = 50$

Solution: (4, 50)

Solution set: $\{(4,50)\}$

41.   Demand model: $N = -25p + 7500$

Supply model: $N = 5p + 6000$

a.   Substitute 40 for p in both models.

$N = -25(40) + 7500 = 6500$

$N = 5(40) + 6000 = 6200$

At \$40 per ticket, 6500 tickets can be sold, but only 6200 tickets will be supplied.

b. To find the price at which supply and demand are equal, solve the demand-supply linear system. Substitute $-25p + 7500$ for N in the supply equation.

$$N = 5p + 6000$$

$$-25p + 7500 = 5p + 6000$$

$$-30p = -1500$$

$$p = 50$$

If $p = 50$,

$$N = 5(50) + 6000 = 6250.$$

Supply and demand are equal when the ticket price is $50. At this price, 6250 tickets are supplied and sold.

43. Weekly costs: $y = 1.2x + 1080$

Weekly revenue: $y = 1.6x$

The station will break even when costs = revenue. Solve the cost-revenue linear system. Substitute $1.6x$ for y in the cost equation.

$$y = 1.2x + 1080$$

$$1.6x = 1.2x + 1080$$

$$0.4x = 1080$$

$$\frac{0.4x}{0.4} = \frac{1080}{0.4}$$

$$x = 2700$$

The station will break even if 2700 gallons of gasoline are sold weekly.

45. Blacks: $M = -0.41x + 22$

Whites: $M = -0.18x + 10$

To find out when infant mortality will be the same for blacks and whites, solve this system. Substitute $-0.41x + 22$ for M in the second equation.

$$M = -0.18x + 10$$

$$-0.41x + 22 = -0.18x + 10$$

$$-0.23x + 22 = 10$$

$$-0.23x = -12$$

$$x \approx 52$$

$x = 52$ corresponds to the year 1980 + 52 = 2032. Substitute 52 for x in either equation of the system.

$$M = -0.18(52) + 10 = 0.6$$

The model projects that the infant mortality for both groups will be about 0.6 deaths per 1000 live births in the year 2032.

47. – 51. Answers will vary.

53.
$$x = 3 - y - z$$

$$2x + y - z = -6$$

$$3x - y + z = 11$$

This is a system of three linear equations with three variables. It can be solved by the substitution method. First substitute $3 - y - z$ for x in the second equation.

$$2x + y - z = -6$$

$$2(3 - y - z) + y - z = -6$$

$$6 - 2y - 2z + y - z = -6$$

$$6 - y - 3z = -6$$

$$6 - y - 3z - 6 = -6 - 6$$

$$-y - 3z = -12$$

Solve this equation for y.

$$-y = -12 + 3z$$

$$y = 12 - 3z$$

Now substitute $3 - y - z$ in the third equation of the given system.

$$3x - y + z = 11$$

$$3(3 - y - z) - y + z = 11$$

$$9 - 3y - 3z - y + z = 11$$

$$9 - 4y - 2z = 11$$

157

Substitute $12-3z$ in the last equation.

$$9-4y-2z=11$$
$$9-4(12-3z)-2z=11$$
$$9-48+12z-2z=11$$
$$-39+10z=11$$
$$10z=50$$
$$z=5$$

Now back-substitute the equation $y=12-3z$ to find the value of y.

$$y=12-3z=12-3(5)=-3$$

Finally, back-substitute in the equation $x=3-y-z$ to find the value of x.

$$x=3-y-z=3-(-3)-5=1$$

Thus, $x=1$, $y=-3$, and $z=5$.

55. $4x+6y=12$

x-intercept: 3
y-intercept: 2

Let $x=-3$: $\quad 4(-3)+6y=12$
$$-12+6y=12$$
$$6y=24$$
$$y=4$$

Checkpoint: $(-3,4)$
Draw a line through $(3,0)$, $(0,2)$, and $(-3,4)$.

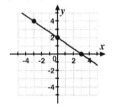

56. $4(x+1)=25+3(x-3)$
$$4x+4=25+3x-9$$
$$x+4=16$$
$$x=12$$

The solution set is $\{12\}$.

57. The integers in the given set are -73, 0, and $\dfrac{3}{1}=3$.

4.3 Exercise Set

1. $x+y=-3$
$x-y=11$

Add the equations to eliminate the y-terms.

$$x+y=-3$$
$$x-y=11$$
$$2x\quad=8$$

Now solve for x.
$$2x=8$$
$$x=4$$

Back-substitute into either of the original equations to solve for y.
$$x+y=-3$$
$$4+y=-3$$
$$y=-7$$

The proposed solution, $(4,-7)$, satisfies both equations of the system since $4+(-7)=-3$ and $4-(-7)=11$.
Solution: $(4,-7)$
Solution set: $\{(4,-7)\}$

3. $2x+3y=6$
$\underline{2x-3y=6}$
$4x=12$
$x=3$

$$2(3)+3y=6$$
$$3y=0$$
$$y=0$$

Solution: $(3,0)$
Solution set: $\{(3,0)\}$

158

5.
$$x + 2y = 7$$
$$\underline{-x + 3y = 18}$$
$$5y = 25$$
$$y = 5$$

$$x + 2(5) = 7$$
$$x + 10 = 7$$
$$x = -3$$

Solution: $(-3, 5)$
Solution set: $\{(-3, 5)\}$

7.
$$5x - y = 14$$
$$\underline{-5x + 2y = -13}$$
$$y = 1$$

$$5x - (1) = 14$$
$$5x = 15$$
$$x = 3$$

Solution: $(3, 1)$
Solution set: $\{(3, 1)\}$

9.
$$3x + y = 7$$
$$2x - 5y = -1$$

Multiply each term of the first equation by 5 and add the equations to eliminate y.

$$15x + 5y = 35$$
$$\underline{2x - 5y = -1}$$
$$17x = 34$$
$$x = 2$$

Substitute 2 for x in one of the original equations and solve for y.

$$3x + y = 7$$
$$3(2) + y = 7$$
$$6 + y = 7$$
$$y = 1$$

Solution: $(2, 1)$
Solution set: $\{(2, 1)\}$

11.
$$x + 3y = 4$$
$$4x + 5y = 2$$

Multiply each term of the first equation by -4 and add the equations to eliminate x.

$$-4x - 12y = -16$$
$$\underline{4x + 5y = 2}$$
$$-7y = -14$$
$$y = 2$$

Substitute 2 for y in one of the original equations and solve for x.

$$x + 3y = 4$$
$$x + 3(2) = 4$$
$$x + 6 = 4$$
$$x = -2$$

Solution: $(-2, 2)$
Solution set: $\{(-2, 2)\}$

13.
$$-3x + 7y = 14$$
$$2x - y = -13$$

Multiply each term of the second equation by 7 and add the equations to eliminate y.

$$-3x + 7y = 14$$
$$\underline{14x - 7y = -91}$$
$$11x = -77$$
$$x = -7$$

Substitute -7 for x in one of the original equations and solve for y.

$$2x - y = -13$$
$$2(-7) - y = -13$$
$$-14 - y = -13$$
$$-y = 1$$
$$y = -1$$

Solution: $(-7, -1)$
Solution set: $\{(-7, -1)\}$

15. $3x - 14y = 6$

$5x + 7y = 10$

Multiply each term of the second equation by 2 and add the equations to eliminate y.

$3x - 14y = 6$

$\underline{10x + 14y = 20}$

$13x \qquad = 26$

$x \qquad = 2$

Substitute 2 for x in one of the original equations and solve for y.

$5x + 7y = 10$

$5(2) + 7y = 10$

$10 + 7y = 10$

$7y = 0$

$y = 0$

Solution: $(2, 0)$

Solution set: $\{(2,0)\}$

17. $3x - 4y = 11$

$2x + 3y = -4$

Multiply the first equation by 3, and the second equation by 4.

$9x - 12y = 33$

$\underline{8x + 12y = -16}$

$17x \qquad = 17$

$x \qquad = 1$

Substitute 1 for x in one of the original equations and solve for y.

$2(1) + 3y = -4$

$3y = -6$

$y = -2$

Solution: $(1, -2)$

Solution set: $\{(1,-2)\}$

19. $3x + 2y = -1$

$-2x + 7y = 9$

Multiply the first equation by 2 and the second equation by 3.

$6x + 4y = -2$

$\underline{-6x + 21y = 27}$

$25y = 25$

$y = 1$

Substitute 1 for y in one of the original equations and solve for x.

$3x + 2(1) = -1$

$3x = -3$

$x = -1$

Solution: $(-1, 1)$

Solution set: $\{(-1,1)\}$

21. $3x = 2y + 7$

$5x = 2y + 13$

Rewrite:

$3x - 2y = 7$

$5x - 2y = 13$

Multiply equation 1 by -1 and add the equations to eliminate y.

$-3x + 2y = -7$

$\underline{5x - 2y = 13}$

$2x = 6$

$x = 3$

Substitute 3 for x in one of the original equations and solve for y.

$3(3) = 2y + 7$

$2 = 2y$

$1 = y$

Solution: $(3, 1)$

Solution set: $\{(3,1)\}$

23. $2x = 3y - 4$

$-6x + 12y = 6$

Rewrite the first equation.

$2x - 3y = -4$

Multiply the first equation by 3 and add to eliminate x.

$6x - 9y = -12$

$\underline{-6x + 12y = 6}$

$3y = -6$

$y = -2$

Substitute -2 for y in one of the original equations and solve for x.

$2x = 3(-2) - 4$

$2x = -6 - 4$

$2x = -10$

$x = -5$

Solution: $(-5, -2)$

Solution set: $\{(-5, -2)\}$

25. $2x - y = 3$

$4x + 4y = -1$

Multiply the first equation by 4 and add to eliminate y.

$8x - 4y = 12$

$\underline{4x + 4y = -1}$

$12x = 11$

$x = \dfrac{11}{12}$

Instead of back-substituting $\dfrac{11}{12}$ and working with fractions, go back to the original system. Multiply the first equation by -2 and add the equations to eliminate x.

$-4x + 2y = -6$

$\underline{4x + 4y = -1}$

$6y = -7$

$y = -\dfrac{7}{6}$

Solution: $\left(\dfrac{11}{12}, -\dfrac{7}{6}\right)$

Solution set: $\left\{\left(\dfrac{11}{12}, -\dfrac{7}{6}\right)\right\}$

27. $4x = 5 + 2y$

$2x + 3y = 4$

Rewrite the first equation, and multiply the second equation by -2.

$4x - 2y = 5$

$\underline{-4x - 6y = -8}$

$-8y = -3$

$y = \dfrac{3}{8}$

Instead of back-substituting $\dfrac{3}{8}$ and working with fractions, go back to the original system. Use the rewritten form of the first equation, and multiply by -3. Solve by addition.

$-12x + 6y = -15$

$\underline{-4x - 6y = -8}$

$-16x = -23$

$x = \dfrac{23}{16}$

Solution: $\left(\dfrac{23}{16}, \dfrac{3}{8}\right)$

Solution set: $\left\{\left(\dfrac{23}{16}, \dfrac{3}{8}\right)\right\}$

29. $3x - y = 1$

$3x - y = 2$

Multiply equation 1 by -1.

$-3x + y = -1$

$\underline{3x - y = 2}$

$\quad 0 = 1 \quad$ false

The false statement $0 = 1$ indicates that the system is inconsistent and has no solution.

Solution set: $\{\ \}$ or $\varnothing$

31. $x + 3y = 2$

$3x + 9y = 6$

Multiply equation 1 by -3.

$-3x - 9y = -6$

$\underline{3x + 9y = 6}$

$\quad 0 = 0 \quad$ true

The true statement $0 = 0$ indicates that the system has infinitely many solutions.

Solution set: $\{(x, y) \mid x + 3y = 2\}$ or $\{(x, y) \mid 3x + 9y = 6\}$

33. $7x - 3y = 4$

$-14x + 6y = -7$

Multiply equation 1 by 2.

$14x - 6y = 8$

$\underline{-14x + 6y = -7}$

$\quad 0 = 1$

The false statement $0 = 1$ indicates that the system has no solution.

Solution set: $\{\ \}$ or $\varnothing$

35. $5x + y = 2$

$3x + y = 1$

Multiply equation 2 by -1.

$\quad 5x + y = 2$

$\underline{-3x - y = -1}$

$\quad 2x = 1$

$x = \dfrac{1}{2}$

Back-substitute $\dfrac{1}{2}$ for x and solve for y.

$3\left(\dfrac{1}{2}\right) + y = 1$

$y = -\dfrac{1}{2}$

Solution: $\left(\dfrac{1}{2}, -\dfrac{1}{2}\right)$

Solution set: $\left\{\left(\dfrac{1}{2}, -\dfrac{1}{2}\right)\right\}$

37. $x = 5 - 3y$

$2x + 6y = 10$

Rewrite equation 1.

$x + 3y = 5$

Multiply this equation by -2.

$-2x - 6y = -10$

$2x + 6y = 10$

$\quad 0 = 0$

The true statement $0 = 0$ indicates that the system has infinitely many solutions.

Solution set: $\{(x, y) \mid x = 5 - 3y\}$ or $\{(x, y) \mid 2x + 6y = 10\}$

39. $4(3x - y) = 0$

$3(x + 3) = 10y$

Rewrite both equations.
$12x - 4y = 0$
$3x - 10y = -9$

Multiply the second equation by -4 and add the equations to eliminate x.

$12x - 4y = 0$

$\underline{-12x + 40y = 36}$

$36y = 36$

$y = 1$

Back-substitute 1 for y in one of the original equations and solve for x.

$12x - 4y = 0$

$12x - 4(1) = 0$

$12x = 4$

$x = \dfrac{1}{3}$

Solution: $\left(\dfrac{1}{3}, 1\right)$

Solution set: $\left\{\left(\dfrac{1}{3}, 1\right)\right\}$

41. $x + y = 11$

$\dfrac{x}{5} + \dfrac{y}{7} = 1$

Multiply the second equation by the LCD, 35, to clear fractions.

$35\left(\dfrac{x}{5} + \dfrac{y}{7}\right) = 35(1)$

$7x + 5y = 35$

Now solve the system.

$x + y = 11$

$7x + 5y = 35$

Multiply the first equation by -5 and add the result to the second equation.

$-5x - 5y = -55$

$\underline{7x + 5y = 35}$

$2x = -20$

$x = -10$

$-10 + y = 11$

$y = 21$

Solution: $(-10, 21)$

Solution set: $\{(-10, 21)\}$

43. $\dfrac{4}{5}x - y = -1$

$\dfrac{2}{5}x + y = 1$

Multiply both equations by 5 to clear fractions.

$4x - 5y = -5$

$\underline{2x + 5y = 5}$

$6x = 0$

$x = 0$

Back-substitute 0 for x and solve for y.

$\dfrac{2}{5}(0) + y = 1$

$y = 1$

Solution: $(0, 1)$

Solution set: $\{(0, 1)\}$

163

45. $3x - 2y = 8$

$x = -2y$

The substitution method is a good choice because the second equation is already solved for x. Substitute $-2y$ for x in the first equation

$3x - 2y = 8$

$3(-2y) - 2y = 8$

$-6y - 2y = 8$

$-8y = 8$

$y = -1$

Back-substitute -1 for y in the second equation.

$x = -2y = -2(-1) = 2$

Solution: $(2, -1)$

Solution set: $\{(2, -1)\}$

47. $3x + 2y = -3$

$2x - 5y = 17$

The addition method is a good choice because both equations are written in the form $Ax + By = C$.

Multiply the first equation by 2 and the second equation by -3.

$6x + 4y = -6$

$\underline{-6x + 15y = -51}$

$19y = -57$

$y = -3$

Back-substitute -3 for y and solve for x.

$3x + 2(-3) = -3$

$3x - 6 = -3$

$3x = 3$

$x = 1$

Solution: $(1, -3)$

Solution set: $\{(1, -3)\}$

49. $3x - 2y = 6$

$y = 3$

The substitution method is a good choice because the second equation is already solved for y. Substitute 3 for y in the first equation.

$3x - 2y = 6$

$3x - 2(3) = 6$

$3x - 6 = 6$

$3x = 12$

$x = 4$

It is not necessary to back-substitute to find the value of y because $y = 3$ is one of the equations of the given system. The solution is $(4, 3)$.

Solution set: $\{(4, 3)\}$

51. $y = 2x + 1$

$y = 2x - 3$

The substitution method is a good choice, because both equations are already solved for y. Substitute $2x + 1$ for y in the second equation.

$y = 2x - 3$

$2x + 1 = 2x - 3$

$2x + 1 - 2x = 2x - 3 - 2x$

$1 = -3$ false

The false statement $1 = -3$ indicates that the system has no solution.

Solution set: $\{\ \}$ or $\varnothing$

53.
$$2(x+2y)=6$$
$$3(x+2y-3)=0$$

The addition method is a good choice since the left-hand sides of the equations can easily be simplified to give equations of the form $Ax+By=C$.

$$2x+4y=6 \qquad 3x+6y-9=0$$
$$3x+6y=9$$

So, solve the system.
$$2x+4y=6$$
$$3x+6y=9$$

Multiply the first equation by -3 and the second by 2 and solve by addition.
$$-6x-12y=-18$$
$$\underline{6x+12y=\ \ 18}$$
$$0=0 \text{ true}$$

The true statement $0=0$ indicates that the original system has infinitely many solutions.

Solution set: $\{(x,y)\,|\,2(x+2y)=6\}$ or $\{(x,y)\,|\,3(x+2y-3)=0\}$

55.
$$3y=2x$$
$$2x+9y=24$$

The substitution method is a good choice because the first equation can easily be solved for one of the variables. Solve this equation for y.
$$3y=2x$$
$$y=\frac{2}{3}x$$

Substitute $\frac{2}{3}x$ for y in the second equation.
$$2x+9y=24$$
$$2x+9\left(\frac{2}{3}x\right)=24$$

$$2x+6x=24$$
$$8x=24$$
$$x=3$$

Back-substitute 3 for x in the equation,
$$y=\frac{2}{3}x.$$
$$y=\frac{2}{3}x=\frac{2}{3}(3)=2$$

Solution: $(3,2)$
Solution set: $\{(3,2)\}$

57.
$$\frac{3x}{5}+\frac{4y}{5}=1$$
$$\frac{x}{4}-\frac{3y}{8}=-1$$

Multiply the first equation by 5 and the second equation by 8 to clear fractions.
$$\frac{3x}{5}+\frac{4y}{5}=1 \qquad \frac{x}{4}-\frac{3y}{8}=-1$$
$$3x+4y=5 \qquad 2x-3y=-8$$

The addition method is a good choice since both equations are of the form $Ax+By=C$.
$$3x+4y=5$$
$$2x-3y=-8$$

Multiply the first equation by 3 and the second equation by 4.
$$9x+12y=\ \ 15$$
$$\underline{8x-12y=-32}$$
$$17x\qquad\ \ =-17$$
$$x\qquad\ \ =-1$$

Back-substitute -1 for x in the equation and solve for y.
$$3x+4y=5$$
$$3(-1)+4y=5$$
$$-3+4y=5$$
$$4y=8$$
$$y=2$$

Solution: $(-1,2)$
Solution set: $\{(-1,2)\}$

58.
$$\frac{x}{3} - \frac{y}{2} = \frac{2}{3}$$
$$\frac{2x}{3} + y = \frac{4}{3}$$

Multiply the first equation by 6 and the second equation by 3 to clear fractions.

$$\frac{x}{3} - \frac{y}{2} = \frac{2}{3} \qquad \frac{2x}{3} + y = \frac{4}{3}$$
$$2x - 3y = 4 \qquad 2x + 3y = 4$$

The addition method is a good choice since both equations are of the form $Ax + By = C$.

$$2x - 3y = 4$$
$$\underline{2x + 3y = 4}$$
$$4x \qquad = 8$$
$$x \qquad = 2$$

Back-substitute 2 for x in the equation and solve for y.

$$2x - 3y = 4$$
$$2(2) - 3y = 4$$
$$4 - 3y = 4$$
$$-3y = 0$$
$$y = 0$$

Solution: $(2, 0)$
Solution set: $\{(2,0)\}$

59.
$$5(x+1) = 7(y+1) - 7$$
$$6(x+1) + 5 = 5(y+1)$$

Simplify both equations.

$$5(x+1) = 7(y+1) - 7$$
$$5x + 5 = 7y + 7 - 7$$
$$5x + 5 = 7y$$
$$5x - 7y + 5 = 0$$
$$5x - 7y = -5$$

$$6(x+1) + 5 = 5(y+1)$$
$$6x + 6 + 5 = 5y + 5$$
$$6x + 11 = 5y + 5$$
$$6x - 5y + 11 = 5$$
$$6x - 5y = -6$$

The rewritten system is as follows.
$$5x - 7y = -5$$
$$6x - 5y = -6$$

Multiply the first equation by -6 and the second equation by 5, and solve by addition.

$$-30x + 42y = 30$$
$$\underline{30x - 25y = -30}$$
$$17y = 0$$
$$y = 0$$

Back-substitute 0 for y to find x.
$$5x - 7y = -5$$
$$5x - 7(0) = -5$$
$$5x - 0 = -5$$
$$5x = -5$$
$$x = -1$$

The solution is $(-1, 0)$.
Solution set: $\{(-1,0)\}$

60.
$$6x = 5(x + y + 3) - x$$
$$3(x - y) + 4y = 5(y+1)$$

Simplify both equations.
$$6x = 5(x + y + 3) - x$$
$$6x = 5x + 5y + 15 - x$$
$$6x = 4x + 5y + 15$$
$$2x - 5y = 15$$

$$3(x - y) + 4y = 5(y+1)$$
$$3x - 3y + 4y = 5y + 5$$
$$3x + y = 5y + 5$$
$$3x - 4y = 5$$

The rewritten system is as follows.

$2x - 5y = 15$

$3x - 4y = 5$

Multiply the first equation by -3 and the second equation by 2, and solve by addition.

$-6x + 15y = -45$

$\underline{6x - 8y = 10}$

$7y = -35$

$y = -5$

Back-substitute -5 for y to find x.

$2x - 5y = 15$

$2x - 5(-5) = 15$

$2x + 25 = 15$

$2x = -10$

$x = -5$

The solution is (−5, −5).

Solution set: $\{(-5, -5)\}$

61. $0.4x + \quad y = 2.2$

$0.5x - 1.2y = 0.3$

Multiply the first equation by 1.2 and solve by addition.

$0.48x + 1.2y = 2.64$

$\underline{0.50x - 1.2y = 0.30}$

$0.98x \qquad = 2.94$

$x \qquad = 3$

Back-substitute 3 for x to find y.

$0.4x + y = 2.2$

$0.4(3) + y = 2.2$

$1.2 + y = 2.2$

$y = 1$

The solution is (3, 1).

Solution set: $\{(3, 1)\}$

62. $1.25x - 1.5y = 2$

$3.5x - 1.75y = 10.5$

Multiply the first equation by −2.8 and solve by addition.

$-3.5x + 4.2y = -5.6$

$\underline{3.5x - 1.75y = 10.5}$

$2.45y = -4.9$

$y = 2$

Back-substitute 2 for y to find x.

$1.25x - 1.5y = 2$

$1.25x - 1.5(2) = 2$

$1.25x - 3 = 2$

$1.25x = 5$

$x = 4$

The solution is (4, 2).

Solution set: $\{(4, 2)\}$

63. $\dfrac{x}{2} = \dfrac{y + 8}{3}$

$\dfrac{x + 2}{2} = \dfrac{y + 11}{3}$

Simplify both equations.

$\dfrac{x}{2} = \dfrac{y + 8}{3}$

$3x = 2(y + 8)$

$3x = 2y + 16$

$3x - 2y = 16$

$\dfrac{x + 2}{2} = \dfrac{y + 11}{3}$

$3(x + 2) = 2(y + 11)$

$3x + 6 = 2y + 22$

$3x - 2y + 6 = 22$

$3x - 2y = 16$

When simplified, the equations are the same. This means that the system is dependent and there are an infinite number of solutions.

167

64.
$$\frac{x}{2} = \frac{y+8}{4}$$
$$\frac{x+3}{2} = \frac{y+5}{4}$$
Simplify both equations.
$$\frac{x}{2} = \frac{y+8}{4}$$
$$4\left(\frac{x}{2}\right) = y+8$$
$$2x = y+8$$
$$2x-8 = y$$
$$y = 2x-8$$

$$\frac{x+3}{2} = \frac{y+5}{4}$$
$$4\left(\frac{x+3}{2}\right) = y+5$$
$$2(x+3) = y+5$$
$$2x+6 = y+5$$
$$2x+1 = y$$
$$y = 2x+1$$
When simplified, the both equations have the same slope, but different y-intercepts. This means that the system is inconsistent and there are no solutions.

65.
$$13x+12y = 992$$
$$-x+y = 16$$
Solve the second equation for y.
$$-x+y = 16$$
$$y = x+16$$
Substitute $x+16$ for y and solve for x.
$$13x+12y = 992$$
$$13x+12(x+16) = 992$$
$$13x+12x+192 = 992$$
$$25x+192 = 992$$
$$25x = 800$$
$$x = 32$$
Back-substitute 32 for x and solve for y.
$$y = x+16 = 32+16 = 48$$
The solution is (32, 48). This means that in the year $1988 + 32 = 2020$, the percent in favor and against the death penalty are both the same at 48%.

67.-71. Answers will vary.

73.
$$x-y = a$$
$$y = 2x+b$$
Substitute $2x+b$ for y and solve for x.
$$x-y = a$$
$$x-(2x+b) = a$$
$$x-2x-b = a$$
$$-x-b = a$$
$$-x = a+b$$
$$x = -a-b$$
Back-substitute $-a-b$ for x to find y.
$$y = 2x+b$$
$$y = 2(-a-b)+b$$
$$y = -2a-2b+b$$
$$y = -2a-b$$
The solution is $x = -a-b$ and $y = -2a-b$.

75. Answers will vary according to the exercises chosen.

77. $x = 5y$

$2x - 3y = 7$

Rewriting the first equation in $Ax + By = C$ form yields $x - 5y = 0$.
The system is as follows.

$x - 5y = 0$

$2x - 3y = 7$

Use the SIMULT (simultaneous equations) function on the TI-85 or higher numbered calculator. Enter 2 for two equations in two variables, then the coefficients and constant terms for each equations, one equation at a time. After entering all the coefficients, press SOLVE and read the solutions displayed on the screen.

Solution: (5, 1)

Solution set: $\{(5,1)\}$

79. Let $x =$ the unknown number.

$5x = x + 40$

$4x = 40$

$x = 10$

The number is 10.

80. Because the x-coordinate is negative and the y-coordinate is positive,

$\left(-\dfrac{3}{2}, 15\right)$ is located in quadrant II.

81. $29,700 + 150x = 5000 + 1100x$

$29,700 - 950x = 5000$

$-950x = -24,700$

$x = 26$

The solution set is {26}.

Mid-Chapter Check Points

1. $3x + 2y = 6$

$2x - y = 4$

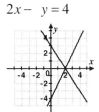

Solution: $(2, 0)$

Solution set: $\{(2,0)\}$

2. $y = 2x - 1$

$y = 3x - 2$

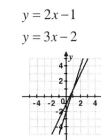

Solution: $(1, 1)$

Solution set: $\{(1,1)\}$

3. $y = 2x - 1$

$6x - 3y = 12$

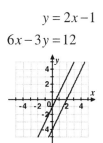

Since the lines are parallel, the system is inconsistent and there is no solution.

Solution set: $\{\ \}$ or $\varnothing$

169

4. $5x - 3y = 1$

$y = 3x - 7$

Substitute $3x - 7$ for y in the first equation and solve for x.

$$5x - 3y = 1$$
$$5x - 3(3x - 7) = 1$$
$$5x - 9x + 21 = 1$$
$$-4x + 21 = 1$$
$$-4x = -20$$
$$x = 5$$

Back-substitute.

$$y = 3x - 7 = 3(5) - 7 = 15 - 7 = 8$$

Solution: $(5, 8)$

Solution set: $\{(5, 8)\}$

5. $6x + 5y = 7$

$3x - 7y = 13$

Multiply the second equation by -2 and add to eliminate x.

$$6x + 5y = 7$$
$$\underline{-6x + 14y = -26}$$
$$19y = -19$$
$$y = -1$$

Back-substitute -1 for y and solve for x.

$$6x + 5y = 7$$
$$6x + 5(-1) = 7$$
$$6x - 5 = 7$$
$$6x = 12$$
$$x = 2$$

Solution: $(2, -1)$

Solution set: $\{(2, -1)\}$

6. $x = \dfrac{y}{3} - 1$

$6x + y = 21$

Substitute $\dfrac{y}{3} - 1$ for x in the second equation and solve for y.

$$6x + y = 21$$
$$6\left(\frac{y}{3} - 1\right) + y = 21$$
$$2y - 6 + y = 21$$
$$3y - 6 = 21$$
$$3y = 27$$
$$y = 9$$

Back-substitute.

$$x = \frac{y}{3} - 1 = \frac{9}{3} - 1 = 3 - 1 = 2$$

Solution: $(2, 9)$

Solution set: $\{(2, 9)\}$

7. $3x - 4y = 6$

$5x - 6y = 8$

Multiply the first equation by -5, the second equation by 3 and add to eliminate x.

$$-15x + 20y = -30$$
$$\underline{15x - 18y = 24}$$
$$2y = -6$$
$$y = -3$$

Back-substitute -3 for y and solve for x.

$$3x - 4y = 6$$
$$3x - 4(-3) = 6$$
$$3x + 12 = 6$$
$$3x = -6$$
$$x = -2$$

Solution: $(-2, -3)$

Solution set: $\{(-2, -3)\}$

170

8. $3x - 2y = 32$

$\dfrac{x}{5} + 3y = -1$

Multiply the second equation by 5 to clear the fraction.

$5\left(\dfrac{x}{5} + 3y\right) = 5(-1)$

$x + 15y = -5$

The system is as follows.

$3x - 2y = 32$

$x + 15y = -5$

Multiply the second equation by -3 and solve by addition.

$\begin{aligned} 3x - 2y &= 32 \\ -3x - 45y &= 15 \\ \hline -47y &= 47 \\ y &= -1 \end{aligned}$

Back-substitute -1 for y and solve for x.

$x + 15y = -5$

$x + 15(-1) = -5$

$x - 15 = -5$

$x = 10$

Solution: $(10, -1)$

9. $x - y = 3$

$2x = 4 + 2y$

Solve the first equation for x.

$x - y = 3$

$x = y + 3$

Substitute $y + 3$ for x in the second equation and solve for y.

$2x = 4 + 2y$

$2(y + 3) = 4 + 2y$

$2y + 6 = 4 + 2y$

$6 = 4$

Note that y has also been eliminated. The false statement $6 = 4$ indicates that the system is inconsistent and has no solution. Solution set: $\{\ \}$ or $\varnothing$

10. $x = 2(y - 5)$

$4x + 40 = y - 7$

Substitute $2(y - 5)$ for x in the second equation and solve for y.

$4x + 40 = y - 7$

$4(2(y - 5)) + 40 = y - 7$

$4(2y - 10) + 40 = y - 7$

$8y - 40 + 40 = y - 7$

$8y = y - 7$

$7y = -7$

$y = -1$

Back-substitute -1 for y and solve for x.

$x = 2(y - 5)$

$\quad = 2(-1 - 5) = 2(-6) = -12$

Solution: $(-12, -1)$

Solution set: $\{(-12, -1)\}$

11. $y = 3x - 2$

$y = 2x - 9$

Substitute $3x - 2$ for y in the second equation and solve for x.

$y = 2x - 9$

$3x - 2 = 2x - 9$

$x - 2 = -9$

$x = -7$

Back-substitute -7 for x and solve for y.

$y = 3(-7) - 2 = -21 - 2 = -23$

Solution: $(-7, -23)$

Solution set: $\{(-7, -23)\}$

12. $2x - 3y = 4$

$3x + 4y = 0$

Multiply the first equation by 4, the second equation by 3 and add to eliminate y.

$8x - 12y = 16$

$\underline{9x + 12y = 0}$

$17x \qquad = 16$

$x \qquad = \dfrac{16}{17}$

Back-substitute $\dfrac{16}{17}$ for x and solve for y.

$3x + 4y = 0$

$3\left(\dfrac{16}{17}\right) + 4y = 0$

$\dfrac{48}{17} + 4y = 0$

$4y = -\dfrac{48}{17}$

$\dfrac{1}{4}(4y) = \dfrac{1}{4}\left(-\dfrac{48}{17}\right)$

$y = -\dfrac{12}{17}$

Solution: $\left(\dfrac{16}{17}, -\dfrac{12}{17}\right)$

Solution set: $\left\{\left(\dfrac{16}{17}, -\dfrac{12}{17}\right)\right\}$

13. $y - 2x = 7$

$4x = 2y - 14$

Solve the first equation for y.

$y - 2x = 7$

$y = 2x + 7$

Substitute $2x + 7$ for y and solve for x.

$4x = 2y - 14$

$4x = 2(2x + 7) - 14$

$4x = 4x + 14 - 14$

$0 = 14 - 14$

$0 = 0$

Notice that x has also been eliminated. The true statement $0 = 0$ indicates that the system is dependent and has infinitely many solutions.

Solution set: $\{(x, y) \mid y - 2x = 7\}$ or $\{(x, y) \mid 4x = 2y - 14\}$

14. $4(x + 3) = 3y + 7$

$2(y - 5) = x + 5$

First, rewrite both equations in the form $Ax + By = C$.

$4(x + 3) = 3y + 7$

$4x + 12 = 3y + 7$

$4x - 3y + 12 = 7$

$4x - 3y = -5$

$2(y - 5) = x + 5$

$2y - 10 = x + 5$

$-x + 2y - 10 = 5$

$-x + 2y = 15$

The system is as follows.

$4x - 3y = -5$

$-x + 2y = 15$

Multiply the second equation by 4 and add to eliminate x.

$4x - 3y = -5$

$\underline{-4x + 8y = 60}$

$5y = 55$

$y = 11$

Back-substitute 11 for y and solve for x.

$$-x+2y=15$$
$$-x+2(11)=15$$
$$-x+22=15$$
$$-x=-7$$
$$x=7$$

Solution: $(7, 11)$

Solution set: $\{(7,11)\}$

15.
$$\frac{x}{2}-\frac{y}{5}=1$$

$$y-\frac{x}{3}=8$$

Multiply the first equation by 10 and the second equation by 3 to clear fractions.

$$10\left(\frac{x}{2}\right)-10\left(\frac{y}{5}\right)=10(1)$$

$$5x-2y=10$$

$$3y-3\left(\frac{x}{3}\right)=3(8)$$

$$3y-x=24$$
$$-x+3y=24$$

The system is as follows.

$$5x-2y=10$$
$$-x+3y=24$$

Multiply the second equation by 5 and solve by addition.

$$5x-\ 2y=\ \ 10$$
$$\underline{-5x+15y=120}$$
$$13y=130$$
$$y=\ \ 10$$

Back-substitute and solve for x.

$$-x+3y=24$$
$$-x+3(10)=24$$
$$-x+30=24$$
$$-x=-6$$
$$x=6$$

Solution: $(6, 10)$

Solution set: $\{(6,10)\}$

4.4 Exercise Set

1. Let x = one number.
Let y = the other number.

$$x+y=17$$
$$\underline{x-y=-3}$$
$$2x\ \ \ \ \ =14$$
$$x\ \ \ \ =\ \ 7$$

Back-substitute 7 for x to find y.

$$x+y=17$$
$$7+y=17$$
$$y=10$$

The numbers are 7 and 10.

3. Let x = one number.
Let y = the other number.

$$3x-\ \ y=-1$$
$$x+2y=23$$

Solve the second equation for x.

$$x+2y=23$$
$$x=-2y+23$$

Substitute $-2y+23$ for x to find y.

$$3x-y=-1$$
$$3(-2y+23)-y=-1$$
$$-6y+69-y=-1$$
$$-7y+69=-1$$
$$-7y=-70$$
$$y=10$$

Back substitute 10 for y to find x.

$$x=-2y+23=-2(10)+23=3$$

The numbers are 3 and 10.

5. Let x = the number of millions of pounds of potato chips.
Let y = the number of millions of pounds of tortilla chips.

$$x + y = 10.4$$
$$\underline{x - y = 1.2}$$
$$2x = 11.6$$
$$x = 5.8$$

Back-substitute to find y.
$$x + y = 10.4$$
$$5.8 + y = 10.4$$
$$y = 4.6$$

On Super Bowl Sunday, 5.8 million pounds of potato chips and 4.6 million pounds of tortilla chips are consumed.

7. Let x = the number of calories in one pan pizza.
Let y = the number of calories in one beef burrito.

$$x + 2y = 1980$$
$$2x + y = 2670$$

To solve this system by the addition method, multiply the first equation by -2 and add the result to the second equation.

$$-2x - 4y = -3960$$
$$\underline{2x + y = 2670}$$
$$-3y = -1290$$
$$y = 430$$

Back-substitute 430 for y and solve for x.

$$x + 2y = 1980$$
$$x + 2(430) = 1980$$
$$x + 860 = 1980$$
$$x = 1120$$

A pan pizza has 1120 calories and a beef burrito has 430 calories.

9. Let x = number of milligrams of cholesterol in scrambled eggs.
Let y = number of milligrams of cholesterol in a Whopper.

$$x + y = 300 + 241$$
$$2x + 3y = 1257$$

Simplify the first equation.

$$x + y = 541$$
$$2x + 3y = 1257$$

Multiply the first equation by -2 and add to second equation.

$$-2x - 2y = -1082$$
$$\underline{2x + 3y = 1257}$$
$$y = 175$$

Back-substitute 175 for y and solve for x.

$$x + y = 541$$
$$x + 175 = 541$$
$$x = 366$$

The scrambled eggs have 366 mg of cholesterol, and the Double Beef Whopper has 175 mg of cholesterol.

11. Let x = the price of one sweater.
Let y = the price of one shirt.

$$x + 3y = 42$$
$$3x + 2y = 56$$

Multiply the first equation by -3 and add the result to the second equation.

$$-3x - 9y = -126$$
$$\underline{3x + 2y = 56}$$
$$-7y = -70$$
$$y = 10$$

Back-substitute 10 for y to solve for x.

$$x + 3y = 42$$
$$x + 3(10) = 42$$
$$x + 30 = 42$$
$$x = 12$$

The price of one sweater is \$12 and the price of one shirt is \$10.

174

13. a. Let x = the number of minutes of long distance calls.
Let y = the monthly cost of a telephone plan.
Plan A: $y = 20 + 0.05x$
Plan B: $y = 5 + 0.10x$
Solve by substitution. Substitute $5 + 0.10x$ for y in the first equation.

$$5 + 0.10x = 20 + 0.05x$$
$$5 + 0.05x = 20$$
$$0.05x = 15$$
$$x = 300$$

Back-substitute 300 for x.
$$y = 20 + 0.05(300) = 35$$

The costs for the two plans will be equal for 300 minutes of long-distance calls per month. The cost for each plan will be $35.

b. $x = 10(20) = 200$

Plan A: $y = 20 + 0.05(200) = 30$
Plan B:
$$y = 5 + 0.10(200) = 25$$

The monthly cost would be $30 for Plan A and $25 for Plan B, so Plan B should be selected to get the lower cost.

15. Let x = the number of dollars of merchandise purchased in a year.
Let y = the total cost for a year.
Plan A: $y = 100 + 0.80x$
Plan B: $y = 40 + 0.90x$
Substitute $40 = 0.90x$ for y in the first equation and solve for x.

$$40 + 0.90x = 100 + 0.80x$$
$$40 + 0.10x = 100$$
$$0.10x = 60$$
$$x = 600$$

Back-substitute 600 for x to find y.
$$y = 100 + 0.80(600) = 580.$$

If you purchase $600 worth of merchandise, you will pay the $580 under both plans.

17. Let x = the number of years after 1985.
Let y = the average high school graduate's weekly earning.
We are interested in the year in which the average college graduate earns twice as much as a high school graduate, so the average college graduate's earnings will be $2y$.
College graduates:
$$2y = 508 + 25x$$
High school graduates:
$$y = 345x + 9x$$
Substitute $345 + 9x$ for y in the first equation and solve for x
$$2(345 + 9x) = 580 + 25x$$
$$690 + 18x = 508 + 25x$$
$$690 - 7x = 508$$
$$-7x = -182$$
$$x = 26$$

Back-substitute 26 for x to find y.
$$y = 345 + 9(26) = 579$$
$$2y = 2(579) = 1158.$$

In $1985 + 26 = 2011$, the average college graduate will earn $1158 per week and the average high school graduate will earn $579 per week.

19. Let x = the number of servings of macaroni.
Let y = the number of servings of broccoli.

$$3x + 2y = 14$$
$$16x + 4y = 48$$

Multiply the first equation by -2 and add to second equation.

$$-6x - 4y = -28$$
$$\underline{16x + 4y = 48}$$
$$10x = 20$$
$$x = 2$$

Back-substitute 2 for x to find y.

$$3(2) + 2y = 14$$
$$2y = 8$$
$$y = 4$$

It would take 2 servings of macaroni and 4 servings of broccoli to get 14 grams of protein and 48 grams of carbohydrate.

21. Let x = the amount invested at 6%.
Let y = the amount invested at 8%.

$$x + y = 7000$$
$$0.06x + 0.08y = 520$$

Solve the first equation for x.

$$x = 7000 - y$$

Substitute this result for x in the second equation.

$$0.06(7000 - y) + 0.08y = 520$$
$$420 - 0.06y + 0.08y = 520$$
$$0.02y = 100$$
$$y = \frac{100}{0.02} = 5000$$

Back-substitute to solve for x.

$$x + y = 7000$$
$$x + 5000 = 7000$$
$$x = 2000$$

$2000 was invested at 6% and $5000 was invested at 8%.

23. Let x = the amount in the first fund
Let y = the amount in the second fund.

$$0.09x + 0.03y = 900$$
$$0.10x + 0.01y = 860$$

Multiply the second equation by -3 and add the two equations.

$$0.09x + 0.03y = 900$$
$$\underline{-0.30x - 0.03y = -2580}$$
$$-0.21x = -1680$$
$$x = 8000$$

Back-substitute to solve for y.

$$0.10x + 0.01y = 860$$
$$0.10(8000) + 0.01y = 860$$
$$800 + 0.01y = 860$$
$$0.01y = 60$$
$$y = \frac{60}{0.01} = 6000$$

$8000 was invested in the first fund and $6000 was invested in the second fund.

25. Let x = amount invested with 12% return.
Let y = amount invested with the 5% loss.

$$x + y = 20,000$$
$$0.12x - 0.05y = 1890$$

Multiply the first equation by 0.05 and add the two equations.

$$0.05x + 0.05y = 1000$$
$$\underline{0.12x - 0.05y = 1890}$$
$$0.17x = 2890$$
$$x = 17,000$$

Back-substitute to solve for y.

$$x + y = 20,000$$
$$17,000 + y = 20,000$$
$$y = 3,000$$

$17,000 was invested at 12% interest and $3,000 was invested at a 5% loss.

27. Let x = gallons of 5% wine.
Let y = gallons of 9% wine.
$$x + y = 200$$
$$0.05x + 0.09y = 0.07(200)$$
or
$$x + y = 200$$
$$0.05x + 0.09y = 14$$

Solve the first equation for x.
$$x + y = 200$$
$$x = 200 - y$$
Substitute this expression for x in the second equation.

$$0.05(200 - y) + 0.09y = 14$$
$$10 - 0.05y + 0.09y = 14$$
$$0.04y = 4$$
$$y = 100$$

Back-substitute and solve for x.
$$x = 200 - y$$
$$= 200 - 100$$
$$= 100$$
The wine company should mix 100 gallons of the 5% California wine with 100 gallons of the 9% French wine.

29. Let x = grams of 18-karat gold.
Let y = grams of 12-karat gold.
$$x + y = 300$$
$$0.75x + 0.5y = 0.58(300)$$
or
$$x + y = 300$$
$$0.75x + 0.5y = 174$$
Solve the first equation for x.
$$x = 300 - y$$
Substitute this result for x into the second equation and solve for y.

$$0.75(300 - y) + 0.5y = 174$$
$$225 - 0.75 + 0.5y = 174$$
$$-0.25y = -51$$
$$y = 204$$
Back-substitute to solve for x.
$$x = 300 - y = 300 - 204 = 96$$
You would need 96 grams of 18-karat gold and 204 grams of 12-karat gold.

31. Let x = pounds of cheaper candy.
Let y = pounds of more expensive candy.
$$x + y = 75$$
$$1.6x + 2.1y = 1.9(75)$$
or
$$x + y = 75$$
$$1.6x + 2.1y = 142.5$$
Multiply the first equation by -1.6 and add the two equations.

$$-1.6x - 1.6y = -120$$
$$\underline{1.6x + 2.1y = 142.5}$$
$$0.5y = 22.5$$
$$y = 45$$
Back-substitute to solve for x.
$$x + 45 = 75$$
$$x = 30$$
The manager should mix 30 pounds of the cheaper candy and 45 pounds of the more expensive candy.

33. Let n = the number of nickels.
Let d = the number of dimes.
$$n + d = 15$$
$$0.05n + 0.1d = 1.10$$
Solve the first equation for n.
$$n = 15 - d$$
$$0.05(15 - d) + 0.1d = 1.10$$
$$0.75 - 0.05d + 0.1d = 1.10$$
$$0.05d = 0.35$$
$$d = 7$$
Back-substitute to solve for n.
$$n + 7 = 15$$
$$n = 8$$
The purse has 8 nickels and 7 dimes.

35. Let x = the speed of the plane in still air
Let y = the speed of the wind

	r $\times$	t =	d
With Wind	$x + y$	5	800
Against Wind	$x - y$	8	800

$$5(x + y) = 800$$
$$8(x - y) = 800$$

$$5x + 5y = 800$$
$$8x - 8y = 800$$
Multiply the first equation by 8 and the second equation by 5.
$$40x + 40y = 6400$$
$$40x - 40y = 4000$$
$$80x = 10400$$
$$x = 130$$
Back-substitute to find y.
$$5x + 5y = 800$$
$$5(130) + 5y = 800$$
$$650 + 5y = 800$$
$$5y = 150$$
$$y = 30$$
The speed of the plane in still air is 130 miles per hour and the speed of the wind is 30 miles per hour.

37. Let x = the crew's rowing rate
Let y = the rate of the current

	r $\times$	t =	d
With Current	$x + y$	2	16
Against Current	$x - y$	4	16

$$2(x + y) = 16$$
$$4(x - y) = 16$$
Rewrite the system is $Ax + By = C$ form.
$$2x + 2y = 16$$
$$4x - 4y = 16$$
Multiply the first equation by –2.
$$-4x - 4y = -32$$
$$\underline{4x - 4y = 16}$$
$$-8y = -16$$
$$y = 2$$
Back-substitute to find x.
$$2x + 2(2) = 16$$
$$2x + 4 = 16$$
$$2x = 12$$
$$x = 6$$
The crew's rowing rate is 6 kilometers per hour and the rate of the current is 2 kilometers per hour.

39. Let x = the speed in still water
Let y = the speed of the current

	r $\cdot$	t =	d
With Current	$x + y$	4	24
Against Current	$x - y$	6	$\frac{3}{4}(24)$

$$4(x + y) = 24$$
$$6(x - y) = \frac{3}{4}(24)$$
Rewrite the system is $Ax + By = C$ form.

178

$4x + 4y = 24$

$6x - 6y = 18$

Multiply the first equation by –3 and the second equation by 2.

$-12x - 12y = -72$

$\underline{12x - 12y = 36}$

$-24y = -36$

$y = 1.5$

Back-substitute to find x.

$4x + 4y = 24$

$4x + 4(1.5) = 24$

$4x + 6 = 24$

$4x = 18$

$x = 4.5$

The speed in still water is 4.5 miles per hour and the speed of the current is 1.5 miles per hour.

41.-43. Answers will vary.

45. Let x = the number of birds.
Let y = the number of lions.
Since each bird has one head and each lion has one head,
$x + y = 30$.
Since each bird has two feet and each lion has four feet,
$2x + 4y = 100$.
Solve the first equation for y.
$y = 30 - x$ Substitute $30 - x$ for y in the second equation.

$2x + 4(30 - x) = 100$

$2x + 120 - 4x = 100$

$-2x + 120 = 100$

$-2x = -20$

$x = 10$

Back-substitute 10 for x to find y.

$10 + y = 30$

$y = 20$

There were 10 birds and 20 lions in the zoo.

47. Let x = the number of people in the downstairs apartment.
Let y = the number of people in the upstairs apartment.
If one of the people in the upstairs apartment goes downstairs, there will be the same number of people in both apartments, so $y - 1 = x + 1$.
If one of the people in the downstairs apartment goes upstairs, there will be twice as many people upstairs as downstairs, so $y + 1 = 2(x - 1)$.
Solve the first equation for y.
$y = x + 2$
Also solve the second equation for y.
$y + 1 = 2x - 2$

$y = 2x - 3$

Substitute $x + 2$ for y in the last equation.

$x + 2 = 2x - 3$

$-x + 2 = -3$

$-x = -5$

$x = 5$

Back-substitute to find y

$y = 5 + 2 = 7$

There are 5 people downstairs and 7 people upstairs.

49. Answers will vary.

50. $(-6, 1)$, $(2, -1)$

$$m = \frac{y_2 - y_1}{x_2 - x_1} = \frac{-1 - 1}{2 - (-6)}$$

$$= \frac{-2}{8} = -\frac{1}{4}$$

The slope is $-\dfrac{1}{4}$.

179

51.
$$\frac{1}{5}+\left(-\frac{3}{4}\right)=\frac{4}{20}+\left(-\frac{15}{20}\right)=\frac{4+(-15)}{20}$$
$$=\frac{-11}{20}=-\frac{11}{20}$$

52. $y=x^2$

x	$y=x^2$	(x,y)
-3	$y=(-3)^2=9$	$(-3,9)$
-2	$y=(-2)^2=4$	$(-2,4)$
-1	$y=(-1)^2=1$	$(-1,1)$
0	$y=(0)^2=0$	$(0,0)$
1	$y=1^2=1$	$(1,1)$
2	$y=2^2=4$	$(2,4)$
3	$y=3^2=9$	$(3,9)$

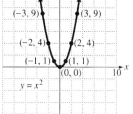

4.5 Exercise Set

1.
$$x+y+z=4$$
$$2-1+3=4$$
$$4=4$$
True
$$x-2y-z=1$$
$$2-2(-1)-3=1$$
$$2+2-3=1$$
$$1=1$$
True

$$2x-y-z=-1$$
$$2(2)-(-1)-3=-1$$
$$4+1-3=-1$$
$$1=-1$$
False

The ordered triple (2, –1, 3) does not make all three equations true, so it is not a solution.

3.
$$x-2y=2 \qquad\qquad 2x+3y=11$$
$$4-2(1)=2 \qquad\quad 2(4)+3(1)=11$$
$$4-2=2 \qquad\qquad\quad 8+3=11$$
$$2=2 \qquad\qquad\qquad 11=11$$
$$\text{True} \qquad\qquad\qquad \text{True}$$

$$y-4z=-7$$
$$1-4(2)=-7$$
$$1-8=-7$$
$$-7=-7$$
True

The ordered triple (4, 1, 2) makes all three equations true, so it is a solution.

5.
$$x+\ y+2z=11$$
$$x+\ y+3z=14$$
$$x+2y-\ z=\ 5$$
Multiply the second equation by –1 and add to the first equation..
$$x+y+2z=\ \ \ 11$$
$$\underline{-x-y-3z=-14}$$
$$-z=-\ 3$$
$$z=\ \ \ 3$$
Back-substitute 3 for z in the first and third equations:
$$x+y+2z=11 \qquad\quad x+2y-z=5$$
$$x+y+2(3)=11 \qquad\quad x+2y-3=5$$
$$x+y+6=11 \qquad\qquad\quad x+2y=8$$
$$x+y=5$$

180

We now have two equations in two variables.

$x + y = 5$

$x + 2y = 8$

Multiply the first equation by -1 and solve by addition.

$-x - y = -5$

$\underline{x + 2y = 8}$

$y = 3$

Back-substitute 3 for y into one of the equations in two variables.

$x + y = 5$

$x + 3 = 5$

$x = 2$

The solution is $(2,3,3)$ and the solution set is $\{(2,3,3)\}$.

7. $\quad 4x - y + 2z = 11$

$x + 2y - z = -1$

$2x + 2y - 3z = -1$

Multiply the second equation by -4 and add to the first equation.

$4x - y + 2z = 11$

$\underline{-4x - 8y + 4z = 4}$

$ -9y + 6z = 15$

Multiply the second equation by -2 and add it to the third equation.

$-2x - 4y + 2z = 2$

$\underline{2x + 2y - 3z = -1}$

$ -2y - z = 1$

We now have two equations in two variables.

$-9y + 6z = 15$

$-2y - z = 1$

Multiply the second equation by 6 and solve by addition.

$-9y + 6z = 15$

$\underline{-12y - 6z = 6}$

$-21y = 21$

$y = 21$

Back-substitute -1 for y in one of the equations in two variables.

$-2y - z = 1$

$-2(-1) - z = 1$

$2 - z = 1$

$-z = -1$

$z = 1$

Back-substitute -1 for y and 1 for z in one of the original equations in three variables.

$x + 2y - z = -1$

$x + 2(-1) - 1 = -1$

$x - 2 - 1 = -1$

$x - 3 = -1$

$x = 2$

The solution is $(2,-1,1)$ and the solution set is $\{(2,-1,1)\}$.

9. $\quad 3x + 2y - 3z = -2$

$2x - 5y + 2z = -2$

$4x - 3y + 4z = 10$

Multiply the second equation by -2 and add to the third equation.

$-4x + 10y - 4z = 4$

$\underline{4x - 3y + 4z = 10}$

$7y = 14$

$y = 2$

Back-substitute 2 for y in the first and third equations to obtain two equations in two unknowns.

$$3x + 2y - 3z = -2$$
$$3x + 2(2) - 3z = -2$$
$$3x + 4 - 3z = -2$$
$$3x - 3z = -6$$
$$4x - 3y + 4z = 10$$
$$4x - 3(2) + 4z = 10$$
$$4x - 6 + 4z = 10$$
$$4x + 4z = 16$$

The system of two equations in two variables becomes:
$$3x - 3z = -6$$
$$4x + 4z = 16$$

Multiply the first equation by –4 and the second equation by 3.
$$-12x + 12z = 24$$
$$\underline{12x + 12z = 48}$$
$$24z = 72$$
$$z = 3$$

Back-substitute 3 for z to find x.
$$3x - 3z = -6$$
$$3x - 3(3) = -6$$
$$3x - 9 = -6$$
$$3x = 3$$
$$x = 1$$

The solution is $(1, 2, 3)$ and the solution set is $\{(1, 2, 3)\}$.

11. $$2x - 4y + 3z = 17$$
$$x + 2y - z = 0$$
$$4x - y - z = 6$$

Multiply the second equation by –1 and add it to the third equation.
$$-x - 2y + z = 0$$
$$\underline{4x - y - z = 6}$$
$$3x - 3y = 6$$

Multiply the second equation by 3 and add it to the first equation.

$$2x - 4y + 3z = 17$$
$$\underline{3x + 6y - 3z = 0}$$
$$5x + 2y = 17$$

The system in two variables becomes:
$$3x - 3y = 6$$
$$5x + 2y = 17$$

Multiply the first equation by 2 and the second equation by 3 and solve by addition.
$$6x - 6y = 12$$
$$\underline{15x + 6y = 51}$$
$$21x = 63$$
$$x = 3$$

Back-substitute 3 for x in one of the equations in two variables.
$$3x - 3y = 6$$
$$3(3) - 3y = 6$$
$$9 - 3y = 6$$
$$-3y = -3$$
$$y = 1$$

Back-substitute 3 for x and 1 for y in one of the original equations in three variables.
$$x + 2y - z = 0$$
$$3 + 2(1) - z = 0$$
$$3 + 2 - z = 0$$
$$5 - z = 0$$
$$5 = z$$

The solution is $(3, 1, 5)$ and the solution set is $\{(3, 1, 5)\}$.

13.

$2x + y = 2$

$x + y - z = 4$

$3x + 2y + z = 0$

Add the second and third equations together to obtain an equation in two variables.

$x + y - z = 4$

$\underline{3x + 2y + z = 0}$

$4x + 3y = 4$

Use this equation and the first equation in the original system to write two equations in two variables.

$2x + y = 2$

$4x + 3y = 4$

Multiply the first equation by –2 and solve by addition.

$-4x - 2y = -4$

$\underline{4x + 3y = 4}$

$y = 0$

Back-substitute 0 for y in one of the equations in two unknowns.

$2x + y = 2$

$2x + 0 = 2$

$2x = 2$

$x = 1$

Back-substitute 1 for x and 0 for y in one of the equations in three unknowns.

$x + y - z = 4$

$1 + 0 - z = 4$

$1 - z = 4$

$-z = 3$

$z = -3$

The solution is $(1, 0, -3)$ and the solution set is $\{(1, 0, -3)\}$.

15.

$x + y = -4$

$y - z = 1$

$2x + y + 3z = -21$

Multiply the first equation by –1 and add to the second equation.

$-x - y = 4$

$\underline{y - z = 1}$

$-x - z = 5$

Multiply the second equation by –1 and add to the third equation.

$-y + z = -1$

$\underline{2x + y + 3z = -21}$

$2x + 4z = -22$

The system of two equations in two variables becomes.

$-x - z = 5$

$2x + 4z = -22$

Multiply the first equation by 2 and add to the second equation.

$-2x - 2z = 10$

$\underline{2x + 4z = -22}$

$2z = -12$

$z = -6$

Back-substitute –6 for z in one of the equations in two variables.

$-x - z = 5$

$-x - (-6) = 5$

$-x + 6 = 5$

$-x = -1$

$x = 1$

Back-substitute 1 for x in the first equation of the original system.

$x + y = -4$

$1 + y = -4$

$y = -5$

The solution is $(1, -5, -6)$ and the solution set is $\{(1, -5, -6)\}$.

183

17. $2x + y + 2z = 1$

$3x - y + z = 2$

$x - 2y - z = 0$

Add the first and second equations to eliminate y.

$2x + y + 2z = 1$

$\underline{3x - y + z = 2}$

$5x \quad + 3z = 3$

Multiply the second equation by -2 and add to the third equation.

$-6x + 2y - 2z = -4$

$\underline{x - 2y - z = 0}$

$-5x \quad - 3z = -4$

We obtain two equations in two variables.

$5x + 3z = 3$

$-5x - 3z = -4$

Adding the two equations, we obtain:

$5x + 3z = 3$

$\underline{-5x - 3z = -4}$

$0 = -1$

The system is inconsistent. There are no values of x, y, and z for which $0 = -1$.

Solution set: $\{ \ \}$ or $\varnothing$

19. $5x - 2y - 5z = 1$

$10x - 4y - 10z = 2$

$15x - 6y - 15z = 3$

Multiply the first equation by -2 and add to the second equation.

$-10x + 4y + 10z = -2$

$\underline{10x - 4y - 10z = 2}$

$0 = 0$

The system is dependent and has infinitely many solutions.

21. $3(2x + y) + 5z = -1$

$2(x - 3y + 4z) = -9$

$4(1 + x) = -3(z - 3y)$

Rewrite each equation and obtain the system of three equations in three variables.

$6x + 3y + 5z = -1$

$2x - 6y + 8z = -9$

$4x - 9y + 3z = -4$

Multiply the second equation by -3 and add to the first equation.

$6x + 3y + 5z = -1$

$\underline{-6x + 18y - 24z = 27}$

$21y - 19z = 26$

Multiply the second equation by -2 and add to the third equation.

$-4x + 12y - 16z = 18$

$\underline{4x - 9y + 3z = -4}$

$3y - 13z = 14$

The system of two variables in two equations is:

$21y - 19z = 26$

$3y - 13z = 14$

Multiply the second equation by -7 and add to the third equation.

$21y - 19z = 26$

$\underline{-21y + 91z = -98}$

$72z = -72$

$z = -1$

Back-substitute -1 for z in one of the equations in two variables to find y.

$3y - 13z = 14$

$3y - 13(-1) = 14$

$3y + 13 = 14$

$3y = 1$

$y = \dfrac{1}{3}$

Back-substitute -1 for z and $\dfrac{1}{3}$ for y in one of the original equations in three variables.

$$6x + 3y + 5z = -1$$
$$6x + 1 - 5 = -1$$
$$6x - 4 = -1$$
$$6x = 3$$
$$x = \dfrac{1}{2}$$

The solution is $\left(\dfrac{1}{2}, \dfrac{1}{3}, -1\right)$ and the

solution set is $\left\{\left(\dfrac{1}{2}, \dfrac{1}{3}, -1\right)\right\}$.

23. Use each ordered pair to write an equation as follows:
$$(x, y) = (-1, 6)$$
$$y = ax^2 + bx + c$$
$$6 = a(-1)^2 + b(-1) + c$$
$$6 = a - b + c$$
$$(x, y) = (1, 4)$$
$$y = ax^2 + bx + c$$
$$4 = a(1)^2 + b(1) + c$$
$$4 = a + b + c$$

$$(x, y) = (2, 9)$$
$$y = ax^2 + bx + c$$
$$9 = a(2)^2 + b(2) + c$$
$$9 = a(4) + 2b + c$$
$$9 = 4a + 2b + c$$

The system of three equations in three variables is:
$$a - b + c = 6$$
$$a + b + c = 4$$
$$4a + 2b + c = 9$$
Add the first and second equations.
$$\begin{array}{r} a - b + c = 6 \\ a + b + c = 4 \\ \hline 2a \quad\; + 2c = 10 \end{array}$$
Multiply the first equation by 2 and add to the third equation.
$$\begin{array}{r} 2a - 2b + 2c = 12 \\ 4a + 2b + \; c = 9 \\ \hline 6a \qquad + 3c = 21 \end{array}$$
The system of two equations in two variables becomes:
$$2a + 2c = 10$$
$$6a + 3c = 21$$
Multiply the first equation by -3 and add to the second equation.
$$\begin{array}{r} -6a - 6c = -30 \\ 6a + 3c = \; 21 \\ \hline -3c = -9 \end{array}$$
$$c = 3$$
Back-substitute 3 for c in one of the equations in two variables.
$$2a + 2c = 10$$
$$2a + 2(3) = 10$$
$$2a + 6 = 10$$
$$2a = 4$$
$$a = 2$$
Back-substitute 3 for c and 2 for a in one of the equations in three variables.
$$a + b + c = 4$$
$$2 + b + 3 = 4$$
$$b + 5 = 4$$
$$b = -1$$
The quadratic equation is
$$y = 2x^2 - x + 3.$$

185

25. Use each ordered pair to write an equation.

$$(x, y) = (-1, -4)$$
$$y = ax^2 + bx + c$$
$$-4 = a(-1)^2 + b(-1) + c$$
$$-4 = a - b + c$$

$$(x, y) = (1, -2)$$
$$y = ax^2 + bx + c$$
$$-2 = a(1)^2 + b(1) + c$$
$$-2 = a + b + c$$

$$(x, y) = (2, 5)$$
$$y = ax^2 + bx + c$$
$$5 = a(2)^2 + b(2) + c$$
$$5 = a(4) + 2b + c$$
$$5 = 4a + 2b + c$$

The system of three equations in three variables is:

$$a - b + c = -4$$
$$a + b + c = -2$$
$$4a + 2b + c = 5$$

Multiply the second equation by -1 and add to the first equation.

$$a - b + c = -4$$
$$\underline{-a - b - c = 2}$$
$$-2b = -2$$
$$b = 1$$

Back-substitute 4 for b in first and third equations to obtain two equations in two variables.

$$a - b + c = -4 \qquad 4a + 2b + c = 5$$
$$a - 1 + c = -4 \qquad 4a + 2(1) + c = 5$$
$$a + c = -3 \qquad 4a + 2 + c = 5$$
$$\qquad\qquad\qquad 4a + c = 3$$

The system of two equations in two variables becomes:

$$a + c = -3$$
$$4a + c = 3$$

Multiply the first equation by -1 and add to the second equation.

$$-a - c = 3$$
$$\underline{4a + c = 3}$$
$$3a = 6$$
$$a = 2$$

Back-substitute 2 for a and 1 for b in one of the equations in three variables.

$$a - b + c = -4$$
$$2 - 1 + c = -4$$
$$1 + c = -4$$
$$c = -5$$

The quadratic equation is
$$y = 2x^2 + x - 5.$$

27. Let x = the first number
Let y = the second number
Let z = the third number

$$x + y + z = 16$$
$$2x + 3y + 4z = 46$$
$$5x - y = 31$$

Multiply the first equation by -4 and add to the second equation.

$$-4x - 4y - 4z = -64$$
$$\underline{2x + 3y + 4z = 46}$$
$$-2x - y = -18$$

The system of two equations in two variables becomes:

$$5x - y = 31$$
$$-2x - y = -18$$

Multiply the first equation by -1 and add to the second equation.

$$-5x + y = -31$$
$$\underline{-2x - y = -18}$$
$$-7x = -49$$
$$x = 7$$

Back-substitute 7 for x in one of the equations in two variables.

$$5x - y = 31$$
$$5(7) - y = 31$$
$$35 - y = 31$$
$$-y = -4$$
$$y = 4$$

Back-substitute 7 for x and 4 for y in one of the equations in two variables.

$$x + y + z = 16$$
$$7 + 4 + z = 16$$
$$11 + z = 16$$
$$z = 5$$

The numbers are 7, 4 and 5.

29.

$$\frac{x+2}{6} - \frac{y+4}{3} + \frac{z}{2} = 0$$

$$6\left(\frac{x+2}{6} - \frac{y+4}{3} + \frac{z}{2}\right) = 6(0)$$

$$(x+2) - 2(y+4) + 3z = 0$$

$$x + 2 - 2y - 8 + 3z = 0$$

$$x - 2y + 3z = 6$$

$$\frac{x+1}{2} + \frac{y-1}{2} - \frac{z}{4} = \frac{9}{2}$$

$$4\left(\frac{x+1}{2} + \frac{y-1}{2} - \frac{z}{4}\right) = 4\left(\frac{9}{2}\right)$$

$$2(x+1) + 2(y-1) - z = 18$$

$$2x + 2 + 2y - 2 - z = 18$$

$$2x + 2y - z = 18$$

$$\frac{x-5}{4} + \frac{y+1}{3} + \frac{z-2}{2} = \frac{19}{4}$$

$$12\left(\frac{x-5}{4} + \frac{y+1}{3} + \frac{z-2}{2}\right) = 12\left(\frac{19}{4}\right)$$

$$3(x-5) + 4(y+1) + 6(z-2) = 57$$

$$3x - 15 + 4y + 4 + 6z - 12 = 57$$

$$3x + 4y + 6z = 80$$

We need to solve the equivalent system:

$$x - 2y + 3z = 6$$
$$2x + 2y - z = 18$$
$$3x + 4y + 6z = 80$$

Add the first two equations together.

$$x - 2y + 3z = 6$$
$$\underline{2x + 2y - z = 18}$$
$$3x + 2z = 24$$

Multiply the second equation by -2 and add it to the third equation.

$$-4x - 4y + 2z = -36$$
$$\underline{3x + 4y + 6z = 80}$$
$$-x + 8z = 44$$

Using the two reduced equations, we solve the system

$$3x + 2z = 24$$
$$-x + 8z = 44$$

Multiply the second equation by 3 and add the equations.

$$3x + 2z = 24$$
$$\underline{-3x + 24z = 132}$$
$$26z = 156$$
$$z = 6$$

Back-substitute to find x.

$$-x + 8(6) = 44$$
$$-x + 48 = 44$$
$$-x = -4$$
$$x = 4$$

187

Back substitute to find y.
$$x - 2y + 3z = 6$$
$$4 - 2y + 3(6) = 6$$
$$-2y = -16$$
$$y = 8$$

The solution is $(4, 8, 6)$ or the solution set is $\{(4, 8, 6)\}$.

30.
$$\frac{x+3}{2} - \frac{y-1}{2} + \frac{z+2}{4} = \frac{3}{2}$$
$$4\left(\frac{x+3}{2} - \frac{y-1}{2} + \frac{z+2}{4}\right) = 4\left(\frac{3}{2}\right)$$
$$2(x+3) - 2(y-1) + (z+2) = 6$$
$$2x + 6 - 2y + 2 + z + 2 = 6$$
$$2x - 2y + z = -4$$

$$\frac{x-5}{2} + \frac{y+1}{3} - \frac{z}{4} = -\frac{25}{6}$$
$$12\left(\frac{x-5}{2} + \frac{y+1}{3} - \frac{z}{4}\right) = 12\left(-\frac{25}{6}\right)$$
$$6(x-5) + 4(y+1) - 3z = -50$$
$$6x - 30 + 4y + 4 - 3z = -50$$
$$6x + 4y - 3z = -24$$

$$\frac{x-3}{4} - \frac{y+1}{2} + \frac{z-3}{2} = -\frac{5}{2}$$
$$4\left(\frac{x-3}{4} - \frac{y+1}{2} + \frac{z-3}{2}\right) = 4\left(-\frac{5}{2}\right)$$
$$(x-3) - 2(y+1) + 2(z-3) = -10$$
$$x - 3 - 2y - 2 + 2z - 6 = -10$$
$$x - 2y + 2z = 1$$

We need to solve the equivalent system:
$$2x - 2y + z = -4$$
$$6x + 4y - 3z = -24$$
$$x - 2y + 2z = 1$$

Multiply the first equation by 2 and add it to the second equation.
$$4x - 4y + 2z = -8$$
$$6x + 4y - 3z = -24$$
$$\overline{\qquad\qquad\qquad}$$
$$10x - z = -32$$

Multiply the third equation by -1 and add to the first equation.
$$2x - 2y + z = -4$$
$$-x + 2y - 2z = -1$$
$$\overline{\qquad\qquad\qquad}$$
$$x - z = -5$$

Using the two reduced equations, we solve the system
$$10x - z = -32$$
$$x - z = -5$$

Multiply the second equation by -1 and add it to the first.
$$10x - z = -32$$
$$-x + z = 5$$
$$\overline{\qquad\qquad\qquad}$$
$$9x = -27$$
$$x = -3$$

Back-substitute to solve for z.
$$x - z = -5$$
$$-3 - z = -5$$
$$-z = -2$$
$$z = 2$$

Back-substitute to solve for y.
$$x - 2y + 2z = 1$$
$$-3 - 2y + 2(2) = 1$$
$$-3 - 2y + 4 = 1$$
$$-2y = 0$$
$$y = 0$$

The solution is $(-3, 0, 2)$ or the solution set is $\{(-3, 0, 2)\}$.

31. Selected points may vary, but the equation will be the same.

$$y = ax^2 + bx + c$$

Use the points $(2,-2)$, $(4,1)$, and $(6,-2)$ to get the system

$$4a + 2b + c = -2$$
$$16a + 4b + c = 1$$
$$36a + 6b + c = -2$$

Multiply the first equation by -1 and add to the second equation.

$$-4a - 2b - c = 2$$
$$\underline{16a + 4b + c = 1}$$
$$12a + 2b = 3$$

Multiply the first equation by -1 and add to the third equation.

$$-4a - 2b - c = 2$$
$$\underline{36a + 6b + c = -2}$$
$$32a + 4b = 0$$

Using the two reduced equations, we get the system

$$12a + 2b = 3$$
$$32a + 4b = 0$$

Multiply the first equation by -2 and add to the second equation.

$$-24a - 4b = -6$$
$$\underline{32a + 4b = 0}$$
$$8a = -6$$
$$a = -\frac{3}{4}$$

Back-substitute to solve for b.

$$12a + 2b = 3$$
$$12\left(-\frac{3}{4}\right) + 2b = 3$$
$$-9 + 2b = 3$$
$$2b = 12$$
$$b = 6$$

Back-substitute to solve for c.

$$4a + 2b + c = -2$$
$$4\left(-\frac{3}{4}\right) + 2(6) + c = -2$$
$$-3 + 12 + c = -2$$
$$c = -11$$

The equation is:

$$y = -\frac{3}{4}x^2 + 6x - 11$$

32. Selected points may vary, but the equation will be the same.

$$y = ax^2 + bx + c$$

Use the points $(3,4)$, $(4,2)$, and $(5,2)$ to get the system

$$9a + 3b + c = 4$$
$$16a + 4b + c = 2$$
$$25a + 5b + c = 2$$

Multiply the first equation by -1 and add to the second equation.

$$-9a - 3b - c = -4$$
$$\underline{16a + 4b + c = 2}$$
$$7a + b = -2$$

Multiply the first equation by -1 and add to the third equation.

$$-9a - 3b - c = -4$$
$$\underline{25a + 5b + c = 2}$$
$$16a + 2b = -2$$

Use the two reduced equations to get the system

$$7a + b = -2$$
$$16a + 2b = -2$$

Multiply the first equation by -2 and add to the second equation.

$$-14a - 2b = 4$$
$$\underline{16a + 2b = -2}$$
$$2a = 2$$
$$a = 1$$

189

Back-substitute to solve for b.

$$7a + b = -2$$
$$7(1) + b = -2$$
$$7 + b = -2$$
$$b = -9$$

Back-substitute to solve for c.

$$9a + 3b + c = 4$$
$$9(1) + 3(-9) + c = 4$$
$$9 - 27 + c = 4$$
$$c = 22$$

The equation is $y = x^2 - 9x + 22$.

33.

$$ax - by - 2cz = 21$$
$$ax + by + cz = 0$$
$$2ax - by + cz = 14$$

Add the first two equations.

$$ax - by - 2cz = 21$$
$$\underline{ax + by + cz = 0}$$
$$2ax - cz = 21$$

Multiply the first equation by -1 and add to the third equation.

$$-ax + by + 2cz = -21$$
$$\underline{2ax - by + cz = 14}$$
$$ax + 3cz = -7$$

Use the two reduced equations to get the following system:

$$2ax - cz = 21$$
$$ax + 3cz = -7$$

Multiply the second equation by -2 and add the equations.

$$2ax - cz = 21$$
$$\underline{-2ax - 6cz = 14}$$
$$-7cz = 35$$
$$z = -\frac{5}{c}$$

Back-substitute to solve for x.

$$ax + 3cz = -7$$
$$ax + 3c\left(-\frac{5}{c}\right) = -7$$
$$ax - 15 = -7$$
$$ax = 8$$
$$x = \frac{8}{a}$$

Back-substitute to solve for y.

$$ax + by + cz = 0$$
$$a\left(\frac{8}{a}\right) + by + c\left(-\frac{5}{c}\right) = 0$$
$$8 + by - 5 = 0$$
$$by = -3$$
$$y = -\frac{3}{b}$$

The solution is $\left(\dfrac{8}{a}, -\dfrac{3}{b}, -\dfrac{5}{c}\right)$.

34.

$$ax - by + 2cz = -4$$
$$ax + 3by - cz = 1$$
$$2ax + by + 3cz = 2$$

Multiply the first equation by -1 and add to the second equation.

$$-ax + by - 2cz = 4$$
$$\underline{ax + 3by - cz = 1}$$
$$4by - 3cz = 5$$

Multiply the first equation by -2 and add to the third equation.

$$-2ax + 2by - 4cz = 8$$
$$\underline{2ax + by + 3cz = 2}$$
$$3by - cz = 10$$

Use the two reduced equations to get the following system:

$$4by - 3cz = 5$$
$$3by - cz = 10$$

Multiply the second equation by -3 and add to the first equation.

190

$$4by - 3cz = 5$$
$$\underline{-9by + 3cz = -30}$$
$$-5by = -25$$
$$y = \frac{5}{b}$$

Back-substitute to solve for z.
$$4by - 3cz = 5$$
$$4b\left(\frac{5}{b}\right) - 3cz = 5$$
$$20 - 3cz = 5$$
$$-3cz = -15$$
$$z = \frac{5}{c}$$

Back-substitute to solve for x.
$$ax - by + 2cz = -4$$
$$ax - b\left(\frac{5}{b}\right) + 2c\left(\frac{5}{c}\right) = -4$$
$$ax - 5 + 10 = -4$$
$$ax = -9$$
$$x = -\frac{9}{a}$$

The solution is $\left(-\dfrac{9}{a}, \dfrac{5}{b}, \dfrac{5}{c}\right)$.

35. **a.** $(0, 13.6)$, $(70, 4.7)$, $(102, 11.5)$

   b.
$$0a + 0b + 0c = 13.6$$
$$4900a + 70b + c = 4.7$$
$$10,404a + 102b + c = 11.5$$

37. **a.** Using the three ordered pairs,
$(1, 224)$, $(3, 176)$, and $(4, 104)$,
we get the following system:
$$a + b + c = 224$$
$$9a + 3b + c = 176$$
$$16a + 4b + c = 104$$
Multiply the first equation by -1
and add to the second equation.
$$-a - b - c = -224$$
$$\underline{9a + 3b + c = 176}$$
$$8a + 2b = -48$$
Multiply the first equation by -1
and add to the third equation.
$$-a - b - c = -224$$
$$\underline{16a + 4b + c = 104}$$
$$15a + 3b = -120$$
Using the two reduced equations,
we get the following system:
$$8a + 2b = -48$$
$$15a + 3b = -120$$
Multiply the first equation by -3
and multiply the second equation
by 2, then add to the equations.
$$-24a - 6b = 144$$
$$\underline{30a + 6b = -240}$$
$$6a = -96$$
$$a = -16$$
Back-substitute to solve for b.
$$8a + 2b = -48$$
$$8(-16) + 2b = -48$$
$$-128 + 2b = -48$$
$$2b = 80$$
$$b = 40$$
Back-substitute to solve for c.
$$a + b + c = 224$$
$$-16 + 40 + c = 224$$
$$c = 200$$
The equation is
$$y = -16x^2 + 40x + 200.$$

b. When $x = 5$, we get
$$y = -16(5)^2 + 40(5) + 200$$
$$= -16(25) + 200 + 200$$
$$= -400 + 400$$
$$= 0$$
After 5 seconds, the ball hits the ground.

39. Let x = estimated wealth of Carnegie.
Let y = estimated wealth of Vanderbilt.
Let z = estimated wealth of Gates.
$$x + y + z = 256$$
$$x - y = 4$$
$$y - z = 36$$
Solve the second equation for x.
$$x - y = 4$$
$$x = y + 4$$
Solve the third equation for z.
$$y - z = 36$$
$$-z = -y + 36$$
$$z = y - 36$$
Substitute the expressions for x and z into the first equation and solve for y.
$$(y + 4) + y + (y - 36) = 256$$
$$y + 4 + y + y - 36 = 256$$
$$3y = 288$$
$$y = 96$$
Back-substitute to solve for x and z.
$$x = y + 4 = 96 + 4 = 100$$
$$z = y - 36 = 96 - 36 = 60$$
The estimated wealth was Carnegie (100 billion), Vanderbilt (96 billion) and Gates (60 billion).

41. Let x = the amount invested at 8%
Let y = the amount invested at 10%
Let z = the amount invested at 12%
$$x + y + z = 6700$$
$$0.08x + 0.10y + 0.12z = 716$$
$$z - x - y = 300$$
Rewrite the system in
$Ax + By + Cz = D$ form.
$$x + y + z = 6700$$
$$0.08x + 0.10y + 0.12z = 716$$
$$-x - y + z = 300$$
Add the first and third equations to find z.
$$x + y + z = 6700$$
$$\underline{-x - y + z = 300}$$
$$2z = 7000$$
$$z = 3500$$
Back-substitute 3500 for z to obtain two equations in two variables.
$$x + y + z = 6700$$
$$x + y + 3500 = 6700$$
$$x + y = 3200$$

$$0.08x + 0.10y + 0.12(3500) = 716$$
$$0.08x + 0.10y + 420 = 716$$
$$0.08x + 0.10y = 296$$
The system of two equations in two variables becomes:
$$x + y = 3200$$
$$0.08x + 0.10y = 296$$
Multiply the second equation by -10 and add it to the first equation.
$$x + y = 3200$$
$$\underline{-0.8x + -y = -2960}$$
$$0.2x = 240$$
$$x = 1200$$

Back-substitute 1200 for x in one of the equations in two variables.

$$x + y = 3200$$
$$1200 + y = 3200$$
$$y = 2000$$

$1200 was invested at 8%, $2000 was invested at 10%, and $3500 was invested at 12%.

43. Let x = the number of $8 tickets
Let y = the number of $10 tickets
Let z = the number of $12 tickets

$$x + y + z = 400$$
$$8x + 10y + 12z = 3700$$
$$x + y = 7z$$

Rewrite the system in
$Ax + By + Cz = D$ form.

$$x + y + z = 400$$
$$8x + 10y + 12z = 3700$$
$$x + y - 7z = 0$$

Multiply the first equation by -1 and add to the third equation.

$$-x - y - z = -400$$
$$\underline{x + y - 7z = 0}$$
$$-8z = -400$$
$$z = 50$$

Back-substitute 50 for z in two of the original equations to obtain two of equations in two variables.

$$x + y + z = 400$$
$$x + y + 50 = 400$$
$$x + y = 350$$
$$8x + 10y + 12z = 3700$$
$$8x + 10y + 12(50) = 3700$$
$$8x + 10y + 600 = 3700$$
$$8x + 10y = 3100$$

The system of two equations in two variables becomes:

$$x + y = 350$$
$$8x + 10y = 3100$$

Multiply the first equation by -8 and add to the second equation.

$$-8x - 8y = -2800$$
$$\underline{8x + 10y = 3100}$$
$$2y = 300$$
$$y = 150$$

Back-substitute 50 for z and 150 for y in one of the original equations in three variables.

$$x + y + z = 400$$
$$x + 150 + 50 = 400$$
$$x + 200 = 400$$
$$x = 200$$

There were 200 $8 tickets, 150 $10 tickets, and 50 $12 tickets sold.

45. Let A = the number of servings of A
Let B = the number of servings of B
Let C = the number of servings of C

$$40A + 200B + 400C = 660$$
$$5A + 2B + 4C = 25$$
$$30A + 10B + 300C = 425$$

Multiply the second equation by -8 and add to the first equation to obtain an equation in two variables.

$$40A + 200B + 400C = 660$$
$$\underline{-40A - 16B - 32C = -200}$$
$$184B + 368C = 460$$

Multiply the second equation by -6 and add to the third equation to obtain an equation in two variables.

$$-30A - 12B - 24C = -150$$
$$\underline{30A + 10B + 300C = 425}$$
$$-2B + 276C = 275$$

The system of two equations in two variables becomes:

$$184B + 368C = 460$$
$$-2B + 276C = 275$$

193

Multiply the second equation by 92 and eliminate B.

$$184B + 368C = 460$$
$$\underline{-184B + 25392C = 25300}$$
$$25760C = 25760$$
$$C = 1$$

Back-substitute 1 for C in one of the equations in two variables.

$$-2B + 276C = 275$$
$$-2B + 276(1) = 275$$
$$-2B + 276 = 275$$
$$-2B = -1$$
$$B = \frac{1}{2}$$

Back-substitute 1 for C and $\frac{1}{2}$ for B in one of the original equations in three variables.

$$5A + 2B + 4C = 25$$
$$5A + 2\left(\frac{1}{2}\right) + 4(1) = 25$$
$$5A + 1 + 4 = 25$$
$$5A + 5 = 25$$
$$5A = 20$$
$$A = 4$$

To meet the requirements, 4 ounces of Food A, $\frac{1}{2}$ ounce of Food B, and 1 ounce of Food C should be used.

47.-53. Answers will vary.

55. Statement **c.** is true. The variable terms of the second equation are multiples of the variable terms in the first equation, but the constants are not. If we multiply the first equation by 2 and add to the second equation, we obtain:

$$-2x - 2y + 2z = -20$$
$$\underline{2x + 2y - 2z = 7}$$
$$0 = -13$$

This is a contradiction, so the system is inconsistent.

Statement **a.** is false. The ordered triple is one solution to the equation, but there are an infinite number of other ordered triples which satisfy the equation.

Statement **b.** is false.
$$x - y - z = -6$$
$$2 - (-3) - 5 = -6$$
$$2 + 3 - 5 = -6$$
$$0 \neq -6$$

Statement **d.** is false. An equation with four variables can be satisfied by real numbers.

57.
$$x + y + z = 180$$
$$(2x + 5) + y = 180$$
$$(2x - 5) + z = 180$$

Rewrite the system in standard form as

$$x + y + z = 180$$
$$2x + y = 175$$
$$2x + z = 185$$

Multiply the first equation by -1 and add to the second equation to obtain an equation with two variables.

$$-x - y - z = -180$$
$$\underline{2x + y = 175}$$
$$x - z = -5$$

Combine this equation with the third equation to make a system of two equations.

$$x - z = -5$$
$$\underline{2x + z = 185}$$
$$3x = 180$$
$$x = 60$$

Back-substitute to find z.

$$x - z = -5$$
$$60 - z = -5$$
$$-z = -65$$
$$z = 65$$

Back-substitute to find y.

$$x + y + z = 180$$
$$60 + 65 + z = 180$$
$$z = 55$$

The angles measure $55°$, $60°$, and $65°$.

59.

$$y = -\frac{3}{4}x + 3$$

Use the slope and the y–intercept to graph the line.

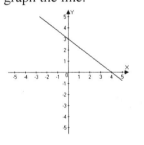

60. $-2x + y = 6$

Rewrite the equation in slope-intercept form.

$$-2x + y = 6$$
$$y = 2x + 6$$

Use the slope and the y–intercept to graph the line.

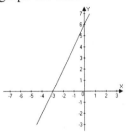

61. $y = -5$ is a horizontal line with y-intercept -5.

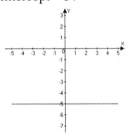

Chapter 4 Review Exercises

1. $4x - y = 9$

$$4(1) - (-5) = 9$$
$$4 + 5 = 9$$
$$9 = 9 \text{ true}$$

$$2x + 3y = -13$$
$$2(1) + 3(-5) = -13$$
$$2 - 15 = -13$$
$$-13 = -13 \text{ true}$$

Since the ordered pair $(1, -5)$ satisfies both equations, it is a solution of the given system.

2.

$$2x + 3y = -4$$
$$2(-5) + 3(2) = -4$$
$$-10 + 6 = -4$$
$$-4 = -4 \text{ true}$$

$$x - 4y = -10$$
$$-5 - 4(-2) = -10$$
$$-5 + 8 = -10$$
$$3 = -10 \text{ false}$$

Since $(-5,2)$ fails to satisfy *both* equations, it is not a solution of the given system.

3.

$$x + y = 2$$
$$-1 + 3 = 2$$
$$2 = 2 \text{ true}$$

$$2x + y = -5$$
$$2(-1) + 3 = -5$$
$$-2 + 3 = -5$$
$$1 = -5 \text{ false}$$

Since $(-1, 3)$ fails to satisfy *both* equations, it is not a solution of the given system. Also, the second equation in the system, which can be rewritten as $y = -2x - 5$, is a line with slope -2 and y-intercept -5, while the graph shows a line with slope 2 and y-intercept 5.

4.

$$x + y = 2$$
$$x - y = 6$$

Graph both lines on the same axes.

$x + y = 2$:
x-intercept = 2; y-intercept 2

$x - y = 6$:
x-intercept = 6, y-intercept = -6

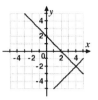

The lines appear to intersect at $(4, -2)$. This apparent solution can be verified by substituting 4 for x and -2 for y in both equations of the original system.

Solution set: $\{(4, -2)\}$

5.

$$2x - 3y = 12$$
$$-2x + y = -8$$

Graph both equations.

$2x - 3y = 12$: x-intercept = 6; y-intercept = -4

$-2x + y = -8$: x-intercept = 4; y-intercept = -8

Solution set: $\{(3, -2)\}$

6.

$$3x + 2y = 6$$
$$3x - 2y = 6$$

Graph both equations.

$3x + 2y = 6$: x-intercept = 2; y-intercept = 3

$3x - 2y = 6$: x-intercept = 2; y-intercept = -3

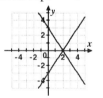

Solution set: $\{(2,0)\}$

7.

$$y = \frac{1}{2}x$$

$$y = 2x - 3$$

Graph both equations.

$y = \frac{1}{2}x$: slope $= \frac{1}{2}$; y-intercept $= 0$

$y = 2x - 3$: slope $= 2$; y-intercept $= -3$

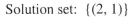

Solution set: $\{(2, 1)\}$

8. $x + 2y = 2$

$$y = x - 5$$

Graph both equations.

$x + 2y = 2$:

x-intercept $= 2$; y-intercept $= 1$

$y = x - 5$:

slope $= 1$; y-intercept $= -5$

Solution set: $\{(4, -1)\}$

9. $x + 2y = 8$

$$3x + 6y = 12$$

Graph both equations.

$x + 2y = 8$:

x-intercept $= 8$; y-intercept $= 4$

$3x + 6y = 12$:

x-intercept $= 4$; y-intercept $= 2$

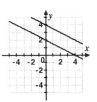

The lines are parallel. The system is inconsistent and has no solution.

Solution set: $\{\ \}$ or $\varnothing$

10. $2x - 4y = 8$

$$x - 2y = 4$$

Graph both equations.

$2x - 4y = 8$:

x-intercept $= 4$; y-intercept $= -2$

$x - 2y = 4$:

x-intercept $= 4$; y-intercept $= -2$

The graphs of the two equations are the same line. The system is dependent and has infinitely many solutions.

Solution set: $\{(x, y) \mid 2x - 4y = 8\}$ or

$\{(x, y) \mid x - 2y = 4\}$

11. $y = 3x - 1$

$$y = 3x + 2$$

Graph both equations.

$y = 3x - 1$: slope $= 3$; y-intercept $= -1$

$y = 3x + 2$: slope $= 3$; y-intercept $= 2$

The lines are parallel, so the system is inconsistent and has no solution.

Solution set: $\{\ \}$ or $\varnothing$

197

12. $x - y = 4$

$\qquad x = -2$

Graph both equations:

$x - y = 4$:

x-intercept = 4; y-intercept = -4

$x = 2$:

vertical line with x-intercept = -2

Solution set: $\{(-2, -6)\}$

13. $x = 2$

$\qquad y = 5$

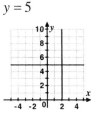

The vertical line and horizontal line intersect at (2,5).

Solution set: $\{(2,5)\}$

14. $x = 2$

$\qquad x = 5$

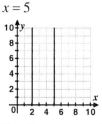

The lines are parallel, so the system inconsistent and has no solution.

Solution set: $\{\ \}$ or $\varnothing$

15. $2x - 3y = 7$

$\qquad y = 3x - 7$

Substitute $3x - 7$ for y in the first equation.

$$2x - 3y = 7$$
$$2x - 3(3x - 7) = 7$$
$$2x - 9x + 21 = 7$$
$$-7x + 21 = 7$$
$$-7x = -14$$
$$x = 2$$

Back-substitute 7 for x into the second equation and solve for y.

$$y = 3x - 7$$
$$y = 3(2) - 7 = -1$$

Solution set: $\{(2, -1)\}$

16. $2x - y = 6$

$\qquad x = 13 - 2y$

Substitute $13 - 2y$ for x into the first equation.

$$2x - y = 6$$
$$2(13 - 2y) - y = 6$$
$$26 - 4y - y = 6$$
$$26 - 5y = 6$$
$$-5y = -20$$
$$y = 4$$

Back-substitute 4 for y in the second equation.

$$x = 13 - 2y$$
$$x = 13 - 2(4) = 5$$

Solution set: $\{(5,4)\}$

17. $2x - 5y = 1$

$3x + y = -7$

Solve the second equation for y.

$3x + y = -7$

$y = -3x - 7$

Substitute $-3x - 7$ in the first equation.

$2x - 5y = 1$

$2x - 5(-3x - 7) = 1$

$2x + 15x + 35 = 1$

$17x + 35 = 1$

$17x = -34$

$x = -2$

Back-substitute in the equation

$y = -3x - 7$.

$y = -3x - 7$

$y = -3(-2) - 7 = -1$

Solution set: $\{(-2, -1)\}$

18. $3x + 4y = -13$

$5y - x = -21$

Solve the second equation for x.

$5y - x = -21$

$-x = -5y - 21$

$x = 5y + 21$

Substitute $5y + 21$ for x in the first equation.

$3x + 4y = -13$

$3(5y + 21) + 4y = -13$

$15y + 63 + 4y = -13$

$19y + 63 = -13$

$19y = -76$

$y = -4$

Back-substitute.

$3x + 4y = -13$

$3x + 4(-4) = -13$

$3x - 16 = -13$

$3x = 3$

$x = 1$

Solution set: $\{(1, -4)\}$

19. $y = 39 - 3x$

$y = 2x - 61$

Substitute $2x - 61$ for y in the first equation.

$2x - 61 = 39 - 3x$

$5x - 61 = 39$

$5x = 100$

$x = 20$

Back-substitute.

$y = 2x - 61 = 2(20) - 61 = -21$

Solution set: $\{(20, -21)\}$

20. $4x + y = 5$

$12x + 3y = 15$

Solve the first equation for y.

$4x + y = 5$

$y = -4x + 5$

Substitute $-4x + 5$ for y in the second equation.

$12x + 3y = 15$

$12x + 3(-4x + 5) = 15$

$12x - 12x + 15 = 15$

$15 = 15$ true

The true statement 15 = 15 indicates that the given system has infinitely many solutions.

Solution set: $\{(x, y) \mid 4x + y = 5\}$ or $\{(x, y) \mid 12x + 3y = 15\}$

199

21. $4x - 2y = 10$

$$y = 2x + 3$$

Substitute $2x + 3$ for y in the first equation.

$$4x - 2y = 10$$
$$4x - 2(2x + 3) = 10$$
$$4x - 4x - 6 = 10$$
$$-6 = 10 \text{ false}$$

The false statement $-6 = 10$ indicates that the system is inconsistent and has no solution.

Solution set: $\{\ \}$ or $\varnothing$

22. $x - 4 = 0$

$$9x - 2y = 0$$

Solve the first equation for x.

$$x - 4 = 0$$
$$x = 4$$

Substitute 4 for x in the second equation.

$$9x - 2y = 0$$
$$9(4) - 2y = 0$$
$$36 - 2y = 0$$
$$-2y = -36$$
$$y = 18$$

Solution set: $\{(4, 18)\}$

23. $8y = 4x$

$$7x + 2y = -8$$

Solve the first equation for y.

$$8y = 4x$$
$$y = \frac{1}{2}x$$

Substitute $\frac{1}{2}x$ for y in the second equation.

$7x + 2y = -8$

$$7x + 2\left(\frac{1}{2}x\right) = -8$$
$$7x + x = -8$$
$$8x = -8$$
$$x = -1$$

Back-substitute.

$$y = \frac{1}{2}x = \frac{1}{2}(-1) = -\frac{1}{2}$$

Solution set: $\left\{\left(-1, -\frac{1}{2}\right)\right\}$

24. Demand model: $N = -60p + 1000$

Supply model: $N = 4p + 200$

Substitute $4p + 200$ for N in the demand equation.

$$N = -60p + 1000$$
$$4p + 200 = -60p + 1000$$
$$64p + 200 = 1000$$
$$64p = 800$$
$$p = 12.5$$

Back-substitute 12.5 for p and find N.

$$N = 4(1.25) + 200 = 250$$

Supply and demand are equal when the price of the video is $12.50. At this price, 250 copies are supplied and sold.

25. $x + y = 6$

$$2x + y = 8$$

Multiply the first equation by -1 and add the result to the second equation to eliminate the y-terms.

$$\begin{array}{r} -x - y = -6 \\ 2x + y = 8 \\ \hline x = 2 \end{array}$$

Back-substitute into either of the original equations to solve for y.

$$x + y = 6$$
$$2 + y = 6$$
$$y = 4$$

Solution set: $\{(2, 4)\}$

26. $3x - 4y = 1$

$12x - y = -11$

Multiply the first equation by -4 and add the result to the second equation.

$-12x + 16y = -4$

$\underline{12x - y = -11}$

$15y = -15$

$y = -1$

Back-substitute.

$3x - 4y = 1$

$3x - 4(-1) = 1$

$3x + 4 = 1$

$3x = -3$

$x = -1$

Solution set: $\{(-1, -1)\}$

27. $3x - 7y = 13$

$6x + 5y = 7$

Multiply the first equation by -2. Don't change the second equation.

$-6x + 14y = -26$

$\underline{6x + 5y = 7}$

$19y = -19$

$y = -1$

Back-substitute.

$3x - 7y = 13$

$3x - 7(-1) = 13$

$3x + 7 = 13$

$3x = 6$

$x = 2$

Solution set: $\{(2, -1)\}$

28. $8x - 4y = 16$

$4x + 5y = 22$

Multiply the second equation by -2. Don't change the first equation.

$8x - 4y = 16$

$\underline{-8x - 10y = -44}$

$-14y = -28$

$y = 2$

Back-substitute.

$8x - 4y = 16$

$8x - 4(2) = 16$

$8x - 8 = 16$

$8x = 24$

$x = 3$

Solution set: $\{(3, 2)\}$

29. $5x - 2y = 8$

$3x - 5y = 1$

Multiply the first equation by 3. Multiply the second equation by -5.

$15x - 6y = 24$

$\underline{-15x + 25y = -5}$

$19y = 19$

$y = 1$

Back-substitute.

$5x - 2y = 8$

$5x - 2(1) = 8$

$5x - 2 = 8$

$5x = 10$

$x = 2$

Solution set: $\{(2,1)\}$

30. $2x + 7y = 0$

$7x + 2y = 0$

Multiply the first equation by 7.
Multiply the second equation by -2.

$14x + 49y = 0$

$\underline{-14x - 4y = 0}$

$45y = 0$

$y = 0$

Back-substitute.

$2x + 7y = 0$

$2x + 7(0) = 0$

$2x = 0$

$x = 0$

Solution set: $\{(0,0)\}$

31. $x + 3y = -4$

$3x + 2y = 3$

Multiply the first equation by -3.

$-3x - 9y = 12$

$\underline{3x + 2y = \ 3}$

$-7y = 15$

$y = -\dfrac{15}{7}$

Instead of back-substituting $-\dfrac{15}{7}$ and
working with fractions, go back to the
original system. Multiply the first
equation by 2 and the second equation
by -3.

$2x + 6y = -8$

$\underline{-9x - 6y = -9}$

$-7x \qquad = -17$

$x \qquad = \dfrac{17}{7}$

Solution set: $\left\{\left(\dfrac{17}{7}, -\dfrac{15}{7}\right)\right\}$

32. $2x + y = 5$

$2x + y = 7$

Multiply the first equation by -1.
Don't change the second equation.

$-2x - y = -5$

$\underline{2x + y = 7}$

$0 = 2$ false

The false statement $0 = 2$ indicates
that the system has no solution.

Solution set: $\{\ \}$ or $\varnothing$

33. $3x - 4y = -1$

$-6x + 8y = 2$

Multiply the first equation by 2.
Don't change the second equation.

$6x - 8y = -2$

$\underline{-6x + 8y = \ 2}$

$0 = 0$ true

The true statement $0 = 0$ indicates that
the system is dependent and has
infinitely many solutions.

Solution set: $\{(x, y) \,|\, 3x - 4y = -1\}$ or

$\{(x, y) \,|\, -6x + 8y = 2\}$

34. $2x = 8y + 24$

$3x + 5y = 2$

Rewrite the first equation in the form
$Ax + By = C$.

$2x - 8y = 24$

Multiply this equation by 3.
Multiply the second equation by -2.

$6x - 24y = 72$

$\underline{-6y - 10y = -4}$

$-34y = 68$

$y = -2$

202

Back-substitute.

$3x + 5y = 2$

$3x + 5(-2) = 2$

$3x - 10 = 2$

$3x = 12$

$x = 4$

Solution set: $\{(4, -2)\}$

35. $5x - 7y = 2$

$3x = 4y$

Rewrite the second equation in the form $Ax + By = C$.

$3x - 4y = 0$

Multiply this equation by -5.

Multiply the first equation by 3.

$15x - 21y = 6$

$\underline{-15x + 20y = 0}$

$-y = 6$

$y = -6$

Back-substitute.

$3x - 4y = 0$

$3x - 4(-6) = 0$

$3x + 24 = 0$

$3x = -24$

$x = -8$

Solution set: $\{(-8, -6)\}$

36. $3x + 4y = -8$

$2x + 3y = -5$

Multiply the first equation by 2.

Multiply the second equation by -3.

$6x + 8y = -16$

$\underline{-6x - 9y = 15}$

$-y = -1$

$y = 1$

Back-substitute.

$3x + 4y = -8$

$3x + 4(1) = -8$

$3x + 4 = -8$

$3x = -12$

$x = -4$

Solution set: $\{(-4, 1)\}$

37. $6x + 8y = 39$

$y = 2x - 2$

Substitute $2x - 2$ for y in the first equation.

$6x + 8y = 39$

$6x + 8(2x - 2) = 39$

$6x + 16x - 16 = 39$

$22x - 16 = 39$

$22x = 55$

$x = \dfrac{55}{22} = \dfrac{5}{2}$

Back-substitute $\dfrac{5}{2}$ for x into the second equation of the system.

$y = 2x - 2$

$y = 2\left(\dfrac{5}{2}\right) - 2 = 5 - 2 = 3$

Solution set: $\left\{\left(\dfrac{5}{2}, 3\right)\right\}$

38. $x + 2y = 7$

$2x + y = 8$

Multiply the first equation by -2.
Don't change the second equation.

$-2x - 4y = -14$

$\underline{2x + y = 8}$

$-3y = -6$

$y = 2$

Back-substitute.

$x + 2y = 7$

$x + 2(2) = 7$

$x + 4 = 7$

$x = 3$

Solution set: $\{(3,2)\}$

39. $y = 2x - 3$

$y = -2x - 1$

Substitute $-2x - 1$ for y in the first equation

$-2x - 1 = 2x - 3$

$-4x - 1 = -3$

$-4x = -2$

$x = \dfrac{1}{2}$

Back-substitute.

$y = 2x - 3$

$y = 2\left(\dfrac{1}{2}\right) - 3 = -2$

Solution set: $\left\{\left(\dfrac{1}{2}, -2\right)\right\}$

40. $3x - 6y = 7$

$3x = 6y$

Solve the second equation for x.

$3x = 6y$

$x = 2y$

Substitute $2y$ for x in the first equation.

$3x - 6y = 7$

$3(2y) - 6y = 7$

$6y - 6y = 7$

$0 = 7$

The false statement $0 = 7$ indicates that the system has no solution.

Solution set: $\{\ \}$ or $\varnothing$

41. $y - 7 = 0$

$7x - 3y = 0$

Solve the first equation for y.

$y - 7 = 0$

$y = 7$

Substitute 7 for y in the second equation.

$7x - 3y = 0$

$7x - 3(7) = 0$

$7x - 21 = 0$

$7x = 21$

$x = 3$

Solution set: $\{(3, 7)\}$

42. Let x = the number of years of healthy life expectancy of people in Japan.
Let y = the number of years of healthy life expectancy of people in Switzerland.

The system to solve is

$x + y = 146.4$

$x - y = 0.8$

Add the two equations:

$x + y = 146.4$

$$x - y = 0.8$$
$$2x = 147.2$$
$$x = 73.6$$
Back substitute to find y:
$$x + y = 146.4$$
$$73.6 + y = 146.4$$
$$y = 72.8$$
The number of years of healthy life expectancy in Japan is 73.6 years and in Switzerland is 72.8 years.

43. Let x = the weight of a gorilla.
Let y = the weight of an orangutan.
$$2x + 3y = 1465$$
$$x + 2y = 815$$
Multiply the second equation by -2.
$$2x + 3y = 1465$$
$$-2x - 4y = -1630$$
$$-y = -165$$
$$y = 165$$
Back-substitute to find x.
$$x + 2(165) = 815$$
$$x + 330 = 815$$
$$x = 485$$
The weight of a gorilla is 485 pounds and the weight of an orangutan is 165 pounds.

44. Let x = the cholesterol content of one ounce of shrimp (in milligrams).
Let y = the cholesterol content in one ounce of scallops.
$$3x + 2y = 156$$
$$5x + 3y = 300 - 45$$
Simplify the second equation.
$$5x + 3y = 255$$
Multiply this equation by -2.
Multiply the first equation by 3.

$$9x + 6y = 468$$
$$-10x - 6y = -510$$
$$-x = -42$$
$$x = 42$$
Back-substitute.
$$3x + 2y = 156$$
$$3(42) + 2y = 156$$
$$126 + 2y = 156$$
$$2y = 30$$
$$y = 15$$
There are 42 mg of cholesterol in an ounce of shrimp and 15 mg in an ounce of scallops.

45. Let x = the length of a tennis table top.
Let y = the width.
Use the formula for perimeter of a rectangle to write the first equation and the other information in the problem to write the second equation.
$$2x + 2y = 28$$
$$4x - 3y = 21$$
Multiply the first equation by -2.
$$-4x + 4y = -56$$
$$4x - 3y = 21$$
$$-7y = -35$$
$$y = 5$$
Back-substitute
$$2x + 2(5) = 28$$
$$2x + 10 = 28$$
$$2x = 18$$
$$x = 9$$
The length is 9 feet and the width is 5 feet, so the dimensions of the table are 9 feet by 5 feet.

46. Let x = daily cost for room.
Let y = daily cost for car.
First plan: $3x + 2y = 360$
Second plan: $4x + 3y = 500$
Multiply the first equation by 3.
Multiply the second equation by –2.

$$9x + 6y = 1080$$
$$\underline{-8x - 6y = -1000}$$
$$x \quad = \quad 80$$

Back-substitute to find y.
$$3(80) + 2y = 360$$
$$240 + 2y = 360$$
$$2y = 120$$
$$y = 60$$

The cost per day is $80 for the room and $60 for the car.

47. Let x = the number of minutes of long-distance calls.
Let y = the monthly cost of a telephone plan.
Plan A: $y = 15 + 0.05x$
Plan B: $y = 10 + 0.075x$
To determine the amount of calling time that will result in the same cost for both plans, solve this system by the substitution method. Substitute $15 + 0.05x$ for y in the first equation.
$$15 + 0.05x = 10 + 0.075x$$
$$15 - 0.025x = 10$$
$$-0.025x = -5$$
$$\frac{-0.025x}{-0.025} = \frac{-5}{-0.025}$$
$$x = 200$$

Back-substitute to find y.
$$y = 15 + 0.05(200) = 25$$

The costs for the two plans will be equal for 200 minutes of long-distance calls per month. The cost of each plan will be $25.

48. Let x = the amount invested at 4%
Let y = the amount invested at 7%
$$x + \quad y = 9000$$
$$0.04x + 0.07y = 555$$
Multiply the first equation by –0.04 and add.
$$-0.04x - 0.04y = -360$$
$$\underline{0.04x + 0.07y = 555}$$
$$0.03y = 195$$
$$y = 6500$$

Back-substitute 6500 for y in one of the original equations to find x.
$$x + y = 9000$$
$$x + 6500 = 9000$$
$$x = 2500$$

There was $2500 invested at 4% and $6500 invested at 7%.

49. Let x = the amount of the 34% solution
Let y = the amount of the 4% solution
$$x + \quad y = 100$$
$$0.34x + 0.04y = 0.07(100)$$
Simplified, the system becomes:
$$x + \quad y = 100$$
$$0.34x + 0.04y = \quad 7$$
Multiply the first equation by –0.34 and add to the second equation.
$$-0.34x - 0.34y = -34$$
$$\underline{0.34x + 0.04y = \quad 7}$$
$$-0.30 = -27$$
$$y = 90$$

Back-substitute 90 for y to find x.
$$x + y = 100$$
$$x + 90 = 100$$
$$x = 10$$

10 ml of the 34% solution and 90 ml of the 4% solution must be used.

50. Let r = the speed of the plane in still air

Let w = the speed of the wind

	$r \cdot$	$t =$	d
With Wind	$r + w$	3	$3(r + w)$
Against Wind	$r - w$	4	$3(r - w)$

$3(r + w) = 2160$

$4(r - w) = 2160$

Simplified, the system becomes:

$3r + 3w = 2160$

$4r - 4w = 2160$

Multiply the first equation by 4, the second equation by 3, and solve by addition.

$12r + 12w = 8640$

$\underline{12r - 12w = 6480}$

$\qquad 24r = 15120$

$\qquad r = 630$

Back-substitute 630 for r to find w.

$3r + 3w = 2160$

$3(630) + 3w = 2160$

$1890 + 3w = 2160$

$3w = 270$

$w = 90$

The speed of the plane in still air is 630 miles per hour and the speed of the wind is 90 miles per hour.

51.

$x + y + z = 0$

$-3 + (-2) + 5 = 0$

$-5 + 5 = 0$

$0 = 0$

True

$2x - 3y + z = 5$

$2(-3) - 3(-2) + 5 = 5$

$-6 + 6 + 5 = 5$

$5 = 5$

True

$4x + 2y + 4z = 3$

$4(-3) + 2(-2) + 4(5) = 3$

$-12 - 4 + 20 = 3$

$4 = 3$

False

The ordered triple $(-3, -2, 5)$ does not satisfy all three equations, so it is not a solution.

52.

$2x - y + z = 1$

$3x - 3y + 4z = 5$

$4x - 2y + 3z = 4$

Multiply the first equation by -2 and add to the third.

$-4x + 2y - 2z = -2$

$\underline{4x - 2y + 3z = 4}$

$\qquad\qquad\qquad z = 2$

Back-substitute 2 for z in two of the original equations to obtain a system of two equations in two variables.

$2x - y + z = 1 \qquad 3x - 3y + 4z = 5$

$2x - y + 2 = 1 \qquad 3x - 3y + 4(2) = 5$

$2x - y = -1 \qquad\quad 3x - 3y + 8 = 5$

$\qquad\qquad\qquad\qquad\quad 3x - 3y = -3$

207

The system of two equations in two variables becomes:

$$2x - y = -1$$
$$3x - 3y = -3$$

Multiply the first equation by –3 and add solve by addition.

$$-6x + 3y = 3$$
$$\underline{3x - 3y = -3}$$
$$-3x = 0$$
$$x = 0$$

Back-substitute 0 for x to find y.

$$2x - y = -1$$
$$2(0) - y = -1$$
$$-y = -1$$
$$y = 1$$

The solution set is $\{(0, 1, 2)\}$.

53.
$$x + 2y - z = 5$$
$$2x - y + 3z = 0$$
$$2y + z = 1$$

Multiply the first equation by –2 and add to the second equation.

$$-2x - 4y + 2z = -10$$
$$\underline{2x - y + 3z = 0}$$
$$-5y + 5z = -10$$

We now have two equations in two variables.

$$2y + z = 1$$
$$-5y + 5z = -10$$

Multiply the first equation by –5 and solve by addition.

$$-10y - 5z = -5$$
$$\underline{-5y + 5z = -10}$$
$$-15y = -15$$
$$y = 1$$

Back-substitute 1 for y to find z.

$$2(1) + z = 1$$
$$2 + z = 1$$
$$z = -1$$

Back-substitute 1 for y and –1 for z to find x.

$$x + 2y - z = 5$$
$$x + 2(1) - (-1) = 5$$
$$x + 2 + 1 = 5$$
$$x + 3 = 5$$
$$x = 2$$

The solution set is $\{(2, 1, -1)\}$.

54.
$$3x - 4y + 4z = 7$$
$$x - y - 2z = 2$$
$$2x - 3y + 6z = 5$$

Multiply the second equation by –3 and add to the third equation.

$$-3x + 3y + 6z = -6$$
$$\underline{2x - 3y + 6z = 5}$$
$$-x + 12z = -1$$

Multiply the second equation by –4 and add to the first equation.

$$3x - 4y + 4z = 7$$
$$\underline{-4x + 4y + 8z = -8}$$
$$-x + 12z = -1$$

The system of two equations in two variables becomes:

$$-x + 12z = -1$$
$$-x + 12z = -1$$

The two equations in two variables are identical. The system is dependent. There are an infinite number of solutions to the system.

55. Use each ordered pair to write an equation as follows:
$$(x, y) = (1, 4)$$
$$y = ax^2 + bx + c$$
$$4 = a(1)^2 + b(1) + c$$
$$4 = a + b + c$$

$$(x, y) = (3, 20)$$
$$y = ax^2 + bx + c$$
$$20 = a(3)^2 + b(3) + c$$
$$20 = a(9) + 3b + c$$
$$20 = 9a + 3b + c$$

$$(x, y) = (-2, 25)$$
$$y = ax^2 + bx + c$$
$$25 = a(-2)^2 + b(-2) + c$$
$$25 = a(4) - 2b + c$$
$$25 = 4a - 2b + c$$

The system of three equations in three variables is:
$$a + b + c = 4$$
$$9a + 3b + c = 20$$
$$4a - 2b + c = 25$$
Multiply the first equation by −1 and add to the second equation.
$$-a - b - c = -4$$
$$\underline{9a + 3b + c = 20}$$
$$8a + 2b = 16$$
Multiply the first equation by −1 and add to the third equation.
$$-a - b - c = -4$$
$$\underline{4a - 2b + c = 25}$$
$$3a - 3b = 21$$
The system of two equations in two variables becomes:
$$8a + 2b = 16$$
$$3a - 3b = 21$$

Multiply the first equation by 3, the second equation by 2 and solve by addition.
$$24a + 6b = 48$$
$$\underline{6a - 6b = 42}$$
$$30a = 90$$
$$a = 3$$
Back-substitute 3 for a to find b.
$$3(3) - 3b = 21$$
$$9 - 3b = 21$$
$$-3b = 12$$
$$b = -4$$
Back-substitute 3 for a and −4 for b to find c.
$$a + b + c = 4$$
$$3 + (-4) + c = 4$$
$$-1 + c = 4$$
$$c = 5$$
The quadratic equation is
$$y = 3x^2 - 4x + 5.$$

56. $$x + y + z = 307$$
$$x - y = 32$$
$$y - z = 16$$
Add the first and third equations to eliminate z.
$$x + y + z = 307$$
$$\underline{y - z = 16}$$
$$x + 2y = 323$$
We obtain a system of two equations in two variables.
$$x - y = 32$$
$$x + 2y = 323$$
Multiply the first equation by 2 and solve by addition.

$$2x - 2y = 64$$
$$\underline{x + 2y = 323}$$
$$3x = 387$$
$$x = 129$$

Back-substitute 129 for x to find y.
$$x - y = 32$$
$$129 - y = 32$$
$$-y = -97$$
$$y = 97$$

Back-substitute 97 for y to find z.
$$y - z = 16$$
$$97 - z = 16$$
$$-z = -81$$
$$z = 81$$

The average yearly cost for veterinary care is \$129 per dog, \$97 per horse, and \$81 per cat.

Chapter 4 Test

1. $(5, -5)$
$$2x + y = 5$$
$$2(5) + (-5) = 5$$
$$10 + (-5) = 5$$
$$5 = 5 \text{ true}$$

$$x + 3y = -10$$
$$5 + 3(-5) = -10$$
$$5 + (-15) = -10$$
$$-10 = -10 \text{ true}$$

Since the ordered pair $(5, -5)$ satisfies both equations, it is a solution of the given system.

2. $(-3, 2)$
$$x + 5y = 7$$
$$-3 + 5(2) = 7$$
$$-3 + 10 = 7$$
$$7 = 7 \text{ true}$$

$$3x - 4y = 1$$
$$3(-3) - 4(2) = 1$$
$$-9 - 8 = 1$$
$$-17 = 1 \text{ false}$$

Since the ordered pair $(-3, 2)$ fails to satisfy *both* equations, it is not a solution of the given system.

3. $$x + y = 6$$
$$4x - y = 4$$
Graph both lines on the same axes.
$x + y = 6$:
x-intercept $= 6$; y-intercept $= 6$

$4x - y = 4$:
x-intercept: 1; y-intercept $= -4$

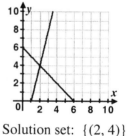

Solution set: $\{(2, 4)\}$

210

4. $2x + y = 8$

     $y = 3x - 2$

Graph both lines on the same axes.

$2x + y = 8$:

x-intercept = 4; y-intercept = 8

$y = 3x - 2$:

slope = 3; y-intercept = -2

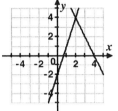

Solution set: $\{(2, 4)\}$

5. $x = y + 4$

     $3x + 7y = -18$

Substitute $y + 4$ for x in the second equation.

$$3x + 7y = -18$$
$$3(y + 4) + 7y = -18$$
$$3y + 12 + 7y = -18$$
$$10y + 12 = -18$$
$$10y = -30$$
$$y = -3$$

Back-substitute -3 for y in the first equation.

$x = y + 4$

$x = -3 + 4 = 1$

Solution set: $\{(1, -3)\}$

6. $2x - y = 7$

     $3x + 2y = 0$

Solve the first equation for y.

$$2x - y = 7$$
$$-y = -2x + 7$$
$$y = 2x - 7$$

Substitute $2x - 7$ for y in the second equation.

$$3x + 2y = 0$$
$$3x + 2(2x - 7) = 0$$
$$3x + 4x - 14 = 0$$
$$7x - 14 = 0$$
$$7x = 14$$
$$x = 2$$

Back-substitute 2 for x in the equation $3x + 2y = 0$.

$$3x + 2y = 0$$
$$3(2) + 2y = 0$$
$$6 + 2y = 0$$
$$2y = -6$$
$$y = -3$$

Solution set: $\{(2, -3)\}$

7. $2x - 4y = 3$

     $x = 2y + 4$

Substitute $2y + 4$ for x in the first equation.

$$2x - 4y = 3$$
$$2(2y + 4) - 4y = 3$$
$$4y + 8 - 4y = 3$$
$$8 = 3 \text{ false}$$

The false statement $8 = 3$ indicates that the system has no solution.

Solution set: $\{\ \}$ or $\varnothing$

8.
$$2x + y = 2$$
$$\underline{4x - y = -8}$$
$$6x \quad\;\; = -6$$
$$x = -1$$
Back-substitute.
$$2x + y = 2$$
$$2(-1) + y = 2$$
$$-2 + y = 2$$
$$y = 4$$
Solution set: $\{(-1, 4)\}$

9.
$$2x + 3y = 1$$
$$3x + 2y = -6$$
Multiply the first equation by 3.
Multiply the second equation by -2.
$$6x + 9y = 3$$
$$\underline{-6x - 4y = 12}$$
$$5y = 15$$
$$y = 3$$
Back-substitute.
$$2x + 3y = 1$$
$$2x + 3(3) = 1$$
$$2x + 9 = 1$$
$$2x = -8$$
$$x = -4$$
Solution set: $\{(-4, 3)\}$

10.
$$3x - 2y = 2$$
$$-9x + 6y = -6$$
Multiply the first equation by 3.
Don't change the second equation.
$$9x - 6y = 6$$
$$\underline{-9x + 6y = -6}$$
$$0 = 0 \text{ true}$$
The true statement $0 = 0$ indicates that the system is dependent and the equation has infinitely many solutions.
Solution set: $\{(x, y) \,|\, 3x - 2y = 2\}$ or $\{(x, y) \,|\, -9x + 6y = -6\}$

11. Let $x =$ the percentage of females named Mary.
Let $y =$ the percentage of females named Patricia.

The system is
$$x + y = 3.7$$
$$x - y = 1.5$$
Add the two equations:
$$x + y = 3.7$$
$$\underline{x - y = 1.5}$$
$$2x \quad\;\; = 5.2$$
$$x \quad\;\; = 2.6$$
Back substitute to find y:
$$2.6 + y = 3.7$$
$$y = 1.1$$
2.6% of females are named Mary.
1.1% of females are named Patricia.

12. Let $x =$ the number of minutes of long-distance calls.
Let $y =$ the monthly cost of a telephone plan.
Plan A: $y = 15 + 0.05x$
Plan B: $y = 5 + 0.07x$
To determine the amount of calling time that will result in the same cost for both plans, solve this system by the substitution method. Substitute $5 + 0.07x$ for y in the first equation.
$$5 + 0.07x = 15 + 0.05x$$
$$5 + 0.02x = 15$$
$$0.02x = 10$$
$$\frac{0.02x}{0.02} = \frac{10}{0.02}$$
$$x = 500$$
If $x = 500$, $y = 15 + 0.05(500) = 40$.

The cost of the two plans will be equal for 500 minutes per month. The cost of each plan will be $40.

13. Let x = the amount invested at 6%
Let y = the amount invested at 7%
$$x + \quad y = 9000$$
$$0.06x + 0.07y = 610$$
Multiply the first equation by –0.06 and add to the second equation.
$$x + \quad y = 9000$$
$$0.06x + 0.07y = 610$$

$$-0.06x - 0.06y = -540$$
$$\underline{0.06x + 0.07y = 610}$$
$$0.01y = 70$$
$$y = 7000$$
Back-substitute 7000 for y to find x.
$$x + y = 9000$$
$$x + 7000 = 9000$$
$$x = 2000$$
There is $2000 invested at 6% and $7000 invested at 7%.

14. Let x = ounces of 6% solution
Let y = ounces of 9% solution
$$x + y = 36$$
$$0.06x + 0.09y = 0.08(36)$$
Rewrite the system in standard form.
$$x + \quad y = 36$$
$$0.06x + 0.09y = 2.88$$
Multiply the first equation by –0.06 and add to the second equation.
$$-0.06x - 0.06y = -2.16$$
$$\underline{0.06x + 0.09y = 2.88}$$
$$0.03y = 0.72$$
$$y = 24$$
Back-substitute 24 for y to find x.
$$x + y = 36$$
$$x + 24 = 36$$
$$x = 12$$
12 ounces of 6% peroxide solution and 24 ounces of 9% peroxide solution must be used.

15. Let r = the speed of the paddleboat in still water.
Let w = the speed of the current.

	r ·	t =	d
With current	$r + w$	3	48
Against current	$r - w$	4	48

$$3(r + w) = 48$$
$$4(r - w) = 48$$
Simplified, the system becomes:
$$3r + 3w = 48$$
$$4r - 4w = 48$$
Multiply the first equation by 4, the second equation by 3, and solve by addition.
$$12r + 12w = 192$$
$$\underline{12r - 12w = 144}$$
$$24r = 336$$
$$r = 14$$
Back-substitute 14 for r to find w.
$$3r + 3w = 48$$
$$3(14) + 3w = 48$$
$$42 + 3w = 48$$
$$3w = 6$$
$$w = 2$$
The speed of the paddleboat in still water is 14 miles per hour and the speed of the current is 2 miles per hour.

16.
$$x + y + z = 6$$
$$3x + 4y - 7z = 1$$
$$2x - y + 3z = 5$$

Multiply the first equation by 7 and add to the second equation.
$$7x + 7y + 7z = 42$$
$$\underline{3x + 4y - 7z = 1}$$
$$10x + 11y = 43$$

Multiply the first equation by –3 and add to the third equation.
$$-3x - 3y - 3z = -18$$
$$\underline{2x - y + 3z = 5}$$
$$-x - 4y = -13$$

The system of two equations in two variables.
$$10x + 11y = 43$$
$$-x - 4y = -13$$

Multiply the second equation by 10 and solve by addition.
$$10x + 11y = 43$$
$$\underline{-10x - 40y = -130}$$
$$-29y = -87$$
$$y = 3$$

Back-substitute 3 for y to find x.
$$-x - 4y = -13$$
$$-x - 4(3) = -13$$
$$-x - 12 = -13$$
$$-x = -1$$
$$x = 1$$

Back-substitute 1 for x and 3 for y to find z.
$$x + y + z = 6$$
$$1 + 3 + z = 6$$
$$4 + z = 6$$
$$z = 2$$

The solution is $(1, 3, 2)$ and the solution set is $\{(1, 3, 2)\}$.

Chapter 4 Cumulative Review Exercises (Chapters 1-4)

1.
$$-14 - \left[18 - (6 - 10)\right]$$
$$= -14 - \left[18 - (-4)\right]$$
$$= -14 - \left[18 + 4\right]$$
$$= -14 - 22$$
$$= -14 + (-22)$$
$$= -36$$

2. $6(3x - 2) - (x - 1) = 18x - 12 - x + 1$
$$= 17x - 11$$

3. $17(x + 3) = 13 + 4(x - 10)$
$$17x + 51 = 13 + 4x - 40$$
$$17x + 51 = 4x - 27$$
$$13x = -78$$
$$x = -6$$

The solution set is $\{-6\}$.

4. $\dfrac{x}{4} - 1 = \dfrac{x}{5}$

To clear fractions, multiply both sides by 20.
$$20\left(\frac{x}{4} - 1\right) = 20\left(\frac{x}{5}\right)$$
$$5x - 20 = 4x$$
$$x - 20 = 0$$
$$x = 20$$

The solution set is $\{20\}$.

5. $A = P + Prt$ for t
$$A = P + Prt$$
$$A - P = Prt$$
$$\frac{A - P}{Pr} = \frac{Prt}{Pr}$$
$$\frac{A - P}{Pr} = t \quad \text{or} \quad t = \frac{A - P}{Pr}$$

214

6. $2x - 5 < 5x - 11$

$-3x - 5 < -11$

$-3x < -6$

$\dfrac{-3x}{-3} > \dfrac{-6}{-3}$

$x > 2$

The solution set is $\{x \mid x > 2\}$.

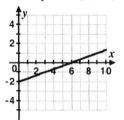

7. $x - 3y = 6$

x-intercept: 6

y-intercept: -2

Check point: $(3, -1)$

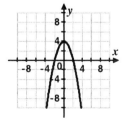

8.

x	$y = 4 - x^2$	(x,y)
-3	$y = 4 - (-3)^2 = -5$	$(-3, -5)$
-2	$y = 4 - (-2)^2 = 0$	$(-2, 0)$
-1	$y = 4 - (-1)^2 = 3$	$(-1, 3)$
0	$y = 4 - 0^2 = 4$	$(0, 4)$
1	$y = 4 - 1^2 = 3$	$(1, 3)$
2	$y = 4 - 2^2 = 0$	$(2, 0)$
3	$y = 4 - 3^2 = -5$	$(3, -5)$

Plot the ordered pairs from the table
and draw a smooth curve through them.

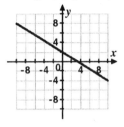

9. $y = -\dfrac{3}{5}x + 2$

slope $= -\dfrac{3}{5} = \dfrac{-3}{5}$; y-intercept $= 2$

Plot the point $(0,2)$. From this point,
move 3 units down (because -3 is
negative) and 5 units to the right to
reach the point $(5, -1)$. Draw a line
through $(0,2)$ and $(5, -1)$.

10. $3x - 4y = 8$

$4x + 5y = -10$

To solve this system by the addition
method, multiply the first equation by 4
and the second equation by -3. Then
add the results.

$12x - 16y = 32$

$\underline{-12x - 15y = 30}$

$-31y = 62$

$y = -2$

Back-substitute.

$3x - 4y = 8$

$3x - 4(-2) = 8$

$3x + 8 = 8$

$3x = 0$

$x = 0$

Solution set: $\{(0, -2)\}$

215

11. $2x - 3y = 9$

$\qquad y = 4x - 8$

To solve this system by the substitution method, substitute $4x - 8$ for y in the first equation.

$$2x - 3y = 9$$
$$2x - 3(4x - 8) = 9$$
$$2x - 12x + 24 = 9$$
$$-10x + 24 = 9$$
$$-10x = -15$$
$$x = \frac{15}{10} = \frac{3}{2}$$

Back-substitute $\dfrac{3}{2}$ for x in the second equation.

$$y = 4x - 8 = 4\left(\frac{3}{2}\right) - 8 = -2$$

Solution set: $\left\{ \left(\dfrac{3}{2}, -2 \right) \right\}$

12. $(5, -6)$ and $(6, -5)$

$$m = \frac{y_2 - y_1}{x_2 - x_1} = \frac{-5 - (-6)}{6 - 5} = \frac{1}{1} = 1$$

13. Passing through $(-1, 6)$ with slope $= -4$

point-slope form:

$$y - y_1 = m(x - x_1)$$
$$y - 6 = -4\left[x - (-1) \right]$$
$$y - 6 = -4(x + 1)$$

slope-intercept form:

$$y - 6 = -4x - 4$$
$$y = -4x + 2$$

14. Let $h =$ the length of the altitude of the triangle.

Use the formula for the area of a triangle.

$$A = \frac{1}{2}bh; \ A = 80, \ b = 16$$

$$80 = \frac{1}{2} \cdot 16 \cdot h$$

$$80 = 8h$$

$$10 = h$$

The altitude is 10 feet.

15. Let $x =$ the cost of one pen.

Let $y =$ the cost of one pad.

$$10x + 15y = 26$$

$$5x + 10y = 16$$

Multiply the second equation by -2, and add the result to the first equation.

$$\begin{array}{r} 10x + 15y = 26 \\ -10x - 20y = -32 \\ \hline -5y = -6 \end{array}$$

$$y = \frac{6}{5} = 1.20$$

Back-substitute 1.20 for y and solve for x.

$$10x + 15(1.20) = 26$$
$$10x + 18 = 26$$
$$10x = 8$$
$$x = \frac{8}{10} = 0.8$$

One pen costs \$0.80 and one pad costs \$1.20.

16. The integers in the given set are -93, 0, $\dfrac{7}{1}$ $(=7)$ and $\sqrt{100}$ $(=10)$.

17. In 2000, 20% of U.S. households had multiple computers.

18. Both lines are rising from left to right and the line for one computer is steeper, so the graph for one computer has the greater slope. This means that the percentage of U.S. households with one computer increased at a faster rate than the percentage with multiple computers over the years 1997 – 2002.

19. Let x = the number of years after 1997. Let y = the percentage of households having one computer.

$$y = 42 + 6x$$

$$90 = 42 + 6x$$

$$48 = 6x$$

$$8 = x$$

90% of U.S. households will have one computer 8 years after 1997, which will be in the year 2005.

20.

$$y = \frac{8}{3}x + 12$$

$$52 = \frac{8}{3}x + 12$$

$$40 = \frac{8}{3}x$$

$$\frac{3}{8}(40) = \frac{3}{8}\left(\frac{8}{3}\right)x$$

$$15 = x$$

52% of U.S. households will have multiple computers 15 years after 1997, which will be in the year 2012.

Chapter 5
Exponents and Polynomials

5.1 Exercise Set

1. $3x+7$ is a binomial of degree 1.

3. x^2-2x is a binomial of degree 3.

5. $8x^2$ is a monomial of degree 2.

7. 5 is a monomial. Because it is a nonzero constant, its degree is 0.

9. x^2-3x+4 is a trinomial of degree 2.

11. $7y^2-9y^4+5$ is a trinomial of degree 4.

13. $15x-7x^3$ is a binomial of degree 3.

15. $-9y^{23}$ is a monomial of degree 23.

17. $(9x+8)+(-17x+5)$

$9x+8+(-17)x+5$

$9x+8-17x+5$

$(9x-17x)+(8+5)$

$-8x+13$

19. $(4x^2+6x-7)+(8x^2+9x-2)$

$4x^2+6x-7+8x^2+9x-2$

$(4x^2+8x^2)+(6x+9x)+(-7-2)$

$12x^2+15x-9$

21. $(7x^2-11x)+(3x^2-x)$

$7x^2-11x+3x^2-x$

$(7x^2+3x^2)+(-11x-x)$

$10x^2-12x$

23. $(4x^2-6x+12)+(x^2+3x+1)$

$4x^2-6x+12+x^2+3x+1$

$(4x^2+x^2)+(-6x+3x)+(12+1)$

$5x^2-3x+13$

25. $(4y^3+7y-5)+(10y^2-6y+3)$

$(4y^3+7y-5)+(10y^2-6y+3)$

$4y^3+7y-5+10y^2-6y+3$

$4y^3+10y^2+(7y-6y)+(-5+3)$

$4y^3+10y^2+y-2$

27. $(2x^2-6x+7)+(3x^3-3x)$

$2x^2-6x+7+3x^3-3x$

$3x^3+2x^2+(-6x-3x)+7$

$3x^3+2x^2-9x+7$

29. $(4y^2+8y+11)+(-2y^3+5y+2)$

$4y^2+8y+11+(-2)y^3+5y+2$

$-2y^3+4y^2+(8y+5y)+(11+2)$

$-2y^3+4y^2+13y+9$

31. $(-2y^6+3y^4-y^2)+(-y^6+5y^4+2y^2)$

$-2y^6+3y^4-y^2-y^6+5y^4+2y^2$

$(-2y^6-y^6)+(3y^4+5y^4)+(-y^2+2y^2)$

$-3y^6+8y^4+y^2$

218

33.

$$\left(9x^3 - x^2 - x - \frac{1}{3}\right) + \left(x^3 + x^2 + x + \frac{4}{3}\right)$$

$$= \left(9x^3 + x^3\right) + \left(-x^2 + x^2\right) + \left(-x + x\right)$$

$$+ \left(-\frac{1}{3} + \frac{4}{3}\right)$$

$$= 10x^3 + \frac{3}{3} = 10x^3 + 1$$

35.

$$\left(\frac{1}{5}x^4 + \frac{1}{3}x^3 + \frac{3}{8}x^2 + 6\right)$$

$$+ \left(-\frac{3}{5}x^4 + \frac{2}{3}x^3 - \frac{1}{2}x^2 - 6\right)$$

$$= \left[\frac{1}{5}x^4 + \left(-\frac{3}{5}x^4\right)\right] + \left(\frac{1}{3}x^2 + \frac{2}{3}x^3\right)$$

$$+ \left[\frac{3}{8}x^2 + \left(-\frac{1}{2}x^2\right)\right] + \left[6 + (-6)\right]$$

$$= -\frac{2}{5}x^4 + x^3 - \frac{1}{8}x^2$$

37.

$$\left(0.03x^5 - 0.1x^3 + x + 0.03\right)$$

$$+ \left(-0.02x^5 + x^4 - 0.7x + 0.3\right)$$

$$= \left(0.03x^5 - 0.02x^5\right) + x^4 - 0.1x^3$$

$$+ \left(x - 0.07x\right) + \left(0.03 + 0.3\right)$$

$$= 0.01x^5 + x^4 - 0.1x^3 + 0.3x + 0.33$$

39. Add:

$$5y^3 - 7y^2$$
$$\underline{6y^3 + 4y^2}$$
$$11y^3 - 3y^2$$

41. Add:

$$3x^2 - 7x + 4$$
$$\underline{-5x^2 + 6x - 3}$$
$$-2x^2 - x + 1$$

43. Add:

$$\frac{1}{4}x^4 - \frac{2}{3}x^3 - 5$$
$$\underline{-\frac{1}{2}x^4 + \frac{1}{5}x^3 + 4.7}$$

$$\frac{1}{4}x^4 - \frac{10}{15}x^3 - 5.0$$
$$\underline{-\frac{1}{2}x^2 + \frac{3}{15}x^3 + 4.7}$$
$$-\frac{1}{4}x^4 - \frac{7}{15}x^3 - 0.3$$

45. Add:

$$y^3 + 5y^2 - 7y - 3$$
$$\underline{-2y^3 + 3y^2 + 4y - 11}$$
$$-y^3 + 8y^2 - 3y - 14$$

47. Add:

$$4x^3 - 6x^2 + 5x - 7$$
$$\underline{-9x^3 \qquad - 4x + 3}$$
$$-5x^3 - 6x^2 + x - 4$$

49. Add:

$$7x^4 - 3x^3 + x^2$$
$$\underline{x^3 - x^2 + 4x - 2}$$
$$7x^4 - 2x^3 \qquad + 4x - 2$$

51. Add:

$$7x^2 - 9x + 3$$
$$4x^2 + 11x - 2$$
$$\underline{-3x^2 + 5x - 6}$$
$$8x^2 + 7x - 5$$

53.

$$1.2x^3 - 3x^2 + 9.1$$
$$7.8x^3 - 3.1x^2 + 8$$
$$\underline{\qquad 1.2x^2 - 6}$$
$$9x^3 - 4.9x^2 + 11.1$$

55.
$$(x-8)-(3x+2)=(x-8)+(-3x-2)$$
$$=(x-3x)+(-8-2)$$
$$=-2x-10$$

57.
$$(x^2-5x-3)-(6x^2-4x+9)$$
$$=(x^2-5x-3)+(-6x^2+4x-9)$$
$$=(x^2-6x^2)+(-5x-4x)+(-3-9)$$
$$=-5x^2-9x-12$$

59.
$$(x^2-5x)-(6x^2-4x)$$
$$=(x^2-5x)+(-6x^2+4x)$$
$$=(x^2-6x^2)+(-5x+4x)$$
$$=-5x^2-x$$

61.
$$(x^2-8x-9)-(5x^2-4x-3)$$
$$=(x^2-8x-9)+(-5x^2+4x+3)$$
$$=-4x^2-4x-6$$

63.
$$(y-8)-(3y-2)=(y-8)+(-3y+2)$$
$$=-2y-6$$

65.
$$(6y^3+2y^2-y-11)-(y^2-8y+9)$$
$$=(6y^3+2y^2-y-11)$$
$$+(-y^2+8y-9)$$
$$=6y^3+y^2+7y-20$$

67.
$$(7n^3-n^7-8)-(6n^3-n^7-10)$$
$$=(7n^3-n^7-8)+(-6n^3+n^7+10)$$
$$=(7n^3-6n^3)+(-n^7+n^7)+(-8+10)$$
$$=n^3+2$$

69.
$$(y^6-y^3)-(y^2-y)$$
$$=(y^6-y^3)+(-y^2+y)$$
$$=y^6-y^3-y^2+y$$

71.
$$(7x^4+4x^2+5x)-(-19x^4-5x^2-x)$$
$$=(7x^4+4x^2+5x)+(19x^4+5x^2+x)$$
$$=26x^4+9x^2+6x$$

73.
$$\left(\frac{3}{7}x^3-\frac{1}{5}x-\frac{1}{3}\right)-\left(-\frac{2}{7}x^3+\frac{1}{4}x-\frac{1}{3}\right)$$
$$=\left(\frac{3}{7}x^3-\frac{1}{5}x-\frac{1}{3}\right)+\left(\frac{2}{7}x^3-\frac{1}{4}x+\frac{1}{3}\right)$$
$$=\left(\frac{3}{7}x^3+\frac{2}{7}x^3\right)+\left(-\frac{1}{5}x-\frac{1}{4}x\right)$$
$$+\left(-\frac{1}{3}+\frac{1}{3}\right)$$
$$=\left(\frac{3}{7}x^3+\frac{2}{7}x^3\right)+\left(-\frac{4}{20}x-\frac{5}{20}x\right)$$
$$=\frac{5}{7}x^3-\frac{9}{20}x$$

75. Subtract:
$$\begin{array}{c}7x+1\\-(3x-5)\end{array} \longrightarrow \begin{array}{c}7x+1\\+\ -3x+5\\\hline 4x+6\end{array}$$

77. Subtract:
$$\begin{array}{c}7x^2-3\\-(-3x^2+4)\end{array} \longrightarrow \begin{array}{c}7x^2-3\\+\ 3x^2-4\\\hline 10x^2-7\end{array}$$

79. Subtract:
$$\begin{array}{c}7y^2-5y+2\\-(11y^2+2y-3)\end{array} \longrightarrow \begin{array}{c}7y^2-5y+2\\+-11y^2-2y+3\\\hline -4y^2-7y+5\end{array}$$

81. Subtract:

$7x^3 + 5x^2 - 3$

$-\left(-2x^3 - 6x^2 + 5\right)$

$\dfrac{\begin{array}{r} 7x^3 + 5x^2 - 3 \\ 2x^3 + 6x^2 - 5 \end{array}}{9x^3 + 11x^2 - 8}$

83. Subtract:

$5y^3 + 6y^2 - 3y + 10$

$-\left(6y^3 - 2y^2 - 4y - 4\right)$

$\begin{array}{r} 5y^3 + 6y^2 - 3y + 10 \\ +{-6y^3 + 2y^2 + 4y + 4} \end{array}$

$\overline{-y^3 + 8y^2 + \quad y + 14}$

85. Subtract:

$7x^4 - 3x^3 + 2x^2$

$-\left(\quad - x^3 - x^2 + x - 2 \right)$

$\begin{array}{r} 7x^4 - 3x^3 + 2x^2 \\ + \quad\quad x^3 + \ x^2 - x + 2 \end{array}$

$7x^4 - 2x^3 + 3x^2 - x + 2$

87. $\quad 0.07x^3 - 0.01x^2 + 0.02x$

$-\left(0.02x^3 - 0.03x^2 - \quad x\right)$

$\begin{array}{r} 0.07x^3 - 0.01x^2 + 0.02x \\ +{-0.02x^3 + 0.03x^2 + \quad x} \end{array}$

$0.05x^3 + 0.02x^2 + 1.02x$

89. $\left[\left(4x^2 + 7x - 5\right) - \left(2x^2 - 10x + 3\right)\right]$

$\quad -\left(x^2 + 5x - 8\right)$

$= \left[2x^2 + 17x - 8\right] - x^2 - 5x + 8$

$= x^2 + 12x$

90. $\left[\left(10x^3 - 5x^2 + 4x + 3\right) - \left(-3x^3 - 4x^2 + x\right)\right]$

$\quad -\left(7x^3 - 5x + 4\right)$

$= \left[13x^3 - x^2 + 3x + 3\right] - 7x^3 + 5x - 4$

$= 6x^3 - x^2 + 8x - 1$

91. $\left[\left(4y^2 - 3y + 8\right) - \left(5y^2 + 7y - 4\right)\right]$

$\quad -\left[\left(8y^2 + 5y - 7\right) + \left(-10y^2 + 4y + 3\right)\right]$

$= \left[-y^2 - 10y + 12\right] - \left[-2y^2 + 9y - 4\right]$

$= y^2 - 19y + 16$

92. $\left[\left(7y^2 - 4y + 2\right) - \left(12y^2 + 3y - 5\right)\right]$

$\quad -\left[\left(5y^2 - 2y - 8\right) + \left(-7y^2 + 10y - 13\right)\right]$

$= \left[-5y^2 - 7y + 7\right] - \left[-2y^2 + 8y - 21\right]$

$= -3y^2 - 15y + 28$

93. $\left[\left(4x^3 + x^2\right) + \left(-x^3 + 7x - 3\right)\right]$

$\quad -\left(x^3 - 2x^2 + 2\right)$

$\left[3x^3 + x^2 + 7x - 3\right] + \left(-x^3 + 2x^2 - 2\right)$

$2x^3 + 3x^2 + 7x - 5$

94. $\left[\left(2x^2 + 4x - 7\right) + \left(-5x^3 - 2x - 3\right)\right]$

$\quad -\left(-3x^3 - 7x + 5\right)$

$\left[-5x^3 + 2x^2 + 2x - 10\right] + \left(3x^3 + 7x - 5\right)$

$-2x^3 + 2x^2 + 9x - 15$

95. $\left[\left(-5y^2 + y^2 + 4y^3\right) - \left(-8 - y + 7y^3\right)\right]$

$\quad -\left(-y^2 + 7y^3\right)$

$\left[-3y^3 + y^2 + y + 3\right] + \left(y^2 - 7y^3\right)$

$-10y^3 + 2y^2 + y + 3$

221

96. $\left[\left(-6+y^2+5y^3\right)-\left(-12-y+13y^3\right)\right]$

$-\left(-2y^2+8y^3\right)$

$\left[-8y^3+y^2+y+6\right]+\left(2y^2-8y^3\right)$

$-16y^3+3y^2+y+6$

97. Let y = the number of viral particles (in billions) .
Let x = the number of days of invasion of the viral particles

$y=-0.75x^4+3x^3+5$

Substitute in $x = 0$ to find the number of particles after 0 days.

$y=-0.75(0)^4+3(0)^3+5=5$

There are 5 billion particles after 0 days.
Substitute in $x = 1$ to find the number of particles after 1 day.

$y=-0.75(1)^4+3(1)^3+5=7.25$

There are 7.25 billion particles after 1 day.
Substitute in $x = 2$ to find the number of particles after 2 days.

$y=-0.75(2)^4+3(2)^3+5=17$

There are 17 billion particles after 2 days.
Substitute in $x = 3$ to find the number of particles after 3 days.

$y=-0.75(3)^4+3(3)^3+5=25.25$

There are 25.25 billion particles after 3 days.
Substitute in $x = 4$ to find the number of particles after 4 days.

$y=-0.75(4)^4+3(4)^3+5=5$

There are 5 billion particles after 4 days.
Maximum number of particles occurs after 3 days.
We should feel better after 4 days since the number of particles decreases back to the original amount.

99. Let y = cigarette consumption
Let x = the number of years after 1940.

$y=-2.3x^2+135.3x+2191$

To find cigarette consumption in the year 2000, substitute $x = 60$ in the formula since $1940 + 60 = 2000$.

$y=-2.3(60)^2+135.3(60)+2191=2029$

To compare the formula and the data, calculate the y-values for the years shown on the graph and compare the these values to the corresponding y-values.

Year	x	y-values from graph	y-values from formula
1940	0	2000	2191
1950	1	3500	2324
1960	2	4200	2452.4
1970	3	4000	2576.2
1980	4	3900	2695.4
1990	5	2800	2810
2000	6	2100	2920

Answers will vary.

101. Let y = median women's earnings as a percentage of median men's earnings.
Let x = the number of years after 1960.

$y=0.012x^2-0.16x+60$

(a) 73%
(b) To find median women's earnings as a percentage of median men's earnings in the year 2000, substitute $x = 40$ in the formula since $1960 + 40 = 2000$.

$y=0.012(40)^2-0.16(40)+60=72.8$

Women's earnings as a percentage of median men's earnings in the year 2000 was 72.8%.

(c) $\left(\dfrac{\$27,355}{\$37,339}\right)100\%=73.3\%$

Answers from parts (a) and (b) are within 0.5% of the actual percentage.

103. Let y = age in human years
Let x = age in dog years
$$y = -0.001618x^4 + 0.077326x^3$$
$$-1.2367x^2 + 11.460x + 2.914$$

(a) A 6 year old dog is 42 human years old according to the graph.
(b) To find age in human years for a 6 year old, substitute $x = 6$ in the formula.
$$y = -0.001618(6)^4 + 0.077326(6)^3$$
$$-1.2367(6)^2 + 11.460(6) + 2.914$$
$$= 41.8$$
To the nearest tenth, a 6 year old dog is 41.8 human years old according to the formula.

105. A 3 year old dog is 25 human years old according to the graph.

117. $5x^2 - 2x + 1 - (-3x^2 - x - 2)$
$$= (5x^2 - 2x + 1) + (3x^2 + x + 2)$$
$$= 8x^2 - x + 3$$
so the polynomial is $-3x^2 - x - 2$.

119. In a polynomial of degree 3, the highest degree term has an exponent of 3. The highest degree term of the sum will be the sum of two terms of degree 3, which will be a term of degree 3 or could be 0. It is impossible to get a term degree of 4, so it is impossible to get a polynomial of degree 4.

120. $(-10)(-7) \div (1 - 8) = (-10)(-7) \div (-7)$
$$= 70 \div (-7) = -10$$

121. $-4.6 - (-10.2) = -4.6 + 10.2 = 5.6$

122.
$$3(x - 2) = 9(x + 2)$$
$$3x - 6 = 9x + 18$$
$$3x - 6 - 9x = 9x + 18 - 9x$$
$$-6x - 6 = 18$$
$$-6x - 6 + 6 = 18 + 6$$
$$-6x = 24$$
$$\frac{-6x}{-6} = \frac{24}{-6}$$
$$x = -4$$
The solution set is $\{-4\}$.

5.2 Exercise Set

1. $x^{15} \cdot x^3 = x^{15+3} = x^{18}$

3. $y \cdot y^{11} = y^1 \cdot y^{11} = y^{1+11} = y^{12}$

5. $x^2 \cdot x^6 \cdot x^3 = x^{2+6+3} = x^{11}$

7. $7^9 \cdot 7^{10} = 7^{9+10} = 7^{19}$

9. $\left(6^9\right)^{10} = 6^{9 \cdot 10} = 6^{90}$

11. $\left(x^{15}\right)^3 = x^{15 \cdot 3} = x^{45}$

13. $\left[(-20)^3\right]^3 = (-20)^{3 \cdot 3} = (-20)^9$

15. $(2x)^3 = 2^3 \cdot x^3 = 8x^3$

17. $(-5x)^2 = (-5)^2 x^2 = 25x^2$

19. $(4x^3)^2 = 4^2 (x^3)^2 = 16x^6$

21. $(-2y^6)^4 = (-2)^4 (y^6)^4 = 16y^{24}$

223

23. $\left(-2x^7\right)^5 = \left(-2\right)^5\left(x^7\right)^5 = -32x^{35}$

25. $\left(7x\right)\left(2x\right) = \left(7\cdot 2\right)\left(x\cdot x\right) = 14x^2$

27. $\left(6x\right)\left(4x^2\right) = \left(6\cdot 4\right)\left(x\cdot x^2\right) = 24x^3$

29. $\left(-5y^4\right)\left(3y^3\right) = \left(-5\cdot 3\right)\left(y^4\cdot y^3\right) = -15y^7$

31. $\left(-\dfrac{1}{2}a^3\right)\left(-\dfrac{1}{4}a^2\right) = \left(-\dfrac{1}{2}\cdot -\dfrac{1}{4}\right)\left(a^3\cdot a^2\right)$

$\qquad = \dfrac{1}{8}a^5$

33. $\left(2x^2\right)\left(-3x\right)\left(8x^4\right)$

$\qquad = \left(2\cdot -3\cdot 8\right)\left(x^2\cdot x\cdot x^4\right) = -48x^7$

35. $4x\left(x+3\right) = 4x\cdot x + 4x\cdot 3$

$\qquad = 4x^2 + 12x$

37. $x\left(x-3\right) = x\cdot x - x\cdot 3$

$\qquad = x^2 - 3x$

39. $2x\left(x-6\right) = 2x\cdot x - 2x\cdot 6$

$\qquad = 2x^2 - 12x$

41. $-4y\left(3y+5\right) = -4y\cdot 3y - 4y\cdot 5$

$\qquad = -12y^2 - 20y$

43. $4x^2\left(x+2\right) = 4x^2\cdot x + 4x^2\cdot 2$

$\qquad = 4x^3 + 8x^2$

45. $2y^2\left(y^2+3y\right) = 2y^2\cdot y^2 + 2y^2\cdot 3y$

$\qquad = 2y^4 + 6y^3$

47. $2y^2\left(3y^2-4y+7\right)$

$\qquad = 2y^2\left(3y^2\right) + 2y^2\left(-4y\right) + 2y^2\left(7\right)$

$\qquad = 6y^4 - 8y^3 + 14y^2$

49. $\left(3x^3+4x^2\right)\left(2x\right) = 3x^3\cdot 2x + 4x^2\cdot 2x$

$\qquad = 6x^4 + 8x^3$

51. $\left(x^2+5x-3\right)\left(-2x\right)$

$\qquad = x^2\left(-2x\right) + 5x\left(-2x\right) - 3\left(-2x\right)$

$\qquad = -2x^3 - 10x^2 + 6x$

53. $-3x^2\left(-4x^2+x-5\right)$

$\qquad = -3x^2\left(-4x^2\right) - 3x^2\left(x\right) - 3x^2\left(-5\right)$

$\qquad = 12x^4 - 3x^3 + 15x^2$

55. $\left(x+3\right)\left(x+5\right)$

$\qquad = x\left(x+5\right) + 3\left(x+5\right)$

$\qquad = x\cdot x + x\cdot 5 + 3\cdot x + 3\cdot 5$

$\qquad = x^2 + 5x + 3x + 15$

$\qquad = x^2 + 8x + 15$

57. $\left(2x+1\right)\left(x+4\right)$

$\qquad = 2x\left(x+4\right) + 1\left(x+4\right)$

$\qquad = 2x^2 + 8x + x + 4$

$\qquad = 2x^2 + 9x + 4$

59. $\left(x+3\right)\left(x-5\right) = x\left(x-5\right) + 3\left(x-5\right)$

$\qquad = x^2 - 5x + 3x - 15$

$\qquad = x^2 - 2x - 15$

61. $\left(x-11\right)\left(x+9\right) = x\left(x+9\right) - 11\left(x+9\right)$

$\qquad = x^2 + 9x - 11x - 99$

$\qquad = x^2 - 2x - 99$

224

63. $(2x-5)(x+4)$

$$= 2x(x+4)-5(x+4)$$
$$= 2x^2+8x-5x-20$$
$$= 2x^2+3x-20$$

65. $\left(\dfrac{1}{4}x+4\right)\left(\dfrac{3}{4}x-1\right)$

$$= \dfrac{1}{4}x\left(\dfrac{3}{4}x-1\right)+4\left(\dfrac{3}{4}x-1\right)$$
$$= \dfrac{1}{4}x\cdot\dfrac{3}{4}x+\dfrac{1}{4}x(-1)$$
$$+4\left(\dfrac{3}{4}x\right)+4(-1)$$
$$= \dfrac{3}{16}x^2-\dfrac{1}{4}x+\dfrac{12}{4}x-4$$
$$= \dfrac{3}{16}x^2+\dfrac{11}{4}x-4$$

67. $(x+1)(x^2+2x+3)$

$$= x(x^2+2x+3)+1(x^2+2x+3)$$
$$= x^3+2x^3+3x+x^2+2x+3$$
$$= x^3+3x^2+5x+3$$

69. $(y-3)(y^2-3y+4)$

$$= y(y^2-3y+4)-3(y^2-3y+4)$$
$$= y^3-3y^2+4y-3y^2+9y-12$$
$$= y^3-6y^2+13y-12$$

71. $(2a-3)(a^2-3a+5)$

$$= 2a(a^2-3a+5)-3(a^2-3a+5)$$
$$= 2a^3-6a^2+10a-3a^2+9a-15$$
$$= 2a^3-9a^2+19a-15$$

73. $(x+1)(x^3+2x^2+3x+4)$

$$= x(x^3+2x^2+3x+4)$$
$$+1(x^3+2x^2+3x+4)$$
$$= x^4+2x^3+3x^2+4x+x^3+2x^2$$
$$+3x+4$$
$$= x^4+(2x^3+x^3)+(3x^2+2x^2)$$
$$+(4x+3x)+4$$
$$= x^4+3x^3+5x^2+7x+4$$

75. $\left(x-\dfrac{1}{2}\right)(4x^3-2x^2+5x-6)$

$$= x(4x^3-2x^2+5x-6)$$
$$-\dfrac{1}{2}(4x^3-2x^2+5x-6)$$
$$= 4x^4-2x^3+5x^2-6x-2x^3+x^2-\dfrac{5}{2}x+3$$
$$= 4x^4-4x^3+6x^2-\dfrac{17}{2}x+3$$

77. $(x^2+2x+1)(x^2-x+2)$

$$= x^2(x^2-x+2)+2x(x^2-x+2)$$
$$+1(x^2-x+2)$$
$$= x^4-x^3+2x^2+2x^3-2x^2+4x$$
$$+x^2-x+2$$
$$= x^4+x^3+x^2+3x+2$$

79.

$$\begin{array}{r}
x^2-5x+3 \\
x+8 \\
\hline
8x^2-40x+24 \\
x^3-5x^2+3x \\
\hline
x^3+3x^2-37x+24
\end{array}$$

225

81.

$$x^2 - 3x + 9$$
$$\underline{2x - 3}$$
$$-3x^2 + 9x - 27$$
$$\underline{2x^3 - 6x^2 + 18x}$$
$$2x^3 - 9x^2 + 27x - 27$$

83.

$$2x^3 + x^2 + 2x + 3$$
$$\underline{x + 4}$$
$$8x^3 + 4x^2 + 8x + 12$$
$$\underline{2x^4 + x^3 + 2x^2 + 3x}$$
$$2x^4 + 9x^3 + 6x^2 + 11x + 12$$

85.

$$4z^3 - 2z^2 + 5z - 4$$
$$\underline{3z - 2}$$
$$-8z^3 + 4z^2 - 10z + 8$$
$$\underline{12z^4 - 5z^3 + 15z^2 - 12z}$$
$$12z^4 - 14z^3 + 19z^2 - 22z + 8$$

87.

$$7x^3 - 5x^2 + 6x$$
$$\underline{3x^2 - 4x}$$
$$-28x^4 + 20x^3 - 24x^2$$
$$\underline{21x^5 - 15x^4 + 18x^3}$$
$$21x^5 - 43x^4 + 38x^3 - 24x^2$$

89.

$$2y^5 -3y^3 + y^2 - 2y + 3$$
$$\underline{2y - 1}$$
$$-2y^5 + 3y^3 - y^2 + 2y - 3$$
$$\underline{4y^6 - 6y^4 + 2y^3 - 4y^2 + 6y}$$
$$4y^6 - 2y^5 - 6y^4 + 5y^3 - 5y^2 + 8y - 3$$

91.

$$x^2 + 7x - 3$$
$$\underline{x^2 - x - 1}$$
$$-x^2 - 7x + 3$$
$$-x^3 - 7x^2 + 3x$$
$$\underline{x^4 + 7x^3 - 3x^2}$$
$$x^4 + 6x^3 - 11x^2 - 4x + 3$$

93. $(x+4)(x-5) - (x+3)(x-6)$

$$= (x^2 - x - 20) - (x^2 - 3x - 18)$$
$$= (x^2 - x - 20) + (-x^2 + 3x + 18)$$
$$= 2x - 2$$

94. $(x+5)(x-6) - (x+2)(x-9)$

$$= (x^2 - x - 30) - (x^2 - 7x - 18)$$
$$= (x^2 - x - 30) + (-x^2 + 7x + 18)$$
$$= 6x - 12$$

95. $4x^2(5x^3 + 3x - 2) - 5x^3(x^2 - 6)$

$$= (20x^5 + 12x^3 - 8x^2) + (-5x^5 + 30x^3)$$
$$= 15x^5 + 42x^3 - 8x^2$$

96. $3x^2(6x^3 + 2x - 3) - 4x^3(x^2 - 5)$

$$= (18x^5 + 6x^3 - 9x^2) + (-4x^5 + 20x^3)$$
$$= 14x^5 + 26x^3 - 9x^2$$

97. $(y+1)(y^2 - y + 1) + (y-1)(y^2 + y + 1)$

$$= y(y^2 - y + 1) + 1(y^2 - y + 1)$$
$$ + y(y^2 + y + 1) - 1(y^2 + y + 1)$$
$$= y^3 - y^2 + y + y^2 - y + 1$$
$$ + y^3 + y^2 + y - y^2 - y - 1$$
$$= 2y^3$$

226

98. $(y+1)(y^2-y+1)-(y-1)(y^2+y+1)$

$= y(y^2-y+1)+1(y^2-y+1)$

$\quad -y(y^2+y+1)+1(y^2+y+1)$

$= y^3-y^2+y+y^2-y+1$

$\quad -y^3-y^2-y+y^2+y+1$

$= 2$

99. $(y+6)^2-(y-2)^2$

$= (y+6)(y+6)-(y-2)(y-2)$

$= (y^2+12y+36)-(y^2-4y+4)$

$= 16y+32$

100. $(y+5)^2-(y-4)^2$

$= (y+5)(y+5)-(y-4)(y-4)$

$= (y^2+10y+25)-(y^2-8y+16)$

$= 18y+9$

101. Use the formula for the area of a rectangle.

$A = l \cdot w$

$A = (x+5)(2x-3)$

$\quad = x(2x-3)+5(2x-3)$

$\quad = 2x^2-3x+10x-15$

$\quad = 2x^2+7x-15$

The area of the rug is $(2x^2+7x-15)$ square feet.

103. **a.** $(x+2)(2x+1)$

b. $x \cdot 2x + 2 \cdot 2x + x \cdot 1 + 2 \cdot 1$

$\quad = 2x^2+4x+x+2$

$\quad = 2x^2+5x+2$

c. $(x+2)(2x+1) = x(2x+1)+2(2x+1)$

$\quad = 2x^2+x+4x+2$

$\quad = 2x^2+5x+2$

105. When multiplying numbers with the same base, keep the base and add the exponents. Example: $2^3 \cdot 2^5 = 2^{3+5} = 2^8$

107. To simplify a product raised to a power, raise each factor of the product to the power, and then multiply the results. Example: $(5 \cdot x)^2 = 5^2 \cdot x^2$

109. To multiply a monomial and a polynomial, distribute the monomial over the polynomial.
Example: $2y^2(3y^2-4y+7)$

$\quad = 2y^2(3y^2)+2y^2(-4y)+2y^2(7)$

$\quad = 6y^4-8y^3+14y^2$

111. The first is addition of two monomials of degree 2.
$2x^2+3x^2 = 5x^2$
The second is the multiplication of two monomials of degree 2.
$(2x^2)(3x^2) = (2 \cdot 3)(x^2 \cdot x^2) = 6x^{2+2} = 6x^4$

113. Answers will vary.

115. The area of the outer square is
$(x+4)(x+4) = x(x+4)+4(x+4)$

$\quad = x^2+4x+4x+16$

$\quad = x^2+8x+16$

The area of the inner square is x^2. The area of the shaded region is the difference between the areas of the two squares, which is

$(x^2+8x+16)-x^2 = 8x+16$

117. $(-8x^4)\left(-\dfrac{1}{4}xy^3\right) = 2x^5y^3$, so the missing factor is $-8x^4$.

227

118.
$$4x - 7 > 9x - 2$$
$$4x - 7 - 9x > 9x - 2 - 9x$$
$$-5x - 7 > -2$$
$$-5x - 7 + 7 > -2 + 7$$
$$-5x > 5$$
$$\frac{-5x}{5} < \frac{5}{-5}$$
$$x < -1$$
Solution: $\{x | x < -1\}$

119. $3x - 2y = 6$
x-intercept: 2
y-intercept: -3
checkpoint: $(4,3)$

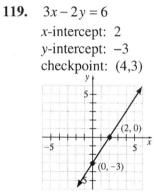

120. $(-2,8)$ and $(1,6)$
$$m = \frac{y_2 - y_1}{x_2 - x_2}$$
$$= \frac{6 - 8}{1 - (-2)} = \frac{-2}{3} = -\frac{2}{3}$$

5.3 Exercise Set

1. $(x + 4)(x + 6) = x^2 + 6x + 4x + 24$
$$= x^2 + 10x + 24$$

3. $(y - 7)(y + 3) = y^2 + 3y - 7y - 21$
$$= y^2 - 4y - 21$$

5. $(2x - 3)(x + 5) = 2x^2 + 10x - 3x - 15$
$$= 2x^2 + 7x - 15$$

7. $(4y + 3)(y - 1) = 4y^2 - 4y + 3y - 3$
$$= 4y^2 - y - 3$$

9. $(2x - 3)(5x + 3) = 10x^2 + 6x - 15x - 9$
$$= 10x^2 - 9x - 9$$

11. $(3y - 7)(4y - 5) = 12y^2 - 15y - 28y + 35$
$$= 12y^2 - 43y + 35$$

13. $(7 + 3x)(1 - 5x) = 7 - 35x + 3x - 15x^2$
$$= -15x^2 - 32x + 7$$

15. $(5 - 3y)(6 - 2y) = 30 - 10y - 18y + 6y^2$
$$= 30 - 28y + 6y^2$$
$$= 6y^2 - 28y + 30$$

17. $(5x^2 - 4)(3x^2 - 7)$
$$= (5x^2)(3x^2) + (5x^2)(-7)$$
$$+ (-4)(3x^2) + (-4)(-7)$$
$$= 15x^4 - 35x^2 - 12x^2 + 28$$
$$= 15x^4 - 47x^2 + 28$$

19. $(6x - 5)(2 - x) = 12x - 6x^2 - 10 + 5x$
$$= -6x^2 + 17x - 10$$

21. $(x + 5)(x^2 + 3) = x^3 + 3x + 5x^2 + 15$
$$= x^3 + 5x^2 + 3x + 15$$

23. $(8x^3 + 3)(x^2 + 5) = 8x^5 + 40x^3 + 3x^2 + 15$

25. $(x + 3)(x - 3) = x^2 - 3^2 = x^2 - 9$

27. $(3x + 2)(3x - 2) = (3x)^2 - 2^2 = 9x^2 - 4$

29. $(3r-4)(3r+4) = (3r)^2 - 4^2$
$$= 9r^2 - 16$$

31. $(3+r)(3-r) = 3^2 - r^2 = 9 - r^2$

33. $(5-7x)(5+7x) = 5^2 - (7x^2) = 25 - 49x^2$

35. $\left(2x+\dfrac{1}{2}\right)\left(2x-\dfrac{1}{2}\right) = (2x)^2 - \left(\dfrac{1}{2}\right)^2$
$$= 4x^2 - \dfrac{1}{4}$$

37. $\left(y^2+1\right)\left(y^2-1\right) = \left(y^2\right)^2 - 1^2 = y^4 - 1$

39. $\left(r^3+2\right)\left(r^3-2\right) = \left(r^3\right)^2 - 2^2 = r^6 - 4$

41. $\left(1-y^4\right)\left(1+y^4\right) = 1^2 - \left(y^4\right)^2 = 1 - y^8$

43. $\left(x^{10}+5\right)\left(x^{10}-5\right) = \left(x^{10}\right)^2 - 5^2$
$$= x^{20} - 25$$

45. $(x+2)^2 = x^2 + 2(2x) + 2^2$
$$= x^2 + 4x + 4$$

47. $(2x+5)^2 = (2x)^2 + 2(2x)(5) + 5^2$
$$= 4x^2 + 20x + 25$$

49. $(x-3)^2 = x^2 - 2(3x) + 3^2$
$$= x^2 - 6x + 9$$

51. $(3y-4)^2 = (3y)^2 - 2(3y)(4) + 4^2$
$$= 9y^2 - 24y + 16$$

53. $\left(4x^2-1\right)^2 = \left(4x^2\right)^2 - 2\left(4x^2\right)(1) + 1^2$
$$= 16x^4 - 8x^2 + 1$$

55. $(7-2x)^2 = 7^2 - 2(7)(2x) + (2x)^2$
$$= 49 - 28x + 4x^2$$

57. $\left(2x+\dfrac{1}{2}\right)^2 = 4x^2 + 2(2x)\left(\dfrac{1}{2}\right) + \left(\dfrac{1}{2}\right)^2$
$$= 4x^2 + 2x + \dfrac{1}{4}$$

59. $\left(4y-\dfrac{1}{4}\right)^2 = (4y)^2 - 2(4y)\left(\dfrac{1}{4}\right) + \left(\dfrac{1}{4}\right)^2$
$$= 16y^2 - 2y + \dfrac{1}{16}$$

61. $\left(x^8+3\right)^2 = \left(x^8\right)^2 + 2\left(x^8\right)(3) + 3^2$
$$= x^{16} + 6x^8 + 9$$

63. $(x-1)\left(x^2+x+1\right)$
$$= x\left(x^2+x+1\right) - 1\left(x^2+x+1\right)$$
$$= x^3 + x^2 + x - x^2 - x - 1$$
$$= x^3 - 1$$

65. $(x-1)^2 = x^2 - 2(x)(1) + 1^2$
$$= x^2 - 2x + 1$$

67. $(3y+7)(3y-7) = \left(3y^2\right) - 7^2$
$$= 9y^2 - 49$$

69. $3x^2\left(4x^2+x+9\right)$
$$= 3x^2\left(4x^2\right) + 3x^2(x) + 3x^2(9)$$
$$= 12x^4 + 3x^3 + 27x^2$$

71. $(7y+3)(10y-4)$
$$= 70y^2 - 28y + 30y - 12$$
$$= 70y^2 + 2y - 12$$

229

73. $\left(x^2+1\right)^2 = \left(x^2\right)^2 + 2\left(x^2\right)(1) + 1^2$
$\qquad = x^4 + 2x^2 + 1$

75. $\left(x^2+1\right)\left(x^2+2\right)$
$\qquad = x^2 \cdot x^2 + x^2 \cdot 2 + 1 \cdot x^2 + 1 \cdot 2$
$\qquad = x^4 + 3x^2 + 2$

77. $\left(x^2+4\right)\left(x^2-4\right) = \left(x^2\right)^2 - 4^2$
$\qquad = x^4 - 16$

79. $\left(2-3x^5\right)^2 = 2^2 - 2(2)\left(3x^5\right) + \left(3x^5\right)^2$
$\qquad = 4 - 12x^5 + 9x^{10}$

81. $\left(\dfrac{1}{4}x^2+12\right)\left(\dfrac{3}{4}x^2-8\right)$

$\qquad = \dfrac{1}{4}x^2\left(\dfrac{3}{4}x^2\right) + \dfrac{1}{4}x^2(-8) + 12\left(\dfrac{3}{4}x^2\right)$

$\qquad + 12(-8)$

$\qquad = \dfrac{3}{16}x^4 - 2x^2 + 9x^2 - 96$

$\qquad = \dfrac{3}{16}x^2 + 7x^2 - 96$

83. $A = \left(x+1\right)^2 = x^2 + 2x + 1$

85. $A = \left(2x-3\right)\left(2x+3\right) = \left(2x\right)^2 - 3^2$
$\qquad = 4x^2 - 9$

87. Area of outer rectangle:
$\qquad \left(x+9\right)\left(x+3\right) = x^2 + 12x + 27$
Area of inner rectangle:
$\qquad \left(x+5\right)\left(x+1\right) = x^2 + 6x + 5$
Area of shaded region:
$\qquad \left(x^2+12x+27\right) - \left(x^2+6x+5\right) = 6x + 22$

89. $\left[(2x+3)(2x-3)\right]^2 = \left[4x^2-9\right]^2$
$\qquad = 16x^4 - 72x^2 + 81$

90. $\left[(3x+2)(3x-2)\right]^2 = \left[9x^2-4\right]^2$
$\qquad = 81x^4 - 72x^2 + 16$

91. $\left(4x^2+1\right)\left[(2x+1)(2x-1)\right]$
$\qquad = \left(4x^2+1\right)\left[4x^2-1\right]$
$\qquad = 16x^4 - 1$

92. $\left(9x^2+1\right)\left[(3x+1)(3x-1)\right]$
$\qquad = \left(9x^2+1\right)\left[9x^2-1\right]$
$\qquad = 81x^4 - 1$

93. $(x+2)^3$
$\qquad = (x+2)(x+2)^2$
$\qquad = (x+2)\left(x^2+4x+4\right)$
$\qquad = x\left(x^2+4x+4\right) + 2\left(x^2+4x+4\right)$
$\qquad = x^3 + 4x^2 + 4x + 2x^2 + 8x + 8$
$\qquad = x^3 + 6x^2 + 12x + 8$

94. $(x+4)^3$
$\qquad = (x+4)(x+4)^2$
$\qquad = (x+4)\left(x^2+8x+16\right)$
$\qquad = x\left(x^2+8x+16\right) + 4\left(x^2+8x+16\right)$
$\qquad = x^3 + 8x^2 + 16x + 4x^2 + 32x + 64$
$\qquad = x^3 + 12x^2 + 48x + 64$

95. $\left[(x+3)-y\right]\left[(x+3)+y\right]$
$\qquad = (x+3)^2 - y^2$
$\qquad = x^2 + 6x + 9 - y^2$

230

96. $\left[(x+5)-y\right]\left[(x+5)+y\right]$

$= (x+5)^2 - y^2$

$= x^2 + 10x + 25 - y^2$

97. $A = (x+1)(x+2)$ yards^2

99. If the original garden measures 6 yards on a side, substitute $x = 6$ in the formula for the larger garden:

$A = (6+1)(6+2) = (7)(8) = 56$

The area of the larger garden will be 56 yards^2. The relationship corresponds to the point (6,56) on the graph.

101. The outer square (square including painting and frame) measures $(x+2)$ inches.

$$(x+2)^2 = x^2 + 4x + 4$$

The area is $\left(x^2 + 4x + 4\right)$ square inches.

103. FOIL - First Outer Inner Last
Example:
$$(4y+3)(y-1) = 4y^2 - 4y + 3y - 3$$
$$= 4y^2 - y - 3$$

105. To square a binomial sum, square the first piece, square the last piece, multiply together and double.
Example:
$$(x+5)^2 = x^2 + 5^2 + 2(5)(x)$$
$$= x^2 + 25 + 10x$$
$$= x^2 + 10x + 25$$

107. The graph for exercises 97-100 is only shown in Quadrant I because the variable x represents the length and width of the original garden. Since length and width cannot be negative, we only have to graph the values of x that are greater than or

equal to zero.

109. To find the correct binomial factors, try different combinations of constants in the binomials that will give a product of -20 as the last term until you find the combination that gives the correct middle term.

$$(x-10)(x+2) = x^2 + 2x - 10x - 20$$
$$= x^2 - 8x - 20$$

so the two binomials are $(x - 10)$ and $(x + 2)$.

111. Divide the figure into two rectangles by drawing a vertical line.

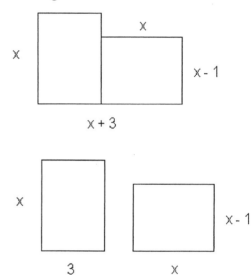

The area of the figure is the sum of the areas of the two rectangles.

$$A = 3 \cdot x + x(x-1)$$
$$= 3x + x^2 - x$$
$$= x^2 + 2x$$

113. Graph $y = (x+2)^2$ and $y = x^2 + 2x + 4$ on the same set of axes.

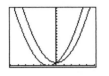

The graphs do not coincide.

$(x+2)^2 = x^2 + 4x + 4$, so $x^2 + 2x + 4$

should be changed to $x^2 + 4x + 4$.

Graph $y = (x+2)^2$ and $y = x^2 + 4x + 4$ on the same set of axes.

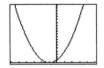

Now the graphs coincide.

115. Graph $y = (x-2)(x+2)+4$ and $y = x^2$ on the same set of axes.

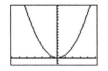

The graphs coincide. We will show that both sides are equivalent.

$$(x-2)(x+2)+4 = x^2$$
$$(x^2 - 4)+4 = x^2$$
$$x^2 = x^2$$

116. $2x + 3y = 1$

$y = 3x - 7$

The substitution method is a good choice because the second equation is already solved for y. Substitute $3x - 7$ for y into the first equation.

$$2x + 3y = 1$$
$$2x + 3(3x - 7) = 1$$
$$2x + 9x - 21 = 1$$
$$11x - 21 = 1$$
$$11x = 22$$
$$x = 2$$

Back-substitute.

$$y = 3x - 7$$
$$y = 3(2) - 7 = 6 + 7 = -1$$

Solution: $\{(2, -1)\}$

117. $3x + 4y = 7$

$2x + 7y = 9$

The addition method is a good choice because both equations are written in the form $Ax + By = C$. To eliminate x, multiply the first equation by 2 and the second equation by -3. Then add the results.

$$6x + 8y = 14$$
$$\underline{-6x - 21y = -27}$$
$$-13y = -13$$
$$y = 1$$

Back-substitute 1 for y in either equation of the original system.

$$3x + 4y = 7$$
$$3x + 4(1) = 7$$
$$3x + 4 = 7$$
$$3x = 3$$
$$x = 1$$

Solution: $\{(1,1)\}$

118. $4x + y + 2z = 6$

$x + y + z = 1$

$x - 3y + z = 5$

Multiply the second equation by –2 and
add to the first equation.

$4x + y + 2z = 6$

$-2x - 2y - 2z = -2$

$\overline{}$

$2x - y = 4$

Multiply the second equation by –1 and
add to the third equation.

$-x - y - z = -1$

$x - 3y + z = 5$

$\overline{}$

$-4y = 4$

$y = -1$

Back-substitute –1 for y in the equation in
two variables to find x.

$2x - y = 4$

$2x - (-1) = 4$

$2x + 1 = 4$

$2x = 3$

$x = \dfrac{3}{2}$

Back-substitute $\dfrac{3}{2}$ for x and –1 for y in

one of the original equations in three
variables to find z.

$4x + y + 2z = 6$

$4\left(\dfrac{3}{2}\right) + (-1) + 2z = 6$

$6 - 1 + 2z = 6$

$2z = 1$

$z = \dfrac{1}{2}$

The solution is $\left(\dfrac{3}{2}, -1, \dfrac{1}{2}\right)$ and the solution

set is $\left\{\left(\dfrac{3}{2}, -1, \dfrac{1}{2}\right)\right\}$.

5.4 Exercise Set

1. $x^2 + 2xy + y^2 = 2^2 + 2(2)(-3) + (-3)^2$

$= 4 - 12 + 9 = 1$

3. $xy^3 - xy + 1 = 2(-3)^3 - 2(-3) + 1$

$= 2(-27) + 6 + 1$

$= -54 + 6 + 1 = -47$

5. $2x^2y - 5y + 3 = 2(2^2)(-3) - 5(-3) + 3$

$= 2(4)(-3) - 5(-3) + 3$

$= -24 + 15 + 3 = -6$

7.

Term	Coefficient	Degree
x^3y^2	1	3+2=5
$-5x^2y^7$	-5	2+7=9
$6y^2$	6	2
-3	-3	0

The degree of the polynomial is the
highest degree of all its terms, which is 9.

9. $\left(5x^2y - 3xy\right) + \left(2x^2y - xy\right)$

$= \left(5x^2y + 2x^2y\right) + \left(-3xy - xy\right)$

$= 7x^2y - 4xy$

11. $\left(4x^2y + 8xy + 11\right) + \left(-2x^2y + 5xy + 2\right)$

$= \left(4x^2y - 2x^2y\right) + \left(8xy + 5xy\right) + \left(11 + 2\right)$

$= 2x^2y + 13xy + 13$

13. $\left(7x^4y^2 - 5x^2y^2 + 3xy\right)$

$+ \left(-18x^4y^2 - 6x^2y^2 - xy\right)$

$= \left(7x^4y^2 - 18x^4y^2\right) + \left(-5x^2y^2 - 6x^2y^2\right)$

$+ \left(3xy - xy\right)$

$= -11x^4y^2 - 11x^2y^2 + 2xy$

15. $\left(x^3+7xy-5y^2\right)-\left(6x^3-xy+4y^2\right)$

$=\left(x^3+7xy-5y^2\right)+\left(-6x^3+xy-4y^2\right)$

$=\left(x^3-6x^3\right)+\left(7xy+xy\right)+\left(-5y^2-4y^2\right)$

$=-5x^3+8xy-9y^2$

17. $\left(3x^4y^2+5x^3y-3y\right)$

$\qquad -\left(2x^4y^2-3x^3y-4y+6x\right)$

$\qquad =\left(3x^4y^2+5x^3y-3y\right)$

$\qquad \quad +\left(-2x^4y^2+3x^3y+4y-6x\right)$

$\qquad =\left(3x^4y^2-2x^4y^2\right)+\left(5x^3y+3x^3y\right)$

$\qquad \quad +\left(-3y+4y\right)+\left(-6x\right)$

$\qquad =x^4y^2+8x^3y+y-6x$

19. $\left(x^3-y^3\right)-\left(-4x^3-x^2y+xy^2+3y^3\right)$

$=\left(x^3-y^3\right)+\left(4x^3+x^2y-xy^2-3y^3\right)$

$=\left(x^3+4x^3\right)+\left(-y^3-3y^3\right)+x^2y-xy^2$

$=5x^3-4y^3+x^2y-xy^2$

$=5x^3+x^2y-xy^2-4y^3$

21. $\quad \begin{aligned} & 5x^2y^2-4xy^2+6y^2 \\ & \underline{-8x^2y^2+5xy^2\ \ -y^2} \\ & -3x^2y^2+\ xy^2\ +5y^2 \end{aligned}$

23. $\quad \begin{aligned} & 3a^2b^4-5ab^2+7ab \\ & -\left(\underline{-5a^2b^4-8ab^2\ -ab}\right) \end{aligned}$

$\qquad \begin{aligned} & 3a^2b^4-5ab^2+\ 7ab \\ & \underline{+5a^2b^4+8ab^2\ +\ ab} \\ & 8a^2b^4+3ab^2\ +8ab \end{aligned}$

25. $\left[\left(7x+13y\right)+\left(-26x+19y\right)\right]-\left(11x-5y\right)$

$=\left[-19x+32y\right]+\left(-11x+5y\right)$

$=-30x+37y$

27. $\left(5x^2y\right)\left(8xy\right)=\left(5\cdot8\right)\left(x^2\cdot x\right)\left(y\cdot y\right)$

$\qquad =40x^3y^2$

29. $\left(-8x^3y^4\right)\left(3x^2y^5\right)=\left(-8\cdot3\right)\left(x^3\cdot x^2\right)\left(y^4\cdot y^5\right)$

$\qquad =-24x^5y^9$

31. $9xy\left(5x+2y\right)=9xy\left(5x\right)+9xy\left(2y\right)$

$\qquad =45x^2y+18xy^2$

33. $5xy^2\left(10x^2-3y\right)$

$\qquad =5xy^2\left(10x^2\right)-5xy^2\left(3y\right)$

$\qquad =50x^3y^2-15xy^3$

35. $4ab^2\left(7a^2b^3+2ab\right)$

$\qquad =4ab^2\left(7a^2b^3\right)+4ab^2\left(2ab\right)$

$\qquad =28a^3b^5+8a^2b^3$

37. $-b\left(a^2-ab+b^2\right)$

$\qquad =-b\left(a^2\right)-b\left(-ab\right)-b\left(b^2\right)$

$\qquad =-a^2b+ab^2-b^3$

39. $\left(x+5y\right)\left(7x+3y\right)$

$\qquad =x\left(7x\right)+x\left(3y\right)+5y\left(7x\right)+5y\left(3y\right)$

$\qquad =7x^2+3xy+35xy+15y^2$

$\qquad =7x^2+38xy+15y^2$

41. $\left(x-3y\right)\left(2x+7y\right)$

$\qquad =x\left(2x\right)+x\left(7y\right)-3y\left(2x\right)-3y\left(7y\right)$

$\qquad =2x^2+7xy-6xy-21y^2$

$\qquad =2x^2+xy-21y^2$

43. $\left(3xy-1\right)\left(5xy+2\right)$

$\qquad =3xy\left(5xy\right)+3xy\left(2\right)-1\left(5xy\right)-1\left(2\right)$

$\qquad =15x^2y^2+6xy-5xy-2$

$\qquad =15x^2y^2+xy-2$

45. $(2x+3y)^2 = (2x)^2 + 2(2x)(3y)+(3y)^2$
$= 4x^2 +12xy+9y^2$

47. $(xy-3)^2 = (xy)^2 - 2(xy)(3)+(-3)^2$
$= x^2y^2 - 6xy+9$

49. $(x^2+y^2)^2 = (x^2)^2 + 2(x^2)(y^2)+(y^2)^2$
$= x^4 + 2x^2y^2 + y^4$

51. $(x^2-2y^2)^2$
$= (x^2)- 2(x^2)(2y^2)+(-2y^2)^2$
$= x^4 - 4x^2y^2 + 4y^4$

53. $(3x+y)(3x-y) = (3x)^2 - y^2 = 9x^2 - y^2$

55. $(ab+1)(ab-1) = (ab)^2 - 1^2 = a^2b^2 -1$

57. $(x+y^2)(x-y^2) = x^2 - (y^2)^2 = x^2 - y^4$

59. $(3a^2b+a)(3a^2b-a) = (3a^2b)^2 - a^2$
$= 9a^4b^2 - a^2$

61. $(3xy^2 - 4y)(3xy^2 + 4y) = (3xy^2)^2 - (4y)^2$
$= 9x^2y^4 - 16y^2$

63. $(a+b)(a^2 -b^2)$
$= a(a^2)+a(-b^2)+b(a^2)+b(-b^2)$
$= a^3 - ab^2 + a^2b - b^3$

65. $(x+y)(x^2 + 3xy + y^2)$
$= x(x^2 + 3xy + y^2)+ y(x^2 + 3xy + y^2)$
$= x^3 + 3x^2y + xy^2 + x^2y + 3xy^2 + y^3$
$= x^3 + 4x^2y + 4xy^2 + y^3$

67. $(x-y)(x^2 -3xy+ y^2)$
$= x(x^2 - 3xy + y^2)- y(x^2 - 3xy + y^2)$
$= x^3 - 3x^2y + xy^2 - x^2y + 3xy^2 - y^3$
$= x^3 - 4x^2y + 4xy^2 - y^3$

69. $(xy+ab)(xy - ab) = (xy)^2 -(ab)^2$
$= x^2y^2 - a^2b^2$

71. $(x^2+1)(x^4y + x^2 +1)$
$x^2(x^4y + x^2 + 1)+1(x^4y + x^2 +1)$
$= x^6y + x^4 + x^2 + x^4y + x^2 + 1$
$= x^6y + x^4y + x^4 + 2x^2 + 1$

73. $(x^2y^2 -3)^2$
$= (x^2y^2)^2 - 2(x^2y^2)(3)+(-3)^2$
$= x^4y^4 - 6x^2y^2 +9$

75. $(x+y+1)(x+y-1)$
$= x(x+y-1)+ y(x+y-1)$
$+1(x+y-1)$
$= x^2 + xy - x + yx + y^2 - y + x + y - 1$
$= x^2 + 2xy + y^2 - 1$

77. $A = (3x+5y)(x+y)$
$= 3x(x)+3x(y)+5y(x)+5y(y)$
$= 3x^2 + 3xy + 5xy + 5y^2$
$= 3x^2 + 8xy + 5y^2$

79. Area of a larger square $= (x+y)^2$
$= x^2 + 2xy + y^2$

Area of a smaller square $= x^2$
Area of shaded region
$= (x^2 + 2xy + y^2)- x^2$
$= 2xy + y^2$

235

81.

$$\left[\left(x^3y^3+1\right)\left(x^3y^3-1\right)\right]^2$$
$$=\left[\left(x^3y^3\right)^2-\left(1\right)^2\right]^2$$
$$=\left[x^6y^6-1\right]^2$$
$$=\left(x^6y^6\right)^2-2\left(x^6y^6\right)\left(1\right)+\left(1\right)^2$$
$$=x^{12}y^{12}-2x^6y^6+1$$

82.

$$\left[\left(1-a^3b^3\right)\left(1+a^3b^3\right)\right]^2$$
$$=\left[\left(1\right)^2-\left(a^3b^3\right)^2\right]^2$$
$$=\left[1-a^6b^6\right]^2$$
$$=\left(1\right)^2-2\left(1\right)\left(a^6b^6\right)+\left(a^6b^6\right)^2$$
$$=1-2a^6b^6+a^{12}b^{12}$$

83.

$$\left(xy-3\right)^2\left(xy+3\right)^2$$
$$=\left[\left(xy-3\right)\left(xy+3\right)\right]^2$$
$$=\left[\left(xy\right)^2-3^2\right]^2$$
$$=\left[x^2y^2-9\right]^2$$
$$=\left(x^2y^2\right)^2-2\left(x^2y^2\right)\left(9\right)+\left(9\right)^2$$
$$=x^4y^4-18x^2y^2+81$$

84.

$$\left(ab-4\right)^2\left(ab+4\right)^2$$
$$=\left[\left(ab-4\right)\left(ab+4\right)\right]^2$$
$$=\left[\left(ab\right)^2-4^2\right]^2$$
$$=\left[a^2b^2-16\right]^2$$
$$=\left(a^2b^2\right)^2-2\left(a^2b^2\right)\left(16\right)+\left(16\right)^2$$
$$=a^4b^4-32a^2b^2+256$$

85.

$$\left[x+y+z\right]\left[x-\left(y+z\right)\right]$$
$$=\left[x+\left(y+z\right)\right]\left[x-\left(y+z\right)\right]$$
$$=x^2-\left(y+z\right)^2$$
$$=x^2-\left(y^2+2yz+z^2\right)$$
$$=x^2-y^2-2yz-z^2$$

86.

$$\left[a-b-c\right]\left[a+b+c\right]$$
$$=\left[a-\left(b+c\right)\right]\left[a+\left(b+c\right)\right]$$
$$=a^2-\left(b+c\right)^2$$
$$=a^2-\left(b^2+2bc+c^2\right)$$
$$=a^2-b^2-2bc-c^2$$

87.

$$N=\frac{1}{4}x^2y-2xy+4y;\ x=10,\ y=16$$
$$N=\frac{1}{4}x^2y-2xy+4y$$
$$=\frac{1}{4}\left(10\right)^2\left(16\right)-2\left(10\right)\left(16\right)+4\left(16\right)$$
$$=\frac{1}{4}\left(100\right)\left(16\right)-2\left(10\right)\left(16\right)+4\left(16\right)$$
$$=400-320+64=144$$

Each tree provides 144 board feet of lumber, so 20 trees will provide 20(144) = 2880 board feet. This is not enough lumber to complete the job. Since 3000 – 2880 = 120, the contractor will need 120 more board feet.

89.

$$s=-16t^2+v_0t+s_0;\ t=2,\ v_0=80,$$
$$s_0=96$$
$$s=-16t^2+v_0t+s_0$$
$$=-16\left(2\right)^2+80\left(2\right)+96$$
$$=-16\left(4\right)+80\left(6\right)+96$$
$$=-64+160+96$$
$$=192$$

The ball will be 192 feet above the ground 2 seconds after being thrown.

91. $s = -16t^2 + v_0 t + s_0; \ t = 6, \ v_0 = 80$

$s_0 = 96$

$$s = -16t^2 + v_0 t + s_0$$
$$= -16(6)^2 + 80(60) + 96$$
$$= -16(36) + 80(6) + 96$$
$$= -576 + 480 + 96 = 0$$

The ball will be 0 feet above the ground after 6 seconds. This means that the ball hits the ground 6 seconds after being thrown.

93. The ball is falling from 2.5 seconds to 6 seconds. The graph is decreasing over this interval.

95. $(2, 192)$

97. The ball reaches its maximum height 2.5 seconds after it is thrown.

$s = -16t^2 + v_0 t + s_0; \ t = 2.5, \ v_0 = 80$

$s_0 = 96$

$$s = -16t^2 + v_0 t + s_0$$
$$= -16(2.5)^2 + 80(2.5) + 96$$
$$= -16(6.25) + 80(2.5) + 96$$
$$= -100 + 200 + 96$$
$$= 196$$

The maximum height is 196 feet.

99. To find the degree of a polynomial in two variables, calculate the degree of each term separately by adding the powers of each variable. The degree is the maximum value of your results.

101. Statement a is false.

The term $-3x^{16}y^9$ has degree 16+9=25.

Statement b is false.

The coefficient of the term is a 1.

Statement c is true.

$$(2x + 3 - 5y)(2x + 3 + 5y)$$
$$= \left[(2x+3) - 5y\right]\left[(2x+3) + 5y\right]$$
$$= (2x+3)^2 - (5y)^2$$
$$= 4x^2 + 12x + 9 - 25y^2$$

Statement d is false.

The right-hand-side of the equation should be $-14xy$, not zero.

103. Area of large rectangle:
$$(3x - 4y)(3x + 4y) = 9x^2 - 16y^2$$

Area of small squares: $(x)(x) = x^2$

Area of shaded region is the area of the large rectangle minus the areas of the 4 small squares:
$$9x^2 - 16y^2 - 4x = 5x^2 - 16y^2$$

105. $R = \dfrac{L + 3W}{2}$; for W

$$R = \frac{L + 3W}{2}$$
$$2R = 2\left(\frac{L + 3W}{2}\right)$$
$$2R = L + 3W$$
$$2R - L = L + 3W - L$$
$$2R - L = 3W$$
$$\frac{2R - L}{3} = \frac{3W}{3}$$
$$\frac{2R - L}{3} = W \ \text{ or } \ W = \frac{2R - L}{3}$$

106. $-6.4 - (-10.2) = -6.4 + 10.2 = 3.8$

107. Through $(-2,5)$ and parallel to the line
$3x - y = 9$.
$$3x - y = 9$$
$$-y = -3x + 9$$
$$y = 3x - 9$$
The slope of the line is 3 since the line is parallel to a line with slope 3. Use the point-slope form to find the equation of the line.
$$y - 5 = 3(x - (-2))$$
$$y - 5 = 3(x + 2)$$
$$y - 5 = 3x + 6$$
$$y = 3x + 11$$

Chapter 5 Mid-Chapter Check Point

1. $\left(11x^2 y^3\right)\left(-5x^2 y^3\right) = -55x^{2+2} y^{3+3}$
$$= -55x^4 y^6$$

2. $11x^2 y^3 - 5x^2 y^3 = 6x^2 y^3$

3. $(3x + 5)(4x - 7) = 12x^2 - 21x + 20x - 35$
$$= 12x^2 - x - 35$$

4. $(3x + 5) - (4x - 7)$
$$= (3x + 5) + (-4x + 7)$$
$$= -x + 12$$

5. $(2x - 5)(x^2 - 3x + 1)$
$$= 2x(x^2 - 3x + 1) - 5(x^2 - 3x + 1)$$
$$= 2x^3 - 6x^2 + 2x - 5x^2 + 15x - 5$$
$$= 2x^3 - 11x^2 + 17x - 5$$

6. $(2x - 5) + (x^2 - 3x + 1) = x^2 - x - 4$

7. $(8x - 3)^2 = (8x)^2 - 2(8x)(3) + 3^2$
$$= 64x^2 - 48x + 9$$

8. $\left(-10x^4\right)\left(-7x^5\right) = 70x^9$

9. $(x^2 + 2)(x^2 - 2) = \left(x^2\right)^2 - 2^2 = x^4 - 4$

10. $(x^2 + 2)^2 = \left(x^2\right)^2 + 2\left(x^2\right)(2) + 2^2$
$$= x^4 + 4x^2 + 4$$

11. $(9a - 10b)(2a + b)$
$$= 18a^2 + 9ab - 20ba - 10b^2$$
$$= 18a^2 + 9ab - 20ab - 10b^2$$
$$= 18a^2 - 11ab - 10b^2$$

12. $7x^2\left(10x^3 - 2x + 3\right) = 70x^5 - 14x^3 + 21x^2$

13. $\left(3a^2 b^3 - ab + 4b^2\right) - \left(-2a^2 b^3 - 3ab + 5b^2\right)$
$$= \left(3a^2 b^3 - ab + 4b^2\right) + \left(2a^2 b^3 + 3ab - 5b^2\right)$$
$$= 5a^2 b^3 + 2ab - b^2$$

14. $2(3y - 5)(3y + 5) = 2\left(9y^2 - 25\right)$
$$= 18y^2 - 50$$

15. $\left(-9x^3 + 5x^2 - 2x + 7\right)$
$$\qquad + \left(11x^3 - 6x^2 + 3x - 7\right)$$
$$= 2x^3 - x^2 + x$$

16. $10x^2 - 8xy - 3\left(y^2 - xy\right)$
$$= 10x^2 - 8xy - 3y^2 + 3xy$$
$$= 10x^2 - 5xy - 3y^2$$

17. $\left(-2x^5 + x^4 - 3x + 10\right)$
$\qquad -\left(2x^5 - 6x^4 + 7x - 13\right)$
$= \left(-2x^5 + x^4 - 3x + 10\right)$
$\qquad + \left(-2x^5 + 6x^4 - 7x + 13\right)$
$= -4x^5 + 7x^4 - 10x + 23$

18. $(x + 3y)\left(x^2 - 3xy + 9y^2\right)$
$= x\left(x^2 - 3xy + 9y^2\right) + 3y\left(x^2 - 3xy + 9y^2\right)$
$= x^3 - 3x^2y + 9xy^2 + 3x^2y - 9xy^2 + 27y^3$
$= x^3 + 27y^3$

19. $\left(5x^4 + 4\right)\left(2x^3 - 1\right) = 10x^7 - 5x^4 + 8x^3 - 4$

20. $(y - 6z)^2 = y^2 - 2(y)(6z) + (6z)^2$
$\qquad = y^2 - 12yz + 36z^2$

21. $(2x + 3)(2x - 3) - (5x + 4)(5x - 4)$
$= \left(4x^2 - 9\right) - \left(25x^2 - 16\right)$
$= \left(4x^2 - 9\right) + \left(-25x^2 + 16\right)$
$= -21x^2 + 7$

5.5 Exercise Set

1. $\dfrac{3^{20}}{3^5} = 3^{20-5} = 3^{15}$

3. $\dfrac{x^6}{x^2} = x^{6-2} = x^4$

5. $\dfrac{y^{13}}{y^5} = y^{13-5} = y^8$

7. $\dfrac{5^6 \cdot 2^8}{5^3 \cdot 2^4} = 5^{6-3} \cdot 2^{8-4} = 5^3 \cdot 2^4$

9. $\dfrac{x^{100} y^{50}}{x^{25} y^{10}} = x^{100-25} y^{50-10} = x^{75} y^{40}$

11. $2^0 = 1$

13. $(-2)^0 = 1$

15. $-2^0 = -\left(2^0\right) = -(1) = -1$

17. $100 y^0 = 100 \cdot 1 = 100$

19. $(100y)^0 = 1$

21. $-5^0 + (-5)^0 = -1 + 1 = 0$

23. $-\pi^0 - (-\pi)^0 = -1 - 1 = -2$

25. $\left(\dfrac{x}{3}\right)^2 = \dfrac{x^2}{3^2} = \dfrac{x^2}{9}$

27. $\left(\dfrac{x^2}{4}\right)^3 = \dfrac{\left(x^2\right)^3}{4^3} = \dfrac{x^{2 \cdot 3}}{4^3} = \dfrac{x^6}{64}$

29. $\left(\dfrac{2x^3}{5}\right)^2 = \dfrac{2^2 \left(x^3\right)^2}{5^2} = \dfrac{4x^6}{25}$

31. $\left(\dfrac{-4}{3a^3}\right)^3 = \dfrac{(-4)^3}{3^3 \left(a^3\right)^3} = \dfrac{-64}{27a^9} = -\dfrac{64}{27a^9}$

33. $\left(\dfrac{-2a^7}{b^4}\right)^5 = \dfrac{\left(-2a^7\right)^5}{\left(b^4\right)^5} = \dfrac{(-2)^5 \left(a^7\right)^5}{\left(b^4\right)^5}$
$\qquad = \dfrac{-32a^{35}}{b^{20}} = -\dfrac{32a^{35}}{b^{20}}$

239

35.

$$\left(\frac{x^2 y^3}{2z}\right)^4 = \frac{\left(x^2\right)^4 \left(y^3\right)^4}{2^4 z^4} = \frac{x^8 y^{12}}{16 z^4}$$

37.

$$\frac{30x^{10}}{10x^5} = \frac{30}{10} x^{10-5} = 3x^5$$

39.

$$\frac{-8x^{22}}{4x^2} = \frac{-8}{4} x^{22-2} = -2x^{20}$$

41.

$$\frac{-9y^8}{18y^5} = \frac{-9}{18} y^{8-5} = -\frac{1}{2} y^3$$

43.

$$\frac{7y^{17}}{5y^5} = \frac{7}{5} y^{17-5} = \frac{7}{5} y^{12}$$

45.

$$\frac{30x^7 y^5}{5x^2 y} = \frac{30}{5} x^{7-2} y^{5-1} = 6x^5 y^4$$

47.

$$\frac{-18x^{14} y^2}{36x^2 y^2} = \frac{-18}{36} x^{14-2} y^{2-2}$$

$$= -\frac{1}{2} x^{12} y^0 = -\frac{1}{2} x^{12} \cdot 1 = -\frac{1}{2} x^{12}$$

49.

$$\frac{9x^{20} y^{20}}{7x^{20} y^{20}} = \frac{9}{7} x^{20-20} y^{20-20}$$

$$= \frac{9}{7} x^0 y^0 = \frac{9}{7} \cdot 1 \cdot 1 = \frac{9}{7}$$

51.

$$\frac{-5x^{10} y^{12} z^6}{50x^2 y^3 z^2} = -\frac{1}{10} x^{10-2} y^{12-3} z^{6-2}$$

$$= -\frac{1}{10} x^8 y^9 z^4$$

53.

$$\frac{10x^4 + 2x^3}{2} = \frac{10x^4}{2} + \frac{2x^3}{2} = 5x^4 + x^3$$

55.

$$\frac{14x^4 - 7x^3}{7x} = \frac{14x^4}{7x} - \frac{7x^3}{7x}$$

$$= 2x^{4-1} - x^{3-1} = 2x^3 - x^2$$

57.

$$\frac{y^7 - 9y^2 + y}{y} = \frac{y^7}{y} - \frac{9y^2}{y} + \frac{y}{y}$$

$$= y^{7-1} - 9y^{2-1} + y^{1-1}$$

$$= y^6 - 9y^1 + y^0$$

$$= y^6 - 9y + 1$$

59.

$$\frac{24x^3 - 15x^2}{-3x} = \frac{24x^3}{-3x} + \frac{-15x^2}{-3x}$$

$$= -8x^{3-1} + 5x^{2-1} = -8x^2 + 5x$$

61.

$$\frac{18x^5 + 6x^4 + 9x^3}{3x^2} = \frac{18x^5}{3x^2} + \frac{6x^4}{3x^2} + \frac{9x^3}{3x^2}$$

$$= 6x^3 + 2x^2 + 3x$$

63.

$$\frac{12x^4 - 8x^3 + 40x^2}{4x} = \frac{12x^4}{4x} - \frac{8x^3}{4x} + \frac{40x^2}{4x}$$

$$= 3x^3 - 2x^2 + 10x$$

65.

$$\left(4x^2 - 6x\right) \div x = \frac{4x^2 - 6x}{x} = \frac{4x^2}{x} - \frac{6x}{x}$$

$$= 4x - 6$$

67.

$$\frac{30z^3 + 10z^2}{-5z} = \frac{30z^3}{-5z} + \frac{10z^2}{-5z} = -6z^2 - 2z$$

69.

$$\frac{8x^3 + 6x^2 - 2x}{2x} = \frac{8x^3}{2x} + \frac{6x^2}{2x} - \frac{2x}{2x}$$

$$= 4x^2 + 3x - 1$$

71.

$$\frac{25x^7 - 15x^5 - 5x^4}{5x^3} = \frac{25x^7}{5x^3} - \frac{15x^5}{5x^3} - \frac{5x^4}{5x^3}$$

$$= 5x^4 - 3x^2 - x$$

73. $\dfrac{18x^7 - 9x^6 + 20x^5 - 10x^4}{-2x^4}$

$= \dfrac{18x^7}{-2x^4} - \dfrac{9x^6}{-2x^4} + \dfrac{20x^5}{-2x^4} - \dfrac{10x^4}{-2x^4}$

$= -9x^3 + \dfrac{9}{2}x^2 - 10x + 5$

75. $\dfrac{12x^2y^2 + 6x^2y - 15xy^2}{3xy}$

$= \dfrac{12x^2y^2}{3xy} + \dfrac{6x^2y}{3xy} - \dfrac{15xy^2}{3xy}$

$= 4xy + 2x - 5y$

77. $\dfrac{20x^7y^4 - 15x^3y^2 - 10x^2y}{-5x^2y}$

$= \dfrac{20x^7y^4}{-5x^2y} + \dfrac{-15x^3y^2}{-5x^2y} + \dfrac{-10x^2y}{-5x^2y}$

$= -4x^5y^3 + 3xy + 2$

79. $\dfrac{2x^3(4x+2) - 3x^2(2x-4)}{2x^2}$

$= \dfrac{8x^4 + 4x^3 - 6x^3 + 12x^2}{2x^2}$

$= \dfrac{8x^4 - 2x^3 + 12x^2}{2x^2}$

$= \dfrac{8x^4}{2x^2} - \dfrac{2x^3}{2x^2} + \dfrac{12x^2}{2x^2} = 4x^2 - x + 6$

80. $\dfrac{6x^3(3x-1) + 5x^2(6x-3)}{3x^2}$

$= \dfrac{18x^4 - 6x^3 + 30x^3 - 15x^2}{3x^2}$

$= \dfrac{18x^4 + 24x^3 - 15x^2}{3x^2}$

$= \dfrac{18x^4}{3x^2} + \dfrac{24x^3}{3x^2} - \dfrac{15x^2}{3x^2} = 6x^2 + 8x - 5$

81. $\left(\dfrac{18x^2y^4}{9xy^2}\right) - \left(\dfrac{15x^5y^6}{5x^4y^4}\right) = 2xy^2 - 3xy^2 = -xy^2$

82. $\left(\dfrac{9x^3 + 6x^2}{3x}\right) - \left(\dfrac{12x^2y^2 - 4xy^2}{2xy^2}\right)$

$= \left(\dfrac{9x^3}{3x} + \dfrac{6x^2}{3x}\right) - \left(\dfrac{12x^2y^2}{2xy^2} - \dfrac{4xy^2}{2xy^2}\right)$

$= 3x^2 + 2x - (6x - 2) = 3x^2 - 4x + 2$

83. $\dfrac{(y+5)^2 + (y+5)(y-5)}{2y}$

$= \dfrac{(y^2 + 10y + 25) + (y^2 - 25)}{2y}$

$= \dfrac{2y^2 + 10y}{2y} = \dfrac{2y^2}{2y} + \dfrac{10y}{2y} = y + 5$

84. $\dfrac{(y+4)^2 + (y+4)(y-4)}{2y}$

$= \dfrac{(y^2 + 8y + 16) + (y^2 - 16)}{2y}$

$= \dfrac{2y^2 + 8y}{2y} = \dfrac{2y^2}{2y} + \dfrac{8y}{2y} = y + 4$

85. $\dfrac{12x^{15n} - 24x^{12n} + 8x^{3n}}{4x^{3n}}$

$= \dfrac{12x^{15n}}{4x^{3n}} - \dfrac{24x^{12n}}{4x^{3n}} + \dfrac{8x^{3n}}{4x^{3n}}$

$= 3x^{12n} - 6x^{9n} + 2$

86. $\dfrac{35x^{10n} - 15x^{8n} + 25x^{2n}}{5x^{2n}}$

$= \dfrac{35x^{10n}}{5x^{2n}} - \dfrac{15x^{8n}}{5x^{2n}} + \dfrac{25x^{2n}}{5x^{2n}}$

$= 7x^{8n} - 3x^{6n} + 5$

87. (a) Divide the expression for the number of convictions by the expression for the number of arrests

$$\frac{6t^4 - 207t^3 + 2128t^2 - 6622t + 15,220}{28t^4 - 711t^3 + 5963t^2 - 1695t + 27,424}$$

(b) No. The denominator is not a monomial.

89. When dividing numbers with the same base, keep the base and subtract the exponents.

Example: $\dfrac{3^6}{3^2} = 3^{6-2} = 3^4$

91. $(-7)^0$ is one number -7 raised to the 0 power. So $(-7)^0 = 1$.

-7^0 is actually $-7^0 = -1 \cdot 7^0 = -1 \cdot 1 = -1$.

93. Divide monomials by dividing coefficients and using the quotient rule on each variable expression.

95. $\dfrac{12x^2 + 6x}{3x}$ and $4x + 2$ are not the same for $x = 0$. The first expression cannot be evaluated at $x = 0$ because this would make the denominator zero.

97. $\dfrac{18x^8 - 27x^6 + 36x^4}{3x^2} = 6x^6 - 9x^4 + 12x^2$

so the required polynomial is
$18x^8 - 27x^6 + 36x^4$.
One way to find this polynomial is to use the relationship between division and multiplication:
$3x^2 \left(6x^6 - 9x^4 + 12x^2 \right)$
$= 18x^8 - 27x^6 + 36x^4$.

99. To get 2 as the coefficient of the middle term of the quotient, the coefficient in the divisor must be -3. To get the exponents shown in the three terms of the quotient, the exponent in the divisor must be 7. Since we now know that the divisor is $-3x^7$, the coefficient of the last term of the dividend must be -9. Therefore,

$$\frac{3x^{14} - 6x^{12} - ?\,x^7}{?\,x^?} = \frac{3x^{14} - 6x^{12} - 9x^7}{-3x^7}$$

100. $|-20.3| = 20.3$

101.
$$\begin{array}{r} 0.875 \\ 8\overline{)7.000} \\ \underline{64} \\ 60 \\ \underline{56} \\ 40 \\ \underline{40} \\ 0 \end{array}$$

$\dfrac{7}{8} = 0.875$

102. $y = \dfrac{1}{3}x + 2$

slope $= \dfrac{1}{3}$; y-intercept $= 2$

Plot $(0,2)$. From this point move 1 unit *up* and 3 units to the *right* to reach the point $(3,3)$. Draw a line through $(0,2)$ and $(3,3)$.

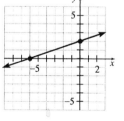

5.6 Exercise Set

1.

$$\begin{array}{r} x+4 \\ x+2\overline{)x^2+6x+8} \\ \underline{x^2+2x} \\ 4x+8 \\ \underline{4x+8} \\ 0 \end{array}$$

$$\frac{x^2+6x+8}{x+2}=x+4$$

3.

$$\begin{array}{r} 2x+5 \\ x-2\overline{)2x^2+x-10} \\ \underline{2x^2-4x} \\ 5x-10 \\ \underline{5x-10} \\ 0 \end{array}$$

$$\frac{2x^2+x-10}{x-2}=2x+5$$

5.

$$\begin{array}{r} x-2 \\ x-3\overline{)x^2-5x+6} \\ \underline{x^2-3x} \\ -2x+6 \\ \underline{-2x+6} \\ 0 \end{array}$$

$$\frac{x^2-5x+6}{x-3}=x-2$$

7.

$$\begin{array}{r} 2y+1 \\ y+2\overline{)2y^2+5y+2} \\ \underline{2y^2+4y} \\ y+2 \\ \underline{y+2} \\ 0 \end{array}$$

$$\frac{2y^2+5y+2}{y+2}=2y+1$$

9.

$$\begin{array}{r} x-5 \\ x+2\overline{)x^2-3x+4} \\ \underline{x^2+2x} \\ -5x+4 \\ \underline{-5x-10} \\ 14 \end{array}$$

$$\frac{x^2-3x+4}{x+2}=x-5+\frac{14}{x+2}$$

11.

$$\begin{array}{r} y+3 \\ y+2\overline{)y^2+5y+10} \\ \underline{y^2+2y} \\ 3y+10 \\ \underline{3y+6} \\ 4 \end{array}$$

$$\frac{5y+10+y^2}{y+2}=\frac{y^2+5y+10}{y+2}$$

$$=y+3+\frac{4}{y+2}$$

13.

$$\begin{array}{r} x^2 - 5x + 2 \\ x-1{\overline{\smash{\big)}\,x^3 - 6x^2 + 7x - 2}} \\ \underline{x^3 -\ x^2} \\ -5x^2 + 7x \\ \underline{-5x^2 + 5x} \\ 2x - 2 \\ \underline{2x - 2} \\ 0 \end{array}$$

$$\frac{x^3 - 6x^2 + 7x - 2}{x-1} = x^2 - 5x + 2$$

15.

$$\begin{array}{r} 6y - 1 \\ 2y-3{\overline{\smash{\big)}\,12y^2 - 20y + 3}} \\ \underline{12y^2 - 18y} \\ -2y + 3 \\ \underline{-2y + 3} \\ 0 \end{array}$$

$$\frac{12y^2 - 20y + 3}{2y-3} = 6y - 1$$

17.

$$\begin{array}{r} 2a + 3 \\ 2a-1{\overline{\smash{\big)}\,4a^2 + 4a - 3}} \\ \underline{4a^2 - 2a} \\ 6a - 3 \\ \underline{6a - 3} \\ 0 \end{array}$$

$$\frac{4a^2 + 4a - 3}{2a-1} = 2a + 3$$

19.

$$\begin{array}{r} y^2 - y + 2 \\ 2y+1{\overline{\smash{\big)}\,2y^3 - y^2 + 3y + 2}} \\ \underline{2y^3 + y^2} \\ -2y^2 + 3y \\ \underline{-2y^2 -\ y} \\ 4y + 2 \\ \underline{4y + 2} \\ 0 \end{array}$$

$$\frac{3y - y^2 + 2y^3 + 2}{2y+1}$$

$$= \frac{2y^3 - y^2 + 3y + 2}{2y+1} = y^2 - y + 2$$

21.

$$\begin{array}{r} 3x + 5 \\ 2x-5{\overline{\smash{\big)}\,6x^2 - 5x - 30}} \\ \underline{6x^2 - 15x} \\ 10x - 30 \\ \underline{10x - 25} \\ -5 \end{array}$$

$$\frac{6x^2 - 5x - 30}{2x-5} = 3x + 5 - \frac{5}{2x-5}$$

23.

$$\begin{array}{r} x^2 + 2x + 8 \\ x-2{\overline{\smash{\big)}\,x^3 + 0x^2 + 4x - 3}} \\ \underline{x^3 - 2x^2} \\ 2x^2 + 4x \\ \underline{2x^2 - 4x} \\ 8x -\ 3 \\ \underline{8x - 16} \\ 13 \end{array}$$

$$\frac{x^2 + 4x - 3}{x-2} = x^2 + 2x + 8 + \frac{13}{x-2}$$

244

25.

$$
\begin{array}{r}
2y^2 + y + 1 \\
2y+3{\overline{\smash{\big)}\,4y^3 + 8y^2 + 5y + 9}} \\
\underline{4y^3 + 6y^2} \\
2y^2 + 5y \\
\underline{2y^2 + 3y} \\
2y + 9 \\
\underline{2y + 3} \\
6
\end{array}
$$

$$\frac{4y^3 + 8y^2 + 5y + 9}{2y+3} = 2y^2 + y + 1 + \frac{6}{2y+3}$$

27.

$$
\begin{array}{r}
2y^2 - 3y + 2 \\
3y+2{\overline{\smash{\big)}\,6y^3 - 5y^2 + 0y + 5}} \\
\underline{6y^3 + 4y^2} \\
-9y^2 + 0y \\
\underline{-9y^2 - 6y} \\
6y + 5 \\
\underline{6y + 4} \\
1
\end{array}
$$

$$\frac{6y^3 - 5y^2 + 5}{3y+2} = 2y^2 - 3y + 2 + \frac{1}{3y+2}$$

29.

$$
\begin{array}{r}
9x^2 + 3x + 1 \\
3x-1{\overline{\smash{\big)}\,27x^3 + 0x^2 + 0x - 1}} \\
\underline{27x^3 - 9x^2} \\
9x^2 + 0x \\
\underline{9x^2 - 3x} \\
3x - 1 \\
\underline{3x - 1} \\
0
\end{array}
$$

$$\frac{27x^3 - 1}{3x-1} = 9x^2 + 3x + 1$$

31.

$$
\begin{array}{r}
y^3 - 9y^2 + 27y - 27 \\
y-3{\overline{\smash{\big)}\,y^4 - 12y^3 + 54y^2 - 108y + 81}} \\
\underline{y^4 - 3y^3} \\
-9y^3 + 54y^2 \\
\underline{-9y^3 + 27y^2} \\
27y^2 - 108y \\
\underline{27y^2 - 81y} \\
-27y + 81 \\
\underline{-27y + 81} \\
0
\end{array}
$$

$$\frac{81 - 12y^3 + 54y^2 + y^4 - 108y}{y-3}$$

$$= \frac{y^4 - 12y^3 + 54y^2 - 108y + 81}{y-3}$$

$$= y^3 - 9y^2 + 27y - 27$$

33.

$$
\begin{array}{r}
2y + 4 \\
2y-1{\overline{\smash{\big)}\,4y^2 + 6y + 0}} \\
\underline{4y^2 - 2y} \\
8y + 0 \\
\underline{8y - 4} \\
4
\end{array}
$$

$$\frac{4y^2 + 6y}{2y-1} = 2y + 4 + \frac{4}{2y-1}$$

245

35.

$$\begin{array}{r} y^3 + y^2 - y - 1 \\ y-1\overline{)y^4 + 0y^3 - 2y^2 + 0y + 5} \\ \underline{y^4 - y^3} \\ y^3 - 2y^2 \\ \underline{y^3 - y^2} \\ -y^2 + 0y \\ \underline{-y^2 + y} \\ -y + 5 \\ \underline{-y + 1} \\ 4 \end{array}$$

$$\frac{y^4 - 2y^2 + 5}{y-1} = y^3 + y^2 - y - 1 + \frac{4}{y-1}$$

37.

$$\begin{array}{r} 4x^2 + 3x - 8 \\ x^2 + 0x + 3\overline{)4x^4 + 3x^3 + 4x^2 + 9x - 6} \\ \underline{4x^4 + 0x^3 + 12x^2} \\ 3x^3 - 8x^2 + 9x \\ \underline{3x^3 + 0x^2 + 9x} \\ -8x^2 + 0x - 6 \\ \underline{-8x^2 + 0x - 24} \\ 18 \end{array}$$

$$\frac{4x^4 + 3x^3 + 4x^2 + 9x - 6}{x^2 + 3}$$
$$= 4x^2 + 3x - 8 + \frac{18}{x^2 + 3}$$

39.

$$\begin{array}{r} 5x^2 + x + 3 \\ 3x^2 + 0x - 1\overline{)15x^4 + 3x^3 + 4x^2 + 0x + 4} \\ \underline{15x^4 + 0x^3 - 5x^2} \\ 3x^3 + 9x^2 + 0x \\ \underline{3x^3 + 0x^2 - x} \\ 9x^2 + x + 4 \\ \underline{9x^2 + 0x - 3} \\ x + 7 \end{array}$$

$$\frac{15x^4 + 3x^3 + 4x^2 + 4}{3x^2 - 1}$$
$$= 5x^2 + x + 3 + \frac{x+7}{3x^2 - 1}$$

41. $\left(2x^2 + x - 10\right) \div \left(x - 2\right)$

$$\begin{array}{r|rrr} 2\rfloor & 2 & 1 & -10 \\ & & 4 & 10 \\ \hline & 2 & 5 & 0 \end{array}$$

$$\left(2x^2 + x - 10\right) \div \left(x - 2\right) = 2x + 5$$

43. $\left(3x^2 + 7x - 20\right) \div \left(x + 5\right)$

$$\begin{array}{r|rrr} -5\rfloor & 3 & 7 & -20 \\ & & -15 & 40 \\ \hline & 3 & -8 & 20 \end{array}$$

$$\left(3x^2 + 7x - 20\right) \div \left(x + 5\right) = 3x - 8 + \frac{20}{x+5}$$

45. $\left(4x^3 - 3x^2 + 3x - 1\right) \div \left(x - 1\right)$

$$\begin{array}{r|rrrr} 1\rfloor & 4 & -3 & 3 & -1 \\ & & 4 & 1 & 4 \\ \hline & 4 & 1 & 4 & 3 \end{array}$$

$$\left(4x^3 - 3x^2 + 3x - 1\right) \div \left(x - 1\right)$$
$$= 4x^2 + x + 4 + \frac{3}{x-1}$$

47. $\left(6x^5 - 2x^3 + 4x^2 - 3x + 1\right) \div \left(x - 2\right)$

$$\begin{array}{r|rrrrrr} 2\rfloor & 6 & 0 & -2 & 4 & -3 & 1 \\ & & 12 & 24 & 44 & 96 & 186 \\ \hline & 6 & 12 & 22 & 48 & 93 & 187 \end{array}$$

$$\left(6x^5 - 2x^3 + 4x^3 - 3x + 1\right) \div \left(x - 2\right)$$
$$= 6x^4 + 12x^3 + 22x^2 + 48x + 93 + \frac{187}{x-2}$$

49. $\left(x^2 - 5x - 5x^3 + x^4\right) \div (5 + x)$

Rewrite the polynomials in descending order.

$\left(x^4 - 5x^3 + x^2 - 5x\right) \div (x + 5)$

$$\underline{-5|} \quad \begin{array}{ccccc} 1 & -5 & 1 & -5 & 0 \\ & -5 & 50 & -255 & 1300 \\ \hline 1 & -10 & 51 & -260 & 1300 \end{array}$$

$\left(x^2 - 5x - 5x^3 + x^4\right) \div (5 + x)$

$= x^3 - 10x^2 + 51x - 260 + \dfrac{1300}{5 + x}$

51. $\left(3x^3 + 2x^2 - 4x + 1\right) \div \left(x - \dfrac{1}{3}\right)$

$$\dfrac{1}{3}\bigg| \quad \begin{array}{cccc} 3 & 2 & -4 & 1 \\ & 1 & 1 & -1 \\ \hline 3 & 3 & -3 & 0 \end{array}$$

$\left(3x^3 + 2x^2 - 4x - 1\right) \div \left(x - \dfrac{1}{3}\right) = 3x^2 + 3x - 3$

53. $\dfrac{x^5 + x^3 - 2}{x - 1}$

$$\underline{1|} \quad \begin{array}{cccccc} 1 & 0 & 1 & 0 & 0 & -2 \\ & 1 & 1 & 2 & 2 & 2 \\ \hline 1 & 1 & 2 & 2 & 2 & 0 \end{array}$$

$\dfrac{x^5 + x^3 - 2}{x - 1} = x^4 + x^3 + 2x^2 + 2x + 2$

55. $\dfrac{x^4 - 256}{x - 4}$

$$\underline{4|} \quad \begin{array}{ccccc} 1 & 0 & 0 & 0 & -256 \\ & 4 & 16 & 64 & 256 \\ \hline 1 & 4 & 16 & 64 & 0 \end{array}$$

$\dfrac{x^4 - 256}{x - 4} = x^3 + 4x^2 + 16x + 64$

57. $\dfrac{2x^5 - 3x^4 + x^3 - x^2 + 2x - 1}{x + 2}$

$$\underline{-2|} \quad \begin{array}{cccccc} 2 & -3 & 1 & -1 & 2 & -1 \\ & -4 & 14 & -30 & 62 & -128 \\ \hline 2 & -7 & 15 & -31 & 64 & -129 \end{array}$$

$\dfrac{2x^5 - 3x^4 + x^3 - x^2 + 2x - 1}{x + 2}$

$= 2x^4 - 7x^3 + 15x^2 - 31x + 64 - \dfrac{129}{x + 2}$

59.

$$\begin{array}{r} x^3 - x^2y + xy^2 - y^3 \\ x + y \,\overline{\smash{\big)}\, x^4 + 0x^3 + 0x^2 + 0x + y^4} \\ \underline{x^4 + x^3y} \\ -x^3y + 0x^2 \\ \underline{-x^3y - x^2y^2} \\ x^2y^2 + 0x \\ \underline{x^2y^2 + xy^3} \\ -xy^3 + y^4 \\ \underline{-xy^3 - y^4} \\ 2y^4 \end{array}$$

$\dfrac{x^4 + y^4}{x + y} = x^3 - x^2y + xy^2 - y^3 + \dfrac{2y^4}{x + y}$

60.

$$x+y \overline{)\begin{array}{l} x^4 - x^3 y + x^2 y^2 - xy^3 + y^4 \\ x^5 + 0x^4 + 0x^3 + 0x^2 + 0x + y^4 \end{array}}$$

$$\underline{x^5 + x^4 y}$$
$$-x^4 y + 0x^3$$
$$\underline{-x^4 y - x^3 y^2}$$
$$x^3 y^2 + 0x^2$$
$$\underline{x^3 y^2 + x^2 y^3}$$
$$-x^2 y^3 + 0x$$
$$\underline{-x^2 y^3 - xy^4}$$
$$xy^4 + y^5$$
$$\underline{xy^4 + y^5}$$
$$0$$

$$\frac{x^5 + y^5}{x+y} = x^4 - x^3 y + x^2 y^2 - xy^3 + y^4$$

61.

$$x^2 + x + 2 \overline{)\begin{array}{l} 3x^2 + 2x - 1 \\ 3x^4 + 5x^3 + 7x^2 + 3x - 2 \end{array}}$$

$$\underline{3x^4 + 3x^3 + 6x^2}$$
$$2x^3 + x^2 + 3x$$
$$\underline{2x^3 + 2x^2 + 4x}$$
$$-x^2 - x - 2$$
$$\underline{-x^2 - x - 2}$$
$$0$$

$$\frac{3x^4 + 5x^3 + 7x^2 + 3x - 2}{x^2 + x + 2} = 3x^2 + 2x - 1$$

62.

$$x^2 - 3x - 2 \overline{)\begin{array}{l} x^2 + 2x + 1 \\ x^4 - x^3 - 7x^2 - 7x - 2 \end{array}}$$

$$\underline{x^4 - 3x^3 - 2x^2}$$
$$2x^3 - 5x^2 - 7x$$
$$\underline{2x^3 - 6x^2 - 4x}$$
$$x^2 - 3x - 2$$
$$\underline{x^2 - 3x - 2}$$
$$0$$

$$\frac{x^4 - x^3 - 7x^2 - 7x - 2}{x^2 - 3x - 2} = x^2 + 2x + 1$$

63.

$$x^2 + x + 1 \overline{)\begin{array}{l} 4x - 7 \\ 4x^3 - 3x^2 + x + 1 \end{array}}$$

$$\underline{4x^3 + 4x^2 + 4x}$$
$$-7x^2 - 3x + 1$$
$$\underline{-7x^2 - 7x - 7}$$
$$4x + 8$$

$$\frac{4x^3 - 3x^2 + x + 1}{x^2 + x + 1} = 4x - 7 + \frac{4x + 8}{x^2 + x + 1}$$

64.

$$x^2 + x + 1 \overline{)\begin{array}{l} x^2 - x - 1 \\ x^4 + 0x^3 - x^2 + 0x + 1 \end{array}}$$

$$\underline{x^4 + x^3 + x^2}$$
$$-x^3 - 2x^2 + 0x$$
$$\underline{-x^3 - x^2 - x}$$
$$-x^2 + x + 1$$
$$\underline{-x^2 - x - 1}$$
$$2x + 2$$

$$\frac{x^4 - x^2 + 1}{x^2 + x + 1} = x^2 - x - 1 + \frac{2x + 2}{x^2 + x + 1}$$

65.

$$
\begin{array}{r}
x^3 + x^2 - x - 3 \\
x^2 - x + 2 \overline{\smash{)}\, x^5 + 0x^4 + 0x^3 + 0x^2 + 0x - 1}
\end{array}
$$

$$
\underline{x^5 - x^4 + 2x^3}
$$
$$
x^4 - 2x^3 + 0x^2
$$
$$
\underline{x^4 - x^3 + 2x^2}
$$
$$
-x^3 - 2x^2 + 0x
$$
$$
\underline{-x^3 + x^2 - 2x}
$$
$$
-3x^2 + 2x - 1
$$
$$
\underline{-3x^2 + 3x - 6}
$$
$$
-x + 5
$$

$$
\frac{x^5 - 1}{x^2 - x + 2} = x^3 + x^2 - x - 3 + \frac{-x + 5}{x^2 - x + 2}
$$

66.

$$
\begin{array}{r}
5x^2 - 7x + 3 \\
x^3 - 4 \overline{\smash{)}\, 5x^5 - 7x^4 + 3x^3 - 20x^2 + 28x - 12}
\end{array}
$$

$$
\underline{5x^5 - 20x^2}
$$
$$
-7x^4 + 3x^3 + 28x
$$
$$
\underline{-7x^4 + 28x}
$$
$$
3x^3 - 12
$$
$$
\underline{3x^3 - 12}
$$
$$
0
$$

$$
\frac{5x^5 - 7x^4 + 3x^3 - 20x^2 + 28x - 12}{x^3 - 4}
$$
$$
= 5x^2 - 7x + 3
$$

67.

$$
\begin{array}{r}
4x^2 + 5xy - y^2 \\
x - 3y \overline{\smash{)}\, 4x^3 - 7x^2y - 16xy^2 + 3y^3}
\end{array}
$$

$$
\underline{4x^3 - 12x^2y}
$$
$$
5x^2y - 16xy^2
$$
$$
\underline{5x^2y - 15xy^2}
$$
$$
-xy^2 + 3y^3
$$
$$
\underline{-xy^2 + 3y^3}
$$
$$
0
$$

$$
\frac{4x^3 - 7x^2y - 16xy^2 + 3y^3}{x - 3y}
$$
$$
= 4x^2 + 5xy - y^2
$$

68.

$$
\begin{array}{r}
3x^2 - xy + 2y^2 \\
4x - 5y \overline{\smash{)}\, 12x^3 - 19x^2y + 13xy^2 - 10y^3}
\end{array}
$$

$$
\underline{12x^3 - 15x^2y}
$$
$$
-4x^2y + 13xy^2
$$
$$
\underline{-4x^2y + 5xy^2}
$$
$$
8xy^2 - 10y^3
$$
$$
\underline{8xy^2 - 10y^3}
$$
$$
0
$$

$$
\frac{12x^3 - 19x^2y + 13xy^2 - 10y^3}{4x - 5y}
$$
$$
= 3x^2 - xy + 2y^2
$$

69. First, compute the difference:

$$\left(4x^3 + x^2 - 2x + 7\right) - \left(3x^3 - 2x^2 - 7x + 4\right)$$
$$= x^3 + 3x^2 + 5x + 3$$

Now, complete the division:

$$\frac{x^3 + 3x^2 + 5x + 3}{x + 1}$$

$$
\begin{array}{r}
x^2 + 2x + 3 \\
x+1\overline{)x^3 + 3x^2 + 5x + 3} \\
\underline{x^3 + x^2} \\
2x^2 + 5x \\
\underline{2x^2 + 2x} \\
3x + 3 \\
\underline{3x + 3} \\
0
\end{array}
$$

$$\frac{x^3 + 3x^2 + 5x + 3}{x + 1} = x^2 + 2x + 3$$

70. First, compute the difference:

$$\left(4x^3 + 2x^2 - x - 1\right) - \left(2x^3 - x^2 + 2x - 5\right)$$
$$= 2x^3 + 3x^2 - 3x + 4$$

Now, complete the division:

$$\frac{2x^3 + 3x^2 - 3x + 4}{x + 2}$$

$$
\begin{array}{r}
2x^2 - x - 1 \\
x+2\overline{)2x^3 + 3x^2 - 3x + 4} \\
\underline{2x^3 + 4x^2} \\
-x^2 - 3x \\
\underline{-x^2 - 2x} \\
-1x + 4 \\
\underline{-x - 2} \\
6
\end{array}
$$

$$\frac{2x^3 + 3x^2 - 3x + 4}{x + 2} = 2x^2 - x - 1 + \frac{6}{x + 2}$$

71.

$$Area = (length)(width)$$
$$x^3 + 3x^2 + 5x + 3 = (length)(x + 1)$$
$$\frac{x^3 + 3x^2 + 5x + 3}{x + 1} = length$$
$$length = \frac{x^3 + 3x^2 + 5x + 3}{x + 1}$$
$$= x^2 + 2x + 3$$

73. a. Substitute $n = 3$ into the formula:

$$\frac{30,000x^3 - 30,000}{x - 1}$$

b. Factor out 30,000 from the numerator:

$$\frac{30,000x^3 - 30,000}{x - 1} = 30,000 \cdot \frac{x^3 - 1}{x - 1}$$

Now, use synthetic division to divide $\frac{x^3 - 1}{x - 1}$:

$$
\begin{array}{r|rrrr}
1 & 1 & 0 & 0 & -1 \\
  &   & 1 & 1 & 1 \\
\hline
  & 1 & 1 & 1 & 0
\end{array}
$$

$$\frac{x^3 - 1}{x - 1} = x^2 + x + 1$$

So, $\dfrac{30,000x^3 - 30,000}{x - 1}$

$$= 30,000 \cdot \frac{x^3 - 1}{x - 1}$$
$$= 30,000\left(x^2 + x + 1\right)$$
$$= 30,000x^2 + 30,000x + 30,000$$

250

c. Substitute in $x = 1.05$ into your formulas from parts (a) and (b) above:

$$\frac{30,000x^3 - 30,000}{x - 1}$$

$$= \frac{30,000(1.05)^3 - 30,000}{(1.05) - 1} = 94,575$$

$$30,000x^2 + 30,000x + 30,000$$

$$= 30,000(1.05)^2 + 30,000(1.05)$$
$$+ 30,000$$

$$= 94,575$$

Total salary over three years is $94,575.

75. Answers will vary.

77. To check a division answer, the following rules must apply:

$$\frac{dividend}{divisor} = quotient + \frac{remainder}{divisor}$$

$$dividend = (quotient)(divisor) + remainder$$

79. **a.** $4x^2 + 25x - 3 = (x + 6)(4x + 1) - 9$

b. True. See second rule in #51 above.

c. False.

d. False.

81. Since the remainder is zero, we have

$$quotient = \frac{dividend}{divisor}$$

$$quotient = \frac{16x^2 - 2x + k}{2x - 1}$$

$$\begin{array}{r} 8x + 3 \\ 2x - 1 \overline{)16x^2 - 2x + k} \\ \underline{16x^2 - 8x} \\ 6x + k \\ \underline{6x - 3} \\ 0 \end{array}$$

To make the remainder zero, we must have $k = -3$.

83. Graph $y = \dfrac{x^2 - 4}{x - 2}$ and $y = x + 2$ on the same set of axes.

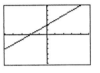

The graphs coincide because

$$\frac{x^2 - 4}{x - 2} = x + 2.$$

85. Graph $y = \dfrac{2x^2 + 13x + 15}{x - 5}$ and $y = 2x + 3$ on the same set of axes.

The graphs do not coincide because

$$\frac{2x^2 + 13x + 15}{x - 5} = 2x + 23 + \frac{130}{x - 5}.$$

Graph $y = \dfrac{2x^2 + 13x + 15}{x - 5}$ and

$y = 2x + 23 + \dfrac{130}{x - 5}$ on the same set of axes. The graphs coincide.

87.
Graph $y = \dfrac{x^3 + 3x^2 + 5x + 3}{x+1}$ and

$y = x^2 - 2x + 3$ on the same set of axes.

The graphs do not coincide because

$\dfrac{x^3 + 3x^2 + 5x + 3}{x+1} \ne x^2 + 2x + 3$.

Graph $y = \dfrac{x^3 + 3x^2 + 5x + 3}{x+1}$ and

$y = x^2 + 2x + 3$ on the same set of axes.
The graphs coincide.

88. $7x - 6y = 17$

$3x + \ y = 18$

The addition method is a good choice because both equations are written in the form $Ax + By = C$. To eliminate y, multiply second equation by 6, and add the result to the first equation.

$$7x - 6y = \ 17$$
$$\underline{18x + 6y = 108}$$
$$25x \qquad = 125$$
$$x = 5$$

Back-substitute 5 for x in either equation of the original system. We choose the original second equation:

$$3x + y = 18$$
$$3(5) + y = 18$$
$$15 + y = 18$$
$$y = 3$$

Solution: $\{(5, 3)\}$

89. $A = PB;\ P = 6\% = 0.06,\ B = 20$

$$A = PB$$
$$A = (0.06)(20)$$
$$1.2$$

Thus, 1.2 is 60% of 20.

90. $\dfrac{x}{3} + \dfrac{2}{5} = \dfrac{x}{5} - \dfrac{2}{5}$

To clear fractions, multiply by the LCD, 15.

$$15\left(\dfrac{x}{3} + \dfrac{2}{5}\right) = 15\left(\dfrac{x}{5} - \dfrac{2}{5}\right)$$
$$15\left(\dfrac{x}{3}\right) + 15\left(\dfrac{2}{5}\right) = 15\left(\dfrac{x}{5}\right) - 15\left(\dfrac{2}{5}\right)$$
$$5x + 6 = 3x - 6$$
$$2x + 6 = -6$$
$$2x = -12$$
$$x = -6$$

The solution set is $\{-6\}$.

5.7 Exercise Set

1. $8^{-2} = \dfrac{1}{8^2} = \dfrac{1}{64}$

3. $5^{-3} = \dfrac{1}{5^3} = \dfrac{1}{125}$

5. $(-6)^{-2} = \dfrac{1}{(-6)^2} = \dfrac{1}{36}$

7. $-6^{-2} = -\dfrac{1}{6^2} = -\dfrac{1}{36}$

9. $4^{-1} = \dfrac{1}{4^1} = \dfrac{1}{4}$

11. $2^{-1} + 3^{-1} = \dfrac{1}{2^1} + \dfrac{1}{3^1} = \dfrac{1}{2} + \dfrac{1}{3} = \dfrac{3}{6} + \dfrac{2}{6} = \dfrac{5}{6}$

13. $\dfrac{1}{3^{-2}} = 3^2 = 9$

15. $\dfrac{1}{(-3)^{-2}} = (-3)^2 = 9$

17. $\dfrac{2^{-3}}{8^{-2}} = \dfrac{8^2}{2^3} = \dfrac{64}{8} = 8$

19. $\left(\dfrac{1}{4}\right)^{-2} = \dfrac{1^{-2}}{4^{-2}} = \dfrac{4^2}{1^2} = \dfrac{16}{1} = 16$

21. $\left(\dfrac{3}{5}\right)^{-3} = \dfrac{3^{-3}}{5^{-3}} = \dfrac{5^3}{3^3} = \dfrac{125}{27}$

23. $\dfrac{1}{6x^{-5}} = \dfrac{1 \cdot x^5}{6} = \dfrac{x^5}{6}$

25. $\dfrac{x^{-8}}{y^{-1}} = \dfrac{y^1}{x^8} = \dfrac{y}{x^8}$

27. $\dfrac{3}{(-5)^{-3}} = 3 \cdot (-5)^3 = 5(-125) = -375$

29. $x^{-8} \cdot x^3 = x^{-8+3} = x^{-5} = \dfrac{1}{x^5}$

31. $\left(4x^{-5}\right)\left(2x^2\right) = 8x^{-5+2} = 8x^{-3} = \dfrac{8}{x^3}$

33. $\dfrac{x^3}{x^9} = x^{3-9} = x^{-6} = \dfrac{1}{x^6}$

35. $\dfrac{y}{y^{100}} = \dfrac{y^1}{y^{100}} = y^{1-100} = y^{-99} = \dfrac{1}{y^{99}}$

37. $\dfrac{30z^5}{10z^{10}} = \dfrac{30}{10} \cdot \dfrac{z^5}{z^{10}} = 3z^{5-10} = -3z^{-5} = \dfrac{3}{z^5}$

39. $\dfrac{-8x^3}{2x^7} = \dfrac{-8}{2} \cdot \dfrac{x^3}{x^7} = -4x^{-4} = -\dfrac{4}{x^4}$

41. $\dfrac{-9a^5}{27a^8} = \dfrac{-9}{27} \cdot \dfrac{a^5}{a^8} = -\dfrac{1}{3}a^{-3} = -\dfrac{1}{3a^3}$

43. $\dfrac{7w^5}{5w^{13}} = \dfrac{7}{5} \cdot \dfrac{w^5}{w^{13}} = \dfrac{7}{5}w^{-8} = \dfrac{7}{5w^8}$

45. $\dfrac{x^3}{\left(x^4\right)^2} = \dfrac{x^3}{x^{4\cdot 2}} = \dfrac{x^3}{x^8} = x^{-5} = \dfrac{1}{x^5}$

47. $\dfrac{y^{-3}}{\left(y^4\right)^2} = \dfrac{y^{-3}}{y^8} = y^{-3-8} = y^{-11} = \dfrac{1}{y^{11}}$

49. $\dfrac{\left(4x^3\right)^2}{x^8} = \dfrac{4^2 x^6}{x^8} = 16x^{-2} = \dfrac{16}{x^2}$

51. $\dfrac{\left(6y^4\right)^3}{y^{-5}} = \dfrac{6^3 y^{12}}{y^{-5}} = 216y^{12-(-5)} = 216y^{17}$

53. $\left(\dfrac{x^4}{x^2}\right)^{-3} = \left(x^2\right)^{-3} = x^{-6} = \dfrac{1}{x^6}$

55. $\left(\dfrac{4x^5}{2x^2}\right)^{-4} = \left(2x^3\right)^{-4}$

$= 2^{-4}x^{-12} = \dfrac{1}{2^4 x^{12}} = \dfrac{1}{16x^{12}}$

57. $\left(3x^{-1}\right)^{-2} = 3^{-2}\left(x^{-1}\right)^{-2} = 3^{-2}x^2 = \dfrac{x^2}{3^2} = \dfrac{x^2}{9}$

59. $\left(-2y^{-1}\right)^{-3} = (-2)^{-3}\left(y^{-1}\right)^{-3}$

$\quad = \dfrac{y^3}{(-2)^3} = \dfrac{y^3}{-8} = -\dfrac{y^3}{8}$

61. $\dfrac{2x^5 \cdot 3x^7}{15x^6} = \dfrac{6x^{12}}{15x^6}$

$\quad = \dfrac{6}{15} \cdot \dfrac{x^{12}}{x^6} = \dfrac{2}{5} \cdot x^6 = \dfrac{2x^6}{5}$

63. $\left(x^3\right)^5 \cdot x^{-7} = x^{15} \cdot x^{-7} = x^{15+(-7)} = x^8$

65. $\left(2y^3\right)^4 y^{-6} = 2^4\left(y^3\right)^4 y^{-6}$

$\quad = 16y^{12}y^{-6} = 16y^6$

67. $\dfrac{\left(y^3\right)^4}{\left(y^2\right)^7} = \dfrac{y^{12}}{y^{14}} = y^{-2} = \dfrac{1}{y^2}$

69. $\left(y^{10}\right)^{-5} = y^{(10)(-5)} = y^{-50} = \dfrac{1}{y^{50}}$

71. $\left(a^4b^5\right)^{-3} = \left(a^4\right)^{-3}\left(b^5\right)^{-3}$

$\quad = a^{-12}b^{-15} = \dfrac{1}{a^{12}b^{15}}$

73. $\left(a^{-2}b^6\right)^{-4} = a^8b^{-24} = \dfrac{a^8}{b^{24}}$

75. $\left(\dfrac{x^2}{2}\right)^{-2} = \dfrac{x^{-4}}{2^{-2}} = \dfrac{2^2}{x^4} = \dfrac{4}{x^4}$

77. $\left(\dfrac{x^2}{y^3}\right)^{-3} = \dfrac{\left(x^2\right)^{-3}}{\left(y^3\right)^{-3}} = \dfrac{x^{-6}}{y^{-9}} = \dfrac{y^9}{x^6}$

79. $8.7 \times 10^2 = 870$ (Move decimal point 2 places to the right.)

81. $9.23 \times 10^5 = 923{,}000$ (Move right 5.)

83. $3.4 \times 10^0 = 3.4$ (Don't move decimal point.)

85. $7.9 \times 10^{-1} = 0.79$ (Move left 1.)

87. $2.15 \times 10^{-2} = 0.0215$ (Move left 2.)

89. $7.86 \times 10^{-4} = 0.000786$ (Move left 4.)

91. $32{,}400 = 3.24 \times 10^4$

93. $220{,}000{,}000 = 2.2 \times 10^8$

95. $713 = 7.13 \times 10^2$

97. $6751 = 6.751 \times 10^3$

99. $0.0027 = 2.7 \times 10^{-3}$

101. $0.000020 = 2.02 \times 10^{-5}$

103. $0.005 = 5 \times 10^{-3}$

105. $3.14159 = 3.14159 \times 10^0$

107. $\left(2 \times 10^3\right)\left(3 \times 10^2\right) = 6 \times 10^{3+2} = 6 \times 10^5$

109. $\left(2 \times 10^5\right)\left(8 \times 10^3\right) = 16 \times 10^{5+3}$

$\quad = 16 \times 10^8 = 1.6 \times 10^9$

111. $\dfrac{12 \times 10^6}{4 \times 10^2} = 3 \times 10^{6-2} = 3 \times 10^4$

113. $\dfrac{15 \times 10^4}{5 \times 10^{-2}} = 3 \times 10^{4+2} = 3 \times 10^6$

115. $\dfrac{15 \times 10^{-4}}{5 \times 10^2} = 3 \times 10^{-4-2} = 3 \times 10^{-6}$

117. $\dfrac{180\times10^6}{2\times10^3}=90\times10^{6-3}$

$$=90\times10^3=9\times10^4$$

119. $\dfrac{3\times10^4}{12\times10^{-3}}=0.25\times10^{4+3}$

$$=0.25\times10^7=2.5\times10^6$$

121. $\left(5\times10^2\right)^3=5^3\times10^{2(3)}$

$$=125\times10^6=1.25\times10^8$$

123. $\left(3\times10^{-2}\right)^4=3^4\times10^{-2(4)}$

$$=81\times10^{-8}=8.1\times10^{-7}$$

125. $\left(4\times10^6\right)^{-1}=4^{-1}\times10^{6(-1)}$

$$=0.25\times10^{-6}=2.6\times10^{-7}$$

127. $\dfrac{\left(x^{-2}y\right)^{-3}}{\left(x^2y^{-1}\right)^3}=\dfrac{x^6y^{-3}}{x^6y^{-3}}=x^{6-6}y^{-3-(-3)}=x^0y^0=1$

128. $\dfrac{\left(xy^{-2}\right)^{-2}}{\left(x^{-2}y\right)^{-3}}=\dfrac{x^{-2}y^4}{x^6y^{-3}}$

$$=x^{-2-6}y^{4-(-3)}=x^{-8}y^7=\dfrac{y^7}{x^8}$$

129. $\left(2x^{-3}yz^{-6}\right)\left(2x\right)^{-5}=2x^{-3}yz^{-6}\cdot2^{-5}x^{-5}$

$$=2^{-4}x^{-8}yz^{-6}$$

$$=\dfrac{y}{2^4x^8z^6}=\dfrac{y}{16x^8z^6}$$

130. $\left(3x^{-4}yz^{-7}\right)\left(3x\right)^{-3}=3x^{-4}yz^{-7}\cdot3^{-3}x^{-3}$

$$=3^{-2}x^{-7}yz^{-7}$$

$$=\dfrac{y}{3^2x^7z^7}=\dfrac{y}{9x^7z^7}$$

131. $\left(\dfrac{x^3y^4z^5}{x^{-3}y^{-4}z^{-5}}\right)^{-2}=\left(x^6y^8z^{10}\right)^{-2}$

$$=x^{-12}y^{-16}z^{-20}=\dfrac{1}{x^{12}y^{16}z^{20}}$$

132. $\left(\dfrac{x^4y^5z^6}{x^{-4}y^{-5}z^{-6}}\right)^{-4}=\left(x^8y^{10}z^{12}\right)^{-4}$

$$=x^{-32}y^{-40}z^{-48}=\dfrac{1}{x^{32}y^{40}z^{48}}$$

133. $\dfrac{\left(2^{-1}x^{-2}y^{-1}\right)^{-2}\left(2x^{-4}y^3\right)^{-2}\left(16x^{-3}y^3\right)^0}{\left(2x^{-3}y^{-5}\right)^2}$

$$=\dfrac{\left(2^2x^2y^2\right)\left(2^{-2}x^8y^{-6}\right)(1)}{\left(2^2x^{-6}y^{-10}\right)}$$

$$=\dfrac{x^{18}y^6}{4}$$

134. $\dfrac{\left(2^{-1}x^{-3}y^{-1}\right)^{-2}\left(2x^{-6}y^4\right)^{-2}\left(9x^3y^{-3}\right)^0}{\left(2x^{-4}y^{-6}\right)^2}$

$$=\dfrac{\left(2^2x^6y^2\right)\left(2^{-2}x^{12}y^{-8}\right)(1)}{\left(2^2x^{-8}y^{-12}\right)}$$

$$=\dfrac{x^{26}y^6}{4}$$

135. $\dfrac{\left(5\times10^3\right)\left(1.2\times10^{-4}\right)}{\left(2.4\times10^2\right)}=2.5\times10^{-3}$

136. $\dfrac{\left(2\times10^2\right)\left(2.6\times10^{-3}\right)}{\left(4\times10^3\right)}=1.3\times10^{-4}$

137. $\dfrac{\left(1.6\times10^4\right)\left(7.2\times10^{-3}\right)}{\left(3.6\times10^8\right)\left(4\times10^{-3}\right)}=0.8\times10^{-4}=8\times10^{-5}$

138. $\dfrac{\left(1.2\times10^{6}\right)\left(8.7\times10^{-2}\right)}{\left(2.9\times10^{6}\right)\left(3\times10^{-3}\right)}=1.2\times10^{1}$

139. $9200=9.2\times10^{3}$

141. $0.0000000000000025=2.5\times10^{-16}$

143. $600\times10^{6}=6\times10^{2}\times10^{6}=6\times10^{8}$

145. $399\times10^{9}=3.99\times10^{2}\times10^{9}=3.99\times10^{11}$

147. $20\%\left(2\times10^{12}\right)=0.2\left(2\times10^{12}\right)$

$\qquad = 2\times10^{-1}\left(2\times10^{12}\right)=4\times10^{11}$

The government spends $\$4\times10^{11}$.

149. $120\left(2.9\times10^{8}\right)=348\times10^{8}$

$\qquad = 3.48\times10^{2}\times10^{8}=3.48\times10^{10}$

The total annual spending in the United States on ice cream is about $\$3.48\times10^{10}$.

151. $\dfrac{2.325\times10^{5}}{1.86\times10^{5}}=1.25$ seconds

153. When moving a base and exponent from numerator to denominator, keep the base and switch the sign of the exponent.

Example: $\dfrac{x^{2}}{y^{-3}}=\dfrac{y^{3}}{x^{-2}}$

155. The number will be written as a number between 1 and 10 (not including 10) times a power of 10.

157. If the number is greater than 1 or less than -1, move the decimal point so it is immediately following the first nonzero digit in the number and raise 10 to the number of places the decimal point moved.

If the number is between -1 and 1, move the decimal point so it is immediately following the first nonzero digit in the number and raise 10 to the negative of the number of places the decimal point moved.

Example:

$123.4567=1.234567\times10^{2}$

$0.0001234567=1.234567\times10^{-4}$

159. Statement b is true.

$5^{-2}=\dfrac{1}{25}$ and $2^{-5}=\dfrac{1}{32}$

Since $\dfrac{1}{25}>\dfrac{1}{32}$, $5^{-2}>2^{-5}$

161. There is no advantage in using scientific notation to represent a number greater than or equal to 1 and less than 10 because the decimal point will not be moved and it is simpler to write it without the zero exponent.

Example: $7.75=7.75\times10^{0}$

163. Students will check their work with a calculator. Results will depend on the exercises chosen.

165. Students will check their work with a calculator. Results will depend on the exercises chosen.

167.
$$8 - 6x > 4x - 12$$
$$8 - 6x - 4x > 4x - 12 - 4x$$
$$-10x + 8 > -12$$
$$-10x + 8 - 8 > -12 - 8$$
$$-10x > -20$$
$$\frac{-10x}{-10} < \frac{-20}{-10}$$
$$x < 2$$
The solution set is $\{x \mid x < 2\}$.

168.
$$24 \div 8 \cdot 3 + 28 \div (-7) = 3 \cdot 3 + 28 \div (-7)$$
$$= 9 + (-4)$$
$$= 5$$

169. The whole numbers in the given set are 0 and $\sqrt{16}\,(= 4)$.

Chapter 5 Review Exercises

1. $7x^4 + 9x$ is a binomial of degree 4.

2. $3x + 5x^2 - 2$ is a trinomial of degree 2.

3. $16x$ is a monomial of degree 1.

4.
$$\left(-6x^3 + 7x^2 - 9x + 3\right)$$
$$+\left(14x^3 + 3x^2 - 11x - 7\right)$$
$$= \left(-6x^3 + 14x^3\right) + \left(7x^2 + 3x^2\right)$$
$$+\left(-9x - 11x\right) + \left(3 - 7\right)$$
$$= 8x^3 + 10x^2 - 20x - 4$$

5.
$$\left(9y^3 - 7y^2 + 5\right) + \left(4y^3 - y^2 + 7y - 10\right)$$
$$= \left(9y^3 + 4y^3\right) + \left(-7y^2 - y^2\right) + 7y$$
$$+\left(5 - 10\right)$$
$$= 13y^3 - 8y^2 + 7y - 5$$

6.
$$\left(5y^2 - y - 8\right) - \left(-6y^2 + 3y - 4\right)$$
$$= \left(5y^2 - y - 8\right) + \left(6y^2 - 3y + 4\right)$$
$$= \left(5y^2 + 6y^2\right) + \left(-y - 3y\right) + \left(-8 + 4\right)$$
$$= 11y^2 - 4y - 4$$

7.
$$\left(13x^4 - 8x^3 + 2x^2\right) - \left(5x^4 - 3x^3 + 2x^2 - 6\right)$$
$$= \left(13x^4 - 8x^3 + 2x^2\right)$$
$$+\left(-5x^4 + 3x^3 - 2x^2 + 6\right)$$
$$= \left(13x^4 - 5x^4\right) + \left(-8x^3 + 3x^3\right)$$
$$+\left(2x^2 - 2x^2\right) + 6$$
$$= 8x^4 - 5x^3 + 6$$

8.
$$\left(-13x^4 - 6x^2 + 5x\right) - \left(x^4 + 7x^2 - 11x\right)$$
$$= \left(-13x^4 - 6x^2 + 5x\right)$$
$$+\left(-x^4 - 7x^2 + 11x\right)$$
$$= \left(-13x^4 - x^4\right) + \left(-6x^2 - 7x^2\right)$$
$$+\left(5x + 11x\right)$$
$$= -14x^4 - 13x^2 + 16x$$

9. Add:

$$7y^4 - 6y^3 + 4y^2 - 4y$$
$$\underline{\qquad\quad y^3 - \ y^2 + 3y - 4}$$
$$7y^4 - 5y^3 + 3y^2 - \ y - 4$$

10. Subtract:

$$7x^2 - 9x + 2$$
$$-\left(4x^2 - 2x - 7\right)$$

Add:

$$7x^2 - 9x + 2$$
$$\underline{-4x^2 + 2x + 7}$$
$$3x^2 - 7x + 9$$

11.

$$5x^3 - 6x^2 - 9x + 14$$
$$-\left(-5x^3 + 3x^2 - 11x + 3\right)$$

Add:

$$5x^3 - 6x^2 - 9x + 14$$
$$\underline{5x^3 - 3x^2 + 11x - 3}$$
$$10x^3 - 9x^2 + 2x + 11$$

12. $104.5x^2 - 1501.5x + 6016; \ x = 10$

$$104.5x^2 - 1501.5x + 6016$$
$$= 104.5(10)^2 - 1501.5(10) + 6016$$
$$= 10,450 - 15,015 + 6016$$
$$= 1451$$

The death rate for men averaging 10 hours of sleep per night is 1451 men per 10,000 men.

13. $x^{20} \cdot x^3 = x^{20+3} = x^{23}$

14. $y \cdot y^5 \cdot y^8 = y^1 \cdot y^5 \cdot y^8 = y^{1+5+8} = y^{14}$

15. $\left(x^{20}\right)^5 = x^{20 \cdot 5} = x^{100}$

16. $\left(10y\right)^2 = 10^2 y^2 = 100 y^2$

17. $\left(-4x^{10}\right)^3 = \left(-4\right)^3 \left(x^{10}\right)^3 = -64x^{30}$

18. $\left(5x\right)\left(10x^3\right) = \left(5 \cdot 10\right)\left(x^1 \cdot x^3\right) = 50x^4$

19. $\left(-12y^7\right)\left(3y^4\right) = -36y^{11}$

20. $\left(-2x^5\right)\left(-3x^4\right)\left(5x^3\right) = 30x^{12}$

21. $7x\left(3x^2 + 9\right) = 7x\left(3x^2\right) + \left(7x\right)\left(9\right)$
$$= 21x^3 + 63x$$

22. $5x^3\left(4x^2 - 11x\right) = 5x^3\left(4x^2\right) - 5x^3\left(11x\right)$
$$= 20x^5 - 55x^4$$

23. $3y^2\left(-7y^2 + 3y - 6\right)$
$$= 3y^2\left(-7y^2\right) + 3y^2\left(3y\right) + 3y^2\left(-6\right)$$
$$= -21y^4 + 9y^3 - 18y^2$$

24. $2y^5\left(8y^3 - 10y^2 + 1\right)$
$$= 2y^5\left(8y^3\right) + 2y^5\left(-10y^2\right) + 2y^5\left(1\right)$$
$$= 16y^8 - 20y^7 + 2y^5$$

25. $\left(x+3\right)\left(x^2 - 5x + 2\right)$
$$= x\left(x^2 - 5x + 2\right) + 3\left(x^2 - 5x + 2\right)$$
$$= x^3 - 5x^2 + 2x + 3x^2 - 15x + 6$$
$$= x^3 - 2x^2 - 13x + 6$$

26. $\left(3y - 2\right)\left(4y^2 + 3y - 5\right)$
$$= 3y\left(4y^2 + 3y - 5\right) - 2\left(4y^2 + 3y - 5\right)$$
$$= 12y^3 + 9y^2 - 15y - 8y^2 - 6y + 10$$
$$= 12y^3 + y^2 - 21y + 10$$

27.

$$y^2 - 4y + 7$$
$$\underline{\quad\quad 3y - 5}$$
$$-5y^2 + 20y - 35$$
$$\underline{3y^3 - 12y^2 + 21y \quad\quad}$$
$$3y^3 - 17y^2 + 41y - 35$$

28.

$$4x^3 - 2x^2 - 6x - 1$$
$$\underline{\quad\quad\quad\quad 2x + 3}$$
$$12x^3 - 6x^2 - 18x - 3$$
$$\underline{8x^4 - 4x^3 - 12x^2 - 2x \quad\quad}$$
$$8x^4 + 8x^3 - 18x^2 - 20x - 3$$

29. $(x+6)(x+2)$

$$= x \cdot x + x \cdot 2 + 6 \cdot x + 6 \cdot 2$$
$$= x^2 + 2x + 6x + 12$$
$$= x^2 + 8x + 12$$

30. $(3y-5)(2y+1) = 6y^2 + 3y - 10y - 5$
$$= 6y^2 - 7y - 5$$

31. $(4x^2 - 2)(x^2 - 3)$

$$= 4x^2 \cdot x^2 + 4x^2(-3) - 2 \cdot x^2 - 2(-3)$$
$$= 4x^4 - 12x^2 - 2x^2 + 6$$
$$= 4x^4 - 14x^2 + 6$$

32. $(5x+4)(5x-4) = (5x)^2 - 4^2$
$$= 25x^2 - 16$$

33. $(7-2y)(7+2y) = 7^2 - (2y)^2 = 49 - 4y^2$

34. $(y^2+1)(y^2-1) = (y^2)^2 - 1^2 = y^4 - 1$

35. $(x+3)^2 = x^2 + 2(x)(3) + 3^2$
$$= x^2 + 6x + 9$$

36. $(3y+4)^2 = (3y)^2 + 2(3y)(4) + 16$
$$= 9y^2 + 24y + 16$$

37. $(y-1)^2 = y^2 - 2y + 1$

38. $(5y-2)^2 = (5y)^2 - 2(5y)(2) + 2^2$
$$= 25y^2 - 20y + 4$$

39. $(x^2+4)^2 = (x^2)^2 + 2(x^2)(4) + 4^2$
$$= x^4 + 8x^2 + 16$$

40. $(x^2+4)(x^2-4) = (x^2)^2 - 4^2 = x^4 - 16$

41. $(x^2+4)(x^2-5) = (x^2)^2 - 5x^2 + 4x^2 - 20$
$$= x^4 - x^2 - 20$$

42. $A = (x+3)(x+4)$
$$= x^2 + 4x + 3x + 12$$
$$= x^2 + 7x + 12$$

43. $A = (x+30)(x+20)$
$$= x^2 + 20x + 30x + 600$$
$$= x^2 + 50x + 600$$

The area of the expanded garage is
$(x^2 + 50x + 500)$ yards^2.

44. $2x^3y - 4xy^2 + 5y + 6; \ x = -1, \ y = 2$
$$2x^3y - 4xy^2 + 5y + 6$$
$$= 2(-1)^3(2) - 4(-1)(2)^2 + 5(2) + 6$$
$$= 2(-1)(2) + 4(1)(4) + 5(2) + 6$$
$$= -4 + 16 + 10 + 6$$
$$= 28$$

45.

Term	Coefficient	Degree
$4x^2y$	4	2+1=3
$9x^3y^2$	9	3+2=5
$-17x^4$	-17	4
-12	-12	0

Degree of the polynomial = 5

46. $\left(7x^2 - 8xy + y^2\right) + \left(-8x^2 - 9xy + 4y^2\right)$

$\quad = \left(7x^2 - 8x^2\right) + \left(-8xy - 9xy\right)$

$\qquad + \left(y^2 + 4y^2\right)$

$\quad = -x^2 - 17xy + 5y^2$

47. $\left(13x^3y^2 - 5x^2y - 9x^2\right)$

$\qquad -\left(11x^3y^2 - 6x^2y - 3x^2 + 4\right)$

$\quad = \left(13x^3y^2 - 5x^2y - 9x^2\right)$

$\qquad + \left(-11x^3y^2 + 6x^2y + 3x^2 - 4\right)$

$\quad = \left(13x^3y^2 - 11x^3y^2\right) + \left(-5x^2y + 6x^2y\right)$

$\qquad + \left(-9x^2 + 3x^2\right) - 4$

$\quad = 2x^3y^3 + x^2y - 6x^2 - 4$

48. $\left(-7x^2y^3\right)\left(5x^4y^6\right)$

$\quad = (-7)(-5)x^{2+4}y^{3+6} = -35x^6y^9$

49. $5ab^2\left(3a^2b^3 - 4ab\right)$

$\quad = 5ab^2\left(3a^2b^3\right) + 5ab^2\left(-4ab\right)$

$\quad = 15a^3b^5 - 20a^2b^3$

50. $(x + 7y)(3x - 5y)$

$\quad = x(3x) + x(-5y) + 7y(3x) + 7y(-5y)$

$\quad = 3x^2 - 5xy + 21xy - 35y^2$

$\quad = 3x^2 + 16xy - 35y^2$

51. $(4xy - 3)(9xy - 1)$

$\quad = 4xy(9xy) + 4xy(-1) - 3(9xy) - 3(-1)$

$\quad = 36x^2y^2 - 4xy - 27xy + 3$

$\quad = 36x^2y^2 - 31xy + 3$

52. $(3x + 5y)^2 = (3x)^2 + 2(3x)(5y) + (5y)^2$

$\qquad = 9x^2 + 30xy + 25y^2$

53. $(xy - 7)^2 = (xy)^2 - 2(xy)(7) + 7^2$

$\qquad = x^2y^2 - 14xy + 49$

54. $(7x + 4y)(7x - 4y) = (7x)^2 - (4y)^2$

$\qquad = 49x^2 - 16y^2$

55. $(a - b)\left(a^2 + ab + b^2\right)$

$\quad = a\left(a^2 + ab + b^2\right) - b\left(a^2 + ab + b^2\right)$

$\quad = a^3 + a^2b + ab^2 - a^2b - ab^2 - b^3$

$\quad = a^3 + \left(a^2b - a^2b\right) + \left(ab^2 - ab^2\right) - b^3$

$\quad = a^3 - b^3$

56. $\dfrac{6^{40}}{6^{10}} = 6^{40-10} = 6^{30}$

57. $\dfrac{x^{18}}{x^3} = x^{18-x} = x^{15}$

58. $(-10)^0 = 1$

59. $-10^0 = -(1) = -1$

60. $400x^0 = 400 \cdot 1 = 400$

61. $\left(\dfrac{x^4}{2}\right)^3 = \dfrac{\left(x^4\right)^3}{2^3} = \dfrac{x^{4 \cdot 3}}{8} = \dfrac{x^{12}}{8}$

62. $\left(\dfrac{-3}{2y^6}\right)^4 = \dfrac{(-3)^4}{\left(2y^6\right)^4} = \dfrac{81}{\left(2^4 y^6\right)^4} = \dfrac{81}{16y^{24}}$

63. $\dfrac{-15y^8}{3y^2} = \dfrac{-15}{3} \cdot \dfrac{y^8}{y^2} = -5y^6$

64. $\dfrac{40x^8 y^6}{5xy^3} = \dfrac{40}{5} \cdot \dfrac{x^8}{x^1} \cdot \dfrac{y^6}{y^3} = 5x^7 y^3$

65. $\dfrac{18x^4 - 12x^2 + 36x}{6x} = \dfrac{18x^4}{6x} - \dfrac{12x^2}{6x} + \dfrac{36x}{6x}$

$= 3x^3 - 2x + 6$

66. $\dfrac{30x^8 - 25x^7 - 40x^5}{-5x^3}$

$= \dfrac{30x^8}{-5x^3} - \dfrac{25x^7}{-5x^3} - \dfrac{40x^5}{-5x^3}$

$= -6x^5 + 5x^4 + 8x^2$

67. $\dfrac{27x^3 y^2 - 9x^2 y - 18xy^2}{3xy}$

$= \dfrac{27x^3 y^2}{3xy} - \dfrac{9x^2 y}{3xy} - \dfrac{18xy^2}{3xy}$

$= 9x^2 y - 3x - 6y$

68.
$$
\begin{array}{r}
2x+7 \\
x-2\overline{\smash{\big)}\,2x^2 + 3x - 14} \\
\underline{2x^2 - 4x} \\
7x - 14 \\
\underline{7x - 14} \\
0
\end{array}
$$

$\dfrac{2x^2 + 3x - 14}{x - 2} = 2x + 7$

69.
$$
\begin{array}{r}
x^2 - 3x + 5 \\
2x+1\overline{\smash{\big)}\,2x^3 - 5x^2 + 7x + 5} \\
\underline{2x^3 + x^2} \\
-6x^2 + 7x \\
\underline{-6x^2 - 3x} \\
10x + 5 \\
\underline{10x + 5} \\
0
\end{array}
$$

$\dfrac{2x^3 - 5x^2 + 7x + 5}{2x + 1} = x^2 - 3x + 5$

70.
$$
\begin{array}{r}
x^2 + 5x + 2 \\
x-7\overline{\smash{\big)}\,x^3 - 2x^2 - 33x - 7} \\
\underline{x^3 - 7x^2} \\
5x^2 - 33x \\
\underline{5x^2 - 35x} \\
2x - 7 \\
\underline{2x - 14} \\
7
\end{array}
$$

$\dfrac{x^3 - 2x^2 - 33x - 7}{x - 7} = x^2 + 5x + 2 + \dfrac{7}{x - 7}$

71.
$$
\begin{array}{r}
y^2 + 3y + 9 \\
y-3\overline{\smash{\big)}\,y^3 + 0y^2 + 0y - 27} \\
\underline{y^3 - 3y^2} \\
3y^2 + 0y \\
\underline{3y^2 - 9y} \\
9y - 27 \\
\underline{9y - 27} \\
0
\end{array}
$$

$\dfrac{y^3 - 27}{y - 3} = y^2 + 3y + 9$

261

72.

$$\begin{array}{r} 2x^2 + 3x - 1 \\ 2x^2 + 0x + 1 \overline{\smash{\big)}\ 4x^4 + 6x^3 + 0x^2 + 3x - 1} \\ \underline{4x^4 + 0x^3 + 2x^2} \\ 6x^3 - 2x^2 + 3x \\ \underline{6x^3 + 0x^2 + 3x} \\ -2x^2 + 0x - 1 \\ \underline{-2x^2 + 0x - 1} \\ 0 \end{array}$$

$$\frac{4x^4 + 6x^3 + 3x - 1}{2x^2 + 1} = 2x^2 + 3x - 1$$

73. $\left(4x^3 - 3x^2 - 2x + 1\right) \div \left(x + 1\right)$

$$\begin{array}{r|rrrr} \underline{-1} & 4 & -3 & -2 & 1 \\ & & -4 & 7 & -5 \\ \hline & 4 & -7 & 5 & -4 \end{array}$$

$$\left(4x^3 - 3x^2 - 2x + 1\right) \div \left(x + 1\right)$$

$$= 4x^2 - 7x + 5 - \frac{4}{x + 1}$$

74. $\left(3x^4 - 2x^2 - 10x - 20\right) \div \left(x - 2\right)$

$$\begin{array}{r|rrrrr} \underline{2} & 3 & 0 & -2 & -10 & -20 \\ & & 6 & 12 & 20 & 20 \\ \hline & 3 & 6 & 10 & 10 & 0 \end{array}$$

$$\left(3x^4 - 2x^2 - 10x - 20\right) \div \left(x - 2\right)$$

$$= 3x^3 + 6x^2 + 10x + 10$$

75. $\left(x^4 + 16\right) \div \left(x + 4\right)$

$$\begin{array}{r|rrrrr} \underline{-4} & 1 & 0 & 0 & 0 & 16 \\ & & -4 & 16 & -64 & 256 \\ \hline & 1 & -4 & 16 & -64 & 272 \end{array}$$

$$\left(x^4 + 16\right) \div \left(x + 4\right)$$

$$= x^3 - 4x^2 + 16x - 64 + \frac{272}{x + 4}$$

76. $7^{-2} = \dfrac{1}{7^2} = \dfrac{1}{49}$

77. $\left(-4\right)^{-3} = \dfrac{1}{\left(-4\right)^3} = \dfrac{1}{-64} = -\dfrac{1}{64}$

78. $2^{-1} + 4^{-1} = \dfrac{1}{2} + \dfrac{1}{4} = \dfrac{3}{4}$

79. $\dfrac{1}{5^{-2}} = 5^2 = 25$

80. $\left(\dfrac{2}{5}\right)^{-3} = \dfrac{2^{-3}}{5^{-3}} = \dfrac{5^3}{2^3} = \dfrac{125}{8}$

81. $\dfrac{x^3}{x^9} = x^{3-9} = x^{-6} = \dfrac{1}{x^6}$

82. $\dfrac{30y^6}{5y^8} = \dfrac{30}{5} \cdot \dfrac{y^6}{y^8} = 6y^{-2} = \dfrac{6}{y^2}$

83. $\left(5x^{-7}\right)\left(6x^2\right) = \left(5 \cdot 6\right)\left(x^{-7+2}\right) = 30x^{-5} = \dfrac{30}{x^5}$

84. $\dfrac{x^4 \cdot x^{-2}}{x^{-6}} = \dfrac{x^{4+(-2)}}{x^{-6}} = \dfrac{x^2}{x^{-6}} = x^{2-(-6)} = x^8$

85. $\dfrac{\left(3y^3\right)^4}{y^{10}} = \dfrac{3^4 y^{3(4)}}{y^{10}} = \dfrac{81y^{12}}{y^{10}} = 81y^{12-10} = 81y^2$

86. $\dfrac{y^{-7}}{\left(y^4\right)^3} = \dfrac{y^{-7}}{y^{12}} = y^{-7-12} = y^{-19} = \dfrac{1}{y^{19}}$

87. $\left(2x^{-1}\right)^{-3} = 2^{-3}\left(x^{-1}\right)^{-3} = 2^{-3}x^3 = \dfrac{x^3}{2^{-3}} = \dfrac{x^3}{8}$

88. $\left(\dfrac{x^7}{x^4}\right)^{-2} = \left(x^3\right)^{-2} = x^{-6} = \dfrac{1}{x^6}$

262

89.
$$\frac{\left(y^3\right)^4}{\left(y^{-2}\right)^4} = \frac{y^{12}}{y^{-8}} = y^{12-(-8)} = y^{20}$$

90. $2.3 \times 10^4 = 23,000$
(Move decimal point to right 4 places.)

91. $1.76 \times 10^{-3} = 0.00176$ (Move left 3 places.)

92. $9 \times 10^{-1} = 0.9$

93. $73,900,000 = 7.39 \times 10^7$

94. $0.00062 = 6.2 \times 10^{-4}$

95. $0.38 = 3.8 \times 10^{-1}$

96. $3.8 = 3.8 \times 10^0$

97.
$$\left(6 \times 10^{-3}\right)\left(1.5 \times 10^6\right) = 6(1.5) \times 10^{-3+6}$$
$$= 9 \times 10^3$$

98.
$$\frac{2 \times 10^2}{4 \times 10^{-3}} = 0.5 \cdot 10^{2+3}$$
$$= 0.5 \times 10^5$$
$$= 5 \times 10^{-1} \times 10^5 = 5.0 \times 10^4$$

99.
$$\left(4 \times 10^{-2}\right) = 4^2 \times 10^{-2(2)}$$
$$= 16 \times 10^{-4}$$
$$= 1.6 \times 10^1 \times 10^{-4}$$
$$= 1.6 \times 10^{1-4} = 1.6 \times 10^{-3}$$

100.
$$\frac{10^{-6}}{10^{-9}} = \frac{10^9}{10^6} = 10^{9-6} = 10^3 = 1000$$
There are 1000 nanoseconds in a microsecond.

101. $2\left(6.3 \times 10^9\right) = 12.6 \times 10^9 = 1.26 \times 10^{10}$
In 40 years, there will be approximately 1.26×10^{10} people in the world.

Chapter 5 Test

1. $9x + 6x^2 - 4$ is a trinomial of degree 2.

2.
$$\left(7x^3 + 3x^2 - 5x - 11\right)$$
$$+ \left(6x^3 - 2x^2 + 4x - 13\right)$$
$$= \left(7x^3 + 6x^3\right) + \left(3x^2 - 2x^2\right)$$
$$+ (-5x + 4x) + (-11 - 13)$$
$$= 13x^3 + x^2 - x - 24$$

3.
$$\left(9x^3 - 6x^2 - 11x - 4\right)$$
$$- \left(4x^3 - 8x^2 - 13x + 5\right)$$
$$= \left(9x^3 - 6x^2 - 11x - 4\right)$$
$$+ \left(-4x^3 + 8x^2 + 13x - 5\right)$$
$$= \left(9x^3 - 4x^3\right) + \left(-6x^2 + 8x^2\right)$$
$$+ (-11x + 13x) + (-4 - 5)$$
$$= 5x^3 + 2x^2 + 2x - 9$$

4. $\left(-7x^3\right)\left(5x^8\right) = (-7 \cdot 5)\left(x^{3+8}\right) = -35x^{11}$

5.
$$6x^2 \left(8x^3 - 5x - 2\right)$$
$$= 6x^2 \left(8x^3\right) + 6x^2 (-5x) + 6x^2 (-2)$$
$$= 48x^5 - 30x^3 - 12x^2$$

6.
$$(3x + 2)\left(x^2 - 4x - 3\right)$$
$$= 3x\left(x^2 - 4x - 3\right) + 2\left(x^2 - 4x - 3\right)$$
$$= 3x^3 - 12x^2 - 9x + 2x^2 - 8x - 6$$
$$= 3x^3 - 10x^2 - 17x - 6$$

7. $(3y+7)(2y-9) = 6y^2 +14y - 27y - 63$
$$= 6y^2 - 13y - 63$$

8. $(7x+5)(7x-5) = (7x)^2 - 5^2 = 49x^2 - 25$

9. $(x^2+3)^2 = (x^2)^2 + 2(x^2)(3) + 3^2$
$$= x^4 + 6x^2 + 9$$

10. $(5x-3)^2 = (5x)^2 - 2(5x)(3) + 3^2$
$$= 25x^2 - 30x + 9$$

11. $4x^2 y + 5xy - 6x;\ x = -2,\ y = 3$
$4x^2 y + 5xy - 6x$
$$= 4(-2)^2 (3) + 5(-2)(3) - 6(-2)$$
$$= 4(4)(3) + 5(-2)(3) - 6(-2)$$
$$= 48 - 30 + 12$$
$$= 30$$

12. $(8x^2 y^3 - xy + 2y^2) - (6x^2 y^3 - 4xy - 10y^2)$
$$= (8x^2 y^3 - xy + 2y^2)$$
$$+ (-6x^2 y^3 + 4xy + 10y^2)$$
$$= (8x^2 y^3 - 6x^2 y^3) + (-xy + 4xy)$$
$$+ (2y^2 + 10y^2)$$
$$= 2x^2 y^3 + 3xy + 12y^2$$

13. $(3a - 7b)(4a + 5b)$
$$= (3a)(4a) + (3a)(5b) - (7b)(4a)$$
$$- (7b)(5b)$$
$$= 12a^2 + 15ab - 28ab - 35b^2$$
$$= 12a^2 - 13ab - 35b^2$$

14. $(2x+3y)^2 = (2x)^2 + 2(2x)(3y) + (3y)^2$
$$= 4x^2 + 12xy + 9y^2$$

15. $\dfrac{-25x^{16}}{5x^4} = \dfrac{-25}{5} \cdot \dfrac{x^{16}}{x^4} = -5x^{16-4}$
$$= -5x^{12}$$

Check by multiplication:
$5x^4(-5x^{12}) = -25x^{4+12} = -25x^{16}$

16. $\dfrac{15x^4 - 10x^3 + 25x^2}{5x}$
$$= \dfrac{15x^4}{5x} - \dfrac{10x^3}{5x} + \dfrac{25x^2}{5x}$$
$$= 3x^3 - 2x^2 + 5x$$

Check by multiplication:
$5x(3x^3 - 2x^2 + 5x)$
$$= 5x(3x^3) + 5x(-2x^2) + 5x(5x)$$
$$= 15x^4 - 10x^3 + 25x^2$$

17.

$$
\begin{array}{r}
x^2 - 2x + 3 \\
2x+1\overline{)2x^3 - 3x^2 + 4x + 4} \\
\underline{2x^3 +\ x^2} \\
-4x^2 + 4x \\
\underline{-4x^2 - 2x} \\
6x + 4 \\
\underline{6x + 3} \\
1
\end{array}
$$

$$\dfrac{2x^3 - 3x^2 + 4x + 4}{2x+1} = x^2 - 2x + 3 + \dfrac{1}{2x+1}$$

Check by multiplication:
$(2x+1)(x^2 - 2x + 3) + 1$
$$= \left[2x(x^2 - 2x + 3) + 1(x^2 - 2x + 3)\right] + 1$$
$$= (2x^3 - 4x^2 + 6x + x^2 - 2x + 3) + 1$$
$$= (2x^3 - 3x^2 + 4x + 3) + 1$$
$$= 2x^3 - 3x^2 + 4x + 4$$

264

18. $\left(3x^4 + 11x^3 - 20x^2 + 7x + 35\right) \div (x+5)$

$$\underline{-5|}\ \ 3\quad 11\quad -20\quad 7\quad 35$$
$$-15\quad 20\quad 0\quad -35$$
$$\overline{3\quad -4\quad 0\quad 7\quad 0}$$

$\left(3x^4 + 11x^3 - 20x^2 + 7x + 35\right) \div (x+5)$

$= 3x^3 - 4x^2 + 7$

19. $10^{-2} = \dfrac{1}{10^2} = \dfrac{1}{100}$

20. $\dfrac{1}{4^{-3}} = 1 \cdot 4^3 = 4^3 = 64$

21. $\left(-3x^2\right)^3 = (-3)^3 \left(x^2\right)^3 = -27x^6$

22. $\dfrac{20x^3}{5x^8} = \dfrac{4}{x^5}$

23. $\left(-7x^{-8}\right)\left(3x^2\right) = -21x^{-8+2} = -\dfrac{21}{x^6}$

24. $\dfrac{\left(2y^3\right)^4}{y^8} = \dfrac{2^4\left(y^3\right)^4}{y^8} = \dfrac{16y^{12}}{y^8} = 16y^4$

25. $\left(5x^{-4}\right)^{-2} = 5^{-2}\left(x^{-4}\right)^{-2} = 5^{-2}x^8 = \dfrac{x^8}{5^2} = \dfrac{x^8}{25}$

26. $\left(\dfrac{x^{10}}{x^5}\right)^{-3} = \left(x^{10-5}\right)^{-3} = \left(x^5\right)^{-3} = x^{-15} = \dfrac{1}{x^{15}}$

27. $3.7 \times 10^{-4} = 0.00037$

28. $7,600,000 = 7.6 \times 10^6$

29. $\left(4.1 \times 10^2\right)\left(3 \times 10^{-5}\right) = (4.1 \cdot 3)\left(10^2 \cdot 10^{-5}\right)$
$$= 12.3 \times 10^{-3}$$
$$= 1.23 \times 10^{-2}$$

30. $\dfrac{8.4 \times 10^6}{4 \times 10^{-2}} = \dfrac{8.4}{4} \times \dfrac{10^6}{10^{-2}}$
$$= 2.1 \times 10^{6-(-2)} = 2.1 \times 10^8$$

31. $A = (x+8)(x+2)$
$$= x^2 + 2x + 8x + 16$$
$$= x^2 + 10x + 16$$

Chapter 5 Cumulative Review Exercises (Chapters 1 – 5)

1. $(-7)(-5) \div (12-3) = (-7)(-5) \div 9$
$$= 35 \div 9 = \dfrac{35}{9}$$

2. $(3-7)^2 (9-11)^3 = (-4)^2(-2)^3$
$$= 16(-8) = -128$$

3. $14,300 - (-750) = 14,300 + 750$
$$= 15,050$$

The difference in elevation between the plane and the submarine is 15,050 feet.

4. $2(x+3) + 2x = x+4$
$$2x + 6 + 2x = x + 4$$
$$4x + 6 = x + 4$$
$$3x + 6 = 4$$
$$3x = -2$$
$$x = -\dfrac{2}{3}$$

The solution set is $\left\{-\dfrac{2}{3}\right\}$.

5.

$$\frac{x}{5} - \frac{1}{3} = \frac{x}{10} - \frac{1}{2}$$

$$30\left(\frac{x}{5} - \frac{1}{3}\right) = 30\left(\frac{x}{10} - \frac{1}{2}\right)$$

$$30\left(\frac{x}{5}\right) - 30\left(\frac{1}{3}\right) = 30\left(\frac{x}{10}\right) - 30\left(\frac{1}{2}\right)$$

$$6x - 10 = 3x - 15$$

$$3x - 10 = -15$$

$$3x = -5$$

$$x = -\frac{5}{3}$$

The solution set is $\left\{-\frac{5}{3}\right\}$.

6. Let x = width of sign.
Then $3x - 2$ = length of sign.

$$2x + 2(3x - 2) = 28$$

$$2x + 6x - 4 = 28$$

$$8x - 4 = 28$$

$$8x = 32$$

$$x = 4$$

$$3x - 2 = 3(4) - 2 = 10$$

The length of the sign is 10 feet and the width is 4 feet, so the dimensions are 10 feet by 4 feet.

7.

$$7 - 8x \leq -6x - 5$$

$$7 - 8x + 6x \leq -6x - 5 + 6x$$

$$-2x + 7 \leq -5$$

$$-2x + 7 - 7 \leq -5 - 7$$

$$-2x \leq -12$$

$$\frac{-2x}{-2} \geq \frac{-12}{-2}$$

$$x \geq 6$$

The solution set is $\left\{x \mid x \geq 6\right\}$.

8. Let x = amount invested at 12%
y = amount invested at 14%

	Amount invested	Interest rate	Interest earned
12%	x	0.12	$0.12x$
14%	y	0.14	$0.14y$

Form a system of equations based on the amount invested and on the amount of interest earned:

$$x + y = 6000$$

$$0.12x + 0.14y = 772$$

Solve the first equation for y and substitute the result into the second equation:

$$x + y = 6000$$

$$y = 6000 - x$$

$$0.12x + 0.14y = 772$$

$$0.12x + 0.14(6000 - x) = 772$$

$$0.12x + 840 - 0.14x = 772$$

$$-0.02x + 840 = 772$$

$$-0.02x = -68$$

$$x = 3400$$

Back-substitute 3400 for x into either of the original equations. We choose the first equation:

$$x + y = 6000$$

$$3400 + y = 6000$$

$$y = 2600$$

Thus, \$3400 was invested at 12%, and \$2600 was invested at 14%.

266

9. Let x = number of liters of 70% antifreeze.
   y = number of liters of 30% antifreeze.

	No. of liters	Percent antifreeze	Amount of antifreeze
70%	x	$70\% = 0.7$	$0.7x$
30%	y	$30\% = 0.3$	$0.3y$
60%	20	$60\% = 0.6$	$0.6(20) = 12$

Form a system of equations based on the number of liters of mixture and on the amount of antifreeze:

$x + y = 20$

$0.7x + 0.3y = 12$

Solve the first equation for y and substitute the result into the second equation:

$x + y = 20$

$y = 20 - x$

$0.7x + 0.3y = 12$

$0.7x + 0.3(20 - x) = 12$

$0.7x + 6 - 0.3x = 12$

$0.4x + 6 = 12$

$0.4x = 6$

$x = 15$

Back-substitute 15 for x into one of the original equations. We choose the first equation:

$x + y = 20$

$15 + y = 20$

$y = 5$

Thus, 15 liters of 70% antifreeze and 5 liters of 30% antifreeze must be used.

10.

$y = -\dfrac{2}{5}x + 2$

slope $= -\dfrac{2}{5} = \dfrac{-2}{5}$; y-intercept $= 2$

Plot (0,2). Move 2 units *down* (since −2 is negative) and 5 units to the *right* to reach the point (5,0).

Draw a line through (0,2) and (5,0).

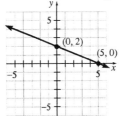

11. $x - 2y = 4$

Let $y = 0$: $\quad x - 2y = 4$

$x - 2(0) = 4$

$x = 4$

The x-intercept is 4.

Let $x = 0$: $x - 2y = 4$

$0 - 2y = 4$

$-2y = 4$

$y = -2$

The y-intercept is -2.

Let $x = -2$: $x - 2y = 4$

$-2 - 2y = 4$

$-2y = 6$

$y = -3$

A checkpoint is $(-2, -3)$.

12. $(-3, 2)$ and $(2, -4)$

$m = \dfrac{y_2 - y_1}{x_2 - x_1}$

$= \dfrac{-4 - 2}{2 - (-3)} = \dfrac{-6}{5} = -\dfrac{6}{5}$

Because the slope is negative, the line is falling.

267

13.
$$y-(-1)=-2(x-3)$$
$$y+1=-2x+6$$
$$y=-2x+5$$

14.
$$3x \;+\; 2y \;=\; 10$$
$$4x \;-\; 3y \;=\; -15$$
Multiply the first equation by 3 and the second equation by –2:
$$9x \;+\; 6y \;=\; 30$$
$$\underline{8x \;-\; 6y \;=\; -30}$$
$$17x \;+\; 0y \;=\; 0$$
$$17x = 0$$
$$x = 0$$
Back-substitute $x = 0$ to find y:
$$3(0)+2y=10$$
$$2y=10$$
$$y=5$$
The solution set is $\{(0, 5)\}$.

15.
$$2x \;+\; 3y \;=\; -6$$
$$y \;=\; 3x \;-\; 13$$
Substitute the second equation in for y in the first equation:
$$2x+3y=-6$$
$$2x+3(3x-13)=-6$$
$$2x+9x-39=-6$$
$$11x-39=-6$$
$$11x=33$$
$$x=3$$
Back-substitute $x = 3$ to find y:
$$y=3x-13=3(3)-13=-4$$
The solution set is $\{(3, -4)\}$.

16. Let y = total charge.
Let x = # of minutes.
Plan A: $y=0.05x+15$
Plan B: $y=0.07x+5$
To find when the plans are the same, substitute the second equation into the first equation:
$$0.07x+5=0.05x+15$$
$$0.02x+5=15$$
$$0.02x=10$$
$$x=500$$
Back-substitute to find y:
$$y=0.07x+5=0.07(500)+5=40$$
The plans will be the same for 500 minutes at $40 a plan.

17. $0.0024 = 2.4 \times 10^{-3}$

18.
$$\left(9x^5-3x^3+2x-7\right)-\left(6x^5+3x^3-7x-9\right)$$
$$=9x^5-3x^3+2x-7-6x^5-3x^3+7x+9$$
$$=3x^5-6x^3+9x+2$$

19.
$$\begin{array}{r} x^2+2x+3 \\ x+1\overline{\smash{\big)}\,x^3+3x^2+5x+3} \end{array}$$
$$\underline{x^3+\;x^2}$$
$$2x^2+5x$$
$$\underline{2x^2+2x}$$
$$3x+3$$
$$\underline{3x+3}$$
$$0$$
$$\frac{x^3+3x^2+5x+3}{x+1}=x^2+2x+3$$

20.
$$\frac{\left(3x^2\right)^4}{x^{10}}=\frac{3^4\left(x^2\right)^4}{x^{10}}-\frac{81x^8}{x^{10}}$$
$$=81x^{8-10}=81x^{-2}=\frac{81}{x^2}$$

268

Chapter 6
Factoring Polynomials

1. Possible answers:
$$8x^3 = (2x)(4x^2)$$
$$8x^3 = (4x)(2x^2)$$
$$8x^3 = (8x)(x^2)$$

3. Possible answers:
$$-12x^5 = (-4x^3)(3x^2)$$
$$-12x^5 = (2x^2)(-6x^3)$$
$$-12x^5 = (-3)(4x^5)$$

5. Possible answers:
$$36x^4 = (6x^2)(6x^2)$$
$$36x^4 = (-2x)(-18x^3)$$
$$36x^4 = (4x^3)(9x)$$

7. The GCF (greatest common factor) of 4 and $8x$ is 4.

9. $12x^2 + 8x$
Since 4 is the numerical coefficient of the GCF, and x is the variable factor of the GCF, the GCF of $12x^2$ and $8x$ is $4x$.

11. The GCF of $-2x^4$ and $6x^3$ is $2x^3$.

13. The GCF of $9y^5, 18y^2$, and $-3y$ is $3y$.

15. The GCF of xy, xy^2, and xy^3 is xy.

17. The GCF of $16x^5y^4, 8x^6y^3$, and $20x^4y^5$ is $4x^4y^3$.

19. $8x + 8 = 8 \cdot x + 8 \cdot 1$
$$= 8(x+1)$$

21. $4y - 4 = 4 \cdot y - 4 \cdot 1$
$$= 4(y-1)$$

23. $5x + 30 = 5 \cdot x + 5 \cdot 6$
$$= 5(x+6)$$

25. $30x - 12 = 6 \cdot 5x - 6 \cdot 2$
$$= 6(5x-2)$$

27. $x^2 + 5x = x \cdot x + x \cdot 5$
$$= x(x+5)$$

29. $18y^2 + 12 = 6 \cdot 3y^2 + 6 \cdot 2$
$$= 6(3y^2+2)$$

31. $14x^3 + 21x^2 = 7x^2 \cdot 2x + 7x^2 \cdot 3$
$$= 7x^2(2x+3)$$

33. $13y^2 - 25y = y \cdot 13y - y \cdot 25$
$$= y(13y-25)$$

35. $9y^4 + 27y^6 = 9y^4 \cdot 1 + 9y^4 \cdot 3y^2$
$$= 9y^4(1+3y^2)$$

37. $8x^2 - 4x^4 = 4x^2(2) - 4x^2(x^2)$
$$= 4x^2(2-x^2)$$

269

39.
$$12y^2 + 16y - 8 = 4(3y^2) + 4(4y) - 4(2)$$
$$= 4(3y^2 + 4y - 2)$$

41.
$$9x^4 + 18x^3 + 6x^2$$
$$= 3x^2(3x^2) + 3x^2(6x) + 3x^2(2)$$
$$= 3x^2(3x^2 + 6x + 2)$$

43.
$$100y^5 - 50y^3 + 100y^2$$
$$= 50y^2(2y^3) - 50y^2(y) + 50y^2(2)$$
$$= 50y^2(2y^3 - y + 2)$$

45.
$$10x - 20x^2 + 5x^3$$
$$= 5x(2) - 5x(4x) + 5x(x^2)$$
$$= 5x(2 - 4x + x^2)$$

47. $11x^2 - 23$ cannot be factored because the two terms have no common factor other than 1.

49.
$$6x^3y^2 + 9xy = 3xy(2x^2 + y) + 3xy(3)$$
$$= 3xy(2x^2y + 3)$$

51.
$$30x^2y^2 - 10xy^2 + 20xy$$
$$= 10xy(3xy^2) - 10xy(y) + 10xy(2)$$
$$= 10xy(3xy^2 - y + 2)$$

53.
$$32x^3y^2 - 24x^3y - 16x^2y$$
$$= 8x^2y(4xy) - 8x^2y(3x) - 8x^2y(2)$$
$$= 8x^2y(4xy - 3x - 2)$$

55.
$$x(x+5) + 3(x+5) = (x+5)(x+3)$$
Here, $(x+5)$ is the greatest common binomial factor.

57. $x(x+2) - 4(x+2) = (x+2)(x-4)$

59. $x(y+6) - 7(y+6) = (y+6)(x-7)$

61.
$$3x(x+y) - (x+y)$$
$$= 3x(x+y) - 1(x+y)$$
$$= (x+y)(3x-1)$$

63.
$$4x(3x+1) + 3x + 1$$
$$= 4x(3x+1) + 1(3x+1)$$
$$= (3x+1)(4x+1)$$

65.
$$7x^2(5x+4) + 5x + 4$$
$$= 7x^2(5x+4) + 1(5x+4)$$
$$= (5x+4)(7x^2+1)$$

67.
$$x^2 + 2x + 4x + 8 = (x^2 + 2x) + (4x+8)$$
$$= x(x+2) + 4(x+2)$$
$$= (x+2)(x+4)$$

69.
$$x^2 + 3x - 5x - 15 = (x^2 + 3x) + (-5x - 15)$$
$$= x(x+3) - 5(x+3)$$
$$= (x+3)(x-5)$$

71.
$$x^3 - 2x^2 + 5x - 10$$
$$= (x^3 - 2x^2) + (5x - 10)$$
$$= x^2(x-2) + 5(x-2)$$
$$= (x-2)(x^2+5)$$

73.
$$x^3 - x^2 + 2x - 2 = x^2(x-1) + 2(x-1)$$
$$= (x-1)(x^2+2)$$

75.
$$xy + 5x + 9y + 45 = x(y+5) + 9(y+5)$$
$$= (y+5)(x+9)$$

270

77. $xy - x + 5y - 5 = x(y-1) + 5(y-1)$
$$= (y-1)(x+5)$$

79. $3x^2 - 6xy + 5xy - 10y^2$
$$= 3x(x-2y) + 5y(x-2y)$$
$$= (x-2y)(3x+5y)$$

81. $3x^3 - 2x^2 - 6x + 4$
$$= x^2(3x-2) - 2(3x-2)$$
$$= (3x-2)(x^2-2)$$

83. $x^2 - ax - bx + ab = x(x-a) - b(x-a)$
$$= (x-a)(x-b)$$

85. $24x^3y^3z^3 + 30x^2y^2z + 18x^2yz^2$
$$= 6x^2yz(4xy^2z^2)$$
$$\quad + 6x^2yz(5y) + 6x^2yz(3z)$$
$$= 6x^2yz(4xy^2z^2 + 5y + 3z)$$

86. $16x^2y^2z^2 + 32x^2yz^2 + 24x^2yz$
$$= 8x^2yz(2yz) + 8x^2yz(4z) + 8x^2yz(3)$$
$$= 8x^2yz(2yz + 4z + 3)$$

87. $x^3 - 4 + 3x^3y - 12y$
$$= 1(x^3 - 4) + 3y(x^3 - 4)$$
$$= (x^3 - 4)(1 + 3y)$$

88. $x^3 - 5 + 2x^3y - 10y$
$$= 1(x^3 - 5) + 2y(x^3 - 5)$$
$$= (x^3 - 5)(1 + 2y)$$

89. $4x^5(x+1) - 6x^3(x+1) - 8x^2(x+1)$
$$= 2x^2(x+1) \cdot 2x^3 - 2x^2(x+1) \cdot 3x$$
$$\quad - 2x^2(x+1) \cdot 4$$
$$= 2x^2(x+1)(2x^3 - 3x - 4)$$

90. $8x^5(x+2) - 10x^3(x+2) - 2x^2(x+2)$
$$= 2x^2(x+2) \cdot 4x^3 - 2x^2 \cdot 5x$$
$$\quad - 2x^2(x+2) \cdot 1$$
$$= 2x^2(x+2)(4x^3 - 5x - 1)$$

91. $3x^5 - 3x^4 + x^3 - x^2 + 5x - 5$
$$= (3x^5 - 3x^4) + (x^3 - x^2) + (5x - 5)$$
$$= 3x^4(x-1) + x^2(x-1) + 5(x-1)$$
$$= (x-1)(3x^4 + x^2 + 5)$$

92 $7x^5 - 7x^4 + x^3 - x^2 + 3x - 3$
$$= (7x^5 - 7x^4) + (x^3 - x^2) + (3x - 3)$$
$$= 7x^4(x-1) + x^2(x-1) + 3(x-1)$$
$$= (x-1)(7x^4 + x^2 + 3)$$

93. The area of the square is $6x \cdot 6x = 36x^2$. The area of the circle is $\pi(2x)^2 = \pi \cdot 4x^2 = 4\pi x^2$. So the shaded area is the area of the square minus the area of the circle, which is $36x^2 - 4\pi x^2 = 4x^2(9 - \pi)$.

94. The area of the square is $4x \cdot 4x = 16x^2$. The area of each circle is πx^2. The area of both circles is $2\pi x^2$. So the shaded area is the area of the square minus the area of the two circles, which is $16x^2 - 2\pi x^2 = 2x^2(8 - \pi)$.

271

95. **a.** Use the formula, $64x - 16x^2$, for the height of the debris above the ground. Substitute 3 for x.

$$64x - 16x^2 = 64(3) - 16(3)^2$$
$$= 192 - 16(9) = 192 - 144 = 48$$

Therefore, the height of the debris after 3 seconds is 48 feet.

b. $64x - 16x^2 = 16x(4 - x)$

c. Substitute 3 for x in the factored polynomial.

$$16 \cdot 3(4 - 3) = 48(1) = 48$$

You do get the same answer as in part (a) but this does not prove your factorization is correct.

97. Use the formula for the area of a rectangle, $A = l \cdot w$. Substitute $5x^4 - 10x$ for A and $5x$ for w.

$$A = l \cdot w$$

$$5x^4 - 10x = l(5x)$$

To find a polynomial representing l, factor $5x^4 - 10x$.

$$5x^4 - 10x = 5x(x^3 - 2) \text{ or } (x^3 - 2) \cdot 5x$$

which is $l \cdot w$.

Therefore, the l, the length, is $(x^3 - 2)$ units.

99. – 103. Answers will vary.

105. Statement d is true.
Either $-4x$ or $4x$ can be used as the GCF.
Multiplying $-4x(x - 3) = -4x^2 + 12x$
and $4x(-x + 3) = -4x^2 + 12x$

107. Answers will vary. One example is $4y^4 - 8y^3 + 2y^2 - 16y$.

109.

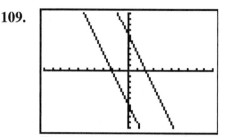

The graphs do not coincide.

Factor out GCF from left side.
$-3x - 6 = -3(x + 2)$. Change the expression on the right side to $-3(x + 2)$.

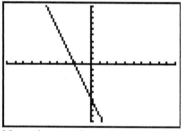

Now the graphs coincide.

111.

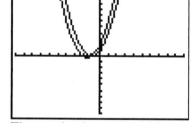

The graphs do not coincide.

Factor by grouping.
$$x^2 + 2x + x + 2 = x(x + 2) + 1(x + 2)$$
$$= (x + 2)(x + 1)$$

Change the expression on the right side to $(x + 2)(x + 1)$.

272

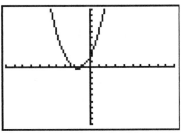

Now the graphs coincide.

112. $(x+7)(x+10) = x^2 + 10x + 7x + 70$
$$= x^2 + 17x + 70$$

113. $2x - y = -4$

$x - 3y = 3$

Graph both equations on the same axes.

$2x - y = -4$:

x-intercept: -2; y-intercept: 4

$x - 3y = 3$:

x-intercept: 3; y-intercept: -1

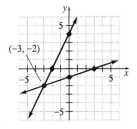

The lines intersect at $(-3, -2)$.

Solution: $\{(-3, -2)\}$

114. Line through $(-7, 2)$ and $(-4, 5)$

First, find the slope

$$m = \frac{5 - 2}{-4 - (-7)} = \frac{3}{3} = 1$$

Write the point-slope equation using $m = 1$ and $(x_1, y_1) = (-7, 2)$ and rewrite this equation in slope-intercept form.

$$y - y_1 = m(x - x_1)$$
$$y - 2 = 1[x - (-7)]$$
$$y - 2 = 1(x + 7)$$
$$y - 2 = x + 7$$
$$y = x + 9$$

Note: If $(-4, 5)$ is used as (x_1, y_1), the point-slope equation will be

$$y - 5 = 1[x - (-4)]$$
$$y - 5 = x + 4$$

This also leads to the slope-intercept equation $y = x + 9$.

6.2 Exercise Set

In Exercises 1-41, each factorization should be checked using FOIL multiplication. The check will be only shown here for Exercise 1.

1. $x^2 + 7x + 6$

Factors of 6	6,1	−6,−1
Sum of Factors	7	−7

The factors of 6 whose sum is 7 are 6 and 1.

Thus, $x^2 + 7x + 6 = (x + 6)(x + 1)$.

Check:
$$(x+6)(x+1) = x^2 + 1x + 6x + 6$$
$$= x^2 + 7x + 6$$

3. $x^2 + 7x + 10 = (x + 5)(x + 2)$

$5(2) = 10; \ 5 + 2 = 7$

5. $x^2 + 11x + 10 = (x + 10)(x + 1)$

$10(1) = 10; \ 10 + 1 = 11$

7. $x^2 - 7x + 12 = (x - 4)(x - 3)$

$-4(-3) = 12; \ -4 + -3 = -7$

273

9. $x^2 - 12x + 36 = (x-6)(x-6)$
$-6(-6) = 36;\ -6 + -6 = -12$

11. $y^2 - 8y + 15 = (y-5)(y-3)$
$-5(-3) = 15;\ -5 + -3 = -8$

13. $x^2 + 3x - 10 = (x+5)(x-2)$
$5(-2) = -10;\ 5 + -2 = 3$

15. $y^2 + 10y - 39 = (y+13)(y-3)$
$(13)(-3) = -39;\ 13 + -3 = 10$

17. $x^2 - 2x - 15 = (x-5)(x+3)$
$(-5)(3) = -15;\ -5 + 3 = -2$

19. $x^2 - 2x - 8 = (x-4)(x+2)$
$(-4)(2) = -8;\ -4 + 2 = -2$

21. $x^2 + 4x + 12$ is prime because there is no pair of integers whose product is 12 and whose sum is 4.

23. $y^2 - 16y + 48 = (y-4)(y-12)$
$(-4)(-12) = 48;\ -4 + -12 = -16$

25. $x^2 - 3x + 6$ is prime because there is no pair of integers whose product is 6 and whose sum is -3.

27. $w^2 - 30w - 64 = (w-32)(w+2)$
$(-32)(2) = -64;\ -32 + 2 = -30$

29. $y^2 - 18y + 65 = (y-5)(y-13)$
$(-5)(-13) = 65;\ -5 + -13 = -18$

31. $r^2 + 12r + 27 = (r+3)(r+9)$
$(3)(9) = 27;\ 3 + 9 = 12$

33. $y^2 - 7y + 5$ is prime because there is no pair of integers whose product is 5 and whose sum is -7.

35. $x^2 + 7xy + 6y^2 = (x+6y)(x+y)$
$(6)(1) = 6;\ 6 + 1 = 7$

37. $x^2 - 8xy + 15y^2 = (x-3y)(x-5y)$
$(-3)(-5) = 15;\ -3 + -5 = -8$

39. $x^2 - 3xy - 18y^2 = (x-6y)(x+3y)$
$(-6)(3) = -18;\ -6 + 3 = -3$

41. $a^2 - 18ab + 45b^2 = (a-15b)(a-3b)$
$(-15)(-3) = 45;\ -15 + -3 = -18$

43. $3x^2 + 15x + 18$
First factor out the GCF, 3. Then factor the resulting binomial.
$3x^2 + 15x + 18 = 3(x^2 + 5x + 6)$
$ = 3(x+2)(x+3)$

45. $4y^2 - 4y - 8 = 4(y^2 - y - 2)$
$ = 4(y-2)(y+1)$

47. $10x^2 - 40x - 600 = 10(x^2 - 4x - 60)$
$ = 10(x-10)(x+6)$

49. $3x^2 - 33x + 54 = 3(x^2 - 11x + 18)$
$ = 3(x-2)(x-9)$

51. $2r^3 + 6r^2 + 4r = 2r(r^2 + 3r + 2)$
$ = 2r(r+2)(r+1)$

53. $4x^3 + 12x^2 - 72x = 4x(x^2 + 3x - 18)$
$ = 4x(x+6)(x-3)$

55. $2r^3 + 8r^2 - 64r = 2r\left(r^2 + 4r - 32\right)$

$\qquad = 2r(r+8)(r-4)$

57. $y^4 + 2y^3 - 80y^2 = y^2\left(y^2 + 2y - 80\right)$

$\qquad = y^2(y+10)(y-8)$

59. $x^4 - 3x^3 - 10x^2 = x^2\left(x^2 - 3x - 10\right)$

$\qquad = x^2(x-5)(x+2)$

61. $2w^4 - 26w^3 - 96w^2$

$\qquad = 2w^2\left(w^2 - 13w - 48\right)$

$\qquad = 2w^2(w-16)(w+3)$

63. $15xy^2 + 45xy - 60x = 15x\left(y^2 + 3y - 4\right)$

$\qquad = 15x(y+4)(y-1)$

65. $x^5 + 3x^4 y - 4x^3 y^2 = x^3\left(x^2 + 3xy - 4y^2\right)$

$\qquad = x^3(x+4y)(x-y)$

67. $2x^2 y^2 - 32x^2 yz + 30x^2 z^2$

$\qquad = 2x^2\left(y^2 - 16yz + 15z^2\right)$

$\qquad = 2x^2(y-15z)(y-z)$

68. $2x^2 y^2 - 30x^2 yz + 28x^2 z^2$

$\qquad = 2x^2\left(y^2 - 15yz + 14z^2\right)$

$\qquad = 2x^2(y-14z)(y-z)$

69. $(a+b)x^2 + (a+b)x - 20(a+b)$

$\qquad = (a+b)\left(x^2 + x - 20\right)$

$\qquad = (a+b)(x+5)(x-4)$

70. $(a+b)x^2 - 13(a+b)x + 36(a+b)$

$\qquad = (a+b)\left(x^2 - 13x + 36\right)$

$\qquad = (a+b)(x-9)(x-4)$

71. $x^2 + 0.5x + 0.06 = (x+0.2)(x+0.3)$

$\qquad 0.2(0.3) = 0.06; \ 0.2 + 0.3 = 0.5$

72. $x^2 - 0.5x - 0.06 = (x-0.6)(x+0.1)$

$\qquad -0.6(0.1) = 0.06; \ -0.6 + 0.1 = -0.5$

73. $x^2 - \dfrac{2}{5}x + \dfrac{1}{25} = \left(x - \dfrac{1}{5}\right)\left(x - \dfrac{1}{5}\right)$

$\qquad \dfrac{1}{5}\left(\dfrac{1}{5}\right) = \dfrac{1}{25}; \ -\dfrac{1}{5} + -\dfrac{1}{5} = -\dfrac{2}{5}$

74. $x^2 + \dfrac{2}{3}x + \dfrac{1}{9} = \left(x + \dfrac{1}{3}\right)\left(x + \dfrac{1}{3}\right)$

$\qquad \left(\dfrac{1}{3}\right)\left(\dfrac{1}{3}\right) = \dfrac{1}{9}; \ \dfrac{1}{3} + \dfrac{1}{3} = \dfrac{2}{3}$

75. $-x^2 - 3x + 40 = -\left(x^2 + 3x - 40\right)$

$\qquad = -(x+8)(x-5)$

$\qquad 8(-5) = -40; \ 8 + -5 = 3$

76. $-x^2 - 4x + 45 = -\left(x^2 + 4x - 45\right)$

$\qquad = -(x+9)(x-5)$

$\qquad 9(-5) = -45; \ 9 + -5 = 4$

77. a. $-16t^2 + 16t + 32 = -16\left(t^2 - t - 2\right)$

$\qquad = -16(t-2)(t+1)$

b. Substitute 2 for t in the original polynomial:

$\qquad -16(2)^2 + 16(2) + 32$

$\qquad = -16(4) + 32 + 32$

$\qquad = -64 + 64 = 0$

Substitute 2 for t in the factored polynomial:

$\qquad -16(2-2)(2+1) = -16(0)(3) = 0$

This answer means that after 2 seconds you hit the water.

79. – 81. Answers will vary.

83. Statement c is true.
$$y^2 + 5y - 24 = (y - 3)(y + 8)$$

85. In order for $x^2 + 4x + b$ to be factorable, b must be an integer with two positive factors whose sum is 4. The only such pairs are 3 and 1, or 2 and 2.
$$(x + 3)(x + 1) = x^2 + 4x + 3$$
$$(x + 2)(x + 2) = x^2 + 4x + 4$$
Therefore, the possible values of b are 3 and 4.

87. $x^3 + 3x^2 + 2x = x(x^2 + 3x + 2)$
$$= x(x + 1)(x + 2)$$
The trinomial represents the product of three consecutive integers.

89.

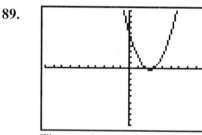

The graphs coincide.
This verifies the factorization
$$x^2 - 5x + 6 = (x - 2)(x - 3).$$

91.

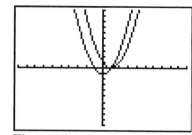

The graphs do not coincide.

$$x^2 - 2x + 1 = (x - 1)(x - 1)$$

Change the polynomial on the right to $(x - 1)(x - 1)$.

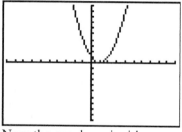

Now the graphs coincide.

93. $(2x + 3)(x - 2) = 2x^2 - 4x + 3x - 6$
$$= 2x^2 - x - 6$$

94. $(3x + 4)(3x + 1) = 9x^2 + 3x + 12x + 4$
$$= 9x^2 + 15x + 4$$

95. $4(x - 2) = 3x + 5$
$$4x - 8 = 3x + 5$$
$$x - 8 = 5$$
$$x = 13$$
The solution set is $\{13\}$.

6.3 Exercise Set

In Exercises 1-57, each trinomial may be factored by either trial and error or by grouping. Both methods will be illustrated here. Each factorization should be checked by FOIL multiplication. The check will be shown here only for Exercise 1. In all answers, the factors may be written in either order.

1. $2x^2 + 5x + 3$

Factor by trial and error.

Step 1 $2x^2 + 5x + 3 = (2x \quad)(x \quad)$

Step 2 The number 3 has pairs of factors that are either both positive or both negative. Because the middle term, $5x$, is positive, both factors must be positive. The only positive factorization is $(1)(3)$.

Step 3

Possible Factors of $2x^2 + 5x + 3$	Sum of Outside and Inside Products
$(2x+1)(x+3)$	$6x + x = 7x$
$(2x+3)(x+1)$	$2x + 3x = 5x$

Thus, $2x^2 + 5x + 3 = (2x+3)(x+1)$.

Check:
$$(2x+3)(x+1) = 2x^2 + 2x + 3x + 3$$
$$= 2x^2 + 5x + 3$$

3. $3x^2 + 13x + 4$

Factor by trial and error.

The only possibility for the first terms is $(3x)(x) = 3x^2$.

Because the middle term is positive and the last term is also positive, the possible factorizations of 4 are $(1)(4)$ and $(2)(2)$.

Possible Factors of $3x^2 + 13x + 4$	Sum of Outside and Inside Products
$(3x+1)(x+4)$	$12x + x = 13x$
$(3x+4)(x+1)$	$3x + 4x = 7x$
$(3x+2)(x+2)$	$6x + 2x = 8x$

Thus, $3x^2 + 13x + 4 = (3x+1)(x+4)$.

5. $2x^2 + 11x + 12$

Factor by grouping.

$a = 2$ and $c = 12$, so $ac = 2(12) = 24$.

The factors of 24 whose sum is 11 are 8 and 3.

$$2x^2 + 11x + 12 = 2x^2 + 8x + 3x + 12$$
$$= 2x(x+4) + 3(x+4)$$
$$= (x+4)(2x+3)$$

7. $5y^2 - 16y + 3$

Factor by trial and error. The first terms must be $5y$ and y. Because the middle term is negative, the factors of 3 must be -3 and -1.

$$(5y-1)(y-3) = 5y^2 - 16y + 3$$
$$(5y-3)(y-1) = 5y^2 - 8y + 3$$

Thus, $y^2 - 16y + 3 = (5y-1)(y-3)$.

9. $3y^2 + y - 4$

Factor by trial and error.

$(3y+1)(y-4) = 3y^2 - 11y - 4$

$(3y-1)(y+4) = 3y^2 + 11y - 4$

$(3y+4)(y-1) = 3y^2 + y - 4$

$(3y-4)(y+1) = 3y^2 - y - 4$

$(3y+2)(y-2) = 3y^2 - 4y - 4$

$(3y-2)(y+2) = 3y^2 + 4y - 4$

Thus, $3y^2 + y - 4 = (3y+4)(y-1)$.

11. $3x^2 + 13x - 10$

Factor by grouping.

$a = 3$ and $c = -10$, so $ac = -30$.

The factors of -30 whose sum is 13 are 15 and -2.

$3x^2 + 13x - 10 = 3x^2 + 15x - 2x - 10$

$\qquad = 3x(x+5) - 2(x+5)$

$\qquad = (x+5)(3x-2)$

13. $3x^2 - 22x + 7$

Factor by trial and error.

$(3x-7)(x-1) = 3x^2 - 10x + 7$

$(3x-1)(x-7) = 3x^2 - 22x + 7$

Thus, $3x^2 - 22x + 7 = (3x-1)(x-7)$.

15. $5y^2 - 16y + 3$

Factor by trial and error.

$(5y-3)(y-1) = 5y^2 - 8y + 3$

$(5y-1)(y-3) = 5y^2 - 16y + 3$

Thus, $5y^2 - 16y + 3 = (5y-1)(y-3)$.

17. $3x^2 - 17x + 10$

Factor by grouping.

$a = 3$ and $c = 10$, so $ac = 30$.

The factors of 30 whose sum is -17 are -15 and -2.

$3x^2 - 17x + 10 = 3x^2 - 15x - 2x + 10$

$\qquad = 3x(x-5) - 2(x-5)$

$\qquad = (x-5)(3x-2)$

19. $6w^2 - 11w + 4$

Factor by grouping.

$a = 6$ and $c = 4$, so $ac = 24$.

The factors of 24 whose sum is -11 are -3 and -8.

$6w^2 - 11w + 4 = 6w^2 - 3w - 8w + 4$

$\qquad = 3w(2w-1) - 4(2w-1)$

$\qquad = (2w-1)(3w-4)$

21. $8x^2 + 33x + 4$

Factor by grouping.

$a = 8$ and $c = 4$, so $ac = 32$.

The factors of 32 whose sum is 33 are 32 and 1.

$8x^2 + 33x + 4 = 8x^2 + 32x + x + 4$

$\qquad = 8x(x+4) + 1(x+4)$

$\qquad = (x+4)(8x+1)$

23. $5x^2 + 33x - 14$

Factor by trial and error.

$(5x-7)(x+2) = 5x^2 + 3x - 14$

$(5x+7)(x-2) = 5x^2 - 3x - 14$

$(5x-2)(x+7) = 5x^2 + 33x - 14$

Because the correct factorization has been found, there is no need to try additional possibilities.

Thus, $5x^2 + 33x - 14 = (5x-2)(x+7)$.

25. $14y^2 + 15y - 9$

Factor by trial and error. The sign in one factor must be positive and the other negative.

$(7y+9)(2y-1) = 14y^2 + 11y - 9$

$(7y+1)(2y-9) = 14y^2 - 61y - 9$

$(7y+3)(2y-3) = 14y^2 - 15y - 9$

$(7y-3)(2y+3) = 14y^2 + 15y - 9$

Thus, $14y^2 + 15y - 9 = (7y-3)(2y+3)$.

27. $6x^2 - 7x + 3$

Factor by trial and error. List all the possibilities in which both signs are negative.

$(6x-1)(x-3) = 6x^2 - 19x + 3$

$(6x-3)(x-1) = 6x^2 - 9x + 3$

$(3x-1)(2x-3) = 6x^2 - 11x + 3$

$(3x-3)(2x-1) = 6x^2 - 9x + 3$

None of these possibilities gives the required middle term, $-7x$, and there are no more possibilities to try, so $6x^2 - 7x + 3$ is prime.

29. $25z^2 - 30z + 9$

Factor by trial and error until the correct factorization is obtained. The signs in both factors must be negative.

$(5z-1)(5z-9) = 25z^2 - 50z + 9$

$(5z-3)(5z-3) = 25z^2 - 30z + 9$

Thus, $25z^2 - 30z + 9 = (5z-3)(5z-3)$.

31. $15y^2 - y - 2$

Factor by grouping.
$a = 15$ and $c = -2$, so $ac = -30$.
The factors of -30 whose sum is -1 are -6 and 5.

$15y^2 - y - 2 = 15y^2 - 6y + 5y - 2$

$\qquad = 3y(5y-2) + 1(5y-2)$

$\qquad = (5y-2)(3y+1)$

33. $5x^2 + 2x + 9$

Factor by trial and error. The signs in both factors must be positive.

$(5x+3)(x+3) = 5x^2 + 18x + 9$

$(5x+9)(x+1) = 5x^2 + 14x + 9$

$(5x+1)(x+9) = 5x^2 + 46x + 9$

None of these possibilities gives the required middle term, $2x$, and there are no more possibilities to try, so $5x^2 + 2x + 9$ is prime.

35. $10y^2 + 43y - 9$

Factor by grouping.
$a = 10$ and $c = -9$ so $ac = -90$.
The factors of -90 whose sum is 43 are 45 and -2.

$10y^2 + 43y - 9 = 10y^2 + 45y - 2y - 9$

$\qquad = 5y(2y+9) - 1(2y+9)$

$\qquad = (2y+9)(5y-1)$

37. $8x^2 - 2x - 1$

Factor by trial and error until the correct factorization is obtained. The sign must be negative in one factor and positive in the other.

$(4x-1)(2x+1) = 8x^2 + 2x - 1$

$(4x+1)(2x-1) = 8x^2 - 2x - 1$

Thus, $8x^2 - 2x - 1 = (4x+1)(2x-1)$.

39. $9y^2 - 9y + 2$

Factor by grouping.
$a = 9$ and $c = 2$, so $ac = 18$.
The factors of 18 whose sum is -9 are -3 and -6.

$9y^2 - 9y + 2 = 9y^2 - 3y - 6y + 2$

$\qquad = 3y(3y-1) - 2(3y-1)$

$\qquad = (3y-1)(3y-2)$

279

41. $20x^2 + 27x - 8$

Factor by grouping.

$a = 20$ and $c = -8$, so $ac = -160$.

The factors of -160 whose sum is 27 are -5 and 32.

$20x^2 + 27x - 8 = 20x^2 - 5x + 32x - 8$

$\qquad = 5x(4x-1) + 8(4x-1)$

$\qquad = (4x-1)(5x+8)$

43. $2x^2 + 3xy + y^2 = (2x+y)(x+y)$

(In this case, there are no other combinations to try.)

45. $3x^2 + 5xy + 2y^2$

Factor by trial and error.

$(3x+y)(x+2y) = 3x^2 + 7xy + 2y^2$

$(3x+2y)(x+y) = 3x^2 + 5xy + 2y^2$

So, $3x^2 + 5xy + 2y^2 = (3x+2y)(x+y)$.

47. $2x^2 - 9xy + 9y^2$

Factor by trial and error until the correct factorization is obtained. The signs in both factors must be negative.

$(2x-9y)(x-y) = 2x^2 - 11xy + 9y^2$

$(2x+9y)(x+y) = 2x^2 + 11xy + 9y^2$

$(2x-3y)(x-3y) = 2x^2 - 9xy + 9y^2$

So, $2x^2 - 9xy + 9y^2 = (2x-3y)(x-3y)$.

49. $6x^2 - 5xy - 6y^2$

Factor by grouping.

$a = 6$ and $c = -6$, so $ac = -36$.

The factors of -36 whose sum is -5 are -9 and 4.

$6x^2 - 5xy - 6y^2$

$= 6x^2 - 9xy + 4xy - 6y^2$

$= 3x(2x-3y) + 2y(2x-3y)$

$= (2x-3y)(3x+2y)$

51. $15x^2 + 11xy - 14y^2$

Factor by grouping.

$a = 15$ and $c = -14$, so $ac = -210$.

The factors of -210 whose sum is 11 are 21 and -10.

$15x^2 + 11xy - 14y^2$

$= 15x^2 + 21xy - 10xy - 14y^2$

$= 3x(5x+7y) - 2y(5x+7y)$

$= (5x+7y)(3x-2y)$

53. $2a^2 + 7ab + 5b^2$

Factor by trial and error.

$(2a+5b)(a+b) = 2a^2 + 7ab + 5b^2$

$(2a+b)(a+5b) = 2a^2 + 11ab + 5b^2$

Thus,

$2a^2 + 7ab + 5b^2 = (2a+5b)(a+b)$.

55. $15a^2 - ab - 6b^2$

Factor by grouping.

$a = 15$ and $c = -6$, so $ac = -90$.

The factors of -90 whose sum is -1 are 9 and -10.

$15a^2 - ab - 6b^2$

$= 15a^2 + 9ab - 10ab - 6b^2$

$= 3a(5a+3b) - 2b(5a+3b)$

$= (5a+3b)(3a-2b)$

57. $12x^2 - 25xy + 12y^2$

Factor by grouping.

$a = 12$ and $c = 12$, so $ac = 144$.

The factors of 144 whose sum is -25 are -9 and -16.

$12x^2 - 25xy + 12y^2$

$= 12x^2 - 9xy - 16xy + 12y^2$

$= 3x(4x-3y) - 4y(4x-3y)$

$= (4x-3y)(3x-4y)$

59. $4x^2 + 26x + 30$

First factor out the GCF, 2. Then factor the resulting trinomial by trial and error or grouping.

$4x^2 + 26x + 30 = 2(2x^2 + 13x + 15)$

$\qquad = 2(2x + 3)(x + 5)$

61. $9x^2 - 6x - 24$

The GCF is 3.

$9x^2 - 6x - 24 = 3(3x^2 - 2x - 8)$

$\qquad = 3(3x + 4)(x - 2)$

63. $4y^2 + 2y - 30 = 2(2y^2 + y - 15)$

$\qquad = 2(2y - 5)(y + 3)$

65. $9y^2 + 33y - 60 = 3(3y^2 + 11y - 20)$

$\qquad = 3(3y - 4)(y + 5)$

67. $3x^3 + 4x^2 + x$

The GCF is x.

$3x^3 + 4x^2 + x = x(3x^2 + 4x + 1)$

$\qquad = x(3x + 1)(x + 1)$

69. $2x^3 - 3x^2 - 5x = x(2x^2 - 3x - 5)$

$\qquad = x(2x - 5)(x + 1)$

71. $9y^3 - 39y^2 + 12y$

The GCF is $3y$.

$9y^3 - 39y^2 + 12y = 3y(3y^2 - 13y + 4)$

$\qquad = 3y(3y - 1)(y - 4)$

73. $60z^3 + 40z^2 + 5z = 5z(12z^2 + 8z + 1)$

$\qquad = 5z(6z + 1)(2z + 1)$

75. $15x^4 - 39x^3 + 18x^2 = 3x^2(5x^2 - 13x + 6)$

$\qquad = 3x^2(5x - 3)(x - 2)$

77. $10x^5 - 17x^4 + 3x^3 = x^3(10x^2 - 17x + 3)$

$\qquad = x^3(2x - 3)(5x - 1)$

79. $6x^2 - 3xy - 18y^2 = 3(2x^2 - xy - 6y^2)$

$\qquad = 3(2x + 3y)(x - 2y)$

81. $12x^2 + 10xy - 8y^2 = 2(6x^2 + 5xy - 4y^2)$

$\qquad = 2(2x - y)(3x + 4y)$

83. $8x^2y + 34xy - 84y = 2y(4x^2 + 17x - 42)$

$\qquad = 2y(4x - 7)(x + 6)$

85. $12a^2b - 46ab^2 + 14b^3$

$\qquad = 2b(6a^2 - 23ab + 7b^2)$

$\qquad = 2b(2a - 7b)(3a - b)$

87. $30(y + 1)x^2 + 10(y + 1)x - 20(y + 1)$

$\qquad = 10(y + 1)(3x^2 + x - 2)$

$\qquad = 10(y + 1)(3x - 2)(x + 1)$

88. $6(y + 1)x^2 + 33(y + 1)x + 15(y + 1)$

$\qquad = 3(y + 1)(2x^2 + 11x + 5)$

$\qquad = 3(y + 1)(2x + 1)(x + 5)$

89. $-32x^2y^4 + 20xy^4 + 12y^4$

$\qquad = -4y^4(8x^2 - 5x - 3)$

$\qquad = -4y^4(8x + 3)(x - 1)$

90. $-10x^2y^4 + 14xy^4 + 12y^4$

$= -2y^4(5x^2 - 7x - 6)$

$= -2y^4(x-2)(5x+3)$

91. **a.** $2x^2 - 5x - 3 = (2x+1)(x-3)$

b. $2(y+1)^2 - 5(y+1) - 3$

$= [2(y+1)+1][(y+1)-3]$

$= [2y+2+1][y+1-3]$

$= (2y+3)(y-2)$

92. **a.** $3x^2 + 5x - 2 = (3x-1)(x+2)$

b. $3(y+1)^2 + 5(y+1) - 2$

$= [3(y+1)-1][(y+1)+2]$

$= [3y+3-1][y+1+2]$

$= (3y+2)(y+3)$

93.

$$\begin{array}{r} 3x^2 - 5x + 2 \\ x-2\overline{\smash{)}3x^3 - 11x^2 + 12x - 4} \\ \underline{3x^3 - 6x^2} \\ -5x^2 + 12x \\ \underline{-5x^2 + 10x} \\ 2x - 4 \\ \underline{2x - 4} \end{array}$$

The quotient $3x^2 - 5x + 2$ into

$(3x-2)(x-1)$.

Thus, $3x^3 - 11x^2 + 12x - 4 =$

$(x-2)(3x-2)(x-1)$.

94.

$$\begin{array}{r} 2x^2 + 5x - 3 \\ x-2\overline{\smash{)}2x^3 + x^2 - 13x + 6} \\ \underline{2x^3 - 4x^2} \\ 5x^2 - 13x \\ \underline{5x^2 - 10x} \\ -3x + 6 \\ \underline{-3x + 6} \end{array}$$

The quotient $2x^2 + 5x - 3$ into

$(2x-1)(x+3)$.

Thus, $3x^3 - 11x^2 + 12x - 4$

$= (x-2)(2x-1)(x+3)$.

95. **a.** $x^2 + 3x + 2$

b. $(x+2)(x+1)$

c. Yes, the pieces are the same in both figures: one large square, three long rectangles, and two small squares. This geometric model illustrates the factorization:

$$x^2 + 3x + 2 = (x+2)(x+1).$$

97. – 99. Answers will vary.

101. Statement *a* is true.

$18y^2 - 6y + 6 = 9(y^2 - 3y + 3)$, and

$y^2 - 3y + 3$ is prime.

103. $2x^2 + bx + 3$

The possible factorizations that will give $2x^2$ as the first term and 3 as the last term are:

$(2x+3)(x+1) = 2x^2 + 5x + 3$

$(2x+1)(x+3) = 2x^2 + 7x + 3$

$(2x-3)(x-1) = 2x^2 - 5x + 3$

$(2x-1)(x-3) = 2x^2 - 7x + 3$

The possible middle terms are

$5x, 7x, -5x$ and $-7x$, so $2x^2 + bx + 3$

can be factored if b is 5, 7, –5, or –7.

105. $2x^{2n} - 7x^n - 4$
Since $x^n \cdot x^n = x^{n+n} = x^{2n}$, the first terms of the factors will be $2x^n$ and x^n. Use trial and error or grouping to obtain the correct factorization.
$2x^{2n} - 7x^n - 4 = \left(2x^n + 1\right)\left(x^n - 4\right)$

106. $(9x + 10)(9x - 10) = (9x)^2 - 10^2$
$$= 81x^2 - 100$$

107. $(4x + 5y)^2 = (4x)^2 + 2(4x)(5y) + (5y)^2$
$$= 16x^2 + 40xy + 25y^2$$

108. $(x + 2)(x^2 - 2x + 4)$
$$= x(x^2 - 2x + 4) + 2(x^2 - 2x + 4)$$
$$= x^3 - 2x^2 + 4x + 2x^2 - 4x + 8$$
$$= x^3 + 8$$

Mid-Chapter Check Point – Chapter 6

1. $x^5 + x^4 = x^4(x + 1)$
GCF is x^4.

2. $x^2 + 7x - 18 = (x - 2)(x + 9)$
Factor by trial and error. The only factors of -18 whose sum is 7 are -2 and 9.

3. $x^2y^3 - x^2y^2 + x^2y = x^2y\left(y^2 - y + 1\right)$
GCF is x^2y. The polynomial in the parentheses is prime because there are no factors of 1 whose sum is -1.

4. $x^2 - 2x + 4$ is prime because there are no factors of 4 whose sum is -2.

5. $7x^2 - 22x + 3$
Factor by grouping.
$a = 7$ and $c = 3$, so $ac = 21$.
The only factors of 21 whose sum is -22 are -21 and -1.
$7x^2 - 22x + 3 = 7x^2 - 21x - x + 3$
$$= 7x(x - 3) - 1(x - 3)$$
$$= (x - 3)(7x - 1)$$

6. $x^3 + 5x^2 + 3x + 15$
Factor by grouping.
$x^3 + 5x^2 + 3x + 15$
$$= \left(x^3 + 5x^2\right) + (3x + 15)$$
$$= x^2(x + 5) + 3(x + 5)$$
$$= (x + 5)\left(x^2 + 3\right)$$

7. $2x^3 - 11x^2 + 5x$
GCF is x.
$2x^3 - 11x^2 + 5x = x\left(2x^2 - 11x + 5\right)$
$$= x(2x - 1)(x - 5)$$

8. $xy - 7x - 4y + 28$
Factor by grouping.
$xy - 7x - 4y + 28$
$$= (xy - 7x) + (-4y + 28)$$
$$= x(y - 7) - 4(y - 7)$$
$$= (y - 7)(x - 4)$$

9. $x^2 - 17xy + 30y^2$
Factor by trial and error. The only factors of 30 whose sum is -17 are -15 and -2.
$x^2 - 17xy + 30y^2 = (x - 15y)(x - 2y)$

10. $25x^2 - 25x - 14$

Factor by trial and error.

$(5x-2)(5x+7) = 25x^2 + 25x - 14$

$(5x+2)(5x-7) = 25x^2 - 25x - 14$

Thus,

$25x^2 - 25x - 14 = (5x+2)(5x-7)$.

Because the correct factorization has been found, there is no need to try additional possibilities.

11. $16x^2 - 70x + 24$

GCF is 2.

$16x^2 - 70x + 24 = 2(8x^2 - 35x + 12)$

Factor the polynomial in parentheses by grouping.

$a = 8$ and $c = 12$, so $ac = 96$.

The only factors of 96 whose sum is -35 are -32 and -3.

$2(8x^2 - 35x + 12)$

$= 2(8x^2 - 32x - 3x + 12)$

$= 2[8x(x-4) - 3(x-4)]$

$= 2(x-4)(8x-3)$

12. $3x^2 + 10xy + 7y^2$

Factor by grouping.

$a = 3$ and $c = 7$, so $ac = 21$.

The only factors of 21 whose sum is 10 are 3 and 7.

$3x^2 + 10xy + 7y^2 = 3x^2 + 3xy + 7xy + 7y^2$

$\qquad = 3x(x+y) + 7y(x+y)$

$\qquad = (x+y)(3x+7y)$

6.4 Exercise Set

1. $x^2 - 25 = x^2 - 5^2 = (x+5)(x-5)$

3. $y^2 - 1 = y^2 - 1^2 = (y+1)(y-1)$

5. $4x^2 - 9 = (2x)^2 - 3^2 = (2x+3)(2x-3)$

7. $25 - x^2 = 5^2 - x^2 = (5+x)(5-x)$

9. $1 - 49x^2 = 1^2 - (7x)^2 = (1+7x)(1-7x)$

11. $9 - 25y^2 = 3^2 - (5y)^2 = (3+5y)(3-5y)$

13. $x^4 - 9 = (x^2)^2 - 3^2 = (x^2+3)(x^2-3)$

15. $49y^4 - 16 = (7y^2)^2 - 4^2$

$\qquad = (7y^2+4)(7y^2-4)$

17. $x^{10} - 9 = (x^5)^2 - 3^2 = (x^5+3)(x^5-3)$

19. $25x^2 - 16y^2 = (5x)^2 - (4y)^2$

$\qquad = (5x+4y)(5x-4y)$

21. $x^4 - y^{10} = (x^2)^2 - (y^5)^2$

$\qquad = (x^2+y^5)(x^2-y^5)$

23. $x^4 - 16 = (x^2)^2 - 4^2 = (x^2+4)(x^2-4)$

Because $x^2 - 4$ is also the difference of two squares, the factorization must be continued. The complete factorization is

$x^4 - 16 = (x^2+4)(x^2-4)$

$\qquad = (x^2+4)(x^2-2^2)$

$\qquad = (x^2+4)(x+2)(x-2)$.

25.
$$16x^4 - 81 = \left(4x^2\right)^2 - 9^2$$
$$= \left(4x^2 + 9\right)\left(4x^2 - 9\right)$$
$$= \left(4x^2 + 9\right)\left[\left(2x\right)^2 - 3^2\right]$$
$$= \left(4x^2 + 9\right)\left(2x + 3\right)\left(2x - 3\right)$$

27. $2x^2 - 18 = 2\left(x^2 - 9\right) = 2\left(x + 3\right)\left(x - 3\right)$

29.
$$2x^3 - 72x = 2x\left(x^2 - 36\right)$$
$$= 2x\left(x + 6\right)\left(x - 6\right)$$

31. $x^2 + 36$ is prime because it is the sum of two squares with no common factor other than 1.

33. $3x^3 + 27x = 3x\left(x^2 + 9\right)$

35. $18 - 2y^2 = 2\left(9 - y^2\right) = 2\left(3 + y\right)\left(3 - y\right)$

37.
$$3y^3 - 48y = 3y\left(y^2 - 16\right)$$
$$= 3y\left(y + 4\right)\left(y - 4\right)$$

39.
$$18x^3 - 2x = 2x\left(9x^2 - 1\right)$$
$$= 2x\left(3x + 1\right)\left(3x - 1\right)$$

41.
$$x^2 + 2x + 1 = x^2 + 2\left(1x\right) + 1^2$$
$$= \left(x + 1\right)^2$$

43.
$$x^2 - 14x + 49 = x^2 - 2\left(7x\right) + 7^2$$
$$= \left(x - 7\right)^2$$

45.
$$x^2 - 2x + 1 = x^2 - 2\left(1x\right) + 1^2$$
$$= \left(x - 1\right)^2$$

47.
$$x^2 + 22x + 121 = x^2 + 2\left(11x\right) + 11^2$$
$$= \left(x + 11\right)^2$$

49.
$$4x^2 + 4x + 1 = \left(2x\right)^2 + 2\left(2x\right) + 1^2$$
$$= \left(2x + 1\right)^2$$

51.
$$25y^2 - 10y + 1 = \left(5y\right)^2 - 2\left(5y\right) + 1^2$$
$$= \left(5y - 1\right)^2$$

53. $x^2 - 10x + 100$ is prime.
To be a perfect square trinomial, the middle term would have to be
$2\left(-10x\right) = -20x$ rather than $-10x$.

55.
$$x^2 + 14xy + 49y^2 = x^2 + 2\left(7xy\right) + \left(7y\right)^2$$
$$= \left(x + 7y\right)^2$$

57.
$$x^2 - 12xy + 36y^2 = x^2 - 2\left(6xy\right) + \left(6y\right)^2$$
$$= \left(x - 6y\right)^2$$

59. $x^2 - 8xy + 64y^2$ is prime.
To be a perfect square trinomial, the middle term would have to be
$2\left(-8xy\right) = -16xy$ rather than $-8xy$.

61.
$$16x^2 - 40xy + 25y^2$$
$$= \left(4x\right)^2 - 2\left(4x \cdot 5y\right) + \left(5y\right)^2$$
$$= \left(4x - 5y\right)^2$$

63.
$$12x^2 - 12x + 3 = 3\left(4x^2 - 4x + 1\right)$$
$$= 3\left[\left(2x\right)^2 - 2\left(2x\right) + 1^2\right]$$
$$= 3\left(2x - 1\right)^2$$

65.
$$9x^3 + 6x^2 + x$$
$$= x\left(9x^2 + 6x + 1\right)$$
$$= x\left[\left(3x\right)^2 + 2\left(3x\right) + 1^2\right]$$
$$= x\left(3x + 1\right)^2$$

67.
$$2y^2 - 4y + 2 = 2(y^2 - 2y + 1)$$
$$= 2(y-1)^2$$

69.
$$2y^3 + 28y^2 + 98y = 2y(y^2 + 14y + 49)$$
$$= 2y(y+7)^2$$

71.
$$x^3 + 1 = x^3 + 1^3$$
$$= (x+1)(x^2 - x \cdot 1 + 1^2)$$
$$= (x+1)(x^2 - x + 1)$$

73.
$$x^3 - 27 = x^3 - 3^3$$
$$= (x-3)(x^2 + x \cdot 3 + 3^2)$$
$$= (x-3)(x^2 + 3x + 9)$$

75.
$$8y^3 - 1 = (2y)^3 - 1^3$$
$$= (2y-1)\left[(2y)^2 + 2y \cdot 1 + 1\right]$$
$$= (2y-1)(4y^2 + 2y + 1)$$

77.
$$27x^3 + 8 = (3x)^3 + 2^3$$
$$= (3x+2)\left[(3x)^2 - 3x \cdot 2 + 2^2\right]$$
$$= (3x+2)(9x^2 - 6x + 4)$$

79.
$$x^3 y^3 - 64 = (xy)^3 - 4^3$$
$$= (xy-4)\left[(xy)^2 + xy \cdot 4 + 4^2\right]$$
$$= (xy-4)(x^2 y^2 + 4xy + 16)$$

81.
$$27y^4 + 8y$$
$$= y(27y^3 + 8)$$
$$= y\left[(3y)^3 + 2^3\right]$$
$$= y(3y+2)\left[(3y)^2 - 3y \cdot 2 + 2^2\right]$$
$$= y(3y+2)(9y^2 - 6y + 4)$$

83.
$$54 - 16y^3$$
$$= 2(27 - 8y^3)$$
$$= 2\left[3^3 - (2y)^3\right]$$
$$= 2(3-2y)\left[3^2 + 3 \cdot 2y + (2y)^2\right]$$
$$= 2(3-2y)(9 + 6y + 4y^2)$$

85.
$$64x^3 + 27y^3$$
$$= (4x)^3 + (3y)^3$$
$$= (4x+3y)\left[(4x)^2 - 4x \cdot 3y + (3y)^2\right]$$
$$= (4x+3y)(16x^2 - 12xy + 9y^2)$$

87.
$$125x^3 - 64y^3$$
$$= (5x)^3 - (4y)^3$$
$$= (5x-4y)\left[(5x)^2 + 5x \cdot 4y + (4y)^2\right]$$
$$= (5x-4y)(25x^2 + 20xy + 16y^2)$$

89.
$$25x^2 - \frac{4}{49} = (5x)^2 - \left(\frac{2}{7}\right)^2$$
$$= \left(5x + \frac{2}{7}\right)\left(5x - \frac{2}{7}\right)$$

90.
$$16x^2 - \frac{9}{25} = (4x)^2 - \left(\frac{3}{5}\right)^2$$
$$= \left(4x + \frac{3}{5}\right)\left(4x - \frac{3}{5}\right)$$

91.
$$y^4 - \frac{y}{1000} = y\left(y^3 - \frac{1}{1000}\right)$$
$$= y\left[y^3 - \left(\frac{1}{10}\right)^3\right]$$
$$= y\left(y - \frac{1}{10}\right)\left[y^2 + y \cdot \frac{1}{10} + \left(\frac{1}{10}\right)^2\right]$$
$$= y\left(y - \frac{1}{10}\right)\left(y^2 + \frac{y}{10} + \frac{1}{100}\right)$$

286

92.

$$y^4 - \frac{y}{8} = y\left(y^3 - \frac{1}{8}\right) = y\left[y^3 - \left(\frac{1}{2}\right)^3\right]$$

$$= y\left(y - \frac{1}{2}\right)\left[y^2 + y \cdot \frac{1}{2} + \left(\frac{1}{2}\right)^2\right]$$

$$= y\left(y - \frac{1}{2}\right)\left(y^2 + \frac{y}{2} + \frac{1}{4}\right)$$

93.

$$0.25x - x^3 = x\left(0.25 - x^2\right)$$

$$= x\left[(0.5)^2 - x^2\right] = x(0.5 + x)(0.5 - x)$$

94.

$$0.64x - x^3 = x\left(0.64 - x^2\right)$$

$$= x\left[(0.8)^2 - x^2\right] = x(0.8 + x)(0.8 - x)$$

95.

$$(x+1)^2 - 25 = (x+1)^2 - 5^2$$

$$= \left[(x+1) + 5\right]\left[(x+1) - 5\right]$$

$$= (x+6)(x-4)$$

96.

$$(x+2)^2 - 49 = (x+2)^2 - 7^2$$

$$= \left[(x+2) + 7\right]\left[(x+2) - 7\right]$$

$$= (x+9)(x-5)$$

97.

$$\begin{array}{r} x^2 + 2x + 1 \\ x-3\overline{)x^3 - x^2 - 5x - 3} \\ \underline{x^3 - 3x^2} \\ 2x^2 - 5x \\ \underline{2x^2 - 6x} \\ x - 3 \\ \underline{x - 3} \end{array}$$

The quotient $x^2 + 2x + 1$ factors further.

$x^2 + 2x + 1 = (x+1)^2$.

Thus, $x^3 - x^2 - 5x - 3 = (x-3)(x+1)^2$.

98.

$$\begin{array}{r} x^2 + 6x + 9 \\ x-2\overline{)x^3 + 4x^2 - 3x - 18} \\ \underline{x^3 - 2x^2} \\ 6x^2 - 3x \\ \underline{6x^2 - 12x} \\ 9x - 18 \\ \underline{9x - 18} \end{array}$$

The quotient $x^2 + 6x + 9$ factors further.

$x^2 + 6x + 9 = (x+3)^2$.

Thus,

$x^3 + 4x^2 - 3x - 18 = (x-2)(x+3)^2$.

99. Area of outer square $= x^2$
Area of inner square $= 5^2 = 25$
Area of shaded region $= x^2 - 25$
$$= (x+5)(x-5)$$

101. Area of large square $= x^2$
Area of each small corner squares
$= 2^2 = 4$
Area of four corner squares $= 4 \cdot 4 = 16$
Area of shaded region $= x^2 - 16$
$$= (x+4)(x-4)$$

103. – 105. Answers will vary.

107. Statement b is true.

109.

$$x^2 - y^2 + 3x + 3y$$

$$= (x+y)(x-y) + 3(x+y)$$

$$= (x+y)((x-y) + 3)$$

$$= (x+y)(x - y + 3)$$

111.

$$4x^{2n} + 12x^n + 9$$

$$= (2x^n)^2 + 2(6x^n) + 3^2$$

$$= (2x^n + 3)^2$$

287

113. $9x^2 + kx + 1$

In order to get $9x^2$ as the first tem of the perfect square trinomial, the possibilities are

$(3x+1)^2 = 9x^2 + 6x + 1$

$(3x-1)^2 = 9x^2 - 6x + 1$

Therefore, for $9x^2 + kx + 1$ to be a perfect square trinomial, k must be -6 or 6.

115.

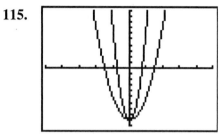

The graphs do not coincide.

$4x^2 - 9 = (2x+3)(2x-3)$

The expression on the right should be changed to $(2x+3)(2x-3)$.

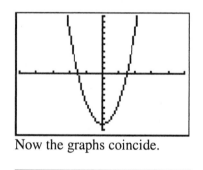

Now the graphs coincide.

117.

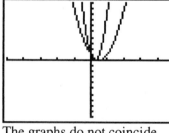

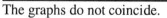

The graphs do not coincide.

$4x^2 - 4x + 1 = (2x)^2 - 2 \cdot 2x \cdot 1 = (2x-1)^2$

The expression on the right should be changed to $(2x-1)^2$.

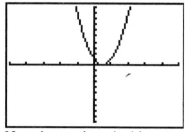

Now the graphs coincide.

119. $\left(2x^2 y^3\right)^4 \left(5xy^2\right)$

$= \left[2^4 \left(x^2\right)^4 \left(y^3\right)^4\right] \cdot \left(5xy^2\right)$

$= \left(16x^8 y^{12}\right)\left(5xy^2\right)$

$= (16 \cdot 5)\left(x^8 \cdot x^1\right)\left(y^{12} \cdot y^2\right)$

$= 80x^9 y^{14}$

120. $\left(10x^2 - 5x + 2\right) - \left(14x^2 - 5x - 1\right)$

$= \left(10x^2 - 5x + 2\right) + \left(-14x^2 + 5x + 1\right)$

$= \left(10x^2 - 14x^2\right) + (-5x + 5x) + (2+1)$

$= -4x^2 + 3$

121.

$$\begin{array}{r} 2x+5 \\ 3x-2\overline{)6x^2 + 11x - 10} \\ \underline{6x^2 - 4x} \\ 15x - 10 \\ \underline{15x - 10} \\ 0 \end{array}$$

$\dfrac{6x^2 + 11x - 10}{3x - 2} = 2x + 5$

288

6.5 Exercise Set

In Exercises 1-61, all factorizations should be checked using multiplication or a graphing utility. Checks will not be shown here.

1.
$$5x^3 - 20x = 5x(x^2 - 4)$$
$$= 5x(x+2)(x-2)$$

3.
$$7x^3 + 7x = 7x(x^2 + 1)$$

5.
$$5x^2 - 5x - 30 = 5(x^2 - x - 6)$$
$$= 5(x+2)(x-3)$$

7.
$$2x^4 - 162 = 2(x^4 - 81)$$
$$= 2(x^2 + 9)(x^2 - 9)$$
$$= 2(x^2 + 9)(x+3)(x-3)$$

9.
$$x^3 + 2x^2 - 9x - 18$$
$$= (x^3 + 2x^2) + (-9x - 18)$$
$$= x^2(x+2) - 9(x+2)$$
$$= (x+2)(x^2 - 9)$$
$$= (x+2)(x+3)(x-3)$$

11.
$$3x^3 - 24x^2 + 48x = 3x(x^2 - 8x + 16)$$
$$= 3x(x-4)^2$$

13.
$$2x^5 + 2x^2 = 2x^2(x^3 + 1)$$
$$= 2x^2(x+1)(x^2 - x + 1)$$

15.
$$6x^2 + 8x = 2x(3x + 4)$$

17.
$$2y^2 - 2y - 112 = 2(y^2 - y - 56)$$
$$= 2(y-8)(y+7)$$

19.
$$7y^4 + 14y^3 + 7y^2 = 7y^2(y^2 + 2y + 1)$$
$$= 7y^2(y+1)^2$$

21.
$y^2 + 8y - 16$ is prime because there are no two integers whose product is -16 and whose sum is 8.

23.
$$16y^2 - 4y - 2 = 2(8y^2 - 2y - 1)$$
$$= 2(4y+1)(2y-1)$$

25.
$r^2 - 25r = r(r - 25)$

27.
$4w^2 + 8w - 5 = (2w+5)(2w-1)$

29.
$x^3 - 4x = x(x^2 - 4) = x(x+2)(x-2)$

31.
$x^2 + 64$ is prime because it is the sum of two squares with no common factor other than 1.

33.
$9y^2 + 13y + 4 = (9y+4)(y+1)$

35.
$$y^3 + 2y^2 - 4y - 8$$
$$= (y^3 + 2y^2) + (-4y - 8)$$
$$= y^2(y+2) - 4(y+2)$$
$$= (y+2)(y^2 - 4)$$
$$= (y+2)(y+2)(y-2)$$
$$\text{or} \quad (y+2)^2(y-2)$$

37.
$$16y^2 + 24y + 9 = (4y)^2 + 2(4y \cdot 3) + 3^2$$
$$= (4y+3)^2$$

39.
$$4y^3 - 28y^2 + 40y = 4y(y^2 - 7y + 10)$$
$$= 4y(y-5)(y-2)$$

289

41. $y^5 - 81y = y(y^4 - 81)$
$$= y(y^2 + 9)(y^2 - 9)$$
$$= y(y^2 + 9)(y + 3)(y - 3)$$

43. $20a^4 - 45a^2 = 5a^2(4a^2 - 9)$
$$= 5a^2(2a + 3)(2a - 3)$$

45. $12y^2 - 11y + 2 = (4y - 1)(3y - 2)$

47. $9y^2 - 64 = (3y)^2 - 8^2$
$$= (3y + 8)(3y - 8)$$

49. $9y^2 + 64$ is prime because it is the sum of two squares with no common factor other than 1.

51. $2y^3 + 3y^2 - 50y - 75$
$$= (2y^3 + 3y^2) + (-50y - 75)$$
$$= y^2(2y + 3) - 25(2y + 3)$$
$$= (2y + 3)(y^2 - 25)$$
$$= (2y + 3)(y + 5)(y - 5)$$

53. $2r^3 + 30r^2 - 68r = 2r(r^2 + 15r - 34)$
$$= 2r(r + 17)(r - 2)$$

55. $8x^5 - 2x^3 = 2x^3(4x^2 - 1)$
$$= 2x^3[(2x)^2 - 1^2]$$
$$= 2x^3(2x + 1)(2x - 1)$$

57. $3x^2 + 243 = 3(x^2 + 81)$

59. $x^4 + 8x = x(x^3 + 8)$
$$= x(x^3 + 2^3)$$
$$= x(x + 2)(x^2 - 2x + 4)$$

61. $2y^5 - 2y^2 = 2y^2(y^3 - 1)$
$$= 2y^2(y - 1)(y^2 + y + 1)$$

63. $6x^2 + 8xy = 2x(3x + 4y)$

65. $xy - 7x + 3y - 21$
$$= (xy - 7x) + (3y - 21)$$
$$= x(y - 7) + 3(y - 7)$$
$$= (y - 7)(x + 3)$$

67. $x^2 - 3xy - 4y^2 = (x - 4y)(x + y)$

69. $72a^3b^2 + 12a^2 - 24a^4b^2$
$$= 12a^2(6ab^2 + 1 - 2a^2b^2)$$

71. $3a^2 + 27ab + 54b^2$
$$= 3(a^2 + 9ab + 18b^2)$$
$$= 3(a + 6b)(a + 3b)$$

73. $48x^4y - 3x^2y = 3x^2y(16x^2 - 1)$
$$= 3x^2y(4x + 1)(4x - 1)$$

75. $6a^2b + ab - 2b = b(6a^2 + a - 2)$
$$= b(3a + 2)(2a - 1)$$

77. $7x^5y - 7xy^5$
$$= 7xy(x^4 - y^4)$$
$$= 7xy(x^2 + y^2)(x^2 - y^2)$$
$$= 7xy(x^2 + y^2)(x + y)(x - y)$$

79. $10x^3y - 14x^2y^2 + 4xy^3$
$$= 2xy(5x^2 - 7xy + 2y^2)$$
$$= 2xy(5x - 2y)(x - y)$$

290

81. $2bx^2 + 44bx + 242b$
$$= 2b(x^2 + 22x + 121)$$
$$= 2b(x^2 + 2(11x) + 11^2)$$
$$= 2b(x + 11)^2$$

83. $15a^2 + 11ab - 14b^2 = (5a + 7b)(3a - 2b)$

85. $36x^3y - 62x^2y^2 + 12xy^3$
$$= 2xy(18x^2 - 31xy + 6y^2)$$
$$= 2xy(9x - 2y)(2x - 3y)$$

87. $a^2y - b^2y - a^2x + b^2x$
$$= (a^2y - b^2y) + (-a^2x + b^2x)$$
$$= y(a^2 - b^2) - x(a^2 - b^2)$$
$$= (a^2 - b^2)(y - x)$$
$$= (a + b)(a - b)(y - x)$$

89. $9ax^3 + 15ax^2 - 14ax$
$$= ax(9x^2 + 15x - 14)$$
$$= ax(3x + 7)(3x - 2)$$

91. $81x^4y - y^5$
$$= y(81x^4 - y^4)$$
$$= y(9x^2 + y^2)(9x^2 - y^2)$$
$$= y(9x^2 + y^2)(3x + y)(3x - y)$$

93. $10x^2(x+1) - 7x(x+1) - 6(x+1)$
$$= (x+1)(10x^2 - 7x - 6)$$
$$= (x+1)(5x - 6)(2x + 1)$$

94. $12x^2(x-1) - 4x(x-1) - 5(x-1)$
$$= (x-1)(12x^2 - 4x - 5)$$
$$= (x-1)(6x - 5)(2x + 1)$$

95. $6x^4 + 35x^2 - 6 = (x^2 + 6)(6x^2 - 1)$

96. $7x^4 + 34x^2 - 5 = (7x^2 - 1)(x^2 + 5)$

97. $(x-7)^2 - 4a^2 = (x-7)^2 - (2a)^2$
$$= [(x-7) + 2a][(x-7) - 2a]$$
$$= (x - 7 + 2a)(x - 7 - 2a)$$

98. $(x-6)^2 - 9a^2 = (x-6)^2 - (3a)^2$
$$= [(x-6) + 3a][(x-6) - 3a]$$
$$= (x - 6 + 3a)(x - 6 - 3a)$$

99. $x^2 + 8x + 16 - 25a^2$
$$= (x^2 + 8x + 16) - (5a)^2$$
$$= (x + 4)^2 - (5a)^2$$
$$= [(x+4) + 5a][(x+4) - 5a]$$
$$= (x + 4 + 5a)(x + 4 - 5a)$$

100. $x^2 + 14x + 49 - 16a^2$
$$= (x^2 + 14x + 49) - (4a)^2$$
$$= (x + 7)^2 - (4a)^2$$
$$= [(x+7) + 4a][(x+7) - 4a]$$
$$= (x + 7 + 4a)(x + 7 - 4a)$$

101. $y^7 + y = y(y^6 + 1) = y[(y^2)^3 + 1^3]$
$$= y(y^2 + 1)(y^4 - y^2 + 1)$$

102. $(y+1)^3 + 1 = (y+1)^3 + 1^3$
$$= [(y+1) + 1][(y+1)^2 - (y+1) + 1]$$
$$= (y+2)[(y^2 + 2y + 1) - y - 1 + 1]$$
$$= (y+2)(y^2 + 2y + 1 - y - 1 + 1)$$
$$= (y+2)(y^2 + y + 1)$$

103.
$$256 - 16t^2 = 16(16 - t^2)$$
$$= 16(4 + t)(4 - t)$$

105. Area of outer circle = πb^2
Area of inner circle = πa^2
Area of shaded ring = $\pi b^2 - \pi a^2$

$$\pi b^2 - \pi a^2 = \pi(b^2 - a^2)$$
$$= \pi(b + a)(b - a)$$

107. Answers will vary.

109. Statement d is true.
$$3x^2 y^3 + 9xy^2 + 21xy$$
$$= 3xy(xy^2 + 3y + 7),$$

and $xy^2 + 3y + 7$ cannot be factored further.

111.
$$5y^5 - 5y^4 - 20y^3 + 20y^2$$
$$= 5y^2(y^3 - y^2 - 4y + 4)$$
$$= 5y^2\left[y^2(y - 1) - 4(y - 1)\right]$$
$$= 5y^2(y - 1)(y^2 - 4)$$
$$= 5y^2(y - 1)(y + 2)(y - 2)$$

113.
$$(x + 5)^2 - 20(x + 5) + 100$$
This is a perfect square trinomial.

$$(x + 5)^2 - 20(x + 5) + 100$$
$$= (x + 5)^2 - 2(x + 5)(10) + 10^2$$
$$= \left[(x + 5) - 10\right]^2$$
$$= (x - 5)^2$$

115.

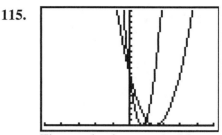

The graphs do not coincide.

$$4x^2 - 12x + 9 = (2x)^2 - 2(2x \cdot 3) + 3^2$$
$$= (2x - 3)^2$$

Change the polynomial on the right side to $(2x - 3)^2$.

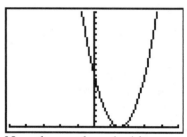

Now the graphs coincide.

117.

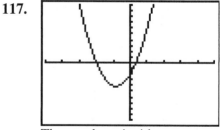

The graphs coincide.

This verifies that the factorization
$$6x^2 + 10x - 4 = 2(3x - 1)(x + 2)$$
is correct.

119.

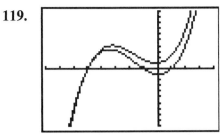

The graphs do not coincide

$$2x^3 + 10x^2 - 2x - 10$$
$$= 2(x^3 + 5x^2 - x - 5)$$
$$= 2\left[(x^3 + 5x^2) + (-x - 5)\right]$$
$$= 2\left[x^2(x + 5) - 1(x + 5)\right]$$
$$= 2(x + 5)(x^2 - 1)$$
$$= 2(x + 5)(x + 1)(x - 1)$$

Change the polynomial on the right side to $2(x + 5)(x + 1)(x - 1)$.

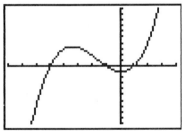

Now the graphs coincide.

120. $9x^2 - 16 = (3x)^2 - 4^2$
$$= (3x + 4)(3x - 4)$$

121. $5x - 2y = 10$
To find the x-intercept, let $y = 0$.
$$5x - 2(0) = 10$$
$$5x = 10$$
$$x = 2$$
To find the y-intercept, let $x = 0$.

$$5(0) - 2y = 10$$
$$-2y = 10$$
$$y = -5$$
checkpoint: $(4, 5)$

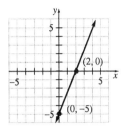

122. Let x = the measure of the first angle.
Then $3x$ = the measure of the second angle;
and $x + 80$ = the measure of the third angle.
$$x + 3x + (x + 80) = 180$$
$$5x + 80 = 180$$
$$5x = 100$$
$$x = 20$$
Measure of first angle, $x = 20°$
Measure of second angle, $3x = 60°$
Measure of third angle, $x + 80 = 100°$

6.6 Exercise Set

1. $x(x + 7) = 0$
$$x = 0 \text{ or } x + 7 = 0$$
$$x = -7$$
The solution set is $\{-7, 0\}$.

3. $(x - 6)(x + 4) = 0$
$$x - 6 = 0 \text{ or } x + 4 = 0$$
$$x = 6 \qquad x = -4$$
The solution set is $\{-4, 6\}$.

5.
$$(x-9)(5x+4)=0$$
$$x-9=0 \text{ or } 5x+4=0$$
$$x=9 \qquad 5x=-4$$
$$x=-\frac{4}{5}$$
The solution set is $\left\{-\frac{4}{5},9\right\}$.

7.
$$10(x-4)(2x+9)=0$$
$$x-4=0 \text{ or } 2x+9=0$$
$$x=4 \qquad 2x=-9$$
$$x=-\frac{9}{2}$$
The solution set is $\left\{-\frac{9}{2},4\right\}$.

In Exercises 9-55, all solutions should be checked by substitution or by using a graphing utility and identifying x-intercepts. The check by substitution will be shown here for Exercise 9 only.

9.
$$x^2+8x+15=0$$
$$(x+5)(x+3)=0$$
$$x+5=0 \text{ or } x+3=0$$
$$x=-5 \qquad x=-3$$

Check -5:
$$x^2+8x+15=0$$
$$(-5)^2+8(-5)+15=0$$
$$25-40+15=0$$
$$0=0 \text{ true}$$
Check -3:
$$x^2+8x+15=0$$
$$(-3)^2+8(-3)+15=0$$
$$9-24+15=0$$
$$0=0 \text{ true}$$
The solution set is $\{-5,-3\}$.

11.
$$x^2-2x-15=0$$
$$(x+3)(x-5)=0$$
$$x+3=0 \text{ or } x-5=0$$
$$x=-3 \qquad x=5$$
The solution set is $\{-3,5\}$.

13.
$$x^2-4x=21$$
$$x^2-4x-21=0$$
$$(x+3)(x-7)=0$$
$$x+3=0 \text{ or } x-7=0$$
$$x=-3 \qquad x=7$$
The solution set is $\{-3,7\}$.

15.
$$x^2+9x=-8$$
$$x^2+9x+8=0$$
$$(x+8)(x+1)=0$$
$$x+8=0 \text{ or } x+1=0$$
$$x=-8 \qquad x=-1$$
The solution set is $\{-8,-1\}$.

17.
$$x^2+4x=0$$
$$x(x+4)=0$$
$$x=0 \text{ or } x+4=0$$
$$x=-4$$
The solution set $\{-4,0\}$.

19.
$$x^2-5x=0$$
$$x(x-5)=0$$
$$x=0 \text{ or } x-5=0$$
$$x=5$$
The solution set is $\{0,5\}$.

21.
$$x^2=4x$$
$$x^2-4x=0$$
$$x(x-4)=0$$
$$x=0 \text{ or } x-4=0$$
$$x=4$$
The solution set is $\{0,4\}$.

23.
$$2x^2 = 5x$$
$$2x^2 - 5x = 0$$
$$x(2x - 5) = 0$$
$$x = 0 \quad \text{or} \quad 2x - 5 = 0$$
$$2x = 5$$
$$x = \frac{5}{2}$$
The solution set is $\left\{0, \frac{5}{2}\right\}$.

25.
$$3x^2 = -5x$$
$$3x^2 + 5x = 0$$
$$x(3x + 5) = 0$$
$$x = 0 \quad \text{or} \quad 3x + 5 = 0$$
$$3x = -5$$
$$x = -\frac{5}{3}$$
The solution set is $\left\{-\frac{5}{3}, 0\right\}$.

27. $x^2 + 4x + 4 = 0$
$$(x - 2)^2 = 0$$
$$x + 2 = 0$$
$$x = -2$$
The solution set is $\{-2\}$.

29.
$$x^2 = 12x - 36$$
$$x^2 - 12x + 36 = 0$$
$$(x - 6)^2 = 0$$
$$x - 6 = 0$$
$$x = 6$$
The solution set is $\{6\}$.

31.
$$4x^2 = 12x - 9$$
$$4x^2 - 12x + 9 = 0$$
$$(2x - 3)^2 = 0$$
$$2x - 3 = 0$$
$$2x = 3$$
$$x = \frac{3}{2}$$
The solution set is $\left\{\frac{3}{2}\right\}$.

33.
$$2x^2 = 7x + 4$$
$$2x^2 - 7x - 4 = 0$$
$$(2x + 1)(x - 4) = 0$$
$$2x + 1 = 0 \quad \text{or} \quad x - 4 = 0$$
$$2x = -1 \qquad x = 4$$
$$x = -\frac{1}{2}$$
The solution set is $\left\{-\frac{1}{2}, 4\right\}$.

35.
$$5x^2 = 18 - x$$
$$5x^2 + x - 18 = 0$$
$$(5x - 9)(x + 2) = 0$$
$$5x - 9 = 0 \quad \text{or} \quad x + 2 = 0$$
$$5x = 9 \qquad x = -2$$
$$x = \frac{9}{5}$$
The solution set is $\left\{-2, \frac{9}{5}\right\}$.

37.
$$x^2 - 49 = 0$$
$$(x + 7)(x - 7) = 0$$
$$x + 7 = 0 \quad \text{or} \quad x - 7 = 0$$
$$x = -7 \qquad x = 7$$
The solution set is $\{-7, 7\}$.

39.

$$4x^2 - 25 = 0$$
$$(2x+5)(2x-5) = 0$$
$$2x+5 = 0 \quad \text{or} \quad 2x-5 = 0$$
$$2x = -5 \qquad\qquad 2x = 5$$
$$x = -\frac{5}{2} \qquad\qquad x = \frac{5}{2}$$

The solution set is $\left\{-\frac{5}{2}, \frac{5}{2}\right\}$.

41.

$$81x^2 = 25$$
$$81x^2 - 25 = 0$$
$$(9x+5)(9x-5) = 0$$
$$9x+5 = 0 \quad \text{or} \quad 9x-5 = 0$$
$$9x = -5 \qquad\qquad 9x = 5$$
$$x = -\frac{5}{9} \qquad\qquad x = \frac{5}{9}$$

The solution set is $\left\{-\frac{5}{9}, \frac{5}{9}\right\}$.

43.

$$x(x-4) = 21$$
$$x^2 - 4x = 21$$
$$x^2 - 4x - 21 = 0$$
$$(x+3)(x-7) = 0$$
$$x+3 = 0 \quad \text{or} \quad x-7 = 0$$
$$x = -3 \qquad\qquad x = 7$$

The solution set is $\{-3, 7\}$.

45.

$$4x(x+1) = 15$$
$$4x^2 + 4x = 15$$
$$4x^2 + 4x - 15 = 0$$
$$(2x+5)(2x-3) = 0$$
$$2x+5 = 0 \quad \text{or} \quad 2x-3 = 0$$
$$2x = -5 \qquad\qquad 2x = 3$$
$$x = -\frac{5}{2} \qquad\qquad x = \frac{3}{2}$$

The solution set is $\left\{-\frac{5}{2}, \frac{3}{2}\right\}$.

47.

$$(x-1)(x+4) = 14$$
$$x^2 + 3x - 4 = 14$$
$$x^2 + 3x - 18 = 0$$
$$(x+6)(x-3) = 0$$
$$x+6 = 0 \quad \text{or} \quad x-3 = 0$$
$$x = -6 \qquad\qquad x = 3$$

The solution set is $\{-6, 3\}$.

49.

$$(x+1)(2x+5) = -1$$
$$2x^2 + 7x + 5 = -1$$
$$2x^2 + 7x + 6 = 0$$
$$(2x+3)(x+2) = 0$$
$$2x+3 = 0 \quad \text{or} \quad x+2 = 0$$
$$2x = -3 \qquad\qquad x = -2$$
$$x = -\frac{3}{2}$$

The solution set is $\left\{-2, -\frac{3}{2}\right\}$.

51.

$$y(y+8) = 16(y-1)$$
$$y^2 + 8y = 16y - 16$$
$$y^2 - 8y + 16 = 0$$
$$(y-4)^2 = 0$$
$$y-4 = 0$$
$$y = 4$$

The solution set is $\{4\}$.

53.

$$4y^2 + 20y + 25 = 0$$
$$(2y+5)^2 = 0$$
$$2y+5 = 0$$
$$2y = -5$$
$$y = -\frac{5}{2}$$

The solution set is $\left\{-\frac{5}{2}\right\}$.

296

55.
$$64w^2 = 48w - 9$$
$$64w^2 - 48w + 9 = 0$$
$$(8w - 3)^2 = 0$$
$$8w - 3 = 0$$
$$8w = 3$$
$$w = \frac{3}{8}$$

The solution set is $\left\{\dfrac{3}{8}\right\}$.

57.
$$(x - 4)(x^2 + 5x + 6) = 0$$
$$(x - 4)(x + 3)(x + 2) = 0$$
$$x - 4 = 0 \ \text{ or } \ x + 3 = 0 \quad \text{ or } \ x + 2 = 0$$
$$\quad x = 4 \qquad\quad x = -3 \qquad\qquad x = -2$$

The solution set is $\{-3, -2, 4\}$.

58.
$$(x - 5)(x^2 - 3x + 2) = 0$$
$$(x - 5)(x - 2)(x - 1) = 0$$
$$x - 5 = 0 \ \text{ or } \ x - 2 = 0 \quad \text{ or } \ x - 1 = 0$$
$$\quad x = 5 \qquad\quad x = 2 \qquad\qquad x = 1$$

The solution set is $\{1, 2, 5\}$.

59.
$$x^3 - 36x = 0$$
$$x(x^2 - 36) = 0$$
$$x(x + 6)(x - 6) = 0$$
$$x = 0 \ \text{ or } \ x + 6 = 0 \ \text{ or } \ x - 6 = 0$$
$$\qquad\qquad x = -6 \qquad\quad x = 6$$

The solution set is $\{-6, 0, 6\}$.

60.
$$x^3 - 4x = 0$$
$$x(x^2 - 4) = 0$$
$$x(x + 2)(x - 2) = 0$$
$$x = 0 \ \text{ or } \ x + 2 = 0 \ \text{ or } \ x - 2 = 0$$
$$\qquad\qquad x = -2 \qquad\quad x = 2$$

The solution set is $\{-2, 0, 2\}$.

61.
$$y^3 + 3y^2 + 2y = 0$$
$$y(y^2 + 3y + 2) = 0$$
$$y(y + 2)(y + 1) = 0$$
$$y = 0 \ \text{ or } \ y + 2 = 0 \ \text{ or } \ y + 1 = 0$$
$$\qquad\qquad\quad y = -2 \qquad\quad y = -1$$

The solution set is $\{-2, -1, 0\}$.

62.
$$y^3 + 2y^2 - 3y = 0$$
$$y(y^2 + 2y - 3) = 0$$
$$y(y + 3)(y - 1) = 0$$
$$y = 0 \ \text{ or } \ y + 3 = 0 \ \text{ or } \ y - 1 = 0$$
$$\qquad\qquad\quad y = -3 \qquad\quad y = 1$$

The solution set is $\{-3, 0, 1\}$.

63.
$$2(x - 4)^2 + x^2 = x(x + 50) - 46x$$
$$2(x^2 - 8x + 16) + x^2 = x^2 + 50x - 46x$$
$$2x^2 - 16x + 32 + x^2 = x^2 + 4x$$
$$3x^2 - 16x + 32 = x^2 + 4x$$
$$2x^2 - 20x + 32 = 0$$
$$2(x^2 - 10x + 16) = 0$$
$$2(x - 8)(x - 2) = 0$$
$$x - 8 = 0 \ \text{ or } \ x - 2 = 0$$
$$\quad x = 8 \qquad\qquad x = 2$$

The solution set is $\{2, 8\}$.

64.
$$(x - 4)(x - 5) + (2x + 3)(x - 1)$$
$$= x(2x - 25) - 13$$
$$x^2 - 9x + 20 + 2x^2 + x - 3$$
$$= 2x^2 - 25x - 13$$
$$3x^2 - 8x + 17 = 2x^2 - 25x - 13$$
$$x^2 + 17x + 30 = 0$$
$$(x + 15)(x + 2) = 0$$
$$x + 15 = 0 \qquad \text{or} \qquad x + 2 = 0$$
$$\quad x = -15 \qquad\qquad\quad x = -2$$

The solution set is $\{-15, -2\}$.

65. $(x-2)^2 - 5(x-2)+6=0$

$[(x-2)-3][(x-2)-2]=0$

$(x-5)(x-4)=0$

$x-5=0$ or $x-4=0$

$\quad x=5 \qquad\qquad x=4$

The solution set is $\{4, 5\}$.

66. $(x-3)^2 + 2(x-3)-8=0$

$[(x-3)-2][(x-3)+4]=0$

$(x-5)(x+1)=0$

$x-5=0$ or $x+1=0$

$\quad x=5 \qquad\qquad x=-1$

The solution set is $\{-1, 5\}$.

67. $h=-16t^2 + 20t + 300$

Substitute 0 for h and solve for t.

$$0=-16t^2 + 20t + 300$$

$-16t^2 + 20t + 300 = 0$

$-4t(4t^2 - 5t - 75)=0$

$-4t(4t+15)(t-5)=0$

$-4t=0$ or $4t+15=0$ or $t-5=0$

$\quad t=0 \qquad 4t=-15 \qquad\quad t=5$

$$t=-\frac{15}{4}=-3.75$$

Discard $t=0$ since this represents the time before the ball was thrown. Also discard $t=-3.75$ since time cannot be negative.

The only solution that makes sense is 5. So it will take 5 seconds for the ball to hit the ground.

Each tick mark represents one second.

69. Substitute 276 for h and solve for t.

$$276=-16t^2 + 20t + 300$$

$16t^2 - 20t - 24 = 0$

$4(4t^2 - 5t - 6)=0$

$4(4t+3)(t-2)=0$

$4t+3=0$ or $t-2=0$

$4t=-3 \qquad\qquad t=2$

$$t=-\frac{3}{4}$$

Discard $t=-\frac{3}{4}$ since time cannot be negative. The ball's height will be 276 feet 2 seconds after it is thrown. This corresponds to the point $(2,276)$ on the graph.

71. $h=-16t^2 + 72t$

Substitute 32 for h and solve for t.

$$32=-16t^2 + 72t$$

$16t^2 - 72t + 32 = 0$

$8(2t^2 - 9t + 4)=0$

$8(2t-1)(t-4)=0$

$2t-1=0$ or $t-4=0$

$\quad t=\frac{1}{2} \qquad\qquad t=4$

The debris will be 32 feet above the ground $\frac{1}{2}$ second after the explosion and 4 seconds after the explosion.

73. $N = 2x^2 + 22x + 320$

Substitute 1100 for N and solve for x.

$1100 = 2x^2 + 22x + 320$

$0 = 2x^2 + 22x - 780$

$0 = 2(x^2 + 11x - 390)$

$0 = 2(x + 26)(x - 15)$

$x + 26 = 0 \quad$ or $\quad x - 15 = 0$

$x = -26 \qquad\qquad x = 15$

Discard $x = -26$ because the model starts at $x = 0$ to represent 1980. Since $x = 15$ represents the year 1995, the model shows that there were 1100 thousand (or 1,100,000) inmates in U.S. state and federal prisons in 1995. This corresponds to the point $(15, 1100)$ on the graph.

75. $P = -10x^2 + 475x + 3500$

Substitute 7250 for P and solve for x.

$7250 = -10x^2 + 475x + 3500$

$10x^2 - 475x + 3750 = 0$

$5(2x^2 - 95x + 750) = 0$

$5(x - 10)(2x - 75) = 0$

$x - 10 = 0 \quad$ or $\quad 2x - 75 = 0$

$x = 10 \qquad\qquad 2x = 75$

$\qquad\qquad\qquad x = \dfrac{75}{2}$ or 37.5

The alligator population will have increased to 7250 after 10 years. (Discard 37.5 because this value is outside of $0 \le x \le 12$.)

77. The solution in Exercise 75 corresponds to the point $(10, 7250)$ on the graph.

79. $N = \dfrac{t^2 - t}{2}$

Substitute 45 for N and solve for t.

$45 = \dfrac{t^2 - t}{2}$

$2 \cdot 45 = 2\left(\dfrac{t^2 - t}{2}\right)$

$90 = t^2 - t$

$0 = t^2 - t - 90$

$0 = (t - 10)(t + 9)$

$t - 10 = 0 \quad$ or $\quad t + 9 = 0$

$t = 10 \qquad\qquad t = -9$

Discard $t = -9$ since the number of teams cannot be negative. If 45 games are scheduled, there are 10 teams in the league.

81. Let $x = $ the width of the parking lot. Then $x + 3 = $ the length.

$l \cdot w = A$

$(x + 3)(x) = 180$

$x^2 + 3x = 180$

$x^2 + 3x - 180 = 0$

$(x + 15)(x - 12) = 0$

$x + 15 = 0 \quad$ or $\quad x - 12 = 0$

$x = -15 \qquad\qquad x = 12$

Discard $x = -15$ since the width cannot be negative. Then $x = 12$ and $x + 3 = 15$, so the length is 15 yards and the width is 12 yards.

83. Use the formula for the area of a triangle where x is the base and $x+1$ is the height.

$$\frac{1}{2}bh = A$$

$$\frac{1}{2}x(x+1) = 15$$

$$2\left[\frac{1}{2}x(x+1)\right] = 2 \cdot 15$$

$$x(x+1) = 30$$

$$x^2 + x = 30$$

$$x^2 + x - 30 = 0$$

$$(x+6)(x-5) = 0$$

$$x+6 = 0 \quad \text{or} \quad x-5 = 0$$

$$x = -6 \qquad\qquad x = 5$$

Discard $x = -6$ since the length of the base cannot be negative.
Then $x = 5$ and $x+1 = 6$, so the base is 5 centimeters and the height is 6 centimeters.

85. **a.** Area of a large rectangle

$$(2x+12)(2x+10)$$

$$= 4x^2 + 20x + 24x + 120$$

$$= 4x^2 + 44x + 120$$

Area of a flower bed =
$10 \cdot 12 = 120$
Area of border

$$= \left(4x^2 + 44x + 120\right) - 120$$

$$= 4x^2 + 44x$$

b. Find the width of the border for which the area of the border would be 168 square feet.

$$4x^2 + 44x = 168$$

$$4x^2 + 44x - 168 = 0$$

$$4\left(x^2 + 11x - 42\right) = 0$$

$$4(x+14)(x-3) = 0$$

$$x+14 = 0 \quad \text{or} \quad x-3 = 0$$

$$x = -14 \qquad\qquad x = 3$$

Discard $x = -14$ since the width of the border cannot be negative. You should prepare a strip that is 3 feet wide for the border.

87. Answers will vary.

89. Statement d is true.

$$x(x+\pi) = 0$$

$$x = 0 \quad \text{or} \quad x + \pi = 0$$

$$x = -\pi$$

The solutions are 0 and π.

91. $x^3 - x^2 - 16x + 16 = 0$

$$\left(x^3 - x^2\right) + \left(-16x + 16\right) = 0$$

$$x^2(x-1) - 16(x-1) = 0$$

$$(x-1)\left(x^2 - 16\right) = 0$$

$$(x-1)(x+4)(x-4) = 0$$

$$x-1 = 0 \quad \text{or} \quad x+4 = 0 \quad \text{or} \quad x-4 = 0$$

$$x = 1 \qquad\qquad x = -4 \qquad\qquad x = 4$$

The solution set is $\{-4,\ 1,\ 4\}$.

93. $\left(x^2 - 5x + 5\right)^3 = 1$

The only number that can be cubed (raised to the third power) to give 1 is 1. Therefore, the given equation is equivalent to the quadratic equation

$$x^2 - 5x + 5 = 1.$$

Solve this equation

$$x^2 - 5x + 4 = 0$$

$$(x-1)(x-4) = 0$$

$$x-1 = 0 \quad \text{or} \quad x-4 = 0$$

$$x = 1 \qquad\qquad x = 4$$

The solution set is $\{1, 4\}$.

95. $y = x^2 + x - 2$

To match this equation with its graph, find the intercepts.

To find the y-intercepts, let $x = 0$ and solve for y.

$y = 0^2 + 0 - 2$

$y = -2$

The y-intercept is -2.

To find the x-intercepts, let $y = 0$ and solve for x.

$0 = x^2 + x - 2$

$0 = (x + 2)(x - 1)$

$x + 2 = 0$ or $x - 1 = 0$

$x = -2$ $x = 1$

The x intercepts are -2 and 1.

The only graph with y-intercept -2 and x-intercepts -2 and 1 is graph a.

97. $y = x^2 - 4x$

To match this equation with its graph, find the intercepts.

To find the y-intercept, let $x = 0$ and solve for y.

$y = 0^2 - 4(0) = 0$

The y-intercept is 0, which means that the graph passes through the origin.

To find the x-intercepts, let $y = 0$ and solve for x.

$0 = x^2 - 4x$

$0 = x(x - 4)$

$x = 0$ or $x - 4 = 0$

               $x = 4$

The x-intercepts are 0 and 4.

The only graph with y-intercept 0 and x-intercepts 0 and 4 is graph b.

99. $y = x^2 + x - 6$

$x^2 + x - 6 = 0$

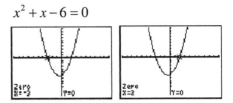

The calculator shows that the x-intercepts for the graph are -3 and 2. This means that the solutions of the equation $x^2 + x - 6 = 0$ are -3 and 2.

Check -3:

$x^2 + x - 6 = 0$

$(-3)^2 + (-3) - 6 = 0$

$9 - 3 - 6 = 0$

$6 - 6 = 0$

$0 = 0$ true

Check 2:

$x^2 + x - 6 = 0$

$2^2 + 2 - 6 = 0$

$4 + 2 - 6 = 0$

$6 - 6 = 0$

$0 = 0$ true

The check verifies that the solution set of $x^2 + x - 6 = 0$ is $\{-3, 2\}$.

101. $y = x^2 - 2x + 1$

$x^2 - 2x + 1 = 0$

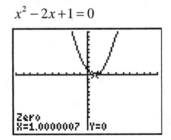

The calculator shows that the graph has one x-intercept, 1. This means that the only solution of the equation $x^2 - 2x + 1 = 0$ is 1.

Check 1:
$$x^2 - 2x + 1 = 0$$
$$1^2 - 2(1) + 1 = 0$$
$$1 - 2 + 1 = 0$$
$$-1 + 1 = 0$$
$$0 = 0 \text{ true}$$

The check verifies that the solution set of $x^2 - 2x + 1$ is $\{1\}$.

103. Answers will vary depending on the exercises chosen.

104. $4x + 2y - z = 12$
$$3x - y + z = 6$$
$$x \qquad + 3z = 14$$

Multiply the second equation by 2 and add to the first equation.
$$4x + 2y - z = 12$$
$$\underline{6x - 2y + 2z = 12}$$
$$10x \qquad + z = 24$$

Multiply this equation by –3 and add the result to the third equation.
$$x + 3z = 14$$
$$\underline{-30x - 3z = -72}$$
$$-29x \qquad = -58$$
$$x \qquad = 2$$

Back-substitute 2 for x in the third equation to find z.
$$x + 3z = 14$$
$$2 + 3z = 14$$
$$3z = 12$$
$$z = 4$$

Back-substitute 2 for x and 4 for z in one of the original equations in three variables to find y.

$$4x + 2y - z = 12$$
$$4(2) + 2y - 4 = 12$$
$$8 + 2y - 4 = 12$$
$$2y + 4 = 12$$
$$2y = 8$$
$$y = 4$$

The solution is $(2, 4, 4)$, and the solution set is $\{(2, 4, 4)\}$.

105.
$$\left(\frac{8x^4}{4x^7}\right)^2 = \left(\frac{8}{4} \cdot x^{4-7}\right) = \left(2x^{-3}\right)^2$$
$$= 2^2 \cdot \left(x^{-3}\right)^2 = 4x^{-6} = \frac{4}{x^6}$$

106.
$$5x + 28 = 6 - 6x$$
$$5x + 6x + 28 = 6 - 6x + 6x$$
$$11x + 28 = 6$$
$$11x + 28 - 28 = 6 - 28$$
$$11x = -22$$
$$\frac{11x}{11} = \frac{-22}{11}$$
$$x = -2$$

The solution set is $\{-2\}$.

Chapter 6 Review Exercises

1. $30x - 45 = 15(2x - 3)$

2. $12x^3 + 16x^2 - 400x$
$$= 4x(3x^2 + 4x - 100)$$

3. $30x^4y + 15x^3y + 5x^2y$
$$= 5x^2y(6x^2 + 3x + 1)$$

302

4. $7(x+3)-2(x+3)$
$=(x+3)(7-2)$
$=(x+3)\cdot 5$ or $5(x+3)$

5. $7x^2(x+y)-(x+y)$
$=7x^2(x+y)-1(x+y)$
$=(x+y)(7x^2-1)$

6. $x^3+3x^2+2x+6=(x^3+3x^2)+(2x+6)$
$=x^2(x+3)+2(x+3)$
$=(x+3)(x^2+2)$

7. $xy+y+4x+4=(xy+y)+(4x+4)$
$=y(x+1)+4(x+1)$
$=(x+1)(y+4)$

8. $x^3+5x+x^2+5=(x^3+5x)+(x^2+5)$
$=x(x^2+5)+1(x^2+5)$
$=(x^2+5)(x+1)$

9. $xy+4x-2y-8=(xy+4x)+(-2y-8)$
$=x(y+4)-2(y+4)$
$=(y+4)(x-2)$

10. $x^2-3x+2=(x-2)(x-1)$

11. $x^2-x-20=(x-5)(x+4)$

12. $x^2+19x+48=(x+3)(x+16)$

13. $x^2-6xy+8y^2=(x-4y)(x-2y)$

14. x^2+5x-9 is prime because there is no pair of integers whose product is -9 and whose sum is 5.

15. $x^2+16xy-17y^2=(x+17y)(x-y)$

16. $3x^2+6x-24=3(x^2+2x-8)$
$=3(x+4)(x-2)$

17. $3x^3-36x^2+33x=3x(x^2-12x+11)$
$=3x(x-11)(x-1)$

18. $3x^2+17x+10$
Factor by trial and error or by grouping. To factor by grouping, find two integers whose product is $ac=3\cdot 10=30$ and whose sum is $b=$ 17. These integers are 15 and 2.
$3x^2+17x+10=3x^2+15x+2x+10$
$=3x(x+5)+2(x+5)$
$=(x+5)(3x+2)$

19. $5y^2-17y+6$
Factor by trial and error or by grouping. To factor by trial and error, start with the First terms, which must be $5y$ and y. Because the middle term is negative, the factors of 6 must both be negative. Try various combinations until the correct middle term is obtained.
$(5y-1)(y-6)=5y^2-31y+6$
$(5y-6)(y-1)=5y^2-11y+6$
$(5y-3)(y-2)=5y^2-13y+6$
$(5y-2)(y-3)=5y^2-17y+6$
Thus, $5y^2-17y+6=(5y-2)(y-3)$.

20. $4x^2+4x-15=(2x+5)(2x-3)$

21. $5y^2 + 11y + 4$

Use trial and error. The first terms must be $5y$ and y. Because the middle term is positive, the factors of 4 must both be positive. Try all the combinations.

$$(5y+2)(y+2) = 5y^2 + 12y + 4$$
$$(5y+4)(y+1) = 5y^2 + 9y + 4$$
$$(5y+1)(y+4) = 5y^2 + 21y + 4$$

None of these possibilities gives the required middle term, $11x$, and there are no more possibilities to try, so $5y^2 + 11y + 4$ is prime.

22. $8x^2 + 8x - 6$

First factor out the GCF, 2. Then factor the resulting trinomial by trial and error or by grouping.

$$8x^2 + 8x - 6 = 2(4x^2 + 4x - 3)$$
$$= 2(2x+3)(2x-1)$$

23. $2x^3 + 7x^2 - 72x = x(2x^2 + 7x - 72)$
$$= x(2x-9)(x+8)$$

24. $12y^3 + 28y^2 + 8y = 4y(3y^2 + 7y + 2)$
$$= 4y(3y+1)(y+2)$$

25. $2x^2 - 7xy + 3y^2 = (2x - y)(x - 3y)$

26. $5x^2 - 6xy - 8y^2 = (5x + 4y)(x - 2y)$

27. $4x^2 - 1 = (2x)^2 - 1^2 = (2x+1)(2x-1)$

28. $81 - 100y^2 = 9^2 - (10y)^2$
$$= (9 + 10y)(9 - 10y)$$

29. $25a^2 - 49b^2 = (5a)^2 - (7b)^2$
$$= (5a + 7b)(5a - 7b)$$

30. $z^4 - 16 = (z^2)^2 - 4^2$
$$= (z^2 + 4)(z^2 - 4)$$
$$= (z^2 + 4)(z + 2)(z - 2)$$

31. $2x^2 - 18 = 2(x^2 - 9) = 2(x+3)(x-3)$

32. $x^2 + 1$ is prime because it is the sum of two squares with no common factor other than 1.

33. $9x^3 - x = x(9x^2 - 1) = x(3x+1)(3x-1)$

34. $18xy^2 - 8x = 2x(9y^2 - 4)$
$$= 2x(3y + 2)(3y - 2)$$

35. $x^2 + 22x + 121 = x^2 + 2(11x) + 11^2$
$$= (x + 11)^2$$

36. $x^2 - 16x + 64 = x^2 - 2(8 \cdot x) + 8^2$
$$= (x - 8)^2$$

37. $9y^2 + 48y + 64 = (3y)^2 + 2(3y \cdot 8) + 8^2$
$$= (3y + 8)^2$$

38. $16x^2 - 40x + 25 = (4x)^2 - 2(4x \cdot 5) + 5^2$
$$= (4x - 5)^2$$

39. $25x^2 + 15x + 9$ is prime. (To be a perfect square trinomial, the middle term would have to be $2(5x \cdot 3) = 30x$.)

304

40. $36x^2 + 60xy + 25y^2$

$= (6x)^2 + 2(6x \cdot 5y) + (5y)^2$

$= (6x + 5y)^2$

41. $25x^2 - 40xy + 16y^2$

$= (5x)^2 - 2(5x \cdot 4y) + (4y)^2$

$= (5x - 4y)^2$

42. $x^3 - 27 = x^3 - 3^2 = (x-3)(x^2 + 3x + 9)$

43. $64x^3 + 1 = (4x)^3 + 1^3$

$= (4x+1)\left[(4x)^2 - 4x \cdot 1 + 1^2\right]$

$= (4x+1)(16x^2 - 4x + 1)$

44. $54x^3 - 16y^3$

$= 2(27x^3 - 8y^3)$

$= 2\left[(3x)^3 - (2y)^3\right]$

$= 2(3x - 2y)\left[(3x)^2 + 3x \cdot 2y + (2y)^2\right]$

$= 2(3x - 2y)(9x^2 + 6xy + 4y^2)$

45. $27x^3y + 8y$

$= y(27x^3 + 8)$

$= y\left[(3x)^3 + 2^3\right]$

$= y(3x+2)\left[(3x)^2 - 3x \cdot 2 + 2^2\right]$

$= y(3x+2)(9x^2 - 6x + 4)$

46. Area of outer square = a^2

Area of inner square = $3^2 = 9$

Area of shaded region $= a^2 - 9$

$= (a+3)(a-3)$

47. Area of large square = a^2

Area of each small corner square = b^2

Area of four corner squares = $4b^2$

Area of shaded region $= a^2 - 4b^2$

$= (a+2b)(a-2b)$

48. Area on the left:

Area of large square = A^2

Area of each rectangle: $A \cdot 1 = A$

Area of two rectangles = $2A$

Area of small square = $1^2 = 1$

Area on the right:

Area of square = $(A+1)^2$

This geometric model illustrates the factorization $A^2 + 2A - 1 = (A+1)^2$

49. $x^3 - 8x^2 + 7x = x(x^2 - 8x + 7)$

$= x(x-7)(x-1)$

50. $10y^2 + 9y + 2 = (5y+2)(2y+1)$

51. $128 - 2y^2 = 2(64 - y^2)$

$= 2(8+y)(8-y)$

52. $9x^2 + 6x + 1 = (3x)^2 + 2(3x) + 1^2$

$= (3x+1)^2$

53. $20x^7 - 36x^3 = 4x^3(5x^4 - 9)$

54. $x^3 - 3x^2 - 9x + 27$

$= (x^3 - 3x^2) + (-9x + 27)$

$= x^2(x-3) - 9(x-3)$

$= (x-3)(x^2 - 9)$

$= (x-3)(x+3)(x-3)$

or $(x-3)^2(x+3)$

55. $y^2 + 16$ is prime because it is the sum of two squares with no common factor other than 1.

56. $2x^3 + 19x^2 + 35x = x(2x^2 + 19x + 35)$
$$= x(2x + 5)(x + 7)$$

57. $3x^3 - 30x^2 + 75x = 3x(x^2 - 10x + 25)$
$$= 3x(x - 5)^2$$

58. $3x^5 - 24x^2 = 3x^2(x^3 - 8)$
$$= 3x^2(x^3 - 2^3)$$
$$= 3x^2(x - 2)(x^2 + 2x + 4)$$

59. $4y^4 - 36y^2 = 4y^2(y^2 - 9)$
$$= 4y^2(y + 3)(y - 3)$$

60. $5x^2 + 20x - 105 = 5(x^2 + 4x - 21)$
$$= 5(x + 7)(x - 3)$$

61. $9x^2 + 8x - 3$ is prime because there are no two integers whose product is $ac = -27$ and whose sum is 8.

62. $10x^5 - 44x^4 + 16x^3 = 2x^3(5x^2 - 22x + 8)$
$$= 2x^3(5x - 2)(x - 4)$$

63. $100y^2 - 49 = (10y)^2 - 7^2$
$$= (10y + 7)(10y - 7)$$

64. $9x^5 - 18x^4 = 9x^4(x - 2)$

65. $x^4 - 1 = (x^2)^2 - 1^2$
$$= (x^2 + 1)(x^2 - 1)$$
$$= (x^2 + 1)(x + 1)(x - 1)$$

66. $2y^3 - 16 = 2(y^3 - 8)$
$$= 2(y^3 - 2^3)$$
$$= 2(y - 2)(y^2 + 2y + 2^2)$$
$$= 2(y - 2)(y^2 + 2y + 4)$$

67. $x^3 + 64 = x^3 + 4^3$
$$= (x + 4)(x^2 - 4x + 4^2)$$
$$= (x + 4)(x^2 - 4x + 16)$$

68. $6x^2 + 11x - 10 = (3x - 2)(2x + 5)$

69. $3x^4 - 12x^2 = 3x^2(x^2 - 4)$
$$= 3x^2(x + 2)(x - 2)$$

70. $x^2 - x - 90 = (x - 10)(x + 9)$

71. $25x^2 + 25xy + 6y^2$
$$= (5x + 2y)(5x + 3y)$$

72. $x^4 + 125x = x(x^3 + 125)$
$$= x(x^3 + 5^3)$$
$$= x(x + 5)(x^2 - 5x + 5^2)$$
$$= x(x + 5)(x^2 - 5x + 25)$$

73. $32y^3 + 32y^2 + 6y = 2y(16y^2 + 16y + 3)$
$$= 2y(4y + 3)(4y + 1)$$

74. $2y^2 - 16y + 32 = 2(y^2 - 8y + 16)$
$$= 2(y - 4)^2$$

75. $x^2 - 2xy - 35y^2 = (x + 5y)(x - 7y)$

76. $x^2 + 7x + xy + 7y = x(x+7) + y(x+7)$
$$= (x+7)(x+y)$$

77. $9x^2 + 24xy + 16y^2$
$$= (3x)^2 + 2(3x \cdot 4y) + (4y)^2$$
$$= (3x + 4y)^2$$

78. $2x^4 y - 2x^2 y = 2x^2 y(x^2 - 1)$
$$= 2x^2 y(x+1)(x-1)$$

79. $100y^2 - 49z^2 = (10y)^2 - (7z)^2$
$$= (10y + 7z)(10y - 7z)$$

80. $x^2 + xy + y^2$ is prime.
(To be a perfect square trinomial, the middle term would have to be $2xy$.)

81. $3x^4 y^2 - 12x^2 y^4$
$$= 3x^2 y^2 (x^2 - 4y^2)$$
$$= 3x^2 y^2 (x+2y)(x-2y)$$

82. $x(x-12) = 0$
$x = 0$ or $x - 12 = 0$
$x = 12$
The solution set is $\{0, 12\}$.

83. $3(x-7)(4x+9) = 0$
$x - 7 = 0$ or $4x + 9 = 0$
$x = 7$ $4x = -9$
$$x = -\frac{9}{4}$$
The solution set is $\left\{ -\frac{9}{4}, 7 \right\}$.

84. $x^2 + 5x - 14 = 0$
$(x+7)(x-2) = 0$
$x + 7 = 0$ or $x - 2 = 0$
$x = -7$ $x = 2$
The solution set is $\{-7, 2\}$.

85. $5x^2 + 20x = 0$
$5x(x+4) = 0$
$5x = 0$ or $x + 4 = 0$
$x = 0$ $x = -4$
The solution set is $\{-4, 0\}$.

86. $2x^2 + 15x = 8$
$2x^2 + 15x - 8 = 0$
$(2x-1)(x+8) = 0$
$2x - 1 = 0$ or $x + 8 = 0$
$2x = 1$ $x = -8$
$$x = \frac{1}{2}$$
The solution set is $\left\{ -8, \frac{1}{2} \right\}$.

87. $x(x-4) = 32$
$x^2 - 4x = 32$
$x^2 - 4x - 32 = 0$
$(x+4)(x-8) = 0$
$x + 4 = 0$ or $x - 8 = 0$
$x = -4$ $x = 8$
The solution set is $\{-4, 8\}$.

88. $(x+3)(x-2) = 50$
$x^2 + x - 6 = 50$
$x^2 + x - 56 = 0$
$(x+8)(x-7) = 0$
$x + 8 = 0$ or $x - 7 = 0$
$x = -8$ $x = 7$
The solution set is $\{-8, 7\}$.

307

89.
$$x^2 = 14x - 49$$
$$x^2 - 14x + 49 = 0$$
$$(x-7)^2 = 0$$
$$x - 7 = 0$$
$$x = 7$$
The solution set is $\{7\}$.

90.
$$9x^2 = 100$$
$$9x^2 - 100 = 0$$
$$(3x+10)(3x-10) = 0$$
$$3x + 10 = 0 \quad \text{or} \quad 3x - 10 = 0$$
$$3x = -10 \qquad\qquad 3x = 10$$
$$x = -\frac{10}{3} \qquad\qquad x = \frac{10}{3}$$
The solution set is $\left\{-\dfrac{10}{3}, \dfrac{10}{3}\right\}$.

91.
$$3x^2 + 21x + 30 = 0$$
$$3(x^2 + 7x + 10) = 0$$
$$3(x+5)(x+2) = 0$$
$$x + 5 = 0 \quad \text{or} \quad x + 2 = 0$$
$$x = -5 \qquad\qquad x = -2$$
The solution set is $\{-5, -2\}$.

92.
$$3x^2 = 22x - 7$$
$$3x^2 - 22x + 7 = 0$$
$$(3x-1)(x-7) = 0$$
$$3x - 1 = 0 \quad \text{or} \quad x - 7 = 0$$
$$3x = 1 \qquad\qquad x = 7$$
$$x = \frac{1}{3}$$
The solution set is $\left\{\dfrac{1}{3}, 7\right\}$.

93.
$$h = -16t^2 + 16t + 32$$
Substitute 0 for h and solve for t.
$$0 = -16t^2 + 16t + 32$$
$$16t^2 - 16t - 32 = 0$$
$$16(t^2 - t - 2) = 0$$
$$16(t+1)(t-2) = 0$$
$$t + 1 = 0 \quad \text{or} \quad t - 2 = 0$$
$$t = -1 \qquad\qquad t = 2$$
Because time cannot be negative, discard the solution $t = -1$. The solution $t = 2$ indicates that you will hit the water after 2 seconds.

94. Let x = the width of the sign. Then $x + 3$ = the length of the sign.

Use the formula for the area of a rectangle.
$$l \cdot w = A$$
$$(x+3)(x) = 40$$
$$x^2 + 3x = 40$$
$$x^2 + 3x - 40 = 0$$
$$(x+8)(x-5) = 0$$
$$x + 8 = 0 \quad \text{or} \quad x - 5 = 0$$
$$x = -8 \qquad\qquad x = 5$$
A rectangle cannot have a negative length. Thus $x = 5$, and $x + 3 = 8$. The length of the sign is 8 feet and the width is 5 feet. This solution checks because
$$A = lw = (8 \text{ feet})(5 \text{ feet})$$
$$= 40 \text{ square feet.}$$

95. Area of garden $= x(x-3) = 88$

$$x(x-3) = 88$$
$$x^2 - 3x = 88$$
$$x^2 - 3x - 88 = 0$$
$$(x-11)(x+8) = 0$$
$$x - 11 = 0 \quad \text{or} \quad x + 8 = 0$$
$$x = 11 \qquad\qquad x = -8$$

Because a length cannot be negative, discard $x = -8$. Each side of the square lot is 11 meters, that is, the dimensions of the square lot are 11 meters by 11 meters.

Chapter 6 Test

1. $x^2 - 9x + 18 = (x-3)(x-6)$

2. $x^2 - 14x + 49 = x^2 - 2(x \cdot 7) + 7^2$
$$= (x-7)^2$$

3. $15y^4 - 35y^3 + 10y^2 = 5y^2(3y^2 - 7y + 2)$
$$= 5y^2(3y-1)(y-2)$$

4. $x^3 + 2x^2 + 3x + 6 = (x^3 + 2x^2) + (3x + 6)$
$$= x^2(x+2) + 3(x+2)$$
$$= (x+2)(x^2+3)$$

5. $x^2 - 9x = x(x-9)$

6. $x^3 + 6x^2 - 7x = x(x^2 + 6x - 7)$
$$= x(x+7)(x-1)$$

7. $14x^2 + 64x - 30 = 2(7x^2 + 32x - 15)$
$$= 2(7x-3)(x+5)$$

8. $25x^2 - 9 = (5x)^2 - 3^2$
$$= (5x+3)(5x-3)$$

9. $x^3 + 8 = x^3 + 2^3$
$$= (x+2)(x^2 - 2x + 2^2)$$
$$= (x+2)(x^2 - 2x + 4)$$

10. $x^2 - 4x - 21 = (x+3)(x-7)$

11. $x^2 + 4$ is prime.

12. $6y^3 + 9y^2 + 3y = 3y(2y^2 + 3y + 1)$
$$= 3y(2y+1)(y+1)$$

13. $4y^2 - 36 = 4(y^2 - 9) = 4(y+3)(y-3)$

14. $16x^2 + 48x + 36$
$$= 4(4x^2 + 12x + 9)$$
$$= 4\left[(2x)^2 + 2(2x \cdot 3) + 3^2\right]$$
$$= 4(2x+3)^2$$

15. $2x^4 - 32 = 2(x^4 - 16)$
$$= 2(x^2+4)(x^2-4)$$
$$= 2(x^2+4)(x+2)(x-2)$$

16. $36x^2 - 84x + 49 = (6x)^2 - 2(6x \cdot 7) + 7^2$
$$= (6x-7)^2$$

17. $7x^2 - 50x + 7 = (7x-1)(x-7)$

18. $x^3 + 2x^2 - 5x - 10$
$$= (x^3 + 2x^2) + (-5x - 10)$$
$$= x^2(x+2) - 5(x+2)$$
$$= (x+2)(x^2 - 5)$$

309

19.
$$12y^3 - 12y^2 - 45y = 3y(4y^2 - 4y - 15)$$
$$= 3y(2y+3)(2y-5)$$

20.
$$y^3 - 125 = y^3 - 5^3$$
$$= (y-5)(y^2 + 5y + 5^2)$$
$$= (y-5)(y^2 + 5y + 25)$$

21.
$$5x^2 - 5xy - 30y^2 = 5(x^2 - xy - 6y^2)$$
$$= 5(x-3y)(x+2y)$$

22.
$$x^2 + 2x - 24 = 0$$
$$(x+6)(x-4) = 0$$
$$x+6 = 0 \quad \text{or} \quad x-4 = 0$$
$$x = -6 \qquad\qquad x = 4$$
The solution set is $\{-6, 4\}$.

23.
$$3x^2 - 5x = 2$$
$$3x^2 - 5x - 2 = 0$$
$$(3x+1)(x-2) = 0$$
$$3x+1 = 0 \quad \text{or} \quad x-2 = 0$$
$$3x = -1 \qquad\qquad x = 2$$
$$x = -\frac{1}{3}$$
The solution set is $\left\{-\dfrac{1}{3}, 2\right\}$.

24.
$$x(x-6) = 16$$
$$x^2 - 6x = 16$$
$$x^2 - 6x - 16 = 0$$
$$(x+2)(x-8) = 0$$
$$x+2 = 0 \quad \text{or} \quad x-8 = 0$$
$$x = -2 \qquad\qquad x = 8$$
The solution set is $\{-2, 8\}$.

25.
$$6x^2 = 21x$$
$$6x^2 - 21x = 0$$
$$3x(2x-7) = 0$$
$$3x = 0 \quad \text{or} \quad 2x-7 = 0$$
$$x = 0 \qquad\qquad 2x = 7$$
$$x = \frac{7}{2}$$
The solution set is $\left\{0, \dfrac{7}{2}\right\}$.

26.
$$16x^2 = 81$$
$$16x^2 - 81 = 0$$
$$(4x+9)(4x-9) = 0$$
$$4x+9 = 0 \quad \text{or} \quad 4x-9 = 0$$
$$4x = -9 \qquad\qquad 4x = 9$$
$$x = -\frac{9}{4} \qquad\qquad x = \frac{9}{4}$$
The solution set is $\left\{-\dfrac{9}{4}, \dfrac{9}{4}\right\}$.

27.
$$(5x+4)(x-1) = 2$$
$$5x^2 - x - 4 = 2$$
$$5x^2 - x - 6 = 0$$
$$(5x-6)(x+1) = 0$$
$$5x-6 = 0 \quad \text{or} \quad x+1 = 0$$
$$5x = 6 \qquad\qquad x = -1$$
$$x = \frac{6}{5}$$
The solution set is $\left\{-1, \dfrac{6}{5}\right\}$.

310

28. Area of large square = x^2
Area of each small (corner) square =
$1^2 = 1$
Area of four corner squares = $4 \cdot 1 = 4$
Area of shaded region = $x^2 - 4$
$$= (x+2)(x-2)$$

29. $h = -16t^2 + 80t + 96$
Substitute 0 for h and solve for t.
$$0 = -16t^2 + 80t + 96$$
$$16t^2 - 80t - 96 = 0$$
$$16(t^2 - 5t - 6) = 0$$
$$16(t-6)(t+1) = 0$$

$t - 6 = 0$ or $t + 1 = 0$
$\quad t = 6 \qquad\qquad t = -1$
Since time cannot be negative,
disregard $t = -1$. The rocket will
reach the ground after 6 seconds.

30. Let x = the width of the garden.
Then $x + 6$ = the length of the garden.
$$(x+6)(x) = 55$$
$$x^2 + 6x = 55$$
$$x^2 + 6x - 55 = 0$$
$$(x+11)(x-5) = 0$$
$x + 11 = 0$ or $x - 5 = 0$
$\quad x = -11 \qquad\quad x = 5$
Since the width cannot be negative,
discard $x = -11$. Then $x = 5$ and
$x + 6 = 11$, so the width is 5 feet and
the length is 11 feet.

**Chapter 6 Cumulative Review Exercises
(Chapters 1 – 6)**

1. $6[5 + 2(3-8) - 3] = 6[5 + 2(-5) - 3]$
$$= 6[5 - 10 - 3]$$
$$= 6(-8)$$
$$= -48$$

2. $4(x-2) = 2(x-4) + 3x$
$$4x - 8 = 2x - 8 + 3x$$
$$4x - 8 = 5x - 8$$
$$-x = 0$$
$$x = 0$$
The solution set is $\{0\}$.

3. $\dfrac{x}{2} - 1 = \dfrac{x}{3} + 1$
$$6\left(\dfrac{x}{2} - 1\right) = 6\left(\dfrac{x}{3} + 1\right)$$
$$3x - 6 = 2x + 6$$
$$x = 12$$
The solution set is $\{12\}$.

4. $5 - 5x > 2(5 - x) + 1$
$$5 - 5x > 10 - 2x + 1$$
$$5 - 5x > 11 - 2x$$
$$5 - 5x + 2x > 11 - 2x + 2x$$
$$5 - 3x > 11$$
$$5 - 3x - 5 > 11 - 5$$
$$-3x > 6$$
$$\dfrac{-3x}{-3} < \dfrac{6}{-3}$$
$$x < -2$$
Solution set: $\{x | x < -2\}$

311

5. Let x = the measure of each of the two base angles.
Then $3x - 10$ = the measure of the third angle.
The three angles of any triangle is $180°$, so
$$x + x + (3x - 10) = 180.$$
Solve this equation.
$$5x - 10 = 180$$
$$5x = 190$$
$$x = 38$$
If $x = 38, 3x - 10 = 3(38) - 10 = 104.$
The measures of the three angles of the triangle are $38°$, $38°$, and $104°$.

6. Let x = the cost of the dinner before tax.
$$x + 0.06x = 159$$
$$1.06x = 159$$
$$\frac{1.06x}{1.06} = \frac{159}{1.06}$$
$$x \approx 150$$
The cost of the dinner before tax was $150.

7.
$$y = -\frac{3}{5}x + 3$$

slope = $-\frac{3}{5} = \frac{-3}{5}$; y-intercept = 3

Plot (0,3). From this point, move 3 units *down* (because −3 is negative) and 5 units to the *right* to reach the point (5,0). Draw a line through (0,3) and (5,0).

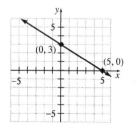

8. Line passing through $(2, -4)$, and $(3,1)$
$$m = \frac{1 - (-4)}{3 - 2} = \frac{5}{1} = 5$$
Use the point $(2, -4)$ in the point-slope equation.
$$y - y_1 = m(x - x_1)$$
$$y - (-4) = 5(x - 2)$$
$$y + 4 = 5(x - 2)$$
Rewrite this equation in slope-intercept form.
$$y + 4 = 5x - 10$$
$$y = 5x - 14$$

9.
$$x - 2y + 2z = 4$$
$$3x - y + 4z = 4$$
$$2x + y - 3z = 5$$
Multiply the third equation by 2 and add to the first equation.
$$x - 2y + 2z = 4$$
$$\underline{4x + 2y - 6z = 10}$$
$$5x \qquad - 4z = 14$$
Add the second and third equations.
$$3x - y + 4z = 4$$
$$\underline{2x + y - 3z = 5}$$
$$5x \qquad + z = 9$$

Multiply this equation by −1 and add the result to the other equation in two variables.
$$5x - 4z = 14$$
$$\underline{-5x - \ z = -9}$$
$$-5z = 5$$
$$z = -1$$
Back-substitute −1 for z in one of the equations in two variables to find x.
$$5x + z = 9$$
$$5x + (-1) = 9$$
$$5x = 10$$
$$x = 2$$

Back-substitute 2 for x and -1 for z in one of the original equations in three variables to find y.

$$2x + y - 3z = 5$$
$$2(2) + y - 3(-1) = 5$$
$$4 + y + 3 = 5$$
$$y + 7 = 5$$
$$y = -2$$

The solution is $(2, -2, -1)$, and the solution set is $\{(2, -2, -1)\}$.

10. $$5x + 2y = 13$$
$$y = 2x - 7$$

The substitution method is a good choice for solving this system because the second equation is already solved for y.

Substitute $2x - 7$ for y in the first equation.

$$5x + 2y = 13$$
$$5x + 2(2x - 7) = 13$$
$$5x + 4x - 14 = 13$$
$$9x - 14 = 13$$
$$9x = 27$$
$$x = 3$$

Back-substitute into the second given equation.

$$y = 2x - 7$$
$$y = 2(3) - 7 = -1$$

The solution is $(3, -1)$, and the solution set is $\{(3, -1)\}$.

11. $$2x + 3y = 5$$
$$3x - 2y = -4$$

The addition method is a good choice for solving this system because both equations are written in the form $Ax + By = C$.

Multiply the first equation by 2 and the second equation by 3; then add the results.

$$
\begin{aligned}
4x + 6y &= 10 \\
9x - 6y &= -12 \\
\hline
13x &= -2 \\
\end{aligned}
$$

$$x = -\frac{2}{13}$$

Instead of back-substituting $-\dfrac{2}{13}$ and working with fractions, go back to the original system and eliminate x. Multiply the first equation by 3 and the second equation by -2; then add the results.

$$
\begin{aligned}
6x + 9y &= 15 \\
-6x + 4y &= 8 \\
\hline
13y &= 23 \\
\end{aligned}
$$

$$y = \frac{23}{3}$$

The solution is $\left(-\dfrac{2}{13}, \dfrac{23}{3}\right)$, and the solution set is $\left\{\left(-\dfrac{2}{13}, \dfrac{23}{3}\right)\right\}$.

12. $$\frac{4}{5} - \frac{9}{8} = \frac{4}{5} \cdot \frac{8}{8} - \frac{9}{8} \cdot \frac{5}{5}$$
$$= \frac{32}{40} - \frac{45}{40} = -\frac{13}{40}$$

13.
$$\frac{6x^5 - 3x^4 + 9x^2 + 27x}{3x}$$
$$= \frac{6x^5}{3x} - \frac{3x^4}{3x} + \frac{9x^2}{3x} + \frac{27x}{3x}$$
$$= 2x^4 - x^3 + 3x + 9$$

14.
$$(3x - 5y)(2x + 9y)$$
$$= 6x^2 + 27xy - 10xy - 45y^2$$
$$= 6x^2 + 17xy - 45y^2$$

15.
$$\begin{array}{r} 2x^2 + 5x - 3 \\ 3x - 5 \overline{\smash{)}6x^3 + 5x^2 - 34x + 13} \\ \underline{6x^3 - 10x^2} \\ 15x^2 - 34x \\ \underline{15x^2 - 25x} \\ -9x + 13 \\ \underline{-9x + 15} \\ -2 \end{array}$$

$$\frac{6x^3 + 5x^2 - 34x + 13}{3x - 5}$$
$$= 2x^2 + 5x - 3 + \frac{-2}{3x - 5}$$
$$\text{or } 2x^2 + 5x - 3 - \frac{2}{3x - 5}$$

16. To write 0.0071 in scientific notation, move the decimal point 3 places to the right. Because the given number is between 0 and 1, the exponent will be negative.
$$0.0071 = 7.1 \times 10^{-3}$$

17. $3x^2 + 11x + 6$
Factor by trial and error or by grouping. To factor by grouping, find two integers whose product is $ac = 3 \cdot 6 = 18$ and whose sum is $b = 11$. These integers are 9 and 2.
$$3x^2 + 11x + 6 = 3x^2 + 9x + 2x + 6$$
$$= 3x(x + 3) + 2(x + 3)$$
$$= (x + 3)(3x + 2)$$

18.
$$y^5 - 16y = y(y^4 - 16)$$
$$= y(y^2 + 4)(y^2 - 4)$$
$$= y(y^2 + 4)(y + 2)(y - 2)$$

19.
$$4x^2 + 12x + 9 = (2x)^2 + 2(2x \cdot 3) + 3x^2$$
$$= (2x + 3)^2$$

20. Let x = the width of the rectangle. Then $x + 2$ = the length of the rectangle.
Use the formula for the area of a rectangle.
$$l \cdot w = A$$
$$(x + 2)(x) = 24$$
$$x^2 + 2x = 24$$
$$x^2 + 2x - 24 = 0$$
$$(x + 6)(x - 4) = 0$$
$$x + 6 = 0 \quad \text{or} \quad x - 4 = 0$$
$$x = -6 \qquad\qquad x = 4$$
Discard -6 because the width cannot be negative. Then $x = 4$ and $x + 2 = 6$, so the width is 4 feet and the length is 6 feet. The dimensions of the rectangle are 6 feet by 4 feet.

314

Chapter 7
Rational Expressions

7.1 Exercise Set

1.
$$\frac{5}{2x}$$
Set the denominator equal to 0 and solve for x.
$$2x = 0$$
$$x = 0$$
The rational expression is undefined for $x = 0$.

3.
$$\frac{x}{x-8}$$
Set the denominator equal to 0 and solve for x.
$$x - 8 = 0$$
$$x = 8$$
The rational expression is undefined for $x = 8$.

5.
$$\frac{13}{5x-20}$$
$$5x - 20 = 0$$
$$5x = 20$$
$$x = 4$$
The rational expression is undefined for $x = 4$.

7.
$$\frac{x+3}{(x+9)(x-2)}$$
$$(x+9)(x-2) = 0$$
$$x + 9 = 0 \quad \text{or} \quad x - 2 = 0$$
$$x = -9 \qquad\qquad x = 2$$
The rational expression is undefined for $x = -9$ and $x = 2$.

9.
$$\frac{4x}{(3x-17)(x+3)}$$
$$(3x-17)(x+3) = 0$$
$$3x - 17 = 0 \quad \text{or} \quad x + 3 = 0$$
$$3x = 17 \qquad\qquad x = -3$$
$$x = \frac{17}{3}$$
The rational expression is undefined for $x = -\dfrac{17}{3}$ and $x = -3$.

11.
$$\frac{x+5}{x^2+x-12}$$
$$x^2 + x - 12 = 0$$
$$(x+4)(x-3) = 0$$
$$x + 4 = 0 \quad \text{or} \quad x - 3 = 0$$
$$x = -4 \qquad\qquad x = 3$$
The rational expression is undefined for $x = -4$ and $x = 3$.

13.
$$\frac{x+5}{5}$$
Because the denominator, 5, is not zero for any value of x, the rational expression is defined for all real numbers.

15.
$$\frac{y+3}{4y^2+y-3}$$
$$4y^2 + y - 3 = 0$$
$$(y+1)(4y-3) = 0$$
$$y + 1 = 0 \quad \text{or} \quad 4y - 3 = 0$$
$$y = -1 \qquad\qquad 4y = 3$$
$$y = \frac{3}{4}$$
The rational expression is undefined for $y = -1$ and $y = \dfrac{3}{4}$.

315

17.
$$\frac{y+5}{y^2-25}$$
$$y^2-25=0$$
$$(y+5)(y-5)=0$$
$$y+5=0 \quad \text{or} \quad y-5=0$$
$$y=-5 \qquad y=5$$
The rational expression is undefined for $y=-5$ and $y=5$.

19.
$$\frac{5}{x^2+1}$$
The smallest possible value of x^2 is 0, so $x^2+1\geq1$ for all real numbers of x. This means that there is no real number x for which $x^2+1=0$. Thus, the rational expression is defined for all real numbers.

21.
$$\frac{14x^2}{7x}=\frac{2\cdot7\cdot x\cdot x}{7\cdot x}=\frac{2x}{1}=2x$$

23.
$$\frac{5x-15}{25}=\frac{5(x-3)}{5\cdot5}=\frac{x-3}{5}$$

25.
$$\frac{2x-8}{4x}=\frac{2(x-4)}{2\cdot2x}=\frac{x-4}{2x}$$

27.
$$\frac{3}{3x-9}=\frac{3}{3(x-3)}=\frac{1}{x-3}$$

29.
$$\frac{-15}{3x-9}=\frac{-15}{3(x-3)}=\frac{-5}{x-3} \text{ or } -\frac{5}{x-3}$$

31.
$$\frac{3x+9}{x+3}=\frac{3(x+3)}{x+3}=\frac{3}{1}=3$$

33.
$$\frac{x+5}{x^2-25}=\frac{x+5}{(x+5)(x-5)}=\frac{1}{x-5}$$

35.
$$\frac{2y-10}{3y-15}=\frac{2(y-5)}{3(y-5)}=\frac{2}{3}$$

37.
$$\frac{x+1}{x^2-2x-3}=\frac{x+1}{(x+1)(x-3)}=\frac{1}{x-3}$$

39.
$$\frac{4x-8}{x^2-4x+4}=\frac{4(x-2)}{(x-2)(x-2)}=\frac{4}{x-2}$$

41.
$$\frac{y^2-3y+2}{y^2+7y-18}=\frac{(y-1)(y-2)}{(y+9)(y-2)}=\frac{y-1}{y+9}$$

43.
$$\frac{2y^2-7y+3}{2y^2-5y+2}=\frac{(2y-1)(y-3)}{(2y-1)(y-2)}=\frac{y-3}{y-2}$$

45.
$$\frac{2x+3}{2x+5}$$
The numerator and denominator have no common factor (other than 1), so this rational expression cannot be simplified.

47.
$$\frac{x^2+12x+36}{x^2-36}=\frac{(x+6)(x+6)}{(x+6)(x-6)}=\frac{x+6}{x-6}$$

49.
$$\frac{x^3-2x^2+x-2}{x-2}=\frac{x^2(x-2)+1(x-2)}{x-2}$$
$$=\frac{(x-2)(x^2+1)}{x-2}$$
$$=x^2+1$$

51.
$$\frac{x^3-8}{x-2}=\frac{(x-2)(x^2+2x+4)}{x-2}$$
$$=x^2+2x+4$$

53.
$$\frac{(x-4)^2}{x^2-16}=\frac{(x-4)(x-4)}{(x+4)(x-4)}=\frac{x-4}{x+4}$$

316

55. $\dfrac{x}{x+1}$

The numerator and denominator have no common factor (other than 1), so this rational expression cannot be simplified.

57. $\dfrac{x+4}{x^2+16}$

The numerator and denominator are both prime polynomials. They have no common factor (other than 1), so this rational expression cannot be simplified.

59. $\dfrac{x-5}{5-x}=\dfrac{-1(5-x)}{5-x}=-1$

Notice that the numerator and denominator of the given rational expression are additive inverses.

61. $\dfrac{2x-3}{3-2x}$

The numerator and denominator of this rational expression are additive inverses, so $\dfrac{2x-3}{3-2x}=-1$.

63. $\dfrac{x-5}{x+5}$

The numerator and denominator have no common factor and they are not additive inverses, so this rational expression cannot be simplified.

65. $\dfrac{4x-6}{3-2x}=\dfrac{2(2x-3)}{3-2x}=\dfrac{-2(3-2x)}{3-2x}=-2$

67. $\dfrac{4-6x}{3x^2-2x}=\dfrac{2(2-3x)}{x(3x-2)}$

$=\dfrac{-2(3x-2)}{x(3x-2)}$

$=-\dfrac{2}{x}$

69. $\dfrac{x^2-1}{1-x}=\dfrac{(x+1)(x-1)}{1-x}$

$=\dfrac{(x+1)\cdot-1(1-x)}{1-x}$

$=-1(x+1)=-x-1$

71. $\dfrac{y^2-y-12}{4-y}=\dfrac{(y-4)(y+3)}{4-y}$

$=\dfrac{-1(4-y)(y+3)}{4-y}$

$=-1(y+3)=-y-3$

73. $\dfrac{x^2y-x^2}{x^3-x^3y}=\dfrac{x^2(y-1)}{x^3(1-y)}$

$=\dfrac{x^2\cdot-1(1-y)}{x^3(1-y)}$

$=-\dfrac{1}{x}$

75. $\dfrac{x^2+2xy-3y^2}{2x^2+5xy-3y^2}=\dfrac{(x-y)(x+3y)}{(2x-y)(x+3y)}$

$=\dfrac{x-y}{2x-y}$

77. $\dfrac{x^2-9x+18}{x^3-27}=\dfrac{(x-3)(x-6)}{(x-3)(x^2+3x+9)}$

$=\dfrac{x-6}{x^2+3x+9}$

78.
$$\frac{x^3 - 8}{x^2 + 2x - 8} = \frac{(x-2)(x^2 + 2x + 4)}{(x-2)(x+4)}$$
$$= \frac{x^2 + 2x + 4}{x + 4}$$

84.
$$\frac{x^3 - 3x^2 + 9x}{x^3 + 27} = \frac{x(x^2 - 3x + 9)}{(x+3)(x^2 - 3x + 9)}$$
$$= \frac{x}{x + 3}$$

79.
$$\frac{9 - y^2}{y^2 - 3(2y - 3)} = \frac{(3+y)(3-y)}{y^2 - 6y + 9}$$
$$= \frac{(3+y)(3-y)}{(y-3)(y-3)} = \frac{(3+y)\cdot -1(y-3)}{(y-3)(y-3)}$$
$$= \frac{-1(3+y)}{y-3} \quad \text{or} \quad \frac{3+y}{-1(y-3)} = \frac{3+y}{3-y}$$

85.
$$\frac{130x}{100 - x}$$

a. $x = 40$:
$$\frac{130x}{100 - x} = \frac{130(40)}{100 - 40}$$
$$= \frac{5200}{60}$$
$$\approx 86.67$$

This means it costs about $86.67 million to inoculate 40% of the population.

$x = 80$:
$$\frac{130x}{100 - x} = \frac{130(80)}{100 - 80}$$
$$= \frac{10,400}{20}$$
$$= 520$$

This means it costs $520 million to inoculate 80% of the population.

80.
$$\frac{16 - y^2}{y(y-8) + 16} = \frac{(4-y)(4+y)}{y^2 - 8y + 16}$$
$$= \frac{-1\cdot(y-4)(4+y)}{(y-4)(y-4)} = \frac{-1(4+y)}{y-4}$$
$$\text{or} \quad \frac{4+y}{-1(y-4)} = \frac{4+y}{4-y}$$

81.
$$\frac{xy + 2y + 3x + 6}{x^2 + 5x + 6} = \frac{y(x+2) + 3(x+2)}{(x+2)(x+3)}$$
$$= \frac{(x+2)(y+3)}{(x+2)(x+3)} = \frac{y+3}{x+3}$$

82.
$$\frac{xy + 4y - 7x - 28}{x^2 + 11x + 28} = \frac{y(x+4) - 7(x+4)}{(x+4)(x+7)}$$
$$= \frac{(x+4)(y-7)}{(x+4)(x+7)} = \frac{y-7}{x+7}$$

$x = 90$:
$$\frac{130x}{100 - x} = \frac{130(90)}{100 - 90}$$
$$= \frac{11,700}{10}$$
$$= 1170$$

This means it costs $1170 million ($1,170,000,000) to inoculate 90% of the population.

83.
$$\frac{8x^2 + 4x + 2}{1 - 8x^3} = \frac{2(4x^2 + 2x + 1)}{(1 - 2x)(1 + 2x + 4x^2)}$$
$$= \frac{2}{1 - 2x}$$

318

b. Set the denominator equal to 0 and solve for x.

$$100 - x = 0$$

$$100 = x$$

The rational expression is undefined for $x = 100$.

c. The cost keeps rising as x approaches 100. No amount of money will be enough to inoculate 100% of the population.

87. $\dfrac{DA}{A+12}$; $D = 1000, A = 8$

$$\frac{DA}{A+12} = \frac{1000 \cdot 8}{8+12} = \frac{8000}{20} = 400$$

The correct dosage for an 8-year old is 400 milligrams.

89. $C = \dfrac{100x + 100,000}{x}$

a. $x = 500$

$$C = \frac{100(500) + 100,000}{500}$$

$$= \frac{150,000}{500} = 300$$

The cost per bicycle when manufacturing 500 bicycles is $300.

b. $x = 4000$

$$C = \frac{100(4000) + 100,000}{4000}$$

$$= \frac{400,000 + 100,000}{4000}$$

$$= \frac{500,000}{4000} = 125$$

The cost per bicycle when manufacturing 4000 bicycles is $125.

c. The cost per bicycle decreases as more bicycles are manufactured. One possible reason for this is that there could be fixed costs for equipment, so the more the equipment is used, the lower the cost per bicycle.

91. $y = \dfrac{5x}{x^2 + 1}$; $x = 3$

$$y = \frac{5 \cdot 3}{3^2 + 1} + \frac{15}{10} = 1.5$$

The equation indicates that the drug's concentration after 3 hours is 1.5 milligram per liter. The point $(3, 1.5)$ on the graph conveys this information.

93. Let $w = 145$ and $h = 70$,

$$\text{BMI} = \frac{703(145)}{70^2} = \frac{101,935}{4900} \approx 20.8$$

This person is not considered underweight.

95. **a.** $\dfrac{-0.4t + 14.2}{3.7t + 257.4}$

b. $t = 7$ for the year 2001

$$\frac{-0.4(7) + 14.2}{3.7(7) + 257.4} = \frac{11.4}{283.3} \approx 0.04$$

This indicates there are about 4 crimes per 100 inhabitants or 4000 crimes per 100,000 inhabitants.

c. The rational expression models this fairly well. There is only a difference of about 161 crimes per 100,000 inhabitants.

97. – 101. Answers will vary.

319

103. Any rational expression in which the numerator and denominator have no common factor other than 1 cannot be simplified. Student examples will vary.

105. $x^2 - x - 6 = (x - 3)(x + 2)$

Therefore,

$$\frac{x^2 - x - 6}{x + 2} = \frac{(x+2)(x-3)}{x+2} = x - 3$$

So $\dfrac{x^2 - x - 6}{x + 2}$ is the desired rational expression.

107.

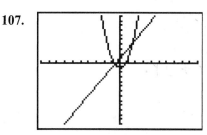

The graphs do not coincide.

$$\frac{2x^2 - x - 1}{x - 1} = \frac{(2x+1)(x-1)}{x-1}$$
$$= 2x + 1, x \neq 1$$

Change the expression on the right from $2x^2 - 1$ to $2x + 1$.

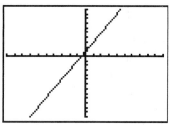

Now the graphs coincide.

109. Answers will vary.

110.

$$\frac{5}{6} \cdot \frac{9}{25} = \frac{\overset{1}{\cancel{5}}}{\underset{2}{\cancel{6}}} \cdot \frac{\overset{3}{\cancel{9}}}{\underset{5}{\cancel{25}}} = \frac{3}{10}$$

111. $\dfrac{2}{3} \div 4 = \dfrac{2}{3} \cdot \dfrac{1}{4} = \dfrac{2}{12} = \dfrac{2 \cdot 1}{2 \cdot 6} = \dfrac{1}{6}$

112. $2x - 5y = -2$

$3x + 4y = 20$

Multiply the first equation by 3 and the second equation by -2; then add the results.

$$6x - 15y = -6$$
$$\underline{-6x - 8y = -40}$$
$$-23y = -46$$
$$y = 2$$

Back-substitute into the first equation of the original system.

$$2x - 5y = -2$$
$$2x - 5(2) = -2$$
$$2x - 10 = -2$$
$$2x = 8$$
$$x = 4$$

The solution set is $\{(4, 2)\}$

7.2 Exercise Set

1. $\dfrac{4}{x+3} \cdot \dfrac{x-5}{9} = \dfrac{4(x-5)}{(x+3)9} = \dfrac{4x-20}{9x+27}$

3. $\dfrac{x}{3} \cdot \dfrac{12}{x+5} = \dfrac{3 \cdot 4x}{3(x+5)} = \dfrac{4x}{x+5}$

5. $\dfrac{3}{x} \cdot \dfrac{4x}{15} = \dfrac{3 \cdot 4x}{3 \cdot 5x} = \dfrac{4}{5}$

7. $\dfrac{x-3}{x+5} \cdot \dfrac{4x+20}{9x-27} = \dfrac{x-3}{x+5} \cdot \dfrac{4(x+5)}{9(x-3)} = \dfrac{4}{9}$

9. $\dfrac{x^2+9x+14}{x+7} \cdot \dfrac{1}{x+2} = \dfrac{(x+7)(x+2) \cdot 1}{(x+7)(x+2)} = 1$

320

11.

$$\frac{x^2-25}{x^2-3x-10}\cdot\frac{x+2}{x}$$

$$=\frac{(x+5)(x-5)}{(x+2)(x-5)}\cdot\frac{(x+2)}{x}=\frac{x+5}{x}$$

13.

$$\frac{4y+30}{y^2-3y}\cdot\frac{y-3}{2y+15}$$

$$=\frac{2(2y+15)}{y(y-3)}\cdot\frac{(y-3)}{(2y+15)}=\frac{2}{y}$$

15.

$$\frac{y^2-7y-30}{y^2-6y-40}\cdot\frac{2y^2+5y+2}{2y^2+7y+3}$$

$$=\frac{(y+3)(y-10)}{(y+4)(y-10)}\cdot\frac{(2y+1)(y+2)}{(2y+1)(y+3)}$$

$$=\frac{y+2}{y+4}$$

17.

$$\left(y^2-9\right)\cdot\frac{4}{y-3}=\frac{y^2-9}{1}\cdot\frac{4}{y-3}$$

$$=\frac{(y+3)(y-3)}{1}\cdot\frac{4}{y-3}$$

$$=4(y+3)\text{ or }4y+12$$

19.

$$\frac{x^2-5x+6}{x^2-2x-3}\cdot\frac{x^2-1}{x^2-4}$$

$$=\frac{(x-2)(x-3)}{(x+1)(x-3)}\cdot\frac{(x+1)(x-1)}{(x+2)(x-2)}$$

$$=\frac{x-1}{x+2}$$

21.

$$\frac{x^3-8}{x^2-4}\cdot\frac{x+2}{3x}$$

$$=\frac{(x-2)(x^2+2x+4)}{(x+2)(x-2)}\cdot\frac{(x+2)}{3x}$$

$$=\frac{x^2+2x+4}{3x}$$

23.

$$\frac{(x-2)^3}{(x-1)^3}\cdot\frac{x^2-2x+1}{x^2-4x+4}$$

$$=\frac{(x-2)^3}{(x-1)^3}\cdot\frac{(x-1)^2}{(x-2)^2}=\frac{x-2}{x-1}$$

25.

$$\frac{6x+2}{x^2-1}\cdot\frac{1-x}{3x^2+x}$$

$$=\frac{2(3x+1)}{(x+1)(x-1)}\cdot\frac{(1-x)}{x(3x+1)}$$

$$=\frac{2(3x+1)}{(x+1)(x-1)}\cdot\frac{-1(x-1)}{x(3x+1)}$$

$$=\frac{-2}{x(x+1)}\text{ or }-\frac{2}{x(x+1)}$$

27.

$$\frac{25-y^2}{y^2-2y-35}\cdot\frac{y^2-8y-20}{y^2-3y-10}$$

$$=\frac{(5+y)(5-y)}{(y+5)(y-7)}\cdot\frac{(y-10)(y+2)}{(y-5)(y+2)}$$

$$=\frac{-(y-10)}{y-7}\text{ or }-\frac{y-10}{y-7}$$

29.

$$\frac{x^2-y^2}{x}\cdot\frac{x^2+xy}{x+y}$$

$$=\frac{(x+y)(x-y)}{x}\cdot\frac{x(x+y)}{(x+y)}$$

$$=(x-y)(x+y)\text{ or }x^2-y^2$$

31.

$$\frac{x^2+2xy+y^2}{x^2-2xy+y^2}\cdot\frac{4x-4y}{3x+3y}$$

$$=\frac{(x+y)(x+y)}{(x-y)(x-y)}\cdot\frac{4(x-y)}{3(x+y)}=\frac{4(x+y)}{3(x-y)}$$

33.

$$\frac{x}{7}\div\frac{5}{3}=\frac{x}{7}\cdot\frac{3}{5}=\frac{3x}{35}$$

321

35. $\dfrac{3}{x} \div \dfrac{12}{x} = \dfrac{3}{x} \cdot \dfrac{x}{12} = \dfrac{1}{4}$

37. $\dfrac{15}{x} \div \dfrac{3}{2x} = \dfrac{15}{x} \cdot \dfrac{2x}{3} = 10$

39. $\dfrac{x+1}{3} \div \dfrac{3x+3}{7} = \dfrac{x+1}{3} \cdot \dfrac{7}{3x+3}$

$\quad = \dfrac{x+1}{3} \cdot \dfrac{7}{3(x+1)} = \dfrac{7}{9}$

41. $\dfrac{7}{x-5} \div \dfrac{28}{3x-15} = \dfrac{7}{x-5} \cdot \dfrac{3x-15}{28}$

$\quad = \dfrac{7}{(x-5)} \cdot \dfrac{3(x-5)}{7 \cdot 4} = \dfrac{3}{4}$

43. $\dfrac{x^2-4}{x} \div \dfrac{x+2}{x-2} = \dfrac{x^2-4}{x} \cdot \dfrac{x-2}{x+2}$

$\quad = \dfrac{(x+2)(x-2)}{x} \cdot \dfrac{x-2}{x+2}$

$\quad = \dfrac{(x-2)^2}{x}$

45. $\left(y^2-16\right) \div \dfrac{y^2+3y-4}{y^2+4}$

$\quad = \dfrac{y^2-16}{1} \cdot \dfrac{y^2+4}{y^2+3y-4}$

$\quad = \dfrac{(y+4)(y-4)}{1} \cdot \dfrac{y^2+4}{(y+4)(y-1)}$

$\quad = \dfrac{(y-4)(y^2+4)}{y-1}$

47. $\dfrac{y^2-y}{15} \div \dfrac{y-1}{5} = \dfrac{y^2-y}{15} \cdot \dfrac{5}{y-1}$

$\quad = \dfrac{y(y-1)}{15} \cdot \dfrac{5}{(y-1)} = \dfrac{y}{3}$

49. $\dfrac{4x^2+10}{x-3} \div \dfrac{6x^2+15}{x^2-9}$

$\quad = \dfrac{4x^2+10}{x-3} \cdot \dfrac{x^2-9}{6x^2+15}$

$\quad = \dfrac{2(2x^2+5)}{(x-3)} \cdot \dfrac{(x+3)(x-3)}{3(2x^2+5)}$

$\quad = \dfrac{2(x+3)}{3}$ or $\dfrac{2x+6}{3}$

51. $\dfrac{x^2-25}{2x-2} \div \dfrac{x^2+10x+25}{x^2+4x-5}$

$\quad = \dfrac{x^2-25}{2x-2} \cdot \dfrac{x^2+4x-5}{x^2+10x+25}$

$\quad = \dfrac{(x+5)(x-5)}{2(x-1)} \cdot \dfrac{(x+5)(x-1)}{(x+5)(x+5)}$

$\quad = \dfrac{x-5}{2}$

53. $\dfrac{y^3+y}{y^2-y} \div \dfrac{y^3-y^2}{y^2-2y+1}$

$\quad = \dfrac{y^3+y}{y^2-y} \cdot \dfrac{y^2-2y+1}{y^3-y^2}$

$\quad = \dfrac{y(y^2+1)}{y(y-1)} \cdot \dfrac{(y-1)(y-1)}{y^2(y-1)}$

$\quad = \dfrac{y^2+1}{y^2}$

55. $\dfrac{y^2+5y+4}{y^2+12y+32} \div \dfrac{y^2-12y+35}{y^2+3y-40}$

$\quad = \dfrac{y^2+5y+4}{y^2+12y+32} \cdot \dfrac{y^2+3y-40}{y^2-12y+35}$

$\quad = \dfrac{(y+4)(y+1)}{(y+4)(y+8)} \cdot \dfrac{(y+8)(y-5)}{(y-7)(y-5)}$

$\quad = \dfrac{y+1}{y-7}$

322

57.
$$\frac{2y^2-128}{y^2+16y+64} \div \frac{y^2-6y-16}{3y^2+30y+48}$$
$$= \frac{2y^2-128}{y^2+16y+64} \cdot \frac{3y^2+30y+48}{y^2-6y-16}$$
$$= \frac{2(y^2-64)}{(y+8)(y+8)} \cdot \frac{3(y^2+10y+16)}{(y+2)(y-8)}$$
$$= \frac{2(y+8)(y-8)}{(y+8)(y+8)} \cdot \frac{3(y+2)(y+8)}{(y+2)(y-8)}$$
$$= 6$$

59.
$$\frac{2x+2y}{3} \div \frac{x^2-y^2}{x-y}$$
$$= \frac{2x+2y}{3} \cdot \frac{x-y}{x^2-y^2}$$
$$= \frac{2(x+y)}{3} \cdot \frac{x-y}{(x+y)(x-y)}$$
$$= \frac{2}{3}$$

61.
$$\frac{x^2-y^2}{8x^2-16xy+8y^2} \div \frac{4x-4y}{x+y}$$
$$= \frac{x^2-y^2}{8x^2-16xy+8y^2} \cdot \frac{x+y}{4x-4y}$$
$$= \frac{(x+y)(x-y)}{8(x^2-2xy+y^2)} \cdot \frac{x+y}{4(x-y)}$$
$$= \frac{(x+y)(x-y)}{8(x-y)(x-y)} \cdot \frac{x+y}{4(x-y)}$$
$$= \frac{(x+y)^2}{32(x-y)^2}$$

63.
$$\frac{xy-y^2}{x^2+2x+1} \div \frac{2x^2+xy-3y^2}{2x^2+5xy+3y^2}$$
$$= \frac{xy-y^2}{x^2+2x+1} \cdot \frac{2x^2+5xy+3y^2}{2x^2+xy-3y^2}$$
$$= \frac{y(x-y)}{(x+1)(x+1)} \cdot \frac{(2x+3y)(x+y)}{(2x+3y)(x-y)}$$
$$= \frac{y(x+y)}{(x+1)^2}$$

65.
$$\left(\frac{y-2}{y^2-9y+18} \cdot \frac{y^2-4y-12}{y+2}\right) \div \frac{y^2-4}{y^2+5y+6} = \left(\frac{y-2}{y^2-9y+18} \cdot \frac{y^2-4y-12}{y+2}\right) \cdot \frac{y^2+5y+6}{y^2-4}$$
$$= \left(\frac{y-2}{(y-6)(y-3)} \cdot \frac{(y-6)(y+2)}{y+2}\right) \cdot \frac{(y+2)(y+3)}{(y+2)(y-2)} = \left(\frac{y-2}{y-3}\right) \cdot \frac{y+3}{y-2} = \frac{y+3}{y-3}$$

66.
$$\left(\frac{6y^2+31y+18}{3y^2-20y+12} \cdot \frac{2y^2-15y+18}{6y^2+35y+36}\right) \div \frac{2y^2-13y+15}{9y^2+15y+4}$$
$$= \left(\frac{6y^2+31y+18}{3y^2-20y+12} \cdot \frac{2y^2-15y+18}{6y^2+35y+36}\right) \cdot \frac{9y^2+15y+4}{2y^2-13y+15}$$
$$= \left(\frac{(3y+2)(2y+9)}{(3y-2)(y-6)} \cdot \frac{(2y-3)(y-6)}{(3y+4)(2y+9)}\right) \cdot \frac{(3y+4)(3y+1)}{(2y-3)(y-5)}$$
$$= \left(\frac{(3y+2)(2y-3)}{(3y-2)(3y+4)}\right) \cdot \frac{(3y+4)(3y+1)}{(2y-3)(y-5)} = \frac{(3y+2)(3y+1)}{(3y-2)(y-5)}$$

67.

$$\frac{3x^2+3x-60}{2x-8} \div \left(\frac{30x^2}{x^2-7x+10} \cdot \frac{x^3+3x^2-10x}{25x^3} \right)$$

$$= \frac{3x^2+3x-60}{2x-8} \div \left(\frac{30x^2}{(x-2)(x-5)} \cdot \frac{x(x^2+3x-10)}{25x^3} \right)$$

$$= \frac{3(x^2+x-20)}{2x-8} \div \left(\frac{30x^2}{(x-2)(x-5)} \cdot \frac{x(x+5)(x-2)}{25x^3} \right)$$

$$= \frac{3(x+5)(x-4)}{2(x-4)} \div \frac{6(x+5)}{5(x-5)}$$

$$= \frac{3(x+5)(x-4)}{2(x-4)} \cdot \frac{5(x-5)}{6(x+5)} = \frac{5(x-5)}{4}$$

68.

$$\frac{5x^2-x}{3x+2} \div \left(\frac{6x^2+x-2}{10x^2+3x-1} \cdot \frac{2x^2-x-1}{2x^2-x} \right) = \frac{x(5x-1)}{3x+2} \div \left(\frac{(2x-1)(3x+2)}{(5x-1)(2x+1)} \cdot \frac{(2x+1)(x-1)}{x(2x-1)} \right)$$

$$= \frac{x(5x-1)}{3x+2} \div \left(\frac{(3x+2)(x-1)}{x(5x-1)} \right) = \frac{x(5x-1)}{3x+2} \cdot \frac{x(5x-1)}{(3x+2)(x-1)} = \frac{x^2(5x-1)^2}{(3x+2)^2(x-1)}$$

69.

$$\frac{x^2+xz+xy+yz}{x-y} \div \frac{x+z}{x+y} = \frac{x(x+z)+y(x+z)}{x-y} \cdot \frac{x+y}{x+z} = \frac{(x+z)(x+y)}{x-y} \cdot \frac{x+y}{x+z} = \frac{(x+y)^2}{x-y}$$

70.

$$\frac{x^2-xz+xy-yz}{x-y} \div \frac{x-z}{y-x} = \frac{x(x-z)+y(x-z)}{x-y} \cdot \frac{y-x}{x-z} = \frac{(x-z)(x+y)}{x-y} \cdot \frac{-1(x-y)}{x-z}$$

$$= -1(x+y) = -x-y$$

71.

$$\frac{3xy+ay+3xb+ab}{9x^2-a^2} \div \frac{y^3+b^3}{6x-2a} = \frac{3xy+ay+3xb+ab}{9x^2-a^2} \cdot \frac{6x-2a}{y^3+b^3}$$

$$= \frac{y(3x+a)+b(3x+a)}{(3x+a)(3x-a)} \cdot \frac{2(3x-a)}{(y+b)(y^2-by+b^2)}$$

$$= \frac{(3x+a)(y+b)}{(3x+a)(3x-a)} \cdot \frac{2(3x-a)}{(y+b)(y^2-by+b^2)} = \frac{2}{y^2-by+b^2}$$

324

72.

$$\frac{5xy - ay - 5xb + ab}{25x^2 - a^2} \div \frac{y^3 - b^3}{15x + 3a} = \frac{5xy - ay - 5xb + ab}{25x^2 - a^2} \cdot \frac{15x + 3a}{y^3 - b^3}$$

$$= \frac{y(5x - a) - b(5x - a)}{(5x + a)(5x - a)} \cdot \frac{3(5x + a)}{(y - b)(y^2 + by + b^2)} = \frac{(5x - a)(y - b)}{(5x + a)(5x - a)} \cdot \frac{3(5x + a)}{(y - b)(y^2 + by + b^2)}$$

$$= \frac{3}{y^2 + by + b^2}$$

73.

$$\frac{1}{2} \cdot \frac{250x}{100 - x} = \frac{125x}{100 - x}$$

The rational expression $\dfrac{125x}{100 - x}$ represents the reduced cost.

75. – 77. Answers will vary.

79.

$$\frac{?}{?} \cdot \frac{3x - 12}{2x} = \frac{3}{2}$$

$$\frac{?}{?} \cdot \frac{3(x - 4)}{2x} = \frac{3}{2}$$

The numerator of the unknown rational expression must contain a factor of x. The denominator of the unknown rational expression must contain a factor of $(x - 4)$. Therefore, the simplest pair of polynomials that will work are x in the numerator and $x - 4$ in the denominator, to give the rational expression $\dfrac{x}{x - 4}$.

Check:

$$\frac{x}{x - 4} \cdot \frac{3x - 12}{2x} = \frac{x}{x - 4} \cdot \frac{3(x - 4)}{2x} = \frac{3}{2}$$

81.

$$\frac{9x^2 - y^2 + 15x - 5y}{3x^2 + xy + 5x} \div \frac{3x + y}{9x^3 + 6x^2y + xy^2} = \frac{9x^2 - y^2 + 15x - 5y}{3x^2 + xy + 5x} \cdot \frac{9x^3 + 6x^2y + xy^2}{3x + y}$$

$$= \frac{(3x + y)(3x - y) + 5(3x - y)}{x(3x + y + 5)} \cdot \frac{x(9x^2 + 6xy + y^2)}{3x + y} = \frac{(3x - y)(3x + y + 5)}{x(3x + y + 5)} \cdot \frac{x(3x + y)(3x + y)}{3x + y}$$

$$= (3x - y)(3x + y)$$

83.

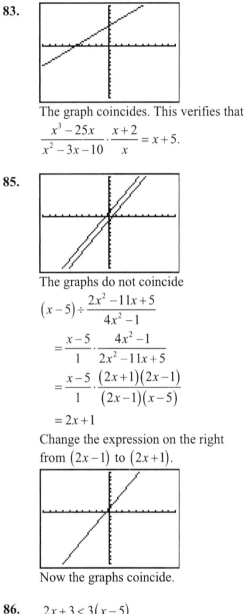

The graph coincides. This verifies that

$$\frac{x^3 - 25x}{x^2 - 3x - 10} \cdot \frac{x+2}{x} = x+5.$$

85.

The graphs do not coincide

$$(x-5) \div \frac{2x^2 - 11x + 5}{4x^2 - 1}$$

$$= \frac{x-5}{1} \cdot \frac{4x^2 - 1}{2x^2 - 11x + 5}$$

$$= \frac{x-5}{1} \cdot \frac{(2x+1)(2x-1)}{(2x-1)(x-5)}$$

$$= 2x+1$$

Change the expression on the right
from $(2x-1)$ to $(2x+1)$.

Now the graphs coincide.

86. $2x+3 < 3(x-5)$

$2x+3 < 3x-15$

$-x+3 < -15$

$-x < -18$

$x > 18$

The solution set is $\{x | x > 18\}$.

87. $3x^2 - 15x - 42 = 3(x^2 - 5x - 14)$

$$= 3(x-7)(x+2)$$

88. $x(2x+9) = 5$

$2x^2 + 9x = 5$

$2x^2 + 9x - 5 = 0$

$(2x-1)(x+5) = 0$

$2x-1 = 0$ or $x+5 = 0$

$2x = 1$ $x = -5$

$$x = \frac{1}{2}$$

The solution set is $\left\{-5, \ \frac{1}{2}\right\}$.

7.3 Exercise Set

1. $\dfrac{7x}{13} + \dfrac{2x}{13} = \dfrac{9x}{13}$

3. $\dfrac{8x}{15} + \dfrac{x}{15} = \dfrac{9x}{15} = \dfrac{3x}{5}$

5. $\dfrac{x-3}{12} + \dfrac{5x+21}{12} = \dfrac{6x+18}{12}$

$$= \frac{6(x+3)}{12}$$

$$= \frac{x+3}{2}$$

7. $\dfrac{4}{x} + \dfrac{2}{x} = \dfrac{6}{x}$

9. $\dfrac{8}{9x} + \dfrac{13}{9x} = \dfrac{21}{9x} = \dfrac{7}{3x}$

11. $\dfrac{5}{x+3} + \dfrac{4}{x+3} = \dfrac{9}{x+3}$

326

13. $\dfrac{x}{x-3} + \dfrac{4x+5}{x-3} = \dfrac{5x+5}{x-3}$

15. $\dfrac{4x+1}{6x+5} + \dfrac{8x+9}{6x+5} = \dfrac{12x+10}{6x+5}$

$\qquad = \dfrac{2(6x+5)}{6x+5} = 2$

17. $\dfrac{y^2+7y}{y^2-5y} + \dfrac{y^2-4y}{y^2-5y} = \dfrac{y^2+7y+y^2-4y}{y^2-5y}$

$\qquad = \dfrac{2y^2+3y}{y^2-5y}$

$\qquad = \dfrac{y(2y+3)}{y(y-5)}$

$\qquad = \dfrac{2y+3}{y-5}$

19. $\dfrac{4y-1}{5y^2} + \dfrac{3y+1}{5y^2} = \dfrac{4y-1+3y+1}{5y^2}$

$\qquad = \dfrac{7y}{5y^2} = \dfrac{7}{5y}$

21. $\dfrac{x^2-2}{x^2+x-2} + \dfrac{2x-x^2}{x^2+x-2}$

$\qquad = \dfrac{x^2-2+2x-x^2}{x^2+x-2}$

$\qquad = \dfrac{2x-2}{x^2+x-2} = \dfrac{2(x-1)}{(x+2)(x-1)} = \dfrac{2}{x+2}$

23. $\dfrac{x^2-4x}{x^2-x-6} + \dfrac{4x-4}{x^2-x-6}$

$\qquad = \dfrac{x^2-4x+4x-4}{x^2-x-6}$

$\qquad = \dfrac{x^2-4}{x^2-x-6} = \dfrac{(x+2)(x-2)}{(x-3)(x+2)} = \dfrac{x-2}{x-3}$

25. $\dfrac{3x}{5x-4} - \dfrac{4}{5x-4} = \dfrac{3x-4}{5x-4}$

27. $\dfrac{4x}{4x-3} - \dfrac{3}{4x-3} = \dfrac{4x-3}{4x-3} = 1$

29. $\dfrac{14y}{7y+2} - \dfrac{7y-2}{7y+2} = \dfrac{14y-(7y-2)}{7y+2}$

$\qquad = \dfrac{14y-7y+2}{7y+2}$

$\qquad = \dfrac{7y+2}{7y+2} = 1$

31. $\dfrac{3x+1}{4x-2} - \dfrac{x+1}{4x-2} = \dfrac{(3x+1)-(x+1)}{4x-2}$

$\qquad = \dfrac{3x+1-x-1}{4x-2}$

$\qquad = \dfrac{2x}{4x-2}$

$\qquad = \dfrac{2x}{2(2x-1)} = \dfrac{x}{2x-1}$

33. $\dfrac{3y^2-1}{3y^3} - \dfrac{6y^2-1}{3y^3}$

$\qquad = \dfrac{(3y^2-1)-(6y^2-1)}{3y^3}$

$\qquad = \dfrac{3y^2-1-6y^2+1}{3y^3} = \dfrac{-3y^2}{3y^3} = -\dfrac{1}{y}$

35. $\dfrac{4y^2+5}{9y^2-64} - \dfrac{y^2-y+29}{9y^2-64}$

$\qquad = \dfrac{(4y^2+5)-(y^2-y+29)}{9y^2-64}$

$\qquad = \dfrac{4y^2+5-y^2+y-29}{9y^2-64}$

$\qquad = \dfrac{3y^2+y-24}{9y^2-64}$

$\qquad = \dfrac{(3y-8)(y+3)}{(3y+8)(3y-8)} = \dfrac{y+3}{3y+8}$

327

37.

$$\frac{6y^2+y}{2y^2-9y+9}-\frac{2y+9}{2y^2-9y+9}$$

$$-\frac{4y-3}{2y^2-9y+9}$$

$$=\frac{\left(6y^2+y\right)-\left(2y+9\right)-\left(4y-3\right)}{2y^2-9y+9}$$

$$=\frac{6y^2+y-2y-9-4y+3}{2y^2-9y+9}$$

$$=\frac{6y^2-5y-6}{2y^2-9y+9}$$

$$=\frac{\left(2y-3\right)\left(3y+2\right)}{\left(2y-3\right)\left(y-3\right)}$$

$$=\frac{3y+2}{y-3}$$

39.

$$\frac{4}{x-3}+\frac{2}{3-x}=\frac{4}{x-3}+\frac{(-1)}{(-1)}\cdot\frac{2}{3-x}$$

$$=\frac{4}{x-3}+\frac{-2}{x-3}$$

$$=\frac{2}{x-3}$$

41.

$$\frac{6x+7}{x-6}+\frac{3x}{6-x}=\frac{6x+7}{x-6}+\frac{(-1)}{(-1)}\cdot\frac{3x}{6-x}$$

$$=\frac{6x+7}{x-6}+\frac{-3x}{x-6}$$

$$=\frac{3x+7}{x-6}$$

43.

$$\frac{5x-2}{3x-4}+\frac{2x-3}{4-3x}=\frac{5x-2}{3x-4}+\frac{(-1)}{(-1)}\cdot\frac{2x-3}{4-3x}$$

$$=\frac{5x-2}{3x-4}+\frac{-2x+3}{3x-4}$$

$$=\frac{5x-2-2x+3}{3x-4}$$

$$=\frac{3x+1}{3x-4}$$

45.

$$\frac{x^2}{x-2}+\frac{4}{2-x}=\frac{x^2}{x-2}+\frac{(-1)}{(-1)}\cdot\frac{4}{2-x}$$

$$=\frac{x^2}{x-2}+\frac{-4}{x-2}$$

$$=\frac{x^2-4}{x-2}$$

$$=\frac{\left(x+2\right)\left(x-2\right)}{x-2}$$

$$=x+2$$

47.

$$\frac{y-3}{y^2-25}+\frac{y-3}{25-y^2}$$

$$=\frac{y-3}{y^2-25}+\frac{(-1)}{(-1)}\cdot\frac{y-3}{25-y^2}$$

$$=\frac{y-3}{y^2-25}+\frac{-y+3}{y^2-25}$$

$$=\frac{y-3-y+3}{y^2-25}$$

$$=\frac{0}{y^2-25}=0$$

49.

$$\frac{6}{x-1}-\frac{5}{1-x}=\frac{6}{x-1}-\frac{(-1)}{(-1)}\cdot\frac{5}{1-x}$$

$$=\frac{6}{x-1}-\frac{-5}{x-1}$$

$$=\frac{6+5}{x-1}=\frac{11}{x-1}$$

51.

$$\frac{10}{x+3}-\frac{2}{-x-3}=\frac{10}{x+3}-\frac{(-1)}{(-1)}\cdot\frac{2}{-x-3}$$

$$=\frac{10}{x+3}-\frac{-2}{x+3}$$

$$=\frac{10+2}{x+3}=\frac{12}{x+3}$$

328

53.

$$\frac{y}{y-1} - \frac{1}{1-y} = \frac{y}{y-1} - \frac{(-1)}{(-1)} \cdot \frac{1}{1-y}$$

$$= \frac{y}{y-1} - \frac{-1}{y-1}$$

$$= \frac{y+1}{y-1}$$

55.

$$\frac{3-x}{x-7} - \frac{2x-5}{7-x} = \frac{3-x}{x-7} - \frac{(-1)}{(-1)} \cdot \frac{2x-5}{7-x}$$

$$= \frac{3-x}{x-7} - \frac{-2x+5}{x-7}$$

$$= \frac{(3-x)-(-2x+5)}{x-7}$$

$$= \frac{3-x+2x-5}{x-7}$$

$$= \frac{x-2}{x-7}$$

57.

$$\frac{x-2}{x^2-25} - \frac{x-2}{25-x^2}$$

$$= \frac{x-2}{x^2-25} - \frac{(-1)}{(-1)} \cdot \frac{x-2}{25-x^2}$$

$$= \frac{x-2}{x^2-25} - \frac{-x+2}{x^2-25}$$

$$= \frac{(x-2)-(-x+2)}{x^2-25}$$

$$= \frac{x-2+x-2}{x^2-25} = \frac{2x-4}{x^2-25}$$

59.

$$\frac{x}{x-y} + \frac{y}{y-x} = \frac{x}{x-y} + \frac{(-1)}{(-1)} \cdot \frac{y}{y-x}$$

$$= \frac{x}{x-y} + \frac{-y}{x-y}$$

$$= \frac{x-y}{x-y} = 1$$

61.

$$\frac{2x}{x^2-y^2} + \frac{2y}{y^2-x^2}$$

$$= \frac{2x}{x^2-y^2} + \frac{(-1)}{(-1)} \cdot \frac{2y}{y^2-x^2}$$

$$= \frac{2x}{x^2-y^2} + \frac{-2y}{x^2-y^2}$$

$$= \frac{2x-2y}{x^2-y^2} = \frac{2(x-y)}{(x+y)(x-y)} = \frac{2}{x+y}$$

63.

$$\frac{x^2-2}{x^2+6x-7} + \frac{19-4x}{7-6x-x^2}$$

$$= \frac{x^2-2}{x^2+6x-7} + \frac{(-1)}{(-1)} \cdot \frac{19-4x}{7-6x-x^2}$$

$$= \frac{x^2-2}{x^2+6x-7} + \frac{-19+4x}{-7+6x+x^2}$$

$$= \frac{x^2-2}{x^2+6x-7} + \frac{-19+4x}{x^2+6x-7}$$

$$= \frac{x^2-2-19+4x}{x^2+6x-7}$$

$$= \frac{x^2+4x-21}{x^2+6x-7}$$

$$= \frac{(x+7)(x-3)}{(x+7)(x-1)} = \frac{x-3}{x-1}$$

65.

$$\frac{6b^2-10b}{16b^2-48b+27} + \frac{7b^2-20b}{16b^2-48b+27}$$

$$- \frac{6b-3b^2}{16b^2-48b+27}$$

$$= \frac{6b^2-10b+7b^2-20b-6b+3b^2}{16b^2-48b+27}$$

$$= \frac{16b^2-36b}{16b^2-48b+27}$$

$$= \frac{4b(4b-9)}{(4b-9)(4b-3)} = \frac{4b}{4b-3}$$

66. $\dfrac{22b+15}{12b^2+52b-9}+\dfrac{30b-20}{12b^2+52b-9}$

$\;-\dfrac{4-2b}{12b^2+52b-9}$

$=\dfrac{22b+15+30b-20-4+2b}{12b^2+52b-9}$

$=\dfrac{54b-9}{12b^2+52b-9}$

$=\dfrac{9(6b-1)}{(6b-1)(2b+9)}=\dfrac{9}{2b+9}$

67. $\dfrac{2y}{y-5}-\left(\dfrac{2}{y-5}+\dfrac{y-2}{y-5}\right)$

$=\dfrac{2y}{y-5}-\left(\dfrac{2+y-2}{y-5}\right)$

$=\dfrac{2y}{y-5}-\dfrac{y}{y-5}=\dfrac{y}{y-5}$

68. $\dfrac{3x}{(x+1)^2}-\left[\dfrac{5x+1}{(x+1)^2}-\dfrac{3x+2}{(x+1)^2}\right]$

$=\dfrac{3x}{(x+1)^2}-\left[\dfrac{5x+1-3x-2}{(x+1)^2}\right]$

$=\dfrac{3x}{(x+1)^2}-\dfrac{2x-1}{(x+1)^2}$

$=\dfrac{3x-2x+1}{(x+1)^2}=\dfrac{x+1}{(x+1)^2}=\dfrac{1}{x+1}$

69. $\dfrac{b}{ac+ad-bc-bd}-\dfrac{a}{ac+ad-bc-bd}$

$=\dfrac{b-a}{ac+ad-bc-bd}$

$=\dfrac{b-a}{a(c+d)-b(c+c)}$

$=\dfrac{b-a}{(c+d)(a-b)}=\dfrac{(-1)}{(-1)}\cdot\dfrac{b-a}{(c+d)(a-b)}$

$=\dfrac{a-b}{-(c+d)(a-b)}=\dfrac{-1}{c+d}$

70. $\dfrac{y}{ax+bx-ay-by}-\dfrac{x}{ax+bx-ay-by}$

$=\dfrac{y-x}{ax+bx-ay-by}$

$=\dfrac{y-x}{x(a+b)-y(a+b)}$

$=\dfrac{y-x}{(a+b)(x-y)}$

$=\dfrac{(-1)}{(-1)}\cdot\dfrac{y-x}{(a+b)(x-y)}$

$=\dfrac{x-y}{-(a+b)(x-y)}=\dfrac{-1}{a+b}$

330

71. $\dfrac{(y-3)(y+2)}{(y+1)(y-4)} - \dfrac{(y+2)(y+3)}{(y+1)(4-y)} - \dfrac{(y+5)(y-1)}{(y+1)(4-y)}$

$= \dfrac{y^2-y-6}{(y+1)(y-4)} - \dfrac{y^2+5y+6}{(y+1)(4-y)} - \dfrac{y^2+4y-5}{(y+1)(4-y)}$

$= \dfrac{y^2-y-6}{(y+1)(y-4)} - \dfrac{(-1)}{(-1)} \cdot \dfrac{y^2+5y+6}{(y+1)(4-y)} - \dfrac{(-1)}{(-1)} \cdot \dfrac{y^2+4y-5}{(y+1)(4-y)}$

$= \dfrac{y^2-y-6}{(y+1)(y-4)} + \dfrac{y^2+5y+6}{(y+1)(y-4)} + \dfrac{y^2+4y-5}{(y+1)(y-4)}$

$= \dfrac{y^2-y-6+y^2+5y+6+y^2+4y-5}{(y+1)(y-4)} = \dfrac{3y^2+8y-5}{(y+1)(y-4)}$

72. $\dfrac{(y+1)(2y-1)}{(y-2)(y-3)} + \dfrac{(y+2)(y-1)}{(y-2)(y-3)} - \dfrac{(y+5)(2y+1)}{(3-y)(2-y)}$

$= \dfrac{2y^2+y-1}{(y-2)(y-3)} + \dfrac{y^2+y-2}{(y-2)(y-3)} - \dfrac{2y^2+11y+5}{-1(y-3)\cdot-1(y-2)}$

$= \dfrac{2y^2+y-1}{(y-2)(y-3)} + \dfrac{y^2+y-2}{(y-2)(y-3)} - \dfrac{2y^2+11y+5}{(y-3)(y-2)}$

$= \dfrac{2y^2+y-1+y^2+y-2-2y^2-11y-5}{(y-2)(y-3)} = \dfrac{y^2-9y-8}{(y-2)(y-3)}$

73. a. $\dfrac{L+60W}{L} - \dfrac{L-40W}{L}$

$= \dfrac{(L+60W)-(L-40W)}{L}$

$= \dfrac{L+60W-L+40W}{L}$

$= \dfrac{100W}{L}$

b. $\dfrac{100W}{L}$; $W=5, L=6$

$\dfrac{100W}{L} = \dfrac{100\cdot5}{6} \approx 83.3$

Since this value is over 80, the skull is round.

75. $P = 2L + 2W$

$= 2\left(\dfrac{5x+10}{x+3}\right) + 2\left(\dfrac{5}{x+3}\right)$

$= \dfrac{10x+20}{x+3} + \dfrac{10}{x+3}$

$= \dfrac{10x+30}{x+3} = \dfrac{10(x+3)}{x+3} = 10$

The perimeter is 10 meters.

77. – 79. Answers will vary.

81. Statement **d** is true.

$\dfrac{2x+1}{x-7} + \dfrac{3x+1}{x-7} - \dfrac{5x+2}{x-7}$

$= \dfrac{5x+2}{x-7} - \dfrac{5x+2}{x-7} = 0$

331

83. $\left(\dfrac{3x^2-4x+4}{3x^2+7x+2}-\dfrac{10x+9}{3x^2+7x+2}\right)\div\dfrac{x-5}{x^2-4}$

$=\left(\dfrac{\left(3x^2-4x+4\right)-\left(10x+9\right)}{3x^2+7x+2}\right)\div\dfrac{x-5}{x^2-4}$

$=\dfrac{3x^2-4x+4-10x-9}{3x^2+7x+2}\div\dfrac{x-5}{x^2-4}$

$=\dfrac{3x^2-14x-5}{3x^2+7x+2}\div\dfrac{x-5}{x^2-4}$

$=\dfrac{3x^2-14x-5}{3x^2+7x+2}\cdot\dfrac{x^2-4}{x-5}$

$=\dfrac{(3x+1)(x-5)}{(3x+1)(x+2)}\cdot\dfrac{(x+2)(x-2)}{(x-5)}$

$=x-2$

85. $\dfrac{3x}{x+2}-\dfrac{?}{x+2}=\dfrac{6-17x}{x+2}$

The difference of the numerators on the left side must be $6-17x$, so the missing expression is $20x-6$.

Check:

$\dfrac{3x}{x+2}-\dfrac{20x-6}{x+2}=\dfrac{3x-(20x-6)}{x+2}$

$=\dfrac{3x-20x+6}{x+2}$

$=\dfrac{-17x+6}{x+2}$

$=\dfrac{6-17x}{x+2}$

87. $\dfrac{a^2}{a-4}-\dfrac{?}{a-4}=a+3$

In order to reduce $a+3$, the difference on the left must be

$\dfrac{(a-4)(a+3)}{a-4}=\dfrac{a^2-a-12}{a-4}$

Since $a^2-(a+12)=a^2-a-12$, the missing expression is $a+12$.

Check:

$\dfrac{a^2}{a-4}-\dfrac{a+12}{a-4}=\dfrac{a^2-(a+12)}{a-4}$

$=\dfrac{a^2-a-12}{a-4}=\dfrac{(a-4)(a-3)}{a-4}=a+3$

89.

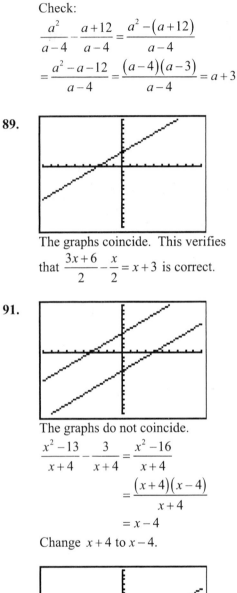

The graphs coincide. This verifies that $\dfrac{3x+6}{2}-\dfrac{x}{2}=x+3$ is correct.

91.

The graphs do not coincide.

$\dfrac{x^2-13}{x+4}-\dfrac{3}{x+4}=\dfrac{x^2-16}{x+4}$

$=\dfrac{(x+4)(x-4)}{x+4}$

$=x-4$

Change $x+4$ to $x-4$.

Now the graphs coincide.

332

92. $\dfrac{13}{15} - \dfrac{8}{45} = \dfrac{13}{15} \cdot \dfrac{3}{3} - \dfrac{8}{45} = \dfrac{39}{45} - \dfrac{8}{45} = \dfrac{31}{45}$

93. $81x^4 - 1 = \left(9x^2 + 1\right)\left(9x^2 - 1\right)$

$\qquad = \left(9x^2 + 1\right)\left(3x + 1\right)\left(3x - 1\right)$

94.
$$x + 3 \,\overline{\smash{\big)}\, 3x^3 + 2x^2 - 26x - 15} \quad \overset{\displaystyle 3x^2 - 7x - 5}{}$$

$\qquad \underline{3x^3 + 9x^2}$

$\qquad\qquad -7x^2 - 26x$

$\qquad\qquad \underline{-7x^2 - 21x}$

$\qquad\qquad\qquad -5x - 15$

$\qquad\qquad\qquad \underline{-5x - 15}$

$\qquad\qquad\qquad\qquad 0$

Thus,

$$\dfrac{3x^3 + 2x^2 - 26x - 15}{x + 3} = 3x^2 - 7x - 5$$

7.4 Exercise Set

1. $\dfrac{7}{15x^2}$ and $\dfrac{13}{24x}$

$15x^2 = 3 \cdot 5x^2$

$24 = 2^3 \cdot 3x$

$\text{LCD} = 2^3 \cdot 3 \cdot 5x^2 = 120x^2$

3. $\dfrac{8}{15x^2}$ and $\dfrac{5}{6x^5}$

$15x^2 = 3 \cdot 5x^2$

$6x^5 = 2 \cdot 3x^5$

$\text{LCD} = 2 \cdot 3 \cdot 5 \cdot x^5 = 30x^5$

5. $\dfrac{4}{x - 3}$ and $\dfrac{7}{x + 1}$

$\text{LCD} = \left(x - 3\right)\left(x + 1\right)$

7. $\dfrac{5}{7(y + 2)}$ and $\dfrac{10}{y}$

$\text{LCD} = 7y\left(y + 2\right)$

9. $\dfrac{17}{x + 4}$ and $\dfrac{18}{x^2 - 16}$

$x + 4 = 1\left(x + 4\right)$

$x^2 - 16 = \left(x + 4\right)\left(x - 4\right)$

$\text{LCD} = \left(x + 4\right)\left(x - 4\right)$

11. $\dfrac{8}{y^2 - 9}$ and $\dfrac{14}{y(y + 3)}$

$y^2 - 9 = \left(y + 3\right)\left(y - 3\right)$

$y\left(y + 3\right) = y\left(y + 3\right)$

$\text{LCD} = y\left(y + 3\right)\left(y - 3\right)$

13. $\dfrac{7}{y^2 - 1}$ and $\dfrac{y}{y^2 - 2y + 1}$

$y^2 - 1 = \left(y + 1\right)\left(y - 1\right)$

$y^2 - 2y + 1 = \left(y - 1\right)\left(y - 1\right)$

$\text{LCD} = \left(y + 1\right)\left(y - 1\right)\left(y - 1\right)$

15. $\dfrac{3}{x^2 - x - 20}$ and $\dfrac{x}{2x^2 + 7x - 4}$

$x^2 - x - 20 = \left(x - 5\right)\left(x + 4\right)$

$2x^2 + 7x - 4 = \left(2x - 1\right)\left(x + 4\right)$

$\text{LCD} = \left(x - 5\right)\left(x + 4\right)\left(2x - 1\right)$

17. $\dfrac{3}{x} + \dfrac{5}{x^2}$

$\text{LCD} = x^2$

$\dfrac{3}{x} + \dfrac{5}{x^2} = \dfrac{3}{x} \cdot \dfrac{x}{x} + \dfrac{5}{x^2} = \dfrac{3x + 5}{x^2}$

333

19.

$$\frac{2}{9x}+\frac{11}{6x}$$

$$\text{LCD} = 18x$$

$$\frac{2}{9x}+\frac{11}{6x}=\frac{2}{9x}\cdot\frac{2}{2}+\frac{11}{6x}\cdot\frac{3}{3}$$

$$=\frac{4}{18x}+\frac{33}{18x}=\frac{37}{18x}$$

21.

$$\frac{4}{x}+\frac{7}{2x^2}$$

$$\text{LCD} = 2x^2$$

$$\frac{4}{x}+\frac{7}{2x^2}=\frac{4}{x}\cdot\frac{2x}{2x}+\frac{7}{2x^2}$$

$$=\frac{8x}{2x^2}+\frac{7}{2x^2}=\frac{8x+7}{2x^2}$$

23.

$$6+\frac{1}{x}$$

$$\text{LCD} = x$$

$$6+\frac{1}{x}=\frac{6}{1}\cdot\frac{x}{x}+\frac{1}{x}=\frac{6x}{x}+\frac{1}{x}=\frac{6x+1}{x}$$

25.

$$\frac{2}{x}+9$$

$$\text{LCD} = x$$

$$\frac{2}{x}+9=\frac{2}{x}+\frac{9}{1}\cdot\frac{x}{x}=\frac{2}{x}+\frac{9x}{x}=\frac{2+9x}{x}$$

27.

$$\frac{x-1}{6}+\frac{x+2}{3}$$

$$\text{LCD} = 6$$

$$\frac{x-1}{6}+\frac{x+2}{3}=\frac{x-1}{6}+\frac{(x+2)}{3}\cdot\frac{2}{2}$$

$$=\frac{x-1}{6}+\frac{2x+4}{6}=\frac{3x+3}{6}=\frac{3(x+1)}{6}$$

$$=\frac{x+1}{2}$$

29.

$$\frac{4}{x}+\frac{3}{x-5}$$

$$\text{LCD} = x(x-5)$$

$$\frac{4}{x}+\frac{3}{x-5}=\frac{4(x-5)}{x(x-5)}+\frac{3}{x-5}\cdot\frac{x}{x}$$

$$=\frac{4(x-5)}{x(x-5)}+\frac{3x}{x(x-5)}$$

$$=\frac{4x-20+3x}{x(x-5)}$$

$$=\frac{7x-20}{x(x-5)}$$

31.

$$\frac{2}{x-1}+\frac{3}{x+2}$$

$$\text{LCD} = (x-1)(x+2)$$

$$\frac{2}{x-1}+\frac{3}{x+2}$$

$$=\frac{2(x+2)}{(x-1)(x+2)}+\frac{3(x-1)}{(x-1)(x+2)}$$

$$=\frac{2x+4+3x-3}{(x-1)(x+2)}$$

$$=\frac{5x+1}{(x-1)(x+2)}$$

33.

$$\frac{2}{y+5}+\frac{3}{4y}$$

$$\text{LCD} = 4y(y+5)$$

$$\frac{2}{y+5}+\frac{3}{4y}=\frac{2(4y)}{(4y)(y+5)}+\frac{3(y+5)}{4y(y+5)}$$

$$=\frac{2(4y)+3(y+5)}{4y(y+5)}$$

$$=\frac{8y+3y+15}{4y(y+5)}$$

$$=\frac{11y+15}{4y(y+5)}$$

334

35.
$$\frac{x}{x+7}-1$$

LCD $= x+7$

$$\frac{x}{x+7}-1=\frac{x}{x+7}-\frac{x+7}{x+7}$$

$$=\frac{x-(x+7)}{x+7}$$

$$=\frac{x-x-7}{x+7}$$

$$=\frac{-7}{x+7} \text{ or } -\frac{7}{x+7}$$

37.
$$\frac{7}{x+5}-\frac{4}{x-5}$$

LCD $= (x+5)(x-5)$

$$\frac{7}{x+5}-\frac{4}{x-5}$$

$$=\frac{7(x-5)}{(x+5)(x-5)}-\frac{4(x+5)}{(x+5)(x-5)}$$

$$=\frac{7(x-5)-4(x+5)}{(x+5)(x-5)}$$

$$=\frac{7x-35-4x-20}{(x+5)(x-5)}$$

$$=\frac{3x-55}{(x+5)(x-5)}$$

39.
$$\frac{2x}{x^2-16}+\frac{x}{x-4}$$

$$x^2-16=(x+4)(x-4)$$

$$x-4=1(x-4)$$

LCD $= (x+4)(x-4)$

$$\frac{2x}{x^2-16}+\frac{x}{x-4}$$

$$=\frac{2x}{(x+4)(x-4)}+\frac{x}{x-4}$$

$$=\frac{2x}{(x+4)(x-4)}+\frac{x(x+4)}{(x+4)(x-4)}$$

$$=\frac{2x+x(x+4)}{(x+4)(x-4)}$$

$$=\frac{2x+x^2+4x}{(x+4)(x-4)}$$

$$=\frac{x^2+6x}{(x+4)(x-4)}$$

41.
$$\frac{5y}{y^2-9}-\frac{4}{y+3}$$

LCD $= (y+3)(y-3)$

$$\frac{5y}{y^2-9}-\frac{4}{y+3}$$

$$=\frac{5y}{(y+3)(y-3)}-\frac{4}{y+3}$$

$$=\frac{5y}{(y+3)(y-3)}-\frac{4(y-3)}{(y+3)(y-3)}$$

$$=\frac{5y-4(y-3)}{(y+3)(y-3)}$$

$$=\frac{5y-4y+12}{(y+3)(y-3)}$$

$$=\frac{y+12}{(y+3)(y-3)}$$

43.
$$\frac{7}{x-1}-\frac{3}{(x-1)(x-1)}$$

LCD $= (x-1)(x-1)$

$$\frac{7}{x-1}-\frac{3}{(x-1)(x-1)}$$

$$=\frac{7(x-1)}{(x-1)(x-1)}-\frac{3}{(x-1)(x-1)}$$

$$=\frac{7x-7-3}{(x-1)(x-1)}$$

$$=\frac{7x-10}{(x-1)(x-1)} \text{ or } \frac{7x-10}{(x-1)^2}$$

335

45.

$$\frac{3y}{4y-20}+\frac{9y}{6y-30}$$

$$4y-20=4(y-5)$$

$$6y-30=6(y-5)$$

$$\text{LCD}=12(y-5)$$

$$\frac{3y}{4y-20}+\frac{9y}{6y-30}$$

$$=\frac{4y}{4(y-5)}+\frac{9y}{6(y-5)}$$

$$=\frac{4y}{4(y-5)}\cdot\frac{3}{3}+\frac{9y}{6(y-5)}\cdot\frac{2}{2}$$

$$=\frac{12y}{12(y-5)}+\frac{18y}{12(y-5)}$$

$$=\frac{9y+18y}{12(y-5)}=\frac{27y}{12(y-5)}$$

$$=\frac{9y}{4(y-5)}$$

47.

$$\frac{y+4}{y}-\frac{y}{y+4}$$

$$\text{LCD}=y(y+4)$$

$$\frac{y+4}{y}-\frac{y}{y+4}$$

$$=\frac{(y+4)(y+4)}{y(y+4)}-\frac{y\cdot y}{y(y+4)}$$

$$=\frac{y^2+8y+16-y^2}{y(y+4)}$$

$$=\frac{8y+16}{y(y+4)}$$

49.

$$\frac{2x+9}{x^2-7x+12}-\frac{2}{x-3}$$

$$x^2-7x+12=(x-3)(x-4)$$

$$x-3=1(x-3)$$

$$\text{LCD}=(x-3)(x-4)$$

$$\frac{2x+9}{x^2-7x+12}-\frac{2}{x-3}$$

$$=\frac{2x+9}{(x-3)(x-4)}-\frac{2}{x-3}$$

$$=\frac{2x+9}{(x-3)(x-4)}-\frac{2(x-4)}{(x-3)(x-4)}$$

$$=\frac{2x+9-2(x-4)}{(x-3)(x-4)}$$

$$=\frac{2x+9-2x+8}{(x-3)(x-4)}$$

$$=\frac{17}{(x-3)(x-4)}$$

51.

$$\frac{3}{x^2-1}+\frac{4}{(x+1)^2}$$

$$x^2-1=(x+1)(x-1)$$

$$(x+1)^2=(x+1)(x+1)$$

$$\text{LCD}=(x+1)(x+1)(x-1)$$

$$\frac{3}{x^2-1}+\frac{4}{(x+1)^2}$$

$$=\frac{3}{(x+1)(x-1)}+\frac{4}{(x+1)(x+1)}$$

$$=\frac{3(x+1)}{(x+1)(x+1)(x-1)}$$

$$+\frac{4(x-1)}{(x+1)(x+1)(x-1)}$$

$$=\frac{3(x+1)+4(x-1)}{(x+1)(x+1)(x-1)}$$

$$=\frac{3x+3+4x-4}{(x+1)(x+1)(x-1)}$$

$$=\frac{7x-1}{(x+1)(x+1)(x-1)}$$

53.

$$\frac{3x}{x^2+3x-10}-\frac{2x}{x^2+x-6}$$

$$x^2+3x-10=(x-2)(x+5)$$

$$x^2+x-6=(x+3)(x-2)$$

$$\text{LCD}=(x+3)(x-2)(x+5)$$

$$\frac{3x}{x^2+3x-10}-\frac{2x}{x^2+x-6}$$

$$=\frac{3x}{(x-2)(x+5)}-\frac{2x}{(x+3)(x-2)}$$

$$=\frac{3x(x+3)}{(x+3)(x-2)(x+5)}$$

$$-\frac{2x(x+5)}{(x+3)(x-2)(x+5)}$$

$$=\frac{3x(x+3)-2x(x+5)}{(x+3)(x-2)(x+5)}$$

$$=\frac{3x^2+9x-2x^2-10x}{(x+3)(x-2)(x+5)}$$

$$=\frac{x^2-x}{(x+3)(x-2)(x+5)}$$

55.

$$\frac{y}{y^2+2y+1}+\frac{4}{y^2+5y+4}$$

$$y^2+2y+1=(y+1)(y+1)$$

$$y^2+5y+4=(y+4)(y+1)$$

$$\text{LCD}=(y+4)(y+1)(y+1)$$

$$\frac{y}{y^2+2y+1}+\frac{4}{y^2+5y+4}$$

$$=\frac{y}{(y+1)(y+1)}+\frac{4}{(y+4)(y+1)}$$

$$=\frac{y(y+4)}{(y+4)(y+1)(y+1)}$$

$$+\frac{4(y+1)}{(y+4)(y+1)(y+1)}$$

$$=\frac{y(y+4)+4(y+1)}{(y+4)(y+1)(y+1)}$$

$$=\frac{y^2+4y+4y+4}{(y+4)(y+1)(y+1)}$$

$$=\frac{y^2+8y+4}{(y+4)(y+1)(y+1)}$$

57.

$$\frac{x-5}{x+3}+\frac{x+3}{x-5}$$

$$\text{LCD}=(x+3)(x-5)$$

$$\frac{x-5}{x+3}+\frac{x+3}{x-5}$$

$$=\frac{(x-5)(x-5)}{(x+3)(x-5)}+\frac{(x+3)(x+3)}{(x-5)(x+3)}$$

$$=\frac{(x-5)(x-5)+(x+3)(x+3)}{(x+3)(x-5)}$$

$$=\frac{(x^2-10x+25)+(x^2+6x+9)}{(x+3)(x-5)}$$

$$=\frac{2x^2-4x+34}{(x+3)(x-5)}$$

59.

$$\frac{5}{2y^2-2y}-\frac{3}{2y-2}$$

$$2y^2-2y=2y(y-1)$$

$$2y-2=2(y-1)$$

$$\text{LCD}=2y(y-1)$$

$$\frac{5}{2y^2-2y}-\frac{3}{2y-2}$$

$$=\frac{5}{2y(y-1)}-\frac{3}{2(y-1)}$$

$$=\frac{5}{2y(y-1)}-\frac{3\cdot y}{2y(y-1)}$$

$$=\frac{5-3y}{2y(y-1)}$$

61. $\dfrac{4x+3}{x^2-9} - \dfrac{x+1}{x-3}$

LCD $= (x+3)(x-3)$

$\dfrac{4x+3}{x^2-9} - \dfrac{x+1}{x-3}$

$= \dfrac{4x+3}{(x+3)(x-3)} - \dfrac{(x+1)(x+3)}{(x+3)(x-3)}$

$= \dfrac{(4x+3)-(x+1)(x+3)}{(x+3)(x-3)}$

$= \dfrac{(4x+3)-(x^2+4x+3)}{(x+3)(x-3)}$

$= \dfrac{4x+3-x^2-4x-3}{(x+3)(x-3)}$

$= \dfrac{-x^2}{(x+3)(x-3)} = -\dfrac{x^2}{(x+3)(x-3)}$

63. $\dfrac{y^2-39}{y^2+3y-10} - \dfrac{y-7}{y-2}$

$y^2+3y-10 = (y-2)(y+5)$

$y-2 = 1(y-2)$

LCD $= (y-2)(y+5)$

$\dfrac{y^2-39}{y^2+3y-10} - \dfrac{y-7}{y-2}$

$= \dfrac{y^2-39}{(y-2)(y+5)} - \dfrac{y-7}{y-2}$

$= \dfrac{y^2-39}{(y-2)(y+5)} - \dfrac{(y-7)(y+5)}{(y-2)(y+5)}$

$= \dfrac{(y^2-39)-(y-7)(y+5)}{(y-2)(y+5)}$

$= \dfrac{(y^2-39)-(y^2-2y-35)}{(y+2)(y+5)}$

$= \dfrac{y^2-39-y^2+2y+35}{(y-2)(y+5)}$

$= \dfrac{2y-4}{(y-2)(y+5)} = \dfrac{2(y-2)}{(y-2)(y+5)}$

$= \dfrac{2}{y+5}$

65. $4 + \dfrac{1}{x-3}$

LCD $= x-3$

$4 + \dfrac{1}{x-3} = \dfrac{4(x-3)}{x-3} + \dfrac{1}{x-3}$

$= \dfrac{4(x-3)+1}{x-3}$

$= \dfrac{4x-12+1}{x-3}$

$= \dfrac{4x-11}{x-3}$

67. $3 - \dfrac{3y}{y+1}$

LCD $= y+1$

$3 - \dfrac{3y}{y+1} = \dfrac{3(y+1)}{y+1} - \dfrac{3y}{y+1}$

$= \dfrac{3(y+1)-3y}{y+1}$

$= \dfrac{3y+3-3y}{y+1}$

$= \dfrac{3}{y+1}$

69. $\dfrac{9x+3}{x^2-x-6} + \dfrac{x}{3-x}$

$x^2-x-6 = (x-3)(x+2)$

$3-x = -1(x-3)$

LCD $= (x-3)(x+2)$

338

$$\frac{9x+3}{x^2-x-6}+\frac{x}{3-x}$$

$$=\frac{9x+3}{(x-3)(x+2)}+\frac{(-1)}{(-1)}\cdot\frac{x}{3-x}$$

$$=\frac{9x+3}{(x-3)(x+2)}+\frac{-x}{x-3}$$

$$=\frac{9x+3}{(x-3)(x+2)}+\frac{-x(x+2)}{(x-3)(x+2)}$$

$$=\frac{9x+3-x(x+2)}{(x-3)(x+2)}$$

$$=\frac{9x+3-x^2-2x}{(x-3)(x+2)}$$

$$=\frac{-x^2+7x+3}{(x-3)(x+2)}$$

71.

$$\frac{x+3}{x^2+x-2}-\frac{2}{x^2-1}$$

$$x^2+x-2=(x-1)(x+2)$$

$$x^2-1=(x+1)(x-1)$$

LCD $=(x+1)(x-1)(x+2)$

$$\frac{x+3}{x^2+x-2}-\frac{2}{x^2-1}$$

$$=\frac{x+3}{(x-1)(x+2)}-\frac{2}{(x+1)(x-1)}$$

$$=\frac{(x+3)(x+1)}{(x+1)(x-1)(x+2)}$$

$$-\frac{2(x+2)}{(x+1)(x-1)(x+2)}$$

$$=\frac{(x+3)(x+1)-2(x+2)}{(x+1)(x-1)(x+2)}$$

$$=\frac{x^2+4x+3-2x-4}{(x+1)(x-1)(x+2)}$$

$$=\frac{x^2+2x-1}{(x+1)(x-1)(x+2)}$$

73.

$$\frac{y+3}{5y^2}-\frac{y-5}{15y}$$

LCD $=15y^2$

$$\frac{y+3}{5y^2}-\frac{y-5}{15y}$$

$$=\frac{(y+3)(3)}{5y^2(3)}-\frac{(y-5)(y)}{15y(y)}$$

$$=\frac{(3y+9)-(y^2-5y)}{15y^2}$$

$$=\frac{3y+9-y^2+5y}{15y^2}$$

$$=\frac{-y^2+8y+9}{15y^2}$$

75.

$$\frac{x+3}{3x+6}+\frac{x}{4-x^2}$$

$$3x+6=3(x+2)$$

$$4-x^2=(2+x)(2-x)$$

Note that $-1(2-x)=x-2$

LCD $=3(x+2)(x-2)$

$$\frac{x+3}{3x+6}+\frac{x}{4-x^2}$$

$$=\frac{x+3}{3(x+2)}+\frac{x}{(2+x)(2-x)}$$

$$=\frac{x+3}{3(x+2)}+\frac{(-1)}{(-1)}\cdot\frac{x}{(2+x)(2-x)}$$

$$=\frac{x+3}{3(x+2)}+\frac{-x}{(x+2)(x-2)}$$

$$=\frac{(x+3)(x-2)}{3(x+2)(x-2)}+\frac{-x(3)}{3(x+2)(x-2)}$$

$$=\frac{x^2+x-6-3x}{3(x+2)(x-2)}$$

$$=\frac{x^2-2x-6}{3(x+2)(x-2)}$$

339

77. $\dfrac{y}{y^2-1}+\dfrac{2y}{y-y^2}$

$y^2-1=(y+1)(y-1)$

$y-y^2=y(1-y)$

Note that $-1(1-y)=y-1$

LCD $= y(y+1)(y-1)$

$\dfrac{y}{y^2-1}+\dfrac{2y}{y-y^2}$

$=\dfrac{y}{(y+1)(y-1)}+\dfrac{2y}{y(1-y)}$

$=\dfrac{y}{(y+1)(y-1)}+\dfrac{(-1)}{(-1)}\cdot\dfrac{2y}{y(1-y)}$

$=\dfrac{y}{(y+1)(y-1)}+\dfrac{-2y}{y(y-1)}$

$=\dfrac{y\cdot y}{y(y+1)(y-1)}+\dfrac{-2y(y+1)}{y(y+1)(y-1)}$

$=\dfrac{y^2-2y(y+1)}{y(y+1)(y-1)}=\dfrac{y^2-2y^2-2y}{y(y+1)(y-1)}$

$=\dfrac{-y^2-2y}{y(y+1)(y-1)}=\dfrac{-y(y+2)}{y(y+1)(y-1)}$

$=\dfrac{-1(y+2)}{(y+1)(y-1)}=\dfrac{-y-2}{(y+1)(y-1)}$

79. $\dfrac{x-1}{x}+\dfrac{y+1}{y}$

LCD $= xy$

$\dfrac{x-1}{x}+\dfrac{y+1}{y}$

$=\dfrac{(x-1)(y)}{xy}+\dfrac{(y+1)(x)}{xy}$

$=\dfrac{xy-y+xy+x}{xy}$

$=\dfrac{x+2xy-y}{xy}$

81. $\dfrac{3x}{x^2-y^2}-\dfrac{2}{y-x}$

$x^2-y^2=(x+y)(x-y)$

Note that $y-x=-1(x-y)$

LCD $=(x+y)(x-y)$

$\dfrac{3x}{x^2-y^2}-\dfrac{2}{y-x}$

$=\dfrac{3x}{(x+y)(x-y)}-\dfrac{(-1)}{(-1)}\cdot\dfrac{2}{y-x}$

$=\dfrac{3x}{(x+y)(x-y)}-\dfrac{-2}{x-y}$

$=\dfrac{3x}{(x+y)(x-y)}-\dfrac{-2(x+y)}{(x+y)(x-y)}$

$=\dfrac{3x+2(x+y)}{(x+y)(x-y)}=\dfrac{3x+2x+2y}{(x+y)(x-y)}$

$=\dfrac{5x+2y}{(x+y)(x-y)}$

83. $\dfrac{x+6}{x^2-4}-\dfrac{x+3}{x+2}+\dfrac{x-3}{x-2}$

LCD $=(x+2)(x-2)$

$\dfrac{x+6}{x^2-4}-\dfrac{x+3}{x+2}+\dfrac{x-3}{x-2}$

$=\dfrac{x+6}{(x+2)(x-2)}-\dfrac{x+3}{x+2}+\dfrac{x-3}{x-2}$

$=\dfrac{x+6}{(x+2)(x-2)}-\dfrac{(x+3)(x-2)}{(x+2)(x-2)}$

$\qquad +\dfrac{(x-3)(x+2)}{(x-2)(x+2)}$

$=\dfrac{x+6-(x+3)(x-2)+(x-3)(x+2)}{(x+2)(x-2)}$

$=\dfrac{x+6-(x^2+x-6)+(x^2-x-6)}{(x+2)(x-2)}$

$$= \frac{x+6-x^2-x+6+x^2-x-6}{(x+2)(x-2)}$$

$$= \frac{-x+6}{(x+2)(x-2)}$$

84. $\dfrac{x+8}{x^2-9} - \dfrac{x+2}{x+3} + \dfrac{x-2}{x-3}$

LCD $= (x+3)(x-3)$

$$\frac{x+8}{x^2-9} - \frac{x+2}{x+3} + \frac{x-2}{x-3}$$

$$= \frac{x+8}{(x+3)(x-3)} - \frac{x+2}{x+3} + \frac{x-2}{x-3}$$

$$= \frac{x+8}{(x+3)(x-3)} - \frac{(x+2)(x-3)}{(x+3)(x-3)}$$
$$\qquad + \frac{(x-2)(x+3)}{(x-3)(x+3)}$$

$$= \frac{x+8-(x+2)(x-3)+(x-2)(x+3)}{(x+3)(x-3)}$$

$$= \frac{x+8-(x^2-x-6)+(x^2+x-6)}{(x+3)(x-3)}$$

$$= \frac{x+8-x^2+x+6+x^2+x-6}{(x+3)(x-3)}$$

$$= \frac{3x+8}{(x+3)(x-3)}$$

85. $\dfrac{5}{x^2-25} + \dfrac{4}{x^2-11x+30} - \dfrac{3}{x^2-x-30}$

$x^2-25 = (x+5)(x-5)$

$x^2-11x+30 = (x-6)(x-5)$

$x^2-x-30 = (x-6)(x+5)$

LCD $= (x+5)(x-5)(x-6)$

$$\frac{5}{x^2-25} + \frac{4}{x^2-11x+30} - \frac{3}{x^2-x-30}$$

$$= \frac{5}{(x+5)(x-5)} + \frac{4}{(x-6)(x-5)}$$

$$\qquad - \frac{3}{(x-6)(x+5)}$$

$$= \frac{5(x-6)}{(x+5)(x-5)(x-6)}$$

$$\qquad + \frac{4(x+5)}{(x-6)(x-5)(x+5)}$$

$$\qquad - \frac{3(x-5)}{(x-6)(x+5)(x-5)}$$

$$= \frac{5(x-6)+4(x+5)-3(x-5)}{(x+5)(x-5)(x-6)}$$

$$= \frac{5x-30+4x+20-3x+15}{(x+5)(x-5)(x-6)}$$

$$= \frac{6x+5}{(x+5)(x-5)(x-6)}$$

86. $\dfrac{3}{x^2-49} + \dfrac{2}{x^2-15x+56} - \dfrac{5}{x^2-x-56}$

$x^2-49 = (x+7)(x-7)$

$x^2-15x+56 = (x-7)(x-8)$

$x^2-x-56 = (x-8)(x+7)$

LCD $= (x+7)(x+7)(x-8)$

$$\frac{3}{x^2-49} + \frac{2}{x^2-15x+56} - \frac{5}{x^2-x-56}$$

$$= \frac{3}{(x+7)(x-7)} + \frac{2}{(x-7)(x-8)}$$

$$\qquad - \frac{5}{(x-8)(x+7)}$$

341

$$= \frac{3(x-8)}{(x+7)(x-7)(x-8)}$$

$$+ \frac{2(x+7)}{(x-7)(x-8)(x+7)}$$

$$- \frac{5(x-7)}{(x-8)(x+7)(x-7)}$$

$$= \frac{3(x-8)+2(x+7)-5(x-7)}{(x+7)(x-7)(x-8)}$$

$$= \frac{3x-24+2x+14-5x+35}{(x+7)(x-7)(x-8)}$$

$$= \frac{25}{(x+7)(x-7)(x-8)}$$

87. $\dfrac{x+6}{x^3-27} - \dfrac{x}{x^3+3x^2+9x}$

$x^3 - 27 = (x-3)(x^2+3x+9)$

$x^3 + 3x^2 + 9x = x(x^2+3x+9)$

$\text{LCD} = x(x-3)(x^2+3x+9)$

$$\frac{x+6}{x^3-27} - \frac{x}{x^3+3x^2+9x}$$

$$= \frac{(x+6)x}{(x-3)(x^2+3x+9)x}$$

$$- \frac{x(x-3)}{x(x^2+3x+9)(x-3)}$$

$$= \frac{x+6}{(x-3)(x^2+3x+9)} - \frac{x}{x(x^2+3x+9)}$$

$$= \frac{x(x+6)-x(x-3)}{x(x-3)(x^2+3x+9)}$$

$$= \frac{x^2+6x-x^2+3x}{x(x-3)(x^2+3x+9)}$$

$$= \frac{9x}{x(x-3)(x^2+3x+9)}$$

$$= \frac{9}{(x-3)(x^2+3x+9)}$$

88. $\dfrac{x+8}{x^3-8} - \dfrac{x}{x^3+2x^2+4x}$

$x^3 - 8 = (x-2)(x^2+2x+4)$

$x^3 + 2x^2 + 4x = x(x^2+2x+4)$

$\text{LCD} = x(x-2)(x^2+2x+4)$

$$\frac{x+8}{x^3-8} - \frac{x}{x^3+2x^2+4x}$$

$$= \frac{x+8}{(x-2)(x^2+2x+4)} - \frac{x}{x(x^2+2x+4)}$$

$$= \frac{(x+8)x}{(x-2)(x^2+2x+4)x}$$

$$- \frac{x(x-2)}{x(x^2+2x+4)(x-2)}$$

$$= \frac{x(x+8)-x(x-2)}{x(x-2)(x^2+2x+4)}$$

$$= \frac{x^2+8x-x^2+2x}{x(x-2)(x^2+2x+4)}$$

$$= \frac{10x}{x(x-2)(x^2+2x+4)}$$

$$= \frac{10}{(x-2)(x^2+2x+4)}$$

89.

$$\frac{9y+3}{y^2-y-6}+\frac{y}{3-y}+\frac{y-1}{y+2}$$

$$y^2-y-6=(y-3)(y+2)$$

$$3-y=-1(y-3)$$

$$y+2=1(y+2)$$

$$\text{LCD}=(y-3)(y+2)$$

$$\frac{9y+3}{y^2-y-6}+\frac{y}{3-y}+\frac{y-1}{y+2}$$

$$=\frac{9y+3}{(y-3)(y+2)}+\frac{y}{-1(y-3)}+\frac{y-1}{y+2}$$

$$=\frac{9y+3}{(y-3)(y+2)}+\frac{-y(y+2)}{(y-3)(y+2)}$$

$$+\frac{(y-1)(y-3)}{(y+2)(y-3)}$$

$$=\frac{9y+3+-y(y+2)+(y-1)(y-3)}{(y-3)(y+2)}$$

$$=\frac{9y+3-y^2-2y+y^2-4y+3}{(y-3)(y+2)}$$

$$=\frac{3y+6}{(y-3)(y+2)}$$

$$=\frac{3(y+2)}{(y-3)(y+2)}$$

$$=\frac{3}{y-3}$$

90.

$$\frac{7y-2}{y^2-y-12}+\frac{2y}{4-y}+\frac{y+1}{y+3}$$

$$y^2-y-12=(y-4)(y+3)$$

$$4-y=-1(y-4)$$

$$y+3=1(y+3)$$

$$\text{LCD}=(y-4)(y+3)$$

$$=\frac{7y-2}{(y-4)(y+3)}+\frac{2y}{-1(y-4)}+\frac{y+1}{y+3}$$

$$=\frac{7y-2}{(y-4)(y+3)}+\frac{-2y(y+3)}{(y-4)(y+3)}$$

$$+\frac{(y+1)(y-4)}{(y+3)(y-4)}$$

$$=\frac{7y-2+-2y(y+3)+(y+1)(y-4)}{(y-4)(y+3)}$$

$$=\frac{7y-2-2y^2-6y+y^2-3y-4}{(y-4)(y+3)}$$

$$=\frac{-y^2-2y-6}{(y-4)(y+3)}\ \text{or}\ -\frac{y^2+2y+6}{(y-4)(y+3)}$$

91.

$$\frac{3}{x^2+4xy+3y^2}-\frac{5}{x^2-2xy-3y^2}$$

$$+\frac{2}{x^2-9y^2}$$

$$x^2+4xy+3y^2=(x+y)(x+3y)$$

$$x^2-2xy-3y^2=(x-3y)(x+y)$$

$$x^2-9y^2=(x+3y)(x-3y)$$

$$\text{LCD}=(x+y)(x+3y)(x-3y)$$

$$\frac{3}{x^2+4xy+3y^2}-\frac{5}{x^2-2xy-3y^2}$$

$$+\frac{2}{x^2-9y^2}$$

$$=\frac{3}{(x+y)(x+3y)}-\frac{5}{(x-3y)(x+y)}$$

$$+\frac{2}{(x+3y)(x-3y)}$$

343

$$= \frac{3(x-3y)}{(x+y)(x+3y)(x-3y)}$$

$$-\frac{5(x+3y)}{(x-3y)(x+y)(x+3y)}$$

$$+\frac{2(x+y)}{(x+3y)(x-3y)(x+y)}$$

$$= \frac{3(x-3y)-5(x+3y)+2(x+y)}{(x+y)(x+3y)(x-3y)}$$

$$= \frac{3x-9y-5x-15y+2x+2y}{(x+y)(x+3y)(x-3y)}$$

$$= \frac{-22y}{(x+y)(x+3y)(x-3y)}$$

$$= \frac{5(x-2y)}{(x+y)(x+2y)(x-2y)}$$

$$-\frac{7(x+2y)}{(x+y)(x-2y)(x+2y)}$$

$$+\frac{4(x+y)}{(x+2y)(x-2y)(x+y)}$$

$$= \frac{5(x-2y)-7(x+2y)+4(x+y)}{(x+y)(x+2y)(x-2y)}$$

$$= \frac{5x-10y-7x-14y+4x+4y}{(x+y)(x+2y)(x-2y)}$$

$$= \frac{2x-20y}{(x+y)(x+2y)(x-2y)}$$

92.

$$\frac{5}{x^2+3xy+2y^2} - \frac{7}{x^2-xy-2y^2}$$

$$+\frac{4}{x^2-4y^2}$$

$$x^2+3xy+2y^2 = (x+y)(x+2y)$$

$$x^2-xy-2y^2 = (x+y)(x-2y)$$

$$x^2-4y^2 = (x+2y)(x-2y)$$

$$\text{LCD} = (x+y)(x+2y)(x-2y)$$

$$\frac{5}{x^2+3xy+2y^2} - \frac{7}{x^2-xy-2y^2}$$

$$+\frac{4}{x^2-4y^2}$$

$$= \frac{5}{(x+y)(x+2y)} - \frac{7}{(x+y)(x-2y)}$$

$$+\frac{4}{(x+2y)(x-2y)}$$

93.

Young's Rule $C = \dfrac{DA}{A+12}$

$A = 8;$

$$C = \frac{D \cdot 8}{8+12} = \frac{8D}{20} = \frac{2D}{5}$$

$A = 3;$

$$C = \frac{D \cdot 3}{3+12} = \frac{3D}{15} = \frac{D}{5}$$

Difference:

$$\frac{2D}{5} - \frac{D}{5} = \frac{D}{5}$$

The difference in dosages for an 8-year-old child and a 3-year-old child is $\dfrac{D}{5}$. This means that an 8-year-old should be given $\dfrac{1}{5}$ of the adult dosage more than a 3-year-old.

344

95. Young's Rule:

$$C = \frac{DA}{A+12}$$

Cowling's Rule:

$$C = \frac{D(A+1)}{24}$$

For $A = 12$, Young's Rule gives

$$C = \frac{D \cdot 12}{12+12} = \frac{12D}{24} = \frac{D}{2}$$

and Cowling's Rule gives

$$C = \frac{D(12+1)}{24} = \frac{13D}{24}$$

The difference between the dosages given by Cowling's Rule and Young's Rule is

$$\frac{13D}{24} - \frac{12D}{24} = \frac{D}{24}.$$

This means that Cowling's Rule says to give a 12-year-old $\frac{1}{24}$ of the adult dose more than Young's Rule says the dosage should be.

97. No, because the graphs cross, neither formula gives a consistently smaller dosage.

99. The difference in dosage is greatest at 5 years. This is where the graphs are farthest apart.

101. $P = 2L + 2W$

$$= 2\left(\frac{x}{x+3}\right) + 2\left(\frac{x}{x-4}\right)$$

$$= \frac{2x}{x+3} + \frac{2x}{x+4}$$

$$= \frac{2x(x+4)}{(x+3)(x+4)} + \frac{2x(x+3)}{(x+3)(x+4)}$$

$$= \frac{2x^2 + 8x + 2x^2 + 6x}{(x+3)(x+4)}$$

$$= \frac{4x^2 + 14x}{(x+3)(x+4)}$$

103. Answers will vary.

105. Explanations will vary. The right side of the equation should be charged from $\dfrac{3}{x+5}$ to $\dfrac{5+2x}{5x}$.

107. Answers will vary.

109. $\dfrac{y^2 + 5y + 4}{y^2 + 2y - 3} \cdot \dfrac{y^2 + y - 6}{y^2 + 2y - 3} - \dfrac{2}{y-1}$

$$= \frac{(y+4)(y+1)}{(y+3)(y-1)} \cdot \frac{(y+3)(y-2)}{(y+3)(y-1)} - \frac{2}{y-1}$$

$$= \frac{(y+4)(y+1)(y-2)}{(y+3)(y-1)(y-1)} - \frac{2}{y-1}$$

$$= \frac{(y+4)(y+1)(y-2)}{(y+3)(y-1)(y-1)}$$

$$- \frac{2(y-1)(y+3)}{(y-1)(y-1)(y+3)}$$

$$= \frac{(y+4)(y^2 - y - 2)}{(y+3)(y-1)(y-1)}$$

$$- \frac{2(y^2 + 2y - 3)}{(y+3)(y-1)(y-1)}$$

$$= \frac{y^3 - y^2 - 2y + 4y^2 - 4y - 8}{(y+3)(y-1)(y-1)}$$

$$- \frac{2y^2 + 4y - 6}{(y+3)(y-1)(y-1)}$$

$$= \frac{y^3 + 3y^2 - 6y - 8}{(y+3)(y-1)(y-1)}$$

$$- \frac{2y^2 + 4y - 6}{(y+3)(y-1)(y-1)}$$

$$= \frac{y^3 + 3y^2 - 6y - 8 - 2y^2 - 4y + 6}{(y+3)(y-1)(y-1)}$$

$$= \frac{y^3 + y^2 - 10y - 2}{(y+3)(y-1)(y-1)}$$

345

111. $\dfrac{2}{x-1} - \dfrac{?}{?} = \dfrac{2x^2 + 3x - 1}{x^2(x-1)}$

If the first rational expression is

multiplied by $\dfrac{x^2}{x^2}$, the result will be

$\dfrac{2}{x-2} \cdot \dfrac{x^2}{x^2} = \dfrac{2x^2}{x^2(x-1)}$.

$\dfrac{2x^2}{x^2(x-1)} + \dfrac{3x-1}{x^2(x-1)} = \dfrac{2x^2 + 3x - 1}{x^2(x-1)}$.

Therefore, the missing rational

expression is $\dfrac{3x-1}{x^2(x-1)}$.

113. $(3x+5)(2x-7) = 6x^2 - 21x + 10x - 35$
$$= 6x^2 - 11x - 35$$

114. $3x - y = 3$
$$-y = -3x + 3$$
$$y = 3x - 3$$
The slope is 3; the y-intercept is -3.

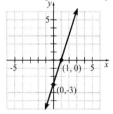

115. Line passing through $(-3, -4)$ and
$(1, 0)$
First find the slope.
$$m = \dfrac{0 - (-4)}{1 - (-3)} = \dfrac{4}{4} = 1$$
Use $m = (1, 0)$ and $(x_1, y_1) = (1, 0)$ in
the point-slope form and simplify to
find the slope-intercept form.
$$y - y_1 = m(x - x_1)$$
$$y - 0 = 1(x - 1)$$
$$y = x - 1$$

Mid-Chapter Check Point – Chapter 7

1. $\dfrac{x^2 - 4}{x^2 - 2x - 8}$
$$x^2 - 2x - 8 = 0$$
$$(x - 4)(x + 2) = 0$$
$$x - 4 = 0 \quad \text{or} \quad x + 2 = 0$$
$$x = 4 \qquad\qquad x = -2$$
The rational expression is undefined
for $x = 4$ and $x = -2$.

2. $\dfrac{3x^2 - 7x + 2}{6x^2 + x - 1} = \dfrac{(3x-1)(x-2)}{(3x-1)(2x+1)} = \dfrac{x-2}{2x+1}$

3. $\dfrac{9 - 3y}{y^2 - 5y + 6} = \dfrac{3(3-y)}{(y-3)(y-2)}$
$$= \dfrac{-3(y-3)}{(y-3)(y-2)} = \dfrac{-3}{y-2}$$

4. $\dfrac{16w^3 - 24w^2}{8w^4 - 12w^3} = \dfrac{8w^2(2w-3)}{4w^3(2w-3)} = \dfrac{2}{w}$

5. $\dfrac{7x-3}{x^2 + 3x - 4} - \dfrac{3x+1}{x^2 + 3x - 4}$
$$= \dfrac{7x - 3 - 3x - 1}{(x-1)(x+4)}$$
$$= \dfrac{4x - 4}{(x-1)(x+4)}$$
$$= \dfrac{4(x-1)}{(x-1)(x+4)} = \dfrac{4}{x+4}$$

6. $\dfrac{x+2}{2x-4} \cdot \dfrac{8}{x^2 - 4}$
$$= \dfrac{x+2}{2(x-2)} \cdot \dfrac{8}{(x+2)(x-2)}$$
$$= \dfrac{4}{(x-2)(x-2)} \quad \text{or} \quad \dfrac{4}{(x-2)^2}$$

346

7.
$$1 + \frac{7}{x-2} = \frac{x-2}{x-2} + \frac{7}{x-2} = \frac{x+5}{x-2}$$

8.
$$\frac{2x^2 + x - 1}{2x^2 - 7x + 3} \div \frac{x^2 - 3x - 4}{x^2 - x - 6}$$

$$= \frac{2x^2 + x - 1}{2x^2 - 7x + 3} \cdot \frac{x^2 - x - 6}{x^2 - 3x - 4}$$

$$= \frac{(2x-1)(x+1)}{(2x-1)(x-3)} \cdot \frac{(x-3)(x+2)}{(x-4)(x+1)}$$

$$= \frac{x+2}{x-4}$$

9.
$$\frac{1}{x^2 + 2x - 3} + \frac{1}{x^2 + 5x + 6}$$

$$x^2 + 2x - 3 = (x+3)(x-1)$$

$$x^2 + 5x + 6 = (x+2)(x+3)$$

$$\text{LCD} = (x+3)(x-1)(x+2)$$

$$\frac{1}{x^2 + 2x - 3} + \frac{1}{x^2 + 5x + 6}$$

$$= \frac{1}{(x+3)(x-1)} + \frac{1}{(x+2)(x+3)}$$

$$= \frac{1(x+2)}{(x+3)(x-1)(x+2)}$$

$$+ \frac{1(x-1)}{(x+2)(x+3)(x-1)}$$

$$= \frac{x+2+x-1}{(x+3)(x-1)(x+2)}$$

$$= \frac{2x+1}{(x+3)(x-1)(x+2)}$$

10.
$$\frac{17}{x-5} + \frac{x+8}{5-x}$$

$$\text{Note: } 5 - x = -1(x-5)$$

$$\text{LCD} = x - 5$$

$$\frac{17}{x-5} + \frac{-1(x+8)}{-1(5-x)} = \frac{17}{x-5} + \frac{-x-8}{x-5}$$

$$= \frac{17-x-8}{x-5} = \frac{9-x}{x-5}$$

11.
$$\frac{4y^2 - 1}{9y - 3y^2} \cdot \frac{y^2 - 7y + 12}{2y^2 - 7y - 4}$$

$$= \frac{(2y+1)(2y-1)}{3y(3-y)} \cdot \frac{(y-4)(y-3)}{(2y+1)(y-4)}$$

$$= \frac{-1(2y+1)(2y-1)}{-1 \cdot 3y(3-y)} \cdot \frac{(y-4)(y-3)}{(2y+1)(y-4)}$$

$$= \frac{-1(2y+1)(2y+1)}{3y(y-3)} \cdot \frac{(y-4)(y-3)}{(2y+1)(y-4)}$$

$$= \frac{-(2y+1)}{3y} = \frac{-2y-1}{3y}$$

12.
$$\frac{y}{y+1} - \frac{2y}{y+2}$$

$$\text{LCD} = (y+1)(y+2)$$

$$\frac{y(y+2)}{(y+1)(y+2)} - \frac{2y(y+1)}{(y+2)(y+1)}$$

$$= \frac{y^2 + 2y - 2y^2 - 2y}{(y+1)(y+2)} = \frac{-y^2}{(y+1)(y+2)}$$

13.
$$\frac{w^2 + 6w + 5}{7w^2 - 63} \div \frac{w^2 + 10w + 25}{7w + 21}$$

$$= \frac{w^2 + 6w + 5}{7w^2 - 63} \cdot \frac{7w + 21}{w^2 + 10w + 25}$$

$$= \frac{(w+5)(w+1)}{7(w^2 - 9)} \cdot \frac{7(w+3)}{(w+5)(w+5)}$$

$$= \frac{(w+5)(w+1)}{7(w+3)(w-3)} \cdot \frac{7(w+3)}{(w+5)(w+5)}$$

$$= \frac{w+1}{(w-3)(w+5)}$$

347

14.

$$\frac{2z}{z^2-9}-\frac{5}{z^2+4z+3}$$

$$z^2-9=(z+3)(z-3)$$

$$z^2+4z+3=(z+3)(z+1)$$

$$\text{LCD}=(z+3)(z-3)(z+1)$$

$$\frac{2z}{z^2-9}-\frac{5}{z^2+4z+3}$$

$$=\frac{2z}{(z+3)(z-3)}-\frac{5}{(z+3)(z+1)}$$

$$\frac{2z(z+1)}{(z+3)(z-3)(z+1)}$$

$$-\frac{5(z-3)}{(z+3)(z+1)(z-3)}$$

$$=\frac{2z^2+2z-5z+15}{(z+3)(z-3)(z+1)}$$

$$=\frac{2z^2-3z+15}{(z+3)(z-3)(z+1)}$$

15.

$$\frac{z+2}{3z-1}+\frac{5}{(3z-1)^2}$$

$$\text{LCD}=(3z-1)(3z-1)$$

$$\frac{(z+2)(3z-1)}{(3z-1)(3z-1)}+\frac{5}{(3z-1)^2}$$

$$=\frac{3z^2+5z-2+5}{(3z-1)^2}=\frac{3z^2+5z+3}{(3z-1)^2}$$

16.

$$\frac{8}{x^2+4x-21}+\frac{3}{x+7}$$

$$x^2+4x-21=(x+7)(x-3)$$

$$x+7=1(x+7)$$

$$\text{LCD}=(x+7)(x-3)$$

$$\frac{8}{x^2+4x-21}+\frac{3}{x+7}$$

$$=\frac{8}{(x+7)(x-3)}+\frac{3}{x+7}$$

$$=\frac{8}{(x+7)(x-3)}+\frac{3(x-3)}{(x+7)(x-3)}$$

$$=\frac{8+3x-9}{(x+7)(x-3)}=\frac{3x-1}{(x+7)(x-3)}$$

17.

$$\frac{x^4-27x}{x^2-9}\cdot\frac{x+3}{x^2+3x+9}$$

$$=\frac{x(x^3-27)}{(x+3)(x-3)}\cdot\frac{x+3}{x^2+3x+9}$$

$$=\frac{x(x-3)(x^2+3x+9)}{(x+3)(x-3)}\cdot\frac{x+3}{x^2+3x+9}$$

$$=\frac{x}{1}=x$$

18.

$$\frac{x-1}{x^2-x-2}-\frac{x+2}{x^2+4x+3}$$

$$x^2-x-2=(x-2)(x+1)$$

$$x^2+4x+3=(x+3)(x+1)$$

$$\text{LCD}=(x-2)(x+1)(x+3)$$

$$\frac{x-1}{x^2-x-2}-\frac{x+2}{x^2+4x+3}$$

$$=\frac{x-1}{(x-2)(x+1)}-\frac{x+2}{(x+1)(x+3)}$$

$$=\frac{(x-1)(x+3)}{(x-2)(x+1)(x+3)}$$

$$-\frac{(x+2)(x-2)}{(x+1)(x+3)(x-2)}$$

$$=\frac{x^2+2x-3-(x^2-4)}{(x-2)(x+1)(x+3)}$$

$$= \frac{x^2 + 2x - 3 - x^2 + 4}{(x-2)(x+1)(x+3)}$$

$$= \frac{2x+1}{(x-2)(x+1)(x+3)}$$

19. $\dfrac{x^2 - 2xy + y^2}{x+y} \div \dfrac{x^2 - xy}{5x + 5y}$

$$= \frac{x^2 - 2xy + y^2}{x+y} \cdot \frac{5x + 5y}{x^2 - xy}$$

$$= \frac{(x-y)(x-y)}{x+y} \cdot \frac{5(x+y)}{x(x-y)}$$

$$= \frac{5(x-y)}{x} = \frac{5x - 5y}{x}$$

20. $\dfrac{5}{x+5} + \dfrac{x}{x-4} - \dfrac{11x - 8}{x^2 + x - 20}$

$x^2 + x - 20 = (x+5)(x-4)$

$\text{LCD} = (x+5)(x-4)$

$$\frac{5}{x+5} + \frac{x}{x-4} - \frac{11x - 8}{x^2 + x - 20}$$

$$= \frac{5}{x+5} + \frac{x}{x-4} - \frac{11x - 8}{(x+5)(x-4)}$$

$$= \frac{5(x-4)}{(x+5)(x-4)} + \frac{x(x+5)}{(x-4)(x+5)}$$

$$- \frac{11x - 8}{(x+5)(x-4)}$$

$$= \frac{5x - 20 + x^2 + 5x - 11x + 8}{(x+5)(x-4)}$$

$$= \frac{x^2 - x - 12}{(x+5)(x-4)} = \frac{(x+3)(x-4)}{(x+5)(x-4)}$$

$$= \frac{x+3}{x+5}$$

7.5 Exercise Set

In Exercises 1-39, each complex rational expression can be simplified by either of the two methods introduced in this section of the textbook. Both methods will be illustrated here.

1. $\dfrac{\dfrac{1}{2} + \dfrac{1}{4}}{\dfrac{1}{2} + \dfrac{1}{3}}$

Add to get a single rational expression in the numerator.

$$\frac{1}{2} + \frac{1}{4} = \frac{2}{4} + \frac{1}{4} = \frac{3}{4}$$

Add to get a single rational expression in the denominator.

$$\frac{1}{2} + \frac{1}{3} = \frac{3}{6} + \frac{2}{6} = \frac{5}{6}$$

Perform the division indicated by the fraction bar. Invert and multiply.

$$\frac{\dfrac{1}{2} + \dfrac{1}{4}}{\dfrac{1}{2} + \dfrac{1}{3}} = \frac{\dfrac{3}{4}}{\dfrac{5}{6}} = \frac{3}{4} \cdot \frac{6}{5} = \frac{9}{10}$$

3. $\dfrac{5 + \dfrac{2}{5}}{7 - \dfrac{1}{10}} = \dfrac{\dfrac{25}{5} + \dfrac{2}{5}}{\dfrac{70}{10} - \dfrac{1}{10}}$

$$= \frac{\dfrac{27}{5}}{\dfrac{69}{10}} = \frac{27}{5} \cdot \frac{10}{69} = \frac{9 \cdot 3 \cdot 2 \cdot 5}{5 \cdot 3 \cdot 23} = \frac{18}{23}$$

349

5.

$$\frac{\dfrac{2}{5}-\dfrac{1}{3}}{\dfrac{2}{3}-\dfrac{3}{4}}$$

LCD = 60

$$\frac{\dfrac{2}{5}-\dfrac{1}{3}}{\dfrac{2}{3}-\dfrac{3}{4}}=\frac{60\cdot\left(\dfrac{2}{5}-\dfrac{1}{3}\right)}{60\cdot\left(\dfrac{2}{3}-\dfrac{3}{4}\right)}$$

$$=\frac{60\cdot\dfrac{2}{5}-60\cdot\dfrac{1}{3}}{60\cdot\dfrac{2}{3}-60\cdot\dfrac{3}{4}}$$

$$=\frac{24-20}{40-45}=\frac{4}{-5}=-\frac{4}{5}$$

7.

$$\frac{\dfrac{3}{4}-x}{\dfrac{3}{4}+x}=\frac{\dfrac{3}{4}-\dfrac{4x}{4}}{\dfrac{3}{4}+\dfrac{4x}{4}}$$

$$=\frac{\dfrac{3-4x}{4}}{\dfrac{3+4x}{4}}$$

$$=\frac{3-4x}{4}\cdot\frac{4}{3+4x}=\frac{3-4x}{3+4x}$$

9.

$$\frac{7-\dfrac{2}{x}}{5+\dfrac{1}{x}}=\frac{\dfrac{7x-2}{x}}{\dfrac{5x+1}{x}}=\frac{7x-2}{x}\cdot\frac{x}{5x+1}=\frac{7x-2}{5x+1}$$

11.

$$\frac{2+\dfrac{3}{y}}{1-\dfrac{7}{y}}=\frac{\dfrac{2y+3}{y}}{\dfrac{y-7}{y}}$$

$$=\frac{2y+3}{y}\cdot\frac{y}{y-7}=\frac{2y+3}{y-7}$$

13.

$$\frac{\dfrac{1}{y}-\dfrac{3}{2}}{\dfrac{1}{y}+\dfrac{3}{4}}=\frac{\dfrac{2-3y}{2y}}{\dfrac{4+3y}{4y}}$$

$$=\frac{2-3y}{2y}\cdot\frac{4y}{4+3y}$$

$$=\frac{2(2-3y)}{4+3y}=\frac{4-6y}{4+3y}$$

15.

$$\frac{\dfrac{x}{5}-\dfrac{5}{x}}{\dfrac{1}{5}+\dfrac{1}{x}}$$

LCD = $5x$

$$\frac{\dfrac{x}{5}-\dfrac{5}{x}}{\dfrac{1}{5}+\dfrac{1}{x}}=\frac{5x\cdot\left(\dfrac{x}{5}-\dfrac{5}{x}\right)}{5x\cdot\left(\dfrac{1}{5}+\dfrac{1}{x}\right)}$$

$$=\frac{5x\cdot\dfrac{x}{5}-5x\cdot\dfrac{5}{x}}{5x\cdot\dfrac{1}{5}+5x\cdot\dfrac{1}{x}}$$

$$=\frac{x^2-25}{x+5}$$

$$=\frac{(x+5)(x-5)}{x+5}=x-5$$

17.

$$\frac{1+\dfrac{1}{x}}{1-\dfrac{1}{x^2}}=\frac{\dfrac{x+1}{x}}{\dfrac{x^2-1}{x^2}}$$

$$=\frac{x+1}{x}\cdot\frac{x^2}{x^2-1}$$

$$=\frac{x+1}{x}\cdot\frac{x^2}{(x+1)(x-1)}$$

$$=\frac{x}{x-1}$$

350

19. $\dfrac{\dfrac{1}{7}-\dfrac{1}{y}}{\dfrac{7-y}{7}}$

LCD $= 7y$

$$\frac{\dfrac{1}{7}-\dfrac{1}{y}}{\dfrac{7-y}{7}} = \frac{7y\left(\dfrac{1}{7}-\dfrac{1}{y}\right)}{7y\left(\dfrac{7-y}{7}\right)}$$

$$= \frac{7y\left(\dfrac{1}{7}\right)-7y\left(\dfrac{1}{y}\right)}{7y\left(\dfrac{7-y}{7}\right)}$$

$$= \frac{y-7}{y(7-y)}$$

$$= \frac{-1(7-y)}{y(7-y)} = -\frac{1}{y}$$

21. $\dfrac{x+\dfrac{2}{y}}{\dfrac{x}{y}} = \dfrac{\dfrac{xy+2}{y}}{\dfrac{x}{y}} = \dfrac{xy+2}{y}\cdot\dfrac{y}{x} = \dfrac{xy+2}{x}$

23. $\dfrac{\dfrac{1}{x}+\dfrac{1}{y}}{xy}$

LCD $= xy$

$$\frac{\dfrac{1}{x}+\dfrac{1}{y}}{xy} = \frac{xy\left(\dfrac{1}{x}+\dfrac{1}{y}\right)}{xy(xy)} = \frac{y+x}{x^2y^2}$$

25. $\dfrac{\dfrac{x}{y}+\dfrac{1}{x}}{\dfrac{y}{x}+\dfrac{1}{x}} = \dfrac{\dfrac{x^2+y}{xy}}{\dfrac{y+1}{x}} = \dfrac{x^2+y}{xy}\cdot\dfrac{x}{y+1}$

$$= \frac{x^2+y}{y(y+1)}$$

27. $\dfrac{\dfrac{1}{y}+\dfrac{2}{y^2}}{\dfrac{2}{y}+1}$

LCD $= y^2$

$$\frac{\dfrac{1}{y}+\dfrac{2}{y^2}}{\dfrac{2}{y}+1} = \frac{y^2\left(\dfrac{1}{y}+\dfrac{2}{y^2}\right)}{y^2\left(\dfrac{2}{y}+1\right)}$$

$$= \frac{y^2\left(\dfrac{1}{y}\right)+y^2\left(\dfrac{2}{y^2}\right)}{y^2\left(\dfrac{2}{y}\right)+y^2(1)}$$

$$= \frac{y+2}{2y+y^2}$$

$$= \frac{(y+2)}{y(2+y)} = \frac{1}{y}$$

29. $\dfrac{\dfrac{12}{x^2}-\dfrac{3}{x}}{\dfrac{15}{x}-\dfrac{9}{x^2}} = \dfrac{\dfrac{12}{x^2}-\dfrac{3x}{x^2}}{\dfrac{15x}{x^2}-\dfrac{9}{x^2}} = \dfrac{\dfrac{12-3x}{x^2}}{\dfrac{15x-9}{x^2}}$

$$= \frac{12-3x}{x^2}\cdot\frac{x^2}{15x-9} = \frac{12-3x}{15x-9}$$

$$= \frac{3(4-x)}{3(5x-3)} = \frac{4-x}{5x-3}$$

351

STOP

31.

$$\dfrac{2+\dfrac{6}{y}}{1-\dfrac{9}{y^2}}$$

$$\text{LCD} = y^2$$

$$\dfrac{2+\dfrac{6}{y}}{1-\dfrac{9}{y^2}} = \dfrac{y^2\left(2+\dfrac{6}{y}\right)}{y^2\left(1-\dfrac{9}{y^2}\right)}$$

$$= \dfrac{2y^2+6y}{y^2-9}$$

$$= \dfrac{2y(y+3)}{(y+3)(y-3)} = \dfrac{2y}{y-3}$$

33.

$$\dfrac{\dfrac{1}{x+2}}{1+\dfrac{1}{x+2}}$$

$$\text{LCD} = x+2$$

$$\dfrac{\dfrac{1}{x+2}}{1+\dfrac{1}{x+2}} = \dfrac{(x+2)\left(\dfrac{1}{x+2}\right)}{(x+2)\left(1+\dfrac{1}{x+2}\right)}$$

$$= \dfrac{1}{x+2+1} = \dfrac{1}{x+3}$$

35.

$$\dfrac{x-5+\dfrac{3}{x}}{x-7+\dfrac{2}{x}}$$

$$\text{LCD} = x$$

$$\dfrac{x-5+\dfrac{3}{x}}{x-7+\dfrac{2}{x}} = \dfrac{x\left(x-5+\dfrac{3}{x}\right)}{x\left(x-7+\dfrac{2}{x}\right)}$$

$$= \dfrac{x^2-5x+3}{x^2-7x+2}$$

37.

$$\dfrac{\dfrac{3}{xy^2}+\dfrac{2}{x^2y}}{\dfrac{1}{x^2y}+\dfrac{2}{xy^3}} = \dfrac{\dfrac{3x}{x^2y^2}+\dfrac{2y}{x^2y^2}}{\dfrac{y^2}{x^2y^3}+\dfrac{2x}{x^2y^3}}$$

$$= \dfrac{\dfrac{3x+2y}{x^2y^2}}{\dfrac{y^2+2x}{x^2y^3}}$$

$$= \dfrac{3x+2y}{x^2y^2} \cdot \dfrac{x^2y^3}{y^2+2x}$$

$$= \dfrac{(3x+2y)(y)}{y^2+2x}$$

$$= \dfrac{3xy+2y^2}{y^2+2x}$$

39.

$$\dfrac{\dfrac{3}{x+1}-\dfrac{3}{x-1}}{\dfrac{5}{x^2-1}}$$

$$= \dfrac{\dfrac{3(x-1)-3(x+1)}{(x+1)(x-1)}}{\dfrac{5}{x^2-1}}$$

$$= \dfrac{\dfrac{3x-3-3x-3}{(x+1)(x-1)}}{\dfrac{5}{x^2-1}}$$

$$= \dfrac{\dfrac{-6}{(x+1)(x-1)}}{\dfrac{5}{x^2-1}}$$

$$= \dfrac{-6}{(x+1)(x-1)} \cdot \dfrac{x^2-1}{5}$$

$$= \dfrac{-6}{(x+1)(x-1)} \cdot \dfrac{(x+1)(x-1)}{5}$$

$$= -\dfrac{6}{5}$$

41.

$$\dfrac{\dfrac{6}{x^2+2x-15}-\dfrac{1}{x-3}}{\dfrac{1}{x+5}+1}$$

$$=\dfrac{\dfrac{6}{(x+5)(x-3)}-\dfrac{1}{x-3}}{\dfrac{1}{x+5}+1}$$

$$LCD=(x+5)(x-3)$$

$$\dfrac{\dfrac{6}{(x+5)(x-3)}-\dfrac{1}{x-3}}{\dfrac{1}{x+5}+1}$$

$$=\dfrac{(x+5)(x-3)\left[\dfrac{6}{(x+5)(x-3)}-\dfrac{1}{x-3}\right]}{(x+5)(x-3)\left[\dfrac{1}{x+5}+1\right]}$$

$$=\dfrac{6-(x+5)}{x-3+(x+5)(x-3)}$$

$$=\dfrac{6-x-5}{x-3+x^2+2x-15}$$

$$=\dfrac{-x+1}{x^2+3x-18}=\dfrac{1-x}{(x-3)(x+6)}$$

42.

$$\dfrac{\dfrac{1}{x-2}-\dfrac{6}{x^2+3x-10}}{1+\dfrac{1}{x-2}}$$

$$=\dfrac{\dfrac{1}{x-2}-\dfrac{6}{(x-2)(x+5)}}{1+\dfrac{1}{x-2}}$$

$$LCD=(x-2)(x+5)$$

$$\dfrac{\dfrac{1}{x-2}-\dfrac{6}{(x-2)(x+5)}}{1+\dfrac{1}{x-2}}$$

$$=\dfrac{(x-2)(x+5)\left[\dfrac{1}{x-2}-\dfrac{6}{(x-2)(x+5)}\right]}{(x-2)(x+5)\left[1+\dfrac{1}{x-2}\right]}$$

$$=\dfrac{x+5-6}{(x-2)(x+5)+x+5}$$

$$=\dfrac{x-1}{x^2+3x-10+x+5}$$

$$=\dfrac{x-1}{x^2+4x-5}=\dfrac{x-1}{(x-1)(x+5)}=\dfrac{1}{x+5}$$

43.

$$\dfrac{y^{-1}-(y+5)^{-1}}{5}=\dfrac{\dfrac{1}{y}-\dfrac{1}{y+5}}{5}$$

$$LCD=y(y+5)$$

$$\dfrac{\dfrac{1}{y}-\dfrac{1}{y+5}}{5}=\dfrac{y(y+5)\left(\dfrac{1}{y}-\dfrac{1}{y+5}\right)}{y(y+5)(5)}$$

$$=\dfrac{y+5-y}{5y(y+5)}=\dfrac{5}{5y(y+5)}=\dfrac{1}{y(y+5)}$$

44.

$$\dfrac{y^{-1}-(y+2)^{-1}}{2}=\dfrac{\dfrac{1}{y}-\dfrac{1}{y+2}}{2}$$

$$LCD=y(y+2)$$

$$\dfrac{\dfrac{1}{y}-\dfrac{1}{y+2}}{2}=\dfrac{y(y+2)\left(\dfrac{1}{y}-\dfrac{1}{y+2}\right)}{y(y+2)(2)}$$

$$=\dfrac{y+2-y}{2y(y+2)}=\dfrac{2}{2y(y+2)}=\dfrac{1}{y(y+2)}$$

45.

$$\frac{1}{1-\frac{1}{x}}-1 = \frac{x(1)}{x\left(1-\frac{1}{x}\right)}-1 = \frac{x}{x-1}-1$$

$$= \frac{x}{x-1}-\frac{x-1}{x-1} = \frac{x-x+1}{x-1} = \frac{1}{x-1}$$

46.

$$\frac{1}{1-\frac{1}{x+1}}-1 = \frac{(x+1)(1)}{(x+1)\left(1-\frac{1}{x+1}\right)}-1$$

$$= \frac{x+1}{x+1-1}-1 = \frac{x+1}{x}-1 = \frac{x+1}{x}-\frac{x}{x}$$

$$= \frac{x+1-x}{x} = \frac{1}{x}$$

47.

$$\frac{1}{1+\frac{1}{1+\frac{1}{x}}} = \frac{1}{1+\frac{x(1)}{x\left(1+\frac{1}{x}\right)}} = \frac{1}{1+\frac{x}{x+1}}$$

$$= \frac{(x+1)(1)}{(x+1)\left(1+\frac{x}{x+1}\right)} = \frac{x+1}{x+1+x} = \frac{x+1}{2x+1}$$

48.

$$\frac{1}{1+\frac{1}{1+\frac{1}{2}}} = \frac{1}{1+\frac{(2)1}{(2)\left(1+\frac{1}{2}\right)}} = \frac{1}{1+\frac{2}{2+1}}$$

$$= \frac{1}{1+\frac{2}{3}} = \frac{1}{\frac{3}{3}+\frac{2}{3}} = \frac{1}{\frac{5}{3}} = 1\cdot\frac{3}{5} = \frac{3}{5}$$

49.

$$\frac{2d}{\frac{d}{r_1}+\frac{d}{r_2}}$$

LCD = $r_1 r_2$

$$\frac{2d}{\frac{d}{r_1}+\frac{d}{r_2}} = \frac{r_1 r_2(2d)}{r_1 r_2\left(\frac{d}{r_1}+\frac{d}{r_2}\right)}$$

$$= \frac{2r_1 r_2 d}{r_2 d + r_1 d}$$

$$= \frac{2r_1 r_2 d}{d(r_2+r_1)} = \frac{2r_1 r_2}{r_2+r_1}$$

If $r_1 = 40$ and $r_2 = 30$, the value
of this expression will be

$$\frac{2\cdot 40\cdot 30}{30+40} = \frac{2400}{70}$$

$$= 34\frac{2}{7}.$$

Your average speed will be $34\frac{2}{7}$

miles per hour.

51. – 53. Answers will vary.

55. Simplify the given complex fraction
LCD = x^5

$$\frac{x^6}{x^6}\cdot\frac{\left(\frac{1}{x}+\frac{1}{x^2}+\frac{1}{x^4}\right)}{\left(\frac{1}{x^4}+\frac{1}{x^5}+\frac{1}{x^6}\right)}$$

$$= \frac{\frac{x^6}{x}+\frac{x^6}{x^2}+\frac{x^6}{x^3}}{\frac{x^6}{x^4}+\frac{x^6}{x^5}+\frac{x^6}{x^6}}$$

$$= \frac{x^5+x^4+x^3}{x^2+x+1}$$

$$= \frac{x^3\left(x^2+x+1\right)}{x^2+x+1}$$

$$= x^3$$

Because the rational expression can
be simplified to x^3, this is what it
does to each number x; it cubes x.

57.

$$\frac{1+\dfrac{1}{y}-\dfrac{6}{y^2}}{1-\dfrac{5}{y}+\dfrac{6}{y^2}}-\frac{1-\dfrac{1}{y}}{1-\dfrac{2}{y}-\dfrac{3}{y^2}}$$

Simplify the first complex rational expression using the LCD method.

$$\frac{y^2}{y^2}\cdot\frac{\left(1+\dfrac{1}{y}-\dfrac{6}{y^2}\right)}{\left(1-\dfrac{5}{y}+\dfrac{6}{y^2}\right)}=\frac{y^2+y-6}{y^2-5y+6}$$

Simplify the second complex algebraic expression by the LCD method.

$$\frac{y^2}{y^2}\cdot\frac{\left(1-\dfrac{1}{y}\right)}{\left(1-\dfrac{2}{y}-\dfrac{3}{y^2}\right)}=\frac{y^2-y}{y^2-2y-3}$$

Now subtract.

$$\frac{y^2+y-6}{y^2-5y+6}-\frac{y^2-y}{y^2-2y-3}$$

$$=\frac{y^2+y-6}{(y-2)(y-3)}-\frac{y^2-y}{(y-3)(y+1)}$$

$$=\frac{(y-2)(y+3)}{(y-2)(y-3)}-\frac{y^2-y}{(y-3)(y+1)}$$

$$=\frac{y+3}{y-3}-\frac{y^2-y}{(y-3)(y+1)}$$

$$=\frac{(y+3)(y+1)}{(y-3)(y+1)}-\frac{y^2-y}{(y-3)(y+1)}$$

$$=\frac{(y+3)(y+1)-(y^2-y)}{(y-3)(y+1)}$$

$$=\frac{(y^2+4y+3)-(y^2-y)}{(y-3)(y+1)}$$

$$=\frac{y^2+4y+3-y^2+y}{(y-3)(y+1)}$$

$$=\frac{5y+3}{(y-3)(y+1)}$$

59.

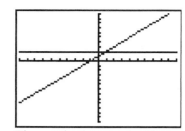

The graphs do not coincide.

$$\frac{\dfrac{1}{x}+1}{\dfrac{1}{x}}=\frac{\dfrac{1}{x}+\dfrac{x}{x}}{\dfrac{1}{x}}=\frac{\dfrac{1+x}{x}}{\dfrac{1}{x}}$$

$$=\frac{1+x}{x}\cdot\frac{x}{1}=1+x$$

Change the expression on the right to $1+x$.

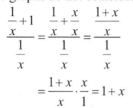

Now the graphs coincide.

61.

$$2x^3-20x^2+50x=2x\left(x^2-10x+25\right)$$
$$=2x(x-5)^2$$

62.

$$2-3(x-2)=5(x+5)-1$$
$$2-3x+6=5x+25-1$$
$$8-3x=5x+24$$
$$8-3x-5x=5x+24-5x$$
$$8-8x=24$$
$$8-8x-8=24-8$$
$$-8x=16$$
$$\frac{-8x}{-8}=\frac{16}{-8}$$
$$x=-2$$

The solution set is $\{-2\}$.

355

63. $(x+y)(x^2 - xy + y^2)$

$$= x(x^2 - xy + y^2) + y(x^2 - xy + y^2)$$
$$= x^3 - x^2 y + xy^2 + x^2 y - xy^2 + y^3$$
$$= x^3 + y^3$$

$$18 \cdot \frac{4x}{3} = 18 \cdot \frac{x}{18} - 18 \cdot \frac{x}{6}$$
$$24x = x - 3x$$
$$24x = -2x$$
$$26x = 0$$
$$x = 0$$

The solution set is $\{0\}$.

7.6 Exercise Set

In Exercises 1-43, all proposed solutions that are on the list of restrictions on the variable should be rejected and all other proposed solutions should be checked in the original equation. Checks will not be shown here.

1. $\dfrac{x}{3} = \dfrac{x}{2} - 2$

There are no restrictions on the variable because the variable does not appear in any denominator.
The LCD is 6.

$$\frac{x}{3} = \frac{x}{2} - 2$$
$$6\left(\frac{x}{3}\right) = 6\left(\frac{x}{2} - 2\right)$$
$$6 \cdot \frac{x}{3} = 6 \cdot \frac{x}{2} - 6 \cdot 2$$
$$2x = 3x - 12$$
$$0 = x - 12$$
$$12 = x$$

The solution set is $\{12\}$.

3. $\dfrac{4x}{3} = \dfrac{x}{18} - \dfrac{x}{6}$

There are no restrictions.
The LCD is 18.

$$\frac{4x}{3} = \frac{x}{18} - \frac{x}{6}$$
$$18\left(\frac{4x}{3}\right) = 18\left(\frac{x}{18} - \frac{x}{6}\right)$$

5. $2 - \dfrac{8}{x} = 6$

The restriction is $x \neq 0$.
The LCD is x.

$$2 - \frac{8}{x} = 6$$
$$x\left(2 - \frac{8}{x}\right) = x \cdot 6$$
$$x \cdot 2 - x \cdot \frac{8}{x} = x \cdot 6$$
$$2x - 8 = 6x$$
$$-8 = 4x$$
$$-2 = x$$

The solution set is $\{-2\}$.

7. $\dfrac{2}{x} + \dfrac{1}{3} = \dfrac{4}{x}$

The restriction is $x \neq 0$.
The LCD is $3x$.

$$\frac{2}{x} + \frac{1}{3} = \frac{4}{x}$$
$$3x\left(\frac{2}{x} + \frac{1}{3}\right) = 3x\left(\frac{4}{x}\right)$$
$$3x \cdot \frac{2}{x} + 3x \cdot \frac{1}{3} = 3x \cdot \frac{4}{x}$$
$$6 + x = 12$$
$$x = 6$$

The solution set is $\{6\}$.

9.

$$\frac{2}{x} + 3 = \frac{5}{2x} + \frac{13}{4}$$

The restriction is $x \neq 0$

The LCD is $4x$.

$$\frac{2}{x} + 3 = \frac{5}{2x} + \frac{13}{4}$$

$$4x\left(\frac{2}{x} + 3\right) = 4x\left(\frac{5}{2x} + \frac{13}{4}\right)$$

$$8 + 12x = 10 + 13x$$

$$8 = 10 + x$$

$$-2 = x$$

The solution set is $\{-2\}$.

11.

$$\frac{2}{3x} + \frac{1}{4} = \frac{11}{6x} - \frac{1}{3}$$

The restriction is $x \neq 0$.

The LCD is $12x$.

$$\frac{2}{3x} + \frac{1}{4} = \frac{11}{6x} - \frac{1}{3}$$

$$12x\left(\frac{2}{3x} + \frac{1}{4}\right) = 12x\left(\frac{11}{6x} - \frac{1}{3}\right)$$

$$8 + 3x = 22 - 4x$$

$$8 + 7x = 22$$

$$7x = 14$$

$$x = 2$$

The solution set is $\{2\}$.

13.

$$\frac{6}{x+3} = \frac{4}{x-3}$$

Restrictions: $x \neq -3, x \neq 3$

LCD $= (x+3)(x-3)$

$$\frac{6}{x+3} = \frac{4}{x-3}$$

$$(x+3)(x-3)\cdot\frac{6}{x+3} = (x+3)(x-3)\cdot\frac{4}{x-3}$$

$$(x-3)\cdot 6 = (x+3)\cdot 4$$

$$6x - 18 = 4x + 12$$

$$2x - 18 = 12$$

$$2x = 30$$

$$x = 15$$

The solution set is $\{15\}$.

15.

$$\frac{x-2}{2x} + 1 = \frac{x+1}{x}$$

Restriction: $x \neq 0$

LCD $= 2x$.

$$\frac{x-2}{2x} + 1 = \frac{x+1}{x}$$

$$2x\left(\frac{x-2}{2x} + 1\right) = 2x\left(\frac{x+1}{x}\right)$$

$$x - 2 + 2x = 2(x+1)$$

$$3x - 2 = 2x + 2$$

$$x - 2 = 2$$

$$x = 4$$

The solution set is $\{4\}$.

17.

$$x + \frac{6}{x} = -7$$

Restriction: $x \neq 0$

LCD $= x$

$$x + \frac{6}{x} = -7$$

$$x\left(x + \frac{6}{x}\right) = x(-7)$$

$$x^2 + 6 = -7x$$

$$x^2 + 7x + 6 = 0$$

$$(x+6)(x+1) = 0$$

$$x + 6 = 0 \quad \text{or} \quad x + 1 = 0$$

$$x = -6 \qquad\qquad x = -1$$

The solution set is $\{-6, -1\}$.

357

19. $\dfrac{x}{5} - \dfrac{5}{x} = 0$

Restriction: $x \neq 0$

LCD $= 5x$

$$\dfrac{x}{5} - \dfrac{5}{x} = 0$$

$$5x\left(\dfrac{x}{5} - \dfrac{5}{x}\right) = 5x \cdot 0$$

$$5x \cdot \dfrac{x}{5} - 5x \cdot \dfrac{5}{x} = 0$$

$$x^2 - 25 = 0$$

$$(x+5)(x-5) = 0$$

$$x+5 = 0 \quad \text{or} \quad x-5 = 0$$

$$x = -5 \qquad\qquad x = 5$$

The solution set is $\{-5, 5\}$.

21. $x + \dfrac{3}{x} = \dfrac{12}{x}$

Restriction: $x \neq 0$

LCD $= x$

$$x + \dfrac{3}{x} = \dfrac{12}{x}$$

$$x\left(x + \dfrac{3}{x}\right) = x\left(\dfrac{12}{x}\right)$$

$$x^2 + 3 = 12$$

$$x^2 - 9 = 0$$

$$(x+3)(x-3) = 0$$

$$x+3 = 0 \quad \text{or} \quad x-3 = 0$$

$$x = -3 \qquad\qquad x = 3$$

The solution set is $\{-3, 3\}$.

23. $\dfrac{4}{y} - \dfrac{y}{2} = \dfrac{7}{2}$

Restrictions: $y \neq 0$

LCD $= 2y$

$$2y\left(\dfrac{4}{y} - \dfrac{y}{2}\right) = 2y\left(\dfrac{7}{2}\right)$$

$$8 - y^2 = 7y$$

$$0 = y^2 + 7y - 8$$

$$0 = (y+8)(y-1)$$

$$y+8 = 0 \quad \text{or} \quad y-1 = 0$$

$$y = -8 \qquad\qquad y = 1$$

The solution set is $\{-8, 1\}$.

25. $\dfrac{x-4}{x} = \dfrac{15}{x+4}$

Restrictions: $x \neq 0, x \neq -4$

LCD $= x(x+4)$

$$\dfrac{x-4}{x} = \dfrac{15}{x+4}$$

$$x(x+4)\left(\dfrac{x-4}{x}\right) = x(x+4)\left(\dfrac{15}{x+4}\right)$$

$$(x+4)(x-4) = x \cdot 15$$

$$x^2 - 16 = 15x$$

$$x^2 - 15x - 16 = 0$$

$$(x+1)(x-16) = 0$$

$$x+1 = 0 \quad \text{or} \quad x-16 = 0$$

$$x = -1 \qquad\qquad x = 16$$

The solution set is $\{-1, 16\}$.

27. $\dfrac{1}{x-1} + 5 = \dfrac{11}{x-1}$

Restriction: $x \neq 1$

LCD $= x-1$

$$\dfrac{1}{x-1} + 5 = \dfrac{11}{x-1}$$

$$(x-1)\left(\dfrac{1}{x-1} + 5\right) = (x-1)\left(\dfrac{11}{x-1}\right)$$

$$1 + (x-1) \cdot 5 = 11$$

$$1 + 5x - 5 = 11$$

$$5x - 4 = 11$$

$$5x = 15$$

$$x = 3$$

The solution set is $\{3\}$.

358

29. $\dfrac{8y}{y+1} = 4 - \dfrac{8}{y+1}$

Restriction: $y \neq -1$

LCD $= y+1$

$$\dfrac{8y}{y+1} = 4 - \dfrac{8}{y+1}$$

$$(y+1)\left(\dfrac{8y}{y+1}\right) = (y+1)\left(4 - \dfrac{8}{y+1}\right)$$

$$8y = (y+1)\cdot 4 - 8$$

$$8y = 4y + 4 - 8$$

$$8y = 4y - 4$$

$$4y = -4$$

$$y = -1$$

The proposed solution, -1, is *not* a solution because of the restriction $x \neq -1$. Notice that -1 makes two of the denominators zero in the original equation. Therefore, the equation has no solution, and the solution set is $\varnothing$.

31. $\dfrac{3}{x-1} + \dfrac{8}{x} = 3$

Restrictions: $x \neq 1, x \neq 0$

LCD $= x(x-1)$

$$\dfrac{3}{x-1} + \dfrac{8}{x} = 3$$

$$x(x-1)\left(\dfrac{3}{x-1} + \dfrac{8}{x}\right) = x(x-1)\cdot 3$$

$$x(x-1)\left(\dfrac{3}{x-1} + \dfrac{8}{x}\right) = 3x(x-1)$$

$$3x + 8(x-1) = 3x^2 - 3x$$

$$3x + 8x - 8 = 3x^2 - 3x$$

$$11x - 8 = 3x^2 - 3x$$

$$0 = 3x^2 - 14x + 8$$

$$0 = (3x-2)(x-4)$$

$3x - 2 = 0 \quad$ or $x - 4 = 0$

$\quad 3x = 2 \qquad\qquad x = 4$

$$x = \dfrac{2}{3}$$

The solution set is $\left\{\dfrac{2}{3},\ 4\right\}$.

33. $\dfrac{3y}{y-4} - 5 = \dfrac{12}{y-4}$

Restriction: $y \neq 4$

LCD $= y-4$

$$\dfrac{3y}{y-4} - 5 = \dfrac{12}{y-4}$$

$$(y-4)\left(\dfrac{3y}{y-4} - 5\right) = (y-4)\left(\dfrac{12}{y-4}\right)$$

$$3y - 5(y-4) = 12$$

$$3y - 5y + 20 = 12$$

$$-2y + 20 = 12$$

$$-2y = -8$$

$$y = 4$$

The proposed solution, 4, is *not* a solution because of the restriction $y \neq 4$. Therefore, this equation has no solution, and the solution set is $\varnothing$.

35. $\dfrac{1}{x} + \dfrac{1}{x-3} = \dfrac{x-2}{x-3}$

Restrictions: $x \neq 0, x \neq 3$

LCD $= x(x-3)$

$$\dfrac{1}{x} + \dfrac{1}{x-3} = \dfrac{x-2}{x-3}$$

$$x(x-3)\left(\dfrac{1}{x} + \dfrac{1}{x-3}\right) = x(x-3)\cdot\dfrac{x-2}{x-3}$$

$$x-3+x = x(x-2)$$

$$2x - 3 = x^2 - 2x$$

$$0 = x^2 - 4x + 3$$

$$0 = (x-3)(x-1)$$

$x - 3 = 0$ or $x - 1 = 0$

$x = 3 \qquad x = 1$

The proposed solution 3 is *not* a solution because of the restriction $x \ne 3$.
The proposed solution 1 checks in the original equation.
The solution set is $\{1\}$.

37. $\dfrac{x+1}{3x+9} + \dfrac{x}{2x+6} = \dfrac{2}{4x+12}$

To find any restrictions and the LCD, factor the denominators.

$\dfrac{x+1}{3(x+3)} + \dfrac{x}{2(x+3)} = \dfrac{2}{4(x+3)}$

Restriction: $x \ne -3$

LCD $= 12(x+3)$

$12(x+3)\left[\dfrac{x+1}{3(x+3)} + \dfrac{x}{2(x+3)}\right]$

$\qquad = 12(x+3)\left[\dfrac{2}{4(x+3)}\right]$

$4(x+1) + 6x = 6$

$4x + 4 + 6x = 6$

$10x + 4 = 6$

$10x = 2$

$x = \dfrac{2}{10} = \dfrac{1}{5}$

The solution set is $\left\{\dfrac{1}{5}\right\}$.

39. $\dfrac{4y}{y^2 - 25} + \dfrac{2}{y-5} = \dfrac{1}{y+5}$

To find any restrictions and the LCD, factor the first denominator.

$\dfrac{4y}{(y+5)(y-5)} + \dfrac{2}{y-5} = \dfrac{1}{y+5}$

Restrictions: $y \ne -5, y \ne 5$

LCD $= (y+5)(y-5)$

$(y+5)(y-5)\left[\dfrac{4y}{(y+5)(y-5)} + \dfrac{2}{y-5}\right]$

$\qquad = (y+5)(y-5) \cdot \dfrac{1}{y+5}$

$4y + 2(y+5) = y - 5$

$4y + 2y + 10 = y - 5$

$6y + 10 = y - 5$

$5y + 10 = -5$

$5y = -15$

$y = -3$

The solution set is $\{-3\}$.

41. $\dfrac{1}{x-4} - \dfrac{5}{x+2} = \dfrac{6}{x^2 - 2x - 8}$

Factor the last denominator.

$\dfrac{1}{x-4} - \dfrac{5}{x+2} = \dfrac{6}{(x-4)(x+2)}$

Restrictions: $x \ne 4, x \ne -2$

LCD $= (x-4)(x+2)$

$(x-4)(x+2)\left[\dfrac{1}{x-4} - \dfrac{5}{x+2}\right]$

$\qquad = (x-4)(x+2)\left[\dfrac{6}{(x-4)(x+2)}\right]$

$(x+2) \cdot 1 - (x-4) \cdot 5 = 6$

$x + 2 - 5x + 20 = 6$

$-4x + 22 = 6$

$-4x = -16$

$x = 4$

The proposed solution 4 is *not* a solution because of the restriction $x \ne 4$. Therefore, the given equation has no solution, and the solution set is $\varnothing$.

43. $\dfrac{2}{x+3} - \dfrac{2x+3}{x-1} = \dfrac{6x-5}{x^2+2x-3}$

Factor the last denominator.

$\dfrac{2}{x+3} - \dfrac{2x+3}{x-1} = \dfrac{6x-5}{(x+3)(x-1)}$

Restrictions: $x \neq -3, x \neq 1$

LCD $= (x+3)(x-1)$

$(x+3)(x-1)\left[\dfrac{2}{x+3} - \dfrac{2x+3}{x-1}\right]$

$\qquad = (x+3)(x-1)\left[\dfrac{6x-5}{(x+3)(x-1)}\right]$

$(x-1)\cdot 2 - (x+3)(2x+3) = 6x-5$

$2x - 2 - \left(2x^2 + 9x + 9\right) = 6x-5$

$2x - 2 - 2x^2 - 9x - 9 = 6x-5$

$-2x^2 - 7x - 11 = 6x-5$

$0 = 2x^2 + 13x + 6$

$0 = (x+6)(2x+1)$

$x+6 = 0 \quad \text{or} \quad 2x+1 = 0$

$x = -6 \qquad\qquad 2x = -1$

$\qquad\qquad\qquad x = -\dfrac{1}{2}$

The solution set is $\left\{-6, -\dfrac{1}{2}\right\}$.

45. $\dfrac{V_1}{V_2} = \dfrac{P_2}{P_1}$

$P_1V_2\left(\dfrac{V_1}{V_2}\right) = P_1V_2\left(\dfrac{P_2}{P_1}\right)$

$P_1(V_1) = V_2(P_2)$

$P_1V_1 = P_2V_2$

$\dfrac{P_1V_1}{V_1} = \dfrac{P_2V_2}{V_1}$

$P_1 = \dfrac{P_2V_2}{V_1}$

47. $\dfrac{1}{p} + \dfrac{1}{q} = \dfrac{1}{f}$

$fpq\left(\dfrac{1}{p} + \dfrac{1}{q}\right) = fpq\left(\dfrac{1}{f}\right)$

$fpq\left(\dfrac{1}{p}\right) + fpq\left(\dfrac{1}{q}\right) = pq$

$fq + fp = pq$

$f(q+p) = pq$

$\dfrac{f(q+p)}{q+p} = \dfrac{pq}{q+p}$

$f = \dfrac{pq}{q+p}$

49. $P = \dfrac{A}{1+r}$

$(1+r)(P) = (1+r)\left(\dfrac{A}{1+r}\right)$

$P + Pr = A$

$Pr = A - P$

$\dfrac{Pr}{P} = \dfrac{A-P}{P}$

$r = \dfrac{A-P}{P}$

51. $F = \dfrac{Gm_1m_2}{d^2}$

$d^2(F) = d^2\left(\dfrac{Gm_1m_2}{d^2}\right)$

$d^2F = Gm_1m_2$

$\dfrac{d^2F}{Gm_2} = \dfrac{Gm_1m_2}{Gm_2}$

$m_1 = \dfrac{d^2F}{Gm_2}$

53.

$$z = \frac{x - \overline{x}}{s}$$

$$s(z) = s\left(\frac{x - \overline{x}}{s}\right)$$

$$zs = x - \overline{x}$$

$$x = \overline{x} + zs$$

55.

$$I = \frac{E}{R + r}$$

$$(R + r)(I) = (R + r)\left(\frac{E}{R + r}\right)$$

$$IR + Ir = E$$

$$IR = E - Ir$$

$$\frac{IR}{I} = \frac{E - Ir}{I}$$

$$R = \frac{E - Ir}{I}$$

57.

$$f = \frac{f_1 f_2}{f_1 + f_2}$$

$$(f_1 + f_2)(f) = (f_1 + f_2)\left(\frac{f_1 f_2}{f_1 + f_2}\right)$$

$$ff_1 + ff_2 = f_1 f_2$$

$$ff_1 = f_1 f_2 - ff_2$$

$$ff_1 + ff_2 = f_1 f_2$$

$$ff_2 = f_1 f_2 - ff_1$$

$$ff_2 = f_1(f_2 - f)$$

$$\frac{ff_2}{f_2 - f} = \frac{f_1(f_2 - f)}{f_2 - f}$$

$$f_1 = \frac{ff_2}{f_2 - f}$$

59.

$$\frac{x^2 - 10}{x^2 - x - 20} = 1 + \frac{7}{x - 5}$$

Factor the first denominator.

$$\frac{x^2 - 10}{(x - 5)(x + 4)} = 1 + \frac{7}{x - 5}$$

Restrictions: $x \neq 5, x \neq -4$

LCD $= (x - 5)(x + 4)$

$$(x - 5)(x + 4)\left(\frac{x^2 - 10}{(x - 5)(x + 4)}\right)$$

$$= (x - 5)(x + 4) \cdot 1 + (x - 5)(x + 4)\left(\frac{7}{x - 5}\right)$$

$$x^2 - 10 = (x - 5)(x + 4) + (x + 4) \cdot 7$$

$$x^2 - 10 = x^2 - x - 20 + 7x + 28$$

$$x^2 - 10 = x^2 + 6x + 8$$

$$-10 = 6x + 8$$

$$-18 = 6x$$

$$-3 = x$$

The solution set is $\{-3\}$.

60.

$$\frac{x^2 + 4x - 2}{x^2 - 2x - 8} = 1 + \frac{4}{x - 4}$$

Factor the first denominator.

$$\frac{x^2 + 4x - 2}{(x - 4)(x + 2)} = 1 + \frac{4}{x - 4}$$

Restrictions: $x \neq 4, x \neq -2$

LCD $= (x - 4)(x + 2)$

$$(x - 4)(x + 2)\left(\frac{x^2 + 4x - 2}{x^2 - 2x - 8}\right)$$

$$= (x - 4)(x + 2) \cdot 1 + (x - 4)(x + 2)\left(\frac{4}{x - 4}\right)$$

$$x^2 + 4x - 2 = x^2 - 2x - 8 + (x + 2) \cdot 4$$

$$x^2 + 4x - 2 = x^2 - 2x - 8 + 4x + 8$$

$$x^2 + 4x - 2 = x^2 + 2x$$

$$4x - 2 = 2x$$

$$2x = 2$$

$$x = 1$$

The solution set is $\{1\}$.

362

61. $\dfrac{x^2-10}{x^2-x-20}-1-\dfrac{7}{x-5}$

Factor the first denominator.

$\dfrac{x^2-10}{(x-5)(x+4)}-1-\dfrac{7}{x-5}$

LCD $=(x-5)(x+4)$

$\dfrac{x^2-10}{(x-5)(x+4)}-\dfrac{(x-5)(x+4)}{(x-5)(x+4)}$

$\qquad\qquad\qquad -\dfrac{7(x+4)}{(x-5)(x+4)}$

$\dfrac{x^2-10-(x-5)(x+4)-7(x+4)}{(x-5)(x+4)}$

$=\dfrac{x^2-10-(x^2-x-20)-7x-28}{(x-5)(x+4)}$

$=\dfrac{x^2-10-x^2+x+20-7x-28}{(x-5)(x+4)}$

$=\dfrac{-6x-8}{(x-5)(x+4)}$

62. $\dfrac{x^2+4x-2}{x^2-2x-8}-1-\dfrac{4}{x-4}$

Factor the first denominator.

$\dfrac{x^2+4x-2}{(x-4)(x+2)}-1-\dfrac{4}{x-4}$

LCD $=(x-4)(x+2)$

$\dfrac{x^2+4x-2}{(x-4)(x+2)}-\dfrac{(x-4)(x+2)}{(x-4)(x+2)}$

$\qquad\qquad\qquad -\dfrac{4(x+2)}{(x-4)(x+2)}$

$\dfrac{x^2+4x-2-(x-4)(x+2)-4(x+2)}{(x-4)(x+2)}$

$=\dfrac{x^2+4x-2-(x^2-2x-8)-4x-8}{(x-4)(x+2)}$

$=\dfrac{x^2+4x-2-x^2+2x+8-4x-8}{(x-4)(x+2)}$

$=\dfrac{2x-2}{(x-4)(x+2)}$

63. $5y^{-2}+1=6y^{-1}$

$\dfrac{5}{y^2}+1=\dfrac{6}{y}$

Restrictions: $y\neq 0$; LCD $=y^2$

$y^2\left(\dfrac{5}{y^2}+1\right)=y^2\left(\dfrac{6}{y}\right)$

$y^2\cdot\dfrac{5}{y^2}+y^2\cdot 1=6y$

$5+y^2=6y$

$y^2-6y+5=0$

$(y-5)(y-1)=0$

$y-5=0\quad$ or $\quad y-1=0$

$y=5\qquad\qquad y=1$

The solution set is $\{1,5\}$.

64. $3y^{-2}+1=4y^{-1}$

$\dfrac{3}{y^2}+1=\dfrac{4}{y}$

Restrictions: $y\neq 0$; LCD $=y^2$

$y^2\left(\dfrac{3}{y^2}+1\right)=y^2\left(\dfrac{4}{y}\right)$

$y^2\cdot\dfrac{3}{y^2}+y^2\cdot 1=4y$

$3+y^2=4y$

$y^2-4y+3=0$

$(y-3)(y-1)=0$

$y-3=0\quad$ or $\quad y-1=0$

$y=3\qquad\qquad y=1$

The solution set is $\{1,3\}$.

65.

$$\frac{3}{y+1} - \frac{1}{1-y} = \frac{10}{y^2 - 1}$$

Factor the denominators.

$$\frac{3}{y+1} - \frac{(-1) \cdot 1}{(-1)(1-y)} = \frac{10}{(y+1)(y-1)}$$

$$\frac{3}{y+1} - \frac{-1}{y-1} = \frac{10}{(y+1)(y-1)}$$

$$\frac{3}{y+1} + \frac{1}{y-1} = \frac{10}{(y+1)(y-1)}$$

Restrictions: $y \neq -1, y \neq 1$

LCD $= (y+1)(y-1)$

$$(y+1)(y-1)\left(\frac{3}{y+1} + \frac{1}{y-1}\right)$$

$$= (y+1)(y-1)\left(\frac{10}{(y+1)(y-1)}\right)$$

$$(y-1) \cdot 3 + (y+1) \cdot 1 = 10$$

$$3y - 3 + y + 1 = 10$$

$$4y - 2 = 10$$

$$4y = 12$$

$$y = 3$$

The solution set is $\{3\}$.

66.

$$\frac{4}{y-2} - \frac{1}{2-y} = \frac{25}{y+6}$$

$$\frac{4}{y-2} + \frac{1}{y-2} = \frac{25}{y+6}$$

Restrictions: $y \neq 2, y \neq -6$

LCD $= (y-2)(y+6)$

$$(y-2)(y+6)\left(\frac{4}{y-2} + \frac{1}{y-2}\right)$$

$$= (y-2)(y+6)\left(\frac{25}{y+6}\right)$$

$$(y+6) \cdot 4 + (y+6) \cdot 1 = (y-2) \cdot 25$$

$$4y + 24 + y + 6 = 25y - 50$$

$$5y + 30 = 25y - 50$$

$$80 = 20y$$

$$4 = y$$

The solution set is $\{4\}$.

67.

$$C = \frac{400x + 500,000}{x}; C = 450$$

$$450 = \frac{400x + 500,000}{x}$$

LCD $= x$

$$x \cdot 450 = x\left(\frac{400x + 500,000}{x}\right)$$

$$450x = 400x + 500,000$$

$$50x = 500,000$$

$$x = 10,000$$

At an average cost of $450 per wheelchair, 10,000 wheelchairs can be produced.

69.

$$C = \frac{2x}{100 - x}; C = 2$$

$$2 = \frac{2x}{100 - x}$$

LCD $= 100 - x$

$$(100 - x) \cdot 2 = (100 - x) \cdot \frac{2x}{100 - x}$$

$$200 - 2x = 2x$$

$$200 = 4x$$

$$50 = x$$

For $2 million, 50% of the contaminants can be removed.

71.
$$C = \frac{DA}{A+12}; C = 300, D = 1000$$

$$300 = \frac{1000A}{A+12}$$

LCD $= A+12$

$$(A+12) \cdot 300 = (A+12)\left(\frac{1000A}{A+12}\right)$$

$$300A + 3600 = 1000A$$

$$3600 = 700A$$

$$\frac{3600}{700} = A$$

$$A = \frac{36}{7} \approx 5.14$$

To the nearest year, the child is 5 years old.

73.
$$C = \frac{10,000}{x} + 3x; C = 350$$

$$350 = \frac{10,000}{x} + 3x$$

LCD $= x$

$$x \cdot 350 = x\left(\frac{10,000}{x} + 3x\right)$$

$$350x = 10,000 + 3x^2$$

$$0 = 3x^2 - 350x + 10,000$$

$$0 = (3x - 200)(x - 50)$$

$$3x - 200 = 0 \quad \text{or} \quad x - 50 = 0$$

$$3x = 200 \qquad\qquad x = 50$$

$$x = \frac{200}{3}$$

$$= 66\frac{2}{3} \approx 67$$

For yearly inventory costs to be $350, the owner should order either 50 or approximately 67 cases. These solutions correspond to the points $(50, 350)$ and $\left(66\frac{2}{3}, 350\right)$ on the graph.

75. Let x = the number of additional hits needed.

After x additional consecutive hits, the player's batting average will be

$$\frac{12+x}{40+x}$$

so solve the equation

$$\frac{12+x}{40+x} = 0.440.$$

Multiply both sides by the LCD, $40 + x$.

$$(40+x)\left(\frac{12+x}{40+x}\right) = (40+x)(0.440)$$

$$12 + x = 17.6 + 0.44x$$

$$12 + x - 12 = 17.6 + 0.44x - 12$$

$$x = 5.6 + 0.44x$$

$$x - 0.44x = 5.6 + 0.44x - 0.44x$$

$$0.56x = 5.6$$

$$\frac{0.56x}{0.56} = \frac{5.6}{0.56}$$

$$x = 10$$

The player must get 10 additional consecutive hits to achieve a batting average of 0.440.

79. – 81. Answers will vary.

83. Statement **b** is true.

$$\frac{a}{x} + 1 = \frac{a}{x}$$

$$x\left(\frac{a}{x} + 1\right) = x\left(\frac{a}{x}\right)$$

$$a + x = a$$

$$x = 0$$

The proposed solution is a restricted value for x, so the given equation has no solution.

85.

$$\left(\frac{x+1}{x+7}\right)^2 \div \left(\frac{x+1}{x+7}\right)^4 = 0$$

$$\left(\frac{x+1}{x+7}\right)^2 \cdot \left(\frac{x+7}{x+1}\right)^4 = 0$$

$$\frac{(x+1)^2}{(x+7)^2} \cdot \frac{(x+7)^4}{(x+1)^4} = 0$$

Restrictions: $x \neq -7, x \neq -1$

$$\frac{(x+7)^2}{(x+1)^2} = 0$$

Multiply both sides by $(x+1)^2$.

$$(x+1)^2 \left[\frac{(x+7)^2}{(x+1)^2}\right] = (x+1)^2 \cdot 0$$

$$(x+7)^2 = 0$$

$$x + 7 = 0$$

$$x = -7$$

The proposed solution, -7, is *not* a solution of the original equation because it is on the list of restrictions. Therefore, the given equation has no solution, and the solution set is $\varnothing$.

87. $\dfrac{x}{2} + \dfrac{x}{4} = 6$

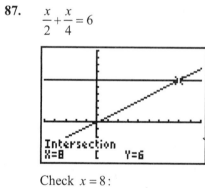

Check $x = 8$:

$$\frac{8}{2} + \frac{8}{4} = 6$$

$$4 + 2 = 6$$

$$6 = 6 \text{ true}$$

The solution set is $\{8\}$.

89. $x + \dfrac{6}{x} = -5$

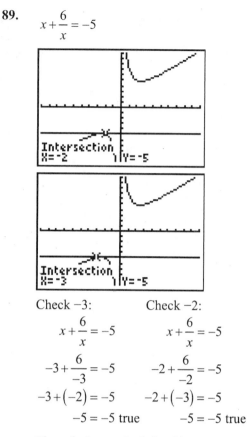

Check -3:   Check -2:

$$x + \frac{6}{x} = -5 \qquad x + \frac{6}{x} = -5$$

$$-3 + \frac{6}{-3} = -5 \qquad -2 + \frac{6}{-2} = -5$$

$$-3 + (-2) = -5 \qquad -2 + (-3) = -5$$

$$-5 = -5 \text{ true} \qquad -5 = -5 \text{ true}$$

The solution set is $\{-3, -2\}$.

90. $x^4 + 2x^3 - 3x - 6$

Factor by grouping.

$$x^4 + 2x^3 - 3x - 6 = \left(x^4 + 2x^3\right) + \left(-3x - 6\right)$$

$$= x^3(x+2) - 3(x+2)$$

$$= (x+2)\left(x^3 - 3\right)$$

91. $\left(3x^2\right)\left(-4x^{-10}\right) = (3 \cdot -4)\left(x^2 \cdot x^{-10}\right)$

$$= -12x^{2+(-10)} = -12x^{-8} = -\frac{12}{x^8}$$

92. $-5\left[4(x-2) - 3\right] = -5\left[4x - 8 - 3\right]$

$$= -5\left[4x - 11\right]$$

$$= -20x + 55$$

366

7.7 Exercise Set

1. The times are equal, so

$$\frac{10}{x} = \frac{15}{x+3}$$

To solve this equation, multiply both sides by the LCD, $x(x+3)$.

$$x(x+3) \cdot \frac{10}{x} = x(x+3) \cdot \frac{15}{x+3}$$

$$10(x+3) = 15x$$

$$10x + 30 = 15x$$

$$30 = 5x$$

$$6 = x$$

If $x = 6$, $x + 3 = 9$.

Note: The equation

$$\frac{10}{x} = \frac{15}{x+3}$$

is a proportion, so it can also be solved by using the cross-products principle.

$$10(x+3) = 15x$$

This allows you to skip the first step of the solution process shown above. The walking rate is 6 miles per hour and the car's rate is 9 miles per hour.

3. Let x = the jogger's rate running uphill

Then $x + 4$ = the jogger's rate running downhill

	Dist	Rate	Time
Down	5	$x+4$	$\dfrac{5}{x+4}$
Up	3	x	$\dfrac{3}{x}$

The times are equal, so

$$\frac{5}{x+4} = \frac{3}{x}.$$

Use the cross-products principle to solve this equation.

$$5x = 3(x+4)$$

$$5x = 3x + 12$$

$$2x = 12$$

$$x = 6$$

If $x = 6$, $x + 4 = 10$.
The jogger runs 10 miles per hour downhill and 6 miles per hour uphill.

5. Let x = the rate of the current.
Then $15 + x$ = the boat's rate with the current.
and $15 - x$ = the boat's rate against the current

	Dist	Rate	Time
With the current	20	$15+x$	$\dfrac{20}{15+x}$
Against the current	10	$15-x$	$\dfrac{10}{15-x}$

$$\frac{20}{15+x} = \frac{10}{15-x}$$

Use the cross-products principle to solve this equation.

$$20(15 - x) = 10(15 + x)$$

$$300 - 20x = 150 + 10x$$

$$300 = 150 + 30x$$

$$150 = 30x$$

$$5 = x$$

The rate of the current is 5 miles per hour.

7. Let x = walking rate.
Then $2x$ = jogging rate.

	Dist	Rate	Time
Walking	2	x	$\dfrac{2}{x}$
Jogging	2	$2x$	$\dfrac{2}{2x}$

The total time is 1 hour, so

$$\frac{2}{x}+\frac{2}{2x}=1$$

$$\frac{2}{x}+\frac{1}{x}=1.$$

To solve this equation, multiply both sides by the LCD, x.

$$x\left(\frac{2}{x}+\frac{1}{x}\right)=x\cdot 1$$

$$2+1=x$$

$$3=x$$

If $x=3$, $2x=6$.
The walking rate is 3 miles per hour
and the jogging rate is 6 miles per hour.

9. Let x = the boat's average rate in still water.
Then $x+2$ = the boat's rate with the current (downstream).
and $x-2$ = the boat's rate against the current (upstream).

	Dist	Rate	Time
Down	6	$x+2$	$\dfrac{6}{x+2}$
Up	4	$x-2$	$\dfrac{4}{x-2}$

The times are equal so solve the following equation.

$$\frac{6}{x+2}=\frac{4}{x-2}$$

$$6(x-2)=4(x+2)$$

$$6x-12=4x+8$$

$$2x=20$$

$$x=10$$

The boat's average rate in still water
is 10 miles per hour.

11. Let x = the time in minutes, for both people to shovel the driveway together.

	Fractional part of job completed in 1 minute	Time working together	Fractional part of job completed in x minutes
You	$\dfrac{1}{20}$	x	$\dfrac{x}{20}$
Your brother	$\dfrac{1}{15}$	x	$\dfrac{x}{15}$

Working together, you and your brother complete the whole job, so

$$\frac{x}{20}+\frac{x}{15}=1.$$

Multiply both sides by the LCD, 60.

$$60\left(\frac{x}{20}+\frac{x}{15}\right)=60\cdot 1$$

$$3x+4x=60$$

$$7x=60$$

$$x=\frac{60}{7}\approx 8.6$$

It will take about 8.6 minutes, which is enough time.

368

13. Let x = the time, in hours, for both teams to clean the streets working together.

	Fractional part of job completed in 1 hour	Time working together	Fractional part of job completed in x hours
First team	$\dfrac{1}{400}$	x	$\dfrac{x}{400}$
Second team	$\dfrac{1}{300}$	x	$\dfrac{x}{300}$

Working together, the two teams complete one whole job, so

$$\frac{x}{400} + \frac{x}{300} = 1.$$

Multiply both sides by the LCD, 1200.

$$1200\left(\frac{x}{400} + \frac{x}{300}\right) = 1200 \cdot 1$$

$$3x + 4x = 1200$$

$$7x = 1200$$

$$x = \frac{1200}{7} \approx 171.4$$

It will take about 171.4 hours for both teams to clean the streets working together. One week is $7 \cdot 24 = 168$ hours, so even if both crews work 24 hours a day, there is not enough time.

15. Let x = the time, in hours, for both pipes to fill in the pool.

$$\frac{x}{4} + \frac{x}{6} = 1$$

$$12\left(\frac{x}{4} + \frac{x}{6}\right) = 12 \cdot 1$$

$$3x + 2x = 12$$

$$5x = 12$$

$$x = \frac{12}{5} = 2.4$$

Using both pipes, it will take 2.4 hours or 2 hours 24 minutes to fill the pool.

17. Let x = the tax on a property with an assessed value of \$162,500.

$$\frac{\text{Tax on } \$62,000 \text{ house}}{\text{Assessed value } (\$62,000)} = \frac{\text{Tax on } \$162,500 \text{ house}}{\text{Assessed value } \$162,500}$$

$$\frac{\$720}{\$65,000} = \frac{\$x}{\$162,500}$$

$$\frac{720}{65,000} = \frac{x}{\$162,500}$$

$$65,000x = (720)(162,500)$$

$$65,000x = 117,000,000$$

$$\frac{65,000x}{65,000} = \frac{117,000,000}{65,000}$$

$$x = 1800$$

The tax on a property assessed at \$162,500 is \$1800.

369

19. Let x = the total number of fur seal pups in the rookery.

$$\frac{\text{Original number tagged fur seal pups}}{\text{Total number fur seal pups}} = \frac{\text{Number tagged fur seal pups in sample}}{\text{Number fur seal pups in sample}}$$

$$\frac{4963}{x} = \frac{218}{900}$$
$$218x = (4963)(900)$$
$$218x = 4,466,700$$
$$\frac{218x}{218} = \frac{4,466,700}{218}$$
$$x \approx 20,489$$

There were approximately 20,489 fur seal pups in the rookery.

21. Let x = the monthly amount of child support for a father earning \$38,000 annually.

$$\frac{x}{\$38,000} = \frac{1}{40}$$
$$40x = 38,000$$
$$x = 950$$

A father earning \$38,000 annually has to pay \$950 in monthly child support.

23. Let x = the height of the critter.

$$\frac{\dfrac{\text{foot length}}{\text{person}}}{\dfrac{\text{height of}}{\text{person}}} = \frac{\dfrac{\text{foot length}}{\text{critter}}}{\dfrac{\text{height of}}{\text{critter}}}$$

$$\frac{10 \text{ inches}}{67 \text{ inches}} = \frac{23 \text{ inches}}{x}$$
$$\frac{10}{67} = \frac{23}{x}$$
$$10x = (67)(23)$$
$$10x = 1541$$
$$x = 154.1$$

The height of the critter is 154.1 in.

25.
$$\frac{18}{9} = \frac{10}{x}$$
$$18x = 9 \cdot 10$$
$$18x = 90$$
$$x = 5$$

The length of the side marked x is 5 inches.

27.
$$\frac{10}{30} = \frac{x}{18}$$
$$30x = 10 \cdot 18$$
$$30x = 180$$
$$x = 6$$

The length of the side marked x is 6 meters.

29.
$$\frac{20}{15} = \frac{x}{12}$$
$$15x = 12 \cdot 20$$
$$15x = 240$$
$$x = 16$$

The length of the side marked x is 16 inches.

31.
$$\frac{8}{6} = \frac{x}{12}$$
$$6x = 8 \cdot 12$$
$$6x = 96$$
$$x = 16$$

The tree is 16 feet tall.

33. – 41. Answers will vary.

370

43. Let x = the usual average rate, in miles per hour, of the bus.

Then $x + 15$ = the average rate, in miles per hour, of the bus in the snowstorm.

	Distance	Rate	Time
Usual conditions	60	x	$\dfrac{60}{x}$
Snowstorm conditions	60	$x - 15$	$\dfrac{60}{x-15}$

Since the time during the snowstorm is 2 hours longer than the usual time solve the following equation.

$$\frac{60}{x} + 2 = \frac{60}{x-15}$$

Multiply both sides of the equation by the LCD, $x(x-15)$

$$x(x-15)\left(\frac{60}{x} + 2\right) = x(x-15)\left(\frac{60}{x-15}\right)$$

$$(x-15)\cdot 60 + x(x-15)\cdot 2 = 60x$$

$$60x - 900 + 2x^2 - 30x = 60x$$

$$2x^2 + 30x - 900 = 60x$$

$$2x^2 - 30x - 900 = 0$$

$$x^2 - 15x - 450 = 0$$

$$(x-30)(x+15) = 0$$

$$x - 30 = 0 \quad \text{or} \quad x + 15 = 0$$

$$x = 30 \qquad\qquad x = -15$$

Since the rate cannot be negative, the solution is 30. Therefore, the usual average rate of the bus is 30 miles per hour.

45. Let x = the time, in hours, it takes to prepare a report working together.

	Fraction of job completed in 1 hour	Time working together	Fraction of job completed in x hours
Ben	$\dfrac{1}{3}$	x	$\dfrac{x}{3}$
Shane	$\dfrac{1}{4.2} = \dfrac{5}{21}$	x	$\dfrac{5x}{21}$

Working together, Ben and Shane prepare one report, so

$$\frac{x}{3} + \frac{5x}{21} = 1$$

To solve this equation, multiply both sides by the LCD, 21.

$$21\cdot\left(\frac{x}{3} + \frac{5x}{21}\right) = 21\cdot 1$$

$$7x + 5x = 21$$

$$12x = 21$$

$$x = \frac{21}{12} = 1.75$$

Ben and Shane can prepare one report in 1.75 hours. Multiply this by four to determine how many hours it takes to prepare four reports. $4(1.75) = 7$.

Therefore, working together Ben and Shane can prepare four reports in 7 hours.

47. Let x = time, in hours, to fill empty swimming pool

$$\frac{x}{2} - \frac{x}{10} = 1$$

Multiply both sides of the equation by the LCD, 20.

$$20 \cdot \left(\frac{x}{2} - \frac{x}{10} \right) = 20 \cdot 1$$

$$10x - 2x = 20$$

$$8x = 20$$

$$x = 2.5$$

It will take 2.5 hours to fill the empty swimming pool.

49. $25x^2 - 81 = (5x)^2 - 9^2$

$$= (5x + 9)(5x - 9)$$

50. $x^2 - 12x + 36 = 0$

$$(x - 6)^2 = 0$$

$$x - 6 = 0$$

$$x = 6$$

The only solution is 6.

51. $y = -\frac{2}{3}x + 4$

slope $= -\frac{2}{3} = \frac{-2}{3}$

y-intercept $= 4$

Plot (0,4). From this point, move 2 units *down* and 3 units to the *right* to reach the point (3,2). Draw a line through (0,4) and (3,2).

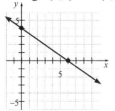

7.8 Exercise Set

1. Since y varies directly with x, we have $y = kx$.

Use the given values to find k.

$$y = kx$$

$$65 = k \cdot 5$$

$$\frac{65}{5} = \frac{k \cdot 5}{5}$$

$$13 = k$$

The equation becomes $y = 13x$.

When $x = 12$, $y = 13x = 13 \cdot 12 = 156$.

3. Since y varies inversely with x, we have $y = \frac{k}{x}$.

Use the given values to find k.

$$y = \frac{k}{x}$$

$$12 = \frac{k}{5}$$

$$5 \cdot 12 = 5 \cdot \frac{k}{5}$$

$$60 = k$$

The equation becomes $y = \frac{60}{x}$.

When $x = 2$, $y = \frac{60}{2} = 30$.

5. Since y varies inversely as x and inversely as the square of z, we have $y = \dfrac{kx}{z^2}$.

Use the given values to find k.

$$y = \frac{kx}{z^2}$$

$$20 = \frac{k(50)}{5^2}$$

$$20 = \frac{k(50)}{25}$$

$$20 = 2k$$

$$10 = k$$

The equation becomes $y = \dfrac{10x}{z^2}$.

When $x = 3$ and $z = 6$,

$$y = \frac{10x}{z^2} = \frac{10(3)}{6^2} = \frac{10(3)}{36} = \frac{30}{36} = \frac{5}{6}.$$

7. Since y varies jointly as x and y, we have $y = kxy$.

Use the given values to find k.

$$y = kxy$$

$$25 = k(2)(5)$$

$$25 = k(10)$$

$$\frac{25}{10} = \frac{k(10)}{10}$$

$$\frac{5}{2} = k$$

The equation becomes $y = \dfrac{5}{2}xy$.

When $x = 8$ and $z = 12$,

$$y = \frac{5}{2}(8)(12) = \frac{5}{\cancel{2}}(\cancel{8}^{4})(12) = 240.$$

9. Since y varies jointly as a and b and inversely as the square root of c, we have $y = \dfrac{kab}{\sqrt{c}}$.

Use the given values to find k.

$$y = \frac{kab}{\sqrt{c}}$$

$$12 = \frac{k(3)(2)}{\sqrt{25}}$$

$$12 = \frac{k(6)}{5}$$

$$12(5) = \frac{k(6)}{5}(5)$$

$$60 = 6k$$

$$\frac{60}{6} = \frac{6k}{6}$$

$$10 = k$$

The equation becomes $y = \dfrac{10ab}{\sqrt{c}}$.

When $a = 5$, $b = 3$, $c = 9$,

$$y = \frac{10ab}{\sqrt{c}} = \frac{10(5)(3)}{\sqrt{9}} = \frac{150}{3} = 50.$$

11. $x = kyz$;

Solving for y:

$$x = kyz$$

$$\frac{x}{kz} = \frac{kyz}{yz}.$$

$$y = \frac{x}{kz}$$

12. $x = kyz^2$;

Solving for y:

$$x = kyz^2$$

$$\frac{x}{kz^2} = \frac{kyz^2}{kz^2}$$

$$y = \frac{x}{kz^2}$$

13.

$$x = \frac{kz^3}{y};$$

Solving for y:

$$x = \frac{kz^3}{y}$$

$$xy = y \cdot \frac{kz^3}{y}$$

$$xy = kz^3$$

$$\frac{xy}{x} = \frac{kz^3}{x}$$

$$y = \frac{kz^3}{x}$$

14.

$$x = \frac{k\sqrt[3]{z}}{y}$$

Solving for y:

$$yx = y \cdot \frac{k\sqrt[3]{z}}{y}$$

$$yx = k\sqrt[3]{z}$$

$$\frac{yx}{x} = \frac{k\sqrt[3]{z}}{x}$$

$$y = \frac{k\sqrt[3]{z}}{x}$$

15.

$$x = \frac{kyz}{\sqrt{w}};$$

Solving for y:

$$x = \frac{kyz}{\sqrt{w}}$$

$$x\left(\sqrt{w}\right) = \left(\sqrt{w}\right)\frac{kyz}{\sqrt{w}}$$

$$x\sqrt{w} = kyz$$

$$\frac{x\sqrt{w}}{kz} = \frac{kyz}{kz}$$

$$y = \frac{x\sqrt{w}}{kz}$$

16.

$$x = \frac{kyz}{w^2}$$

$$\left(\frac{w^2}{kz}\right)x = \frac{w^2}{kz}\frac{kyz}{w^2}$$

$$y = \frac{xw^2}{kz}$$

17.

$$x = kz(y + w);$$

Solving for y:

$$x = kz(y + w)$$

$$x = kzy + kzw$$

$$x - kzw = kzy$$

$$\frac{x - kzw}{kz} = \frac{kzy}{kz}$$

$$y = \frac{x - kzw}{kz}$$

18.

$$x = kz(y - w)$$

$$x = kzy - kzw$$

$$x + kzw = kzy$$

$$\frac{x + kzw}{kz} = \frac{kzy}{kz}$$

$$y = \frac{x + kzw}{kz}$$

19.

$$x = \frac{kz}{y - w};$$

Solving for y:

$$x = \frac{kz}{y - w}$$

$$(y - w)x = (y - w)\frac{kz}{y - w}$$

$$xy - wx = kz$$

$$xy = kz + wx$$

$$\frac{xy}{x} = \frac{kz + wx}{x}$$

$$y = \frac{kz + wx}{x}$$

374

20.

$$x = \frac{kz}{y + w}$$

$$(y + w)x = (y + w)\frac{kz}{y + w}$$

$$yx + xw = kz$$

$$yz = kz - xw$$

$$\frac{yz}{z} = \frac{kz - xw}{z}$$

$$y = \frac{kz - xw}{z}.$$

21. Since T varies directly as B, we have
$T = kB$.
Use the given values to find k.
$$T = kB$$
$$3.6 = k(4)$$
$$\frac{3.6}{4} = \frac{k(4)}{4}$$
$$0.9 = k$$
The equation becomes $T = 0.9B$.
When $B = 6$, $T = 0.9(6) = 5.4$. The
tail length is 5.4 feet.

23. Since B varies directly as D, we have
$B = kD$.
Use the given values to find k.
$$B = kD$$
$$8.4 = k(12)$$
$$\frac{8.4}{12} = \frac{k(12)}{12}$$
$$k = \frac{8.4}{12} = 0.7$$
The equation becomes $B = 0.7D$.
When $B = 56$,
$$56 = 0.7D$$
$$\frac{56}{0.7} = \frac{0.7D}{0.7}$$
$$D = \frac{56}{0.7} = 80$$
It was dropped from 80 inches.

25. Since a man's weight varies directly as
the cube of his height, we have
$w = kh^3$.
Use the given values to find k.
$$w = kh^3$$
$$170 = k(70)^3$$
$$170 = k(343,000)$$
$$\frac{170}{343,000} = \frac{k(343,000)}{343,000}$$
$$0.000496 = k$$
The equation becomes
$w = 0.000496h^3$.
When $h = 107$,
$$w = 0.000496(107)^3$$
$$= 0.000496(1,225,043) \approx 607.$$
Robert Wadlow's weight was
approximately 607 pounds.

27. Since the banking angle varies
inversely as the turning radius, we
have $B = \frac{k}{r}$.
Use the given values to find k.
$$B = \frac{k}{r}$$
$$28 = \frac{k}{4}$$
$$28(4) = 28\left(\frac{k}{4}\right)$$
$$112 = k$$
The equation becomes $B = \frac{112}{r}$.
When $r = 3.5$, $B = \frac{112}{r} = \frac{112}{3.5} = 32$.
The banking angle is $32°$ when the
turning radius is 3.5 feet.

29. Since intensity varies inversely as the square of the distance, we have pressure, we have $I = \dfrac{k}{d}$.

Use the given values to find k.

$$I = \dfrac{k}{d^2}.$$

$$62.5 = \dfrac{k}{3^2}$$

$$62.5 = \dfrac{k}{9}$$

$$9(62.5) = 9\left(\dfrac{k}{9}\right)$$

$$562.5 = k$$

The equation becomes $I = \dfrac{562.5}{d^2}$.

When $d = 2.5$,

$$I = \dfrac{562.5}{2.5^2} = \dfrac{562.5}{6.25} = 90$$

The intensity is 90 milliroentgens per hour.

31. Since index varies directly as weight and inversely as the square of one's height, we have $I = \dfrac{kw}{h^2}$.

Use the given values to find k.

$$I = \dfrac{kw}{h^2}$$

$$35.15 = \dfrac{k(180)}{60^2}$$

$$35.15 = \dfrac{k(180)}{3600}$$

$$(3600)35.15 = \dfrac{k(180)}{3600}$$

$$126540 = k(180)$$

$$k = \dfrac{126540}{180} = 703$$

The equation becomes $I = \dfrac{703w}{h^2}$.

When $w = 170$ and $h = 70$,

$$I = \dfrac{703(170)}{(70)^2} \approx 24.4.$$

This person has a BMI of 24.4 and is not overweight.

33. Since heat loss varies jointly as the area and temperature difference, we have $L = kAD$.

Use the given values to find k.

$$L = kAD$$

$$1200 = k(3 \cdot 6)(20)$$

$$1200 = 360k$$

$$\dfrac{1200}{360} = \dfrac{360k}{360}$$

$$k = \dfrac{10}{3}$$

The equation becomes $L = \dfrac{10}{3}AD$

When $A = 6 \cdot 9 = 54$, $D = 10$,

$$L = \dfrac{10}{3}(9 \cdot 6)(10) = 1800.$$

The heat loss is 1800 Btu.

35. Since intensity varies inversely as the square of the distance from the sound source, we have $I = \dfrac{k}{d^2}$. If you move to a seat twice as far, then $d = 2d$. So we have $I = \dfrac{k}{(2d)^2} = \dfrac{k}{4d^2} = \dfrac{1}{4} \cdot \dfrac{k}{d^2}$.

The intensity will be multiplied by a factor of $\dfrac{1}{4}$. So the sound intensity is $\dfrac{1}{4}$ of what it was originally.

37. a. Since the average number of phone calls varies jointly as the product of the populations and inversely as the square of the distance, we have $C = \dfrac{kP_1P_2}{d^2}$.

b. Use the given values to find k.

$$C = \frac{kP_1P_2}{d^2}$$

$$326,000 = \frac{k(777,000)(3,695,000)}{(420)^2}$$

$$326,000 = \frac{k(2.87 \times 10^{12})}{176,400}$$

$$326,000 = 16269841.27k$$

$$0.02 \approx k$$

The equation becomes

$$C = \frac{0.02P_1P_2}{d^2}.$$

c. $$C = \frac{0.02(650,000)(490,000)}{(400)^2}$$

$$\approx 39813$$

The average number of calls is approximately 39,813 daily phone calls.

39. a.

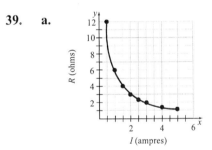

I (ampres)

b. Current varies inversely as resistance. Answers will vary.

c. Since the current varies inversely as resistance we have $R = \frac{k}{I}$.

Using one of the given ordered pairs to find k.

$$12 = \frac{k}{0.5}$$

$$12(0.5) = \frac{k}{0.5}(0.5)$$

$$k = 6$$

The equation becomes $R = \frac{6}{I}$.

41. – 43. Answers will vary.

45. z varies directly as the square root of x and inversely as the square of y.

47. Answers will vary.

49. Since wind pressure varies directly as the square of the wind velocity, we have $P = kv^2$. If the wind speed doubles then the value of v has been multiplied by two. In the formula, $P = k(2v)^2 = k(4v^2) = 4kv^2$. Then the wind pressure will be multiplied by a factor of 4. So if the wind speed doubles, the wind pressure is 4 times more destructive.

51. Since the brightness of a source point varies inversely as the square of its distance from an observer, we have $B = \frac{k}{d^2}$. We can now see things that are only $\frac{1}{50}$ as bright.

$$B = \frac{1}{50} \cdot \frac{k}{d^2} = \frac{k}{50d^2} = \frac{k}{\left(\sqrt{50}d\right)^2}$$

The distance that can be seen is $\sqrt{50}$, or about 7.07, times farther with the space telescope.

52.

$$8(2-x) = -5x$$
$$16 - 8x = -5x$$
$$16 = 3x$$
$$\frac{16}{3} = x$$

The solution set is $\left\{\dfrac{16}{3}\right\}$.

53.

$$\begin{array}{r} 9x^2 - 6x + 4 \\ 3x+2\overline{)27x^3 + 0x^2 + 0x - 8} \\ \underline{27x^3 + 18x^2} \\ -18x^2 + 0x \\ \underline{-18x^2 - 12x} \\ 12x - 8 \\ \underline{12x + 8} \\ -16 \end{array}$$

$$\frac{27x^3 + 8}{3x+2} = 9x^2 - 6x + 4 - \frac{16}{3x+2}$$

54.

$$6x^3 - 6x^2 - 120x = 6x(x^2 - x - 20)$$
$$= 6x(x-5)(x+4)$$

Chapter 7 Review Exercises

1. $\dfrac{5x}{6x-24}$

Set the denominator equal to 0 and solve for x.

$$6x - 24 = 0$$
$$6x = 24$$
$$x = 4$$

The rational expression is undefined for $x = 4$.

2. $\dfrac{x+3}{(x-2)(x+5)}$

Set the denominator equal to 0 and solve for x.

$$(x-2)(x+5) = 0$$
$$x - 2 = 0 \quad \text{or} \quad x + 5 = 0$$
$$x = 2 \qquad\qquad x = -5$$

The rational expression is undefined for $x = 2$ and $x = -5$.

3. $\dfrac{x^2+3}{x^2-3x+2}$

$$x^2 - 3x + 2 = 0$$
$$(x-1)(x-2) = 0$$
$$x - 1 = 0 \quad \text{or} \quad x - 2 = 0$$
$$x = 1 \qquad\qquad x = 2$$

The rational expression is undefined for $x = 1$ and $x = 2$.

4. $\dfrac{7}{x^2+81}$

The smallest possible value of x^2 is 0, so $x^2 + 81 \ge 81$ for all real numbers x. This means that there is no real number for x for which $x^2 + 81 = 0$. Thus, the rational expression is defined for all real numbers.

5. $\dfrac{16x^2}{12x} = \dfrac{4 \cdot 4 \cdot x \cdot x}{4 \cdot 3 \cdot x} = \dfrac{4x}{3}$

6. $\dfrac{x^2-4}{x-2} = \dfrac{(x+2)(x-2)}{(x-2)} = x+2$

7. $\dfrac{x^3+2x^2}{x+2} = \dfrac{x^2(x+2)}{(x+2)} = x^2$

8. $\dfrac{x^2+3x-18}{x^2-36} = \dfrac{(x+6)(x-3)}{(x+6)(x-6)} = \dfrac{x-3}{x-6}$

378

9. $\dfrac{x^2-4x-5}{x^2+8x+7}=\dfrac{(x+1)(x-5)}{(x+1)(x+7)}=\dfrac{x-5}{x+7}$

10. $\dfrac{y^2+2y}{y^2+4y+4}=\dfrac{y(y+2)}{(y+2)(y+2)}=\dfrac{y}{y+2}$

11. $\dfrac{x^2}{x^2+4}$

The numerator and denominator have no common factor, so this rational expression cannot be simplified.

12. $\dfrac{2x^2-18y^2}{3y-x}=\dfrac{2(x^2-9y^2)}{3y-x}$

$=\dfrac{2(x+3y)(x-3y)}{(3y-x)}$

$=\dfrac{2(x+3y)(-1)(3y-x)}{(3y-x)}$

$=-2(x+3y) \text{ or } -2x-6y$

13. $\dfrac{x^2-4}{12x}\cdot\dfrac{3x}{x+2}=\dfrac{(x+2)(x-2)}{12x}\cdot\dfrac{3x}{(x+2)}$

$=\dfrac{x-2}{4}$

14. $\dfrac{5x+5}{6}\cdot\dfrac{3x}{x^2+x}=\dfrac{5(x+1)}{6}\cdot\dfrac{3x}{x(x+1)}$

$=\dfrac{5}{2}$

15. $\dfrac{x^2+6x+9}{x^2-4}\cdot\dfrac{x-2}{x+3}=\dfrac{(x+3)(x+3)}{(x+2)(x-2)}\cdot\dfrac{x-2}{x+3}$

$=\dfrac{x+3}{x+2}$

16. $\dfrac{y^2-2y+1}{y^2-1}\cdot\dfrac{2y^2+y-1}{5y-5}$

$=\dfrac{(y-1)(y-1)}{(y+1)(y-1)}\cdot\dfrac{(2y-1)(y+1)}{5(y-1)}$

$=\dfrac{2y-1}{5}$

17. $\dfrac{2y^2+y-3}{4y^2-9}\cdot\dfrac{3y+3}{5y-5y^2}$

$=\dfrac{(2y+3)(y-1)}{(2y+3)(2y-3)}\cdot\dfrac{3(y+1)}{5y(1-y)}$

$=\dfrac{-3(y+1)}{5y(2y-3)} \text{ or } -\dfrac{3(y+1)}{5y(2y-3)}$

18. $\dfrac{x^2+x-2}{10}\div\dfrac{2x+4}{5}$

$=\dfrac{x^2+x-2}{10}\cdot\dfrac{5}{2x+4}$

$=\dfrac{(x-1)(x+2)}{10}\cdot\dfrac{5}{2(x+2)}=\dfrac{x-1}{4}$

19. $\dfrac{6x+2}{x^2-1}\div\dfrac{3x^2+x}{x-1}$

$=\dfrac{6x+2}{x^2-1}\cdot\dfrac{x-1}{3x^2+x}$

$=\dfrac{2(3x+1)}{(x+1)(x-1)}\cdot\dfrac{(x-1)}{x(3x+1)}=\dfrac{2}{x(x+1)}$

20. $\dfrac{1}{y^2+8y+15}\div\dfrac{7}{y+5}$

$=\dfrac{1}{y^2+8y+15}\cdot\dfrac{y+5}{7}$

$=\dfrac{1}{(y+3)(y+5)}\cdot\dfrac{(y+5)}{7}=\dfrac{1}{7(y+3)}$

379

21.

$$\frac{y^2 + y - 42}{y - 3} \div \frac{y + 7}{(y - 3)^2}$$

$$= \frac{y^2 + y - 42}{y - 3} \cdot \frac{(y - 3)^2}{y + 7}$$

$$= \frac{(y + 7)(y - 6)}{(y - 3)} \cdot \frac{(y - 3)(y - 3)}{y + 7}$$

$$= (y - 6)(y - 3) \text{ or } y^2 - 9y + 18$$

22.

$$\frac{8x + 8y}{x^2} \div \frac{x^2 - y^2}{x^2}$$

$$= \frac{8x + 8y}{x^2} \cdot \frac{x^2}{x^2 - y^2}$$

$$= \frac{8(x + y)}{x^2} \cdot \frac{x^2}{(x + y)(x - y)} = \frac{8}{x - y}$$

23.

$$\frac{4x}{x + 5} + \frac{20}{x + 5} = \frac{4x + 20}{x + 5} = \frac{4(x + 5)}{x + 5} = 4$$

24.

$$\frac{8x - 5}{3x - 1} + \frac{4x + 1}{3x - 1} = \frac{8x - 5 + 4x + 1}{3x - 1}$$

$$= \frac{12x - 4}{3x - 1}$$

$$= \frac{4(3x - 1)}{3x - 1} = 4$$

25.

$$\frac{3x^2 + 2x}{x - 1} - \frac{10x - 5}{x - 1}$$

$$= \frac{(3x^2 + 2x) - (10x - 5)}{x - 1}$$

$$= \frac{3x^2 + 2x - 10x + 5}{x - 1}$$

$$= \frac{3x^2 - 8x + 5}{x - 1}$$

$$= \frac{(3x - 5)(x - 1)}{x - 1} = 3x - 5$$

26.

$$\frac{6y^2 - 4y}{2y - 3} - \frac{12 - 3y}{2y - 3}$$

$$= \frac{(6y^2 - 4y) - (12 - 3y)}{2y - 3}$$

$$= \frac{6y^2 - 4y - 12 + 3y}{2y - 3}$$

$$= \frac{6y^2 - y - 12}{2y - 3}$$

$$= \frac{(2y - 3)(3y + 4)}{2y - 3} = 3y + 4$$

27.

$$\frac{x}{x - 2} + \frac{x - 4}{2 - x} = \frac{x}{x - 2} + \frac{(-1)}{(-1)} \cdot \frac{x - 4}{x - 2}$$

$$= \frac{x}{x - 2} + \frac{-x + 4}{x - 2}$$

$$= \frac{x - x + 4}{x - 2} = \frac{4}{x - 2}$$

28.

$$\frac{x + 5}{x - 3} - \frac{x}{3 - x} = \frac{x + 5}{x - 3} - \frac{(-1)}{(-1)} \cdot \frac{x}{3 - x}$$

$$= \frac{x + 5}{x - 3} + \frac{x}{x - 3}$$

$$= \frac{x + 5 + x}{x - 3} = \frac{2x + 5}{x - 5}$$

29.

$$\frac{7}{9x^3} \text{ and } \frac{5}{12x}$$

$$9x^3 = 3^2 x^3$$

$$12x = 2^2 \cdot 3x$$

$$\text{LCD} = 2^2 \cdot 3^2 \cdot x^3 = 36x^3$$

30.

$$\frac{3}{x^2(x - 1)} \text{ and } \frac{11}{x(x - 1)^2}$$

$$\text{LCD} = x^2(x - 1)^2$$

380

31. $\dfrac{x}{x^2+4x+3}$ and $\dfrac{17}{x^2+10x+21}$

$x^2+4x+3=(x+3)(x+1)$

$x^2+10x+21=(x+3)(x+7)$

$LCD = (x+3)(x+1)(x+7)$

32. $\dfrac{7}{3x}+\dfrac{5}{2x^2}$

$LCD = 6x^2$

$\dfrac{7}{3x}+\dfrac{6}{2x^2}=\dfrac{7}{3x}\cdot\dfrac{2x}{2x}+\dfrac{5}{2x^2}\cdot\dfrac{3}{3}=\dfrac{14x+15}{6x^2}$

33. $\dfrac{5}{x+1}+\dfrac{2}{x}$

$LCD = x(x+1)$

$\dfrac{5}{x+1}+\dfrac{2}{x}=\dfrac{5x}{x(x+1)}+\dfrac{2(x+1)}{x(x+1)}$

$=\dfrac{5x+2(x+1)}{x(x+1)}$

$=\dfrac{5x+2x+2}{x(x+1)}=\dfrac{7x+2}{x(x+1)}$

34. $\dfrac{7}{x+3}+\dfrac{4}{(x+3)^2}$

$LCD = (x+3)^2$ or $(x+3)(x+3)$

$\dfrac{7}{x+3}+\dfrac{4}{(x+3)^2}$

$=\dfrac{7}{x+3}+\dfrac{4}{(x+3)(x+3)}$

$=\dfrac{7(x+3)}{(x+3)(x+3)}+\dfrac{4}{(x+3)(x+3)}$

$=\dfrac{7(x+3)+4}{(x+3)(x+3)}=\dfrac{7x+21+4}{(x+3)(x+3)}$

$=\dfrac{7x+25}{(x+3)(x+3)}$ or $\dfrac{7x+25}{(x+3)^2}$

35. $\dfrac{6y}{y^2-4}-\dfrac{3}{y+2}$

$y^2-4=(y+2)(y-2)$

$y+2=1(y+2)$

$LCD = (y+2)(y-2)$

$\dfrac{6y}{y^2-4}-\dfrac{3}{y+2}$

$=\dfrac{6y}{(y+2)(y-2)}-\dfrac{3}{y+2}$

$=\dfrac{6y}{(y+2)(y-2)}-\dfrac{3(y-2)}{(y+2)(y-2)}$

$=\dfrac{6y-3(y-2)}{(y+2)(y-2)}$

$=\dfrac{6y-3y+6}{(y+2)(y-2)}$

$=\dfrac{3y+6}{(y+2)(y-2)}$

$=\dfrac{3(y+2)}{(y+2)(y-2)}=\dfrac{3}{y-2}$

36. $\dfrac{y-1}{y^2-2y+1}-\dfrac{y+1}{y-1}$

$=\dfrac{y-1}{(y-1)(y-1)}-\dfrac{y+1}{y-1}$

$=\dfrac{1}{y-1}-\dfrac{y+1}{y-1}$

$=\dfrac{1-(y+1)}{y-1}$

$=\dfrac{1-y-1}{y-1}=\dfrac{-y}{y-1}$ or $-\dfrac{y}{y-1}$

381

37.

$$\frac{x+y}{y} - \frac{y-x}{x}$$

LCD $= xy$

$$\frac{x+y}{y} - \frac{y-x}{x}$$

$$= \frac{(x+y)}{y} \cdot \frac{x}{x} - \frac{(x-y)}{x} \cdot \frac{y}{y}$$

$$= \frac{x^2 + xy}{xy} - \frac{xy - y^2}{xy}$$

$$= \frac{\left(x^2 + xy\right) - \left(xy - y^2\right)}{xy}$$

$$= \frac{x^2 + xy - xy + y^2}{xy} = \frac{x^2 + y^2}{xy}$$

38.

$$\frac{2x}{x^2 + 2x + 1} + \frac{x}{x^2 - 1}$$

$$x^2 + 2x + 1 = (x+1)(x+1)$$

$$x^2 - 1 = (x+1)(x-1)$$

LCD $= (x+1)(x+1)(x-1)$

$$\frac{2x}{x^2 + 2x + 1} + \frac{x}{x^2 - 1}$$

$$= \frac{2x}{(x+1)(x+1)} + \frac{x}{(x+1)(x-1)}$$

$$= \frac{2x(x-1)}{(x+1)(x+1)(x-1)}$$

$$\qquad + \frac{x(x+1)}{(x+1)(x-1)(x+1)}$$

$$= \frac{2x(x-1) + x(x+1)}{(x+1)(x+1)(x-1)}$$

$$= \frac{2x^2 - 2x + x^2 + x}{(x+1)(x+1)(x-1)}$$

$$= \frac{3x^2 - x}{(x+1)(x+1)(x-1)}$$

39.

$$\frac{5x}{x+1} - \frac{2x}{1-x^2}$$

$$x + 1 = 1(x+1)$$

$$1 - x^2 = -1\left(x^2 - 1\right) = -(x+1)(x-1)$$

LCD $= (x+1)(x-1)$

$$\frac{5x}{x+1} - \frac{2x}{1-x^2}$$

$$= \frac{5x}{x+1} - \frac{(-1)}{(-1)} \cdot \frac{2x}{1-x^2}$$

$$= \frac{5x}{x+1} - \frac{-2x}{x^2 - 1}$$

$$= \frac{5x(x-1)}{(x+1)(x-1)} - \frac{-2x}{(x+1)(x-1)}$$

$$= \frac{5x(x-1) + 2x}{(x+1)(x-1)}$$

$$= \frac{5x^2 - 5x + 2x}{(x+1)(x-1)} = \frac{5x^2 - 3x}{(x+1)(x-1)}$$

40.

$$\frac{4}{x^2 - x - 6} - \frac{4}{x^2 - 4}$$

$$x^2 - x - 6 = (x+2)(x-3)$$

$$x^2 - 4 = (x+2)(x-2)$$

LCD $= (x+2)(x-3)(x-2)$

$$\frac{4}{x^2 - x - 6} - \frac{4}{x^2 - 4}$$

$$= \frac{4}{(x+2)(x-3)} - \frac{4}{(x+2)(x-2)}$$

$$= \frac{4(x-2)}{(x+2)(x-3)(x-2)}$$

$$\qquad - \frac{4(x-3)}{(x+2)(x-3)(x-2)}$$

$$= \frac{4(x-2) - 4(x-3)}{(x+2)(x-3)(x-2)}$$

$$= \frac{4x - 8 - 4x + 12}{(x+2)(x-3)(x-2)}$$

$$= \frac{4}{(x+2)(x-3)(x-2)}$$

41.
$$\frac{7}{x+3}+2$$
$$LCD = x+3$$
$$\frac{7}{x+3}+2 = \frac{7}{x+3}+\frac{2(x+3)}{x+3}$$
$$= \frac{7+2(x+3)}{x+3}$$
$$= \frac{7+2x+6}{x+3} = \frac{2x+13}{x+3}$$

42.
$$\frac{2y-5}{6y+9}-\frac{4}{2y^2+3y}$$
$$6y+9 = 3(2y+3)$$
$$2y^2+3y = y(2y+3)$$
$$LCD = 3y(2y+3)$$
$$\frac{2y-5}{6y+9}-\frac{4}{2y^2+3y}$$
$$= \frac{2y-5}{3(2y+3)}-\frac{4}{y(2y+3)}$$
$$= \frac{(2y-5)(y)}{3(2y+3)(y)}-\frac{4(3)}{y(2y+3)(3)}$$
$$= \frac{2y^2-5y-12}{3y(2y+3)}$$
$$= \frac{(2y+3)(y-4)}{3y(2y+3)} = \frac{y-4}{3y}$$

In Exercises 43-47, each complex rational expression can be simplified by either of the two methods introduced in Section 8.5 of the textbook. Both methods will be illustrated here.

43.
$$\frac{\frac{1}{2}+\frac{3}{8}}{\frac{3}{4}-\frac{1}{2}} = \frac{\frac{4}{8}+\frac{3}{8}}{\frac{3}{4}-\frac{2}{4}} = \frac{\frac{7}{8}}{\frac{1}{4}} = \frac{7}{8}\cdot\frac{4}{1} = \frac{7}{2}$$

44.
$$\frac{\frac{1}{x}}{1-\frac{1}{x}}$$
$$LCD = x$$
$$\frac{\frac{1}{x}}{1-\frac{1}{x}} = \frac{x}{x}\cdot\frac{\left(\frac{1}{x}\right)}{\left(1-\frac{1}{x}\right)} = \frac{x\cdot\frac{1}{x}}{x\cdot1-x\cdot\frac{1}{x}} = \frac{1}{x-1}$$

45.
$$\frac{\frac{1}{x}+\frac{1}{y}}{\frac{1}{xy}}$$
$$LCD = xy$$
$$\frac{\frac{1}{x}+\frac{1}{y}}{\frac{1}{xy}} = \frac{xy}{xy}\cdot\frac{\left(\frac{1}{x}+\frac{1}{y}\right)}{\left(\frac{1}{xy}\right)}$$
$$= \frac{xy\cdot\frac{1}{x}+xy\cdot\frac{1}{y}}{xy\cdot\frac{1}{xy}}$$
$$= \frac{y+x}{1} = y+x \text{ or } x+y$$

46.
$$\frac{\frac{1}{x}-\frac{1}{2}}{\frac{1}{3}-\frac{x}{6}} = \frac{\frac{2}{2x}-\frac{x}{2x}}{\frac{2}{6}-\frac{x}{6}}$$
$$= \frac{\frac{2-x}{2x}}{\frac{2-x}{6}} = \frac{2-x}{2x}\cdot\frac{6}{2-x} = \frac{3}{x}$$

47.

$$\dfrac{3+\dfrac{12}{x}}{1-\dfrac{16}{x^2}}$$

$$\text{LCD} = x^2$$

$$\dfrac{3+\dfrac{12}{x}}{1-\dfrac{16}{x^2}} = \dfrac{x^2}{x^2} \cdot \dfrac{\left(3+\dfrac{12}{x}\right)}{\left(1-\dfrac{16}{x^2}\right)}$$

$$= \dfrac{3x^2+12x}{x^2-16}$$

$$= \dfrac{3x(x+4)}{(x+4)(x-4)} = \dfrac{3x}{x-4}$$

48.

$$\dfrac{3}{x}-\dfrac{1}{6}=\dfrac{1}{x}$$

The restriction is $x \neq 0$.
The LCD is $6x$.

$$\dfrac{3}{x}-\dfrac{1}{6}=\dfrac{1}{x}$$

$$6x\left(\dfrac{3}{x}-\dfrac{1}{6}\right)=6x\left(\dfrac{1}{x}\right)$$

$$18-x=6$$

$$-x=-12$$

$$x=12$$

The solution set is $\{12\}$.

49.

$$\dfrac{3}{4x}=\dfrac{1}{x}+\dfrac{1}{4}$$

The restriction is $x \neq 0$.
The LCD is $4x$.

$$\dfrac{3}{4x}=\dfrac{1}{x}+\dfrac{1}{4}$$

$$4x\left(\dfrac{3}{4x}\right)=4x\left(\dfrac{1}{x}+\dfrac{1}{4}\right)$$

$$3=4+x$$

$$-1=x$$

The solution set is $\{-1\}$.

50.

$$x+5=\dfrac{6}{x}$$

The restriction is $x \neq 0$.
The LCD is x.

$$x+5=\dfrac{6}{x}$$

$$x(x+5)=x\left(\dfrac{6}{x}\right)$$

$$x^2+5x=6$$

$$x^2+5x-6=0$$

$$(x+6)(x-1)=0$$

$$x+6=0 \quad \text{or} \quad x-1=0$$

$$x=-6 \qquad \qquad x=1$$

The solution set is $\{-6,\ 1\}$.

51.

$$4-\dfrac{x}{x+5}=\dfrac{5}{x+5}$$

The restriction is $x \neq -5$.
The LCD is $x+5$.

$$(x+5)\left(4-\dfrac{x}{x+5}\right)=(x+5)\left(\dfrac{5}{x+5}\right)$$

$$(x+5)\cdot 4-(x+5)\left(\dfrac{x}{x+5}\right)=(x+5)\left(\dfrac{5}{x+5}\right)$$

$$4x+20-x=5$$

$$3x+20=5$$

$$3x=-15$$

$$x=-5$$

The only proposed solution, -5, is *not* a solution because of the restriction $x \neq -5$. Notice that -5 makes two of the denominators zero in the original equation. Therefore, the given equation has no solution. The solution set is $\varnothing$.

52. $\dfrac{2}{x-3} = \dfrac{4}{x+3} + \dfrac{8}{x^2-9}$

To find any restrictions and the LCD, all denominators should be written in factored form.

$$\dfrac{2}{x-3} = \dfrac{4}{x+3} + \dfrac{8}{(x+3)(x-3)}$$

Restrictions: $x \neq 3, x \neq -3$

LCD $= (x+3)(x-3)$

$$(x+3)(x-3) \cdot \dfrac{2}{x-3}$$

$$= (x+3)(x-3)\left(\dfrac{4}{x+3} + \dfrac{8}{(x+3)(x-3)}\right)$$

$$2(x+3) = 4(x-3) + 8$$
$$2x+6 = 4x-12+8$$
$$2x+6 = 4x-4$$
$$10 = 2x$$
$$5 = x$$

The solution set is $\{5\}$.

53. $\dfrac{2}{x} = \dfrac{2}{3} + \dfrac{x}{6}$

Restriction: $x \neq 0$

LCD $= 6x$

$$6x\left(\dfrac{2}{x}\right) = 6x\left(\dfrac{2}{3} + \dfrac{x}{6}\right)$$

$$12 = 4x + x^2$$
$$0 = x^2 + 4x - 12$$
$$0 = (x+6)(x-2)$$
$$x+6 = 0 \quad \text{or} \quad x-2 = 0$$
$$x = -6 \qquad\quad x = 2$$

The solution set is $\{-6, 2\}$.

54. $\dfrac{13}{y-1} - 3 = \dfrac{1}{y-1}$

Restrictions: $y \neq 1$

LCD $= y-1$

$$(y-1)\left(\dfrac{13}{y-1} - 3\right) = (y-1)\left(\dfrac{1}{y-1}\right)$$

$$13 - 3(y-1) = 1$$
$$13 - 3y + 3 = 1$$
$$16 - 3y = 1$$
$$-3y = -15$$
$$y = 5$$

The solution set is $\{5\}$.

55. $\dfrac{1}{x+3} - \dfrac{1}{x-1} = \dfrac{x+1}{x^2+2x-3}$

$$\dfrac{1}{x+3} - \dfrac{1}{x-1} = \dfrac{x+1}{(x+3)(x-1)}$$

Restrictions: $x \neq -3, x \neq 1$

LCD $= (x+3)(x-1)$

$$(x+3)(x-1)\left[\dfrac{1}{x+3} - \dfrac{1}{x-1}\right]$$

$$= (x+3)(x-1) \cdot \left[\dfrac{x+1}{(x+3)(x-1)}\right]$$

$$(x-1) - (x+3) = x+1$$
$$x-1-x-3 = x+1$$
$$-4 = x+1$$
$$-5 = x$$

The solution is $\{-5\}$.

56.
$$P = \frac{250(3t+5)}{t+25}; P = 125$$

$$125 = \frac{250(3t+5)}{t+25}$$

$$125(t+25) = \frac{250(3t+5)}{t+25} \cdot (t+25)$$

$$125t + 3125 = 250(3t+5)$$

$$125t + 3125 = 750t + 1250$$

$$3125 = 625t + 1250$$

$$1875 = 625t$$

$$3 = t$$

It will take 3 years for the population to reach 125 elk.

57.
$$S = \frac{C}{1-r}; S = 200, \ C = 140$$

$$200 = \frac{140}{1-r}$$

$$200(1-r) = \frac{140}{1-r} \cdot 1 - r$$

$$200 - 200r = 140$$

$$-200r = -60$$

$$r = \frac{-60}{-200} = \frac{3}{10} = 30\%$$

The markup is 30%.

58.
$$P = \frac{R-C}{n}$$

$$n(P) = n\left(\frac{R-C}{n}\right)$$

$$nP = R - C$$

$$nP + C = R$$

$$C = R - nP$$

59.
$$\frac{P_1 V_1}{T_1} = \frac{P_2 V_2}{T_2}$$

$$T_1 T_2 \left(\frac{P_1 V_1}{T_1}\right) = T_1 T_2 \left(\frac{P_2 V_2}{T_2}\right)$$

$$T_2 (P_1 V_1) = T_1 (P_2 V_2)$$

$$P_1 T_2 V_1 = P_2 T_1 V_2$$

$$\frac{P_1 T_2 V_1}{P_2 V_2} = \frac{P_2 T_1 V_2}{P_2 V_2}$$

$$T_1 = \frac{P_1 T_2 V_1}{P_2 V_2}$$

60.
$$T = \frac{A-P}{Pr}$$

$$Pr(T) = Pr\left(\frac{A-P}{Pr}\right)$$

$$PrT = A - P$$

$$PrT + P = A$$

$$P(rT+1) = A$$

$$\frac{P(rT+1)}{rT+1} = \frac{A}{rT+1}$$

$$P = \frac{A}{rT+1}$$

61.
$$\frac{1}{R} = \frac{1}{R_1} + \frac{1}{R_2}$$

$$RR_1 R_2 \left(\frac{1}{R}\right) = RR_1 R_2 \left(\frac{1}{R_1} + \frac{1}{R_2}\right)$$

$$R_1 R_2 = RR_1 R_2 \left(\frac{1}{R_1}\right) + RR_1 R_2 \left(\frac{1}{R_2}\right)$$

$$R_1 R_2 = RR_2 + RR_1$$

$$R_1 R_2 = R(R_2 + R_1)$$

$$\frac{R_1 R_2}{R_2 + R_1} = \frac{R(R_2 + R_1)}{R_2 + R_1}$$

$$R = \frac{R_1 R_2}{R_2 + R_1}$$

62.

$$I = \frac{nE}{R + nr}$$

$$(R + nr)(I) = (R + nr)\left(\frac{nE}{R + nr}\right)$$

$$IR + Inr = nE$$

$$IR = nE - Inr$$

$$IR = n(E - Ir)$$

$$\frac{IR}{E - Ir} = \frac{n(E - Ir)}{E - Ir}$$

$$n = \frac{IR}{E - Ir}$$

63. Let $x =$ the rate of the current.
$20 + x =$ the rate of the boat with the
current
$20 - x =$ the rate of the boat against the
the current.

	Distance	Rate	Time
With Current	72	$20 + x$	$\dfrac{72}{20 + x}$
Against Current	48	$20 - x$	$\dfrac{48}{20 - x}$

The times are equal, so
$$\frac{72}{20 + x} = \frac{48}{20 - x}$$
This equation is a proportion, so it can
be solved using the cross-products
principle.
$$72(20 - x) = 48(20 + x)$$
$$1440 - 72x = 960 + 48x$$
$$1440 = 960 + 120x$$
$$480 = 120x$$
$$4 = x$$
The rate of the current is 4 miles per
hour

64. Let $x =$ the rate of the slower car.
$x + 10 =$ the rate of the faster car.

	Distance	Rate	Time
Slower car	60	x	$\dfrac{60}{x}$
Faster car	90	$x + 10$	$\dfrac{90}{x + 10}$

$$\frac{60}{x} = \frac{90}{x + 10}$$
$$60(x + 10) = 90x$$
$$60x + 600 = 90x$$
$$600 = 30x$$
$$20 = x$$
If $x = 20$, $x + 10 = 30$.
The rate of the slower car is 20 miles
per hour and the rate of the faster car is
30 miles per hour.

65. Let $x =$ the time, in hours, for both people to
paint the fence together.

	Fractional part of job completed in 1 hour	Time working together	Fractional part of job completed in x hour
Painter	$\dfrac{1}{6}$	x	$\dfrac{x}{6}$
Apprentice	$\dfrac{1}{12}$	x	$\dfrac{x}{12}$

Working together, the two people complete
one whole job, so
$$\frac{x}{6} + \frac{x}{12} = 1.$$
$$12\left(\frac{x}{6} + \frac{x}{12}\right) = 12 \cdot 1$$
$$2x + x = 12$$
$$3x = 12$$
$$x = 4$$
It would take them 4 hours to paint the
fence working together.

66. Let x = number of teachers needed for 5400 students.

$$\frac{3}{50} = \frac{x}{5400}$$

$$50 \cdot x = 3 \cdot 5400$$

$$50x = 16,200$$

$$x = 324$$

For an enrollment of 5400 students, 324 teachers are needed.

67. Let x = number of trout in the lake.

$$\frac{\text{Original Number}\atop\text{Tagged Deer}}{\text{Total Number}\atop\text{of Deer}} = \frac{\text{Number Tagged}\atop\text{Deer in Sample}}{\text{Total Number}\atop\text{Deer in Sample}}$$

$$\frac{112}{x} = \frac{32}{82}$$

$$32 \cdot x = 112 \cdot 82$$

$$32x = 9184$$

$$x = 287$$

There are 287 trout in the lake.

68.

$$\frac{8}{4} = \frac{10}{x}$$

$$8x = 40$$

$$x = 5$$

The length of the side marked with an x is 5 feet.

69. Write a proportion relating the corresponding sides of the large and small triangle. Notice that the length of the base of the larger triangle is 9 ft + 6 ft = 15 ft.

$$\frac{x}{5} = \frac{15}{6}$$

$$6x = 5 \cdot 15$$

$$6x = 75$$

$$x = \frac{75}{6} = 12.5$$

The height of the lamppost is 12.5 feet.

70. Since the profit varies directly as the number of products sold, we have $p = kn$.

Use the given values to find k.

$$p = kn.$$

$$1175 = k(25)$$

$$\frac{1175}{25} = \frac{k(25)}{25}$$

$$47 = k$$

The equation becomes $p = 47n$

When $n = 105$ products,

$$p = 47(105) = 4935.$$

If 105 products are sold, the company's profit is $4935.

71. Since distance varies directly as the square of the time, we have $d = kt^2$.

Use the given values to find k.

$$d = kt^2$$

$$144 = k(3)^2$$

$$144 = k(9)$$

$$\frac{144}{9} = \frac{k(9)}{9}$$

$$16 = k$$

The equation becomes $d = 16t^2$.

The equation becomes $d = 16t^2$.

When $t = 10$,

$$d = 16(10)^2 = 16(100) = 1600.$$

A skydiver will fall 1600 feet in 10 seconds.

72. Since the pitch of a musical tone varies inversely as its wavelength, we have $p = \dfrac{k}{w}$.

Use the given values to find k.

$$p = \frac{k}{w}$$

$$660 = \frac{k}{1.6}$$

$$660(1.6) = 1.6\left(\frac{k}{1.6}\right)$$

$$1056 = k$$

The equation becomes $p = \dfrac{1056}{w}$.

When $w = 2.4$, $p = \dfrac{1056}{2.4} = 440$.

The tone's pitch is 440 vibrations per second.

73. Since loudness varies inversely as the square of the distance, we have

$$l = \frac{k}{d^2}.$$

Use the given values to find k.

$$l = \frac{k}{d^2}$$

$$28 = \frac{k}{8^2}$$

$$28 = \frac{k}{64}$$

$$64(28) = 64\left(\frac{k}{64}\right)$$

$$1792 = k$$

The equation becomes $l = \dfrac{1792}{d^2}$.

When $d = 4$, $l = \dfrac{1792}{(4)^2} = \dfrac{1792}{16} = 112$.

At a distance of 4 feet, the loudness of the stereo is 112 decibels.

74. Since time varies directly as the number of computers and inversely as the number of workers, we have

$$t = \frac{kn}{w}.$$

Use the given values to find k.

$$t = \frac{kn}{w}$$

$$10 = \frac{k(30)}{6}$$

$$10 = 5k$$

$$\frac{10}{5} = \frac{5k}{5}$$

$$2 = k$$

The equation becomes $t = \dfrac{2n}{w}$. When $n = 40$ and $w = 5$,

$$t = \frac{2(40)}{5} = \frac{80}{5} = 16.$$

It will take 16 hours for 5 workers to assemble 40 computers.

75. Since the volume varies jointly as height and the area of the base, we have $v = kha$.

Use the given values to find k.

$$175 = k(15)(35)$$

$$175 = k(525)$$

$$\frac{175}{525} = \frac{k(525)}{525}$$

$$\frac{1}{3} = k$$

The equation becomes $v = \dfrac{1}{3}ha$.

When $h = 20$ feet and $a = 120$ square feet, $v = \dfrac{1}{3}(20)(120) = 800$.

If the height is 20 feet and the area is 120 square feet, the volume will be 800 cubic feet.

389

Chapter 7 Test

1.

$$\frac{x+7}{x^2+5x-36}$$

Set the denominator equal to 0 and solve for x.

$$x^2+5x-36=0$$
$$(x+9)(x-4)=0$$
$$x+9=0 \quad \text{or} \quad x-4=0$$
$$x=-9 \qquad\qquad x=4$$

The rational expression is undefined for $x=-9$ and $x=4$.

2.

$$\frac{x^2+2x-3}{x^2-3x+2}=\frac{(x-1)(x+3)}{(x-1)(x-2)}=\frac{x+3}{x-2}$$

3.

$$\frac{4x^2-20x}{x^2-4x-5}=\frac{4x(x-5)}{(x+1)(x-5)}=\frac{4x}{x+1}$$

4.

$$\frac{x^2-16}{10}\cdot\frac{5}{x+4}=\frac{(x+4)(x-4)}{10}\cdot\frac{5}{(x+4)}$$
$$=\frac{x-4}{2}$$

5.

$$\frac{x^2-7x+12}{x^2-4x}\cdot\frac{x^2}{x^2-9}$$
$$=\frac{(x-3)(x-4)}{x(x-4)}\cdot\frac{x^2}{(x+3)(x-3)}=\frac{x}{x+3}$$

6.

$$\frac{2x+8}{x-3}\div\frac{x^2+5x+4}{x^2-9}$$
$$=\frac{2x+8}{x-3}\cdot\frac{x^2-9}{x^2+5x+4}$$
$$=\frac{2(x+4)}{(x-3)}\cdot\frac{(x+3)(x-3)}{(x+4)(x+1)}$$
$$=\frac{2(x+3)}{x+1}=\frac{2x+6}{x+1}$$

7.

$$\frac{5y+5}{(y-3)^2}\div\frac{y^2-1}{y-3}$$
$$=\frac{5y+5}{(y-3)^2}\cdot\frac{y-3}{y^2-1}$$
$$=\frac{5(y+1)}{(y-3)(y-3)}\cdot\frac{(y-3)}{(y+1)(y-1)}$$
$$=\frac{5}{(y-3)(y-1)}$$

8.

$$\frac{2y^2+5}{y+3}+\frac{6y-5}{y+3}$$
$$=\frac{(2y^2+5)+(6y-5)}{y+3}$$
$$=\frac{2y^2+5+6y-5}{y+3}$$
$$=\frac{2y^2+6y}{y+3}=\frac{2y(y+3)}{y+3}=2y$$

9.

$$\frac{y^2-2y+3}{y^2+7y+12}-\frac{y^2-4y-5}{y^2+7y+12}$$
$$=\frac{(y^2-2y+3)-(y^2-4y-5)}{y^2+7y+12}$$
$$=\frac{y^2-2y+3-y^2+4y+5}{y^2+7y+12}$$
$$=\frac{2y+8}{y^2+7y+12}$$
$$=\frac{2(y+4)}{(y+3)(y+4)}=\frac{2}{y+3}$$

10. $\dfrac{x}{x+3}+\dfrac{5}{x-3}$

$LCD=(x+3)(x-3)$

$\dfrac{x}{x+3}+\dfrac{5}{x-3}$

$=\dfrac{x(x-3)}{(x+3)(x-3)}+\dfrac{5(x+3)}{(x+3)(x-3)}$

$=\dfrac{x(x-3)+5(x+3)}{(x+3)(x-3)}$

$=\dfrac{x^2-3x+5x+15}{(x+3)(x-3)}$

$=\dfrac{x^2+2x+15}{(x+3)(x-3)}$

11. $\dfrac{2}{x^2-4x+3}+\dfrac{6}{x^2+x-2}$

$x^2-4x+3=(x-1)(x-3)$

$x^2+x-2=(x-1)(x+2)$

$LCD=(x-1)(x-3)(x+2)$

$\dfrac{2}{x^2-4x+3}+\dfrac{6}{x^2+x-2}$

$=\dfrac{2}{(x-1)(x-3)}+\dfrac{6}{(x-1)(x+2)}$

$=\dfrac{2(x+2)}{(x-1)(x-3)(x+2)}$

$\quad+\dfrac{6(x-3)}{(x-1)(x-3)(x+2)}$

$=\dfrac{2(x+2)+6(x-3)}{(x-1)(x-3)(x+2)}$

$=\dfrac{2x+4+6x-18}{(x-1)(x-3)(x+2)}$

$=\dfrac{8x-14}{(x-1)(x-3)(x+2)}$

12. $\dfrac{4}{x-3}+\dfrac{x+5}{3-x}$

$3-x=-1(x-3)$

$LCD=x-3$

$\dfrac{4}{x-3}+\dfrac{x+5}{3-x}=\dfrac{4}{x-3}+\dfrac{(-1)}{(-1)}\cdot\dfrac{(x+5)}{(3-x)}$

$=\dfrac{4}{x-3}+\dfrac{-x-5}{x-3}$

$=\dfrac{4-x-5}{x-3}$

$=\dfrac{-x-1}{x-3}$

13. $1+\dfrac{3}{x-1}$

$LCD=x-1$

$1+\dfrac{3}{x-1}=\dfrac{1(x-1)}{x-1}+\dfrac{3}{x-1}$

$=\dfrac{x-1+3}{x-1}=\dfrac{x+2}{x-1}$

14. $\dfrac{2x+3}{x^2-7x+12}-\dfrac{2}{x-3}$

$x^2-7x+12=(x-3)(x-4)$

$x-3=1(x-3)$

$LCD=(x-3)(x-4)$

$\dfrac{2x+3}{x^2-7x+12}-\dfrac{2}{x-3}$

$=\dfrac{2x+3}{(x-3)(x-4)}-\dfrac{2(x-4)}{(x-3)(x-4)}$

$=\dfrac{2x+3-2(x-4)}{(x-3)(x-4)}$

$=\dfrac{2x+3-2x+8}{(x-3)(x-4)}$

$=\dfrac{11}{(x-3)(x-4)}$

391

15.

$$\frac{8y}{y^2-16}-\frac{4}{y-4}$$

$$y^2-16=(y+4)(y-4)$$

$$y-4=1(y-4)$$

$$\text{LCD}=(y+4)(y-4)$$

$$\frac{8y}{y^2-16}-\frac{4}{y-4}$$

$$=\frac{8y}{(y+4)(y-4)}-\frac{4}{y-4}$$

$$=\frac{8y}{(y+4)(y-4)}-\frac{4(y+4)}{(y+4)(y-4)}$$

$$=\frac{8y-4(y+4)}{(y+4)(y-4)}$$

$$=\frac{8y-4y-16}{(y+4)(y-4)}$$

$$=\frac{4y-16}{(y+4)(y-4)}$$

$$=\frac{4(y-4)}{(y+4)(y-4)}=\frac{4}{y+4}$$

16.

$$\frac{(x-y)^2}{x+y}\div\frac{x^2-xy}{3x+3y}$$

$$=\frac{(x-y)^2}{x+y}\cdot\frac{3x+3y}{x^2-xy}$$

$$=\frac{(x-y)(x-y)}{(x+y)}\cdot\frac{3(x+y)}{x(x-y)}$$

$$=\frac{3(x-y)}{x}=\frac{3x-3y}{x}$$

17.

$$\frac{5+\dfrac{5}{x}}{2+\dfrac{1}{x}}=\frac{\dfrac{5x}{x}+\dfrac{5}{x}}{\dfrac{2x}{x}+\dfrac{1}{x}}$$

$$=\frac{\dfrac{5x+5}{x}}{\dfrac{2x+1}{x}}$$

$$=\frac{5x+5}{x}\cdot\frac{x}{2x+1}=\frac{5x+5}{2x+1}$$

18.

$$\frac{\dfrac{1}{x}-\dfrac{1}{y}}{\dfrac{1}{x}}$$

$$\text{LCD}=xy$$

$$\frac{xy\cdot\left(\dfrac{1}{x}-\dfrac{1}{y}\right)}{xy\cdot\left(\dfrac{1}{x}\right)}=\frac{xy\cdot\dfrac{1}{x}-xy\cdot\dfrac{1}{y}}{xy\cdot\dfrac{1}{x}}=\frac{y-x}{y}$$

19.

$$\frac{5}{x}+\frac{2}{3}=2-\frac{2}{x}-\frac{1}{6}$$

Restriction: $x\neq0$

$$\text{LCD}=6x$$

$$6x\left(\frac{5}{x}+\frac{2}{3}\right)=6x\left(2-\frac{2}{x}-\frac{1}{6}\right)$$

$$6x\cdot\frac{5}{x}+6x\cdot\frac{2}{3}=6x\cdot2-6x\cdot\frac{2}{x}-6x\cdot\frac{1}{6}$$

$$30+4x=12x-12-x$$

$$30+4x=11x-12$$

$$30=7x-12$$

$$42=7x$$

$$6=x$$

The solution set is $\{6\}$.

20.

$$\frac{3}{y+5} - 1 = \frac{4-y}{2y+10}$$

$$\frac{3}{y+5} - 1 = \frac{4-y}{2(y+5)}$$

Restriction: $y \neq -5$

LCD $= 2(y+5)$

$$2(y+5)\left(\frac{3}{y+5} - 1\right) = 2(y+5)\left[\frac{4-y}{2(y+5)}\right]$$

$$6 - 2(y+5) = 4 - y$$

$$6 - 2y - 10 = 4 - y$$

$$-4 - 2y = 4 - y$$

$$-4 = 4 + y$$

$$-8 = y$$

The solution set is $\{-8\}$.

21.

$$\frac{2}{x-1} = \frac{3}{x^2-1} + 1$$

$$\frac{2}{x-1} = \frac{3}{(x+1)(x-1)} + 1$$

Restrictions: $x \neq 1, x \neq -1$

LCD $= (x+1)(x-1)$

$$(x+1)(x-1)\left(\frac{2}{x-1}\right)$$

$$= (x+1)(x-1)\left[\frac{3}{(x+1)(x-1)} + 1\right]$$

$$2(x+1) = 3 + (x+1)(x-1)$$

$$2x + 2 = 3 + x^2 - 1$$

$$2x + 2 = 2 + x^2$$

$$0 = x^2 - 2x$$

$$0 = x(x-2)$$

$$x = 0 \text{ or } x - 2 = 0$$

$$x = 2$$

The solution set is $\{0, 2\}$.

22.

$$R = \frac{as}{a+s}$$

$$(a+s)R = (a+s)\left(\frac{as}{a+s}\right)$$

$$aR + Rs = as$$

$$aR = as - Rs$$

$$aR - as = -Rs$$

$$a(R-s) = -Rs$$

$$\frac{a(R-s)}{R-s} = -\frac{Rs}{R-s}$$

$$a = -\frac{Rs}{R-s} \text{ or } \frac{Rs}{s-R}$$

23. Let $x =$ the rate of the current
$30 + x =$ the rate of the boat with the current
$30 - x =$ the rate of the boat against the the current

	Distance	Rate	Time
With current	16	$30+x$	$\frac{16}{30+x}$
Against current	14	$30-x$	$\frac{14}{30-x}$

$$\frac{16}{30+x} = \frac{14}{30-x}$$

$$16(30-x) = 14(30+x)$$

$$480 - 16x = 420 + 14x$$

$$480 = 420 + 30x$$

$$60 = 30x$$

$$2 = x$$

The rate of the current is 2 miles per hour.

24. Let x = the time (in minutes) for both pipes to fill the hot tub.

$$\frac{x}{20} + \frac{x}{30} = 1$$

LCD = 60

$$60\left(\frac{x}{20} + \frac{x}{30}\right) = 60 \cdot 1$$

$$3x + 2x = 60$$

$$5x = 60$$

$$x = 12$$

It will take 12 minutes for both pipes to fill the hot tub.

25. Let x = number of tule elk in the park.

$$\frac{200}{x} = \frac{5}{150}$$

$$5x = 30,000$$

$$x = 6000$$

There are 6000 tule elk in the park.

26.

$$\frac{10}{4} = \frac{8}{x}$$

$$10x = 8 \cdot 4$$

$$10x = 32$$

$$x = 3.2$$

The length of the side marked with an x is 3.2 inches.

27. Let C = the current (in amperes). Then R = the resistance (in ohms).

Step 1 $C = \dfrac{k}{R}$

Step 2 To find k, substitute 42 for C and 5 for R.

$$42 = \frac{k}{5}$$

$$42 \cdot 5 = \frac{k}{5} \cdot 5$$

$$210 = k$$

Step 3 $C = \dfrac{210}{R}$

Step 4 Substitute 4 for R and solve for C.

$$C = \frac{210}{4} = 52.5$$

When the resistance is 4 ohms, the current is 52.5 amperes.

Chapter 7 Cumulative Review Exercises (Chapters 1 – 7)

1.

$$2(x-3) + 5x = 8(x-1)$$

$$2x - 6 + 5x = 8x - 8$$

$$7x - 6 = 8x - 8$$

$$-6 = x - 8$$

$$2 = x$$

The solution set is $\{2\}$.

2.

$$-3(2x-4) > 2(6x-12)$$

$$-6x + 12 > 12x - 24$$

$$-18x + 12 > -24$$

$$-18x > -36$$

$$\frac{-18x}{-18} < \frac{-36}{-18}$$

$$x < 2$$

The solution set is $\{x \mid x < 2\}$.

3.

$$x^2 + 3x = 18$$

$$x^2 + 3x - 18 = 0$$

$$(x+6)(x-3) = 0$$

$$x + 6 = 0 \quad \text{or} \quad x - 3 = 0$$

$$x = -6 \qquad x = 3$$

The solution set is $\{-6, 3\}$.

4.
$$\frac{2x}{x^2 - 4} + \frac{1}{x - 2} = \frac{2}{x + 2}$$
$$x^2 - 4 = (x + 2)(x - 2)$$
Restrictions: $x \neq 2, x \neq -2$
$$LCD = (x + 2)(x - 2)$$
$$(x+2)(x-2)\left[\frac{2x}{(x+2)(x-2)} + \frac{1}{x-2}\right]$$
$$= (x+2)(x-2) \cdot \frac{2}{x+2}$$
$$2x + (x+2) = 2(x-2)$$
$$3x + 2 = 2x - 4$$
$$x = -6$$
The solution set is $\{-6\}$.

5.
$$y = 2x - 3$$
$$x + 2y = 9$$
To solve this system by the substitution method, substitute $2x - 3$ for y in the second equation.
$$x + 2y = 9$$
$$x + 2(2x - 3) = 9$$
$$x + 4x - 6 = 9$$
$$5x - 6 = 9$$
$$5x = 15$$
$$x = 3$$
Back-substitute 3 for x into the first equation.
$$y = 2x - 3$$
$$y = 2 \cdot 3 - 3 = 3$$
The solution set is $\{(3, 3)\}$.

6.
$$3x + 2y = -2$$
$$-4x + 5y = 18$$
To solve this system by the addition method, multiply the first equation by 4 and the second equation by 3. Then add the equations.
$$12x + 8y = -8$$
$$-12x + 15y = 54$$
$$\overline{23y = 46}$$
$$y = 2$$
Back-substitute 2 for y in the first equation of the original system.
$$3x + 2y = -2$$
$$3x + 2(2) = -2$$
$$3x + 4 = -2$$
$$3x = -6$$
$$x = -2$$
The solution set is $\{(-2, 2)\}$.

7.
$$3x - 2y = 6$$
x-intercept: 2
y-intercept: -3
checkpoint: $(4, 3)$
Draw a line through $(2, 0)$, $(0, -3)$ and $(4, 3)$.

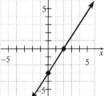

8. $y = -2x + 3$

The slope of the line is $-2 = \dfrac{-2}{1}$, and the y-intercept is 3. Begin at the point $(0, 3)$, and move down 2 units and to the right 1 unit to the point $(1, 1)$. Connect the points with a solid line.

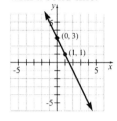

9. $y = -3$

The graph is a horizontal line with y-intercept -3.

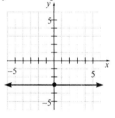

10. $\begin{aligned} -21 - 16 - 3(2 - 8) &= -21 - 16 - 3(-6) \\ &= -21 - 16 + 18 \\ &= -37 + 18 = -19 \end{aligned}$

11. $\left(\dfrac{4x^5}{2x^2}\right)^3 = \left(2x^3\right)^3 = 2^3 \cdot \left(x^3\right)^3 = 8x^9$

12. $\dfrac{\dfrac{1}{x} - 2}{4 - \dfrac{1}{x}}$

LCD $= x$

$\dfrac{\dfrac{1}{x} - 2}{4 - \dfrac{1}{x}} = \dfrac{x\left(\dfrac{1}{x} - 2\right)}{x\left(4 - \dfrac{1}{x}\right)}$

$= \dfrac{x \cdot \dfrac{1}{x} - x \cdot 2}{x \cdot 4 - x \cdot \dfrac{1}{x}} = \dfrac{1 - 2x}{4x - 1}$

13. $4x^2 - 13x + 3$

Factor by trial and error. Try various combinations until the correct one is found

$4x^2 - 13x + 3 = (4x - 1)(x - 3)$

14. $\begin{aligned} 4x^2 - 20x + 25 &= \left(2x\right)^2 - 2\left(2x \cdot 5\right) + 5^2 \\ &= \left(2x - 5\right)^2 \end{aligned}$

15. $\begin{aligned} 3x^2 - 75 &= 3\left(x^2 - 25\right) \\ &= 3(x + 5)(x - 5) \end{aligned}$

16. $\begin{aligned} &\left(4x^2 - 3x + 2\right) - \left(5x^2 - 7x - 6\right) \\ &= \left(4x^2 - 3x + 2\right) + \left(-5x^2 + 7x + 6\right) \\ &= -x^2 + 4x + 8 \end{aligned}$

17. $\begin{aligned} \dfrac{-8x^6 + 12x^4 - 4x^2}{4x^2} &= \dfrac{-8x^6}{4x^2} + \dfrac{12x^4}{4x^2} - \dfrac{4x^2}{4x^2} \\ &= -2x^4 + 3x^2 - 1 \end{aligned}$

18. $\dfrac{x+6}{x-2} + \dfrac{2x+1}{x+3}$

$\text{LCD} = (x-2)(x+3)$

$\dfrac{x+6}{x-2} + \dfrac{2x+1}{x+3}$

$= \dfrac{(x+6)(x+3)}{(x-2)(x+3)} + \dfrac{(2x+1)(x-2)}{(x-2)(x+3)}$

$= \dfrac{(x+6)(x+3)+(2x+1)(x-2)}{(x-2)(x+3)}$

$= \dfrac{x^2 +9x+18+2x^2 -3x-2}{(x-2)(x+3)}$

$= \dfrac{3x^2 +6x+16}{(x-2)(x+3)}$

19. Let x = the amount invested at 5%
$4000 - x$ = the amount invested at 9%

$0.05x + 0.09(4000-x) = 311$

$0.05x + 360 - 0.09x = 311$

$-0.04x + 360 = 311$

$-0.04x = -49$

$x = \dfrac{-49}{-0.04}$

$x = 1225$

If x = 1225, then $4000 - x = 2775$.
$1225 was invested at 5% and $2775 at
9%.

20. Let x = the length of the shorter piece.
Then $3x$ = the length of the larger piece.

$x + 3x = 68$

$4x = 68$

$x = 17$

If x = 17, then $3x = 51$.
The lengths of the pieces are 17 inches
and 51 inches.

Mid-Textbook Check Point

1.
$$2 - 4(x+2) = 5 - 3(2x+1)$$
$$2 - 4x - 8 = 5 - 6x - 3$$
$$-4x - 6 = -6x + 2$$
$$-4x - 6 + 6x = -6x + 2 + 6x$$
$$2x - 6 = 2$$
$$2x - 6 + 6 = 2 + 6$$
$$2x = 8$$
$$\frac{2x}{2} = \frac{8}{2}$$
$$x = 4$$
The solution set it $\{4\}$.

2.
$$\frac{x}{2} - 3 = \frac{x}{5}$$
Multiply both sides by the least common denominator of the fractions, 10:
$$10\left(\frac{x}{2} - 3\right) = 10\left(\frac{x}{5}\right)$$
$$5x - 30 = 2x$$
$$3x - 30 = 0$$
$$3x = 30$$
$$x = 10$$
The solution set it $\{10\}$.

3.
$$3x + 9 \geq 5(x-1)$$
$$3x + 9 \geq 5x - 5$$
$$3x + 9 - 5x \geq 5x - 5 - 5x$$
$$-2x + 9 \geq -5$$
$$-2x + 9 - 9 \geq -5 - 9$$
$$-2x \geq -14$$
$$\frac{-2x}{-2} \leq \frac{-14}{-2}$$
$$x \leq 7$$
The solution set is $\{x \mid x \leq 7\}$ or $(-\infty, 7]$.

4.
$$2x + 3y = 6$$
$$x + 2y = 5$$
Multiply the second equation by -2 and add the result to the first equation.
$$2x + 3y = 6$$
$$\underline{-2x - 4y = -10}$$
$$-y = -4$$
$$y = 4$$
Back-substitute 4 for y into either of the original equations to find x. We choose to use the second equation:
$$x + 2y = 5$$
$$x + 2(4) = 5$$
$$x + 8 = 5$$
$$x = -3$$
The solution set is $\{(-3, 4)\}$.

5.
$$3x - 2y = 1$$
$$y = 10 - 2x$$
Substitute the expression $10 - 2x$ for y into the first equation and solve for x.
$$3x - 2(10 - 2x) = 1$$
$$3x - 20 + 4x = 1$$
$$7x - 20 = 1$$
$$7x = 21$$
$$x = 3$$
Back-substitute 3 for x into either of the original equations to find y. We choose to use the second equation:
$$y = 10 - 2x$$
$$y = 10 - 2(3)$$
$$y = 10 - 6$$
$$y = 4$$
The solution set is $\{(3, 4)\}$.

398

6. $\dfrac{3}{x+5}-1=\dfrac{4-x}{2x+10}$

$\dfrac{3}{x+5}-1=\dfrac{4-x}{2(x+5)}$

Multiply both sides of the equation by the LCD, $2(x+5)$.

$2(x+5)\left(\dfrac{3}{x+5}-1\right)=2(x+5)\left(\dfrac{4-x}{2(x+5)}\right)$

$2(3)-2(x+5)(1)=4-x$

$6-2x-10=4-x$

$-2x-4=4-x$

$-x-4=4$

$-x=8$

$x=-8$

This proposed solution checks, so the solution set is $\{-8\}$.

7. $x+\dfrac{6}{x}=-5$

Multiply both sides of the equation by the LCD, x.

$x\left(x+\dfrac{6}{x}\right)=x(-5)$

$x^2+6=-5x$

$x^2+5x+6=0$

$(x+3)(x+2)=0$

$x+3=0$ or $x+2=0$

$x=-3$ $\qquad$ $x=-2$

Both proposed solutions check, so the solution set is $\{-3,-2\}$.

8. $\dfrac{12x^3}{3x^{12}}=\dfrac{12}{3}\cdot\dfrac{x^3}{x^{12}}=4x^{3-12}=4x^{-9}=\dfrac{4}{x^9}$

9. $4\cdot6\div2\cdot3+(-5)=24\div2\cdot3+(-5)$

$=12\cdot3+(-5)$

$=36+(-5)$

$=31$

10. $(6x^2-8x+3)-(-4x^2+x-1)$

$=6x^2-8x+3+4x^2-x+1$

$=10x^2-4x+4$

11. $(7x+4)(3x-5)$

$=7x(3x)-7x(5)+4(3x)-4(5)$

$=21x^2-35x+12x-20$

$=21x^2-23x-20$

12. $(5x-2)^2=(5x)^2-2(5x)(2)+2^2$

$=25x^2-20x+4$

13. $(x+y)(x^2-xy+y^2)$

$=x(x^2)-x(xy)+x(y^2)$

$\qquad\qquad +y(x^2)-y(xy)+y(y^2)$

$=x^3-x^2y+xy^2+x^2y-xy^2+y^3$

$=x^3+y^3$

14. $\dfrac{x^2+6x+8}{x^2}\div(3x^2+6x)$

$=\dfrac{x^2+6x+8}{x^2}\cdot\dfrac{1}{3x^2+6x}$

$=\dfrac{(x+4)(x+2)}{x^2}\cdot\dfrac{1}{3x(x+2)}$

$=\dfrac{(x+4)\cancel{(x+2)}}{x^2}\cdot\dfrac{1}{3x\cancel{(x+2)}}$

$=\dfrac{x+4}{3x^3}$

15.

$$\frac{x}{x^2+2x-3} - \frac{x}{x^2-5x+4}$$

$$= \frac{x}{(x+3)(x-1)} - \frac{x}{(x-4)(x-1)}$$

The LCD is $(x+3)(x-1)(x-4)$

$$\frac{x(x-4)}{(x+3)(x-1)(x-4)} - \frac{x(x+3)}{(x-4)(x-1)(x+3)}$$

$$= \frac{x(x-4)-x(x+3)}{(x+3)(x-1)(x-4)}$$

$$= \frac{x^2-4x-x^2-3x}{(x+3)(x-1)(x-4)}$$

$$= \frac{-7x}{(x+3)(x-1)(x-4)}$$

16.

$$\frac{x-\dfrac{1}{5}}{5-\dfrac{1}{x}}$$

Multiply the numerator and denominator by the LCD, $5x$.

$$\frac{5x}{5x} \cdot \frac{x-\dfrac{1}{5}}{5-\dfrac{1}{x}} = \frac{5x\cdot x-5x\cdot\dfrac{1}{5}}{5x\cdot5-5x\cdot\dfrac{1}{x}}$$

$$= \frac{5x^2-x}{25x-5} = \frac{x(5x-1)}{5(5x-1)} = \frac{x}{5}$$

17. $4x^2-49 = (2x)^2-7^2$

$$= (2x+7)(2x-7)$$

18. $x^3+3x^2-x-3 = x^2(x+3)-1(x+3)$

$$= (x+3)(x^2-1)$$

$$= (x+3)(x+1)(x-1)$$

19. $2x^2+8x-42 = 2(x^2+4x-21)$

$$= 2(x-3)(x+7)$$

20. $x^5-16x = x(x^4-16)$

$$= x(x^2+4)(x^2-4)$$

$$= x(x^2+4)(x+2)(x-2)$$

21. $x^3-10x^2+25x = x(x^2-10x+25)$

$$= x(x-5)^2$$

22. $x^3-8 = x^3-2^3$

$$= (x-2)(x^2+x\cdot2+2^2)$$

$$= (x-2)(x^2+2x+4)$$

23.

$$y = \frac{1}{3}x-1$$

The slope is $\dfrac{1}{3}$, and the y-intercept is -1. Plot the point $(0,-1)$. We move up 1 unit and to the right 3 units to the point $(3,0)$. Find additional points as needed and connect with a line.

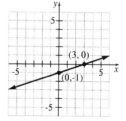

400

24. $3x + 2y = -6$

Let $x = 0$: $3(0) + 2y = -6$
$$2y = -6$$
$$y = -3$$

The y-intercept is -3, so the line passes through the point $(0, -3)$.

Let $y = 0$: $3x + 2(0) = -6$
$$3x = -6$$
$$x = -2$$

The x-intercept is -2, so the line passes through the point $(-2, 0)$. Find additional points to check and connect them with a straight line.

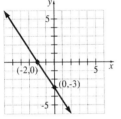

25. $y = -2$

The graph is a horizontal line that passes through the point $(0, -2)$.

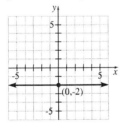

26. $m = \dfrac{y_2 - y_1}{x_2 - x_1} = \dfrac{-3 - 3}{2 - (-1)} = \dfrac{-6}{3} = -2$

27. $m = \dfrac{y_2 - y_1}{x_2 - x_1} = \dfrac{6 - 2}{3 - 1} = \dfrac{4}{2} = 2$

The point-slope equation is
$$y - y_1 = m(x - x_1)$$
$$y - 2 = 2(x - 1) \quad \text{or} \quad y - 6 = 2(x - 3)$$

The slope-intercept equation is
$$y - 2 = 2(x - 1)$$
$$y - 2 = 2x - 2$$
$$y = 2x$$

28. Let $x =$ the number.
$$5x - 7 = 208$$
$$5x = 215$$
$$x = 43$$

The number is 43.

29. Let $x =$ the price before the reduction.
$$x - 0.20x = 256$$
$$0.80x = 256$$
$$x = 320$$

The price of the digital camera before the reduction is $320.

30. Let $x =$ the width of the field.
$3x =$ the length of the field.
$$2x + 2(3x) = 400$$
$$2x + 6x = 400$$
$$8x = 400$$
$$x = 50$$
$$3x = 150$$

The width of the field is 50 yards, and the length of the field is 150 yards.

31. Let $x =$ the amount invested at 7%.
$y =$ the amount invested at 9%.

	Principal	Rate	Interest
7%	x	0.07	$0.07x$
9%	y	0.09	$0.09y$
	20,000		1550

$x + y = 20,000$
$0.07x + 0.09y = 1550$

Multiply the first equation by -0.07 and add the result to the second equation.

$$-0.07x - 0.07y = -1400$$
$$\underline{0.07x + 0.09y = 1550}$$
$$0.02y = 150$$
$$y = 7500$$

Back-substitute 7500 for y into one of the original equations. We use the first equation.

$x + 7500 = 20,000$
$x = 12,500$

$12,500 was invested at 7% and $7500 was invested at 9%.

32. Let $x =$ the number of liters of 40% acid solution.
$y =$ the number of liters of 70% acid solution.

	No. of liters	Percent of acid	Amount of acid
40% Sol	x	40% = 0.4	$0.4x$
70% Sol	y	70% = 0.7	$0.7y$
50% Mix	12	50% = 0.5	$0.5(12) = 6$

$x + y = 12$
$0.4x + 0.7y = 6$

Multiply the first equation by -0.4 and add the result to the second equation.

$$-0.4x - 0.4y = -4.8$$
$$\underline{0.4x + 0.7y = 6}$$
$$0.3y = 1.2$$
$$y = 4$$

Back-substitute 4 for y into one of the original equations. We use the first equation.

$x + 4 = 12$
$x = 8$

The chemist should mix 8 liters of 40% acid solution with 4 liters of 70% acid solution.

33. Let $x =$ the height.

$$\frac{1}{2} \cdot 15 \cdot x = 120$$
$$\frac{15x}{2} = 120$$
$$15x = 240$$
$$x = 16$$

The triangular sail is 16 feet high.

34. Let $x =$ the measure of the 2nd angle.
$x + 10 =$ the measure of the 1st angle.
$4x + 20 =$ the measure of the 3rd angle.

$$x + (x + 10) + (4x + 20) = 180$$
$$6x + 30 = 180$$
$$6x = 150$$
$$x = 25$$
$$x + 10 = 35$$
$$4x + 20 = 120$$

The 1st angle measures $35°$; the 2nd angle measures $25°$, and the 3rd angle measures $120°$.

35. Let x = the price of a TV.

   y = the price of a stereo.

$3x + 4y = 2530$

$4x + 3y = 2510$

Multiply the first equation by 4, multiply the second equation by -3, and add the results.

$12x + 16y = 10,120$

$\underline{-12x - 9y = -7530}$

$7y = 2590$

$y = 370$

Back-substitute 370 for y into one of the original equations. We use the first equation.

$3x + 4(370) = 2530$

$3x + 1480 = 2530$

$3x = 1050$

$x = 350$

The price of the TV is $350, and the price of the stereo is $370.

36. Let x = the width of the rectangle.

$x + 6$ = the length of the rectangle.

$x(x + 6) = 55$

$x^2 + 6x = 55$

$x^2 + 6x - 55 = 0$

$(x + 11)(x - 5) = 0$

$x + 11 = 0 \quad$ of $\quad x - 5 = 0$

$x = -11 \qquad x = 5$

Disregard -11 because the witdth of a rectangle cannot be negative. So $x = 5$ and $x + 6 = 11$.

The width of the rectangle is 5 meters, and the length is 11 meters.

Chapter 8
Basics of Functions

8.1 Exercise Set

1. The relation is a function.
   The domain is $\{1, 3, 5\}$.
   The range is $\{2, 4, 5\}$.

3. The relation is not a function.
   The domain is $\{3, 4\}$.
   The range is $\{4, 5\}$.

5. The relation is a function.
   The domain is $\{-3, -2, -1, 0\}$.
   The range is $\{-3, -2, -1, 0\}$.

7. The relation is not a function.
   The domain is $\{1\}$.
   The range is $\{4, 5, 6\}$.

9. a. $f(0) = 0 + 1 = 1$

   b. $f(5) = 5 + 1 = 6$

   c. $f(-8) = -8 + 1 = -7$

   d. $f(2a) = 2a + 1$

   e. $f(a+2) = (a+2) + 1$
   $= a + 2 + 1 = a + 3$

11. a. $g(0) = 3(0) - 2 = 0 - 2 = -2$

   b. $g(-5) = 3(-5) - 2$
   $= -15 - 2 = -17$

   c. $g\left(\dfrac{2}{3}\right) = 3\left(\dfrac{2}{3}\right) - 2 = 2 - 2 = 0$

   d. $g(4b) = 3(4b) - 2 = 12b - 2$

e. $g(b+4) = 3(b+4) - 2$
   $= 3b + 12 - 2 = 3b + 10$

13. a. $h(0) = 3(0)^2 + 5 = 3(0) + 5$
   $= 0 + 5 = 5$

   b. $h(-1) = 3(-1)^2 + 5 = 3(1) + 5$
   $= 3 + 5 = 8$

   c. $h(4) = 3(4)^2 + 5 = 3(16) + 5$
   $= 48 + 5 = 53$

   d. $h(-3) = 3(-3)^2 + 5 = 3(9) + 5$
   $= 27 + 5 = 32$

   e. $h(4b) = 3(4b)^2 + 5 = 3(16b^2) + 5$
   $= 48b^2 + 5$

15. a. $f(0) = 2(0)^2 + 3(0) - 1$
   $= 0 + 0 - 1 = -1$

   b. $f(3) = 2(3)^2 + 3(3) - 1$
   $= 2(9) + 9 - 1$
   $= 18 + 9 - 1 = 26$

   c. $f(-4) = 2(-4)^2 + 3(-4) - 1$
   $= 2(16) - 12 - 1$
   $= 32 - 12 - 1 = 19$

   d. $f(b) = 2(b)^2 + 3(b) - 1$
   $= 2b^2 + 3b - 1$

404

e. $f(5a) = 2(5a)^2 + 3(5a) - 1$

$\qquad = 2(25a^2) + 15a - 1$

$\qquad = 50a^2 + 15a - 1$

17. a. $f(0) = \dfrac{2(0) - 3}{(0) - 4} = \dfrac{0 - 3}{0 - 4}$

$\qquad = \dfrac{-3}{-4} = \dfrac{3}{4}$

b. $f(3) = \dfrac{2(3) - 3}{(3) - 4} = \dfrac{6 - 3}{3 - 4}$

$\qquad = \dfrac{3}{-1} = -3$

c. $f(-4) = \dfrac{2(-4) - 3}{(-4) - 4} = \dfrac{-8 - 3}{-8}$

$\qquad = \dfrac{-11}{-8} = \dfrac{11}{8}$

d. $f(-5) = \dfrac{2(-5) - 3}{(-5) - 4} = \dfrac{-10 - 3}{-9}$

$\qquad = \dfrac{-13}{-9} = \dfrac{13}{9}$

e. $f(a + h) = \dfrac{2(a + h) - 3}{(a + h) - 4}$

$\qquad = \dfrac{2a + 2h - 3}{a + h - 4}$

f. Four must be excluded from the domain, because four would make the denominator zero. Division by zero is undefined.

19. The vertical line test shows that the graph represents a function.

21. The vertical line test shows that the graph does not represent a function.

23. The vertical line test shows that the graph represents a function.

25. The vertical line test shows that the graph does not represent a function.

27. $f(-2) = -4$

29. $f(4) = 4$

31. $f(-3) = 0$

33. $g(-4) = 2$

35. $g(-10) = 2$

37. When $x = -2$, $g(x) = 1$.

39. The domain is $\{x \mid 0 \le x < 5\}$.
The range is $\{y \mid -1 \le y < 5\}$.

41. The domain is $\{x \mid x \ge 0\}$.
The range is $\{y \mid y \ge 1\}$.

43. The domain is $\{x \mid -2 \le x \le 6\}$.
The range is $\{y \mid -2 \le y \le 6\}$.

45. The domain is $\{x \mid x \text{ is a real number}\}$.
The range is $\{y \mid y \le -2\}$.

47. The domain is $\{x \mid x = -5, -2, 0, 1, 3\}$.
The range is $\{y \mid y = 2\}$.

49.
$$g(1) = 3(1) - 5 = 3 - 5 = -2$$
$$f(g(1)) = f(-2) = (-2)^2 - (-2) + 4$$
$$= 4 + 2 + 4 = 10$$

60.
$$g(-1) = 3(-1) - 5 = -3 - 5 = -8$$
$$f(g(-1)) = f(-8) = (-8)^2 - (-8) + 4$$
$$= 64 + 8 + 4 = 76$$

51.
$$\sqrt{3 - (-1)} - (-6)^2 + 6 \div (-6) \cdot 4$$
$$= \sqrt{3 + 1} - 36 + 6 \div (-6) \cdot 4$$
$$= \sqrt{4} - 36 + -1 \cdot 4$$
$$= 2 - 36 + -4$$
$$= -34 + -4$$
$$= -38$$

52.
$$|-4 - (-1)| - (-3)^2 + -3 \div 3 \cdot -6$$
$$= |-4 + 1| - 9 + -3 \div 3 \cdot -6$$
$$= |-3| - 9 + -1 \cdot -6$$
$$= 3 - 9 + 6 = -6 + 6 = 0$$

53. $f(-x) - f(x)$
$$= (-x)^3 + (-x) - 5 - (x^3 + x - 5)$$
$$= -x^3 - x - 5 - x^3 - x + 5 = -2x^3 - 2x$$

54. $f(-x) - f(x)$
$$= (-x)^2 - 3(-x) + 7 - (x^2 - 3x + 7)$$
$$= x^2 + 3x + 7 - x^2 + 3x - 7$$
$$= 6x$$

55. a. $f(-2) = 3(-2) + 5 = -6 + 5 = -1$

b. $f(0) = 4(0) + 7 = 0 + 7 = 7$

c. $f(3) = 4(3) + 7 = 12 + 7 = 19$

d. $f(-100) + f(100)$
$$= 3(-100) + 5 + 4(100) + 7$$
$$= -300 + 5 + 400 + 7$$
$$= 100 + 12$$
$$= 112$$

56. a. $f(-3) = 6(-3) - 1 = -18 - 1 = -19$

b. $f(0) = 7(0) + 3 = 0 + 3 = 3$

c. $f(4) = 7(4) + 3 = 28 + 3 = 31$

d. $f(-100) + f(100)$
$$= 6(-100) - 1 + 7(100) + 3$$
$$= -600 - 1 + 700 + 3$$
$$= 100 + 2 = 102$$

57. The domain is $\{x \mid x \neq 1\}$.
The range is $\{y \mid y \neq 0\}$.

58. The domain is $\{x \mid x \text{ is a real number}\}$.
The range is $\{y \mid y > 0\}$.

59. a. {(EL,1%),(L,7%),(SL,11%),
(M,52%),(SC,13%),(C,13%),
(EC,3%)}

b. Yes, the relation in part (a) is a function because each ideology corresponds to exactly one percentage.

c. {(1%,EL),(7%,L),(11%,SL),
(52%,M),(13%,SC),(13%,C),
(3%,EC)}

d. No, the relation in part (b) is not a function because 13% in the domain corresponds to two ideologies, SC and C, in the range.

61. $W(16) = 0.07(16) + 4.1$

$$= 1.12 + 4.1 = 5.22$$

In 2000 there were 5.22 million women enrolled in U.S. colleges.
$(2000, 5.22)$

63. $W(20) = 0.07(20) + 4.1$

$$= 1.4 + 4.1 = 5.5$$
$$M(20) = 0.01(20) + 3.9$$
$$= 0.2 + 3.9 = 4.1$$
$$W(20) - M(20) = 5.5 - 4.1 = 1.4$$

In 2004, there will be 1.4 million more women than men enrolled in U.S. colleges.

65. $f(20) = 0.4(20)^2 - 36(20) + 1000$

$$= 0.4(400) - 720 + 1000$$
$$= 160 - 720 + 1000$$
$$= -560 + 1000 = 440$$

Twenty-year-old drivers have 440 accidents per 50 million miles driven.
$(20, 440)$

67. The graph reaches its lowest point at $x = 45$.

$$f(45) = 0.4(45)^2 - 36(45) + 1000$$
$$= 0.4(2025) - 1620 + 1000$$
$$= 810 - 1620 + 1000$$
$$= -810 + 1000 = 190$$

Drivers at age 45 have 190 accidents per 50 million miles driven. This is the least number of accidents for any driver between ages 16 and 74.

69. $f(60) \approx 3.1$

In 1960, 3.1% of the U.S. population was made up of Jewish Americans.

71. In 1919 and 1964, $f(x) = 3$. This means that in 1919 and 1964, 3% of the U.S. population was made up of Jewish Americans.

73. The percentage of Jewish Americans in the U.S. population reached a maximum in 1940. Using the graph to estimate, approximately 3.7% of the U.S. population was Jewish American.

75. Each year is paired with exactly one percentage. This means that each member of the domain is paired with one member of the range.

77. $f(3) = 0.83$

The cost of mailing a first-class letter weighing 3 ounces is $0.83.

79. The cost to mail a letter weighing 1.5 ounces is $0.60.

81. - 87. Answers will vary.

91. $f(x) = 3x + 7$

$$\frac{f(a+h) - f(a)}{h}$$

$$= \frac{[3(a+h) + 7] - [3a + 7]}{h}$$

$$= \frac{3a + 3h + 7 - 3a - 7}{h}$$

$$= \frac{3h}{h} = 3$$

93. $f(x + y) = f(x) + f(y); \quad f(1) = 3$

$$f(2) = f(1+1)$$
$$= f(1) + f(1)$$
$$= 3 + 3$$
$$= 6$$

$f(3) = f(1+2)$

$\quad = f(1) + f(2)$

$\quad = 3 + 6$

$\quad = 9$

$f(4) = f(1+3)$

$\quad = f(1) + f(3)$

$\quad = 3 + 9$

$\quad = 12$

No; $f(x+y)$ is not equal to $f(x) + f(y)$ for all functions. For example, consider $f(x) = x^2$.

94.

$24 \div 4\left[2 - (5-2)\right]^2 - 6$

$= 24 \div 4\left[2 - (3)\right]^2 - 6$

$= 24 \div 4[-1]^2 - 6$

$= 6[1] - 6 = 6 - 6 = 0$

95.

$\left(\dfrac{3x^2 y^{-2}}{y^3}\right)^{-2} = \left(\dfrac{3x^2}{y^5}\right)^{-2} = \left(\dfrac{y^5}{3x^2}\right)^2 = \dfrac{y^{10}}{9x^4}$

96.

$\dfrac{x}{3} = \dfrac{3x}{5} + 4$

$15\left(\dfrac{x}{3}\right) = 15\left(\dfrac{3x}{5} + 4\right)$

$15\left(\dfrac{x}{3}\right) = 15\left(\dfrac{3x}{5}\right) + 15(4)$

$5x = 3(3x) + 60$

$5x = 9x + 60$

$5x - 9x = 9x - 9x + 60$

$-4x = 60$

$\dfrac{-4x}{-4} = \dfrac{60}{-4}$

$x = -15$

The solution is -15 and the solution set is $\{-15\}$.

8.2 Exercise Set

1. The domain of f is $\{x \mid x \text{ is a real number}\}$.

3. The domain of g is $\{x \mid x \text{ is a real number and } x \neq -4\}$.

5. The domain of f is $\{x \mid x \text{ is a real number and } x \neq 3\}$.

7. The domain of g is $\{x \mid x \text{ is a real number and } x \neq 5\}$.

9. The domain of f is $\{x \mid x \text{ is a real number and } x \neq -7 \text{ and } x \neq 9\}$.

11. a. $(f+g)(x) = (3x+1) + (2x-6)$

$\quad = 3x + 1 + 2x - 6$

$\quad = 5x - 5$

b. $(f+g)(5) = 5(5) - 5$

$\quad = 25 - 5 = 20$

13. a. $(f+g)(x) = (x-5) + (3x^2)$

$\quad = x - 5 + 3x^2$

$\quad = 3x^2 + x - 5$

b. $(f+g)(5) = 3(5)^2 + 5 - 5$

$\quad = 3(25) = 75$

15. a. $(f+g)(x)$

$\quad = (2x^2 - x - 3) + (x+1)$

$\quad = 2x^2 - x - 3 + x + 1 = 2x^2 - 2$

408

b. $(f+g)(5) = 2(5)^2 - 2$
$$= 2(25) - 2$$
$$= 50 - 2 = 48$$

17. The domain of $f+g$ is $\{x|x$ is a real number$\}$.

19. The domain of $f+g$ is $\{x|x$ is a real number and $x \neq 5\}$.

21. The domain of $f+g$ is $\{x|x$ is a real number and $x \neq 0$ and $x \neq 5\}$.

23. The domain of $f+g$ is $\{x|x$ is a real number and $x \neq 2$ and $x \neq -3\}$.

25. Domain of $f+g$ is $\{x|x$ is a real number and $x \neq 2\}$.

27. Domain of $f+g$ is $\{x|x$ is a real number$\}$.

29. $(f+g)(x) = f(x) + g(x)$
$$= x^2 + 4x + 2 - x$$
$$= x^2 + 3x + 2$$
$(f+g)(3) = (3)^2 + 3(3) + 2$
$$= 9 + 9 + 2 = 20$$

31. $f(-2) = (-2)^2 + 4(-2)$
$$= 4 + (-8) = -4$$
$g(-2) = 2 - (-2) = 2 + 2 = 4$
$f(-2) + g(-2) = -4 + 4 = 0$

33. $(f-g)(x) = f(x) - g(x)$
$$= (x^2 + 4x) - (2 - x)$$
$$= x^2 + 4x - 2 + x$$
$$= x^2 + 5x - 2$$
$(f-g)(5) = (5)^2 + 5(5) - 2$
$$= 25 + 25 - 2 = 48$$

35. From Exercise 31, we know
$f(-2) = -4$, and $g(-2) = 4$.
$f(-2) - g(-2) = -4 - 4 = -8$

37. $(fg)(x) = f(x) \cdot g(x)$
$$= (x^2 + 4x)(2 - x)$$
$$= 2x^2 - x^3 + 8x - 4x^2$$
$$= -x^3 - 2x^2 + 8x$$
$(fg)(2) = -(2)^3 - 2(2)^2 + 8(2)$
$$= -8 - 2(4) + 16$$
$$= -8 - 8 + 16$$
$$= 0$$

39. $f(5) = (5)^2 + 4(5) = 25 + 20 = 45$
$g(5) = 2 - 5 = -3$
$(fg)(5) = f(5) \cdot g(5)$
$$= 45(-3) = -135$$

41. $\left(\dfrac{f}{g}\right)(x) = \dfrac{f(x)}{g(x)} = \dfrac{x^2 + 4x}{2 - x}$
$\left(\dfrac{f}{g}\right)(1) = \dfrac{(1)^2 + 4(1)}{2 - (1)} = \dfrac{1+4}{1} = \dfrac{5}{1} = 5$

43. $\left(\dfrac{f}{g}\right)(-1) = \dfrac{(-1)^2 + 4(-1)}{2 - (-1)}$
$$= \dfrac{1-4}{3} = \dfrac{-3}{3} = -1$$

409

45. The domain of $f + g$ is $\{x \mid x$ is a real number$\}$.

47. $\left(\dfrac{f}{g}\right)(x) = \dfrac{f(x)}{g(x)} = \dfrac{x^2 + 4x}{2 - x}$

The domain of $\dfrac{f}{g}$ is $\{x \mid x$ is a real number and $x \neq 2\}$.

49. $(f + g)(-3) = f(-3) + g(-3)$

$4 + 1 = 5$

50. $(g - f)(-2) = g(-2) - f(-2)$

$= 2 - 3 = -1$

51. $(fg)(2) = f(2)g(2) = (-1)(1) = -1$

52. $\left(\dfrac{g}{f}\right)(3) = \dfrac{g(3)}{f(3)} = \dfrac{0}{-3} = 0$

53. The domain of $f + g$ is $\{x \mid -4 \le x \le 3\}$.

54. The domain of $\dfrac{f}{g}$ is $\{x \mid -4 < x < 3\}$

55. The graph of $f + g$

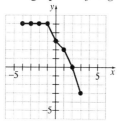

56. The graph of $f - g$

57. $(f + g)(1) - (g - f)(-1)$

$= f(1) + g(1) - [g(-1) - f(-1)]$

$= f(1) + g(1) - g(-1) + f(-1)$

$= -6 + -3 - (-2) + 3$

$= -6 + -3 + 2 + 3 = -4$

58. $(f + g)(-1) - (g - f)(0)$

$= f(-1) + g(-1) - \left[g(0) - f(0)\right]$

$= 3 + (-2) - \left[4 - (-2)\right]$

$= 3 + -2 - (4 + 2) = 3 + -2 - 6 = -5$

59.

$(fg)(-2) - \left[\left(\dfrac{f}{g}\right)(1)\right]^2$

$= f(-2)g(-2) - \left[\dfrac{f(1)}{g(1)}\right]^2$

$= 5 \cdot 0 - \left[\dfrac{-6}{-3}\right]^2 = 0 - 2^2 = 0 - 4 = -4$

60.

$(fg)(2) - \left[\left(\dfrac{g}{f}\right)(0)\right]^2$

$= f(2)g(2) - \left[\dfrac{g(0)}{f(0)}\right]^2$

$= 0(1) - \left(\dfrac{4}{-2}\right)^2 = 0 - (-2)^2$

$= 0 - 4 = -4$

410

61. The domain is $[x \mid x = 0, 1, 2, ..., 7]$.

63. **a.** $(B - D)(x)$

$= 24,770x + 3,873,266$

$\qquad - (20,205x + 2,294,970)$

$= 24,770x + 3,873,266$

$\qquad - 20,205x - 2,294,970$

$= 4565x + 1,578,296$

This function represents the change in population; i.e. the difference between births and deaths in the U.S.

b. $(B - D)(6) = 4565(6) + 1,578,296$

$= 1,605,686$

This means there was an increase in the population of 1,605,686 in 2001.

c. Using the table,

$(B - D)(6) = 4,025,933 - 2,416,425$

$= 1,609,508$

This function models the data in the table fairly well since the difference in the answers to part (b) and part (c) is fairly small.

65. $(f + g)(x)$ represents the total world population, $h(x)$.

67. $(f + g)(2000) = f(2000) + g(2000)$

$= h(2000) = 7.5$

This means that the total world population is 7.5 billion.

69. First, find $(R - C)(x)$.

$(R - C)(x) = 65x - (600,000 + 45x)$

$= 65x - 600,000 - 45x$

$= 20x - 600,000$

$(R - C)(20,000)$

$= 20(20,000) - 600,000$

$= 400,000 - 600,000 = -200,000$

This means that if the company produces and sells 20,000 radios, it will lose $200,000.

$(R - C)(30,000)$

$= 20(30,000) - 600,000$

$= 600,000 - 600,000 = 0$

If the company produces and sells 30,000 radios, it will break even with its costs equal to its revenue.

$(R - C)(40,000)$

$= 20(40,000) - 600,000$

$= 800,000 - 600,000 = 200,000$

This means that if the company produces and sells 40,000 radios, it will make a profit of $200,000.

71. – 75. Answers will vary.

77. $y_1 = x - 4 \qquad\qquad y_2 = 2x$

$y_3 = y_1 - y_2$

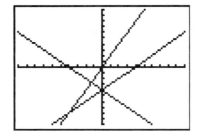

79. $y_1 = x^2 - 2x$ $\qquad$ $y_2 = x$

$y_3 = \dfrac{y_1}{y_2}$

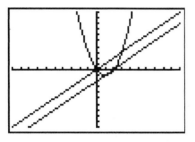

81. Statement **d.** is false. If $(fg)(a) = 0$, then $f(a) = 0$ or $g(a) = 0$. If $g(a) = 0$, $(fg)(a) = 0$ regardless of the value of $f(a)$.

Statement **a.** is true. If $(f + g)(a) = 0$, then $f(a) + g(a) = 0$ and $f(a) = -g(a)$. This means that $f(a)$ and $g(a)$ are additive inverses.

Statement **b.** is true. If $(f - g)(a) = 0$, then $f(a) - g(a) = 0$ and $f(a) = g(a)$.

Statement **c.** is true. If $\left(\dfrac{f}{g}\right)(a) = 0$,

then $\dfrac{f(a)}{g(a)} = 0$. The only way that

$\dfrac{f(a)}{g(a)}$ can equal zero is if $f(a)$ equals

zero. (Recall: $g(a)$ cannot equal zero because division by zero is meaningless.)

83. $\begin{cases} 11x + 4y = -3 \\ -13x + y = 15 \end{cases}$

Multiply both sides of the second equation by -4 and add the two equations.

$$11x + 4y = -3$$
$$\underline{52x - 4y = -60}$$
$$63x \qquad = -63$$
$$x \qquad = -1$$

Back-substitute $x = -1$ in the second equation and solve for y.

$$-13x + y = 15$$
$$-13(-1) + y = 15$$
$$13 + y = 15$$
$$y = 2$$

The solution is $(-1, 2)$, and the solution set is $\{(-1, 2)\}$.

84. $3(6 - x) = 3 - 2(x - 4)$

$$18 - 3x = 3 - 2x + 8$$
$$18 - 3x = 11 - 2x$$
$$18 = 11 + x$$
$$7 = x$$

The solution is 7, and the solution set is $\{7\}$.

85. $f(b + 2) = 6(b + 2) - 4$
$$= 6b + 12 - 4 = 6b + 8$$

Mid-Chapter Check Point

1. The relation is not a function.
The domain is $\{1, 2\}$.
The range is $\{-6, 4, 6\}$.

2. The relation is a function.
The domain is $\{0, 2, 3\}$.
The range is $\{1, 4\}$.

3. The relation is a function.
The domain is $\{x \mid -2 \le x < 2\}$.
The range is $\{y \mid 0 \le y \le 3\}$.

4. The relation is not a function.
The domain is $\{x \mid -3 < x \le 4\}$.
The range is $\{y \mid -1 \le y \le 2\}$.

5. The relation is not a function.
The domain is $\{-2, -1, 0, 1, 2\}$.
The range is $\{-2, -1, 1, 3\}$.

6. The relation is a function.
The domain is $\{x \mid x \le 1\}$.
The range is $\{y \mid y \ge -1\}$.

7. The graph of f represents the graph of a function because every element in the domain is corresponds to exactly one element in the range. It passes the vertical line test.

8. $f(-4) = 3$

9. The function $f(x) = 4$ when $x = -2$.

10. The function $f(x) = 0$ when $x = 2$ and $x = -6$.

11. The domain of f is $\{x \mid x \text{ is a real number}\}$.

12. The range of f is $\{y \mid y \le 4\}$.

13. The domain is $\{x \mid x \text{ is a real number}\}$.

14. The domain of g is $\{x \mid x \text{ is a real number and } x \ne -2 \text{ and } x \ne 2\}$.

15. $f(0) = 0^2 - 3(0) + 8 = 8$

$g(-10) = -2(-10) - 5 = 20 - 5 = 15$

$f(0) + g(-10) = 8 + 15 = 23$

16. $f(-1) = (-1)^2 - 3(-1) + 8$
$\qquad = 1 + 3 + 8 = 12$

$g(3) = -2(3) - 5 = -6 - 5 = -11$

$f(-1) - g(3) = 12 - (-11)$
$\qquad = 12 + 11 = 23$

17. $f(a) = a^2 - 3a + 8$

$g(a+3) = -2(a+3) - 5$
$\qquad = -2a - 6 - 5 = -2a - 11$

$f(a) + g(a+3) = a^2 - 3a + 8 + -2a - 11$
$\qquad = a^2 - 5a - 3$

18. $(f+g)(x) = x^2 - 3x + 8 + -2x - 5$
$\qquad = x^2 - 5x + 3$

$(f+g)(-2) = (-2)^2 - 5(-2) + 3$
$\qquad = 4 + 10 + 3 = 17$

19. $(f-g)(x) = x^2 - 3x + 8 - (-2x - 5)$
$\qquad = x^2 - 3x + 8 + 2x + 5$
$\qquad = x^2 - x + 13$

$(f-g)(5) = (5)^2 - 5 + 13$
$\qquad = 25 - 5 + 13 = 33$

20. $(fg)(x) = f(x) \cdot g(x)$
$\qquad = (x^2 - 3x + 8)(-2x - 5)$
$\qquad = -2x^3 + 6x^2 - 16x - 5x^2 + 15x - 40$
$\qquad = -2x^3 + x^2 - x - 40$

$(fg)(-1) = -2(-1)^3 + (-1)^2 - (-1) - 40$
$\qquad = 2 + 1 + 1 - 40 = -36$

413

21.

$$\left(\frac{f}{g}\right)(x) = \frac{x^2 - 3x + 8}{-2x - 5}$$

$$\left(\frac{f}{g}\right)(-4) = \frac{(-4)^2 - 3(-4) + 8}{-2(-4) - 5}$$

$$= \frac{16 + 12 + 8}{8 - 5} = \frac{36}{3} = 12$$

22.

The domain of $\dfrac{f}{g}$ is

$$\left\{ x \mid x \text{ is a real number and } x \neq -\frac{5}{2} \right\}.$$

8.3 Exercise Set

1.   **a.** $(f \circ g)(x) = f(g(x))$

$$= f(x + 7)$$

$$= 2(x + 7) = 2x + 14$$

b. $(g \circ f)(x) = g(f(x))$

$$= g(2x) = 2x + 7$$

c. $(f \circ g)(2) = 2(2) + 14$

$$= 4 + 14 = 18$$

3.   **a.** $(f \circ g)(x) = f(g(x))$

$$= f(2x + 1)$$

$$= (2x + 1) + 4 = 2x + 5$$

b. $(g \circ f)(x) = g(f(x))$

$$= g(x + 4)$$

$$= 2(x + 4) + 1$$

$$= 2x + 8 + 1 = 2x + 9$$

c. $(f \circ g)(2) = 2(2) + 5 = 4 + 5 = 9$

5.   **a.** $(f \circ g)(x) = f(g(x))$

$$= f(5x^2 - 2)$$

$$= 4(5x^2 - 2) - 3$$

$$= 20x^2 - 8 - 3$$

$$= 20x^2 - 11$$

b. $(g \circ f)(x) = g(f(x))$

$$= g(4x - 3)$$

$$= 5(4x - 3)^2 - 2$$

$$= 5(16x^2 - 24x + 9) - 2$$

$$= 80x^2 - 120x + 45 - 2$$

$$= 80x^2 - 120x + 43$$

c. $(f \circ g)(2) = 20(2)^2 - 11$

$$= 20(4) - 11$$

$$= 80 - 11 = 69$$

7.   **a.** $(f \circ g)(x) = f(g(x))$

$$= f(x^2 - 2)$$

$$= (x^2 - 2)^2 + 2$$

$$= x^4 - 4x^2 + 4 + 2$$

$$= x^4 - 4x^2 + 6$$

b. $(g \circ f)(x) = g(f(x))$

$$= g(x^2 + 2)$$

$$= (x^2 + 2)^2 - 2$$

$$= x^4 + 4x^2 + 4 - 2$$

$$= x^4 + 4x^2 + 2$$

c. $(f \circ g)(2) = 2^4 - 4(2)^2 + 6$

$$= 16 - 4(4) + 6$$

$$= 16 - 16 + 6 = 6$$

9. **a.** $(f \circ g)(x) = f(g(x))$

$= f(x-1) = \sqrt{x-1}$

b. $(g \circ f)(x) = g(f(x))$

$= g(\sqrt{x}) = \sqrt{x} - 1$

c. $(f \circ g)(2) = \sqrt{2-1} = \sqrt{1} = 1$

11. **a.** $(f \circ g)(x) = f(g(x))$

$= f\left(\dfrac{x+3}{2}\right)$

$= 2\left(\dfrac{x+3}{2}\right) - 3$

$= x + 3 - 3 = x$

b. $(g \circ f)(x) = g(f(x))$

$= g(2x-3)$

$= \dfrac{(2x-3)+3}{2}$

$= \dfrac{2x-3+3}{2} = \dfrac{2x}{2} = x$

c. $(f \circ g)(2) = 2$

13. **a.** $(f \circ g)(x) = f(g(x))$

$= f\left(\dfrac{1}{x}\right)$

$= \dfrac{1}{\frac{1}{x}} = 1 \cdot \dfrac{x}{1} = x$

b. $(g \circ f)(x) = g(f(x))$

$= g\left(\dfrac{1}{x}\right)$

$= \dfrac{1}{\frac{1}{x}} = 1 \cdot \dfrac{x}{1} = x$

c. $(f \circ g)(2) = 2$

15. $f(g(x)) = f\left(\dfrac{x}{4}\right) = 4\left(\dfrac{x}{4}\right) = x$

$g(f(x)) = g(4x) = \dfrac{4x}{4} = x$

The functions are inverses.

17. $f(g(x)) = f\left(\dfrac{x-8}{3}\right)$

$= 3\left(\dfrac{x-8}{3}\right) + 8$

$= x - 8 + 8 = x$

$g(f(x)) = g(3x+8)$

$= \dfrac{(3x+8)-8}{3}$

$= \dfrac{3x+8-8}{3} = \dfrac{3x}{3} = x$

The functions are inverses.

19. $f(g(x)) = f\left(\dfrac{x+5}{9}\right)$

$= 5\left(\dfrac{x+5}{9}\right) - 9$

$= \dfrac{5x+25}{9} - \dfrac{81}{9}$

$= \dfrac{5x+25-81}{9} = \dfrac{5x-56}{9}$

$g(f(x)) = g(5x-9)$

$= \dfrac{(5x-9)+5}{9} = \dfrac{5x-4}{9}$

Since $f(g(x)) \neq g(f(x)) \neq x$, we conclude the functions are not inverses.

415

21.

$$f\left(g\left(x\right)\right) = f\left(\frac{3}{x}+4\right)$$

$$= \frac{3}{\left(\frac{3}{x}+4\right)-4}$$

$$= \frac{3}{\frac{3}{x}+4-4} = \frac{3}{\frac{3}{x}} = 3 \cdot \frac{x}{3} = x$$

$$g\left(f\left(x\right)\right) = g\left(\frac{3}{x-4}\right)$$

$$= \frac{3}{\frac{3}{x-4}}+4$$

$$= 3 \cdot \frac{x-4}{3}+4 = x-4+4 = x$$

The functions are inverses.

23. $f\left(g\left(x\right)\right) = f\left(-x\right) = -\left(-x\right) = x$

$g\left(f\left(x\right)\right) = g\left(-x\right) = -\left(-x\right) = x$

The functions are inverses.

25. **a.** $f\left(x\right) = x+3$

$y = x+3$

Interchange x and y and solve for y.

$x = y+3$

$x-3 = y$

$f^{-1}\left(x\right) = x-3$

b. $f\left(f^{-1}\left(x\right)\right) = f\left(x-3\right)$

$= \left(x-3\right)+3$

$= x-3+3 = x$

$f^{-1}\left(f\left(x\right)\right) = f\left(x+3\right)$

$= \left(x+3\right)-3$

$= x+3-3 = x$

27. **a.** $f\left(x\right) = 2x$

$y = 2x$

Interchange x and y and solve for y.

$x = 2y$

$\frac{x}{2} = y$

$f^{-1}\left(x\right) = \frac{x}{2}$

b. $f\left(f^{-1}\left(x\right)\right) = f\left(\frac{x}{2}\right) = 2\left(\frac{x}{2}\right) = x$

$f^{-1}\left(f\left(x\right)\right) = f\left(2x\right) = \frac{2x}{2} = x$

29. **a.** $f\left(x\right) = 2x+3$

$y = 2x+3$

Interchange x and y and solve for y.

$x = 2y+3$

$x-3 = 2y$

$\frac{x-3}{2} = y$

$f^{-1}\left(x\right) = \frac{x-3}{2}$

b. $f\left(f^{-1}\left(x\right)\right) = f\left(\frac{x-3}{2}\right)$

$= 2\left(\frac{x-3}{2}\right)+3$

$= x-3+3 = x$

$f^{-1}\left(f\left(x\right)\right) = f^{-1}\left(2x+3\right)$

$= \frac{\left(2x+3\right)-3}{2}$

$= \frac{2x+3-3}{2} = \frac{2x}{2} = x$

416

31. **a.**

$$f(x) = \frac{1}{x}$$

$$y = \frac{1}{x}$$

Interchange x and y and solve for y.

$$x = \frac{1}{y}$$

$$xy = 1$$

$$y = \frac{1}{x}$$

$$f^{-1}(x) = \frac{1}{x}$$

b.

$$f\left(f^{-1}(x)\right) = f\left(\frac{1}{x}\right) = \frac{1}{\frac{1}{x}} = 1 \cdot \frac{x}{1} = x$$

$$f^{-1}\left(f(x)\right) = f^{-1}\left(\frac{1}{x}\right)$$

$$= \frac{1}{\frac{1}{x}} = 1 \cdot \frac{x}{1} = x$$

33. **a.**

$$f(x) = \frac{2x+1}{x-3}$$

$$y = \frac{2x+1}{x-3}$$

Interchange x and y and solve for y.

$$x = \frac{2y+1}{y-3}$$

$$x(y-3) = 2y+1$$

$$xy - 3x = 2y+1$$

$$xy - 2y = 3x+1$$

$$(x-2)y = 3x+1$$

$$y = \frac{3x+1}{x-2}$$

$$f^{-1}(x) = \frac{3x+1}{x-2}$$

b. $f\left(f^{-1}(x)\right)$

$$= f\left(\frac{3x+1}{x-2}\right)$$

$$= \frac{2\left(\frac{3x+1}{x-2}\right)+1}{\left(\frac{3x+1}{x-2}\right)-3}$$

$$= \frac{x-2}{x-2} \cdot \frac{2\left(\frac{3x+1}{x-2}\right)+1}{\left(\frac{3x+1}{x-2}\right)-3}$$

$$= \frac{2(3x+1)+1(x-2)}{(3x+1)-3(x-2)}$$

$$= \frac{6x+2+x-2}{3x+1-3x+6} = \frac{7x}{7} = x$$

$$f^{-1}\left(f(x)\right)$$

$$= f^{-1}\left(\frac{2x+1}{x-3}\right)$$

$$= \frac{3\left(\frac{2x+1}{x-3}\right)+1}{\left(\frac{2x+1}{x-3}\right)-2}$$

$$= \frac{x-3}{x-3} \cdot \frac{3\left(\frac{2x+1}{x-3}\right)+1}{\left(\frac{2x+1}{x-3}\right)-2}$$

$$= \frac{3(2x+1)+1(x-3)}{(2x+1)-2(x-3)}$$

$$= \frac{6x+3+x-3}{2x+1-2x+6} = \frac{7x}{7} = x$$

417

35. The graph does not satisfy the horizontal line test so the function does not have an inverse.

37. The graph does not satisfy the horizontal line test so the function does not have an inverse.

39. The graph satisfies the horizontal line test so the function has an inverse.

41.

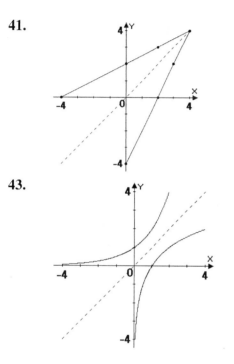

43.

45. $f(g(1)) = f(1) = 5$

46. $f(g(4)) = f(2) = -1$

47. $(g \circ f)(-1) = g(f(-1)) = g(1) = 1$

48. $(g \circ f)(0) = g(f(0)) = g(4) = 2$

49. $f^{-1}(g(10)) = f^{-1}(-1) = 2$, since $f(2) = -1$.

50. $f^{-1}(g(1)) = f^{-1}(1) = -1$, since $f(-1) = 1$.

51. $(f \circ g)(-1) = f(g(-1)) = f(-3) = 1$

52. $(f \circ g)(1) = f(g(1)) = f(-5) = 3$

53. $(g \circ f)(0) = g(f(0)) = g(2) = -6$

54. $(g \circ f)(-1) = g(f(-1)) = g(1) = -5$

55.
$$(f \circ g)(0) = f(g(0))$$
$$= f(4 \cdot 0 - 1)$$
$$= f(-1) = 2(-1) - 5 = -7$$

56.
$$(g \circ f)(0) = g(f(0))$$
$$= g(2 \cdot 0 - 5)$$
$$= g(-5) = 4(-5) - 1 = -21$$

57. Let $f^{-1}(1) = x$. Then
$$f(x) = 1$$
$$2x - 5 = 1$$
$$2x = 6$$
$$x = 3$$
Thus, $f^{-1}(1) = 3$

58. Let $g^{-1}(7) = x$. Then
$$g(x) = 7$$
$$4x - 1 = 7$$
$$4x = 8$$
$$x = 2$$
Thus, $g^{-1}(7) = 2$

59.
$$g\left(f\left[h(1)\right]\right) = g\left(f\left[1^2 + 1 + 2\right]\right)$$
$$= g\left(f(4)\right)$$
$$= g\left(2 \cdot 4 - 5\right)$$
$$= g(3)$$
$$= 4 \cdot 3 - 1 = 11$$

60.
$$f\left(g\left[h(1)\right]\right) = f\left(g\left[1^2 + 1 + 2\right]\right)$$
$$= f\left(g(4)\right)$$
$$= f\left(4 \cdot 4 - 1\right)$$
$$= f(15)$$
$$= 2 \cdot 15 - 5 = 25$$

61. **a.** f represents the price after a $400 discount; g represents the price after a 25% discount (75% of the regular price).

b.
$$(f \circ g)(x) = f\left(g(x)\right)$$
$$= f(0.75x)$$
$$= 0.75x - 400$$
$f \circ g$ represents and additional $400 discount on a price that has already been reduced by 25%.

c.
$$(g \circ f)(x) = g\left(f(x)\right)$$
$$= g(x - 400)$$
$$= 0.75(x - 400)$$
$$= 0.75x - 300$$
$g \circ f$ represents an additional 25% discount on a price that has already been reduced by $400.

d. $0.75x - 400 < 0.75x - 300$, so $f \circ g$ models the greater discount. It has a savings of $100 over $g \circ f$.

e. $f(x) = x - 400$
$$y = x - 400$$
Interchange x and y and solve for y.
$$x = y - 400$$
$$x + 400 = y$$
$$f^{-1}(x) = x + 400$$
f^{-1} represents the regular price of the computer, since the value of x here is the price after a $400 discount.

63. **a.** f: {(Zambia, 4.2), (Columbia, 4.5), (Poland, 3.3), (Italy, 3.3), (U.S., 2.5)}

b. Inverse: {(4.2, Zambia), (4.5, Columbia), (3.3, Poland), (3.3, Italy), (2.5, U.S.)}; The inverse is not a function because the input 3.3 is associated with two different outputs: Poland and Italy.

65. **a.** We know that f has an inverse because no horizontal line intersects the graph of f in more than one point.

b. $f^{-1}(0.25)$, or approximately 15, represents the number of people who must be in a room so that the probability of two sharing a birthday would be 0.25; $f^{-1}(0.5)$, or approximately 23, represents the number of people who must be in a room so that the probability of 2 sharing a birthday would be 0.5;

$f^{-1}(0.7)$, or approximately 30, represents the number of people who must be in a room so that the probability of two sharing a birthday would be 0.70.

419

67. – 71. Answers will vary.

73. $f(x) = x^2 - 1$

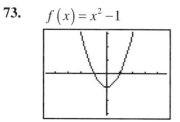

f does not have an inverse function.

75. $f(x) = \dfrac{x^3}{2}$

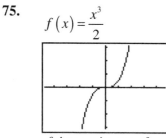

f has an inverse function.

77. $f(x) = |x - 2|$

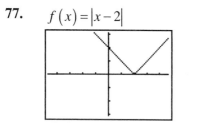

f does not have an inverse function.

79. $f(x) = -\sqrt{16 - x^2}$

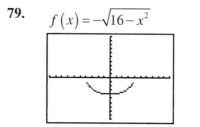

f does not have an inverse function.

81. $f(x) = 4x + 4$

$g(x) = 0.25x - 1$

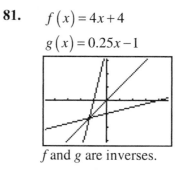

f and g are inverses.

83. $f(x) = \sqrt[3]{x} - 2$

$g(x) = (x + 2)^3$

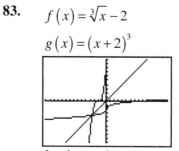

f and g are inverses.

85. Answers will vary. One example is
$f(x) = \sqrt{x} + 5$ and $g(x) = 3x^2$.

87.

$$f(f(x)) = \frac{3(f(x)) - 2}{5(f(x)) - 3}$$

$$= \frac{3\left(\dfrac{3x-2}{5x-3}\right) - 2}{5\left(\dfrac{3x-2}{5x-3}\right) - 3}$$

$$= \frac{3\left(\dfrac{3x-2}{5x-3}\right) - 2}{5\left(\dfrac{3x-2}{5x-3}\right) - 3} \cdot \frac{5x-3}{5x-3}$$

$$= \frac{3(3x-2) - 2(5x-3)}{5(3x-2) - 3(5x-3)}$$

$$= \frac{9x - 6 - 10x + 6}{15x - 10 - 15x + 9}$$

$$= \frac{-x}{-1} = x$$

Since $f(f(x)) = x$, f is it own inverse.

89.

$$\frac{4.3\times10^5}{8.6\times10^{-4}}=\frac{4.3}{8.6}\times\frac{10^5}{10^{-4}}$$

$$=0.5\times10^9$$

$$=5\times10^{-1}\times10^9=5\times10^8$$

90.

$$\require{enclose}\begin{array}{r}x^2+9x+16\\x-2\enclose{longdiv}{x^3-7x^2-20x+3}\end{array}$$

$$\underline{x^3-2x^2}$$
$$9x^2-\;2x$$
$$\underline{9x^2-18x}$$
$$16x+\;3$$
$$\underline{16x-32}$$
$$35$$

$$\frac{x^3+7x^2-20x+3}{x-2}=x^2+9x+16+\frac{35}{x-2}$$

92. $3x+2y=6$

$8x-3y=1$

To solve this system by the addition method, multiply the first equation by 3 and then second equation by 2; then add the equations.

$$9x+6y=18$$
$$\underline{16x-6y=\;\;2}$$
$$25x=20$$

$$x=\frac{20}{25}=\frac{4}{5}$$

Instead of substituting $\dfrac{4}{5}$ for x for

working with fractions, go back to the original system and eliminate x.
To do this, multiply the first equation by 8 and the second equation by -3; then add.

$$24x+16y=48$$
$$\underline{-24x+\;9y=-3}$$
$$25y=45$$

$$y=\frac{45}{25}=\frac{9}{5}$$

The solution is $\left(\dfrac{4}{5},\dfrac{9}{5}\right)$, and the

solution set is $\left\{\left(\dfrac{4}{5},\dfrac{9}{5}\right)\right\}$.

Chapter 8 Review Exercises

1.   The relation is a function.
Domain $\{3, 4, 5\}$
Range $\{10\}$

2.   The relation is a function.
Domain $\{1, 2, 3, 4\}$
Range $\{-6, \pi, 12, 100\}$

3.   The relation is not a function.
Domain $\{13, 15\}$
Range $\{14, 16, 17\}$

4.   **a.** $f(0)=7(0)-5=0-5=-5$

   b. $f(3)=7(3)-5=21-5=16$

   c. $f(-10)=7(-10)-5$
$$=-70-5=-75$$

   d. $f(2a)=7(2a)-5=14a-5$

   e. $f(a+2)=7(a+2)-5$
$$=7a+14-5=7a+9$$

5.   **a.** $g(0)=3(0)^2-5(0)+2$
$$=0-0+2=2$$

b.
$$g(5) = 3(5)^2 - 5(5) + 2$$
$$= 3(25) - 25 + 2$$
$$= 75 - 25 + 2 = 52$$

c.
$$g(-4) = 3(-4)^2 - 5(-4) + 2$$
$$= 3(16) + 20 + 2$$
$$= 48 + 20 + 2 = 70$$

d.
$$g(b) = 3(b)^2 - 5(b) + 2$$
$$= 3b^2 - 5b + 2$$

e.
$$g(4a) = 3(4a)^2 - 5(4a) + 2$$
$$= 3(16a^2) - 20a + 2$$
$$= 48a^2 - 20a + 2$$

6. The vertical line test shows that this is not the graph of a function.

7. The vertical line test shows that this is the graph of a function.

8. The vertical line test shows that this is the graph of a function.

9. The vertical line test shows that this is not the graph of a function.

10. The vertical line test shows that this is not the graph of a function.

11. The vertical line test shows that this is the graph of a function.

12. $f(-2) = -3$

13. $f(0) = -2$

14. When $x = 3$, $f(x) = -5$.

15. The domain of f is $\{x \mid -3 \leq x < 5\}$.

16. The range of f is $\{y \mid -5 \leq y \leq 0\}$.

17. a. The vulture's height is a function of its time in flight because every time, t, is associated with at most one height.

b. $f(15) = 0$

At time $t = 15$ seconds, the vulture is at height zero. This means that after 15 seconds, the vulture is on the ground.

c. The vulture's maximum height is 45 meters.

d. For $x = 7$ and 22, $f(x) = 20$. This means that at times 7 seconds and 22 seconds, the vulture is at a height of 20 meters.

e. The vulture began the flight at 45 meters and remained there for approximately 3 seconds. At that time, the vulture descended for 9 seconds. It landed on the ground and stayed there for 5 seconds. The vulture then began to climb back up to a height of 44 meters.

18. The domain of f is $\{x \mid x \text{ is a real number}\}$.

19. The domain of f is $\{x \mid x \text{ is a real number and } x \neq -8\}$.

20. The domain of f is $\{x \mid x \text{ is a real number and } x \neq 5\}$.

21. a.
$$(f + g)(x) = (4x - 5) + (2x + 1)$$
$$= 4x - 5 + 2x + 1$$
$$= 6x - 4$$

b. $(f+g)(3) = 6(3) - 4$

$\qquad = 18 - 4 = 14$

22. a. $(f+g)(x)$

$= (5x^2 - x + 4) + (x - 3)$

$= 5x^2 - x + 4 + x - 3 = 5x^2 + 1$

b. $(f+g)(3) = 5(3)^2 + 1 = 5(9) + 1$

$\qquad = 45 + 1 = 46$

23. The domain of $f + g$ is

$\{x | x \text{ is a real number and } x \neq 4\}$

24. The domain of $f + g$ is

$\{x \mid x \text{ is a real number and}$

$x \neq -6 \text{ and } x \neq -1\}$.

25. $f(x) = x^2 - 2x, \quad g(x) = x - 5$

$(f+g)(x) = (x^2 - 2x) + (x - 5)$

$\qquad = x^2 - 2x + x - 5$

$\qquad = x^2 - x - 5$

$(f+g)(-2) = (-2)^2 - (-2) - 5$

$\qquad = 4 + 2 - 5 = 1$

26. From Exercise 25 we know

$(f+g)(x) = x^2 - x - 5$. We can use

this to find $f(3) + g(3)$.

$f(3) + g(3) = (f+g)(3)$

$\qquad = (3)^2 - (3) - 5$

$\qquad = 9 - 3 - 5 = 1$

27. $f(x) = x^2 - 2x, \quad g(x) = x - 5$

$(f-g)(x) = (x^2 - 2x) - (x - 5)$

$\qquad = x^2 - 2x - x + 5$

$\qquad = x^2 - 3x + 5$

$(f-g)(x) = x^2 - 3x + 5$

$(f-g)(1) = (1)^2 - 3(1) + 5$

$\qquad = 1 - 3 + 5 = 3$

28. From Exercise 27 we know

$(f-g)(x) = x^2 - 3x + 5$. We can use

this to find $f(4) - g(4)$.

$f(4) - g(4) = (f-g)(4)$

$\qquad = (4)^2 - 3(4) + 5$

$\qquad = 16 - 12 + 5 = 9$

29. $(fg)(x) = (x^2 - 2x)(x - 5)$

$\qquad = x^3 - 5x^2 - 2x^2 + 10x$

$\qquad = x^3 - 7x^2 + 10x$

$(fg)(-3) = (-3)^3 - 7(-3)^2 + 10(-3)$

$\qquad = -27 - 63 - 30$

$\qquad = -120$

30. $f(x) = x^2 - 2x, \quad g(x) = x - 5$

$\left(\dfrac{f}{g}\right)(x) = \dfrac{x^2 - 2x}{x - 5}$

$\left(\dfrac{f}{g}\right)(4) = \dfrac{(4)^2 - 2(4)}{4 - 5} = \dfrac{16 - 8}{-1}$

$\qquad = \dfrac{8}{-1} = -8$

31. $(f-g)(x) = x^2 - 3x + 5$

The domain of $f - g$ is $\{x | x \text{ is a real}$

$\text{number}\}$.

423

32.
$$\left(\frac{f}{g}\right)(x) = \frac{x^2 - 2x}{x - 5}$$

The domain of

$\dfrac{f}{g}$ is $\{x | x \text{ is a real number and } x \neq 5\}$.

33. a.
$$(f \circ g)(x) = f(g(x))$$
$$= f(4x - 1)$$
$$= (4x - 1)^2 + 3$$
$$= 16x^2 - 8x + 1 + 3$$
$$= 16x^2 - 8x + 4$$

b.
$$(g \circ f)(x) = g(f(x))$$
$$= g(x^2 + 3)$$
$$= 4(x^2 + 3) - 1$$
$$= 4x^2 + 12 - 1$$
$$= 4x^2 + 11$$

c.
$$(f \circ g)(3) = 16(3)^2 - 8(3) + 4$$
$$= 16(9) - 24 + 4$$
$$= 144 - 24 + 4$$
$$= 124$$

34. a.
$$(f \circ g)(x) = f(g(x))$$
$$= f(x + 1) = \sqrt{x + 1}$$

b.
$$(g \circ f)(x) = g(f(x))$$
$$= g(\sqrt{x}) = \sqrt{x} + 1$$

c. $(f \circ g)(3) = \sqrt{3 + 1} = \sqrt{4} = 2$

35.
$$f(x) = \frac{3}{5}x + \frac{1}{2} \text{ and } g(x) = \frac{5}{3}x - 2$$

$$f(g(x)) = f\left(\frac{5}{3}x - 2\right)$$
$$= \frac{3}{5}\left(\frac{5}{3}x - 2\right) + \frac{1}{2}$$
$$= \frac{3}{5}\left(\frac{5}{3}x\right) - \left(\frac{3}{5}\right)2 + \frac{1}{2}$$
$$= x - \frac{6}{5} + \frac{1}{2}$$
$$= x - \frac{7}{10}$$

$$g(f(x)) = g\left(\frac{3}{5}x + \frac{1}{2}\right)$$
$$= \frac{5}{3}\left(\frac{3}{5}x + \frac{1}{2}\right) - 2$$
$$= \frac{5}{3}\left(\frac{3}{5}x\right) + \left(\frac{5}{3}\right)\frac{1}{2} - 2$$
$$= x + \frac{5}{6} - 2$$
$$= x - \frac{7}{6}$$

The functions are not inverses.

36.
$$f(x) = 2 - 5x \text{ and } g(x) = \frac{2 - x}{5}$$

$$f(g(x)) = f\left(\frac{2 - x}{5}\right)$$
$$= 2 - 5\left(\frac{2 - x}{5}\right)$$
$$= 2 - (2 - x) = 2 - 2 + x = x$$

$$g(f(x)) = g(2 - 5x)$$
$$= \frac{2 - (2 - 5x)}{5}$$
$$= \frac{2 - 2 + 5x}{5} = \frac{5x}{5} = x$$

The functions are inverses.

37. a. $f(x) = 4x - 3$

$y = 4x - 3$

Interchange x and y and solve for y.

$x = 4y - 3$

$x + 3 = 4y$

$\dfrac{x+3}{4} = y$

$f^{-1}(x) = \dfrac{x+3}{4}$

b. $f\left(f^{-1}(x)\right) = f\left(\dfrac{x+3}{4}\right)$

$= 4\left(\dfrac{x+3}{4}\right) - 3$

$= x + 3 - 3 = x$

$f^{-1}\left(f(x)\right) = f(4x - 3)$

$= \dfrac{(4x-3)+3}{4}$

$= \dfrac{4x-3+3}{4} = \dfrac{4x}{4} = x$

38. a. $f(x) = -\dfrac{1}{x}$

$y = -\dfrac{1}{x}$

Interchange x and y and solve for y.

$x = -\dfrac{1}{y}$

$y = -\dfrac{1}{x}$

$f^{-1}(x) = -\dfrac{1}{x}$

b. $f\left(f^{-1}(x)\right) = f\left(-\dfrac{1}{x}\right)$

$= -\dfrac{1}{\left(-\dfrac{1}{x}\right)} = x$

$f^{-1}\left(f(x)\right) = f^{-1}\left(-\dfrac{1}{x}\right)$

$= -\dfrac{1}{\left(-\dfrac{1}{x}\right)} = x$

39. Since the graph satisfies the horizontal line test, its inverse is a function.

40. Since the graph does not satisfy the horizontal line test, its inverse in not a function.

41. Since the graph satisfies the horizontal line test, its inverse is a function.

42. Since the graph does not satisfy the horizontal line test, its inverse is not a function.

43. Since the points $(-3, -1), (0, 0)$ and $(2, 4)$ lie on the graph of the function, the points $(-1, -3)$, $(0, 0)$ and $(4, 2)$ lie on the inverse function.

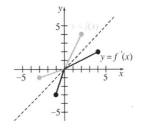

425

Chapter 8 Test

1. The relation is a function.
   Domain $\{1, 3, 5, 6\}$
   Range $\{2, 4, 6\}$

2. The relation is not a function.
   Domain $\{2, 4, 6\}$
   Range $\{1, 3, 5, 6\}$

3. $f(a+4) = 3(a+4) - 2$
   $$= 3a + 12 - 2 = 3a + 10$$

4. $f(-2) = 4(-2)^2 - 3(-2) + 6$
   $$= 4(4) + 6 + 6 = 16 + 6 + 6 = 28$$

5. The vertical line test shows that this is the graph of a function.

6. The vertical line test shows that this is not the graph of a function.

7. $f(6) = -3$

8. $f(x) = 0$ when $x = -2$ and $x = 3$.

9. The domain of f is
   $\{x \mid x \text{ is a real number}\}$

10. The range of f is $\{y \mid y \le 3\}$.

11. The domain of f is
    $\{x \mid x \text{ is a real number and } x \neq 10\}$.

12. $f(x) = x^2 + 4x \qquad g(x) = x + 2$
    $(f+g)(x) = f(x) + g(x)$
    $$= (x^2 + 4x) + (x + 2)$$
    $$= x^2 + 4x + x + 2$$
    $$= x^2 + 5x + 2$$
    $(f+g)(3) = (3)^2 + 5(3) + 2$
    $$= 9 + 15 + 2 = 26$$

13. $f(x) = x^2 + 4x \qquad g(x) = x + 2$
    $(f-g)(x) = f(x) - g(x)$
    $$= (x^2 + 4x) - (x + 2)$$
    $$= x^2 + 4x - x - 2$$
    $$= x^2 + 3x - 2$$
    $(f-g)(-1) = (-1)^2 + 3(-1) - 2$
    $$= 1 - 3 - 2 = -4$$

14. We know that $(fg)(x) = f(x) \cdot g(x)$.

    $(fg)(x) = (x^2 + 4x)(x + 2)$
    $$= x^3 + 2x^2 + 4x^2 + 8x$$
    $$= x^3 + 6x^2 + 8x$$
    So,
    $(fg)(-5) = (-5)^3 + 6(-5)^2 + 8(-5)$
    $$= -125 + 150 - 40$$
    $$= -15$$

15. $f(x) = x^2 + 4x \qquad g(x) = x + 2$
    $$\left(\frac{f}{g}\right)(x) = \frac{x^2 + 4x}{x + 2}$$
    $$\left(\frac{f}{g}\right)(2) = \frac{(2)^2 + 4(2)}{2 + 2} = \frac{4 + 8}{4} = \frac{12}{4} = 3$$

426

16. The domains of f and g are both all real numbers, so we only need to exclude values where $g(x) = 0$. That is, give $\left(\dfrac{f}{g}\right)(x) = \dfrac{x^2 + 4x}{x + 2}$, we need to solve $x + 2 = 0$ and exclude the solution(s) from the domain.

$$x + 2 = 0$$
$$x = -2$$

So, the domain of $\dfrac{f}{g}$ is all real numbers except $x = -2$.

Domain:
$\{x \mid x \text{ is a real number and } x \neq -2\}$

17. $f(x) = x^2 + x$ and $g(x) = 3x - 1$

$$(f \circ g)(x) = f(g(x)) = f(3x - 1)$$
$$= (3x - 1)^2 + (3x - 1)$$
$$= 9x^2 - 6x + 1 + 3x - 1$$
$$= 9x^2 - 3x$$

$$(g \circ f)(x) = g(f(x))$$
$$= g(x^2 + x)$$
$$= 3(x^2 + x) - 1$$
$$= 3x^2 + 3x - 1$$

18. $f(x) = 5x - 7$

$$y = 5x - 7$$

Interchange x and y and solve for y.

$$x = 5y - 7$$
$$x + 7 = 5y$$
$$\frac{x + 7}{5} = y$$
$$f^{-1}(x) = \frac{x + 7}{5}$$

19. a. The function passes the horizontal line test (i.e., no horizontal line intersects the graph of f in more than one point), so we know its inverse is a function.

b. $f(80) = 2000$

c. $f^{-1}(2000)$ represents the income, $80 thousand, of a family that gives $2000 to charity.

Cumulative Review Exercises (Chapters 1-8)

1. $2x + 3x - 5 + 7 = 10x + 3 - 6x - 4$
$$5x + 2 = 4x - 1$$
$$x + 2 = -1$$
$$x = -3$$
The solution set is $\{-3\}$.

2. $2x^2 + 5x = 12$
$$2x^2 + 5x - 12 = 0$$
$$(2x - 3)(x + 4) = 0$$
$$2x - 3 = 0 \quad \text{or} \quad x + 4 = 0$$
$$2x = 3 \qquad\qquad x = -4$$
$$x = \frac{3}{2}$$
The solution set is $\left\{-4, \dfrac{3}{2}\right\}$.

3. $8x - 5y = -4$
$$2x + 15y = -66$$
Eliminate y by multiplying both sides of the first equation by 3 and adding the two equations.
$$24x - 15y = -12$$
$$\underline{2x + 15y = -66}$$
$$26x \qquad = -78$$
$$x \qquad = -3$$

427

Let $x = -3$ in the first equation and solve for y.

$$8(-3) - 5y = -4$$
$$-24 - 5y = -4$$
$$-5y = 20$$
$$y = -4$$

The solution is $(-3, -4)$ and the solution set is $\{(-3, -4)\}$.

4. $\dfrac{15}{x} - 4 = \dfrac{6}{x} + 3$

Multiply both sides of the equation by x to eliminate the fractions.

$$x\left(\frac{15}{x} - 4\right) = x\left(\frac{6}{x} + 3\right)$$
$$15 - 4x = 6 + 3x$$
$$15 = 6 + 7x$$
$$9 = 7x$$
$$\frac{9}{7} = x$$

The solution set is $\left\{\dfrac{9}{7}\right\}$.

5. $-3x - 7 = 8$
$$-3x = 15$$
$$x = -5$$

The solution set is $\{-5\}$.

6. $f(x) = 2x^2 - 5x + 2$;
$g(x) = x^2 - 2x + 3$
$(f - g)(x)$
$= f(x) - g(x)$
$= (2x^2 - 5x + 2) - (x^2 - 2x + 3)$
$= 2x^2 - 5x + 2 - x^2 + 2x - 3$
$= x^2 - 3x - 1$

$(f - g)(3) = (3)^2 - 3(3) - 1$
$$= 9 - 9 - 1$$
$$= -1$$

7. $\dfrac{8x^3}{-4x^7} = \dfrac{8}{-4} \cdot \dfrac{x^3}{x^7} = -2x^{3-7}$

$$= -2x^{-4} = -\frac{2}{x^4}$$

8. $-8 - (-3) \cdot 4 = -8 - (-12)$
$$= -8 + 12$$
$$= 4$$

9. $\dfrac{\dfrac{1}{x} - \dfrac{1}{2}}{\dfrac{1}{3} - \dfrac{x}{6}} = \dfrac{\dfrac{2}{2x} - \dfrac{x}{2x}}{\dfrac{2}{6} - \dfrac{x}{6}} = \dfrac{\dfrac{2-x}{2x}}{\dfrac{2-x}{6}}$

$$= \frac{2-x}{2x} \cdot \frac{6}{2-x}$$

$$= \frac{6}{2x} = \frac{3}{x}$$

10. $\dfrac{4 - x^2}{3x^2 - 5x - 2} = \dfrac{(2-x)(2+x)}{(3x+1)(x-2)}$

$$= \frac{-1(x-2)(2+x)}{(3x+1)(x-2)}$$

$$= \frac{-(2+x)}{3x+1} \quad \text{or} \quad -\frac{2+x}{3x+1}$$

11. $-5 - (-8) - (4 - 6)$
$$= -5 - (-8) - (-2)$$
$$= -5 + 8 + 2$$
$$= 3 + 2$$
$$= 5$$

428

12. $x^2 - 18x + 77$

We need two factors of 77 whose sum is -18. Since the product is positive, the factors have the same sign, and since the sum is negative, they are both negative.

Since $-11 \cdot -7 = 77$ and $-11 + (-7) = -18$, we get

$x^2 - 18x + 77 = (x - 11)(x - 7)$

13. $x^3 - 25x = x\left(x^2 - 25\right)$

$\qquad = x(x - 5)(x + 5)$

14.

$$\begin{array}{r} 6x^2 - 7x + 2 \\ x - 2\overline{\smash)6x^3 - 19x^2 + 16x - 4} \\ \underline{6x^3 - 12x^2} \\ -7x^2 + 16x \\ \underline{-7x^2 + 14x} \\ 2x - 4 \\ \underline{2x - 4} \\ 0 \end{array}$$

$\dfrac{6x^3 - 19x^2 + 16x - 4}{x - 2} = 6x^2 - 7x + 2$

15. $(2x - 3)\left(4x^2 + 6x + 9\right)$

$= (2x)\left(4x^2\right) + (2x)(6x) + (2x)(9)$

$-3\left(4x^2\right) - 3(6x) - 3(9)$

$= 8x^3 + 12x^2 + 18x - 12x^2 - 18x - 27$

$= 8x^3 - 27$

16. $\dfrac{3x}{x^2 + x - 2} - \dfrac{2}{x + 2}$

$= \dfrac{3x}{(x + 2)(x - 1)} - \dfrac{2(x - 1)}{(x + 2)(x - 1)}$

$= \dfrac{3x - 2(x - 1)}{(x + 2)(x - 1)}$

$= \dfrac{3x - 2x + 2}{(x + 2)(x - 1)}$

$= \dfrac{x + 2}{(x + 2)(x - 1)}$

$= \dfrac{1}{x - 1}$

17. $\dfrac{5x^2 - 6x + 1}{x^2 - 1} \div \dfrac{16x^2 - 9}{4x^2 + 7x + 3}$

$= \dfrac{5x^2 - 6x + 1}{x^2 - 1} \cdot \dfrac{4x^2 + 7x + 3}{16x^2 - 9}$

$= \dfrac{(5x - 1)(x - 1)}{(x + 1)(x - 1)} \cdot \dfrac{(4x + 3)(x + 1)}{(4x - 3)(4x + 3)}$

$= \dfrac{(5x - 1)\cancel{(x - 1)}}{\cancel{(x + 1)}\cancel{(x - 1)}} \cdot \dfrac{\cancel{(4x + 3)}\cancel{(x + 1)}}{(4x - 3)\cancel{(4x + 3)}}$

$= \dfrac{5x - 1}{4x - 3}$

18.
$$x + 3y - z = 5$$
$$-x + 2y + 3z = 13$$
$$2x - 5y - z = -8$$

Eliminate x from the second equation by adding the first two equations together.
$$x + 3y - z = 5$$
$$\underline{-x + 2y + 3z = 13}$$
$$5y + 2z = 18$$

Eliminate x from the third equation by multiplying both sides of the second equation by 2 and adding to the third equation.
$$-2x + 4y + 6z = 26$$
$$\underline{2x - 5y - z = -8}$$
$$-y + 5z = 18$$

Using the two reduced equations, we can form the following system of linear equations in two variables:
$$5y + 2z = 18$$
$$-y + 5z = 18$$

Multiply the second equation by 5 and add to the first equation.
$$5y + 2z = 18$$
$$\underline{-5y + 25z = 90}$$
$$27z = 108$$
$$z = 4$$

Back-substitute this value to solve for y.
$$5y + 2z = 18$$
$$5y + 2(4) = 18$$
$$5y + 8 = 18$$
$$5y = 10$$
$$y = 2$$

Back-substitute the values for y and z to solve for x.

$$x + 3y - z = 5$$
$$x + 3(2) - (4) = 5$$
$$x + 6 - 4 = 5$$
$$x + 2 = 5$$
$$x = 3$$

The solution is $(3, 2, 4)$ and the solution set is $\{(3, 2, 4)\}$.

19.
$$2x - y = 4$$
$$-y = -2x + 4$$
$$y = 2x - 4$$

The slope is $m = \dfrac{2}{1} = 2$ and the y-intercept is $b = -4$.

One point is $(0, -4)$ and using the slope, we can get a second point: $(1, -2)$

Let $x = -1$. $y = 2(-1) - 4 = -6$, so the point $(-1, -6)$ must be on the graph as well.

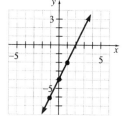

20.

$$y = -\frac{2}{3}x$$

The slope is $m = -\frac{2}{3} = \frac{-2}{3}$ and the y-intercept is 0.

One point is $(0,0)$ and using the slope we can get a second point: $(3,-2)$.

Let $x = -3$. $y = -\frac{2}{3}(-3) = 2$, so the

point $(-3,2)$ should be on the graph.

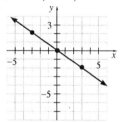

21. Since each element from the domain corresponds to exactly one element of the range, the relation is a function.

Domain: $\{1,2,3,4,6\}$

Range: $\{5\}$

22. $m = \frac{y_2 - y_1}{x_2 - x_1} = \frac{-3-5}{2-(-1)} = \frac{-8}{3} = -\frac{8}{3}$

23. $m = 5$; $(x_1, y_1) = (-2,-3)$

$$y - y_1 = m(x - x_1)$$
$$y - (-3) = 5(x - (-2))$$
$$y + 3 = 5(x + 2)$$

To obtain the slope-intercept form, solve this equation for y.

$$y + 3 = 5(x + 2)$$
$$y + 3 = 5x + 10$$
$$y = 5x + 7$$

24. $\left(7 \times 10^{-8}\right)\left(3 \times 10^{2}\right)$

$$= (7 \cdot 3) \times \left(10^{-8} \cdot 10^{2}\right)$$
$$= 21 \times 10^{-6}$$
$$= 2.1 \times 10^{1} \times 10^{-6}$$
$$= 2.1 \times 10^{-5}$$

25. $f(x) = \frac{1}{15 - x}$

This is a rational function so the domain is all real numbers except where the denominator equals 0.

$$15 - x = 0$$
$$15 = x$$

Therefore, the domain is $\{x \mid x \text{ is a real number and } x \neq 15\}$.

431

Chapter 9
Inequalities and Problem Solving

9.1 Exercise Set

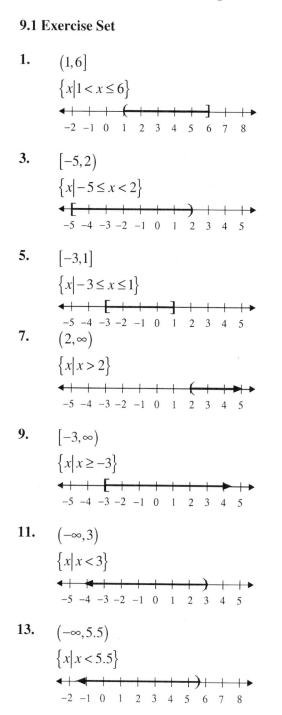

1. $(1,6]$

$\{x \mid 1 < x \le 6\}$

3. $[-5,2)$

$\{x \mid -5 \le x < 2\}$

5. $[-3,1]$

$\{x \mid -3 \le x \le 1\}$

7. $(2,\infty)$

$\{x \mid x > 2\}$

9. $[-3,\infty)$

$\{x \mid x \ge -3\}$

11. $(-\infty,3)$

$\{x \mid x < 3\}$

13. $(-\infty,5.5)$

$\{x \mid x < 5.5\}$

15. $5x + 11 < 26$

$5x < 15$

$x < 3$

The solution set is $\{x \mid x < 3\}$ or $(-\infty,3)$.

17. $3x - 8 \ge 13$

$3x \ge 21$

$x \ge 7$

The solution set is $\{x \mid x \ge 7\}$ or $[7,\infty)$.

19. $-9x \ge 36$

$x \le -4$

The solution set is $\{x \mid x \le -4\}$ or $(-\infty,-4]$.

21. $8x - 11 \le 3x - 13$

$5x - 11 \le -13$

$5x \le -2$

$x \le -\dfrac{2}{5}$

The solution set is $\left\{x \mid x \le -\dfrac{2}{5}\right\}$ or $\left(-\infty,-\dfrac{2}{5}\right]$.

432

23. $4(x+1)+2 \geq 3x+6$

$4x+4+2 \geq 3x+6$

$4x+6 \geq 3x+6$

$x+6 \geq 6$

$x \geq 0$

The solution set is $\{x | x \geq 0\}$ or $[0, \infty)$.

25. $2x-11 < -3(x+2)$

$2x-11 < -3x-6$

$5x-11 < -6$

$5x < 5$

$x < 1$

The solution set is $\{x | x < 1\}$ or $(-\infty, 1)$.

27. $1-(x+3) \geq 4-2x$

$1-x-3 \geq 4-2x$

$-x-2 \geq 4-2x$

$x-2 \geq 4$

$x \geq 6$

The solution set is $\{x | x \geq 6\}$ or $[6, \infty)$.

29. $\dfrac{x}{4} - \dfrac{1}{2} \leq \dfrac{x}{2} + 1$

$4\left(\dfrac{x}{4}\right) - 4\left(\dfrac{1}{2}\right) \leq 4\left(\dfrac{x}{2}\right) + 4(1)$

$x-2 \leq 2x+4$

$-x-2 \leq 4$

$-x \leq 6$

$x \geq -6$

The solution set is $\{x | x \geq -6\}$ or $[-6, \infty)$.

31. $1 - \dfrac{x}{2} > 4$

$2(1) - 2\left(\dfrac{x}{2}\right) > 2(4)$

$2-x > 8$

$-x > 6$

$x < -6$

The solution set is $\{x | x < -6\}$ or $(-\infty, -6)$.

33. $\dfrac{x-4}{6} \geq \dfrac{x-2}{9} + \dfrac{5}{18}$

$18\left(\dfrac{x-4}{6}\right) \geq 18\left(\dfrac{x-2}{9}\right) + 18\left(\dfrac{5}{18}\right)$

$3(x-4) \geq 2(x-2)+5$

$3x-12 \geq 2x-4+5$

$3x-12 \geq 2x+1$

$x-12 \geq 1$

$x \geq 13$

The solution set is $\{x | x \geq 13\}$ or $[13, \infty)$.

35. $7(y+4)-13 < 12+13(3+y)$

$7y+28-13 < 12+39+13y$

$7y+15 < 13y+51$

$-6y+15 < 51$

$-6y < 36$

$\dfrac{-6y}{-6} > \dfrac{36}{-6}$

$y > -6$

$\{y | y > -6\}$ or $(-6, \infty)$

433

37.

$$6 - \frac{2}{3}(3x - 12) \le \frac{2}{5}(10x + 50)$$

$$6 - 2x + 8 \le 4x + 20$$

$$-2x + 14 \le 4x + 20$$

$$-6x + 14 \le 20$$

$$-6x \le 6$$

$$x \ge -1$$

$$\{x \mid x \ge -1\} \quad \text{or} \quad [-1, \infty)$$

39.

$$3\big[3(y+5)+8y+7\big]$$

$$+5\big[3(y-6)-2(y-5)\big] < 2(4y+3)$$

$$3\big[3y+15+8y+7\big]$$

$$+5\big[3y-18-2y+10\big] < 8y+6$$

$$3[11y+22]+5[y-8] < 8y+6$$

$$33y+66+5y-40 < 8y+6$$

$$28y+26 < 8y+6$$

$$20y+26 < 6$$

$$20y < -20$$

$$y < -2$$

$$\{y \mid y < -2\} \quad \text{or} \quad (-\infty, -2)$$

41.

$$f(x) > g(x)$$

$$3x+2 > 5x-8$$

$$-2x+2 > -8$$

$$-2x > -10$$

$$\frac{-2x}{-2} < \frac{-10}{-2}$$

$$x < 5$$

$$\{x \mid x < 5\} \quad \text{or} \quad (-\infty, 5)$$

43.

$$g(x) \le f(x)$$

$$\frac{1}{4}(8-12x) \le \frac{2}{5}(10x+15)$$

$$20 \cdot \frac{1}{4}(8-12x) \le 20 \cdot \frac{2}{5}(10x+15)$$

$$5(8-12x) \le 8(10x+15)$$

$$40-60x \le 80x+120$$

$$-80-60x \le 80x$$

$$-80 \le 140x$$

$$\frac{-80}{140} \le x$$

$$-\frac{4}{7} \le x$$

$$\left\{x \mid x \ge -\frac{4}{7}\right\} \quad \text{or} \quad \left[-\frac{4}{7}, \infty\right)$$

45. **a.**

$$P(x) = R(x) - C(x)$$

$$= 32x - (25,500 + 15x)$$

$$= 32x - 25,500 - 15x$$

$$= 17x - 25,500$$

b.

$$P(x) > 0$$

$$17x - 25,500 > 0$$

$$17x > 25,500$$

$$\frac{17x}{17} > \frac{25,500}{17}$$

$$x > 1500$$

More than 1500 units must be produced and sold to have a profit.

434

47.   **a.**

$$P(x) = R(x) - C(x)$$
$$= 245x - (105x + 70,000)$$
$$= 245x - 105x - 70,000$$
$$= 140x - 70,000$$

  b.

$$P(x) > 0$$
$$140x - 70,000 > 0$$
$$140x > 70,000$$
$$\frac{140x}{140} > \frac{70,000}{140}$$
$$x > 500$$

More than 500 units must be produced and sold to have a profit.

49.

$$2(x+3) > 6 - \left\{ 4\left[x - (3x - 4) - x \right] + 4 \right\}$$
$$2x + 6 > 6 - \left\{ 4\left[x - 3x + 4 - x \right] + 4 \right\}$$
$$2x + 6 > 6 - \left\{ 4\left[-3x + 4 \right] + 4 \right\}$$
$$2x + 6 > 6 - \left\{ -12x + 16 + 4 \right\}$$
$$2x + 6 > 6 - \left\{ -12x + 20 \right\}$$
$$2x + 6 > 6 + 12x - 20$$
$$2x + 6 > 12x - 14$$
$$6 > 10x - 14$$
$$20 > 10x$$
$$2 > x$$
$$x < 2$$

$\{x \mid x < 2\}$ or $(-\infty, 2)$

50.

$$3(4x - 6) < 4 - \left\{ 5x - \left[6x - (4x - (3x + 2)) \right] \right\}$$
$$12x - 18 < 4 - \left\{ 5x - \left[6x - (4x - 3x - 2) \right] \right\}$$
$$12x - 18 < 4 - \left\{ 5x - \left[6x - (x - 2) \right] \right\}$$
$$12x - 18 < 4 - \left\{ 5x - \left[6x - x + 2 \right] \right\}$$
$$12x - 18 < 4 - \left\{ 5x - \left[5x + 2 \right] \right\}$$
$$12x - 18 < 4 - \left\{ 5x - 5x - 2 \right\}$$
$$12x - 18 < 4 - \left\{ -2 \right\}$$
$$12x - 18 < 6$$
$$12x < 24$$
$$x < 2$$

$\{x \mid x < 2\}$ or $(-\infty, 2)$

51.

$$ax + b > c, a < 0$$
$$ax + b - b > c - b$$
$$ax > c - b$$
$$\frac{ax}{a} < \frac{c - b}{a}, a < 0$$
$$x < \frac{c - b}{a}$$

52.

$$\frac{ax + b}{c} > b, c < 0$$
$$ax + b < bc$$
$$ax + b - b < bc - b$$
$$ax < bc - b$$
$$x < \frac{bc - b}{a}$$

53. $\{x \mid x \le -3\}$ or $(-\infty, -3]$

54. $\{x \mid x \ge -3\}$ or $[-3, \infty)$

55. $\{x \mid x > -1.4\}$ or $(-1.4, \infty)$

56. $\{x \mid x < -1.4\}$ or $(-\infty, -1.4)$

57. $(0, 4)$

59. passion $\leq$ intimacy

61. passion<commitment

63. 9, after 3 years

65. $3.1x + 25.8 > 63$

$3.1x > 37.2$

$x > 12$

Since x is the number of years after 1994, we calculate 1994+12=2006. 63% of voters will use electronic systems after 2006.

67. $W < M$

$-0.19t + 57 < -0.15t + 50$

$-0.04t + 57 < 50$

$-0.04t < -7$

$t > 175$

The women's winning time will be less than the men's winning time after 1900 + 175 = 2075.

69. **a.** cost = fixed costs + variable cost

$C(x) = 18,000 + 20x$

b. revenue = price $\cdot$ quantity

$R(x) = 80x$

c. $P(x) = R(x) - C(x)$

$= 80x - (18,000 + 20x)$

$= 80x - 18,000 - 20x$

$= 60x - 18,000$

d. $P(x) > 0$

$60x - 18,000 > 0$

$60x > 18,000$

$\dfrac{60x}{60} > \dfrac{18,000}{60}$

$x > 300$

More than 300 canoes need to be produced and sold in order to make a profit.

71. **a.** cost = overhead + per show cost

$C(x) = 30,000 + 2500x$

b. revenue = (receipts) $\cdot$ (# of sell-outs)

$R(x) = 3125x$

c. $P(x) = R(x) - C(x)$

$= 3125x - (30,000 + 2500x)$

$= 3125 - 30,000 - 2500x$

$= 625x - 30,000$

d. $P(x) > 0$

$625x - 30,000 > 0$

$625x > 30,000$

$\dfrac{625x}{625} > \dfrac{30,000}{625}$

$x > 48$

More than 48 sold-out performances are needed to make a profit.

73. Let x = number of tapes produced and sold each week.

$$P(x) > 0$$

$$R(x) - C(x) > 0$$

$$2x - (10,000 + 0.40x) > 0$$

$$2x - 10,000 - 0.40x > 0$$

$$1.60x - 10,000 > 0$$

$$1.60x > 10,000$$

$$x > 6250$$

More than 6250 tapes need to be produced and sold each week to make a profit.

75. Let x = number of minutes of long-distance calls in a month.
Plan A will be a better deal if the cost of Plan A is less than the cost of Plan B.

$$\text{Cost}_A < \text{Cost}_B$$

$$15 + 0.08x < 3 + 0.12x$$

$$12 + 0.08x < 0.12x$$

$$12 < 0.04x$$

$$\frac{12}{0.04} < \frac{0.04x}{0.04}$$

$$300 < x \qquad \text{or} \qquad x > 300$$

Plan A is a better deal if you have more than 300 minutes of long-distance calls.

77. A parenthesis signifies that a number is not included in the solution set, bracket signifies that the number is included in the solution set.

79. Answers will vary.

81. Answers will vary.

83. $-2(x+4) > 6x + 16$

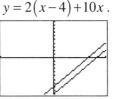

Moving from left to right on the graphing calculator screen, we see that the graph of $-2(x+4)$ is above the graph of $6x + 16$ from $-\infty$ to -3. The solution set is $\{x | x < -3\}$ or $(-\infty, -3)$.

85. Graph $y = 12x - 10$ and
$y = 2(x - 4) + 10x$.

The lines are parallel. They do not intersect. There is no solution. When solving the inequality algebraically, we arrive at a *false* statement:

$$12x - 10 > 2(x - 4) + 10x$$

$$12x - 10 > 2x - 8 + 10x$$

$$12x - 10 > 12x - 8$$

$$-10 > -8 \text{ false}$$

There are no x-values that solve the inequality. The solution set is $\varnothing$.

87. a. Plan A: $4 + 0.10x$
Plan B: $2 + 0.15x$

b.

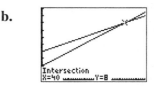

c. Plan A is better than Plan B for more than 40 checks per month.

437

d.
$$A < B$$
$$4 + 0.10x < 2 + 0.15x$$
$$4 < 2 + 0.05x$$
$$0.05x + 2 > 4$$
$$0.05x > 2$$
$$x > 40$$

89. Since $x < y \Rightarrow y - x < 0$. When multiplying both sides of the inequality by $(y - x)$, remember to *flip* the inequality.
$$2 > 1$$
$$2(y - x) < 1(y - x)$$
$$2y - 2x < y - x$$
$$y - 2x < -x$$
$$y < x$$

91.
$$f(x) = x^2 - 2x + 5$$
$$f(-4) = (-4)^2 - 2(-4) + 5$$
$$= 16 + 8 + 5$$
$$= 29$$

92.
$$2x - y - z = -3$$
$$3x - 2y - 2z = -5$$
$$-x + y + 2z = 4$$

Add the first and third equations to eliminate y.
$$2x - y - z = -3$$
$$\underline{-x + y + 2z = 4}$$
$$x + z = 1$$

Multiply the third equation by 2 and add to the second equation.
$$3x - 2y - 2z = -5$$
$$\underline{-2x + 2y + 4z = 8}$$
$$x + 2z = 3$$

The system of two equations in two variables becomes:

$$x + z = 1$$
$$x + 2z = 3$$

Multiply the second equation by -1 and solve for z.

$$x + z = 1$$
$$\underline{-x - 2z = -3}$$
$$-z = -2$$
$$z = 2$$

Back-substitute 2 for z to find x.
$$x + z = 1$$
$$x + 2 = 1$$
$$x = -1$$

Back-substitute 2 for z and -1 and x in one of the original equations in three variables to find y.
$$2x - y - z = -3$$
$$2(-1) - y - 2 = -3$$
$$-2 - y - 2 = -3$$
$$-y - 4 = -3$$
$$-y = 1$$
$$y = -1$$

The solution is $(-1, -1, 2)$ and the solution set is $\{(-1, -1, 2)\}$.

93.
$$25x^2 - 81 = (5x)^2 - (9)^2$$
$$= (5x + 9)(5x - 9)$$

9.2 Exercise Set

1. $\{1, 2, 3, 4\} \cap \{2, 4, 5\} = \{2, 4\}$

3. $\{1, 3, 5, 7\} \cap \{2, 4, 6, 8, 10\} = \{ \ \ \}$

The empty set is also denoted by $\varnothing$.

5. $\{a, b, c, d\} \cap \varnothing = \varnothing$

7. $x > 3$, $x > 6$, $x > 3$ and $x > 6$

The solution set is $\{x|x > 6\}$ or $(6, \infty)$.

9. $x \le 5$, $x \le 1$, $x \le 5$ and $x \le 1$

The solution set is $\{x|x \le 1\}$ or $(-\infty, 1]$.

11. $x < 2$, $x \ge -1$, $x < 2$ and $x \ge -1$

The solution set is $\{x|-1 \le x < 2\}$ or $[-1, 2)$.

13. $x > 2$, $x < -1$, $x > 2$ and $x < -1$

Since the two sets do not intersect, the solution set is $\varnothing$ or $\{\ \}$.

15. $5x < -20$, $3x > -18$,

$x < -4 \qquad x > -6$

$x < -4$ and $x > -6$

The solution set is $\{x|-6 < x < -4\}$ or $(-6, -4)$.

17. $x - 4 \le 2$ and $3x + 1 > -8$

$x \le 6 \qquad 3x > -9$

$\qquad\qquad x > -3$

$x \le 6$, $x > -3$, $x \le 6$ and $x > -3$

The solution set is $\{x|-3 < x \le 6\}$ or $(-3, 6]$.

19. $2x > 5x - 15$ and $7x > 2x + 10$

$-3x > -15 \qquad 5x > 10$

$x < 5 \qquad\qquad x > 2$

$x < 5$, $x > 2$, $x < 5$ and $x > 2$

The solution set is $\{x|2 < x < 5\}$ or $(2, 5)$.

439

21.

$$4(1-x) < -6$$
$$4 - 4x < -6$$
$$-4x < -10$$
$$x > \frac{5}{2}$$

$$\frac{x-7}{5} \le -2$$
$$5\left(\frac{x-7}{5}\right) \le 5(-2)$$
$$x - 7 \le -10$$
$$x \le -3$$

$$x > \frac{5}{2}, \quad x \le -3, \quad x > \frac{5}{2} \text{ and } x \le -3$$

Since the two sets do not intersect, the solution set is $\varnothing$ or $\{\ \}$.

23.

$$x - 1 \le 7x - 1 \quad \text{and} \quad 4x - 7 < 3 - x$$
$$-1 \le 6x - 1 \qquad\qquad 5x - 7 < 3$$
$$0 \le 6x \qquad\qquad\qquad 5x < 10$$
$$0 \le x \qquad\qquad\qquad\quad x < 2$$
$$x \ge 0$$

$$x < 2, \quad x \ge 0, \quad x < 2 \text{ and } x \ge 0$$

The solution set is $\{x | 0 \le x < 2\}$ or $[0, 2)$.

25.

$$6 < x + 3 < 8$$
$$6 - 3 < x + 3 - 3 < 8 - 3$$
$$3 < x < 5$$

The solution set is $\{x | 3 < x < 5\}$ or $(3, 5)$.

27.

$$-3 \le x - 2 < 1$$
$$-3 + 2 \le x - 2 + 2 < 1 + 2$$
$$-1 \le x < 3$$

The solution set is $\{x | -1 \le x < 3\}$ or $[-1, 3)$.

29.

$$-11 < 2x - 1 \le -5$$
$$-11 + 1 < 2x - 1 + 1 \le -5 + 1$$
$$-10 < 2x \le -4$$
$$-5 < x \le -2$$

The solution set is $\{x | -5 < x \le -2\}$ or $(-5, -2]$.

31.

$$-3 \le \frac{2x}{3} - 5 < -1$$
$$-3 + 5 \le \frac{2x}{3} - 5 + 5 < -1 + 5$$
$$2 \le \frac{2x}{3} < 4$$
$$3(2) \le 3\left(\frac{2x}{3}\right) < 3(4)$$
$$6 \le 2x < 12$$
$$3 \le x < 6$$

The solution set is $\{x | 3 \le x < 6\}$ or $[3, 6)$.

33. $\{1,2,3,4\}\cup\{2,4,5\}=\{1,2,3,4,5\}$

35. $\{1,3,5,7\}\cup\{2,4,6,8,10\}$
$=\{1,2,3,4,5,6,7,8,10\}$

37. $\{a,e,i,o,u\}\cup\varnothing=\{a,e,i,o,u\}$

39. $x>3$, $x>6$, $x>3$ or $x>6$

The solution set is $\{x|x>3\}$ or $(3,\infty)$.

41. $x\le5$, $x\le1$, $x\le5$ or $x\le1$

The solution set is $\{x|x\le5\}$ or $(-\infty,5]$.

43. $x<2$, $x\ge-1$, $x<2$ or $x\ge-1$

The solution set is $\mathbb{R}$, $(-\infty,\infty)$ or $\{x|x$ is a real number$\}$.

45. $x\ge2$, $x<-1$, $x\ge2$ or $x<-1$

The solution set is $\{x|x<-1$ or $x\ge2\}$ or $(-\infty,-1)\cup[2,\infty)$.

47. $3x>12$ or $2x<-6$
$x>4$ $\qquad x<-3$

$x>4$, $x<-3$, $x>4$ or $x<-3$

The solution set is $\{x|x<-3$ or $x>4\}$ or $(-\infty,-3)\cup(4,\infty)$.

49. $3x+2\le5$ or $5x-7\ge8$
$3x\le3$ $\qquad 5x\ge15$
$x\le1$ $\qquad x\ge3$

$x\le1$, $x\ge3$, $x\le1$ or $x\ge3$

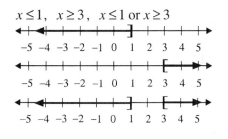

The solution set is $\{x|x\le1$ or $x\ge3\}$ or $(-\infty,1]\cup[3,\infty)$.

441

51. $4x+3<-1$ or $2x-3\geq-11$

$$4x<-4 \qquad\qquad 2x\geq-8$$
$$x<-1 \qquad\qquad x\geq-4$$

$x<-1$, $x\geq-4$, $x<-1$ or $x\geq-4$

The solution set is $\mathbb{R}$, $(-\infty,\infty)$ or $\{x\,|\,x$ is a real number$\}$.

53. $-2x+5>7$ or $-3x+10>2x$

$$-2x>2 \qquad\qquad -5x+10>0$$
$$x<-1 \qquad\qquad -5x>-10$$
$$\qquad\qquad\qquad\qquad x<2$$

$x<-1$, $x<2$, $x<-1$ or $x<2$

The solution set is $\{x\,|\,x<2\}$ or $(-\infty,2)$.

55. $2x+3\geq5$ and $3x-1>11$

$$2x\geq2 \qquad\qquad 3x>12$$
$$x\geq1 \qquad\qquad x>4$$

The solution set is $\{x\,|\,x>4\}$ or $(4,\infty)$.

57. $3x-1<-1$ and $4-x<-2$

$$3x<0 \qquad\qquad 4<-2+x$$
$$x<0 \qquad\qquad 6<x$$

The solution set is $\{x\,|\,x<0$ or $x>6\}$ or $(-\infty,0)\cup(6,\infty)$.

59. $a>0, b>0, c>0$

$$-c<ax-b<c$$
$$b-c<ax<b+c$$
$$\frac{b-c}{a}<x<\frac{b+c}{a}$$

60. $a>0, b>0, c>0$

$$-2<\frac{ax-b}{c}<2$$
$$-2c<ax-b<2c$$
$$b-2c<ax<b+2c$$
$$\frac{b-2c}{a}<x<\frac{b+2c}{a}$$

61. $\{x\,|-1\leq x\leq3\}$ or $[-1,3]$

62. $\{x\,|-1<x<3\}$ or $(-1,3)$

63.   Solving in separate pieces:

$$x-2<2x-1 \qquad\qquad 2x-1<x+2$$
$$-2<x-1 \qquad \text{or} \qquad x-1<2$$
$$-1<x \qquad\qquad\qquad x<3$$

Since both exterior pieces of the inequality have the same number of x's, we can solve this inequality all in one piece:

$$x-2<2x-1<x+2$$
$$x-2-x<2x-1-x<x+2-x$$
$$-2<x-1<2$$
$$-1<x<3$$

The solution set is $\{x\,|-1<x<3\}$ or $(-1,3)$.

442

64. Solving in separate pieces:

$$x \le 3x - 10$$
$$0 \le 2x - 10$$
$$10 \le 2x$$
$$5 \le x$$

or

$$3x - 10 \le 2x$$
$$x - 10 \le 0$$
$$x \le 10$$

The solution set is $\{x | 5 \le x \le 10\}$ or $[5, 10]$.

65. The solution set is $\{x | -1 \le x < 2\}$ or $[-1, 2)$.

66. The solution set is $\{x | 1 < x \le 4\}$ or $(1, 4]$.

67.

$$5 - 4x \ge 1$$
$$-4x \ge -4$$
$$x \le 1$$

and

$$3 - 7x < 31$$
$$3 < 7x + 31$$
$$-28 < 7x$$
$$-4 < x$$

The solution set is $\{x | -4 < x \le 1\}$ or $(-4, 1]$. The set of negative integers that fall within this set are $\{-3, -2, -1\}$.

68. $-5 < 3x + 4 \le 16$

$$-9 < 3x \le 12$$
$$-3 < x \le 4$$

The solution set is $\{x | -3 < x \le 4\}$ or $(-3, 4]$. The set of negative integers that fall within this set are $\{-2, -1\}$.

69. toys cars and trucks
sports equipment
spatial-temporal toys

71. toys cars and trucks
sports equipment
spatial-temporal toys
doll houses}

73. No toys were requested by more than 40% of the boys and more than 10% of the girls.

75. $28 \le 20 + 0.40(x - 60) \le 40$

$$28 \le 20 + 0.40x - 24 \le 40$$
$$28 \le 0.40x - 4 \le 40$$
$$32 \le 0.40x \le 44$$
$$80 \le x \le 110$$

Between 80 and 110 ten minutes, inclusive.

77. Let x = the score on the fifth exam

$$80 \le \frac{70 + 75 + 87 + 92 + x}{5} < 90$$

$$80 \le \frac{324 + x}{5} < 90$$

$$5(80) \le 5\left(\frac{324 + x}{5}\right) < 5(90)$$

$$400 \le 324 + x < 450$$

$$400 - 324 \le 324 - 324 + x < 450 - 324$$

$$76 \le x < 126$$

A grade between 76 and 125 is needed on the fifth exam. (Because the inequality states the score must be less than 126, we say 125 is the highest possible score. In interval notation, we can use parentheses to exclude the maximum value. The range of scores can be expressed as $[76, 126)$.) If the highest grade is 100, the grade would need to be between 76 and 100.

443

79. Let x = the number of times the bridge is crossed per three month period

The cost with the 3-month pass is
$C_3 = 7.50 + 0.50x.$

The cost with the 6-month pass is
$C_6 = 30.$

Because we need to buy two 3-month passes per 6-month pass, we multiply the cost with the 3-month pass by 2.
$$2(7.50 + 0.50x) < 30$$
$$15 + x < 30$$
$$x < 15$$

We also must consider the cost without purchasing a pass. We need this cost to be less than the cost with a 3-month pass.
$$3x > 7.50 + 0.50x$$
$$2.50x > 7.50$$
$$x > 3$$

The 3-month pass is the best deal when making more than 3 but less than 15 crossings per 3-month period.

81.-87. Answers will vary.

89. $-1 < \dfrac{x+4}{2} < 3$

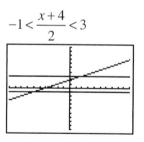

We need to find the range of the x-values of the points lying between the two constant functions. Using the intersection feature, we can determine the x-values of the endpoints of the range.

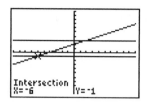

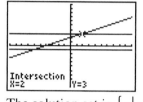

The solution set is $\{x|-6 < x < 2\}$ or $(-6, 2).$

91. $2 \le 4 - x \le 7$

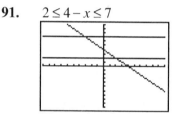

We need to find the range of the x-values of the points lying between the two constant functions. Using the intersection feature, we can determine the x-values of the endpoints of the range.

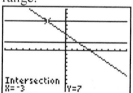

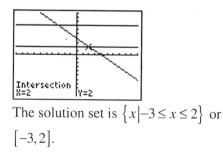

The solution set is $\{x|-3 \le x \le 2\}$ or $[-3, 2].$

444

93. $-7 \le 8 - 3x \le 20$ $\qquad$ $-7 < 6x - 1 < 41$

$\qquad$ $-15 \le -3x \le 12$ $\qquad$ $-6 < 6x < 42$

$\qquad\qquad$ $5 \ge x \ge -4$ $\qquad\qquad$ $-1 < x < 7$

$\qquad\qquad$ $-4 \le x \le 5$

The intersection of the above two sets is the solution set: $\{x | -1 < x \le 5\}$ or $(-1, 5]$.

95. $[-1, \infty)$

97. $(-1, 4]$

99. $f(x) = x^2 - 3x + 4$ $\qquad$ $g(x) = 2x - 5$

$(g - f)(x) = g(x) - f(x)$

$\qquad = (2x - 5) - (x^2 - 3x + 4)$

$\qquad = 2x - 5 - x^2 + 3x - 4$

$\qquad = -x^2 + 5x - 9$

$(g - f)(x) = -x^2 + 5x - 9$

$(g - f)(-1) = -(-1)^2 + 5(-1) - 9$

$\qquad = -1 - 5 - 9$

$\qquad = -15$

100. Passing through (4, 2) and perpendicular to the line $4x - 2y = 8$

The slope of the line $4x - 2y = 8$ can be found by rewriting the equation in slope-intercept form.

$4x - 2y = 8$

$\qquad -2y = -4x + 8$

$\qquad y = 2x - 4$

The slope of this line is 2. The slope of the line perpendicular to this line is $-\dfrac{1}{2}$.

Use the slope and the point to write the equation of the line in point-slope form. Then, solve for y and rewrite the equation using function notation.

$y - y_1 = m(x - x_1)$

$y - 2 = -\dfrac{1}{2}(x - 4)$

$y - 2 = -\dfrac{1}{2}x + 2$

$y = -\dfrac{1}{2}x + 4$

$f(x) = -\dfrac{1}{2}x + 4$

101. $4 - [2(x - 4) - 5] = 4 - [2x - 8 - 5]$

$\qquad\qquad\qquad\qquad = 4 - [2x - 13]$

$\qquad\qquad\qquad\qquad = 4 - 2x + 13$

$\qquad\qquad\qquad\qquad = 17 - 2x$

9.3 Exercise Set

1. $|x| = 8$

$\qquad x = 8$ or $x = -8$

The solutions are −8 and 8 and the solution set is $\{-8, 8\}$.

3. $|x - 2| = 7$

$\qquad x - 2 = 7$ or $x - 2 = -7$

$\qquad\quad x = 9$ $\qquad\qquad x = -5$

The solutions are −5 and 9 and the solution set is $\{-5, 9\}$.

5. $|2x-1|=7$

$2x-1=7$ or $2x-1=-7$

$2x=8$ $\qquad$ $2x=-6$

$x=4$ $\qquad$ $x=-3$

The solutions are -3 and 4 and the solution set is $\{-3,4\}$.

7. $\left|\dfrac{4x-2}{3}\right|=2$

$\dfrac{4x-2}{3}=2$ or $\dfrac{4x-2}{3}=-2$

$4x-2=3(2)$ $\qquad$ $4x-2=3(-2)$

$4x-2=6$ $\qquad$ $4x-2=-6$

$4x=8$ $\qquad$ $4x=-4$

$x=2$ $\qquad$ $x=-1$

The solutions are -1 and 2 and the solution set is $\{-1,2\}$.

9. $|x|=-8$

The solution set is $\varnothing$ or $\{\ \}$. There are no values of x for which the absolute value of x is a negative number. By definition, absolute values are always zero or positive.

11. $|x+3|=0$

Since the absolute value of the expression equals zero, we set the expression equal to zero and solve.

$x+3=0$

$x=-3$

The solution is -3 and the solution set is $\{-3\}$.

13. $2|y+6|=10$

$|y+6|=5$

$y+6=5$ or $y+6=-5$

$y=-1$ $\qquad$ $y=-11$

The solutions are -11 and -1 and the solution set is $\{-11,-1\}$.

15. $3|2x-1|=21$

$|2x-1|=7$

$2x-1=7$ or $2x-1=-7$

$2x=8$ $\qquad$ $2x=-6$

$x=4$ $\qquad$ $x=-3$

The solutions are -3 and 4 and the solution set is $\{-3,4\}$.

17. $|6y-2|+4=32$

$|6y-2|=28$

$6y-2=28$ or $6y-2=-28$

$6y=30$ $\qquad$ $6y=-26$

$y=5$ $\qquad$ $y=-\dfrac{26}{6}$

$\qquad\qquad\qquad y=-\dfrac{13}{3}$

The solutions are $-\dfrac{13}{3}$ and 5 and the

solution set is $\left\{-\dfrac{13}{3},5\right\}$.

446

19. $7|5x| + 2 = 16$

$7|5x| = 14$

$|5x| = 2$

$5x = 2$ or $5x = -2$

$x = \dfrac{2}{5}$ $x = -\dfrac{2}{5}$

The solutions are $-\dfrac{2}{5}$ and $\dfrac{2}{5}$ and the

solution set is $\left\{-\dfrac{2}{5}, \dfrac{2}{5}\right\}$.

21. $|x + 1| + 5 = 3$

$|x + 1| = -2$

The solution set is $\varnothing$ or $\{\ \ \}$. By definition, absolute values are always zero or positive.

23. $|4y + 1| + 10 = 4$

$|4y + 1| = -6$

The solution set is $\varnothing$ or $\{\ \ \}$. By definition, absolute values are always zero or positive.

25. $|2x - 1| + 3 = 3$

$|2x - 1| = 0$

Since the absolute value of the expression equals zero, we set the expression equal to zero and solve.

$2x - 1 = 0$

$2x = 1$

$x = \dfrac{1}{2}$

The solution is $\dfrac{1}{2}$ and the solution set

is $\left\{\dfrac{1}{2}\right\}$.

27. $|5x - 8| = |3x + 2|$

$5x - 8 = 3x + 2$ or $5x - 8 = -3x - 2$

$2x - 8 = 2$ $8x - 8 = -2$

$2x = 10$ $8x = 6$

$x = 5$ $x = \dfrac{6}{8} = \dfrac{3}{4}$

The solutions are $\dfrac{3}{4}$ and 5 and the

solution set is $\left\{\dfrac{3}{4}, 5\right\}$.

29. $|2x - 4| = |x - 1|$

$2x - 4 = x - 1$ or $2x - 4 = -x + 1$

$x - 4 = -1$ $3x - 4 = 1$

$x = 3$ $3x = 5$

                   $x = \dfrac{5}{3}$

The solutions are $\dfrac{5}{3}$ and 3 and the

solution set is $\left\{\dfrac{5}{3}, 3\right\}$.

31. $|2x - 5| = |2x + 5|$

$2x - 5 = 2x + 5$ or $2x - 5 = -2x - 5$

$-5 \neq 5$ $4x - 5 = -5$

                 $4x = 0$

                 $x = 0$

The solution is 0 and the solution set is $\{0\}$.

33. $|x - 3| = |5 - x|$

$x - 3 = 5 - x$ or $x - 3 = -(5 - x)$

$2x - 3 = 5$ $x - 3 = -5 + x$

$2x = 8$ $-3 \neq -5$

$x = 4$

The solution is 4 and the solution set is $\{4\}$.

447

35. $|2y-6|=|10-2y|$

$2y-6=10-2y \quad$ or $\quad 2y-6=-10+2y$

$4y-6=10 \qquad\qquad -6 \neq -10$

$\qquad 4y=16$

$\qquad y=4$

he solution is 4 and the solution set is $\{4\}$.

T

37. $\left|\dfrac{2x}{3}-2\right|=\left|\dfrac{x}{3}+3\right|$

$\dfrac{2x}{3}-2=\dfrac{x}{3}+3$

$3\left(\dfrac{2x}{3}\right)-3(2)=3\left(\dfrac{x}{3}\right)+3(3)$

$2x-6=x+9$

$x-6=9$

$x=15$

or

$\dfrac{2x}{3}-2=-\left(\dfrac{x}{3}+3\right)$

$\dfrac{2x}{3}-2=-\dfrac{x}{3}-3$

$3\left(\dfrac{2x}{3}\right)-3(2)=3\left(-\dfrac{x}{3}\right)-3(3)$

$2x-6=-x-9$

$3x-6=-9$

$3x=-3$

$x=-1$

The solutions are -1 and 15 and the solution set is $\{-1,15\}$.

39. $|x|<3$

$-3<x<3$

The solution set is $\{x|-3<x<3\}$ or $(-3,3)$.

41. $|x-2|<1$

$-1<x-2<1$

$-1+2<x-2+2<1+2$

$1<x<3$

The solution set is $\{x|1<x<3\}$ or $(1,3)$.

43. $|x+2|\leq 1$

$-1\leq x+2\leq 1$

$-1-2\leq x+2-2\leq 1-2$

$-3\leq x\leq -1$

The solution set is $\{x|-3\leq x\leq -1\}$ or $[-3,-1]$.

45. $|2x-6|<8$

$-8<2x-6<8$

$-8+6<2x-6+6<8+6$

$-2<2x<14$

$-1<x<7$

The solution set is $\{x|-1<x<7\}$ or $(-1,7)$.

47. $|x| > 3$

$x < -3 \quad \text{or} \quad x > 3$

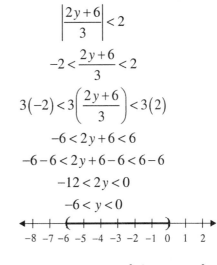

The solution set is $\{x | x < -3 \text{ and }$

$x > 3\}$ or $(-\infty, -3) \cup (3, \infty)$.

49. $|x + 3| > 1$

$x + 3 < -1 \quad \text{or} \quad x + 3 > 1$

$x < -4 \qquad\qquad x > -2$

The solution set is $\{x | x < -4 \text{ and }$

$x > -2\}$ or $(-\infty, -4) \cup (-2, \infty)$.

51. $|x - 4| \geq 2$

$x - 4 \leq -2 \quad \text{or} \quad x - 4 \geq 2$

$x \leq 2 \qquad\qquad x \geq 6$

The solution set is $\{x | x \leq 2 \text{ and }$

$x \geq 6\}$ or $(-\infty, 2] \cup [6, \infty)$.

53. $|3x - 8| > 7$

$3x - 8 < -7 \quad \text{or} \quad 3x - 8 > 7$

$3x < 1 \qquad\qquad 3x > 15$

$x < \dfrac{1}{3} \qquad\qquad x > 5$

The solution set is $\left\{ x \middle| x < \dfrac{1}{3} \text{ and } \right.$

$x > 5\}$ or $\left(-\infty, \dfrac{1}{3} \right) \cup (5, \infty)$.

55. $|2(x - 1) + 4| \leq 8$

$|2x - 2 + 4| \leq 8$

$|2x + 2| \leq 8$

$-8 \leq 2x + 2 \leq 8$

$-8 - 2 \leq 2x + 2 - 2 \leq 8 - 2$

$-10 \leq 2x \leq 6$

$-5 \leq x \leq 3$

The solution set is $\{x | -5 \leq x \leq 3\}$ or

$[-5, 3]$.

57. $\left| \dfrac{2y + 6}{3} \right| < 2$

$-2 < \dfrac{2y + 6}{3} < 2$

$3(-2) < 3\left(\dfrac{2y + 6}{3} \right) < 3(2)$

$-6 < 2y + 6 < 6$

$-6 - 6 < 2y + 6 - 6 < 6 - 6$

$-12 < 2y < 0$

$-6 < y < 0$

The solution set is $\{x | -6 < x < 0\}$ or

$(-6, 0)$.

449

59. $\left|\dfrac{2x+2}{4}\right| \geq 2$

$\dfrac{2x+2}{4} \leq -2$ or $\dfrac{2x+2}{4} \geq 2$

$2x+2 \leq -8$ $2x+2 \geq 8$

$2x \leq -10$ $2x \geq 6$

$x \leq -5$ $x \geq 3$

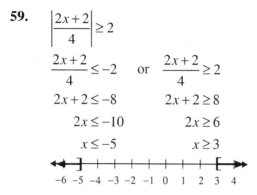

The solution set is $\{x \mid x \leq -5$ and $x \geq 3\}$ or $(-\infty, -5] \cup [3, \infty)$.

61. $\left|3 - \dfrac{2x}{3}\right| > 5$

$3 - \dfrac{2x}{3} < -5$ or $3 - \dfrac{2x}{3} > 5$

$-\dfrac{2x}{3} < -8$ $-\dfrac{2x}{3} > 2$

$-2x < -24$ $-2x > 6$

$x > 12$ $x < -3$

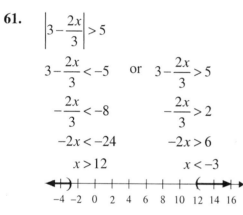

The solution set is $\{x \mid x < -3$ and $x > 12\}$ or $(-\infty, -3) \cup (12, \infty)$.

63. $|x-2| < -1$

The solution set is $\varnothing$ or $\{\ \ \}$. Since all absolute values are zero or positive, there are no values of x that will make the absolute value of the expression less than -1.

65. $|x+6| > -10$

Since all absolute values are zero or positive, we know that when simplified, the left hand side will be a positive number. We also know that any positive number is greater than any negative number. This means that regardless of the value of x, the left hand side will be greater than the right hand side of the inequality. The solution set is $\{x \mid x$ is a real number$\}$, $\mathbb{R}$ or $(-\infty, \infty)$.

67. $|x+2| + 9 \leq 16$

$|x+2| \leq 7$

$-7 \leq x+2 \leq 7$

$-7-2 \leq x+2-2 \leq 7-2$

$-9 \leq x \leq 5$

The solution set is $\{x \mid -9 \leq x \leq 5\}$ or $[-9, 5]$.

69. $2|2x-3| + 10 > 12$

$2|2x-3| > 2$

$|2x-3| > 1$

$2x-3 < -1$ $2x-3 > 1$

$2x < 2$ or $2x > 4$

$x < 1$ $x > 2$

The solution set is $\{x \mid x < 1$ and $x > 2\}$ or $(-\infty, 1) \cup (2, \infty)$.

71. $|5-4x|=11$

$5-4x=11$ or $5-4x=-11$

$-4x=6$ $\qquad$ $-4x=-16$

$x=-\dfrac{3}{2}$ $\qquad$ $y=4$

The solutions are $-\dfrac{3}{2}$ and 4 and the

solution set is $\left\{-\dfrac{3}{2},4\right\}$.

73. $|3-x|=|3x+11|$

$3-x=3x+11$

$-4x+3=11$

$-4x=8$

$x=-2$

or

$3-x=-(3x+11)$

$3-x=-3x-11$

$2x+3=-11$

$2x=-14$

$x=-7$

The solutions are -2 and -7 and the
solution set is $\{-7,-2\}$.

75. $|-1+3(x+1)|\le 5$

$-5\le -1+3x+3\le 5$

$-5\le 3x+2\le 5$

$-7\le 3x\le 3$

$-\dfrac{7}{3}\le x\le 1$

The solution set is $\left\{x\,\middle|\,-\dfrac{7}{3}\le x\le 1\right\}$ or

$\left[-\dfrac{7}{3},1\right]$.

77. $|2x-3|+1>6$

$|2x-3|>5$

$2x-3>5$ $\qquad$ $2x-3<-5$

$2x>8$ or $\qquad$ $2x<-2$

$x>4$ $\qquad$ $x<-1$

The solution set is $\{x\,|\,x<-1 \text{ or } x>4\}$
or $(-\infty,-1)\cup(4,\infty)$.

79. Let x be the number.

$|4-3x|\ge 5$ or $|3x-4|\ge 5$

$3x-4\ge 5$ $\qquad$ $3x-4\le -5$

$3x\ge 9$ or $\qquad$ $3x\le -1$

$x\ge 3$ $\qquad$ $x\le -\dfrac{1}{3}$

The solution set is

$\left\{x\,\middle|\,x\le -\dfrac{1}{3} \text{ or } x\ge 3\right\}$ or

$\left(-\infty,-\dfrac{1}{3}\right]\cup[3,\infty)$.

80. Let x be the number.

$|5-4x|\le 13$ or $|4x-5|\le 13$

$-13\le 4x-5\le 13$

$-8\le 4x\le 18$

$-2\le x\le \dfrac{9}{2}$

The solution set is $\left\{x\,\middle|\,-2\le x\le \dfrac{9}{2}\right\}$ or

$\left[-2,\dfrac{9}{2}\right]$.

81. $|ax+b| < c$

When solving, we do not "flip" the inequality symbol when dividing by a since $a > 0$.

$$-c < ax + b < c$$

$$-c - b < ax < c - b$$

$$\frac{-c-b}{a} < x < \frac{c-b}{a}$$

The solution set is

$$\left\{ x \mid \frac{-c-b}{a} < x < \frac{c-b}{a} \right\}.$$

82. $|ax+b| \geq c$

$ax + b \geq c$	$ax + b \leq -c$
$ax \geq c - b$ or	$ax \leq -c - b$
$x \geq \dfrac{c-b}{a}$	$x \leq \dfrac{-c-b}{a}$

The solution set is

$$\left\{ x \mid x \leq \frac{-c-b}{a} \text{ or } x \geq \frac{c-b}{a} \right\}.$$

83. $|4-x| = 1$

$4 - x = 1$	$4 - x = -1$
$-x = -3$ or	$-x = -5$
$x = 3$	$x = 5$

The solution set is $\{3, 5\}$.

84. $|4-x| < 5$ or $|x-4| < 5$

$$-5 < x - 4 < 5$$

$$-1 < x < 9$$

The solution set is $\{x \mid -1 < x < 9\}$.

85. The solution set is $\{x \mid -2 \leq x \leq 1\}$.

86. The solution set is

$\{x \mid x \leq -2 \text{ or } x \geq 1\}$.

87.
$$|x - 60.2| \leq 1.6$$

$$-1.6 \leq x - 60.2 \leq 1.6$$

$$-1.6 + 60.2 \leq x - 60.2 + 60.2 \leq 1.6 + 60.2$$

$$58.6 \leq x \leq 61.8$$

The percentage of the U.S. population that watched M*A*S*H is between 58.6% and 61.8%, inclusive. The margin of error is 1.6%.

89.
$$|T - 57| \leq 7$$

$$-7 \leq T - 57 \leq 7$$

$$-7 + 57 \leq T - 57 + 57 \leq 7 + 57$$

$$50 \leq T \leq 64$$

The monthly average temperature for San Francisco, California ranges from $50°F$ to $64°F$, inclusive.

91.
$$|x - 8.6| \leq 0.01$$

$$-0.01 \leq x - 8.6 \leq 0.01$$

$$-0.01 + 8.6 \leq x - 8.6 + 8.6 \leq 0.01 + 8.6$$

$$8.59 \leq x \leq 8.61$$

The length of the machine part must be between 8.59 and 8.61 centimeters, inclusive.

93.
$$\left| \frac{h-50}{5} \right| \geq 1.645$$

$$\frac{h-50}{5} \leq -1.645$$

$$h - 50 \leq 5(-1.645)$$

$$h - 50 \leq -8.225$$

$$h \leq 41.775$$

or

$$\frac{h-50}{5} \geq 1.645$$

$$h - 50 \geq 5(1.645)$$

$$h - 50 \geq 8.225$$

$$h \geq 58.225$$

The coin would be considered unfair if the tosses resulted in 41 or less heads, or 59 or more heads.

94.-101. Answers will vary.

103. $|3(x+4)|=12$

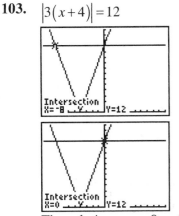

The solutions are –8 and 0 and the
solution set is $\{-8,0\}$.

105. $|2x+3|<5$

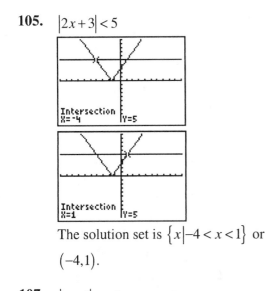

The solution set is $\{x|-4<x<1\}$ or
$(-4,1)$.

107. $|x+4|<-1$

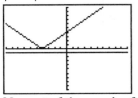

No part of the graph of the absolute
value lies below the graph of the
constant. The solution set is
$\varnothing$ or $\{\ \}$.

109. $|0.1x-0.4|+0.4>0.6$

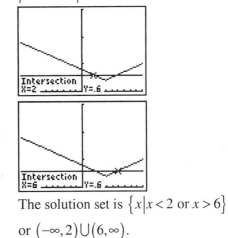

The solution set is $\{x|x<2 \text{ or } x>6\}$
or $(-\infty,2)\cup(6,\infty)$.

111. Answers will vary. For example,
consider Exercise 5.
$|2x-1|=5$

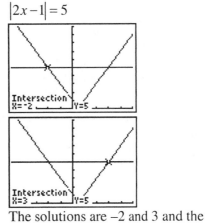

The solutions are –2 and 3 and the
solution set is $\{-2,3\}$.

113. a. $|x-4|<3$

b. $|x-4|\geq3$

453

115. $|2x+5| = 3x+4$

$2x+5 = 3x+4$ or $2x+5 = -(3x+4)$

$-x+5 = 4$ $\qquad$ $2x+5 = -3x-4$

$\quad -x = -1$ $\qquad$ $5x+5 = -4$

$\qquad x = 1$ $\qquad\qquad$ $5x = -9$

$\qquad\qquad\qquad\qquad x = -\dfrac{9}{5}$

Check:

$|2(1)+5| = 3(1)+4$

$\qquad |7| = 7$

$\qquad 7 = 7$ true

$\left|2\left(-\dfrac{9}{5}\right)+5\right| = 3\left(-\dfrac{9}{5}\right)+4$

$\qquad \left|\dfrac{7}{5}\right| = -\dfrac{7}{5}$

$\qquad \dfrac{7}{5} = -\dfrac{7}{5}$ false

Therefore, the solution set is $\{1\}$.

116. Solve for y to obtain slope-intercept form.

$3x-5y = 15$

$\quad -5y = -3x+15$

$\qquad y = \dfrac{3}{5}x-3$

The y-intercept is -3 and the slope is $\dfrac{3}{5}$.

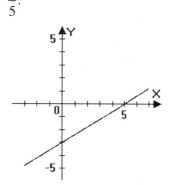

117.

$f(x) = -\dfrac{2}{3}x$

$y = -\dfrac{2}{3}x$

The y-intercept is 0 and the slope is $-\dfrac{2}{3}$.

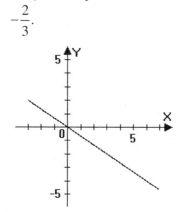

118. $f(x) = -2$

$\quad y = -2$

When graphed, an equation of the form $y = b$ is a horizontal line. $f(x) = -2$ is the horizontal line positioned at $y = -2$.

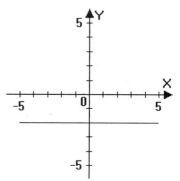

454

Mid-Chapter 9 Check Point

1. $4 - 3x \geq 12 - x$

$4 \geq 12 + 2x$

$-8 \geq 2x$

$-4 \geq x$

$x \leq -4$

$\{x \mid x \leq -4\}$ or $(-\infty, 4]$

2. $5 \leq 2x - 1 < 9$

$6 \leq 2x < 10$

$3 \leq x < 5$

$\{x \mid 3 \leq x < 5\}$ or $[3, 5)$

3. $|4x - 7| = 5$

$4x - 7 = 5 \qquad 4x - 7 = -5$

$\quad 4x = 12 \quad$ or $\quad 4x = 2$

$\quad x = 3 \qquad\qquad x = \dfrac{1}{2}$

The solution set is $\left\{\dfrac{1}{2}, 3\right\}$.

4. $-10 - 3(2x + 1) > 8x + 1$

$-10 - 6x - 3 > 8x + 1$

$-6x - 13 > 8x + 1$

$-13 > 14x + 1$

$-14 > 14x$

$-1 > x$

$x < -1$

$\{x \mid x < -1\}$ or $(-\infty, -1)$

5. $2x + 7 < -11 \quad$ or $\quad -3x - 2 < 13$

$\quad 2x < -18 \qquad\qquad -3x < 15$

$\quad\quad x < -9 \qquad\qquad\quad x > -5$

$\{x \mid x < -9 \ \text{or} \ x > -5\}$

$\quad$ or $(-\infty, -9) \cup (-5, \infty)$

6. $|3x - 2| \leq 4$

$-4 \leq 3x - 2 \leq 4$

$-2 \leq 3x \leq 6$

$-\dfrac{2}{3} \leq x \leq 2$

$\left\{x \mid -\dfrac{2}{3} \leq x \leq 2\right\}$ or $\left[-\dfrac{2}{3}, 2\right]$

7. $|x + 5| = |5x - 8|$

$x + 5 = 5x - 8 \quad$ or $\quad x + 5 = -(5x - 8)$

$-4x + 5 = -8 \qquad\qquad x + 5 = -5x + 8$

$\quad -4x = -13 \qquad\qquad\quad 6x + 5 = 8$

$\quad\quad x = \dfrac{13}{4} \qquad\qquad\qquad 6x = 3$

$\qquad\qquad\qquad\qquad\qquad\quad x = \dfrac{1}{2}$

The solution set is $\left\{\dfrac{1}{2}, \dfrac{13}{4}\right\}$.

8. $5 - 2x \geq 9 \qquad$ and $\quad 5x + 3 > -17$

$\quad 5 \geq 2x + 9 \qquad\qquad 5x > -20$

$\quad -4 \geq 2x \qquad\qquad\quad x > -4$

$\quad -2 \geq x$

$\quad\quad x \leq -2$

$\{x \mid -4 < x \leq -2\}$ or $(-4, -2]$

9. $3x - 2 > -8 \qquad\quad 2x + 1 < 9$

$\quad 3x > -6 \quad$ or $\quad 2x < 8$

$\quad\quad x > -2 \qquad\qquad x < 4$

The union of these sets is the entire number line. The solution set is $\{x \mid x \ \text{is a real number}\}$ or $(-\infty, \infty)$.

455

10.
$$\frac{x}{2}+3\le\frac{x}{3}+\frac{5}{2}$$
$$6\left(\frac{x}{2}+3\right)\le6\left(\frac{x}{3}+\frac{5}{2}\right)$$
$$3x+18\le2x+15$$
$$x+18\le15$$
$$x\le-3$$
$$\{x\mid x\le-3\}\quad\text{or}\quad(-\infty,-3]$$

11.
$$\frac{2}{3}(6x-9)+4>5x+1$$
$$4x-6+4>5x+1$$
$$4x-2>5x+1$$
$$-2>x+1$$
$$-3>x$$
$$x<-3$$
$$\{x\mid x<-3\}\quad\text{or}\quad(-\infty,-3)$$

12.
$$|5x+3|>2$$
$$5x+3>2\quad\text{or}\quad5x+3<-2$$
$$5x>-1\qquad\qquad5x<-4$$
$$x>-\frac{1}{5}\qquad\qquad x<-1$$
$$\left\{x\mid x<-1\text{ or }x>-\frac{1}{5}\right\}$$
$$\text{or}\quad(-\infty,-1)\cup\left(-\frac{1}{5},\infty\right)$$

13.
$$7-\left|\frac{x}{2}+2\right|\le4$$
$$-\left|\frac{x}{2}+2\right|\le-3$$
$$\left|\frac{x}{2}+2\right|\ge3$$
$$|x+4|\ge6$$

$$\begin{array}{ccc}x+4\ge6 & & x+4\le-6\\ & \text{or} & \\ x\ge2 & & x\le-10\end{array}$$

$$\{x\mid x\le-10\text{ or }x\ge2\}$$
$$\text{or}\quad(-\infty,-10]\cup[2,\infty)$$

14.
$$\frac{x+3}{4}<\frac{1}{3}$$
$$3x+9<4$$
$$3x<-5$$
$$x<-\frac{5}{3}$$
$$\left\{x\mid x<-\frac{5}{3}\right\}\quad\text{or}\quad\left(-\infty,-\frac{5}{3}\right)$$

15.
$$\begin{array}{ccc}5x+1\ge4x-2 & & 2x-3>5\\ x+1\ge-2 & \text{and} & 2x>8\\ x\ge-3 & & x>4\end{array}$$

The solution set is $\{x\mid x>4\}$ or $(4,\infty)$.

16.
$$3-|2x-5|=-6$$
$$-|2x-5|=-9$$
$$|2x-5|=9$$
$$\begin{array}{cc}2x-5=9 & 2x-5=-9\\ 2x=14\quad\text{or} & 2x=-4\\ x=7 & x=-2\end{array}$$
The solution set is $\{-2,7\}$.

17. $3+|2x-5|=-6$

$|2x-5|=-9$

Since absolute values cannot be negative, there are no solutions. The solution set is $\varnothing$.

18. a. cost = fixed costs + variable cost

$C(x)=60,000+0.18x$

b. revenue = price $\cdot$ quantity

$R(x)=0.30x$

c. profit = revenue − cost

$P(x)=R(x)-C(x)$

$=0.30x-(60,000+0.18x)$

$=0.30x-60,000-0.18x$

$=0.12x-60,000$

d. Let x = number of compact discs. We need

$0.30x-(60,000+0.18x)\ge 30,000$

$0.30x-60,000-0.18x\ge 30,000$

$0.12x-60,000\ge 30,000$

$0.12x\ge 90,000$

$x\ge 750,000$

The company should produce and sell at least 750,000 compact discs.

19. Let x = number of miles.

$24+0.20x\le 40$

$0.20x\le 16$

$x\le 80$

No more than 80 miles per day.

20. Let x = grade on the fifth exam.

$80\le \dfrac{95+79+91+86+x}{5}<90$

$80\le \dfrac{351+x}{5}<90$

$400\le x+351<450$

$49\le x<98$

$[49,98)$

21. Let x = amount invested.

$x(0.075)\ge 9000$

$x\ge 120,000$

The retiree should invest at least $120,000.

9.4 Exercise Set

1. $x+y\ge 3$

First, graph the equation $x+y=3$.

Rewrite the equation in slope-intercept form by solving for y.

$x+y=3$

$y=-x+3$

$y-$intercept $=3$

slope $=-1$

Next, use the origin as a test point.

$x+y\ge 3$

$0+0\ge 3$

$0\ge 3$

This is a false statement. This means that the point $(0,0)$ will not fall in the shaded half-plane.

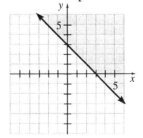

3. $x - y < 5$

First, graph the equation $x - y = 5$.
Rewrite the equation in slope-intercept
form by solving for y.

$x - y = 5$

$\quad -y = -x + 5$

$\quad\ \ y = x - 5$

y-intercept $= -5$

slope $= 1$

Next, use the origin as a test point.

$x - y < 5$

$0 - 0 < 5$

$\quad\ \ 0 < 5$

This is a true statement. This means
that the point $(0,0)$ will fall in the
shaded half-plane.

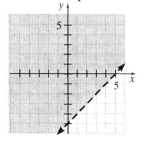

5. $x + 2y > 4$

First, graph the equation $x + 2y = 4$.
Rewrite the equation in slope-intercept
form by solving for y.

$x + 2y = 4$

$\quad 2y = -x + 4$

$\quad\ \ y = -\dfrac{1}{2}x + 2$

y-intercept $= 2$

slope $= -\dfrac{1}{2}$

Next, use the origin as a test point.

$0 + 2(0) > 4$

$\quad 0 + 0 > 4$

$\quad\quad\ \ 0 > 4$

This is a false statement. This means
that the point $(0,0)$ will not fall in the
shaded half-plane.

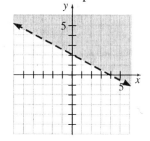

7. $3x - y \le 6$

First, graph the equation $3x - y = 6$.
Rewrite the equation in slope-intercept
form by solving for y.

$3x - y = 6$

$\quad -y = -3x + 6$

$\quad\ \ y = 3x - 6$

y-intercept $= -6$ \quad slope $= 3$

Next, use the origin as a test point.

$3(0) - 0 \le 6$

$\quad 0 - 0 \le 6$

$\quad\quad\ \ 0 \le 6$

This is a true statement. This means
that the point $(0,0)$ will fall in the
shaded half-plane.

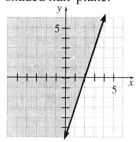

458

9.

$$\frac{x}{2}+\frac{y}{3}<1$$

First, graph the equation $\frac{x}{2}+\frac{y}{3}=1$.

Rewrite the equation in slope-intercept form by solving for y.

$$\frac{x}{2}+\frac{y}{3}=1$$

$$6\left(\frac{x}{2}\right)+6\left(\frac{y}{3}\right)=6(1)$$

$$3x+2y=6$$

$$2y=-3x+6$$

$$y=-\frac{3}{2}x+3$$

y-intercept $= 3$ slope $= -\frac{3}{2}$

Next, use the origin as a test point.

$$\frac{0}{2}+\frac{0}{3}<1$$

$$0+0<1$$

$$0<1$$

This is a true statement. This means that the point $(0,0)$ will fall in the shaded half-plane.

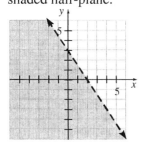

11.

$$y>\frac{1}{3}x$$

Replacing the inequality symbol with an equal sign, we have $y>\frac{1}{3}x$. Since the equation is in slope-intercept form, use the slope and the intercept to graph the equation. The y–intercept is 0 and the slope is $\frac{1}{3}$.

Next, we need to find a test point. We cannot use the origin this time, because it lies on the line. Use $(1,1)$ as a test point.

$$1>\frac{1}{3}(1)$$

$$1>\frac{1}{3}$$

This is a true statement, so we know the point $(1,1)$ lies in the shaded half-plane.

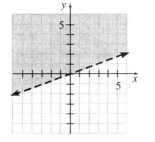

459

13. $y \le 3x + 2$

First, graph the equation $y = 3x + 2$.
Since the equation is in slope-intercept
form, use the slope and the intercept to
graph the equation. The y–intercept is 2
and the slope is 3.
Next, use the origin as a test point.

$0 \le 3(0) + 2$

$0 \le 2$

This is a true statement. This means
that the point $(0,0)$ will fall in the
shaded half-plane.

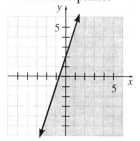

15.

$y < -\dfrac{1}{4}x$

Replacing the inequality symbol with an

equal sign, we have $y = -\dfrac{1}{4}x$. Since

the equation is in slope-intercept form,
use the slope and the intercept to graph
the equation. The y–intercept is 0 and

the slope is $-\dfrac{1}{4}$.

Next, we need to find a test point. We
cannot use the origin this time, because
it lies on the line. Use $(1,1)$ as a test
point.

$1 < -\dfrac{1}{4}(1)$

$1 < -\dfrac{1}{4}$

This is a false statement, so we know
the point $(1,1)$ does not lie in the

shaded half-plane.

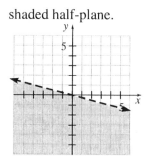

17. $x \le 2$

Replacing the inequality symbol with an
equal sign, we have $x = 2$. We know
that equations of the form $x = a$ are
vertical lines with x–intercept $= a$.
Next, use the origin as a test point.

$x \le 2$

$0 \le 2$

This is a true statement, so we know the
point $(0,0)$ lies in the shaded half-
plane.

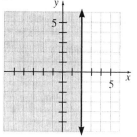

460

19. $y > -4$

Replacing the inequality symbol with an equal sign, we have $y = -4$. We know that equations of the form $y = b$ are horizontal lines with y–intercept $= b$.

Next, use the origin as a test point.

$y > -4$

$0 > -4$

This is a true statement, so we know the point $(0,0)$ lies in the shaded half-plane.

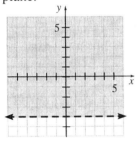

21. $y \geq 0$

Replacing the inequality symbol with an equal sign, we have $y = 0$. We know that equations of the form $y = b$ are vertical lines with y–intercept $= b$. In this case, we have $y = 0$, the equation of the x–axis.

Next, we need to find a test point. We cannot use the origin, because it lies on the line. Use $(1,1)$ as a test point.

$y \geq 0$

$1 \geq 0$

This is a true statement, so we know the point $(1,1)$ lies in the shaded half-plane.

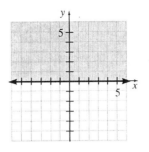

23. $3x + 6y \leq 6$

$2x + y \leq 8$

Graph the equations using the intercepts.

$3x + 6y = 6$ $\qquad$ $2x + y = 8$

x–intercept $= 2$ $\qquad$ x–intercept $= 4$ U

y–intercept $= 1$ $\qquad$ y–intercept $= 8$

se the origin as a test point to determine shading.

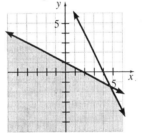

The solution set is the intersection of the shaded half-planes.

25. $2x - 5y \leq 10$

$3x - 2y > 6$

Graph the equations using the intercepts.

$2x - 5y = 10$ $\qquad$ $3x - 2y = 6$

$x-\text{intercept} = 5$ $\qquad$ $x-\text{intercept} = 2$ U

$y-\text{intercept} = 2$ $\qquad$ $y-\text{intercept} = -3$

se the origin as a test point to determine shading.

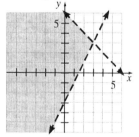

The solution set is the intersection of the shaded half-planes.

27. $y > 2x - 3$

$y < -x + 6$

Graph the equations using the intercepts.

$y = 2x - 3$ $\qquad$ $y = -x + 6$

$x-\text{intercept} = \dfrac{3}{2}$ $\qquad$ $x-\text{intercept} = 6$ U

$\qquad\qquad\qquad\qquad$ $y-\text{intercept} = 6$

$y-\text{intercept} = -3$

se the origin as a test point to determine shading.

The solution set is the intersection of the shaded half-planes.

29. $x + 2y \leq 4$

$y \geq x - 3$

Graph the equations using the intercepts.

$x + 2y = 4$ $\qquad$ $y = x - 3$

$x-\text{intercept} = 4$ $\qquad$ $x-\text{intercept} = 3$ U

$y-\text{intercept} = 2$ $\qquad$ $y-\text{intercept} = -3$

se the origin as a test point to determine shading.

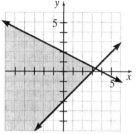

The solution set is the intersection of the shaded half-planes.

31. $x \leq 2$

$y \geq -1$

Graph the vertical line, $x = 2$, and the horizontal line, $y = -1$. Use the origin as a test point to determine shading.

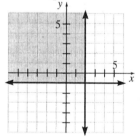

The solution set is the intersection of the shaded half-planes.

33. $-2 \le x < 5$

Since x lies between –2 and 5, graph the two vertical lines, $x = -2$ and $x = 5$. Since x lies between –2 and 5, shade between the two vertical lines.

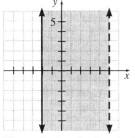

The solution is the shaded region.

35. $x - y \le 1$

$x \ge 2$

Graph the equations.

$x - y = 1$ $\qquad$ $x = 2$

$x - \text{intercept} = 1$ $\qquad$ $x - \text{intercept} = 2\,\text{U}$

$y - \text{intercept} = -1$ $\qquad$ vertical line

se the origin as a test point to determine shading.

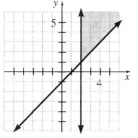

The solution set is the intersection of the shaded half-planes.

37. $x + y > 4$

$x + y < -1$

Graph the equations using the intercepts.

$x + y = 4$ $\qquad$ $x + y = -1$

$x - \text{intercept} = 4$ $\qquad$ $x - \text{intercept} = -1$

$y - \text{intercept} = 4$ $\qquad$ $y - \text{intercept} = -1$

Use the origin as a test point to determine shading.

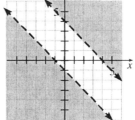

The solution set is the intersection of the shaded half-planes. Since the shaded half-planes do not intersect, there is no solution.

39. $x + y > 4$

$x + y > -1$

Graph the equations using the intercepts.

$x + y = 4$ $\qquad$ $x + y = -1$

$x - \text{intercept} = 4$ $\qquad$ $x - \text{intercept} = -1\,\text{U}$

$y - \text{intercept} = 4$ $\qquad$ $y - \text{intercept} = -1$

se the origin as a test point to determine shading.

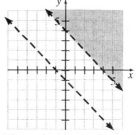

The solution set is the intersection of the shaded half-planes.

463

41. $x - y \leq 2$

$x \geq -2$

$y \leq 3$

Graph the equations using the intercepts.

$x - y = 2$ $y = 3$

$x-\text{intercept} = 2$ $y-\text{intercept} = 3$

$y-\text{intercept} = -2$ horizontal line

$x = -2$

$x-\text{intercept} = -2$

vertical line

Use the origin as a test point to determine shading.

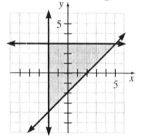

The solution set is the intersection of the shaded half-planes.

43. $x \geq 0$

$y \geq 0$

$2x + 5y \leq 10$

$3x + 4y \leq 12$

Since both x and y are greater than 0, we are concerned only with the first quadrant. Graph the other equations using the intercepts.

$2x + 5y = 10$ $3x + 4y = 12$

$x-\text{intercept} = 5$ $x-\text{intercept} = 4$ U

$y-\text{intercept} = 2$ $y-\text{intercept} = 3$

se the origin as a test point to determine shading.

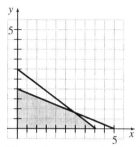

The solution set is the intersection of the shaded half-planes.

45. $3x + y \leq 6$

$2x - y \leq -1$

$x \geq -2$

$y \leq 4$

Graph the equations using the intercepts.

$3x + y = 6$ $x = -2$

$x-\text{intercept} = 2$ $x-\text{intercept} = -2$

$y-\text{intercept} = 6$ vertical line

$2x - y = -1$ $y = 4$

$x-\text{intercept} = -\dfrac{1}{2}$ $y-\text{intercept} = 4$

                      horizontal line

$y-\text{intercept} = 1$

Use the origin as a test point to determine shading.

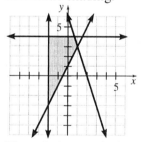

The solution set is the intersection of the shaded half-planes. Because all inequalities are greater than or equal to or less than or equal to, the boundaries of the shaded half-planes are also included in the solution set.

464

47. $y \geq -2x + 4$

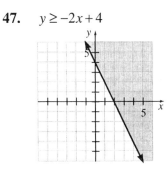

48. $y \geq -3x + 2$

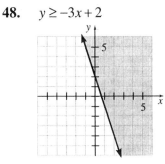

49. $x + y \leq 4$ and $3x + y \leq 6$

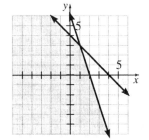

50. $x + y \leq 3$ and $4x + y \leq 6$

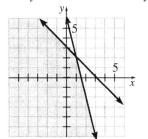

51. $-2 \leq x \leq 2$ and $-3 \leq y \leq 3$

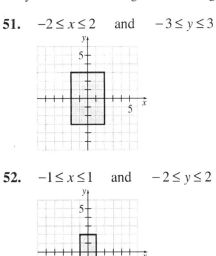

52. $-1 \leq x \leq 1$ and $-2 \leq y \leq 2$

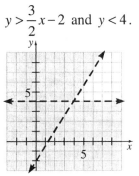

53. Find the union of solutions of
$y > \dfrac{3}{2}x - 2$ and $y < 4$.

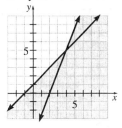

54. Find the union of solutions of
$x - y \geq -1$ and $5x - 2y \leq 10$.

465

55. The system

$$3x + 3y < 9$$

$$3x + 3y > 9$$

has no solution. The number $3x + 3y$ cannot both be less than 9 and greater than 9 at the same time.

56. The system

$$6x - y \le 24$$

$$6x - y > 24$$

has no solution. The number $6x - y$ cannot both be less than or equal to 24 and greater than 24 at the same time.

57. The system

$$3x + y \le 9$$

$$3x + y \ge 9$$

has infinitely many solutions. The solutions are all points on the line $3x + y = 9$.

58. The system

$$6x - y \le 24$$

$$6x - y \ge 24$$

has infinitely many solutions. The solutions are all points on the line $6x - y = 24$.

59. a. The coordinates of point A are $(20, 150)$. This means that a 20 year-old person with a pulse rate of 150 beats per minute falls within the target zone.

b. $10 \le a \le 70$

$10 \le 20 \le 70$ True

$150 \ge 0.7(220 - 20)$ True

$150 \le 0.8(220 - 20)$ True

Since point A makes all three inequalities true, it is a solution of the system.

61. $10 \le a \le 70$

$$H \ge 0.6(220 - a)$$

$$H \le 0.7(220 - a)$$

63. a.

$$y \ge 0$$
$$x + y \ge 5$$
$$x \ge 1$$
$$200x + 100y \le 700$$

b.

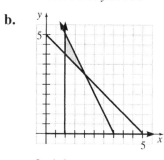

c.   2 nights

65.-73.   Answers will vary.

75. $y \le 4x + 4$

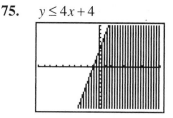

77. $2x + y \le 6$

$$y \le -2x + 6$$

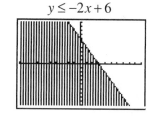

79.   Answers will vary.

466

81. Answers will vary. For example, verify
Exercise 23.
$$3x + 6y \le 6$$
$$2x + y \le 8$$
First solve both inequalities for y.

$$3x + 6y \le 6 \qquad\qquad 2x + y \le 8$$
$$6y \le -3x + 6 \qquad\qquad y \le -2x + 8$$
$$y \le -\frac{1}{2}x + 1$$

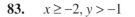

83. $x \ge -2,\ y > -1$

85. Answers will vary.
One simple example is
$$x \ge 0.$$
$$x < 0$$

87. $3x - y = 8$
$$x - 5y = -2$$
Solve the first equation for y.
$$3x - y = 8$$
$$-y = -3x + 8$$
$$y = 3x - 8$$
Substitute this expression for y in the
second equation and solve for x.
$$x - 5(3x - 8) = -2$$
$$x - 15x + 40 = -2$$
$$-14x + 40 = -2$$
$$-14x = -42$$
$$x = 3$$
Let $x = 3$ in the above substitution and
solve for y.

$$y = 3x - 8$$
$$= 3(3) - 8$$
$$= 9 - 8$$
$$= 1$$
The solution is $(3,1)$ and the solution
set is $\{(3,1)\}$.

88. $y = 3x - 2$
$$y = -2x + 8$$
Both equations are in slope-intercept
form, so use the slopes and
$y-$intercepts to graph the lines.

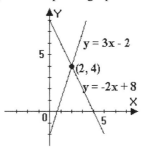

The solution is the intersection point
$(2,4)$ and the solution set is $\{(2,4)\}$.

89.
$$2x^6 + 20x^5 y + 50x^4 y^2$$
$$= 2x^4 \left(x^2 + 10xy + 25y^2 \right)$$
$$= 2x^4 \left(x^2 + 2 \cdot x \cdot 5y + (5y)^2 \right)$$
$$= 2x^4 (x + 5y)^2$$

9.5 Exercise Set

1.

Corner (x, y)	Objective Function $z = 5x + 6y$
(1, 2)	$z = 5x + 6y$ $= 5(1) + 6(2)$ $= 5 + 12 = 17$
(8, 3)	$z = 5x + 6y$ $= 5(8) + 6(3)$ $= 40 + 18 = 58$
(7, 5)	$z = 5x + 6y$ $= 5(7) + 6(5)$ $= 35 + 30 = 65$
(2, 10)	$z = 5x + 6y$ $= 5(2) + 6(10)$ $= 10 + 60 = 70$

The maximum value is 70 and the minimum is 17.

3.

Corner (x, y)	Objective Function $z = 40x + 50y$
(0, 0)	$z = 40x + 50y$ $= 40(0) + 50(0)$ $= 0 + 0 = 0$
(8, 0)	$z = 40x + 50y$ $= 40(8) + 50(0) = 320$
(4, 9)	$z = 40x + 50y$ $= 40(4) + 50(9)$ $= 160 + 450 = 610$
(0, 8)	$z = 40x + 50y$ $= 40(0) + 50(8) = 400$

The maximum value is 610 and the minimum value is 0.

5. Objective Function: $z = 3x + 2y$

Constraints:
$$x \geq 0, \quad y \geq 0$$
$$2x + y \leq 8$$
$$x + y \geq 4$$

a.

/////// 2x+y<=8

\\\\\\ x+y>=4

b.

Corner (x, y)	Objective Function $z = 3x + 2y$
(4, 0)	$z = 3x + 2y$ $= 3(4) + 2(0) = 12$
(0, 8)	$z = 3x + 2y$ $= 3(0) + 2(8) = 16$
(0, 4)	$z = 3x + 2y$ $= 3(0) + 2(4) = 8$

c. The maximum value is 16. It occurs at the point (0, 8).

468

7. Objective Function: $z = 4x + y$

Constraints: $x \geq 0, \; y \geq 0$

$2x + 3y \leq 12$

$x + y \geq 3$

a.

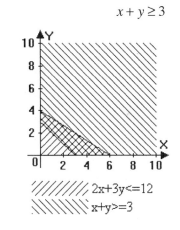

$$\text{///////} \; 2x{+}3y{<}{=}12$$
$$\text{\\\\\\\\} \; x{+}y{>}{=}3$$

b.

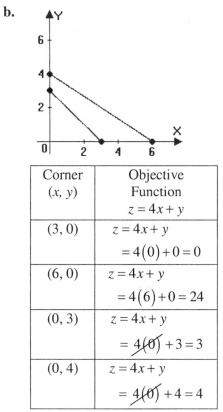

Corner (x, y)	Objective Function $z = 4x + y$
$(3, 0)$	$z = 4x + y$ $= 4(0) + 0 = 0$
$(6, 0)$	$z = 4x + y$ $= 4(6) + 0 = 24$
$(0, 3)$	$z = 4x + y$ $= 4(0) + 3 = 3$
$(0, 4)$	$z = 4x + y$ $= 4(0) + 4 = 4$

c. The maximum value is 24. It occurs at the point (6, 0).

9. Objective Function: $z = 3x - 2y$

Constraints: $1 \leq x \leq 5$

$y \geq 2$

$x - y \geq -3$

a.

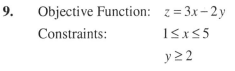

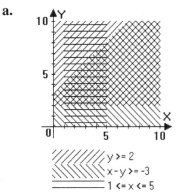

$$\text{//////} \; y >= 2$$
$$\text{\\\\\\} \; x{-}y >= {-}3$$
$$\text{———} \; 1 <= x <= 5$$

b.

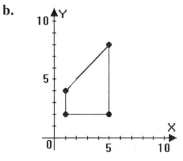

Corner (x, y)	Objective Function $z = 3x - 2y$
$(1, 2)$	$z = 3x - 2y$ $= 3(1) - 2(2) = -1$
$(5, 2)$	$z = 3x - 2y$ $= 3(5) - 2(2) = 11$
$(5, 8)$	$z = 3x - 2y$ $= 3(5) - 2(8) = -1$
$(1, 4)$	$z = 3x - 2y$ $= 3(1) - 2(4) = -5$

c. The maximum value is 11. It occurs at the point (5, 2).

11. Objective Function: $z = 4x + 2y$

Constraints: $x \geq 0, \ y \geq 0$

$$2x + 3y \leq 12$$
$$3x + 2y \leq 12$$
$$x + y \geq 2$$

a.

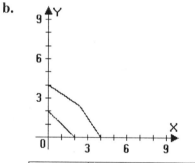

2x+3y<=12
3x+2y<=12
x+y>=2

b.

Corner (x, y)	Objective Function $z = 4x + 2y$
(2, 0)	$z = 4x + 2y$ $= 4(2) + 2(0) = 8$
(4, 0)	$z = 4x + 2y$ $= 4(4) + 2(0) = 16$
(2.4, 2.4)	$z = 4x + 2y$ $= 4(2.4) + 2(2.4)$ $= 9.6 + 4.8 = 14.4$
(0, 4)	$z = 4x + 2y$ $= 4(0) + 2(4) = 8$
(0, 2)	$z = 4x + 2y$ $= 4(0) + 2(2) = 4$

c. The maximum value is 16. It occurs at the point (4, 0).

13. Objective Function: $z = 10x + 12y$

Constraints: $x \geq 0, \ y \geq 0$

$$x + y \leq 7$$
$$2x + y \leq 10$$
$$2x + 3y \leq 18$$

a.

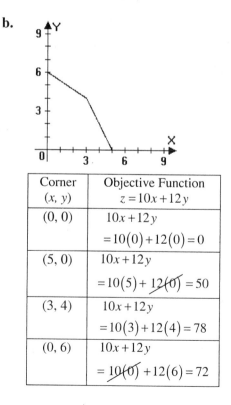

2x+y<=10
2x+3y<=18
x+y<=7

b.

Corner (x, y)	Objective Function $z = 10x + 12y$
(0, 0)	$10x + 12y$ $= 10(0) + 12(0) = 0$
(5, 0)	$10x + 12y$ $= 10(5) + 12(0) = 50$
(3, 4)	$10x + 12y$ $= 10(3) + 12(4) = 78$
(0, 6)	$10x + 12y$ $= 10(0) + 12(6) = 72$

470

c. The maximum value is 78 and it occurs at the point (3, 4)

15. a. The objective function is
$z = 125x + 200y$.

b. Since we can make at most 450 console televisions, we have
$x \leq 450$.
Since we can make at most 200 wide screen televisions, we have
$y \leq 200$.
Since we can spend at most $360,000 per month, we have
$600x + 900y \leq 360,000$.

Corner (x, y)	Objective Function $z = 125x + 200y$
(0, 0)	$125x + 200y$ $= 125(0) + 200(0) = 0$
(0, 200)	$125x + 200y$ $= 125(0) + 200(200)$ $= 40,000$
(300, 200)	$125x + 200y$ $= 125(300) + 200(200)$ $= 37,500 + 40,000$ $= 77,500$
(450, 100)	$125x + 200y$ $= 125(450) + 200(100)$ $= 56,250 + 20,000$ $= 76,250$
(450, 0)	$125x + 200y$ $= 125(450) + 200(0)$ $= 56,250$

c.

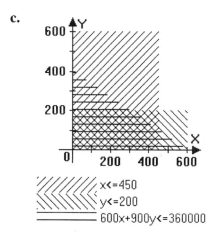

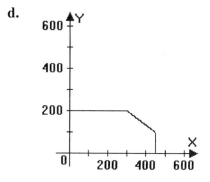

x<=450
y<=200
600x+900y<=360000

e. The television manufacturer will make the greatest profit by manufacturing 300 console televisions each month and 200 wide screen televisions each month. The maximum monthly profit is $77,500.

d.

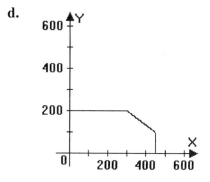

17. Let x = the number of model A bicycles produced
Let y = the number of model B bicycles produced
The objective function is
$z = 25x + 15y$.
The assembling constraint is
$5x + 4y \leq 200$.
The painting constraint is
$2x + 3y \leq 108$.

We also know that x and y must either

471

be zero or a positive number. We cannot make a negative number of bicycles.
Next, graph the constraints.

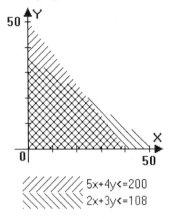

Using the graph, find the value of the objective function at each of the corner points.

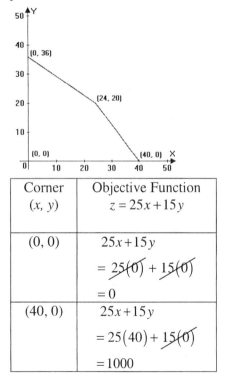

Corner (x, y)	Objective Function $z = 25x + 15y$
(0, 0)	$25x + 15y$ $= 25(0) + 15(0)$ $= 0$
(40, 0)	$25x + 15y$ $= 25(40) + 15(0)$ $= 1000$

(24, 20)	$25x + 15y$ $= 25(24) + 15(20)$ $= 600 + 300$ $= 900$
(0, 36)	$25x + 15y$ $= 25(0) + 15(36)$ $= 540$

The maximum of 1000 occurs at the point (40, 0). This means that the company should produce 40 of model A and none of model B each week for a profit of $1000.

19. Let x = the number of cartons of food
Let y = the number of cartons of clothing
The objective function is $z = 12x + 5y$.
The weight constraint is $50x + 20y \leq 19,000$.
The volume constraint is $20x + 10y \leq 8000$.
We also know that x and y must either be zero or a positive number. We cannot have a negative number of cartons of food or clothing.
Next, graph the constraints.

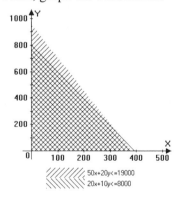

Using the graph, find the value of the objective function at each of the corner points.

472

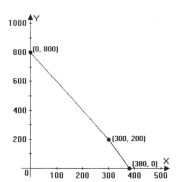

Corner (x, y)	Objective Function $z = 12x + 5y$
$(0, 0)$	$12x + 5y$ $= 12(0) + 5(0) = 0$
$(380, 0)$	$12x + 5y$ $= 12(380) + 5(0)$ $= 4560$
$(300, 200)$	$12x + 5y$ $= 12(300) + 5(200)$ $= 3600 + 1000 = 4600$
$(0, 600)$	$12x + 5y$ $= 12(0) + 5(600)$ $= 3000$

The maximum of 4600 occurs at the point (300, 200). This means that to maximize the number of people who are helped, 300 boxes of food and 200 boxes of clothing should be sent.

21. Let x = the number of students
Let y = the number of parents
The objective function is $z = x + 2y$.
The seating constraint is $x + y \leq 150$.
The two parents per student constraint is $y \leq 2x$.

We also know that x and y must either be zero or a positive number. We cannot have a negative number of parents or students.
Next, graph the constraints.

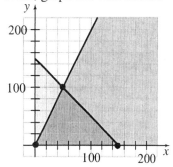

Using the graph, find the value of the objective function at each of the corner points.

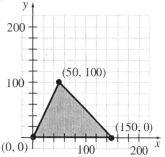

Corner (x, y)	Objective Function $z = x + 2y$
$(0, 0)$	$x + 2y = 0 + 2(0) = 0$
$(50, 100)$	$x + 2y = 50 + 2(100)$ $= 50 + 200 = 250$
$(150, 0)$	$x + 2y = 150 + 2(0) = 150$

The maximum of 250 occurs at the point (50, 100). This means that to maximize the amount of money raised, 50 students and 100 parents should attend.

23. Let x = the number of Boeing 727s
Let y = the number of Falcon 20s
The objective function is $z = x + y$.
The hourly operating cost constraint is
$1400x + 500y \leq 35000$.
The total payload constraint is
$42000x + 6000y \geq 672,000$.
The 727 constraint is $x \leq 20$.
We also know that x and y must either
be zero or a positive number. We
cannot have a negative number of
aircraft.
Next, graph the constraints.

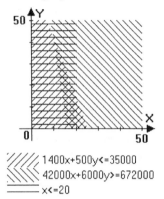

1400x+500y<=35000
42000x+6000y>=672000
x<=20

Using the graph, find the value of the
objective function at each of the corner
points.

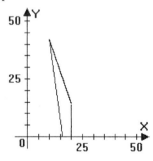

Corner (x, y)	Objective Function $z = x + y$
(16, 0)	$z = x + y$ $= 16 + 0 = 16$
(20, 0)	$z = x + y$ $= 20 + 0 = 20$
(20, 14)	$z = x + y$ $= 20 + 14 = 34$
(10, 42)	$z = x + y$ $= 10 + 42 = 52$

The maximum of 52 occurs at the point
(10, 42). This means that to maximize
the number of aircraft, 10 Boeing 727s
and 42 Falcon 20s should be
purchased.

24.-28. Answers will vary.

29. Let x = the amount invested in stocks
Let y = the amount invested in bonds
The objective function is
$z = 0.12x + 0.08y$.
The total money constraint is
$x + y \leq 10000$.
The minimum bond investment
constraint is $y \geq 3000$.
The minimum stock investment
constraint is $x \geq 2000$.
The stock versus bond constraint is
$y \geq x$.
We also know that x and y must either
be zero or a positive number. We
cannot invest a negative amount of
money.

Next, graph the constraints.

474

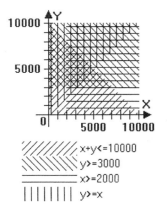

x+y<=10000
y>=3000
x>=2000
y>=x

Using the graph, find the value of the objective function at each of the corner points.

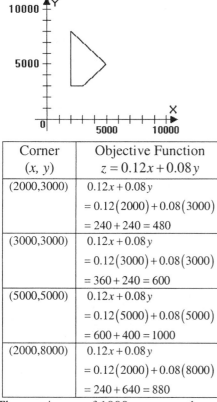

Corner (x, y)	Objective Function $z = 0.12x + 0.08y$
(2000,3000)	$0.12x + 0.08y$
	$= 0.12(2000) + 0.08(3000)$
	$= 240 + 240 = 480$
(3000,3000)	$0.12x + 0.08y$
	$= 0.12(3000) + 0.08(3000)$
	$= 360 + 240 = 600$
(5000,5000)	$0.12x + 0.08y$
	$= 0.12(5000) + 0.08(5000)$
	$= 600 + 400 = 1000$
(2000,8000)	$0.12x + 0.08y$
	$= 0.12(2000) + 0.08(8000)$
	$= 240 + 640 = 880$

The maximum of 1000 occurs at the point (5000, 5000). This means that to maximize the return on the investment, $5000 should be invested in stocks and $5000 should be invested in bonds.

31.
$$x^2 - 12x + 36 = 0$$
$$(x-6)^2 = 0$$
$$x - 6 = 0$$
$$x = 6$$
The solution set is $\{6\}$.

32.
$$\frac{1}{x^2 - 17x + 30} \div \frac{1}{x^2 + 7x - 18}$$
$$= \frac{1}{x^2 - 17x + 30} \cdot \frac{x^2 + 7x - 18}{1}$$
$$= \frac{x^2 + 7x - 18}{x^2 - 17x + 30}$$
$$= \frac{(x+9)(x-2)}{(x-15)(x-2)}$$
$$= \frac{x+9}{x-15}$$

33.
$$f(x) = x^3 + 2x^2 - 5x + 4$$
$$f(-1) = (-1)^3 + 2(-1)^2 - 5(-1) + 4$$
$$= -1 + 2(1) + 5 + 4$$
$$= -1 + 2 + 5 + 4 = 10$$

Chapter 9 Review

1. $\{x | -2 < x \le 3\}$

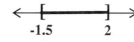

-2   3

2. $\{x | -1.5 \le x \le 2\}$

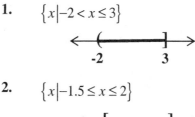

-1.5   2

3. $\{x | x > -1\}$

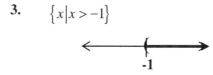

-1

4.
$$-6x + 3 \le 15$$
$$-6x \le 12$$
$$\frac{-6x}{-6} \ge \frac{12}{-6}$$
$$x \ge -2$$

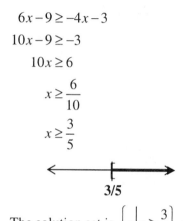

-2

The solution set is $\{x | x \ge -2\}$ or

$[2, \infty)$.

5.
$$6x - 9 \ge -4x - 3$$
$$10x - 9 \ge -3$$
$$10x \ge 6$$
$$x \ge \frac{6}{10}$$
$$x \ge \frac{3}{5}$$

3/5

The solution set is $\left\{x \middle| x \ge \frac{3}{5}\right\}$ or

$\left[\frac{3}{5}, \infty\right)$.

6.
$$\frac{x}{3} - \frac{3}{4} - 1 > \frac{x}{2}$$
$$12\left(\frac{x}{3}\right) - 12\left(\frac{3}{4}\right) - 12(1) > 12\left(\frac{x}{2}\right)$$
$$4x - 3(3) - 12 > 6x$$
$$4x - 9 - 12 > 6x$$
$$4x - 21 > 6x$$
$$-2x - 21 > 0$$
$$-2x > 21$$
$$x < -\frac{21}{2}$$

-21/2

The solution set is $\left\{x \middle| x < -\frac{21}{2}\right\}$ or

$\left(-\infty, -\frac{21}{2}\right)$.

7.
$$6x + 5 > -2(x - 3) - 25$$
$$6x + 5 > -2x + 6 - 25$$
$$6x + 5 > -2x - 19$$
$$8x + 5 > -19$$
$$8x > -24$$
$$x > -3$$

-3

The solution set is $\{x | x > -3\}$ or

$(-3, \infty)$.

8.
$$3(2x - 1) - 2(x - 4) \ge 7 + 2(3 + 4x)$$
$$6x - 3 - 2x + 8 \ge 7 + 6 + 8x$$
$$4x + 5 \ge 13 + 8x$$
$$-4x + 5 \ge 13$$
$$-4x \ge 8$$
$$x \le -2$$

-2

The solution set is $\{x | x \le -2\}$ or

$(-\infty, -2)$.

476

9. **a.** $P(x) = R(x) - C(x)$

$$= 125x - (40x + 357,000)$$

$$= 125x - 40x - 357,000$$

$$= 85x - 357,000$$

b. $P(x) > 0$

$$85x - 357,000 > 0$$

$$85x > 357,000$$

$$x > 4200$$

More than 4200 toaster ovens need to be produced and sold to make a profit.

10. cost = fixed costs + variable cost

$$C(x) = 360,000 + 850x$$

11. revenue = price · quantity

$$R(x) = 1150x$$

12. profit = revenue − cost

$$P(x) = R(x) - C(x)$$

$$= 1150x - (360,000 + 850x)$$

$$= 1150x - 360,000 - 850x$$

$$= 300x - 360,000$$

13. $P(x) > 0$

$$300x - 360,000 > 0$$

$$300x > 360,000$$

$$x > 1200$$

More than 1200 computers need to be produced and sold to make a profit.

14. Let x = the number of checks written per month

The cost using the first method is $c_1 = 11 + 0.06x$.

The cost using the second method is $c_2 = 4 + 0.20x$.

The first method is a better deal if it costs less than the second method.

$$c_1 < c_2$$

$$11 + 0.06x < 4 + 0.20x$$

$$11 - 0.14x < 4$$

$$-0.14x < -7$$

$$\frac{-0.14x}{-0.14} > \frac{-7}{-0.14}$$

$$x > 50$$

The first method is a better deal when more than 50 checks per month are written.

15. Let x = the amount of sales per month in dollars

The salesperson's commission is $c = 500 + 0.20x$.

We are looking for the amount of sales, x, the salesman must make to receive more than $3200 in income.

$$c > 3200$$

$$500 + 0.20x > 3200$$

$$0.20x > 2700$$

$$x > 13500$$

The salesman must sell at least $13,500 to receive a total income that exceeds $3200 per month.

16. $A \cap B = \{a, c\}$

17. $A \cap C = \{a\}$

18. $A \cup B = \{a, b, c, d, e\}$

477

19. $A \cup C = \{a, b, c, d, f, g\}$

20. $x \le 3$

$x < 6$

$x \le 3$ and $x < 6$

The solution set is $\{x | x \le 3\}$ or $(-\infty, 3]$.

21. $x \le 3$

$x < 6$

$x \le 3$ or $x < 6$

The solution set is $\{x | x < 6\}$ or $(-\infty, 6)$.

22.
$$-2x < -12 \quad \text{and} \quad x - 3 < 5$$
$$\frac{-2x}{-2} > \frac{-12}{-2} \qquad x < 8$$
$$x > 6$$

$x < 8$

$x > 6$

$x < 8$ and $x > 6$

The solution set is $\{x | 6 < x < 8\}$ or $(6, 8)$.

23.
$$5x + 3 \le 18 \quad \text{and} \quad 2x - 7 \le -5$$
$$5x \le 15 \qquad\qquad 2x \le 2$$
$$x \le 3 \qquad\qquad x \le 1$$

$x \le 3$

$x \le 1$

$x \le 3$ and $x \le 1$

The solution set is $\{x | x \le 1\}$ or $(-\infty, 1]$.

24.
$$2x - 5 > -1 \quad \text{and} \quad 3x < 3$$
$$2x > 4 \qquad\qquad x < 1$$
$$x > 2$$

$x > 2$

$x < 1$

$x > 2$ and $x < 1$

Since the two sets do not intersect, the solution set is $\varnothing$ or $\{\ \}$.

25.
$$2x - 5 > -1 \quad \text{or} \quad 3x < 3$$
$$2x > 4 \qquad\qquad x < 1$$
$$x > 2$$

$x > 2$

$x < 1$

$x > 2$ or $x < 1$

The solution set is $\{x | x < 1 \text{ or } x > 2\}$ or $(-\infty, 1) \cup (2, \infty)$.

26. $x+1 \le -3$ or $-4x+3 < -5$
$x \le -4 \qquad\quad -4x < -8$
$x > 2$

$x \le -4$

-4   2

$x > 2$

-4   2

$x \le -4$ or $x > 2$

-4   2

The solution set is $\{x | x \le -4$
and $x > 2\}$ or $(-\infty, -4] \cup (2, \infty)$.

27. $5x-2 \le -22$ or $-3x-2 > 4$
$5x \le -20 \qquad\quad -3x > 6$
$x \le -4 \qquad\quad\;\; x < -2$

$x \le -4$

-4   -2

$x < -2$

-4   -2

$x \le -4$ or $x < -2$

-4   -2

The solution set is $\{x | x < -2\}$ or
$(-\infty, -2)$.

28. $5x+4 \ge -11$ or $1-4x \ge 9$
$5x \ge -15 \qquad\quad -4x \ge 8$
$x \ge -3 \qquad\quad\;\; x \le -2$

$x \ge -3$

-3   2

$x \le -2$

-3   -2

$x \ge -3$ or $x \le -2$

-3   -2

The solution set is $\mathbb{R}$, $(-\infty, \infty)$ or
$\{x | x \text{ is a real number}\}$.

29. $-3 < x+2 \le 4$
$-3-2 < x+2-2 \le 4-2$
$-5 < x \le 2$

-5   2

The solution set is $\{x | -5 < x \le 2\}$ or
$(-5, 2]$.

30. $-1 \le 4x+2 \le 6$
$-1-2 \le 4x+2-2 \le 6-2$
$-3 \le 4x \le 4$
$-\dfrac{3}{4} \le \dfrac{4x}{4} \le \dfrac{4}{4}$
$-\dfrac{3}{4} \le x \le 1$

-3/4   1

The solution set is $\left\{x \left| -\dfrac{3}{4} \le x \le 1 \right.\right\}$ or
$\left[-\dfrac{3}{4}, 1\right]$.

479

31. Let x = the grade on the fifth exam

$$80 \le \frac{72 + 73 + 94 + 80 + x}{5} < 90$$

$$80 \le \frac{319 + x}{5} < 90$$

$$5(80) \le 5\left(\frac{319 + x}{5}\right) < 5(90)$$

$$400 \le 319 + x < 450$$

$$400 - 319 \le 319 - 319 + x < 450 - 319$$

$$81 \le x < 131$$

You need to score at least 81 and less than 131 on the exam to receive a B. In interval notation, the range is $[81, 131)$. If the highest score is 100, the range is $[81, 100]$.

32. $|2x + 1| = 7$

$$2x + 1 = 7 \quad \text{or} \quad 2x + 1 = -7$$
$$2x = 6 \qquad\qquad 2x = -8$$
$$x = 3 \qquad\qquad x = -4$$

The solutions are –4 and 3 and the solution set is $\{-4, 3\}$.

33. $|3x + 2| = -5$

There are no values of x for which the absolute value of $3x + 2$ is a negative number. By definition, absolute values are always positive. The solution set is $\varnothing$ or $\{\ \}$.

34. $2|x - 3| - 7 = 10$

$$2|x - 3| = 17$$
$$|x - 3| = 8.5$$
$$x - 3 = 8.5 \quad \text{or} \quad x - 3 = -8.5$$
$$x = 11.5 \qquad\qquad x = -5.5$$

The solutions are –5.5 and 11.5 and the solution set is $\{-5.5, 11.5\}$.

35. $|4x - 3| = |7x + 9|$

$$4x - 3 = 7x + 9$$
$$-3x - 3 = 9$$
$$-3x = 12$$
$$x = -4$$

or

$$4x - 3 = -7x - 9$$
$$11x - 3 = -9$$
$$11x = -6$$
$$x = -\frac{6}{11}$$

The solutions are -4 and $-\frac{6}{11}$ and the solution set is $\left\{-4, -\frac{6}{11}\right\}$.

36.
$$|2x + 3| \le 15$$
$$-15 \le 2x + 3 \le 15$$
$$-15 - 3 \le 2x + 3 - 3 \le 15 - 3$$
$$-18 \le 2x \le 12$$
$$-\frac{18}{2} \le \frac{2x}{2} \le \frac{12}{2}$$
$$-9 \le x \le 6$$

The solution set is $\{x | -9 \le x \le 6\}$ or $[-9, 6]$.

480

37. $\left|\dfrac{2x+6}{3}\right| > 2$

$\dfrac{2x+6}{3} < -2$ or $\dfrac{2x+6}{3} > 2$

$2x+6 < -6$ $2x+6 > 6$

$2x < -12$ $2x > 0$

$x < -6$ $x > 0$

The solution set is $\{x \,|\, x < -6$
or $x > 0\}$ or $(-\infty, -6) \cup (0, \infty)$.

38. $|2x+5| - 7 < -6$

$|2x+5| < 1$

$-1 < 2x+5 < 1$

$-1-5 < 2x+5-5 < 1-5$

$-6 < 2x < -4$

$-3 < x < -2$

The solution set is $\{x \,|\, -3 < x < -2\}$ or
$(-3, -2)$.

39. $|2x-3| + 4 \le -10$

$|2x-3| \le -14$

There are no values of x for which the
absolute value of $2x-3$ is a negative
number. By definition, absolute
values are always positive. The
solution set is $\varnothing$ or $\{\ \ \}$.

40. $|h-6.5| \le 1$

$-1 \le h-6.5 \le 1$

$5.5 \le h \le 7.5$

Approximately 90% of the population
sleeps between 5.5 hours and 7.5
hours daily, inclusive.

41. $3x-4y > 12$

First, find the intercepts to the
equation $3x-4y = 12$.
Find the x–intercept by setting $y = 0$.

$3x-4y = 12$

$3x - 4(0) = 12$

$3x = 12$

$x = 4$

Find the y–intercept by setting $x = 0$.

$3x-4y = 12$

$3(0) - 4y = 12$

$-4y = 12$

$y = -3$

Next, use the origin as a test point.

$3x-4y > 12$

$3(0) - 4(0) > 12$

$0 > 12$

This is a false statement. This means
that the point, $(0,0)$, will not fall in
the shaded half-plane.

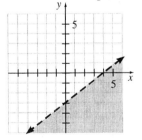

42. $x - 3y \leq 6$

First, find the intercepts to the equation $x - 3y = 6$.

Find the x–intercept by setting $y = 0$, find the y–intercept by setting $x = 0$.

$$x - 3y = 6 \qquad x - 3y = 6$$
$$x - 3(0) = 6 \qquad 0 - 3y = 6$$
$$x = 6 \qquad -3y = 6$$
$$y = -2$$

Next, use the origin as a test point.

$$0 - 3(0) \leq 6$$
$$0 \leq 6$$

This is a true statement. This means that the point, $(0,0)$, will fall in the shaded half-plane.

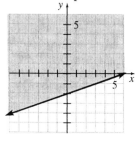

43.

$$y \leq -\frac{1}{2}x + 2$$

Replacing the inequality symbol with an equal sign, we have $y = -\frac{1}{2}x + 2$.

Since the equation is in slope-intercept form, use the slope and the intercept to graph the equation. The y–intercept is 2 and the slope is $-\frac{1}{2}$.

Next, use the origin as a test point.

$$y \leq -\frac{1}{2}x + 2$$
$$0 \leq -\frac{1}{2}(0) + 2$$
$$0 \leq 2$$

This is a true statement. This means that the point $(0,0)$ will fall in the shaded half-plane.

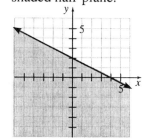

44.

$$y > \frac{3}{5}x$$

Replacing the inequality symbol with an equal sign, we have $y = \frac{3}{5}x$. Since the equation is in slope-intercept form, use the slope and the intercept to graph the equation. The y–intercept is 0 and the slope is $\frac{3}{5}$.

Next, we need to find a test point. We cannot use the origin this time, because it lies on the line. Use $(1,1)$ as a test point.

$$1 > \frac{3}{5}(1)$$
$$1 > \frac{3}{5}$$

This is a true statement, so we know the point $(1,1)$ lies in the shaded half-plane.

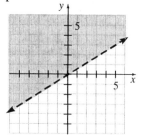

45. $x \le 2$

Replacing the inequality symbol with an equal sign, we have $x = 2$. We know that equations of the form $x = a$ are vertical lines with x-intercept $= a$. Next, use the origin as a test point.

$x \le 2$

$0 \le 2$

This is a true statement, so we know the point $(0,0)$ lies in the shaded half-plane.

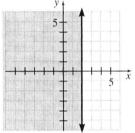

46. $y > -3$

Replacing the inequality symbol with an equal sign, we have $y = -3$. We know that equations of the form $y = b$ are horizontal lines with y-intercept $= b$.

Next, use the origin as a test point.

$y > -3$

$0 > -3$

This is a true statement, so we know the point $(0,0)$ lies in the shaded half-plane.

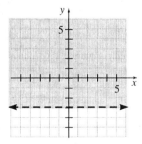

47. $3x - y \le 6$

$x + y \ge 2$

First consider $3x - y \le 6$. If we solve for y in $3x - y = 6$, we can graph the line using the slope and the y-intercept.

$3x - y = 6$

$-y = -3x + 6$

$y = 3x - 6$

y-intercept $= -6$

slope $= 3$

Now, use the origin as a test point.

$3(0) - 0 \le 6$

$0 \le 6$

This is a true statement. This means that the point $(0,0)$ will fall in the shaded half-plane.

Next consider $x + y \ge 2$. If we solve for y in $x + y = 2$, we can graph using the slope and the y-intercept.

$x + y = 2$

$y = -x + 2$

y-intercept $= 2$

slope $= -1$

Now, use the origin as a test point.

$0 + 0 \ge 2$

$0 \ge 2$

This is a false statement. This means that the point $(0,0)$ will not fall in the shaded half-plane.

Next, graph each of the inequalities. The solution to the system is the intersection of the shaded half-planes.

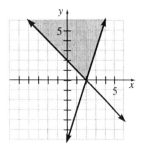

48. $y < -x + 4$

$y > x - 4$

First consider $y < -x + 4$. Change the
inequality symbol to an equal sign.
The line $y = -x + 4$ is in slope-
intercept form and can be graphed
using the slope and the y-intercept.
y-intercept $= 4$
slope $= -1$
Now, use the origin as a test point.
$0 < -0 + 4$

$0 < 4$
This is a true statement. This means
that the point $(0,0)$ will fall in the
shaded half-plane.
Next consider $y > x - 4$. Change the
inequality symbol to an equal sign.
The line $y = x - 4$ is in slope-intercept
form and can be graphed using the
slope and the y-intercept.
y-intercept $= -4$
slope $= 1$
Now, use the origin as a test point.
$0 > 0 - 4$

$0 > 4$
This is a false statement. This means
that the point $(0,0)$ will not fall in

the shaded half-plane.
Next, graph each of the inequalities.
The solution to the system is the
intersection of the shaded half-planes.

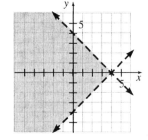

49. $-3 \le x < 5$
Rewrite the three part inequality as
two separate inequalities. We have
$-3 \le x$ and $x < 5$. We replace the
inequality symbols with equal signs
and obtain $-3 = x$ and $x = 5$.
Equations of the form $x = a$ are
vertical lines with x-intercept $= a$.
We know the shading in the graph will
be between $x = -3$ and $x = 5$ because
in the original inequality we see that x
lies between -3 and 5.

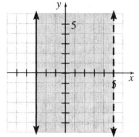

50. $-2 < y \le 6$
Rewrite the three part inequality as
two separate inequalities. We have
$-2 < y$ and $y \le 6$. We replace the
inequality symbols with equal signs
and obtain $-2 = y$ and $y = 6$.
Equations of the form $y = b$ are
vertical lines with y-intercept $= b$.
We know the shading in the graph will
be between $y = -2$ and $y = 6$

484

because in the original inequality we see that y lies between -2 and 6.

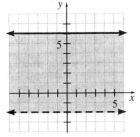

51. $x \geq 3$

   $y \leq 0$

First consider $x \geq 3$. Change the inequality symbol to an equal sign and

we obtain the vertical line $x = 3$. Because we have $x \geq 3$, we know the shading is to the right of the line $x = 3$.
Next consider $y \leq 0$. Change the inequality symbol to an equal sign and we obtain the horizontal line $y = 0$. (Recall that this is the equation of the x–axis.) Because we have $y \leq 0$, we know that the shading will be below the x–axis.
Next, graph each of the inequalities. The solution to the system is the intersection of the shaded half-planes.

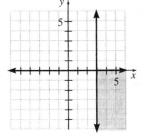

52. $2x - y > -4$

   $x \geq 0$

First consider $2x - y > -4$. Replace the inequality symbol with an equal sign and we have $2x - y = -4$. Solve for y to obtain slope-intercept form.

$$2x - y = -4$$
$$-y = -2x - 4$$
$$y = 2x + 4$$

y–intercept $= 4$
slope $= 2$

Now, use the origin as a test point.
$$2x - y > -4$$
$$2(0) - 0 > -4$$
$$0 > -4$$

This is a false statement. This means that the point $(0,0)$ will not fall in the shaded half-plane.
Next consider $x \geq 0$. Change the inequality symbol to an equal sign and we obtain the horizontal line $x = 0$. (Recall that this is the equation of the y–axis.) Because we have $x \geq 0$, we know that the shading will be above the y–axis.
Next, graph each of the inequalities. The solution to the system is the intersection of the shaded half-planes.

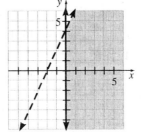

53. $x + y \le 6$

$y \ge 2x - 3$

First consider $x + y \le 6$. Replace the inequality symbol with an equal sign and we have $x + y = 6$. Solve for y to obtain slope-intercept form.

$x + y = 6$

$y = -x + 6$

y-intercept $= 6$

slope $= -1$

Now, use the origin as a test point.

$0 + 0 \le 6$

$0 \le 6$

This is a true statement. This means that the point $(0,0)$ will fall in the shaded half-plane.

Next consider $y \ge 2x - 3$. Replace the inequality symbol with an equal sign and we have $y = 2x - 3$. The equation is in slope-intercept form, so we can use the slope and the y-intercept to graph the line.

y-intercept $= -3$

slope $= 2$

Now, use the origin as a test point.

$y \ge 2x - 3$

$0 \ge 2(0) - 3$

$0 \ge -3$

This is a true statement. This means that the point $(0,0)$ will fall in the shaded half-plane.

Next, graph each of the inequalities. The solution to the system is the intersection of the shaded half-planes.

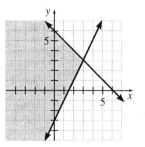

54. $3x + 2y \ge 4$

$x - y \le 3$

$x \ge 0, \ y \ge 0$

First consider $3x + 2y \ge 4$. Replace the inequality symbol with an equal sign and we have $3x + 2y = 4$. Solve for y to obtain slope-intercept form.

$3x + 2y = 4$

$2y = -3x + 4$

$y = -\dfrac{3}{2}x + 2$

y-intercept $= 2$ slope $= -\dfrac{3}{2}$

Now, use the origin as a test point.

$3x + 2y \ge 4$

$3(0) + 2(0) \ge 4$

$0 \ge 4$

This is a false statement. This means that the point $(0,0)$ will not fall in the shaded half-plane.

Now consider $x - y \le 3$. Replace the inequality symbol with an equal sign and we have $x - y = 3$. Solve for y to obtain slope-intercept form.

$x - y = 3$

$-y = -x + 3$

$y = x - 3$

y-intercept $= -3$ slope $= 1$

Now, use the origin as a test point.

$x - y \le 3$

$0 - 0 \le 3$

$0 \le 3$

This is a true statement. This means that the point $(0,0)$ will fall in the shaded half-plane.

Now consider the inequalities $x \ge 0$ and $y \ge 0$. The inequalities mean that both x and y will be positive. This means that we only need to consider quadrant I.

Next, graph each of the inequalities. The solution to the system is the intersection of the shaded half-planes.

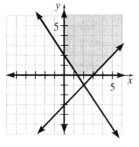

55. $2x - y > 2$

$2x - y < -2$

First consider $2x - y > 2$. Replace the inequality symbol with an equal sign and we have $2x - y = 2$. Solve for y to obtain slope-intercept form.

$2x - y = 2$

$-y = -2x + 2$

$y = 2x - 2$

y-intercept $= -2$ slope $= 2$

Now, use the origin as a test point.

$2x - y > 2$

$2(0) - 0 > 2$

$0 > 2$

This is a false statement. This means that the point $(0,0)$ will not fall in the shaded half-plane.

Now consider $2x - y < -2$. Replace the inequality symbol with an equal sign and we have $2x - y = -2$. Solve for y to obtain slope-intercept form.

$2x - y = -2$

$-y = -2x - 2$

$y = 2x + 2$

y-intercept $= 2$ slope $= 2$

Now, use the origin as a test point.

$2x - y < -2$

$2(0) - 0 < -2$

$0 < -2$

This is a false statement. This means that the point $(0,0)$ will not fall in the shaded half-plane.

Next, graph each of the inequalities. The solution to the system is the intersection of the shaded half-planes.

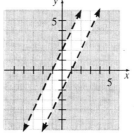

The graphs of the inequalities do not intersect, so there is no solution. The solution set is $\varnothing$ or $\{\ \}$.

56.

Corner (x, y)	Objective Function $z = 2x + 3y$
$(1, 0)$	$z = 2x + 3y$ $= 2(1) + 3(0) = 2$
$(4, 0)$	$z = 2x + 3y$ $= 2(4) + 3(0) = 8$
$(2, 2)$	$z = 2x + 3y$ $= 2(2) + 3(2)$ $= 4 + 6 = 10$
$\left(\dfrac{1}{2}, \dfrac{1}{2}\right)$	$z = 2x + 3y$ $= 2\left(\dfrac{1}{2}\right) + 3\left(\dfrac{1}{2}\right)$ $= \dfrac{2}{2} + \dfrac{3}{2} = \dfrac{5}{2}$

The maximum value is 10 and the minimum is 2.

57. Objective Function: $z = 2x + 3y$

Constraints: $x \geq 0, \quad y \geq 0$

$x + y \leq 8$

$3x + 2y \geq 6$

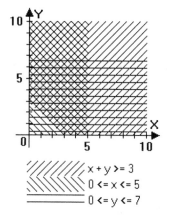

Using the graph, find the value of the objective function at each of the corner points.

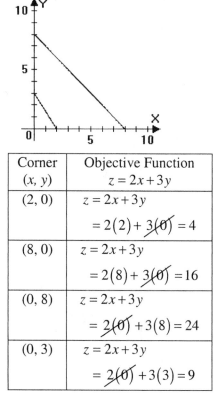

Corner (x, y)	Objective Function $z = 2x + 3y$
$(2, 0)$	$z = 2x + 3y$ $= 2(2) + 3(0) = 4$
$(8, 0)$	$z = 2x + 3y$ $= 2(8) + 3(0) = 16$
$(0, 8)$	$z = 2x + 3y$ $= 2(0) + 3(8) = 24$
$(0, 3)$	$z = 2x + 3y$ $= 2(0) + 3(3) = 9$

The maximum of 24 occurs at the point $(0, 8)$.

58. Objective Function: $z = x + 4y$

Constraints: $0 \leq x \leq 5$

$0 \leq y \leq 7$

$x + y \geq 3$

Using the graph, find the value of the

488

objective function at each of the
corner points.

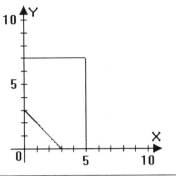

Corner (x, y)	Objective Function $z = x + 4y$
$(3, 0)$	$z = x + 4y$ $= 3 + 4(0) = 3$
$(5, 0)$	$z = x + 4y$ $= 5 + 4(0) = 5$
$(5, 7)$	$z = x + 4y$ $= 5 + 4(7)$ $= 5 + 28 = 33$
$(0, 7)$	$z = x + 4y$ $= 0 + 4(7) = 28$
$(0, 3)$	$z = x + 4y$ $= 0 + 4(3) = 12$

The maximum of 33 occurs at the
point $(5, 7)$.

59. Objective Function: $z = 5x + 6y$

Constraints: $x \geq 0, \ y \geq 0$

$y \leq x$

$2x + y \leq 12$

$2x + 3y \geq 6$

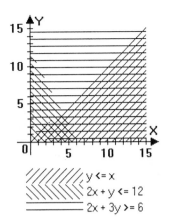

$y \mathrel{<=} x$

$2x + y \mathrel{<=} 12$

$2x + 3y \mathrel{>=} 6$

Using the graph, find the value of the
objective function at each of the
corner points.

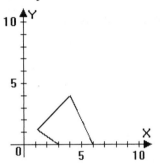

Corner (x, y)	Objective Function $z = 5x + 6y$
$(3, 0)$	$z = 5x + 6y$ $= 5(3) + 6(0) = 15$
$(6, 0)$	$z = 5x + 6y$ $= 5(6) + 6(0) = 30$
$(4, 4)$	$z = 5x + 6y$ $= 5(4) + 6(4)$ $= 20 + 24 = 44$
$(1.2, 1.2)$	$z = 5x + 6y$ $= 5(1.2) + 6(1.2)$ $= 6 + 7.2 = 13.2$

The maximum of 44 occurs at the
point $(4, 4)$.

60. **a.** The objective function is
$z = 500x + 350y$.

b. The paper constraint is
$x + y \leq 200$.

The minimum writing paper constraint is $x \geq 10$.

The minimum newsprint constraint is $y \geq 80$.

c.

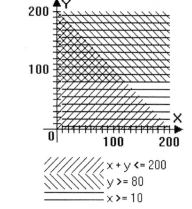

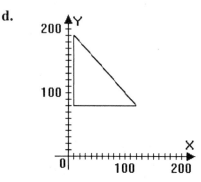

$x + y <= 200$
$y >= 80$
$x >= 10$

d.

Corner (x, y)	Objective Function $z = 500x + 350y$
(10, 80)	$z = 500x + 350y$ $= 500(10) + 350(80)$ $= 5000 + 28000$ $= 33000$
(120, 80)	$z = 500x + 350y$ $= 500(120) + 350(80)$ $= 60000 + 28000$ $= 88000$
(10, 190)	$z = 500x + 350y$ $= 500(10) + 350(190)$ $= 5000 + 66500$ $= 71500$

e. The company will make the greatest profit by producing <u>120</u> units of writing paper and <u>80</u> units of newsprint each day. The maximum daily profit is <u>$88,000</u>.

61. Let x = the number of model A produced
Let y = the number of model B produced
The objective function is
$z = 25x + 40y$.
The cutting department labor constraint is $0.9x + 1.8y \leq 864$.
The assembly department labor constraint is $0.8x + 1.2y \leq 672$.
We also know that x and y are either zero or a positive number. We cannot have a negative number of units produced.

490

Next, graph the constraints.

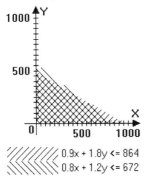

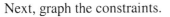

0.9x + 1.8y <= 864
0.8x + 1.2y <= 672

Using the graph, find the value of the objective function at each of the corner points.

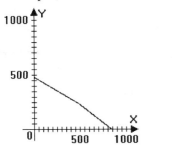

Corner (x, y)	Objective Function $z = 25x + 40y$
(0, 0)	$25x + 40y$ $= 25(0) + 40(0)$ $= 0$
(840, 0)	$25x + 40y$ $= 25(840) + 40(0)$ $= 21000$
(480, 240)	$25x + 40y$ $= 25(480) + 40(240)$ $= 12000 + 9600$ $= 21600$
(0, 480)	$25x + 40y$ $= 25(0) + 40(480)$ $= 19200$

The maximum of 21,600 occurs at the point (480, 240). This means that to maximize the profit, 480 of model A and 240 of model B should be manufactured monthly. This would result in a profit of $21,600.

Chapter 9 Test

1.　　$[-3, 2)$

　　$\{x | -3 \le x < 2\}$

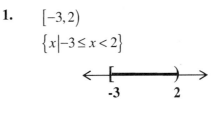

2.　　$(-\infty, -1]$

　　$\{x | x \le -1\}$

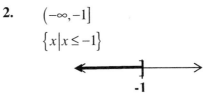

3.　　$3(x + 4) \ge 5x - 12$

　　$3x + 12 \ge 5x - 12$

　　$-2x + 12 \ge -12$

　　　$-2x \ge -24$

　　　$\dfrac{-2x}{-2} \le \dfrac{-24}{-2}$

　　　$x \le 12$

The solution set is $\{x | x \le 12\}$ or $(-\infty, 12]$.

491

4.

$$\frac{x}{6}+\frac{1}{8}\le\frac{x}{2}-\frac{3}{4}$$

$$24\left(\frac{x}{6}\right)+24\left(\frac{1}{8}\right)\le24\left(\frac{x}{2}\right)-24\left(\frac{3}{4}\right)$$

$$4x+3\le12x-6(3)$$

$$4x+3\le12x-18$$

$$-8x+3\le-18$$

$$-8x\le-21$$

$$\frac{-8x}{-8}\ge\frac{-21}{-8}$$

$$x\ge\frac{21}{8}$$

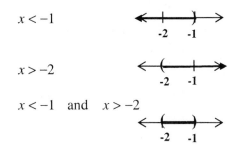

21/8

The solution set is $\left\{x\middle|x\ge\frac{21}{8}\right\}$ or

$$\left[\frac{21}{8},\infty\right).$$

5. **a.** cost = fixed costs + variable cost

$C(x)=60,000+200x$

b. revenue = price · quantity

$R(x)=450x$

c. profit = revenue − cost

$P(x)=R(x)-C(x)$

$=450x-(60,000+200x)$

$=450x-60,000-200x$

$=250x-60,000$

d. $P(x)>0$

$250x-60,000>0$

$250x>60,000$

$x>240$

More than 240 computer desks
need to be produced and sold to
make a profit.

6. $\{2,4,6,8,10\}\cap\{4,6,12,14\}=\{4,6\}$

7. $\{2,4,6,8,10\}\cup\{4,6,12,14\}$

$=\{2,4,6,8,10,12,14\}$

8. $2x+4<2$ and $x-3>-5$

$2x<-2$ $x>-2$

$x<-1$

$x<-1$

-2   -1

$x>-2$

-2   -1

$x<-1$ and $x>-2$

-2   -1

The solution set is $\{x|-2<x<-1\}$ or

$(-2,-1)$.

9. $x+6\ge4$ and $2x+3\ge-2$

$x\ge-2$ $2x\ge-5$

$x\ge-\frac{5}{2}$

$x\ge-2$

-5/2   -2

$x\ge-\frac{5}{2}$

-5/2   -2

$x\ge-2$ and $x\ge-\frac{5}{2}$

-5/2   -2

The solution set is $\{x|x\ge-2\}$ or

$[-2,\infty)$.

492

10. $2x - 3 < 5$ or $3x - 6 \leq 4$

$\qquad 2x < 8 \qquad\qquad 3x \leq 10$

$\qquad\quad x < 4 \qquad\qquad x \leq \dfrac{10}{3}$

$x < 4$

10/3   4

$x \leq \dfrac{10}{3}$

10/3   4

$x < 4$ or $x \leq \dfrac{10}{3}$

10/3   4

The solution set is $\{x | x < 4\}$ or $(-\infty, 4)$.

11. $x + 3 \leq -1$ or $-4x + 3 < -5$

$\qquad x \leq -4 \qquad\qquad -4x < -8$

$\qquad\qquad\qquad\qquad\quad x > 2$

$x \leq -4$

-4   2

$x > 8$

-4   2

$x \leq -4$ or $x > 2$

-4   2

The solution set is $\{x | x \leq -4$ or $x > 2\}$ or $(-\infty, -4] \cup (2, \infty)$.

12.

$$-3 \leq \dfrac{2x + 5}{3} < 6$$

$$3(-3) \leq 3\left(\dfrac{2x + 5}{3}\right) < 3(6)$$

$$-9 \leq 2x + 5 < 18$$

$$-9 - 5 \leq 2x + 5 - 5 < 18 - 5$$

$$-14 \leq 2x < 13$$

$$-7 \leq x < \dfrac{13}{2}$$

-7   13/2

The solution set is $\left\{x \middle| -7 \leq x < \dfrac{13}{2}\right\}$ or $\left[-7, \dfrac{13}{2}\right)$.

13. $|5x + 3| = 7$

$\qquad 5x + 3 = 7$ or $5x + 3 = -7$

$\qquad\quad 5x = 4 \qquad\qquad 5x = -10$

$\qquad\quad x = \dfrac{4}{5} \qquad\qquad x = -2$

The solutions are -2 and $\dfrac{4}{5}$ and the solution set is $\left\{-2, \dfrac{4}{5}\right\}$.

14. $|6x + 1| = |4x + 15|$

$6x + 1 = 4x + 15$ or $6x + 1 = -(4x + 15)$

$\quad 2x + 1 = 15 \qquad\qquad 6x + 1 = -4x - 15$

$\qquad 2x = 14 \qquad\qquad 10x + 1 = -15$

$\qquad\quad x = 7 \qquad\qquad\quad 10x = -16$

$\qquad\qquad\qquad\qquad\qquad x = -\dfrac{16}{10} = -\dfrac{8}{5}$

The solutions are $-\dfrac{8}{5}$ and 7 and the solution set is $\left\{-\dfrac{8}{5}, 7\right\}$.

493

15.
$$|2x-1|<7$$
$$-7<2x-1<7$$
$$-7+1<2x-1+1<7+1$$
$$-6<2x<8$$
$$-3<x<4$$

The solution set is $\{x|-3<x<4\}$ or $(-3,4)$.

16. $|2x-3|\ge 5$
$$2x-3\le -5 \quad \text{or} \quad 2x-3\ge 5$$
$$2x\le -2 \qquad\qquad 2x\ge 8$$
$$x\le -1 \qquad\qquad x\ge 4$$

The solution set is $\{x|x\le -1 \text{ or } x\ge 4\}$ or $(-\infty,-1]\cup[4,\infty)$.

17. $|b-98.6|>8$
$$b-98.6<-8 \quad \text{or} \quad b-98.6>8$$
$$b<90.6 \qquad\qquad b>106.6$$
Hypothermia occurs when the body temperature is below 90.6°F and Hyperthermia occurs when the body temperature is above 106.6°F.

18. $3x-2y<6$
First, find the intercepts to the equation $3x-2y=6$.
Find the x–intercept by setting $y=0$.
$$3x-2y=6$$
$$3x-2(0)=6$$
$$3x=6$$
$$x=2$$
Find the y–intercept by setting $x=0$.

$$3x-2y=6$$
$$3(0)-2y=6$$
$$-2y=6$$
$$y=-3$$
Next, use the origin as a test point.
$$3x-2y<6$$
$$3(0)-2(0)<6$$
$$0<6$$
This is a true statement. This means that the point will fall in the shaded half-plane.

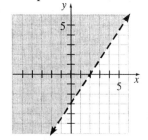

19. $y\ge \dfrac{1}{2}x-1$

Replacing the inequality symbol with an equal sign, we have $y=\dfrac{1}{2}x-1$.

The equation is in slope-intercept form, so graph the line using the slope and the y-intercept.

$$y\text{-intercept} = -1 \quad \text{slope} = \frac{1}{2}$$

Now, use the origin, $(0,0)$, as a test point.

$$y\ge \frac{1}{2}x-1$$
$$0\ge \frac{1}{2}(0)-1$$
$$0\ge -1$$

This is a true statement. This means that the point will fall in the shaded half-plane.

494

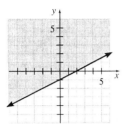

20. $y \leq -1$

Replacing the inequality symbol with an equal sign, we have $y = -1$. Equations of the form $y = b$ are horizontal lines with y–intercept $= b$, so this is a horizontal line at $y = -1$.

Next, use the origin as a test point.

$y \leq -1$

$0 \leq -1$

This is a false statement, so we know the point $(0,0)$ does not lie in the shaded half-plane.

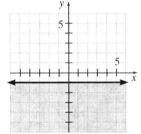

21. $x + y \geq 2$

$x - y \geq 4$

First consider $x + y \geq 2$. If we solve for y in $x + y = 2$, we can graph the line using the slope and the y–intercept.

$x + y = 2$

$y = -x + 2$

y-intercept $= 2$ slope $= -1$

Now, use the origin as a test point.

$x + y \geq 2$

$0 + 0 \geq 2$

$0 \geq 2$

This is a false statement. This means that the point will not fall in the shaded half-plane.

Next consider $x - y \geq 4$. If we solve for y in $x - y = 4$, we can graph using the slope and the y-intercept.

$x - y = 4$

$-y = -x + 4$

$y = x - 4$

y-intercept $= -4$ slope $= 1$

Now, use the origin as a test point.

$x - y \geq 4$

$0 - 0 \geq 4$

$0 \geq 4$

This is a false statement. This means that the point will not fall in the shaded half-plane.

Next, graph each of the inequalities. The solution to the system is the intersection of the shaded half-planes.

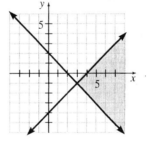

22. $3x + y \leq 9$

$2x + 3y \geq 6$

$x \geq 0, \ y \geq 0$

First consider $3x + y \leq 9$. If we solve for y in $3x + y = 9$, we can graph the line using the slope and the y–intercept.

$3x + y = 9$

$y = -3x + 9$

y-intercept $= 9$ slope $= -3$

Now, use the origin as a test point.

495

$$3x + y \le 9$$

$$3(\cancel{0}) + 0 \le 9$$

$$0 \le 9$$

This is a true statement. This means that the point will fall in the shaded half-plane.

Next consider $2x + 3y \ge 6$. If we solve for y in $2x + 3y = 6$, we can graph using the slope and the y-intercept.

$$2x + 3y = 6$$

$$3y = -2x + 6$$

$$y = -\frac{2}{3}x + 2$$

y-intercept $= 2$ slope $= -\dfrac{2}{3}$

Now, use the origin as a test point.

$$2x + 3y \ge 6$$

$$2(\cancel{0}) + 3(\cancel{0}) \ge 6$$

$$0 \ge 6$$

This is a false statement. This means that the point will not fall in the shaded half-plane.

Next consider the inequalities $x \ge 0$ and $y \ge 0$. When x and y are both positive, we are only concerned with the first quadrant of the coordinate system.

Graph each of the inequalities. The solution to the system is the intersection of the shaded half-planes.

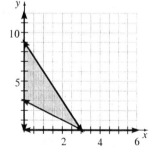

23. $-2 < x \le 4$

Rewrite the three part inequality as two separate inequalities. We have $-2 < x$ and $x \le 4$. We replace the inequality symbols with equal signs and obtain $-2 = x$ and $x = 4$. Equations of the form $x = a$ are vertical lines with x-intercept $= a$. We know the shading will be between $x = -2$ and $x = 4$ because in the original inequality we see that x lies between -2 and 4.

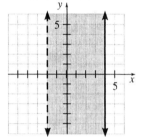

24.   Objective Function: $z = 3x + 5y$

Constraints: $x \ge 0,\ y \ge 0$

$$x + y \le 6$$

$$x \ge 2$$

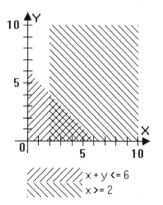

Using the graph, find the value of the objective function at each of the corner points.

496

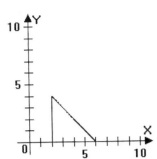

Corner (x, y)	Objective Function $z = 3x + 5y$
$(2, 0)$	$z = 3x + 5y$ $= 3(2) + 5(0) = 6$
$(6, 0)$	$z = 3x + 5y$ $= 3(6) + 5(0) = 18$
$(2, 4)$	$z = 3x + 5y$ $= 3(2) + 5(4)$ $= 6 + 20 = 26$

The maximum of 26 occurs at the point $(2, 4)$.

25. Let x = the number of regular jet skis produced
Let y = the number of deluxe jet skis produced
The objective function is
$z = 200x + 250y$.
The regular jet ski demand constraint is $x \geq 50$.
The deluxe jet ski demand constraint is $y \geq 75$.
The quality constraint is $x + y \leq 150$.

We also know that x and y are either zero or a positive number. We cannot have a negative number of units produced.
Next, graph the constraints.

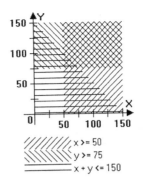

$x >= 50$
$y >= 75$
$x + y <= 150$

Using the graph, find the value of the objective function at each of the corner points.

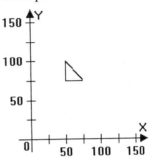

Corner (x, y)	Objective Function $z = 200x + 250y$
$(50, 75)$	$z = 200x + 250y$ $= 200(50) + 250(75)$ $= 10000 + 18750$ $= 28750$
$(75, 75)$	$z = 200x + 250y$ $= 200(75) + 250(75)$ $= 15000 + 18750$ $= 33750$
$(50, 100)$	$z = 200x + 250y$ $= 200(50) + 250(100)$ $= 10000 + 25000$ $= 35000$

The maximum of 35,000 occurs at the point $(50, 100)$. This means that to maximize the profit, 50 regular jet skis and 100 deluxe jet skis should be manufactured weekly. This would result in a profit of $35,000.

Cumulative Review Exercises
(Chapters 1-9)

1. $5(x+1)+2 = x-3(2x+1)$

$5x+5+2 = x-6x-3$

$5x+7 = -5x-3$

$10x+7 = -3$

$10x = -10$

$x = -1$

The solution is -1 and the solution set is $\{-1\}$.

2. $\dfrac{2(x+6)}{3} = 1 + \dfrac{4x-7}{3}$

$3\left(\dfrac{2(x+6)}{3}\right) = 3(1)+3\left(\dfrac{4x-7}{3}\right)$

$2(x+6) = 3+4x-7$

$2x+12 = 4x-4$

$-2x+12 = -4$

$-2x = -16$

$x = 8$

The solution is 8 and the solution set is $\{8\}$.

3. $\dfrac{-10x^2 y^4}{15x^7 y^{-3}} = \dfrac{-10}{15}x^{2-7}y^{4-(-3)}$

$= -\dfrac{2}{3}x^{-5}y^7 = -\dfrac{2y^7}{3x^5}$

4. $f(x) = x^2 - 3x + 4$

$f(-3) = (-3)^2 - 3(-3)+4$

$= 9+9+4 = 22$

$f(2a) = (2a)^2 - 3(2a)+4$

$= 4a^2 - 6a + 4$

5. $f(x) = 3x^2 - 4x + 1$

$g(x) = x^2 - 5x - 1$

$(f-g)(x) = f(x) - g(x)$

$= (3x^2 - 4x + 1) - (x^2 - 5x - 1)$

$= 3x^2 - 4x + 1 - x^2 + 5x + 1$

$= 2x^2 + x + 2$

$(f-g)(2) = 2(2)^2 + 2 + 2$

$= 2(4) + 2 + 2$

$= 8 + 2 + 2 = 12$

6. Since the line we are concerned with is perpendicular to the line, $y = 2x - 3$, we know the slopes are negative reciprocals. The slope of the line will be the negative reciprocal of 2 which is $-\dfrac{1}{2}$. Using the slope and the point, $(2,3)$, write the equation of the line in point-slope form.

$y - y_1 = m(x - x_1)$

$y - 3 = -\dfrac{1}{2}(x - 2)$

Solve for y to write the equation in function notation.

$y - 3 = -\dfrac{1}{2}(x - 2)$

$y - 3 = -\dfrac{1}{2}x + 1$

$y = -\dfrac{1}{2}x + 4$

$f(x) = -\dfrac{1}{2}x + 4$

498

7. $f(x) = 2x + 1$

$y = 2x + 1$

Find the x–intercept by setting $y = 0$,
and the y–intercept by setting $x = 0$.

$y = 2x + 1$ $y = 2x + 1$

$0 = 2x + 1$ $y = 2(0) + 1$

$-1 = 2x$ $y = 1$

$-\dfrac{1}{2} = x$

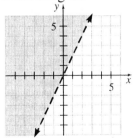

8. $y > 2x$

Consider the line $y = 2x$. Since the
line is in slope-intercept form, we

know that the slope is 2 and the y–
intercept is 0. Use this information to
graph the line.
Since the origin, (0, 0), lies on the line,
we cannot use it as a test point.
Instead, use the point (1, 1).

$y > 2x$

$1 > 2(1)$

$1 > 2$

This is a false statement. This means
that the point (1, 1) does not lie in the
shaded region.

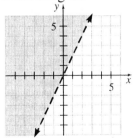

9. $2x - y \geq 6$

Graph the equation using the intercepts.

$2x - y = 6$

$x - \text{intercept} = 3$

$y - \text{intercept} = -6$

Use the origin as a test point to
determine shading.

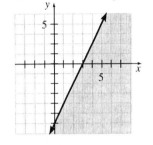

10. $f(x) = -1$

$y = -1$

Equations of the form $y = b$ are
horizontal lines with $y-\text{intercept} = b$.
This is the horizontal line at $y = -1$.

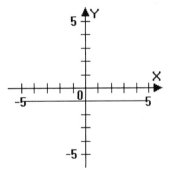

11. $3x - y + z = -15$

$\qquad x + 2y - z = 1$

$\qquad 2x + 3y - 2z = 0$

Add the first two equations to eliminate z.

$3x - y + z = -15$

$\underline{x + 2y - z = 1}$

$\qquad 4x + y = -14$

Multiply the first equation by 2 and add to the third equation.

$6x - 2y + 2z = -30$

$\underline{2x + 3y - 2z = 0}$

$\qquad 8x + y = -30$

The system of two equations in two variables becomes is as follows.

$4x + y = -14$

$8x + y = -30$

Multiply the first equation by -1 and add to the second equation.

$-4x - y = 14$

$\underline{8x + y = -30}$

$\qquad 4x = -16$

$\qquad x = -4$

Back-substitute -4 for x to find y.

$4(-4) + y = -14$

$\qquad -16 + y = -14$

$\qquad y = 2$

Back-substitute 2 for y and -4 for x to find z.

$\qquad 3x - y + z = -15$

$3(-4) - 2 + z = -15$

$\quad -12 - 2 + z = -15$

$\qquad -14 + z = -15$

$\qquad z = -1$

The solution is $(-4, 2, -1)$ and the solution set is $\{(-4, 2, -1)\}$.

12. $f(x) = \dfrac{x}{3} - 4$

$y = \dfrac{x}{3} - 4$

Start by switching x and y, and solve for y.

$x = \dfrac{y}{3} - 4$

$x + 4 = \dfrac{y}{3}$

$3(x + 4) = y$

$y = 3x + 12 = f^{-1}(x)$

Check:

$f\left(f^{-1}(x)\right) = \dfrac{(3x - 12)}{3} - 4$

$\qquad\qquad = x - 4 + 4 = x$

$f^{-1}(f(x)) = 3\left(\dfrac{x}{3} - 4\right) + 12$

$\qquad\qquad = x - 12 + 12 = x$

13. $f(x) = 3x^2 - 1$ and $g(x) = x + 2$

$f(g(x)) = 3(x + 2)^2 - 1$

$\qquad\quad = 3(x^2 + 4x + 4) - 1$

$\qquad\quad = 3x^2 + 12x + 12 - 1$

$\qquad\quad = 3x^2 + 12x + 11$

$g(f(x)) = (3x^2 - 1) + 2$

$\qquad\quad = 3x^2 + 1$

14. Let x = the number of rooms with a kitchen

Let y = the number of rooms without a kitchen

$\qquad x + y = 60$

$90x + 80y = 5260$

Solve the first equation for y.

500

$x + y = 60$

$y = 60 - x$

Substitute $60 - x$ for y to find x.

$90x + 80y = 5260$

$90x + 80(60 - x) = 5260$

$90x + 4800 - 80x = 5260$

$10x + 4800 = 5260$

$10x = 460$

$x = 46$

Back-substitute 46 for x to find y.

$y = 60 - x = 60 - 46 = 14$

There are 46 rooms with kitchens and 14 rooms without kitchens.

15. Using the vertical line test, we see that graphs a. and b. are functions.

16.

$$\frac{x}{4} - \frac{3}{4} - 1 \leq \frac{x}{2}$$

$$4\left(\frac{x}{4}\right) - 4\left(\frac{3}{4}\right) - 4(1) \leq 4\left(\frac{x}{2}\right)$$

$$x - 3 - 4 \leq 2x$$

$$x - 7 \leq 2x$$

$$x \leq 2x + 7$$

$$-x \leq 7$$

$$x \geq -7$$

The solution set is $\{x | x \geq -7\}$ or $(-7, \infty)$.

17. $2x + 5 \leq 11$ and $-3x > 18$

$\qquad 2x \leq 6 \qquad\qquad x < -6$

$\qquad\ x \leq 3$

$x \leq 3$

$x < -6$

$x \leq 3$ and $x < -6$

The solution set is $\{x | x < -6\}$ or $(-\infty, -6)$.

18. $x - 4 \geq 1$ or $-3x + 1 \geq -5 - x$

$\qquad x \geq 5 \qquad\qquad -2x + 1 \geq -5$

$\qquad\qquad\qquad\qquad\ -2x \geq -6$

$\qquad\qquad\qquad\qquad\qquad x \leq 3$

$x \geq 5$

$x \leq 3$

$x \geq 5$ or $x \leq 3$

The solution set is $\{x | x \leq 3 \text{ or } x \geq 5\}$ or $(-\infty, 3] \cup [5, \infty)$.

19.

$$|2x+3| \le 17$$

$$-17 \le 2x+3 \le 17$$

$$-20 \le 2x \le 14$$

$$-10 \le x \le 7$$

The solution set is $\{x \mid -10 \le x \le 7\}$ or $[-10, 7]$.

20.

$$|3x-8| > 7$$

$$3x-8 < -7 \quad \text{or} \quad 3x-8 > 7$$

$$3x < 1 \qquad\qquad 3x > 15$$

$$x < \frac{1}{3} \qquad\qquad x > 5$$

$$x < \frac{1}{3}$$

$$x > 5$$

$$x < \frac{1}{3} \text{ or } x > 5$$

The solution set is $\left\{x \mid x < \dfrac{1}{3} \text{ or } x > 5\right\}$

or $\left(-\infty, \dfrac{1}{3}\right) \cup (5, \infty)$.

502

Chapter 10
Radicals, Radical Functions, and Rational Exponents

10.1 Exercise Set

1. $\sqrt{36} = 6$ because $6^2 = 36$

3. $-\sqrt{36} = -6$ because $6^2 = 36$

5. $\sqrt{-36}$
Not a real number

7. $\sqrt{\dfrac{1}{25}} = \dfrac{1}{5}$ because $\left(\dfrac{1}{5}\right)^2 = \dfrac{1}{25}$

9. $-\sqrt{\dfrac{9}{16}} = -\dfrac{3}{4}$ because $\left(\dfrac{3}{4}\right)^2 = \dfrac{9}{16}$

11. $\sqrt{0.81} = 0.9$ because $(0.9)^2 = 0.81$

13. $-\sqrt{0.04} = -0.2$ because $(0.2)^2 = 0.04$

15. $\sqrt{25 - 16} = \sqrt{9} = 3$

17. $\sqrt{25} - \sqrt{16} = 5 - 4 = 1$

19. $\sqrt{16 - 25} = \sqrt{-9}$
Not a real number

21. $f(x) = \sqrt{x - 2}$
$f(18) = \sqrt{18 - 2} = \sqrt{16} = 4$
$f(3) = \sqrt{3 - 2} = \sqrt{1} = 1$
$f(2) = \sqrt{2 - 2} = \sqrt{0} = 0$
$f(-2) = \sqrt{-2 - 2} = \sqrt{-4}$
Not a real number

23. $g(x) = -\sqrt{2x + 3}$
$g(11) = -\sqrt{2(11) + 3}$
$\quad = -\sqrt{22 + 3}$
$\quad = -\sqrt{25} = -5$
$g(1) = -\sqrt{2(1) + 3}$
$\quad = -\sqrt{2 + 3}$
$\quad = -\sqrt{5} \approx -2.24$
$g(-1) = -\sqrt{2(-1) + 3}$
$\quad = -\sqrt{-2 + 3}$
$\quad = -\sqrt{1} = -1$
$g(-2) = -\sqrt{2(-2) + 3}$
$\quad = -\sqrt{-4 + 3} = -\sqrt{-1}$
Not a real number

25. $h(x) = \sqrt{(x-1)^2}$
$h(5) = \sqrt{(5-1)^2} = \sqrt{(4)^2} = |4| = 4$
$h(3) = \sqrt{(3-1)^2} = \sqrt{(2)^2} = |2| = 2$
$h(0) = \sqrt{(0-1)^2} = \sqrt{(-1)^2} = |-1| = 1$
$h(-5) = \sqrt{(-5-1)^2} = \sqrt{(-6)^2}$
$\quad = |-6| = 6$

27. To find the domain, set the radicand greater than or equal to zero and solve.
$x - 3 \geq 0$
$x \geq 3$
The domain of f is $\{x \mid x \geq 3\}$ or $[3, \infty)$. This corresponds to graph (c).

503

29. To find the domain, set the radicand greater than or equal to zero and solve.

$$3x + 15 \geq 0$$
$$3x \geq -15$$
$$x \geq -5$$

The domain of f is $\{x \mid x \geq -5\}$ or $[-5, \infty)$. This corresponds to graph (d).

31. To find the domain, set the radicand greater than or equal to zero and solve.

$$6 - 2x \geq 0$$
$$-2x \geq -6$$
$$x \leq 3$$

The domain of f is $\{x \mid x \leq 3\}$ or $(-\infty, 3]$. This corresponds to graph (e).

33. $\sqrt{5^2} = |5| = 5$

35. $\sqrt{(-4)^2} = |-4| = 4$

37. $\sqrt{(x-1)^2} = |x-1|$

39. $\sqrt{36x^4} = \sqrt{(6x^2)^2} = |6x^2| = 6x^2$

41. $-\sqrt{100x^6} = -\sqrt{(10x^3)^2}$
$$= -|10x^3| = -10|x^3|$$

43. $\sqrt{x^2 + 12x + 36} = \sqrt{(x+6)^2} = |x+6|$

45. $-\sqrt{x^2 - 8x + 16} = -\sqrt{(x-4)^2}$
$$= -|x-4|$$

47. $\sqrt[3]{27} = 3$ because $3^3 = 27$

49. $\sqrt[3]{-27} = -3$ because $(-3)^3 = -27$

51. $\sqrt[3]{\dfrac{1}{125}} = \dfrac{1}{5}$ because $\left(\dfrac{1}{5}\right)^3 = \dfrac{1}{125}$

53. $f(x) = \sqrt[3]{x-1}$
$$f(28) = \sqrt[3]{28-1} = \sqrt[3]{27} = 3$$
$$f(9) = \sqrt[3]{9-1} = \sqrt[3]{8} = 2$$
$$f(0) = \sqrt[3]{0-1} = \sqrt[3]{-1} = -1$$
$$f(-63) = \sqrt[3]{-63-1} = \sqrt[3]{-64} = -4$$

55. $g(x) = -\sqrt[3]{8x-8}$
$$g(2) = -\sqrt[3]{8(2)-8} = -\sqrt[3]{16-8}$$
$$= -\sqrt[3]{8} = -2$$
$$g(1) = -\sqrt[3]{8(1)-8} = -\sqrt[3]{8-8}$$
$$= -\sqrt[3]{0} = -0 = 0$$
$$g(0) = -\sqrt[3]{8(0)-8} = -\sqrt[3]{-8}$$
$$= -(-2) = 2$$

57. $\sqrt[4]{1} = 1$ because $1^4 = 1$

59. $\sqrt[4]{16} = 2$ because $2^4 = 16$

61. $-\sqrt[4]{16} = -2$ because $2^4 = 16$

63. $\sqrt[4]{-16}$
Not a real number

65. $\sqrt[5]{-1} = -1$ because $(-1)^5 = -1$

67. $\sqrt[6]{-1}$
Not a real number

504

69. $-\sqrt[4]{256} = -4$ because $4^4 = 256$

71. $\sqrt[6]{64} = 2$ because $2^6 = 64$

73. $-\sqrt[5]{32} = -2$ because $2^5 = 32$

75. $\sqrt[3]{x^3} = x$

77. $\sqrt[4]{y^4} = |y|$

79. $\sqrt[3]{-8x^3} = -2x$

81. $\sqrt[3]{(-5)^3} = -5$

83. $\sqrt[4]{(-5)^4} = |-5| = 5$

85. $\sqrt[4]{(x+3)^4} = |x+3|$

87. $\sqrt[5]{-32(x-1)^5} = -2(x-1)$

89.

x	$f(x) = \sqrt{x} + 3$
0	$f(0) = \sqrt{0} + 3 = 0 + 3 = 3$
1	$f(1) = \sqrt{1} + 3 = 1 + 3 = 4$
4	$f(4) = \sqrt{4} + 3 = 2 + 3 = 5$
9	$f(9) = \sqrt{9} + 3 = 3 + 3 = 6$

Domain: $\{x \mid x \geq 0\}$ or $[0, \infty)$
Range: $\{y \mid y \geq 3\}$ or $[3, \infty)$

90.

x	$f(x) = \sqrt{x} - 2$
0	$f(0) = \sqrt{0} - 2 = 0 - 2 = -2$
1	$f(1) = \sqrt{1} - 2 = 1 - 2 = -1$
4	$f(4) = \sqrt{4} - 2 = 2 - 2 = 0$
9	$f(9) = \sqrt{9} - 2 = 3 - 2 = 1$

Domain: $\{x \mid x \geq 0\}$ or $[0, \infty)$
Range: $\{y \mid y \geq -2\}$ or $[-2, \infty)$

91.

x	$f(x) = \sqrt{x - 3}$
3	$f(3) = \sqrt{3 - 3} = \sqrt{0} = 0$
4	$f(4) = \sqrt{4 - 3} = \sqrt{1} = 1$
7	$f(7) = \sqrt{7 - 3} = \sqrt{4} = 2$
12	$f(12) = \sqrt{12 - 3} = \sqrt{9} = 3$

Domain: $\{x \mid x \geq 3\}$ or $[3, \infty)$
Range: $\{y \mid y \geq 0\}$ or $[0, \infty)$

92.

x	$f(x) = \sqrt{4-x}$
-5	$f(-5) = \sqrt{4-(-5)} = \sqrt{9} = 3$
0	$f(0) = \sqrt{4-0} = \sqrt{4} = 2$
3	$f(3) = \sqrt{4-3} = \sqrt{1} = 1$
4	$f(4) = \sqrt{4-4} = \sqrt{0} = 0$

Domain: $\{x \mid x \le 4\}$ or $(-\infty, 4]$

Range: $\{y \mid y \ge 0\}$ or $[0, \infty)$

93. The domain of the cube root function is all real numbers, so we only need to worry about the square root in the denominator. We need the radicand of the square root to be ≥ 0, but we also cannot divide by 0. Therefore, we have

$$30 - 2x > 0$$
$$-2x > -30$$
$$x < 15$$

The domain of f is $\{x \mid x < 15\}$ or $(-\infty, 15)$.

94. The domain of the cube root function is all real numbers, so we only need to worry about the square root in the denominator. We need the radicand of the square root to be ≥ 0, but we also cannot divide by 0. Therefore, we have

$$80 - 5x > 0$$
$$-5x > -80$$
$$x < 16$$

The domain of f is $\{x \mid x < 16\}$ or $(-\infty, 16)$.

95. From the numerator, we need $x - 1 \ge 0$. From the denominator, we need $3 - x > 0$. We need to solve the two inequalities. The domain of the function is the overlap of the two solution sets.

$$x - 1 \ge 0 \quad \text{and} \quad 3 - x > 0$$
$$x \ge 1 \qquad\qquad -x > -3$$
$$\qquad\qquad\qquad x < 3$$

We need $x \ge 1$ and $x < 3$. Therefore, the domain of f is $\{x \mid 1 \le x < 3\}$ or $[1, 3)$.

96. From the numerator, we need $x - 2 \ge 0$. From the denominator, we need $7 - x > 0$. We need to solve the two inequalities. The domain of the function is the overlap of the two solution sets.

$$x - 2 \ge 0 \quad \text{and} \quad 7 - x > 0$$
$$x \ge 2 \qquad\qquad -x > -7$$
$$\qquad\qquad\qquad x < 7$$

We need $x \ge 2$ and $x < 7$. Therefore, the domain of f is $\{x \mid 2 \le x < 7\}$ or $[2, 7)$.

97. $\sqrt[3]{\sqrt[4]{16} + \sqrt{625}} = \sqrt[3]{2 + 25} = \sqrt[3]{27} = 3$

98. $\sqrt[3]{\sqrt{\sqrt{169} + \sqrt{9}} + \sqrt{\sqrt[3]{1000} + \sqrt[3]{216}}}$

$$= \sqrt[3]{\sqrt{13 + 3} + \sqrt{10 + 6}}$$
$$= \sqrt[3]{\sqrt{16} + \sqrt{16}}$$
$$= \sqrt[3]{4 + 4} = \sqrt[3]{8}$$
$$= 2$$

99.
$$f(48) = 2.9\sqrt{48} + 20.1$$
$$= 2.9(6.9) + 20.1$$
$$= 20.1 + 20.1 \approx 40.2$$

The model predicts the median height of boys who are 48 months old to be 40.2 inches. The model predicts the median height very well. According to the table, the median height is 40.8.

101.
$$f(245) = \sqrt{20(245)} = \sqrt{4900} = 70$$

The officer should not believe the motorist. The model predicts that the motorist's speed was 70 miles per hour. This is well above the 50 miles per hour speed limit.

103. Answers will vary.

105. Answers will vary.

107. Answers will vary.

109. Answers will vary.

111. Answers will vary.

113. Answers will vary.

115.
$$y = \sqrt{x}$$
$$y = \sqrt{x} + 4$$
$$y = \sqrt{x} - 3$$

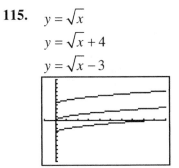

The graphs start at the y-axis, are increasing, and have the same shape. They differ in where they begin on the y-axis (i.e. different y-intercepts).

117.
$$y_1 = \sqrt{x^2}$$
$$y_2 = -x$$

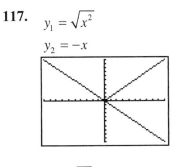

a. $\sqrt{x^2} = -x$ for $\{x | x \le 0\}$.

b. $\sqrt{x^2} \ne -x$ for $\{x | x > 0\}$.

119. Answers will vary. One example is $f(x) = \sqrt{5 - x}$.

121.
$$\sqrt{(2x+3)^{10}} = \sqrt{\left((2x+3)^5\right)^2}$$
$$= \left|(2x+3)^5\right|$$

123. $h(x) = \sqrt{x+3}$

x	$h(x) = \sqrt{x+3}$
-3	$h(-3) = \sqrt{-3+3} = \sqrt{0} = 0$
-2	$h(-2) = \sqrt{-2+3} = \sqrt{1} = 1$
1	$h(1) = \sqrt{1+3} = \sqrt{4} = 2$
6	$h(6) = \sqrt{6+3} = \sqrt{9} = 3$

The graph of h is the graph of f shifted three units to the left.

124. $3x - 2[x - 3(x+5)]$
$= 3x - 2[x - 3x - 15]$
$= 3x - 2[-2x - 15]$
$= 3x + 4x + 30$
$= 7x + 30$

125. $\left(-3x^{-4}y^3\right)^{-2} = (-3)^{-2}\left(x^{-4}\right)^{-2}\left(y^3\right)^{-2}$

$$= \frac{1}{(-3)^2}x^8 y^{-6}$$

$$= \frac{x^8}{(-3)^2 y^6} = \frac{x^8}{9y^6}$$

126. $|3x - 4| > 11$

$3x - 4 < -11$ or $3x - 4 > 11$
$3x < -7$ $\qquad$ $3x > 15$
$x < -\dfrac{7}{3}$ $\qquad$ $x > 5$

The solution set is
$\left\{ x \mid x < -\frac{7}{3} \text{ or } x > 5 \right\}$
or $\left(-\infty, -\dfrac{7}{3} \right) \cup (5, \infty)$.

10.2 Exercise Set

1. $49^{1/2} = \sqrt{49} = 7$

3. $(-27)^{1/3} = \sqrt[3]{-27} = -3$

5. $-16^{1/4} = -\sqrt[4]{16} = -2$

7. $(xy)^{1/3} = \sqrt[3]{xy}$

9. $\left(2xy^3\right)^{1/5} = \sqrt[5]{2xy^3}$

11. $81^{3/2} = \left(\sqrt{81}\right)^3 = 9^3 = 729$

13. $125^{2/3} = \left(\sqrt[3]{125}\right)^2 = 5^2 = 25$

15. $(-32)^{3/5} = \left(\sqrt[5]{-32}\right)^3 = (-2)^3 = -8$

17. $27^{2/3} + 16^{3/4} = \left(\sqrt[3]{27}\right)^2 + \left(\sqrt[4]{16}\right)^3$
$= 3^2 + 2^3$
$= 9 + 8 = 17$

19. $(xy)^{4/7} = \left(\sqrt[7]{xy}\right)^4$ or $\sqrt[7]{(xy)^4}$

21. $\sqrt{7} = 7^{1/2}$

23. $\sqrt[3]{5} = 5^{1/3}$

25. $\sqrt[5]{11x} = (11x)^{1/5}$

27. $\sqrt{x^3} = x^{3/2}$

29. $\sqrt[5]{x^3} = x^{3/5}$

31. $\sqrt[5]{x^2 y} = \left(x^2 y\right)^{1/5}$

33. $\left(\sqrt{19xy}\right)^3 = (19xy)^{3/2}$

35. $\left(\sqrt[6]{7xy^2}\right)^5 = \left(7xy^2\right)^{5/6}$

37. $2x\sqrt[3]{y^2} = 2xy^{2/3}$

39. $49^{-1/2} = \dfrac{1}{49^{1/2}} = \dfrac{1}{\sqrt{49}} = \dfrac{1}{7}$

508

41. $27^{-1/3} = \dfrac{1}{27^{1/3}} = \dfrac{1}{\sqrt[3]{27}} = \dfrac{1}{3}$

43. $16^{-3/4} = \dfrac{1}{16^{3/4}} = \dfrac{1}{\left(\sqrt[4]{16}\right)^3} = \dfrac{1}{2^3} = \dfrac{1}{8}$

45. $8^{-2/3} = \dfrac{1}{8^{2/3}} = \dfrac{1}{\left(\sqrt[3]{8}\right)^2} = \dfrac{1}{2^2} = \dfrac{1}{4}$

47. $\left(\dfrac{8}{27}\right)^{-1/3} = \left(\dfrac{27}{8}\right)^{1/3} = \sqrt[3]{\dfrac{27}{8}} = \dfrac{3}{2}$

49. $(-64)^{-2/3} = \dfrac{1}{(-64)^{2/3}} = \dfrac{1}{\left(\sqrt[3]{-64}\right)^2}$

$\qquad = \dfrac{1}{(-4)^2} = \dfrac{1}{16}$

51. $(2xy)^{-7/10} = \dfrac{1}{(2xy)^{7/10}}$

$\qquad = \dfrac{1}{\sqrt[10]{(2xy)^7}} \text{ or } \dfrac{1}{\left(\sqrt[10]{2xy}\right)^7}$

53. $5xz^{-1/3} = \dfrac{5xz^{-1/3}}{1} = \dfrac{5x}{z^{1/3}}$

55. $3^{3/4} \cdot 3^{1/4} = 3^{(3/4)+(1/4)}$

$\qquad = 3^{4/4} = 3^1 = 3$

57. $\dfrac{16^{3/4}}{16^{1/4}} = 16^{(3/4)-(1/4)} = 16^{2/4}$

$\qquad = 16^{1/2} = \sqrt{16} = 4$

59. $x^{1/2} \cdot x^{1/3} = x^{(1/2)+(1/3)}$

$\qquad = x^{(3/6)+(2/6)} = x^{5/6}$

61. $\dfrac{x^{4/5}}{x^{1/5}} = x^{(4/5)-(1/5)} = x^{3/5}$

63. $\dfrac{x^{1/3}}{x^{3/4}} = x^{(1/3)-(3/4)} = x^{(4/12)-(9/12)}$

$\qquad = x^{-5/12} = \dfrac{1}{x^{5/12}}$

65. $\left(5^{\frac{2}{3}}\right)^3 = 5^{\frac{2}{3}\cdot 3} = 5^2 = 25$

67. $\left(y^{-2/3}\right)^{1/4} = y^{(-2/3)\cdot(1/4)} = y^{-2/12}$

$\qquad = y^{-1/6} = \dfrac{1}{y^{1/6}}$

69. $\left(2x^{1/5}\right)^5 = 2^5 x^{(1/5)\cdot 5} = 32x^1 = 32x$

71. $\left(25x^4 y^6\right)^{1/2} = 25^{1/2}\left(x^4\right)^{1/2}\left(y^6\right)^{1/2}$

$\qquad = \sqrt{25}\,x^{4(1/2)} y^{6(1/2)}$

$\qquad = 5x^2 y^3$

73. $\left(x^{1/2} y^{-3/5}\right)^{1/2} = \left(\dfrac{x^{1/2} y^{-3/5}}{1}\right)^{1/2}$

$\qquad = \left(\dfrac{x^{1/2}}{y^{3/5}}\right)^{1/2}$

$\qquad = \dfrac{x^{(1/2)\cdot(1/2)}}{y^{(3/5)\cdot(1/2)}} = \dfrac{x^{1/4}}{y^{3/10}}$

75. $\dfrac{3^{1/2} \cdot 3^{3/4}}{3^{1/4}} = 3^{(1/2)+(3/4)-(1/4)}$

$\qquad = 3^{(2/4)+(3/4)-(1/4)}$

$\qquad = 3^{4/4} = 3^1 = 3$

509

77.
$$\frac{\left(3y^{1/4}\right)^3}{y^{1/12}} = \frac{3^3 \, y^{(1/4)\cdot3}}{y^{1/12}} = \frac{27 \, y^{3/4}}{y^{1/12}}$$
$$= 27 \, y^{(3/4)-(1/12)}$$
$$= 27 \, y^{(9/12)-(1/12)}$$
$$= 27 \, y^{8/12} = 27 \, y^{2/3}$$

79.
$$\sqrt[8]{x^2} = x^{2/8} = x^{1/4} = \sqrt[4]{x}$$

81.
$$\sqrt[3]{8a^6} = 8^{1/3} a^{6/3} = 2a^2$$

83.
$$\sqrt[5]{x^{10} y^{15}} = x^{10/5} y^{15/5} = x^2 y^3$$

85.
$$\left(\sqrt[3]{xy}\right)^{18} = (xy)^{18/3} = (xy)^6 = x^6 y^6$$

87.
$$\sqrt[10]{(3y)^2} = (3y)^{2/10} = (3y)^{1/5} = \sqrt[5]{3y}$$

89.
$$\left(\sqrt[6]{2a}\right)^4 = (2a)^{4/6} = (2a)^{2/3}$$
$$= \left(4a^2\right)^{1/3} = \sqrt[3]{4a^2}$$

91.
$$\sqrt[9]{x^6 y^3} = x^{6/9} y^{3/9}$$
$$= x^{2/3} y^{1/3} = \sqrt[3]{x^2 y}$$

93.
$$\sqrt{2} \cdot \sqrt[3]{2} = 2^{1/2} \cdot 2^{1/3} = 2^{(1/2)+(1/3)}$$
$$= 2^{(3/6)+(2/6)} = 2^{5/6}$$
$$= \sqrt[6]{2^5} \text{ or } \sqrt[6]{32}$$

95.
$$\sqrt[5]{x^2} \cdot \sqrt{x} = \left(x^2\right)^{1/5} \cdot x^{1/2}$$
$$= x^{2/5} \cdot x^{1/2} = x^{(2/5)+(1/2)}$$
$$= x^{(4/10)+(5/10)} = x^{9/10}$$
$$= \sqrt[10]{x^9}$$

97.
$$\sqrt[4]{a^2 b} \cdot \sqrt[3]{ab} = \left(a^2 b\right)^{1/4} \cdot (ab)^{1/3}$$
$$= a^{1/2} b^{1/4} \cdot a^{1/3} b^{1/3}$$
$$= a^{(1/2)+(1/3)} b^{(1/4)+(1/3)}$$
$$= a^{(6/12)+(4/12)} b^{(3/12)+(4/12)}$$
$$= a^{10/12} b^{7/12}$$
$$= \sqrt[12]{a^{10} b^7}$$

99.
$$\frac{\sqrt[4]{x}}{\sqrt[5]{x}} = \frac{x^{1/4}}{x^{1/5}} = x^{(1/4)-(1/5)}$$
$$= x^{(5/20)-(4/20)}$$
$$= x^{1/20} = \sqrt[20]{x}$$

101.
$$\frac{\sqrt[3]{y^2}}{\sqrt[6]{y}} = \frac{y^{2/3}}{y^{1/6}} = y^{(2/3)-(1/6)}$$
$$= y^{(4/6)-(1/6)} = y^{3/6}$$
$$= y^{1/2} = \sqrt{y}$$

103.
$$\sqrt[4]{\sqrt{x}} = \sqrt[4]{x^{1/2}} = \left(x^{1/2}\right)^{1/4}$$
$$= x^{(1/2)\cdot(1/4)} = x^{1/8}$$
$$= \sqrt[8]{x}$$

105.
$$\sqrt{\sqrt{x^2 y}} = \sqrt{\left(x^2 y\right)^{1/2}} = \left(\left(x^2 y\right)^{1/2}\right)^{1/2}$$
$$= \left(x^2 y\right)^{(1/2)\cdot(1/2)} = \left(x^2 y\right)^{1/4}$$
$$= \sqrt[4]{x^2 y}$$

107.
$$\sqrt[4]{\sqrt[3]{2x}} = \sqrt[4]{(2x)^{1/3}} = \left((2x)^{1/3}\right)^{1/4}$$
$$= (2x)^{(1/3)\cdot(1/4)} = (2x)^{1/12}$$
$$= \sqrt[12]{2x}$$

109. $\left(\sqrt[4]{x^3 y^5}\right)^{12} = \left(\left(x^3 y^5\right)^{1/4}\right)^{12}$

$$= \left(x^3 y^5\right)^{(1/4)\cdot 12}$$

$$= \left(x^3 y^5\right)^{12/4} = \left(x^3 y^5\right)^3$$

$$= x^{3\cdot 3} y^{5\cdot 3} = x^9 y^{15}$$

111. $\dfrac{\sqrt[4]{a^5 b^5}}{\sqrt{ab}} = \dfrac{a^{5/4} b^{5/4}}{a^{1/2} b^{1/2}}$

$$= a^{(5/4)-(1/2)} b^{(5/4)-(1/2)}$$

$$= a^{(5/4)-(2/4)} b^{(5/4)-(2/4)}$$

$$= a^{3/4} b^{3/4} = \left(a^3 b^3\right)^{1/4}$$

$$= \sqrt[4]{a^3 b^3}$$

113. $x^{1/3}\left(x^{1/3} - x^{2/3}\right)$

$$= x^{1/3} \cdot x^{1/3} - x^{1/3} \cdot x^{2/3}$$

$$= x^{(1/3)+(1/3)} - x^{(1/3)+(2/3)}$$

$$= x^{2/3} - x^{3/3}$$

$$= x^{2/3} - x$$

114. $x^{-1/4}\left(x^{9/4} - x^{1/4}\right)$

$$= x^{-1/4} \cdot x^{9/4} - x^{-1/4} \cdot x^{1/4}$$

$$= x^{(-1/4)+(9/4)} - x^{(-1/4)+(1/4)}$$

$$= x^{8/4} - x^0$$

$$= x^2 - 1$$

115. $\left(x^{1/2} - 3\right)\left(x^{1/2} + 5\right)$

$$= x^{1/2} \cdot x^{1/2} + x^{1/2} \cdot 5 - 3 \cdot x^{1/2} - 3 \cdot 5$$

$$= x^{(1/2)+(1/2)} + 5x^{1/2} - 3x^{1/2} - 15$$

$$= x^{2/2} + 2x^{1/2} - 15$$

$$= x + 2x^{1/2} - 15$$

116. $\left(x^{1/3} - 2\right)\left(x^{1/3} + 6\right)$

$$= x^{1/3} \cdot x^{1/3} + x^{1/3} \cdot 6 - 2 \cdot x^{1/3} - 2 \cdot 6$$

$$= x^{(1/3)+(1/3)} + 6x^{1/3} - 2x^{1/3} - 12$$

$$= x^{2/3} + 4x^{1/3} - 12$$

117. $6x^{1/2} + 2x^{3/2}$

$$= 3 \cdot 2x^{1/2} + 2x^{(1/2)+(2/2)}$$

$$= 3 \cdot 2x^{1/2} + 2x^{1/2} \cdot x^{2/2}$$

$$= 3 \cdot 2x^{1/2} + 2x^{1/2} \cdot x$$

$$= 2x^{1/2}\left(3 + x\right)$$

118. $8x^{1/4} + 4x^{5/4}$

$$= 2 \cdot 4x^{1/4} + 4x^{(1/4)+(4/4)}$$

$$= 2 \cdot 4x^{1/4} + 4x^{1/4} \cdot x^{4/4}$$

$$= 2 \cdot 4x^{1/4} + 4x^{1/4} \cdot x^1$$

$$= 4x^{1/4}\left(2 + x\right)$$

119. $15x^{1/3} - 60x = 15x^{1/3} - 60x^{3/3}$

$$= 15x^{1/3} - 60x^{(1/3)+(2/3)}$$

$$= 15x^{1/3} - 60x^{1/3} x^{2/3}$$

$$= 15x^{1/3} \cdot 1 - 15x^{1/3} \cdot 4x^{2/3}$$

$$= 15x^{1/3}\left(1 - 4x^{2/3}\right)$$

120. $7x^{1/3} - 70x = 7x^{1/3} - 70x^{3/3}$

$$= 7x^{1/3} - 70x^{(1/3)+(2/3)}$$

$$= 7x^{1/3} - 70x^{1/3} \cdot x^{2/3}$$

$$= 7x^{1/3} \cdot 1 - 7x^{1/3} \cdot 10x^{2/3}$$

$$= 7x^{1/3}\left(1 - 10x^{2/3}\right)$$

511

121. $\left(49x^{-2}y^4\right)^{-1/2}\left(xy^{1/2}\right)$

$= (49)^{-1/2}\left(x^{-2}\right)^{-1/2}\left(y^4\right)^{-1/2}\left(xy^{1/2}\right)$

$= \dfrac{1}{49^{1/2}}x^{(-2)(-1/2)}y^{(4)(-1/2)}\left(xy^{1/2}\right)$

$= \dfrac{1}{7}x^1y^{-2}\cdot xy^{1/2}$

$= \dfrac{1}{7}x^{1+1}y^{-2+(1/2)}$

$= \dfrac{1}{7}x^2y^{-3/2}$

$= \dfrac{x^2}{7y^{3/2}}$

122. $\left(8x^{-6}y^3\right)^{1/3}\left(x^{5/6}y^{-1/3}\right)^6$

$= 8^{1/3}x^{(-6)(1/3)}y^{(3)(1/3)}x^{(5/6)(6)}y^{(-1/3)(6)}$

$= 2x^{-2}y^1x^5y^{-2}$

$= 2x^{-2+5}y^{1+(-2)}$

$= 2x^3y^{-1}$

$= \dfrac{2x^3}{y}$

123. $\left(\dfrac{x^{-5/4}y^{1/3}}{x^{-3/4}}\right)^{-6}$

$= \left(x^{(-5/4)-(-3/4)}y^{1/3}\right)^{-6}$

$= \left(x^{-2/4}y^{1/3}\right)^{-6}$

$= x^{(-2/4)(-6)}y^{(1/3)(-6)}$

$= x^3y^{-2}$

$= \dfrac{x^3}{y^2}$

124. $\left(\dfrac{x^{1/2}y^{-7/4}}{y^{-5/4}}\right)^{-4}$

$= \left(x^{1/2}y^{(-7/4)-(-5/4)}\right)^{-4}$

$= \left(x^{1/2}y^{-2/4}\right)^{-4}$

$= x^{(1/2)(-4)}y^{(-2/4)(-4)}$

$= x^{-2}y^2$

$= \dfrac{y^2}{x^2}$

125. $f(8) = 29(8)^{1/3}$

$= 29\sqrt[3]{8}$

$= 29(2) = 58$

There are 58 plant species on an 8 square mile island.

127. $f(x) = 70x^{3/4}$

$f(80) = 70(80)^{3/4} \approx 1872$

A person who weighs 80 kilograms needs about 1872 calories per day to maintain life.

129. $C = 35.74 + 0.6215t - 35.74v^{4/25} + 0.4275t \cdot v^{4/25}$

    a. For $t = 0$, we get

      $C(v) = 35.74 - 35.74v^{4/25}$

    b. $C(25) = 35.74 - 35.74(25)^{4/25} \approx -24$

      When the air temperature is $0°F$ and the wind speed is 25 miles per hour, the windchill temperature is $-24°F$.

    c. The solution to part (b) is represented by the point $(25, -24)$ on the graph.

131. $L + 1.25\sqrt{S} - 9.8\sqrt[3]{D} \le 16.296$

    a. $L + 1.25S^{1/2} - 9.8D^{1/3} \le 16.296$

    b.

$$L + 1.25S^{1/2} - 9.8D^{1/3} \le 16.296$$
$$20.85 + 1.25(276.4)^{1/2} - 9.8(18.55)^{1/3} \le 16.296$$
$$20.85 + 1.25\sqrt{276.4} - 9.8\sqrt[3]{18.55} \le 16.296$$
$$20.85 + 1.25(16.625) - 9.8(2.647) \le 16.296$$
$$20.85 + 20.781 - 25.941 \le 16.296$$
$$15.69 \le 16.296$$

    The yacht is eligible to enter the America's Cup.

133. – 139. Answers will vary.

141. Answers will vary depending on exercises selected. For example, consider Exercise 45.

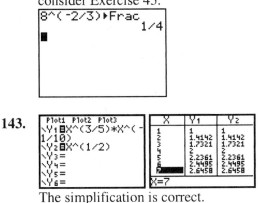

143.

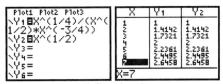

The simplification is correct.

145.

The simplification is not correct.

$$\frac{x^{1/4}}{x^{1/2} \cdot x^{-3/4}} = x^{(1/4) - [(1/2) + (-3/4)]}$$
$$= x^{(1/4) - (2/4) + (3/4)}$$
$$= x^{2/4}$$
$$= x^{1/2}$$

The new simplification is correct.

147. $2^{5/2} \cdot 2^{3/4} \div 2^{1/4} = 2^{(5/2)+(3/4)-(1/4)}$

$$= 2^{(10/4)+(3/4)-(1/4)}$$

$$= 2^{12/4} = 2^3 = 8$$

The son is 8 years old.

149. $\left[3+\left(27^{2/3}+32^{2/5}\right)\right]^{3/2} - 9^{1/2}$

$$= \left[3+\left(\left(\sqrt[3]{27}\right)^2+\left(\sqrt[5]{32}\right)^2\right)\right]^{3/2} - \sqrt{9}$$

$$= \left[3+\left(3^2+2^2\right)\right]^{3/2} - 3$$

$$= \left[3+\left(9+4\right)\right]^{3/2} - 3$$

$$= \left[3+\left(13\right)\right]^{3/2} - 3 = \left[16\right]^{3/2} - 3$$

$$= \left(\sqrt{16}\right)^3 - 3 = \left(4\right)^3 - 3$$

$$= 64-3 = 61$$

151. First, find the slope.

$$m = \frac{y_2 - y_1}{x_2 - x_1} = \frac{3-1}{4-5} = \frac{2}{-1} = -2$$

Use the slope and one of the points to write the equation of the line in point-slope form.

$$y - y_1 = m\left(x - x_1\right)$$

$$y - 3 = -2\left(x - 4\right)$$

Solve for y to write the equation in slope–intercept form.

$$y - 3 = -2\left(x - 4\right)$$

$$y - 3 = -2x + 8$$

$$y = -2x + 11 \text{ or } f\left(x\right) = -2x + 11$$

152. $y \le -\dfrac{3}{2}x + 3$

First graph the line, $y = -\dfrac{3}{2}x + 3$.

Since the line is in slope–intercept form we can identify the slope and y–intercept.

slope $= -\dfrac{3}{2}$ $\qquad$ y–intercept $= 3$

Now, use the origin, $\left(0,0\right)$, as a test point.

$$0 \le -\frac{3}{2}\left(0\right) + 3$$

$$0 \le 3$$

This is a true statement. This means that the point $\left(0,0\right)$ will fall in the shaded half-plane.

Next, graph the inequality.

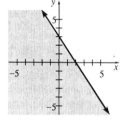

153. $f\left(x\right) = 3x^2 - 5x + 4$;

$f\left(a+h\right)$

$$= 3\left(a+h\right)^2 - 5\left(a+h\right) + 4$$

$$= 3\left(a^2 + 2ah + h^2\right) - 5\left(a+h\right) + 4$$

$$= 3a^2 + 6ah + 3h^2 - 5a - 5h + 4$$

514

10.3 Exercise Set

1. $\sqrt{3} \cdot \sqrt{5} = \sqrt{3 \cdot 5} = \sqrt{15}$

3. $\sqrt[3]{2} \cdot \sqrt[3]{9} = \sqrt[3]{2 \cdot 9} = \sqrt[3]{18}$

5. $\sqrt[4]{11} \cdot \sqrt[4]{3} = \sqrt[4]{11 \cdot 3} = \sqrt[4]{33}$

7. $\sqrt{3x} \cdot \sqrt{11y} = \sqrt{3x \cdot 11y} = \sqrt{33xy}$

9. $\sqrt[5]{6x^3} \cdot \sqrt[5]{4x} = \sqrt[5]{6x^3 \cdot 4x} = \sqrt[5]{24x^4}$

11. $\sqrt{x+3} \cdot \sqrt{x-3} = \sqrt{(x+3)(x-3)}$
$$= \sqrt{x^2 - 9}$$

13. $\sqrt[6]{x-4} \cdot \sqrt[6]{(x-4)^4}$
$$= \sqrt[6]{(x-4)(x-4)^4} = \sqrt[6]{(x-4)^5}$$

15. $\sqrt{\dfrac{2x}{3}} \cdot \sqrt{\dfrac{3}{2}} = \sqrt{\dfrac{2x}{3} \cdot \dfrac{3}{2}}$
$$= \sqrt{\dfrac{1\cancel{2}x}{1\cancel{3}} \cdot \dfrac{1\cancel{3}}{1\cancel{2}}}$$
$$= \sqrt{x}$$

17. $\sqrt[4]{\dfrac{x}{7}} \cdot \sqrt[4]{\dfrac{3}{y}} = \sqrt[4]{\dfrac{x}{7} \cdot \dfrac{3}{y}} = \sqrt[4]{\dfrac{3x}{7y}}$

19. $\sqrt[7]{7x^2 y} \cdot \sqrt[7]{11x^3 y^2} = \sqrt[7]{7x^2 y \cdot 11x^3 y^2}$
$$= \sqrt[7]{7 \cdot 11 x^2 x^3 y y^2}$$
$$= \sqrt[7]{77 x^5 y^3}$$

21. $\sqrt{50} = \sqrt{25 \cdot 2} = \sqrt{25} \cdot \sqrt{2} = 5\sqrt{2}$

23. $\sqrt{45} = \sqrt{9 \cdot 5} = \sqrt{9} \cdot \sqrt{5} = 3\sqrt{5}$

25. $\sqrt{75x} = \sqrt{25 \cdot 3x}$
$$= \sqrt{25} \cdot \sqrt{3x} = 5\sqrt{3x}$$

27. $\sqrt[3]{16} = \sqrt[3]{8 \cdot 2} = \sqrt[3]{8} \cdot \sqrt[3]{2} = 2\sqrt[3]{2}$

29. $\sqrt[3]{27x^3} = \sqrt[3]{27 \cdot x^3} = \sqrt[3]{27} \cdot \sqrt[3]{x^3} = 3x$

31. $\sqrt[3]{-16x^2 y^3} = \sqrt[3]{-8 \cdot 2x^2 y^3}$
$$= \sqrt[3]{-8y^3} \cdot \sqrt[3]{2x^2}$$
$$= -2y\sqrt[3]{2x^2}$$

33. $f(x) = \sqrt{36(x+2)^2} = 6|x+2|$

35. $f(x) = \sqrt[3]{32(x+2)^3}$
$$= \sqrt[3]{8 \cdot 4(x+2)^3}$$
$$= \sqrt[3]{8(x+2)^3} \cdot \sqrt[3]{4}$$
$$= 2(x+2)\sqrt[3]{4}$$

37. $f(x) = \sqrt{3x^2 - 6x + 3}$
$$= \sqrt{3(x^2 - 2x + 1)}$$
$$= \sqrt{3(x-1)^2}$$
$$= |x-1|\sqrt{3}$$

39. $\sqrt{x^7} = \sqrt{x^6 \cdot x} = \sqrt{x^6} \cdot \sqrt{x} = x^3\sqrt{x}$

41. $\sqrt{x^8 y^9} = \sqrt{x^8 y^8 y}$
$$= \sqrt{x^8 y^8} \sqrt{y} = x^4 y^4 \sqrt{y}$$

43. $\sqrt{48x^3} = \sqrt{16 \cdot 3x^2 x}$
$$= \sqrt{16x^2} \cdot \sqrt{3x} = 4x\sqrt{3x}$$

515

45. $\sqrt[3]{y^8} = \sqrt[3]{y^6 \cdot y^2} = \sqrt[3]{y^6} \cdot \sqrt[3]{y^2} = y^2 \sqrt[3]{y^2}$

47. $\sqrt[3]{x^{14} y^3 z} = \sqrt[3]{x^{12} x^2 y^3 z}$

$= \sqrt[3]{x^{12} y^3} \cdot \sqrt[3]{x^2 z}$

$= x^4 y \sqrt[3]{x^2 z}$

49. $\sqrt[3]{81 x^8 y^6} = \sqrt[3]{27 \cdot 3 x^6 x^2 y^6}$

$= \sqrt[3]{27 x^6 y^6} \cdot \sqrt[3]{3 x^2}$

$= 3 x^2 y^2 \sqrt[3]{3 x^2}$

51. $\sqrt[3]{(x+y)^5} = \sqrt[3]{(x+y)^3 \cdot (x+y)^2}$

$= \sqrt[3]{(x+y)^3} \cdot \sqrt[3]{(x+y)^2}$

$= (x+y) \sqrt[3]{(x+y)^2}$

53. $\sqrt[5]{y^{17}} = \sqrt[5]{y^{15} \cdot y^2} = \sqrt[5]{y^{15}} \cdot \sqrt[5]{y^2} = y^3 \sqrt[5]{y^2}$

55. $\sqrt[5]{64 x^6 y^{17}} = \sqrt[5]{32 \cdot 2 x^5 x y^{15} y^2}$

$= \sqrt[5]{32 x^5 y^{15}} \cdot \sqrt[5]{2 x y^2}$

$= 2 x y^3 \sqrt[5]{2 x y^2}$

57. $\sqrt[4]{80 x^{10}} = \sqrt[4]{16 \cdot 5 x^8 x^2}$

$= \sqrt[4]{16 x^8} \cdot \sqrt[4]{5 x^2} = 2 x^2 \sqrt[4]{5 x^2}$

59. $\sqrt[4]{(x-3)^{10}} = \sqrt[4]{(x-3)^8 (x-3)^2}$

$= \sqrt[4]{(x-3)^8} \cdot \sqrt[4]{(x-3)^2}$

$= (x-3)^2 \sqrt[4]{(x-3)^2}$

or

$= (x-3)^2 \sqrt{x-3}$

61. $\sqrt{12} \cdot \sqrt{2} = \sqrt{12 \cdot 2}$

$= \sqrt{24}$

$= \sqrt{4 \cdot 6}$

$= \sqrt{4} \cdot \sqrt{6} = 2\sqrt{6}$

63. $\sqrt{5x} \cdot \sqrt{10 y} = \sqrt{5x \cdot 10 y}$

$= \sqrt{50 xy}$

$= \sqrt{25 \cdot 2 xy} = 5\sqrt{2 xy}$

65. $\sqrt{12 x} \cdot \sqrt{3 x} = \sqrt{12 x \cdot 3 x}$

$= \sqrt{36 x^2} = 6 x$

67. $\sqrt{50 xy} \cdot \sqrt{4 xy^2} = \sqrt{50 xy \cdot 4 xy^2}$

$= \sqrt{200 x^2 y^3}$

$= \sqrt{100 \cdot 2 x^2 y^2 y}$

$= \sqrt{100 x^2 y^2} \cdot \sqrt{2 y}$

$= 10 xy \sqrt{2 y}$

69. $2\sqrt{5} \cdot 3\sqrt{40} = 2 \cdot 3 \sqrt{5 \cdot 40}$

$= 6\sqrt{200}$

$= 6\sqrt{100 \cdot 2}$

$= 6\sqrt{100} \cdot \sqrt{2}$

$= 6 \cdot 10\sqrt{2} = 60\sqrt{2}$

71. $\sqrt[3]{12} \cdot \sqrt[3]{4} = \sqrt[3]{12 \cdot 4}$

$= \sqrt[3]{48}$

$= \sqrt[3]{8 \cdot 6}$

$= \sqrt[3]{8} \cdot \sqrt[3]{6} = 2\sqrt[3]{6}$

73.
$$\sqrt{5x^3} \cdot \sqrt{8x^2} = \sqrt{5x^3 \cdot 8x^2}$$
$$= \sqrt{40x^5}$$
$$= \sqrt{4 \cdot 10x^4 x}$$
$$= \sqrt{4x^4} \cdot \sqrt{10x}$$
$$= 2x^2 \sqrt{10x}$$

75.
$$\sqrt[3]{25x^4 y^2} \cdot \sqrt[3]{5xy^{12}}$$
$$= \sqrt[3]{25x^4 y^2 \cdot 5xy^{12}}$$
$$= \sqrt[3]{125x^5 y^{14}}$$
$$= \sqrt[3]{125x^3 x^2 y^{12} y^2}$$
$$= \sqrt[3]{125x^3 y^{12}} \cdot \sqrt[3]{x^2 y^2}$$
$$= 5xy^4 \sqrt[3]{x^2 y^2}$$

77.
$$\sqrt[4]{8x^2 y^3 z^6} \cdot \sqrt[4]{2x^4 yz}$$
$$= \sqrt[4]{8x^2 y^3 z^6 \cdot 2x^4 yz}$$
$$= \sqrt[4]{16x^6 y^4 z^7}$$
$$= \sqrt[4]{16x^4 x^2 y^4 z^4 z^3}$$
$$= \sqrt[4]{16x^4 y^4 z^4} \cdot \sqrt[4]{x^2 z^3}$$
$$= 2xyz \sqrt[4]{x^2 z^3}$$

79.
$$\sqrt[5]{8x^4 y^6 z^2} \cdot \sqrt[5]{8xy^7 z^4}$$
$$= \sqrt[5]{8x^4 y^6 z^2 \cdot 8xy^7 z^4}$$
$$= \sqrt[5]{64x^5 y^{13} z^6}$$
$$= \sqrt[5]{32 \cdot 2x^5 y^{10} z^5 z}$$
$$= \sqrt[5]{32x^5 y^{10} z^5} \cdot \sqrt[5]{2y^3 z}$$
$$= 2xy^2 z \sqrt[5]{2y^3 z}$$

81.
$$\sqrt[3]{x-y} \cdot \sqrt[3]{(x-y)^7}$$
$$= \sqrt[3]{(x-y) \cdot (x-y)^7}$$
$$= \sqrt[3]{(x-y)^8}$$
$$= \sqrt[3]{(x-y)^6 (x-y)^2}$$
$$= \sqrt[3]{(x-y)^6} \cdot \sqrt[3]{(x-y)^2}$$
$$= (x-y)^2 \sqrt[3]{(x-y)^2}$$

83.
$$-2x^2 y \left(\sqrt[3]{54x^3 y^7 z^2} \right)$$
$$= -2x^2 y \sqrt[3]{27 \cdot 2x^3 y^6 yz^2}$$
$$= -2x^2 y \sqrt[3]{27x^3 y^6} \cdot \sqrt[3]{2yz^2}$$
$$= -2x^2 y \cdot 3xy^2 \cdot \sqrt[3]{2yz^2}$$
$$= -6x^3 y^3 \sqrt[3]{2yz^2}$$

84.
$$\frac{-x^2 y^7}{2} \left(\sqrt[3]{-32x^4 y^9 z^7} \right)$$
$$= \frac{-x^2 y^7}{2} \sqrt[3]{-8 \cdot 4x^3 xy^9 z^6 z}$$
$$= \frac{-x^2 y^7}{2} \sqrt[3]{-8x^3 y^9 z^6} \cdot \sqrt[3]{4xz}$$
$$= \frac{-x^2 y^7}{2} \cdot \left(-2xy^3 z^2 \right) \cdot \sqrt[3]{4xz}$$
$$= x^3 y^{10} z^2 \sqrt[3]{4xz}$$

85.
$$-3y \left(\sqrt[5]{64x^3 y^6} \right)$$
$$= -3y \sqrt[5]{32 \cdot 2x^3 y^5 y}$$
$$= -3y \sqrt[5]{32y^5} \cdot \sqrt[5]{2x^3 y}$$
$$= -3y \cdot 2y \sqrt[5]{2x^3 y}$$
$$= -6y^2 \sqrt[5]{2x^3 y}$$

86.

$$-4x^2y^7\left(\sqrt[5]{-32x^{11}y^{17}}\right)$$

$$=-4x^2y^7\sqrt[5]{-32x^{10}xy^{15}y^2}$$

$$=-4x^2y^7\sqrt[5]{-32x^{10}y^{15}}\cdot\sqrt[5]{xy^2}$$

$$=-4x^2y^7\left(-2x^2y^3\right)\sqrt[5]{xy^2}$$

$$=8x^4y^{10}\sqrt[5]{xy^2}$$

87.

$$\left(-2xy^2\sqrt{3x}\right)\left(xy\sqrt{6x}\right)$$

$$=-2x^2y^3\sqrt{3x\cdot 6x}$$

$$=-2x^2y^3\sqrt{18x^2}$$

$$=-2x^2y^3\sqrt{9x^2\cdot 2}$$

$$=-2x^2y^3\sqrt{9x^2}\cdot\sqrt{2}$$

$$=-2x^2y^3\left(3x\right)\sqrt{2}=-6x^3y^3\sqrt{2}$$

88.

$$\left(-5x^2y^3z\sqrt{2xyz}\right)\left(-x^4z\sqrt{10xz}\right)$$

$$=5x^6y^3z^2\sqrt{2xyz\cdot 10xz}$$

$$=5x^6y^3z^2\sqrt{20x^2yz^2}$$

$$=5x^6y^3z^2\sqrt{4x^2z^2\cdot 5y}$$

$$=5x^6y^3z^2\sqrt{4x^2z^2}\cdot\sqrt{5y}$$

$$=5x^6y^3z^2\left(2xz\right)\sqrt{5y}$$

$$=10x^7y^3z^3\sqrt{5y}$$

89.

$$\left(2x^2y\sqrt[4]{8xy}\right)\left(-3xy^2\sqrt[4]{2x^2y^3}\right)$$

$$=-6x^3y^3\sqrt[4]{8xy\cdot 2x^2y^3}$$

$$=-6x^3y^3\sqrt[4]{16x^3y^4}$$

$$=-6x^3y^3\sqrt[4]{16y^4\cdot x^3}$$

$$=-6x^3y^3\left(2y\right)\sqrt[4]{x^3}$$

$$=-12x^3y^4\sqrt[4]{x^3}$$

90.

$$\left(5a^2b\sqrt[4]{8a^2b}\right)\left(4ab\sqrt[4]{4a^3b^2}\right)$$

$$=20a^3b^2\sqrt[4]{8a^2b\cdot 4a^3b^2}$$

$$=20a^3b^2\sqrt[4]{32a^5b^3}$$

$$=20a^3b^2\sqrt[4]{16a^4\cdot 2ab^3}$$

$$=20a^3b^2\left(2a\right)\sqrt[4]{2ab^3}$$

$$=40a^4b^2\sqrt[4]{2ab^3}$$

91.

$$\sqrt[5]{8x^4y^6}\left(\sqrt[5]{2xy^7}+\sqrt[5]{4x^6y^9}\right)$$

$$=\sqrt[5]{8x^4y^6\cdot 2xy^7}+\sqrt[5]{8x^4y^6\cdot 4x^6y^9}$$

$$=\sqrt[5]{16x^5y^{13}}+\sqrt[5]{32x^{10}y^{15}}$$

$$=\sqrt[5]{x^5y^{10}\cdot 16y^3}+\sqrt[5]{32x^{10}y^{15}}$$

$$=xy^2\sqrt[5]{16y^3}+2x^2y^3$$

92.

$$\sqrt[4]{2x^3y^2}\left(\sqrt[4]{6x^5y^6}+\sqrt[4]{8x^5y^7}\right)$$

$$=\sqrt[4]{2x^3y^2\cdot 6x^5y^6}+\sqrt[4]{2x^3y^2\cdot 8x^5y^7}$$

$$=\sqrt[4]{12x^8y^8}+\sqrt[4]{16x^8y^9}$$

$$=\sqrt[4]{x^8y^8\cdot 12}+\sqrt[4]{16x^8y^8\cdot y}$$

$$=x^2y^2\sqrt[4]{12}+2x^2y^2\sqrt[4]{y}$$

93.

$$d(x)=\sqrt{\frac{3x}{2}}$$

$$d(72)=\sqrt{\frac{3(72)}{2}}$$

$$=\sqrt{3(36)}$$

$$=\sqrt{3}\cdot\sqrt{36}$$

$$=6\sqrt{3}\approx 10.4 \text{ miles}$$

A passenger on the pool deck can see roughly 10.4 miles.

95. $W(x) = 4\sqrt{2x}$

$W(6) = 4\sqrt{2(6)} = 4\sqrt{12}$

$\qquad = 4\sqrt{4 \cdot 3} = 4\sqrt{4} \cdot \sqrt{3}$

$\qquad = 4 \cdot 2\sqrt{3}$

$\qquad = 8\sqrt{3} \approx 14$ feet per second

A dinosaur with a leg length of 6 feet has a walking speed of about 14 feet per second.

97. a. $C(32) = \dfrac{7.644}{\sqrt[4]{32}} = \dfrac{7.644}{\sqrt[4]{16 \cdot 2}}$

$\qquad = \dfrac{7.644}{2\sqrt[4]{2}} = \dfrac{3.822}{\sqrt[4]{2}}$

The cardiac index of a 32-year-old is $\dfrac{3.822}{\sqrt[4]{2}}$.

b. $\dfrac{3.822}{\sqrt[4]{2}} = \dfrac{3.822}{1.189} = \dfrac{3.822}{1.189} \approx 3.21$

The cardiac index of a 32-year-old is 3.21 liters per minute per square meter. This is shown on the graph as the point (32, 3.21).

99. – 103. Answers will vary.

105. $\sqrt{x^4} = x^2$

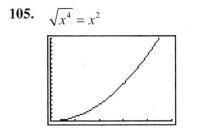

The graphs coincide, so the simplification is correct.

107. $\sqrt{3x^2 - 6x + 3} = (x-1)\sqrt{3}$

The graphs do not coincide.

To correct the simplification:

$$\sqrt{3x^2 - 6x + 3} = \sqrt{3(x^2 - 2x + 1)}$$

$$= \sqrt{3(x-1)^2} = |x-1|\sqrt{3}$$

The graphs coincide. The simplification is correct.

109. Statement **d.** is true.

$\sqrt[5]{3^{25}} = 3^5 = 243$

Statement **a.** is false.

$2\sqrt{5} \cdot 6\sqrt{5} = 12\sqrt{5 \cdot 5} = 12 \cdot 5 = 60$

Statement **b.** is false.

$\sqrt[3]{4} \cdot \sqrt[3]{4} = \sqrt[3]{4 \cdot 4} = \sqrt[3]{16}$

Statement **c.** is false.

$\sqrt{12} = \sqrt{4 \cdot 3} = 2\sqrt{3}$

111. Assume the cube root of a number is x. Triple the cube root and work in reverse to find the number.

$$3x = \sqrt[3]{(3x)^3} = \sqrt[3]{27x^3}$$

The number must be multiplied by 27 for the cube root to be tripled.

113. $f(x) = \sqrt{(x-1)^2}$

x	$f(x) = \sqrt{(x-1)^2}$
-3	$f(-3) = \sqrt{(-3-1)^2} = \sqrt{16} = 4$
-2	$f(-2) = \sqrt{(-2-1)^2} = \sqrt{9} = 3$
-1	$f(-1) = \sqrt{(-1-1)^2} = \sqrt{4} = 2$
0	$f(0) = \sqrt{(0-1)^2} = \sqrt{1} = 1$
1	$f(1) = \sqrt{(1-1)^2} = \sqrt{0} = 0$
2	$f(2) = \sqrt{(2-1)^2} = \sqrt{1} = 1$
3	$f(3) = \sqrt{(3-1)^2} = \sqrt{4} = 2$

114. $2x - 1 \le 21$ and $2x + 2 \ge 12$

$\qquad 2x \le 22 \qquad\qquad 2x \ge 10$

$\qquad\quad x \le 11 \qquad\qquad\quad x \ge 5$

The solution set is $\{x | 5 \le x \le 11\}$ or $[5,11]$.

115. $5x + 2y = 2$

$4x + 3y = -4$

Multiply the first equation by -3, the second equation by 2 and solve by addition.

$$-15x - 6y = -6$$
$$\underline{8x + 6y = -8}$$
$$-7x = -14$$
$$x = 2$$

Back-substitute 2 for x to find y.

$$5x + 2y = 2$$
$$5(2) + 2y = 2$$
$$10 + 2y = 2$$
$$2y = -8$$
$$y = -4$$

The solution set is $\{(2, -4)\}$.

116. $64x^3 - 27$

$$= (4x)^3 - (3)^3$$
$$= (4x - 3)\left((4x)^2 + 4x \cdot 3 + 3^2\right)$$
$$= (4x - 3)(16x^2 + 12x + 9)$$

10.4 Exercise Set

1. $8\sqrt{5} + 3\sqrt{5} = (8+3)\sqrt{5} = 11\sqrt{5}$

3. $9\sqrt[3]{6} - 2\sqrt[3]{6} = (9-2)\sqrt[3]{6} = 7\sqrt[3]{6}$

5. $4\sqrt[5]{2} + 3\sqrt[5]{2} - 5\sqrt[5]{2} = (4+3-5)\sqrt[5]{2}$

$$= 2\sqrt[5]{2}$$

7. $3\sqrt{13} - 2\sqrt{5} - 2\sqrt{13} + 4\sqrt{5}$

$$= 3\sqrt{13} - 2\sqrt{13} - 2\sqrt{5} + 4\sqrt{5}$$
$$= (3-2)\sqrt{13} + (-2+4)\sqrt{5}$$
$$= \sqrt{13} + 2\sqrt{5}$$

9.

$$3\sqrt{5} - \sqrt[3]{x} + 4\sqrt{5} + 3\sqrt[3]{x}$$
$$= 3\sqrt{5} + 4\sqrt{5} - \sqrt[3]{x} + 3\sqrt[3]{x}$$
$$= (3+4)\sqrt{5} + (-1+3)\sqrt[3]{x}$$
$$= 7\sqrt{5} + 2\sqrt[3]{x}$$

11.

$$\sqrt{3} + \sqrt{27} = \sqrt{3} + \sqrt{9 \cdot 3}$$
$$= \sqrt{3} + 3\sqrt{3}$$
$$= (1+3)\sqrt{3} = 4\sqrt{3}$$

13.

$$7\sqrt{12} + \sqrt{75} = 7\sqrt{4 \cdot 3} + \sqrt{25 \cdot 3}$$
$$= 7 \cdot 2\sqrt{3} + 5\sqrt{3}$$
$$= 14\sqrt{3} + 5\sqrt{3}$$
$$= (14+5)\sqrt{3} = 19\sqrt{3}$$

15.

$$3\sqrt{32x} - 2\sqrt{18x}$$
$$= 3\sqrt{16 \cdot 2x} - 2\sqrt{9 \cdot 2x}$$
$$= 3 \cdot 4\sqrt{2x} - 2 \cdot 3\sqrt{2x}$$
$$= 12\sqrt{2x} - 6\sqrt{2x} = 6\sqrt{2x}$$

17.

$$5\sqrt[3]{16} + \sqrt[3]{54} = 5\sqrt[3]{8 \cdot 2} + \sqrt[3]{27 \cdot 2}$$
$$= 5 \cdot 2\sqrt[3]{2} + 3\sqrt[3]{2}$$
$$= 10\sqrt[3]{2} + 3\sqrt[3]{2}$$
$$= (10+3)\sqrt[3]{2} = 13\sqrt[3]{2}$$

19.

$$3\sqrt{45x^3} + \sqrt{5x} = 3\sqrt{9 \cdot 5x^2 x} + \sqrt{5x}$$
$$= 3 \cdot 3x\sqrt{5x} + \sqrt{5x}$$
$$= 9x\sqrt{5x} + \sqrt{5x}$$
$$= (9x+1)\sqrt{5x}$$

21.

$$\sqrt[3]{54xy^3} + y\sqrt[3]{128x}$$
$$= \sqrt[3]{27 \cdot 2xy^3} + y\sqrt[3]{64 \cdot 2x}$$
$$= 3y\sqrt[3]{2x} + 4y\sqrt[3]{2x}$$
$$= (3y+4y)\sqrt[3]{2x} = 7y\sqrt[3]{2x}$$

23.

$$\sqrt[3]{54x^4} - \sqrt[3]{16x} = \sqrt[3]{27 \cdot 2x^3 x} - \sqrt[3]{8 \cdot 2x}$$
$$= 3x\sqrt[3]{2x} - 2\sqrt[3]{2x}$$
$$= (3x-2)\sqrt[3]{2x}$$

25.

$$\sqrt{9x-18} + \sqrt{x-2} = \sqrt{9(x-2)} + \sqrt{x-2}$$
$$= 3\sqrt{x-2} + \sqrt{x-2}$$
$$= (3+1)\sqrt{x-2}$$
$$= 4\sqrt{x-2}$$

27.

$$2\sqrt[3]{x^4 y^2} + 3x\sqrt[3]{xy^2} = 2\sqrt[3]{x^3 xy^2} + 3x\sqrt[3]{xy^2}$$
$$= 2x\sqrt[3]{xy^2} + 3x\sqrt[3]{xy^2}$$
$$= (2x+3x)\sqrt[3]{xy^2}$$
$$= 5x\sqrt[3]{xy^2}$$

29.

$$\sqrt{\frac{11}{4}} = \frac{\sqrt{11}}{\sqrt{4}} = \frac{\sqrt{11}}{2}$$

31.

$$\sqrt[3]{\frac{19}{27}} = \frac{\sqrt[3]{19}}{\sqrt[3]{27}} = \frac{\sqrt[3]{19}}{3}$$

33.

$$\sqrt{\frac{x^2}{36y^8}} = \frac{\sqrt{x^2}}{\sqrt{36y^8}} = \frac{x}{6y^4}$$

35.

$$\sqrt{\frac{8x^3}{25y^6}} = \frac{\sqrt{8x^3}}{\sqrt{25y^6}} = \frac{\sqrt{4 \cdot 2x^2 x}}{5y^3} = \frac{2x\sqrt{2x}}{5y^3}$$

521

37. $\sqrt[3]{\dfrac{x^4}{8y^3}} = \dfrac{\sqrt[3]{x^4}}{\sqrt[3]{8y^3}} = \dfrac{\sqrt[3]{x^3 x}}{2y} = \dfrac{x\sqrt[3]{x}}{2y}$

39. $\sqrt[3]{\dfrac{50x^8}{27y^{12}}} = \dfrac{\sqrt[3]{50x^8}}{\sqrt[3]{27y^{12}}}$

$= \dfrac{\sqrt[3]{50x^6 x^2}}{3y^4} = \dfrac{x^2\sqrt[3]{50x^2}}{3y^4}$

41. $\sqrt[4]{\dfrac{9y^6}{x^8}} = \dfrac{\sqrt[4]{9y^6}}{\sqrt[4]{x^8}} = \dfrac{\sqrt[4]{9y^4 y^2}}{x^2} = \dfrac{y\sqrt[4]{9y^2}}{x^2}$

43. $\sqrt[5]{\dfrac{64x^{13}}{y^{20}}} = \dfrac{\sqrt[5]{64x^{13}}}{\sqrt[5]{y^{20}}}$

$= \dfrac{\sqrt[5]{32 \cdot 2x^{10}x^3}}{y^4} = \dfrac{2x^2\sqrt[5]{2x^3}}{y^4}$

45. $\dfrac{\sqrt{40}}{\sqrt{5}} = \sqrt{\dfrac{40}{5}} = \sqrt{8} = \sqrt{4 \cdot 2} = 2\sqrt{2}$

47. $\dfrac{\sqrt[3]{48}}{\sqrt[3]{6}} = \sqrt[3]{\dfrac{48}{6}} = \sqrt[3]{8} = 2$

49. $\dfrac{\sqrt{54x^3}}{\sqrt{6x}} = \sqrt{\dfrac{54x^3}{6x}} = \sqrt{9x^2} = 3x$

51. $\dfrac{\sqrt{x^5 y^3}}{\sqrt{xy}} = \sqrt{\dfrac{x^5 y^3}{xy}} = \sqrt{x^4 y^2} = x^2 y$

53. $\dfrac{\sqrt{200x^3}}{\sqrt{10x^{-1}}} = \sqrt{\dfrac{200x^3}{10x^{-1}}}$

$= \sqrt{20x^{3-(-1)}}$

$= \sqrt{20x^4}$

$= \sqrt{4 \cdot 5x^4} = 2x^2\sqrt{5}$

55. $\dfrac{\sqrt{48a^8 b^7}}{\sqrt{3a^{-2}b^{-3}}} = \sqrt{\dfrac{48a^8 b^7}{3a^{-2}b^{-3}}}$

$= \sqrt{16a^{10}b^{10}} = 4a^5 b^5$

57. $\dfrac{\sqrt{72xy}}{2\sqrt{2}} = \dfrac{1}{2}\sqrt{\dfrac{72xy}{2}}$

$= \dfrac{1}{2}\sqrt{36xy}$

$= \dfrac{1}{2} \cdot 6\sqrt{xy} = 3\sqrt{xy}$

59. $\dfrac{\sqrt[3]{24x^3 y^5}}{\sqrt[3]{3y^2}} = \sqrt[3]{\dfrac{24x^3 y^5}{3y^2}} = \sqrt[3]{8x^3 y^3} = 2xy$

61. $\dfrac{\sqrt[4]{32x^{10}y^8}}{\sqrt[4]{2x^2 y^{-2}}} = \sqrt[4]{\dfrac{32x^{10}y^8}{2x^2 y^{-2}}}$

$= \sqrt[4]{16x^8 y^{8-(-2)}}$

$= \sqrt[4]{16x^8 y^{10}}$

$= \sqrt[4]{16x^8 y^8 y^2}$

$= 2x^2 y^2 \sqrt[4]{y^2}$ or $2x^2 y^2 \sqrt{y}$

63. $\dfrac{\sqrt[3]{x^2 + 5x + 6}}{\sqrt[3]{x+2}} = \sqrt[3]{\dfrac{x^2 + 5x + 6}{x+2}}$

$= \sqrt[3]{\dfrac{\cancel{(x+2)}(x+3)}{\cancel{x+2}}}$

$= \sqrt[3]{x+3}$

65. $\dfrac{\sqrt[3]{a^3 + b^3}}{\sqrt[3]{a+b}} = \sqrt[3]{\dfrac{a^3 + b^3}{a+b}}$

$= \sqrt[3]{\dfrac{(a+b)(a^2 - ab + b^2)}{a+b}}$

$= \sqrt[3]{a^2 - ab + b^2}$

522

67.

$$\frac{\sqrt{32}}{5}+\frac{\sqrt{18}}{7}=\frac{\sqrt{16\cdot 2}}{5}+\frac{\sqrt{9\cdot 2}}{7}$$

$$=\frac{\sqrt{16}\cdot\sqrt{2}}{5}+\frac{\sqrt{9}\cdot\sqrt{2}}{7}$$

$$=\frac{4\sqrt{2}}{5}+\frac{3\sqrt{2}}{7}$$

$$=\frac{28\sqrt{2}}{35}+\frac{15\sqrt{2}}{35}$$

$$=\frac{28\sqrt{2}+15\sqrt{2}}{35}$$

$$=\frac{(28+15)\sqrt{2}}{35}$$

$$=\frac{43\sqrt{2}}{35}$$

68.

$$\frac{\sqrt{27}}{2}+\frac{\sqrt{75}}{7}=\frac{\sqrt{9\cdot 3}}{2}+\frac{\sqrt{25\cdot 3}}{7}$$

$$=\frac{\sqrt{9}\cdot\sqrt{3}}{2}+\frac{\sqrt{25}\cdot\sqrt{3}}{7}$$

$$=\frac{3\sqrt{3}}{2}+\frac{5\sqrt{3}}{7}$$

$$=\frac{21\sqrt{3}}{14}+\frac{10\sqrt{3}}{14}$$

$$=\frac{(21+10)\sqrt{3}}{14}$$

$$=\frac{31\sqrt{3}}{14}$$

69.

$$3x\sqrt{8xy^2}-5y\sqrt{32x^3}+\sqrt{18x^3y^2}$$

$$=3x\sqrt{4y^2\cdot 2x}-5y\sqrt{16x^2\cdot 2x}$$

$$\quad+\sqrt{9x^2y^2\cdot 2x}$$

$$=3x(2y)\sqrt{2x}-5y(4x)\sqrt{2x}+3xy\sqrt{2x}$$

$$=6xy\sqrt{2x}-20xy\sqrt{2x}+3xy\sqrt{2x}$$

$$=(6-20+3)xy\sqrt{2x}$$

$$=-11xy\sqrt{2x}$$

70.

$$6x\sqrt{3xy^2}-4x^2\sqrt{27xy}-5\sqrt{75x^5y}$$

$$=6x\sqrt{y^2\cdot 3x}-4x^2\sqrt{9\cdot 3xy}$$

$$\quad-5\sqrt{25x^4\cdot 3xy}$$

$$=6x(y)\sqrt{3x}-4x^2(3)\sqrt{3xy}$$

$$\quad-5(5x^2)\sqrt{3xy}$$

$$=6xy\sqrt{3x}-12x^2\sqrt{3xy}-25x^2\sqrt{3xy}$$

$$=6xy\sqrt{3x}-(12+25)x^2\sqrt{3xy}$$

$$=6xy\sqrt{3x}-37x^2\sqrt{3xy}$$

71.

$$5\sqrt{2x^3}+\frac{30x^3\sqrt{24x^2}}{3x^2\sqrt{3x}}$$

$$=5\sqrt{2x^3}+10x\sqrt{\frac{24x^2}{3x}}$$

$$=5\sqrt{2x^3}+10x\sqrt{8x}$$

$$=5\sqrt{x^2\cdot 2x}+10x\sqrt{4\cdot 2x}$$

$$=5x\sqrt{2x}+10x(2)\sqrt{2x}$$

$$=5x\sqrt{2x}+20x\sqrt{2x}$$

$$=(5+20)x\sqrt{2x}=25x\sqrt{2x}$$

72.

$$7\sqrt{2x^3} + \frac{40x^3\sqrt{150x^2}}{5x^2\sqrt{3x}}$$

$$= 7\sqrt{2x^3} + 8x\sqrt{\frac{150x^2}{3x}}$$

$$= 7\sqrt{2x^3} + 8x\sqrt{50x}$$

$$= 7\sqrt{x^2 \cdot 2x} + 8x\sqrt{25 \cdot 2x}$$

$$= 7x\sqrt{2x} + 8x(5)\sqrt{2x}$$

$$= 7x\sqrt{2x} + 40x\sqrt{2x}$$

$$= (7+40)x\sqrt{2x} = 47x\sqrt{2x}$$

73.

$$2x\sqrt{75xy} - \frac{\sqrt{81xy^2}}{\sqrt{3x^{-2}y}}$$

$$= 2x\sqrt{75xy} - \sqrt{\frac{81xy^2}{3x^{-2}y}}$$

$$= 2x\sqrt{75xy} - \sqrt{27x^3y}$$

$$= 2x\sqrt{25 \cdot 3xy} - \sqrt{9x^2 \cdot 3xy}$$

$$= 2x(5)\sqrt{3xy} - 3x\sqrt{3xy}$$

$$= 10x\sqrt{3xy} - 3x\sqrt{3xy}$$

$$= (10-3)x\sqrt{3xy}$$

$$= 7x\sqrt{3xy}$$

74.

$$5\sqrt{8x^2y^3} - \frac{9x^2\sqrt{64y}}{3x\sqrt{2y^{-2}}}$$

$$= 5\sqrt{8x^2y^3} - 3x\sqrt{\frac{64y}{2y^{-2}}}$$

$$= 5\sqrt{8x^2y^3} - 3x\sqrt{32y^3}$$

$$= 5\sqrt{4x^2y^2 \cdot 2y} - 3x\sqrt{16y^2 \cdot 2y}$$

$$= 5(2xy)\sqrt{2y} - 3x(4y)\sqrt{2y}$$

$$= 10xy\sqrt{2y} - 12xy\sqrt{2y}$$

$$= (10-12)xy\sqrt{2y} = -2xy\sqrt{2y}$$

75.

$$\frac{15x^4\sqrt[3]{80x^3y^2}}{5x^3\sqrt[3]{2x^2y}} - \frac{75\sqrt[3]{5x^3y}}{25\sqrt[3]{x^{-1}}}$$

$$= 3x\sqrt[3]{\frac{80x^3y^2}{2x^2y}} - 3\sqrt[3]{\frac{5x^3y}{x^{-1}}}$$

$$= 3x\sqrt[3]{40xy} - 3\sqrt[3]{5x^4y}$$

$$= 3x\sqrt[3]{8 \cdot 5xy} - 3\sqrt[3]{x^3 \cdot 5xy}$$

$$= 3x(2)\sqrt[3]{5xy} - 3x\sqrt[3]{5xy}$$

$$= 6x\sqrt[3]{5xy} - 3x\sqrt[3]{5xy}$$

$$= (6-3)x\sqrt[3]{5xy} = 3x\sqrt[3]{5xy}$$

76.

$$\frac{16x^4\sqrt[3]{48x^3y^2}}{8x^3\sqrt[3]{3x^2y}} - \frac{20\sqrt[3]{2x^3y}}{4\sqrt[3]{x^{-1}}}$$

$$= 2x\sqrt[3]{\frac{48x^3y^2}{3x^2y}} - 5\sqrt[3]{\frac{2x^3y}{x^{-1}}}$$

$$= 2x\sqrt[3]{16xy} - 5\sqrt[3]{2x^4y}$$

$$= 2x\sqrt[3]{8 \cdot 2xy} - 5\sqrt[3]{x^3 \cdot 2xy}$$

$$= 2x(2)\sqrt[3]{2xy} - 5x\sqrt[3]{2xy}$$

$$= 4x\sqrt[3]{2xy} - 5x\sqrt[3]{2xy}$$

$$= (4-5)x\sqrt[3]{2xy} = -x\sqrt[3]{2xy}$$

77.

$$\left(\frac{f}{g}\right)(x) = \frac{\sqrt{48x^5}}{\sqrt{3x^2}}$$

$$= \sqrt{\frac{48x^5}{3x^2}}$$

$$= \sqrt{16x^3}$$

$$= \sqrt{16x^2 \cdot x} = 4x\sqrt{x}$$

To get the domain, we need $x \geq 0$ and $3x^2 > 0$. Combining these restrictions gives us $x > 0$.

Domain: $\{x \mid x > 0\}$ or $(0, \infty)$

78.
$$\left(\frac{f}{g}\right)(x) = \frac{\sqrt{x^2 - 25}}{\sqrt{x+5}}$$

$$= \sqrt{\frac{x^2 - 25}{x+5}}$$

$$= \sqrt{\frac{(x-5)(x+5)}{x+5}} = \sqrt{x-5}$$

To get the domain, we need
$x+5 > 0$ and $x - 5 \geq 0$
$x > -5$ $x \geq 5$
Therefore, we need $x \geq 5$.
Domain: $\{x \mid x \geq 5\}$ or $[5, \infty)$

79.
$$\left(\frac{f}{g}\right)(x) = \frac{\sqrt[3]{32x^6}}{\sqrt[3]{2x^2}} = \sqrt[3]{\frac{32x^6}{2x^2}}$$

$$= \sqrt[3]{16x^4} = \sqrt[3]{8x^3 \cdot 2x}$$

$$= 2x\sqrt[3]{2x}$$

Our only restriction here is that we
cannot divide by 0. Thus, we need
$x \neq 0$.
Domain: $\{x \mid x \neq 0\}$ or
$(-\infty, 0) \cup (0, \infty)$

80.
$$\left(\frac{f}{g}\right)(x) = \frac{\sqrt[3]{2x^6}}{\sqrt[3]{16x}}$$

$$= \sqrt[3]{\frac{2x^6}{16x}}$$

$$= \sqrt[3]{\frac{x^5}{8}} = \frac{\sqrt[3]{x^3 \cdot x^2}}{\sqrt[3]{8}} = \frac{x\sqrt[3]{x^2}}{2}$$

Our only restriction here is that we
cannot divide by 0. Thus, we need
$x \neq 0$.
Domain: $\{x \mid x \neq 0\}$ or
$(-\infty, 0) \cup (0, \infty)$

81. a.
$$R_f \frac{\sqrt{c^2 - v^2}}{\sqrt{c^2}} = R_f \sqrt{\frac{c^2 - v^2}{c^2}}$$

$$= R_f \sqrt{\frac{c^2}{c^2} - \frac{v^2}{c^2}}$$

$$= R_f \sqrt{1 - \left(\frac{v}{c}\right)^2}$$

b.
$$R_f \sqrt{1 - \left(\frac{v}{c}\right)^2} = R_f \sqrt{1 - \left(\frac{c}{c}\right)^2}$$

$$= R_f \sqrt{1 - (1)^2}$$

$$= R_f \sqrt{1 - 1}$$

$$= R_f \sqrt{0}$$

$$= R_f \cdot 0 = 0$$

Your aging rate is zero. This
means that a person moving
close to the speed of light does
not age relative to a friend on
Earth.

83.
$$P = 2l + 2w$$

$$= 2\left(2\sqrt{20}\right) + 2\left(\sqrt{125}\right)$$

$$= 4\sqrt{20} + 2\sqrt{125}$$

$$= 4\sqrt{4 \cdot 5} + 2\sqrt{25 \cdot 5}$$

$$= 4 \cdot 2\sqrt{5} + 2 \cdot 5\sqrt{5}$$

$$= 8\sqrt{5} + 10\sqrt{5}$$

$$= (8 + 10)\sqrt{5} = 18\sqrt{5}$$

The perimeter is $18\sqrt{5}$ feet.
$$A = lw = 2\sqrt{20} \cdot \sqrt{125}$$

$$= 2\sqrt{20 \cdot 125} = 2\sqrt{2500}$$

$$= 2 \cdot 50 = 100$$

The area is 100 square feet.

85. Answers will vary.

87. We can add $\sqrt{2}$ and $\sqrt{8}$ because we can simplify $\sqrt{8} = \sqrt{4 \cdot 2} = 2\sqrt{2}$.

89. Answers will vary.

91. Answers will vary. For example, consider Exercise 11.

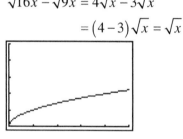

93. $\sqrt{16x} - \sqrt{9x} = \sqrt{7x}$

The graphs do not coincide.
Correct the simplification.

$$\sqrt{16x} - \sqrt{9x} = 4\sqrt{x} - 3\sqrt{x}$$
$$= (4-3)\sqrt{x} = \sqrt{x}$$

95. Statement **d.** is true.

Statement **a.** is false.
$$\sqrt{5} + \sqrt{5} = 2\sqrt{5}$$

Statement **b.** is false.
$$4\sqrt{3} + 5\sqrt{3} = 9\sqrt{3}$$

Statement **c.** is false. In order for two radical expressions to be combined, both the index and the radicand must be the same. Just because two radical expressions are completely simplified does guarantee that the index and radicands match.

97.
$$\frac{\sqrt{20}}{3} + \frac{\sqrt{45}}{4} - \sqrt{80}$$
$$= \frac{\sqrt{4 \cdot 5}}{3} + \frac{\sqrt{9 \cdot 5}}{4} - \sqrt{16 \cdot 5}$$
$$= \frac{2\sqrt{5}}{3} + \frac{3\sqrt{5}}{4} - 4\sqrt{5}$$
$$= \frac{2}{3}\sqrt{5} + \frac{3}{4}\sqrt{5} - 4\sqrt{5}$$
$$= \left(\frac{2}{3} + \frac{3}{4} - 4\right)\sqrt{5}$$
$$= \left(\frac{2}{3} \cdot \frac{4}{4} + \frac{3}{4} \cdot \frac{3}{3} - \frac{4}{1} \cdot \frac{12}{12}\right)\sqrt{5}$$
$$= \left(\frac{8}{12} + \frac{9}{12} - \frac{48}{12}\right)\sqrt{5}$$
$$= -\frac{31}{12}\sqrt{5} \text{ or } -\frac{31\sqrt{5}}{12}$$

99.
$$2(3x-1) - 4 = 2x - (6-x)$$
$$6x - 2 - 4 = 2x - 6 + x$$
$$6x - 6 = x - 6$$
$$5x = 0$$
$$x = 0$$
The solution set is $\{0\}$.

100. $x^2 - 8xy + 12y^2 = (x - 6y)(x - 2y)$

101.
$$\frac{2}{x^2 + 5x + 6} + \frac{3x}{x^2 + 6x + 9}$$
$$= \frac{2}{(x+3)(x+2)} + \frac{3x}{(x+3)^2}$$
$$= \frac{2(x+3)}{(x+3)^2(x+2)} + \frac{3x(x+2)}{(x+3)^2(x+2)}$$
$$= \frac{2(x+3) + 3x(x+2)}{(x+3)^2(x+2)}$$
$$= \frac{2x + 6 + 3x^2 + 6x}{(x+3)^2(x+2)}$$
$$= \frac{3x^2 + 8x + 6}{(x+3)^2(x+2)}$$

Mid-Chapter 7 Check Point

1.
$$\sqrt{100} - \sqrt[3]{-27} = 10 - (-3)$$
$$= 10 + 3$$
$$= 13$$

2.
$$\sqrt{8x^5 y^7} = \sqrt{4x^4 y^6 \cdot 2xy}$$
$$= 2x^2 y^3 \sqrt{2xy}$$

3.
$$3\sqrt[3]{4x^2} + 2\sqrt[3]{4x^2} = (3+2)\sqrt[3]{4x^2}$$
$$= 5\sqrt[3]{4x^2}$$

4.
$$\left(3\sqrt[3]{4x^2}\right)\left(2\sqrt[3]{4x^2}\right) = 6\sqrt[3]{4x^2 \cdot 4x^2}$$
$$= 6\sqrt[3]{16x^4}$$
$$= 6\sqrt[3]{8x^3 \cdot 2x}$$
$$= 6(2x)\sqrt[3]{2x}$$
$$= 12x\sqrt[3]{2x}$$

5.
$$27^{2/3} + (-32)^{3/5} = \left(\sqrt[3]{27}\right)^2 + \left(\sqrt[5]{-32}\right)^3$$
$$= (3)^2 + (-2)^3$$
$$= 9 + (-8)$$
$$= 1$$

6.
$$\left(64x^3 y^{1/4}\right)^{1/3} = (64)^{1/3} \left(x^3\right)^{1/3} \left(y^{1/4}\right)^{1/3}$$
$$= \sqrt[3]{64} \cdot x^{3(1/3)} \cdot y^{(1/4)(1/3)}$$
$$= 4xy^{1/12}$$

7.
$$5\sqrt{27} - 4\sqrt{48} = 5\sqrt{9 \cdot 3} - 4\sqrt{16 \cdot 3}$$
$$= 5(3)\sqrt{3} - 4(4)\sqrt{3}$$
$$= 15\sqrt{3} - 16\sqrt{3}$$
$$= (15 - 16)\sqrt{3}$$
$$= -\sqrt{3}$$

8.
$$\sqrt{\frac{500x^3}{4y^4}} = \frac{\sqrt{500x^3}}{\sqrt{4y^4}}$$
$$= \frac{\sqrt{100x^2 \cdot 5x}}{\sqrt{4y^4}}$$
$$= \frac{10x\sqrt{5x}}{2y^2} = \frac{5x\sqrt{5x}}{y^2}$$

9.
$$\frac{x}{\sqrt[4]{x}} = \frac{x}{x^{1/4}}$$
$$= x^{1-(1/4)} = x^{(4/4)-(1/4)} = x^{3/4} = \sqrt[4]{x^3}$$

10.
$$\sqrt[3]{54x^5} = \sqrt[3]{27x^3 \cdot 2x^2} = 3x\sqrt[3]{2x^2}$$

11.
$$\frac{\sqrt[3]{160}}{\sqrt[3]{2}} = \sqrt[3]{\frac{160}{2}} = \sqrt[3]{80} = \sqrt[3]{8 \cdot 10} = 2\sqrt[3]{10}$$

12.
$$\sqrt[5]{\frac{x^{10}}{y^{20}}} = \left(\frac{x^{10}}{y^{20}}\right)^{1/5} = \frac{\left(x^{10}\right)^{1/5}}{\left(y^{20}\right)^{1/5}} = \frac{x^{10(1/5)}}{y^{20(1/5)}} = \frac{x^2}{y^4}$$

13.
$$\frac{\left(x^{2/3}\right)^2}{\left(x^{1/4}\right)^3} = \frac{x^{(2/3)\cdot 2}}{x^{(1/4)\cdot 3}}$$
$$= \frac{x^{4/3}}{x^{3/4}}$$
$$= x^{(4/3)-(3/4)}$$
$$= x^{(16/12)-(9/12)} = x^{7/12}$$

14.
$$\sqrt[6]{x^6 y^4} = \left(x^6 y^4\right)^{1/6}$$
$$= \left(x^6\right)^{1/6} \left(y^4\right)^{1/6}$$
$$= x^{6(1/6)} y^{4(1/6)}$$
$$= x^1 y^{2/3} = x\sqrt[3]{y^2}$$

15.
$$\sqrt[7]{(x-2)^3} \cdot \sqrt[7]{(x-2)^6} = \sqrt[7]{(x-2)^3 \cdot (x-2)^6}$$
$$= \sqrt[7]{(x-2)^9}$$
$$= \sqrt[7]{(x-2)^7 \cdot (x-2)^2}$$
$$= (x-2)\sqrt[7]{(x-2)^2}$$

16.
$$\sqrt[4]{32x^{11}y^{17}} = \sqrt[4]{16x^8 y^{16} \cdot 2x^3 y}$$
$$= \sqrt[4]{16x^8 y^{16}} \cdot \sqrt[4]{2x^3 y}$$
$$= 2x^2 y^4 \sqrt[4]{2x^3 y}$$

17.
$$4\sqrt[3]{16} + 2\sqrt[3]{54} = 4\sqrt[3]{8 \cdot 2} + 2\sqrt[3]{27 \cdot 2}$$
$$= 4\sqrt[3]{8} \cdot \sqrt[3]{2} + 2\sqrt[3]{27} \cdot \sqrt[3]{2}$$
$$= 4(2)\sqrt[3]{2} + 2(3)\sqrt[3]{2}$$
$$= 8\sqrt[3]{2} + 6\sqrt[3]{2}$$
$$= (8+6)\sqrt[3]{2} = 14\sqrt[3]{2}$$

18.
$$\frac{\sqrt[7]{x^4 y^9}}{\sqrt[7]{x^{-5} y^7}} = \sqrt[7]{\frac{x^4 y^9}{x^{-5} y^7}}$$
$$= \sqrt[7]{x^9 y^2}$$
$$= \sqrt[7]{x^7 \cdot x^2 y^2} = x\sqrt[7]{x^2 y^2}$$

19.
$$(-125)^{-2/3} = \frac{1}{(-125)^{2/3}}$$
$$= \frac{1}{\left(\sqrt[3]{-125}\right)^2} = \frac{1}{(-5)^2} = \frac{1}{25}$$

20.
$$\sqrt{2} \cdot \sqrt[3]{2} = 2^{1/2} \cdot 2^{1/3}$$
$$= 2^{(1/2)+(1/3)}$$
$$= 2^{(3/6)+(2/6)} = 2^{5/6} = \sqrt[6]{2^5} = \sqrt[6]{32}$$

21.
$$\sqrt[3]{\frac{32x}{y^4}} \cdot \sqrt[3]{\frac{2x^2}{y^2}} = \sqrt[3]{\frac{32x}{y^4} \cdot \frac{2x^2}{y^2}}$$
$$= \sqrt[3]{\frac{64x^3}{y^6}}$$
$$= \frac{\sqrt[3]{64x^3}}{\sqrt[3]{y^6}} = \frac{4x}{y^2}$$

22.
$$\sqrt{32xy^2} \cdot \sqrt{2x^3 y^5} = \sqrt{32xy^2 \cdot 2x^3 y^5}$$
$$= \sqrt{64x^4 y^7}$$
$$= \sqrt{64x^4 y^6 \cdot y}$$
$$= 8x^2 y^3 \sqrt{y}$$

23.
$$4x\sqrt{6x^4 y^3} - 7y\sqrt{24x^6 y}$$
$$= 4x\sqrt{x^4 y^2 \cdot 6y} - 7y\sqrt{4x^6 \cdot 6y}$$
$$= 4x\left(x^2 y\right)\sqrt{6y} - 7y\left(2x^3\right)\sqrt{6y}$$
$$= 4x^3 y\sqrt{6y} - 14x^3 y\sqrt{6y}$$
$$= (4-14)x^3 y\sqrt{6y}$$
$$= -10x^3 y\sqrt{6y}$$

24.
$$f(x) = \sqrt{30-5x}$$
Do find the domain, we set the integrand greater than or equal to 0.
$$30-5x \geq 0$$
$$-5x \geq -30$$
$$x \leq 6$$
Domain: $\{x \mid x \leq 6\}$ or $(-\infty, 6]$

25.
$$g(x) = \sqrt[3]{3x-15}$$
The domain of a cube root is all real numbers. Since there are no other restrictions, we have
Domain: $\{x \mid x \text{ is a real number}\}$ or $(-\infty, \infty)$

528

10.5 Exercise Set

1.
$$\sqrt{2}\left(x+\sqrt{7}\right)=\sqrt{2}\cdot x+\sqrt{2}\sqrt{7}$$
$$=x\sqrt{2}+\sqrt{14}$$

3.
$$\sqrt{6}\left(7-\sqrt{6}\right)=\sqrt{6}\cdot 7-\sqrt{6}\sqrt{6}$$
$$=7\sqrt{6}-\sqrt{36}$$
$$=7\sqrt{6}-6$$

5.
$$\sqrt{3}\left(4\sqrt{6}-2\sqrt{3}\right)=\sqrt{3}\cdot 4\sqrt{6}-\sqrt{3}\cdot 2\sqrt{3}$$
$$=4\sqrt{18}-2\sqrt{9}$$
$$=4\sqrt{9\cdot 2}-2\cdot 3$$
$$=4\cdot 3\sqrt{2}-6$$
$$=12\sqrt{2}-6$$

7.
$$\sqrt[3]{2}\left(\sqrt[3]{6}+4\sqrt[3]{5}\right)=\sqrt[3]{2}\cdot\sqrt[3]{6}+\sqrt[3]{2}\cdot 4\sqrt[3]{5}$$
$$=\sqrt[3]{12}+4\sqrt[3]{10}$$

9.
$$\sqrt[3]{x}\left(\sqrt[3]{16x^2}-\sqrt[3]{x}\right)=\sqrt[3]{x}\cdot\sqrt[3]{16x^2}-\sqrt[3]{x}\cdot\sqrt[3]{x}$$
$$=\sqrt[3]{x}\cdot\sqrt[3]{8\cdot 2x^2}-\sqrt[3]{x^2}$$
$$=\sqrt[3]{8\cdot 2x^3}-\sqrt[3]{x^2}$$
$$=2x\sqrt[3]{2}-\sqrt[3]{x^2}$$

11.
$$\left(5+\sqrt{2}\right)\left(6+\sqrt{2}\right)$$
$$=5\cdot 6+5\sqrt{2}+6\sqrt{2}+\sqrt{2}\sqrt{2}$$
$$=30+(5+6)\sqrt{2}+2$$
$$=32+11\sqrt{2}$$

13.
$$\left(6+\sqrt{5}\right)\left(9-4\sqrt{5}\right)$$
$$=6\cdot 9-6\cdot 4\sqrt{5}+9\sqrt{5}-4\sqrt{5}\sqrt{5}$$
$$=54-24\sqrt{5}+9\sqrt{5}-4\cdot 5$$
$$=54+(-24+9)\sqrt{5}-20$$
$$=34+(-15)\sqrt{5}$$
$$=34-15\sqrt{5}$$

15.
$$\left(6-3\sqrt{7}\right)\left(2-5\sqrt{7}\right)$$
$$=6\cdot 2-6\cdot 5\sqrt{7}-2\cdot 3\sqrt{7}+3\sqrt{7}\cdot 5\sqrt{7}$$
$$=12-30\sqrt{7}-6\sqrt{7}+15\cdot 7$$
$$=12+(-30-6)\sqrt{7}+105$$
$$=117+(-36)\sqrt{7}$$
$$=117-36\sqrt{7}$$

17.
$$\left(\sqrt{2}+\sqrt{7}\right)\left(\sqrt{3}+\sqrt{5}\right)$$
$$=\sqrt{2}\sqrt{3}+\sqrt{2}\sqrt{5}+\sqrt{7}\sqrt{3}+\sqrt{7}\sqrt{5}$$
$$=\sqrt{6}+\sqrt{10}+\sqrt{21}+\sqrt{35}$$

19.
$$\left(\sqrt{2}-\sqrt{7}\right)\left(\sqrt{3}-\sqrt{5}\right)$$
$$=\sqrt{2}\sqrt{3}-\sqrt{2}\sqrt{5}-\sqrt{7}\sqrt{3}+\sqrt{7}\sqrt{5}$$
$$=\sqrt{6}-\sqrt{10}-\sqrt{21}+\sqrt{35}$$

21.
$$\left(3\sqrt{2}-4\sqrt{3}\right)\left(2\sqrt{2}+5\sqrt{3}\right)$$
$$=3\sqrt{2}\left(2\sqrt{2}\right)+3\sqrt{2}\left(5\sqrt{3}\right)$$
$$\qquad -4\sqrt{3}\left(2\sqrt{2}\right)-4\sqrt{3}\left(5\sqrt{3}\right)$$
$$=6\cdot 2+15\sqrt{6}-8\sqrt{6}-20\cdot 3$$
$$=12+7\sqrt{6}-60$$
$$=7\sqrt{6}-48 \ \text{ or } \ -48+7\sqrt{6}$$

529

23. $\left(\sqrt{3}+\sqrt{5}\right)^{2} = \left(\sqrt{3}\right)^{2}+2\sqrt{3}\sqrt{5}+\left(\sqrt{5}\right)^{2}$

$$= 3+2\sqrt{15}+5$$
$$= 8+2\sqrt{15}$$

25. $\left(\sqrt{3x}-\sqrt{y}\right)^{2}$

$$= \left(\sqrt{3x}\right)^{2}-2\sqrt{3x}\sqrt{y}+\left(\sqrt{y}\right)^{2}$$
$$= 3x-2\sqrt{3xy}+y$$

27. $\left(\sqrt{5}+7\right)\left(\sqrt{5}-7\right)$

$$= \sqrt{5}\sqrt{5}-7\sqrt{5}+7\sqrt{5}-7\cdot7$$
$$= 5-7\sqrt{5}+7\sqrt{5}-49$$
$$= 5-49$$
$$= -44$$

29. $\left(2-5\sqrt{3}\right)\left(2+5\sqrt{3}\right)$

$$= 2\cdot2+2\cdot5\sqrt{3}-2\cdot5\sqrt{3}-5\sqrt{3}\cdot5\sqrt{3}$$
$$= 4+10\sqrt{3}-10\sqrt{3}-25\cdot3$$
$$= 4-75$$
$$= -71$$

31. $\left(3\sqrt{2}+2\sqrt{3}\right)\left(3\sqrt{2}-2\sqrt{3}\right)$

$$= 3\sqrt{2}\cdot3\sqrt{2}-3\sqrt{2}\cdot2\sqrt{3}$$
$$\quad +3\sqrt{2}\cdot2\sqrt{3}-2\sqrt{3}\cdot2\sqrt{3}$$
$$= 9\cdot2-6\sqrt{6}+6\sqrt{6}-4\cdot3$$
$$= 18-12$$
$$= 6$$

33. $\left(3-\sqrt{x}\right)\left(2-\sqrt{x}\right)$

$$= 3\cdot2-3\sqrt{x}-2\sqrt{x}+\sqrt{x}\sqrt{x}$$
$$= 6+\left(-3-2\right)\sqrt{x}+x$$
$$= 6+\left(-5\right)\sqrt{x}+x$$
$$= 6-5\sqrt{x}+x$$

35. $\left(\sqrt[3]{x}-4\right)\left(\sqrt[3]{x}+5\right)$

$$= \sqrt[3]{x}\sqrt[3]{x}+5\sqrt[3]{x}-4\sqrt[3]{x}-4\cdot5$$
$$= \sqrt[3]{x^2}+\left(5-4\right)\sqrt[3]{x}-20$$
$$= \sqrt[3]{x^2}+\sqrt[3]{x}-20$$

37. $\left(x+\sqrt[3]{y^2}\right)\left(2x-\sqrt[3]{y^2}\right)$

$$= x\cdot2x-x\sqrt[3]{y^2}+2x\sqrt[3]{y^2}-\sqrt[3]{y^2}\sqrt[3]{y^2}$$
$$= 2x^2+\left(-x+2x\right)\sqrt[3]{y^2}-\sqrt[3]{y^4}$$
$$= 2x^2+x\sqrt[3]{y^2}-\sqrt[3]{y^3 y}$$
$$= 2x^2+x\sqrt[3]{y^2}-y\sqrt[3]{y}$$

39. $\dfrac{\sqrt{2}}{\sqrt{5}}=\dfrac{\sqrt{2}}{\sqrt{5}}\cdot\dfrac{\sqrt{5}}{\sqrt{5}}=\dfrac{\sqrt{2\cdot5}}{\sqrt{5\cdot5}}=\dfrac{\sqrt{10}}{5}$

41. $\sqrt{\dfrac{11}{x}}=\dfrac{\sqrt{11}}{\sqrt{x}}=\dfrac{\sqrt{11}}{\sqrt{x}}\cdot\dfrac{\sqrt{x}}{\sqrt{x}}=\dfrac{\sqrt{11x}}{\sqrt{x^2}}=\dfrac{\sqrt{11x}}{x}$

43. $\dfrac{9}{\sqrt{3y}}=\dfrac{9}{\sqrt{3y}}\cdot\dfrac{\sqrt{3y}}{\sqrt{3y}}$

$$= \dfrac{9\sqrt{3y}}{\sqrt{3y\cdot3y}}=\dfrac{\overset{3}{\cancel{9}}\sqrt{3y}}{\underset{1}{\cancel{3}}\,y}=\dfrac{3\sqrt{3y}}{y}$$

45. $\dfrac{1}{\sqrt[3]{2}}=\dfrac{1}{\sqrt[3]{2}}\cdot\dfrac{\sqrt[3]{2^2}}{\sqrt[3]{2^2}}=\dfrac{\sqrt[3]{2^2}}{\sqrt[3]{2^3}}=\dfrac{\sqrt[3]{4}}{2}$

530

47.
$$\frac{6}{\sqrt[3]{4}} = \frac{6}{\sqrt[3]{4}} \cdot \frac{\sqrt[3]{4^2}}{\sqrt[3]{4^2}} = \frac{6\sqrt[3]{4^2}}{\sqrt[3]{4}\sqrt[3]{4^2}}$$

$$= \frac{6\sqrt[3]{16}}{\sqrt[3]{4^3}} = \frac{6\sqrt[3]{8 \cdot 2}}{4} = \frac{6 \cdot 2\sqrt[3]{2}}{4}$$

$$= \frac{\overset{3}{\cancel{12}}\sqrt[3]{2}}{\underset{1}{\cancel{4}}} = 3\sqrt[3]{2}$$

49.
$$\sqrt[3]{\frac{2}{3}} = \frac{\sqrt[3]{2}}{\sqrt[3]{3}} = \frac{\sqrt[3]{2}}{\sqrt[3]{3}} \cdot \frac{\sqrt[3]{3^2}}{\sqrt[3]{3^2}} = \frac{\sqrt[3]{2 \cdot 3^2}}{\sqrt[3]{3^3}}$$

$$= \frac{\sqrt[3]{2 \cdot 9}}{3} = \frac{\sqrt[3]{18}}{3}$$

51.
$$\frac{4}{\sqrt[3]{x}} = \frac{4}{\sqrt[3]{x}} \cdot \frac{\sqrt[3]{x^2}}{\sqrt[3]{x^2}} = \frac{4\sqrt[3]{x^2}}{\sqrt[3]{x}\sqrt[3]{x^2}}$$

$$= \frac{4\sqrt[3]{x^2}}{\sqrt[3]{x^3}} = \frac{4\sqrt[3]{x^2}}{x}$$

53.
$$\sqrt[3]{\frac{2}{y^2}} = \frac{\sqrt[3]{2}}{\sqrt[3]{y^2}} = \frac{\sqrt[3]{2}}{\sqrt[3]{y^2}} \cdot \frac{\sqrt[3]{y}}{\sqrt[3]{y}}$$

$$= \frac{\sqrt[3]{2y}}{\sqrt[3]{y^3}} = \frac{\sqrt[3]{2y}}{y}$$

55.
$$\frac{7}{\sqrt[3]{2x^2}} = \frac{7}{\sqrt[3]{2x^2}} \cdot \frac{\sqrt[3]{2^2 x}}{\sqrt[3]{2^2 x}} = \frac{7\sqrt[3]{2^2 x}}{\sqrt[3]{2x^2}\sqrt[3]{2^2 x}}$$

$$= \frac{7\sqrt[3]{4x}}{\sqrt[3]{2^3 x^3}} = \frac{7\sqrt[3]{4x}}{2x}$$

57.
$$\sqrt[3]{\frac{2}{xy^2}} = \frac{\sqrt[3]{2}}{\sqrt[3]{xy^2}} = \frac{\sqrt[3]{2}}{\sqrt[3]{xy^2}} \cdot \frac{\sqrt[3]{x^2 y}}{\sqrt[3]{x^2 y}}$$

$$= \frac{\sqrt[3]{2}\sqrt[3]{x^2 y}}{\sqrt[3]{xy^2}\sqrt[3]{x^2 y}} = \frac{\sqrt[3]{2x^2 y}}{\sqrt[3]{x^3 y^3}}$$

$$= \frac{\sqrt[3]{2x^2 y}}{xy}$$

59.
$$\frac{3}{\sqrt[4]{x}} = \frac{3}{\sqrt[4]{x}} \cdot \frac{\sqrt[4]{x^3}}{\sqrt[4]{x^3}} = \frac{3\sqrt[4]{x^3}}{\sqrt[4]{xx^3}}$$

$$= \frac{3\sqrt[4]{x^3}}{\sqrt[4]{x^4}} = \frac{3\sqrt[4]{x^3}}{x}$$

61.
$$\frac{6}{\sqrt[5]{8x^3}} = \frac{6}{\sqrt[5]{2^3 x^3}} \cdot \frac{\sqrt[5]{2^2 x^2}}{\sqrt[5]{2^2 x^2}} = \frac{6\sqrt[5]{4x^2}}{\sqrt[5]{2^5 x^5}}$$

$$= \frac{6\sqrt[5]{4x^2}}{2x} = \frac{3\sqrt[5]{4x^2}}{x}$$

63.
$$\frac{2x^2 y}{\sqrt[5]{4x^2 y^4}} = \frac{2x^2 y}{\sqrt[5]{2^2 x^2 y^4}} \cdot \frac{\sqrt[5]{2^3 x^3 y}}{\sqrt[5]{2^3 x^3 y}}$$

$$= \frac{2x^2 y\sqrt[5]{8x^3 y}}{\sqrt[5]{2^5 x^5 y^5}}$$

$$= \frac{\cancel{2}x^2 \cancel{y}\sqrt[5]{8x^3 y}}{\cancel{2} \cancel{x} \cancel{y}}$$

$$= x\sqrt[5]{8x^3 y}$$

65.
$$\frac{9}{\sqrt{3x^2 y}} = \frac{9}{\sqrt{x^2 \cdot 3y}} = \frac{9}{x\sqrt{3y}}$$

$$= \frac{9}{x\sqrt{3y}} \cdot \frac{\sqrt{3y}}{\sqrt{3y}}$$

$$= \frac{9\sqrt{3y}}{x\sqrt{(3y)^2}} = \frac{9\sqrt{3y}}{x(3y)}$$

$$= \frac{\cancel{3} \cdot 3\sqrt{3y}}{\cancel{3}xy} = \frac{3\sqrt{3y}}{xy}$$

67.
$$-\sqrt{\frac{75a^5}{b^3}} = -\frac{\sqrt{75a^5}}{\sqrt{b^3}} = -\frac{\sqrt{25a^4 \cdot 3a}}{\sqrt{b^2 \cdot b}}$$
$$= -\frac{5a^2\sqrt{3a}}{b\sqrt{b}} = -\frac{5a^2\sqrt{3a}}{b\sqrt{b}} \cdot \frac{\sqrt{b}}{\sqrt{b}}$$
$$= -\frac{5a^2\sqrt{3ab}}{b\sqrt{b^2}} = -\frac{5a^2\sqrt{3ab}}{b(b)}$$
$$= -\frac{5a^2\sqrt{3ab}}{b^2}$$

69.
$$\sqrt{\frac{7m^2n^3}{14m^3n^2}} = \sqrt{\frac{n}{2m}} = \frac{\sqrt{n}}{\sqrt{2m}}$$
$$= \frac{\sqrt{n}}{\sqrt{2m}} \cdot \frac{\sqrt{2m}}{\sqrt{2m}} = \frac{\sqrt{2mn}}{\sqrt{(2m)^2}}$$
$$= \frac{\sqrt{2mn}}{2m}$$

71.
$$\frac{3}{\sqrt[4]{x^5y^3}} = \frac{3}{\sqrt[4]{x^4 \cdot xy^3}} = \frac{3}{x\sqrt[4]{xy^3}}$$
$$= \frac{3}{x\sqrt[4]{xy^3}} \cdot \frac{\sqrt[4]{x^3y}}{\sqrt[4]{x^3y}} = \frac{3\sqrt[4]{x^3y}}{x\sqrt[4]{x^4y^4}}$$
$$= \frac{3\sqrt[4]{x^3y}}{x(xy)} = \frac{3\sqrt[4]{x^3y}}{x^2y}$$

73.
$$\frac{12}{\sqrt[3]{-8x^5y^8}} = \frac{12}{\sqrt[3]{-8x^3y^6 \cdot x^2y^2}}$$
$$= \frac{12}{-2xy^2\sqrt[3]{x^2y^2}}$$
$$= \frac{12}{-2xy^2\sqrt[3]{x^2y^2}} \cdot \frac{\sqrt[3]{xy}}{\sqrt[3]{xy}}$$
$$= \frac{12\sqrt[3]{xy}}{-2xy^2\sqrt[3]{x^3y^3}} = \frac{12\sqrt[3]{xy}}{-2xy^2(xy)}$$
$$= \frac{12\sqrt[3]{xy}}{-2x^2y^3} = -\frac{6\sqrt[3]{xy}}{x^2y^3}$$

75.
$$\frac{8}{\sqrt{5}+2} = \frac{8}{\sqrt{5}+2} \cdot \frac{\sqrt{5}-2}{\sqrt{5}-2}$$
$$= \frac{8\sqrt{5}-8\cdot 2}{\sqrt{5}\sqrt{5}-2\sqrt{5}+2\sqrt{5}-2\cdot 2}$$
$$= \frac{8\sqrt{5}-16}{5-2\sqrt{5}+2\sqrt{5}-4}$$
$$= \frac{8\sqrt{5}-16}{5-4} = \frac{8\sqrt{5}-16}{1}$$
$$= 8\sqrt{5}-16$$

77.
$$\frac{13}{\sqrt{11}-3} = \frac{13}{\sqrt{11}-3} \cdot \frac{\sqrt{11}+3}{\sqrt{11}+3}$$
$$= \frac{13(\sqrt{11}+3)}{(\sqrt{11}-3)(\sqrt{11}+3)}$$
$$= \frac{13\sqrt{11}+13\cdot 3}{\sqrt{11}\cdot\sqrt{11}+3\sqrt{11}-3\sqrt{11}-3\cdot 3}$$
$$= \frac{13\sqrt{11}+39}{11+3\sqrt{11}-3\sqrt{11}-9}$$
$$= \frac{13\sqrt{11}+39}{11-9} = \frac{13\sqrt{11}+39}{2}$$

79.
$$\frac{6}{\sqrt{5}+\sqrt{3}} = \frac{6}{\sqrt{5}+\sqrt{3}} \cdot \frac{\sqrt{5}-\sqrt{3}}{\sqrt{5}-\sqrt{3}}$$
$$= \frac{6(\sqrt{5}-\sqrt{3})}{(\sqrt{5}+\sqrt{3})(\sqrt{5}-\sqrt{3})}$$
$$= \frac{6\sqrt{5}-6\sqrt{3}}{\sqrt{5}\sqrt{5}-\sqrt{3}\sqrt{5}+\sqrt{3}\sqrt{5}-\sqrt{3}\sqrt{3}}$$
$$= \frac{6\sqrt{5}-6\sqrt{3}}{5-\sqrt{15}+\sqrt{15}-3}$$
$$= \frac{6\sqrt{5}-6\sqrt{3}}{5-3} = \frac{6\sqrt{5}-6\sqrt{3}}{2}$$
$$= \frac{2(3\sqrt{5}-3\sqrt{3})}{2} = 3\sqrt{5}-3\sqrt{3}$$

532

81.

$$\frac{\sqrt{a}}{\sqrt{a}-\sqrt{b}} = \frac{\sqrt{a}}{\sqrt{a}-\sqrt{b}} \cdot \frac{\sqrt{a}+\sqrt{b}}{\sqrt{a}+\sqrt{b}} = \frac{\sqrt{a}\left(\sqrt{a}+\sqrt{b}\right)}{\left(\sqrt{a}-\sqrt{b}\right)\left(\sqrt{a}+\sqrt{b}\right)} = \frac{\sqrt{a}\sqrt{a}+\sqrt{a}\sqrt{b}}{\sqrt{a}\sqrt{a}+\sqrt{a}\sqrt{b}-\sqrt{a}\sqrt{b}-\sqrt{b}\sqrt{b}}$$

$$= \frac{a+\sqrt{ab}}{a-b}$$

83.

$$\frac{25}{5\sqrt{2}-3\sqrt{5}} = \frac{25}{5\sqrt{2}-3\sqrt{5}} \cdot \frac{5\sqrt{2}+3\sqrt{5}}{5\sqrt{2}+3\sqrt{5}} = \frac{25\left(5\sqrt{2}+3\sqrt{5}\right)}{\left(5\sqrt{2}-3\sqrt{5}\right)\left(5\sqrt{2}+3\sqrt{5}\right)}$$

$$= \frac{125\sqrt{2}+75\sqrt{5}}{5\cdot5\sqrt{2\cdot2}+5\cdot3\sqrt{2\cdot5}-5\cdot3\sqrt{2\cdot5}-3\cdot3\sqrt{5\cdot5}} = \frac{125\sqrt{2}+75\sqrt{5}}{25\cdot2-9\cdot5}$$

$$= \frac{125\sqrt{2}+75\sqrt{5}}{50-45} = \frac{125\sqrt{2}+75\sqrt{5}}{5} = \frac{5\left(25\sqrt{2}+15\sqrt{5}\right)}{5} = 25\sqrt{2}+15\sqrt{5}$$

85.

$$\frac{\sqrt{5}+\sqrt{3}}{\sqrt{5}-\sqrt{3}} = \frac{\sqrt{5}+\sqrt{3}}{\sqrt{5}-\sqrt{3}} \cdot \frac{\sqrt{5}+\sqrt{3}}{\sqrt{5}+\sqrt{3}} = \frac{\left(\sqrt{5}+\sqrt{3}\right)^2}{\left(\sqrt{5}-\sqrt{3}\right)\left(\sqrt{5}+\sqrt{3}\right)}$$

$$= \frac{\left(\sqrt{5}\right)^2+2\sqrt{5}\sqrt{3}+\left(\sqrt{3}\right)^2}{\sqrt{5}\cdot\sqrt{5}+\sqrt{5}\cdot\sqrt{3}-\sqrt{5}\cdot\sqrt{3}-\sqrt{3}\sqrt{3}} = \frac{5+2\sqrt{15}+3}{5+\sqrt{15}-\sqrt{15}-3}$$

$$= \frac{8+2\sqrt{15}}{5-3} = \frac{2\left(4+\sqrt{15}\right)}{2} = 4+\sqrt{15}$$

87.

$$\frac{\sqrt{x}+1}{\sqrt{x}+3} = \frac{\sqrt{x}+1}{\sqrt{x}+3} \cdot \frac{\sqrt{x}-3}{\sqrt{x}-3} = \frac{\sqrt{x}\cdot\sqrt{x}-3\sqrt{x}+1\sqrt{x}-3\cdot1}{\sqrt{x}\cdot\sqrt{x}-3\sqrt{x}+3\sqrt{x}-3\cdot3} = \frac{\sqrt{x^2}+\left(-3+1\right)\sqrt{x}-3}{\sqrt{x^2}-9}$$

$$= \frac{x+\left(-2\right)\sqrt{x}-3}{x-9} = \frac{x-2\sqrt{x}-3}{x-9}$$

89.

$$\frac{5\sqrt{3}-3\sqrt{2}}{3\sqrt{2}-2\sqrt{3}} = \frac{5\sqrt{3}-3\sqrt{2}}{3\sqrt{2}-2\sqrt{3}} \cdot \frac{3\sqrt{2}+2\sqrt{3}}{3\sqrt{2}+2\sqrt{3}} = \frac{5\sqrt{3}\cdot3\sqrt{2}+5\sqrt{3}\cdot2\sqrt{3}-3\sqrt{2}\cdot3\sqrt{2}-3\sqrt{2}\cdot2\sqrt{3}}{3\sqrt{2}\cdot3\sqrt{2}+3\sqrt{2}\cdot2\sqrt{3}-3\sqrt{2}\cdot2\sqrt{3}-2\sqrt{3}\cdot2\sqrt{3}}$$

$$= \frac{15\sqrt{6}+10\cdot3-9\cdot2-6\sqrt{6}}{9\cdot2+6\sqrt{6}-6\sqrt{6}-4\cdot3} = \frac{15\sqrt{6}+30-18-6\sqrt{6}}{18-12} = \frac{9\sqrt{6}+12}{6} = \frac{3\left(3\sqrt{6}+4\right)}{3\cdot2}$$

$$= \frac{3\sqrt{6}+4}{2}$$

91.

$$\frac{2\sqrt{x}+\sqrt{y}}{\sqrt{y}-2\sqrt{x}}=\frac{2\sqrt{x}+\sqrt{y}}{\sqrt{y}-2\sqrt{x}}\cdot\frac{\sqrt{y}+2\sqrt{x}}{\sqrt{y}+2\sqrt{x}}=\frac{2\sqrt{x}\sqrt{y}+2\sqrt{x}\cdot2\sqrt{x}+\sqrt{y}\sqrt{y}+2\sqrt{x}\sqrt{y}}{\sqrt{y}\sqrt{y}+2\sqrt{x}\sqrt{y}-2\sqrt{x}\sqrt{y}-2\sqrt{x}\cdot2\sqrt{x}}$$

$$=\frac{2\sqrt{xy}+4\sqrt{x^2}+\sqrt{y^2}+2\sqrt{xy}}{\sqrt{y^2}+2\sqrt{xy}-2\sqrt{xy}-4\sqrt{x^2}}=\frac{2\sqrt{xy}+4x+y+2\sqrt{xy}}{y-4x}=\frac{4\sqrt{xy}+4x+y}{y-4x}$$

93.

$$\sqrt{\frac{3}{2}}=\frac{\sqrt{3}}{\sqrt{2}}\cdot\frac{\sqrt{3}}{\sqrt{3}}=\frac{\sqrt{3}\sqrt{3}}{\sqrt{2}\sqrt{3}}=\frac{3}{\sqrt{6}}$$

95.

$$\frac{\sqrt[3]{4x}}{\sqrt[3]{y}}=\frac{\sqrt[3]{4x}}{\sqrt[3]{y}}\cdot\frac{\sqrt[3]{4^2x^2}}{\sqrt[3]{4^2x^2}}=\frac{\sqrt[3]{4^3x^3}}{\sqrt[3]{4^2x^2y}}=\frac{4x}{\sqrt[3]{16x^2y}}=\frac{4x}{\sqrt[3]{8\cdot2x^2y}}=\frac{4x}{2\sqrt[3]{2x^2y}}=\frac{2x}{\sqrt[3]{2x^2y}}$$

97.

$$\frac{\sqrt{x}+3}{\sqrt{x}}=\frac{\sqrt{x}+3}{\sqrt{x}}\cdot\frac{\sqrt{x}-3}{\sqrt{x}-3}=\frac{\sqrt{x}\cdot\sqrt{x}-3\sqrt{x}+3\sqrt{x}-3\cdot3}{\sqrt{x}\cdot\sqrt{x}-3\sqrt{x}}=\frac{\sqrt{x^2}-9}{\sqrt{x^2}-3\sqrt{x}}=\frac{x-9}{x-3\sqrt{x}}$$

99.

$$\frac{\sqrt{a}+\sqrt{b}}{\sqrt{a}-\sqrt{b}}=\frac{\sqrt{a}+\sqrt{b}}{\sqrt{a}-\sqrt{b}}\cdot\frac{\sqrt{a}-\sqrt{b}}{\sqrt{a}-\sqrt{b}}=\frac{\sqrt{a}\cdot\sqrt{a}-\sqrt{a}\sqrt{b}+\sqrt{a}\sqrt{b}-\sqrt{b}\sqrt{b}}{\sqrt{a}\cdot\sqrt{a}-\sqrt{a}\sqrt{b}-\sqrt{a}\sqrt{b}+\sqrt{b}\sqrt{b}}$$

$$=\frac{\sqrt{a^2}-\sqrt{ab}+\sqrt{ab}-\sqrt{b^2}}{\sqrt{a^2}-\sqrt{ab}-\sqrt{ab}+\sqrt{b^2}}=\frac{a-b}{a-2\sqrt{ab}+b}$$

101.

$$\frac{\sqrt{x+5}-\sqrt{x}}{5}=\frac{\sqrt{x+5}-\sqrt{x}}{5}\cdot\frac{\sqrt{x+5}+\sqrt{x}}{\sqrt{x+5}+\sqrt{x}}=\frac{\left(\sqrt{x+5}\right)^2+\sqrt{x+5}\cdot\sqrt{x}-\sqrt{x+5}\cdot\sqrt{x}-\left(\sqrt{x}\right)^2}{5\left(\sqrt{x+5}+\sqrt{x}\right)}$$

$$=\frac{x+5+\sqrt{x(x+5)}-\sqrt{x(x+5)}-x}{5\left(\sqrt{x+5}+\sqrt{x}\right)}=\frac{5}{5\left(\sqrt{x+5}+\sqrt{x}\right)}=\frac{1}{\sqrt{x+5}+\sqrt{x}}$$

103.

$$\frac{\sqrt{x}+\sqrt{y}}{x^2-y^2}=\frac{\sqrt{x}+\sqrt{y}}{x^2-y^2}\cdot\frac{\sqrt{x}-\sqrt{y}}{\sqrt{x}-\sqrt{y}}=\frac{\left(\sqrt{x}\right)^2-\sqrt{xy}+\sqrt{xy}-\left(\sqrt{y}\right)^2}{x^2\sqrt{x}-x^2\sqrt{y}-y^2\sqrt{x}+y^2\sqrt{y}}$$

$$=\frac{x-y}{x^2\left(\sqrt{x}-\sqrt{y}\right)-y^2\left(\sqrt{x}-\sqrt{y}\right)}=\frac{x-y}{\left(\sqrt{x}-\sqrt{y}\right)\left(x^2-y^2\right)}$$

$$=\frac{x-y}{\left(\sqrt{x}-\sqrt{y}\right)(x+y)(x-y)}=\frac{1}{\left(\sqrt{x}-\sqrt{y}\right)(x+y)}$$

105.

$$\sqrt{2} + \frac{1}{\sqrt{2}} = \sqrt{2} + \frac{1}{\sqrt{2}} \cdot \frac{\sqrt{2}}{\sqrt{2}}$$

$$= \sqrt{2} + \frac{\sqrt{2}}{2}$$

$$= \frac{2\sqrt{2}}{2} + \frac{\sqrt{2}}{2}$$

$$= \frac{2\sqrt{2} + \sqrt{2}}{2}$$

$$= \frac{3\sqrt{2}}{2}$$

106.

$$\sqrt{5} + \frac{1}{\sqrt{5}} = \sqrt{5} + \frac{1}{\sqrt{5}} \cdot \frac{\sqrt{5}}{\sqrt{5}}$$

$$= \sqrt{5} + \frac{\sqrt{5}}{5}$$

$$= \frac{5\sqrt{5}}{5} + \frac{\sqrt{5}}{5}$$

$$= \frac{5\sqrt{5} + \sqrt{5}}{5}$$

$$= \frac{6\sqrt{5}}{5}$$

107.

$$\sqrt[3]{25} - \frac{15}{\sqrt[3]{5}} = \sqrt[3]{25} - \frac{15}{\sqrt[3]{5}} \cdot \frac{\sqrt[3]{5^2}}{\sqrt[3]{5^2}}$$

$$= \sqrt[3]{25} - \frac{15\sqrt[3]{25}}{5}$$

$$= \sqrt[3]{25} - 3\sqrt[3]{25}$$

$$= -2\sqrt[3]{25}$$

108.

$$\sqrt[4]{8} - \frac{20}{\sqrt[4]{2}} = \sqrt[4]{8} - \frac{20}{\sqrt[4]{2}} \cdot \frac{\sqrt[4]{2^3}}{\sqrt[4]{2^3}}$$

$$= \sqrt[4]{8} - \frac{20\sqrt[4]{8}}{2}$$

$$= \sqrt[4]{8} - 10\sqrt[4]{8}$$

$$= -9\sqrt[4]{8}$$

109.

$$\sqrt{6} - \sqrt{\frac{1}{6}} + \sqrt{\frac{2}{3}}$$

$$= \sqrt{6} - \frac{\sqrt{1}}{\sqrt{6}} + \frac{\sqrt{2}}{\sqrt{3}}$$

$$= \sqrt{6} - \frac{1}{\sqrt{6}} \cdot \frac{\sqrt{6}}{\sqrt{6}} + \frac{\sqrt{2}}{\sqrt{3}} \cdot \frac{\sqrt{3}}{\sqrt{3}}$$

$$= \sqrt{6} - \frac{\sqrt{6}}{6} + \frac{\sqrt{6}}{3}$$

$$= \frac{6\sqrt{6}}{6} - \frac{\sqrt{6}}{6} + \frac{2\sqrt{6}}{6}$$

$$= \frac{6\sqrt{6} - \sqrt{6} + 2\sqrt{6}}{6}$$

$$= \frac{7\sqrt{6}}{6}$$

110.

$$\sqrt{15} - \sqrt{\frac{5}{3}} + \sqrt{\frac{3}{5}}$$

$$= \sqrt{15} - \frac{\sqrt{5}}{\sqrt{3}} + \frac{\sqrt{3}}{\sqrt{5}}$$

$$= \sqrt{15} - \frac{\sqrt{5}}{\sqrt{3}} \cdot \frac{\sqrt{3}}{\sqrt{3}} + \frac{\sqrt{3}}{\sqrt{5}} \cdot \frac{\sqrt{5}}{\sqrt{5}}$$

$$= \sqrt{15} - \frac{\sqrt{15}}{3} + \frac{\sqrt{15}}{5}$$

$$= \frac{15\sqrt{15}}{15} - \frac{5\sqrt{15}}{15} + \frac{3\sqrt{15}}{15}$$

$$= \frac{15\sqrt{15} - 5\sqrt{15} + 3\sqrt{15}}{15}$$

$$= \frac{13\sqrt{15}}{15}$$

111.

$$\frac{2}{\sqrt{2}+\sqrt{3}}+\sqrt{75}-\sqrt{50}$$

$$=\frac{2}{\sqrt{2}+\sqrt{3}}\cdot\frac{\sqrt{2}-\sqrt{3}}{\sqrt{2}-\sqrt{3}}+\sqrt{25\cdot3}-\sqrt{25\cdot2}$$

$$=\frac{2\sqrt{2}-2\sqrt{3}}{\left(\sqrt{2}\right)^2-\left(\sqrt{3}\right)^2}+5\sqrt{3}-5\sqrt{2}$$

$$=\frac{2\sqrt{2}-2\sqrt{3}}{2-3}+5\sqrt{3}-5\sqrt{2}$$

$$=\frac{2\sqrt{2}-2\sqrt{3}}{-1}+5\sqrt{3}-5\sqrt{2}$$

$$=2\sqrt{3}-2\sqrt{2}+5\sqrt{3}-5\sqrt{2}$$

$$=7\sqrt{3}-7\sqrt{2}$$

112.

$$\frac{5}{\sqrt{2}+\sqrt{7}}-2\sqrt{32}+\sqrt{28}$$

$$=\frac{5}{\sqrt{2}+\sqrt{7}}\cdot\frac{\sqrt{2}-\sqrt{7}}{\sqrt{2}-\sqrt{7}}-2\sqrt{16\cdot2}+\sqrt{4\cdot7}$$

$$=\frac{5\sqrt{2}-5\sqrt{7}}{\left(\sqrt{2}\right)^2-\left(\sqrt{7}\right)^2}-2(4)\sqrt{2}+2\sqrt{7}$$

$$=\frac{5\sqrt{2}-5\sqrt{7}}{2-7}-8\sqrt{2}+2\sqrt{7}$$

$$=\frac{5\sqrt{2}-5\sqrt{7}}{-5}-8\sqrt{2}+2\sqrt{7}$$

$$=\sqrt{7}-\sqrt{2}-8\sqrt{2}+2\sqrt{7}$$

$$=3\sqrt{7}-9\sqrt{2}$$

113. $f(x)=x^2-6x-4$

$f\left(3-\sqrt{13}\right)$

$$=\left(3-\sqrt{13}\right)^2-6\left(3-\sqrt{13}\right)-4$$

$$=9-6\sqrt{13}+13-18+6\sqrt{13}-4$$

$$=0$$

114. $f(x)=x^2+4x-2$

$f\left(-2+\sqrt{6}\right)$

$$=\left(-2+\sqrt{6}\right)^2+4\left(-2+\sqrt{6}\right)-2$$

$$=4-4\sqrt{6}+6-8+4\sqrt{6}-2$$

$$=0$$

115. $f(x)=\sqrt{9+x}$

$f\left(3\sqrt{5}\right)\cdot f\left(-3\sqrt{5}\right)$

$$=\sqrt{9+3\sqrt{5}}\cdot\sqrt{9-3\sqrt{5}}$$

$$=\sqrt{\left(9+3\sqrt{5}\right)\left(9-3\sqrt{5}\right)}$$

$$=\sqrt{9^2-\left(3\sqrt{5}\right)^2}$$

$$=\sqrt{81-9\cdot5}$$

$$=\sqrt{81-45}$$

$$=\sqrt{36}$$

$$=6$$

116. $f(x)=x^2$

$f\left(\sqrt{a+1}-\sqrt{a-1}\right)$

$$=\left(\sqrt{a+1}-\sqrt{a-1}\right)^2$$

$$=\left(\sqrt{a+1}\right)^2-2\sqrt{a+1}\cdot\sqrt{a-1}+\left(\sqrt{a-1}\right)^2$$

$$=a+1-2\sqrt{(a+1)(a-1)}+a-1$$

$$=2a-2\sqrt{a^2-1}$$

117. $P(t) = 15.92\sqrt{t} + 19$

$P(4) = 15.92\sqrt{4} + 19$

$\quad = 15.92(2) + 19$

$\quad = 50.84$

$\quad \approx 51\%$

In 2001 (4 years after 1997), the percentage of U.S. households online was roughly 51%. This answer models the data well. According to the graph, 51% of U.S. households were online in 2001.

119.

$\text{a.r.c.} = \dfrac{\text{change in percent}}{\text{change in time}}$

$= \dfrac{\left[15.92\sqrt{6} + 19\right] - \left[15.92\sqrt{0} + 19\right]}{2003 - 1997}$

$= \dfrac{15.92\sqrt{6} + 19 - 19}{6}$

$= \dfrac{15.92\sqrt{6}}{6} \approx 6.5\%$

The average yearly increase in the percentage of online households from 1997 to 2003 was about 6.5%.

121.

$15.92\left(\dfrac{\sqrt{0+6} - \sqrt{0}}{6}\right) = \dfrac{15.92\sqrt{6}}{6}$

This is exactly the same result as that obtained in Exercise 119. This answer models the actual yearly percentage increase very well.

123. a.

$15.92\left(\dfrac{\sqrt{t+h} - \sqrt{t}}{h}\right)$

$= 15.92\left(\dfrac{\sqrt{t+h} - \sqrt{t}}{h} \cdot \dfrac{\sqrt{t+h} + \sqrt{t}}{\sqrt{t+h} + \sqrt{t}}\right)$

$= 15.92\left(\dfrac{\left(\sqrt{t+h}\right)^2 - \left(\sqrt{t}\right)^2}{h\left(\sqrt{t+h} + \sqrt{t}\right)}\right)$

$= 15.92\left(\dfrac{t+h-t}{h\left(\sqrt{t+h} + \sqrt{t}\right)}\right)$

$= \dfrac{15.92h}{h\left(\sqrt{t+h} + \sqrt{t}\right)}$

$= \dfrac{15.92}{\sqrt{t+h} + \sqrt{t}}$

b.

$\dfrac{15.92}{\sqrt{t+0} + \sqrt{t}} = \dfrac{15.92}{\sqrt{t} + \sqrt{t}}$

$= \dfrac{15.92}{2\sqrt{t}}$

$= \dfrac{7.96}{\sqrt{t}}$

c. In 2003, we have $t = 6$.

$\dfrac{7.96}{\sqrt{6}} \approx 3.2497\%$

The rate of change in the percentage of households online in 2003 was roughly 3.2%.

125. Perimeter $= 2l + 2w$

$$= 2\left(\sqrt{8}+1\right)+2\left(\sqrt{8}-1\right)$$

$$= 2\sqrt{8}+\cancel{2}+2\sqrt{8}-\cancel{2}$$

$$= (2+2)\sqrt{8} = 4\sqrt{8}$$

$$= 4\sqrt{4\cdot 2} = 4\cdot 2\sqrt{2} = 8\sqrt{2}$$

The perimeter is $8\sqrt{2}$ inches.

Area $= lw = \left(\sqrt{8}+1\right)\left(\sqrt{8}-1\right)$

$$= \left(\sqrt{8}\right)^2 - \cancel{\sqrt{8}} + \cancel{\sqrt{8}} - 1$$

$$= 8 - 1 = 7$$

The area is 7 square inches.

127. $\dfrac{7\sqrt{2\cdot 2\cdot 3}}{6} = \dfrac{7\cdot 2\sqrt{3}}{6}$

$$= \dfrac{7\cdot \cancel{2}\sqrt{3}}{\cancel{2}\cdot 3} = \dfrac{7}{3}\sqrt{3}$$

129. Answers will vary. You will need to distribute the $\sqrt{2}$ across the sum.

131. Answers will vary. Use the form $(a+b)^2 = a^2 + 2ab + b^2$.

133. Answers will vary. One approach is to FOIL like you would when multiplying two binomials.

135. Answers will vary. The value remains the same because we are just multiplying by 1. However, we do so in a way that changes the *form*, not the value.

137. Answers will vary. The percentage has been increasing each year, but the rate of increase began to slow.

139. $\left(\sqrt{x}+2\right)\left(\sqrt{x}-2\right) = x^2 - 4$ for $x \ge 0$

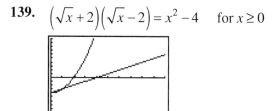

The graphs do not coincide.
Correct the simplification:

$\left(\sqrt{x}+2\right)\left(\sqrt{x}-2\right) = x - 4$ for $x \ge 0$

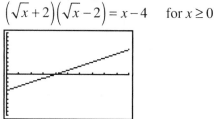

The graphs coincide. The new simplification is correct.

141. $\dfrac{3}{\sqrt{x+3}-\sqrt{x}} = \sqrt{x+3}+\sqrt{x}$

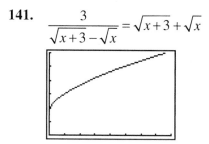

The graphs coincide, so the simplification is correct.

143. $7\left[(2x-5)-(x+1)\right] = \left(\sqrt{7}+2\right)\left(\sqrt{7}-2\right)$

$$7\left[2x-5-x-1\right] = \left(\sqrt{7}\right)^2 - (2)^2$$

$$7(x-6) = 7-4$$

$$7x - 42 = 3$$

$$7x = 45$$

$$x = \dfrac{45}{7}$$

The solution is $\dfrac{45}{7}$ and the solution set is $\left\{\dfrac{45}{7}\right\}$.

145.

$$\frac{1}{\sqrt{2}+\sqrt{3}+\sqrt{4}}$$

$$=\frac{1}{\left(\sqrt{2}+\sqrt{3}\right)+2}\cdot\frac{\left(\sqrt{2}+\sqrt{3}\right)-2}{\left(\sqrt{2}+\sqrt{3}\right)-2}$$

$$=\frac{\sqrt{2}+\sqrt{3}-2}{\left(\sqrt{2}+\sqrt{3}\right)^{2}-2^{2}}=\frac{\sqrt{2}+\sqrt{3}-2}{2+2\sqrt{6}+3-4}$$

$$=\frac{\sqrt{2}+\sqrt{3}-2}{2\sqrt{6}+1}\cdot\frac{2\sqrt{6}-1}{2\sqrt{6}-1}$$

$$=\frac{2\sqrt{12}+2\sqrt{18}-4\sqrt{6}-\sqrt{2}-\sqrt{3}+2}{\left(2\sqrt{6}\right)^{2}-1^{2}}$$

$$=\frac{4\sqrt{3}+6\sqrt{2}-4\sqrt{6}-\sqrt{2}-\sqrt{3}+2}{4\cdot6-1}$$

$$=\frac{3\sqrt{3}+5\sqrt{2}-4\sqrt{6}+2}{24+1}$$

$$=\frac{3\sqrt{3}+5\sqrt{2}-4\sqrt{6}+2}{24-1}$$

$$=\frac{3\sqrt{3}+5\sqrt{2}-4\sqrt{6}+2}{23}$$

146.

$$\frac{2}{x-2}+\frac{3}{x^{2}-4}$$

$$=\frac{2}{x-2}+\frac{3}{\left(x+2\right)\left(x-2\right)}$$

$$=\frac{2}{x-2}\cdot\frac{\left(x+2\right)}{\left(x+2\right)}+\frac{3}{\left(x+2\right)\left(x-2\right)}$$

$$=\frac{2\left(x+2\right)}{\left(x-2\right)\left(x+2\right)}+\frac{3}{\left(x+2\right)\left(x-2\right)}$$

$$=\frac{2\left(x+2\right)+3}{\left(x-2\right)\left(x+2\right)}$$

$$=\frac{2x+4+3}{\left(x-2\right)\left(x+2\right)}$$

$$=\frac{2x+7}{\left(x-2\right)\left(x+2\right)}\text{ or }\frac{2x+7}{x^{2}-4}$$

147.

$$3x-4\leq2\quad\text{and}\quad4x+5\geq5$$
$$3x\leq6\quad\text{and}\quad\quad4x\geq0$$
$$x\leq2\quad\text{and}\quad\quad x\geq0$$
$$0\leq x\leq2$$

The solution set is $\left\{x\,|\,0\leq x\leq2\right\}$ or $[0, 2]$.

148. $\left\{(-1,1),(1,1),(-2,4),(2,4)\right\}$

Since each element in the domain corresponds to exactly one element in the range, the relation is a function.

The inverse of the relation is $\left\{(1,-1),(1,1),(4,-2),(4,2)\right\}$.

Since the elements in the domain of the inverse relation are paired with more than one element in the range, the inverse is not a function.

10.6 Exercise Set

1.

$$\sqrt{3x-2}=4$$
$$\left(\sqrt{3x-2}\right)^{2}=4^{2}$$
$$3x-2=16$$
$$3x=18$$
$$x=6$$

Check:
$$\sqrt{3(6)-2}=4$$
$$\sqrt{18-2}=4$$
$$\sqrt{16}=4$$
$$4=4$$

The solution set is $\{6\}$.

539

3.
$$\sqrt{5x-4}-9=0$$
$$\sqrt{5x-4}=9$$
$$\left(\sqrt{5x-4}\right)^2=9^2$$
$$5x-4=81$$
$$5x=85$$
$$x=17$$
Check:
$$\sqrt{5(17)-4}-9=0$$
$$\sqrt{81}-9=0$$
$$9-9=0$$
$$0=0$$
The solution set is $\{17\}$.

5.
$$\sqrt{3x+7}+10=4$$
$$\sqrt{3x+7}=-6$$
Since the square root of a number is always positive, the solution set is $\{\ \}$ or $\varnothing$.

7.
$$x=\sqrt{7x+8}$$
$$x^2=\left(\sqrt{7x+8}\right)^2$$
$$x^2=7x+8$$
$$x^2-7x-8=0$$
$$(x-8)(x+1)=0$$
Apply the zero product principle.
$$x-8=0 \qquad x+1=0$$
$$x=8 \qquad\quad x=-1$$
Check:
$$8=\sqrt{7(8)+8} \qquad -1=\sqrt{7(-1)+8}$$
$$8=\sqrt{64}$$
$$8=8$$
We disregard -1 because square roots are always positive. The solution set is $\{8\}$.

9.
$$\sqrt{5x+1}=x+1$$
$$\left(\sqrt{5x+1}\right)^2=(x+1)^2$$
$$5x+1=x^2+2x+1$$
$$0=x^2-3x$$
$$0=x(x-3)$$
Apply the zero product principle.
$$x=0 \qquad x-3=0$$
$$x=3$$
Both check. The solution set is $\{0,3\}$.

11.
$$x=\sqrt{2x-2}+1$$
$$x-1=\sqrt{2x-2}$$
$$(x-1)^2=\left(\sqrt{2x-2}\right)^2$$
$$x^2-2x+1=2x-2$$
$$x^2-4x+3=0$$
$$(x-3)(x-1)=0$$
Apply the zero product principle.
$$x-3=0 \qquad x-1=0$$
$$x=3 \qquad\quad x=1$$
Both check. The solution set is $\{1,3\}$.

13.
$$x-2\sqrt{x-3}=3$$
$$x-3=2\sqrt{x-3}$$
$$(x-3)^2=\left(2\sqrt{x-3}\right)^2$$
$$x^2-6x+9=4(x-3)$$
$$x^2-6x+9=4x-12$$
$$x^2-10x+21=0$$
$$(x-7)(x-3)=0$$
Apply the zero product principle.
$$x-7=0 \qquad x-3=0$$
$$x=7 \qquad\quad x=3$$
Both check. The solution set is $\{3,7\}$.

540

15. $\sqrt{2x-5} = \sqrt{x+4}$

$\left(\sqrt{2x-5}\right)^2 = \left(\sqrt{x+4}\right)^2$

$2x - 5 = x + 4$

$x - 5 = 4$

$x = 9$

The solution checks. The solution set is $\{9\}$.

17. $\sqrt[3]{2x+11} = 3$

$\left(\sqrt[3]{2x+11}\right)^3 = 3^3$

$2x + 11 = 27$

$2x = 16$

$x = 8$

The solution checks. The solution set is $\{8\}$.

19. $\sqrt[3]{2x-6} - 4 = 0$

$\sqrt[3]{2x-6} = 4$

$\left(\sqrt[3]{2x-6}\right)^3 = 4^3$

$2x - 6 = 64$

$2x = 70$

$x = 35$

The solution checks. The solution set is $\{35\}$.

21. $\sqrt{x-7} = 7 - \sqrt{x}$

$\left(\sqrt{x-7}\right)^2 = \left(7 - \sqrt{x}\right)^2$

$\cancel{x} - 7 = 49 - 14\sqrt{x} + \cancel{x}$

$-7 = 49 - 14\sqrt{x}$

$-56 = -14\sqrt{x}$

$\dfrac{-56}{-14} = \dfrac{-14\sqrt{x}}{-14}$

$4 = \sqrt{x}$

$4^2 = \left(\sqrt{x}\right)^2$

$16 = x$

The solution checks. The solution set is $\{16\}$.

23. $\sqrt{x+2} + \sqrt{x-1} = 3$

$\sqrt{x+2} = 3 - \sqrt{x-1}$

$\left(\sqrt{x+2}\right)^2 = \left(3 - \sqrt{x-1}\right)^2$

$\cancel{x} + 2 = 9 - 6\sqrt{x-1} + \cancel{x} - 1$

$2 = 8 - 6\sqrt{x-1}$

$-6 = -6\sqrt{x-1}$

$\dfrac{-6}{-6} = \dfrac{-6\sqrt{x-1}}{-6}$

$1 = \sqrt{x-1}$

$1^2 = \left(\sqrt{x-1}\right)^2$

$1 = x - 1$

$2 = x$

The solution checks. The solution set is $\{2\}$.

25. $2\sqrt{4x+1} - 9 = x - 5$

$2\sqrt{4x+1} = x + 4$

$\left(2\sqrt{4x+1}\right)^2 = (x+4)^2$

$2^2\left(\sqrt{4x+1}\right)^2 = x^2 + 8x + 16$

$4(4x+1) = x^2 + 8x + 16$

$16x + 4 = x^2 + 8x + 16$

$0 = x^2 - 8x + 12$

$0 = (x-6)(x-2)$

$x - 6 = 0 \quad \text{or} \quad x - 2 = 0$

$x = 6 \qquad\qquad x = 2$

Both check. The solution set is $\{2, 6\}$.

27.
$$(2x+3)^{1/3} + 4 = 6$$
$$(2x+3)^{1/3} = 2$$
$$\left((2x+3)^{1/3}\right)^3 = 2^3$$
$$2x+3 = 8$$
$$2x = 5$$
$$x = \frac{5}{2}$$
The solution checks. The solution set is
$$\left\{\frac{5}{2}\right\}.$$

29.
$$(3x+1)^{1/4} + 7 = 9$$
$$(3x+1)^{1/4} = 2$$
$$\left((3x+1)^{1/4}\right)^4 = 2^4$$
$$3x+1 = 16$$
$$3x = 15$$
$$x = 5$$
The solution checks. The solution set is
$$\{5\}.$$

31.
$$(x+2)^{1/2} + 8 = 4$$
$$(x+2)^{1/2} = -4$$
$$\sqrt{x+2} = -4$$
The square root of a number must be
positive. The solution set is $\varnothing$.

33.
$$\sqrt{2x-3} - \sqrt{x-2} = 1$$
$$\sqrt{2x-3} = \sqrt{x-2} + 1$$
$$\left(\sqrt{2x-3}\right)^2 = \left(\sqrt{x-2}+1\right)^2$$
$$2x-3 = x-2 + 2\sqrt{x-2} + 1$$
$$2x-3 = x-1 + 2\sqrt{x-2}$$
$$x-2 = 2\sqrt{x-2}$$
$$(x-2)^2 = \left(2\sqrt{x-2}\right)^2$$
$$x^2 - 4x + 4 = 4(x-2)$$
$$x^2 - 4x + 4 = 4x - 8$$
$$x^2 - 8x + 12 = 0$$
$$(x-6)(x-2) = 0$$
$$x-6 = 0 \quad \text{or} \quad x-2 = 0$$
$$x = 6 \qquad\qquad x = 2$$
Both check. The solution set is $\{2,6\}$.

35.
$$3x^{1/3} = \left(x^2 + 17x\right)^{1/3}$$
$$\left(3x^{1/3}\right)^3 = \left(\left(x^2+17x\right)^{1/3}\right)^3$$
$$3^3 x = x^2 + 17x$$
$$27x = x^2 + 17x$$
$$0 = x^2 - 10x$$
$$0 = x(x-10)$$
$$x = 0 \quad \text{or} \quad x-10 = 0$$
$$x = 10$$
Both check. The solution set is $\{0,10\}$.

37.
$$(x+8)^{1/4} = (2x)^{1/4}$$
$$\left((x+8)^{1/4}\right)^4 = \left((2x)^{1/4}\right)^4$$
$$x+8 = 2x$$
$$8 = x$$
The solution checks. The solution set is
$$\{8\}.$$

39. $f(x) = x + \sqrt{x+5}$

$$7 = x + \sqrt{x+5}$$
$$7 - x = \sqrt{x+5}$$
$$(7-x)^2 = (\sqrt{x+5})^2$$
$$49 - 14x + x^2 = x+5$$
$$x^2 - 15x + 44 = 0$$
$$(x-11)(x-4) = 0$$
$$x - 11 = 0 \quad \text{or} \quad x - 4 = 0$$
$$x = 11 \qquad\qquad x = 4$$

Check $x = 11$: $11 + \sqrt{11+5} = 11 + \sqrt{16}$
$$= 15 \neq 7$$
Check $x = 4$: $4 + \sqrt{4+5} = 4 + \sqrt{9}$
$$= 7$$
Discard 11. The solution set is 4.

40. $f(x) = x - \sqrt{x-2}$

$$4 = x - \sqrt{x-2}$$
$$\sqrt{x-2} = x - 4$$
$$(\sqrt{x-2})^2 = (x-4)^2$$
$$x - 2 = x^2 - 8x + 16$$
$$0 = x^2 - 9x + 18$$
$$0 = (x-6)(x-3)$$
$$x - 6 = 0 \quad \text{or} \quad x - 3 = 0$$
$$x = 6 \qquad\qquad x = 3$$

Check $x = 6$: $6 - \sqrt{6-2} = 6 - \sqrt{4}$
$$= 4$$
Check $x = 3$: $3 - \sqrt{3-2} = 3 - \sqrt{1}$
$$= 2 \neq 4$$
Discard 3. The solution is 6.

41. $f(x) = (5x+16)^{1/3}$; $g(x) = (x-12)^{1/3}$

$$(5x+16)^{1/3} = (x-12)^{1/3}$$
$$\left[(5x+16)^{1/3}\right]^3 = \left[(x-12)^{1/3}\right]^3$$
$$5x + 16 = x - 12$$
$$4x = -28$$
$$x = -7$$
The solution is -7.

42. $f(x) = (9x+2)^{1/4}$; $g(x) = (5x+18)^{1/4}$

$$(9x+2)^{1/4} = (5x+18)^{1/4}$$
$$\left[(9x+2)^{1/4}\right]^4 = \left[(5x+18)^{1/4}\right]^4$$
$$9x + 2 = 5x + 18$$
$$4x = 16$$
$$x = 4$$
Check:
$$(9(4)+2)^{1/4} = (5(4)+18)^{1/4}$$
$$(36+2)^{1/4} = (20+18)^{1/4}$$
$$38^{1/4} = 38^{1/4}$$
The solution is 4.

43.
$$r = \sqrt{\frac{3V}{\pi h}}$$
$$r^2 = \left(\sqrt{\frac{3V}{\pi h}}\right)^2$$
$$r^2 = \frac{3V}{\pi h}$$
$$\pi r^2 h = 3V$$
$$\frac{\pi r^2 h}{3} = V \quad \text{or} \quad V = \frac{\pi r^2 h}{3}$$

543

44.
$$r = \sqrt{\frac{A}{4\pi}}$$

$$r^2 = \left(\sqrt{\frac{A}{4\pi}}\right)^2$$

$$r^2 = \frac{A}{4\pi}$$

$$4\pi r^2 = A \quad \text{or} \quad A = 4\pi r^2$$

45.
$$t = 2\pi\sqrt{\frac{l}{32}}$$

$$\frac{t}{2\pi} = \sqrt{\frac{l}{32}}$$

$$\left(\frac{t}{2\pi}\right)^2 = \left(\sqrt{\frac{l}{32}}\right)^2$$

$$\frac{t^2}{4\pi^2} = \frac{l}{32}$$

$$\frac{32t^2}{4\pi^2} = l$$

$$\frac{8t^2}{\pi^2} = l \quad \text{or} \quad l = \frac{8t^2}{\pi^2}$$

46.
$$v = \sqrt{\frac{FR}{m}}$$

$$v^2 = \left(\sqrt{\frac{FR}{m}}\right)^2$$

$$v^2 = \frac{FR}{m}$$

$$mv^2 = FR$$

$$m = \frac{FR}{v^2}$$

47. Let $x =$ the number.
$$\sqrt{5x-4} = x-2$$
$$\left(\sqrt{5x-4}\right)^2 = (x-2)^2$$
$$5x-4 = x^2 - 4x + 4$$
$$0 = x^2 - 9x + 8$$
$$0 = (x-8)(x-1)$$
$$x-8 = 0 \quad \text{or} \quad x-1 = 0$$
$$x = 8 \qquad\qquad x = 1$$

Check $x = 8$: $\sqrt{5(8)-4} = 8-2$
$$\sqrt{40-4} = 6$$
$$\sqrt{36} = 6$$
$$6 = 6$$
Check $x = 1$: $\sqrt{5(1)-4} = 1-2$
$$\sqrt{5-4} = -1$$
$$\sqrt{-1} \neq -1$$
Discard $x = 1$. The number is 8.

48. Let $x =$ the number.
$$\sqrt{x-3} = x-5$$
$$\left(\sqrt{x-3}\right)^2 = (x-5)^2$$
$$x-3 = x^2 - 10x + 25$$
$$0 = x^2 - 11x + 28$$
$$0 = (x-7)(x-4)$$
$$x-7 = 0 \quad \text{or} \quad x-4 = 0$$
$$x = 7 \qquad\qquad x = 4$$

Check $x = 7$: $\sqrt{7-3} = 7-5$
$$\sqrt{4} = 2$$
$$2 = 2$$
Check $x = 4$: $\sqrt{4-3} = 4-5$
$$\sqrt{1} = -1$$
$$1 \neq -1$$
Discard 4. The number is 7.

544

49. $f(x) = \sqrt{x+16} - \sqrt{x} - 2$

To find the x-intercepts, set the function equal to 0 and solve for x.

$$0 = \sqrt{x+16} - \sqrt{x} - 2$$

$$\sqrt{x} + 2 = \sqrt{x+16}$$

$$\left(\sqrt{x}+2\right)^2 = \left(\sqrt{x+16}\right)^2$$

$$x + 4\sqrt{x} + 4 = x + 16$$

$$4\sqrt{x} = 12$$

$$\sqrt{x} = 3$$

$$\left(\sqrt{x}\right)^2 = 3^2$$

$$x = 9$$

Check $x = 9$:

$$\sqrt{9+16} - \sqrt{9} - 2$$

$$= \sqrt{25} - \sqrt{9} - 2$$

$$= 5 - 3 - 2$$

$$= 0$$

The only x-intercept is 9.

50. $f(x) = \sqrt{2x-3} - \sqrt{2x} + 1$

To find the x-intercepts, set the function equal to 0 and solve for x.

$$0 = \sqrt{2x-3} - \sqrt{2x} + 1$$

$$\sqrt{2x} - 1 = \sqrt{2x-3}$$

$$\left(\sqrt{2x}-1\right)^2 = \left(\sqrt{2x-3}\right)^2$$

$$2x - 2\sqrt{2x} + 1 = 2x - 3$$

$$-2\sqrt{2x} = -4$$

$$\sqrt{2x} = 2$$

$$\left(\sqrt{2x}\right)^2 = 2^2$$

$$2x = 4$$

$$x = 2$$

Check $x = 2$:

$$\sqrt{2(2)-3} - \sqrt{2(2)} + 1$$

$$= \sqrt{4-3} - \sqrt{4} + 1$$

$$= \sqrt{1} - \sqrt{4} + 1$$

$$= 1 - 2 + 1$$

$$= 0$$

The only x-intercept is 2.

51. For the year 2100, we use $x = 98$.

$$f(98) = 0.083(98) + 57.9$$

$$= 66.034$$

$$g(98) = 0.36\sqrt{98} + 57.9$$

$$\approx 61.464$$

In the year 2100, the projected high end temperature is about $66.0°$ and the projected low end temperature is about $61.5°$.

53. Using f:

$$0.083x = 1$$

$$x = \frac{1}{0.083} \approx 12.05$$

The projected global temperature will exceed the 2002 average by 1 degree in 2014 (12 years after 2002).

Using g:

$$0.36\sqrt{x} = 1$$

$$\sqrt{x} = \frac{1}{0.36}$$

$$\left(\sqrt{x}\right)^2 = \left(\frac{1}{0.36}\right)^2$$

$$x \approx 7.716 \quad \text{(roughly 8)}$$

The projected global temperature will exceed the 2002 average by 1 degree in 2010 (8 years after 2002).

55.
$$40000 = 5000\sqrt{100 - x}$$
$$\frac{40000}{5000} = \frac{5000\sqrt{100 - x}}{5000}$$
$$8 = \sqrt{100 - x}$$
$$8^2 = \left(\sqrt{100 - x}\right)^2$$
$$64 = 100 - x$$
$$-36 = -x$$
$$36 = x$$
40,000 people in the group will survive to age 36. This is shown on the graph as the point $(36,\ 40,000)$.

57.
$$87 = 29x^{1/3}$$
$$\frac{87}{29} = \frac{29x^{1/3}}{29}$$
$$3 = x^{1/3}$$
$$3^3 = \left(x^{1/3}\right)^3$$
$$27 = x$$
A Galápagos island with an area of 27 square miles will have 87 plant species.

59.
$$365 = 0.2x^{3/2}$$
$$\frac{365}{0.2} = \frac{0.2x^{3/2}}{0.2}$$
$$1825 = x^{3/2}$$
$$1825^2 = \left(x^{3/2}\right)^2$$
$$3,330,625 = x^3$$
$$\sqrt[3]{3,330,625} = \sqrt[3]{x^3}$$
$$149.34 \approx x$$
The average distance of the Earth from the sun is approximately 149 million kilometers.

61. Answers will vary.

63. Answers will vary. An extraneous solution is a solution to an equation that does not satisfy the equation in its original form. Typically these arise due to some manipulation of the original equation.

65. Answers will vary.

67. Answers will vary. The graph indicates that the number of survivors at a given age decreases at a faster rate as the age increases. The decrease is most rapid just before the last of the survivors die.

69. $\sqrt{x} + 3 = 5$

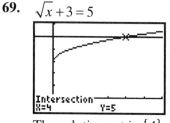

The solution set is $\{4\}$.

71. $4\sqrt{x} = x + 3$

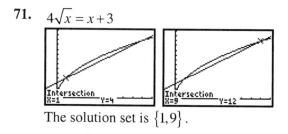

The solution set is $\{1, 9\}$.

73. Statement **c.** is true. To show this, substitute for T in the equation for L and simplify.

$$L = \frac{8T^2}{\pi^2} = \frac{8\left(2\pi\sqrt{\dfrac{L}{32}}\right)^2}{\pi^2} = \frac{8\left(4\pi^2\dfrac{L}{32}\right)}{\pi^2}$$

$$= \frac{\cancel{32}\pi^2\dfrac{L}{\cancel{32}}}{\pi^2} = \frac{\cancel{\pi^2}L}{\cancel{\pi^2}} = L$$

Statement **a.** is false. The first step is to square both sides, obtaining
$x+6 = x^2 + 4x + 4$.

Statement **b.** is false. The equation $\sqrt{x+4} = -5$ has no solution. By definition, absolute values are positive.

Statement **d.** is false. We know that an equation with an absolute value equal to a negative number has no solution. In this case, however, we do not know that $-x$ represents a negative number. If x is negative, then $-x$ is positive.

75.
$$\sqrt[3]{x\sqrt{x}} = 9$$
$$\left(\sqrt[3]{x\sqrt{x}}\right)^3 = 9^3$$
$$x\sqrt{x} = 729$$
$$\left(x\sqrt{x}\right)^2 = 729^2$$
$$x^2 x = 531441$$
$$x^3 = 531441$$
$$x = 81$$
Check:
$$\sqrt[3]{81\sqrt{81}} = 9$$
$$9 = 9$$
The solution checks. The solution set is $\{81\}$.

77.
$$(x-4)^{2/3} = 25$$
$$\left((x-4)^{2/3}\right)^{3/2} = 25^{3/2}$$
$$x-4 = \left(\sqrt{25}\right)^3$$
$$x-4 = 5^3$$
$$x-4 = 125$$
$$x = 129$$

Check:
$$(129-4)^{2/3} = 25$$
$$(125)^{2/3} = 25$$
$$\left(\sqrt[3]{125}\right)^2 = 25$$
$$5^2 = 25$$
$$25 = 25$$
The solution checks. The solution set is $\{129\}$.

78.
$$\frac{4x^4 - 3x^3 + 2x^2 - x - 1}{x+3}$$
$$= \frac{4x^4 - 3x^3 + 2x^2 - x - 1}{x-(-3)}$$

$$
\begin{array}{r|rrrrr}
-3 & 4 & -3 & 2 & -1 & -1 \\
   &   & -12 & 45 & -141 & 426 \\
\hline
   & 4 & -15 & 47 & -142 & 425
\end{array}
$$

$$\frac{4x^4 - 3x^3 + 2x^2 - x - 1}{x+3}$$
$$= 4x^3 - 15x^2 + 47x - 142 + \frac{425}{x+3}$$

79.

$$\frac{3x^2-12}{x^2+2x-8} \div \frac{6x+18}{x+4}$$

$$= \frac{3x^2-12}{x^2+2x-8} \cdot \frac{x+4}{6x+18}$$

$$= \frac{3(x^2-4)}{(x+4)(x-2)} \cdot \frac{x+4}{6(x+3)}$$

$$= \frac{3(x+2)(x-2)}{(x-2)} \cdot \frac{1}{6(x+3)}$$

$$= \frac{3(x+2)}{1} \cdot \frac{1}{6(x+3)}$$

$$= \frac{3(x+2)}{6(x+3)} = \frac{x+2}{2(x+3)}$$

80.

$$y^2-6y+9-25x^2$$

$$= (y^2-6y+9)-25x^2$$

$$= (y-3)^2-(5x)^2$$

$$= ((y-3)+5x)((y-3)-5x)$$

$$= (y-3+5x)(y-3-5x)$$

10.7 Exercise Set

1. $\sqrt{-100} = \sqrt{100 \cdot -1} = \sqrt{100} \cdot \sqrt{-1} = 10i$

3. $\sqrt{-23} = \sqrt{23 \cdot -1} = \sqrt{23} \cdot \sqrt{-1} = \sqrt{23}\,i$

5. $\sqrt{-18} = \sqrt{9 \cdot 2 \cdot -1}$

$$= \sqrt{9} \cdot \sqrt{2} \cdot \sqrt{-1}$$

$$= 3\sqrt{2}\,i$$

7. $\sqrt{-63} = \sqrt{9 \cdot 7 \cdot -1}$

$$= \sqrt{9} \cdot \sqrt{7} \cdot \sqrt{-1}$$

$$= 3\sqrt{7}\,i$$

9. $-\sqrt{-108} = -\sqrt{36 \cdot 3 \cdot -1}$

$$= -\sqrt{36} \cdot \sqrt{3} \cdot \sqrt{-1}$$

$$= -6\sqrt{3}\,i$$

11. $5+\sqrt{-36} = 5+\sqrt{36 \cdot -1}$

$$= 5+\sqrt{36} \cdot \sqrt{-1}$$

$$= 5+6i$$

13. $15+\sqrt{-3} = 15+\sqrt{3 \cdot -1}$

$$= 15+\sqrt{3} \cdot \sqrt{-1}$$

$$= 15+\sqrt{3}\,i$$

15. $-2-\sqrt{-18} = -2-\sqrt{9 \cdot 2 \cdot -1}$

$$= -2-\sqrt{9} \cdot \sqrt{2} \cdot \sqrt{-1}$$

$$= -2-3\sqrt{2}\,i$$

17. $(3+2i)+(5+i)$

$$= 3+2i+5+i = 3+5+2i+i$$

$$= (3+5)+(2+1)i = 8+3i$$

19. $(7+2i)+(1-4i)$

$$= 7+2i+1-4i = 7+1+2i-4i$$

$$= (7+1)+(2-4)i = 8-2i$$

21. $(10+7i)-(5+4i)$

$$= 10+7i-5-4i = 10-5+7i-4i$$

$$= (10-5)+(7-4)i = 5+3i$$

23. $(9-4i)-(10+3i)$

$$= 9-4i-10-3i = 9-10-4i-3i$$

$$= (9-10)+(-4-3)i$$

$$= -1+(-7)i = -1-7i$$

25. $(3+2i)-(5-7i)$

$=3+2i-5+7i=3-5+2i+7i$

$=(3-5)+(2+7)i=-2+9i$

27. $(-5+4i)-(-13-11i)$

$=-5+4i+13+11i$

$=-5+13+4i+11i$

$=(-5+13)+(4+11)i=8+15i$

29. $8i-(14-9i)$

$=8i-14+9i=-14+8i+9i$

$=-14+(8+9)i=-14+17i$

31. $\left(2+\sqrt{3}\,i\right)+\left(7+4\sqrt{3}\,i\right)$

$=2+\sqrt{3}\,i+7+4\sqrt{3}\,i$

$=2+7+\sqrt{3}\,i+4\sqrt{3}\,i$

$=(2+7)+\left(\sqrt{3}+4\sqrt{3}\right)i=9+5\sqrt{3}\,i$

33. $2i(5+3i)$

$=2i\cdot5+2i\cdot3i=10i+6i^2$

$=10i+6(-1)=-6+10i$

35. $3i(7i-5)$

$=3i\cdot7i-3i\cdot5=21i^2-15i$

$=21(-1)-15i=-21-15i$

37. $-7i(2-5i)$

$=-7i\cdot2-(-7i)5i=-14i+35i^2$

$=-14i+35(-1)=-35-14i$

39. $(3+i)(4+5i)=12+15i+4i+5i^2$

$=12+15i+4i+5(-1)$

$=12-5+15i+4i$

$=7+19i$

41. $(7-5i)(2-3i)$

$=14-21i-10i+15i^2$

$=14-21i-10i+15(-1)$

$=14-15-21i-10i=-1-31i$

43. $(6-3i)(-2+5i)$

$=-12+30i+6i-15i^2$

$=-12+30i+6i-15(-1)$

$=-12+15+30i+6i=3+36i$

45. $(3+5i)(3-5i)$

$=9-\cancel{15i}+\cancel{15i}-25i^2$

$=9-25(-1)=9+25$

$=34=34+0i$

47. $(-5+3i)(-5-3i)$

$=25+\cancel{15i}-\cancel{15i}-9i^2$

$=25-9(-1)=25+9$

$=34=34+0i$

49. $\left(3-\sqrt{2}\,i\right)\left(3+\sqrt{2}\,i\right)$

$=9+\cancel{3\sqrt{2}\,i}-\cancel{3\sqrt{2}\,i}-2i^2$

$=9-2(-1)=9+2$

$=11=11+0i$

51. $(2+3i)^2$

$=4+2\cdot6i+9i^2=4+12i+9(-1)$

$=4-9+12i=-5+12i$

53. $(5-2i)^2=25-2\cdot10i+4i^2$

$=25-20i+4(-1)$

$=25-4-20i=21-20i$

55. $\sqrt{-7} \cdot \sqrt{-2} = \sqrt{7}\sqrt{-1} \cdot \sqrt{2}\sqrt{-1}$

$\qquad = \sqrt{7}\ i \cdot \sqrt{2}\ i = \sqrt{14}\ i^2$

$\qquad = \sqrt{14}(-1)$

$\qquad = -\sqrt{14} = -\sqrt{14} + 0i$

57. $\sqrt{-9} \cdot \sqrt{-4}$

$= \sqrt{9}\sqrt{-1} \cdot \sqrt{4}\sqrt{-1} = 3i \cdot 2i = 6i^2$

$= 6(-1) = -6 = -6 + 0i$

59. $\sqrt{-7} \cdot \sqrt{-25} = \sqrt{7}\sqrt{-1} \cdot \sqrt{25}\sqrt{-1}$

$\qquad = \sqrt{7}\ i \cdot 5i = 5\sqrt{7}\ i^2$

$\qquad = 5\sqrt{7}(-1) = -5\sqrt{7}$

$\qquad = -5\sqrt{7} + 0i$

61. $\sqrt{-8} \cdot \sqrt{-3} = \sqrt{4 \cdot 2}\sqrt{-1} \cdot \sqrt{3}\sqrt{-1}$

$\qquad = 2\sqrt{2}\ i \cdot \sqrt{3}\ i = 2\sqrt{6}\ i^2$

$\qquad = 2\sqrt{6}(-1) = -2\sqrt{6}$

$\qquad = -2\sqrt{6} + 0i$

63. $\dfrac{2}{3+i} = \dfrac{2}{3+i} \cdot \dfrac{3-i}{3-i} = \dfrac{6-2i}{3^2-i^2}$

$\qquad = \dfrac{6-2i}{9-(-1)} = \dfrac{6-2i}{9+1}$

$\qquad = \dfrac{6-2i}{10} = \dfrac{6}{10} - \dfrac{2i}{10}$

$\qquad = \dfrac{3}{5} - \dfrac{1}{5}i$

65. $\dfrac{2i}{1+i} = \dfrac{2i}{1+i} \cdot \dfrac{1-i}{1-i} = \dfrac{2i-2i^2}{1^2-i^2}$

$\qquad = \dfrac{2i-2(-1)}{1-(-1)} = \dfrac{2+2i}{1+1}$

$\qquad = \dfrac{2+2i}{2} = \dfrac{2}{2} + \dfrac{2i}{2} = 1+i$

67. $\dfrac{7}{4-3i} = \dfrac{7}{4-3i} \cdot \dfrac{4+3i}{4+3i} = \dfrac{28+21i}{4^2-(3i)^2}$

$\qquad = \dfrac{28+21i}{16-9i^2} = \dfrac{28+21i}{16-9(-1)}$

$\qquad = \dfrac{28+21i}{16+9} = \dfrac{28+21i}{25}$

$\qquad = \dfrac{28}{25} + \dfrac{21}{25}i$

69. $\dfrac{6i}{3-2i} = \dfrac{6i}{3-2i} \cdot \dfrac{3+2i}{3+2i} = \dfrac{18i+12i^2}{3^2-(2i)^2}$

$\qquad = \dfrac{18i+12(-1)}{9-4i^2} = \dfrac{-12+18i}{9-4(-1)}$

$\qquad = \dfrac{-12+18i}{9+4} = \dfrac{-12+18i}{13}$

$\qquad = -\dfrac{12}{13} + \dfrac{18}{13}i$

71. $\dfrac{1+i}{1-i} = \dfrac{1+i}{1-i} \cdot \dfrac{1+i}{1+i} = \dfrac{1+2i+i^2}{1^2-i^2}$

$\qquad = \dfrac{1+2i+(-1)}{1-(-1)} = \dfrac{2i}{2}$

$\qquad = i$ or $0+i$

73. $\dfrac{2-3i}{3+i} = \dfrac{2-3i}{3+i} \cdot \dfrac{3-i}{3-i}$

$\qquad = \dfrac{6-2i-9i+3i^2}{3^2-i^2}$

$\qquad = \dfrac{6-11i+3(-1)}{9-(-1)}$

$\qquad = \dfrac{6-3-11i}{9+1}$

$\qquad = \dfrac{3-11i}{10} = \dfrac{3}{10} - \dfrac{11}{10}i$

75.
$$\frac{5-2i}{3+2i} = \frac{5-2i}{3+2i} \cdot \frac{3-2i}{3-2i}$$
$$= \frac{15-10i-6i+4i^2}{3^2-(2i)^2}$$
$$= \frac{15-10i-6i+4i^2}{3^2-(2i)^2}$$
$$= \frac{15-16i+4(-1)}{9-4i^2}$$
$$= \frac{15-4-16i}{9-4(-1)}$$
$$= \frac{11-16i}{9+4}$$
$$= \frac{11-16i}{13} = \frac{11}{13} - \frac{16}{13}i$$

77.
$$\frac{4+5i}{3-7i} = \frac{4+5i}{3-7i} \cdot \frac{3+7i}{3+7i}$$
$$= \frac{12+28i+15i+35i^2}{3^2-(7i)^2}$$
$$= \frac{12+43i+35(-1)}{9-49i^2}$$
$$= \frac{12-35+43i}{9-49(-1)}$$
$$= \frac{-23+43i}{9+49} = \frac{-23+43i}{58}$$
$$= -\frac{23}{58} + \frac{43}{58}i$$

79.
$$\frac{7}{3i} = \frac{7}{3i} \cdot \frac{-3i}{-3i} = \frac{-21i}{-9i^2} = \frac{-21i}{-9(-1)}$$
$$= \frac{-21i}{9} = -\frac{7}{3}i \text{ or } 0 - \frac{7}{3}i$$

81.
$$\frac{8-5i}{2i} = \frac{8-5i}{2i} \cdot \frac{-2i}{-2i} = \frac{-16i+10i^2}{-4i^2}$$
$$= \frac{-16i+10(-1)}{-4(-1)} = \frac{-10-16i}{4}$$
$$= -\frac{10}{4} - \frac{16}{4}i = -\frac{5}{2} - 4i$$

83.
$$\frac{4+7i}{-3i} = \frac{4+7i}{-3i} \cdot \frac{3i}{3i} = \frac{12i+21i^2}{-9i^2}$$
$$= \frac{12i+21(-1)}{-9(-1)} = \frac{-21+12i}{9}$$
$$= -\frac{21}{9} + \frac{12}{9}i = -\frac{7}{3} + \frac{4}{3}i$$

85. $i^{10} = (i^2)^5 = (-1)^5 = -1$

87. $i^{11} = (i^2)^5 i = (-1)^5 i = -i$

89. $i^{22} = (i^2)^{11} = (-1)^{11} = -1$

91. $i^{200} = (i^2)^{100} = (-1)^{100} = 1$

93. $i^{17} = (i^2)^8 i = (-1)^8 i = i$

95. $(-i)^4 = (-1)^4 i^4 = i^4 = (i^2)^2$
$$= (-1)^2 = 1$$

97. $(-i)^9 = (-1)^9 i^9 = (-1)(i^2)^4 i$
$$= (-1)(-1)^4 i = (-1)i$$
$$= -i$$

99. $i^{24} + i^2 = (i^2)^{12} + (-1)$
$$= (-1)^{12} + (-1)$$
$$= 1 + (-1) = 0$$

551

101. $(2-3i)(1-i)-(3-i)(3+i)$

$\quad = \left(2 - 2i - 3i + 3i^2\right) - \left(3^2 - i^2\right)$

$\quad = 2 - 5i + 3i^2 - 9 + i^2$

$\quad = -7 - 5i + 4i^2$

$\quad = -7 - 5i + 4(-1)$

$\quad = -11 - 5i$

102. $(8+9i)(2-i)-(1-i)(1+i)$

$\quad = \left(16 - 8i + 18i - 9i^2\right) - \left(1^2 - i^2\right)$

$\quad = 16 + 10i - 9i^2 - 1 + i^2$

$\quad = 15 + 10i - 8i^2$

$\quad = 15 + 10i - 8(-1)$

$\quad = 23 + 10i$

103. $(2+i)^2 - (3-i)^2$

$\quad = \left(4 + 4i + i^2\right) - \left(9 - 6i + i^2\right)$

$\quad = 4 + 4i + i^2 - 9 + 6i - i^2$

$\quad = -5 + 10i$

104. $(4-i)^2 - (1+2i)^2$

$\quad = \left(16 - 8i + i^2\right) - \left(1 + 4i + 4i^2\right)$

$\quad = 16 - 8i + i^2 - 1 - 4i - 4i^2$

$\quad = 15 - 12i - 3i^2$

$\quad = 15 - 12i - 3(-1)$

$\quad = 18 - 12i$

105. $5\sqrt{-16} + 3\sqrt{-81}$

$\quad = 5\sqrt{16}\sqrt{-1} + 3\sqrt{81}\sqrt{-1}$

$\quad = 5 \cdot 4i + 3 \cdot 9i$

$\quad = 20i + 27i$

$\quad = 47i \quad \text{or} \quad 0 + 47i$

106. $5\sqrt{-8} + 3\sqrt{-18}$

$\quad = 5\sqrt{4}\sqrt{2}\sqrt{-1} + 3\sqrt{9}\sqrt{2}\sqrt{-1}$

$\quad = 5 \cdot 2\sqrt{2}\,i + 3 \cdot 3\sqrt{2}\,i$

$\quad = 10\sqrt{2}\,i + 9\sqrt{2}\,i$

$\quad = (10+9)\sqrt{2}\,i$

$\quad = 19\sqrt{2}\,i \quad \text{or} \quad 0 + 19\sqrt{2}\,i$

107. $\dfrac{i^4 + i^{12}}{i^8 - i^7} = \dfrac{i^4 + \left(i^4\right)^3}{\left(i^4\right)^2 - \left(i^2\right)^3 i}$

$\quad\quad\quad\quad = \dfrac{1 + 1^3}{1^2 - (-1)^3 i} = \dfrac{1+1}{1+i}$

$\quad\quad\quad\quad = \dfrac{2}{1+i} = \dfrac{2}{1+i} \cdot \dfrac{1-i}{1-i}$

$\quad\quad\quad\quad = \dfrac{2-2i}{1^2 - i^2} = \dfrac{2-2i}{1+1}$

$\quad\quad\quad\quad = \dfrac{2-2i}{2} = 1 - i$

108. $\dfrac{i^8 + i^{40}}{i^4 + i^3} = \dfrac{\left(i^4\right)^2 + \left(i^4\right)^{10}}{i^4 + i^2 \cdot i}$

$\quad\quad\quad\quad = \dfrac{1^2 + 1^{10}}{1 + (-1)i} = \dfrac{1+1}{1-i}$

$\quad\quad\quad\quad = \dfrac{2}{1-i} = \dfrac{2}{1-i} \cdot \dfrac{1+i}{1+i}$

$\quad\quad\quad\quad = \dfrac{2+2i}{1^2 - i^2} = \dfrac{2+2i}{1+1}$

$\quad\quad\quad\quad = \dfrac{2+2i}{2} = 1 + i$

109. $f(x) = x^2 - 2x + 2$

$\quad f(1+i) = (1+i)^2 - 2(1+i) + 2$

$\quad\quad\quad\quad = 1 + 2i + i^2 - 2 - 2i + 2$

$\quad\quad\quad\quad = 1 + i^2$

$\quad\quad\quad\quad = 1 - 1 = 0$

110. $f(x) = x^2 - 2x + 5$

$f(1-2i) = (1-2i)^2 - 2(1-2i) + 5$

$\qquad = 1 - 4i + 4i^2 - 2 + 4i + 5$

$\qquad = 4 + 4i^2$

$\qquad = 4 - 4$

$\qquad = 0$

111. $f(x) = x - 3i$; $g(x) = 4x + 2i$

$f(-1) = -1 - 3i$

$g(-1) = -4 + 2i$

$(fg)(-1) = (-1 - 3i)(-4 + 2i)$

$\qquad = 4 - 2i + 12i - 6i^2$

$\qquad = 4 + 10i - 6(-1)$

$\qquad = 4 + 10i + 6$

$\qquad = 10 + 10i$

112. $f(x) = 12x - i$; $g(x) = 6x + 3i$

$f\left(-\dfrac{1}{3}\right) = 12\left(-\dfrac{1}{3}\right) - i = -4 - i$

$g\left(-\dfrac{1}{3}\right) = 6\left(-\dfrac{1}{3}\right) + 3i = -2 + 3i$

$(fg)\left(-\dfrac{1}{3}\right) = (-4 - i)(-2 + 3i)$

$\qquad = 8 - 12i + 2i - 3i^2$

$\qquad = 8 - 10i - 3(-1)$

$\qquad = 8 - 10i + 3$

$\qquad = 11 - 10i$

113. $f(x) = \dfrac{x^2 + 19}{2 - x}$

$f(3i) = \dfrac{(3i)^2 + 19}{2 - 3i} = \dfrac{9i^2 + 19}{2 - 3i}$

$\qquad = \dfrac{9(-1) + 19}{2 - 3i} = \dfrac{10}{2 - 3i}$

$\qquad = \dfrac{10}{2 - 3i} \cdot \dfrac{2 + 3i}{2 + 3i}$

$\qquad = \dfrac{20 + 30i}{2^2 - (3i)^2} = \dfrac{20 + 30i}{4 - 9i^2}$

$\qquad = \dfrac{20 + 30i}{4 - 9(-1)} = \dfrac{20 + 30i}{13}$

$\qquad = \dfrac{20}{13} + \dfrac{30}{13}i$

114. $f(x) = \dfrac{x^2 + 11}{3 - x}$

$f(4i) = \dfrac{(4i)^2 + 11}{3 - 4i} = \dfrac{16i^2 + 11}{3 - 4i}$

$\qquad = \dfrac{16(-1) + 11}{3 - 4i} = \dfrac{-5}{3 - 4i}$

$\qquad = \dfrac{-5}{3 - 4i} \cdot \dfrac{3 + 4i}{3 + 4i}$

$\qquad = \dfrac{-15 - 20i}{3^2 - (4i)^2} = \dfrac{-15 - 20i}{9 - 16i^2}$

$\qquad = \dfrac{-15 - 20i}{9 - 16(-1)} = \dfrac{-15 - 20i}{25}$

$\qquad = \dfrac{-15}{25} - \dfrac{20}{25}i$

$\qquad = -\dfrac{3}{5} - \dfrac{4}{5}i$

115. $E = IR = (4-5i)(3+7i)$

$= 12 + 28i - 15i - 35i^2$

$= 12 + 13i - 35(-1)$

$= 12 + 35 + 13i = 47 + 13i$

The voltage of the circuit is
$(47 + 13i)$ volts.

117. Sum:

$\left(5 + \sqrt{15}\,i\right) + \left(5 - \sqrt{15}\,i\right)$

$= 5 + \sqrt{15}\,i + 5 - \sqrt{15}\,i$

$= 5 + 5 = 10$

Product:

$\left(5 + \sqrt{15}\,i\right)\left(5 - \sqrt{15}\,i\right)$

$= 25 - 5\sqrt{15}\,i + 5\sqrt{15}\,i - 15i^2$

$= 25 - 15(-1) = 25 + 15 = 40$

119. Answers will vary.
Write -64 as the product of 64 and
-1. Then split up the radical as
$\sqrt{-64} = \sqrt{64 \cdot -1} = \sqrt{64}\sqrt{-1} = 8i$

121. Answers will vary. Add corresponding
real parts and corresponding
imaginary parts.

123. Answers will vary. Use the
distributive property to distribute $2i$.
Then simplify by converting powers of
i as appropriate and collecting like
terms.

125. Answers will vary. The product is in
the form $(a+b)(a-b)$ so the result is
the difference of two squares. Simplify
by converting powers of i as
appropriate and collecting like terms.

127. The conjugate of $2 + 3i$ is $2 - 3i$.
Answers may vary. When you
multiply conjugates, the result is a
pure real number.

129. Answers will vary.

131. Answers may vary. The two radicands
were incorrectly added together. First
write the numbers in terms of i and
then see if they can be combined.
$\sqrt{-9} + \sqrt{-16} = \sqrt{9}\sqrt{-1} + \sqrt{16}\sqrt{-1}$

$= 3i + 4i$

$= 7i$

133. Statement **d.** is true.

$(x + yi)(x - yi)$

$= x^2 - xyi + xyi - y^2i^2$

$= x^2 - y^2(-1)$

$= x^2 + y^2$

Statement **a.** is false. All irrational
numbers are complex numbers.

Statement **b.** is false.

$(3 + 7i)(3 - 7i)$

$= 3^2 - (7i)^2 = 9 - 49i^2$

$= 9 - 49(-1)$

$= 9 + 49 = 58$

Statement **c.** is false.

$\dfrac{7 + 3i}{5 + 3i} = \dfrac{7 + 3i}{5 + 3i} \cdot \dfrac{5 - 3i}{5 - 3i}$

$= \dfrac{35 - 21i + 15i - 9i^2}{5^2 - (3i)^2} = \dfrac{35 - 6i - 9(-1)}{25 - 9i^2}$

$= \dfrac{35 - 6i + 9}{25 - 9(-1)} = \dfrac{44 - 6i}{25 + 9} = \dfrac{44 - 6i}{34}$

$= \dfrac{44}{34} - \dfrac{6}{34}i = \dfrac{22}{17} - \dfrac{3}{17}i$

554

135.

$$\frac{1+i}{1+2i}+\frac{1-i}{1-2i}$$

$$=\frac{(1+i)(1-2i)}{(1+2i)(1-2i)}+\frac{(1-i)(1+2i)}{(1+2i)(1-2i)}$$

$$=\frac{(1+i)(1-2i)+(1-i)(1+2i)}{(1+2i)(1-2i)}$$

$$=\frac{1-2i+i-2i^2+1+2i-i-2i^2}{1^2-(2i)^2}$$

$$=\frac{2-4i^2}{1-4i^2}=\frac{2-4(-1)}{1-4(-1)}$$

$$=\frac{2+4}{1+4}=\frac{6}{5}=\frac{6}{5}+0i$$

137.

$$\frac{\dfrac{x}{y^2}+\dfrac{1}{y}}{\dfrac{y}{x^2}+\dfrac{1}{x}}=\frac{\dfrac{x}{y^2}+\dfrac{1}{y}}{\dfrac{y}{x^2}+\dfrac{1}{x}}\cdot\frac{x^2y^2}{x^2y^2}$$

$$=\frac{\dfrac{x}{y^2}\cdot x^2 y^2+\dfrac{1}{y}\cdot x^2 y^2}{\dfrac{y}{x^2}\cdot x^2 y^2+\dfrac{1}{x}\cdot x^2 y^2}$$

$$=\frac{x^3+x^2 y}{y^3+xy^2}=\frac{x^2(x+y)}{y^2(y+x)}$$

$$=\frac{x^2}{y^2}$$

138.

$$\frac{1}{x}+\frac{1}{y}=\frac{1}{z}$$

$$\frac{1}{x}\cdot xyz+\frac{1}{y}\cdot xyz=\frac{1}{z}\cdot xyz$$

$$yz+xz=xy$$

$$yz=xy-xz$$

$$yz=x(y-z)$$

$$x=\frac{yz}{y-z}$$

139.
$$(g-f)(x)=g(x)-f(x)$$
$$=(x-6)-(2x^2-x)$$
$$=x-6-2x^2+x$$
$$=-2x^2+2x-6$$
$$(g-f)(3)=-2(3)^2+2(3)-6$$
$$=-2(9)+2(3)-6$$
$$=-18+6-6$$
$$=-18$$

Chapter 10 Review Exercises

1. $\sqrt{81}=9$ because $9^2=81$

2. $-\sqrt{\dfrac{1}{100}}=-\dfrac{1}{10}$ because $\left(\dfrac{1}{10}\right)^2=\dfrac{1}{100}$

3. $\sqrt[3]{-27}=-3$ because $(-3)^3=-27$

4. $\sqrt[4]{-16}$
Not a real number
The index is even and the radicand is
negative.

5. $\sqrt[5]{-32}=-2$ because $(-2)^5=-32$

6. $f(15)=\sqrt{2(15)-5}=\sqrt{30-5}$
$$=\sqrt{25}=5$$
$f(4)=\sqrt{2(4)-5}=\sqrt{8-5}=\sqrt{3}$
$f\left(\dfrac{5}{2}\right)=\sqrt{2\left(\dfrac{5}{2}\right)-5}=\sqrt{5-5}$
$$=\sqrt{0}=0$$
$f(1)=\sqrt{2(1)-5}=\sqrt{2-5}=\sqrt{-3}$
Not a real number

7.
$$g(4) = \sqrt[3]{4(4)-8} = \sqrt[3]{16-8} = \sqrt[3]{8} = 2$$
$$g(0) = \sqrt[3]{4(0)-8} = \sqrt[3]{-8} = -2$$
$$g(-14) = \sqrt[3]{4(-14)-8} = \sqrt[3]{-56-8}$$
$$= \sqrt[3]{-64} = -4$$

8. To find the domain, set the radicand greater than or equal to zero and solve the resulting inequality.
$$x - 2 \geq 0$$
$$x \geq 2$$
The domain of f is $\{x | x \geq 2\}$ or $[2, \infty)$.

9. To find the domain, set the radicand greater than or equal to zero and solve the resulting inequality.
$$100 - 4x \geq 0$$
$$-4x \geq -100$$
$$\frac{-4x}{-4} \leq \frac{-100}{-4}$$
$$x \leq 25$$
The domain of g is $\{x | x \leq 25\}$ or $(-\infty, 25]$.

10. $\sqrt{25x^2} = 5|x|$

11. $\sqrt{(x+14)^2} = |x+14|$

12. $\sqrt{x^2 - 8x + 16} = \sqrt{(x-4)^2} = |x-4|$

13. $\sqrt[3]{64x^3} = 4x$

14. $\sqrt[4]{16x^4} = 2|x|$

15. $\sqrt[5]{-32(x+7)^5} = -2(x+7)$

16. $(5xy)^{\frac{1}{3}} = \sqrt[3]{5xy}$

17. $16^{\frac{3}{2}} = \left(\sqrt{16}\right)^3 = (4)^3 = 64$

18. $32^{\frac{4}{5}} = \left(\sqrt[5]{32}\right)^4 = (2)^4 = 16$

19. $\sqrt{7x} = (7x)^{\frac{1}{2}}$

20. $\left(\sqrt[3]{19xy}\right)^5 = (19xy)^{\frac{5}{3}}$

21. $8^{-\frac{2}{3}} = \frac{1}{8^{\frac{2}{3}}} = \frac{1}{\left(\sqrt[3]{8}\right)^2} = \frac{1}{(2)^2} = \frac{1}{4}$

22.
$$3x(ab)^{-\frac{4}{5}} = \frac{3x}{(ab)^{\frac{4}{5}}}$$
$$= \frac{3x}{\left(\sqrt[5]{ab}\right)^4} \text{ or } \frac{3x}{\sqrt[5]{(ab)^4}}$$

23. $x^{\frac{1}{3}} \cdot x^{\frac{1}{4}} = x^{\frac{1}{3} + \frac{1}{4}} = x^{\frac{4}{12} + \frac{3}{12}} = x^{\frac{7}{12}}$

24. $\dfrac{5^{\frac{1}{2}}}{5^{\frac{1}{3}}} = 5^{\frac{1}{2} - \frac{1}{3}} = 5^{\frac{3}{6} - \frac{2}{6}} = 5^{\frac{1}{6}}$

25. $\left(8x^6 y^3\right)^{\frac{1}{3}} = 8^{\frac{1}{3}} x^{6 \cdot \frac{1}{3}} y^{3 \cdot \frac{1}{3}} = 2x^2 y$

26. $\left(x^{-\frac{2}{3}} y^{\frac{1}{4}}\right)^{\frac{1}{2}} = x^{-\frac{2}{3} \cdot \frac{1}{2}} y^{\frac{1}{4} \cdot \frac{1}{2}} = x^{-\frac{1}{3}} y^{\frac{1}{8}} = \dfrac{y^{\frac{1}{8}}}{x^{\frac{1}{3}}}$

27.
$$\sqrt[3]{x^9 y^{12}} = \left(x^9 y^{12}\right)^{\frac{1}{3}} = x^{9 \cdot \frac{1}{3}} y^{12 \cdot \frac{1}{3}} = x^3 y^4$$

28.
$$\sqrt[9]{x^3 y^9} = \left(x^3 y^9\right)^{\frac{1}{9}} = x^{3 \cdot \frac{1}{9}} y^{9 \cdot \frac{1}{9}}$$
$$= x^{\frac{1}{3}} y = y\sqrt[3]{x}$$

29.
$$\sqrt{x} \cdot \sqrt[3]{x} = x^{\frac{1}{2}} x^{\frac{1}{3}} = x^{\frac{1}{2}+\frac{1}{3}} = x^{\frac{3}{6}+\frac{2}{6}}$$
$$= x^{\frac{5}{6}} = \sqrt[6]{x^5}$$

30.
$$\frac{\sqrt[3]{x^2}}{\sqrt[4]{x^2}} = \frac{x^{\frac{2}{3}}}{x^{\frac{2}{4}}} = x^{\frac{2}{3}-\frac{1}{2}} = x^{\frac{4}{6}-\frac{3}{6}} = x^{\frac{1}{6}} = \sqrt[6]{x}$$

31.
$$\sqrt[5]{\sqrt[3]{x}} = \sqrt[5]{x^{\frac{1}{3}}} = \left(x^{\frac{1}{3}}\right)^{\frac{1}{5}} = x^{\frac{1}{3} \cdot \frac{1}{5}}$$
$$= x^{\frac{1}{15}} = \sqrt[15]{x}$$

32. Since 2012 is 27 years after 1985, find $f(27)$.
$$f(27) = 350(27)^{\frac{2}{3}} = 350\left(\sqrt[3]{27}\right)^2$$
$$= 350(3)^2 = 350(9) = 3150$$
Expenditures will be $3150 million or $3,150,000,000 in the year 2012.

33.
$$\sqrt{3x} \cdot \sqrt{7y} = \sqrt{21xy}$$

34.
$$\sqrt[5]{7x^2} \cdot \sqrt[5]{11x} = \sqrt[5]{77x^3}$$

35.
$$\sqrt[6]{x-5} \cdot \sqrt[6]{(x-5)^4} = \sqrt[6]{(x-5)^5}$$

36.
$$f(x) = \sqrt{7x^2 - 14x + 7}$$
$$= \sqrt{7\left(x^2 - 2x + 1\right)}$$
$$= \sqrt{7(x-1)^2} = \sqrt{7}\,|x-1|$$

37.
$$\sqrt{20x^3} = \sqrt{4 \cdot 5 \cdot x^2 \cdot x} = \sqrt{4x^2 \cdot 5x}$$
$$= 2x\sqrt{5x}$$

38.
$$\sqrt[3]{54x^8 y^6} = \sqrt[3]{27 \cdot 2 \cdot x^6 \cdot x^2 y^6}$$
$$= \sqrt[3]{27x^6 y^6 \cdot 2x^2}$$
$$= 3x^2 y^2 \sqrt[3]{2x^2}$$

39.
$$\sqrt[4]{32x^3 y^{11} z^5} = \sqrt[4]{16 \cdot 2 \cdot x^3 y^8 \cdot y^3 \cdot z^5 \cdot z}$$
$$= \sqrt[4]{16 y^8 z^4 \cdot 2x^3 y^3 z}$$
$$= 2y^2 z \sqrt[4]{2x^3 y^3 z}$$

40.
$$\sqrt{6x^3} \cdot \sqrt{4x^2} = \sqrt{24x^5} = \sqrt{4 \cdot 6 \cdot x^4 \cdot x}$$
$$= \sqrt{4x^4 \cdot 6x} = 2x^2 \sqrt{6x}$$

41.
$$\sqrt[3]{4x^2 y} \cdot \sqrt[3]{4xy^4} = \sqrt[3]{16x^3 y^5}$$
$$= \sqrt[3]{8 \cdot 2 \cdot x^3 \cdot y^3 \cdot y^2}$$
$$= \sqrt[3]{8x^3 y^3 \cdot 2y^2}$$
$$= 2xy\sqrt[3]{2y^2}$$

42.
$$\sqrt[5]{2x^4 y^3 z^4} \cdot \sqrt[5]{8xy^6 z^7}$$
$$= \sqrt[5]{16x^5 y^9 z^{11}}$$
$$= \sqrt[5]{16 \cdot x^5 \cdot y^5 \cdot y^4 \cdot z^{10} \cdot z}$$
$$= \sqrt[5]{x^5 y^5 z^{10} \cdot 16 y^4 z}$$
$$= xyz^2 \sqrt[5]{16 y^4 z}$$

43. $\sqrt{x+1} \cdot \sqrt{x-1} = \sqrt{(x+1)(x-1)}$

$$= \sqrt{x^2 - 1}$$

44. $6\sqrt[3]{3} + 2\sqrt[3]{3} = (6+2)\sqrt[3]{3} = 8\sqrt[3]{3}$

45. $5\sqrt{18} - 3\sqrt{8} = 5\sqrt{9 \cdot 2} - 3\sqrt{4 \cdot 2}$

$$= 5 \cdot 3\sqrt{2} - 3 \cdot 2\sqrt{2}$$
$$= 15\sqrt{2} - 6\sqrt{2}$$
$$= (15 - 6)\sqrt{2} = 9\sqrt{2}$$

46. $\sqrt[3]{27x^4} + \sqrt[3]{xy^6}$

$$= \sqrt[3]{27x^3 x} + \sqrt[3]{xy^6}$$
$$= 3x\sqrt[3]{x} + y^2 \sqrt[3]{x}$$
$$= (3x + y^2)\sqrt[3]{x}$$

47. $2\sqrt[3]{6} - 5\sqrt[3]{48} = 2\sqrt[3]{6} - 5\sqrt[3]{8 \cdot 6}$

$$= 2\sqrt[3]{6} - 5 \cdot 2\sqrt[3]{6}$$
$$= 2\sqrt[3]{6} - 10\sqrt[3]{6}$$
$$= (2 - 10)\sqrt[3]{6} = -8\sqrt[3]{6}$$

48. $\sqrt[3]{\dfrac{16}{125}} = \sqrt[3]{\dfrac{8 \cdot 2}{125}} = \dfrac{2}{5}\sqrt[3]{2}$

49. $\sqrt{\dfrac{x^3}{100y^4}} = \sqrt{\dfrac{x^2 \cdot x}{100y^4}}$

$$= \dfrac{x}{10y^2}\sqrt{x} \text{ or } \dfrac{x\sqrt{x}}{10y^2}$$

50. $\sqrt[4]{\dfrac{3y^5}{16x^{20}}} = \sqrt[4]{\dfrac{y^4 \cdot 3y}{16x^{20}}}$

$$= \dfrac{y}{2x^5}\sqrt[4]{3y} \text{ or } \dfrac{y\sqrt[4]{3y}}{2x^5}$$

51. $\dfrac{\sqrt{48}}{\sqrt{2}} = \sqrt{\dfrac{48}{2}} = \sqrt{24} = \sqrt{4 \cdot 6} = 2\sqrt{6}$

52. $\dfrac{\sqrt[3]{32}}{\sqrt[3]{2}} = \sqrt[3]{\dfrac{32}{2}} = \sqrt[3]{16} = \sqrt[3]{8 \cdot 2} = 2\sqrt[3]{2}$

53. $\dfrac{\sqrt[4]{64x^7}}{\sqrt[4]{2x^2}} = \sqrt[4]{\dfrac{64x^7}{2x^2}} = \sqrt[4]{32x^5}$

$$= \sqrt[4]{16 \cdot 2 \cdot x^4 \cdot x}$$
$$= \sqrt[4]{16x^4 \cdot 2x} = 2x\sqrt[4]{2x}$$

54. $\dfrac{\sqrt{200x^3 y^2}}{\sqrt{2x^{-2}y}} = \sqrt{\dfrac{200x^3 y^2}{2x^{-2}y}} = \sqrt{100x^5 y}$

$$= \sqrt{100x^4 xy} = 10x^2 \sqrt{xy}$$

55. $\sqrt{3}\left(2\sqrt{6} + 4\sqrt{15}\right) = 2\sqrt{18} + 4\sqrt{45}$

$$= 2\sqrt{9 \cdot 2} + 4\sqrt{9 \cdot 5}$$
$$= 2 \cdot 3\sqrt{2} + 4 \cdot 3\sqrt{5}$$
$$= 6\sqrt{2} + 12\sqrt{5}$$

56. $\sqrt[3]{5}\left(\sqrt[3]{50} - \sqrt[3]{2}\right) = \sqrt[3]{250} - \sqrt[3]{10}$

$$= \sqrt[3]{125 \cdot 2} - \sqrt[3]{10}$$
$$= 5\sqrt[3]{2} - \sqrt[3]{10}$$

57. $\left(\sqrt{7} - 3\sqrt{5}\right)\left(\sqrt{7} + 6\sqrt{5}\right)$

$$= 7 + 6\sqrt{35} - 3\sqrt{35} - 18 \cdot 5$$
$$= 7 + 3\sqrt{35} - 90$$
$$= 3\sqrt{35} - 83 \text{ or } -83 + 3\sqrt{35}$$

58. $\left(\sqrt{x} - \sqrt{11}\right)\left(\sqrt{y} - \sqrt{11}\right)$

$$= \sqrt{xy} - \sqrt{11x} - \sqrt{11y} + 11$$

59.
$$\left(\sqrt{5}+\sqrt{8}\right)^2 = 5 + 2\cdot\sqrt{5}\cdot\sqrt{8} + 8$$
$$= 13 + 2\sqrt{40}$$
$$= 13 + 2\sqrt{4\cdot 10}$$
$$= 13 + 2\cdot 2\sqrt{10}$$
$$= 13 + 4\sqrt{10}$$

60.
$$\left(2\sqrt{3}-\sqrt{10}\right)^2$$
$$= 4\cdot 3 - 2\cdot 2\sqrt{3}\cdot\sqrt{10} + 10$$
$$= 12 - 4\sqrt{30} + 10 = 22 - 4\sqrt{30}$$

61.
$$\left(\sqrt{7}+\sqrt{13}\right)\left(\sqrt{7}-\sqrt{13}\right)$$
$$= \left(\sqrt{7}\right)^2 - \left(\sqrt{13}\right)^2 = 7 - 13 = -6$$

62.
$$\left(7-3\sqrt{5}\right)\left(7+3\sqrt{5}\right) = 7^2 - \left(3\sqrt{5}\right)^2$$
$$= 49 - 9\cdot 5$$
$$= 49 - 45 = 4$$

63.
$$\frac{4}{\sqrt{6}} = \frac{4}{\sqrt{6}}\cdot\frac{\sqrt{6}}{\sqrt{6}} = \frac{4\sqrt{6}}{6} = \frac{2\sqrt{6}}{3}$$

64.
$$\sqrt{\frac{2}{7}} = \frac{\sqrt{2}}{\sqrt{7}} = \frac{\sqrt{2}}{\sqrt{7}}\cdot\frac{\sqrt{7}}{\sqrt{7}} = \frac{\sqrt{14}}{7}$$

65.
$$\frac{12}{\sqrt[3]{9}} = \frac{12}{\sqrt[3]{3^2}}\cdot\frac{\sqrt[3]{3}}{\sqrt[3]{3}} = \frac{12\sqrt[3]{3}}{\sqrt[3]{3^3}}$$
$$= \frac{12\sqrt[3]{3}}{3} = 4\sqrt[3]{3}$$

66.
$$\sqrt{\frac{2x}{5y}} = \frac{\sqrt{2x}}{\sqrt{5y}}\cdot\frac{\sqrt{5y}}{\sqrt{5y}} = \frac{\sqrt{10xy}}{\sqrt{5^2 y^2}} = \frac{\sqrt{10xy}}{5y}$$

67.
$$\frac{14}{\sqrt[3]{2x^2}} = \frac{14}{\sqrt[3]{2x^2}}\cdot\frac{\sqrt[3]{2^2 x}}{\sqrt[3]{2^2 x}} = \frac{14\sqrt[3]{2^2 x}}{\sqrt[3]{2^3 x^3}}$$
$$= \frac{14\sqrt[3]{4x}}{2x} = \frac{7\sqrt[3]{4x}}{x}$$

68.
$$\sqrt[4]{\frac{7}{3x}} = \frac{\sqrt[4]{7}}{\sqrt[4]{3x}} = \frac{\sqrt[4]{7}}{\sqrt[4]{3x}}\cdot\frac{\sqrt[4]{3^3 x^3}}{\sqrt[4]{3^3 x^3}}$$
$$= \frac{\sqrt[4]{7\cdot 3^3 x^3}}{\sqrt[4]{3^4 x^4}} = \frac{\sqrt[4]{7\cdot 27x^3}}{3x}$$
$$= \frac{\sqrt[4]{189x^3}}{3x}$$

69.
$$\frac{5}{\sqrt[5]{32x^4 y}} = \frac{5}{\sqrt[5]{2^5 x^4 y}}\cdot\frac{\sqrt[5]{xy^4}}{\sqrt[5]{xy^4}}$$
$$= \frac{5\sqrt[5]{xy^4}}{\sqrt[5]{2^5 x^5 y^5}} = \frac{5\sqrt[5]{xy^4}}{2xy}$$

70.
$$\frac{6}{\sqrt{3}-1} = \frac{6}{\sqrt{3}-1}\cdot\frac{\sqrt{3}+1}{\sqrt{3}+1}$$
$$= \frac{6\left(\sqrt{3}+1\right)}{\left(\sqrt{3}\right)^2 - 1^2} = \frac{6\left(\sqrt{3}+1\right)}{3-1}$$
$$= \frac{6\left(\sqrt{3}+1\right)}{2} = 3\left(\sqrt{3}+1\right)$$
$$= 3\sqrt{3}+3$$

71.
$$\frac{\sqrt{7}}{\sqrt{5}+\sqrt{3}} = \frac{\sqrt{7}}{\sqrt{5}+\sqrt{3}}\cdot\frac{\sqrt{5}-\sqrt{3}}{\sqrt{5}-\sqrt{3}}$$
$$= \frac{\sqrt{35}-\sqrt{21}}{\left(\sqrt{5}\right)^2 - \left(\sqrt{3}\right)^2}$$
$$= \frac{\sqrt{35}-\sqrt{21}}{5-3} = \frac{\sqrt{35}-\sqrt{21}}{2}$$

72.

$$\frac{10}{2\sqrt{5}-3\sqrt{2}} = \frac{10}{2\sqrt{5}-3\sqrt{2}} \cdot \frac{2\sqrt{5}+3\sqrt{2}}{2\sqrt{5}+3\sqrt{2}}$$

$$= \frac{10\left(2\sqrt{5}+3\sqrt{2}\right)}{\left(2\sqrt{5}\right)^2 - \left(3\sqrt{2}\right)^2}$$

$$= \frac{10\left(2\sqrt{5}+3\sqrt{2}\right)}{4\cdot 5 - 9\cdot 2}$$

$$= \frac{10\left(2\sqrt{5}+3\sqrt{2}\right)}{20-18}$$

$$= \frac{10\left(2\sqrt{5}+3\sqrt{2}\right)}{2}$$

$$= 5\left(2\sqrt{5}+3\sqrt{2}\right)$$

$$= 10\sqrt{5}+15\sqrt{2}$$

73.

$$\frac{\sqrt{x}+5}{\sqrt{x}-3} = \frac{\sqrt{x}+5}{\sqrt{x}-3} \cdot \frac{\sqrt{x}+3}{\sqrt{x}+3}$$

$$= \frac{x+3\sqrt{x}+5\sqrt{x}+15}{\left(\sqrt{x}\right)^2 - 3^2}$$

$$= \frac{x+8\sqrt{x}+15}{x-9}$$

74.

$$\frac{\sqrt{7}+\sqrt{3}}{\sqrt{7}-\sqrt{3}} = \frac{\sqrt{7}+\sqrt{3}}{\sqrt{7}-\sqrt{3}} \cdot \frac{\sqrt{7}+\sqrt{3}}{\sqrt{7}+\sqrt{3}}$$

$$= \frac{7+2\cdot\sqrt{7}\cdot\sqrt{3}+3}{\left(\sqrt{7}\right)^2 - \left(\sqrt{3}\right)^2}$$

$$= \frac{10+2\sqrt{21}}{7-3}$$

$$= \frac{10+2\sqrt{21}}{4}$$

$$= \frac{2\left(5+\sqrt{21}\right)}{4} = \frac{5+\sqrt{21}}{2}$$

75.

$$\frac{2\sqrt{3}+\sqrt{6}}{2\sqrt{6}+\sqrt{3}} = \frac{2\sqrt{3}+\sqrt{6}}{2\sqrt{6}+\sqrt{3}} \cdot \frac{2\sqrt{6}-\sqrt{3}}{2\sqrt{6}-\sqrt{3}}$$

$$= \frac{4\sqrt{18}-2\cdot 3+2\cdot 6-\sqrt{18}}{\left(2\sqrt{6}\right)^2 - \left(\sqrt{3}\right)^2}$$

$$= \frac{3\sqrt{18}-6+12}{4\cdot 6 - 3}$$

$$= \frac{3\sqrt{9\cdot 2}+6}{24-3} = \frac{3\cdot 3\sqrt{2}+6}{21}$$

$$= \frac{9\sqrt{2}+6}{21} = \frac{3\left(3\sqrt{2}+2\right)}{21}$$

$$= \frac{3\sqrt{2}+2}{7}$$

76.

$$\sqrt{\frac{2}{7}} = \frac{\sqrt{2}}{\sqrt{7}} = \frac{\sqrt{2}}{\sqrt{7}} \cdot \frac{\sqrt{2}}{\sqrt{2}} = \frac{2}{\sqrt{14}}$$

77.

$$\frac{\sqrt[3]{3x}}{\sqrt[3]{y}} = \frac{\sqrt[3]{3x}}{\sqrt[3]{y}} \cdot \frac{\sqrt[3]{3^2 x^2}}{\sqrt[3]{3^2 x^2}}$$

$$= \frac{\sqrt[3]{3^3 x^3}}{\sqrt[3]{3^2 x^2 y}} = \frac{3x}{\sqrt[3]{9x^2 y}}$$

78.

$$\frac{\sqrt{7}}{\sqrt{5}+\sqrt{3}} = \frac{\sqrt{7}}{\sqrt{5}+\sqrt{3}} \cdot \frac{\sqrt{7}}{\sqrt{7}} = \frac{7}{\sqrt{35}+\sqrt{21}}$$

79.

$$\frac{\sqrt{7}+\sqrt{3}}{\sqrt{7}-\sqrt{3}} = \frac{\sqrt{7}+\sqrt{3}}{\sqrt{7}-\sqrt{3}} \cdot \frac{\sqrt{7}-\sqrt{3}}{\sqrt{7}-\sqrt{3}}$$

$$= \frac{\left(\sqrt{7}\right)^2 - \left(\sqrt{3}\right)^2}{7-2\sqrt{7}\sqrt{3}+3}$$

$$= \frac{7-3}{10-2\sqrt{21}} = \frac{4}{10-2\sqrt{21}}$$

$$= \frac{4}{2\left(5-\sqrt{21}\right)} = \frac{2}{5-\sqrt{21}}$$

80.

$$\sqrt{2x+4} = 6$$

$$\left(\sqrt{2x+4}\right)^2 = 6^2$$

$$2x+4 = 36$$

$$2x = 32$$

$$x = 16$$

The solution checks. The solution set is $\{16\}$.

81. $\sqrt{x-5} + 9 = 4$

$$\sqrt{x-5} = -5$$

The square root of a number is always positive. The solution set is $\varnothing$ or $\{\ \ \}$.

82. $\sqrt{2x-3} + x = 3$

$$\sqrt{2x-3} = 3 - x$$

$$\left(\sqrt{2x-3}\right)^2 = (3-x)^2$$

$$2x-3 = 9 - 6x + x^2$$

$$0 = 12 - 8x + x^2$$

$$0 = x^2 - 8x + 12$$

$$0 = (x-6)(x-2)$$

Apply the zero product principle.

$x-6=0 \qquad x-2=0$

$\qquad x = 6 \qquad\qquad x = 2$

6 is an extraneous solution. The solution set is $\{2\}$.

83. $\sqrt{x-4} + \sqrt{x+1} = 5$

$$\sqrt{x-4} = 5 - \sqrt{x+1}$$

$$\left(\sqrt{x-4}\right)^2 = \left(5 - \sqrt{x+1}\right)^2$$

$$x-4 = 25 - 10\sqrt{x+1} + x + 1$$

$$-30 = -10\sqrt{x+1}$$

$$\frac{-30}{-10} = \frac{-10\sqrt{x+1}}{-10}$$

$$3 = \sqrt{x+1}$$

$$3^2 = \left(\sqrt{x+1}\right)^2$$

$$9 = x + 1$$

$$8 = x$$

The solution checks. The solution set is $\{8\}$.

84.

$$\left(x^2 + 6x\right)^{\frac{1}{3}} + 2 = 0$$

$$\left(x^2 + 6x\right)^{\frac{1}{3}} = -2$$

$$\sqrt[3]{x^2 + 6x} = -2$$

$$\left(\sqrt[3]{x^2 + 6x}\right)^3 = (-2)^3$$

$$x^2 + 6x = -8$$

$$x^2 + 6x + 8 = 0$$

$$(x+4)(x+2) = 0$$

Apply the zero product principle.

$x+4=0 \qquad x+2=0$

$\quad x = -4 \qquad\qquad x = -2$

Both check. The solution set is $\{-4, -2\}$.

85.

$$4 = \sqrt{\frac{x}{16}}$$

$$4^2 = \left(\sqrt{\frac{x}{16}}\right)^2$$

$$16 = \frac{x}{16}$$

$$256 = x$$

The hammer was dropped from a height of 256 feet.

561

86.
$$20,000 = 5000\sqrt{100 - x}$$
$$\frac{20,000}{5000} = \frac{5000\sqrt{100 - x}}{5000}$$
$$4 = \sqrt{100 - x}$$
$$4^2 = \left(\sqrt{100 - x}\right)^2$$
$$16 = 100 - x$$
$$-84 = -x$$
$$84 = x$$
20,000 people in the group will survive to 84 years old.

87. $\sqrt{-81} = \sqrt{81 \cdot -1} = \sqrt{81}\sqrt{-1} = 9i$

88.
$$\sqrt{-63} = \sqrt{9 \cdot 7 \cdot -1}$$
$$= \sqrt{9}\sqrt{7}\sqrt{-1} = 3\sqrt{7}i$$

89.
$$-\sqrt{-8} = -\sqrt{4 \cdot 2 \cdot -1}$$
$$= -\sqrt{4}\sqrt{2}\sqrt{-1} = -2\sqrt{2}i$$

90.
$$(7 + 12i) + (5 - 10i)$$
$$= 7 + 12i + 5 - 10i = 12 + 2i$$

91.
$$(8 - 3i) - (17 - 7i) = 8 - 3i - 17 + 7i$$
$$= -9 + 4i$$

92.
$$4i(3i - 2) = 4i \cdot 3i - 4i \cdot 2$$
$$= 12i^2 - 8i$$
$$= 12(-1) - 8i$$
$$= -12 - 8i$$

93.
$$(7 - 5i)(2 + 3i) = 14 + 21i - 10i - 15i^2$$
$$= 14 + 11i - 15(-1)$$
$$= 14 + 11i + 15$$
$$= 29 + 11i$$

94.
$$(3 - 4i)^2 = 3^2 - 2 \cdot 3 \cdot 4i + (4i)^2$$
$$= 9 - 24i + 16i^2$$
$$= 9 - 24i + 16(-1)$$
$$= 9 - 24i - 16$$
$$= -7 - 24i$$

95.
$$(7 + 8i)(7 - 8i) = 7^2 - (8i)^2$$
$$= 49 - 64i^2$$
$$= 49 - 64(-1)$$
$$= 49 + 64$$
$$= 113 = 113 + 0i$$

96.
$$\sqrt{-8} \cdot \sqrt{-3} = \sqrt{4 \cdot 2 \cdot -1} \cdot \sqrt{3 \cdot -1}$$
$$= 2\sqrt{2}i \cdot \sqrt{3}i = 2\sqrt{6}i^2$$
$$= 2\sqrt{6}(-1) = -2\sqrt{6}$$
$$= -2\sqrt{6} + 0i$$

97.
$$\frac{6}{5 + i} = \frac{6}{5 + i} \cdot \frac{5 - i}{5 - i} = \frac{30 - 6i}{25 - i^2}$$
$$= \frac{30 - 6i}{25 - (-1)} = \frac{30 - 6i}{25 + 1}$$
$$= \frac{30 - 6i}{26} = \frac{30}{26} - \frac{6}{26}i$$
$$= \frac{15}{13} - \frac{3}{13}i$$

98.
$$\frac{3 + 4i}{4 - 2i} = \frac{3 + 4i}{4 - 2i} \cdot \frac{4 + 2i}{4 + 2i}$$
$$= \frac{12 + 6i + 16i + 8i^2}{16 - 4i^2}$$
$$= \frac{12 + 22i + 8(-1)}{16 - 4(-1)}$$
$$= \frac{12 + 22i - 8}{16 + 4} = \frac{4 + 22i}{20}$$
$$= \frac{4}{20} + \frac{22}{20}i = \frac{1}{5} + \frac{11}{10}i$$

99.
$$\frac{5+i}{3i} = \frac{5+i}{3i} \cdot \frac{i}{i} = \frac{5i+i^2}{3i^2}$$
$$= \frac{5i+(-1)}{3(-1)} = \frac{5i-1}{-3}$$
$$= \frac{-1}{-3} + \frac{5}{-3}i = \frac{1}{3} - \frac{5}{3}i$$

100. $\quad i^{16} = \left(i^2\right)^8 = (-1)^8 = 1$

101. $\quad i^{23} = i^{22} \cdot i = \left(i^2\right)^{11} i = (-1)^{11} i$
$$= (-1)i = -i$$

Chapter 10 Test

1. a.
$$f(-14) = \sqrt{8-2(-14)}$$
$$= \sqrt{8+28} = \sqrt{36} = 6$$

b. To find the domain, set the radicand greater than or equal to zero and solve the resulting inequality.
$$8 - 2x \geq 0$$
$$-2x \geq -8$$
$$x \leq 4$$
The domain of f is $\{x | x \leq 4\}$ or $(-\infty, 4]$.

2.
$$27^{-\frac{4}{3}} = \frac{1}{27^{\frac{4}{3}}} = \frac{1}{\left(\sqrt[3]{27}\right)^4} = \frac{1}{(3)^4} = \frac{1}{81}$$

3.
$$\left(25x^{-\frac{1}{2}}y^{\frac{1}{4}}\right)^{\frac{1}{2}} = 25^{\frac{1}{2}} x^{-\frac{1}{4}} y^{\frac{1}{8}} = 5x^{-\frac{1}{4}} y^{\frac{1}{8}}$$
$$= \frac{5y^{\frac{1}{8}}}{x^{\frac{1}{4}}} = \frac{5\sqrt[8]{y}}{\sqrt[4]{x}}$$

4.
$$\sqrt[8]{x^4} = \left(x^4\right)^{\frac{1}{8}} = x^{4 \cdot \frac{1}{8}} = x^{\frac{1}{2}} = \sqrt{x}$$

5.
$$\sqrt[4]{x} \cdot \sqrt[5]{x} = x^{\frac{1}{4}} \cdot x^{\frac{1}{5}} = x^{\frac{1}{4}+\frac{1}{5}} = x^{\frac{5}{20}+\frac{4}{20}}$$
$$= x^{\frac{9}{20}} = \sqrt[20]{x^9}$$

6.
$$\sqrt{75x^2} = \sqrt{25 \cdot 3x^2} = 5|x|\sqrt{3}$$

7.
$$\sqrt{x^2-10x+25} = \sqrt{(x-5)^2} = |x-5|$$

8.
$$\sqrt[3]{16x^4y^8} = \sqrt[3]{8 \cdot 2 \cdot x^3 \cdot x \cdot y^6 \cdot y^2}$$
$$= \sqrt[3]{8x^3y^6 \cdot 2xy^2}$$
$$= 2xy^2\sqrt[3]{2xy^2}$$

9.
$$\sqrt[5]{-\frac{32}{x^{10}}} = \sqrt[5]{-\frac{2^5}{\left(x^2\right)^5}} = -\frac{2}{x^2}$$

10. $\quad \sqrt[3]{5x^2} \cdot \sqrt[3]{10y} = \sqrt[3]{50x^2y}$

11.
$$\sqrt[4]{8x^3y} \cdot \sqrt[4]{4xy^2} = \sqrt[4]{32x^4y^3}$$
$$= \sqrt[4]{16 \cdot 2 \cdot x^4 \cdot y^3}$$
$$= \sqrt[4]{16x^4 \cdot 2y^3}$$
$$= 2x\sqrt[4]{2y^3}$$

12.
$$3\sqrt{18} - 4\sqrt{32} = 3\sqrt{9 \cdot 2} - 4\sqrt{16 \cdot 2}$$
$$= 3 \cdot 3\sqrt{2} - 4 \cdot 4\sqrt{2}$$
$$= 9\sqrt{2} - 16\sqrt{2} = -7\sqrt{2}$$

13.
$$\sqrt[3]{8x^4} + \sqrt[3]{xy^6} = \sqrt[3]{8x^3 \cdot x} + \sqrt[3]{xy^6}$$
$$= 2x\sqrt[3]{x} + y^2\sqrt[3]{x}$$
$$= \left(2x + y^2\right)\sqrt[3]{x}$$

14.

$$\frac{\sqrt[3]{16x^8}}{\sqrt[3]{2x^4}} = \sqrt[3]{\frac{16x^8}{2x^4}} = \sqrt[3]{8x^4}$$

$$= \sqrt[3]{8x^3 \cdot x} = 2x\sqrt[3]{x}$$

15.

$$\sqrt{3}\left(4\sqrt{6} - \sqrt{5}\right) = \sqrt{3} \cdot 4\sqrt{6} - \sqrt{3} \cdot \sqrt{5}$$

$$= 4\sqrt{18} - \sqrt{15}$$

$$= 4\sqrt{9 \cdot 2} - \sqrt{15}$$

$$= 4 \cdot 3\sqrt{2} - \sqrt{15}$$

$$= 12\sqrt{2} - \sqrt{15}$$

16.

$$\left(5\sqrt{6} - 2\sqrt{2}\right)\left(\sqrt{6} + \sqrt{2}\right)$$

$$= 5 \cdot 6 + 5\sqrt{12} - 2\sqrt{12} - 2 \cdot 2$$

$$= 30 + 3\sqrt{12} - 4 = 26 + 3\sqrt{4 \cdot 3}$$

$$= 26 + 3 \cdot 2\sqrt{3} = 26 + 6\sqrt{3}$$

17.

$$\left(7 - \sqrt{3}\right)^2 = 49 - 2 \cdot 7 \cdot \sqrt{3} + 3$$

$$= 52 - 14\sqrt{3}$$

18.

$$\sqrt{\frac{5}{x}} = \frac{\sqrt{5}}{\sqrt{x}} \cdot \frac{\sqrt{x}}{\sqrt{x}} = \frac{\sqrt{5x}}{x}$$

19.

$$\frac{5}{\sqrt[3]{5x^2}} = \frac{5}{\sqrt[3]{5x^2}} \cdot \frac{\sqrt[3]{5^2 x}}{\sqrt[3]{5^2 x}} = \frac{5\sqrt[3]{5^2 x}}{\sqrt[3]{5^3 x^3}}$$

$$= \frac{5\sqrt[3]{25x}}{5x} = \frac{\sqrt[3]{25x}}{x}$$

20.

$$\frac{\sqrt{2} - \sqrt{3}}{\sqrt{2} + \sqrt{3}} = \frac{\sqrt{2} - \sqrt{3}}{\sqrt{2} + \sqrt{3}} \cdot \frac{\sqrt{2} - \sqrt{3}}{\sqrt{2} - \sqrt{3}}$$

$$= \frac{2 - 2\sqrt{2}\sqrt{3} + 3}{2 - 3}$$

$$= \frac{5 - 2\sqrt{6}}{-1} = -5 + 2\sqrt{6}$$

21.

$$3 + \sqrt{2x - 3} = x$$

$$\sqrt{2x - 3} = x - 3$$

$$\left(\sqrt{2x - 3}\right)^2 = (x - 3)^2$$

$$2x - 3 = x^2 - 6x + 9$$

$$0 = x^2 - 8x + 12$$

$$0 = (x - 6)(x - 2)$$

Apply the zero product rule.

$$x - 6 = 0 \qquad x - 2 = 0$$

$$x = 6 \qquad x = 2$$

2 is an extraneous solution. The solution set is $\{6\}$.

22.

$$\sqrt{x + 9} - \sqrt{x - 7} = 2$$

$$\sqrt{x + 9} = 2 + \sqrt{x - 7}$$

$$\left(\sqrt{x + 9}\right)^2 = \left(2 + \sqrt{x - 7}\right)^2$$

$$x + 9 = 4 + 2 \cdot 2 \cdot \sqrt{x - 7} + x - 7$$

$$x + 9 = 4\sqrt{x - 7} + x - 3$$

$$12 = 4\sqrt{x - 7}$$

$$3 = \sqrt{x - 7}$$

$$3^2 = \left(\sqrt{x - 7}\right)^2$$

$$9 = x - 7$$

$$16 = x$$

The solution set is $\{16\}$.

23.

$$(11x + 6)^{\frac{1}{3}} + 3 = 0$$

$$(11x + 6)^{\frac{1}{3}} = -3$$

$$\sqrt[3]{11x + 6} = -3$$

$$\left(\sqrt[3]{11x + 6}\right)^3 = (-3)^3$$

$$11x + 6 = -27$$

$$11x = -33$$

$$x = -3$$

The solution set is $\{-3\}$.

564

24.
$$40.4 = 2.9\sqrt{x} + 20.1$$
$$20.3 = 2.9\sqrt{x}$$
$$7 = \sqrt{x}$$
$$7^2 = \left(\sqrt{x}\right)^2$$
$$49 = x$$

Boys who are 49 months of age have an average height of 40.4 inches.

25.
$$\sqrt{-75} = \sqrt{25 \cdot 3 \cdot -1}$$
$$= \sqrt{25} \cdot \sqrt{3} \cdot \sqrt{-1} = 5\sqrt{3}i$$

26.
$$\left(5 - 3i\right) - \left(6 - 9i\right) = 5 - 3i - 6 + 9i$$
$$= 5 - 6 - 3i + 9i$$
$$= -1 + 6i$$

27.
$$\left(3 - 4i\right)\left(2 + 5i\right) = 6 + 15i - 8i - 20i^2$$
$$= 6 + 7i - 20(-1)$$
$$= 6 + 7i + 20$$
$$= 26 + 7i$$

28.
$$\sqrt{-9} \cdot \sqrt{-4} = \sqrt{9 \cdot -1} \cdot \sqrt{4 \cdot -1}$$
$$= \sqrt{9} \cdot \sqrt{-1} \cdot \sqrt{4} \cdot \sqrt{-1}$$
$$= 3 \cdot i \cdot 2 \cdot i = 6i^2 = 6(-1)$$
$$= -6 \text{ or } -6 + 0i$$

29.
$$\frac{3+i}{1-2i} = \frac{3+i}{1-2i} \cdot \frac{1+2i}{1+2i} = \frac{3+6i+i+2i^2}{1-4i^2}$$
$$= \frac{3+7i+2(-1)}{1-4(-1)} = \frac{3+7i-2}{1+4}$$
$$= \frac{1+7i}{5} = \frac{1}{5} + \frac{7}{5}i$$

30.
$$i^{35} = i^{34} \cdot i = \left(i^2\right)^{17} \cdot i = (-1)^{17} \cdot i$$
$$= (-1)i = -i$$

Cumulative Review Exercises (Chapters 1-10)

1.
$$2x - y + z = -5$$
$$x - 2y - 3z = 6$$
$$x + y - 2z = 1$$

Add the first and third equations to eliminate y.
$$2x - y + z = -5$$
$$\underline{x + y - 2z = 1}$$
$$3x \qquad - z = -4$$

Multiply the third equation by 2 and add to the second equation.
$$x - 2y - 3z = 6$$
$$\underline{2x + 2y - 4z = 2}$$
$$3x \qquad - 7z = 8$$

We now have a system of two equations in two variables.
$$3x - z = -4$$
$$3x - 7z = 8$$

Multiply the first equation by -1 and add to the second equation.
$$-3x + z = 4$$
$$\underline{3x - 7z = 8}$$
$$-6z = 12$$
$$z = -2$$

Back-substitute -2 for z to find x.
$$-3x + z = 4$$
$$-3x + (-2) = 4$$
$$-3x = 6$$
$$x = -2$$

Back-substitute -2 for x and z in one of the original equations to find y.
$$2x - y + z = -5$$
$$2(-2) - y + (-2) = -5$$
$$-4 - y - 2 = -5$$
$$-y = 1$$
$$y = -1$$

The solution set is $\left\{(-2, -1, -2)\right\}$.

2.

$$3x^2 - 11x = 4$$
$$3x^2 - 11x - 4 = 0$$
$$(3x+1)(x-4) = 0$$

Apply the zero product principle.

$$3x+1 = 0 \qquad x-4 = 0$$
$$3x = -1 \qquad x = 4$$
$$x = -\frac{1}{3}$$

The solution set is $\left\{-\dfrac{1}{3}, 4\right\}$.

3.

$$2(x+4) < 5x + 3(x+2)$$
$$2x + 8 < 5x + 3x + 6$$
$$2x + 8 < 8x + 6$$
$$-6x + 8 < 6$$
$$-6x < -2$$
$$\frac{-6x}{-6} > \frac{-2}{-6}$$
$$x > \frac{1}{3}$$

The solution set is $\left\{ x \,\middle|\, x > \dfrac{1}{3} \right\}$ or $\left(\dfrac{1}{3}, \infty\right)$.

4.

$$\frac{1}{x+2} + \frac{15}{x^2-4} = \frac{5}{x-2}$$

$$\frac{1}{x+2} + \frac{15}{(x+2)(x-2)} = \frac{5}{x-2}$$

So that denominators will not equal zero, x cannot equal 2 or –2. To eliminate fractions, multiply by the LCD, $(x+2)(x-2)$.

$$(x+2)(x-2)\left(\frac{1}{x+2} + \frac{15}{(x+2)(x-2)}\right) = (x+2)(x-2)\left(\frac{5}{x-2}\right)$$

$$(x+2)(x-2)\left(\frac{1}{x+2}\right) + (x+2)(x-2)\left(\frac{15}{(x+2)(x-2)}\right) = (x+2)(5)$$

$$x - 2 + 15 = 5x + 10$$
$$x + 13 = 5x + 10$$
$$-4x + 13 = 10$$
$$-4x = -3$$
$$x = \frac{3}{4}$$

The solution set is $\left\{\dfrac{3}{4}\right\}$.

5. $\sqrt{x+2} - \sqrt{x+1} = 1$

$$\sqrt{x+2} = 1 + \sqrt{x+1}$$

$$\left(\sqrt{x+2}\right)^2 = \left(1 + \sqrt{x+1}\right)^2$$

$$x+2 = 1 + 2\sqrt{x+1} + x + 1$$

$$x+2 = 2 + 2\sqrt{x+1} + x$$

$$0^2 = \left(2\sqrt{x+1}\right)^2$$

$$0 = 4(x+1)$$

$$0 = 4x+4$$

$$-4 = 4x$$

$$-1 = x$$

The solution checks. The solution set is $\{-1\}$.

6. $x+2y < 2$

$2y - x > 4$

First consider $x+2y < 2$. Replace the inequality symbol with an equal sign and we have $x+2y = 2$. Solve for y to put the equation in slope-intercept form.

$$x+2y = 2$$

$$2y = -x+2$$

$$y = -\frac{1}{2}x+1$$

slope $= -\dfrac{1}{2}$ y–intercept $= 1$

Now, use the origin as a test point.

$$0 + 2(0) < 2$$

$$0 < 2$$

This is a true statement. This means that the point $(0,0)$ will fall in the shaded half-plane.

Next consider $2y - x > 4$. Replace the inequality symbol with an equal sign and we have $2y - x = 4$. Solve for y to put the equation in slope-intercept form.

$$2y - x = 4$$

$$2y = x+4$$

$$y = \frac{1}{2}x+2$$

slope $= \dfrac{1}{2}$ y–intercept $= 2$

Now, use the origin as a test point.

$$2(0) - 0 > 4$$

$$0 > 4$$

This is a false statement. This means that the point $(0,0)$ will not fall in the shaded half-plane.

Next, graph each of the inequalities. The solution to the system is the intersection of the shaded half-planes.

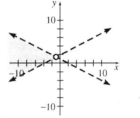

7. $\dfrac{8x^2}{3x^2-12} \div \dfrac{40}{x-2}$

$$= \frac{8x^2}{3x^2-12} \cdot \frac{x-2}{40}$$

$$= \frac{8x^2}{3(x^2-4)} \cdot \frac{x-2}{40}$$

$$= \frac{\overset{1}{\cancel{8}}x^2}{3(x+2)(\cancel{x-2})} \cdot \frac{\cancel{x-2}}{\underset{5}{\cancel{40}}}$$

$$= \frac{x^2}{3 \cdot 5(x+2)}$$

$$= \frac{x^2}{15(x+2)}$$

8.

$$\frac{x+\dfrac{1}{y}}{y+\dfrac{1}{x}} = \frac{x+\dfrac{1}{y}}{y+\dfrac{1}{x}}\cdot\frac{xy}{xy} = \frac{xy\cdot x+xy\cdot\dfrac{1}{y}}{xy\cdot y+xy\cdot\dfrac{1}{x}}$$

$$= \frac{x^2y+x}{xy^2+y} = \frac{x(xy+1)}{y(xy+1)} = \frac{x}{y}$$

9. $(2x-3)\left(4x^2-5x-2\right)$

$$= 2x\cdot 4x^2 - 2x\cdot 5x - 2x\cdot 2 - 3\cdot 4x^2$$
$$\quad +3\cdot 5x+3\cdot 2$$
$$= 8x^3 - 10x^2 - 4x - 12x^2 + 15x + 6$$
$$= 8x^3 - 22x^2 + 11x + 6$$

10. $\dfrac{7x}{x^2-2x-15} - \dfrac{2}{x-5}$

$$= \frac{7x}{(x-5)(x+3)} - \frac{2}{x-5}$$

$$= \frac{7x}{(x-5)(x+3)} - \frac{2(x+3)}{(x-5)(x+3)}$$

$$= \frac{7x-2(x+3)}{(x-5)(x+3)} = \frac{7x-2x-6}{(x-5)(x+3)}$$

$$= \frac{5x-6}{(x-5)(x+3)}$$

11. $7(8-10)^3 - 7 + 3\div(-3)$

$$= 7(-2)^3 - 7 + 3\div(-3)$$
$$= 7(-8) - 7 + 3\div(-3)$$
$$= -56 - 7 + (-1) = -64$$

12. $\sqrt{80x} - 5\sqrt{20x} + 2\sqrt{45x}$

$$= \sqrt{16\cdot 5x} - 5\sqrt{4\cdot 5x} + 2\sqrt{9\cdot 5x}$$
$$= 4\sqrt{5x} - 5\cdot 2\sqrt{5x} + 2\cdot 3\sqrt{5x}$$
$$= 4\sqrt{5x} - 10\sqrt{5x} + 6\sqrt{5x} = 0$$

13. $\dfrac{\sqrt{3}-2}{2\sqrt{3}+5} = \dfrac{\sqrt{3}-2}{2\sqrt{3}+5}\cdot\dfrac{2\sqrt{3}-5}{2\sqrt{3}-5}$

$$= \frac{2\cdot 3 - 5\sqrt{3} - 4\sqrt{3} + 10}{4\cdot 3 - 25}$$

$$= \frac{6 - 9\sqrt{3} + 10}{12 - 25}$$

$$= \frac{16 - 9\sqrt{3}}{-13}$$

$$= -\frac{16 - 9\sqrt{3}}{13}$$

14.

$$\require{enclose}\begin{array}{r}2x^2+x+5 \\ x-2\enclose{longdiv}{2x^3-3x^2+3x-4} \\ \underline{2x^3-4x^2} \\ x^2+3x \\ \underline{x^2-2x} \\ 5x-4 \\ \underline{5x-10} \\ 6 \end{array}$$

$$\frac{2x^3-3x^2+3x-4}{x-2} = 2x^2+x+5+\frac{6}{x-2}$$

15. $\left(2\sqrt{3}+5\sqrt{2}\right)\left(\sqrt{3}-4\sqrt{2}\right)$

$$= 2\cdot 3 - 8\sqrt{6} + 5\sqrt{6} - 20\cdot 2$$
$$= 6 - 3\sqrt{6} - 40$$
$$= -34 - 3\sqrt{6}$$

16. $24x^2 + 10x - 4 = 2\left(12x^2 + 5x - 2\right)$

$$= 2(3x+2)(4x-1)$$

17. $16x^4 - 1 = \left(4x^2+1\right)\left(4x^2-1\right)$

$$= \left(4x^2+1\right)(2x+1)(2x-1)$$

568

18. Since light varies inversely as the square of the distance, we have $l = \dfrac{k}{d^2}$.

Use the given values to find k.

$$l = \frac{k}{d^2}$$

$$120 = \frac{k}{10^2}$$

$$120 = \frac{k}{100}$$

$$12,000 = k$$

The equation becomes $l = \dfrac{12,000}{d^2}$.

When $d = 15$, $l = \dfrac{12,000}{15^2} \approx 53.3$.

At a distance of 15 feet, approximately 53 lumens are provided.

19. Let $x =$ the amount invested at 7%
Let $y =$ the amount invested at 9%

$$x + \quad y = 6000$$

$$0.07x + 0.09y = \ 510$$

Solve the first equation for y.

$$x + y = 6000$$

$$y = 6000 - x$$

Substitute and solve.

$$0.07x + 0.09(6000 - x) = 510$$

$$0.07x + 540 - 0.09x = 510$$

$$540 - 0.02x = 510$$

$$-0.02x = -30$$

$$x = 1500$$

Back-substitute 1500 for x to find y.

$$y = 6000 - x$$

$$y = 6000 - 1500 = 4500$$

$1500 was invested at 7% and $4500 was invested at 9%.

20. Let $x =$ the number of students enrolled last year

$$x - 0.12x = 2332$$

$$0.88x = 2332$$

$$x = 2650$$

2650 students were enrolled last year.

569

Chapter 11
Quadratic Equations and Functions

11.1 Exercise Set

1. $3x^2 = 75$

$x^2 = 25$

Apply the square root property.

$x = \pm\sqrt{25}$

$x = \pm5$

The solutions are ±5 and the solution st is $\{\pm5\}$.

3. $7x^2 = 42$

$x^2 = 6$

Apply the square root property.

$x = \pm\sqrt{6}$

The solutions are $\pm\sqrt{6}$ and the solution set is $\{\pm\sqrt{6}\}$.

5. $16x^2 = 25$

$x^2 = \dfrac{25}{16}$

Apply the square root property.

$x = \pm\sqrt{\dfrac{25}{16}}$

$x = \pm\dfrac{5}{4}$

The solutions are $\pm\dfrac{5}{4}$ and the

solution set is $\left\{\pm\dfrac{5}{4}\right\}$.

7. $3x^2 - 2 = 0$

$3x^2 = 2$

$x^2 = \dfrac{2}{3}$

Apply the square root property.

$x = \pm\sqrt{\dfrac{2}{3}}$

Because the proposed solutions are opposites, rationalize both denominators at once.

$x = \pm\sqrt{\dfrac{2}{3}} = \pm\dfrac{\sqrt{2}}{\sqrt{3}}\cdot\dfrac{\sqrt{3}}{\sqrt{3}} = \pm\dfrac{\sqrt{6}}{3}$

The solutions are $\pm\dfrac{\sqrt{6}}{3}$ and the

solution set is $\left\{\pm\dfrac{\sqrt{6}}{3}\right\}$.

9. $25x^2 + 16 = 0$

$25x^2 = -16$

$x^2 = -\dfrac{16}{25}$

Apply the square root property.

$x = \pm\sqrt{-\dfrac{16}{25}}$

$x = \pm\sqrt{\dfrac{16}{25}}\sqrt{-1}$

$x = \pm\dfrac{4}{5}i$

$x = 0 \pm \dfrac{4}{5}i = \pm\dfrac{4}{5}i$

The solutions are $\pm\dfrac{4}{5}i$ and the

solution set is $\left\{\pm\dfrac{4}{5}i\right\}$.

570

11. $(x+7)^2 = 9$

Apply the square root property.

$x+7 = \sqrt{9}$ or $x+7 = -\sqrt{9}$

$x+7 = 3$ $\qquad$ $x+7 = -3$

$x = -4$ $\qquad$ $x = -10$

The solutions are -4 and -10 and the solution set is $\{-10, -4\}$.

13. $(x-3)^2 = 5$

Apply the square root property.

$x-3 = \pm\sqrt{5}$

$x = 3 \pm \sqrt{5}$

The solutions are $3 \pm \sqrt{5}$ and the solution set is $\{3 \pm \sqrt{5}\}$.

15. $2(x+2)^2 = 16$

$(x+2)^2 = 8$

Apply the square root property.

$x+2 = \pm\sqrt{8}$

$x+2 = \pm\sqrt{4 \cdot 2}$

$x+2 = \pm 2\sqrt{2}$

$x = -2 \pm 2\sqrt{2}$

The solutions are $-2 \pm 2\sqrt{2}$ and the solution set is $\{-2 \pm 2\sqrt{2}\}$.

17. $(x-5)^2 = -9$

Apply the square root property.

$x-5 = \pm\sqrt{-9}$

$x-5 = \pm 3i$

$x = 5 \pm 3i$

The solutions are $5 \pm 3i$ and the solution set is $\{5 \pm 3i\}$.

19. $\left(x + \dfrac{3}{4}\right)^2 = \dfrac{11}{16}$

Apply the square root property.

$x + \dfrac{3}{4} = \pm\sqrt{\dfrac{11}{16}}$

$x + \dfrac{3}{4} = \pm\dfrac{\sqrt{11}}{4}$

$x = -\dfrac{3}{4} \pm \dfrac{\sqrt{11}}{4} = \dfrac{-3 \pm \sqrt{11}}{4}$

The solutions are $\dfrac{-3 \pm \sqrt{11}}{4}$ and the

solution set is $\left\{\dfrac{-3 \pm \sqrt{11}}{4}\right\}$.

21. $x^2 - 6x + 9 = 36$

$(x-3)^2 = 36$

Apply the square root property.

$x-3 = \sqrt{36}$ or $x-3 = -\sqrt{36}$

$x-3 = 6$ $\qquad$ $x-3 = -6$

$x = 9$ $\qquad$ $x = -3$

The solutions are 9 and -3 and the solution set is $\{-3, 9\}$.

23. $x^2 + 2x + \underline{\quad}$

Since $b = 2$, we add

$\left(\dfrac{b}{2}\right)^2 = \left(\dfrac{2}{2}\right)^2 = (1)^2 = 1$.

$x^2 + 2x + 1 = (x+1)^2$

25. $x^2 - 14x + \underline{\quad}$

Since $b = -14$, we add

$\left(\dfrac{b}{2}\right)^2 = \left(\dfrac{-14}{2}\right)^2 = (-7)^2 = 49$.

$x^2 - 14x + 49 = (x-7)^2$

27. $x^2 + 7x +$ _____

Since $b = 7$, we add

$$\left(\frac{b}{2}\right)^2 = \left(\frac{7}{2}\right)^2 = \frac{49}{4}.$$

$$x^2 + 7x + \frac{49}{4} = \left(x + \frac{7}{2}\right)^2$$

29. $x^2 - \frac{1}{2}x +$ _____

Since $b = -\frac{1}{2}$, we add

$$\left(\frac{b}{2}\right)^2 = \left(\frac{-1}{2} \div 2\right)^2$$

$$= \left(\frac{-1}{2} \cdot \frac{1}{2}\right)^2 = \left(\frac{-1}{4}\right)^2 = \frac{1}{16}.$$

$$x^2 - \frac{1}{2}x + \frac{1}{16} = \left(x - \frac{1}{4}\right)^2$$

31. $x^2 + \frac{4}{3}x +$ _____

Since $b = \frac{4}{3}$, we add

$$\left(\frac{b}{2}\right)^2 = \left(\frac{4}{3} \div 2\right)^2 = \left(\frac{4}{3} \cdot \frac{1}{2}\right)^2 = \left(\frac{2}{3}\right)^2 = \frac{4}{9}.$$

$$x^2 + \frac{4}{3}x + \frac{4}{9} = \left(x + \frac{2}{3}\right)^2$$

33. $x^2 - \frac{9}{4}x +$ _____

Since $b = -\frac{9}{4}$, we add

$$\left(\frac{b}{2}\right)^2 = \left(-\frac{9}{4} \div 2\right)^2$$

$$= \left(-\frac{9}{4} \cdot \frac{1}{2}\right)^2 = \left(-\frac{9}{8}\right)^2 = \frac{81}{64}.$$

$$x^2 - \frac{9}{4}x + \frac{81}{64} = \left(x - \frac{9}{8}\right)^2$$

35. $x^2 + 4x = 32$

$$x^2 + 4x \qquad = 32$$

Since $b = 4$, we add

$$\left(\frac{b}{2}\right)^2 = \left(\frac{4}{2}\right)^2 = (2)^2 = 4.$$

$$x^2 + 4x + 4 = 32 + 4$$

$$(x + 2)^2 = 36$$

Apply the square root property.

$$x + 2 = \sqrt{36} \qquad x + 2 = -\sqrt{36}$$
$$\text{or}$$
$$x + 2 = 6 \qquad x + 2 = -6$$

$$x = 4 \qquad x = -8$$

The solutions are 4 and -8 and the solution set is $\{-8, \ 4\}$.

37. $x^2 + 6x = -2$

$$x^2 + 6x \qquad = -2$$

Since $b = 6$, we add

$$\left(\frac{b}{2}\right)^2 = \left(\frac{6}{2}\right)^2 = (3)^2 = 9.$$

$$x^2 + 6x + 9 = -2 + 9$$

$$(x + 3)^2 = 7$$

Apply the square root property.

$$x + 3 = \pm\sqrt{7}$$

$$x = -3 \pm \sqrt{7}$$

The solutions are $-3 \pm \sqrt{7}$ and the solution set is $\left\{-3 \pm \sqrt{7}\right\}$.

39. $x^2 - 8x + 1 = 0$

$$x^2 - 8x \qquad = -1$$

Since $b = -8$, we add

$$\left(\frac{b}{2}\right)^2 = \left(\frac{-8}{2}\right)^2 = (-4)^2 = 16.$$

$$x^2 - 8x + 16 = -1 + 16$$

$$(x - 4)^2 = 15$$

Apply the square root property.

$$x - 4 = \pm\sqrt{15}$$

$$x = 4 \pm \sqrt{15}$$

The solutions are $4 \pm \sqrt{15}$ and the solution set is $\{4 \pm \sqrt{15}\}$.

41. $x^2 + 2x + 2 = 0$

$$x^2 + 2x = -2$$

Since $b = 2$, we add

$$\left(\frac{b}{2}\right)^2 = \left(\frac{2}{2}\right)^2 = (1)^2 = 1.$$

$$x^2 + 2x + 1 = -2 + 1$$

$$(x + 1)^2 = -1$$

Apply the square root property.

$$x + 1 = \pm\sqrt{-1} = \pm i$$

$$x = -1 \pm i$$

The solutions are $-1 \pm i$ and the solution set is $\{-1 \pm i\}$.

43. $x^2 + 3x - 1 = 0$

$$x^2 + 3x = 1$$

Since $b = 3$, we add

$$\left(\frac{b}{2}\right)^2 = \left(\frac{3}{2}\right)^2 = \frac{9}{4}.$$

$$x^2 + 3x + \frac{9}{4} = 1 + \frac{9}{4}$$

$$\left(x + \frac{3}{2}\right)^2 = \frac{13}{4}$$

Apply the square root property.

$$x + \frac{3}{2} = \pm\sqrt{\frac{13}{4}} = \pm\frac{\sqrt{13}}{2}$$

$$x = -\frac{3}{2} \pm \frac{\sqrt{13}}{2} = \frac{-3 \pm \sqrt{13}}{2}$$

The solutions are $\dfrac{-3 \pm \sqrt{13}}{2}$ and the solution set is $\left\{\dfrac{-3 \pm \sqrt{13}}{2}\right\}$.

45. $x^2 + \dfrac{4}{7}x + \dfrac{3}{49} = 0$

$$x^2 + \frac{4}{7}x = -\frac{3}{49}$$

Since $b = \dfrac{4}{7}$, we add

$$\left(\frac{1}{2}b\right)^2 = \left(\frac{1}{2} \cdot \frac{4}{7}\right)^2 \left(\frac{2}{7}\right)^2 = \frac{4}{49}.$$

$$x^2 + \frac{4}{7}x + \frac{4}{49} = -\frac{3}{49} + \frac{4}{49}$$

$$\left(x + \frac{2}{7}\right)^2 = \frac{1}{49}$$

Apply the square root property.

$$x + \frac{2}{7} = \pm\sqrt{\frac{1}{49}}$$

$$x + \frac{2}{7} = \pm\frac{1}{7}$$

$$x = -\frac{2}{7} \pm \frac{1}{7}$$

$$x = -\frac{2}{7} + \frac{1}{7} = -\frac{1}{7} \quad \text{or} \quad -\frac{2}{7} - \frac{1}{7} = -\frac{3}{7}$$

The solutions are $-\dfrac{1}{7}$ and $-\dfrac{3}{7}$, and the solution set is $\left\{-\dfrac{3}{7}, -\dfrac{1}{7}\right\}$.

47. $x^2 + x - 1 = 0$

$$x^2 + x = 1$$

Since $b = 1$, we add

$$\left(\frac{b}{2}\right)^2 = \left(\frac{1}{2}\right)^2 = \frac{1}{4}.$$

$$x^2 + x + \frac{1}{4} = 1 + \frac{1}{4}$$

$$\left(x + \frac{1}{2}\right)^2 = \frac{5}{4}$$

Apply the square root property.

573

$$x + \frac{1}{2} = \pm\sqrt{\frac{5}{4}}$$

$$x + \frac{1}{2} = \pm\frac{\sqrt{5}}{2}$$

$$x = -\frac{1}{2} \pm \frac{\sqrt{5}}{2} = \frac{-1 \pm \sqrt{5}}{2}$$

The solutions are $\dfrac{-1 \pm \sqrt{5}}{2}$ and the

solution set is $\left\{ \dfrac{-1 \pm \sqrt{5}}{2} \right\}$.

49. $2x^2 + 3x - 5 = 0$

$$x^2 + \frac{3}{2}x - \frac{5}{2} = 0$$

$$x^2 + \frac{3}{2}x \quad = \frac{5}{2}$$

Since $b = \dfrac{3}{2}$, we add

$$\left(\frac{1}{2}b\right)^2 = \left(\frac{1}{2} \cdot \frac{3}{2}\right)^2 = \left(\frac{3}{4}\right)^2 = \frac{9}{16}.$$

$$x^2 + \frac{3}{2}x + \frac{9}{16} = \frac{5}{2} + \frac{9}{16}$$

$$\left(x + \frac{3}{4}\right)^2 = \frac{40}{16} + \frac{9}{16} = \frac{49}{16}$$

Apply the square root property.

$$x + \frac{3}{4} = \pm\sqrt{\frac{49}{16}} = \pm\frac{7}{4}$$

$$x = -\frac{3}{4} \pm \frac{7}{4}$$

$$x = -\frac{3}{4} + \frac{7}{4} \quad \text{or} \quad x = -\frac{3}{4} - \frac{7}{4}$$

$$x = \frac{4}{4} = 1 \quad \text{or} \quad x = -\frac{10}{4} = -\frac{5}{2}$$

The solutions are $-\dfrac{5}{2}$ and 1, and the

solution set is $\left\{ -\dfrac{5}{2}, 1 \right\}$.

51. $3x^2 + 6x + 1 = 0$

$$x^2 + 2x + \frac{1}{3} = 0$$

$$x^2 + 2x \quad = -\frac{1}{3}$$

Since $b = 2$, we add

$$\left(\frac{b}{2}\right)^2 = \left(\frac{2}{2}\right)^2 = 1^2 = 1.$$

$$x^2 + 2x + 1 = -\frac{1}{3} + 1$$

$$\left(x + 1\right)^2 = -\frac{1}{3} + \frac{3}{3} = \frac{2}{3}$$

Apply the square root property.

$$x + 1 = \pm\sqrt{\frac{2}{3}}$$

$$x + 1 = \pm\frac{\sqrt{2}}{\sqrt{3}} \cdot \frac{\sqrt{3}}{\sqrt{3}} = \pm\frac{\sqrt{6}}{3}$$

$$x = -1 \pm \frac{\sqrt{6}}{3} = \frac{-3 \pm \sqrt{6}}{3}$$

The solutions are $\dfrac{-3 \pm \sqrt{6}}{3}$ and the

solution set is $\left\{ \dfrac{-3 \pm \sqrt{6}}{3} \right\}$.

53. $3x^2 - 8x + 1 = 0$

$$x^2 - \frac{8}{3}x + \frac{1}{3} = 0$$

$$x^2 - \frac{8}{3}x \quad = -\frac{1}{3}$$

Since $b = -\dfrac{8}{3}$, we add

$$\left(\frac{1}{2}b\right)^2 = \left[\frac{1}{2}\left(-\frac{8}{3}\right)\right]^2 = \left(-\frac{4}{3}\right)^2 = \frac{16}{9}.$$

$$x^2 - \frac{8}{3}x + \frac{16}{9} = -\frac{1}{3} + \frac{16}{9}$$

$$\left(x - \frac{4}{3}\right)^2 = -\frac{3}{9} + \frac{16}{9} = \frac{13}{9}$$

Apply the square root property.

$$x - \frac{4}{3} = \pm\sqrt{\frac{13}{9}}$$

$$x - \frac{4}{3} = \pm\frac{\sqrt{13}}{3}$$

$$x = \frac{4}{3} \pm \frac{\sqrt{13}}{3} = \frac{4 \pm \sqrt{13}}{3}$$

The solutions are $\dfrac{4 \pm \sqrt{13}}{3}$ and the

solution set is $\left\{ \dfrac{4 \pm \sqrt{13}}{3} \right\}$.

55. $8x^2 - 4x + 1 = 0$

$$x^2 - \frac{1}{2}x + \frac{1}{8} = 0$$

$$x^2 - \frac{1}{2}x \quad = -\frac{1}{8}$$

Since $b = -\dfrac{1}{2}$, we add

$$\left(\frac{1}{2}b\right)^2 = \left[\frac{1}{2}\left(-\frac{1}{2}\right)\right]^2 = \left(-\frac{1}{4}\right)^2 = \frac{1}{16}.$$

$$x^2 - \frac{1}{2}x + \frac{1}{16} = -\frac{1}{8} + \frac{1}{16}$$

$$\left(x - \frac{1}{4}\right)^2 = -\frac{2}{16} + \frac{1}{16} = -\frac{1}{16}$$

Apply the square root property.

$$x - \frac{1}{4} = \pm\sqrt{-\frac{1}{16}}$$

$$x - \frac{1}{4} = \pm\frac{1}{4}i$$

$$x = \frac{1}{4} \pm \frac{1}{4}i$$

The solutions are $\dfrac{1}{4} \pm \dfrac{1}{4}i$ and the

solution set is $\left\{ \dfrac{1}{4} \pm \dfrac{1}{4}i \right\}$.

57. $f(x) = 36$

$$(x-1)^2 = 36$$

Apply the square root property.

$$x - 1 = \pm\sqrt{36}$$

$$x - 1 = \pm 6$$

$$x = 1 \pm 6$$

$$x = 1 + 6 = 7 \text{ or } 1 - 6 = -5$$

The values are -5 and 7.

59. $$g(x) = \frac{9}{25}$$

$$\left(x - \frac{2}{5}\right)^2 = \frac{9}{25}$$

Apply the square root property.

$$x - \frac{2}{5} = \pm\sqrt{\frac{9}{25}} = \pm\frac{3}{5}$$

$$x = \frac{2}{5} \pm \frac{3}{5}$$

$$x = \frac{2}{5} + \frac{3}{5} \text{ or } x = \frac{2}{5} - \frac{3}{5}$$

$$x = \frac{5}{5} = 1 \text{ or } x = -\frac{1}{5}$$

The values are $-\dfrac{1}{5}$ and 1.

61. $h(x) = -125$

$$5(x+2)^2 = -125$$

$$(x+2)^2 = -25$$

Apply the square root property.

$$x + 2 = \pm\sqrt{-25}$$

$$x + 2 = \pm 5i$$

$$x = -2 \pm 5i$$

The values are $-2 \pm 5i$.

63.
$$d = \sqrt{(14-2)^2 + (8-3)^2}$$
$$= \sqrt{12^2 + 5^2} = \sqrt{144 + 25}$$
$$= \sqrt{169} = 13$$
The distance is 13 units.

65.
$$d = \sqrt{(6-4)^2 + (3-1)^2}$$
$$= \sqrt{2^2 + 2^2} = \sqrt{4+4}$$
$$= \sqrt{8} = \sqrt{4 \cdot 2} = 2\sqrt{2} \approx 2.83$$
The distance is $2\sqrt{2}$ or 2.83 units.

67.
$$d = \sqrt{(-3-0)^2 + (4-0)^2}$$
$$= \sqrt{(-3)^2 + 4^2} = \sqrt{9+16}$$
$$= \sqrt{25} = 5$$
The distance is 5 units.

69.
$$d = \sqrt{(3-(-2))^2 + (-4-(-6))^2}$$
$$= \sqrt{5^2 + 2^2} = \sqrt{25+4}$$
$$= \sqrt{29} \approx 5.39$$
The distance is $\sqrt{29}$ or 5.39 units.

71.
$$d = \sqrt{(4-0)^2 + (1-(-3))^2}$$
$$= \sqrt{4^2 + 4^2} = \sqrt{16+16}$$
$$= \sqrt{32} = \sqrt{16 \cdot 2} = 4\sqrt{2} \approx 5.66$$
The distance is $4\sqrt{2}$ or 5.66 units.

73.
$$d = \sqrt{(3.5-(-0.5))^2 + (8.2-6.2)^2}$$
$$= \sqrt{4^2 + 2^2} = \sqrt{16+4}$$
$$= \sqrt{20} = \sqrt{4 \cdot 5} = 2\sqrt{5} \approx 4.47$$
The distance is $2\sqrt{5}$ or 4.47 units.

75.
$$d = \sqrt{(\sqrt{5}-0)^2 + (0-(-\sqrt{3}))^2}$$
$$= \sqrt{(\sqrt{5})^2 + (\sqrt{3})^2} = \sqrt{5+3}$$
$$= \sqrt{8} = \sqrt{4 \cdot 2} = 2\sqrt{2} \approx 2.83$$
The distance is $2\sqrt{2}$ or 2.83 units.

77.
$$d = \sqrt{(3\sqrt{3}-(-\sqrt{3}))^2 + (\sqrt{5}-4\sqrt{5})^2}$$
$$= \sqrt{(4\sqrt{3})^2 + (-3\sqrt{5})^2}$$
$$= \sqrt{16 \cdot 3 + 9 \cdot 5} = \sqrt{48+45}$$
$$= \sqrt{93} \approx 9.64$$
The distance is $\sqrt{93}$ or 9.64 units.

79.
$$d = \sqrt{\left(\frac{7}{3}-\frac{1}{3}\right)^2 + \left(\frac{1}{5}-\frac{6}{5}\right)^2}$$
$$= \sqrt{\left(\frac{6}{3}\right)^2 + \left(-\frac{5}{5}\right)^2}$$
$$= \sqrt{2^2 + (-1)^2} = \sqrt{4+1}$$
$$= \sqrt{5} \approx 2.24$$
The distance is $\sqrt{5}$ or 2.24 units.

81.
$$\text{Midpoint} = \left(\frac{6+2}{2}, \frac{8+4}{2}\right)$$
$$= \left(\frac{8}{2}, \frac{12}{2}\right) = (4,6)$$
The midpoint is $(4,6)$.

83.
$$\text{Midpoint} = \left(\frac{-2+(-6)}{2}, \frac{-8+(-2)}{2}\right)$$
$$= \left(\frac{-8}{2}, \frac{-10}{2}\right) = (-4,-5)$$
The midpoint is $(-4,-5)$.

85.
$$\text{Midpoint} = \left(\frac{-3+6}{2}, \frac{-4+(-8)}{2}\right)$$
$$= \left(\frac{3}{2}, \frac{-12}{2}\right) = \left(\frac{3}{2}, -6\right)$$
The midpoint is $\left(\frac{3}{2}, -6\right)$.

87.
$$\text{Midpoint} = \left(\frac{-\frac{7}{2}+\left(-\frac{5}{2}\right)}{2}, \frac{\frac{3}{2}+\left(-\frac{11}{2}\right)}{2}\right)$$
$$= \left(\frac{-\frac{12}{2}}{2}, \frac{-\frac{8}{2}}{2}\right)$$
$$= \left(-\frac{12}{2}\cdot\frac{1}{2}, -\frac{8}{2}\cdot\frac{1}{2}\right)$$
$$= \left(-\frac{12}{4}, -\frac{8}{4}\right) = (-3, -2)$$
The midpoint is $(-3, -2)$.

89.
$$\text{Midpoint} = \left(\frac{8+(-6)}{2}, \frac{3\sqrt{5}+7\sqrt{5}}{2}\right)$$
$$= \left(\frac{2}{2}, \frac{10\sqrt{5}}{2}\right) = \left(1, 5\sqrt{5}\right)$$
The midpoint is $\left(1, 5\sqrt{5}\right)$.

91.
$$\text{Midpoint} = \left(\frac{\sqrt{18}+\sqrt{2}}{2}, \frac{-4+4}{2}\right)$$
$$= \left(\frac{\sqrt{9\cdot2}+\sqrt{2}}{2}, \frac{0}{2}\right)$$
$$= \left(\frac{3\sqrt{2}+\sqrt{2}}{2}, 0\right)$$
$$= \left(\frac{4\sqrt{2}}{2}, 0\right) = \left(2\sqrt{2}, 0\right)$$
The midpoint is $\left(2\sqrt{2}, 0\right)$.

93. Let x = the number.
$$3(x-2)^2 = -12$$
$$(x-2)^2 = -4$$
Apply the square root property.
$$x-2 = \pm\sqrt{-4} = \pm2i$$
$$x = 2 \pm 2i$$
The values are $2+2i$ and $2-2i$.

94. Let x = the number.
$$3(x-9)^2 = -27$$
$$(x-9)^2 = -9$$
Apply the square root property.
$$x-9 = \pm\sqrt{-9} = \pm3i$$
$$x = 9 \pm 3i$$
The values are $9+3i$ and $9-3i$.

95.
$$h = \frac{v^2}{2g}$$
$$2gh = v^2$$
Apply the square root property and keep only the principal square root.
$$v = \sqrt{2gh}$$

96.
$$s = \frac{kwd^2}{l}$$
$$sl = kwd^2$$
$$\frac{sl}{kw} = d^2$$
Apply the square root property and keep only the principal square root.
$$d = \sqrt{\frac{sl}{kw}} = \frac{\sqrt{sl}}{\sqrt{kw}} \cdot \frac{\sqrt{kw}}{\sqrt{kw}} = \frac{\sqrt{slkw}}{kw}$$

97.
$$A = P(1+r)^2$$
$$\frac{A}{P} = (1+r)^2$$
Apply the square root property and keep only the principal square root.

577

$$1 + r = \sqrt{\dfrac{A}{P}}$$

$$1 + r = \dfrac{\sqrt{A}}{\sqrt{P}} \cdot \dfrac{\sqrt{P}}{\sqrt{P}} = \dfrac{\sqrt{AP}}{P}$$

$$r = \dfrac{\sqrt{AP}}{P} - 1$$

98.

$$C = \dfrac{kP_1P_2}{d^2}$$

$$Cd^2 = kP_1P_2$$

$$d^2 = \dfrac{kP_1P_2}{C}$$

Apply the square root property and keep only the principal square root.

$$d = \sqrt{\dfrac{kP_1P_2}{C}}$$

$$d = \dfrac{\sqrt{kP_1P_2}}{\sqrt{C}} \cdot \dfrac{\sqrt{C}}{\sqrt{C}} = \dfrac{\sqrt{kP_1P_2C}}{C}$$

99.

$$\dfrac{x^2}{3} + \dfrac{x}{9} - \dfrac{1}{6} = 0$$

$$3\left(\dfrac{x^2}{3} + \dfrac{x}{9} - \dfrac{1}{6}\right) = 3(0)$$

$$x^2 + \dfrac{1}{3}x - \dfrac{1}{2} = 0$$

$$x^2 + \dfrac{1}{3}x \quad = \dfrac{1}{2}$$

Since $b = \dfrac{1}{3}$, we add

$$\left(\dfrac{1}{2}b\right)^2 = \left(\dfrac{1}{2} \cdot \dfrac{1}{3}\right)^2 = \left(\dfrac{1}{6}\right)^2 = \dfrac{1}{36}.$$

$$x^2 + \dfrac{1}{3}x + \dfrac{1}{36} = \dfrac{1}{2} + \dfrac{1}{36}$$

$$\left(x + \dfrac{1}{6}\right)^2 = \dfrac{18}{36} + \dfrac{1}{36} = \dfrac{19}{36}$$

Apply the square root property.

$$x + \dfrac{1}{6} = \pm\sqrt{\dfrac{19}{36}} = \pm\dfrac{\sqrt{19}}{6}$$

$$x = -\dfrac{1}{6} \pm \dfrac{\sqrt{19}}{6} = \dfrac{-1 \pm \sqrt{19}}{6}$$

The solutions are $\dfrac{-1 \pm \sqrt{19}}{6}$ and the

solution set is $\left\{\dfrac{-1 \pm \sqrt{19}}{6}\right\}$.

100.

$$\dfrac{x^2}{2} - \dfrac{x}{6} - \dfrac{3}{4} = 0$$

$$2\left(\dfrac{x^2}{2} - \dfrac{x}{6} - \dfrac{3}{4}\right) = 2(0)$$

$$x^2 - \dfrac{1}{3}x - \dfrac{3}{2} = 0$$

$$x^2 - \dfrac{1}{3}x \quad = \dfrac{3}{2}$$

Since $b = -\dfrac{1}{3}$, we add

$$\left(\dfrac{1}{2}b\right)^2 = \left[\dfrac{1}{2}\left(-\dfrac{1}{3}\right)\right]^2 = \left(-\dfrac{1}{6}\right)^2 = \dfrac{1}{36}.$$

$$x^2 - \dfrac{1}{3}x + \dfrac{1}{36} = \dfrac{3}{2} + \dfrac{1}{36}$$

$$\left(x - \dfrac{1}{6}\right)^2 = \dfrac{54}{36} + \dfrac{1}{36} = \dfrac{55}{36}$$

Apply the square root property.

$$x - \dfrac{1}{6} = \pm\sqrt{\dfrac{55}{36}} = \pm\dfrac{\sqrt{55}}{6}$$

$$x = \dfrac{1}{6} \pm \dfrac{\sqrt{55}}{6} = \dfrac{1 \pm \sqrt{55}}{6}$$

The solutions are $\dfrac{1 \pm \sqrt{55}}{6}$ and the

solution set is $\left\{\dfrac{1 \pm \sqrt{55}}{6}\right\}$.

578

101.
$$x^2 - bx = 2b^2$$

$$x^2 - bx \qquad = 2b^2$$

Since $-b$ is the linear coefficient, we add

$$\left(\frac{-b}{2}\right)^2 = \frac{b^2}{4}.$$

$$x^2 - bx + \frac{b^2}{4} = 2b^2 + \frac{b^2}{4}$$

$$\left(x - \frac{b}{2}\right)^2 = \frac{8b^2}{4} + \frac{b^2}{4} = \frac{9b^2}{4}$$

Apply the square root property.

$$x - \frac{b}{2} = \pm\sqrt{\frac{9b^2}{4}} = \pm\frac{3b}{2}$$

$$x = \frac{b}{2} \pm \frac{3b}{2}$$

$$x = \frac{b}{2} + \frac{3b}{2} \quad \text{or} \quad x = \frac{b}{2} - \frac{3b}{2}$$

$$x = \frac{4b}{2} = 2b \quad \text{or} \quad x = -\frac{2b}{2} = -b$$

The solutions are $2b$ and $-b$, and the solution set is $\{-b,\ 2b\}$.

102.
$$x^2 - bx = 6b^2$$

$$x^2 - bx \qquad = 6b^2$$

Since $-b$ is the linear coefficient, we add

$$\left(\frac{-b}{2}\right)^2 = \frac{b^2}{4}.$$

$$x^2 - bx + \frac{b^2}{4} = 6b^2 + \frac{b^2}{4}$$

$$\left(x - \frac{b}{2}\right)^2 = \frac{24b^2}{4} + \frac{b^2}{4} = \frac{25b^2}{4}$$

Apply the square root property.

$$x - \frac{b}{2} = \pm\sqrt{\frac{25b^2}{4}} = \pm\frac{5b}{2}$$

$$x = \frac{b}{2} \pm \frac{5b}{2}$$

$$x = \frac{b}{2} + \frac{5b}{2} \quad \text{or} \quad x = \frac{b}{2} - \frac{5b}{2}$$

$$x = \frac{6b}{2} = 3b \quad \text{or} \quad x = -\frac{4b}{2} = -2b$$

The solutions are $3b$ and $-2b$, and the solution set is $\{-2b,\ 3b\}$.

103.
$$2880 = 2000(1+r)^2$$

$$\frac{2880}{2000} = (1+r)^2$$

$$1.44 = (1+r)^2$$

Apply the square root property.

$$1 + r = \pm\sqrt{1.44}$$

$$1 + r = \pm 1.2$$

$$r = -1 \pm 1.2$$

$$r = -1 + 1.2 \quad \text{or} \quad -1 - 1.2$$

$$r = 0.2 \quad \text{or} \quad -2.2$$

We reject –2.2 because we cannot have a negative interest rate. The solution is 0.2 and we conclude that the annual interest rate is 20%.

105.
$$1445 = 1280(1+r)^2$$

$$\frac{1445}{1280} = (1+r)^2$$

$$1.12890625 = (1+r)^2$$

Apply the square root property.

$$1 + r = \pm\sqrt{1.12890625}$$

$$1 + r = \pm 1.0625$$

$$r = -1 \pm 1.0625$$

$$r = -1 + 1.0625 \quad \text{or} \quad -1 - 1.0625$$

$$r = 0.0625 \quad \text{or} \quad -2.0625$$

We reject –2.0625 because we cannot have a negative interest rate. The solution is 0.0625 and we conclude that the annual interest rate is 6.25%.

579

107.
$$92,000 = 62.2x^2 + 7000$$
$$85,000 = 62.2x^2$$
$$\frac{85,000}{62.2} = x^2$$
Apply the square root property.
$$x = \pm\sqrt{\frac{85,000}{62.2}} \approx \pm 37$$
We disregard –37 because we can't have a negative number of years. The solution is 37 and we conclude that there will be 92,000 multinational corporation in $1970 + 37 = 2007$.

109.
$$4800 = 16t^2$$
$$\frac{4800}{16} = t^2$$
$$300 = t^2$$
Apply the square root property.
$$t = \pm\sqrt{300}$$
$$t = \pm 10\sqrt{3} \approx \pm 17.3$$
We disregard –17.3 because we can't have a negative time measurement. The solution is 17.3 and we conclude that the sky diver was in a free fall for $10\sqrt{3}$ or approximately 17.3 seconds.

111.

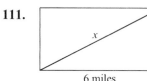

$$x^2 = 6^2 + 3^2 = 36 + 9 = 45$$
Apply the square root property.
$$x = \pm\sqrt{45} = \pm\sqrt{9\cdot 5} = \pm 3\sqrt{5}$$
We disregard $-3\sqrt{5}$ because we can't have a negative length measurement. The solution is $3\sqrt{5}$ and we conclude that the pedestrian route is $3\sqrt{5}$ or approximately 6.7 miles long.

113.
$$x^2 + 10^2 = 30^2$$
$$x^2 + 100 = 900$$
$$x^2 = 800$$
Apply the square root property.
$$x = \pm\sqrt{800} = \pm\sqrt{400\cdot 2} = \pm 20\sqrt{2}$$
We disregard $-20\sqrt{2}$ because we can't have a negative length measurement. The solution is $20\sqrt{2}$. We conclude that the ladder reaches $20\sqrt{2}$ feet, or approximately 28.3 feet, up the house.

115.

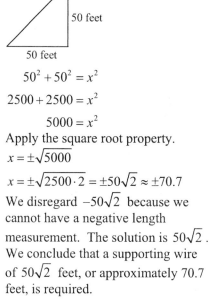

$$50^2 + 50^2 = x^2$$
$$2500 + 2500 = x^2$$
$$5000 = x^2$$
Apply the square root property.
$$x = \pm\sqrt{5000}$$
$$x = \pm\sqrt{2500\cdot 2} = \pm 50\sqrt{2} \approx \pm 70.7$$
We disregard $-50\sqrt{2}$ because we cannot have a negative length measurement. The solution is $50\sqrt{2}$. We conclude that a supporting wire of $50\sqrt{2}$ feet, or approximately 70.7 feet, is required.

117.
$$A = lw$$
$$196 = (x+2+2)(x+2+2)$$
$$196 = (x+4)(x+4)$$
$$196 = x^2 + 8x + 16$$
$$180 = x^2 + 8x$$
$$x^2 + 8x \qquad = 180$$
Since $b = 8$, we add

$$\left(\frac{b}{2}\right)^2 = \left(\frac{8}{2}\right)^2 = 4^2 = 16.$$

$$x^2 + 8x + 16 = 180 + 16$$

$$(x+4)^2 = 196$$

Apply the square root property.

$$x + 4 = \pm\sqrt{196} = \pm 14$$

$$x = -4 \pm 14$$

$$x = -4 + 14 = 10 \ \text{ or } \ x = -4 - 14 = -18$$

We disregard -18 because we can't have a negative length measurement. The solution is 10. We conclude that the length of the original square is 10 meters.

119. First find the distance from Bangkok to Phnom Penh.

$$d = \sqrt{\left(65 - (-115)\right)^2 + \left(70 - 170\right)^2}$$

$$= \sqrt{180^2 + (-100)^2}$$

$$= \sqrt{32400 + 10000}$$

$$= \sqrt{42400} \approx 205.9$$

The distance is approximately 205.9 miles.

$$t = \frac{d}{r} = \frac{205.9}{400} \approx 0.5$$

It will take approximately 0.5 hours or 30 minutes to make the flight.

121. – 123. Answers will vary.

125. $a^2 + b^2 = c^2$

Where a and b are the lengths of the legs of a right triangle, and c is the length of the hypotenuse.

127. Answers will vary.

129. $4 - (x+1)^2 = 0$

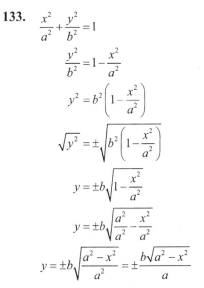

The solutions are -3 and 1, and the solution set is $\{-3, 1\}$.

Check:

$x = -3$	$x = 1$
$4 - (-3+1)^2 = 0$	$4 - (1+1)^2 = 0$
$4 - (-2)^2 = 0$	$4 - 2^2 = 0$
$4 - 4 = 0$	$4 - 4 = 0$
$0 = 0$	$0 = 0$
True	True

131. Answers will vary

133.

$$\frac{x^2}{a^2} + \frac{y^2}{b^2} = 1$$

$$\frac{y^2}{b^2} = 1 - \frac{x^2}{a^2}$$

$$y^2 = b^2\left(1 - \frac{x^2}{a^2}\right)$$

$$\sqrt{y^2} = \pm\sqrt{b^2\left(1 - \frac{x^2}{a^2}\right)}$$

$$y = \pm b\sqrt{1 - \frac{x^2}{a^2}}$$

$$y = \pm b\sqrt{\frac{a^2}{a^2} - \frac{x^2}{a^2}}$$

$$y = \pm b\sqrt{\frac{a^2 - x^2}{a^2}} = \pm\frac{b\sqrt{a^2 - x^2}}{a}$$

135. $x^2 + bx + c = 0$

$x^2 + bx = -c$

$x^2 + bx + \dfrac{b^2}{4} = -c + \dfrac{b^2}{4}$

$\left(x + \dfrac{b}{2}\right)^2 = -c + \dfrac{b^2}{4}$

$x + \dfrac{b}{2} = \pm\sqrt{-c + \dfrac{b^2}{4}}$

$x = -\dfrac{b}{2} \pm \sqrt{-\dfrac{4c}{4} + \dfrac{b^2}{4}}$

$x = -\dfrac{b}{2} \pm \sqrt{\dfrac{4c + b^2}{4}}$

$x = -\dfrac{b}{2} \pm \dfrac{\sqrt{-4c + b^2}}{2}$

$x = \dfrac{-b \pm \sqrt{b^2 - 4c}}{2}$

137. Distance from A to B:

$d = \sqrt{(3-1)^2 + ((3+d) - (1+d))^2}$

$= \sqrt{(2)^2 + (3 + d - 1 - d)^2} = \sqrt{4 + (2)^2}$

$= \sqrt{4 + 4} = \sqrt{8} = \sqrt{4 \cdot 2} = 2\sqrt{2}$

Distance from B to C:

$d = \sqrt{(6-3)^2 + ((6+d) - (3+d))^2}$

$= \sqrt{(3)^2 + (6 + d - 3 - d)^2} = \sqrt{9 + (3)^2}$

$= \sqrt{9 + 9} = \sqrt{18} = \sqrt{9 \cdot 2} = 3\sqrt{2}$

Distance from A to C.

$d = \sqrt{(6-1)^2 + ((6+d) - (1+d))^2}$

$= \sqrt{(5)^2 + (6 + d - 1 - d)^2} = \sqrt{25 + (5)}$

$= \sqrt{25 + 25} = \sqrt{50} = \sqrt{25 \cdot 2} = 5\sqrt{2}$

If the points are collinear,

$d_{AB} + d_{BC} = d_{AC}$.

$d_{AB} + d_{BC} = 2\sqrt{2} + 3\sqrt{2} = 5\sqrt{2}$

Since this is the same as the distance from A to C, we know that the points are collinear.

139.

$d = \sqrt{(x_2 - x_1)^2 + (y_2 - y_1)^2}$

$5 = \sqrt{(x-2)^2 + (2 - (-1))^2}$

$5^2 = (x-2)^2 + 3^2$

$25 = (x-2)^2 + 9$

$16 = (x-2)^2$

$\pm 4 = x - 2$

$2 \pm 4 = x$

Therefore, $x = 2 - 4 = -2$ or $x = 2 + 4 = 6$. There are two points with y-coordinate 2 whose distance is 5 units from the point $(2, -1)$. The two points are $(-2, 2)$ and $(6, 2)$.

140. $4x - 2 - 3\left[4 - 2(3 - x)\right]$

$= 4x - 2 - 3\left[4 - 6 + 2x\right]$

$= 4x - 2 - 3\left[-2 + 2x\right]$

$= 4x - 2 + 6 - 6x$

$= 4 - 2x$

141. $1 - 8x^3 = 1^3 - (2x)^3$

$= (1 - 2x)\left(1^2 + 1 \cdot 2x + (2x)^2\right)$

$= (1 - 2x)\left(1 + 2x + 4x^2\right)$

142. $\left(x^4 - 5x^3 + 2x^2 - 6\right) \div (x - 3)$

3⌋	1	−5	2	0	−6
		3	−6	−12	−36
	1	−2	−4	−12	−42

$\left(x^4 - 5x^3 + 2x^2 - 6\right) \div (x - 3)$

$= x^3 - 2x^2 - 4x - 12 - \dfrac{42}{x - 3}$

11.2 Exercise Set

1. $x^2 + 8x + 12 = 0$

$a = 1 \quad b = 8 \quad c = 12$

$x = \dfrac{-8 \pm \sqrt{8^2 - 4(1)(12)}}{2(1)}$

$= \dfrac{-8 \pm \sqrt{64 - 48}}{2}$

$= \dfrac{-8 \pm \sqrt{16}}{2} = \dfrac{-8 \pm 4}{2}$

Evaluate the expression to obtain two solutions.

$x = \dfrac{-8 - 4}{2} = -6 \quad \text{or} \quad x = \dfrac{-8 + 4}{2} = -2$

The solutions are –2 and –6 and the solution set is $\{-6, -2\}$.

3. $2x^2 - 7x = -5$

$2x^2 - 7x + 5 = 0$

$a = 2 \quad b = -7 \quad c = 5$

$x = \dfrac{-(-7) \pm \sqrt{(-7)^2 - 4(2)(5)}}{2(2)}$

$= \dfrac{7 \pm \sqrt{49 - 40}}{4} = \dfrac{7 \pm \sqrt{9}}{4} = \dfrac{7 \pm 3}{4}$

Evaluate the expression to obtain two solutions.

$x = \dfrac{7 - 3}{4} = 1 \quad \text{or} \quad x = \dfrac{7 + 3}{4} = \dfrac{5}{2}$

The solutions are 1 and $\dfrac{5}{2}$ and the

solution set is $\left\{ 1, \dfrac{5}{2} \right\}$.

5. $x^2 + 3x - 20 = 0$

$a = 1 \quad b = 3 \quad c = -20$

$x = \dfrac{-3 \pm \sqrt{3^2 - 4(1)(-20)}}{2(1)}$

$= \dfrac{-3 \pm \sqrt{9 - (-80)}}{2} = \dfrac{-3 \pm \sqrt{89}}{2}$

The solutions are $\dfrac{-3 \pm \sqrt{89}}{2}$ and the

solution set is $\left\{ \dfrac{-3 \pm \sqrt{89}}{2} \right\}$.

7. $3x^2 - 7x = 3$

$3x^2 - 7x - 3 = 0$

$a = 3 \quad b = -7 \quad c = -3$

$x = \dfrac{-(-7) \pm \sqrt{(-7)^2 - 4(3)(-3)}}{2(3)}$

$= \dfrac{7 \pm \sqrt{49 - (-36)}}{6} = \dfrac{7 \pm \sqrt{85}}{6}$

The solutions are $\dfrac{7 \pm \sqrt{85}}{6}$ and the

solution set is $\left\{ \dfrac{7 \pm \sqrt{85}}{6} \right\}$.

9. $6x^2 = 2x + 1$

$6x^2 - 2x - 1 = 0$

$a = 6 \quad b = -2 \quad c = -1$

$x = \dfrac{-(-2) \pm \sqrt{(-2)^2 - 4(6)(-1)}}{2(6)}$

$= \dfrac{2 \pm \sqrt{28}}{12} = \dfrac{2 \pm 2\sqrt{7}}{12} = \dfrac{1 \pm \sqrt{7}}{6}$

The solutions are $\dfrac{1 \pm \sqrt{7}}{6}$ and the

solution set is $\left\{ \dfrac{1 \pm \sqrt{7}}{6} \right\}$.

11.

$$4x^2 - 3x = -6$$
$$4x^2 - 3x + 6 = 0$$
$$a = 4 \quad b = -3 \quad c = 6$$
$$x = \frac{-(-3) \pm \sqrt{(-3)^2 - 4(4)(6)}}{2(4)}$$
$$= \frac{3 \pm \sqrt{9 - 96}}{8}$$
$$= \frac{3 \pm \sqrt{-87}}{8}$$
$$= \frac{3 \pm \sqrt{87(-1)}}{8}$$
$$= \frac{3 \pm \sqrt{87}i}{8} = \frac{3}{8} \pm \frac{\sqrt{87}}{8}i$$

The solutions are $\dfrac{3}{8} \pm \dfrac{\sqrt{87}}{8}i$ and the

solution set is $\left\{ \dfrac{3}{8} \pm \dfrac{\sqrt{87}}{8}i \right\}$.

13.

$$x^2 - 4x + 8 = 0$$
$$a = 1 \quad b = -4 \quad c = 8$$
$$x = \frac{-(-4) \pm \sqrt{(-4)^2 - 4(1)(8)}}{2(1)}$$
$$= \frac{4 \pm \sqrt{16 - 32}}{2}$$
$$= \frac{4 \pm \sqrt{-16}}{2}$$
$$= \frac{4 \pm 4i}{2} = \frac{4}{2} \pm \frac{4}{2}i = 2 \pm 2i$$

The solutions are $2 \pm 2i$ and the
solution set is $\{2 \pm 2i\}$.

15.

$$3x^2 = 8x - 7$$
$$3x^2 - 8x + 7 = 0$$
$$a = 3 \quad b = -8 \quad c = 7$$
$$x = \frac{-(-8) \pm \sqrt{(-8)^2 - 4(3)(7)}}{2(3)}$$
$$= \frac{8 \pm \sqrt{64 - 84}}{6}$$
$$= \frac{8 \pm \sqrt{-20}}{6}$$
$$= \frac{8 \pm \sqrt{4 \cdot 5(-1)}}{6}$$
$$= \frac{8 \pm 2\sqrt{5}i}{6} = \frac{8}{6} \pm \frac{2}{6}\sqrt{5}i = \frac{4}{3} \pm \frac{\sqrt{5}}{3}i$$

The solutions are $\dfrac{4}{3} \pm \dfrac{\sqrt{5}}{3}i$ and the

solution set is $\left\{ \dfrac{4}{3} \pm \dfrac{\sqrt{5}}{3}i \right\}$.

17.

$$2x(x - 2) = x + 12$$
$$2x^2 - 4x = x + 12$$
$$2x^2 - 5x - 12 = 0$$
$$a = 2 \quad b = -5 \quad c = -12$$
$$x = \frac{-(-5) \pm \sqrt{(-5)^2 - 4(2)(-12)}}{2(2)}$$
$$= \frac{5 \pm \sqrt{25 + 96}}{4} = \frac{5 \pm \sqrt{121}}{4} = \frac{5 \pm 11}{4}$$

Evaluate the expression to obtain two
solutions.

$$x = \frac{5 - 11}{4} = -\frac{3}{2} \quad \text{or} \quad x = \frac{5 + 11}{4} = 4$$

The solutions are $-\dfrac{3}{2}$ and 4, and the

solution set is $\left\{ -\dfrac{3}{2}, \ 4 \right\}$.

584

19.
$$x^2 + 8x + 3 = 0$$
$$a = 1 \quad b = 8 \quad c = 3$$
$$b^2 - 4ac = 8^2 - 4(1)(3) = 64 - 12 = 52$$
Since the discriminant is positive and not a perfect square, there are two irrational solutions.

21.
$$x^2 + 6x + 8 = 0$$
$$a = 1 \quad b = 6 \quad c = 8$$
$$b^2 - 4ac = (6)^2 - 4(1)(8) = 36 - 32 = 4$$
Since the discriminant is greater than zero, there are two unequal real solutions. Also, since the discriminant is a perfect square, the solutions are rational.

23.
$$2x^2 + x + 3 = 0$$
$$a = 2 \quad b = 1 \quad c = 3$$
$$b^2 - 4ac = 1^2 - 4(2)(3) = 1 - 24 = -23$$
Since the discriminant is negative, there are no real solutions. There are two imaginary solutions that are complex conjugates.

25.
$$2x^2 + 6x = 0$$
$$a = 2 \quad b = 6 \quad c = 0$$
$$b^2 - 4ac = (6)^2 - 4(1)(0)$$
$$= 36 - 0 = 36$$
Since the discriminant is greater than zero, there are two unequal real solutions. Also, since the discriminant is a perfect square, the solutions are rational.

27.
$$5x^2 + 3 = 0$$
$$a = 5 \quad b = 0 \quad c = 3$$
$$b^2 - 4ac = 0^2 - 4(5)(3) = 0 - 60 = -60$$
Since the discriminant is negative, there are no real solutions. There are two imaginary solutions that are complex conjugates.

29.
$$9x^2 = 12x - 4$$
$$9x^2 - 12x + 4 = 0$$
$$a = 9 \quad b = -12 \quad c = 4$$
$$b^2 - 4ac = (-12)^2 - 4(9)(4)$$
$$= 144 - 144 = 0$$
Since the discriminant is zero, there is one repeated rational solution.

31.
$$3x^2 - 4x = 4$$
$$3x^2 - 4x - 4 = 0$$
$$(3x + 2)(x - 2) = 0$$
Apply the zero product principle.
$$3x + 2 = 0 \quad \text{or} \quad x - 2 = 0$$
$$3x = -2 \qquad\qquad x = 2$$
$$x = -\frac{2}{3}$$

The solutions are $-\frac{2}{3}$ and 2, and the solution set is $\left\{-\frac{2}{3}, 2\right\}$.

33.
$$x^2 - 2x = 1$$
Since $b = -2$, we add
$$\left(\frac{b}{2}\right)^2 = \left(\frac{-2}{2}\right)^2 = (-1)^2 = 1.$$
$$x^2 - 2x + 1 = 1 + 1$$
$$(x - 1)^2 = 2$$
Apply the square root principle.
$$x - 1 = \pm\sqrt{2}$$
$$x = 1 \pm \sqrt{2}$$

The solutions are $1 \pm \sqrt{2}$, and the solution set is $\left\{1 \pm \sqrt{2}\right\}$.

35. $(2x-5)(x+1)=2$

$2x^2+2x-5x-5=2$

$2x^2-3x-7=0$

Apply the quadratic formula.

$a=2 \quad b=-3 \quad c=-7$

$x=\dfrac{-(-3)\pm\sqrt{(-3)^2-4(2)(-7)}}{2(2)}$

$=\dfrac{3\pm\sqrt{9-(-56)}}{4}=\dfrac{3\pm\sqrt{65}}{4}$

The solutions are $\dfrac{3\pm\sqrt{65}}{4}$, and the

solution set is $\left\{\dfrac{3\pm\sqrt{65}}{4}\right\}$.

37. $(3x-4)^2=16$

Apply the square root property.

$3x-4=\sqrt{16} \quad$ or $\quad 3x-4=-\sqrt{16}$

$3x-4=4 \qquad\qquad 3x-4=-4$

$3x=8 \qquad\qquad\quad 3x=0$

$x=\dfrac{8}{3} \qquad\qquad\quad x=0$

The solutions are $\dfrac{8}{3}$ and 0, and the

solution set is $\left\{0,\dfrac{8}{3}\right\}$.

39. $\dfrac{x^2}{2}+2x+\dfrac{2}{3}=0$

Multiply both sides of the equation by 6 to clear fractions.

$3x^2+12x+4=0$

Apply the quadratic formula.

$a=3 \quad b=12 \quad c=4$

$x=\dfrac{-12\pm\sqrt{12^2-4(3)(4)}}{2(3)}$

$=\dfrac{-12\pm\sqrt{144-48}}{6}$

$=\dfrac{-12\pm\sqrt{96}}{6}$

$=\dfrac{-12\pm\sqrt{16\cdot 6}}{6}$

$=\dfrac{-12\pm 4\sqrt{6}}{6}$

$=\dfrac{2\left(-6\pm 2\sqrt{6}\right)}{6}=\dfrac{-6\pm 2\sqrt{6}}{3}$

The solutions are $\dfrac{-6\pm 2\sqrt{6}}{3}$, and the

solution set is $\left\{\dfrac{-6\pm 2\sqrt{6}}{3}\right\}$.

41. $(3x-2)^2=10$

Apply the square root property.

$3x-2=\pm\sqrt{10}$

$3x=2\pm\sqrt{10}$

$x=\dfrac{2\pm\sqrt{10}}{3}$

The solutions are $\dfrac{2\pm\sqrt{10}}{3}$, and the

solution set is $\left\{\dfrac{2\pm\sqrt{10}}{3}\right\}$.

43.

$$\frac{1}{x} + \frac{1}{x+2} = \frac{1}{3}$$

The LCD is $3x(x+2)$.

$$3x(x+2)\left(\frac{1}{x} + \frac{1}{x+2}\right) = 3x(x+2)\left(\frac{1}{3}\right)$$

$$3(x+2) + 3x = x(x+2)$$

$$3x + 6 + 3x = x^2 + 2x$$

$$0 = x^2 - 4x - 6$$

Apply the quadratic formula.

$a = 1 \quad b = -4 \quad c = -6$

$$x = \frac{-(-4) \pm \sqrt{(-4)^2 - 4(1)(-6)}}{2(1)}$$

$$= \frac{4 \pm \sqrt{16 - (-24)}}{2}$$

$$= \frac{4 \pm \sqrt{40}}{2} = \frac{4 \pm 2\sqrt{10}}{2} = 2 \pm \sqrt{10}$$

The solutions are $2 \pm \sqrt{10}$, and the solution set is $\left\{2 \pm \sqrt{10}\right\}$.

45.

$$(2x-6)(x+2) = 5(x-1) - 12$$

$$2x^2 + 4x - 6x - 12 = 5x - 5 - 12$$

$$2x^2 - 2x - 12 = 5x - 17$$

$$2x^2 - 7x + 5 = 0$$

$$(2x-5)(x-1) = 0$$

Apply the zero product principle.

$2x - 5 = 0 \quad \text{or} \quad x - 1 = 0$

$2x = 5 \qquad\qquad x = 1$

$x = \dfrac{5}{2}$

The solutions are 1 and $\dfrac{5}{2}$, and the

solution set is $\left\{1, \dfrac{5}{2}\right\}$.

47. Because the solution set is $\{-3, 5\}$,

we have

$x = -3 \quad \text{or} \qquad x = 5$

$x + 3 = 0 \qquad\qquad x - 5 = 0.$

Use the zero-product principle in reverse.

$$(x+3)(x-5) = 0$$

$$x^2 - 5x + 3x - 15 = 0$$

$$x^2 - 2x - 15 = 0$$

49. Because the solution set is $\left\{-\dfrac{2}{3}, \dfrac{1}{4}\right\}$,

we have

$x = -\dfrac{2}{3} \quad \text{or} \qquad x = \dfrac{1}{4}$

$3x = -2 \qquad\qquad 4x = 1$

$3x + 2 = 0 \qquad\qquad 4x - 1 = 0.$

Use the zero-product principle in reverse.

$$(3x+2)(4x-1) = 0$$

$$12x^2 - 3x + 8x - 2 = 0$$

$$12x^2 + 5x - 2 = 0$$

51. Because the solution set is $\{-6i, 6i\}$,

we have

$x = 6i \quad \text{or} \qquad x = -6i$

$x - 6i = 0 \qquad\qquad x + 6i = 0.$

Use the zero-product principle in reverse.

$$(x-6i)(x+6i) = 0$$

$$x^2 + 6i - 6i - 36i^2 = 0$$

$$x^2 - 36(-1) = 0$$

$$x^2 + 36 = 0$$

53. Because the solution set is
$\left\{-\sqrt{2}, \sqrt{2}\right\}$, we have

$$x = \sqrt{2} \quad \text{or} \quad x = -\sqrt{2}$$
$$x - \sqrt{2} = 0 \qquad x + \sqrt{2} = 0.$$

Use the zero-product principle in reverse.

$$\left(x - \sqrt{2}\right)\left(x + \sqrt{2}\right) = 0$$
$$x^2 + x\sqrt{2} - x\sqrt{2} - 2 = 0$$
$$x^2 - 2 = 0$$

55. Because the solution set is
$\left\{-2\sqrt{5}, \ 2\sqrt{5}\right\}$ we have

$$x = 2\sqrt{5} \quad \text{or} \quad x = -2\sqrt{5}$$
$$x - 2\sqrt{5} = 0 \qquad x + 2\sqrt{5} = 0.$$

Use the zero-product principle in reverse.

$$\left(x - 2\sqrt{5}\right)\left(x + 2\sqrt{5}\right) = 0$$
$$x^2 + 2x\sqrt{5} - 2x\sqrt{5} - 4 \cdot 5 = 0$$
$$x^2 - 20 = 0$$

57. Because the solution set is
$\left\{1 + i, \ 1 - i\right\}$, we have

$$x = 1 + i \quad \text{or} \quad x = 1 - i$$
$$x - (1 + i) = 0 \qquad x - (1 - i) = 0.$$

Use the zero-product principle in reverse.

$$\left[x - (1 + i)\right]\left[x - (1 - i)\right] = 0$$
$$x^2 - x(1 - i) - x(1 + i) + (1 + i)(1 - i) = 0$$
$$x^2 - x + xi - x - xi + 1 - i^2 = 0$$
$$x^2 - x - x + 1 - (-1) = 0$$
$$x^2 - 2x + 2 = 0$$

59. Because the solution set is
$\left\{1 + \sqrt{2}, 1 - \sqrt{2}\right\}$, we have

$$x = 1 + \sqrt{2} \quad \text{or} \quad x = 1 - \sqrt{2}$$
$$x - \left(1 + \sqrt{2}\right) = 0 \qquad x - \left(1 - \sqrt{2}\right) = 0.$$

Use the zero-product principle in reverse.

$$\left(x - \left(1 + \sqrt{2}\right)\right)\left(x - \left(1 - \sqrt{2}\right)\right) = 0$$
$$x^2 - x\left(1 - \sqrt{2}\right) - x\left(1 + \sqrt{2}\right)$$
$$+ \left(1 + \sqrt{2}\right)\left(1 - \sqrt{2}\right) = 0$$
$$x^2 - x + x\sqrt{2} - x - x\sqrt{2} + 1 - 2 = 0$$
$$x^2 - 2x - 1 = 0$$

61. b. If the solutions are imaginary number, then the graph will not cross the x-axis.

62. c. If the discriminant is 0, then the equation has one real solution (a repeated solution). Thus, the graph only touches the x-axis at one point.

63. a. The equation has two non-integer solutions $3 \pm \sqrt{2}$, so the graph crosses the x-axis at $3 - \sqrt{2}$ and $3 + \sqrt{2}$.

64. d. The equation has two integer solutions, so the graph has two integer x-intercepts.

588

65. Let x = the number.

$$x^2 - (6 + 2x) = 0$$

$$x^2 - 2x - 6 = 0$$

Apply the quadratic formula.

$$a = 1 \quad b = -2 \quad c = -6$$

$$x = \frac{-(-2) \pm \sqrt{(-2)^2 - 4(1)(-6)}}{2(1)}$$

$$= \frac{2 \pm \sqrt{4 - (-24)}}{2}$$

$$= \frac{2 \pm \sqrt{28}}{2}$$

$$= \frac{2 \pm \sqrt{4 \cdot 7}}{2} = \frac{2 \pm 2\sqrt{7}}{2} = 1 \pm \sqrt{7}$$

We disregard $1 - \sqrt{7}$ because it is negative, and we are looking for a positive number.

Thus, the number is $1 + \sqrt{7}$.

66. Let x = the number.

$$2x^2 - (1 + 2x) = 0$$

$$2x^2 - 2x - 1 = 0$$

Apply the quadratic formula.

$$a = 2 \quad b = -2 \quad c = -1$$

$$x = \frac{-(-2) \pm \sqrt{(-2)^2 - 4(2)(-1)}}{2(2)}$$

$$= \frac{2 \pm \sqrt{4 - (-8)}}{4}$$

$$= \frac{2 \pm \sqrt{12}}{4} = \frac{2 \pm \sqrt{4 \cdot 3}}{4} = \frac{2 \pm 2\sqrt{3}}{4} = \frac{1 \pm \sqrt{3}}{2}$$

We disregard $\dfrac{1 + \sqrt{3}}{2}$ because it is positive,

and we are looking for a negative number.

The number is $\dfrac{1 - \sqrt{3}}{2}$.

67.

$$\frac{1}{x^2-3x+2}=\frac{1}{x+2}+\frac{5}{x^2-4}$$

$$\frac{1}{(x-1)(x-2)}=\frac{1}{x+2}+\frac{5}{(x+2)(x-2)}$$

Multiply both sides of the equation by the least common denominator $(x-1)(x-2)(x+2)$:

$$(x-1)(x-2)(x+2)\left[\frac{1}{(x-1)(x-2)}\right]=(x-1)(x-2)(x+2)\left[\frac{1}{x+2}+\frac{5}{(x-2)(x+2)}\right]$$

$$x+2=(x-1)(x-2)+5(x-1)$$

$$x+2=x^2-2x-x+2+5x-5$$

$$x+2=x^2+2x-3$$

$$0=x^2+x-5$$

Apply the quadratic formula: $a=1 \quad b=1 \quad c=-5$.

$$x=\frac{-1\pm\sqrt{1^2-4(1)(-5)}}{2(1)}=\frac{-1\pm\sqrt{1-(-20)}}{2}=\frac{-1\pm\sqrt{21}}{2}$$

The solutions are $\dfrac{-1\pm\sqrt{21}}{2}$, and the solution set is $\left\{\dfrac{-1\pm\sqrt{21}}{2}\right\}$.

68.

$$\frac{x-1}{x-2}+\frac{x}{x-3}=\frac{1}{x^2-5x+6}$$

$$\frac{x-1}{x-2}+\frac{x}{x-3}=\frac{1}{(x-2)(x-3)}$$

Multiply both sides of the equation by the least common denominator $(x-2)(x-3)$:

$$(x-2)(x-3)\left[\frac{x-1}{x-2}+\frac{x}{x-3}\right]=(x-2)(x-3)\left[\frac{1}{(x-2)(x-3)}\right]$$

$$(x-3)(x-1)+x(x-2)=1$$

$$x^2-x-3x+3+x^2-2x=1$$

$$2x^2-6x+3=1$$

$$2x^2-6x+2=0$$

Apply the quadratic formula: $a=2 \quad b=-6 \quad c=2$.

$$x=\frac{-(-6)\pm\sqrt{(-6)^2-4(2)(2)}}{2(2)}=\frac{6\pm\sqrt{36-16}}{4}=\frac{6\pm\sqrt{20}}{4}=\frac{6\pm\sqrt{4\cdot5}}{4}=\frac{6\pm2\sqrt{5}}{4}=\frac{3\pm\sqrt{5}}{2}$$

The solutions are $\dfrac{3\pm\sqrt{5}}{2}$, and the solution set is $\left\{\dfrac{3\pm\sqrt{5}}{2}\right\}$.

69. $\sqrt{2}x^2 + 3x - 2\sqrt{2} = 0$

Apply the quadratic formula:

$a = \sqrt{2} \quad b = 3 \quad c = -2\sqrt{2}$

$x = \dfrac{-3 \pm \sqrt{3^2 - 4\left(\sqrt{2}\right)\left(-2\sqrt{2}\right)}}{2\left(\sqrt{2}\right)}$

$= \dfrac{-3 \pm \sqrt{9 - (-16)}}{2\sqrt{2}}$

$= \dfrac{-3 \pm \sqrt{25}}{2\sqrt{2}} = \dfrac{-3 \pm 5}{2\sqrt{2}}$

Evaluate the expression to obtain two solutions.

$x = \dfrac{-3 - 5}{2\sqrt{2}} \quad$ or $\quad x = \dfrac{-3 + 5}{2\sqrt{2}}$

$= \dfrac{-8}{2\sqrt{2}} \cdot \dfrac{\sqrt{2}}{\sqrt{2}} \qquad = \dfrac{2}{2\sqrt{2}} \cdot \dfrac{\sqrt{2}}{\sqrt{2}}$

$= \dfrac{-8\sqrt{2}}{4} \qquad\quad = \dfrac{2\sqrt{2}}{4}$

$= -2\sqrt{2} \qquad\quad = \dfrac{\sqrt{2}}{2}$

The solutions are $-2\sqrt{2}$ and $\dfrac{\sqrt{2}}{2}$,

and the solution set is $\left\{-2\sqrt{2}, \dfrac{\sqrt{2}}{2}\right\}$.

70. $\sqrt{3}x^2 + 6x + 7\sqrt{3} = 0$

Apply the quadratic formula:

$a = \sqrt{3} \quad b = 6 \quad c = 7\sqrt{3}$

$x = \dfrac{-6 \pm \sqrt{6^2 - 4\left(\sqrt{3}\right)\left(7\sqrt{3}\right)}}{2\left(\sqrt{3}\right)}$

$= \dfrac{-6 \pm \sqrt{36 - 84}}{2\sqrt{3}}$

$= \dfrac{-6 \pm \sqrt{-48}}{2\sqrt{3}}$

$= \dfrac{-6 \pm \sqrt{16 \cdot 3 \cdot (-1)}}{2\sqrt{3}}$

$= \dfrac{-6 \pm 4\sqrt{3}i}{2\sqrt{3}}$

$= \dfrac{-6}{2\sqrt{3}} \pm \dfrac{4\sqrt{3}i}{2\sqrt{3}} = -\sqrt{3} \pm 2i$

The solutions are $-\sqrt{3} \pm 2i$, and the solution set is $\left\{-\sqrt{3} \pm 2i\right\}$.

71. $\left|x^2 + 2x\right| = 3$

$x^2 + 2x = -3 \quad$ or $\quad x^2 + 2x = 3$

$x^2 + 2x + 3 = 0 \qquad\quad x^2 + 2x - 3 = 0$

Apply the quadratic formula to solve $x^2 + 2x + 3 = 0$:

$a = 1 \quad b = 2 \quad c = 3$.

$x = \dfrac{-2 \pm \sqrt{2^2 - 4(1)(3)}}{2(1)}$

$= \dfrac{-2 \pm \sqrt{4 - 12}}{2}$

$= \dfrac{-2 \pm \sqrt{-8}}{2}$

$= \dfrac{-2 \pm \sqrt{2 \cdot 4 \cdot (-1)}}{2}$

$= \dfrac{-2 \pm 2\sqrt{2}i}{2} = -1 \pm \sqrt{2}i$

Apply the zero product principle to solve $x^2 + 2x - 3 = 0$:

$(x + 3)(x - 1) = 0$

$x + 3 = 0 \quad$ or $\quad x - 1 = 0$

$x = -3 \quad$ or $\qquad x = 1$

The solutions are $-1 \pm \sqrt{2}i$, -3, and 1, and the solution set is $\left\{-3, \ 1, \ -1 \pm \sqrt{2}i\right\}$.

591

72. $\left| x^2 + 3x \right| = 2$

$x^2 + 3x = -2$ or $\quad x^2 + 3x = 2$

$x^2 + 3x + 2 = 0$ $\qquad x^2 + 3x - 2 = 0$

Apply the zero product principle to solve $x^2 + 3x + 2 = 0$:

$(x + 2)(x + 1) = 0$

$x + 2 = 0$ or $\quad x + 1 = 0$

$x = -2$ or $\qquad x = -1$

Apply the quadratic formula to solve $x^2 + 3x - 2 = 0$:

$a = 1 \quad b = 3 \quad c = -2$.

$$x = \frac{-3 \pm \sqrt{3^2 - 4(1)(-2)}}{2(1)}$$

$$= \frac{-3 \pm \sqrt{9 - (-8)}}{2} = \frac{-3 \pm \sqrt{17}}{2}$$

The solutions are -2, -1, and $\dfrac{-3 \pm \sqrt{17}}{2}$, and the solution set is

$$\left\{ -2, \ -1, \ \frac{-3 \pm \sqrt{17}}{2} \right\}.$$

73. $f(x) = 0.013x^2 - 1.19x + 28.24$

$3 = 0.013x^2 - 1.19x + 28.24$

$0 = 0.013x^2 - 1.19x + 25.24$

Apply the quadratic formula:

$a = 0.013 \quad b = -1.19 \quad c = 25.24$

$$x = \frac{-(-1.19) \pm \sqrt{(-1.19)^2 - 4(0.013)(25.24)}}{2(0.013)}$$

$$= \frac{1.19 \pm \sqrt{1.4161 - 1.31248}}{0.026}$$

$$= \frac{1.19 \pm \sqrt{0.10362}}{0.026}$$

$$\approx \frac{1.19 \pm 0.32190}{0.026}$$

$$\approx 58.15 \text{ or } 33.39$$

The solutions are approximately 33.39 and 58.15. Thus, 33 year olds and 58 year olds are expected to be in 3 fatal crashes per 100 million miles driven. The function models the actual data well.

75. Let $y_1 = -0.01x^2 + 0.7x + 6.1$

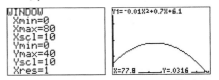

Using the TRACE feature, we find that the height of the shot put is approximately 0 feet when the distance is 77.8 feet. Graph (b) shows the shot' path.

77. Let x = the width of the rectangle; $x + 4$ = the length of the rectangle

$A = lw$

$8 = x(x + 4)$

$0 = x^2 + 4x - 8$

Apply the quadratic formula:

$a = 1 \quad b = 4 \quad c = -8$

$$x = \frac{-4 \pm \sqrt{4^2 - 4(1)(-8)}}{2(1)}$$

$$= \frac{-4 \pm \sqrt{16 - (-32)}}{2}$$

$$= \frac{-4 \pm \sqrt{48}}{2}$$

$$= \frac{-4 \pm 4\sqrt{3}}{2}$$

$$= -2 \pm 2\sqrt{3} \approx 1.5 \text{ or } -5.5$$

Disregard -5.5 because the width of a rectangle cannot be negative. Thus, the solution is 1.5, and we conclude that the rectangle's dimensions are 1.5 meters by $1.5 + 4 = 5.5$ meters.

79. Let x = the length of the longer leg;
$x-1$ = the length of the shorter leg;
$x+7$ = the length of the hypotenuse.

$$x^2 + (x-1)^2 = (x+7)^2$$

$$x^2 + x^2 - 2x + 1 = x^2 + 14x + 49$$

$$2x^2 - 2x + 1 = x^2 + 14x + 49$$

$$x^2 - 16x - 48 = 0$$

Apply the quadratic formula:
$a = 1 \quad b = -16 \quad c = -48$

$$x = \frac{-(-16) \pm \sqrt{(-16)^2 - 4(1)(-48)}}{2(1)}$$

$$= \frac{16 \pm \sqrt{256 - (-192)}}{2}$$

$$= \frac{16 \pm \sqrt{448}}{2}$$

$$= \frac{16 \pm 8\sqrt{7}}{2}$$

$$= 8 \pm 4\sqrt{7} \approx 18.6 \text{ or } -2.6$$

Disregard −2.6 because the length of a leg cannot be negative. The solution is 18.6, and we conclude that the lengths of the triangle's legs are approximately 18.6 inches and $18.6 - 1 = 17.6$ inches.

81. $x(20 - 2x) = 13$

$$20x - 2x^2 = 13$$

$$0 = 2x^2 - 20x + 13$$

Apply the quadratic formula:
$a = 2 \quad b = -20 \quad c = 13$

$$x = \frac{-(-20) \pm \sqrt{(-20)^2 - 4(2)(13)}}{2(2)}$$

$$= \frac{20 \pm \sqrt{400 - 104}}{4}$$

$$= \frac{20 \pm \sqrt{296}}{4}$$

$$= \frac{20 \pm 2\sqrt{74}}{4} = \frac{10 \pm \sqrt{74}}{2} \approx 9.3 \text{ or } 0.7$$

A gutter with depth 9.3 or 0.7 inches will have a cross-sectional area of 13 square inches.

83. Let x = the time for the first person to mow the yard alone;
$x+1$ = the time for the second person to mow the yard alone.

	Fractional part of job completed in 1 hour	Time working together	Fractional part of job completed in 4 hour
1st person	$\dfrac{1}{x}$	4	$\dfrac{4}{x}$
2nd person	$\dfrac{1}{x+1}$	4	$\dfrac{1}{x+1}$

$$\frac{4}{x} + \frac{4}{x+1} = 1$$

$$x(x+1)\left(\frac{4}{x} + \frac{4}{x+1}\right) = x(x+1)1$$

$$4(x+1) + 4x = x^2 + x$$

$$4x + 4 + 4x = x^2 + x$$

$$0 = x^2 - 7x - 4$$

Apply the quadratic formula:
$a = 1 \quad b = -7 \quad c = -4$

$$x = \frac{-(-7) \pm \sqrt{(-7)^2 - 4(1)(-4)}}{2(1)}$$

$$= \frac{7 \pm \sqrt{49 - (-16)}}{2}$$

$$= \frac{7 \pm \sqrt{65}}{2} \approx 7.5 \text{ or } -0.5$$

Disregard −0.5 because time cannot be negative. Thus, the solution is 7.5, and we conclude that the first person can mow the lawn alone in 7.5 hours, and the second can mow the lawn alone in 7.5 + 1 = 8.5 hours.

85. – 91. Answers will vary.

93. Answers will vary. For example, consider Exercise 23.

$$2x^2 + x + 3 = 0$$

The graph does not cross the x–axis and we conclude that there are 2 imaginary solutions which are complex conjugates.

95. Statement **d** is true. Any quadratic equation that can be solved by completing the square can be solved by the quadratic formula.

Statement **a** is false. The quadratic equation is developed by completing the square and the zero product principle.

Statement **b** is false. Before using the quadratic equation to solve $5x^2 = 2x - 7$, the equation must be rewritten in standard form.

$$5x^2 = 2x - 7$$

$$5x^2 - 2x + 7 = 0$$

We now have, $a = 5$, $b = -2$, and $c = 7$.

Statement **c** is false. The quadratic equation can be used to solve $x^2 - 9 = 0$, with $a = 1$, $b = 0$ and $c = -9$. (It would be easier, however, to factor or use the square root property.)

97. The dimensions of the pool are 12 meters by 8 meters. With the tile, the dimensions will be $12 + 2x$ meters by $8 + 2x$ meters. If we take the area of the pool with the tile and subtract the area of the pool without the tile, we are left with the area of the tile only.

$$(12 + 2x)(8 + 2x) - 12(8) = 120$$

$$\cancel{96} + 24x + 16x + 4x^2 - \cancel{96} = 120$$

$$4x^2 + 40x - 120 = 0$$

$$x^2 + 10x - 30 = 0$$

$$a = 1 \qquad b = 10 \qquad c = -30$$

$$x = \frac{-10 \pm \sqrt{10^2 - 4(1)(-30)}}{2(1)}$$

$$= \frac{-10 \pm \sqrt{100 + 120}}{2}$$

$$= \frac{-10 \pm \sqrt{220}}{2} \approx \frac{-10 \pm 14.8}{2}$$

Evaluate the expression to obtain two solutions.

$$x = \frac{-10 + 14.8}{2} \quad \text{or} \quad x = \frac{-10 - 14.8}{2}$$

$$x = \frac{4.8}{2} \qquad\qquad x = \frac{-24.8}{2}$$

$$x = 2.4 \qquad\qquad x = -12.4$$

We disregard –12.4 because we can't have a negative width measurement. The solution is 2.4 and we conclude that the width of the uniform tile border is 2.4 meters. This is more than the 2-meter requirement, so the tile meets the zoning laws.

99. $|5x+2| = |4-3x|$

$5x+2 = 4-3x$ or $5x+2 = -(4-3x)$

$8x+2 = 4$ $\qquad\qquad 5x+2 = -4+3x$

$\quad 8x = 2$ $\qquad\qquad\quad 2x+2 = -4$

$\quad x = \dfrac{1}{4}$ $\qquad\qquad\quad\; 2x = -6$

$\qquad\qquad\qquad\qquad\qquad x = -3$

The solutions are $\dfrac{1}{4}$ and -3, and the

solution set is $\left\{-3, \dfrac{1}{4}\right\}$.

100. $\sqrt{2x-5} - \sqrt{x-3} = 1$

$\sqrt{2x-5} = \sqrt{x-3}+1$

$\left(\sqrt{2x-5}\right)^2 = \left(\sqrt{x-3}+1\right)^2$

$2x-5 = x-3+2\sqrt{x-3}+1$

$2x-5 = x-2+2\sqrt{x-3}$

$x-3 = 2\sqrt{x-3}$

$(x-3)^2 = \left(2\sqrt{x-3}\right)^2$

$x^2 - 6x + 9 = 4(x-3)$

$x^2 - 6x + 9 = 4x - 12$

$x^2 - 10x + 21 = 0$

$(x-7)(x-3) = 0$

Apply the zero product principle.

$x-7 = 0$ or $x-3 = 0$

$\quad x = 7$ $\qquad\quad x = 3$

Both check. The solutions are 3 and
7, and the solution set is $\{3, 7\}$.

101.

$\dfrac{5}{\sqrt{3}+x} = \dfrac{5}{\sqrt{3}+x} \cdot \dfrac{\sqrt{3}-x}{\sqrt{3}-x}$

$= \dfrac{5\left(\sqrt{3}-x\right)}{3-x^2} = \dfrac{5\sqrt{3}-5x}{3-x^2}$

11.3 Exercise Set

1. The vertex of the graph is the point
$(1, 1)$. This means that the equation
is $h(x) = (x-1)^2 + 1$.

3. The vertex of the graph is the point
$(1, -1)$. This means that the equation
is $j(x) = (x-1)^2 - 1$.

5. The vertex of the graph is the point
$(0, -1)$. This means that the equation
is $h(x) = (x-0)^2 - 1 = x^2 - 1$.

7. The vertex of the graph is the point
$(1, 0)$. This means that the equation
is $g(x) = (x-1)^2 + 0$

$\qquad\qquad = (x-1)^2 = x^2 - 2x + 1$

9. $f(x) = 2(x-3)^2 + 1$
The vertex is $(3, 1)$.

11. $f(x) = -2(x+1)^2 + 5$
The vertex is $(-1, 5)$.

13. $f(x) = 2x^2 - 8x + 3$
The x–coordinate of the vertex of the

parabola is $-\dfrac{b}{2a} = -\dfrac{-8}{2(2)} = -\dfrac{-8}{4} = 2$,

and the y–coordinate of the vertex of
the parabola is

$f\left(-\dfrac{b}{2a}\right) = f(2) = 2(2)^2 - 8(2) + 3$

$\qquad\qquad = 2(4) - 16 + 3$

$\qquad\qquad = 8 - 16 + 3 = -5.$

The vertex is $(2, -5)$.

595

15. $f(x) = -x^2 - 2x + 8$

The x–coordinate of the vertex of the parabola is

$$-\frac{b}{2a} = -\frac{-2}{2(-1)} = -\frac{-2}{-2} = -1,$$

and the y–coordinate of the vertex of the parabola is

$$f\left(-\frac{b}{2a}\right) = f(-1)$$

$$= -(-1)^2 - 2(-1) + 8$$

$$= -1 + 2 + 8 = 9.$$

The vertex is $(-1, 9)$.

17. $f(x) = (x-4)^2 - 1$

Since $a = 1$ is positive, the parabola opens upward. The vertex of the parabola is $(h, k) = (4, -1)$. Replace $f(x)$ with 0 to find x–intercepts.

$$0 = (x-4)^2 - 1$$

$$1 = (x-4)^2$$

Apply the square root property.

$$x - 4 = \pm\sqrt{1} = \pm 1$$

$$x = 4 \pm 1 = 5 \text{ or } 3$$

The x–intercepts are 5 and 3.

Set $x = 0$ and solve for y to obtain the y–intercept. $y = (0-4)^2 - 1 = 15$

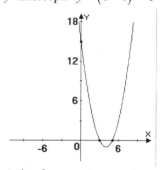

Axis of symmetry: $x = 4$.
Range: $\{y \mid y \geq -1\}$ or $[-1, \infty)$.

19. $f(x) = (x-1)^2 + 2$

Since $a = 1$ is positive, the parabola opens upward. The vertex of the parabola is $(h, k) = (1, 2)$. Replace $f(x)$ with 0 to find x–intercepts.

$$0 = (x-1)^2 + 2$$

$$-2 = (x-1)^2$$

Because the solutions to the equation are imaginary, we know that there are no x–intercepts. Set $x = 0$ and solve for y to obtain the y–intercept.

$$y = (0-1)^2 + 2 = (-1)^2 + 2 = 1 + 2 = 3$$

The y–intercept is 3.

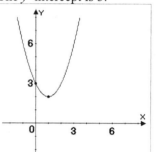

Axis of symmetry: $x = 1$.
Range: $\{y \mid y \geq 2\}$ or $[2, \infty)$.

21.
$$y - 1 = (x-3)^2$$

$$y = (x-3)^2 + 1$$

$$f(x) = (x-3)^2 + 1$$

Since $a = 1$ is positive, the parabola opens upward. The vertex of the parabola is $(h, k) = (3, 1)$. Replace $f(x)$ with 0 to find x–intercepts.

$$0 = (x-3)^2 + 1$$

$$-1 = (x-3)^2$$

Because the solutions to the equation are imaginary, we know that there are no x–intercepts. Set $x = 0$ and solve for y to obtain the y–intercept.

$$y = (0-3)^2 + 1 = (-3)^2 + 1 = 9 + 1 = 10$$

The y–intercept is 10.

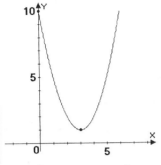

Axis of symmetry: $x = 3$.
Range: $\{y \mid y \geq 1\}$ or $[1, \infty)$.

23. $f(x) = 2(x+2)^2 - 1$

Since $a = 2$ is positive, the parabola opens upward. The vertex of the parabola is $(h, k) = (-2, -1)$. Replace $f(x)$ with 0 to find x–intercepts.

$$0 = 2(x+2)^2 - 1$$
$$1 = 2(x+2)^2$$
$$\frac{1}{2} = (x+2)^2$$

Apply the square root property.

$$x + 2 = \pm\sqrt{\frac{1}{2}}$$
$$x = -2 \pm \sqrt{\frac{1}{2}}$$
$$x \approx -2 - \sqrt{\frac{1}{2}} \quad \text{or} \quad -2 + \sqrt{\frac{1}{2}}$$
$$x \approx -2.7 \quad \text{or} \quad -1.3$$

The x–intercepts are -1.3 and -2.7.
Set $x = 0$ and solve for y to obtain the y–intercept.

$$y = 2(0+2)^2 - 1$$
$$= 2(2)^2 - 1 = 2(4) - 1 = 8 - 1 = 7$$

The y–intercept is 7.

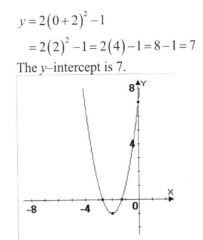

Axis of symmetry: $x = -2$.
Range: $\{y \mid y \geq -1\}$ or $[-1, \infty)$.

25. $f(x) = 4 - (x-1)^2$

$$f(x) = -(x-1)^2 + 4$$

Since $a = -1$ is negative, the parabola opens downward. The vertex of the parabola is $(h, k) = (1, 4)$. Replace $f(x)$ with 0 to find x–intercepts.

$$0 = -(x-1)^2 + 4$$
$$-4 = -(x-1)^2$$
$$4 = (x-1)^2$$

Apply the square root property.

$$\sqrt{4} = x-1 \quad \text{or} \quad -\sqrt{4} = x-1$$
$$2 = x-1 \qquad\qquad -2 = x-1$$
$$3 = x \qquad\qquad\quad -1 = x$$

The x–intercepts are -1 and 3.
Set $x = 0$ and solve for y to obtain the y–intercept.

$$y = -(0-1)^2 + 4$$
$$= -(-1)^2 + 4 = -1 + 4 = 3$$

The y–intercept is 3.

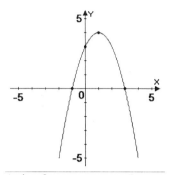

Axis of symmetry: $x = 1$.
Range: $\{y \mid y \leq 4\}$ or $(-\infty, 4]$.

27. $f(x) = x^2 - 2x - 3$

Since $a = 1$ is positive, the parabola opens upward. The x–coordinate of the vertex of the parabola is

$-\dfrac{b}{2a} = -\dfrac{(-2)}{2(1)} = \dfrac{2}{2} = 1$ and the

y–coordinate of the vertex of the parabola is

$f\left(-\dfrac{b}{2a}\right) = f(1)$

$= (1)^2 - 2(1) - 3$

$= 1 - 2 - 3 = -4.$

The vertex is $(1, -4)$. Replace $f(x)$ with 0 to find x–intercepts.

$0 = x^2 - 2x - 3$

$0 = (x - 3)(x + 1)$

Apply the zero product principle.

$x - 3 = 0 \quad$ or $\quad x + 1 = 0$

$x = 3 \qquad\qquad x = -1$

The x–intercepts are 3 and -1. Set $x = 0$ and solve for y to obtain the y–intercept.

$y = (0)^2 - 2(0) - 3 = -3$

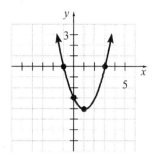

Axis of symmetry: $x = 1$.
Range: $\{y \mid y \geq -4\}$ or $[-4, \infty)$.

29. $f(x) = x^2 + 3x - 10$

Since $a = 1$ is positive, the parabola opens upward. The x–coordinate of the vertex of the parabola is

$-\dfrac{b}{2a} = -\dfrac{3}{2(1)} = -\dfrac{3}{2}$ and the

y–coordinate of the vertex of the parabola is

$f\left(-\dfrac{b}{2a}\right) = f\left(-\dfrac{3}{2}\right)$

$= \left(-\dfrac{3}{2}\right)^2 + 3\left(-\dfrac{3}{2}\right) - 10$

$= \dfrac{9}{4} - \dfrac{9}{2} - 10 = -\dfrac{49}{4}.$

The vertex is $\left(-\dfrac{3}{2}, -\dfrac{49}{4}\right)$.

Replace $f(x)$ with 0 to find the x–intercepts.

$0 = x^2 + 3x - 10$

$0 = (x + 5)(x - 2)$

Apply the zero product principle.

$x + 5 = 0 \quad$ or $\quad x - 2 = 0$

$x = -5 \qquad\qquad x = 2$

The x–intercepts are -5 and 2.

Set $x = 0$ and solve for y to obtain the y–intercept.

$y = 0^2 + 3(0) - 10 = -10$

598

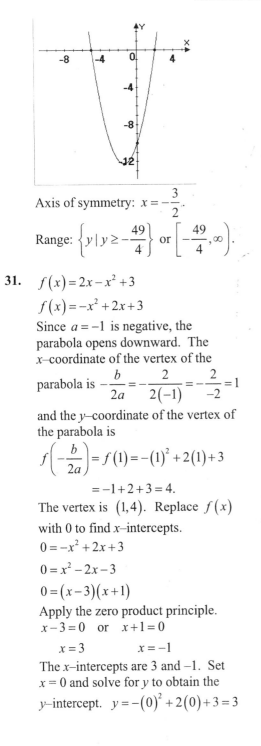

Axis of symmetry: $x = -\dfrac{3}{2}$.

Range: $\left\{ y \mid y \geq -\dfrac{49}{4} \right\}$ or $\left[-\dfrac{49}{4}, \infty \right)$.

31. $f(x) = 2x - x^2 + 3$

$f(x) = -x^2 + 2x + 3$

Since $a = -1$ is negative, the parabola opens downward. The x–coordinate of the vertex of the parabola is $-\dfrac{b}{2a} = -\dfrac{2}{2(-1)} = -\dfrac{2}{-2} = 1$

and the y–coordinate of the vertex of the parabola is

$f\left(-\dfrac{b}{2a}\right) = f(1) = -(1)^2 + 2(1) + 3$

$= -1 + 2 + 3 = 4.$

The vertex is $(1,4)$. Replace $f(x)$ with 0 to find x–intercepts.

$0 = -x^2 + 2x + 3$

$0 = x^2 - 2x - 3$

$0 = (x - 3)(x + 1)$

Apply the zero product principle.

$x - 3 = 0 \quad$ or $\quad x + 1 = 0$

$\qquad x = 3 \qquad\qquad x = -1$

The x–intercepts are 3 and -1. Set $x = 0$ and solve for y to obtain the y–intercept. $y = -(0)^2 + 2(0) + 3 = 3$

Axis of symmetry: $x = 1$.

Range: $\{ y \mid y \leq 4 \}$ or $(-\infty, 4]$.

33. $f(x) = 2x - x^2 - 2$

$f(x) = -x^2 + 2x - 2$

Since $a = -1$ is negative, the parabola opens downward. The x–coordinate of the vertex is

$-\dfrac{b}{2a} = -\dfrac{2}{2(-1)} = -\dfrac{2}{-2} = 1$

and the y–coordinate of the vertex is

$f\left(-\dfrac{b}{2a}\right) = f(1)$

$= -(1)^2 + 2(1) - 2$

$= -1 + 2 - 2 = -1.$

The vertex is $(1,-1)$. Replace $f(x)$ with 0 to find x–intercepts.

$0 = -x^2 + 2x - 2$

$x^2 - 2x = -2$

Since $b = -2$, we add

$\left(\dfrac{b}{2}\right)^2 = \left(\dfrac{-2}{2}\right)^2 = (-1)^2 = 1$

$x^2 - 2x + 1 = -2 + 1$

$(x - 1)^2 = -1$

Because the solutions to the equation are imaginary, we know that there are no x–intercepts. Set $x = 0$ and solve for y to obtain the y–intercept.

599

$$y = 2(0) - 0^2 - 2 = -2$$

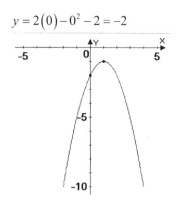

Axis of symmetry: $x = 1$.

Range: $\{y \mid y \le -1\}$ or $(-\infty, -1]$.

35. $f(x) = 3x^2 - 12x - 1$

Since $a = 3$, the parabola opens upward and has a minimum. The x–coordinate of the minimum is

$$-\frac{b}{2a} = -\frac{-12}{2(3)} = -\frac{-12}{6} = 2 \text{ and the}$$

y–coordinate of the minimum is

$$f\left(-\frac{b}{2a}\right) = f(2)$$
$$= 3(2)^2 - 12(2) - 1$$
$$= 12 - 24 - 1 = -13.$$

The minimum is $(2, -13)$.

37. $f(x) = -4x^2 + 8x - 3$

Since $a = -4$, the parabola opens downward and has a maximum. The x–coordinate of the maximum is

$$-\frac{b}{2a} = -\frac{8}{2(-4)} = -\frac{8}{-8} = 1 \text{ and the}$$

y–coordinate of the maximum is

$$f\left(-\frac{b}{2a}\right) = f(1)$$
$$= -4(1)^2 + 8(1) - 3$$
$$= -4 + 8 - 3 = 1.$$

The maximum is $(1, 1)$.

39. $f(x) = 5x^2 - 5x$

Since $a = 5$, the parabola opens upward and has a minimum. The x–coordinate of the minimum is

$$-\frac{b}{2a} = -\frac{-5}{2(5)} = -\frac{-5}{10} = \frac{1}{2} \text{ and the}$$

y–coordinate of the minimum is

$$f\left(-\frac{b}{2a}\right) = f\left(\frac{1}{2}\right)$$
$$= 5\left(\frac{1}{2}\right)^2 - 5\left(\frac{1}{2}\right)$$
$$= 5\left(\frac{1}{4}\right) - \frac{5}{2} = \frac{5}{4} - \frac{10}{4} = -\frac{5}{4}.$$

The minimum is $\left(\frac{1}{2}, -\frac{5}{4}\right)$.

41. Since the parabola opens up, the vertex $(-1, -2)$ is a minimum point. The domain is $\{x \mid x \text{ is a real number}\}$ or $(-\infty, \infty)$. The range is $\{y \mid y \ge -2\}$ or $[-2, \infty)$.

42. Since the parabola opens down, the vertex $(-3, -4)$ is a maximum point. The domain is $\{x \mid x \text{ is a real number}\}$ or $(-\infty, \infty)$. The range is $\{y \mid y \le -4\}$ or $(-\infty, -4]$.

43. Since the parabola has a maximum point of $(10, 3)$, it opens down. The domain is $\{x \mid x \text{ is a real number}\}$ or $(-\infty, \infty)$. The range is $\{y \mid y \le 3\}$ or $(-\infty, 3]$.

44. Since the parabola has a minimum point of $(5, 12)$, it opens up. The domain is $\{x|x \text{ is a real number}\}$ or $(-\infty, \infty)$. The range is $\{y \mid y \geq 12\}$ or $[12, \infty)$.

45. $(h, k) = (5, 3)$

$f(x) = 2(x - h)^2 + k = 2(x - 5)^2 + 3$

46. $(h, k) = (7, 4)$

$f(x) = 2(x - h)^2 + k = 2(x - 7)^2 + 4$

47. $(h, k) = (-10, -5)$

$f(x) = 2(x - h)^2 + k$

$= 2[x - (-10)]^2 + (-5)$

$= 2(x + 10)^2 - 5$

48. $(h, k) = (-8, -6)$

$f(x) = 2(x - h)^2 + k$

$= 2[x - (-8)]^2 + (-6)$

$= 2(x + 8)^2 - 6$

49. Since the vertex is a maximum, the parabola opens down and $a = -3$.

$(h, k) = (-2, 4)$

$f(x) = -3(x - h)^2 + k$

$= -3[x - (-2)]^2 + 4$

$= -3(x + 2)^2 + 4$

50. Since the vertex is a maximum, the parabola opens down and $a = -3$.

$(h, k) = (5, -7)$

$f(x) = -3(x - h)^2 + k$

$= -3(x - 5)^2 + (-7)$

$= -3(x - 5)^2 - 7$

51. Since the vertex is a minimum, the parabola opens up and $a = 3$.

$(h, k) = (11, 0)$

$f(x) = 3(x - h)^2 + k$

$= 3(x - 11)^2 + 0$

$= 3(x - 11)^2$

52. Since the vertex is a minimum, the parabola opens up and $a = 3$.

$(h, k) = (9, 0)$

$f(x) = 3(x - h)^2 + k$

$= 3(x - 9)^2 + 0$

$= 3(x - 9)^2$

53. From the graph, the vertex (maximum point) appears to be approximately $(14, 19.5)$. This means that in the year 2016, the projected mortality from *HCV* will reach a maximum of 19,500.

55. $s(t) = -16t^2 + 64t + 160$

a. The t-coordinate of the minimum is

$t = -\dfrac{b}{2a} = -\dfrac{64}{2(-16)} = -\dfrac{64}{-32} = 2.$

The s-coordinate of the minimum is

$s(2) = -16(2)^2 + 64(2) + 160$

$= -16(4) + 128 + 160$

$= -64 + 128 + 160 = 224$

The ball reaches a maximum height of 244 feet 2 seconds after it is thrown.

b.
$$0 = -16t^2 + 64t + 160$$
$$0 = t^2 - 4t - 10$$
$$a = 1 \quad b = -4 \quad c = -10$$
$$t = \frac{-(-4) \pm \sqrt{(-4)^2 - 4(1)(-10)}}{2(1)}$$
$$= \frac{4 \pm \sqrt{16 + 40}}{2}$$
$$= \frac{4 \pm \sqrt{56}}{2} \approx \frac{4 \pm 7.48}{2}$$

Evaluate the expression to obtain two solutions.

$$x = \frac{4 + 7.48}{2} \quad \text{or} \quad x = \frac{4 - 7.48}{2}$$
$$x = \frac{11.48}{2} \qquad\qquad x = \frac{-3.48}{2}$$
$$x = 5.74 \qquad\qquad x = -1.74$$

We disregard –1.74 because we can't have a negative time measurement. The solution is 5.74 and we conclude that the ball will hit the ground in approximately 5.7 seconds.

c.
$$s(0) = -16(0)^2 + 64(0) + 160$$
$$= -16(0) + 0 + 160 = 160$$

At $t = 0$, the ball has not yet been thrown and is at a height of 160 feet. This is the height of the building.

d.

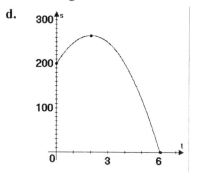

57. $f(x) = 104.5x^2 - 1501.5x + 6016$

The x-coordinate of the minimum is

$$x = -\frac{b}{2a} = -\frac{-1501.5}{2(104.5)} \approx 7.2.$$

$$f(7.2)$$
$$= 104.5(7.2)^2 - 1501.5(7.2) + 6016$$
$$= 104.5(51.84) - 10810.8 + 6016$$
$$= 622.48$$

The minimum death rate is about 622 per year per 100,000 males among U.S. men who average 7.2 hours of sleep per night.

59. Let x = one of the numbers;
$16 - x$ = the other number.
The product is
$$f(x) = x(16 - x)$$
$$= 16x - x^2 = -x^2 + 16x$$
The x-coordinate of the maximum is
$$x = -\frac{b}{2a} = -\frac{16}{2(-1)} = -\frac{16}{-2} = 8.$$

$$f(8) = -8^2 + 16(8) = -64 + 128 = 64$$

The vertex is (8, 64). The maximum product is 64. This occurs when the two number are 8 and $16 - 8 = 8$.

61. Let x = one of the numbers;
$x - 16$ = the other number.
The product is
$$f(x) = x(x - 16) = x^2 - 16x$$
The x-coordinate of the minimum is
$$x = -\frac{b}{2a} = -\frac{16}{2(1)} = -\frac{16}{2} = -8.$$

$$f(-8) = (-8)^2 + 16(-8)$$
$$= 64 - 128 = -64$$

The vertex is $(-8, -64)$. The minimum product is -64. This occurs when the two number are -8 and $-8 + 16 = 8$.

602

63. Maximize the area of a rectangle constructed along a river with 600 feet of fencing.
Let x = the width of the rectangle;
$600 - 2x$ = the length of the rectangle
We need to maximize.
$$A(x) = x(600 - 2x)$$
$$= 600x - 2x^2 = -2x^2 + 600x$$
Since $a = -2$ is negative, we know the function opens downward and has a maximum at
$$x = -\frac{b}{2a} = -\frac{600}{2(-2)} = -\frac{600}{-4} = 150.$$
When the width is $x = 150$ feet, the length is
$600 - 2(150) = 600 - 300 = 300$ feet.

The dimensions of the rectangular plot with maximum area are 150 feet by 300 feet. This gives an area of $150 \cdot 300 = 45{,}000$ square feet.

65. Maximize the area of a rectangle constructed with 50 yards of fencing.
Let x = the length of the rectangle.
Let y = the width of the rectangle.
Since we need an equation in one variable, use the perimeter to express y in terms of x.
$$2x + 2y = 50$$
$$2y = 50 - 2x$$
$$y = \frac{50 - 2x}{2} = 25 - x$$
We need to maximize
$A = xy = x(25 - x)$. Rewrite A as a function of x.
$$A(x) = x(25 - x) = -x^2 + 25x$$
Since $a = -1$ is negative, we know the function opens downward and has a maximum at
$$x = -\frac{b}{2a} = -\frac{25}{2(-1)} = -\frac{25}{-2} = 12.5.$$

When the length x is 12.5, the width y is $y = 25 - x = 25 - 12.5 = 12.5$.
The dimensions of the rectangular region with maximum area are 12.5 yards by 12.5 yards. This gives an area of $12.5 \cdot 12.5 = 156.25$ square feet.

67. Maximize the cross-sectional area of the gutter:
$$A(x) = x(20 - 2x)$$
$$= 20x - 2x^2 = -2x^2 + 20x.$$
Since $a = -2$ is negative, we know the function opens downward and has a maximum at
$$x = -\frac{b}{2a} = -\frac{20}{2(-2)} = -\frac{20}{-4} = 5.$$
When the height x is 5, the width is
$20 - 2x = 20 - 2(5) = 20 - 10 = 10$.
$$A(5) = -2(5)^2 + 20(5)$$
$$= -2(25) + 100 = -50 + 100 = 50$$
The maximum cross-sectional area is 50 square inches. This occurs when the gutter is 5 inches deep and 10 inches wide.

69. a. $C(x) = 525 + 0.55x$

b. $P(x) = R(x) - C(x)$
$$= \left(-0.001x^2 + 3x\right) - \left(525 + 0.55x\right)$$
$$= -0.001x^2 + 3x - 525 - 0.55x$$
$$= -0.001x^2 + 2.45x - 525$$

c. $P(x) = R(x) - C(x)$
$$= \left(-0.001x^2 + 3x\right) - \left(525 + 0.55x\right)$$
$$= -0.001x^2 + 3x - 525 - 0.55x$$
$$= -0.001x^2 + 2.45x - 525$$
Since $a = -0.001$ is negative, we know the function opens down and has a maximum at

603

$$x = -\frac{b}{2a}$$

$$= -\frac{2.45}{2(-0.001)} = -\frac{2.45}{-0.002} = 1225.$$

When the number of units x is 1225, the profit is

$P(1225)$

$= -0.001(1225)^2 + 2.45(1225) - 525$

$= -0.001(1500625) + 3001.25 - 525$

$= -1500.625 + 3001.25 - 525$

$= 975.625$

The store maximizes its weekly profit when 1225 roast beef sandwiches are made and sold, resulting in a profit of \$975.63.

71. – 75. Answers will vary.

77. a. $y = 2x^2 - 82x + 720$

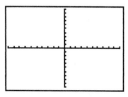

The function has no values that fall within the window.

b. $y = 2x^2 - 82x + 720$

The x–coordinate of the vertex of the parabola is

$$-\frac{b}{2a} = -\frac{-82}{2(2)} = -\frac{-82}{4} = 20.5$$

and the y–coordinate of the vertex of the parabola is

$$f\left(-\frac{b}{2a}\right) = f(20.5)$$

$= 2(20.5)^2 - 82(20.5) + 720$

$= 2(420.25) - 1681 + 720$

$= 840.5 - 1681 + 720 = -120.5.$

The vertex is $(20.5, -120.5)$.

c. Using the viewing window $[0, 30, 10]$ by $[-130, 10, 20]$, we have the following.

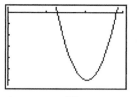

d. Answers will vary.

79. $y = -4x^2 + 20x + 160$

The x–coordinate of the vertex of the parabola is

$$-\frac{b}{2a} = -\frac{20}{2(-4)} = -\frac{20}{-8} = 2.5$$

and the y–coordinate of the vertex of the parabola is

$$f\left(-\frac{b}{2a}\right) = f(2.5)$$

$= -4(2.5)^2 + 20(2.5) + 160$

$= -4(6.25) + 50 + 160$

$= -25 + 50 + 160$

$= 185.$

The vertex is $(2.5, 185)$.
Using the viewing window $[-20, 20, 10]$ by $[0, 200, 20]$, we have the following.

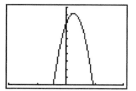

81. $y = 0.01x^2 + 0.6x + 100$

The x–coordinate of the vertex of the parabola is

$$-\frac{b}{2a} = -\frac{0.6}{2(0.01)} = -\frac{0.6}{0.02} = -30$$

and the y–coordinate of the vertex of the parabola is

$$f\left(-\frac{b}{2a}\right) = f(-30)$$

$$= 0.01(-30)^2 + 0.6(-30) + 100$$

$$= 0.01(900) - 18 + 100$$

$$= 9 - 18 + 100 = 91.$$

The vertex is $(-30, 91)$.

Using the viewing window $[-150, 150, 20]$ by $[0, 200, 20]$, we have the following.

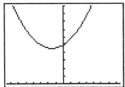

83. Statement **a** is true. Since quadratic functions represent parabolas, we know that the function has a maximum or a minimum. This means that the range cannot be $(-\infty, \infty)$.

Statement **b** is false. The vertex is $(5, -1)$.

Statement **c** is false. The graph has no x–intercepts. To find x–intercepts, set $y = 0$ and solve for x.

$$0 = -2(x + 4)^2 - 8$$

$$2(x + 4)^2 = -8$$

$$(x + 4)^2 = -4$$

Because the solutions to the equation are imaginary, we know that there are no x–intercepts.

Statement **d** is false. The x–coordinate of the maximum is

$$-\frac{b}{2a} = -\frac{1}{2(-1)} = -\frac{1}{-2} = \frac{1}{2}$$ and the

y–coordinate of the vertex of the parabola is

$$f\left(-\frac{b}{2a}\right) = f\left(\frac{1}{2}\right)$$

$$= -\left(\frac{1}{2}\right)^2 + \frac{1}{2} + 1$$

$$= -\frac{1}{4} + \frac{1}{2} + 1$$

$$= -\frac{1}{4} + \frac{2}{4} + \frac{4}{4} = \frac{5}{4}.$$

The maximum y–value is $\frac{5}{4}$.

85. $f(x) = (x - 3)^2 + 2$

Since the vertex is $(3, 2)$, we know that the axis of symmetry is the line $x = 3$. The point $(6, 11)$ is on the parabola and lies three units to the right of the axis of symmetry. This means that the point $(0, 11)$ will also lie on the parabola since it lies 3 units to the right of the axis of symmetry.

87. We know $(h, k) = (-3, -4)$, so the equation is of the form

$$f(x) = a(x - h)^2 + k$$

$$= a[x - (-3)]^2 + (-1)$$

$$= a(x + 3)^2 - 1$$

We use the point $(-2,-3)$ on the graph to determine the value of a:

$$f(x) = a(x+3)^2 - 1$$
$$-3 = a(-2+3)^2 - 1$$
$$-3 = a(1)^2 - 1$$
$$-3 = a - 1$$
$$-2 = a$$

Thus, the equation of the parabola is

$$f(x) = -2(x+3)^2 - 1.$$

89. Let x = the number of trees over 50 that will be planted.
The function describing the annual yield per lemon tree when $x+50$ trees are planted per acre is

$$f(x) = (x+50)(320-4x)$$
$$= 320x - 4x^2 + 16000 - 200x$$
$$= -4x^2 + 120x + 16000.$$

This represents the number of lemon trees planted per acre multiplied by yield per tree.

The x–coordinate of the maximum is

$$-\frac{b}{2a} = -\frac{120}{2(-4)} = -\frac{120}{-8} = 15 \text{ and the}$$

y–coordinate of the vertex of the parabola is

$$f\left(-\frac{b}{2a}\right) = f(15)$$
$$= -4(15)^2 + 120(15) + 16000$$
$$= -4(225) + 1800 + 16000$$
$$= -900 + 1800 + 16000$$
$$= 16900$$

The maximum lemon yield is 16,900 pounds when $50 + 15 = 65$ lemon trees are planted per acre.

90.

$$\frac{2}{x+5}+\frac{1}{x-5}=\frac{16}{x^2-25}$$

$$\frac{2}{x+5}+\frac{1}{x-5}=\frac{16}{(x+5)(x-5)}$$

The LCD is $(x+5)(x-5)$, so multiply each side of the equation by the LCD and clear fractions.

$$(x+5)(x-5)\left(\frac{2}{x+5}+\frac{1}{x-5}\right)=(x+5)(x-5)\left[\frac{16}{(x+5)(x-5)}\right]$$

$$(x-5)(2)+(x+5)(1)=16$$

$$2x-10+x+5=16$$

$$3x-5=16$$

$$3x=21$$

$$x=7$$

Since $x = 7$ will not make any of the denominators zero, the solution is 7, and the solution set is $\{7\}$.

91.

$$\frac{1+\frac{2}{x}}{1-\frac{4}{x^2}}=\frac{x^2}{x^2}\cdot\frac{1+\frac{2}{x}}{1-\frac{4}{x^2}}$$

$$=\frac{x^2\cdot1+x^2\cdot\frac{2}{x}}{x^2\cdot1-x^2\cdot\frac{4}{x^2}}$$

$$=\frac{x^2+x\cdot2}{x^2-4}$$

$$=\frac{x^2+2x}{(x+2)(x-2)}$$

$$=\frac{x(x+2)}{(x+2)(x-2)}=\frac{x}{x-2}$$

92.

$$2x+3y=6$$

$$x-4y=14$$

$$D=\begin{vmatrix}2 & 3\\1 & -4\end{vmatrix}$$

$$=2(-4)-1(3)=-8-3=-11$$

$$D_x=\begin{vmatrix}6 & 3\\14 & -4\end{vmatrix}$$

$$=6(-4)-14(3)=-24-42=-66$$

$$D_y=\begin{vmatrix}2 & 6\\1 & 14\end{vmatrix}$$

$$=2(14)-1(6)=28-6=22$$

$$x=\frac{D_x}{D}=\frac{-66}{-11}=6;\ y=\frac{D_y}{D}=\frac{22}{-11}=-2$$

The solution is $(6,-2)$, and the solution set is $\{(6,-2)\}$.

Mid-Chapter 11 Check Point

1. $(3x-5)^2 = 36$

Apply the square root principle:

$3x-5 = \pm\sqrt{36} = \pm 6$

$3x = 5 \pm 6$

$x = \dfrac{5 \pm 6}{3} = \dfrac{11}{3}$ or $-\dfrac{1}{3}$

The solutions are $\dfrac{11}{3}$ and $-\dfrac{1}{3}$, and the

solution set is $\left\{\dfrac{11}{3}, -\dfrac{1}{3}\right\}$.

2. $5x^2 - 2x = 7$

$5x^2 - 2x - 7 = 0$

$(5x-7)(x+1) = 0$

Apply the zero-product principle:

$5x - 7 = 0$ or $x + 1 = 0$

$5x = 7$ $\qquad\qquad x = -1$

$x = \dfrac{7}{5}$

The solutions are -1 and $\dfrac{7}{5}$, and the

solution set is $\left\{-1, \dfrac{7}{5}\right\}$.

3. $3x^2 - 6x - 2 = 0$

Apply the quadratic formula:

$a = 3 \quad b = -6 \quad c = -2$

$x = \dfrac{-(-6) \pm \sqrt{(-6)^2 - 4(3)(-2)}}{2(3)}$

$= \dfrac{6 \pm \sqrt{36 - (-24)}}{6} = \dfrac{6 \pm \sqrt{60}}{6}$

$= \dfrac{6 \pm \sqrt{4 \cdot 15}}{6} = \dfrac{6 \pm 2\sqrt{15}}{6} = \dfrac{3 \pm \sqrt{15}}{3}$

The solutions are $\dfrac{3 \pm \sqrt{15}}{3}$, and the

solution set is $\left\{\dfrac{3 \pm \sqrt{15}}{3}\right\}$.

4. $x^2 + 6x = -2$

$x^2 + 6x + 2 = 0$

Apply the quadratic formula:

$a = 1 \quad b = 6 \quad c = 2$

$x = \dfrac{-6 \pm \sqrt{6^2 - 4(1)(2)}}{2(1)}$

$= \dfrac{-6 \pm \sqrt{36 - 8}}{2}$

$= \dfrac{-6 \pm \sqrt{28}}{2}$

$= \dfrac{-6 \pm \sqrt{4 \cdot 7}}{2} = \dfrac{-6 \pm 2\sqrt{7}}{2} = -3 \pm \sqrt{7}$

The solutions are $-3 \pm \sqrt{7}$, and the

solution set is $\left\{-3 \pm \sqrt{7}\right\}$.

5. $5x^2 + 1 = 37$

$5x^2 = 36$

$x^2 = \dfrac{36}{5}$

Apply the square root principle:

$x = \pm\sqrt{\dfrac{36}{5}} = \pm\dfrac{6}{\sqrt{5}} \cdot \dfrac{\sqrt{5}}{\sqrt{5}} = \pm\dfrac{6\sqrt{5}}{5}$

The solutions are $\pm\dfrac{6\sqrt{5}}{5}$, and the

solution set is $\left\{\pm\dfrac{6\sqrt{5}}{5}\right\}$.

608

6. $x^2 - 5x + 8 = 0$

Apply the quadratic formula:

$a = 1 \quad b = -5 \quad c = 8$

$x = \dfrac{-(-5) \pm \sqrt{(-5)^2 - 4(1)(8)}}{2(1)}$

$= \dfrac{5 \pm \sqrt{25 - 32}}{2}$

$= \dfrac{5 \pm \sqrt{-7}}{2}$

$= \dfrac{5 \pm \sqrt{7 \cdot (-1)}}{2} = \dfrac{5 \pm \sqrt{7}i}{2} = \dfrac{5}{2} \pm \dfrac{\sqrt{7}}{2}i$

The solutions are $\dfrac{5}{2} \pm \dfrac{\sqrt{7}}{2}i$, and the

solution set is $\left\{ \dfrac{5}{2} \pm \dfrac{\sqrt{7}}{2}i \right\}$.

7. $2x^2 + 26 = 0$

$2x^2 = -26$

$x^2 = -13$

Apply the square root principle:

$x = \pm\sqrt{-13} = \pm\sqrt{13(-1)} = \pm\sqrt{13}i$.

The solutions are $\pm\sqrt{13}i$, and the

solution set is $\left\{ \pm\sqrt{13}i \right\}$.

8. $(2x + 3)(x + 2) = 10$

$2x^2 + 4x + 3x + 6 = 10$

$2x^2 + 7x - 4 = 0$

$(2x - 1)(x + 4) = 0$

Apply the zero-product principle:

$2x - 1 = 0 \quad$ or $\quad x + 4 = 0$

$2x = 1 \qquad\qquad x = -4$

$x = \dfrac{1}{2}$

The solutions are -4 and $\dfrac{1}{2}$, and the

solution set is $\left\{ -4, \ \dfrac{1}{2} \right\}$.

9. $(x + 3)^2 = 24$

Apply the square root principle:

$x + 3 = \pm\sqrt{24}$

$x + 3 = \pm\sqrt{4 \cdot 6} = \pm 2\sqrt{6}$

$x = -3 \pm 2\sqrt{6}$

The solutions are $-3 \pm 2\sqrt{6}$, and the

solution set is $\left\{ -3 \pm 2\sqrt{6} \right\}$.

10. $\dfrac{1}{x^2} - \dfrac{4}{x} + 1 = 0$

Multiply both sides of the equation by
the least common denominator x^2.

$x^2\left(\dfrac{1}{x^2} - \dfrac{4}{x} + 1 \right) = x^2(0)$

$1 - 4x + x^2 = 0$

$x^2 - 4x + 1 = 0$

Apply the quadratic formula:

$a = 1 \quad b = -4 \quad c = 1$

$x = \dfrac{-(-4) \pm \sqrt{(-4)^2 - 4(1)(1)}}{2(1)}$

$= \dfrac{4 \pm \sqrt{16 - 4}}{2}$

$= \dfrac{4 \pm \sqrt{12}}{2}$

$= \dfrac{4 \pm \sqrt{4 \cdot 3}}{2} = \dfrac{4 \pm 2\sqrt{3}}{2} = 2 \pm \sqrt{3}$

The solutions are $2 \pm \sqrt{3}$, and the

solution set is $\left\{ 2 \pm \sqrt{3} \right\}$.

11. $x(2x-3) = -4$

$2x^2 - 3x = -4$

$2x^2 - 3x + 4 = 0$

Apply the quadratic formula:

$a = 2 \quad b = -3 \quad c = 4$

$x = \dfrac{-(-3) \pm \sqrt{(-3)^2 - 4(2)(4)}}{2(2)}$

$= \dfrac{3 \pm \sqrt{9 - 32}}{4}$

$= \dfrac{3 \pm \sqrt{-23}}{4}$

$= \dfrac{3 \pm \sqrt{23(-1)}}{4} = \dfrac{3 \pm \sqrt{23}i}{4} = \dfrac{3}{4} \pm \dfrac{\sqrt{23}}{4}i$

The solutions are $\dfrac{3}{4} \pm \dfrac{\sqrt{23}}{4}i$, and the

solution set is $\left\{ \dfrac{3}{4} \pm \dfrac{\sqrt{23}}{4}i \right\}$.

12. $\dfrac{x^2}{3} + \dfrac{x}{2} = \dfrac{2}{3}$

Multiply both sides of the equation by the least common denominator 6.

$6\left(\dfrac{x^2}{3} + \dfrac{x}{2} \right) = 6\left(\dfrac{2}{3} \right)$

$2x^2 + 3x = 4$

$2x^2 + 3x - 4 = 0$

Apply the quadratic formula:

$a = 3 \quad b = 3 \quad c = -4$

$x = \dfrac{-3 \pm \sqrt{3^2 - 4(2)(-4)}}{2(2)}$

$= \dfrac{-3 \pm \sqrt{9 - (-32)}}{4} = \dfrac{-3 \pm \sqrt{41}}{4}$

The solutions are $\dfrac{-3 \pm \sqrt{41}}{4}$, and the

solution set is $\left\{ \dfrac{-3 \pm \sqrt{41}}{4} \right\}$

13.

$\dfrac{2x}{x^2 + 6x + 8} = \dfrac{x}{x+4} - \dfrac{2}{x+2}$

$\dfrac{2x}{(x+4)(x+2)} = \dfrac{x}{x+4} - \dfrac{2}{x+2}$

Multiply both sides of the equation by the least common denominator $(x+4)(x+2)$.

$(x+4)(x+2)\left[\dfrac{2x}{(x+4)(x+2)} \right] = (x+4)(x+2)\left[\dfrac{x}{x+4} - \dfrac{2}{x+2} \right]$

$2x = x(x+2) - 2(x+4)$

$2x = x^2 + 2x - 2x - 8$

$0 = x^2 - 2x - 8$

$0 = (x-4)(x+2)$

Apply the zero-product principle:

$x - 4 = 0 \quad \text{or} \quad x + 2 = 0$

$x = 4 \qquad\qquad x = -2$

The solutions are -2 and 4, and the solution set is $\{-2, \, 4\}$.

610

14. $x^2 + 10x - 3 = 0$

$x^2 + 10x \quad = 3$

Since $b = 10$, we add $\left(\dfrac{10}{2}\right)^2 = 5^2 = 25$.

$x^2 + 10x + 25 = 3 + 25$

$(x + 5)^2 = 28$

Apply the square root principle:

$x + 5 = \pm\sqrt{28}$

$x + 5 = \pm\sqrt{4 \cdot 7} = \pm 2\sqrt{7}$

$x = -5 \pm 2\sqrt{7}$

The solutions are $-5 \pm 2\sqrt{7}$, and the solution set is $\left\{-5 \pm 2\sqrt{7}\right\}$.

15. $d = \sqrt{(-2-2)^2 + \left(2-(-2)\right)^2}$

$= \sqrt{(-4)^2 + (4)^2} = \sqrt{16 + 16} = \sqrt{32}$

$= \sqrt{16 \cdot 2} = 4\sqrt{2} \approx 5.66$ units

$\left(\dfrac{2 + (-2)}{2}, \dfrac{-2 + 2}{2}\right) = \left(\dfrac{0}{2}, \dfrac{0}{2}\right) = (0, 0)$

The length of the segment is $4\sqrt{2} \approx 5.66$ units and the midpoint is the origin, $(0, 0)$.

16. $d = \sqrt{\left(-10 - (-5)\right)^2 + (14 - 8)^2}$

$= \sqrt{(-5)^2 + (6)^2} = \sqrt{25 + 36}$

$= \sqrt{61} \approx 7.81$ units

$\left(\dfrac{-5 + (-10)}{2}, \dfrac{8 + 14}{2}\right) = \left(\dfrac{-15}{2}, \dfrac{22}{2}\right)$

$= \left(-\dfrac{15}{2}, 11\right)$

The length of the segment is $\sqrt{61} \approx 7.81$ units and the midpoint is $\left(-\dfrac{15}{2}, 11\right)$.

17. $f(x) = (x - 3)^2 - 4$

Since $a = 1$ is positive, the parabola opens upward. The vertex of the parabola is $(h, k) = (3, -4)$. Replace $f(x)$ with 0 to find x–intercepts.

$0 = (x - 3)^2 - 4$

$4 = (x - 3)^2$

Apply the square root property.

$x - 3 = \pm\sqrt{4} = \pm 2$

$x = 3 \pm 2 = 5$ or 1

The x–intercepts are 5 and 1.
Set $x = 0$ and solve for y to obtain the y–intercept. $y = (0 - 3)^2 - 4 = 5$

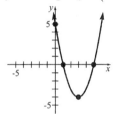

Domain: $\{x|x$ is a real number$\}$ or $(-\infty, \infty)$

Range: $\{y \mid y \geq -4\}$ or $[-4, \infty)$.

18. $g(x) = 5 - (x + 2)^2$

$g(x) = -\left[x - (-2)\right]^2 + 5$

Since $a = -1$ is negative, the parabola opens downward. The vertex of the parabola is $(h, k) = (-2, 5)$. Replace $g(x)$ with 0 to find x–intercepts.

$0 = -(x + 2)^2 + 5$

$-5 = -(x + 2)^2$

$5 = (x + 2)^2$

Apply the square root property.

$$\sqrt{5} = x + 2 \quad \text{or} \quad -\sqrt{5} = x + 2$$

$$-2 + \sqrt{5} = x \qquad\qquad -2 - \sqrt{5} = x$$

$$0.24 \approx x \qquad\qquad -4.24 \approx x$$

The x–intercepts are $-2 + \sqrt{5} \approx 0.24$ and $-2 - \sqrt{5} \approx -4.24$.

Set $x = 0$ and solve for y to obtain the y–intercept.

$$y = 5 - (0 + 2)^2 = 5 - 4 = 1$$

The y–intercept is 1.

Domain: $\{x | x$ is a real number$\}$ or $(-\infty, \infty)$

Range: $\{y | y \leq 5\}$ or $(-\infty, 5]$.

19. $h(x) = -x^2 - 4x + 5$

Since $a = -1$ is negative, the parabola opens downward. The x–coordinate of the vertex of the parabola is

$$-\frac{b}{2a} = -\frac{-4}{2(-1)} = -\frac{-4}{-2} = -2 \text{ and the}$$

y–coordinate of the vertex of the parabola is

$$h\left(-\frac{b}{2a}\right) = h(-2)$$

$$= -(-2)^2 - 4(-2) + 5$$

$$= -4 + 8 + 5 = 9$$

The vertex is $(-2, 9)$. Replace $h(x)$ with 0 to find the x–intercepts:

$$0 = -x^2 - 4x + 5$$

$$0 = x^2 + 4x - 5$$

$$0 = (x + 5)(x - 1)$$

Apply the zero product principle.

$$x + 5 = 0 \quad \text{or} \quad x - 1 = 0$$

$$x = -5 \qquad\qquad x = 1$$

The x–intercepts are -5 and 1. Set $x = 0$ and solve for y to obtain the y–intercept. $y = -(0)^2 - 4(0) + 5 = 5$

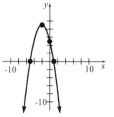

Domain: $\{x | x$ is a real number$\}$ or $(-\infty, \infty)$

Range: $\{y | y \leq 9\}$ or $(-\infty, 9]$.

20. $f(x) = 3x^2 - 6x + 1$

Since $a = 3$, the parabola opens upward. The x–coordinate of the vertex of the parabola is

$$-\frac{b}{2a} = -\frac{-6}{2(3)} = -\frac{-6}{6} = 1 \text{ and the}$$

y–coordinate of the minimum is

$$f\left(-\frac{b}{2a}\right) = f(1)$$

$$= 3(1)^2 - 6(1) + 1$$

$$= 3 - 6 + 1 = -2$$

The vertex $(1, 1)$. Replace $f(x)$ with 0 to find the x–intercepts:

$$0 = 3x^2 - 6x + 1$$

Apply the quadratic formula:

$$a = 3 \quad b = -6 \quad c = 1$$

$$x = \frac{-(-6) \pm \sqrt{(-6)^2 - 4(3)(1)}}{2(3)}$$

$$= \frac{6 \pm \sqrt{36 - 12}}{6} = \frac{6 \pm \sqrt{24}}{6}$$

$$= \frac{6 \pm 2\sqrt{6}}{6} = \frac{3 \pm \sqrt{6}}{3} \approx 0.18 \text{ or } 1.82$$

612

Set $x = 0$ and solve for y to obtain the y-intercept: $y = 3(0)^2 - 6(0) + 1 = 1$

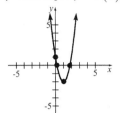

Domain: $\{x | x$ is a real number$\}$ or $(-\infty, \infty)$

Range: $\{y \,|\, y \geq -2\}$ or $[-2, \infty)$.

21. $2x^2 + 5x + 4 = 0$

$a = 2 \quad b = 5 \quad c = 4$

$b^2 - 4ac = 5^2 - 4(2)(4)$

$\qquad = 25 - 32 = -7$

Since the discriminant is negative, there are no real solutions. There are two imaginary solutions that are complex conjugates.

22. $10x(x + 4) = 15x - 15$

$\qquad 10x^2 + 40x = 15x - 15$

$10x^2 - 25x + 15 = 0$

$a = 10 \quad b = -25 \quad c = 15$

$b^2 - 4ac = (-25)^2 - 4(10)(15)$

$\qquad = 625 - 600 = 25$

Since the discriminant is positive and a perfect square, there are two rational solutions.

23.

Because the solution set is $\left\{-\dfrac{1}{2}, \dfrac{3}{4}\right\}$, we have

$$x = -\frac{1}{2} \quad \text{or} \quad x = \frac{3}{4}$$
$$2x = -1 \qquad\qquad 4x = 3$$
$$2x + 1 = 0 \qquad\quad 4x - 3 = 0$$

Use the zero-product principle in reverse.

$(2x + 1)(4x - 3) = 0$

$8x^2 - 6x + 4x - 3 = 0$

$8x^2 - 2x - 3 = 0$

24.   Because the solution set is $\left\{-2\sqrt{3}, 2\sqrt{3}\right\}$ we have

$$x = -2\sqrt{3} \quad \text{or} \quad x = 2\sqrt{3}$$
$$x + 2\sqrt{3} = 0 \qquad\quad x - 2\sqrt{3} = 0$$

Use the zero-product principle in reverse.

$$\left(x + 2\sqrt{3}\right)\left(x - 2\sqrt{3}\right) = 0$$

$x^2 + 2x\sqrt{3} - 2x\sqrt{3} - 4 \cdot 3 = 0$

$x^2 - 12 = 0$

25. $P(x) = -x^2 + 150x - 4425$

Since $a = -1$ is negative, we know the function opens down and has a maximum at

$$x = -\frac{b}{2a} = -\frac{150}{2(-1)} = -\frac{150}{-2} = 75.$$

$P(75) = -75^2 + 150(75) - 4425$

$\qquad = -5625 + 11{,}250 - 4425 = 1200$

The company will maximize its profit by manufacturing and selling 75 cabinets per day. The maximum daily profit is $1200.

26. Let x = one of the numbers;
$-18-x$ = the other number
The product is
$$f(x) = x(-18-x) = -x^2 - 18x$$
The x-coordinate of the maximum is
$$x = -\frac{b}{2a} = -\frac{-18}{2(-1)} = -\frac{-18}{-2} = -9.$$
$$f(-9) = -9\left[-18-(-9)\right]$$
$$= -9(-18+9) = -9(-9) = 81$$
The vertex is $(-9, 81)$. The maximum product is 81. This occurs when the two number are -9 and $-18-(-9) = -9$.

27. Let x = the measure of the height;
$40 - 2x$ = the measure of the base.
$$A = \frac{1}{2}bh$$
$$A(x) = \frac{1}{2}(40-2x)x$$
$$A(x) = -x^2 + 20x$$
Since $a = -1$ is negative, we know the function opens down and has a maximum at
$$x = -\frac{b}{2a} = -\frac{20}{2(-1)} = -\frac{20}{-2} = 10.$$
$$A(10) = -10^2 + 20(10)$$
$$= -100 + 200 = 100$$
A height of 10 inches will maximize the area of the triangle. The maximum area will be 100 square inches.

11.4 Exercise Set

1. Let $t = x^2$.
$$x^4 - 5x^2 + 4 = 0$$
$$\left(x^2\right)^2 - 5x^2 + 4 = 0$$
$$t^2 - 5t + 4 = 0$$
$$(t-4)(t-1) = 0$$
Apply the zero product principle.
$$t - 4 = 0 \quad \text{or} \quad t - 1 = 0$$
$$t = 4 \qquad\qquad t = 1$$
Replace t by x^2.
$$x^2 = 4 \quad \text{or} \quad x^2 = 1$$
$$x = \pm 2 \qquad\qquad x = \pm 1$$
The solutions are ± 1 and ± 2, and the solution set is $\{-2, -1, 1, 2\}$.

3. Let $t = x^2$.
$$x^4 - 11x^2 + 18 = 0$$
$$\left(x^2\right)^2 - 11x^2 + 18 = 0$$
$$t^2 - 11t + 18 = 0$$
$$(t-9)(t-2) = 0$$
Apply the zero product principle.
$$t - 9 = 0 \quad \text{or} \quad t - 2 = 0$$
$$t = 9 \qquad\qquad t = 2$$
Replace t by x^2.
$$x^2 = 9 \quad \text{or} \quad x^2 = 2$$
$$x = \pm 3 \qquad\qquad x = \pm\sqrt{2}$$
The solutions are $\pm\sqrt{2}$ and ± 3, and the solution set is $\left\{-3, -\sqrt{2}, \sqrt{2}, 3\right\}$.

5. Let $t = x^2$.

$$x^4 + 2x^2 = 8$$

$$x^4 + 2x^2 - 8 = 0$$

$$\left(x^2\right)^2 + 2x^2 - 8 = 0$$

$$t^2 + 2t - 8 = 0$$

$$(t+4)(t-2) = 0$$

Apply the zero product principle.

$$t + 4 = 0 \quad \text{or} \quad t - 2 = 0$$
$$t = -4 \qquad\qquad t = 2$$

Replace t by x^2.

$$x^2 = -4 \quad \text{or} \quad x^2 = 2$$
$$x = \pm\sqrt{-4} \qquad x = \pm\sqrt{2}$$
$$x = \pm 2i$$

The solutions are $\pm 2i$ and $\pm\sqrt{2}$, and the solution set is

$$\left\{-2i, -\sqrt{2}, \sqrt{2}, 2i\right\}.$$

7. Let $t = \sqrt{x}$.

$$x + \sqrt{x} - 2 = 0$$

$$\left(\sqrt{x}\right)^2 + \sqrt{x} - 2 = 0$$

$$t^2 + t - 2 = 0$$

$$(t+2)(t-1) = 0$$

Apply the zero product principle.

$$t + 2 = 0 \quad \text{or} \quad t - 1 = 0$$
$$t = -2 \qquad\qquad t = 1$$

Replace t by $\sqrt{x}$.

$$\cancel{\sqrt{x} = -2} \quad \text{or} \quad \sqrt{x} = 1$$
$$x = 1$$

We disregard –2 because the square root of x cannot be a negative number. We need to check the solution, 1, because both sides of the equation were raised to an even power.

Check:

$$1 + \sqrt{1} - 2 = 0$$
$$1 + 1 - 2 = 0$$
$$2 - 2 = 0$$
$$0 = 0$$

The solution is 1, and the solution set is $\{1\}$.

9. Let $t = x^{\frac{1}{2}}$.

$$x - 4x^{\frac{1}{2}} - 21 = 0$$

$$\left(x^{\frac{1}{2}}\right)^2 - 4x^{\frac{1}{2}} - 21 = 0$$

$$t^2 - 4t - 21 = 0$$

$$(t-7)(t+3) = 0$$

Apply the zero product principle.

$$t - 7 = 0 \quad \text{or} \quad t + 3 = 0$$
$$t = 7 \qquad\qquad t = -3$$

Replace t by $x^{\frac{1}{2}}$.

$$x^{\frac{1}{2}} = 7 \quad \text{or} \quad x^{\frac{1}{2}} = -3$$
$$\sqrt{x} = 7 \qquad \cancel{\sqrt{x} = -3}$$
$$x = 49$$

We disregard –2 because the square root of x cannot be a negative number. We need to check the solution, 49, because both sides of the equation were raised to an even power.

Check:

$$49 - 4(49)^{\frac{1}{2}} - 21 = 0$$
$$49 - 4(7) - 21 = 0$$
$$49 - 28 - 21 = 0$$
$$49 - 49 = 0$$
$$0 = 0$$

The solution is 49, and the solution set is $\{49\}$.

615

11. Let $t = \sqrt{x}$.
$$x - 13\sqrt{x} + 40 = 0$$
$$\left(\sqrt{x}\right)^2 - 13\sqrt{x} + 40 = 0$$
$$t^2 - 13t + 40 = 0$$
$$(t - 5)(t - 8) = 0$$

Apply the zero product principle.
$$t - 5 = 0 \quad \text{or} \quad t - 8 = 0$$
$$t = 5 \qquad\qquad t = 8$$

Replace t by $\sqrt{x}$.
$$\sqrt{x} = 5 \quad \text{or} \quad \sqrt{x} = 8$$
$$x = 25 \qquad\qquad x = 64$$

Both solutions must be checked since both sides of the equation were raised to an even power.
$$x = 25$$
$$25 - 13\sqrt{25} + 40 = 0$$
$$25 - 13(5) + 40 = 0$$
$$25 - 65 + 40 = 0$$
$$65 - 65 = 0$$
$$0 = 0$$
$$x = 64$$
$$64 - 13\sqrt{64} + 40 = 0$$
$$64 - 13(8) + 40 = 0$$
$$64 - 104 + 40 = 0$$
$$104 - 104 = 0$$
$$0 = 0$$

Both solutions check. The solutions are 25 and 64, and the solution set is $\{25, 64\}$.

13. Let $t = x - 5$.
$$(x - 5)^2 - 4(x - 5) - 21 = 0$$
$$t^2 - 4t - 21 = 0$$
$$(t - 7)(t + 3) = 0$$

Apply the zero product principle.
$$t - 7 = 0 \quad \text{or} \quad t + 3 = 0$$
$$t = 7 \qquad\qquad t = -3$$

Replace t by $x - 5$.
$$x - 5 = 7 \quad \text{or} \quad x - 5 = -3$$
$$x = 12 \qquad\qquad x = 2$$

The solutions are 2 and 12, and the solution set is $\{2, 12\}$.

15. Let $t = x^2 - 1$.
$$\left(x^2 - 1\right)^2 - \left(x^2 - 1\right) = 2$$
$$\left(x^2 - 1\right)^2 - \left(x^2 - 1\right) - 2 = 0$$
$$t^2 - t - 2 = 0$$
$$(t - 2)(t + 1) = 0$$

Apply the zero product principle.
$$t - 2 = 0 \quad \text{or} \quad t + 1 = 0$$
$$t = 2 \qquad\qquad t = -1$$

Replace t by $x^2 - 1$.
$$x^2 - 1 = 2 \quad \text{or} \quad x^2 - 1 = -1$$
$$x^2 = 3 \qquad\qquad x^2 = 0$$
$$x = \pm\sqrt{3} \qquad\qquad x = 0$$

The solutions are $\pm\sqrt{3}$ and 0, and the solution set is $\left\{-\sqrt{3}, 0, \sqrt{3}\right\}$.

17. Let $t = x^2 + 3x$.

$$\left(x^2 + 3x\right)^2 - 8\left(x^2 + 3x\right) - 20 = 0$$

$$t^2 - 8t - 20 = 0$$

$$(t-10)(t+2) = 0$$

Apply the zero product principle.

$$t - 10 = 0 \quad \text{or} \quad t + 2 = 0$$

$$t = 10 \qquad\qquad t = -2$$

Replace t by $x^2 + 3x$.

First, consider $t = 10$.

$$x^2 + 3x = 10$$

$$x^2 + 3x - 10 = 0$$

$$(x+5)(x-2) = 0$$

Apply the zero product principle.

$$x + 5 = 0 \quad \text{or} \quad x - 2 = 0$$

$$x = -5 \qquad\qquad x = 2$$

Next, consider $t = -2$.

$$x^2 + 3x = -2$$

$$x^2 + 3x + 2 = 0$$

$$(x+2)(x+1) = 0$$

Apply the zero product principle.

$$x + 2 = 0 \quad \text{or} \quad x + 1 = 0$$

$$x = -2 \qquad\qquad x = -1$$

The solutions are $-5, -2, -1$, and 2, and the solution set is
$\{-5, -2, -1, 2\}$.

19. Let $t = x^{-1}$.

$$x^{-2} - x^{-1} - 20 = 0$$

$$\left(x^{-1}\right)^2 - x^{-1} - 20 = 0$$

$$t^2 - t - 20 = 0$$

$$(t-5)(t+4) = 0$$

Apply the zero product principle.

$$t - 5 = 0 \quad \text{or} \quad t + 4 = 0$$

$$t = 5 \qquad\qquad t = -4$$

Replace t by x^{-1}.

$$x^{-1} = 5 \quad \text{or} \quad x^{-1} = -4$$

$$\frac{1}{x} = 5 \qquad\qquad \frac{1}{x} = -4$$

$$5x = 1 \qquad\qquad -4x = 1$$

$$x = \frac{1}{5} \qquad\qquad x = -\frac{1}{4}$$

The solutions are $-\dfrac{1}{4}$ and $\dfrac{1}{5}$, and

the solution set is $\left\{-\dfrac{1}{4}, \dfrac{1}{5}\right\}$.

21. Let $t = x^{-1}$.

$$2x^{-2} - 7x^{-1} + 3 = 0$$

$$2\left(x^{-1}\right)^2 - 7x^{-1} + 3 = 0$$

$$2t^2 - 7t + 3 = 0$$

$$(2t-1)(t-3) = 0$$

Apply the zero product principle.

$$2t - 1 = 0 \quad \text{or} \quad t - 3 = 0$$

$$2t = 1 \qquad\qquad t = 3$$

$$t = \frac{1}{2}$$

Replace t by x^{-1}.

$$x^{-1} = \frac{1}{2} \quad \text{or} \quad x^{-1} = 3$$

$$\frac{1}{x} = \frac{1}{2} \qquad\qquad \frac{1}{x} = 3$$

$$x = 2 \qquad\qquad 3x = 1$$

$$x = \frac{1}{3}$$

The solutions are $\dfrac{1}{3}$ and 2, and the

solution set is $\left\{\dfrac{1}{3}, 2\right\}$.

617

23. Let $t = x^{-1}$.

$$x^{-2} - 4x^{-1} = 3$$
$$x^{-2} - 4x^{-1} - 3 = 0$$
$$\left(x^{-1}\right)^2 - 4x^{-1} - 3 = 0$$
$$t^2 - 4t - 3 = 0$$

$$a = 1 \qquad b = -4 \qquad c = -3$$

Use the quadratic formula.

$$t = \frac{-(-4) \pm \sqrt{(-4)^2 - 4(1)(-3)}}{2(1)}$$

$$= \frac{4 \pm \sqrt{16 + 12}}{2} = \frac{4 \pm \sqrt{28}}{2}$$

$$= \frac{4 \pm 2\sqrt{7}}{2} = \frac{2\left(2 \pm \sqrt{7}\right)}{2} = 2 \pm \sqrt{7}$$

Replace t by x^{-1}.

$$x^{-1} = 2 \pm \sqrt{7}$$
$$\frac{1}{x} = 2 \pm \sqrt{7}$$
$$\left(2 \pm \sqrt{7}\right)x = 1$$
$$x = \frac{1}{2 \pm \sqrt{7}}$$

Rationalize the denominator.

$$x = \frac{1}{2 \pm \sqrt{7}} \cdot \frac{2 \mp \sqrt{7}}{2 \mp \sqrt{7}} = \frac{2 \mp \sqrt{7}}{2^2 - \left(\sqrt{7}\right)^2}$$

$$= \frac{2 \mp \sqrt{7}}{4 - 7} = \frac{2 \mp \sqrt{7}}{-3} = \frac{-2 \pm \sqrt{7}}{3}$$

The solutions are $\dfrac{-2 \pm \sqrt{7}}{3}$, and the

solution set is $\left\{\dfrac{-2 \pm \sqrt{7}}{3}\right\}$.

25. Let $t = x^{\frac{1}{3}}$.

$$x^{\frac{2}{3}} - x^{\frac{1}{3}} - 6 = 0$$
$$\left(x^{\frac{1}{3}}\right)^2 - x^{\frac{1}{3}} - 6 = 0$$
$$t^2 - t - 6 = 0$$
$$(t - 3)(t + 2) = 0$$

Apply the zero product principle.

$$t - 3 = 0 \quad \text{or} \quad t + 2 = 0$$
$$t = 3 \qquad\qquad t = -2$$

Replace t by $x^{\frac{1}{3}}$.

$$x^{\frac{1}{3}} = 3 \quad \text{or} \quad x^{\frac{1}{3}} = -2$$

$$\left(x^{\frac{1}{3}}\right)^3 = 3^3 \qquad \left(x^{\frac{1}{3}}\right)^3 = (-2)^3$$

$$x = 27 \qquad\qquad x = -8$$

The solutions are -8 and 27, and
the solution set is $\{-8, 27\}$.

27. Let $t = x^{\frac{1}{5}}$.

$$x^{\frac{2}{5}} + x^{\frac{1}{5}} - 6 = 0$$
$$\left(x^{\frac{1}{5}}\right)^2 + x^{\frac{1}{5}} - 6 = 0$$
$$t^2 + t - 6 = 0$$
$$(t + 3)(t - 2) = 0$$

Apply the zero product principle.

$$t + 3 = 0 \quad \text{or} \quad t - 2 = 0$$
$$t = -3 \qquad\qquad t = 2$$

Replace t by $x^{\frac{1}{5}}$.

$$x^{\frac{1}{5}} = -3 \quad \text{or} \quad x^{\frac{1}{5}} = 2$$

$$\left(x^{\frac{1}{5}}\right)^5 = (-3)^5 \qquad \left(x^{\frac{1}{5}}\right)^5 = (2)^5$$

$$x = -243 \qquad\qquad x = 32$$

The solutions are -243 and 32, and
the solution set is $\{-243, 32\}$.

29.

Let $t = x^{\frac{1}{4}}$.

$$2x^{\frac{1}{2}} - x^{\frac{1}{4}} = 1$$

$$2\left(x^{\frac{1}{4}}\right)^2 - x^{\frac{1}{4}} - 1 = 0$$

$$2t^2 - t - 1 = 0$$

$$(2t + 1)(t - 1) = 0$$

Apply the zero product principle.

$$2t + 1 = 0 \quad \text{or} \quad t - 1 = 0$$

$$2t = -1 \qquad\qquad t = 1$$

$$t = -\frac{1}{2}$$

Replace t by $x^{\frac{1}{4}}$.

$$x^{\frac{1}{4}} = -\frac{1}{2} \quad \text{or} \quad x^{\frac{1}{4}} = 1$$

$$\left(x^{\frac{1}{4}}\right)^4 = \left(-\frac{1}{2}\right)^4 \qquad \left(x^{\frac{1}{4}}\right)^4 = 1^4$$

$$x = 1$$

$$x = \frac{1}{16}$$

Since both sides of the equations were raised to an even power, the solutions must be checked.

First, check $x = \frac{1}{16}$.

$$2\left(\frac{1}{16}\right)^{\frac{1}{2}} - \left(\frac{1}{16}\right)^{\frac{1}{4}} = 1$$

$$2\left(\frac{1}{4}\right) - \frac{1}{2} = 1$$

$$\frac{1}{2} - \frac{1}{2} = 1$$

$$0 \neq 1$$

The solution does not check, so disregard $x = \frac{1}{16}$.

Next, check $x = 1$.

$$2(1)^{\frac{1}{2}} - (1)^{\frac{1}{4}} = 1$$

$$2(1) - 1 = 1$$

$$1 = 1$$

The solution checks. The solution is 1, and the solution set is $\{1\}$.

31.

Let $t = x - \frac{8}{x}$.

$$\left(x - \frac{8}{x}\right)^2 + 5\left(x - \frac{8}{x}\right) - 14 = 0$$

$$t^2 + 5t - 14 = 0$$

$$(t + 7)(t - 2) = 0$$

Apply the zero product principle.

$$t + 7 = 0 \quad \text{or} \quad t - 2 = 0$$

$$t = -7 \qquad\qquad t = 2$$

Replace t by $x - \frac{8}{x}$.

First, consider $t = -7$.

$$x - \frac{8}{x} = -7$$

$$x\left(x - \frac{8}{x}\right) = x(-7)$$

$$x^2 - 8 = -7x$$

$$x^2 + 7x - 8 = 0$$

$$(x + 8)(x - 1) = 0$$

Apply the zero product principle.

$$x + 8 = 0 \quad \text{or} \quad x - 1 = 0$$

$$x = -8 \qquad\qquad x = 1$$

Next, consider $t = 2$.

$$x - \frac{8}{x} = 2$$

$$x\left(x - \frac{8}{x}\right) = x(2)$$

$$x^2 - 8 = 2x$$

$$x^2 - 2x - 8 = 0$$

$$(x-4)(x+2) = 0$$

Apply the zero product principle.

$$x - 4 = 0 \quad \text{or} \quad x + 2 = 0$$

$$x = 4 \qquad\qquad x = -2$$

The solutions are $-8, -2, 1,$ and $4,$
and the solution set is $\{-8, -2, 1, 4\}$.

33. $f(x) = x^4 - 5x^2 + 4$

$$y = x^4 - 5x^2 + 4$$

Set $y = 0$ to find the x–intercept(s).

$$0 = x^4 - 5x^2 + 4$$

Let $t = x^2$.

$$x^4 - 5x^2 + 4 = 0$$

$$\left(x^2\right)^2 - 5x^2 + 4 = 0$$

$$t^2 - 5t + 4 = 0$$

$$(t-4)(t-1) = 0$$

Apply the zero product principle.

$$t - 1 = 0 \quad \text{or} \quad t - 4 = 0$$

$$t = 1 \qquad\qquad t = 4$$

Substitute x^2 for t.

$$x^2 = 1 \quad \text{or} \quad x^2 = 4$$

$$x = \pm 1 \qquad\qquad x = \pm 2$$

The intercepts are ± 1 and ± 2. The
corresponding graph is graph **c.**

35. $f(x) = x^{\frac{1}{3}} + 2x^{\frac{1}{6}} - 3$

$$y = x^{\frac{1}{3}} + 2x^{\frac{1}{6}} - 3$$

Set $y = 0$ to find the x–intercept(s).

$$0 = x^{\frac{1}{3}} + 2x^{\frac{1}{6}} - 3$$

Let $t = x^{\frac{1}{6}}$.

$$x^{\frac{1}{3}} + 2x^{\frac{1}{6}} - 3 = 0$$

$$\left(x^{\frac{1}{6}}\right)^2 + 2x^{\frac{1}{6}} - 3 = 0$$

$$t^2 + 2t - 3 = 0$$

$$(t+3)(t-1) = 0$$

Apply the zero product principle.

$$t + 3 = 0 \quad \text{or} \quad t - 1 = 0$$

$$t = -3 \qquad\qquad t = 1$$

Substitute $x^{\frac{1}{6}}$ for t.

$$x^{\frac{1}{6}} = -3 \quad \text{or} \quad x^{\frac{1}{6}} = 1$$

$$\left(x^{\frac{1}{6}}\right)^6 = (-3)^6 \qquad \left(x^{\frac{1}{6}}\right)^6 = (1)^6$$

$$x = 729 \qquad\qquad x = 1$$

Since both sides of the equations
were raised to an even power, the
solutions must be checked.

First check $x = 729$.

$$(729)^{\frac{1}{3}} + 2(729)^{\frac{1}{6}} - 3 = 0$$

$$9 + 2(3) - 3 = 0$$

$$9 + 6 - 3 = 0$$

$$12 \neq 0$$

Next check $x = 1$.

$$(1)^{\frac{1}{3}} + 2(1)^{\frac{1}{6}} - 3 = 0$$

$$1 + 2(1) - 3 = 0$$

$$1 + 2 - 3 = 0$$

$$0 = 0$$

Since 729 does not check, we
disregard it. The intercept is 1. The
corresponding graph is graph **e.**

37. $f(x) = (x+2)^2 - 9(x+2) + 20$

$y = (x+2)^2 - 9(x+2) + 20$

Set $y = 0$ to find the x–intercept(s).

$(x+2)^2 - 9(x+2) + 20 = 0$

Let $t = x + 2$.

$(x+2)^2 - 9(x+2) + 20 = 0$

$t^2 - 9t + 20 = 0$

$(t-5)(t-4) = 0$

Apply the zero product principle.

$t - 5 = 0$ or $t - 4 = 0$

$t = 5$ $\qquad$ $t = 4$

Substitute $x + 2$ for t.

$x + 2 = 5$ or $x + 2 = 4$

$x = 3$ $\qquad$ $x = 2$

The intercepts are 2 and 3. The corresponding graph is graph **f**.

39. Let $t = x^2 + 3x - 2$

$f(x) = -16$

$(x^2 + 3x - 2)^2 - 10(x^2 + 3x - 2) = -16$

$t^2 - 10t = -16$

$t^2 - 10t + 16 = 0$

$(t-8)(t-2) = 0$

Apply the zero product principle:

$t - 8 = 0$ or $t - 2 = 0$

$t = 8$ $\qquad$ $t = 2$

Replace t by $x^2 + 3x - 2$.

First, consider $t = 8$.

$x^2 + 3x - 2 = 8$

$x^2 + 3x - 10 = 0$

$(x+5)(x-2) = 0$

Apply the zero product principle.

$x + 5 = 0$ or $x - 2 = 0$

$x = -5$ $\qquad$ $x = 2$

Next, consider $t = 2$.

$x^2 + 3x - 2 = 2$

$x^2 + 3x - 4 = 0$

$(x+4)(x-1) = 0$

Apply the zero product principle.

$x + 4 = 0$ or $x - 1 = 0$

$x = -4$ $\qquad$ $x = 1$

The solutions are $-5, -4, 1$, and 2.

40. Let $t = x^2 + 2x - 2$

$f(x) = -6$

$(x^2 + 2x - 2)^2 - 7(x^2 + 2x - 2) = -6$

$t^2 - 7t = -6$

$t^2 - 7t + 6 = 0$

$(t-1)(t-6) = 0$

Apply the zero product principle:

$t - 1 = 0$ or $t - 6 = 0$

$t = 1$ $\qquad$ $t = 6$

Replace t by $x^2 + 2x - 2$.

First, consider $t = 1$.

$x^2 + 2x - 2 = 1$

$x^2 + 2x - 3 = 0$

$(x+3)(x-1) = 0$

Apply the zero product principle.

$x + 3 = 0$ or $x - 1 = 0$

$x = -3$ $\qquad$ $x = 1$

Next, consider $t = 6$.

$x^2 + 2x - 2 = 6$

$x^2 + 2x - 8 = 0$

$(x+4)(x-2) = 0$

Apply the zero product principle.

$x + 4 = 0$ or $x - 2 = 0$

$x = -4$ $\qquad$ $x = 2$

The solutions are $-4, -3, 1$, and 2.

41.

Let $t = \dfrac{1}{x} + 1$.

$$f(x) = 2$$

$$3\left(\dfrac{1}{x}+1\right)^2 + 5\left(\dfrac{1}{x}+1\right) = 2$$

$$3t^2 + 5t = 2$$

$$3t^2 + 5t - 2 = 0$$

$$(3t - 1)(t + 2) = 0$$

Apply the zero product principle.

$$3t - 1 = 0 \quad \text{or} \quad t + 2 = 0$$

$$3t = 1 \qquad\qquad t = -2$$

$$t = \dfrac{1}{3}$$

Replace t by $\dfrac{1}{x} + 1$.

First, consider $t = \dfrac{1}{3}$.

$$\dfrac{1}{x} + 1 = \dfrac{1}{3}$$

$$3x\left(\dfrac{1}{x}+1\right) = 3x\left(\dfrac{1}{3}\right)$$

$$3 + 3x = x$$

$$2x = -3$$

$$x = -\dfrac{3}{2}$$

Next, consider $t = -2$.

$$\dfrac{1}{x} + 1 = -2$$

$$3x\left(\dfrac{1}{x}+1\right) = 3x(-2)$$

$$3 + 3x = -6x$$

$$9x = -3$$

$$x = -\dfrac{3}{9} = -\dfrac{1}{3}$$

The solutions are $-\dfrac{3}{2}$ and $-\dfrac{1}{3}$.

42.

Let $t = x^{\frac{1}{3}}$.

$$f(x) = 2$$

$$2x^{\frac{2}{3}} + 3x^{\frac{1}{3}} = 2$$

$$2\left(x^{\frac{1}{3}}\right)^2 + 3x^{\frac{1}{3}} = 2$$

$$2t^2 + 3t - 2 = 0$$

$$(2t - 1)(t + 2) = 0$$

Apply the zero product principle.

$$2t - 1 = 0 \quad \text{or} \quad t + 2 = 0$$

$$2t = 1 \qquad\qquad t = -2$$

$$t = \dfrac{1}{2}$$

Replace t by $x^{\frac{1}{3}}$.

$$x^{\frac{1}{3}} = \dfrac{1}{2} \qquad \text{or} \qquad x^{\frac{1}{3}} = -2$$

$$\left(x^{\frac{1}{3}}\right)^3 = \left(\dfrac{1}{2}\right)^3 \qquad \left(x^{\frac{1}{3}}\right)^3 = (-2)^3$$

$$x = \dfrac{1}{8} \qquad\qquad\qquad x = -8$$

The solutions are -8 and $\dfrac{1}{8}$.

43.

Let $t = \sqrt{\dfrac{x}{x-4}}$.

$$f(x) = g(x)$$

$$\dfrac{x}{x-4} = 13\sqrt{\dfrac{x}{x-4}} - 36$$

$$\left(\sqrt{\dfrac{x}{x-4}}\right)^2 = 13\sqrt{\dfrac{x}{x-4}} - 36$$

$$t^2 = 13t - 36$$

$$t^2 - 13t + 36 = 0$$

$$(t - 9)(t - 4) = 0$$

Apply the zero product principle:

$$t - 9 = 0 \quad \text{or} \quad t - 4 = 0$$

$$t = 9 \qquad\qquad t = 4$$

Replace t by $\sqrt{\dfrac{x}{x-4}}$.

First, consider $t = 9$:

$$\sqrt{\frac{x}{x-4}} = 9$$

$$\left(\sqrt{\frac{x}{x-4}}\right)^2 = 9^2$$

$$\frac{x}{x-4} = 81$$

$$81(x-4) = x$$

$$81x - 324 = x$$

$$80x = 324$$

$$x = \frac{324}{80} = \frac{81}{20}$$

Next, consider $t = 4$:

$$\sqrt{\frac{x}{x-4}} = 4$$

$$\left(\sqrt{\frac{x}{x-4}}\right)^2 = 4^2$$

$$\frac{x}{x-4} = 16$$

$$16(x-4) = x$$

$$16x - 64 = x$$

$$15x = 64$$

$$x = \frac{64}{15}$$

Since both sides of the equations were raised to an even power, the solutions must be checked. In this case, both check, so the solutions are $\dfrac{81}{20}$ and $\dfrac{64}{15}$.

44. Let $t = \sqrt{\dfrac{x}{x-2}}$.

$$f(x) = g(x)$$

$$\frac{x}{x-2} + 10 = -11\sqrt{\frac{x}{x-2}}$$

$$\left(\sqrt{\frac{x}{x-2}}\right)^2 + 10 = -11\sqrt{\frac{x}{x-2}}$$

$$t^2 + 10 = -11t$$

$$t^2 + 11t + 10 = 0$$

$$(t+10)(t+1) = 0$$

Apply the zero product principle:

$$t + 10 = 0 \quad \text{or} \quad t + 1 = 0$$
$$t = -10 \qquad\qquad t = -1$$

Replace t by $\sqrt{\dfrac{x}{x-2}}$.

First, consider $t = -10$:

$$\sqrt{\frac{x}{x-2}} = -10$$

We disregard -10 because the square root cannot be a negative number.

Next, consider $t = -1$:

$$\sqrt{\frac{x}{x-2}} = -1$$

We disregard -1 because the square root cannot be a negative number. Thus, there are no values of x that satisfy $f(x) = g(x)$.

623

45. Let $t = (x-4)^{-1}$

$$f(x) = g(x) + 12$$
$$3(x-4)^{-2} = 16(x-4)^{-1} + 12$$
$$3\left[(x-4)^{-1}\right]^2 = 16(x-4)^{-1} + 12$$
$$3t^2 = 16t + 12$$
$$3t^2 - 16t - 12 = 0$$
$$(3t+2)(t-6) = 0$$

Apply the zero product principle:

$$3t + 2 = 0 \quad \text{or} \quad t - 6 = 0$$
$$3t = -2 \qquad\qquad t = 6$$
$$t = -\frac{2}{3}$$

Replace t by $(x-4)^{-1}$.

First, consider $t = -\frac{2}{3}$.

$$(x-4)^{-1} = -\frac{2}{3}$$
$$\frac{1}{x-4} = -\frac{2}{3}$$
$$-2(x-4) = 1(3)$$
$$-2x + 8 = 3$$
$$-2x = -5$$
$$x = \frac{-5}{-2} = \frac{5}{2}$$

Next, consider $t = 6$.

$$(x-4)^{-1} = 6$$
$$\frac{1}{x-4} = 6$$
$$6(x-4) = 1$$
$$6x - 24 = 1$$
$$6x = 25$$
$$x = \frac{25}{6}$$

The solutions are $\frac{5}{2}$ and $\frac{25}{6}$.

46. Let $t = \frac{2x}{x-3}$

$$f(x) = g(x) + 6$$
$$6\left(\frac{2x}{x-3}\right)^2 = 5\left(\frac{2x}{x-3}\right) + 6$$
$$6t^2 = 5t + 6$$
$$6t^2 - 5t - 6 = 0$$
$$(3t+2)(2t-3) = 0$$

Apply the zero product principle:

$$3t + 2 = 0 \quad \text{or} \quad 2t - 3 = 0$$
$$3t = -2 \qquad\qquad 2t = 3$$
$$t = -\frac{2}{3} \qquad\qquad t = \frac{3}{2}$$

Replace t by $\frac{2x}{x-3}$.

First, consider $t = -\frac{2}{3}$.

$$\frac{2x}{x-3} = -\frac{2}{3}$$
$$-2(x-3) = 2x(3)$$
$$-2x + 6 = 6x$$
$$-8x = -6$$
$$x = \frac{-6}{-8} = \frac{3}{4}$$

Next, consider $t = \frac{3}{2}$.

$$\frac{2x}{x-3} = \frac{3}{2}$$
$$3(x-3) = 2x(2)$$
$$3x - 9 = 4x$$
$$-9 = x$$

The solutions are -9 and $\frac{3}{4}$.

624

47.

$$P(x) = 0.04(x+40)^2 - 3(x+40) + 104$$
$$60 = 0.04(x+40)^2 - 3(x+40) + 104$$
$$0 = 0.04(x+40)^2 - 3(x+40) + 44$$

Let $t = x + 40$.

$$0.04(x+40)^2 - 3(x+40) + 44 = 0$$
$$0.04t^2 - 3t + 44 = 0$$

Solve using the quadratic formula.

$$a = 0.04 \quad b = -3 \quad c = 44$$

$$t = \frac{-(-3) \pm \sqrt{(-3)^2 - 4(0.04)(44)}}{2(0.04)}$$

$$= \frac{3 \pm \sqrt{9 - 7.04}}{0.08}$$

$$= \frac{3 \pm \sqrt{1.96}}{0.08} = \frac{3 \pm 1.4}{0.08} = 55 \text{ or } 20$$

Since x represents the number of years a person's age is above or below 40, $t = x + 40$ is the percentage we are looking for. The ages at which 60% of us feel that having a clean house is very important are 20 and 55. From the graph, we see that at 20, 58%, and at 55, 52% feel that a clean house if very important. The function models the data fairly well.

49. – 51. Answers will vary.

53. $x^6 - 7x^3 - 8 = 0$

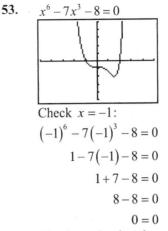

Check $x = -1$:

$$(-1)^6 - 7(-1)^3 - 8 = 0$$
$$1 - 7(-1) - 8 = 0$$
$$1 + 7 - 8 = 0$$
$$8 - 8 = 0$$
$$0 = 0$$

Check $x = 2$ using the same method. The solutions are -1 and 2, and the solution set is $\{-1, 2\}$.

55. $x^4 - 10x^2 + 9 = 0$

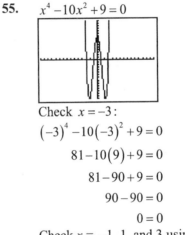

Check $x = -3$:

$$(-3)^4 - 10(-3)^2 + 9 = 0$$
$$81 - 10(9) + 9 = 0$$
$$81 - 90 + 9 = 0$$
$$90 - 90 = 0$$
$$0 = 0$$

Check $x = -1$, 1, and 3 using the same method. The solutions are -3, -1, 1 and 3, and the solution set is $\{-3, -1, 1, 3\}$.

57.
$$2(x+1)^2 = 5(x+1)+3$$
$$2(x+1)^2 - 5(x+1) - 3 = 0$$

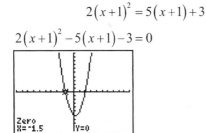

Because -1.5 is not an integer, the calculate zero feature was used to determine the intercept.
Check: $x = -1.5$:
$$2(-1.5+1)^2 = 5(-1.5+1)+3$$
$$2(-0.5)^2 = 5(-0.5)+3$$
$$2(0.25) = -2.5+3$$
$$0.5 = 0.5$$
Check $x = 2$ using the same method.

The solutions are $-1.5 = -\dfrac{3}{2}$ and 2,

and the solution set is $\left\{-\dfrac{3}{2}, 2\right\}$.

59.
$$x^{\frac{1}{2}} + 4x^{\frac{1}{4}} = 5$$
$$x^{\frac{1}{2}} + 4x^{\frac{1}{4}} - 5 = 0$$

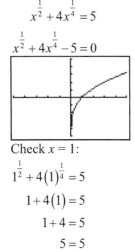

Check $x = 1$:
$$1^{\frac{1}{2}} + 4(1)^{\frac{1}{4}} = 5$$
$$1 + 4(1) = 5$$
$$1 + 4 = 5$$
$$5 = 5$$
The solution is 1, and the solution set is $\{1\}$.

61. Statement **b.** is true.

Statement **a.** is false. Any method that can be used to solve a quadratic equation can also be used to solve a quadratic-in-form equation.

Statement **c.** is false. The equation would be quadratic in form if the third term were a constant.

Statement **d.** is false. To solve the equation, let $t = \sqrt{x}$.

63.
$$5x^6 + x^3 = 18$$
$$5x^6 + x^3 - 18 = 0$$
Let $t = x^3$.
$$5x^6 + x^3 - 18 = 0$$
$$5(x^3)^2 + x^3 - 18 = 0$$
$$5t^2 + t - 18 = 0$$
$$(5t-9)(t+2) = 0$$
Apply the zero product principle.
$$5t - 9 = 0 \quad \text{or} \quad t + 2 = 0$$
$$5t = 9 \qquad\qquad t = -2$$
$$t = \dfrac{9}{5}$$
Substitute x^3 for t.
$$x^3 = \dfrac{9}{5} \quad \text{or} \quad x^3 = -2$$
$$\qquad\qquad\qquad x = \sqrt[3]{-2}$$
$$x = \sqrt[3]{\dfrac{9}{5}}$$
Rationalize the denominator.
$$\sqrt[3]{\dfrac{9}{5}} = \dfrac{\sqrt[3]{9}}{\sqrt[3]{5}} \cdot \dfrac{\sqrt[3]{5^2}}{\sqrt[3]{5^2}} = \dfrac{\sqrt[3]{9 \cdot 5^2}}{\sqrt[3]{5^3}} = \dfrac{\sqrt[3]{225}}{5}$$
The solutions are $\sqrt[3]{-2}$ and $\dfrac{\sqrt[3]{225}}{5}$,

and the solution set is
$$\left\{\sqrt[3]{-2}, \dfrac{\sqrt[3]{225}}{5}\right\}.$$

65.
$$\frac{2x^2}{10x^3 - 2x^2} = \frac{2x^2}{2x^2(5x-1)} = \frac{1}{5x-1}$$

66.
$$\frac{2+i}{1-i} = \frac{2+i}{1-i} \cdot \frac{1+i}{1+i}$$
$$= \frac{2+2i+i+i^2}{1^2 - i^2}$$
$$= \frac{2+3i-1}{1-(-1)} = \frac{1+3i}{2} = \frac{1}{2} + \frac{3}{2}i$$

67.
$$f(x) = \sqrt{x+1}$$
$$f(3) - f(24) = \sqrt{3+1} - \sqrt{24+1}$$
$$= \sqrt{4} - \sqrt{25}$$
$$= 2 - 5$$
$$= -3$$

11.5 Exercise Set

1. $(x-4)(x+2) > 0$

Solve the related quadratic equation.
$(x-4)(x+2) = 0$

Apply the zero product principle.
$x - 4 = 0$ or $x + 2 = 0$
$\quad x = 4 \qquad\qquad x = -2$

The boundary points are -2 and 4.

Test Interval	Test Number	Test	Conclusion
$(-\infty, -2)$	-3	$(-3-4)(-3+2) > 0$ $7 > 0$, true	$(-\infty, -2)$ belongs to the solution set.
$(-2, 4)$	0	$(0-4)(0+2) > 0$ $-8 > 0$, false	$(-2, 4)$ does not belong to the solution set.
$(4, \infty)$	5	$(5-4)(5+2) > 0$ $7 > 0$, true	$(4, \infty)$ belongs to the solution set.

The solution set is $(-\infty, -2) \cup (4, \infty)$ or $\{x | x < -2 \text{ or } x > 4\}$.

3. $(x-7)(x+3) \le 0$

Solve the related quadratic equation.

$(x-7)(x+3) = 0$

Apply the zero product principle.

$x - 7 = 0$ or $x + 3 = 0$

$\qquad x = 7 \qquad\qquad x = -3$

The boundary points are -3 and 7.

Test Interval	Test Number	Test	Conclusion
$(-\infty, -3)$	-4	$(-4-7)(-4+3) \le 0$ $11 \le 0$, false	$(-\infty, -3)$ does not belong to the solution set.
$(-3, 7)$	0	$(0-7)(0+3) \le 0$ $-21 \le 0$, true	$(-3, 7)$ belongs to the solution set.
$(7, \infty)$	8	$(8-7)(8+3) \le 0$ $11 \le 0$, false	$(7, \infty)$ does not belong to the solution set.

The solution set is $[-3, 7]$ or $\{x|-3 \le x \le 7\}$.

5. $x^2 - 5x + 4 > 0$

Solve the related quadratic equation.

$\qquad x^2 - 5x + 4 = 0$

$(x-4)(x-1) = 0$

Apply the zero product principle.

$x - 4 = 0$ or $x - 1 = 0$

$\qquad x = 4 \qquad\qquad x = 1$

The boundary points are 1 and 4.

Test Interval	Test Number	Test	Conclusion
$(-\infty, 1)$	0	$0^2 - 5(0) + 4 > 0$ $4 > 0$, true	$(-\infty, 1)$ belongs to the solution set.
$(1, 4)$	2	$2^2 - 5(2) + 4 > 0$ $-2 > 0$, false	$(1, 4)$ does not belong to the solution set.
$(4, \infty)$	5	$5^2 - 5(5) + 4 > 0$ $4 > 0$, true	$(4, \infty)$ belongs to the solution set.

The solution set is $(-\infty, 1) \cup (4, \infty)$ or $\{x|x < 1 \text{ or } x > 4\}$.

628

7. $x^2 + 5x + 4 > 0$

Solve the related quadratic equation.

$x^2 + 5x + 4 = 0$

$(x+4)(x+1) = 0$

Apply the zero product principle.

$x + 4 = 0$ or $x + 1 = 0$

$x = -4$ $x = -1$

The boundary points are -1 and -4.

Test Interval	Test Number	Test	Conclusion
$(-\infty, -4)$	-5	$(-5)^2 + 5(-5) + 4 > 0$ $4 > 0$, true	$(-\infty, -4)$ belongs to the solution set.
$(-4, -1)$	-2	$(-2)^2 + 5(-2) + 4 > 0$ $-2 > 0$, false	$(-4, -1)$ does not belong to the solution set.
$(-1, \infty)$	0	$0^2 + 5(0) + 4 > 0$ $4 > 0$, true	$(-1, \infty)$ belongs to the solution set.

The solution set is $(-\infty, -4) \cup (-1, \infty)$ or $\{x \mid x < -4 \text{ or } x > -1\}$.

9. $x^2 - 6x + 8 \leq 0$

Solve the related quadratic equation.

$x^2 - 6x + 8 = 0$

$(x-4)(x-2) = 0$

Apply the zero product principle.

$x - 4 = 0$ or $x - 2 = 0$

$x = 4$ $x = 2$

The boundary points are 2 and 4.

Test Interval	Test Number	Test	Conclusion
$(-\infty, 2)$	0	$0^2 - 6(0) + 8 \leq 0$ $8 \leq 0$, false	$(-\infty, 2)$ does not belong to the solution set.
$(2, 4)$	3	$3^2 - 6(3) + 8 \leq 0$ $-1 \leq 0$, true	$(2, 4)$ belongs to the solution set.
$(4, \infty)$	5	$5^2 - 6(5) + 8 \leq 0$ $3 \leq 0$, false	$(4, \infty)$ does not belong to the solution set.

The solution set is $[2, 4]$ or $\{x \mid 2 \leq x \leq 4\}$.

629

11. $3x^2 + 10x - 8 \le 0$

Solve the related quadratic equation.

$3x^2 + 10x - 8 = 0$

$(3x - 2)(x + 4) = 0$

Apply the zero product principle.

$3x - 2 = 0$ or $x + 4 = 0$

$3x = 2$ $\qquad x = -4$

$x = \dfrac{2}{3}$

The boundary points are -4 and $\dfrac{2}{3}$.

Test Interval	Test Number	Test	Conclusion
$(-\infty, -4)$	-5	$3(-5)^2 + 10(-5) - 8 \le 0$ $17 \le 0$, false	$(-\infty, -4)$ does not belong to the solution set.
$\left(-4, \dfrac{2}{3}\right)$	0	$3(0)^2 + 10(0) - 8 \le 0$ $-8 \le 0$, true	$\left(-4, \dfrac{2}{3}\right)$ belongs to the solution set.
$\left(\dfrac{2}{3}, \infty\right)$	1	$3(1)^2 + 10(1) - 8 \le 0$ $5 \le 0$, false	$\left(\dfrac{2}{3}, \infty\right)$ does not belong to the solution set.

The solution set is $\left[-4, \dfrac{2}{3}\right]$ or $\left\{x \middle| -4 \le x \le \dfrac{2}{3}\right\}$.

13. $2x^2 + x < 15$

$2x^2 + x - 15 < 0$

Solve the related quadratic equation.

$2x^2 + x - 15 = 0$

$(2x - 5)(x + 3) = 0$

Apply the zero product principle.

$2x - 5 = 0$ or $x + 3 = 0$

$2x = 5$ $\qquad x = -3$

$x = \dfrac{5}{2}$

The boundary points are -3 and $\dfrac{5}{2}$.

630

Test Interval	Test Number	Test	Conclusion
$(-\infty, -3)$	-4	$2(-4)^2 + (-4) < 15$ $28 < 15$, false	$(-\infty, -3)$ does not belong to the solution set.
$\left(-3, \dfrac{5}{2}\right)$	0	$2(0)^2 + 0 < 15$ $0 < 15$, true	$\left(-3, \dfrac{5}{2}\right)$ belongs to the solution set.
$\left(\dfrac{5}{2}, \infty\right)$	3	$2(3)^2 + 3 < 15$ $21 < 15$, false	$\left(\dfrac{5}{2}, \infty\right)$ does not belong to the solution set.

The solution set is $\left(-3, \dfrac{5}{2}\right)$ or $\left\{x \middle| -3 < x < \dfrac{5}{2}\right\}$.

15. $\quad 4x^2 + 7x < -3$

$4x^2 + 7x + 3 < 0$

Solve the related quadratic equation.

$\quad 4x^2 + 7x + 3 = 0$

$(4x + 3)(x + 1) = 0$

Apply the zero product principle.

$4x + 3 = 0 \quad$ or $\quad x + 1 = 0$

$\quad 4x = -3 \qquad\qquad x = -1$

$\qquad x = -\dfrac{3}{4}$

The boundary points are -1 and $-\dfrac{3}{4}$.

Test Interval	Test Number	Test	Conclusion
$(-\infty, -1)$	-2	$4(-2)^2 + 7(-2) < -3$ $2 < -3$, false	$(-\infty, -1)$ does not belong to the solution set.
$\left(-1, -\dfrac{3}{4}\right)$	$-\dfrac{7}{8}$	$4\left(-\dfrac{7}{8}\right)^2 + 7\left(-\dfrac{7}{8}\right) < -3$ $-3\dfrac{1}{16} < -3$, true	$\left(-1, -\dfrac{3}{4}\right)$ belongs to the solution set.
$\left(-\dfrac{3}{4}, \infty\right)$	0	$4(0)^2 + 7(0) < -3$ $0 < -3$, false	$\left(-\dfrac{3}{4}, \infty\right)$ does not belong to the solution set.

The solution set is $\left(-1, -\dfrac{3}{4}\right)$ or $\left\{x \middle| -1 < x < -\dfrac{3}{4}\right\}$.

631

17. $x^2 - 4x \geq 0$

Solve the related quadratic equation.

$x^2 - 4x = 0$

$x(x - 4) = 0$

Apply the zero product principle.

$x = 0$ or $x - 4 = 0$

$x = 4$

The boundary points are 0 and 4.

Test Interval	Test Number	Test	Conclusion
$(-\infty, 0)$	-1	$(-1)^2 - 4(-1) \geq 0$ $5 \geq 0$, true	$(-\infty, 0)$ belongs to the solution set.
$(0, 4)$	1	$(1)^2 - 4(1) \geq 0$ $-3 \geq 0$, false	$(0, 4)$ does not belong to the solution set.
$(4, \infty)$	5	$(5)^2 - 4(5) \geq 0$ $5 \geq 0$, true	$(4, \infty)$ belongs to the solution set.

The solution set is $(-\infty, 0] \cup [4, \infty)$ or $\{x \mid x \leq 0 \text{ or } x \geq 4\}$.

19. $2x^2 + 3x > 0$

Solve the related quadratic equation.

$2x^2 + 3x = 0$

$x(2x + 3) = 0$

Apply the zero product principle.

$x = 0$ or $2x + 3 = 0$

$2x = -3$

$x = -\dfrac{3}{2}$

The boundary points are $-\dfrac{3}{2}$ and 0.

Test Interval	Test Number	Test	Conclusion
$\left(-\infty, -\dfrac{3}{2}\right)$	-2	$2(-2)^2 + 3(-2) > 0$ $2 > 0$, true	$\left(-\infty, -\dfrac{3}{2}\right)$ belongs to the solution set.
$\left(-\dfrac{3}{2}, 0\right)$	-1	$2(-1)^2 + 3(-1) > 0$ $-1 > 0$, false	$\left(-\dfrac{3}{2}, 0\right)$ does not belong to the solution set.
$(0, \infty)$	1	$2(1)^2 + 3(1) > 0$ $5 > 0$, true	$(0, \infty)$ belongs to the solution set.

The solution set is $\left(-\infty, -\dfrac{3}{2}\right) \cup (0, \infty)$ or $\left\{ x \,\middle|\, x < -\dfrac{3}{2} \text{ or } x > 0 \right\}$.

21. $-x^2 + x \geq 0$

Solve the related quadratic equation.

$-x^2 + x = 0$

$-x(x - 1) = 0$

Apply the zero product principle.

$-x = 0 \quad \text{or} \quad x - 1 = 0$

$x = 0 \qquad\qquad x = 1$

The boundary points are 0 and 1.

Test Interval	Test Number	Test	Conclusion
$(-\infty, 0)$	-1	$-(-1)^2 + (-1) \geq 0$ $-2 \geq 0$, false	$(-\infty, 0)$ does not belong to the solution set.
$(0, 1)$	$\dfrac{1}{2}$	$-\left(\dfrac{1}{2}\right)^2 + \dfrac{1}{2} \geq 0$ $\dfrac{1}{4} \geq 0$, true	$(0, 1)$ belongs to the solution set.
$(1, \infty)$	2	$-(2)^2 + 2 \geq 0$ $-2 \geq 0$, false	$(1, \infty)$ does not belong to the solution set.

The solution set is $[0, 1]$ or $\{ x \mid 0 \leq x \leq 1 \}$.

23.
$$x^2 \leq 4x - 2$$

$x^2 - 4x + 2 \leq 0$

Solve the related quadratic equation, using the quadratic formula.

$x^2 - 4x + 2 = 0$

$a = 1 \quad b = -4 \quad c = 2$

$$x = \frac{-(-4) \pm \sqrt{(-4)^2 - 4(1)(2)}}{2(1)} = \frac{4 \pm \sqrt{16-8}}{2} = \frac{4 \pm \sqrt{8}}{2} = \frac{4 \pm 2\sqrt{2}}{2} = \frac{2(2 \pm \sqrt{2})}{2} = 2 \pm \sqrt{2}$$

The boundary points are $2 - \sqrt{2}$ and $2 + \sqrt{2}$.

Test Interval	Test Number	Test	Conclusion
$\left(-\infty, 2-\sqrt{2}\right)$	0	$0^2 \leq 4(0) - 2$ $0 \leq -2$, false	$\left(-\infty, 2-\sqrt{2}\right)$ does not belong to the solution set.
$\left(2-\sqrt{2}, 2+\sqrt{2}\right)$	2	$2^2 \leq 4(2) - 2$ $4 \leq 6$, true	$\left(2-\sqrt{2}, 2+\sqrt{2}\right)$ belongs to the solution set.
$\left(2+\sqrt{2}, \infty\right)$	4	$4^2 \leq 4(4) - 2$ $16 \leq 14$, false	$\left(2+\sqrt{2}, \infty\right)$ does not belong to the solution set.

The solution set is $\left[2-\sqrt{2}, 2+\sqrt{2}\right]$ or $\left\{x \mid 2-\sqrt{2} \leq x \leq 2+\sqrt{2}\right\}$.

25. $x^2 - 6x + 9 < 0$

Solve the related quadratic equation.

$x^2 - 6x + 9 = 0$

$(x-3)^2 = 0$

Apply the zero product principle to obtain the double root.

$x - 3 = 0$

$x = 3$

The boundary point is 3.

Test Interval	Test Number	Test	Conclusion
$(-\infty, 3)$	0	$0^2 - 6(0) + 9 < 0$ $9 < 0$, false	$(-\infty, 3)$ does not belong to the solution set.
$(3, \infty)$	4	$4^2 - 6(4) + 9 < 0$ $1 < 0$, false	$(3, \infty)$ does not belong to the solution set.

There is no solution. The solution set is $\varnothing$ or $\{\ \}$.

634

27. $(x-1)(x-2)(x-3) \geq 0$

Solve the related quadratic equation.

$(x-1)(x-2)(x-3) = 0$

Apply the zero product principle.

$x-1=0$ or $x-2=0$ or $x-3=0$

$\quad x=1 \qquad\quad x=2 \qquad\quad x=3$

The boundary points are 1, 2, and 3.

Test Interval	Test Number	Test	Conclusion
$(-\infty,1)$	0	$(0-1)(0-2)(0-3) \geq 0$ $-6 \geq 0$, False	$(-\infty,1)$ does not belong to the solution set.
$(1,2)$	1.5	$(1.5-1)(1.5-2)(1.5-3) \geq 0$ $0.375 \geq 0$, True	$(1,2)$ belongs to the solution set.
$(2,3)$	2.5	$(2.5-1)(2.5-2)(2.5-3) \geq 0$ $-0.375 \geq 0$, False	$(2,3)$ does not belong to the solution set.
$(3,\infty)$	4	$(4-1)(4-2)(4-3) \geq 0$ $6 \geq 0$, True	$(3,\infty)$ belongs to the solution set.

The solution set is $[1,2] \cup [3,\infty)$ or $\{x | 1 \leq x \leq 2 \text{ or } x \geq 3\}$.

29. $x^3 + 2x^2 - x - 2 \geq 0$

Solve the related quadratic equation.

$\quad x^3 + 2x^2 - x - 2 = 0$

$x^2(x+2) - 1(x+2) = 0$

$\quad (x^2 - 1)(x+2) = 0$

$(x-1)(x+1)(x+2) = 0$

Apply the zero product principle.

$x-1=0$ or $x+1=0$ or $x+2=0$

$\quad x=1 \qquad\quad x=-1 \qquad\quad x=-2$

The boundary points are $-2, -1$, and 1.

635

Test Interval	Test Number	Test	Conclusion
$(-\infty, -2)$	-3	$(-3)^3 + 2(-3)^2 - (-3) - 2 \geq 0$ $-8 \geq 0$, False	$(-\infty, -2)$ does not belong to the solution set.
$(-2, -1)$	-1.5	$(-1.5)^3 + 2(-1.5)^2 - (-1.5) - 2 \geq 0$ $0.625 \geq 0$, True	$(-2, -1)$ belongs to the solution set.
$(-1, 1)$	0	$0^3 + 2(0)^2 - 0 - 2 \geq 0$ $-2 \geq 0$, False	$(-1, 1)$ does not belong to the solution set.
$(1, \infty)$	2	$2^3 + 2(2)^2 - 2 - 2 \geq 0$ $12 \geq 0$, True	$(1, \infty)$ belongs to the solution set.

The solution set is $[-2, -1] \cup [1, \infty)$ or $\{x \mid -2 \leq x \leq -1 \ \text{or} \ x \geq 1\}$.

31. $x^3 - 3x^2 - 9x + 27 < 0$

Solve the related quadratic equation.

$$x^3 - 3x^2 - 9x + 27 = 0$$
$$x^2(x-3) - 9(x-3) = 0$$
$$(x^2 - 9)(x-3) = 0$$
$$(x-3)(x+3)(x-3) = 0$$
$$(x-3)^2(x+3) = 0$$

Apply the zero product principle.

$x - 3 = 0$ or $x + 3 = 0$

$\quad x = 3 \qquad\qquad x = -3$

The boundary points are -3 and 3.

Test Interval	Test Number	Test	Conclusion
$(-\infty, -3)$	-4	$(-4)^3 - 3(-4)^2 - 9(-4) + 27 < 0$ $-49 < 0$, True	$(-\infty, -3)$ belongs to the solution set.
$(-3, 3)$	0	$0^3 - 3(0)^2 - 9(0) + 27 < 0$ $27 < 0$, False	$(-3, 3)$ does not belong to the solution set.
$(3, \infty)$	4	$4^3 - 3(4)^2 - 9(4) + 27 < 0$ $7 < 0$, False	$(3, \infty)$ does not belong to the solution set.

The solution set is $(-\infty, -3)$ or $\{x \mid x < -3\}$.

636

33. $x^3 + x^2 + 4x + 4 > 0$

Solve the related quadratic equation.

$$x^3 + x^2 + 4x + 4 = 0$$

$$x^2(x+1) + 4(x+1) = 0$$

$$(x^2 + 4)(x+1) = 0$$

Apply the zero product principle.

$x^2 + 4 = 0 \qquad$ or $\quad x + 1 = 0$

$\qquad x^2 = -4 \qquad\qquad\quad x = -1$

$\qquad x = \pm\sqrt{-4}$

$\qquad\quad = \pm 2i$

The imaginary solutions will not be boundary points, so the only boundary point is -1.

Test Interval	Test Number	Test	Conclusion
$(-\infty, -1)$	-2	$(-2)^3 + (-2)^2 + 4(-2) + 4 > 0$ $-8 > 0$, False	$(-\infty, -1)$ does not belong to the solution set.
$(-1, \infty)$	0	$0^3 + 0^2 + 4(0) + 4 > 0$ $4 > 0$, True	$(-1, \infty)$ belongs to the solution set.

The solution set is $(-1, \infty)$ or $\{x \mid x > -1\}$.

35. $x^3 \geq 9x^2$

$x^3 - 9x^2 \geq 0$

Solve the related quadratic equation.

$$x^3 - 9x^2 = 0$$

$$x^2(x-9) = 0$$

Apply the zero product principle.

$x^2 = 0 \qquad$ or $\quad x - 9 = 0$

$x = \pm\sqrt{0} = 0 \qquad\quad x = 9$

The boundary points are 0 and 9.

Test Interval	Test Number	Test	Conclusion
$(-\infty, 0)$	-1	$(-1)^3 \geq 9(-1)^2$ $-1 \geq 9$, False	$(-\infty, 0)$ does not belong to the solution set.
$(0, 9)$	1	$1^3 \geq 9(1)^2$ $1 \geq 9$, False	$(0, 9)$ does not belong to the solution set.
$(9, \infty)$	10	$10^3 \geq 9(10)^2$ $1000 \geq 900$, True	$(9, \infty)$ belongs to the solution set.

The solution set is $\{0\} \cup [9, \infty)$ or $\{x | x = 0 \text{ or } x \geq 9\}$.

37. $\dfrac{x - 4}{x + 3} > 0$

Find the values of x that make the numerator and denominator zero.

$$x - 4 = 0 \qquad x + 3 = 0$$
$$x = 4 \qquad x = -3$$

The boundary points are -3 and 4. We exclude -3 from the solution set, since this would make the denominator zero.

Test Interval	Test Number	Test	Conclusion
$(-\infty, -3)$	-4	$\dfrac{-4 - 4}{-4 + 3} > 0$ $8 > 0$, true	$(-\infty, -3)$ belongs to the solution set.
$(-3, 4)$	0	$\dfrac{0 - 4}{0 + 3} > 0$ $\dfrac{-4}{3} > 0$, false	$(-3, 4)$ does not belong to the solution set.
$(4, \infty)$	5	$\dfrac{5 - 4}{5 + 3} > 0$ $\dfrac{1}{8} > 0$, true	$(4, \infty)$ belongs to the solution set.

The solution set is $(-\infty, -3) \cup (4, \infty)$ or $\{x | x < -3 \text{ or } x > 4\}$.

638

39. $\dfrac{x+3}{x+4} < 0$

Find the values of x that make the numerator and denominator zero.

$x + 3 = 0 \qquad x + 4 = 0$

$\quad x = -3 \qquad\quad x = -4$

The boundary points are -4 and -3.

Test Interval	Test Number	Test	Conclusion
$(-\infty, -4)$	-5	$\dfrac{-5+3}{-5+4} < 0$ $2 < 0$, false	$(-\infty, -4)$ does not belong to the solution set.
$(-4, -3)$	-3.5	$\dfrac{-3.5+3}{-3.5+4} < 0$ $-1 < 0$, true	$(-4, -3)$ belongs to the solution set.
$(-3, \infty)$	0	$\dfrac{0+3}{0+4} < 0$ $\dfrac{3}{4} < 0$, false	$(-3, \infty)$ does not belong to the solution set.

The solution set is $(-4, -3)$ or $\left\{x \middle| -4 < x < -3\right\}$.

$-7\ -6\ -5\ -4\ -3\ -2\ -1\ \ 0\ \ 1\ \ 2\ \ 3$

41. $\dfrac{-x+2}{x-4} \geq 0$

Find the values of x that make the numerator and denominator zero.

$-x + 2 = 0 \quad \text{and} \quad x - 4 = 0$

$\quad x = 2 \qquad\qquad\quad x = 4$

The boundary points are 2 and 4.

Test Interval	Test Number	Test	Conclusion
$(-\infty, 2)$	0	$\dfrac{-0+2}{0-4} \geq 0$ $-\dfrac{1}{2} \geq 0$, false	$(-\infty, 2)$ does not belong to the solution set.
$(2, 4)$	3	$\dfrac{-3+2}{3-4} \geq 0$ $1 \geq 0$, true	$(2, 4)$ belongs to the solution set.
$(4, \infty)$	5	$\dfrac{-5+2}{5-4} \geq 0$ $-3 \geq 0$, false	$(4, \infty)$ does not belong to the solution set.

We exclude 4 from the solution set because 4 would make the denominator zero. The solution set is $[2, 4)$ or $\left\{x \middle| 2 \leq x < 4\right\}$.

$-5\ -4\ -3\ -2\ -1\ \ 0\ \ 1\ \ 2\ \ 3\ \ 4\ \ 5$

639

43. $\dfrac{4-2x}{3x+4} \le 0$

Find the values of x that make the numerator and denominator zero.

$$4 - 2x = 0 \quad \text{and} \quad 3x + 4 = 0$$

$$-2x = -4 \qquad\qquad 3x = -4$$

$$x = 2 \qquad\qquad x = -\dfrac{4}{3}$$

The boundary points are $-\dfrac{4}{3}$ and 2.

Test Interval	Test Number	Test	Conclusion
$\left(-\infty, -\dfrac{4}{3}\right)$	-2	$\dfrac{4-2(-2)}{3(-2)+4} \le 0$ $-4 \le 0$, true	$\left(-\infty, -\dfrac{4}{3}\right)$ belongs to the solution set.
$\left(-\dfrac{4}{3}, 2\right)$	0	$\dfrac{4-2(0)}{3(0)+4} \le 0$ $1 \le 0$, false	$\left(-\dfrac{4}{3}, 2\right)$ does not belong to the solution set.
$[2, \infty)$	3	$\dfrac{4-2(3)}{3(3)+4} \le 0$ $-\dfrac{2}{13} \le 0$, true	$[2, \infty)$ belongs to the solution set.

We exclude $-\dfrac{4}{3}$ from the solution set because $-\dfrac{4}{3}$ would make the denominator zero. The solution set is $\left(-\infty, -\dfrac{4}{3}\right) \cup [2, \infty)$ or $\left\{x \middle| x < -\dfrac{4}{3} \text{ or } x \ge 2\right\}$.

45. $\dfrac{x}{x-3} > 0$

Find the values of x that make the numerator and denominator zero.

$x = 0$ and $x - 3 = 0$

$\qquad\qquad\quad x = 3$

The boundary points are 0 and 3.

Test Interval	Test Number	Test	Conclusion
$(-\infty, 0)$	-1	$\dfrac{-1}{-1-3} > 0$ $\dfrac{1}{4} > 0$, true	$\left(-\infty, -\dfrac{4}{3}\right)$ belongs to the solution set.
$(0, 3)$	1	$\dfrac{1}{1-3} > 0$ $-\dfrac{1}{2} > 0$, false	$(0, 3)$ does not belong to the solution set.
$(3, \infty)$	4	$\dfrac{4}{4-3} > 0$ $4 > 0$, true	$(3, \infty)$ belongs to the solution set.

The solution set is $(-\infty, 0) \cup (3, \infty)$ or $\{x \mid x < 0 \text{ or } x > 3\}$.

47. $\dfrac{x+1}{x+3} < 2$

Express the inequality so that one side is zero.

$$\dfrac{x+1}{x+3} - 2 < 0$$

$$\dfrac{x+1}{x+3} - \dfrac{2(x+3)}{x+3} < 0$$

$$\dfrac{x+1-2(x+3)}{x+3} < 0$$

$$\dfrac{x+1-2x-6}{x+3} < 0$$

$$\dfrac{-x-5}{x+3} < 0$$

Find the values of x that make the numerator and denominator zero.

$-x - 5 = 0 \qquad\quad x + 3 = 0$

$\quad -x = 5 \qquad\qquad\quad x = -3$

$\quad\quad x = -5$

The boundary points are –5 and –3.

641

Test Interval	Test Number	Test	Conclusion
$(-\infty, -5)$	-6	$\dfrac{-6+1}{-6+3} < 2$ $\dfrac{5}{3} < 2$, true	$(-\infty, -5)$ belongs to the solution set.
$(-5, -3)$	-4	$\dfrac{-4+1}{-4+3} < 2$ $3 < 2$, false	$(-5, -3)$ does not belong to the solution set.
$(-3, \infty)$	0	$\dfrac{0+1}{0+3} < 2$ $\dfrac{1}{3} < 2$, true	$(-3, \infty)$ belongs to the solution set.

The solution set is $(-\infty, -5) \cup (-3, \infty)$ or $\{x \mid x < -5 \text{ or } x > -3\}$.

49. $\dfrac{x+4}{2x-1} \le 3$

Express the inequality so that one side is zero.

$$\frac{x+4}{2x-1} - 3 \le 0$$

$$\frac{x+4}{2x-1} - \frac{3(2x-1)}{2x-1} \le 0$$

$$\frac{x+4-3(2x-1)}{2x-1} \le 0$$

$$\frac{x+4-6x+3}{2x-1} \le 0$$

$$\frac{-5x+7}{2x-1} \le 0$$

Find the values of x that make the numerator and denominator zero.

$$
\begin{array}{ll}
-5x + 7 = 0 & 2x - 1 = 0 \\
-5x = -7 & 2x = 1 \\
x = \dfrac{7}{5} & x = \dfrac{1}{2}
\end{array}
$$

The boundary points are $\dfrac{1}{2}$ and $\dfrac{7}{5}$.

642

Test Interval	Test Number	Test	Conclusion
$\left(-\infty, \dfrac{1}{2}\right)$	0	$\dfrac{0+4}{2(0)-1} \le 3$ $-4 \le 3$, true	$\left(-\infty, \dfrac{1}{2}\right)$ belongs to the solution set.
$\left(\dfrac{1}{2}, \dfrac{7}{5}\right)$	1	$\dfrac{1+4}{2(1)-1} \le 3$ $5 \le 3$, false	$\left(\dfrac{1}{2}, \dfrac{7}{5}\right)$ does not belong to the solution set.
$\left(\dfrac{7}{5}, \infty\right)$	2	$\dfrac{2+4}{2(2)-1} \le 3$ $2 \le 3$, true	$\left(\dfrac{7}{5}, \infty\right)$ belongs to the solution set.

We exclude $\dfrac{1}{2}$ from the solution set because $\dfrac{1}{2}$ would make the denominator zero. The solution

set is $\left(-\infty, \dfrac{1}{2}\right) \cup \left[\dfrac{7}{5}, \infty\right)$ or $\left\{ x \middle| x < \dfrac{1}{2} \text{ or } x \ge \dfrac{7}{5} \right\}$.

51. $\dfrac{x-2}{x+2} \le 2$

Express the inequality so that one side is zero.

$$\dfrac{x-2}{x+2} - 2 \le 0$$

$$\dfrac{x-2}{x+2} - \dfrac{2(x+2)}{x+2} \le 0$$

$$\dfrac{x-2-2(x+2)}{x+2} \le 0$$

$$\dfrac{x-2-2x-4}{x+2} \le 0$$

$$\dfrac{-x-6}{x+2} \le 0$$

Find the values of x that make the numerator and denominator zero.

$$
\begin{array}{ll}
-x-6 = 0 & x+2 = 0 \\
\quad -x = 6 & \quad x = -2 \\
\quad\ \ x = -6 &
\end{array}
$$

The boundary points are -6 and -2.

643

Test Interval	Test Number	Test	Conclusion
$(-\infty, -6)$	-7	$\dfrac{-7-2}{-7+2} \le 2$ $\dfrac{9}{5} \le 2$, true	$(-\infty, -6)$ belongs to the solution set.
$(-6, -2)$	-3	$\dfrac{-3-2}{-3+2} \le 2$ $5 \le 2$, false	$(-6, -2)$ does not belong to the solution set.
$(-2, \infty)$	0	$\dfrac{0-2}{0+2} \le 2$ $-1 \le 2$, true	$(-2, \infty)$ belongs to the solution set.

We exclude -2 from the solution set because -2 would make the denominator zero. The solution set is $(-\infty, -6] \cup (-2, \infty)$ or $\{x \mid x \le -6 \text{ or } x > -2\}$.

53.

$$f(x) \ge g(x)$$

$$2x^2 \ge 5x - 2$$

$$2x^2 - 5x + 2 \ge 0$$

Solve the related quadratic equation.

$$2x^2 - 5x + 2 = 0$$

$$(2x - 1)(x - 2) = 0$$

Apply the zero product principle.

$$2x - 1 = 0 \quad \text{or} \quad x - 2 = 0$$

$$2x = 1 \qquad\qquad x = 2$$

$$x = \frac{1}{2}$$

The boundary points are $\frac{1}{2}$ and 2.

Test Interval	Test Number	Test	Conclusion
$\left(-\infty, \dfrac{1}{2}\right)$	0	$2(0)^2 \ge 5(0) - 2$ $0 \ge -2$, True	$\left(-\infty, \dfrac{1}{2}\right)$ belongs to the solution set.
$\left(\dfrac{1}{2}, 2\right)$	1	$2(1)^2 \ge 5(1) - 2$ $2 \ge 3$, False	$\left(\dfrac{1}{2}, 2\right)$ does not belong to the solution set.
$(2, \infty)$	3	$2(3)^2 \ge 5(3) - 2$ $18 \ge 13$, True	$(2, \infty)$ does not belong to the solution set.

The solution set is $\left(-\infty, \dfrac{1}{2}\right] \cup [2, \infty)$ or $\left\{x \mid x \le \dfrac{1}{2} \text{ or } x \ge 2\right\}$.

55. $f(x) \le g(x)$

$$\frac{2x}{x+1} \le 1$$

Express the inequality so that one side is zero.

$$\frac{2x}{x+1} - 1 \le 0$$

$$\frac{2x}{x+1} - \frac{x+1}{x+1} \le 0$$

$$\frac{2x-x-1}{x+1} \le 0$$

$$\frac{x-1}{x+1} \le 0$$

Find the values of x that make the numerator and denominator zero.

$x - 1 = 0$ or $x + 1 = 0$

$\quad x = 1 \qquad\qquad x = -1$

The boundary points are -1 and 1.

Test Interval	Test Number	Test	Conclusion
$(-\infty, -1)$	-3	$\dfrac{2(-3)}{-3+1} \le 1$ $3 \le 1$, false	$(-\infty, -1)$ does not belong to the solution set.
$(-1, 1)$	0	$\dfrac{2(0)}{0+1} \le 1$ $0 \le 1$, true	$(-1, 1)$ belongs to the solution set.
$(1, \infty)$	2	$\dfrac{2(3)}{3+1} \le 1$ $\dfrac{3}{2} \le 1$, false	$(1, \infty)$ does not belong to the solution set.

The solution set is $(-1, 1)$ or $\{x \mid -1 < x < 1\}$.

57. $\left|x^2 + 2x - 36\right| > 12$

Express the inequality without the absolute value symbol:

$x^2 + 2x - 36 < -12$　or　$x^2 + 2x - 36 > 12$

$x^2 + 2x - 24 < 0$　　　　$x^2 + 2x - 48 > 0$

Solve the related quadratic equations.

$x^2 + 2x - 24 = 0$　or　$x^2 + 2x - 48 = 0$

$(x+6)(x-4) = 0$　　　$(x+8)(x-6) = 0$

Apply the zero product principle.

$x + 6 = 0$　or　$x - 4 = 0$　or　$x + 8 = 0$　or　$x - 6 = 0$

$x = -6$　　　　$x = 4$　　　　$x = -8$　　　　$x = 6$

The boundary points are -8, -6, 4 and 6.

Test Interval	Test Number	Test	Conclusion
$(-\infty, -8)$	-9	$\left|(-9)^2 + 2(-9) - 36\right| > 12$ $27 > 12$, True	$(-\infty, -8)$ belongs to the solution set.
$(-8, -6)$	-7	$\left|(-7)^2 + 2(-7) - 36\right| > 12$ $1 > 12$, False	$(-8, -6)$ does not belong to the solution set.
$(-6, 4)$	0	$\left|0^2 + 2(0) - 36\right| > 12$ $36 > 12$, True	$(-6, 4)$ belongs to the solution set.
$(4, 6)$	5	$\left|5^2 + 2(5) - 36\right| > 12$ $1 > 12$, False	$(4, 6)$ does not belong to the solution set.
$(6, \infty)$	7	$\left|7^2 + 2(7) - 36\right| > 12$ $27 > 12$, True	$(6, \infty)$ belongs to the solution set.

The solution set is $(-\infty, -8) \cup (-6, 4) \cup (6, \infty)$ or $\{x \mid x < -8$ or $-6 < x < 4$ or $x > 6\}$.

$$-10\;-8\;-6\;-4\;-2\;\;0\;\;2\;\;4\;\;6\;\;8\;\;10$$

58. $\left|x^2 + 6x + 1\right| > 8$

Express the inequality without the absolute value symbol:

$x^2 + 6x + 1 < -8$ or $x^2 + 6x + 1 > 8$

$x^2 + 6x + 9 < 0$ $\qquad$ $x^2 + 6x - 7 > 0$

Solve the related quadratic equations.

$x^2 + 6x + 9 = 0$ or $x^2 + 6x - 7 = 0$

$(x+3)^2 = 0$ $\qquad$ $(x+7)(x-1) = 0$

$x + 3 = \pm\sqrt{0}$ or $x + 7 = 0$ or $x - 1 = 0$

$x + 3 = 0$ $\qquad$ $x = -7$ $\qquad$ $x = 1$

$\qquad x = -3$

The boundary points are $-7, -3,$ and 1.

Test Interval	Test Number	Test	Conclusion
$(-\infty, -7)$	-8	$\left|(-8)^2 + 6(-8) + 1\right| > 8$ $17 \geq 8$, True	$(-\infty, -7)$ belongs to the solution set.
$(-7, -3)$	-5	$\left|(-5)^2 + 6(-5) + 1\right| > 8$ $4 \geq 8$, False	$(-7, -3)$ does not belong to the solution set.
$(-3, 1)$	0	$\left|0^2 + 6(0) + 1\right| > 8$ $1 \geq 8$, False	$(-3, 1)$ does not belong to the solution set.
$(1, \infty)$	2	$\left|2^2 + 6(2) + 1\right| > 8$ $17 \geq 8$, True	$(1, \infty)$ belongs to the solution set.

The solution set is $(-\infty, -7) \cup (1, \infty)$ or $\left\{x \mid x < -7 \text{ or } x > 1\right\}$.

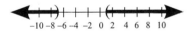

$\begin{array}{ccccccccccc} -10 & -8 & -6 & -4 & -2 & 0 & 2 & 4 & 6 & 8 & 10 \end{array}$

59. $\dfrac{3}{x+3} > \dfrac{3}{x-2}$

Express the inequality so that one side is zero.

$$\frac{3}{x+3} - \frac{3}{x-2} > 0$$

$$\frac{3(x-2)}{(x+3)(x-2)} - \frac{3(x+3)}{(x+3)(x-2)} > 0$$

$$\frac{3x-6-3x-9}{(x+3)(x-2)} < 0$$

$$\frac{-15}{(x+3)(x-2)} < 0$$

Find the values of x that make the denominator zero.

$$x+3=0 \qquad x-2=0$$
$$x=-3 \qquad x=2$$

The boundary points are -3 and 2.

Test Interval	Test Number	Test	Conclusion
$(-\infty,-3)$	-4	$\dfrac{3}{-4+3} > \dfrac{3}{-4-2}$ $-3 > \dfrac{1}{2}$, False	$(-\infty,-3)$ does not belong to the solution set.
$(-3,2)$	0	$\dfrac{3}{0+3} > \dfrac{3}{0-2}$ $1 > -\dfrac{3}{2}$, True	$(-3,2)$ belongs to the solution set.
$(2,\infty)$	3	$\dfrac{3}{3+3} > \dfrac{3}{3-2}$ $\dfrac{1}{2} > 3$, False	$(2,\infty)$ does not belong to the solution set.

The solution set is $(-3,2)$ or $\{x|-3<x<2\}$.

$$-5\ -4\ -3\ -2\ -1\ \ 0\ \ 1\ \ 2\ \ 3\ \ 4\ \ 5$$

648

60. $\dfrac{1}{x+1} > \dfrac{2}{x-1}$

Express the inequality so that one side is zero.

$$\frac{1}{x+1} - \frac{2}{x-1} > 0$$

$$\frac{x-1}{(x+1)(x-1)} - \frac{2(x+1)}{(x+1)(x-1)} > 0$$

$$\frac{x-1-2x-2}{(x+1)(x-1)} < 0$$

$$\frac{-x-3}{(x+1)(x-1)} < 0$$

Find the values of x that make the numerator and denominator zero.

$$-x-3 = 0 \qquad x+1 = 0 \qquad x-1 = 0$$
$$-3 = x \qquad\quad x = -1 \qquad\quad x = 1$$

The boundary points are -3, -1, and 1.

Test Interval	Test Number	Test	Conclusion
$(-\infty, -3)$	-4	$\dfrac{1}{-4+1} > \dfrac{2}{-3-1}$ $-\dfrac{1}{3} > -\dfrac{1}{2}$, True	$(-\infty, -3)$ belongs to the solution set.
$(-3, -1)$	-2	$\dfrac{1}{-2+1} > \dfrac{2}{-2-1}$ $-1 > -\dfrac{2}{3}$, False	$(-3, -1)$ does not belong to the solution set.
$(-1, 1)$	0	$\dfrac{1}{0+1} > \dfrac{2}{0-1}$ $1 > -2$, True	$(-3, 1)$ belongs to the solution set.
$(1, \infty)$	2	$\dfrac{1}{2+1} > \dfrac{2}{2-1}$ $\dfrac{1}{3} > 1$, False	$(1, \infty)$ does not belong to the solution set.

The solution set is $(-\infty, -3) \cup (-1, 1)$ or $\{x \mid x < -3 \text{ or } -1 < x < 1\}$.

649

61.
$$\frac{x^2 - x - 2}{x^2 - 4x + 3} > 0$$

Find the values of x that make the numerator and denominator zero.

$$x^2 - x - 2 = 0 \qquad x^2 - 4x + 3 = 0$$
$$(x - 2)(x + 1) = 0 \qquad (x - 3)(x - 1) = 0$$

Apply the zero product principle.

$$x - 2 = 0 \quad \text{or} \quad x + 1 = 0 \qquad x - 3 = 0 \quad \text{or} \quad x - 1 = 0$$
$$x = 2 \qquad \qquad x = -1 \qquad \qquad x = 3 \qquad \qquad x = 1$$

The boundary points are $-1, 1, 2$ and 3.

Test Interval	Test Number	Test	Conclusion
$(-\infty, -1)$	-2	$\dfrac{(-2)^2 - (-2) - 2}{(-2)^2 - 4(-2) + 3} > 0$ $\dfrac{4}{15} > 0$, True	$(-\infty, -1)$ belongs to the solution set.
$(-1, 1)$	0	$\dfrac{0^2 - 0 - 2}{0^2 - 4(0) + 3} > 0$ $-\dfrac{2}{3} > 0$, False	$(-1, 1)$ does not belong to the solution set.
$(1, 2)$	1.5	$\dfrac{1.5^2 - 1.5 - 2}{1.5^2 - 4(1.5) + 3} > 0$ $\dfrac{5}{3} > 0$, True	$(1, 2)$ belongs to the solution set.
$(2, 3)$	2.5	$\dfrac{2.5^2 - 2.5 - 2}{2.5^2 - 4(2.5) + 3} > 0$ $-\dfrac{7}{3} > 0$, False	$(2, 3)$ does not belong to the solution set.
$(3, \infty)$	4	$\dfrac{4^2 - 4 - 2}{4^2 - 4(4) + 3} > 0$ $\dfrac{10}{3} > 0$, True	$(3, \infty)$ belongs to the solution set.

The solution set is $(-\infty, -1) \cup (1, 2) \cup (3, \infty)$ or $\{x \mid x < -1 \text{ or } 1 < x < 2 \text{ or } x > 3\}$.

650

62. $\dfrac{x^2 - 3x + 2}{x^2 - 2x - 3} > 0$

Find the values of x that make the numerator and denominator zero.

$x^2 - 3x + 2 = 0 \qquad x^2 - 2x - 3 = 0$

$(x-2)(x-1) = 0 \qquad (x-3)(x+1) = 0$

Apply the zero product principle.

$x - 2 = 0 \quad \text{or} \quad x - 1 = 0 \qquad x - 3 = 0 \quad \text{or} \quad x + 1 = 0$

$\qquad x = 2 \qquad\qquad x = 1 \qquad\qquad x = 3 \qquad\qquad x = -1$

The boundary points are -1, 1, 2 and 3.

Test Interval	Test Number	Test	Conclusion
$(-\infty, -1)$	-2 $\dfrac{x^2 - 3x + 2}{x^2 - 2x - 3} > 0$	$\dfrac{(-2)^2 - 3(-2) + 2}{(-2)^2 - 2(-2) - 3} > 0$ $\dfrac{12}{5} > 0$, True	$(-\infty, -1)$ belongs to the solution set.
$(-1, 1)$	0	$\dfrac{0^2 - 3(0) + 2}{0^2 - 2(0) - 3} > 0$ $-\dfrac{2}{3} > 0$, False	$(-1, 1)$ does not belong to the solution set.
$(1, 2)$	1.5	$\dfrac{1.5^2 - 3(1.5) + 2}{1.5^2 - 2(1.5) - 3} > 0$ $\dfrac{1}{15} > 0$, True	$(1, 2)$ belongs to the solution set.
$(2, 3)$	2.5	$\dfrac{2.5^2 - 3(2.5) + 2}{2.5^2 - 2(2.5) - 3} > 0$ $-\dfrac{3}{7} > 0$, False	$(2, 3)$ does not belong to the solution set.
$(3, \infty)$	4	$\dfrac{4^2 - 3(4) + 2}{4^2 - 2(4) - 3} > 0$ $\dfrac{6}{5} > 0$, True	$(3, \infty)$ belongs to the solution set.

The solution set is $(-\infty, -1) \cup (1, 2) \cup (3, \infty)$ or $\{x \mid x < -1 \text{ or } 1 < x < 2 \text{ or } x > 3\}$.

651

63.
$$2x^3 + 11x^2 \geq 7x + 6$$
$$2x^3 + 11x^2 - 7x - 6 \geq 0$$

The graph of $f(x) = 2x^3 + 11x^2 - 7x - 6$ appears to cross the x-axis at -6, $-\frac{1}{2}$, and 1. We verify this numerically by substituting these values into the function:

$$f(-6) = 2(-6)^3 + 11(-6)^2 - 7(-6) - 6 = 2(-216) + 11(36) - (-42) - 6 = -432 + 396 + 42 - 6 = 0$$

$$f\left(-\frac{1}{2}\right) = 2\left(-\frac{1}{2}\right)^3 + 11\left(-\frac{1}{2}\right)^2 - 7\left(-\frac{1}{2}\right) - 6 = 2\left(-\frac{1}{8}\right) + 11\left(\frac{1}{4}\right) - \left(-\frac{7}{2}\right) - 6 = -\frac{1}{4} + \frac{11}{4} + \frac{7}{2} - 6 = 0$$

$$f(1) = 2(1)^3 + 11(1)^2 - 7(1) - 6 = 2(1) + 11(1) - 7 - 6 = 2 + 11 - 7 - 6 = 0$$

Thus, the boundaries are -6, $-\frac{1}{2}$, and 1. We need to find the intervals on which $f(x) \geq 0$. These intervals are indicated on the graph where the curve is above the x-axis. Now, the curve is above the x-axis when $-6 < x < -\frac{1}{2}$ and when $x > 1$. Thus, the solution set is

$$\left\{x \middle| -6 \leq x \leq -\frac{1}{2} \text{ or } x \geq 1\right\} \text{ or } \left[-6, -\frac{1}{2}\right] \cup [1, \infty).$$

64.
$$2x^3 + 11x^2 < 7x + 6$$
$$2x^3 + 11x^2 - 7x - 6 < 0$$

In Problem 63, we verified that the boundaries are -6, $-\frac{1}{2}$, and 1. We need to find the intervals on which $f(x) < 0$. These intervals are indicated on the graph where the curve is below the x-axis. Now, the curve is below the x-axis when $x < -6$ and when $-\frac{1}{2} < x < 1$.

Thus, the solution set is $\left\{x \middle| x < -6 \text{ or } -\frac{1}{2} < x < 1\right\}$ or $(-\infty, -6) \cup \left(-\frac{1}{2}, 1\right)$.

65.
$$\frac{1}{4(x+2)} \leq -\frac{3}{4(x-2)}$$

$$\frac{1}{4(x+2)} + \frac{3}{4(x-2)} \leq 0$$

Simplify the left side of the inequality:

$$\frac{x-2}{4(x+2)} + \frac{3(x+2)}{4(x-2)} = \frac{x-2+3x+6}{4(x+2)(x-2)} = \frac{4x+4}{4(x+2)(x-2)} = \frac{4(x+1)}{4(x+2)(x-2)} = \frac{x+1}{x^2-4}.$$

The graph of $f(x) = \frac{x+1}{x^2-4}$ crosses the x-axis at -1, and has vertical asymptotes at $x = -2$ and $x = 2$. Thus, the boundaries are -2, -1, and 1. We need to find the intervals on which $f(x) \leq 0$. These intervals are indicated on the graph where the curve is below the x-axis. Now, the curve is below the x-axis when $x < -2$ and when $-1 < x < 2$. Thus, the solution set is $\{x \mid x < -2 \text{ or } -1 \leq x < 2\}$ or $(-\infty, -2) \cup [-1, 2)$.

66.
$$\frac{1}{4(x+2)} > -\frac{3}{4(x-2)}$$

$$\frac{1}{4(x+2)} + \frac{3}{4(x-2)} > 0$$

In Problem 65, we found that the boundaries are -2, -1, and 1. We need to find the intervals on which $f(x) > 0$. These intervals are indicated on the graph where the curve is above the x-axis. Now, the curve is above the x-axis when $-2 < x < -1$ and when $x > 2$. Thus, the solution set is $\{x | -2 < x < -1 \text{ or } x > 2\}$ or $(-2, -1) \cup (2, \infty)$.

67. $s(t) = -16t^2 + 48t + 160$

To find when the height exceeds the height of the building, solve the inequality
$-16t^2 + 48t + 160 > 160$.
Solve the related quadratic equation.
$-16t^2 + 48t + 160 = 160$

$$-16t^2 + 48t = 0$$

$$t^2 - 3t = 0$$

$$t(t-3) = 0$$

Apply the zero product principle.
$t = 0$ or $t - 3 = 0$

$$t = 3$$

The boundary points are 0 and 3.

Test Interval	Test Number	Test	Conclusion
$(0,3)$	1	$-16(1)^2 + 48(1) + 160 > 160$ $192 > 160$, true	$(0,3)$ belongs to the solution set.
$(3,\infty)$	4	$-16(4)^2 + 48(4) + 160 > 160$ $96 > 160$, true	$(3,\infty)$ does not belong to the solution set.

The solution set is $(0,3)$. This means that the ball exceeds the height of the building between 0 and 3 seconds.

69. $f(8) = 27(8) + 163 = 216 + 163 = 379$

$g(8) = 1.2(8)^2 + 15.2(8) + 181.4 = 1.2(64) + 121.6 + 181.4$

$\quad = 76.8 + 121.6 + 181.4 = 379.8$

Since the graph indicates that Medicare spending will reach $379 billion, we conclude that both functions model the data quite well.

653

71. $g(x) = 1.2x^2 + 15.2x + 181.4$

To find when spending exceeds \$536.6 billion, solve the inequality
$1.2x^2 + 15.2x + 181.4 > 536.6$.
Solve the related quadratic equation using the quadratic formula.
$1.2x^2 + 15.2x + 181.4 = 536.6$

$1.2x^2 + 15.2x - 355.2 = 0$
$a = 1.2 \qquad b = 15.2 \qquad c = -355.2$

$$x = \frac{-15.2 \pm \sqrt{15.2^2 - 4(1.2)(-355.2)}}{2(1.2)} = \frac{-15.2 \pm \sqrt{231.04 + 1704.96}}{2.4}$$

$$= \frac{-15.2 \pm \sqrt{1936}}{2.4} = \frac{-15.2 \pm 44}{2.4}$$

$$= \frac{-15.2 - 44}{2.4} \quad \text{or} \quad \frac{-15.2 + 44}{2.4} = -24\frac{2}{3} \quad \text{or} \quad 12$$

We disregard $-24\frac{2}{3}$ since x represents the number of years after 1995 and cannot be negative.
The boundary point is 12.

Test Interval	Test Number	Test	Conclusion
$(0,12)$	1	$1.2(1)^2 + 15.2(1) + 181.4 > 536.6$ $197.8 > 536.6$, false	$(0,12)$ does not belong to the solution set.
$(12,\infty)$	13	$1.2(13)^2 + 15.2(13) + 181.4 > 536.6$ $581.8 > 536.6$, true	$(12,\infty)$ belongs to the solution set.

The solution set is $(12,\infty)$. This means that spending will exceed \$536.6 billion after $1995 + 12 = 2007$.

73. $\overline{C}(x) = \frac{500,000 + 400x}{x}$

To find when the cost of producing each wheelchair does not exceed \$425, solve the inequality
$\frac{500,000 + 400x}{x} \le 425$.
Express the inequality so that one side is zero.

$$\frac{500,000 + 400x}{x} - 425 \le 0$$

$$\frac{500,000 + 400x}{x} - \frac{425x}{x} \le 0$$

$$\frac{500,000 + 400x - 425x}{x} \le 0$$

$$\frac{500,000 - 25x}{x} \le 0$$

654

Find the values of x that make the numerator and denominator zero.

$$500,000 - 25x = 0 \qquad x = 0$$
$$500,000 = 25x$$
$$20,000 = x$$

The boundary points are 0 and 20,000.

Test Interval	Test Number	Test	Conclusion
$[0, 20000]$	1	$\dfrac{500,000 + 400(1)}{1} \leq 425$ $500,400 \leq 425$, false	$[0, 20000]$ does not belong to the solution set.
$[20000, \infty)$	25,000	$\dfrac{500,000 + 400(25,000)}{25,000} \leq 425$ $420 \leq 425$, true	$[20000, \infty)$ belongs to the solution set.

The solution set is $[20000, \infty)$. This means that the company's production level will have to be at least 20,000 wheelchairs per week. The boundary corresponds to the point (20,000, 425) on the graph. When production is 20,000 or more per month, the average cost is $425 or less.

75. Let $x =$ the length of the rectangle.

Since Perimeter $= 2(\text{length}) + 2(\text{width})$, we know

$$50 = 2x + 2(\text{width})$$
$$50 - 2x = 2(\text{width})$$
$$\text{width} = \frac{50 - 2x}{2} = 25 - x$$

Now, $A = (\text{length})(\text{width})$, so we have that

$$A(x) \leq 114$$
$$x(25 - x) \leq 114$$
$$25x - x^2 \leq 114$$

Solve the related equation

$$25x - x^2 = 114$$
$$0 = x^2 - 25x + 114$$
$$0 = (x - 19)(x - 6)$$

Apply the zero product principle:

$$x - 19 = 0 \quad \text{or} \quad x - 6 = 0$$
$$x = 19 \qquad\qquad x = 6$$

The boundary points are 6 and 19.

Test Interval	Test Number	Test	Conclusion
$(-\infty,6)$	0	$25(0)-0^2 \le 114$ $0 \le 114$, True	$(-\infty,6)$ belongs to the solution set.
$(6,19)$	10	$25(10)-10^2 \le 114$ $150 \le 114$, False	$(6,19)$ does not belong to the solution set.
$(19,\infty)$	20	$25(20)-20^2 \le 114$ $100 \le 114$, True	$(19,\infty)$ belongs to the solution set.

If the length is 6 feet, then the width is 19 feet. If the length is less than 6 feet, then the width is greater than 19 feet. Thus, if the area of the rectangle is not to exceed 114 square feet, the length of the shorter side must be 6 feet or less.

77. – 79. Answers will vary.

81. $2x^2 + 5x - 3 \le 0$

Let $y_1 = 2x^2 + 5x - 3$.

```
WINDOW
 Xmin=-10
 Xmax=10
 Xscl=1
 Ymin=-10
 Ymax=10
 Yscl=1
 Xres=1
```

The graph is crosses the x-axis at -3 and $\frac{1}{2}$. The graph is below the x-axis when $-3 < x < \frac{1}{2}$. Thus, the solution set is $\left\{ x \middle| -3 \le x \le \frac{1}{2} \right\}$ or $\left[-3, \frac{1}{2} \right]$.

83. $\frac{x+2}{x-3} \le 2$

$\frac{x+2}{x-3} - 2 \le 0$

Let $y_1 = \frac{x+2}{x-3} - 2$.

```
WINDOW
 Xmin=-10
 Xmax=10
 Xscl=1
 Ymin=-10
 Ymax=10
 Yscl=1
 Xres=1
```
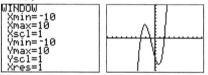

The graph is crosses the x-axis at 8.

The function has a vertical asymptote at $x = 3$. The graph is below the x-axis when $x < 3$ and when $x > 8$. Thus, the solution set is $\{ x \mid x < 3$ or $x \ge 8 \}$ or $(-\infty, 3) \cup [8, \infty)$.

85. $x^3 + 2x^2 - 5x - 6 > 0$

Let $y_1 = x^3 + 2x^2 - 5x - 6$

```
WINDOW
 Xmin=-10
 Xmax=10
 Xscl=1
 Ymin=-10
 Ymax=10
 Yscl=1
 Xres=1
```

The graph is crosses the x-axis at -3, -1, and 2. The graph is above the x-axis when $-3 < x < -1$ and when $x > 2$. Thus, the solution set is $\{ x \mid -3 < x < -1$ or $x > 2 \}$ or $(-3, -1) \cup (2, \infty)$.

87. Answers will vary. An example is as follows.

$$x = -3 \qquad x = 5$$
$$x + 3 = 0 \qquad x - 5 = 0$$
$$(x+3)(x-5) = 0$$
$$x^2 - 2x - 15 = 0.$$

Since x falls between two numbers the inequality symbol should be less than or equal to, so the inequality is $x^2 - 2x - 15 \le 0$.

89. The left hand side of the inequality is zero when x is 2, so the solution set is $\{x \mid x \text{ is a real number and } x \neq 2\}$ or $(-\infty, 2) \cup (2, \infty)$.

91. There is no value of x for which the left hand side will be less than -1. The solution set is $\varnothing$ or $\{\ \}$.

93. a. The x–axis is the divider between y–values that are positive and y–values that are negative. Since the entire graph falls above the x–axis, we know that all of the corresponding y–values are positive. Since the inequality is greater than zero, the solution set is $\{x \mid x \text{ is a real number}\}$ or $(-\infty, \infty)$.

b. Since the entire graph falls above the x–axis, we know that all of the corresponding y–values are negative. Since the inequality is less than zero, the solution set is $\varnothing$ or $\{\ \}$.

c. First, consider $4x^2 - 8x + 7 > 0$ from part **a.**

$$4x^2 - 8x + 7 = 0$$
$$a = 4 \qquad b = -8 \qquad c = 7$$
$$x = \frac{-(-8) \pm \sqrt{(-8)^2 - 4(4)(7)}}{2(4)}$$
$$= \frac{8 \pm \sqrt{64 - 112}}{8}$$
$$= \frac{8 \pm \sqrt{-48}}{8}$$
$$= \frac{8 \pm \sqrt{-16 \cdot 3}}{8}$$
$$= \frac{8 \pm 4\sqrt{3}i}{8} = \frac{8}{8} \pm \frac{4\sqrt{3}i}{8} = 1 \pm \frac{\sqrt{3}}{2}i$$

The graph of $4x^2 - 8x + 7 = 0$ is a parabola. Since the values of x are complex numbers, we know there are no x–intercepts. This means that the entire graph lies above the x–axis and the value of $4x^2 - 8x + 7$ will always be greater than zero. As a result, the solution set is $\{x \mid x \text{ is a real number}\}$ or $(-\infty, \infty)$.

Next, consider $4x^2 - 8x + 7 < 0$ from part **b.** From above, we know that $4x^2 - 8x + 7$ will always be greater than zero and never less than zero. As a result, the solution set is the solution set is $\varnothing$ or $\{\ \}$.

95.
$$\left| \frac{x - 5}{3} \right| < 8$$
$$-8 < \frac{x - 5}{3} < 8$$
$$-24 < x - 5 < 24$$
$$-19 < x < 29$$

The solution set is $\{x \mid -19 < x < 29\}$ or $(-19, 29)$.

96.
$$\frac{2x + 6}{x^2 + 8x + 16} \div \frac{x^2 - 9}{x^2 + 3x - 4}$$
$$= \frac{2x + 6}{x^2 + 8x + 16} \cdot \frac{x^2 + 3x - 4}{x^2 - 9}$$
$$= \frac{2\cancel{(x+3)}}{\cancel{(x+4)}(x+4)} \cdot \frac{\cancel{(x+4)}(x-1)}{\cancel{(x+3)}(x-3)}$$
$$= \frac{2(x - 1)}{(x + 4)(x - 3)}$$

97. $x^4 - 16y^4$
$$= (x^2 + 4y^2)(x^2 - 4y^2)$$
$$= (x^2 + 4y^2)(x + 2y)(x - 2y)$$

Chapter 11 Review Exercises

1.
$$2x^2 - 3 = 125$$
$$2x^2 = 128$$
$$x^2 = 64$$
$$x = \pm 8$$
The solutions are -8 and 8, and the solution set is $\{-8, 8\}$.

2.
$$3x^2 - 150 = 0$$
$$3x^2 = 150$$
$$x^2 = 50$$
$$x = \pm\sqrt{50}$$
$$x = \pm\sqrt{25 \cdot 2}$$
$$x = \pm 5\sqrt{2}$$
The solutions are $-5\sqrt{2}$ and $5\sqrt{2}$, and the solution set is $\{-5\sqrt{2}, 5\sqrt{2}\}$.

3.
$$3x^2 - 2 = 0$$
$$3x^2 = 2$$
$$x^2 = \frac{2}{3}$$
$$x = \pm\sqrt{\frac{2}{3}}$$
Rationalize the denominator.
$$x = \pm\frac{\sqrt{2}}{\sqrt{3}} \cdot \frac{\sqrt{3}}{\sqrt{3}} = \pm\frac{\sqrt{6}}{3}$$
The solutions are $-\dfrac{\sqrt{6}}{3}$ and $\dfrac{\sqrt{6}}{3}$, and

the solution set is $\left\{-\dfrac{\sqrt{6}}{3}, \dfrac{\sqrt{6}}{3}\right\}$.

4.
$$(x-4)^2 = 18$$
$$x - 4 = \pm\sqrt{18}$$
$$x = 4 \pm \sqrt{9 \cdot 2}$$
$$x = 4 \pm 3\sqrt{2}$$
The solutions are $4 - 3\sqrt{2}$ and $4 + 3\sqrt{2}$, and the solution set is $\{4 - 3\sqrt{2}, 4 + 3\sqrt{2}\}$.

5.
$$(x+7)^2 = -36$$
$$x + 7 = \pm\sqrt{-36}$$
$$x = -7 \pm 6i$$
The solutions are $-7 - 6i$ and $-7 + 6i$, and the solution set is $\{-7 - 6i, -7 + 6i\}$.

6.
$$x^2 + 20x + \underline{\quad\quad}$$
Since $b = 20$, we add
$$\left(\frac{b}{2}\right)^2 = \left(\frac{20}{2}\right)^2 = (10)^2 = 100.$$
$$x^2 + 20x + 100 = (x + 10)^2$$

7.
$$x^2 - 3x + \underline{\quad\quad}$$
Since $b = 3$, we add $\left(\dfrac{b}{2}\right)^2 = \left(\dfrac{3}{2}\right)^2 = \dfrac{9}{4}$.
$$x^2 - 3x + \frac{9}{4} = \left(x - \frac{3}{2}\right)^2$$

8. $x^2 - 12x + 27 = 0$

$x^2 - 12x \quad = -27$

Since $b = -12$, we add

$\left(\dfrac{b}{2}\right)^2 = \left(\dfrac{-12}{2}\right)^2 = (-6)^2 = 36$.

$x^2 - 12x + 27 = 0$

$x^2 - 12x + 36 = -27 + 36$

$(x - 6)^2 = 9$

Apply the square root property.

$x - 6 = 3 \qquad x - 6 = -3$

$x = 9 \qquad x = 3$

The solutions are 3 and 9 and the solution set is $\{3, 9\}$.

9. $x^2 - 7x - 1 = 0$

$x^2 - 7x \quad = 1$

Since $b = -7$, we add

$\left(\dfrac{b}{2}\right)^2 = \left(\dfrac{-7}{2}\right)^2 = \dfrac{49}{4}$.

$x^2 - 7x + \dfrac{49}{4} = 1 + \dfrac{49}{4}$

$\left(x - \dfrac{7}{2}\right)^2 = \dfrac{4}{4} + \dfrac{49}{4}$

$\left(x - \dfrac{7}{2}\right)^2 = \dfrac{53}{4}$

Apply the square root property.

$x - \dfrac{7}{2} = \pm\sqrt{\dfrac{53}{4}}$

$x = \dfrac{7}{2} \pm \dfrac{\sqrt{53}}{2} = \dfrac{7 \pm \sqrt{53}}{2}$

The solutions are $\dfrac{7 \pm \sqrt{53}}{2}$ and the

solution set is $\left\{\dfrac{7 \pm \sqrt{53}}{2}\right\}$.

10. $2x^2 + 3x - 4 = 0$

$x^2 + \dfrac{3}{2}x - 2 = 0$

$x^2 + \dfrac{3}{2}x \quad = 2$

Since $b = \dfrac{3}{2}$, we add

$\left(\dfrac{b}{2}\right)^2 = \left(\dfrac{\frac{3}{2}}{2}\right)^2 = \left(\dfrac{3}{2} \div 2\right)^2$

$= \left(\dfrac{3}{2} \cdot \dfrac{1}{2}\right)^2 = \left(\dfrac{3}{4}\right)^2 = \dfrac{9}{16}$.

$x^2 + \dfrac{3}{2}x + \dfrac{9}{16} = 2 + \dfrac{9}{16}$

$\left(x + \dfrac{3}{4}\right)^2 = \dfrac{32}{16} + \dfrac{9}{16}$

$\left(x + \dfrac{3}{4}\right)^2 = \dfrac{41}{16}$

Apply the square root property.

$x + \dfrac{3}{4} = \pm\sqrt{\dfrac{41}{16}}$

$x = -\dfrac{3}{4} \pm \dfrac{\sqrt{41}}{4}$

$x = \dfrac{-3 \pm \sqrt{41}}{4}$

The solutions are $\dfrac{-3 \pm \sqrt{41}}{4}$ and the

solution set is $\left\{\dfrac{-3 \pm \sqrt{41}}{4}\right\}$.

11.
$$A = P(1+r)^t$$
$$2916 = 2500(1+r)^2$$
$$\frac{2916}{2500} = (1+r)^2$$
Apply the square root property.
$$1+r = \pm\sqrt{\frac{2916}{2500}}$$
$$r = -1 \pm \sqrt{1.1664}$$
$$r = -1 \pm 1.08$$
The solutions are $-1 - 1.08 = -2.08$ and $-1 + 1.08 = 0.08$. We disregard -2.08 since we cannot have a negative interest rate. The interest rate is 0.08 or 8%.

12.
$$W(t) = 3t^2$$
$$588 = 3t^2$$
$$196 = t^2$$
Apply the square root property.
$$t^2 = 196$$
$$t = \pm\sqrt{196}$$
$$t = \pm 14$$
The solutions are -14 and 14. We disregard -14, because we cannot have a negative time measurement. The fetus will weigh 588 grams after 14 weeks.

13.

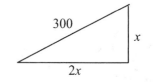

Use the Pythagorean Theorem.
$$(2x)^2 + x^2 = 300^2$$
$$4x^2 + x^2 = 90,000$$
$$5x^2 = 90,000$$
$$x^2 = 18,000$$
$$x = \pm\sqrt{18,000}$$
$$x = \pm\sqrt{3600 \cdot 5}$$
$$x = \pm 60\sqrt{5}$$
The solutions are $\pm 60\sqrt{5}$ meters. We disregard $-60\sqrt{5}$ meters, because we can't have a negative length measurement. Therefore, the building is $60\sqrt{5}$ meters, or approximately 134.2 meters high.

14.
$$d = \sqrt{(3-(-2))^2 + (9-(-3))^2}$$
$$= \sqrt{(3+2)^2 + (9+3)^2}$$
$$= \sqrt{5^2 + 12^2} = \sqrt{25+144}$$
$$= \sqrt{169} = 13$$
The distance between the points is 13 units.

15.
$$d = \sqrt{(-2-(-4))^2 + (5-3)^2}$$
$$= \sqrt{(-2+4)^2 + 2^2} = \sqrt{2^2 + 4}$$
$$= \sqrt{4+4} = \sqrt{8} = \sqrt{4 \cdot 2} = 2\sqrt{2}$$
The distance between the points is $2\sqrt{2}$ or approximately 2.83 units.

660

16.

$$\text{Midpoint} = \left(\frac{2+(-12)}{2}, \frac{6+4}{2}\right)$$

$$= \left(\frac{-10}{2}, \frac{10}{2}\right) = (-5,5)$$

The midpoint is $(-5,5)$.

17.

$$\text{Midpoint} = \left(\frac{4+(-15)}{2}, \frac{-6+2}{2}\right)$$

$$= \left(\frac{-11}{2}, \frac{-4}{2}\right) = \left(-\frac{11}{2}, -2\right)$$

The midpoint is $\left(-\frac{11}{2}, -2\right)$.

18.

$$x^2 = 2x+4$$

$$x^2 - 2x - 4 = 0$$

$$a=1 \quad b=-2 \quad c=-4$$

$$x = \frac{-(-2) \pm \sqrt{(-2)^2 - 4(1)(-4)}}{2(1)}$$

$$= \frac{2 \pm \sqrt{4+16}}{2}$$

$$= \frac{2 \pm \sqrt{20}}{2}$$

$$= \frac{2 \pm \sqrt{4\cdot 5}}{2}$$

$$= \frac{2 \pm 2\sqrt{5}}{2} = \frac{2(1\pm\sqrt{5})}{2} = 1\pm\sqrt{5}$$

The solutions are $1\pm\sqrt{5}$, and the solution set is $\{1\pm\sqrt{5}\}$.

19.

$$x^2 - 2x + 19 = 0$$

$$a=1 \quad b=-2 \quad c=19$$

$$x = \frac{-(-2) \pm \sqrt{(-2)^2 - 4(1)(19)}}{2(1)}$$

$$= \frac{2 \pm \sqrt{4-76}}{2}$$

$$= \frac{2 \pm \sqrt{-72}}{2}$$

$$= \frac{2 \pm \sqrt{-36\cdot 2}}{2}$$

$$= \frac{2 \pm 6\sqrt{2}i}{2} = \frac{2(1\pm 3\sqrt{2}i)}{2} = 1\pm 3\sqrt{2}i$$

The solutions are $1\pm 3\sqrt{2}i$, and the solution set is $\{1\pm 3\sqrt{2}i\}$.

20.

$$2x^2 = 3-4x$$

$$2x^2 + 4x - 3 = 0$$

$$a=2 \quad b=4 \quad c=-3$$

$$x = \frac{-4 \pm \sqrt{4^2 - 4(2)(-3)}}{2(2)}$$

$$= \frac{-4 \pm \sqrt{16+24}}{4}$$

$$= \frac{-4 \pm \sqrt{40}}{4}$$

$$= \frac{-4 \pm \sqrt{4\cdot 10}}{4}$$

$$= \frac{-4 \pm 2\sqrt{10}}{4}$$

$$= \frac{2(-2\pm\sqrt{10})}{4} = \frac{-2\pm\sqrt{10}}{2}$$

The solutions are $\dfrac{-2\pm\sqrt{10}}{2}$, and the

solution set is $\left\{\dfrac{-2\pm\sqrt{10}}{2}\right\}$.

661

21. $x^2 - 4x + 13 = 0$

$a = 1 \quad b = -4 \quad c = 13$

Find the discriminant.

$b^2 - 4ac = (-4)^2 - 4(1)(13)$

$\qquad = 16 - 52 = -36$

Since the discriminant is negative, there are two imaginary solutions which are complex conjugates.

22. $9x^2 = 2 - 3x$

$9x^2 + 3x - 2 = 0$

$a = 9 \quad b = 3 \quad c = -2$

Find the discriminant.

$b^2 - 4ac = 3^2 - 4(9)(-2)$

$\qquad = 9 + 72 = 81$

Since the discriminant is greater than zero, there are two unequal real solutions. Also, since the discriminant is a perfect square, the solutions are rational.

23. $2x^2 + 4x = 3$

$2x^2 + 4x - 3 = 0$

$a = 2 \quad b = 4 \quad c = -3$

Find the discriminant.

$b^2 - 4ac = 4^2 - 4(2)(-3)$

$\qquad = 16 + 24 = 40$

Since the discriminant is greater than zero, there are two unequal real solutions. Also, since the discriminant is not a perfect square, the solutions are irrational.

24. $3x^2 - 10x - 8 = 0$

$(3x + 2)(x - 4) = 0$

Apply the zero product principle.

$3x + 2 = 0 \quad$ and $\quad x - 4 = 0$

$3x = -2 \qquad\qquad x = 4$

$x = -\dfrac{2}{3}$

The solutions are $-\dfrac{2}{3}$ and 4, and the

solution set is $\left\{ -\dfrac{2}{3}, 4 \right\}$.

25. $(2x - 3)(x + 2) = x^2 - 2x + 4$

$2x^2 + 4x - 3x - 6 = x^2 - 2x + 4$

$x^2 + 3x - 10 = 0$

Use the quadratic formula.

$a = 1 \quad b = 3 \quad c = -10$

$x = \dfrac{-3 \pm \sqrt{3^2 - 4(1)(-10)}}{2(1)}$

$\quad = \dfrac{-3 \pm \sqrt{9 - (-40)}}{2}$

$\quad = \dfrac{-3 \pm \sqrt{49}}{2} = \dfrac{-3 \pm 7}{2} = -5 \text{ or } 2$

The solutions are -5 and 2, and the solution set is $\{-5, 2\}$.

26. $5x^2 - x - 1 = 0$

Use the quadratic formula.

$a = 5 \quad b = -1 \quad c = -1$

$x = \dfrac{-(-1) \pm \sqrt{(-1)^2 - 4(5)(-1)}}{2(5)}$

$\quad = \dfrac{1 \pm \sqrt{1 - (-20)}}{10} = \dfrac{1 \pm \sqrt{21}}{10}$

The solutions are $\dfrac{1 \pm \sqrt{21}}{10}$, and the

solution set is $\left\{ \dfrac{1 \pm \sqrt{21}}{10} \right\}$.

27. $x^2 - 16 = 0$

$x^2 = 16$

Apply the square root principle.

$x = \pm\sqrt{16} = \pm 4$

The solutions are -4 and 4, and the solution set is $\{-4, 4\}$.

28. $(x-3)^2 - 8 = 0$

$(x-3)^2 = 8$

Apply the square root principle.

$x - 3 = \pm\sqrt{8}$

$x = 3 \pm \sqrt{4 \cdot 2}$

$x = 3 \pm 2\sqrt{2}$

The solutions are $3 \pm 2\sqrt{2}$, and the solution set is $\{3 \pm 2\sqrt{2}\}$.

29. $3x^2 - x + 2 = 0$

Use the quadratic formula.

$a = 3 \quad b = -1 \quad c = 2$

$x = \dfrac{-(-1) \pm \sqrt{(-1)^2 - 4(3)(2)}}{2(3)}$

$= \dfrac{1 \pm \sqrt{1 - 24}}{6}$

$= \dfrac{1 \pm \sqrt{-23}}{6} = \dfrac{1}{6} \pm \dfrac{\sqrt{23}}{6} i$

The solutions are $\dfrac{1}{6} \pm \dfrac{\sqrt{23}}{6} i$, and the

solution set is $\left\{ \dfrac{1}{6} \pm \dfrac{\sqrt{23}}{6} i \right\}$.

30.

$\dfrac{5}{x+1} + \dfrac{x-1}{4} = 2$

$4(x+1)\left(\dfrac{5}{x+1} + \dfrac{x-1}{4} \right) = 4(x+1)(2)$

$20 + (x+1)(x-1) = 8x + 8$

$20 + x^2 - 1 = 8x + 8$

$x^2 - 8x + 11 = 0$

Use the quadratic formula.

$a = 1 \quad b = -8 \quad c = 11$

$x = \dfrac{-(-8) \pm \sqrt{(-8)^2 - 4(1)(11)}}{2(1)}$

$= \dfrac{8 \pm \sqrt{64 - 44}}{2} = \dfrac{8 \pm \sqrt{20}}{2}$

$= \dfrac{8 \pm \sqrt{4 \cdot 5}}{2} = \dfrac{8 \pm 2\sqrt{5}}{2}$

$= \dfrac{2(4 \pm \sqrt{5})}{2} = 4 \pm \sqrt{5}$

The solutions are $4 \pm \sqrt{5}$, and the solution set is $\{4 \pm \sqrt{5}\}$.

31. Because the solution set is $\left\{ -\dfrac{1}{3}, \dfrac{3}{5} \right\}$,

we have

$x = -\dfrac{1}{3} \quad$ or $\quad x = \dfrac{3}{5}$

$3x = -1 \qquad\qquad 5x = 3$

$3x + 1 = 0 \qquad\quad 5x - 3 = 0.$

Apply the zero-product principle in reverse.

$(3x+1)(5x-3) = 0$

$15x^2 - 9x + 5x - 3 = 0$

$15x^2 - 4x - 3 = 0$

32. Because the solution set is $\{-9i, 9i\}$,

we have

$x = -9i \quad$ or $\quad x = 9i$

$x + 9i = 0 \qquad\quad x - 9i = 0.$

Apply the zero-product principle in reverse.

$(x+9i)(x-9i) = 0$

$x^2 - 9ix + 9ix - 81i^2 = 0$

$x^2 - 81(-1) = 0$

$x^2 + 81 = 0$

33. Because the solution set is $\left\{-4\sqrt{3}, 4\sqrt{3}\right\}$, we have

$$x = -4\sqrt{3} \quad \text{or} \quad x = 4\sqrt{3}$$
$$x + 4\sqrt{3} = 0 \qquad x - 4\sqrt{3} = 0.$$

Apply the zero product principle in reverse.

$$\left(x + 4\sqrt{3}\right)\left(x - 4\sqrt{3}\right) = 0$$
$$x^2 - \left(4\sqrt{3}\right)^2 = 0$$
$$x^2 - 16 \cdot 3 = 0$$
$$x^2 - 48 = 0$$

34. $1020 = 23x^2 - 259x + 816$

$$0 = 23x^2 - 259x - 204$$

Apply the Pythagorean Theorem.

$$a = 23 \quad b = -259 \quad c = -204$$

$$x = \frac{-(-259) \pm \sqrt{(-259)^2 - 4(23)(-204)}}{2(23)}$$

$$= \frac{259 \pm \sqrt{67,081 - (-18,768)}}{46}$$

$$= \frac{259 \pm \sqrt{85,849}}{46}$$

$$= \frac{259 \pm 293}{46} = 12 \quad \text{or} \quad -\frac{17}{23}$$

We disregard $-\dfrac{17}{23}$ because we cannot

have a negative number of years. The solution is 12. We conclude that 1020 police officers were convicted in the year $1990 + 12 = 2002$.

35. $0 = -16t^2 + 140t + 3$

Apply the Pythagorean Theorem.

$$a = -16 \quad b = 140 \quad c = 3$$

$$= \frac{-140 \pm \sqrt{19,600 + 192}}{-32}$$

$$= \frac{-140 \pm \sqrt{19,792}}{-32}$$

$$\approx \frac{-140 \pm 140.7}{-32}$$

$$\approx \frac{-140 - 140.7}{-32} \quad \text{or} \quad \frac{-140 + 140.7}{-32}$$

$$\approx \frac{-280.7}{-32} \quad \text{or} \quad \frac{0.7}{-32}$$

$$\approx 8.8 \quad \text{or} \quad -0.02$$

We disregard -0.02 because we cannot have a negative time measurement. The solution is approximately 8.8. We conclude that the ball will hit the ground in about 8.8 seconds.

36. $f(x) = -(x+1)^2 + 4$

Since $a = -1$ is negative, the parabola opens downward. The vertex of the parabola is $(h, k) = (-1, 4)$ and the axis of symmetry is $x = -1$. Replace $f(x)$ with 0 to find x–intercepts.

$$0 = -(x+1)^2 + 4$$
$$(x+1)^2 = 4$$

Apply the square root property.

$$x + 1 = \sqrt{4} \quad \text{or} \quad x + 1 = -\sqrt{4}$$
$$x + 1 = 2 \qquad\qquad x + 1 = -2$$
$$x = 1 \qquad\qquad\quad x = -3$$

The x–intercepts are 1 and –3. Set $x = 0$ and solve for y to obtain the y–intercept.

$$y = -(0+1)^2 + 4$$
$$y = -(1)^2 + 4$$
$$y = -1 + 4 = 3$$

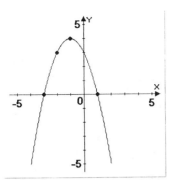

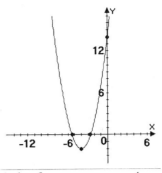

Axis of symmetry: $x = -1$.

Axis of symmetry: $x = -4$.

37. $f(x) = (x+4)^2 - 2$

Since $a = 1$ is positive, the parabola opens upward. The vertex of the parabola is $(h, k) = (-4, -2)$ and the axis of symmetry is $x = -4$. Replace $f(x)$ with 0 to find x–intercepts.

$0 = (x+4)^2 - 2$

$2 = (x+4)^2$

Apply the square root property.

$x + 4 = \sqrt{2}$ or $x + 4 = -\sqrt{2}$

$x = -4 + \sqrt{2}$ $x = -4 - \sqrt{2}$

The x–intercepts are $-4 - \sqrt{2}$ and $-4 + \sqrt{2}$. Set $x = 0$ and solve for y to obtain the y–intercept.

$y = (0+4)^2 - 2$

$y = 4^2 - 2$

$y = 16 - 2$

$y = 14$

38. $f(x) = -x^2 + 2x + 3$

Since $a = -1$ is negative, the parabola opens downward. The x–coordinate of the vertex of the parabola is

$-\dfrac{b}{2a} = -\dfrac{2}{2(-1)} = -\dfrac{2}{-2} = 1$ and the

y–coordinate of the vertex of the

parabola is $f\left(-\dfrac{b}{2a}\right) = f(1)$

$= -1^2 + 2(1) + 3$

$= -1 + 2 + 3 = 4.$

The vertex is (1, 4). Replace $f(x)$ with 0 to find x–intercepts.

$0 = -x^2 + 2x + 3$

$0 = x^2 - 2x - 3$

$0 = (x-3)(x+1)$

Apply the zero product principle.

$x - 3 = 0$ or $x + 1 = 0$

$x = 3$ $x = -1$

The x–intercepts are -1 and 3. Set $x = 0$ and solve for y to obtain the y–intercept.

$y = -0^2 + 2(0) + 3$

$y = 0 + 0 + 3$

$y = 3$

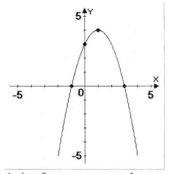

Axis of symmetry: $x = 1$.

39. $f(x) = 2x^2 - 4x - 6$

Since $a = 2$ is positive, the parabola opens upward. The x–coordinate of the vertex of the parabola is

$$-\frac{b}{2a} = -\frac{-4}{2(2)} = -\frac{-4}{4} = 1 \text{ and the}$$

y–coordinate of the vertex of the

$$f\left(-\frac{b}{2a}\right) = f(1)$$

parabola is
$$= 2(1)^2 - 4(1) - 6$$
$$= 2(1) - 4 - 6$$
$$= 2 - 4 - 6 = -8.$$

The vertex is $(1, -8)$. Replace $f(x)$ with 0 to find x–intercepts.

$0 = 2x^2 - 4x - 6$

$0 = x^2 - 2x - 3$

$0 = (x - 3)(x + 1)$

Apply the zero product principle.

$x - 3 = 0$ or $x + 1 = 0$

$x = 3$ $x = -1$

The x–intercepts are –1 and 3. Set $x = 0$ and solve for y to obtain the y–intercept.

$y = 2(0)^2 - 4(0) - 6$

$y = 2(0) - 0 - 6$

$y = 0 - 0 - 6 = -6$

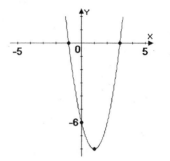

Axis of symmetry: $x = 1$.

40. $f(x) = -0.02x^2 + x + 1$

Since $a = -0.02$ is negative, we know the function opens downward and has a maximum at

$$x = -\frac{b}{2a} = -\frac{1}{2(-0.02)} = -\frac{1}{-0.04} = 25.$$

When 25 inches of rain falls, the maximum growth will occur. The maximum growth is

$$f(25) = -0.02(25)^2 + 25 + 1$$
$$= -0.02(625) + 25 + 1$$
$$= -12.5 + 25 + 1 = 13.5.$$

A maximum yearly growth of 13.5 inches occurs when 25 inches of rain falls per year.

41. $s(t) = -16t^2 + 400t + 40$

Since $a = -16$ is negative, we know the function opens downward and has a maximum at

$$x = -\frac{b}{2a} = -\frac{400}{2(-16)} = -\frac{400}{-32} = 12.5.$$

At 12.5 seconds, the rocket reaches its maximum height. The maximum height is

$$s(12.5) = -16(12.5)^2 + 400(12.5) + 40$$
$$= -16(156.25) + 5000 + 40$$
$$= -2500 + 5000 + 40 = 2540.$$

The rocket reaches a maximum height of 2540 feet in 12.5 seconds.

666

42. According to the graph, the vertex (maximum point) is (25, 5). This means that the maximum divorce rate of 5 divorces per 1000 people occurred in the year $1960 + 25 = 1985$.

43. Maximize the area using $A = lw$.

$$A(x) = x(1000 - 2x)$$
$$A(x) = -2x^2 + 1000x$$

Since $a = -2$ is negative, we know the function opens downward and has a maximum at

$$x = -\frac{b}{2a} = -\frac{1000}{2(-2)} = -\frac{1000}{-4} = 250.$$

The maximum area is achieved when the width is 250 yards. The maximum area is

$$A(250) = 250(1000 - 2(250))$$
$$= 250(1000 - 500)$$
$$= 250(500) = 125,000.$$

The area is maximized at 125,000 square yards when the width is 250 yards and the length is $1000 - 2 \cdot 250 = 500$ yards.

44. Let x = one of the numbers
Let $14 + x$ = the other number

We need to minimize the function
$$P(x) = x(14 + x)$$
$$= 14x + x^2$$
$$= x^2 + 14x.$$
The minimum is at
$$x = -\frac{b}{2a} = -\frac{14}{2(1)} = -\frac{14}{2} = -7.$$

The other number is
$$14 + x = 14 + (-7) = 7.$$

The numbers which minimize the product are -7 and 7. The minimum product is $-7 \cdot 7 = -49$.

45. Let $t = x^2$.
$$x^4 - 6x^2 + 8 = 0$$
$$\left(x^2\right)^2 - 6x^2 + 8 = 0$$
$$t^2 - 6t + 8 = 0$$
$$(t - 4)(t - 2) = 0$$
Apply the zero product principle.
$$t - 4 = 0 \quad \text{or} \quad t - 2 = 0$$
$$t = 4 \qquad\qquad t = 2$$
Replace t by x^2.
$$x^2 = 4 \quad \text{or} \quad x^2 = 2$$
$$x = \pm 2 \qquad\quad x = \pm\sqrt{2}$$
The solutions are $\pm\sqrt{2}$ and ± 2, and the solution set is $\left\{-2, -\sqrt{2}, \sqrt{2}, 2\right\}$.

46. Let $t = \sqrt{x}$.
$$x + 7\sqrt{x} - 8 = 0$$
$$\left(\sqrt{x}\right)^2 + 7\sqrt{x} - 8 = 0$$
$$t^2 + 7t - 8 = 0$$
$$(t + 8)(t - 1) = 0$$
Apply the zero product principle.
$$t + 8 = 0 \quad \text{or} \quad t - 1 = 0$$
$$t = -8 \qquad\qquad t = 1$$
Replace t by $\sqrt{x}$.
$$\cancel{\sqrt{x} = -8} \quad \text{or} \quad \sqrt{x} = 1$$
$$x = 1$$

We disregard -8 because the square root of x cannot be a negative number. We need to check this solution because both sides of the equation were raised to an even power.
Check: $1 + 7\sqrt{1} - 8 = 0$
$$1 + 7(1) - 8 = 0$$
$$1 + 7 - 8 = 0$$
$$0 = 0$$
The solution is 1 and the solution set is $\{1\}$.

47. Let $t = x^2 + 2x$.
$$\left(x^2 + 2x\right)^2 - 14\left(x^2 + 2x\right) = 15$$
$$\left(x^2 + 2x\right)^2 - 14\left(x^2 + 2x\right) - 15 = 0$$
$$t^2 - 14t - 15 = 0$$
$$(t - 15)(t + 1) = 0$$
Apply the zero product principle.
$$t - 15 = 0 \quad \text{or} \quad t + 1 = 0$$
$$t = 15 \qquad\qquad t = -1$$
Replace t by $x^2 + 2x$.
First, consider $t = 15$.
$$x^2 + 2x = 15$$
$$x^2 + 2x - 15 = 0$$
$$(x + 5)(x - 3) = 0$$
Apply the zero product principle.
$$x + 5 = 0 \quad \text{or} \quad x - 3 = 0$$
$$x = -5 \qquad\qquad x = 3$$

Next, consider $t = -1$.
$$x^2 + 2x = -1$$
$$x^2 + 2x + 1 = 0$$
$$(x + 1)^2 = 0$$
Apply the zero product principle to find the double root.
$$x + 1 = 0$$
$$x = -1$$
The solutions are $-5, -1$, and 3, and the solution set is $\{-5, -1, 3\}$.

48. Let $t = x^{-1}$.
$$x^{-2} + x^{-1} - 56 = 0$$
$$\left(x^{-1}\right)^2 + x^{-1} - 56 = 0$$
$$t^2 + t - 56 = 0$$
$$(t + 8)(t - 7) = 0$$
Apply the zero product principle.

$$t + 8 = 0 \quad \text{or} \quad t - 7 = 0$$
$$t = -8 \qquad\qquad t = 7$$
Replace t by x^{-1}.
$$x^{-1} = -8 \quad \text{or} \quad x^{-1} = 7$$
$$\frac{1}{x} = -8 \qquad\qquad \frac{1}{x} = 7$$
$$-8x = 1 \qquad\qquad 7x = 1$$
$$x = -\frac{1}{8} \qquad\qquad x = \frac{1}{7}$$
The solutions are $-\dfrac{1}{8}$ and $\dfrac{1}{7}$, and the solution set is $\left\{-\dfrac{1}{8}, \dfrac{1}{7}\right\}$.

49. Let $t = x^{\frac{1}{3}}$.
$$x^{\frac{2}{3}} - x^{\frac{1}{3}} - 12 = 0$$
$$\left(x^{\frac{1}{3}}\right)^2 - x^{\frac{1}{3}} - 12 = 0$$
$$t^2 - t - 12 = 0$$
$$(t - 4)(t + 3) = 0$$
Apply the zero product principle.
$$t - 4 = 0 \quad \text{or} \quad t + 3 = 0$$
$$t = 4 \qquad\qquad t = -3$$
Replace t by $x^{\frac{1}{3}}$.
$$x^{\frac{1}{3}} = 4 \qquad\quad \text{or} \qquad x^{\frac{1}{3}} = -3$$
$$\left(x^{\frac{1}{3}}\right)^3 = 4^3 \qquad\qquad \left(x^{\frac{1}{3}}\right)^3 = (-3)^3$$
$$x = 64 \qquad\qquad x = -27$$

The solutions are -27 and 64, and the solution set is $\{-27, 64\}$.

668

50.

Let $t = x^{\frac{1}{4}}$.

$$x^{\frac{1}{2}} + 3x^{\frac{1}{4}} - 10 = 0$$

$$\left(x^{\frac{1}{4}}\right)^2 + 3x^{\frac{1}{4}} - 10 = 0$$

$$t^2 + 3t - 10 = 0$$

$$(t + 5)(t - 2) = 0$$

Apply the zero product principle.

$$t + 5 = 0 \quad \text{or} \quad t - 2 = 0$$
$$t = -5 \qquad\qquad t = 2$$

Replace t by $x^{\frac{1}{4}}$.

$$x^{\frac{1}{4}} = -5 \quad \text{or} \quad x^{\frac{1}{4}} = 2$$

$$\cancel{\sqrt[4]{x} = -5} \qquad \left(x^{\frac{1}{4}}\right)^4 = 2^4$$

$$x = 16$$

We disregard –5 because the fourth root of x cannot be a negative number.
We need to check the solution, 16, because both sides of the equation were raised to an even power.

Check $x = 16$.

$$16^{\frac{1}{2}} + 3(16)^{\frac{1}{4}} - 10 = 0$$
$$4 + 3(2) - 10 = 0$$
$$4 + 6 - 10 = 0$$
$$10 - 10 = 0$$
$$0 = 0$$

The solution checks. The solution is 16 and the solution set is $\{16\}$.

51. $2x^2 + 5x - 3 < 0$

Solve the related quadratic equation.

$$2x^2 + 5x - 3 = 0$$
$$(2x - 1)(x + 3) = 0$$

Apply the zero product principle.

$2x - 1 = 0$ or $x + 3 = 0$
$\quad 2x = 1 \qquad\qquad x = -3$
$$x = \frac{1}{2}$$

The boundary points are -3 and $\frac{1}{2}$.

Test Interval	Test Number	Test	Conclusion
$(-\infty, -3)$	-4	$2(-4)^2 + 5(-4) - 3 < 0$ $9 < 0$, false	$(-\infty, -3)$ does not belong to the solution set.
$\left(-3, \frac{1}{2}\right)$	0	$2(0)^2 + 5(0) - 3 < 0$ $-3 < 0$, true	$\left(-3, \frac{1}{2}\right)$ belongs to the solution set.
$\left(\frac{1}{2}, \infty\right)$	1	$2(1)^2 + 5(1) - 3 < 0$ $4 < 0$, false	$\left(\frac{1}{2}, \infty\right)$ does not belong to the solution set.

The solution set is $\left(-3, \frac{1}{2}\right)$ or $\left\{ x \mid -3 < x < \frac{1}{2} \right\}$.

52. $2x^2 + 9x + 4 \geq 0$

Solve the related quadratic equation.

$$2x^2 + 9x + 4 = 0$$
$$(2x + 1)(x + 4) = 0$$

Apply the zero product principle.

$2x + 1 = 0$ or $x + 4 = 0$
$\quad 2x = -1 \qquad\qquad x = -4$
$$x = -\frac{1}{2}$$

The boundary points are -4 and $-\frac{1}{2}$.

670

Test Interval	Test Number	Test	Conclusion
$(-\infty, -4]$	-5	$2(-5)^2 + 9(-5) + 4 \geq 0$ $9 \geq 0$, true	$(-\infty, -4]$ belongs to the solution set.
$\left[-4, -\dfrac{1}{2}\right]$	-1	$2(-1)^2 + 9(-1) + 4 \geq 0$ $-3 \geq 0$, false	$\left[-4, -\dfrac{1}{2}\right]$ does not belong to the solution set.
$\left[-\dfrac{1}{2}, \infty\right)$	0	$2(0)^2 + 9(0) + 4 \geq 0$ $4 \geq 0$, true	$\left[-\dfrac{1}{2}, \infty\right)$ belongs to the solution

The solution set is $(-\infty, -4] \cup \left[-\dfrac{1}{2}, \infty\right)$ or $\left\{ x \mid x \leq -4 \text{ or } x \geq -\dfrac{1}{2} \right\}$.

53. $x^3 + 2x^2 > 3x$

Solve the related quadratic equation.

$$x^3 + 2x^2 = 3x$$

$$x^3 + 2x^2 - 3x = 0$$

$$x(x^2 + 2x - 3) = 0$$

$$x(x+3)(x-1) = 0$$

Apply the zero product principle.

$x = 0$ or $x + 3 = 0$ or $x - 1 = 0$

$\qquad\qquad x = -3 \qquad\quad x = 1$

The boundary points are -3, 0, and 1.

Test Interval	Test Number	Test	Conclusion
$(-\infty, -3)$	-4	$(-4)^3 + 2(-4)^2 > 3(-4)$ $-32 > -12$, False	$(-\infty, -3)$ does not belong to the solution set.
$(-3, 0)$	-2	$(-2)^3 + 2(-2)^2 > 3(-2)$ $0 > -6$, True	$(-3, 0)$ belongs to the solution set.
$(0, 1)$	0.5	$0.5^3 + 2(0.5)^2 > 3(0.5)$ $0.625 > 1.5$, False	$(0, 1)$ does not belong to the solution set.
$(1, \infty)$	2	$2^3 + 2(2)^2 > 3(2)$ $16 > 6$, True	$(1, \infty)$ belongs to the solution set.

The solution set is $(-3, 0) \cup (1, \infty)$ or $\{ x \mid -3 < x < 0 \text{ or } x > 1 \}$.

671

54. $\dfrac{x-6}{x+2} > 0$

Find the values of x that make the numerator and denominator zero.

$x - 6 = 0 \qquad x + 2 = 0$

$\quad x = 6 \qquad\quad x = -2$

The boundary points are -2 and 6.

Test Interval	Test Number	Test	Conclusion
$(-\infty, -2)$	-3	$\dfrac{-3-6}{-3+2} > 0$ $9 > 0$, true	$(-\infty, -2)$ belongs to the solution set.
$(-2, 6)$	0	$\dfrac{0-6}{0+2} > 0$ $-3 > 0$, false	$(-2, 6)$ does not belong to the solution set.
$(6, \infty)$	7	$\dfrac{7-6}{7+2} > 0$ $\dfrac{1}{9} > 0$, true	$(6, \infty)$ belongs to the solution set.

The solution set is $(-\infty, -2) \cup (6, \infty)$ or $\{x \mid x < -2 \text{ or } x > 6\}$.

55. $\dfrac{x+3}{x-4} \le 5$

Express the inequality so that one side is zero.

$$\frac{x+3}{x-4} - 5 \le 0$$

$$\frac{x+3}{x-4} - \frac{5(x-4)}{x-4} \le 0$$

$$\frac{x+3-5(x-4)}{x-4} \le 0$$

$$\frac{x+3-5x+20}{x-4} \le 0$$

$$\frac{-4x+23}{x-4} \le 0$$

Find the values of x that make the numerator and denominator zero.

$-4x + 23 = 0 \qquad \text{and} \quad x - 4 = 0$

$\quad -4x = -23 \qquad\qquad x = 4$

$\qquad x = \dfrac{23}{4}$

The boundary points are 4 and $\dfrac{23}{4}$. We exclude 4 from the solution set, since this would make the denominator zero.

672

Test Interval	Test Number	Test	Conclusion
$(-\infty, 4)$	0	$\dfrac{0+3}{0-4} \le 5$ $\dfrac{3}{-4} \le 5$, true	$(-\infty, 4)$ belongs to the solution set.
$\left(4, \dfrac{23}{4}\right]$	5	$\dfrac{5+3}{5-4} \le 5$ $8 \le 5$, false	$\left(4, \dfrac{23}{4}\right]$ does not belong to the solution set.
$\left[\dfrac{23}{4}, \infty\right)$	6	$\dfrac{6+3}{6-4} \le 5$ $\dfrac{9}{2} \le 5$, true	$\left[\dfrac{23}{4}, \infty\right)$ belongs to the solution set.

The solution set is $(-\infty, 4) \cup \left[\dfrac{23}{4}, \infty\right)$ or $\left\{x \,\middle|\, x < 4 \text{ or } x \ge \dfrac{23}{4}\right\}$.

56. $s(t) = -16t^2 + 48t$

To find when the height is more than 32 feet above the ground, solve the inequality $-16t^2 + 48t > 32$.

Solve the related quadratic equation.

$$-16t^2 + 48t = 32$$

$$-16t^2 + 48t - 32 = 0$$

$$t^2 - 3t + 2 = 0$$

$$(t-2)(t-1) = 0$$

Apply the zero product principle.

$t - 2 = 0$ or $t - 1 = 0$

$t = 2$ $t = 1$

The boundary points are 1 and 2.

Test Interval	Test Number	Test	Conclusion
$(0, 1)$	0.5	$-16(0.5)^2 + 48(0.5) > 32$ $20 > 32$, false	$(0, 1)$ does not belong to the solution set.
$(1, 2)$	1.5	$-16(1.5)^2 + 48(1.5) > 32$ $36 > 32$, true	$(1, 2)$ belongs to the solution set.
$(2, \infty)$	3	$-16(3)^2 + 48(3) > 32$ $0 > 32$, false	$(2, \infty)$ does not belong to the solution set.

The solution set is $(1, 2)$. This means that the ball will be more than 32 feet above the graph between 1 and 2 seconds.

673

57. a.

$$H(0) = \frac{15}{8}(0)^2 - 30(0) + 200 = \frac{15}{8}(0) - 0 + 200 = 0 - 0 + 200 = 200$$

The heart rate is 200 beats per minute immediately following the workout.

b.

$$\frac{15}{8}x^2 - 30x + 200 > 110$$

$$\frac{15}{8}x^2 - 30x + 90 > 0$$

$$\frac{8}{15}\left(\frac{15}{8}x^2 - 30x + 90\right) > \frac{8}{15}(0)$$

$$x^2 - \frac{8}{15}(30x) + \frac{8}{15}(90) > 0$$

$$x^2 - 16x + 48 > 0$$

$$(x-12)(x-4) > 0$$

Apply the zero product principle.

$$x - 12 = 0 \quad \text{or} \quad x - 4 = 0$$
$$x = 12 \qquad\qquad x = 4$$

The boundary points are 4 and 12.

Test Interval	Test Number	Test	Conclusion
$(0,4)$	1	$\frac{15}{8}(1)^2 - 30(1) + 200 > 110$ $171\frac{7}{8} > 110$, true	$(0,4)$ belongs to the solution set.
$(4,12)$	5	$\frac{15}{8}(5)^2 - 30(5) + 200 > 110$ $96\frac{7}{8} > 110$, false	$(4,\infty)$ does not belong to the solution set.
$(12,\infty)$	13	$\frac{15}{8}(13)^2 - 30(13) + 200 > 110$ $126\frac{7}{8} > 110$, false	$(12,\infty)$ does not belong to the solution set.

The solution set is $(0,4) \cup (12,\infty)$. This means that the heart rate exceeds 110 beats per minute between 0 and 4 minutes after the workout and more than 12 minutes after the workout. Between 0 and 4 minutes provides a more realistic answer since it is unlikely that the heart rate will begin to climb again without further exertion. Model breakdown occurs for the interval $(12,\infty)$.

Chapter 11 Test

1. $2x^2 - 5 = 0$

$$2x^2 = 5$$

$$x^2 = \frac{5}{2}$$

$$x = \pm\sqrt{\frac{5}{2}}$$

Rationalize the denominators.

$$x = \pm\frac{\sqrt{5}}{\sqrt{2}} \cdot \frac{\sqrt{2}}{\sqrt{2}} = \pm\frac{\sqrt{10}}{2}$$

The solutions are $\pm\dfrac{\sqrt{10}}{2}$, and the

solution set is $\left\{\pm\dfrac{\sqrt{10}}{2}\right\}$.

2. $(x-3)^2 = 20$

$$x - 3 = \pm\sqrt{20}$$

$$x = 3 \pm \sqrt{4 \cdot 5}$$

$$x = 3 \pm 2\sqrt{5}$$

The solutions are $3 \pm 2\sqrt{5}$, and the
solution set is $\left\{3 \pm 2\sqrt{5}\right\}$.

3. $x^2 - 16x + \underline{\hspace{1cm}}$

Since $b = -16$, we add

$$\left(\frac{b}{2}\right)^2 = \left(\frac{-16}{2}\right)^2 = (-8)^2 = 64.$$

$$x^2 - 16x + 64 = (x-8)^2$$

4. $x^2 + \dfrac{2}{5}x + \underline{\hspace{1cm}}$

Since $b = \dfrac{2}{5}$, we add

$$\left(\frac{1}{2}b\right)^2 = \left(\frac{1}{2} \cdot \frac{2}{5}\right)^2 = \left(\frac{1}{5}\right)^2 = \frac{1}{25}.$$

$$x^2 + \frac{2}{5}x + \frac{1}{25} = \left(x + \frac{1}{5}\right)^2$$

5. $x^2 - 6x + 7 = 0$

$$x^2 - 6x = -7$$

Since $b = -6$, we add

$$\left(\frac{b}{2}\right)^2 = \left(\frac{-6}{2}\right)^2 = (-3)^2 = 9.$$

$$x^2 - 6x + 9 = -7 + 9$$

$$(x-3)^2 = 2$$

Apply the square root property.

$$x - 3 = \pm\sqrt{2}$$

$$x = 3 \pm \sqrt{2}$$

The solutions are $3 \pm \sqrt{2}$ and the
solution set is $\left\{3 \pm \sqrt{2}\right\}$.

6. Use the Pythagorean Theorem.

$$50^2 + 50^2 = x^2$$

$$2500 + 2500 = x^2$$

$$5000 = x^2$$

$$\pm\sqrt{5000} = x$$

$$\pm\sqrt{2500 \cdot 2} = x$$

$$\pm 50\sqrt{2} = x$$

The solutions are $\pm 50\sqrt{2}$ feet. We
disregard $-50\sqrt{2}$ feet because we can't
have a negative length measurement.
The width of the pond is $50\sqrt{2}$ feet.

7. $d = \sqrt{\left(2 - (-1)\right)^2 + \left(-3 - 5\right)^2}$

$$= \sqrt{(3)^2 + (-8)^2}$$

$$= \sqrt{9 + 64} = \sqrt{73} \approx 8.54$$

The distance between the points is
$\sqrt{73}$ or 8.54 units.

675

8.
$$\text{Midpoint} = \left(\frac{-5+12}{2}, \frac{-2+(-6)}{2}\right)$$
$$= \left(\frac{7}{2}, \frac{-8}{2}\right) = \left(\frac{7}{2}, -4\right)$$
The midpoint is $\left(\frac{7}{2}, -4\right)$.

9.
$$3x^2 + 4x - 2 = 0$$
$a = 3 \quad b = 4 \quad c = -2$
Find the discriminant.
$$b^2 - 4ac = 4^2 - 4(3)(-2)$$
$$= 16 + 24 = 40$$
Since the discriminant is greater than zero, there are two unequal real solutions. Also, since the discriminant is not a perfect, the solutions are irrational.

10.
$$x^2 = 4x - 8$$
$$x^2 - 4x + 8 = 0$$
$a = 1 \quad b = -4 \quad c = 8$
Find the discriminant.
$$b^2 - 4ac = (-4)^2 - 4(1)(8)$$
$$= 16 - 32 = -16$$
Since the discriminant is negative, there are two imaginary solutions which are complex conjugates.

11.
$$2x^2 + 9x = 5$$
$$2x^2 + 9x - 5 = 0$$
$$(2x - 1)(x + 5) = 0$$
Apply the zero product principle.
$$2x - 1 = 0 \quad \text{and} \quad x + 5 = 0$$
$$2x = 1 \qquad\qquad x = -5$$
$$x = \frac{1}{2}$$
The solutions are $\frac{1}{2}$ and -5, and the solution set is $\left\{-5, \frac{1}{2}\right\}$.

12. $x^2 + 8x + 5 = 0$
Solve using the quadratic formula.
$a = 1 \quad b = 8 \quad c = 5$
$$x = \frac{-8 \pm \sqrt{8^2 - 4(1)(5)}}{2(1)}$$
$$= \frac{-8 \pm \sqrt{64 - 20}}{2}$$
$$= \frac{-8 \pm \sqrt{44}}{2}$$
$$= \frac{-8 \pm \sqrt{4 \cdot 11}}{2}$$
$$= \frac{-8 \pm 2\sqrt{11}}{2}$$
$$= \frac{2\left(-4 \pm \sqrt{11}\right)}{2} = -4 \pm \sqrt{11}$$
The solutions are $-4 \pm \sqrt{11}$, and the solution set is $\left\{-4 \pm \sqrt{11}\right\}$.

13. $(x + 2)^2 + 25 = 0$
$$(x + 2)^2 = -25$$
Apply the square root principle.
$$x + 2 = \pm\sqrt{-25}$$
$$x = -2 \pm 5i$$
The solutions are $-2 \pm 5i$, and the solution set is $\left\{-2 \pm 5i\right\}$.

676

14. $2x^2 - 6x + 5 = 0$

$a = 2 \quad b = -6 \quad c = 5$

$x = \dfrac{-(-6) \pm \sqrt{(-6)^2 - 4(2)(5)}}{2(2)}$

$= \dfrac{6 \pm \sqrt{36 - 40}}{4}$

$= \dfrac{6 \pm \sqrt{-4}}{4}$

$= \dfrac{6 \pm 2i}{4} = \dfrac{6}{4} \pm \dfrac{2}{4}i = \dfrac{3}{2} \pm \dfrac{1}{2}i$

The solutions are $\dfrac{3}{2} \pm \dfrac{1}{2}i$, and the

solution set is $\left\{\dfrac{3}{2} \pm \dfrac{1}{2}i\right\}$.

15. Because the solution set is $\{-3, 7\}$, we
have

$\quad x = -3 \quad$ or $\quad\quad x = 7$

$x + 3 = 0 \quad\quad\quad\quad x - 7 = 0$

Apply the zero-product principle in
reverse.

$\quad (x + 3)(x - 7) = 0$

$\quad x^2 - 7x + 3x - 21 = 0$

$\quad\quad x^2 - 4x - 21 = 0$

16. Because the solution set is $\{-10i, 10i\}$,
we have

$\quad x = -10i \quad$ or $\quad\quad x = 10i$

$x + 10i = 0 \quad\quad\quad\quad x - 10i = 0$

Apply the zero-product principle in
reverse.

$(x + 10i)(x - 10i) = 0$

$\quad\quad x^2 - 100i^2 = 0$

$\quad x^2 - 100(-1) = 0$

$\quad\quad\quad x^2 + 100 = 0$

17. $f(x) = -0.5x^2 + 4x + 19$

$\quad 20 = -0.5x^2 + 4x + 19$

$0.5x^2 - 4x + 1 = 0$

Solve using the quadratic formula.

$a = 0.5 \quad b = -4 \quad c = 1$

$x = \dfrac{-(-4) \pm \sqrt{(-4)^2 - 4(0.5)(1)}}{2(0.5)}$

$= \dfrac{4 \pm \sqrt{16 - 2}}{1}$

$= 4 \pm \sqrt{14}$

$= 7.7$ or 0.3

≈ 8 or 0

In the years 1900 and 1998, 20 million
people were receiving food stamps.

18. $f(x) = (x + 1)^2 + 4$

Since $a = 1$ is negative, the parabola
opens upward. The vertex of the
parabola is $(h, k) = (-1, 4)$ and the axis
of symmetry is $x = -1$. Replace $f(x)$
with 0 to find x–intercepts.

$0 = (x + 1)^2 + 4$

$-4 = (x + 1)^2$

This will be result in complex solutions.
As a result, there are no
x–intercepts. Set $x = 0$ and solve for y
to obtain the y–intercept.

$y = (0 + 1)^2 + 4 = 1 + 4 = 5$

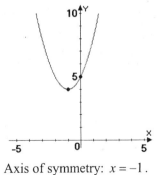

Axis of symmetry: $x = -1$.

19. $f(x) = x^2 - 2x - 3$

Since $a = 1$ is positive, the parabola opens upward. The x–coordinate of the vertex of the parabola is

$$-\frac{b}{2a} = -\frac{-2}{2(1)} = -\frac{-2}{2} = 1 \text{ and the}$$

y–coordinate of the vertex of the parabola is

$$f\left(-\frac{b}{2a}\right) = f(1) = 1^2 - 2(1) - 3$$
$$= 1 - 2 - 3 = -4.$$

The vertex is $(1, -4)$. Replace $f(x)$ with 0 to find x–intercepts.

$$0 = x^2 - 2x - 3$$
$$0 = (x - 3)(x + 1)$$

Apply the zero product principle.

$$x - 3 = 0 \quad \text{or} \quad x + 1 = 0$$
$$x = 3 \qquad\qquad x = -1$$

The x–intercepts are -1 and 3. Set $x = 0$ and solve for y to obtain the y–intercept.

$$y = 0^2 - 2(0) - 3 = -3$$

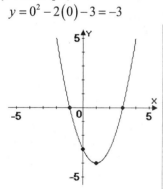

Axis of symmetry: $x = 1$.

20. $s(t) = -16t^2 + 64t + 5$

Since $a = -16$ is negative, we know the function opens downward and has a maximum at

$$x = -\frac{b}{2a} = -\frac{64}{2(-16)} = -\frac{64}{-32} = 2.$$

The ball reaches its maximum height a two seconds. The maximum height is

$$s(2) = -16(2)^2 + 64(2) + 5$$
$$= -16(4) + 128 + 5$$
$$= -64 + 128 + 5 = 69.$$

The baseball reaches a maximum height of 69 feet after 2 seconds.

21. $0 = -16t^2 + 64t + 5$

Solve using the quadratic formula.

$$a = -16 \quad b = 64 \quad c = 5$$

$$x = \frac{-64 \pm \sqrt{64^2 - 4(-16)(5)}}{2(-16)}$$

$$= \frac{-64 \pm \sqrt{4096 + 320}}{-32}$$

$$= \frac{-64 \pm \sqrt{4416}}{-32}$$

$$\approx \frac{-64 - 66.5}{-32} \quad \text{or} \quad \frac{-64 + 66.5}{-32}$$

$$\approx \frac{-130.5}{-32} \quad \text{or} \quad \frac{2.5}{-32}$$

$$\approx 4.1 \quad \text{or} \quad -0.1$$

We disregard -0.1 since we cannot have a negative time measurement. The solution is 4.1 and we conclude that the baseball hits the ground in approximately 4.1 seconds.

22. $f(x) = -x^2 + 46x - 360$

Since $a = -1$ is negative, we know the function opens downward and has a maximum at

$$x = -\frac{b}{2a} = -\frac{46}{2(-1)} = -\frac{46}{-2} = 23.$$

$$f(23) = -23^2 + 46(23) - 360 = 169$$

Profit is maximized when 23 computers are manufactured. This produces a profit of $169 hundreds or $16,900.

23. Let $t = 2x - 5$.

$$(2x-5)^2 + 4(2x-5) + 3 = 0$$
$$t^2 + 4t + 3 = 0$$
$$(t+3)(t+1) = 0$$

Apply the zero product principle.

$t + 3 = 0 \quad$ or $\quad t + 1 = 0$

$\quad t = -3 \qquad\qquad t = -1$

Replace t by $2x - 5$.

First, consider $t = 15$.

$2x - 5 = -3 \quad$ or $\quad 2x - 5 = -1$

$\quad 2x = 2 \qquad\qquad 2x = 4$

$\quad x = 1 \qquad\qquad x = 2$

The solutions are 1 and 2 and the solution set is $\{1, 2\}$.

24. Let $t = x^2$.

$$x^4 - 13x^2 + 36 = 0$$
$$(x^2)^2 - 13x^2 + 36 = 0$$
$$t^2 - 13t + 36 = 0$$
$$(t-9)(t-4) = 0$$

Apply the zero product principle.

$t - 9 = 0 \quad$ or $\quad t - 4 = 0$

$\quad t = 9 \qquad\qquad t = 4$

Replace t by x^2.

$x^2 = 9 \quad$ or $\quad x^2 = 4$

$\quad x = \pm 3 \qquad\qquad x = \pm 2$

The solutions are ± 2 and ± 3 and the solution set is $\{-3, -2, 2, 3\}$.

25. Let $t = x^{1/3}$.

$$x^{2/3} - 9x^{1/3} + 8 = 0$$
$$(x^{1/3})^2 - 9x^{1/3} + 8 = 0$$
$$t^2 - 9t + 8 = 0$$
$$(t-8)(t-1) = 0$$

Apply the zero product principle.

$t - 8 = 0 \quad$ or $\quad t - 1 = 0$

$\quad t = 8 \qquad\qquad t = 1$

Replace t by $x^{1/3}$.

$x^{1/3} = 8 \qquad\qquad$ or $\qquad x^{1/3} = 1$

$\quad x = 8^3 = 512 \qquad\qquad x = 1^3 = 1$

The solutions are 1 and 512 and the solution set is $\{1, \ 512\}$.

26. $x^2 - x - 12 < 0$

Solve the related quadratic equation.

$x^2 - x - 12 = 0$

$(x-4)(x+3) = 0$

Apply the zero product principle.

$x - 4 = 0$ or $x + 3 = 0$

$x = 4$ $x = -3$

The boundary points are -3 and 4.

Test Interval	Test Number	Test	Conclusion
$(-\infty, -3)$	-4	$(-4)^2 - (-4) - 12 < 0$ $8 < 0$, false	$(-\infty, -3)$ does not belong to the solution set.
$(-3, 4)$	0	$0^2 - 0 - 12 < 0$ $-12 < 0$, true	$(-3, 4)$ belongs to the solution set.
$(4, \infty)$	5	$5^2 - 5 - 12 < 0$ $8 < 0$, false	$(4, \infty)$ does not belong to the solution set.

The solution set is $(-3, 4)$ or $\{x | -3 < x < 4\}$.

27. $\dfrac{2x+1}{x-3} \le 3$

Express the inequality so that one side is zero.

$$\frac{2x+1}{x-3} - 3 \le 0$$

$$\frac{2x+1}{x-3} - \frac{3(x-3)}{x-3} \le 0$$

$$\frac{2x+1-3(x-3)}{x-3} \le 0$$

$$\frac{2x+1-3x+9}{x-3} \le 0$$

$$\frac{-x+10}{x-3} \le 0$$

Find the values of x that make the numerator and denominator zero.

$-x + 10 = 0$ and $x - 3 = 0$

$-x = -10$ $x = 3$

$x = 10$

The boundary points are 3 and 10. We exclude 3 from the solution set(s), since this would make the denominator zero.

Test Interval	Test Number	Test	Conclusion
$(-\infty, 3)$	0	$\dfrac{2(0)+1}{0-3} \leq 3$ $-\dfrac{1}{3} \leq 3$, true	$(-\infty, 3)$ belongs to the solution set.
$(3, 10]$	4	$\dfrac{2(4)+1}{4-3} \leq 3$ $9 \leq 3$, false	$(3, 10]$ does not belong to the solution set.
$[10, \infty)$	11	$\dfrac{2(10)+1}{10-3} \leq 3$ $3 \leq 3$, true	$[10, \infty)$ belongs to the solution set.

The solution set is $(-\infty, 3) \cup [10, \infty)$ or $\{x \mid x < 3 \text{ or } x \geq 10\}$.

Cumulative Review Exercises (Chapters 1 – 11)

1.
$$8 - (4x - 5) = x - 7$$
$$8 - 4x + 5 = x - 7$$
$$13 - 4x = x - 7$$
$$13 = 5x - 7$$
$$20 = 5x$$
$$4 = x$$
The solution is 4, and the solution set is $\{4\}$.

2.
$$5x + 4y = 22$$
$$3x - 8y = -18$$
Multiply the first equation by 2 and solve by addition.
$$10x + 8y = 44$$
$$\underline{3x - 8y = -18}$$
$$13x = 26$$
$$x = 2$$
Back-substitute 2 for x to find y.

$$5(2) + 4y = 22$$
$$10 + 4y = 22$$
$$4y = 12$$
$$y = 3$$
The solution is $(2, 3)$ and the solution set is $\{(2, 3)\}$.

3.
$$-3x + 2y + 4z = 6$$
$$7x - y + 3z = 23$$
$$2x + 3y + z = 7$$
Multiply the second equation by 2 and add to the first equation to eliminate y.
$$-3x + 2y + 4z = 6$$
$$\underline{14x - 2y + 6z = 46}$$
$$11x + 10z = 52$$
Multiply the second equation by 3 and add to the second equation to eliminate y.
$$21x - 3y + 9z = 69$$
$$\underline{2x + 3y + z = 7}$$
$$23x + 10z = 76$$

681

The system of two variables in two equations is:

$$11x + 10z = 52$$

$$23x + 10z = 76$$

Multiply the first equation by -1 and add to the second equation.

$$-11x - 10z = -52$$

$$\underline{23x + 10z = \ \ 76}$$

$$12x = 24$$

$$x = 2$$

Back-substitute 2 for x to find z.

$$11(2) + 10z = 52$$

$$22 + 10z = 52$$

$$10z = 30$$

$$z = 3$$

Back-substitute 2 for x and 3 for z to find y.

$$-3(2) + 2y + 4(3) = 6$$

$$-6 + 2y + 12 = 6$$

$$2y = 0$$

$$y = 0$$

The solution is $(2, 0, 3)$, and the solution set is $\{(2, 0, 3)\}$.

4. $|x - 1| > 3$

$$x - 1 < -3 \quad \text{or} \quad x - 1 > 3$$

$$x < -2 \qquad\qquad x > 4$$

The solution set is $\{x | x < -2$ and $x > 4\}$ or $(-\infty, -2) \cup (4, \infty)$.

5. $\sqrt{x + 4} - \sqrt{x - 4} = 2$

$$\sqrt{x + 4} = 2 + \sqrt{x - 4}$$

$$\left(\sqrt{x + 4}\right)^2 = \left(2 + \sqrt{x - 4}\right)^2$$

$$x + 4 = 4 + 4\sqrt{x - 4} + x - 4$$

$$\cancel{x} + 4 = 4\sqrt{x - 4} + \cancel{x}$$

$$4 = 4\sqrt{x - 4}$$

$$1 = \sqrt{x - 4}$$

$$1^2 = \left(\sqrt{x - 4}\right)^2$$

$$1 = x - 4$$

$$5 = x$$

The solution is 5, and the solution set is $\{5\}$.

6. $x - 4 \geq 0$ and $-3x \leq -6$

$$x \geq 4 \qquad\qquad x \geq 2$$

For a value to be in the solution set, it must satisfy both of the conditions $x \geq 4$ and $x \geq 2$. Now any value that is 4 or larger is also larger than 2. But values between 2 and 4 do not satisfy both conditions. Therefore, only values that are 4 or larger will be in the solution set. Thus, the solution set is $\{x | x \geq 4\}$ or $[4, \infty)$.

7.
$$2x^2 = 3x - 2$$

$$2x^2 - 3x + 2 = 0$$

Solve using the quadratic formula.

$$a = 2 \qquad b = -3 \qquad c = 2$$

$$x = \frac{-(-3) \pm \sqrt{(-3)^2 - 4(2)(2)}}{2(2)}$$

$$= \frac{3 \pm \sqrt{9 - 16}}{4}$$

$$= \frac{3 \pm \sqrt{-7}}{4} = \frac{3 \pm \sqrt{7}i}{4} = \frac{3}{4} \pm \frac{\sqrt{7}}{4}i$$

The solutions are $\dfrac{3}{4} \pm \dfrac{\sqrt{7}}{4}i$, and the

solution set is $\left\{ \dfrac{3}{4} - \dfrac{\sqrt{7}}{4}i, \dfrac{3}{4} + \dfrac{\sqrt{7}}{4}i \right\}$.

8. $3x = 15 + 5y$

Find the x–intercept by setting $y = 0$
and solving.

$$3x = 15 + 5(0)$$

$$3x = 15$$

$$x = 5$$

Find the y–intercept by setting $x = 0$
and solving.

$$3(0) = 15 + 5y$$

$$0 = 15 + 5y$$

$$-15 = 5y$$

$$-3 = y$$

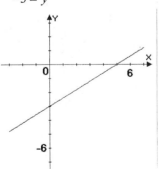

9. $2x - 3y > 6$

First, find the intercepts to the
equation $2x - 3y = 6$.
Find the x–intercept by setting $y = 0$
and solving.

$$2x - 3(0) = 6$$

$$2x = 6$$

$$x = 3$$

Find the y–intercept by setting $x = 0$
and solving.

$$2(0) - 3y = 6$$

$$-3y = 6$$

$$y = -2$$

Next, use the origin as a test point.

$$2(0) - 3(0) > 6$$

$$0 > 6$$

This is a false statement. This means
that the origin will not fall in the
shaded half-plane.

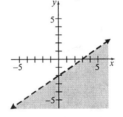

10. $f(x) = -\dfrac{1}{2}x + 1$

$m = -\dfrac{1}{2}$; y–intercept $= 1$

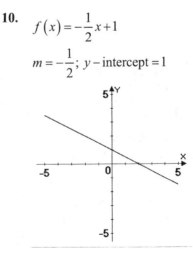

683

11. $f(x) = x^2 + 6x + 8$

Since $a = 1$ is positive, the parabola opens upward. The x-coordinate of the vertex of the parabola is
$$-\frac{b}{2a} = -\frac{6}{2(1)} = -\frac{6}{2} = -3 \text{ and the}$$
y-coordinate of the vertex of the parabola is
$$f\left(-\frac{b}{2a}\right) = f(-3) = (-3)^2 + 6(-3) + 8$$
$$= 9 - 18 + 8 = -1.$$

The vertex is $(-3, -1)$. Replace $f(x)$ with 0 to find x-intercepts.
$$0 = x^2 + 6x + 8$$
$$0 = (x + 4)(x + 2)$$
Apply the zero product principle.
$$x + 4 = 0 \quad \text{or} \quad x + 2 = 0$$
$$x = -4 \qquad\qquad x = -2$$
The x-intercepts are -4 and -2. Set $x = 0$ and solve for y to obtain the y-intercept.
$$y = 0^2 + 6(0) + 8$$
$$y = 0 + 0 + 8$$
$$y = 8$$

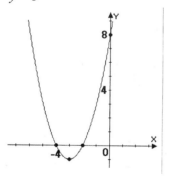

12. $f(x) = (x - 3)^2 - 4$

Since $a = 1$ is positive, the parabola opens upward. The vertex of the parabola is $(h, k) = (3, -4)$ and the axis of symmetry is $x = 3$. Replace $f(x)$ with 0 to find x-intercepts.
$$0 = (x - 3)^2 - 4$$
$$4 = (x - 3)^2$$
Apply the square root property.
$$x - 3 = -2 \quad \text{and} \quad x - 3 = 2$$
$$x = 1 \qquad\qquad x = 5$$
The x-intercepts are 1 and 5.

Set $x = 0$ and solve for y to obtain the y-intercept.
$$y = (0 - 3)^2 - 4$$
$$y = (-3)^2 - 4$$
$$y = 9 - 4$$
$$y = 5$$

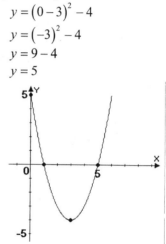

13. $f(x) = \sqrt[3]{x + 1}$

$$y = \sqrt[3]{x + 1}$$
Begin by switching x and y, then solve for y.
$$x = \sqrt[3]{y + 1}$$
$$x^3 = \left(\sqrt[3]{y + 1}\right)^3$$
$$x^3 = y + 1$$
$$x^3 - 1 = y \qquad \text{so } f^{-1}(x) = x^3 - 1$$

14.

$$A = \frac{cd}{c+d}$$

$$A(c+d) = cd$$

$$Ac + Ad = cd$$

$$Ac - cd = -Ad$$

$$c(A-d) = -Ad$$

$$c = -\frac{Ad}{A-d} \text{ or } \frac{Ad}{d-A}$$

15. First, solve for y to obtain the slope of the line whose equation is $2x + y = 10$.

$$2x + y = 10$$

$$y = -2x + 10$$

The slope is -2. The line we want to find is perpendicular to this line, so we know the slope will be $\frac{1}{2}$.

Using the point, $(-2, 4)$, and the slope, $\frac{1}{2}$, we can write the equation in point-slope form.

$$y - y_1 = m(x - x_1)$$

$$y - 4 = \frac{1}{2}(x - (-2))$$

$$y - 4 = \frac{1}{2}(x + 2)$$

Solve for y to obtain slope-intercept form.

$$y - 4 = \frac{1}{2}(x + 2)$$

$$y - 4 = \frac{1}{2}x + 1$$

$$y = \frac{1}{2}x + 5$$

$$f(x) = \frac{1}{2}x + 5$$

16. $\dfrac{-5x^3 y^7}{15x^4 y^{-2}} = \dfrac{-y^7 y^2}{3x} = \dfrac{-y^9}{3x} = -\dfrac{y^9}{3x}$

17. $(4x^2 - 5y)^2$

$$= (4x^2)^2 + 2(4x^2)(-5y) + (-5y)^2$$

$$= 16x^4 - 40x^2 y + 25y^2$$

18.

$$\begin{array}{r} x^2 - 5x + 1 \\ 5x+1 \overline{)5x^3 - 24x^2 + 0x + 9} \\ \underline{5x^3 + x^2} \\ -25x^2 + 0x \\ \underline{-25x^2 - 5x} \\ 5x + 9 \\ \underline{5x + 1} \\ 8 \end{array}$$

$$\frac{5x^3 - 24x^2 + 9}{5x + 1} = x^2 - 5x + 1 + \frac{8}{5x + 1}$$

19. $\dfrac{\sqrt[3]{32xy^{10}}}{\sqrt[3]{2xy^2}} = \sqrt[3]{\dfrac{32xy^{10}}{2xy^2}}$

$$= \sqrt[3]{16y^8}$$

$$= \sqrt[3]{8 \cdot 2y^6 y^2} = 2y^2 \sqrt[3]{2y^2}$$

20.
$$\frac{x+2}{x^2-6x+8}+\frac{3x-8}{x^2-5x+6}=\frac{x+2}{(x-4)(x-2)}+\frac{3x-8}{(x-2)(x-3)}$$
$$=\frac{(x+2)(x-3)}{(x-4)(x-2)(x-3)}+\frac{(3x-8)(x-4)}{(x-4)(x-2)(x-3)}$$
$$=\frac{x^2-3x+2x-6+3x^2-12x-8x+32}{(x-4)(x-2)(x-3)}$$
$$=\frac{4x^2-21x+26}{(x-4)(x-2)(x-3)}$$
$$=\frac{(4x-13)\cancel{(x-2)}}{(x-4)\cancel{(x-2)}(x-3)}=\frac{4x-13}{(x-4)(x-3)}$$

21.
$$x^4-4x^3+8x-32$$
$$=x^3(x-4)+8(x-4)$$
$$=(x-4)(x^3+8)$$
$$=(x-4)(x+2)(x^2-2x+4)$$

22.
$$2x^2+12xy+18y^2$$
$$=2(x^2+6xy+9y^2)=2(x+3y)^2$$

23. Let $x=$ the width of the carpet
Let $2x+4=$ the length of the carpet
$$x(2x+4)=48$$
$$2x^2+4x=48$$
$$2x^2+4x-48=0$$
$$x^2+2x-24=0$$
$$(x+6)(x-4)=0$$
Apply the zero product principle.
$$x+6=0\quad\text{and}\quad x-4=0$$
$$x=-6\qquad\qquad x=4$$
We disregard –6 because we can't have a negative length measurement. The width of the carpet is 4 feet and the length of the carpet is
$$2x+4=2(4)+4=8+4=12\text{ feet.}$$

24.

	Part Done in 1 Hour	Time Working Together	Part Done in x Hours
You	$\dfrac{1}{2}$	x	$\dfrac{x}{2}$
Your Sister	$\dfrac{1}{3}$	x	$\dfrac{x}{3}$

$$\frac{x}{2}+\frac{x}{3}=1$$
$$6\left(\frac{x}{2}+\frac{x}{3}\right)=6(1)$$
$$6\left(\frac{x}{2}\right)+6\left(\frac{x}{3}\right)=6$$
$$3x+2x=6$$
$$5x=6$$
$$x=\frac{6}{5}$$

If you and your sister work together, it will take $\dfrac{6}{5}$ hours, or 1 hour and 12 minutes, to clean the house.

25.

	d	r	$t = \dfrac{d}{r}$
Down Stream	20	$15 + x$	$\dfrac{20}{15 + x}$
Up Stream	10	$15 - x$	$\dfrac{10}{15 - x}$

$$\frac{20}{15+x} = \frac{10}{15-x}$$

$$20(15-x) = 10(15+x)$$

$$300 - 20x = 150 + 10x$$

$$300 = 150 + 30x$$

$$150 = 30x$$

$$5 = x$$

The rate of the current is 5 miles per hour.

Chapter 12
Exponential and Logarithmic Functions

12.1 Exercise Set

1. $2^{3.4} \approx 10.556$

3. $3^{\sqrt{5}} \approx 11.665$

5. $4^{-1.5} = 0.125$

7. $e^{2.3} \approx 9.974$

9. $e^{-0.95} \approx 0.387$

11. $f(x) = 3^x$

x	$f(x)$
-2	$3^{-2} = \dfrac{1}{3^2} = \dfrac{1}{9}$
-1	$3^{-1} = \dfrac{1}{3^1} = \dfrac{1}{3}$
0	$3^0 = 1$
1	$3^1 = 3$
2	$3^2 = 9$

This functions matches graph (**d**).

13. $f(x) = 3^x - 1$

x	$f(x)$
-2	$3^{-2} - 1 = \dfrac{1}{3^2} - 1 = \dfrac{1}{9} - 1 = -\dfrac{8}{9}$
-1	$3^{-1} - 1 = \dfrac{1}{3^1} - 1 = \dfrac{1}{3} - 1 = -\dfrac{2}{3}$
0	$3^0 - 1 = 1 - 1 = 0$
1	$3^1 - 1 = 3 - 1 = 2$
2	$3^2 - 1 = 9 - 1 = 8$

This functions matches graph (**e**).

15. $f(x) = 3^{-x}$

x	$f(x)$
-2	$3^{-(-2)} = 3^2 = 9$
-1	$3^{-(-1)} = 3^1 = 3$
0	$3^{-(0)} = 3^0 = 1$
1	$3^{-(1)} = 3^{-1} = \dfrac{1}{3}$
2	$3^{-(2)} = 3^{-2} = \dfrac{1}{3^2} = \dfrac{1}{9}$

This functions matches graph (**f**).

17. $f(x) = 4^x$

x	$f(x)$
-2	$4^{-2} = \dfrac{1}{4^2} = \dfrac{1}{16}$
-1	$4^{-1} = \dfrac{1}{4^1} = \dfrac{1}{4}$
0	$4^0 = 1$
1	$4^1 = 4$
2	$4^2 = 16$

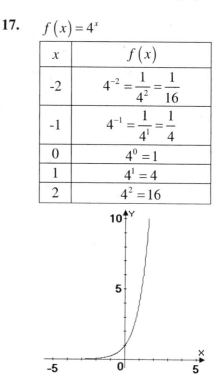

688

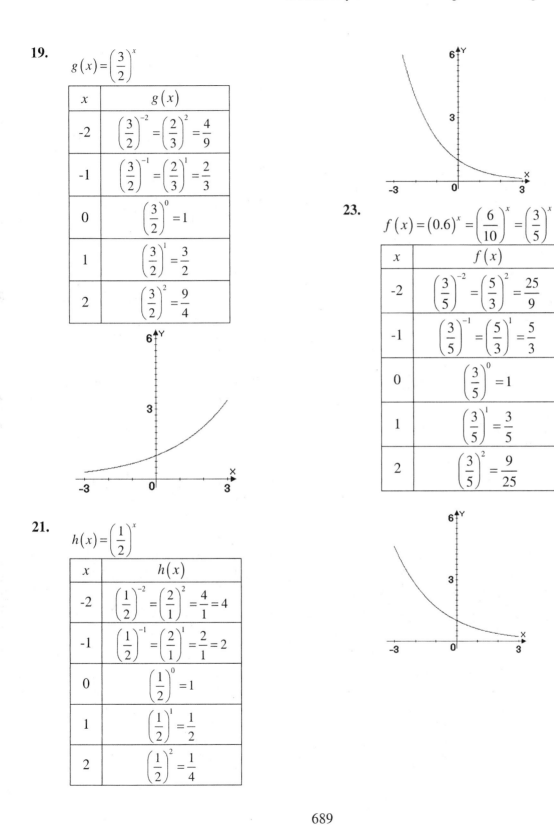

19.

$$g(x) = \left(\frac{3}{2}\right)^x$$

x	$g(x)$
-2	$\left(\frac{3}{2}\right)^{-2} = \left(\frac{2}{3}\right)^{2} = \frac{4}{9}$
-1	$\left(\frac{3}{2}\right)^{-1} = \left(\frac{2}{3}\right)^{1} = \frac{2}{3}$
0	$\left(\frac{3}{2}\right)^{0} = 1$
1	$\left(\frac{3}{2}\right)^{1} = \frac{3}{2}$
2	$\left(\frac{3}{2}\right)^{2} = \frac{9}{4}$

21.

$$h(x) = \left(\frac{1}{2}\right)^x$$

x	$h(x)$
-2	$\left(\frac{1}{2}\right)^{-2} = \left(\frac{2}{1}\right)^{2} = \frac{4}{1} = 4$
-1	$\left(\frac{1}{2}\right)^{-1} = \left(\frac{2}{1}\right)^{1} = \frac{2}{1} = 2$
0	$\left(\frac{1}{2}\right)^{0} = 1$
1	$\left(\frac{1}{2}\right)^{1} = \frac{1}{2}$
2	$\left(\frac{1}{2}\right)^{2} = \frac{1}{4}$

23.

$$f(x) = (0.6)^x = \left(\frac{6}{10}\right)^x = \left(\frac{3}{5}\right)^x$$

x	$f(x)$
-2	$\left(\frac{3}{5}\right)^{-2} = \left(\frac{5}{3}\right)^{2} = \frac{25}{9}$
-1	$\left(\frac{3}{5}\right)^{-1} = \left(\frac{5}{3}\right)^{1} = \frac{5}{3}$
0	$\left(\frac{3}{5}\right)^{0} = 1$
1	$\left(\frac{3}{5}\right)^{1} = \frac{3}{5}$
2	$\left(\frac{3}{5}\right)^{2} = \frac{9}{25}$

689

25.

x	$f(x) = 2^x$	$g(x) = 2^{x+1}$
-2	$\dfrac{1}{4}$	$\dfrac{1}{2}$
-1	$\dfrac{1}{2}$	1
0	1	2
1	2	4
2	4	8

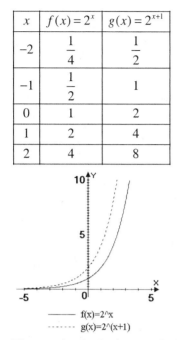

The graph of g is the graph of f shifted 1 unit to the left.

29.

x	$f(x) = 2^x$	$g(x) = 2^x + 1$
-2	$\dfrac{1}{4}$	$\dfrac{5}{4}$
-1	$\dfrac{1}{2}$	$\dfrac{3}{2}$
0	1	2
1	2	3
2	4	5

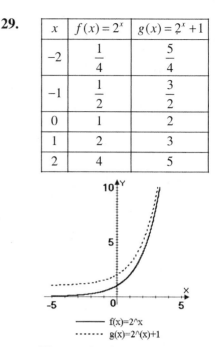

The graph of g is the graph of f shifted up 1 unit.

27.

x	$f(x) = 2^x$	$g(x) = 2^{x-2}$
-2	$\dfrac{1}{4}$	$\dfrac{1}{16}$
-1	$\dfrac{1}{2}$	$\dfrac{1}{8}$
0	1	$\dfrac{1}{2}$
1	2	1
2	4	2

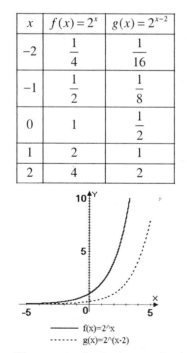

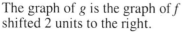

The graph of g is the graph of f shifted 2 units to the right.

31.

x	$f(x) = 2^x$	$g(x) = 2^x - 2$
-2	$\dfrac{1}{4}$	$-\dfrac{7}{4}$
-1	$\dfrac{1}{2}$	$-\dfrac{3}{2}$
0	1	-1
1	2	0
2	4	2

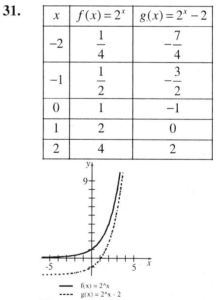

The graph of g is the graph of f shifted down 2 units.

690

33.

x	$f(x) = 3^x$	$g(x) = -3^x$
-2	$\dfrac{1}{9}$	$-\dfrac{1}{9}$
-1	$\dfrac{1}{3}$	$-\dfrac{1}{3}$
0	1	-1
1	3	-3
2	9	-9

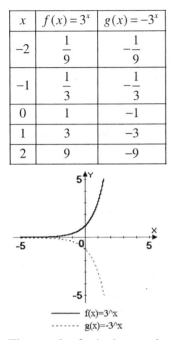

The graph of g is the graph of f reflected across the x–axis.

35.

x	$f(x) = 2^x$	$g(x) = 2^{x+1} - 1$
-2	$\dfrac{1}{4}$	$-\dfrac{1}{2}$
-1	$\dfrac{1}{2}$	0
0	1	1
1	2	3
2	4	7

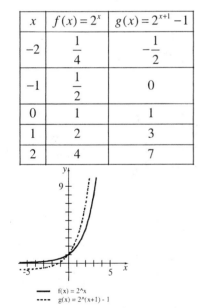

The graph of g is the graph of f shifted 1 unit down and 1 unit to the left.

37.

x	$f(x) = 3^x$	$g(x) = \dfrac{1}{3} \cdot 3^x$
-2	$\dfrac{1}{9}$	$\dfrac{1}{27}$
-1	$\dfrac{1}{3}$	$\dfrac{1}{9}$
0	1	$\dfrac{1}{3}$
1	3	1
2	9	3

The graph of g is the graph of f compressed vertically by a factor of $\dfrac{1}{3}$.

39. a.

$$A = 10{,}000\left(1 + \frac{0.055}{2}\right)^{2(5)}$$

$$= 10{,}000(1.0275)^{10}$$

$$= 13116.51$$

The balance in the account is $13,116.51 after 5 years of semiannual compounding.

b.

$$A = 10{,}000\left(1 + \frac{0.055}{12}\right)^{12(5)}$$

$$= 10{,}000(1.0045833)^{60}$$

$$= 13157.04$$

The balance in the account is $13,157.04 after 5 years of monthly compounding.

691

c. $A = Pe^{rt} = 10,000e^{0.055(5)}$

$= 10,000e^{0.275} = 13165.31$

The balance in the account is $13,165.31 after 5 years of continuous compounding.

41. Monthly Compounding

$A = 12,000\left(1 + \dfrac{0.07}{12}\right)^{12(3)}$

$= 10,000(1 + 0.0058333)^{36}$

$= 10,000(1.0058333)^{36}$

$= 12329.24$

Continuous Compounding

$A = 12,000e^{0.0685(3)}$

$= 10,000e^{0.2055} = 12281.39$

Monthly compounding at 7% yields the greatest return.

43. Domain: $\{x \mid x \text{ is a real number}\}$ or $(-\infty, \infty)$

Range: $\{y \mid y > -2\}$ or $(-2, \infty)$

44. Domain: $\{x \mid x \text{ is a real number}\}$ or $(-\infty, \infty)$

Range: $\{y \mid y > -3\}$ or $(-3, \infty)$

45. Domain: $\{x \mid x \text{ is a real number}\}$ or $(-\infty, \infty)$

Range: $\{y \mid y > 1\}$ or $(1, \infty)$

46. Domain: $\{x \mid x \text{ is a real number}\}$ or $(-\infty, \infty)$

Range: $\{y \mid y > 2\}$ or $(2, \infty)$

47. Domain: $\{x \mid x \text{ is a real number}\}$ or $(-\infty, \infty)$

Range: $\{y \mid y > 0\}$ or $(0, \infty)$

48. Domain: $\{x \mid x \text{ is a real number}\}$ or $(-\infty, \infty)$

Range: $\{y \mid y > 0\}$ or $(0, \infty)$

49.

x	$f(x) = 2^x$	$g(x) = 2^{-x}$
-2	$\dfrac{1}{4}$	4
-1	$\dfrac{1}{2}$	2
0	1	1
1	2	$\dfrac{1}{2}$
2	4	$\dfrac{1}{4}$

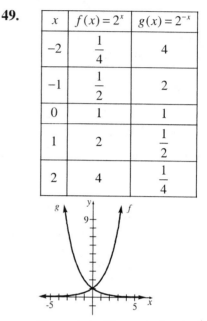

The point of intersection is $(0,1)$.

50.

x	$f(x) = 2^{x+1}$	$g(x) = 2^{-x+1}$
-2	$\dfrac{1}{2}$	8
-1	1	4
0	2	2
1	4	1
2	8	$\dfrac{1}{2}$

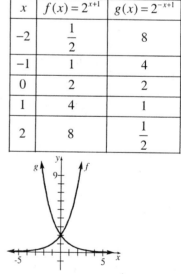

The point of intersection is $(0,1)$.

51.

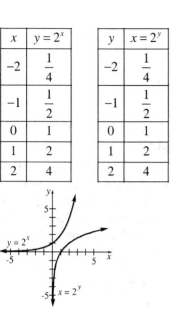

x	$y = 2^x$
-2	$\dfrac{1}{4}$
-1	$\dfrac{1}{2}$
0	1
1	2
2	4

y	$x = 2^y$
-2	$\dfrac{1}{4}$
-1	$\dfrac{1}{2}$
0	1
1	2
2	4

52.

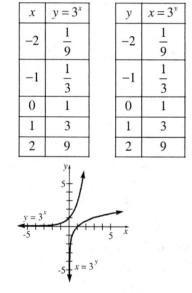

x	$y = 3^x$
-2	$\dfrac{1}{9}$
-1	$\dfrac{1}{3}$
0	1
1	3
2	9

y	$x = 3^y$
-2	$\dfrac{1}{9}$
-1	$\dfrac{1}{3}$
0	1
1	3
2	9

53. **a.** $f(0) = 574(1.026)^0$

$$= 574(1) = 574$$

India's population in 1974 was 574 million.

b. $f(27) = 574(1.026)^{27} \approx 1148$

India's population in 2001 will be 1148 million.

c. Since $2028 - 1974 = 54$, find
$$f(54) = 574(1.026)^{54} \approx 2295.$$
India's population in 2028 will be 2295 million.

d. $2055 - 1974 = 81$, find
$$f(54) = 574(1.026)^{81} \approx 4590.$$
India's population in 2055 will be 4590 million.

e. India's population appears to be doubling every 27 years.

55. $S = 65,000(1 + 0.06)^{10}$

$$= 65,000(1.06)^{10} \approx 116,405$$

In 10 years, the house will be worth $116,405.

57. Since $2001 - 1995 = 6$, find
$$f(6) = 35.86e^{0.207(6)}$$
$$= 35.86e^{1.242} \approx 124.2$$
According to the model, there were 124.2 million cellular telephone subscribers in 2001. The actual number of cellular telephone subscribers was 128.4 million, so the model describes the actual data fairly well.

59. **a.** $f(0) = 80e^{-0.5(0)} + 20$

$$= 80e^0 + 20$$
$$= 80(1) + 20$$
$$= 80 + 20 = 100$$

100% of information is remembered at the moment it is first learned.

b. $f(1) = 80e^{-0.5(1)} + 20$

$$= 80e^{-0.5} + 20 \approx 68.522$$

About 68.5% of information is remembered after one week.

693

c. $f(4) = 80e^{-0.5(4)} + 20$

$$= 80e^{-2} + 20$$

$$= 10.827 + 20 = 30.827$$

Approximately 30.8% of information is remembered after four weeks.

d. $f(52) = 80e^{-0.5(52)} + 20$

$$= 80e^{-26} + 20$$

$$= (4.087 \times 10^{-10}) + 20$$

$$\approx 20$$

Approximately 20% of information is remembered after one year. (4.087×10^{-10} will be eliminated in rounding.)

61.

$$f(30) = \frac{90}{1 + 270e^{-0.122(30)}}$$

$$= \frac{90}{1 + 270e^{-3.66}}$$

$$= \frac{90}{1 + 6.948} = \frac{90}{7.948} \approx 11.3$$

Approximately 11.3% of 30-year-olds have some coronary heart disease.

63. **a.**

$$N(0) = \frac{30,000}{1 + 20e^{-1.5(0)}}$$

$$= \frac{30,000}{1 + 20e^{0}}$$

$$= \frac{30,000}{1 + 20(1)}$$

$$= \frac{30,000}{1 + 20}$$

$$= \frac{30,000}{21} \approx 1428.6$$

Approximately 1429 people became ill with the flu when the epidemic began.

b.

$$N(3) = \frac{30,000}{1 + 20e^{-1.5(3)}}$$

$$= \frac{30,000}{1 + 20e^{-4.5}} \approx 24,546$$

Approximately 24,546 people became ill with the flu by the end of the third week.

c. The epidemic cannot grow indefinitely because there are a limited number of people that can become ill. Because there are 30,000 people in the town, the limit is 30,000.

65. – 69. Answers will vary

71. **a.**

$$Q(t) = 10000\left(1 + \frac{0.05}{4}\right)^{4t}$$

$$M(t) = 10000\left(1 + \frac{0.045}{12}\right)^{12t}$$

b.

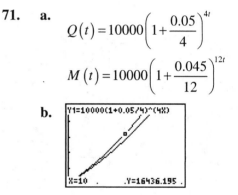

The bank paying 5% compounded quarterly offers a better return.

73. Statement **d** is true.

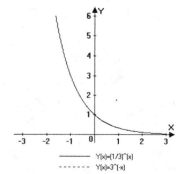

The graphs coincide, so the functions are equivalent.

Statement **a** is false. The amount of money will not increase without bound.

Statement **b** is false.

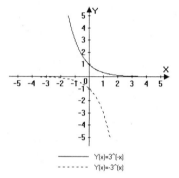

$$\text{---- } Y(x)=3^{(-x)}$$
$$\text{- - - } Y(x)=-3^{(x)}$$

The graphs do not coincide.

Statement **c** is false. 2.718 is an approximation of e.

75. $(\cosh x)^2 - (\sinh x)^2$

$$= \left(\frac{e^x + e^{-x}}{2}\right)^2 - \left(\frac{e^x - e^{-x}}{2}\right)^2$$

$$= \frac{e^{2x} + 2e^x e^{-x} + e^{-2x}}{4} - \frac{e^{2x} - 2e^x e^{-x} + e^{-2x}}{4}$$

$$= \frac{\left(e^{2x} + 2e^x e^{-x} + e^{-2x}\right) - \left(e^{2x} - 2e^x e^{-x} + e^{-2x}\right)}{4}$$

$$= \frac{e^{2x} + 2e^x e^{-x} + e^{-2x} - e^{2x} + 2e^x e^{-x} - e^{-2x}}{4}$$

$$= \frac{2e^x e^{-x} + 2e^x e^{-x}}{4} = \frac{4e^x e^{-x}}{4} = e^x e^{-x} = \frac{e^x}{e^x} = 1$$

76.
$$D = \frac{ab}{a+b}$$
$$D(a+b) = ab$$
$$Da + Db = ab$$
$$Da = ab - Db$$
$$Da = (a - D)b$$
$$b = \frac{Da}{a - D}$$

77.
$$\frac{2x+3}{x^2 - 7x + 12} - \frac{2}{x-3}$$
$$= \frac{2x+3}{(x-3)(x-4)} - \frac{2}{x-3}$$
$$= \frac{2x+3}{(x-3)(x-4)} - \frac{2(x-4)}{(x-3)(x-4)}$$
$$= \frac{2x+3 - 2(x-4)}{(x-3)(x-4)}$$
$$= \frac{2x+3 - 2x + 8}{(x-3)(x-4)}$$
$$= \frac{11}{(x-3)(x-4)}$$

78.
$$x(x-3) = 10$$
$$x^2 - 3x = 10$$
$$x^2 - 3x - 10 = 0$$
$$(x-5)(x+2) = 0$$
Apply the zero product principle.
$$x - 5 = 0 \quad \text{or} \quad x + 2 = 0$$
$$x = 5 \qquad\qquad x = -2$$
The solutions are 5 and –2, and the solution set is $\{-2, 5\}$.

12.2 Exercise Set

1. $4 = \log_2 16$
$$2^4 = 16$$

3. $2 = \log_3 x$
$$3^2 = x$$

5. $5 = \log_b 32$
$$b^5 = 32$$

7. $\log_6 216 = y$
$$6^y = 216$$

9. $\quad 2^3 = 8$

$\log_2 8 = 3$

11. $\quad 2^{-4} = \dfrac{1}{16}$

$\log_2 \dfrac{1}{16} = -4$

13. $\quad \sqrt[3]{8} = 2$

$8^{\frac{1}{3}} = 2$

$\log_8 2 = \dfrac{1}{3}$

15. $\quad 13^2 = x$

$\log_{13} x = 2$

17. $\quad b^3 = 1000$

$\log_b 1000 = 3$

19. $\quad 7^y = 200$

$\log_7 200 = y$

21. $\quad \log_4 16 = y$

$4^y = 16$

$4^y = 4^2$

$y = 2$

23. $\quad \log_2 64 = y$

$2^y = 64$

$2^y = 2^6$

$y = 6$

25. $\quad \log_5 \dfrac{1}{5} = y$

$5^y = \dfrac{1}{5}$

$5^y = 5^{-1}$

$y = -1$

27. $\quad \log_2 \dfrac{1}{8} = y$

$2^y = \dfrac{1}{8}$

$2^y = \dfrac{1}{2^3}$

$2^y = 2^{-3}$

$y = -3$

29. $\quad \log_7 \sqrt{7} = y$

$7^y = \sqrt{7}$

$7^y = 7^{\frac{1}{2}}$

$y = \dfrac{1}{2}$

31. $\quad \log_2 \dfrac{1}{\sqrt{2}} = y$

$2^y = \dfrac{1}{\sqrt{2}}$

$2^y = \dfrac{1}{2^{\frac{1}{2}}}$

$2^y = 2^{-\frac{1}{2}}$

$y = -\dfrac{1}{2}$

33. $\log_{64} 8 = y$

$64^y = 8$

$64^y = 64^{\frac{1}{2}}$

$y = \frac{1}{2}$

35. $\log_5 5 = y$

$5^y = 5^1$

$y = 1$

37. $\log_4 1 = y$

$4^y = 1$

$4^y = 4^0$

$y = 0$

39. $\log_5 5^7 = y$

$5^y = 5^7$

$y = 7$

41. Since $b^{\log_b x} = x$, $8^{\log_8 19} = 19$.

43. $f(x) = 4^x$

$g(x) = \log_4 x$

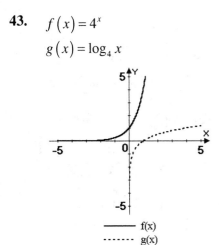

45.
$$f(x) = \left(\frac{1}{2}\right)^x$$

$$g(x) = \log_{\frac{1}{2}} x$$

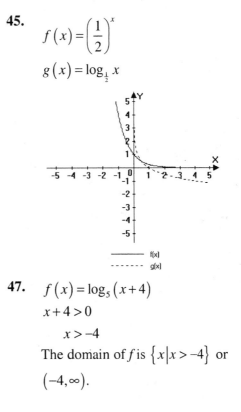

47. $f(x) = \log_5(x+4)$

$x + 4 > 0$

$x > -4$

The domain of f is $\{x \mid x > -4\}$ or

$(-4, \infty)$.

49. $f(x) = \log_5(2-x)$

$2 - x > 0$

$-x > -2$

$x < 2$

The domain of f is $\{x \mid x < 2\}$ or

$(-\infty, 2)$.

51. $f(x) = \ln(x-2)^2$

The domain of g is all real numbers
for which $(x-2)^2 > 0$. The only
number that must be excluded is 2.
The domain of f is $\{x \mid x \neq 2\}$ or

$(-\infty, 2) \cup (2, \infty)$.

53. $\log 100 = y$

$\qquad 10^y = 100$

$\qquad 10^y = 10^2$

$\qquad y = 2$

55. $\log 10^7 = y$

$\qquad 10^y = 10^7$

$\qquad y = 7$

57. Since $10^{\log x} = x$, $10^{\log 33} = 33$.

59. $\ln 1 = y$

$\qquad e^y = 1$

$\qquad e^y = e^0$

$\qquad y = 0$

61. Since $\ln e^x = x$, $\ln e^6 = 6$.

63. $\ln \dfrac{1}{e^6} = \ln e^{-6}$

Since $\ln e^x = x$, $\ln e^{-6} = -6$.

65. Since $e^{\ln x} = x$, $e^{\ln 125} = 125$.

67. Since $\ln e^x = x$, $\ln e^{9x} = 9x$.

69. Since $e^{\ln x} = x$, $e^{\ln 5x^2} = 5x^2$.

71. Since $10^{\log x} = x$, $10^{\log \sqrt{x}} = \sqrt{x}$.

73. $\log_3 (x-1) = 2$

$\qquad 3^2 = x - 1$

$\qquad 9 = x - 1$

$\qquad 10 = x$

The solution set is $\{10\}$.

74. $\log_5 (x+4) = 2$

$\qquad 5^2 = x + 4$

$\qquad 25 = x + 4$

$\qquad 21 = x$

The solution set is $\{21\}$.

75. $\log_4 x = -3$

$\qquad 4^{-3} = x$

$\qquad x = \dfrac{1}{4^3} = \dfrac{1}{64}$

The solution set is $\left\{ \dfrac{1}{64} \right\}$.

76. $\log_{64} x = \dfrac{2}{3}$

$\qquad 64^{\frac{2}{3}} = x$

$\qquad x = \left(\sqrt[3]{64} \right)^2 = 4^2 = 16$

The solution set is $\{16\}$.

77. $\log_3 (\log_7 7) = \log_3 1 = 0$

78. $\log_5 (\log_2 32) = \log_5 \left(\log_2 2^5 \right)$

$\qquad\qquad\qquad\quad = \log_5 5 = 1$

79. $\log_2 (\log_3 81) = \log_2 \left(\log_3 3^4 \right)$

$\qquad\qquad\qquad\quad = \log_2 4 = \log_2 2^2 = 2$

80. $\log (\ln e) = \log 1 = 0$

81. **(d)** The graph is similar to that of $y = \ln x$, but shifted left 2 units.

82. **(f)** The graph is similar to that of $y = \ln x$, but shifted right 2 units.

83. **(c)** The graph is similar to that of $y = \ln x$, but shifted up 2 units.

84. **(a)** The graph is similar to that of $y = \ln x$, but shifted down 2 units.

85. **(b)** The graph is similar to that of $y = \ln x$, but reflected across the y-axis and then shifted right 1 unit.

86. **(e)** The graph is similar to that of $y = \ln x$, but reflected across the y-axis and then shifted right 2 units.

87. $f(13) = 62 + 35\log(13 - 4)$

$= 62 + 35\log(9) \approx 95.4$

A 13-year-old girl is approximately 95.4% of her adult height.

89. Since $2003 - 1997 = 6$, we find $f(6)$:

$f(6) = -4.9\ln 6 + 73.8 \approx 65$

In 2003, approximately 65% of U.S. companies performed drug tests. The function modeled the actual number very well. It gives the actual percent.

91. $D = 10\log\left(10^{12}\left(6.3\times10^6\right)\right)$

$= 10\log\left(6.3\times10^{18}\right) \approx 188.0$

The decibel level of a blue whale is approximately 188 decibels. At close range, the sound could rupture the human ear drum.

93. **a.** The original exam was at time, $t = 0$.

$f(0) = 88 - 15\ln(0 + 1)$

$= 88 - 15\ln(1) \approx 88$

The average score on the original exam was 88.

b. $f(2) = 88 - 15\ln(2 + 1)$

$= 88 - 15\ln(3) \approx 71.5$

$f(4) = 88 - 15\ln(4 + 1)$

$= 88 - 15\ln(5) \approx 63.9$

$f(6) = 88 - 15\ln(6 + 1)$

$= 88 - 15\ln(7) \approx 58.8$

$f(8) = 88 - 15\ln(8 + 1)$

$= 88 - 15\ln(9) \approx 55.0$

$f(10) = 88 - 15\ln(10 + 1)$

$= 88 - 15\ln(11) \approx 52.0$

$f(12) = 88 - 15\ln(12 + 1)$

$= 88 - 15\ln(13) \approx 49.5$

The average score for the tests is as follows:

2 months: 71.5
4 months: 63.9
6 months: 58.8
8 months: 55.0
10 months: 52.0
12 months: 49.5

c.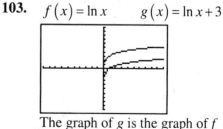

The students remembered less of the material over time.

95. – 101. Answers will vary.

103. $f(x) = \ln x$ $\qquad g(x) = \ln x + 3$

The graph of g is the graph of f shifted up 3 units.

105. $f(x) = \log x \qquad g(x) = \log(x-2)+1$

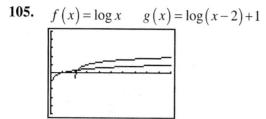

The graph of g is the graph of f shifted 2 units to the right and 1 unit up.

107. a. $f(x) = \ln(3x)$

$g(x) = \ln 3 + \ln x$

The graphs coincide.

b. $f(x) = \log(5x^2)$

$g(x) = \log 5 + \log x^2$

The graphs coincide.

c. $f(x) = \ln(2x^3)$

$g(x) = \ln 2 + \ln x^3$

The graphs coincide.

d. In each case, the function, f, is equivalent to g. This means that

$$\log_b(MN) = \log_b M + \log_b N.$$

e. The logarithm of a product is equal to <u>the sum of the logarithms of the factors</u>.

109. Statement **d.** is true. Recall:
$b^{\log_b x} = x.$

Statement **a.** is false. To evaluate $\dfrac{\log_2 8}{\log_2 4}$, evaluate each term independently.

$\log_2 8 = y$	$\log_2 4 = y$
$2^y = 8$	$2^y = 4$
$2^y = 2^3$	$2^y = 2^2$
$y = 3$	$y = 2$

Now substitute these values in the original expression.

$$\frac{\log_2 8}{\log_2 4} = \frac{3}{2}$$

Statement **b.** is false. We cannot take the log of a negative number.

Statement **c.** is false. The domain of $f(x) = \log_2 x$ is $(0, \infty)$.

111. $\log_4\left[\log_3\left(\log_2 8\right)\right]$

$= \log_4\left[\log_3\left(\log_2 2^3\right)\right]$

$= \log_4\left[\log_3 3\right] = \log_4 1 = 0$

113. $\qquad 2x = 11 - 5y$

$3x - 2y = -12$

Rewrite the equations.

$2x + 5y = \ \ 11$

$3x - 2y = -12$

Multiply the first equation by 2 and the second equation by 5, and solve by addition.

$$4x + 10y = 22$$
$$\underline{15x - 10y = -60}$$
$$19x = -38$$
$$x = -2$$

Back-substitute -2 for x to find y.

$$2(-2) + 5y = 11$$
$$-4 + 5y = 11$$
$$5y = 15$$
$$y = 3$$

The solution set is $\{(-2, 3)\}$.

114. $6x^2 - 8xy + 2y^2 = 2(3x^2 - 4xy + y^2)$
$$= 2(3x - y)(x - y)$$

115. $x + 3 \le -4$ or $2 - 7x \le 16$
$$x \le -7 \qquad\qquad -7x \le 14$$
$$x \ge -2$$

The solution set is $\{x \mid x \le -7$ or

$x \ge -2\}$ or $(-\infty, -7] \cup [-2, \infty)$.

12.3 Exercise Set

1. $\log_5(7 \cdot 3) = \log_5 7 + \log_5 3$

3. $\log_7(7x) = \log_7 7 + \log_7 x = 1 + \log_7 x$

5. $\log(1000x) = \log 1000 + \log x$
$$= 3 + \log x$$

7. $\log_7\left(\dfrac{7}{x}\right) = \log_7 7 - \log_7 x = 1 - \log_7 x$

9. $\log\left(\dfrac{x}{100}\right) = \log x - \log 100 = \log x - 2$

11. $\log_4\left(\dfrac{64}{y}\right) = \log_4 64 - \log_4 y$
$$= 3 - \log_4 y$$

13. $\ln\left(\dfrac{e^2}{5}\right) = \ln e^2 - \ln 5 = 2 - \ln 5$

15. $\log_b x^3 = 3\log_b x$

17. $\log N^{-6} = -6\log N$

19. $\ln \sqrt[5]{x} = \ln x^{\frac{1}{5}} = \dfrac{1}{5}\ln x$

21. $\log_b x^2 y = \log_b x^2 + \log_b y$
$$= 2\log_b x + \log_b y$$

23. $\log_4\left(\dfrac{\sqrt{x}}{64}\right) = \log_4 \sqrt{x} - \log_4 64$
$$= \log_4 x^{\frac{1}{2}} - 3$$
$$= \dfrac{1}{2}\log_4 x - 3$$

25. $\log_6\left(\dfrac{36}{\sqrt{x+1}}\right) = \log_6 36 - \log_6 \sqrt{x+1}$
$$= 2 - \log_6(x+1)^{\frac{1}{2}}$$
$$= 2 - \dfrac{1}{2}\log_6(x+1)$$

27. $\log_b\left(\dfrac{x^2 y}{z^2}\right) = \log_b x^2 y - \log_b z^2$
$$= \log_b x^2 + \log_b y - 2\log_b z$$
$$= 2\log_b x + \log_b y - 2\log_b z$$

29.
$$\log \sqrt{100x} = \log (100x)^{\frac{1}{2}}$$
$$= \frac{1}{2}\log (100x)$$
$$= \frac{1}{2}(\log 100 + \log x)$$
$$= \frac{1}{2}(2 + \log x)$$
$$= 1 + \frac{1}{2}\log x$$

31.
$$\log \sqrt[3]{\frac{x}{y}} = \log \left(\frac{x}{y}\right)^{\frac{1}{3}}$$
$$= \frac{1}{3}\log \left(\frac{x}{y}\right)$$
$$= \frac{1}{3}(\log x - \log y)$$
$$= \frac{1}{3}\log x - \frac{1}{3}\log y$$

33.
$$\log_b \left(\frac{\sqrt{x}y^3}{z^3}\right)$$
$$= \log_b \left(\frac{x^{\frac{1}{2}}y^3}{z^3}\right)$$
$$= \log_b \left(x^{\frac{1}{2}}y^3\right) - \log_b z^3$$
$$= \log_b x^{\frac{1}{2}} + \log_b y^3 - \log_b z^3$$
$$= \frac{1}{2}\log_b x + 3\log_b y - 3\log_b z$$

35.
$$\log_5 \sqrt[3]{\frac{x^2y}{25}}$$
$$= \log_5 \left(\frac{x^2y}{25}\right)^{\frac{1}{3}}$$
$$= \frac{1}{3}\log_5 \left(\frac{x^2y}{25}\right)$$
$$= \frac{1}{3}\left(\log_5 \left[x^2y\right] - \log_5 25\right)$$
$$= \frac{1}{3}\left(\log_5 x^2 + \log_5 y - \log_5 5^2\right)$$
$$= \frac{1}{3}(2\log_5 x + \log_5 y - 2)$$
$$= \frac{2}{3}\log_5 x + \frac{1}{3}\log_5 y - \frac{2}{3}$$

37. $\log 5 + \log 2 = \log (5 \cdot 2) = \log 10 = 1$

39. $\ln x + \ln 7 = \ln (x \cdot 7) = \ln (7x)$

41.
$$\log_2 96 - \log_2 3 = \log_2 \frac{96}{3} = \log_2 32 = 5$$

43.
$$\log (2x+5) - \log x = \log \left(\frac{2x+5}{x}\right)$$

45. $\log x + 3\log y = \log x + \log y^3$
$$= \log (xy^3)$$

47. $\frac{1}{2}\ln x + \ln y = \ln x^{\frac{1}{2}} + \ln y$
$$= \ln \left(x^{\frac{1}{2}}y\right) = \ln \left(y\sqrt{x}\right)$$

49. $2\log_b x + 3\log_b y = \log_b x^2 + \log_b y^3$
$$= \log_b (x^2y^3)$$

702

51.
$$5\ln x - 2\ln y = \ln x^5 - \ln y^2 = \ln\left(\frac{x^5}{y^2}\right)$$

53.
$$3\ln x - \frac{1}{3}\ln y = \ln x^3 - \ln y^{\frac{1}{3}}$$
$$= \ln\left(\frac{x^3}{y^{\frac{1}{3}}}\right) = \ln\left(\frac{x^3}{\sqrt[3]{y}}\right)$$

55.
$$4\ln(x+6) - 3\ln x = \ln(x+6)^4 - \ln x^3$$
$$= \ln\left[\frac{(x+6)^4}{x^3}\right]$$

57.
$$3\ln x + 5\ln y - 6\ln z$$
$$= \ln x^3 + \ln y^5 - \ln z^6$$
$$= \ln(x^3 y^5) - \ln z^6 = \ln\left(\frac{x^3 y^5}{z^6}\right)$$

59.
$$\frac{1}{2}(\log_5 x + \log_5 y) - 2\log_5(x+1)$$
$$= \frac{1}{2}\log_5(xy) - \log_5(x+1)^2$$
$$= \log_5(xy)^{\frac{1}{2}} - \log_5(x+1)^2$$
$$= \log_5 \sqrt{xy} - \log_5(x+1)^2$$
$$= \log_5\left[\frac{\sqrt{xy}}{(x+1)^2}\right]$$

61.
$$\log_5 13 = \frac{\log 13}{\log 5} \approx 1.5937$$

63.
$$\log_{14} 87.5 = \frac{\log 87.5}{\log 14} \approx 1.6944$$

65.
$$\log_{0.1} 17 = \frac{\log 17}{\log 0.1} \approx -1.2304$$

67.
$$\log_\pi 63 = \frac{\log 63}{\log \pi} \approx 3.6193$$

69.
$$\log_b \frac{3}{2} = \log_b 3 - \log_b 2 = C - A$$

70.
$$\log_b 6 = \log_b(2\cdot 3)$$
$$= \log_b 2 + \log_b 3 = A + C$$

71.
$$\log_b 8 = \log_b 2^3 = 3\log_b 2 = 3A$$

72.
$$\log_b 81 = \log_b 3^4 = 4\log_b 3 = 4C$$

73.
$$\log_b \sqrt{\frac{2}{27}} = \log_b\left(\frac{2}{27}\right)^{\frac{1}{2}}$$
$$= \frac{1}{2}\log_b\left(\frac{2}{3^3}\right)$$
$$= \frac{1}{2}\left(\log_b 2 - \log_b 3^3\right)$$
$$= \frac{1}{2}\left(\log_b 2 - 3\log_b 3\right)$$
$$= \frac{1}{2}\log_b 2 - \frac{3}{2}\log_b 3$$
$$= \frac{1}{2}A - \frac{3}{2}C$$

74.
$$\log_b \sqrt{\frac{3}{16}} = \log_b\left(\frac{\sqrt{3}}{4}\right)$$
$$= \log_b \sqrt{3} - \log_b 4$$
$$= \log_b 3^{\frac{1}{2}} - \log 2^2$$
$$= \frac{1}{2}\log_b 3 - 2\log 2$$
$$= \frac{1}{2}C - 2A$$

75.
$$\log_3 x = \log_3 5 + \log_3 7$$
$$\log_3 x = \log_3(5\cdot 7)$$
$$\log_3 x = \log_3 35$$
$$x = 35$$
The solution set is $\{35\}$.

76. $\log_7 x = \log_7 3 + \log_7 5$

$\log_7 x = \log_7 (3 \cdot 5)$

$\log_7 x = \log_7 15$

$x = 15$

The solution set is $\{15\}$.

77. $\log_5 x = 4 \log_5 2 - \log_5 8$

$\log_5 x = \log_5 2^4 - \log_5 8$

$\log_5 x = \log_5 16 - \log_5 8$

$\log_5 x = \log_5 \dfrac{16}{8}$

$\log_5 x = \log_5 2$

$x = 2$

The solution set is $\{2\}$.

78. $\log_5 x = 5 \log_5 2 - \log_5 4$

$\log_5 x = \log_5 2^5 - \log_5 4$

$\log_5 x = \log_5 32 - \log_5 4$

$\log_5 x = \log_5 \dfrac{32}{4}$

$\log_5 x = \log_5 8$

$x = 8$

The solution set is $\{8\}$.

79. $(f - g)(x)$

$= f(x) - g(x)$

$= \log x + \log 7 + \log(x^2 - 1) - \log(x + 1)$

$= \log(7x) + \log(x^2 - 1) - \log(x + 1)$

$= \log\left[7x(x^2 - 1)\right] - \log(x + 1)$

$= \log\left[\dfrac{7x(x^2 - 1)}{x + 1}\right]$

$= \log\left[\dfrac{7x(x - 1)(x + 1)}{x + 1}\right]$

$= \log\left[7x(x - 1)\right]$

80. $(f - g)(x)$

$= f(x) - g(x)$

$= \log x + \log 15 + \log(x^2 - 4) - \log(x + 2)$

$= \log(15x) + \log(x^2 - 4) - \log(x + 2)$

$= \log\left[15x(x^2 - 4)\right] - \log(x + 2)$

$= \log\left[\dfrac{15x(x^2 - 4)}{x + 2}\right]$

$= \log\left[\dfrac{15x(x - 2)(x + 2)}{x + 2}\right]$

$= \log\left[15x(x - 2)\right]$

81. **a.** $D = 10\left(\log I - \log I_0\right)$

$= 10\left(\log \dfrac{I}{I_0}\right)$

b. $D = 10\left(\log \dfrac{100}{1}\right) = 10\left(\log 100\right)$

$= 10(2) = 20$

The sound is 20 decibels louder on the decibel scale.

83. – 89. Answers will vary.

91. **a.** $y = \log_3 x = \dfrac{\log x}{\log 3}$

b. $y = 2 + \log_3 x$

$y = \log_3 (x + 2)$

$y = -\log_3 x$

$y = \log_3 x$

704

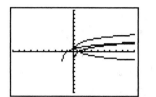

The graph of $y = 2 + \log_3 x$ is the graph of $y = \log_3 x$ shifted up two units.

The graph of $y = \log_3 (x + 2)$ is the graph of $y = \log_3 x$ shifted 2 units to the left.

The graph of $y = -\log_3 x$ is the graph of $y = \log_3 x$ reflected about the x–axis.

93. $y = \log_3 x$

$y = \log_{25} x$

$y = \log_{100} x$

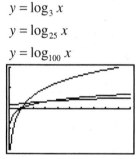

a.   Change the window to focus on the (0, 1) interval.

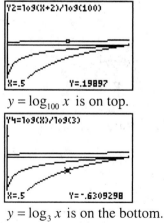

$y = \log_{100} x$ is on top.

$y = \log_3 x$ is on the bottom.

b.   Change the window to focus on the (1, 10) interval.

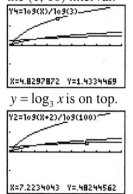

$y = \log_3 x$ is on top.

$y = \log_{100} x$ is on the bottom.

c.   If $y = \log_b x$ is graphed for two different values of b, the graph of the one with the larger base will be on top in the interval (0, 1) and the one with the smaller base will be on top in the interval $(1, \infty)$. Likewise, if $y = \log_b x$ is graphed for two different values of b, the graph of the one with the smaller base will be on the bottom in the interval (0, 1) and the one with the larger base will be on the bottom in the interval $(1, \infty)$.

95.   Answers will vary. One example follows. To disprove the statement $\log \dfrac{x}{y} = \dfrac{\log x}{\log y}$, let $y = 3$.

Graph $y = \log \dfrac{x}{3}$ and $y = \dfrac{\log x}{\log 3}$.

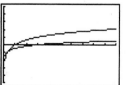

The graphs do not coincide, so the expressions are not equivalent.

97. Answers will vary. One example follows. To disprove the statement $\ln(xy) = (\ln x)(\ln y)$, let $y = 3$.

Graph $y = \ln(x \cdot 3)$ and $y = (\ln x)(\ln 3)$.

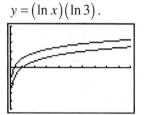

The graphs do not coincide, so the expressions are not equivalent.

99. Statement **d.** is true.

$$\ln \sqrt{2} = \ln 2^{\frac{1}{2}} = \frac{1}{2}\ln 2 = \frac{\ln 2}{2}$$

Statement **a.** is false.

$$\frac{\log_7 49}{\log_7 7} = \frac{\log_7 49}{1} = \log_7 49 = 2$$

Statement **b.** is false.

$\log_b(x^3 + y^3)$ cannot be simplified.

If we were taking the logarithm of a product and not a sum, we would have been able to simplify as follows.

$$\log_b(x^3 y^3) = \log_b x^3 + \log_b y^3$$
$$= 3\log_b x + 3\log_b y$$

Statement **c.** is false.

$$\log_b(xy)^5 = 5\log_b(xy)$$
$$= 5(\log_b x + \log_b y)$$
$$= 5\log_b x + 5\log_b y$$

101.
$$\log_7 9 = \frac{\log 9}{\log 7} = \frac{\log 3^2}{\log 7} = \frac{2\log 3}{\log 7} = \frac{2A}{B}$$

103. $5x - 2y > 10$

First, find the intercepts to the equation $5x - 2y = 10$.

Find the x–intercept by setting $y = 0$.
$$5x - 2(0) = 10$$
$$5x = 10$$
$$x = 2$$

Find the y–intercept by setting $x = 0$.
$$5(0) - 2y = 10$$
$$-2y = 10$$
$$y = -5$$

Next, use the origin as a test point.
$$5(0) - 2(0) > 10$$
$$0 - 0 > 10$$
$$0 > 10$$

This is a false statement. This means that the origin will not fall in the shaded half-plane.

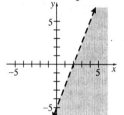

104. $x - 2(3x - 2) > 2x - 3$
$$x - 6x + 4 > 2x - 3$$
$$-5x + 4 > 2x - 3$$
$$-7x + 4 > -3$$
$$-7x > -7$$
$$x < 1$$

The solution set is $\{x \mid x < 1\}$ or $(-\infty, 1)$.

105.
$$\frac{\sqrt[3]{40x^2 y^6}}{\sqrt[3]{5xy}} = \sqrt[3]{\frac{40x^2 y^6}{5xy}} = \sqrt[3]{8xy^5}$$
$$= \sqrt[3]{8xy^3 y^2} = 2y\sqrt[3]{xy^2}$$

Mid-Chapter Check Point – Chapter 12

1.

x	$f(x) = 2^x - 3$
-2	$-\frac{11}{4} = -2.75$
-1	$-\frac{5}{2} = -2.5$
0	-3
1	-1
2	1
3	5

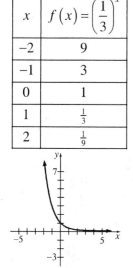

Domain: $\{x \mid x$ is a real number$\}$ or $(-\infty, \infty)$;

Range: $\{x \mid x > -3\}$ or $(-3, \infty)$.

2.

x	$f(x) = \left(\frac{1}{3}\right)^x$
-2	9
-1	3
0	1
1	$\frac{1}{3}$
2	$\frac{1}{9}$

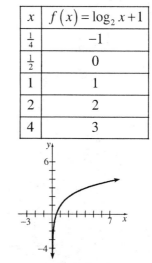

Domain: $\{x \mid x$ is a real number$\}$ or $(-\infty, \infty)$;

Range: $\{x \mid x > 0\}$ or $(0, \infty)$.

3.

x	$f(x) = \log_2 x$
$\frac{1}{4}$	-2
$\frac{1}{2}$	-1
1	0
2	1
4	2

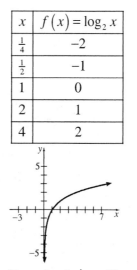

Domain: $\{x \mid x > 0\}$ or $(0, \infty)$;

Range: $\{x \mid x$ is a real number$\}$ or $(-\infty, \infty)$.

4.

x	$f(x) = \log_2 x + 1$
$\frac{1}{4}$	-1
$\frac{1}{2}$	0
1	1
2	2
4	3

Domain: $\{x \mid x > 0\}$ or $(0, \infty)$;

Range: $\{x \mid x$ is a real number$\}$ or $(-\infty, \infty)$.

707

5. $f(x) = \log_3(x+6)$

The argument of the logarithm must be positive:

$x + 6 > 0$

$x > -6$

Domain: $\{x \mid x > -6\}$ or $(-6, \infty)$.

6. $f(x) = \log_3 x + 6$

The argument of the logarithm must be positive: $x > 0$

Domain: $\{x \mid x > 0\}$ or $(0, \infty)$.

7. $\log_3(x+6)^2$

The argument of the logarithm must be positive. Now $(x+6)^2$ is always positive, except when $x = -6$

Domain: $\{x \mid x \neq 0\}$ or

$(-\infty - 6) \cup (-6, \infty)$.

8. $f(x) = 3^{x+6}$

Domain: $\{x \mid x \text{ is a real number}\}$ or $(-\infty, \infty)$.

9. $\log_2 8 + \log_5 25 = \log_2 2^3 + \log_5 5^2$

$= 3 + 2 = 5$

10. $\log_3 \dfrac{1}{9} = \log_3 \dfrac{1}{3^2} = \log_3 3^{-2} = -2$

11. Let $\log_{100} 10 = y$

$100^y = 10$

$(10^2)^y = 10^1$

$10^{2y} = 10^1$

$2y = 1$

$y = \dfrac{1}{2}$

12. $\log \sqrt[3]{10} = \log 10^{\frac{1}{3}} = \dfrac{1}{3}$

13. $\log_2(\log_3 81) = \log_2(\log_3 3^4)$

$= \log_2 4 = \log_2 2^2 = 2$

14. $\log_3\left(\log_2 \dfrac{1}{8}\right) = \log_3\left(\log_2 \dfrac{1}{2^3}\right)$

$= \log_3\left(\log_2 2^{-3}\right)$

$= \log_3(-3)$

$= \text{not possible}$

This expression is impossible to evaluate.

15. $6^{\log_6 5} = 5$

16. $\ln e^{\sqrt{7}} = \sqrt{7}$

17. $10^{\log 13} = 13$

18. $\log_{100} 0.1 = y$

$100^y = 0.1$

$(10^2)^y = \dfrac{1}{10}$

$10^{2y} = 10^{-1}$

$2y = -1$

$y = -\dfrac{1}{2}$

19. $\log_\pi \pi^{\sqrt{\pi}} = \sqrt{\pi}$

708

20.

$$\log\left(\frac{\sqrt{xy}}{1000}\right) = \log\left(\sqrt{xy}\right) - \log 1000$$

$$= \log\left(xy\right)^{\frac{1}{2}} - \log 10^3$$

$$= \frac{1}{2}\log\left(xy\right) - 3$$

$$= \frac{1}{2}\left(\log x + \log y\right) - 3$$

$$= \frac{1}{2}\log x + \frac{1}{2}\log y - 3$$

21.

$$\ln\left(e^{19}x^{20}\right) = \ln e^{19} + \ln x^{20}$$

$$= 19 + 20\ln x$$

22.

$$8\log_7 x - \frac{1}{3}\log_7 y = \log_7 x^8 - \log_7 y^{\frac{1}{3}}$$

$$= \log_7\left(\frac{x^8}{y^{\frac{1}{3}}}\right)$$

$$= \log_7\left(\frac{x^8}{\sqrt[3]{y}}\right)$$

23.

$$7\log_5 x + 2\log_5 x = \log_5 x^7 + \log_5 x^2$$

$$= \log_5\left(x^7 \cdot x^2\right)$$

$$= \log_5 x^9$$

24.

$$\frac{1}{2}\ln x - 3\ln y - \ln\left(z - 2\right)$$

$$= \ln x^{\frac{1}{2}} - \ln y^2 - \ln\left(z - 2\right)$$

$$= \ln \sqrt{x} - \left[\ln y^2 + \ln\left(z - 2\right)\right]$$

$$= \ln \sqrt{x} - \ln\left[y\left(z - 2\right)\right]$$

$$= \ln\left[\frac{\sqrt{x}}{y\left(z - 2\right)}\right]$$

25. Continuously: $A = 8000e^{0.08(3)}$

$$\approx 10{,}170$$

Monthly: $A = 8000\left(1 + \dfrac{0.08}{12}\right)^{12 \cdot 3}$

$$\approx 10{,}162$$

$$10{,}170 - 10{,}162 = 8$$

Interest returned will be $8 more if compounded continuously.

12.4 Exercise Set

1.

$$2^x = 64$$

$$2^x = 2^6$$

$$x = 6$$

The solution set is $\{6\}$.

3.

$$5^x = 125$$

$$5^x = 5^3$$

$$x = 3$$

The solution set is $\{3\}$.

5.

$$2^{2x-1} = 32$$

$$2^{2x-1} = 2^5$$

$$2x - 1 = 5$$

$$2x = 6$$

$$x = 3$$

The solution set is $\{3\}$.

7.

$$4^{2x-1} = 64$$

$$4^{2x-1} = 4^3$$

$$2x - 1 = 3$$

$$2x = 4$$

$$x = 2$$

The solution set is $\{2\}$.

9.

$$32^x = 8$$
$$\left(2^5\right)^x = 2^3$$
$$2^{5x} = 2^3$$
$$5x = 3$$
$$x = \frac{3}{5}$$

The solution set is $\left\{\dfrac{3}{5}\right\}$.

11.

$$9^x = 27$$
$$\left(3^2\right)^x = 3^3$$
$$3^{2x} = 3^3$$
$$2x = 3$$
$$x = \frac{3}{2}$$

The solution set is $\left\{\dfrac{3}{2}\right\}$.

13.

$$3^{1-x} = \frac{1}{27}$$
$$3^{1-x} = \frac{1}{3^3}$$
$$3^{1-x} = 3^{-3}$$
$$1 - x = -3$$
$$-x = -2$$
$$x = 2$$

The solution set is $\{2\}$.

15.

$$6^{\frac{x-3}{4}} = \sqrt{6}$$
$$6^{\frac{x-3}{4}} = 6^{\frac{1}{2}}$$
$$\frac{x-3}{4} = \frac{1}{2}$$
$$2(x-3) = 4(1)$$
$$2x - 6 = 4$$
$$2x = 10$$
$$x = 5$$

The solution set is $\{5\}$.

17.

$$4^x = \frac{1}{\sqrt{2}}$$
$$\left(2^2\right)^x = \frac{1}{2^{\frac{1}{2}}}$$
$$2^{2x} = 2^{-\frac{1}{2}}$$
$$2x = -\frac{1}{2}$$
$$x = \frac{1}{2}\left(-\frac{1}{2}\right) = -\frac{1}{4}$$

The solution set is $\left\{-\dfrac{1}{4}\right\}$.

19.

$$10^x = 3.91$$
$$\ln 10^x = \ln 3.91$$
$$x \ln 10 = \ln 3.91$$
$$x = \frac{\ln 3.91}{\ln 10} \approx 0.59$$

The solution set is $\left\{\dfrac{\ln 3.91}{\ln 10} \approx 0.59\right\}$.

21.

$$e^x = 5.7$$
$$\ln e^x = \ln 5.7$$
$$x = \ln 5.7 \approx 1.74$$

The solution set is $\{\ln 5.7 \approx 1.74\}$.

23.

$$5^x = 17$$
$$\ln 5^x = \ln 17$$
$$x \ln 5 = \ln 17$$
$$x = \frac{\ln 17}{\ln 5} \approx 1.76$$

The solution set is $\left\{\dfrac{\ln 17}{\ln 5} \approx 1.76\right\}$.

25.

$$5e^x = 25$$
$$e^x = 5$$
$$\ln e^x = \ln 5$$
$$x = \ln 5 \approx 1.61$$

The solution set is $\{\ln 5 \approx 1.61\}$.

27.
$$3e^{5x} = 1977$$
$$e^{5x} = 659$$
$$\ln e^{5x} = \ln 659$$
$$5x = \ln 659$$
$$x = \frac{\ln 659}{5} \approx 1.30$$

The solution set is $\left\{ \dfrac{\ln 659}{5} \approx 1.30 \right\}$.

29.
$$e^{0.7x} = 13$$
$$\ln e^{0.7x} = \ln 13$$
$$0.7x = \ln 13$$
$$x = \frac{\ln 13}{0.7} \approx 3.66$$

The solution set is $\left\{ \dfrac{\ln 13}{0.7} \approx 3.66 \right\}$.

31.
$$1250e^{0.055x} = 3750$$
$$e^{0.055x} = 3$$
$$\ln e^{0.055x} = \ln 3$$
$$0.055x = \ln 3$$
$$x = \frac{\ln 3}{0.055} \approx 19.97$$

The solution set is $\left\{ \dfrac{\ln 3}{0.055} \approx 19.97 \right\}$.

33.
$$30 - (1.4)^x = 0$$
$$-1.4^x = -30$$
$$1.4^x = 30$$
$$\ln 1.4^x = \ln 30$$
$$x \ln 1.4 = \ln 30$$
$$x = \frac{\ln 30}{\ln 1.4} \approx 10.11$$

The solution set is $\left\{ \dfrac{\ln 30}{\ln 1.4} \approx 10.11 \right\}$.

35.
$$e^{1-5x} = 793$$
$$\ln e^{1-5x} = \ln 793$$
$$1 - 5x = \ln 793$$
$$-5x = \ln 793 - 1$$
$$x = \frac{-(\ln 793 - 1)}{5}$$
$$x = \frac{1 - \ln 793}{5} \approx -1.14$$

The solution set is $\left\{ \dfrac{1 - \ln 793}{5} \approx -1.14 \right\}$.

37.
$$7^{x+2} = 410$$
$$\ln 7^{x+2} = \ln 410$$
$$(x+2)\ln 7 = \ln 410$$
$$x + 2 = \frac{\ln 410}{\ln 7}$$
$$x = \frac{\ln 410}{\ln 7} - 2 \approx 1.09$$

The solution set is $\left\{ \dfrac{\ln 410}{\ln 7} - 2 \approx 1.09 \right\}$.

39.
$$2^{x+1} = 5^x$$
$$\ln 2^{x+1} = \ln 5^x$$
$$(x+1)\ln 2 = x \ln 5$$
$$x \ln 2 + \ln 2 = x \ln 5$$
$$x \ln 2 = x \ln 5 - \ln 2$$
$$x \ln 2 - x \ln 5 = -\ln 2$$
$$x(\ln 2 - \ln 5) = -\ln 2$$
$$x = \frac{-\ln 2}{\ln 2 - \ln 5}$$
$$x = \frac{\ln 2}{\ln 5 - \ln 2} \approx 0.76$$

The solution set is $\left\{ \dfrac{\ln 2}{\ln 5 - \ln 2} \approx 0.76 \right\}$.

41. $\log_3 x = 4$

$\quad x = 3^4$

$\quad x = 81$

The solution set is $\{81\}$.

43. $\log_2 x = -4$

$\quad x = 2^{-4}$

$\quad x = \dfrac{1}{2^4} = \dfrac{1}{16}$

The solution set is $\left\{\dfrac{1}{16}\right\}$.

45. $\log_9 x = \dfrac{1}{2}$

$\quad x = 9^{\frac{1}{2}}$

$\quad x = \sqrt{9} = 3$

The solution set is $\{3\}$.

47. $\log x = 2$

$\quad x = 10^2$

$\quad x = 100$

The solution set is $\{100\}$.

49. $\log_4(x + 5) = 3$

$\quad x + 5 = 4^3$

$\quad x + 5 = 64$

$\quad x = 59$

The solution set is $\{59\}$.

51. $\log_3(x - 4) = -3$

$\quad x - 4 = 3^{-3}$

$\quad x - 4 = \dfrac{1}{3^3}$

$\quad x - 4 = \dfrac{1}{27}$

$\quad x = \dfrac{1}{27} + 4$

$\quad x = \dfrac{1}{27} + \dfrac{108}{27} = \dfrac{109}{27}$

The solution set is $\left\{\dfrac{109}{27}\right\}$.

53. $\log_4(3x + 2) = 3$

$\quad 3x + 2 = 4^3$

$\quad 3x + 2 = 64$

$\quad 3x = 62$

$\quad x = \dfrac{62}{3}$

The solution set is $\left\{\dfrac{62}{3}\right\}$.

55. $\log_5 x + \log_5(4x - 1) = 1$

$\quad \log_5(x(4x - 1)) = 1$

$\quad x(4x - 1) = 5^1$

$\quad 4x^2 - x = 5$

$\quad 4x^2 - x - 5 = 0$

$(4x - 5)(x + 1) = 0$

Apply the zero product principle.

$4x - 5 = 0 \quad$ and $\quad x + 1 = 0$

$\quad 4x = 5 \qquad\qquad x = -1$

$\quad x = \dfrac{5}{4}$

We disregard -1 because it would result in taking the logarithm of a negative number in the original equation. The solution set is $\left\{\dfrac{5}{4}\right\}$.

712

57. $\log_3(x-5)+\log_3(x+3)=2$

$$\log_3((x-5)(x+3))=2$$

$$(x-5)(x+3)=3^2$$

$$x^2-2x-15=9$$

$$x^2-2x-24=0$$

$$(x-6)(x+2)=0$$

Apply the zero product principle.

$x-6=0$ and $x+2=0$

$\quad x=6 \qquad\qquad x=-2$

We disregard –2 because it would result in taking the logarithm of a negative number in the original equation. The solution set is $\{6\}$.

59. $\log_2(x+2)-\log_2(x-5)=3$

$$\log_2\frac{x+2}{x-5}=3$$

$$\frac{x+2}{x-5}=2^3$$

$$\frac{x+2}{x-5}=8$$

$$x+2=8(x-5)$$

$$x+2=8x-40$$

$$-7x+2=-40$$

$$-7x=-42$$

$$x=6$$

The solution set is $\{6\}$.

61. $\log(3x-5)-\log(5x)=2$

$$\log\frac{3x-5}{5x}=2$$

$$\frac{3x-5}{5x}=10^2$$

$$\frac{3x-5}{5x}=100$$

$$3x-5=500x$$

$$-5=497x$$

$$-\frac{5}{497}=x$$

We disregard $-\dfrac{5}{497}$ because it would result in taking the logarithm of a negative number in the original equation. Therefore, the equation has no solution. The solution set is $\varnothing$ or $\{\ \}$.

63. $\ln x=2$

$$e^{\ln x}=e^2$$

$$x=e^2\approx 7.39$$

The solution set is $\{e^2\approx 7.39\}$.

65. $\ln x=-3$

$$x=e^{-3}=\frac{1}{e^3}$$

The solution set is $\left\{e^{-3}=\dfrac{1}{e^3}\approx 0.05\right\}$.

67. $5\ln(2x)=20$

$$\ln(2x)=4$$

$$e^{\ln(2x)}=e^4$$

$$2x=e^4$$

$$x=\frac{e^4}{2}\approx 27.30$$

The solution set is $\left\{\dfrac{e^4}{2}\approx 27.30\right\}$.

69. $6+2\ln x=5$

$$2\ln x=-1$$

$$e^{\ln x}=e^{-\frac{1}{2}}$$

$$x=e^{-\frac{1}{2}}\approx 0.61$$

The solution set is $\left\{e^{-\frac{1}{2}}\approx 0.61\right\}$.

71.

$$\ln \sqrt{x+3} = 1$$

$$\ln (x+3)^{\frac{1}{2}} = 1$$

$$\frac{1}{2}\ln (x+3) = 1$$

$$\ln (x+3) = 2$$

$$e^{\ln (x+3)} = e^2$$

$$x+3 = e^2$$

$$x = e^2 - 3 \approx 4.39$$

The solution set is $\{e^2 - 3 \approx 4.39\}$.

73.

$$\ln (x+1) - \ln x = 1$$

$$\ln \left(\frac{x+1}{x}\right) = 1$$

$$\frac{x+1}{x} = e^1$$

$$x+1 = ex$$

$$1 = ex - x$$

$$1 = (e-1)x$$

$$x = \frac{1}{e-1} \approx 0.58$$

The solution set is $\left\{\frac{1}{e-1} \approx 0.58\right\}$.

75.

$$5^{2x} \cdot 5^{4x} = 125$$

$$5^{2x+4x} = 5^3$$

$$5^{6x} = 5^3$$

$$6x = 3$$

$$x = \frac{1}{2}$$

The solution set is $\left\{\frac{1}{2}\right\}$.

76.

$$3^{x+2} \cdot 3^x = 81$$

$$3^{(x+2)+x} = 3^4$$

$$3^{2x+2} = 3^4$$

$$2x+2 = 4$$

$$2x = 2$$

$$x = 1$$

The solution set is $\{1\}$.

77.

$$2\log_3 (x+4) = \log_3 9 + 2$$

$$2\log_3 (x+4) = \log_3 3^2 + 2$$

$$2\log_3 (x+4) = 2 + 2$$

$$2\log_3 (x+4) = 4$$

$$\log_3 (x+4) = 2$$

$$x+4 = 3^2$$

$$x+4 = 9$$

$$x = 5$$

The solution set is $\{5\}$.

78.

$$3\log_2 (x-1) = 5 - \log_2 4$$

$$3\log_2 (x-1) = 5 - \log_2 2^2$$

$$3\log_2 (x-1) = 5 - 2$$

$$3\log_2 (x-1) = 3$$

$$\log_2 (x-1) = 1$$

$$x-1 = 2^1$$

$$x-1 = 2$$

$$x = 3$$

The solution set is $\{3\}$.

79.

$$3^{x^2} = 45$$

$$\ln 3^{x^2} = \ln 45$$

$$x^2 \ln 3 = \ln 45$$

$$x^2 = \frac{\ln 45}{\ln 3}$$

$$x = \pm\sqrt{\frac{\ln 45}{\ln 3}} \approx \pm 1.86$$

The solution set is $\left\{\pm\sqrt{\dfrac{\ln 45}{\ln 3}} \approx \pm 1.86\right\}$.

80.

$$5^{x^2} = 50$$

$$\ln 5^{x^2} = \ln 50$$

$$x^2 \ln 5 = \ln 50$$

$$x^2 = \frac{\ln 50}{\ln 5}$$

$$x = \pm\sqrt{\frac{\ln 50}{\ln 5}} \approx \pm 1.56$$

The solution set is $\left\{\pm\sqrt{\dfrac{\ln 50}{\ln 5}} \approx \pm 1.56\right\}$.

81.

$$\log_2(x-6) + \log_2(x-4) - \log_2 x = 2$$

$$\log_2\left[(x-6)(x-4)\right] - \log_2 x = 2$$

$$\log_2\left[\frac{(x-6)(x-4)}{x}\right] = 2$$

$$\log_2\left(\frac{x^2 - 10x + 24}{x}\right) = 2$$

$$\frac{x^2 - 10x + 24}{x} = 2^2$$

$$\frac{x^2 - 10x + 24}{x} = 4$$

$$x^2 - 10x + 24 = 4x$$

$$x^2 - 14x + 24 = 0$$

$$(x-12)(x-2) = 0$$

Apply the zero product property:

$$x - 12 = 0 \quad \text{or} \quad x - 2 = 0$$

$$x = 12 \qquad\qquad x = 2$$

We disregard 2 because it would result in taking the logarithm of a negative number in the original equation. The solution set is $\{12\}$.

82.

$$\log_2(x-3) + \log_2 x - \log_2(x+2) = 2$$

$$\log_2\left[(x-3)x\right] - \log_2(x+2) = 2$$

$$\log_2\left[\frac{(x-3)x}{x+2}\right] = 2$$

$$\log_2\left(\frac{x^2 - 3x}{x+2}\right) = 2$$

$$\frac{x^2 - 3x}{x+2} = 2^2$$

$$\frac{x^2 - 3x}{x+2} = 4$$

$$x^2 - 3x = 4(x+2)$$

$$x^2 - 3x = 4x + 8$$

$$x^2 - 7x - 8 = 0$$

$$(x-8)(x+1) = 0$$

Apply the zero product property:

$$x - 8 = 0 \quad \text{or} \quad x + 1 = 0$$

$$x = 8 \qquad\qquad x = -1$$

We disregard -1 because it would result in taking the logarithm of a negative number in the original equation. The solution set is $\{8\}$.

83.

$$5^{x^2-12} = 25^{2x}$$

$$5^{x^2-12} = \left(5^2\right)^{2x}$$

$$5^{x^2-12} = 5^{4x}$$

$$x^2 - 12 = 4x$$

$$x^2 - 4x - 12 = 0$$

$$(x-6)(x+2) = 0$$

Apply the zero product property:

$$x - 6 = 0 \quad \text{or} \quad x + 2 = 0$$

$$x = 6 \qquad\qquad x = -2$$

The solution set is $\{-2,\ 6\}$.

84.

$$3^{x^2-12} = 9^{2x}$$

$$3^{x^2-12} = \left(3^2\right)^{2x}$$

$$3^{x^2-12} = 3^{4x}$$

$$x^2 - 12 = 4x$$

$$x^2 - 4x - 12 = 0$$

$$(x-6)(x+2) = 0$$

Apply the zero product property:

$$x - 6 = 0 \quad \text{or} \quad x + 2 = 0$$

$$x = 6 \qquad\qquad x = -2$$

The solution set is $\{-2,\ 6\}$.

85.

$$R = 6e^{12.77x}$$

$$6e^{12.77x} = 100$$

$$e^{12.77x} = \frac{100}{6}$$

$$\ln e^{12.77x} = \ln \frac{100}{6}$$

$$12.77x = \ln \frac{100}{6}$$

$$x = \frac{\ln \dfrac{100}{6}}{12.77} \approx 0.22$$

A blood alcohol concentration of 0.22 corresponds to a 100% risk.

87. **a.** Since 2000 is 0 years after 2000, find $f(0)$.

$$f(0) = 18.9e^{0.0055(0)}$$

$$= 18.9e^0 = 18.9(1) = 18.9$$

The population of New York was 18.9 million in 2000.

b.

$$19.54 = 18.9e^{0.0055t}$$

$$e^{0.0055t} = \frac{19.54}{18.9}$$

$$\ln e^{0.0055t} = \ln \frac{19.54}{18.9}$$

$$0.0055t = \ln \frac{19.54}{18.9}$$

$$t = \frac{\ln \dfrac{19.54}{18.9}}{0.0055} \approx 6$$

$$2000 + 6 = 2006$$

The population of New York will reach 19.54 million in approximately the year 2006.

89.

$$20000 = 12500\left(1 + \frac{0.0575}{4}\right)^{4t}$$

$$20000 = 12500(1 + 0.014375)^{4t}$$

$$20000 = 12500(1.014375)^{4t}$$

$$\frac{20000}{12500} = (1.014375)^{4t}$$

$$1.6 = (1.014375)^{4t}$$

$$\ln 1.6 = \ln(1.014375)^{4t}$$

$$\ln 1.6 = 4t \ln 1.014375$$

$$\frac{4t \ln 1.014375}{4 \ln 1.014375} = \frac{\ln 1.6}{4 \ln 1.014375}$$

$$t = \frac{\ln 1.6}{4 \ln 1.014375} \approx 8.2$$

It will take approximately 8.2 years.

91.

$$1400 = 1000\left(1 + \frac{r}{360}\right)^{360(2)}$$

$$\frac{1400}{1000} = \left(1 + \frac{r}{360}\right)^{720}$$

$$1.4 = \left(1 + \frac{r}{360}\right)^{720}$$

$$\ln 1.4 = \ln\left(1 + \frac{r}{360}\right)^{720}$$

$$\ln 1.4 = 720\ln\left(1 + \frac{r}{360}\right)$$

$$\frac{\ln 1.4}{720} = \ln\left(1 + \frac{r}{360}\right)$$

$$e^{\frac{\ln 1.4}{720}} = e^{\ln\left(1 + \frac{r}{360}\right)}$$

$$e^{\frac{\ln 1.4}{720}} = 1 + \frac{r}{360}$$

$$1 + \frac{r}{360} = e^{\frac{\ln 1.4}{720}}$$

$$\frac{r}{360} = e^{\frac{\ln 1.4}{720}} - 1$$

$$r = 360\left(e^{\frac{\ln 1.4}{720}} - 1\right) \approx 0.168$$

The annual interest rate is approximately 16.8%.

93.

$$16000 = 8000e^{0.08t}$$

$$\frac{16000}{8000} = e^{0.08t}$$

$$2 = e^{0.08t}$$

$$\ln 2 = \ln e^{0.08t}$$

$$\ln 2 = 0.08t$$

$$t = \frac{\ln 2}{0.08} \approx 8.7$$

It will take approximately 8.7 years to double the money.

95.

$$7050 = 2350e^{r7}$$

$$\frac{7050}{2350} = e^{7r}$$

$$3 = e^{7r}$$

$$\ln 3 = \ln e^{7r}$$

$$\ln 3 = 7r$$

$$r = \frac{\ln 3}{7} \approx 0.157$$

The annual interest rate would have to be 15.7% to triple the money.

97.

$$1270 = 2246 - 501.4\ln x$$

$$1270 + 501.4\ln x = 2246$$

$$501.4\ln x = 976$$

$$\ln x = \frac{976}{501.4}$$

$$e^{\ln x} = e^{\frac{976}{501.4}}$$

$$x = e^{\frac{976}{501.4}} \approx 7$$

$$1995 + 7 = 2002$$

The average price of a new computer was $1270 in approximately the year 2002

99.

$$50 = 95 - 30\log_2 x$$

$$-45 = -30\log_2 x$$

$$\frac{-45}{-30} = \log_2 x$$

$$\log_2 x = \frac{3}{2}$$

$$x = 2^{\frac{3}{2}} \approx 2.8$$

After approximately 2.8 days, only half the students recall the important features of the lecture. This is represented by the point (2.8, 50).

101.
$$\text{pH} = -\log x$$
$$2.4 = -\log x$$
$$-2.4 = \log x$$
$$x = 10^{-2.4} \approx .004$$

The hydrogen ion concentration is $10^{-2.4}$, or approximately 0.004, moles per liter.

103. – 107. Answers will vary.

109. $2^{x+1} = 8$

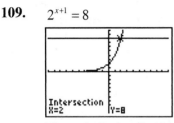

The solution set is $\{2\}$.
Verify the solution algebraically:
$$2^{2+1} = 8$$
$$2^3 = 8$$
$$8 = 8$$

111. $\log_3(4x - 7) = 2$

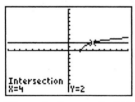

The solution set is $\{4\}$.
Verify the solution algebraically:
$$\log_3(4 \cdot 4 - 7) = 2$$
$$\log_3(16 - 7) = 2$$
$$\log_3 9 = 2$$
$$\log_3 3^2 = 2$$
$$2 = 2$$

113. $\log(x+3) + \log x = 1$

The solution set is $\{2\}$.
Verify the solution algebraically:
$$\log(2+3) + \log 2 = 1$$
$$\log 5 + \log 2 = 1$$
$$\log(5 \cdot 2) = 1$$
$$\log 10 = 1$$
$$1 = 1$$

115. $3^x = 2x + 3$

The solution set is $\{-1.39, 1.69\}$.
The solutions check algebraically.

117. $f(x) = 0.48\ln(x+1) + 27$

The barometric air pressure increases as the distance from the eye increases. It increases quickly at first, and the more slowly over time.

718

119. $P(t) = 145e^{-0.092t}$

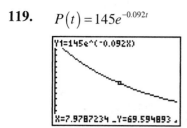

The runner's pulse will be 70 beats per minute after approximately 7.9 minutes.
Verifying algebraically:
$P(7.9) = 145e^{-0.092(7.9)}$
$= 145e^{-07268} \approx 70$

121. Statement **c.** is true.
$x = \dfrac{1}{k} \ln y$
$kx = \ln y$
$e^{kx} = e^{\ln y}$
$y = e^{kx}$

Statement **a.** is false. If
$\log(x+3) = 2$, then $10^2 = x+3$.

Statement **b.** is false. If
$\log(7x+3) - \log(2x+5) = 4$, then
$\log\left(\dfrac{7x+3}{2x+5}\right) = 4$, and $10^4 = \dfrac{7x+3}{2x+5}$.

Statement **d.** is false. $x^{10} = 5.71$ is not an exponential equation, because there is not a variable in an exponent.

123. $(\ln x)^2 = \ln x^2$
$(\ln x)^2 = 2\ln x$
Let $t = \ln x$.
$t^2 = 2t$
$t^2 - 2t = 0$
$t(t-2) = 0$

$t = 0$ and $t - 2 = 0$
$t = 2$
Substitute $\ln x$ for t.
$\ln x = 0$ and $\ln x = 2$
$x = e^0$ $\qquad$ $x = e^2$
$x = 1$
The solution set is $\{1, e^2\}$.

125. $\ln(\ln x) = 0$
Let $t = \ln x$.
$\ln(t) = 0$
$t = e^0$
$t = 1$
Substitute $\ln x$ for t.
$\ln(x) = 1$
$x = e^1$
$x = e$
The solution set is $\{e\}$.

126. $\sqrt{x+4} - \sqrt{x-1} = 1$
$\sqrt{x+4} = 1 + \sqrt{x-1}$
$\left(\sqrt{x+4}\right)^2 = \left(1 + \sqrt{x-1}\right)^2$
$x+4 = 1 + 2\sqrt{x-1} + x - 1$
$4 = 2\sqrt{x-1}$
$2 = \sqrt{x-1}$
$2^2 = \left(\sqrt{x-1}\right)^2$
$4 = x - 1$
$5 = x$
This value checks, so the solution set is $\{5\}$.

719

127.

$$\frac{3}{x+1} - \frac{5}{x} = \frac{19}{x^2 + x}$$

$$\frac{3}{x+1} - \frac{5}{x} = \frac{19}{x(x+1)}$$

$$x(x+1)\left(\frac{3}{x+1} - \frac{5}{x}\right) = x(x+1)\left(\frac{19}{x(x+1)}\right)$$

$$x(3) - 5(x+1) = 19$$

$$3x - 5x - 5 = 19$$

$$-2x - 5 = 19$$

$$-2x = 24$$

$$x = -12$$

The solution set is $\{-12\}$.

128.

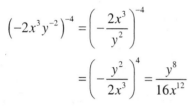

$$\left(-2x^3 y^{-2}\right)^{-4} = \left(-\frac{2x^3}{y^2}\right)^{-4}$$

$$= \left(-\frac{y^2}{2x^3}\right)^4 = \frac{y^8}{16x^{12}}$$

12.5 Exercise Set

1. Since 2003 is 0 years after 2003, find A when $t = 0$:

$$A = 127.2e^{0.001t}$$

$$A = 127.2e^{0.001(0)}$$

$$A = 127.2e^0$$

$$A = 127.2(1)$$

$$A = 127.2$$

In 2003, the population was 127.2 million.

3. Iraq has the greatest growth rate at 2.8% per year.

5. Substitute $A = 1238$ into the model for India and solve for t:

$$1238 = 1049.7e^{0.015t}$$

$$\frac{1238}{1049.7} = e^{0.015t}$$

$$\ln\frac{1238}{1049.7} = \ln e^{0.015t}$$

$$\ln\frac{1238}{1049.7} = 0.015t$$

$$t = \frac{\ln\dfrac{1238}{1049.7}}{0.015} \approx 11$$

Now, $2003 + 11 = 2014$. The population of India will be 1238 million in approximately the year 2014.

7. a. $A_0 = 6.04$. Since 2050 is 50 years after 2000, when $t = 50$, $A = 10$.

$$A = A_0 e^{kt}$$

$$10 = 6.04e^{k(50)}$$

$$\frac{10}{6.04} = e^{50k}$$

$$\ln\left(\frac{10}{6.04}\right) = \ln e^{50k}$$

$$\ln\left(\frac{10}{6.04}\right) = 50k$$

$$k = \frac{\ln\left(\dfrac{10}{6.04}\right)}{50} \approx 0.01$$

Thus, the growth function is $A = 6.04e^{0.01t}$.

b.
$$9 = 6.04e^{0.01t}$$

$$\frac{9}{6.04} = e^{0.01t}$$

$$\ln\left(\frac{9}{6.04}\right) = \ln e^{0.01t}$$

$$\ln\left(\frac{9}{6.04}\right) = 0.01t$$

$$t = \frac{\ln\left(\frac{9}{6.04}\right)}{0.01} \approx 40$$

Now, $2000 + 40 = 2040$, so the population will be 9 million is approximately the year 2040.

9.
$$A = 16e^{-0.000121t}$$

$$A = 16e^{-0.000121(5715)}$$

$$A = 16e^{-0.691515}$$

$$A \approx 8.01$$

Approximately 8 grams of carbon-14 will be present in 5715 years.

11. After 10 seconds, there will be $16 \cdot \frac{1}{2} = 8$ grams present. After 20 seconds, there will be $8 \cdot \frac{1}{2} = 4$ grams present. After 30 seconds, there will be $4 \cdot \frac{1}{2} = 2$ grams present. After 40 seconds, there will be $2 \cdot \frac{1}{2} = 1$ grams present. After 50 seconds, there will be $1 \cdot \frac{1}{2} = \frac{1}{2}$ gram present.

13.
$$A = A_0 e^{-0.000121t}$$

$$15 = 100e^{-0.000121t}$$

$$\frac{15}{100} = e^{-0.000121t}$$

$$\ln 0.15 = \ln e^{-0.000121t}$$

$$\ln 0.15 = -0.000121t$$

$$t = \frac{\ln 0.15}{-0.000121} \approx 15{,}679$$

The paintings are approximately 15,679 years old.

15. a.
$$\frac{1}{2} = 1e^{k1.31}$$

$$\ln\frac{1}{2} = \ln e^{1.31k}$$

$$\ln\frac{1}{2} = 1.31k$$

$$k = \frac{\ln\frac{1}{2}}{1.31} \approx -0.52912$$

The exponential model is given by $A = A_0 e^{-0.52912t}$.

b.
$$A = A_0 e^{-0.52912t}$$

$$0.945A_0 = A_0 e^{-0.52912t}$$

$$0.945 = e^{-0.52912t}$$

$$\ln 0.945 = \ln e^{-0.52912t}$$

$$\ln 0.945 = -0.52912t$$

$$t = \frac{\ln 0.945}{-0.52912} \approx 0.1069$$

The age of the dinosaur ones is approximately 0.1069 billion or 106,900,000 years old.

17.
$$2A_0 = A_0 e^{kt}$$
$$2 = e^{kt}$$
$$\ln 2 = \ln e^{kt}$$
$$\ln 2 = kt$$
$$t = \frac{\ln 2}{k}$$

The population will double in
$$t = \frac{\ln 2}{k} \text{ years.}$$

19. $A = e^{0.007t}$

a. $k = 0.007$, so New Zealand's growth rate is 0.7%.

b.
$$t = \frac{\ln 2}{k}$$
$$t = \frac{\ln 2}{0.007} \approx 99$$
New Zealand's population will double in approximately 99 years.

21. **a.**

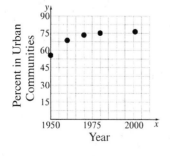

Woman's Age

b. An exponential function appears to be the best choice for modeling the data.

23. **a.**

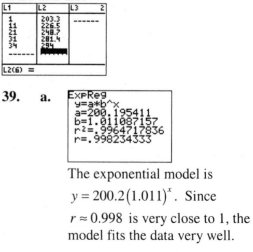

b. A logarithmic function appears to be the best choice for modeling the data.

25. **a.**

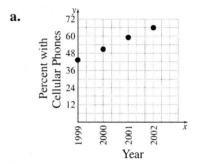

b. A linear function appears to be the best choice for modeling the data.

27.
$$y = 100(4.6)^x$$
$$y = 100e^{(\ln 4.6)x}$$
$$y = 100e^{1.526x}$$

29.
$$y = 2.5(0.7)^x$$
$$y = 2.5e^{(\ln 0.7)x}$$
$$y = 100e^{-0.357x}$$

31. – 37. Answers will vary.

For Exercises 39. – 43, we enter the data in L1 and L2:

L1	L2	L3	2
1	203.3	------	
11	226.5		
21	248.7		
31	281.4		
34	284		

L2(6) =

39. **a.**

ExpReg
y=a*b^x
a=200.195411
b=1.011087157
r²=.9964717836
r=.998234333

The exponential model is
$$y = 200.2(1.011)^x . \text{ Since}$$
$r \approx 0.998$ is very close to 1, the model fits the data very well.

722

b. $y = 200.2(1.011)^x$

$y = 200.2e^{(\ln 1.011)x}$

$y = 200.2e^{0.0109x}$

Since $k = .0109$, the population of the United States is increasing by about 1% each year.

41.

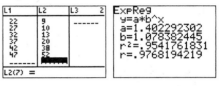

The linear model is $y = 2.714x + 197.586$. Since $r \approx 0.995$ is close to 1, the model fits the data very well.

43. Using r, the model of best fit is the exponential model $y = 200.2(1.011)^x$. The model of second best fit is the linear model $y = 2.714x + 197.586$.

Using the exponential model:

$$315 = 200.2(1.011)^x$$

$$\frac{315}{200.2} = (1.011)^x$$

$$\ln\left(\frac{315}{200.2}\right) = \ln(1.011)^x$$

$$\ln\left(\frac{315}{200.2}\right) = x\ln(1.011)$$

$$x = \frac{\ln\left(\dfrac{315}{200.2}\right)}{\ln(1.011)} \approx 41$$

$1969 + 41 = 2010$

Using the linear model:

$$315 = 2.714x + 197.586$$

$$117.414 = 2.714x$$

$$x = \frac{117.414}{2.714} \approx 43$$

$1969 + 43 = 2012$

According to the exponential model, the U.S. population will reach 315 million around the year 2010. According to the linear model, the U.S. population will reach 315 million around the year 2012. Both results are reasonably close to the result found in Example 1 (2010).

Explanations will vary.

45. For Exercise 21, we use an exponential model:

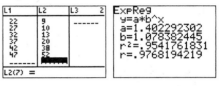

The model is $y = 1.402(1.078)^x$.

For Exercise 23, we use a logarithmic model with $x =$ the number of years after 1949:

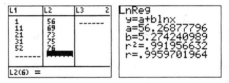

The model is $y = 56.269 + 5.274\ln x$.

For Exercise 25, we use a linear model with $x =$ the number of years after 1998:

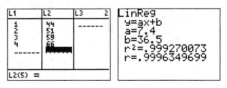

The model is $y = 7.4x + 36.5$.

Predictions will vary.

47. Use $T_0 = 210$, $C = 70$, $t = 30$, and $T = 140$ to determine the constant k:

$$T = C + (T_0 - C)e^{-kt}$$
$$140 = 70 + (210 - 70)e^{-k(30)}$$
$$140 = 70 + 140e^{-30k}$$
$$70 = 140e^{-30k}$$
$$\frac{70}{140} = \frac{140e^{-30k}}{140}$$
$$0.5 = e^{-30k}$$
$$\ln 0.5 = \ln e^{-30k}$$
$$\ln 0.5 = -30k$$
$$k = \frac{\ln 0.5}{-30} \approx 0.0231$$

Thus, the model for these conditions is $T = 70 + 140e^{-0.0231t}$.

Evaluate the model for $t = 40$:
$$T = 70 + 140e^{-0.0231(40)} \approx 126$$

Thus, the temperature of the cake after 40 minutes will be approximately $126°F$.

48.
$$\frac{x^2 - 9}{2x^2 + 7x + 3} \div \frac{x^2 - 3x}{2x^2 + 11x + 5}$$
$$= \frac{x^2 - 9}{2x^2 + 7x + 3} \cdot \frac{2x^2 + 11x + 5}{x^2 - 3x}$$
$$= \frac{(x+3)(x-3)}{(2x+1)(x+3)} \cdot \frac{(2x+1)(x+5)}{x(x-3)}$$
$$= \frac{x+5}{x}$$

49.
$$x^{\frac{2}{3}} + 2x^{\frac{1}{3}} - 3 = 0$$

Let $t = x^{\frac{1}{3}}$.
$$\left(x^{\frac{1}{3}}\right)^2 + 2x^{\frac{1}{3}} - 3 = 0$$
$$t^2 + 2t - 3 = 0$$
$$(t+3)(t-1) = 0$$

Apply the zero product principle.

$t + 3 = 0$ and $t - 1 = 0$

$\qquad t = -3 \qquad\qquad t = 1$

Substitute $x^{\frac{1}{3}}$ for t.

$\qquad x^{\frac{1}{3}} = -3 \qquad$ and $\qquad x^{\frac{1}{3}} = 1$

$\left(x^{\frac{1}{3}}\right)^3 = (-3)^3 \qquad \left(x^{\frac{1}{3}}\right)^3 = (1)^3$

$\qquad x = -27 \qquad\qquad\qquad x = 1$

The solution set is $\{-27, 1\}$.

50.
$$6\sqrt{2} - 2\sqrt{50} + 3\sqrt{98}$$
$$= 6\sqrt{2} - 2\sqrt{25 \cdot 2} + 3\sqrt{49 \cdot 2}$$
$$= 6\sqrt{2} - 2 \cdot 5\sqrt{2} + 3 \cdot 7\sqrt{2}$$
$$= 6\sqrt{2} - 10\sqrt{2} + 21\sqrt{2} = 17\sqrt{2}$$

Chapter 12 Review Exercises

1. $f(x) = 4^x$

x	$f(x)$
-2	$4^{-2} = \dfrac{1}{4^2} = \dfrac{1}{16}$
-1	$4^{-1} = \dfrac{1}{4^1} = \dfrac{1}{4}$
0	$4^0 = 1$
1	$4^1 = 4$
2	$4^2 = 16$

The coordinates match graph **d**.

2. $f(x) = 4^{-x}$

x	$f(x)$
-2	$4^{-(-2)} = 4^2 = 16$
-1	$4^{-(-1)} = 4^1 = 4$
0	$4^{-0} = 4^0 = 1$
1	$4^{-1} = \dfrac{1}{4^1} = \dfrac{1}{4}$
2	$4^{-2} = \dfrac{1}{4^2} = \dfrac{1}{16}$

The coordinates match graph **a.**

3. $f(x) = -4^{-x}$

x	$f(x)$
-2	$-4^{-(-2)} = -4^2 = -16$
-1	$-4^{-(-1)} = -4^1 = -4$
0	$-4^{-0} = -4^0 = -1$
1	$-4^{-1} = -\dfrac{1}{4^1} = -\dfrac{1}{4}$
2	$-4^{-2} = -\dfrac{1}{4^2} = -\dfrac{1}{16}$

The coordinates match graph **b.**

4. $f(x) = -4^{-x} + 3$

x	$f(x)$
−2	$-4^{-(-2)} + 3 = -4^2 + 3 = -16 + 3 = -13$
−1	$-4^{-(-1)} + 3 = -4^1 + 3 = -4 + 3 = -1$
0	$-4^{-0} + 3 = -4^0 + 3 = -1 + 3 = 2$
1	$-4^{-1} + 3 = -\dfrac{1}{4^1} + 3 = -\dfrac{1}{4} + 3 = \dfrac{11}{4}$
2	$-4^{-2} + 3 = -\dfrac{1}{4^2} + 3 = -\dfrac{1}{16} + 3 = \dfrac{47}{16}$

The coordinates match graph **c.**

5. $f(x) = 2^x$ and $g(x) = 2^{x-1}$

x	$f(x)$	$g(x)$
-2	$\dfrac{1}{4}$	$\dfrac{1}{8}$
-1	$\dfrac{1}{2}$	$\dfrac{1}{4}$
0	1	$\dfrac{1}{2}$
1	2	1
2	4	2

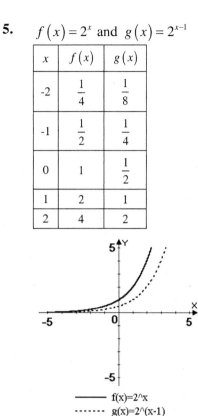

——— f(x)=2^x

········ g(x)=2^(x-1)

The graph of g is the graph of f shifted 1 unit to the right.

6. $f(x) = 2^x$ and $g(x) = \left(\dfrac{1}{2}\right)^x$

x	$f(x)$	$g(x)$
-2	$\dfrac{1}{4}$	4
-1	$\dfrac{1}{2}$	2
0	1	1
1	2	$\dfrac{1}{2}$
2	4	$\dfrac{1}{4}$

725

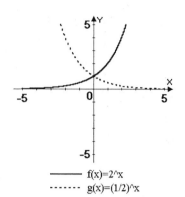

$f(x)=2^x$
$g(x)=(1/2)^x$

The graph of g is the graph of f reflected across the y–axis.

7. $f(x)=3^x$ and $g(x)=3^x-1$

x	$f(x)$	$g(x)$
-2	$\dfrac{1}{9}$	$-\dfrac{8}{9}$
-1	$\dfrac{1}{3}$	$-\dfrac{2}{3}$
0	1	0
1	3	2
2	9	8

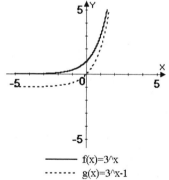

$f(x)=3^x$
$g(x)=3^x-1$

The graph of g is the graph of f shifted down 1 unit.

8. $f(x)=3^x$ and $g(x)=-3^x$

x	$f(x)$	$g(x)$
-2	$\dfrac{1}{9}$	$-\dfrac{1}{9}$
-1	$\dfrac{1}{3}$	$-\dfrac{1}{3}$
0	1	-1
1	3	-3
2	9	-9

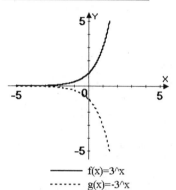

$f(x)=3^x$
$g(x)=-3^x$

The graph of g is the graph of f reflected across the x–axis.

9. 5.5% Compounded Semiannually:

$$A = 5000\left(1+\frac{0.055}{2}\right)^{2\cdot5}$$
$$= 5000(1+0.0275)^{10}$$
$$= 5000(1.0275)^{10} \approx 6558.26$$

5.25% Compounded Monthly:

$$A = 5000\left(1+\frac{0.0525}{12}\right)^{12\cdot5}$$
$$= 5000(1+0.004375)^{60}$$
$$= 5000(1.004375)^{60} \approx 6497.16$$

5.5% compounded semiannually yields the greater return.

10. 7.0% Compounded Monthly:

$$A = 14000\left(1 + \frac{0.07}{12}\right)^{12 \cdot 10}$$

$$= 14000\left(1 + \frac{7}{1200}\right)^{120}$$

$$= 14000\left(\frac{1207}{1200}\right)^{120} \approx 28135.26$$

6.85% Compounded Continuously:
$$A = 14000e^{0.0685 \cdot 10}$$

$$= 14000e^{0.685} \approx 27772.81$$

7.0% compounded monthly yields the greater return.

11. a. The coffee was $200°F$ when it was first taken out of the microwave.

    b. After 20 minutes, the temperature is approximately $119°F$.

    c. The coffee will cool to a low of $70°F$. This means that the temperature of the room is $70°F$.

12. $\dfrac{1}{2} = \log_{49} 7$

$$49^{\frac{1}{2}} = 7$$

13. $3 = \log_4 x$

$$4^3 = x$$

14. $\log_3 81 = y$

$$3^y = 81$$

15. $6^3 = 216$

$$\log_6 216 = 3$$

16. $b^4 = 625$

$$\log_b 625 = 4$$

17. $13^y = 874$

$$\log_{13} 874 = y$$

18. $\log_4 64 = \log_4 4^3 = 3$ because $\log_b b^x = x$.

19. $\log_5 \dfrac{1}{25} = \log_5 \dfrac{1}{5^2} = \log_5 5^{-2} = -2$

because $\log_b b^x = x$.

20. $\log_3(-9)$

This logarithm cannot be evaluated because -9 is not in the domain of $y = \log_3(-9)$.

21. $\log_{16} 4 = y$

$$16^y = 4$$

$$\left(4^2\right)^y = 4$$

$$4^{2y} = 4^1$$

$$2y = 1$$

$$y = \frac{1}{2}$$

22. $\log_{17} 17 = 1$ because $17^1 = 17$.

23. $\log_3 3^8 = 8$ because $\log_b b^x = x$.

24. Because $\ln e^x = x$, we conclude that $\ln e^5 = 5$.

25. $\log_3 \dfrac{1}{\sqrt{3}} = \log_3 \dfrac{1}{3^{\frac{1}{2}}} = \log_3 3^{-\frac{1}{2}} = -\dfrac{1}{2}$

because $\log_b b^x = x$.

26. $\ln \dfrac{1}{e^2} = \ln e^{-2} = -2$ because $\log_b b^x = x$.

27. $\log \dfrac{1}{1000} = \log \dfrac{1}{10^3} = \log 10^{-3} = -3$

because $\log_b b^x = x$.

28. Recall that $\log_b b = 1$ and $\log_b 1 = 0$ for all $b > 0$, $b \neq 1$. Therefore,

$$\log_3\left(\log_8 8\right) = \log_3 1 = 0.$$

29. $f(x) = 2^x;\ g(x) = \log_2 x$

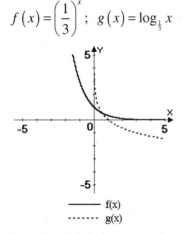

—— f(x)
······ g(x)

Domain of f: $\{x \mid x$ is a real number$\}$ or $(-\infty, \infty)$.

Range of f: $\{y \mid y > 0\}$ or $(0, \infty)$

Domain of g: $\{x \mid x > 0\}$ or $(0, \infty)$

Range of g: $\{y \mid y$ is a real number$\}$ or $(-\infty, \infty)$.

30.

$f(x) = \left(\dfrac{1}{3}\right)^x;\ g(x) = \log_{\frac{1}{3}} x$

—— f(x)
······ g(x)

Domain of f: $\{x \mid x$ is a real number$\}$ or $(-\infty, \infty)$.

Range of f: $\{y \mid y > 0\}$ or $(0, \infty)$

Domain of g: $\{x \mid x > 0\}$ or $(0, \infty)$

Range of g: $\{y \mid y$ is a real number$\}$ or $(-\infty, \infty)$.

31. $f(x) = \log_8 (x + 5)$

$x + 5 > 0$

$x > -5$

The domain of f is $\{x \mid x > -5\}$ or $(-5, \infty)$.

32. $f(x) = \log (3 - x)$

$3 - x > 0$

$-x > -3$

$x < 3$

The domain of f is $\{x \mid x < 3\}$ or $(-\infty, 3)$.

33. $f(x) = \ln (x - 1)^2$

The domain of g is all real numbers for which $(x - 1)^2 > 0$. The only number that must be excluded is 1. The domain of f is $\{x \mid x \neq 1\}$ or $(-\infty, 1) \cup (1, \infty)$.

34. Since $\ln e^x = x,\ \ln e^{6x} = 6x$.

35. Since $e^{\ln x} = x,\ e^{\ln \sqrt{x}} = \sqrt{x}$.

36. Since $10^{\log x} = x,\ 10^{\log 4x^2} = 4x^2$.

37.

$$R = \log \frac{I}{I_0}$$

$$R = \log \frac{1000 I_0}{I_0}$$

$$R = \log 1000$$

$$10^R = 1000$$

$$10^R = 10^3$$

$$R = 3$$

The magnitude on the Richter scale is 3.

38. a. $f(0) = 76 - 18\log(0+1)$

$\qquad = 76 - 18\log(1)$

$\qquad = 76 - 18(0) = 76 - 0 = 76$

The average score when the exam was first given was 76.

$f(2) = 76 - 18\log(2+1)$

$\qquad = 76 - 18\log(3) \approx 67.4$

$f(4) = 76 - 18\log(4+1)$

$\qquad = 76 - 18\log(5) \approx 63.4$

$f(6) = 76 - 18\log(6+1)$

$\qquad = 76 - 18\log(7) \approx 60.8$

$f(8) = 76 - 18\log(8+1)$

$\qquad = 76 - 18\log(9) \approx 58.8$

$f(12) = 76 - 18\log(12+1)$

$\qquad = 76 - 18\log(13) \approx 55.9$

The average scores were as follows:

2 months	67.4
4 months	63.4
6 months	60.8
8 months	58.8
12 months	55.9.

c.

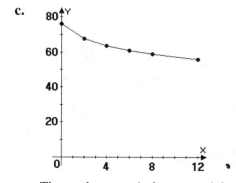

The students retain less material over time.

39. $t = \dfrac{1}{0.06}\ln\left(\dfrac{12}{12-5}\right)$

$\qquad = \dfrac{1}{0.06}\ln\left(\dfrac{12}{7}\right) \approx 9.0$

It will take approximately 9 weeks for the man to run 5 miles per hour.

40. $\log_6\left(36x^3\right) = \log_6 36 + \log_6 x^3$

$\qquad = 2 + 3\log_6 x$

41. $\log_4 \dfrac{\sqrt{x}}{64} = \log_4 \sqrt{x} - \log_4 64$

$\qquad = \log_4 x^{\frac{1}{2}} - 3 = \dfrac{1}{2}\log_4 x - 3$

42. $\log_2\left(\dfrac{xy^2}{64}\right) = \log_2 xy^2 - \log_2 64$

$\qquad = \log_2 x + \log_2 y^2 - 6$

$\qquad = \log_2 x + 2\log_2 y - 6$

43. $\ln\sqrt[3]{\dfrac{x}{e}} = \ln\left(\dfrac{x}{e}\right)^{\frac{1}{3}} = \dfrac{1}{3}\ln\left(\dfrac{x}{e}\right)$

$\qquad = \dfrac{1}{3}\left(\ln x - \ln e\right)$

$\qquad = \dfrac{1}{3}\left(\ln x - 1\right) = \dfrac{1}{3}\ln x - \dfrac{1}{3}$

44. $\log_b 7 + \log_b 3 = \log_b\left(7 \cdot 3\right) = \log_b 21$

45. $\log 3 - 3\log x = \log 3 - \log x^3 = \log \dfrac{3}{x^3}$

46. $3\ln x + 4\ln y = \ln x^3 + \ln y^4 = \ln\left(x^3 y^4\right)$

47. $\dfrac{1}{2}\ln x - \ln y = \ln x^{\frac{1}{2}} - \ln y$

$\qquad = \ln\sqrt{x} - \ln y = \ln\left(\dfrac{\sqrt{x}}{y}\right)$

48.
$$\log_6 72,348 = \frac{\log 72,348}{\log 6} \approx 6.2448$$

49.
$$\log_4 0.863 = \frac{\log 0.863}{\log 4} \approx -0.1063$$

50.
$$2^{4x-2} = 64$$
$$2^{4x-2} = 2^6$$
$$4x - 2 = 6$$
$$4x = 8$$
$$x = 2$$
The solution is 2, and the solution set is $\{2\}$.

51.
$$125^x = 25$$
$$\left(5^3\right)^x = 5^2$$
$$5^{3x} = 5^2$$
$$3x = 2$$
$$x = \frac{2}{3}$$
The solution is $\frac{2}{3}$, and the solution set is $\left\{\frac{2}{3}\right\}$.

52.
$$9^x = \frac{1}{27}$$
$$\left(3^2\right)^x = 3^{-3}$$
$$3^{2x} = 3^{-3}$$
$$2x = -3$$
$$x = -\frac{3}{2}$$
The solution is $-\frac{3}{2}$, and the solution set is $\left\{-\frac{3}{2}\right\}$.

53.
$$8^x = 12,143$$
$$\ln 8^x = \ln 12,143$$
$$x \ln 8 = \ln 12,143$$
$$x = \frac{\ln 12,143}{\ln 8} \approx 4.52$$
The solution set is $\left\{\frac{\ln 12,143}{\ln 8} \approx 4.52\right\}$.

54.
$$9e^{5x} = 1269$$
$$e^{5x} = \frac{1269}{9}$$
$$\ln e^{5x} = \ln 141$$
$$5x = \ln 141$$
$$x = \frac{\ln 141}{5} \approx 0.99$$
The solution set is $\left\{\frac{\ln 141}{5} \approx 0.99\right\}$.

55.
$$30e^{0.045x} = 90$$
$$e^{0.045x} = \frac{90}{30}$$
$$\ln e^{0.045x} = \ln 3$$
$$0.045x = \ln 3$$
$$x = \frac{\ln 3}{0.045} \approx 24.41$$
The solution set is $\left\{\frac{\ln 3}{0.045} \approx 24.41\right\}$.

56. $\log_5 x = -3$
$$x = 5^{-3}$$
$$x = \frac{1}{125}$$
The solution set is $\left\{\frac{1}{125}\right\}$.

57. $\log x = 2$
$$x = 10^2$$
$$x = 100$$
The solution set is $\{100\}$.

730

58. $\log_4(3x-5)=3$

$$3x-5=4^3$$
$$3x-5=64$$
$$3x=69$$
$$x=23$$

The solution set is $\{23\}$.

59. $\log_2(x+3)+\log_2(x-3)=4$

$$\log_2\big((x+3)(x-3)\big)=4$$
$$\log_2(x^2-9)=4$$
$$x^2-9=2^4$$
$$x^2-9=16$$
$$x^2=25$$
$$x=\pm 5$$

We disregard -5 because it would result in taking the logarithm of a negative number in the original equation. The solution set is $\{5\}$.

60. $\log_3(x-1)-\log_3(x+2)=2$

$$\log_3\frac{x-1}{x+2}=2$$
$$\frac{x-1}{x+2}=3^2$$
$$\frac{x-1}{x+2}=9$$
$$x-1=9(x+2)$$
$$x-1=9x+18$$
$$-8x-1=18$$
$$-8x=19$$
$$x=-\frac{19}{8}$$

We disregard $-\dfrac{19}{8}$ because it would result in taking the logarithm of a negative number in the original equation. There is no solution. The solution set is $\varnothing$ or $\{\ \}$.

61. $\ln x=-1$

$$x=e^{-1}$$
$$x=\frac{1}{e}$$

The solution set is $\left\{\dfrac{1}{e}\right\}$.

62. $3+4\ln 2x=15$

$$4\ln 2x=12$$
$$\ln 2x=3$$
$$2x=e^3$$
$$x=\frac{e^3}{2}$$

The solution set is $\left\{\dfrac{e^3}{2}\right\}$.

63. $P(x)=14.7e^{-0.21x}$

$$4.6=14.7e^{-0.21x}$$
$$\frac{4.6}{14.7}=e^{-0.21x}$$
$$\ln\frac{4.6}{14.7}=\ln e^{-0.21x}$$
$$\ln\frac{4.6}{14.7}=-0.21x$$
$$t=\frac{\ln\dfrac{4.6}{14.7}}{-0.21}\approx 5.5$$

The peak of Mt. Everest is about 5.5 miles above sea level.

731

64.
$$f(t) = 364(1.005)^t$$
$$560 = 364(1.005)^t$$
$$\frac{560}{364} = (1.005)^t$$
$$\ln\frac{560}{364} = \ln(1.005)^t$$
$$\ln\frac{560}{364} = t\ln 1.005$$
$$t = \frac{\ln\frac{560}{364}}{\ln 1.005} \approx 86.4$$

The carbon dioxide concentration will be double the pre-industrial level approximately 86 years after the year 2000 in the year 2086.

65. $W(x) = 0.37\ln x + 0.05$
$$3.38 = 0.37\ln x + 0.05$$
$$3.33 = 0.37\ln x$$
$$\frac{3.33}{0.37} = \ln x$$
$$9 = \ln x$$
$$e^9 = e^{\ln x}$$
$$x = e^9 \approx 8103$$

The population of New Your City is approximately 8103 thousand, or 8,103,000

66.
$$20,000 = 12,500\left(1 + \frac{0.065}{4}\right)^{4t}$$
$$20,000 = 12,500(1 + 0.01625)^{4t}$$
$$20,000 = 12,500(1.01625)^{4t}$$
$$\frac{20,000}{12,500} = (1.01625)^{4t}$$
$$1.6 = (1.01625)^{4t}$$
$$\ln 1.6 = \ln(1.01625)^{4t}$$
$$\ln 1.6 = 4t\ln 1.01625$$

$$\frac{\ln 1.6}{4\ln 1.01625} = \frac{4t\ln 1.01625}{4\ln 1.01625}$$
$$t = \frac{\ln 1.6}{4\ln 1.01625} \approx 7.3$$

It will take approximately 7.3 years.

67. $3(50,000) = 50,000e^{0.075t}$
$$\frac{3(50,000)}{50,000} = e^{0.075t}$$
$$3 = e^{0.075t}$$
$$\ln 3 = \ln e^{0.075t}$$
$$\ln 3 = 0.075t$$
$$t = \frac{\ln 3}{0.075} \approx 14.6$$

The money will triple in approximately 14.6 years.

68. $3 = e^{r5}$
$$\ln 3 = \ln e^{5r}$$
$$\ln 3 = 5r$$
$$r = \frac{\ln 3}{5} \approx 0.220$$

The money will triple in 5 years if the interest rate is approximately 22%.

69. a. $t = 2000 - 1990 = 10$
$$A = 22.4e^{kt}$$
$$35.3 = 22.46e^{k(10)}$$
$$\frac{35.3}{22.46} = e^{10k}$$
$$\ln\frac{35.3}{22.46} = \ln e^{10k}$$
$$\ln\frac{35.3}{22.46} = 10k$$
$$k = \frac{\ln\frac{35.3}{22.46}}{10} \approx 0.045$$

732

b. Note that 2010 is 20 years after 1990, find A for $t = 25$.

$A = 22.4e^{0.045(20)} = 22.4e^{0.9} \approx 55.1$

The population will be about 55.1 million the year 2010.

c.
$$60 = 22.4e^{0.045t}$$

$$\frac{60}{22.4} = e^{0.045t}$$

$$\ln\frac{60}{22.4} = \ln e^{0.045t}$$

$$\ln\frac{60}{22.4} = 0.045t$$

$$t = \frac{\ln\dfrac{60}{22.4}}{0.045t} \approx 22$$

Now, $1990 + 22 = 2012$, so the Hispanic resident population will reach 60 million approximately 30 years after 1990, in the year 2012.

70.
$$A = A_0 e^{-0.000121t}$$

$$15 = 100e^{-0.000121t}$$

$$\frac{15}{100} = e^{-0.000121t}$$

$$\ln\frac{3}{20} = \ln e^{-0.000121t}$$

$$\ln\frac{3}{20} = -0.000121t$$

$$t = \frac{\ln\dfrac{3}{20}}{-0.000121} \approx 15,679$$

The paintings are approximately 15,679 years old.

71. a.

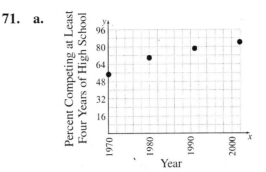

b. A logarithmic function appears to be the best choice for modeling the data.

72. a.

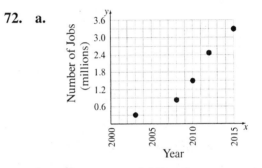

b. An exponential function appears to be the best choice for modeling the data.

73.
$$y = 73(2.6)^x$$
$$y = 73e^{(\ln 2.6)x}$$
$$y = 73e^{0.956x}$$

74.
$$y = 6.5(0.43)^x$$
$$y = 6.5e^{(\ln 0.43)x}$$
$$y = 6.5e^{-0.844x}$$

75. Answers will vary.

733

Chapter 12 Test

1. $f(x) = 2^x$

$g(x) = 2^{x+1}$

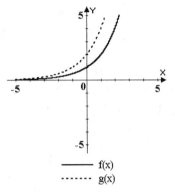

—— f(x)

······ g(x)

2. Semiannual Compounding:

$$A = 3000\left(1 + \frac{0.065}{2}\right)^{2(10)}$$

$$= 3000(1.0325)^{20} \approx 5687.51$$

Continuous Compounding:

$A = 3000e^{0.06(10)} = 3000e^{0.6} \approx 5466.36$

Semiannual compounding at 6.5% yields a greater return. The difference in the yields is $221.

3. $\log_5 125 = 3$

$5^3 = 125$

4. $\sqrt{36} = 6$

$36^{\frac{1}{2}} = 6$

$\log_{36} 6 = \frac{1}{2}$

5. $f(x) = 3^x$

$g(x) = \log_3 x$

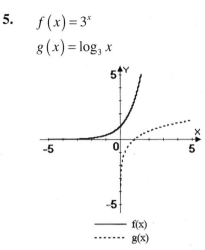

—— f(x)

······ g(x)

Domain of f: $\{x \mid x \text{ is a real number}\}$ or $(-\infty, \infty)$.

Range of f: $\{y \mid y > 0\}$ or $(0, \infty)$

Domain of g: $\{x \mid x > 0\}$ or $(0, \infty)$

Range of g: $\{y \mid y \text{ is a real number}\}$ or $(-\infty, \infty)$.

6. Since $\ln e^x = x$, $\ln e^{5x} = 5x$.

7. $\log_b b = 1$ because $b^1 = b$.

8. $\log_6 1 = 0$ because $6^0 = 1$.

9. $f(x) = \log_5(x - 7)$

$x - 7 > 0$

$x > 7$

The domain of f is $\{x \mid x > 7\}$ or $(7, \infty)$.

10.

$$D = 10\log\frac{I}{I_0}$$

$$D = 10\log\frac{10^{12} I_0}{I_0}$$

$$= 10\log 10^{12} = 10(12) = 120$$

The sound has a loudness of 120 decibels.

11. $\log_4\left(64x^5\right) = \log_4 64 + \log_4 x^5$

$\qquad = 3 + 5\log_4 x$

12. $\log_3 \dfrac{\sqrt[3]{x}}{81} = \log_3 \sqrt[3]{x} - \log_3 81$

$\qquad = \log_3 x^{\frac{1}{3}} - 4 = \dfrac{1}{3}\log_3 x - 4$

13. $6\log x + 2\log y = \log x^6 + \log y^2$

$\qquad = \log x^6 y^2$

14. $\ln 7 - 3\ln x = \ln 7 - \ln x^3 = \ln\left(\dfrac{7}{x^3}\right)$

15. $\log_{15} 71 = \dfrac{\ln 71}{\ln 15} \approx 1.5741$

16. $3^{x-2} = 81$

$3^{x-2} = 3^4$

$x - 2 = 4$

$x = 6$

The solution set is $\{6\}$.

17. $5^x = 1.4$

$\ln 5^x = \ln 1.4$

$x\ln 5 = \ln 1.4$

$x = \dfrac{\ln 1.4}{\ln 5} \approx 0.21$

The solution set is $\left\{\dfrac{\ln 1.4}{\ln 5} \approx 0.21\right\}$.

18. $400e^{0.005x} = 1600$

$e^{0.005x} = \dfrac{1600}{400}$

$\ln e^{0.005x} = \ln 4$

$0.005x = \ln 4$

$x = \dfrac{\ln 4}{0.005} \approx 277.26$

The solution set is $\left\{\dfrac{\ln 4}{0.005} \approx 277.26\right\}$.

19. $\log_{25} x = \dfrac{1}{2}$

$x = 25^{\frac{1}{2}} = \sqrt{25} = 5$

The solution set is $\{5\}$.

20. $\log_6\left(4x - 1\right) = 3$

$4x - 1 = 6^3$

$4x - 1 = 216$

$4x = 217$

$x = \dfrac{217}{4}$

The solution set is $\left\{\dfrac{217}{4}\right\}$.

21. $\log x + \log\left(x + 15\right) = 2$

$\log\left(x\left(x + 15\right)\right) = 2$

$x\left(x + 15\right) = 10^2$

$x^2 + 15 = 100$

$x^2 + 15 - 100 = 0$

$\left(x + 20\right)\left(x - 5\right) = 0$

Apply the zero product principle.

$x + 20 = 0 \qquad$ and $\quad x - 5 = 0$

$\qquad x = -20 \qquad\qquad\quad x = 5$

We disregard -20 because it would result in taking the logarithm of a negative number in the original equation. The solution set is $\{5\}$.

22. $2\ln 3x = 8$

$\ln 3x = \dfrac{8}{2}$

$e^{\ln 3x} = e^4$

$3x = e^4$

$x = \dfrac{e^4}{3}$

The solution set is $\left\{\dfrac{e^4}{3}\right\}$.

735

23. a. $P(0) = 82.3e^{-0.002(0)}$

$= 82.3e^0 = 82.3(1) = 82.3$

In 2003, the population of Germany was 82.3 million.

b. The population of Germany is decreasing. We can tell the model has a negative, $k = -0.002$.

c. $81.5 = 82.3e^{-0.002t}$

$\dfrac{81.5}{82.3} = e^{-0.002t}$

$\ln \dfrac{81.5}{82.3} = \ln e^{-0.002t}$

$\ln \dfrac{81.5}{82.3} = -0.002t$

$t = \dfrac{\ln \dfrac{81.5}{82.3}}{-0.002} \approx 5$

The population of Germany will be 81.5 million approximately 5 years after 2003 in the year 2008.

24.

$8000 = 4000\left(1 + \dfrac{0.05}{4}\right)^{4t}$

$\dfrac{8000}{4000} = (1 + 0.0125)^{4t}$

$2 = (1.0125)^{4t}$

$\ln 2 = \ln (1.0125)^{4t}$

$\ln 2 = 4t \ln (1.0125)$

$\dfrac{\ln 2}{4\ln (1.0125)} = \dfrac{4t \ln (1.0125)}{4\ln (1.0125)}$

$t = \dfrac{\ln 2}{4\ln (1.0125)} \approx 13.9$

It will take approximately 13.9 years for the money to grow to $8000.

25. $2 = 1e^{r10}$

$2 = e^{10r}$

$\ln 2 = \ln e^{10r}$

$\ln 2 = 10r$

$r = \dfrac{\ln 2}{10} \approx 0.069$

The money will double in 10 years with an interest rate of approximately 6.9%.

26. Substitute $A_0 = 509$, $A = 729$, and $t = 2000 - 1990 = 10$ into the general growth function to determine the growth rate k:

$A = A_0 e^{kt}$

$729 = 509e^{k(10)}$

$\dfrac{729}{509} = e^{10k}$

$\ln \dfrac{729}{509} = \ln e^{10k}$

$\ln \dfrac{729}{509} = 10k$

$k = \dfrac{\ln \dfrac{729}{509}}{10} \approx 0.036$

The exponential growth function is $A = 484e^{0.005t}$.

27. $A = A_0 e^{-0.000121t}$

$5 = 100e^{-0.000121t}$

$\dfrac{5}{100} = e^{-0.000121t}$

$\ln 0.05 = \ln e^{-0.000121t}$

$\ln 0.05 = -0.000121t$

$t = \dfrac{\ln 0.05}{-0.000121} \approx 24758$

The man died approximately 24,758 years ago.

28.

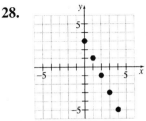

The values appear to belong to a linear function.

29.

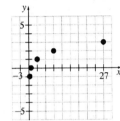

The values appear to belong to a logarithmic function.

30.

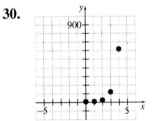

The values appear to belong to an exponential function.

31.

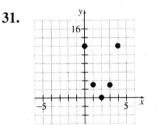

The values appear to belong to a quadratic function.

32.

$$y = 96(0.38)^x$$

$$y = 96e^{(\ln 0.38)x}$$

$$y = 96e^{-0.968x}$$

Cumulative Review Exercises
(Chapters 1 – 12)

1. $9(x-1) = 1 + 3(x-2)$

$$9x - 9 = 1 + 3x - 6$$

$$9x - 9 = 3x - 5$$

$$6x - 9 = -5$$

$$6x = 4$$

$$x = \frac{4}{6} = \frac{2}{3}$$

The solution set is $\left\{\dfrac{2}{3}\right\}$.

2. $3x + 4y = -7$

$x - 2y = -9$

Multiply the second equation by 2 and add the result to the first equation:

$3x + 4y = -7$

$\underline{2x - 4y = -18}$

$5x \qquad = -25$

$x = -5$

Back substitute into the second equation:

$$-5 - 2y = -9$$

$$-2y = -4$$

$$y = 2$$

The solution set is $\{(-5, 2)\}$.

3. $x - y + 3z = -9$

$2x + 3y - z = 16$

$5x + 2y - z = 15$

Multiply the second equation by 3 and add to the first equation to eliminate z.

$x - y + 3z = -9$

$\underline{6x + 9y - 3z = 48}$

$7x + 8y \qquad = 39$

Multiply the second equation by -1 and add to the third equation.

$-2x - 3y + z = -16$

$\underline{5x + 2y - z = 15}$

$3x - y \quad = -1$

We now have a system of two equations in two variables.

$7x + 8y = 39$

$3x - y = -1$

Multiply the second equation by 8 and add to the second equation.

$7x + 8y = 39$

$\underline{24x - 8y = -8}$

$31x \quad = 31$

$x = 1$

Back-substitute 1 for x to find y.

$3x - y = -1$

$3(1) - y = -1$

$3 - y = -1$

$-y = -4$

$y = 4$

Back-substitute 1 for x and 4 for y to find z.

$x - y + 3z = -9$

$1 - 4 + 3z = -9$

$-3 + 3z = -9$

$3z = -6$

$z = -2$

The solution set is $\{(1, 4, -2)\}$.

4. $7x + 18 \le 9x - 2$

$-2x + 18 \le -2$

$-2x \le -20$

$\dfrac{-2x}{-2} \ge \dfrac{-20}{-2}$

$x \ge 10$

The solution set is $\{x \mid x \ge 10\}$ or $[10, \infty)$.

5. $4x - 3 < 13$ and $-3x - 4 \ge 8$

$4x < 16 \qquad -3x \ge 12$

$x < 4 \qquad x \le -4$

For a value to be in the solution set, it must be both less than 4 and less than or equal to -4. Now only values that are less than or equal to -4 meet both conditions. Therefore, the solution set is $\{x \mid x \le -4\}$ or $(-\infty, -4]$.

6. $2x + 4 > 8$ or $x - 7 \ge 3$

$2x > 4 \qquad x \ge 10$

$x > 2$

For a value to be in the solution set, it must either one of the conditions. Now, all numbers that are greater than or equal to 10 are also greater than 2. Therefore, the solution set is $\{x \mid x > 2\}$ or $(2, \infty)$.

7. $|2x - 1| < 5$

$-5 < 2x - 1 < 5$

$-4 < 2x < 6$

$-2 < x < 3$

The solution set is $\{x \mid -2 < x < 3\}$ or $(-2, 3)$.

8. $\left| \dfrac{2}{3}x - 4 \right| = 2$

$\dfrac{2}{3}x - 4 = -2$ or $\dfrac{2}{3}x - 4 = 2$

$3\left(\dfrac{2}{3}x - 4\right) = 3(-2) \qquad 3\left(\dfrac{2}{3}x - 4\right) = 3(2)$

$2x - 12 = -6 \qquad 2x - 12 = 6$

$2x = 6 \qquad 2x = 18$

$x = 3 \qquad x = 9$

The solution set is $\{3, 9\}$.

9.

$$\frac{4}{x-3} - \frac{6}{x+3} = \frac{24}{x^2 - 9}$$

$$\frac{4}{x-3} - \frac{6}{x+3} = \frac{24}{(x-3)(x+3)}$$

$$(x-3)(x+3)\left[\frac{4}{x-3} - \frac{6}{x+3}\right] = (x-3)(x+3)\left[\frac{24}{(x-3)(x+3)}\right]$$

$$4(x+3) - 6(x-3) = 24$$

$$4x + 12 - 6x + 18 = 24$$

$$-2x + 30 = 24$$

$$-2x = -6$$

$$x = 3$$

We disregard 3 since it cause a result of 0 in the denominator of a fraction. Thus, the equation has no solution. The solution set is $\varnothing$ or $\{\ \}$.

10. $\sqrt{x+4} - \sqrt{x-3} = 1$

$$\sqrt{x+4} = \sqrt{x-3} + 1$$

$$\left(\sqrt{x+4}\right)^2 = \left(\sqrt{x-3} + 1\right)^2$$

$$x + 4 = (x-3) + 2\sqrt{x-3} + 1$$

$$x + 4 = x - 2 + 2\sqrt{x-3}$$

$$6 = 2\sqrt{x-3}$$

$$3 = \sqrt{x-3}$$

$$(3)^2 = \left(\sqrt{x-3}\right)^2$$

$$9 = x - 3$$

$$12 = x$$

Since we square both sides of the equation, we must check to make sure 12 is not extraneous:

$$\sqrt{12+4} - \sqrt{12-3} = 1$$

$$\sqrt{16} - \sqrt{9} = 1$$

$$4 - 3 = 1$$

$$1 = 1 \quad \text{True}$$

Thus, the solution set is $\{12\}$.

11.

$$2x^2 = 5 - 4x$$

$$2x^2 + 4x - 5 = 0$$

Apply the quadratic formula:

$$a = 2 \quad b = 4 \quad c = -5$$

$$x = \frac{-4 \pm \sqrt{4^2 - 4(2)(-5)}}{2(2)}$$

$$= \frac{-4 \pm \sqrt{56}}{4}$$

$$= \frac{-4 \pm \sqrt{4 \cdot 14}}{4}$$

$$= \frac{-4 \pm 2\sqrt{14}}{4} = \frac{-2 \pm \sqrt{14}}{2}$$

The solutions are $\dfrac{-2 \pm \sqrt{14}}{2}$, and the

solution set is $\left\{\dfrac{-2 \pm \sqrt{14}}{2}\right\}$.

12. $x^{\frac{2}{3}} - 5x^{\frac{1}{3}} + 6 = 0$

$$\left(x^{\frac{1}{3}}\right)^2 - 5x^{\frac{1}{3}} + 6 = 0$$

Let $t = x^{\frac{1}{3}}$.

$$t^2 - 5t + 6 = 0$$

$$(t-3)(t-2) = 0$$

Apply the zero-product principle:

$t - 3 = 0$ or $t - 2 = 0$

$\quad t = 3 \qquad\qquad t = 2$

Substitute $x^{\frac{1}{3}}$ back in for t.

$\quad x^{\frac{1}{3}} = 3 \qquad$ or $\qquad x^{\frac{1}{3}} = 2$

$\left(x^{\frac{1}{3}}\right)^3 = 3^3 \qquad \left(x^{\frac{1}{3}}\right)^3 = 2^3$

$\quad x = 27 \qquad\qquad x = 8$

The solution set is $\{8, 27\}$.

13. $2x^2 + x - 6 \le 0$

Solve the related quadratic equation.

$$2x^2 + x - 6 = 0$$

$$(2x-3)(x+2) = 0$$

Apply the zero product principle.

$2x - 3 = 0 \quad$ or $\quad x + 2 = 0$

$\quad 2x = 3 \qquad\qquad x = -2$

$\quad x = \dfrac{3}{2}$

The boundary points are -2 and $\dfrac{3}{2}$.

Test Interval	Test No.	Test	Conclusion
$(-\infty, -2)$	-3	$2(-3)^2 + (-3) - 6 \le 0$ $9 \le 0,$ False	$(-\infty, -2)$ does not belong to the solution set.
$\left(-2, \dfrac{3}{2}\right)$	0	$2(0)^2 + 0 - 6 \le 0$ $-6 \le 0,$ True	$\left(-2, \dfrac{3}{2}\right)$ belongs to the solution set.
$\left(\dfrac{3}{2}, \infty\right)$	2	$2(2)^2 + 2 - 6 \le 0$ $4 \le 0,$ False	$\left(\dfrac{3}{2}, \infty\right)$ does not belong to the solution set.

The solution set is $\left[-2, \dfrac{3}{2}\right]$ or $\left\{x \middle| -2 \le x \le \dfrac{3}{2}\right\}$.

14. $\log_8 x + \log_8(x+2) = 1$

$$\log_8\left[x(x+2)\right] = 1$$

$$\log_8\left[x^2 + 2x\right] = 1$$

$$x^2 + 2x = 8^1$$

$$x^2 + 2x - 8 = 0$$

$$(x+4)(x-2) = 0$$

Apply the zero product principle.

$x + 4 = 0 \quad$ and $\quad x - 2 = 0$

$\quad x = -4 \qquad\qquad x = 2$

We disregard -4 because it would result in taking the logarithm of a negative number in the original equation. The solution set is $\{2\}$.

15. $5^{2x+3} = 125$

$$5^{2x+3} = 5^3$$

$$2x + 3 = 3$$

$$2x = 0$$

$$x = 0$$

The solution set is $\{0\}$.

16. $x - 3y = 6$

$$-3y = -x + 6$$

$$y = \frac{-x + 6}{-3}$$

$$y = \frac{1}{3}x - 2$$

The slope is $m = \frac{1}{3}$ and the y-intercept

is $b = -2$.

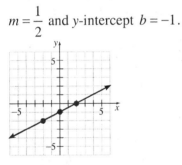

17.

$$f(x) = \frac{1}{2}x - 1$$

This is a linear function with slope

$m = \frac{1}{2}$ and y-intercept $b = -1$.

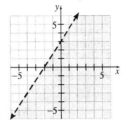

18. $3x - 2y > -6$

First, graph the equation $3x - 2y = -6$
as a dashed line.

$$3x - 2y = -6$$

$$-2y = -3x - 6$$

$$y = \frac{-3x - 6}{-2}$$

$$y = \frac{3}{2}x + 3$$

The slope is $m = \frac{3}{2}$ and the y-intercept

is $b = 3$. Use the origin as a test point.

$$3(0) - 2(0) > -6$$

$$0 > -6$$

This is a true statement. This means
that the point, $(0,0)$, will fall in the
shaded half-plane.

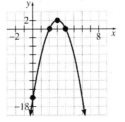

19. $f(x) = -2(x - 3)^2 + 2$

Since $a = -2$ is negative, the parabola
opens downward. The vertex of the
parabola is $(h, k) = (3, 2)$. Replace

$f(x)$ with 0 to find x–intercepts.

$$0 = -2(x - 3)^2 + 2$$

$$2(x - 3)^2 = 2$$

$$(x - 3)^2 = 1$$

$$x - 3 = \pm 1$$

$$x = 3 \pm 1$$

$$x = 3 - 1 \text{ or } 3 + 1$$

$$x = 2 \text{ or } 4$$

The x–intercepts are -1 and 4.

Set $x = 0$ to obtain the y–intercept.

$$f(0) = -2(0 - 3)^2 + 2$$

$$= -2(-3)^2 + 2$$

$$= -2(9) + 2 = -18 + 2 = -16$$

The y-intercept is -16.

741

20. $y = \log_2 x$

x	$y = \log_2 x$
$\dfrac{1}{4}$	-2
$\dfrac{1}{2}$	-1
1	0
2	1
4	2

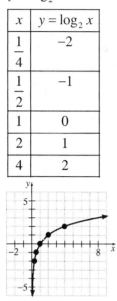

21. $4\big[2x - 6(x-y)\big] = 4(2x - 6x + 6y)$

$$= 4(-4x + 6y)$$
$$= -16x + 24y$$

22. $\left(-5x^3 y^2\right)\left(4x^4 y^{-6}\right) = -20x^{3+4} y^{2+(-6)}$

$$= -20x^7 y^{-4}$$
$$= -\frac{20x^7}{y^4}$$

23. $\left(8x^2 - 9xy - 11y^2\right) - \left(7x^2 - 4xy + 5y^2\right)$

$$= 8x^2 - 9xy - 11y^2 - 7x^2 + 4xy - 5y^2$$
$$= x^2 - 5xy - 16y^2$$

24. $(3x - 1)(2x + 5) = 6x^2 + 15x - 2x - 1$

$$= 6x^2 + 13x - 1$$

25. $\left(3x^2 - 4y\right)^2$

$$= \left(3x^2\right)^2 - 2\left(3x^2\right)(4y) + (4y)^2$$
$$= 9x^4 - 24x^2 y + 16y^2$$

26. $\dfrac{3x}{x+5} - \dfrac{2}{x^2 + 7x + 10}$

$$= \frac{3x}{x+5} - \frac{2}{(x+5)(x+2)}$$
$$= \frac{3x}{x+5} \cdot \frac{(x+2)}{(x+2)} - \frac{2}{(x+5)(x+2)}$$
$$= \frac{3x^2 + 6x}{(x+5)(x+2)} - \frac{2}{(x+5)(x+2)}$$
$$= \frac{3x^2 + 6x - 2}{(x-5)(x+2)}$$

27. $\dfrac{1 - \dfrac{9}{x^2}}{1 + \dfrac{3}{x}} = \dfrac{1 - \dfrac{9}{x^2}}{1 + \dfrac{3}{x}} \cdot \dfrac{x^2}{x^2}$

$$= \frac{x^2 - 9}{x^2 + 3x}$$
$$= \frac{(x-3)(x+3)}{x(x+3)} = \frac{x-3}{x}$$

28. $\dfrac{x^2 - 6x + 8}{3x + 9} \div \dfrac{x^2 - 4}{x + 3}$

$$= \frac{x^2 - 6x + 8}{3x + 9} \cdot \frac{x + 3}{x^2 - 4}$$
$$= \frac{(x-4)(x-2)}{3(x+3)} \cdot \frac{x+3}{(x-2)(x+2)}$$
$$= \frac{x-4}{3(x+2)} \quad \text{or} \quad \frac{x-4}{3x+6}$$

29. $\sqrt{5xy} \cdot \sqrt{10x^2 y} = \sqrt{50x^3 y^2}$

$$= \sqrt{25 \cdot 2 \cdot x^2 \cdot x \cdot y^2}$$
$$= 5xy\sqrt{2x}$$

30.
$$4\sqrt{72} - 3\sqrt{50} = 4\sqrt{36\cdot 2} - 3\sqrt{25\cdot 2}$$
$$= 4\cdot 6\sqrt{2} - 3\cdot 5\sqrt{2}$$
$$= 45\sqrt{2} - 15\sqrt{2}$$
$$= 9\sqrt{2}$$

31.
$$(5+3i)(7-3i) = 35 - 15i + 21i - 9i^2$$
$$= 35 + 6i - 9(-1)$$
$$= 35 + 6i + 9$$
$$= 44 + 6i$$

32.
$$81x^4 - 1 = (9x^2 + 1)(9x^2 - 1)$$
$$= (9x^2 + 1)(3x+1)(3x-1)$$

33.
$$24x^3 - 22x^2 + 4x = 2x(12x^2 - 11x + 2)$$
$$= 2x(4x-1)(3x-2)$$

34.
$$x^3 + 27y^3 = x^3 + (3y)^3$$
$$= (x+3y)\left[x^2 - x(3y) + (3y)^2\right]$$
$$= (x+3y)(x^2 - 3xy + 9y^2)$$

35.
$$(f-g)(x) = f(x) - g(x)$$
$$= (x^2 + 3x - 15) - (x-2)$$
$$= x^2 + 3x - 15 - x + 2$$
$$= x^2 + 2x - 13$$
$$(f-g)(5) = 5^2 + 2\cdot 5 - 13$$
$$= 25 + 10 - 13 = 22$$

36.
$$\left(\frac{f}{g}\right)(x) = \frac{f(x)}{g(x)} = \frac{x^2 + 3x - 15}{x-2}$$

The domain of $\dfrac{f}{g}$ is
$\{x \mid x \text{ is a real number and } x \neq 2\}$ or
$(-\infty, 2) \cup (2, \infty)$.

37.
$$f(g(x)) = \left[g(x)\right]^2 + 3\left[g(x)\right] - 15$$
$$= (x-2)^2 + 3(x-2) - 15$$
$$= x^2 - 4x + 4 + 3x - 6 - 15$$
$$= x^2 - x - 17$$

38.
$$g(f(x)) = f(x) - 2$$
$$= (x^2 + 3x - 15) - 2$$
$$= x^2 + 3 - 17$$

39.
$$f(x) = 7x - 3$$
$$y = 7x - 3$$
Interchange x and y, and solve for y.
$$x = 7y - 3$$
$$x + 3 = 7y$$
$$\frac{x+3}{7} = y$$
Thus, $f^{-1}(x) = \dfrac{x+3}{7}$.

40.

$$\begin{array}{r|rrrr} -2 & 3 & -1 & 4 & 8 \\ & & -6 & 14 & -36 \\ \hline & 3 & -7 & 18 & -28 \end{array}$$

$$(3x^3 - x^2 + 4x + 8) \div (x+2)$$
$$= 3x^2 - 7x + 18 - \frac{28}{x+2}$$

41.
$$I = \frac{R}{R+r}$$
$$I(R+r) = R$$
$$IR + Ir = R$$
$$Ir = R - IR$$
$$Ir = (1-I)R$$
$$\frac{Ir}{1-I} = R \quad \text{or} \quad R = -\frac{Ir}{I-1}$$

743

42. $3x + y = 9$

$y = -3x + 9$

The line whose equation we want to find has a slope of $m = -3$, the same as that of the line above. Using this slope with the point through with the line passes, $(-2, 5)$, we first find the point-slope equation and then put it in slope-intercept form.

$y - y_1 = m(x - x_1)$

$y - 5 = -3(x - (-2))$

$y - 5 = -3(x + 2)$

$y - 5 = -3x - 6$

$y = -3x - 1$

The slope-intercept equation of the line is through $(-2, 5)$ and parallel to $3x + y = 9$ is $y = -3x - 1$.

43.

$2 \ln x - \dfrac{1}{2} \ln y = \ln x^2 - \ln y^{\frac{1}{2}}$

$= \ln \left(\dfrac{x^2}{y^{\frac{1}{2}}} \right) = \ln \left(\dfrac{x^2}{\sqrt{y}} \right)$

44.

$f(x) = \dfrac{x - 2}{x^2 - 3x + 2}$

Since a denominator cannot equal zero, exclude from the domain all values which make $x^2 - 3x + 2 = 0$.

$x^2 - 3x + 2 = 0$

$(x - 2)(x - 1) = 0$

Apply the zero-product principle.

$x - 2 = 0$ or $x - 1 = 0$

$x = 2$ $x = 1$

The domain of f is $\{x \mid x$ is a real number and $x \neq 1$ and $x \neq 2\}$ or $(-\infty, 1) \cup (1, 2) \cup (2, \infty)$.

45. $f(x) = \ln(2x - 8)$

To find the domain, find all values of x for which $2x - 8$ is greater than zero.

$2x - 8 > 0$

$2x > 8$

$x > 4$

The domain of f is $\{x \mid x > 4\}$ or $(4, \infty)$.

46. Let $x = $ the computer's original price.

$x - 0.30x = 434$

$0.70x = 434$

$x = \dfrac{434}{0.70} = 620$

The original price of the computer was $620.

47. Let $x = $ the width of the rectangle; $3x + 1 = $ the length of the rectangle.

$x(3x + 1) = 52$

$3x^2 + x - 52 = 0$

$(3x + 13)(x - 4) = 0$

Apply the zero-product principle:

$3x + 13 = 0$ or $x - 4 = 0$

$x = -\dfrac{13}{3}$ $x = 4$

Disregard $-\dfrac{13}{3}$ because the width of a rectangle cannot be negative. If $x = 4$, then $3x + 1 = 3(4) + 1 = 13$. Thus, the length of the rectangle is 13 yards and the width is 4 yards.

744

48. Let x = the amount invested at 12%;
$4000 - x$ = the amount invested at 14%.

$$0.12x + 0.14(4000 - x) = 508$$
$$0.12x + 560 - 0.14x = 508$$
$$-0.02x + 560 = 508$$
$$-0.02x = -52$$
$$x = 2600$$

$4000 - x = 4000 - 2600 = 1400$

Thus, $2600 was invested at 12% and $1400 was invested at 14%.

49.
$$A = Pe^{rt}$$
$$18,000 = 6000e^{r(10)}$$
$$3 = e^{10r}$$
$$\ln 3 = \ln e^{10r}$$
$$\ln 3 = 10r$$
$$r = \frac{\ln 3}{10} \approx 0.11$$

An interest rate of approximately 11% compounded continuously would be required for $6000 to grow to $18,000 in 10 years.

50. Because I varies inversely as R, we have the following for a constant k:

$$I = \frac{k}{R}$$

Use the fact that $I = 5$ when $R = 22$ to find k:

$$5 = \frac{k}{22}$$
$$k = 22 \cdot 5 = 110$$

Thus, the equation relating I and R is

$$I = \frac{110}{R}.$$

If $R = 10$, then $I = \frac{110}{10} = 11$.

A current of 11 amperes is required when the resistance is 10 ohms.

Chapter 13
Conic Sections and Systems of Nonlinear Equations

13.1 Exercise Set

1.
$$(x-h)^2 + (y-k)^2 = r^2$$
$$(x-0)^2 + (y-0)^2 = 7^2$$
$$x^2 + y^2 = 49$$

3.
$$(x-h)^2 + (y-k)^2 = r^2$$
$$(x-3)^2 + (y-2)^2 = 5^2$$
$$(x-3)^2 + (y-2)^2 = 25$$

5.
$$(x-h)^2 + (y-k)^2 = r^2$$
$$(x-(-1))^2 + (y-4)^2 = 2^2$$
$$(x+1)^2 + (y-4)^2 = 4$$

7.
$$(x-h)^2 + (y-k)^2 = r^2$$
$$(x-(-3))^2 + (y-(-1))^2 = \left(\sqrt{3}\right)^2$$
$$(x+3)^2 + (y+1)^2 = 3$$

9.
$$(x-h)^2 + (y-k)^2 = r^2$$
$$(x-(-4))^2 + (y-0)^2 = 10^2$$
$$(x+4)^2 + y^2 = 100$$

11.
$$x^2 + y^2 = 16$$
$$(x-0)^2 + (y-0)^2 = 4^2$$

The center is $(0,0)$ and the radius is 4 units.

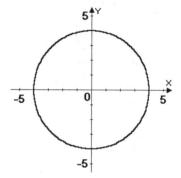

13.
$$(x-3)^2 + (y-1)^2 = 36$$
$$(x-3)^2 + (y-1)^2 = 6^2$$

The center is $(3,1)$ and the radius is 6 units.

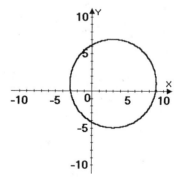

746

15.
$$(x+3)^2 + (y-2)^2 = 4$$
$$(x-(-3))^2 + (y-2)^2 = 2^2$$

The center is $(-3,2)$ and the radius is 2 units.

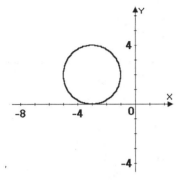

$$(x^2 + 6x + 9) + (y^2 + 2y + 1) = -6 + 9 + 1$$
T
$$(x+3)^2 + (y+1)^2 = 4$$

he center is $(-3,-1)$ and the radius is 2 units.

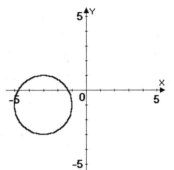

17.
$$(x+2)^2 + (y+2)^2 = 4$$
$$(x-(-2))^2 + (y-(-2))^2 = 2^2$$

The center is $(-2,-2)$ and the radius is 2 units.

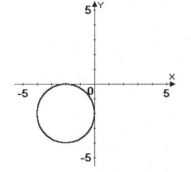

21.
$$x^2 + y^2 - 10x - 6y - 30 = 0$$
$$(x^2 - 10x \quad) + (y^2 - 6y \quad) = 30$$

Complete the squares.

$$\left(\frac{b}{2}\right)^2 = \left(\frac{-10}{2}\right)^2 = (-5)^2 = 25$$

$$\left(\frac{b}{2}\right)^2 = \left(\frac{-6}{2}\right)^2 = (-3)^2 = 9$$

$$(x^2 - 10x + 25) + (y^2 - 6y + 9) = 30 + 25 + 9$$

$$(x-5)^2 + (y-3)^2 = 64$$

The center is $(5,3)$ and the radius is 8 units.

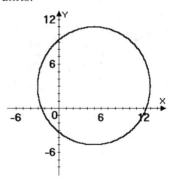

19.
$$x^2 + y^2 + 6x + 2y + 6 = 0$$
$$(x^2 + 6x \quad) + (y^2 + 2y \quad) = -6$$

Complete the squares.

$$\left(\frac{b}{2}\right)^2 = \left(\frac{6}{2}\right)^2 = (3)^2 = 9$$

$$\left(\frac{b}{2}\right)^2 = \left(\frac{2}{2}\right)^2 = (1)^2 = 1$$

23.
$$x^2 + y^2 + 8x - 2y - 8 = 0$$
$$\left(x^2 + 8x \quad\right) + \left(y^2 - 2y \quad\right) = 8$$
Complete the squares.
$$\left(\frac{b}{2}\right)^2 = \left(\frac{8}{2}\right)^2 = (4)^2 = 16$$
$$\left(\frac{b}{2}\right)^2 = \left(\frac{-2}{2}\right)^2 = (-1)^2 = 4$$
$$\left(x^2 + 8x + 16\right) + \left(y^2 - 2y + 1\right) = 8 + 16 + 1$$
$$\left(x + 4\right)^2 + \left(y - 1\right)^2 = 25$$
The center is $(-4, 1)$ and the radius is 5 units.

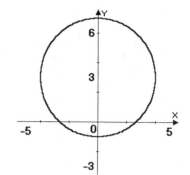

27.

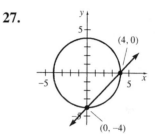

Intersection points: $(0, -4)$ and $(4, 0)$

Check $(0, -4)$:
$$0^2 + (-4)^2 = 16 \qquad 0 - (-4) = 4$$
$$16 = 16 \text{ true} \qquad 4 = 4 \text{ true}$$

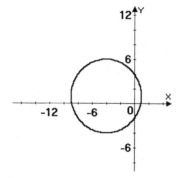

25.
$$x^2 - 2x + y^2 - 15 = 0$$
$$\left(x^2 - 2x \quad\right) + y^2 = 15$$
Complete the squares.
$$\left(\frac{b}{2}\right)^2 = \left(\frac{-2}{2}\right)^2 = (-1)^2 = 1$$
$$\left(x^2 - 2x + 1\right) + y^2 = 15 + 1$$
$$\left(x - 1\right)^2 + y^2 = 16$$
The center is $(1, 0)$ and the radius is 4 units.

Check $(4, 0)$:
$$4^2 + 0^2 = 16 \qquad 4 - 0 = 4$$
$$16 = 16 \text{ true} \qquad 4 = 4 \text{ true}$$
The solution set is $\{(0, -4), (4, 0)\}$.

28.

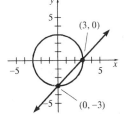

Intersection points: $(0,-3)$ and $(3,0)$

Check $(0,-3)$:

$0^2 + (-3)^2 = 9 \qquad 0 - (-3) = 3$

$\qquad 9 = 9$ true $\qquad 3 = 3$ true

Check $(3,0)$:

$3^2 + 0^2 = 9 \qquad 3 - 0 = 3$

$\qquad 9 = 9$ true $\qquad 3 = 3$ true

The solution set is $\{(0,-3),(3,0)\}$.

29.

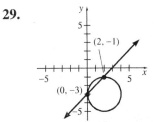

Intersection points: $(0,-3)$ and $(2,-1)$

Check $(0,-3)$:

$(0-2)^2 + (-3+3)^2 = 9 \qquad -3 = 0 - 3$

$\qquad (-2)^2 + 0^2 = 4 \qquad -3 = -3$ true

$\qquad\qquad 4 = 4$

$\qquad\qquad\qquad$ true

Check $(2,-1)$:

$(2-2)^2 + (-1+3)^2 = 4 \qquad -1 = 2 - 3$

$\qquad 0^2 + 2^2 = 4 \qquad -1 = -1$ true

$\qquad\qquad 4 = 4$

$\qquad\qquad\qquad$ true

The solution set is $\{(0,-3),(2,-1)\}$.

30.

Intersection points: $(0,-1)$ and $(3,2)$

Check $(0,-1)$:

$(0-3)^2 + (-1+1)^2 = 9 \qquad -1 = 0 - 1$

$\qquad (-3)^2 + 0^2 = 9 \qquad -1 = -1$ true

$\qquad\qquad 9 = 9$

$\qquad\qquad\qquad$ true

Check $(3,2)$:

$(3-3)^2 + (2+1)^2 = 9 \qquad 2 = 3 - 1$

$\qquad 0^2 + 3^2 = 9 \qquad 2 = 2$ true

$\qquad\qquad 9 = 9$

$\qquad\qquad\qquad$ true

The solution set is $\{(0,-1),(3,2)\}$.

31. From the graph we can see that the center of the circle is at $(2,-1)$ and the radius is 2 units. Therefore, the equation is

$$(x-2)^2 + (y-(-1))^2 = 2^2$$
$$(x-2)^2 + (y+1)^2 = 4$$

32. From the graph we can see that the center of the circle is at $(3,-1)$ and the radius is 3 units. Therefore, the equation is

$$(x-3)^2 + (y-(-1))^2 = 3^2$$
$$(x-3)^2 + (y+1)^2 = 9$$

33. From the graph we can see that the center of the circle is at $(-3, -2)$ and the radius is 1 unit. Therefore, the equation is

$$\left(x - (-3)\right)^2 + \left(y - (-2)\right)^2 = 1^2$$
$$\left(x + 3\right)^2 + \left(y + 2\right)^2 = 1$$

34. From the graph we can see that the center of the circle is at $(-1, 1)$ and the radius is 4 units. Therefore, the equation is

$$\left(x - (-1)\right)^2 + \left(y - 1\right)^2 = 4^2$$
$$\left(x + 1\right)^2 + \left(y - 1\right)^2 = 16$$

35. a. Since the line segment passes through the center, the center is the midpoint of the segment.

$$M = \left(\frac{x_1 + x_2}{2}, \frac{y_1 + y_2}{2}\right)$$
$$= \left(\frac{3 + 7}{2}, \frac{9 + 11}{2}\right) = \left(\frac{10}{2}, \frac{20}{2}\right)$$
$$= (5, 10)$$

The center is $(5, 10)$.

b. The radius is the distance from the center to one of the points on the circle. Using the point $(3, 9)$, we get:

$$d = \sqrt{(5 - 3)^2 + (10 - 9)^2}$$
$$= \sqrt{2^2 + 1^2} = \sqrt{4 + 1}$$
$$= \sqrt{5}$$

The radius is $\sqrt{5}$ units.

c. $\left(x - 5\right)^2 + \left(y - 10\right)^2 = \left(\sqrt{5}\right)^2$
$\left(x - 5\right)^2 + \left(y - 10\right)^2 = 5$

36. a. Since the line segment passes through the center, the center is the midpoint of the segment.

$$M = \left(\frac{x_1 + x_2}{2}, \frac{y_1 + y_2}{2}\right)$$
$$= \left(\frac{3 + 5}{2}, \frac{6 + 4}{2}\right) = \left(\frac{8}{2}, \frac{10}{2}\right)$$
$$= (4, 5)$$

The center is $(4, 5)$.

b. The radius is the distance from the center to one of the points on the circle. Using the point $(3, 6)$, we get:

$$d = \sqrt{(4 - 3)^2 + (5 - 6)^2}$$
$$= \sqrt{1^2 + (-1)^2} = \sqrt{1 + 1}$$
$$= \sqrt{2}$$

The radius is $\sqrt{2}$ units.

c. $\left(x - 4\right)^2 + \left(y - 5\right)^2 = \left(\sqrt{2}\right)^2$
$\left(x - 4\right)^2 + \left(y - 5\right)^2 = 2$

37. If we place L.A. at the origin, then we want the equation of a circle with center at $(-2.4, -2.7)$ and radius 30.

$$\left(x - (-2.4)\right)^2 + \left(y - (-2.7)\right)^2 = 30^2$$
$$\left(x + 2.4\right)^2 + \left(y + 2.7\right)^2 = 900$$

39. Answers will vary.

41. Answers will vary.

43. Answers will vary.

45.
$$(y+1)^2 = 36-(x-3)^2$$
$$y+1 = \pm\sqrt{36-(x-3)^2}$$
$$y = -1\pm\sqrt{36-(x-3)^2}$$

```
Plot1 Plot2 Plot3      WINDOW
\Y1■-1+√(36-(X-3       Xmin=-11.16129…
)²)                    Xmax=19.161290…
\Y2■-1-√(36-(X-3       Xscl=1
)²)                    Ymin=-10
\Y3=                   Ymax=10
\Y4=                   Yscl=1
\Y5=                   Xres=1
```

47. **a** is not true. The equation of the circle with radius 16 and whose center is at the origin is $x^2 + y^2 = 16^2$.

b is not true. The graph of $(x-3)^2 + (y+5)^2 = 36$ is a circle with radius 6 and whose center is at $(3,-5)$.

c is not true.
$$(x-4)+(y+6) = 25$$
$$x-4+y+6 = 25$$
$$x+y = 23$$
$$y = -x+23$$
The graph of $(x-4)+(y+6) = 25$ is a line with slope -1 and y-intercept 23.

Therefore, the correct answer is **d**, none of the above is true.

49. The center of the circle with equation, $x^2 + y^2 = 25$, is the point $(0,0)$. First, find the slope of the line going through the center and the point, $(3, -4)$.
$$m = \frac{y_2 - y_1}{x_2 - x_1} = \frac{-4-0}{3-0} = -\frac{4}{3}$$
Since the tangent line is perpendicular to the line going through the center and the point, $(3, -4)$, we know that its slope will be $\frac{3}{4}$. We can now write the point-slope equation of the line.
$$y-(-4) = \frac{3}{4}(x-3)$$
$$y+4 = \frac{3}{4}(x-3)$$

50.
$$f(g(x)) = f(3x+4) = (3x+4)^2 - 2$$
$$= 9x^2 + 24x + 16 - 2$$
$$= 9x^2 + 24x + 14$$
$$g(f(x)) = g(x^2-2) = 3(x^2-2)+4$$
$$= 3x^2 - 6 + 4 = 3x^2 - 2$$

51.
$$2x = \sqrt{7x-3}+3$$
$$2x-3 = \sqrt{7x-3}$$
$$(2x-3)^2 = 7x-3$$
$$4x^2 - 12x + 9 = 7x - 3$$
$$4x^2 - 19x + 12 = 0$$
$$(4x-3)(x-4) = 0$$
Apply the zero product principle.
$$4x-3 = 0 \qquad x-4 = 0$$
$$4x = 3 \qquad\quad x = 4$$
$$x = \frac{3}{4}$$
The solution $\frac{3}{4}$ does not check. The solution is 4 and the solution set is $\{4\}$.

52.
$$|2x-5|<10$$
$$-10<2x-5<10$$
$$-10+5<2x-5+5<10+5$$
$$-5<2x<15$$
$$-\frac{5}{2}<x<\frac{15}{2}$$

The solution set is $\left\{x\middle|-\frac{5}{2}<x<\frac{15}{2}\right\}$

or $\left(-\frac{5}{2},\frac{15}{2}\right)$.

13.2 Exercise Set

1. $\frac{x^2}{16}+\frac{y^2}{4}=1$

Because the denominator of the x^2 – term is greater than the denominator of the y^2 – term, the major axis is horizontal. Since $a^2=16$, $a=4$ and the vertices are $(-4,0)$ and $(4,0)$. Since $b^2=4$, $b=2$ and endpoints of the minor axis are $(0,-2)$ and $(0,2)$.

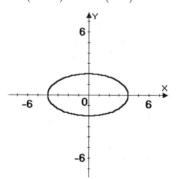

3. $\frac{x^2}{9}+\frac{y^2}{36}=1$

Because the denominator of the y^2 – term is greater than the denominator of the x^2 – term, the

major axis is vertical. Since $a^2=36$, $a=6$ and the vertices are $(0,-6)$ and $(0,6)$. Since $b^2=9$, $b=3$ and endpoints of the minor axis are $(-3,0)$ and $(3,0)$.

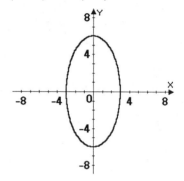

5. $\frac{x^2}{25}+\frac{y^2}{64}=1$

Because the denominator of the y^2 – term is greater than the denominator of the x^2 – term, the major axis is vertical. Since $a^2=64$, $a=8$ and the vertices are $(0,-8)$ and $(0,8)$. Since $b^2=25$, $b=5$ and endpoints of the minor axis are $(-5,0)$ and $(5,0)$.

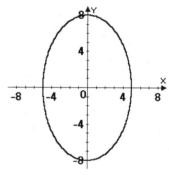

752

7. $\dfrac{x^2}{49}+\dfrac{y^2}{81}=1$

Because the denominator of the
y^2 – term is greater than the
denominator of the x^2 – term, the
major axis is vertical. Since $a^2=81$,
$a=9$ and the vertices are
$(0,-9)$ and $(0,9)$. Since $b^2=49$,
$b=7$ and endpoints of the minor axis
are $(-7,0)$ and $(7,0)$.

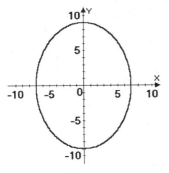

9. $25x^2+4y^2=100$

$\dfrac{25x^2}{100}+\dfrac{4y^2}{100}=\dfrac{100}{100}$

$\dfrac{x^2}{4}+\dfrac{y^2}{25}=1$

Because the denominator of the
y^2 – term is greater than the
denominator of the x^2 – term, the
major axis is vertical. Since $a^2=25$,
$a=5$ and the vertices are
$(0,-5)$ and $(0,5)$. Since $b^2=4$, $b=2$
and endpoints of the minor axis are
$(-2,0)$ and $(2,0)$.

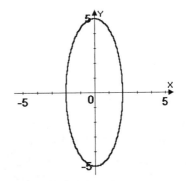

11. $4x^2+16y^2=64$

$\dfrac{4x^2}{64}+\dfrac{16y^2}{64}=\dfrac{64}{64}$

$\dfrac{x^2}{16}+\dfrac{y^2}{4}=1$

Because the denominator of the
x^2 – term is greater than the
denominator of the y^2 – term, the
major axis is horizontal. Since
$a^2=16$, $a=4$ and the vertices are
$(-4,0)$ and $(4,0)$. Since $b^2=4$,
$b=2$ and endpoints of the minor axis
are $(0,-2)$ and $(0,2)$.

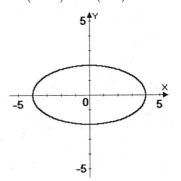

753

13. $25x^2 + 9y^2 = 225$

$$\frac{25x^2}{225} + \frac{9y^2}{225} = \frac{225}{225}$$

$$\frac{x^2}{9} + \frac{y^2}{25} = 1$$

Because the denominator of the y^2 – term is greater than the denominator of the x^2 – term, the major axis is vertical. Since $a^2 = 9$, $a = 3$ and the vertices are $(0, -3)$ and $(0, 3)$. Since $b^2 = 25$, $b = 5$ and endpoints of the minor axis are $(-5, 0)$ and $(5, 0)$.

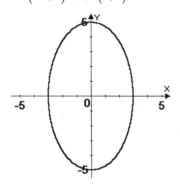

15. $x^2 + 2y^2 = 8$

$$\frac{x^2}{8} + \frac{2y^2}{8} = \frac{8}{8}$$

$$\frac{x^2}{8} + \frac{y^2}{4} = 1$$

Because the denominator of the x^2 – term is greater than the denominator of the y^2 – term, the major axis is horizontal. Since $a^2 = 8$, $a = \sqrt{8} = 2\sqrt{2}$ and the vertices are $\left(-2\sqrt{2}, 0\right)$ and $\left(2\sqrt{2}, 0\right)$. Since $b^2 = 4$, $b = 2$ and endpoints of the minor axis are $(0, -2)$ and $(0, 2)$.

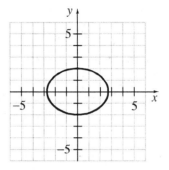

17. From the graph, we see that the center of the ellipse is the origin, the major axis is horizontal with $a = 2$, and $b = 1$.

$$\frac{x^2}{2^2} + \frac{y^2}{1^2} = 1$$

$$\frac{x^2}{4} + \frac{y^2}{1} = 1$$

19. From the graph, we see that the center of the ellipse is the origin, the major axis is vertical with $a = 2$, and $b = 1$.

$$\frac{x^2}{1^2} + \frac{y^2}{2^2} = 1$$

$$\frac{x^2}{1} + \frac{y^2}{4} = 1$$

21. $\dfrac{(x-2)^2}{9}+\dfrac{(y-1)^2}{4}=1$

The center of the ellipse is $(2,1)$. Because the denominator of the x^2 – term is greater than the denominator of the y^2 – term, the major axis is horizontal. Since $a^2=9$, $a=3$ and the vertices lie 3 units to the left and right of the center. Since $b^2=4$, $b=2$ and endpoints of the minor axis lie two units above and below the center.

Center	Vertices	Endpoints of Minor Axis
$(2,1)$	$(2-3,1)$ $=(-1,1)$	$(2,1-2)$ $=(2,-1)$
	$(2+3,1)$ $=(5,1)$	$(2,1+2)$ $=(2,3)$

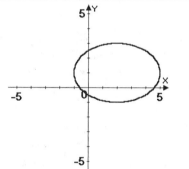

23. $(x+3)^2+4(y-2)^2=16$

$\dfrac{(x+3)^2}{16}+\dfrac{4(y-2)^2}{16}=\dfrac{16}{16}$

$\dfrac{(x+3)^2}{16}+\dfrac{(y-2)^2}{4}=1$

The center of the ellipse is $(-3,2)$. Because the denominator of the x^2 – term is greater than the denominator of the y^2 – term, the

major axis is horizontal. Since $a^2=16$, $a=4$ and the vertices lie 4 units to the left and right of the center. Since $b^2=4$, $b=2$ and endpoints of the minor axis lie two units above and below the center.

Center	Vertices	Endpoints of Minor Axis
$(-3,2)$	$(-3-4,2)$ $=(-7,2)$	$(-3,2-2)$ $=(-3,0)$
	$(-3+4,2)$ $=(1,2)$	$(-3,2+2)$ $=(-3,4)$

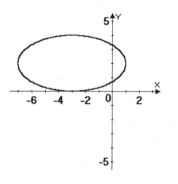

25. $\dfrac{(x-4)^2}{9}+\dfrac{(y+2)^2}{25}=1$

The center of the ellipse is $(4,-2)$. Because the denominator of the y^2 – term is greater than the denominator of the x^2 – term, the major axis is vertical. Since $a^2=25$, $a=5$ and the vertices lie 5 units to the above and below the center. Since $b^2=9$, $b=3$ and endpoints of the minor axis lie 3 units to the right and left of the center.

755

Center	Vertices	Endpoints Minor Axis
$(4,-2)$	$(4,-2-5)$ $=(4,-7)$	$(4-3,-2)$ $=(1,-2)$
	$(4,-2+5)$ $=(4,3)$	$(4+3,-2)$ $=(7,-2)$

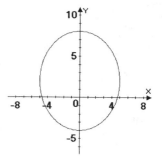

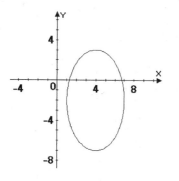

27. $\dfrac{x^2}{25}+\dfrac{(y-2)^2}{36}=1$

The center of the ellipse is $(0,2)$. Because the denominator of the y^2- term is greater than the denominator of the x^2- term, the major axis is vertical. Since $a^2=36$, $a=6$ and the vertices lie 6 units to the above and below the center. Since $b^2=25$, $b=5$ and endpoints of the minor axis lie 5 units to the left and right of the center.

Center	Vertices	Endpoint Minor Axis
$(0,2)$	$(0,2-6)$ $=(0,-4)$	$(0-5,2)$ $=(-5,2)$
	$(0,2+6)$ $=(0,8)$	$(0+5,2)$ $=(5,2)$

29. $\dfrac{(x+3)^2}{9}+(y-2)^2=1$

$\dfrac{(x+3)^2}{9}+\dfrac{(y-2)^2}{1}=1$

The center of the ellipse is $(-3,2)$. Because the denominator of the x^2- term is greater than the denominator of the y^2- term, the major axis is horizontal. Since $a^2=9$, $a=3$ and the vertices lie 3 units to the left and right of the center. Since $b^2=1$, $b=1$ and endpoints of the minor axis lie two units above and below the center.

Center	Vertices	Endpoints of Minor Axis
$(-3,2)$	$(-3+3,2)$ $=(0,2)$	$(-3,2-1)$ $=(-3,1)$
	$(-3-3,2)$ $=(-6,2)$	$(-3,2+1)$ $=(-3,3)$

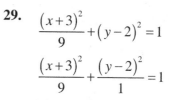

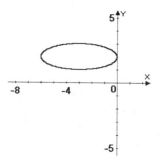

31.

$$9(x-1)^2 + 4(y+3)^2 = 36$$

$$\frac{9(x-1)^2}{36} + \frac{4(y+3)^2}{36} = \frac{36}{36}$$

$$\frac{(x-1)^2}{4} + \frac{(y+3)^2}{9} = 1$$

The center of the ellipse is $(1,-3)$. Because the denominator of the y^2-term is greater than the denominator of the x^2-term, the major axis is vertical. Since $a^2 = 9$, $a = 3$ and the vertices lie 3 units to the above and below the center. Since $b^2 = 9$, $b = 3$ and endpoints of the minor axis lie 3 units to the right and left of the center.

Center	Vertices	Endpoints of Minor Axis
$(1,-3)$	$(1,-3-3)$ $= (1,-6)$	$(1-3,-3)$ $= (-2,-3)$
	$(1,-3+3)$ $= (1,0)$	$(1+3,-3)$ $= (4,-3)$

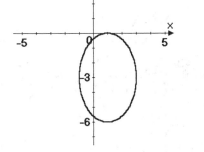

33. From the graph we see that the center of the ellipse is $(h,k) = (-1,1)$. We also see that the major axis is horizontal so we have $a > b$. The length of the major axis is 4 units, so $a = 2$. The length of the minor axis is 2 units so $b = 1$. Therefore, the equation of the ellipse is

$$\frac{(x-(-1))^2}{2^2} + \frac{(y-1)^2}{1^2} = 1$$

$$\frac{(x+1)^2}{4} + \frac{(y-1)^2}{1} = 1$$

34. From the graph we see that the center of the ellipse is $(h,k) = (-1,-1)$. We also see that the major axis is vertical so we have $b > a$. The length of the major axis is 4 units, so $b = 2$. The length of the minor axis is 2 units so $a = 1$. Therefore, the equation of the ellipse is

$$\frac{(x-(-1))^2}{1^2} + \frac{(y-(-1))^2}{2^2} = 1$$

$$\frac{(x+1)^2}{1} + \frac{(y+1)^2}{4} = 1$$

35.

$$x^2 + y^2 = 1 \qquad x^2 + 9y^2 = 9$$

$$\frac{x^2}{9} + \frac{9y^2}{9} = \frac{9}{9}$$

$$\frac{x^2}{9} + \frac{y^2}{1} = 1$$

The first equation is that of a circle with center at the origin and $r = 1$. The second equation is that of an ellipse with center at the origin, horizontal major axis of length 6 units $(a = 3)$, and vertical minor axis of length 2 units $(b = 1)$.

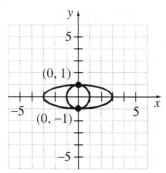

Check each intersection point.

The solutions set is $\{(0,-1),(0,1)\}$.

36. $x^2 + y^2 = 25 \qquad 25x^2 + y^2 = 25$

$$\frac{25x^2}{25} + \frac{y^2}{25} = \frac{25}{25}$$

$$\frac{x^2}{1} + \frac{y^2}{25} = 1$$

The first equation is for a circle with center at the origin and $r = 5$. The second is for an ellipse with center at the origin, vertictal major axis of length 10 units $(b = 5)$, and horizontal minor axis of length 2 units $(a = 1)$.

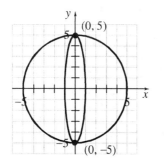

Check each intersection point.

The solutions set is $\{(0,-5),(0,5)\}$.

37. $\dfrac{x^2}{25} + \dfrac{y^2}{9} = 1 \qquad y = 3$

The first equation is for an ellipse centered at the origin with horizontal major axis of length 10 units and vertical minor axis of length 6 units. The second equation is for a horizontal line with a y-intercept of 3.

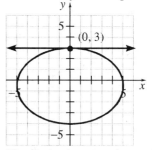

Check the intersection point.

The solution set is $\{(0,3)\}$.

38. $\dfrac{x^2}{4} + \dfrac{y^2}{36} = 1 \qquad x = -2$

The first equation is for an ellipse centered at the origin with vertical major axis of length 12 units and horizontal minor axis of length 4 units. The second equation is for a horizontal line with an x-intercept of -2.

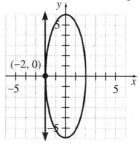

Check the intersection point.

The solution set is $\{(-2,0)\}$.

39.

$$4x^2 + y^2 = 4 \qquad 2x - y = 2$$

$$\frac{4x^2}{4} + \frac{y^2}{4} = \frac{4}{4} \qquad \begin{aligned} -y &= -2x + 2 \\ y &= 2x - 2 \end{aligned}$$

$$\frac{x^2}{1} + \frac{y^2}{4} = 1$$

The first equation is for an ellipse centered at the origin with vertical major axis of length 4 units ($b = 2$) and horizontal minor axis of length 2 units ($a = 1$). The second equation is for a line with slope 2 and y-intercept -2.

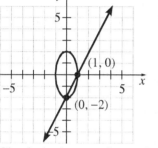

Check the intersection points.
The solution set is $\{(0, -2), (1, 0)\}$.

40.

$$4x^2 + y^2 = 4 \qquad x + y = 3$$

$$\frac{4x^2}{4} + \frac{y^2}{4} = \frac{4}{4} \qquad y = -x + 3$$

$$\frac{x^2}{1} + \frac{y^2}{4} = 1$$

The first equation is for an ellipse centered at the origin with vertical major axis of length 4 units ($b = 2$) and horizontal minor axis of length 2 units ($a = 1$). The second equation is for a line with slope -1 and y-intercept 3.

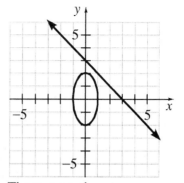

The two graphs never cross, so there are no intersection points.
The solution set is $\{\ \}$ or $\varnothing$.

41.

$$y = -\sqrt{16 - 4x^2}$$

$$y^2 = \left(-\sqrt{16 - 4x^2}\right)^2$$

$$y^2 = 16 - 4x^2$$

$$4x^2 + y^2 = 16$$

$$\frac{x^2}{4} + \frac{y^2}{16} = 1$$

We want to graph the bottom half of an ellipse centered at the origin with a vertical major axis of length 8 units ($b = 4$) and horizontal minor axis of length 4 units ($a = 2$).

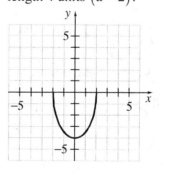

759

42.

$$y = -\sqrt{4 - 4x^2}$$

$$y^2 = \left(-\sqrt{4 - 4x^2}\right)^2$$

$$y^2 = 4 - 4x^2$$

$$4x^2 + y^2 = 4$$

$$\frac{x^2}{1} + \frac{y^2}{4} = 1$$

We want to graph the bottom half of an ellipse centered at the origin with a vertical major axis of length 4 units $(b = 2)$ and horizontal minor axis of length 2 units $(a = 1)$.

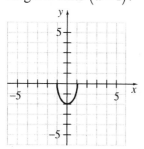

43. From the figure, we see that the major axis is horizontal with $a = 15$, and $b = 10$.

$$\frac{x^2}{15^2} + \frac{y^2}{10^2} = 1$$

$$\frac{x^2}{225} + \frac{y^2}{100} = 1$$

Since the truck is 8 feet wide, we need to determine the height of the archway at $\frac{8}{2} = 4$ feet from the center.

$$\frac{4^2}{225} + \frac{y^2}{100} = 1$$

$$\frac{16}{225} + \frac{y^2}{100} = 1$$

$$900\left(\frac{16}{225} + \frac{y^2}{100}\right) = 900(1)$$

$$4(16) + 9y^2 = 900$$

$$64 + 9y^2 = 900$$

$$9y^2 = 836$$

$$y^2 = \frac{836}{9}$$

$$y = \sqrt{\frac{836}{9}} \approx 9.64$$

The height of the archway 4 feet from the center is approximately 9.64 feet. Since the truck is 7 feet high, the truck will clear the archway.

45. a.

$$\frac{x^2}{48^2} + \frac{y^2}{23^2} = 1$$

$$\frac{x^2}{2304} + \frac{y^2}{529} = 1$$

b.

$$c^2 = a^2 - b^2$$

$$c^2 = 48^2 - 23^2$$

$$c^2 = 2304 - 529$$

$$c^2 = 1775$$

$$c = \sqrt{1775} \approx 42.1$$

The desk was situated approximately 42 feet from the center of the ellipse.

47. Answers will vary.

49. Answers will vary.

51. Answers will vary.

53. Answers will vary. For example, consider Exercise 21.

$$\frac{(x-2)^2}{9} + \frac{(y-1)^2}{4} = 1$$

$$\frac{(y-1)^2}{4} = 1 - \frac{(x-2)^2}{9}$$

$$(y-1)^2 = 4\left(1 - \frac{(x-2)^2}{9}\right)$$

$$(y-1)^2 = 4 - \frac{4(x-2)^2}{9}$$

$$y - 1 = \pm\sqrt{4 - \frac{4(x-2)^2}{9}}$$

$$y = 1 \pm \sqrt{4 - \frac{4(x-2)^2}{9}}$$

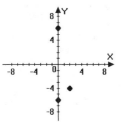

55. Graphing the points, we see that the center of the ellipse is at the origin and the major axis is vertical. We have $a = 6$.

Using a and the given point, we can solve for b.

$$\frac{x^2}{b^2} + \frac{y^2}{a^2} = 1$$

$$\frac{2^2}{b^2} + \frac{(-4)^2}{6^2} = 1$$

$$\frac{4}{b^2} + \frac{16}{36} = 1$$

$$36b^2\left(\frac{4}{b^2} + \frac{16}{36}\right) = 36b^2(1)$$

$$36(4) + 16b^2 = 36b^2$$

$$144 + 16b^2 = 36b^2$$

$$144 = 20b^2$$

$$\frac{144}{20} = b^2$$

$$\frac{36}{5} = b^2$$

The equation ellipse in standard form is

$$\frac{x^2}{\frac{36}{5}} + \frac{y^2}{36} = 1.$$

761

57.
$$4x^2 + 9y^2 - 32x + 36y + 64 = 0$$
$$\left(4x^2 - 32x \quad\right) + \left(9y^2 + 36y \quad\right) = -64$$
$$4\left(x^2 - 8x \quad\right) + 9\left(y^2 + 4y \quad\right) = -64$$

Complete the squares.

$$\left(\frac{b}{2}\right)^2 = \left(\frac{-8}{2}\right)^2 = (-4)^2 = 16$$

$$\left(\frac{b}{2}\right)^2 = \left(\frac{4}{2}\right)^2 = (2)^2 = 4$$

$$4\left(x^2 - 8x + 16\right) + 9\left(y^2 + 4y + 4\right) = -64 + 4(16) + 9(4)$$

$$4(x - 4)^2 + 9(y + 2)^2 = -64 + 64 + 36$$

$$4(x - 4)^2 + 9(y + 2)^2 = 36$$

$$\frac{4(x - 4)^2}{36} + \frac{9(y + 2)^2}{36} = \frac{36}{36}$$

$$\frac{(x - 4)^2}{9} + \frac{(y + 2)^2}{4} = 1$$

$$\frac{(x - 4)^2}{9} + \frac{(y + 2)^2}{4} = 1$$

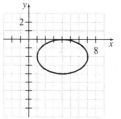

59. The ellipse's vertices lie on the larger circle. This means that a is the radius of the circle. The equation of the larger circle is $x^2 + y^2 = 25$. The endpoints of the ellipse's minor axis lie on the smaller circle. This means that b is the radius of the smaller circle. The equation of the smaller circle is $x^2 + y^2 = 9$.

60. $x^3 + 2x^2 - 4x - 8 = x^2(x + 2) - 4(x + 2) = (x + 2)(x^2 - 4)$
$$= (x + 2)(x + 2)(x - 2) = (x + 2)^2(x - 2)$$

61. $\sqrt[3]{40x^4y^7} = \sqrt[3]{8 \cdot 5x^3xy^6y} = 2xy^2\sqrt[3]{5xy}$

62.

$$\frac{2}{x+2} + \frac{4}{x-2} = \frac{x-1}{x^2-4}$$

$$\frac{2}{x+2} + \frac{4}{x-2} = \frac{x-1}{(x+2)(x-2)}$$

$$(x+2)(x-2)\left(\frac{2}{x+2} + \frac{4}{x-2}\right) = (x+2)(x-2)\left(\frac{x-1}{(x+2)(x-2)}\right)$$

$$2(x-2) + 4(x+2) = x-1$$

$$2x - 4 + 4x + 8 = x - 1$$

$$6x + 4 = x - 1$$

$$5x = -5$$

$$x = -1$$

The solution is –1 and the solution set is $\{-1\}$.

13.3 Exercise Set

1. Since the x^2–term is positive, the transverse axis lies along the x–axis. Also, since $a^2 = 4$ and $a = 2$, the vertices are $(-2,0)$ and $(2,0)$. This corresponds to graph (b).

3. Since the y^2–term is positive, the transverse axis lies along the y–axis. Also, since $a^2 = 4$ and $a = 2$, the vertices are $(0,-2)$ and $(0,2)$. This corresponds to graph (a).

5. $$\frac{x^2}{9} - \frac{y^2}{25} = 1$$

The equation is in the form $\frac{x^2}{a^2} - \frac{y^2}{b^2} = 1$ with $a^2 = 9$, and $b^2 = 25$. We know the transverse axis lies on the x-axis and the vertices are $(-3,0)$ and $(3,0)$.

Because $a^2 = 9$ and $b^2 = 25$, $a = 3$ and $b = 5$. Construct a rectangle using –3 and 3 on the x–axis, and –5 and 5 on the y–axis. Draw extended diagonals to obtain the asymptotes. Graph the hyperbola.

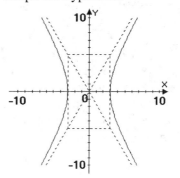

763

7. $\dfrac{x^2}{100} - \dfrac{y^2}{64} = 1$

The equation is in the form $\dfrac{x^2}{a^2} - \dfrac{y^2}{b^2} = 1$ with $a^2 = 100$, and $b^2 = 64$. We know the transverse axis lies on the x-axis and the vertices are $(-10,0)$ and $(10,0)$.

Because $a^2 = 100$ and $b^2 = 64$, $a = 10$ and $b = 8$. Construct a rectangle using -10 and 10 on the x–axis, and -8 and 8 on the y–axis. Draw extended diagonals to obtain the asymptotes. Graph the hyperbola.

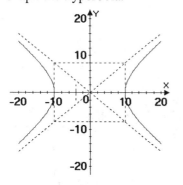

9. $\dfrac{y^2}{16} - \dfrac{x^2}{36} = 1$

The equation is in the form $\dfrac{y^2}{a^2} - \dfrac{x^2}{b^2} = 1$ with $a^2 = 16$, and $b^2 = 36$. We know the transverse axis lies on the y-axis and the vertices are $(0,-4)$ and $(0,4)$.

Because $a^2 = 16$ and $b^2 = 36$, $a = 4$ and $b = 6$. Construct a rectangle using -4 and 4 on the x–axis, and -6 and 6 on the y–axis. Draw extended diagonals to obtain the asymptotes. Graph the hyperbola.

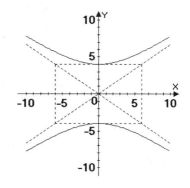

11. $\dfrac{y^2}{36} - \dfrac{x^2}{25} = 1$

The equation is in the form $\dfrac{y^2}{a^2} - \dfrac{x^2}{b^2} = 1$ with $a^2 = 36$, and $b^2 = 25$. We know the transverse axis lies on the y-axis and the vertices are $(0,-6)$ and $(0,6)$.

Because $a^2 = 36$ and $b^2 = 25$, $a = 6$ and $b = 5$. Construct a rectangle using -5 and 5 on the x–axis, and -6 and 6 on the y–axis. Draw extended diagonals to obtain the asymptotes. Graph the hyperbola.

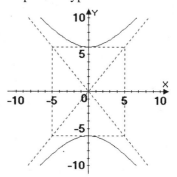

13. $9x^2 - 4y^2 = 36$

$$\frac{9x^2}{36} - \frac{4y^2}{36} = \frac{36}{36}$$

$$\frac{x^2}{4} - \frac{y^2}{9} = 1$$

The equation is in the form $\dfrac{x^2}{a^2} - \dfrac{y^2}{b^2} = 1$

with $a^2 = 4$ and $b^2 = 9$. We know the transverse axis lies on the x-axis and the vertices are $(-2,0)$ and $(2,0)$.

Because $a^2 = 4$ and $b^2 = 9$,

$a = 2$ and $b = 3$. Construct a rectangle using -2 and 2 on the x–axis, and -3 and 3 on the y–axis. Draw extended diagonals to obtain the asymptotes. Graph the hyperbola.

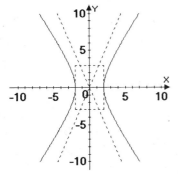

15. $9y^2 - 25x^2 = 225$

$$\frac{9y^2}{225} - \frac{25x^2}{225} = \frac{225}{225}$$

$$\frac{y^2}{25} - \frac{x^2}{9} = 1$$

The equation is in the form $\dfrac{y^2}{a^2} - \dfrac{x^2}{b^2} = 1$

with $a^2 = 25$ and $b^2 = 9$. We know the transverse axis lies on the y-axis and the vertices are $(0,-5)$ and $(0,5)$.

Because $a^2 = 25$ and $b^2 = 9$,

$a = 5$ and $b = 3$. Construct a rectangle using -3 and 3 on the x-axis, and -5 and 5 on the y-axis. Draw extended diagonals to obtain the asymptotes. Graph the hyperbola.

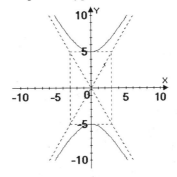

17. $4x^2 = 4 + y^2$

$$4x^2 - y^2 = 4$$

$$\frac{4x^2}{4} - \frac{y^2}{4} = \frac{4}{4}$$

$$\frac{x^2}{1} - \frac{y^2}{4} = 1$$

The equation is in the form $\dfrac{x^2}{a^2} - \dfrac{y^2}{b^2} = 1$

with $a^2 = 1$ and $b^2 = 4$. We know the transverse axis lies on the x-axis and the vertices are $(-1,0)$ and $(1,0)$. Because $a^2 = 1$ and $b^2 = 4$, $a = 1$ and $b = 2$. Construct a rectangle using -1 and 1 on the x–axis, and -2 and 2 on the y–axis. Draw extended diagonals to obtain the asymptotes. Graph the hyperbola.

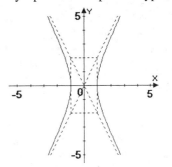

765

19. From the graph we see that the transverse axis lies along the x–axis and the vertices are $(-3,0)$ and $(3,0)$. This means that $a = 3$. We also see that $b = 5$.

$$\frac{x^2}{a^2} - \frac{y^2}{b^2} = 1$$

$$\frac{x^2}{3^2} - \frac{y^2}{5^2} = 1$$

$$\frac{x^2}{9} - \frac{y^2}{25} = 1$$

21. From the graph we see that the transverse axis lies along the y–axis and the vertices are $(0,-2)$ and $(0,2)$. This means that $a = 2$. We also see that $b = 3$.

$$\frac{y^2}{a^2} - \frac{x^2}{b^2} = 1$$

$$\frac{y^2}{2^2} - \frac{x^2}{3^2} = 1$$

$$\frac{y^2}{4} - \frac{x^2}{9} = 1$$

23. $\dfrac{x^2}{9} - \dfrac{y^2}{16} = 1$

The equation is for a hyperbola in standard form with the transverse axis on the x-axis. We have $a^2 = 9$ and $b^2 = 16$, so $a = 3$ and $b = 4$. Therefore, the vertices are at $(\pm a, 0)$ or $(\pm 3, 0)$.

Using a dashed line, we construct a rectangle using the ± 3 on the x-axis and ± 4 on the y-axis. Then use dashed lines to draw extended diagonals for the rectangle. These represent the asymptotes of the graph.

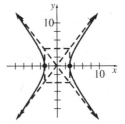

From the graph we determine the following:

Domain: $\{x \mid x \le -3 \text{ or } x \ge 3\}$ or $(-\infty, -3] \cup [3, \infty)$

Range: $\{y \mid y \text{ is a real number}\}$ or $(-\infty, \infty)$

24. $\dfrac{x^2}{25} - \dfrac{y^2}{4} = 1$

The equation is for a hyperbola in standard form with the transverse axis on the x-axis. We have $a^2 = 25$ and $b^2 = 4$, so $a = 5$ and $b = 2$. Therefore, the vertices are at $(\pm a, 0)$ or $(\pm 5, 0)$.

Using a dashed line, we construct a rectangle using the ± 5 on the x-axis and ± 2 on the y-axis. Then use dashed lines to draw extended diagonals for the rectangle. These represent the asymptotes of the graph.

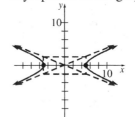

From the graph we determine the following:

Domain: $\{x \mid x \le -5 \text{ or } x \ge 5\}$ or $(-\infty, -5] \cup [5, \infty)$

Range: $\{y \mid y \text{ is a real number}\}$ or $(-\infty, \infty)$

25. $\dfrac{x^2}{9} + \dfrac{y^2}{16} = 1$

The equation is for an ellipse in standard form with major axis along the y-axis. We have $a^2 = 16$ and $b^2 = 9$, so $a = 4$ and $b = 3$. Therefore, the vertices are $(0, \pm a)$ or $(0, \pm 4)$. The endpoints of the minor axis are $(\pm b, 0)$ or $(\pm 3, 0)$.

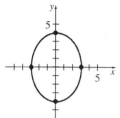

From the graph we determine the following:

Domain: $\{x \mid -3 \le x \le 3\}$ or $[-3, 3]$

Range: $\{y \mid -4 \le y \le 4\}$ or $[-4, 4]$.

26. $\dfrac{x^2}{25} + \dfrac{y^2}{4} = 1$

The equation is for an ellipse in standard form with major axis along the y-axis. We have $a^2 = 25$ and $b^2 = 4$, so $a = 5$ and $b = 2$. Therefore, the vertices are $(\pm a, 0)$ or $(\pm 5, 0)$. The endpoints of the minor axis are $(0, \pm b)$ or $(0, \pm 2)$.

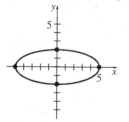

From the graph we determine the following:

Domain: $\{x \mid -5 \le x \le 5\}$ or $[-5, 5]$

Range: $\{y \mid -2 \le y \le 2\}$ or $[-2, 2]$.

27. $\dfrac{y^2}{16} - \dfrac{x^2}{9} = 1$

The equation is in standard form with the transverse axis on the y-axis. We have $a^2 = 16$ and $b^2 = 9$, so $a = 4$ and $b = 3$. Therefore, the vertices are at $(0, \pm a)$ or $(0, \pm 4)$. Using a dashed line, we construct a rectangle using the ± 4 on the y-axis and ± 3 on the x-axis. Then use dashed lines to draw extended diagonals for the rectangle. These represent the asymptotes of the graph.

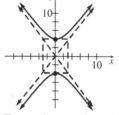

From the graph we determine the following:

Domain: $\{x \mid x \text{ is a real number}\}$ or $(-\infty, \infty)$

Range: $\{y \mid y \le -4 \text{ or } y \ge 4\}$ or $(-\infty, -4] \cup [4, \infty)$

28. $\dfrac{y^2}{4} - \dfrac{x^2}{25} = 1$

The equation is in standard form with the transverse axis on the y-axis. We have $a^2 = 4$ and $b^2 = 25$, so $a = 2$ and $b = 5$. Therefore, the vertices are at $(0, \pm a)$ or $(0, \pm 2)$. Using a dashed line, we construct a rectangle using the ± 2 on the y-axis and ± 5 on the x-axis. Then use dashed lines to draw extended diagonals for the rectangle. These represent the asymptotes of the graph.

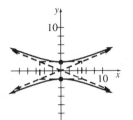

From the graph we determine the following:

Domain: $\{x \mid x \text{ is a real number}\}$ or

$(-\infty, \infty)$

Range: $\{y \mid y \le -2 \text{ or } y \ge 2\}$ or

$(-\infty, -2] \cup [2, \infty)$

29. $x^2 - y^2 = 4$

$x^2 + y^2 = 4$

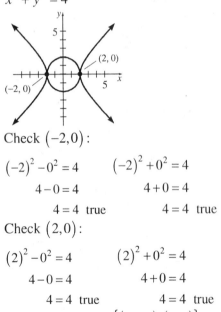

Check $(-2, 0)$:

$$(-2)^2 - 0^2 = 4 \qquad (-2)^2 + 0^2 = 4$$
$$4 - 0 = 4 \qquad\qquad 4 + 0 = 4$$
$$4 = 4 \text{ true} \qquad\qquad 4 = 4 \text{ true}$$

Check $(2, 0)$:

$$(2)^2 - 0^2 = 4 \qquad (2)^2 + 0^2 = 4$$
$$4 - 0 = 4 \qquad\qquad 4 + 0 = 4$$
$$4 = 4 \text{ true} \qquad\qquad 4 = 4 \text{ true}$$

The solution set is $\{(-2, 0), (2, 0)\}$.

30. $x^2 - y^2 = 9$

$x^2 + y^2 = 9$

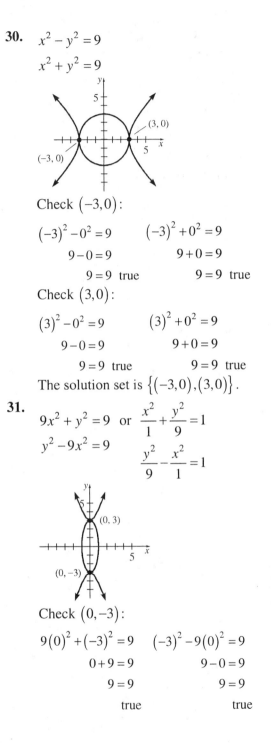

Check $(-3, 0)$:

$$(-3)^2 - 0^2 = 9 \qquad (-3)^2 + 0^2 = 9$$
$$9 - 0 = 9 \qquad\qquad 9 + 0 = 9$$
$$9 = 9 \text{ true} \qquad\qquad 9 = 9 \text{ true}$$

Check $(3, 0)$:

$$(3)^2 - 0^2 = 9 \qquad (3)^2 + 0^2 = 9$$
$$9 - 0 = 9 \qquad\qquad 9 + 0 = 9$$
$$9 = 9 \text{ true} \qquad\qquad 9 = 9 \text{ true}$$

The solution set is $\{(-3, 0), (3, 0)\}$.

31. $9x^2 + y^2 = 9$ or $\dfrac{x^2}{1} + \dfrac{y^2}{9} = 1$

$y^2 - 9x^2 = 9$ $\qquad \dfrac{y^2}{9} - \dfrac{x^2}{1} = 1$

Check $(0, -3)$:

$$9(0)^2 + (-3)^2 = 9 \qquad (-3)^2 - 9(0)^2 = 9$$
$$0 + 9 = 9 \qquad\qquad 9 - 0 = 9$$
$$9 = 9 \qquad\qquad 9 = 9$$
$$\text{true} \qquad\qquad\qquad \text{true}$$

Check $(0,3)$:

$$9(0)^2 + (3)^2 = 9 \qquad (3)^2 - 9(0)^2 = 9$$
$$0 + 9 = 9 \qquad\qquad 9 - 0 = 9$$
$$9 = 9 \qquad\qquad 9 = 9$$
$$\text{true} \qquad\qquad \text{true}$$

The solution set is $\{(0,-3),(0,3)\}$.

32.

$4x^2 + y^2 = 4$ or $\dfrac{x^2}{1} + \dfrac{y^2}{4} = 1$

$y^2 - 4x^2 = 4 \qquad \dfrac{y^2}{4} - \dfrac{x^2}{1} = 1$

Check $(0,-2)$:

$$4(0)^2 + (-2)^2 = 4 \qquad (-2)^2 - 4(0)^2 = 4$$
$$0 + 4 = 4 \qquad\qquad 4 - 0 = 4$$
$$4 = 4 \qquad\qquad 4 = 4$$
$$\text{true} \qquad\qquad \text{true}$$

Check $(0,2)$:

$$4(0)^2 + (2)^2 = 4 \qquad (2)^2 - 4(0)^2 = 4$$
$$0 + 4 = 4 \qquad\qquad 4 - 0 = 4$$
$$4 = 4 \qquad\qquad 4 = 4$$
$$\text{true} \qquad\qquad \text{true}$$

The solution set is $\{(0,-2),(0,2)\}$.

33.

$$625y^2 - 400x^2 = 250,000$$

$$\frac{625y^2}{250,000} - \frac{400x^2}{250,000} = \frac{250,000}{250,000}$$

$$\frac{y^2}{400} - \frac{x^2}{625} = 1$$

Since the houses at the vertices of the hyperbola will be closest, find the distance between the vertices. Since $a^2 = 400$, $a = 20$. The houses are $20 + 20 = 40$ yards apart.

35. Answers will vary.

37. Answers will vary.

39. Answers will vary.

41.

$$\frac{x^2}{4} - \frac{y^2}{9} = 0$$

Solve the equation for y.

$$\frac{x^2}{4} = \frac{y^2}{9}$$

$$9x^2 = 4y^2$$

$$\frac{9}{4}x^2 = y^2$$

$$\pm\sqrt{\frac{9}{4}x^2} = y$$

$$\pm\frac{3}{2}x = y$$

The graph is not a hyperbola. The graph is two lines.

43.

Statement **c.** is true. Since $y = -\dfrac{2}{3}$ is an asymptote, the graph of the hyperbola does not intersect it.

Statement **a.** is false. If a hyperbola has a transverse axis along the y–axis and one of the branches is removed, the remaining branch does not define a function of x.

Statement **b.** is false. The points on the hyperbola's asymptotes do not satisfy the hyperbola's equation.

Statement **d.** is false. See Exercise 32 for two different hyperbolas that share the same asymptotes.

45. $\dfrac{(x+2)^2}{9} - \dfrac{(y-1)^2}{25} = 1$

This is the graph of a hyperbola with center $(-2,1)$. The equation is in the form $\dfrac{(x-h)^2}{a^2} - \dfrac{(y-k)^2}{b^2} = 1$ with $a^2 = 9$ and $b^2 = 25$. We know the transverse axis is horizontal and the vertices lie 3 units to the right and left of $(-2,1)$ at $(-2-3,1) = (-5,1)$ and $(-2+3,1) = (1,1)$. Because $a^2 = 9$ and $b^2 = 25$, $a = 3$ and $b = 5$. Construct two sides of a rectangle using -5 and 1 (the x–coordinates of the vertices) on the x–axis. The remaining two sides of the rectangle are constructed 5 units above and 5 units below the center, $(-2,1)$, at $1-5 = -4$ and $1+5 = 6$. Draw extended diagonals to obtain the asymptotes. Graph the hyperbola.

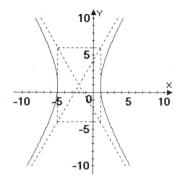

47. $x^2 - y^2 - 2x - 4y - 4 = 0$

Rearrange and complete the squares.
$$x^2 - 2x \quad - y^2 - 4y \quad = 4$$
$$\left(x^2 - 2x \quad\right) - \left(y^2 + 4y \quad\right) = 4$$

Complete the squares.
$$\left(\frac{b}{2}\right)^2 = \left(\frac{-2}{2}\right)^2 = (-1)^2 = 1$$
$$\left(\frac{b}{2}\right)^2 = \left(\frac{4}{2}\right)^2 = 2^2 = 4$$
$$\left(x^2 - 2x + 1\right) - \left(y^2 + 4y + 4\right) = 4 + 1 - 4$$
$$(x-1)^2 - (y+2)^2 = 1$$
$$\frac{(x-1)^2}{1} - \frac{(y+2)^2}{1} = 1$$

This is the graph of a hyperbola with center $(1,-2)$. The equation is in the form $\dfrac{(x-h)^2}{a^2} - \dfrac{(y-k)^2}{b^2} = 1$ with $a^2 = 1$ and $b^2 = 1$. We know the transverse axis is horizontal and the vertices lie 3 units to the right and left of $(1,-2)$ at $(1-1,-2) = (0,-2)$ and $(1+1,-2) = (2,-2)$. Because $a^2 = 1$ and $b^2 = 1$, $a = 1$ and $b = 1$. Construct two sides of a rectangle using 0 and 2 (the x–coordinates of the vertices) on the x–axis. The remaining two sides of the rectangle are constructed 1 unit above and 1 unit below the center, $(1,-2)$, at $-2-1=-3$ and $-2+1=-1$. Draw extended diagonals to obtain the asymptotes. Graph the hyperbola

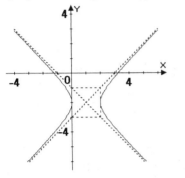

49. Since the vertices are $(0,7)$ and $(0,-7)$, we know that the transverse axis lies along the y–axis and $a = 7$. Use the equation of the asymptote, $y = 5x$, to find b. We need to find the x–coordinate that corresponds with $y = 7$.

$7 = 5x$

$\dfrac{7}{5} = x$

This means that $b = \pm\dfrac{7}{5}$. Using a and b, write the equation of the hyperbola.

$$\dfrac{y^2}{7^2} - \dfrac{x^2}{\left(\dfrac{7}{5}\right)^2} = 1$$

$$\dfrac{y^2}{49} - \dfrac{x^2}{\dfrac{49}{25}} = 1$$

50. $y = -x^2 - 4x + 5$

Since $a = -1$ is negative, the parabola opens downward. The x–coordinate of the vertex of the parabola is

$$-\dfrac{b}{2a} = -\dfrac{-4}{2(-1)} = -2$$ and the y–coordinate of the vertex of the parabola is

$$f\left(-\dfrac{b}{2a}\right) = f(-2)$$
$$= -(-2)^2 - 4(-2) + 5$$
$$= -4 + 8 + 5 = 9.$$
The vertex is at $(-2, 9)$.

Replace y with 0 to find x–intercepts.
$0 = -x^2 - 4x + 5$
$0 = x^2 + 4x - 5$
$0 = (x+5)(x-1)$
Apply the zero product principle.
$x + 5 = 0$　　or　　$x - 1 = 0$
　　$x = -5$　　　　　$x = 1$

The x–intercepts are –5 and 1.
Set $x = 0$ and solve for y to obtain the y–intercept.
$y = -0^2 - 4(0) + 5 = 5$

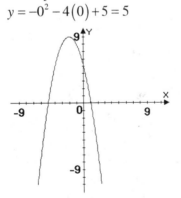

51. $3x^2 - 11x - 4 \geq 0$

Solve the related quadratic equation.

$$3x^2 - 11x - 4 = 0$$

$$(3x + 1)(x - 4) = 0$$

Use the zero product principle.

$$3x + 1 = 0 \quad \text{or} \quad x - 4 = 0$$
$$3x = -1 \qquad\qquad x = 4$$
$$x = -\frac{1}{3}$$

The boundary points are $-\frac{1}{3}$ and 4.

Test Interval	Test Number	Substitution	Conclusion
$\left(-\infty, -\dfrac{1}{3}\right]$	-1	$3(-1)^2 - 11(-1) - 4 \geq 0$ $10 \geq 0$, true	$\left(-\infty, -\dfrac{1}{3}\right]$ belongs in the solution set
$\left[-\dfrac{1}{3}, 4\right]$	0	$3(0)^2 - 11(0) - 4 \geq 0$ $-4 \geq 0$, false	$\left[-\dfrac{1}{3}, 4\right]$ does not belong in the solution set.
$[4, \infty)$	5	$3(5)^2 - 11(5) - 4 \geq 0$ $16 \geq 0$, true	$[4, \infty)$ belongs in the solution set.

The solution set is $\left(-\infty, -\dfrac{1}{3}\right] \cup [4, \infty)$ or $\left\{x \,\middle|\, x \leq -\dfrac{1}{3} \text{ or } x \geq 4\right\}$.

52. $\log_4(3x + 1) = 3$

$$3x + 1 = 4^3$$
$$3x + 1 = 64$$
$$3x = 63$$
$$x = 21$$

The solution is 21 and the solution set is $\{21\}$.

Mid-Chapter 13 Check Point

1. $x^2 + y^2 = 9$

Center: $(0,0)$

Radius: $r = \sqrt{9} = 3$
We plot points that are 3 units to the left, right, above, and below the center. These points are $(-3,0)$, $(3,0)$, $(0,3)$ and $(0,-3)$.

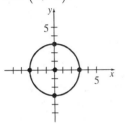

2. $(x-3)^2 + (y+2)^2 = 25$

Center: $(3,-2)$

Radius: $r = \sqrt{25} = 5$
We plot the points that are 5 units to the left, right, above and below the center.

These points are $(-2,-2)$, $(8,-2)$, $(3,3)$, and $(3,-7)$.

3. $x^2 + (y-1)^2 = 4$

Center: $(0,1)$

Radius: $r = \sqrt{4} = 2$
We plot the points that are 2 units to the left, right, above, and below the center. These points are $(-2,1)$, $(2,1)$, $(0,3)$, and $(0,-1)$.

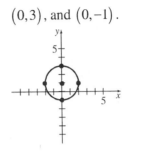

4. $x^2 + y^2 - 4x - 2y - 4 = 0$
Complete the square in both x and y to get the equation in standard form.
$$\left(x^2 - 4x\right) + \left(y^2 - 2y\right) = 4$$
$$\left(x^2 - 4x + 4\right) + \left(y^2 - 2y + 1\right) = 4 + 4 + 1$$
$$(x-2)^2 + (y-1)^2 = 9$$

Center: $(2,1)$

Radius: $r = \sqrt{9} = 3$
We plot the points that are 3 units to the left, right, above, and below the center. These points are $(-1,1)$, $(5,1)$, $(2,4)$, and $(2,-2)$.

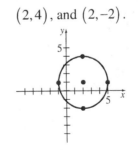

773

5. $\dfrac{x^2}{25}+\dfrac{y^2}{4}=1$

Center: $(0,0)$

Because the denominator of the x^2-term is greater than the denominator of the y^2-term, the major axis is horizontal. Since $a^2=25$, $a=5$ and the vertices are $(-5,0)$ and $(5,0)$. Since $b^2=4$, $b=2$ and endpoints of the minor axis are $(0,-2)$ and $(0,2)$.

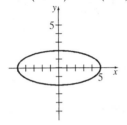

6. $9x^2+4y^2=36$

Divide both sides by 36 to get the standard form:

$\dfrac{x^2}{4}+\dfrac{y^2}{9}=1$

Center: $(0,0)$

Because the denominator of the y^2-term is greater than the denominator of the x^2-term, the major axis is vertical. Since $a^2=9$, $a=3$ and the vertices are $(0,-3)$ and $(0,3)$. Since $b^2=4$, $b=2$ and endpoints of the minor axis are $(-2,0)$ and $(2,0)$.

7. $\dfrac{(x-2)^2}{16}+\dfrac{(y+1)^2}{25}=1$

Center: $(2,-1)$

Because the denominator of the y^2-term is greater than the denominator of the x^2-term, the major axis is vertical. We have $a^2=25$ and $b^2=16$, so $a=5$ and $b=4$. The vertices lie 5 units above and below the center. The endpoints of the minor axis lie 4 units to the left and right of the center.

Vertices: $(2,4)$ and $(2,-6)$

Minor endpoints: $(-2,-1)$ and $(6,-1)$

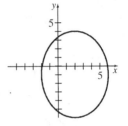

8. $\dfrac{(x+2)^2}{25}+\dfrac{(y-1)^2}{16}=1$

Center: $(-2,1)$

Because the denominator of the x^2-term is greater than the denominator of the y^2-term, the major axis is horizontal. We have $a^2=25$ and $b^2=16$, so $a=5$ and $b=4$. The vertices lie 5 units to the left and right of the center. The endpoints of the minor axis lie 4 units above and below the center.

Vertices: $(-7,1)$ and $(3,1)$

Minor endpoints: $(-2,5)$ and $(-2,-3)$

774

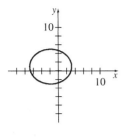

9. $\dfrac{x^2}{9} - y^2 = 1$

The equation is for a hyperbola in standard form with the transverse axis on the x-axis. We have $a^2 = 9$ and $b^2 = 1$, so $a = 3$ and $b = 1$. Therefore, the vertices are at $(\pm a, 0)$ or $(\pm 3, 0)$.

Using a dashed line, we construct a rectangle using the ± 3 on the x-axis and ± 1 on the y-axis. Then use dashed lines to draw extended diagonals for the rectangle. These represent the asymptotes of the graph.
Graph the hyperbola.

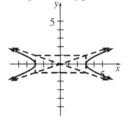

10. $\dfrac{y^2}{9} - x^2 = 1$

The equation is in the form $\dfrac{y^2}{a^2} - \dfrac{x^2}{b^2} = 1$ with $a^2 = 9$, and $b^2 = 1$. We know the transverse axis lies on the y-axis and the vertices are $(0, -3)$ and $(0, 3)$.

Because $a^2 = 9$ and $b^2 = 1$, $a = 3$ and $b = 1$. Construct a rectangle using -1 and 1 on the x–axis, and -3 and 3 on the y–axis. Draw extended diagonals to obtain the asymptotes.

Graph the hyperbola.

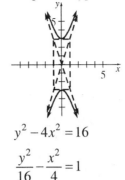

11. $y^2 - 4x^2 = 16$

$\dfrac{y^2}{16} - \dfrac{x^2}{4} = 1$

The equation is in the form $\dfrac{y^2}{a^2} - \dfrac{x^2}{b^2} = 1$ with $a^2 = 16$, and $b^2 = 4$. We know the transverse axis lies on the y-axis and the vertices are $(0, -4)$ and $(0, 4)$.

Because $a^2 = 16$ and $b^2 = 4$, $a = 4$ and $b = 2$. Construct a rectangle using -2 and 2 on the x–axis, and -4 and 4 on the y–axis. Draw extended diagonals to obtain the asymptotes.
Graph the hyperbola.

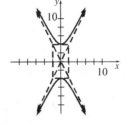

775

12. $4x^2 - 49y^2 = 196$

$$\frac{x^2}{49} - \frac{y^2}{4} = 1$$

The equation is for a hyperbola in standard form with the transverse axis on the x-axis. We have $a^2 = 49$ and $b^2 = 4$, so $a = 7$ and $b = 2$. Therefore, the vertices are at $(\pm a, 0)$ or $(\pm 7, 0)$.

Using a dashed line, we construct a rectangle using the ± 7 on the x-axis and ± 2 on the y-axis. Then use dashed lines to draw extended diagonals for the rectangle. These represent the asymptotes of the graph.
Graph the hyperbola.

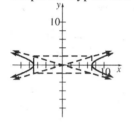

13. $x^2 + y^2 = 4$

This is the equation of a circle centered at the origin with radius $r = \sqrt{4} = 2$. We can plot points that are 2 units to the left, right, above, and below the origin and then graph the circle. The points are $(-2, 0)$, $(2, 0)$, $(0, 2)$, and $(0, -2)$.

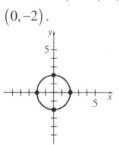

14. $x + y = 4$

$y = -x + 4$

This is the equation of a line with slope $m = -1$ and a y-intercept of 4. We can plot the point $(0, 4)$, use the slope to get an additional point, connect the points with a straight line and then extend the line to represent the graph of the equation.

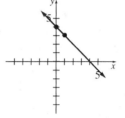

15. $x^2 - y^2 = 4$

$$\frac{x^2}{4} - \frac{y^2}{4} = 1$$

The equation is for a hyperbola in standard form with the transverse axis on the x-axis. We have $a^2 = 4$ and $b^2 = 4$, so $a = 2$ and $b = 2$. Therefore, the vertices are at $(\pm a, 0)$ or $(\pm 2, 0)$.

Using a dashed line, we construct a rectangle using the ± 2 on the x-axis and ± 2 on the y-axis. Then use dashed lines to draw extended diagonals for the rectangle. These represent the asymptotes of the graph.
Graph the hyperbola.

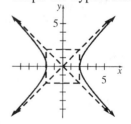

16. $x^2 + 4y^2 = 4$

$$\frac{x^2}{4} + \frac{y^2}{1} = 1$$

Center: $(0,0)$

Because the denominator of the x^2 – term is greater than the denominator of the y^2 – term, the major axis is horizontal. We have $a^2 = 4$ and $b^2 = 1$, so $a = 2$ and $b = 1$. The vertices lie 2 units to the left and right of the center. The endpoints of the minor axis lie 1 unit above and below the center.

Vertices: $(-2,0)$ and $(2,0)$

Minor endpoints: $(0,-1)$ and $(0,1)$

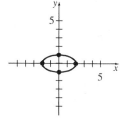

17. $(x+1)^2 + (y-1)^2 = 4$

Center: $(-1,1)$

Radius: $r = \sqrt{4} = 2$

We plot the points that are 2 units to the left, right, above and below the center.

These points are $(-3,1)$, $(1,1)$, $(-1,3)$, and $(-1,-1)$.

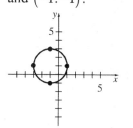

18. $x^2 + 4(y-1)^2 = 4$

$$\frac{x^2}{4} + \frac{(y-1)^2}{1} = 1$$

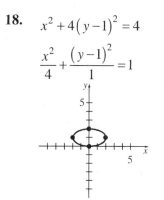

13.4 Exercise Set

1. Since $a = 1$, the parabola opens to the right.
The vertex of the parabola is $(-1,2)$.
Graph **b.** is the equation's graph.

3. Since $a = 1$, the parabola opens to the right.
The vertex of the parabola is $(1,-2)$.
Graph **f** .is the equation's graph.

5. Since $a = -1$, the parabola opens to the left.
The vertex of the parabola is $(1,2)$.
Graph **a.** is the equation's graph.
Either graph a or graph e will match this. One will be changed to open to the left.

7. $x = 2y^2$

$x = 2(y-0)^2 + 0$

The vertex is the point $(0,0)$.

9. $x = (y-2)^2 + 3$

The vertex is the point $(3,2)$.

11. $x = -4(y+2)^2 - 1$

The vertex is the point $(-1, -2)$.

13. $x = 2(y-6)^2$

$x = 2(y-6)^2 + 0$

The vertex is the point $(0, 6)$.

15. $x = y^2 - 6y + 6$

The y–coordinate of the vertex is

$$-\frac{b}{2a} = -\frac{-6}{2(1)} = -\frac{-6}{2} = 3.$$

The x–coordinate of the vertex is

$f(3) = 3^2 - 6(3) + 6 = 9 - 18 + 6 = -3$.

The vertex is the point $(-3, 3)$.

17. $x = 3y^2 + 6y + 7$

The y–coordinate of the vertex is

$$-\frac{b}{2a} = -\frac{6}{2(3)} = -\frac{6}{6} = -1.$$

The x–coordinate of the vertex is

$f(-1) = 3(-1)^2 + 6(-1) + 7$

$\quad = 3(1) - 6 + 7 = 3 - 6 + 7 = 4$.

The vertex is the point $(4, -1)$.

19. $x = (y-2)^2 - 4$

This is a parabola of the form $x = a(y-k)^2 + h$. Since $a = 1$ is positive, the parabola opens to the right. The vertex of the parabola is $(-4, 2)$. The axis of symmetry is $y = 2$. Replace y with 0 to find the x–intercept.

$x = (0-2)^2 - 4 = 4 - 4 = 0$

The x–intercept is 0. Replace x with 0 to find the y–intercepts.

$0 = (y-2)^2 - 4$

$0 = y^2 - 4y + 4 - 4$

$0 = y^2 - 4y$

$0 = y(y-4)$

Apply the zero product principle.

$y = 0$ and $y - 4 = 0$

$\qquad\qquad y = 4$

The y–intercepts are 0 and 4.

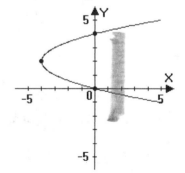

21. $x = (y-3)^2 - 5$

This is a parabola of the form $x = a(y-k)^2 + h$. Since $a = 1$ is positive, the parabola opens to the right. The vertex of the parabola is $(-5,3)$. The axis of symmetry is $y = 3$. Replace y with 0 to find the x–intercept.

$x = (0-3)^2 - 5 = (-3)^2 - 5 = 9 - 5 = 4$

The x–intercept is 0. Replace x with 0 to find the y–intercepts.

$0 = (y-3)^2 - 5$

$0 = y^2 - 6y + 9 - 5$

$0 = y^2 - 6y + 4$

Solve using the quadratic formula.

$x = \dfrac{-b \pm \sqrt{b^2 - 4ac}}{2a}$

$= \dfrac{-(-6) \pm \sqrt{(-6)^2 - 4(1)4}}{2(1)}$

$= \dfrac{6 \pm \sqrt{36 - 16}}{2} = \dfrac{6 \pm \sqrt{20}}{2}$

$= \dfrac{6 \pm 2\sqrt{5}}{2} = 3 \pm \sqrt{5}$

The y–intercepts are $3 - \sqrt{5}$ and $3 + \sqrt{5}$.

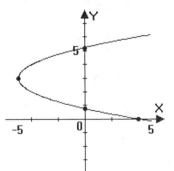

23. $x = -(y-5)^2 + 4$

This is a parabola of the form $x = a(y-k)^2 + h$. Since $a = -1$ is negative, the parabola opens to the left. The vertex of the parabola is $(4,5)$. The axis of symmetry is $y = 5$. Replace y with 0 to find the x–intercept.

$x = -(0-5)^2 + 4 = -(-5)^2 + 4$

$\quad = -25 + 4 = -21$

The x–intercept is 0. Replace x with 0 to find the y–intercepts.

$0 = -(y-5)^2 + 4$

$0 = -(y^2 - 10y + 25) + 4$

$0 = -y^2 + 10y - 25 + 4$

$0 = -y^2 + 10y - 21$

$0 = y^2 - 10y + 21$

$0 = (y-7)(y-3)$

Apply the zero product principle.

$y - 7 = 0 \quad$ and $\quad y - 3 = 0$

$\quad y = 7 \qquad\qquad y = 3$

The y–intercepts are 3 and 7.

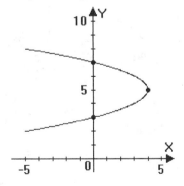

779

25. $x = (y-4)^2 + 1$

This is a parabola of the form $x = a(y-k)^2 + h$. Since $a = 1$ is positive, the parabola opens to the right. The vertex of the parabola is $(1,4)$. The axis of symmetry is $y = 4$. Replace y with 0 to find the x–intercept.

$x = (0-4)^2 + 1 = (-4)^2 + 1 = 16 + 1 = 17$

The x–intercept is 0. Replace x with 0 to find the y–intercepts.

$0 = (y-4)^2 + 1$

$0 = y^2 - 8y + 16 + 1$

$0 = y^2 - 8y + 17$

Solve using the quadratic formula.

$$y = \frac{-b \pm \sqrt{b^2 - 4ac}}{2a}$$

$$= \frac{-(-8) \pm \sqrt{(-8)^2 - 4(1)(17)}}{2(1)}$$

$$= \frac{8 \pm \sqrt{64-68}}{2} = \frac{8 \pm \sqrt{-4}}{2}$$

$$= \frac{8 \pm 2i}{2} = 4 \pm i$$

The solutions are complex, so there are no y–intercepts.

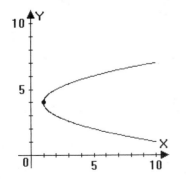

27. $x = -3(y-5)^2 + 3$

This is a parabola of the form $x = a(y-k)^2 + h$. Since $a = -3$ is negative, the parabola opens to the left. The vertex of the parabola is $(3,5)$. The axis of symmetry is $y = 5$. Replace y with 0 to find the x–intercept.

$x = -3(0-5)^2 + 3 = -3(-5)^2 + 3$

$\quad = -3(25) + 3 = -75 + 3 = -72$

The x–intercept is 0. Replace x with 0 to find the y–intercepts.

$0 = -3(y-5)^2 + 3$

$0 = -3(y^2 - 10y + 25) + 3$

$0 = -3y^2 + 30y - 75 + 3$

$0 = -3y^2 + 30y - 72$

$0 = y^2 - 10y + 24$

$0 = (y-6)(y-4)$

Apply the zero product principle.

$y - 6 = 0 \quad$ and $\quad y - 4 = 0$

$\quad\quad y = 6 \quad\quad\quad\quad\quad y = 4$

The y–intercepts are 4 and 6.

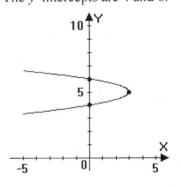

29. $x = -2(y+3)^2 - 1$

This is a parabola of the form $x = a(y-k)^2 + h$. Since $a = -2$ is negative, the parabola opens to the left. The vertex of the parabola is $(-1, -3)$.

The axis of symmetry is $y = -3$. Replace y with 0 to find the x–intercept.

$$x = -2(0+3)^2 - 1 = -2(3)^2 - 1$$

$$= -2(9) - 1 = -18 - 1 = -19$$

The x–intercept is 0. Replace x with 0 to find the y–intercepts.

$$0 = -2(y+3)^2 - 1$$

$$0 = -2(y^2 + 6x + 9) - 1$$

$$0 = -2y^2 - 12x - 18 - 1$$

$$0 = -2y^2 - 12x - 19$$

$$0 = 2y^2 + 12x + 19$$

Solve using the quadratic formula.

$$y = \frac{-12 \pm \sqrt{12^2 - 4(2)(19)}}{2(2)}$$

$$= \frac{-12 \pm \sqrt{144 - 152}}{4}$$

$$= \frac{-12 \pm \sqrt{-8}}{4}$$

Since the solutions will be complex, there are no y–intercepts.

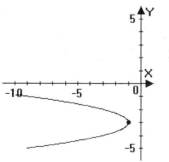

31. $x = \frac{1}{2}(y+2)^2 + 1$

This is a parabola of the form $x = a(y-k)^2 + h$. Since $a = \frac{1}{2}$ is positive, the parabola opens to the right. The vertex of the parabola is $(1, -2)$. The axis of symmetry is $y = -2$. Replace y with 0 to find the x–intercept.

$$x = \frac{1}{2}(0+2)^2 + 1$$

$$= \frac{1}{2}(4) + 1 = 2 + 1 = 3$$

The x–intercept is 0. Replace x with 0 to find the y–intercepts.

$$0 = \frac{1}{2}(y+2)^2 + 1$$

$$0 = \frac{1}{2}(y^2 + 2y + 4) + 1$$

$$0 = \frac{1}{2}y^2 + y + 2 + 1$$

$$0 = \frac{1}{2}y^2 + y + 3$$

$$0 = y^2 + 2y + 6$$

Solve using the quadratic formula.

$$y = \frac{-2 \pm \sqrt{2^2 - 4(1)(6)}}{2(1)} = \frac{-2 \pm \sqrt{4 - 24}}{2}$$

$$= \frac{-2 \pm \sqrt{-20}}{2}$$

Since the solutions will be complex, there are no y–intercepts.

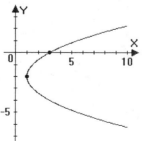

33. $x = y^2 + 2y - 3$

This is a parabola of the form $x = ay^2 + by + c$. Since $a = 1$ is positive, the parabola opens to the right. The y–coordinate of the vertex is

$$-\frac{b}{2a} = -\frac{2}{2(1)} = -\frac{2}{2} = -1.$$ The

x–coordinate of the vertex is

$$x = (-1)^2 + 2(-1) - 3 = 1 - 2 - 3 = -4.$$

The vertex of the parabola is $(-4, -1)$.

The axis of symmetry is $y = -1$.
Replace y with 0 to find the x–intercept.

$$x = 0^2 + 2(0) - 3 = 0 + 0 - 3 = -3$$

The x–intercept is –3. Replace x with 0 to find the y–intercepts.

$$0 = y^2 + 2y - 3$$

$$0 = (y + 3)(y - 1)$$

Apply the zero product principle.

$$y + 3 = 0 \quad \text{and} \quad y - 1 = 0$$

$$y = -3 \qquad\qquad y = 1$$

The y–intercepts are –3 and 1.

35. $x = -y^2 - 4y + 5$

This is a parabola of the form $x = ay^2 + by + c$. Since $a = -1$ is negative, the parabola opens to the left. The y–coordinate of the vertex is

$$-\frac{b}{2a} = -\frac{-4}{2(-1)} = -\frac{-4}{-2} = -2.$$ The

x–coordinate of the vertex is

$$x = -(-2)^2 - 4(-2) + 5 = -4 + 8 + 5 = 9.$$

The vertex of the parabola is $(9, -2)$.

The axis of symmetry is $y = -2$.
Replace y with 0 to find the x–intercept.

$$x = -0^2 - 4(0) + 5 = 0 - 0 + 5 = 5$$

The x–intercept is 5. Replace x with 0 to find the y–intercepts.

$$0 = -y^2 - 4y + 5$$

$$0 = y^2 + 4y - 5$$

$$0 = (y + 5)(y - 1)$$

Apply the zero product principle.

$$y + 5 = 0 \quad \text{and} \quad y - 1 = 0$$

$$y = -5 \qquad\qquad y = 1$$

The y–intercepts are –5 and 1.

37. $x = y^2 + 6y$

This is a parabola of the form $x = ay^2 + by + c$. Since $a = 1$ is positive, the parabola opens to the right. The y–coordinate of the vertex is

$$-\frac{b}{2a} = -\frac{6}{2(1)} = -\frac{6}{2} = -3.$$

The x–coordinate of the vertex is

$$x = (-3)^2 + 6(-3) = 9 - 18 = -9.$$

The vertex of the parabola is $(-9, -3)$.

The axis of symmetry is $y = -3$.

Replace y with 0 to find the x–intercept.

$$x = 0^2 + 6(0) = 0$$

The x–intercept is 0. Replace x with 0 to find the y–intercepts.

$$0 = y^2 + 6y$$

$$0 = y(y + 6)$$

Apply the zero product principle.

$$y = 0 \quad \text{and} \quad y + 6 = 0$$
$$y = -6$$

The y–intercepts are –6 and 0.

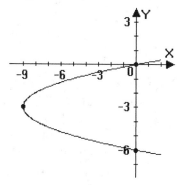

39. $x = -2y^2 - 4y$

This is a parabola of the form $x = ay^2 + by + c$. Since $a = -2$ is negative, the parabola opens to the left. The y–coordinate of the vertex is

$$-\frac{b}{2a} = -\frac{-4}{2(-2)} = -\frac{-4}{-4} = -1. \text{ The}$$

x–coordinate of the vertex is

$$x = -2(-1)^2 - 4(-1) = -2(1) + 4$$
$$= -2 + 4 = 2$$

The vertex of the parabola is $(2, -1)$.

The axis of symmetry is $y = -1$.

Replace y with 0 to find the x–intercept.

$$x = -2(0)^2 - 4(0) = -2(0) - 0 = 0$$

The x–intercept is 0. Replace x with 0 to find the y–intercepts.

$$0 = -2y^2 - 4y$$

$$0 = y^2 + 2y$$

$$0 = y(y + 2)$$

Apply the zero product principle.

$$y = 0 \quad \text{and} \quad y + 2 = 0$$
$$y = -2$$

The y–intercepts are –2 and 0.

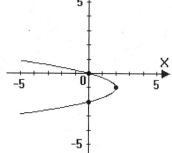

41. $x = -2y^2 - 4y + 1$

This is a parabola of the form
$x = ay^2 + by + c.$ Since $a = -2$ is
negative, the parabola opens to the left.
The y–coordinate of the vertex is
$$-\frac{b}{2a} = -\frac{-4}{2(-2)} = -\frac{-4}{-4} = -1.$$
The x–coordinate of the vertex is
$$x = -2(-1)^2 - 4(-1) + 1 = -2(1) + 4 + 1$$
$$= -2 + 4 + 1 = 3$$
The vertex of the parabola is $(3, -1)$.

The axis of symmetry is $y = -1$.
Replace y with 0 to find the x–
intercept.
$$x = -2(0)^2 - 4(0) + 1 = -2(0) - 0 + 1$$
$$= 0 - 0 + 1 = 1$$
The x–intercept is 0. Replace x with 0
to find the y–intercepts.
$$0 = -2y^2 - 4y + 1$$
Solve using the quadratic formula.
$$y = \frac{-b \pm \sqrt{b^2 - 4ac}}{2a}$$
$$= \frac{-(-4) \pm \sqrt{(-4)^2 - 4(-2)(1)}}{2(-2)}$$
$$= \frac{4 \pm \sqrt{16 + 8}}{-4} = \frac{4 \pm \sqrt{24}}{-4} = \frac{4 \pm 2\sqrt{6}}{-4}$$
$$= \frac{2(2 \pm \sqrt{6})}{-4} = \frac{2 \pm \sqrt{6}}{-2} = \frac{-(2 \pm \sqrt{6})}{2}$$
$$= \frac{-2 \pm \sqrt{6}}{2}$$
The y–intercepts are $\dfrac{-2 \pm \sqrt{6}}{2}$.

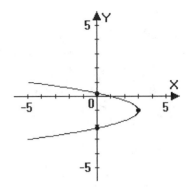

43. a. Since the squared term is y, the
parabola is horizontal.

b. Since $a = 2$ is positive, the
parabola opens to the right.

c. The vertex is the point $(2, 1)$.

45. a. Since the squared term is x, the
parabola is vertical.

b. Since $a = 2$ is positive, the
parabola opens up.

c. The vertex is the point $(1, 2)$.

47. a. Since the squared term is x, the
parabola is vertical.

b. Since $a = -1$ is negative, the
parabola opens down.

c. The vertex is the point $(-3, 4)$.

49. a. Since the squared term is y, the
parabola is horizontal.

b. Since $a = -1$ is negative, the
parabola opens to the left.

c. The vertex is the point $(4, -3)$.

51. **a.** Since the squared term is x, the parabola is vertical.

   b. Since $a = 1$ is positive, the parabola opens up.

   c. The x–coordinate of the vertex is
   $$-\frac{b}{2a} = -\frac{-4}{2(1)} = -\frac{-4}{2} = 2.$$
   The y–coordinate of the vertex is
   $$f(2) = 2^2 - 4(2) - 1$$
   $$= 4 - 8 - 1 = -5.$$
   The vertex is the point $(2, -5)$.

53. **a.** Since the squared term is y, the parabola is horizontal.

   b. Since $a = -1$ is negative, the parabola opens to the left.

   c. The y–coordinate of the vertex is
   $$-\frac{b}{2a} = -\frac{4}{2(-1)} = -\frac{4}{-2} = 2.$$
   The x–coordinate of the vertex is
   $$f(2) = -(2)^2 + 4(2) + 1$$
   $$= -4 + 8 + 1 = 5.$$
   The vertex is the point $(5, 2)$.

55. $x - 7 - 8y = y^2$
   Since only one variable is squared, the graph of the equation is a parabola.

57. $$4x^2 = 36 - y^2$$
   $$4x^2 + y^2 = 36$$
   Because x^2 and y^2 have different positive coefficients, the equation's graph is an ellipse.

59. $$x^2 = 36 + 4y^2$$
   $$x^2 - 4y^2 = 36$$
   Because x^2 and y^2 have opposite signs, the equation's graph is a hyperbola.

61. $$3x^2 = 12 - 3y^2$$
   $$3x^2 + 3y^2 = 12$$
   Because x^2 and y^2 have the same positive coefficient, the equation's graph is a circle.

63. $$3x^2 = 12 + 3y^2$$
   $$3x^2 - 3y^2 = 12$$
   Because x^2 and y^2 have opposite signs, the equation's graph is a hyperbola.

65. $x^2 - 4y^2 = 16$
   Because x^2 and y^2 have opposite signs, the equation's graph is a hyperbola.
   $$\frac{x^2}{16} - \frac{4y^2}{16} = \frac{16}{16}$$
   $$\frac{x^2}{16} - \frac{y^2}{4} = 1$$
   The equation is in the form $\dfrac{x^2}{a^2} - \dfrac{y^2}{b^2} = 1$ with $a^2 = 16$, and $b^2 = 4$. We know the transverse axis lies on the x-axis and the vertices are $(-4, 0)$ and $(4, 0)$.
   Because $a^2 = 16$ and $b^2 = 4$, $a = 4$ and $b = 2$. Construct a rectangle using -4 and 4 on the x–axis, and -2 and 2 on the y–axis. Draw extended diagonals to obtain the asymptotes. Graph the hyperbola.

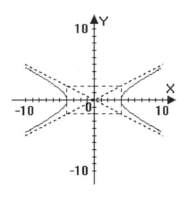

67. $4x^2 + 4y^2 = 16$

Because x^2 and y^2 have the same positive coefficient, the equation's graph is a circle.

$$\frac{4x^2}{4} + \frac{4y^2}{4} = \frac{16}{4}$$

$$x^2 + y^2 = 4$$

The center is $(0,0)$ and the radius is 2 units.

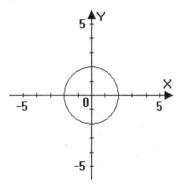

69. $x^2 + 4y^2 = 16$

Because x^2 and y^2 have different positive coefficients, the equation's graph is an ellipse.

$$\frac{x^2}{16} + \frac{4y^2}{16} = \frac{16}{16}$$

$$\frac{x^2}{16} + \frac{y^2}{4} = 1$$

Because the denominator of the $x^2 -$ term is greater than the denominator of the $y^2 -$ term, the major axis is horizontal. Since $a^2 = 16$, $a = 4$ and the vertices are $(-4,0)$ and $(4,0)$. Since $b^2 = 4$, $b = 2$ and endpoints of the minor axis are $(0,-2)$ and $(0,2)$.

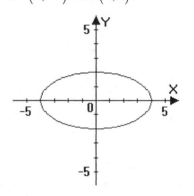

71. $x = (y-1)^2 - 4$

Since only one variable is squared, the graph of the equation is a parabola. This is a parabola of the form $x = a(y-k)^2 + h$. Since $a = 1$ is positive, the parabola opens to the right. The vertex of the parabola is $(-4,1)$. The axis of symmetry is $y = 1$. Replace y with 0 to find the x–intercept.

$$x = (0-1)^2 - 4 = (-1)^2 - 4 = 1 - 4 = -3$$

The x–intercept is 0. Replace x with 0 to find the y–intercepts.

$$0 = (y-1)^2 - 4$$

$$0 = y^2 - 2y + 1 - 4$$

$$0 = y^2 - 2y - 3$$

$$0 = (y-3)(y+1)$$

Apply the zero product principle.

$y - 3 = 0$ and $y + 1 = 0$

$y = 3 \qquad\qquad y = -1$

The y–intercepts are -1 and 3.

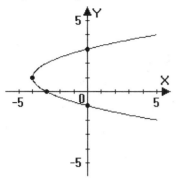

73. $(x - 2)^2 + (y + 1)^2 = 16$

Because x^2 and y^2 have the same positive coefficient, the equation's graph is a circle.

The center is $(2, -1)$ and the radius is 4 units.

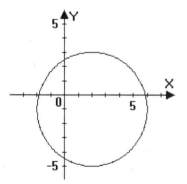

75. The y-coordinate of the vertex is

$$y = -\frac{b}{2a} = -\frac{6}{2(1)} = -3$$

The x-coordinate of the vertex is

$$x = (-3)^2 + 6(-3) + 5$$
$$= 9 - 18 + 5$$
$$= -4$$

The vertex is $(-4, -3)$.

Since the squared term is y and $a > 0$,

the graph opens to the right.

Domain: $\{x \mid x \geq -4\}$ or $[-4, \infty)$

Range: $\{y \mid y$ is a real number$\}$ or $(-\infty, \infty)$

The relation is not a function.

76. The y-coordinate of the vertex is

$$y = -\frac{b}{2a} = -\frac{(-2)}{2(1)} = 1$$

The x-coordinate of the vertex is

$$x = (1)^2 - 2(1) - 5$$
$$= 1 - 2 - 5$$
$$= -6$$

The vertex is $(-6, 1)$.

Since the squared term is y and $a > 0$, the graph opens to the right.

Domain: $\{x \mid x \geq -6\}$ or $[-6, \infty)$

Range: $\{y \mid y$ is a real number$\}$ or $(-\infty, \infty)$

The relation is not a function.

77. The x-coordinate of the vertex is

$$x = -\frac{b}{2a} = -\frac{(4)}{2(-1)} = 2$$

The y-coordinate of the vertex is

$$y = -(2)^2 + 4(2) - 3$$
$$= -4 + 8 - 3$$
$$= 1$$

The vertex is $(2, 1)$.

Since the squared term is x and $a < 0$, the graph opens down.

Domain: $\{x \mid x$ is a real number$\}$ or $(-\infty, \infty)$

Range: $\{y \mid y \leq 1\}$ or $(-\infty, 1]$

The relation is a function.

78. The x-coordinate of the vertex is

$$x = -\frac{b}{2a} = -\frac{(-4)}{2(-1)} = -2$$

The y-coordinate of the vertex is

$$y = -(-2)^2 - 4(-2) + 4$$
$$= -4 + 8 + 4$$
$$= 8$$

The vertex is $(-2, 8)$.

Since the squared term is x and $a < 0$, the graph opens down.

Domain: $\{x \mid x \text{ is a real number}\}$ or $(-\infty, \infty)$

Range: $\{y \mid y \le 8\}$ or $(-\infty, 8]$

The relation is a function.

79. The equation is in the form

$$x = a(y - k)^2 + h$$

From the equation, we can see that the vertex is $(3, 1)$.

Since the squared term is y and $a < 0$, the graph opens to the left.

Domain: $\{x \mid x \le 3\}$ or $(-\infty, 3]$

Range: $\{y \mid y \text{ is a real number}\}$ or $(-\infty, \infty)$

The relation is not a function.

80. The equation is in the form

$$x = a(y - k)^2 + h$$

From the equation, we can see that the vertex is $(-2, 1)$.

Since the squared term is y and $a < 0$, the graph opens to the left.

Domain: $\{x \mid x \le -2\}$ or $(-\infty, -2]$

Range: $\{y \mid y \text{ is a real number}\}$ or $(-\infty, \infty)$

The relation is not a function.

81.
$$x = (y - 2)^2 - 4$$
$$y = -\frac{1}{2}x$$

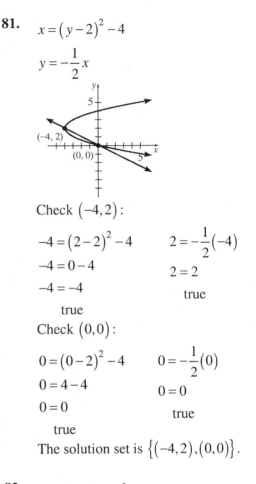

Check $(-4, 2)$:

$$-4 = (2-2)^2 - 4 \qquad 2 = -\frac{1}{2}(-4)$$
$$-4 = 0 - 4 \qquad\qquad 2 = 2$$
$$-4 = -4 \qquad\qquad\quad \text{true}$$
$$\text{true}$$

Check $(0, 0)$:

$$0 = (0-2)^2 - 4 \qquad 0 = -\frac{1}{2}(0)$$
$$0 = 4 - 4 \qquad\qquad 0 = 0$$
$$0 = 0 \qquad\qquad\quad \text{true}$$
$$\text{true}$$

The solution set is $\{(-4, 2), (0, 0)\}$.

82.
$$x = (y - 3)^2 + 2$$
$$x + y = 5$$

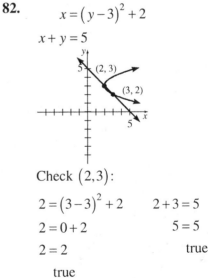

Check $(2, 3)$:

$$2 = (3-3)^2 + 2 \qquad 2 + 3 = 5$$
$$2 = 0 + 2 \qquad\qquad 5 = 5$$
$$2 = 2 \qquad\qquad\quad \text{true}$$
$$\text{true}$$

Check $(3,2)$:

$3 = (2-3)^2 + 2 \qquad 3+2=5$

$3 = 1+2 \qquad\qquad 5 = 5$

$3 = 3 \qquad\qquad\qquad$ true

$\qquad$ true

The solution set is $\{(2,3),(3,2)\}$.

83. $x = y^2 - 3$

$x = y^2 - 3y$

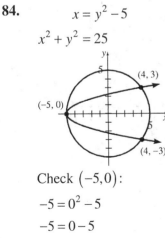

Check $(-2,1)$:

$-2 = (1)^2 - 3 \qquad -2 = (1)^2 - 3(1)$

$-2 = 1-3 \qquad\qquad -2 = 1-3$

$-2 = -2$ true $\qquad -2 = -2$ true

The solution set is $\{(-2,1)\}$.

84. $\qquad x = y^2 - 5$

$x^2 + y^2 = 25$

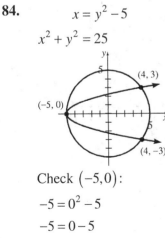

Check $(-5,0)$:

$-5 = 0^2 - 5$

$-5 = 0 - 5$

$-5 = -5$ true

$(-5)^2 + 0^2 = 25$

$25 + 0 = 25$

$25 = 25$ true

Check $(4,-3)$:

$4 = (-3)^2 - 5$

$4 = 9-5$

$4 = 4$ true

$(4)^2 + (-3)^2 = 25$

$16 + 9 = 25$

$25 = 25$ true

Check $(4,3)$:

$4 = (3)^2 - 5 \qquad (4)^2 + (3)^2 = 25$

$4 = 9-5 \qquad\qquad 16 + 9 = 25$

$4 = 4$ true $\qquad\qquad 25 = 25$ true

The solution set is

$\{(-5,0),(4,-3),(4,3)\}$.

85. $\qquad\qquad x = (y+2)^2 - 1$

$(x-2)^2 + (y+2)^2 = 1$

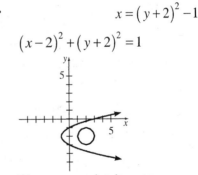

The two graphs do not cross.
Therefore, the solution set is the empty
set, $\{\ \}$ or $\varnothing$.

86.

$$x = 2y^2 + 4y + 5$$

$$(x+1)^2 + (y-2)^2 = 1$$

The two graphs do not cross.
Therefore, the solution set is the empty set, $\{\ \}$ or $\varnothing$.

87. a.

$$y = ax^2$$

$$316 = a(1750)^2$$

$$316 = a(3062500)$$

$$\frac{316}{3062500} = a$$

$$0.0001032 = a$$

The equation is $y = 0.0001032x^2$.

b. To find the height of the cable 1000 feet from the tower, find y when $x = 1750 - 1000 = 750$.

$$y = 0.0001032(750)^2$$

$$= 0.0001032(562,500) = 58.05$$

The height of the cable is about 58 feet.

89. a.

$$y = ax^2$$

$$2 = a(6)^2$$

$$2 = a(36)$$

$$\frac{2}{36} = a$$

$$\frac{1}{18} = a$$

The equation is $y = \frac{1}{18}x^2$.

b.

$$a = \frac{1}{4p}$$

$$\frac{1}{18} = \frac{1}{4p}$$

$$4p = 18$$

$$p = \frac{18}{4} = 4.5$$

The receiver should be placed 4.5 feet from the base of the dish.

91. Answers will vary.

93. Answers will vary.

95. Answers will vary.

97. Answers will vary.

99.

$$y^2 + 2y - 6x + 13 = 0$$

$$y^2 + 2y + (-6x + 13) = 0$$

$$a = 1 \qquad b = 2 \qquad c = -6x + 13$$

$$y = \frac{-2 \pm \sqrt{2^2 - 4(1)(-6x+13)}}{2(1)}$$

$$= \frac{-2 \pm \sqrt{4 - 4(-6x+13)}}{2}$$

$$= \frac{-2 \pm \sqrt{4 + 24x - 52}}{2}$$

$$= \frac{-2 \pm \sqrt{24x - 48}}{2} = \frac{-2 \pm \sqrt{4(6x-12)}}{2}$$

$$= \frac{-2 \pm 2\sqrt{6x-12}}{2}$$

$$= -1 \pm \sqrt{6x - 12}$$

101. Answers will vary. For example, consider Exercise 19.

$$x = (y-2)^2 - 4$$
$$x + 4 = (y-2)^2$$
$$\pm\sqrt{x+4} = y - 2$$
$$2 \pm \sqrt{x+4} = y$$

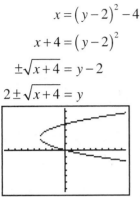

103. Answers will vary.

105. $f(x) = 2^{1-x}$

x	$f(x)$
-2	8
-1	4
0	2
1	1
2	$\dfrac{1}{2}$

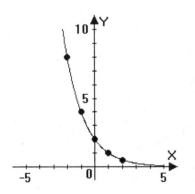

106.

$$f(x) = \frac{1}{3}x - 5$$
$$y = \frac{1}{3}x - 5$$

Interchange x and y and solve for y.

$$x = \frac{1}{3}y - 5$$
$$x + 5 = \frac{1}{3}y$$
$$3x + 15 = y$$
$$f^{-1}(x) = 3x + 15$$

107. $4x - 3y = 12$

$3x - 4y = 2$

Multiply the first equation by –3 and the second equation by 4.

$$-12x + 9y = -36$$
$$\underline{12x - 16y = 8}$$
$$-7y = -28$$
$$y = 4$$

Back-substitute 4 for y to find x.

$$4x - 3(4) = 12$$
$$4x - 12 = 12$$
$$4x = 24$$
$$x = 6$$

The solution is $(6,4)$ and the solution set is $\{(6,4)\}$.

13.5 Exercise Set

1. $x + y = 2$

$\quad y = x^2 - 4$

Substitute $x^2 + 4$ for y in the first equation and solve for x.

$\quad x + (x^2 - 4) = 2$

$\quad x + x^2 - 4 = 2$

$\quad x^2 + x - 6 = 0$

$\quad (x + 3)(x - 2) = 0$

Apply the zero product principle.

$\quad x + 3 = 0 \quad$ or $\quad x - 2 = 0$

$\quad\quad x = -3 \quad\quad\quad\quad x = 2$

Substitute -3 and 2 for x in the second equation to find y.

$\quad x = -3 \quad\quad$ or $\quad x = 2$

$\quad y = (-3)^2 - 4 \quad\quad y = 2^2 - 4$

$\quad y = 9 - 4 \quad\quad\quad\quad y = 4 - 4$

$\quad y = 5 \quad\quad\quad\quad\quad y = 0$

The solutions are $(-3, 5)$ and $(2, 0)$ and the solution set is $\{(-3, 5),\ (2, 0)\}$.

3. $x + y = 2$

$\quad y = x^2 - 4x + 4$

Substitute $x^2 - 4x + 4$ for y in the first equation and solve for x.

$\quad x + x^2 - 4x + 4 = 2$

$\quad x^2 - 3x + 4 = 2$

$\quad x^2 - 3x + 2 = 0$

$\quad (x - 2)(x - 1) = 0$

Apply the zero product principle.

$\quad x - 2 = 0 \quad$ or $\quad x - 1 = 0$

$\quad\quad x = 2 \quad\quad\quad\quad x = 1$

Substitute 1 and 2 for x to find y.

$\quad x = 2 \quad$ or $\quad x = 1$

$\quad x + y = 2 \quad\quad x + y = 2$

$\quad 2 + y = 2 \quad\quad 1 + y = 2$

$\quad\quad y = 0 \quad\quad\quad\quad y = 1$

The solutions are $(2, 0)$ and $(1, 1)$ and the solution set is $\{(1, 1), (2, 0)\}$.

5. $y = x^2 - 4x - 10$

$\quad y = -x^2 - 2x + 14$

Substitute $-x^2 - 2x + 14$ for y in the first equation and solve for x.

$\quad -x^2 - 2x + 14 = x^2 - 4x - 10$

$\quad\quad 0 = 2x^2 - 2x - 24$

$\quad\quad 0 = x^2 - x - 12$

$\quad\quad 0 = (x - 4)(x + 3)$

Apply the zero product principle.

$\quad x - 4 = 0 \quad$ or $\quad x + 3 = 0$

$\quad\quad x = 4 \quad\quad\quad\quad x = -3$

Substitute 3 and 4 for x to find y.

$\quad x = 4$

$\quad y = 4^2 - 4(4) - 10$

$\quad\quad = 16 - 16 - 10 = -10$

$\quad x = -3$

$\quad y = (-3)^2 - 4(-3) - 10$

$\quad\quad = 9 + 12 - 10 = 11$

The solutions are $(4, -10)$ and $(-3, 11)$ and the solution set is $\{(-3, 11), (4, -10)\}$.

7. $x^2 + y^2 = 25$

$x - y = 1$

Solve the second equation for x.

$x - y = 1$

$x = y + 1$

Substitute $y + 1$ for x to find y.

$x^2 + y^2 = 25$

$(y+1)^2 + y^2 = 25$

$y^2 + 2y + 1 + y^2 = 25$

$2y^2 + 2y + 1 = 25$

$2y^2 + 2y - 24 = 0$

$y^2 + y - 12 = 0$

$(y+4)(y-3) = 0$

Apply the zero product principle.

$y + 4 = 0$ or $y - 3 = 0$

$y = -4$ $\qquad\qquad y = 3$

Substitute –4 and 3 for y to find x.

$y = -4$ $\qquad\qquad y = 3$

$x = -4 + 1$ $\qquad x = 3 + 1$

$x = -3$ $\qquad\quad x = 4$

The solutions are $(-3, -4)$ and $(4, 3)$

and the solution set it $\{(-3, -4),$

$(4, 3)\}$.

9. $xy = 6$

$2x - y = 1$

Solve the first equation for y.

$xy = 6$

$y = \dfrac{6}{x}$

Substitute $\dfrac{6}{x}$ for y in the second

equation and solve for x.

$2x - \dfrac{6}{x} = 1$

$x\left(2x - \dfrac{6}{x}\right) = x(1)$

$2x^2 - 6 = x$

$2x^2 - x - 6 = 0$

$(2x + 3)(x - 2) = 0$

Apply the zero product principle.

$x - 2 = 0$ or $2x + 3 = 0$

$x = 2$ $\qquad\qquad 2x = -3$

$\qquad\qquad\qquad x = -\dfrac{3}{2}$

Substitute 2 and $-\dfrac{3}{2}$ for x to find y.

$x = 2$ or $\qquad\qquad x = -\dfrac{3}{2}$

$2y = 6$

$y = 3$ $\qquad\qquad -\dfrac{3}{2}y = 6$

$\qquad\quad -\dfrac{2}{3}\left(-\dfrac{3}{2}\right)y = \left(-\dfrac{2}{3}\right)6$

$\qquad\qquad\qquad y = -4$

The solutions are $(2, 3)$ and $\left(-\dfrac{3}{2}, -4\right)$

and the solution set is

$\left\{(2, 3), \left(-\dfrac{3}{2}, -4\right)\right\}$.

11. $y^2 = x^2 - 9$

$2y = x - 3$

Solve the second equation for x.

$2y = x - 3$

$2y + 3 = x$

Substitute $2y + 3$ for x to find y.

$y^2 = (2y + 3)^2 - 9$

$y^2 = 4y^2 + 12y + 9 - 9$

$y^2 = 4y^2 + 12y$

$0 = 3y^2 + 12y$

$0 = 3y(y + 4)$

793

Apply the zero product principle.

$3y = 0$ or $y + 4 = 0$

$y = 0$ $\qquad\qquad$ $y = -4$

Substitute -4 and 0 for y to find x.

$\qquad y = 0$ or $\qquad\qquad y = -4$

$2(0) + 3 = x$ $\qquad\quad 2(-4) + 3 = x$

$\qquad 3 = x$ $\qquad\qquad\quad -8 + 3 = x$

$\qquad\qquad\qquad\qquad\qquad\quad -5 = x$

The solutions are $(3, 0)$ and $(-5, -4)$

and the solution set is $\{(-5, -4),$

$(3, 0)\}$.

13. $\quad xy = 3$

$x^2 + y^2 = 10$

Solve the first equation for y.

$xy = 3$

$y = \dfrac{3}{x}$

Substitute $\dfrac{3}{x}$ for y to find x.

$$x^2 + \left(\dfrac{3}{x}\right)^2 = 10$$

$$x^2 + \dfrac{9}{x^2} = 10$$

$$x^2\left(x^2 + \dfrac{9}{x^2}\right) = x^2(10)$$

$$x^4 + 9 = 10x^2$$

$$x^4 - 10x^2 + 9 = 0$$

$$\left(x^2 - 9\right)\left(x^2 - 1\right) = 0$$

$(x + 3)(x - 3)(x + 1)(x - 1) = 0$

Apply the zero product principle.

$x + 3 = 0 \qquad\quad x - 3 = 0$

$\quad x = -3 \qquad\qquad x = 3$

$x + 1 = 0 \qquad\quad x - 1 = 0$

$\quad x = -1 \qquad\qquad x = 1$

Substitute ± 1 and ± 3 for x to find y.

$x = -3 \qquad\qquad\qquad x = 3$

$y = \dfrac{3}{-3} \qquad\qquad\qquad y = \dfrac{3}{3}$

$y = -1 \qquad\qquad\qquad\quad y = 1$

$x = -1 \qquad\qquad\qquad x = 1$

$y = \dfrac{3}{-1} \qquad\qquad\qquad y = \dfrac{3}{1}$

$y = -3 \qquad\qquad\qquad\quad y = 3$

The solution set is

$\{(-3, -1), (-1, -3), (1, 3), (3, 1)\}$.

15. $\qquad\qquad x + y = 1$

$\quad x^2 + xy - y^2 = -5$

Solve the first equation for y.

$x + y = 1$

$\quad y = -x + 1$

Substitute $-x + 1$ for y and solve for x.

$x^2 + x(-x + 1) - (-x + 1)^2 = -5$

$x^2 - x^2 + x - \left(x^2 - 2x + 1\right) = -5$

$x^2 - x^2 + x - x^2 + 2x - 1 = -5$

$\qquad\qquad\qquad -x^2 + 3x - 1 = -5$

$\qquad\qquad\qquad -x^2 + 3x + 4 = 0$

$\qquad\qquad\qquad\quad x^2 - 3x - 4 = 0$

$\qquad\qquad\qquad (x - 4)(x + 1) = 0$

Apply the zero product principle.

$x - 4 = 0$ or $x + 1 = 0$

$\quad x = 4 \qquad\qquad x = -1$

Substitute -1 and 4 for x to find y.

$x = 4 \qquad$ or $\qquad x = -1$

$y = -4 + 1 \qquad\quad y = -(-1) + 1$

$y = -3 \qquad\qquad\quad y = 1 + 1$

$\qquad\qquad\qquad\qquad\quad y = 2$

The solution set is $\{(4, -3),\ (-1, 2)\}$.

17.
$$x + y = 1$$
$$(x-1)^2 + (y+2)^2 = 10$$

Solve the first equation for y.

$$x + y = 1$$
$$y = -x + 1$$

Substitute $-x+1$ for y to find x.

$$(x-1)^2 + ((-x+1)+2)^2 = 10$$
$$(x-1)^2 + (-x+1+2)^2 = 10$$
$$(x-1)^2 + (-x+3)^2 = 10$$
$$x^2 - 2x + 1 + x^2 - 6x + 9 = 10$$
$$2x^2 - 8x + 10 = 10$$
$$2x^2 - 8x = 0$$
$$2x(x-4) = 0$$

Apply the zero product principle.

$$2x = 0 \quad \text{or} \quad x - 4 = 0$$
$$x = 0 \qquad\qquad x = 4$$

Substitute 0 and 4 for x to find y.

$$x = 0 \qquad \text{or} \qquad x = 4$$
$$y = -0 + 1 \qquad y = -4 + 1$$
$$y = 1 \qquad\qquad y = -3$$

The solutions are $(0,1)$ and $(4,-3)$

and the solution set is $\{(0,1),\ (4,-3)\}$.

19. Solve the system by addition.

$$x^2 + y^2 = 13$$
$$\underline{x^2 - y^2 = \ 5}$$
$$2x^2 = 18$$
$$x^2 = 9$$
$$x = \pm 3$$

Substitute ± 3 for x to find y.

$$x = \pm 3$$
$$(\pm 3)^2 + y^2 = 13$$
$$9 + y^2 = 13$$
$$y^2 = 4$$
$$y = \pm 2$$

The solutions are $(-3,-2),(-3,2),$

$(3,-2)$ and $(3,2)$ and the solution set is

$\{(-3,-2),(-3,2),(3,-2),(3,2)\}$.

21.
$$x^2 - 4y^2 = -7$$
$$3x^2 + \ y^2 = 31$$

Multiply the first equation by –3 and add to the second equation.

$$-3x^2 + 12y^2 = 21$$
$$\underline{3x^2 + \ y^2 = 31}$$
$$13y^2 = 52$$
$$y^2 = 4$$
$$y = \pm 2$$

Substitute –2 and 2 for y to find x.

$$y = \pm 2$$
$$3x^2 + (\pm 2)^2 = 31$$
$$3x^2 + 4 = 31$$
$$3x^2 = 27$$
$$x^2 = 9$$
$$x = \pm 3$$

The solutions are $(-3,-2),(-3,2),$

$(3,-2)$ and $(3,2)$ and the solution set is

$\{(-3,-2),(-3,2),(3,-2),(3,2)\}$.

23. $3x^2 + 4y^2 - 16 = 0$

$2x^2 - 3y^2 - 5 = 0$

Multiply the first equation by 3 and the second equation by 4 and solve by addition.

$9x^2 + 12y^2 - 48 = 0$

$\underline{8x^2 - 12y^2 - 20 = 0}$

$17x^2 - 68 = 0$

$\qquad 17x^2 = 68$

$\qquad x^2 = 4$

$\qquad x = \pm 2$

Substitute ± 2 for x to find y.

$x = \pm 2$

$2(\pm 2)^2 - 3y^2 - 5 = 0$

$2(4) - 3y^2 - 5 = 0$

$8 - 3y^2 - 5 = 0$

$3 - 3y^2 = 0$

$3 = 3y^2$

$1 = y^2$

$\pm 1 = y$

The solution set is

$\{(-2,-1),(-2,1),(2,-1),(2,1)\}$.

25. $x^2 + y^2 = 25$

$(x-8)^2 + y^2 = 41$

Multiply the first equation by -1 and solve by addition.

$-x^2 \qquad - y^2 = -25$

$\underline{(x-8)^2 + y^2 = \quad 41}$

$-x^2 + (x-8)^2 = 16$

$-x^2 + x^2 - 16x + 64 = 16$

$-16x + 64 = 16$

$-16x = -48$

$x = 3$

Substitute 3 for x to find y.

$x = 3$

$3^2 + y^2 = 25$

$6 + y^2 = 25$

$y^2 = 16$

$y = \pm 4$

The solutions are $(3,-4)$ and $(3,4)$

and the solution set is $\{(3,-4),\ (3,4)\}$.

27. $y^2 - x = 4$

$x^2 + y^2 \quad = 4$

Multiply the first equation by -1 and solve by addition.

$-y^2 + x = -4$

$\underline{x^2 + y^2 \qquad = \quad 4}$

$x^2 + x = 0$

$x(x+1) = 0$

Apply the zero product principle.

$x = 0 \quad$ or $\quad x + 1 = 0$

$x = -1$

Substitute -1 and 0 for x to find y.

$x = 0 \qquad$ or $\quad x = -1$

$y^2 - 0 = 4 \qquad\qquad y^2 - (-1) = 4$

$y^2 = 4 \qquad\qquad\quad y^2 + 1 = 4$

$y = \pm 2 \qquad\qquad\quad y^2 = 3$

$\qquad\qquad\qquad\qquad y = \pm\sqrt{3}$

The solutions are $(0,-2),(0,2)$,

$\left(-1,-\sqrt{3}\right)$ and $\left(-1,\sqrt{3}\right)$ and the

solution set is $\{\left(-1,-\sqrt{3}\right),\left(-1,\sqrt{3}\right),$

$(0,-2),(0,2)\}$.

29. $3x^2 + 4y^2 = 16$

$2x^2 - 3y^2 = 5$

Multiply the first equation by -2 and the second equation by 3 and solve by addition.

$-6x^2 - 8y^2 = -32$

$\underline{6x^2 - 9y^2 = 15}$

$-17y^2 = -17$

$y^2 = 1$

$y = \pm 1$

Substitute ± 1 for y to find x.

$y = \pm 1$

$3x^2 + 4(\pm 1)^2 = 16$

$3x^2 + 4(1) = 16$

$3x^2 + 4 = 16$

$3x^2 = 12$

$x^2 = 4$

$x = \pm 2$

The solutions are $(-2,1), (2,1),$

$(-2,-1)$ and $(2,-1)$ and the solution

set is $\{(-2,-1), (-2,1), (2,-1), (2,1)\}$.

31. $2x^2 + y^2 = 18$

$xy = 4$

Solve the second equation for y.

$xy = 4 \ \rightarrow \ y = \dfrac{4}{x}$

Substitute $\dfrac{4}{x}$ for y in the second equation and solve for x.

$2x^2 + \left(\dfrac{4}{x}\right)^2 = 18$

$2x^2 + \dfrac{16}{x^2} = 18$

$x^2\left(2x^2 + \dfrac{16}{x^2}\right) = x^2(18)$

$2x^4 + 16 = 18x^2$

$2x^4 - 18x^2 + 16 = 0$

$x^4 - 9x^2 + 8 = 0$

$(x^2 - 8)(x^2 - 1) = 0$

$(x^2 - 8)(x+1)(x-1) = 0$

Apply the zero product principle.

$x^2 - 8 = 0 \qquad x + 1 = 0 \qquad x - 1 = 0$

$x^2 = 8 \qquad\qquad x = -1 \qquad x = 1$

$x = \pm\sqrt{8}$

$x = \pm 2\sqrt{2}$

Substitute $\pm 2\sqrt{2}$ and for x to find y.

$x = 1 \qquad\qquad x = -1$

$y = \dfrac{4}{1} \qquad\qquad y = \dfrac{4}{-1}$

$y = 4 \qquad\qquad y = -4$

$x = 2\sqrt{2} \qquad\qquad x = -2\sqrt{2}$

$y = \dfrac{4}{2\sqrt{2}} \qquad\qquad y = \dfrac{4}{-2\sqrt{2}}$

$y = \dfrac{2\sqrt{2}}{2} \qquad\qquad y = -\dfrac{2\sqrt{2}}{2}$

$y = \sqrt{2} \qquad\qquad y = -\sqrt{2}$

The solutions are $\left(2\sqrt{2}, \sqrt{2}\right),$

$\left(-2\sqrt{2}, -\sqrt{2}\right),$ $(1,4)$ and $(-1,-4)$ and the

solution set is $\left\{\left(-2\sqrt{2}, -\sqrt{2}\right),\right.$

$\left.(-1,-4), (1,4), \left(2\sqrt{2}, \sqrt{2}\right)\right\}.$

33. $x^2 + 4y^2 = 20$

$x + 2y = 6$

Solve the second equation for x.

$x + 2y = 6$

$x = 6 - 2y$

Substitute $6 - 2y$ for x to find y.

$(6 - 2y)^2 + 4y^2 = 20$

$36 - 24y + 4y^2 + 4y^2 = 20$

$36 - 24y + 8y^2 = 20$

$8y^2 - 24y + 16 = 0$

$y^2 - 3y + 2 = 0$

$(y - 2)(y - 1) = 0$

Apply the zero product principle.

$y - 2 = 0$ or $y - 1 = 0$

$y = 2$ $\qquad$ $y = 1$

Substitute 1 and 2 for y to find x.

$y = 2$ $\qquad$ or $\quad y = 1$

$x = 6 - 2(2)$ $\qquad$ $x = 6 - 2(1)$

$x = 6 - 4$ $\qquad$ $x = 6 - 2$

$x = 2$ $\qquad$ $x = 4$

The solutions are $(2, 2)$ and $(4, 1)$ and

the solution set is $\{(2, 2), (4, 1)\}$.

35. Eliminate y by adding the two equations.

$x^3 + y = 0$

$\underline{x^2 - y = 0}$

$x^3 + x^2 = 0$

$x^2(x + 1) = 0$

Apply the zero product principle.

$x = 0$ or $x = -1$

Substitute -1 and 0 for x to find y.

$x = 0$ $\quad$ or $\qquad$ $x = -1$

$0^2 - y = 0$ $\qquad$ $(-1)^2 - y = 0$

$-y = 0$ $\qquad$ $1 - y = 0$

$y = 0$ $\qquad$ $-y = -1$

$\qquad\qquad\qquad$ $y = 1$

The solutions are $(0, 0)$ and $(-1, 1)$ and

the solution set is $\{(-1, 1), (0, 0)\}$.

37. $x^2 + (y - 2)^2 = 4$

$x^2 - 2y = 0$

Solve the second equation for x^2.

$x^2 - 2y = 0$

$x^2 = 2y$

Substitute $2y$ for x^2 in the first equation and solve for y.

$2y + (y - 2)^2 = 4$

$2y + y^2 - 4y + 4 = 4$

$y^2 - 2y + 4 = 4$

$y^2 - 2y = 0$

$y(y - 2) = 0$

Apply the zero product principle.

$y = 0$ or $y - 2 = 0$

$\qquad\qquad\qquad$ $y = 2$

Substitute 0 and $\dfrac{4}{5}$ for y to find x.

$y = 0$ $\qquad$ or $\quad y = 2$

$x^2 = 2(0)$ $\qquad$ $x^2 = 2(2)$

$x^2 = 0$ $\qquad\quad$ $x^2 = 4$

$x = 0$ $\qquad\qquad$ $x = \pm 2$

The solutions are $(0, 0), (-2, 2)$ and

$(2, 2)$ and the solution set is $\{(0, 0),$

$(-2, 2), (2, 2)\}$.

39.

$$y = (x+3)^2$$
$$x + 2y = -2$$

Substitute $(x+3)^2$ for y in the second equation.

$$x + 2(x+3)^2 = -2$$
$$x + 2(x^2 + 6x + 9) = -2$$
$$x + 2x^2 + 12x + 18 = -2$$
$$2x^2 + 13x + 18 = -2$$
$$2x^2 + 13x + 20 = 0$$
$$(2x+5)(x+4) = 0$$

Apply the zero product principle.

$$2x + 5 = 0 \quad \text{or} \quad x + 4 = 0$$
$$x = -\frac{5}{2} \qquad x = -4$$

Substitute $-\frac{5}{2}$ and -4 for x to find y.

$$x = -\frac{5}{2} \quad \text{or} \quad x = -4$$
$$-\frac{5}{2} + 2y = -2 \qquad -4 + 2y = -2$$
$$-5 + 4y = -4 \qquad 2y = 2$$
$$4y = 1 \qquad y = 1$$
$$y = \frac{1}{4}$$

The solutions are $\left(-\frac{5}{2}, \frac{1}{4}\right)$ and $(-4,1)$ and the solution set is
$$\left\{(-4,1), \left(-\frac{5}{2}, \frac{1}{4}\right)\right\}.$$

41.

$$x^2 + y^2 + 3y = 22$$
$$2x + y = -1$$

Solve the second equation for y.
$$2x + y = -1$$
$$y = -2x - 1$$

Substitute $-2x - 1$ for y to find x.

$$x^2 + (-2x-1)^2 + 3(-2x-1) = 22$$
$$x^2 + 4x^2 + 4x + 1 - 6x - 3 = 22$$
$$5x^2 - 2x - 2 = 22$$
$$5x^2 - 2x - 24 = 0$$
$$(5x-12)(x+2) = 0$$

Apply the zero product principle.

$$5x - 12 = 0 \quad \text{or} \quad x + 2 = 0$$
$$5x = 12 \qquad x = -2$$
$$x = \frac{12}{5}$$

Substitute -2 and $\frac{12}{5}$ for x to find y.

$$x = \frac{12}{5} \qquad \text{or} \quad x = -2$$
$$y = -2\left(\frac{12}{5}\right) - 1 \qquad y = -2(-2) - 1$$
$$y = -\frac{24}{5} - \frac{5}{5} \qquad y = 4 - 1$$
$$y = -\frac{29}{5} \qquad y = 3$$

The solutions are $\left(\frac{12}{5}, -\frac{29}{5}\right)$ and $(-2,3)$ and the solution set is
$$\left\{\left(\frac{12}{5}, -\frac{29}{5}\right), (-2,3)\right\}.$$

43. Let x = one of the numbers
Let y = the other number
$$x + y = 10$$
$$xy = 24$$
Solve the second equation for y.
$$xy = 24$$
$$y = \frac{24}{x}$$

Substitute $\frac{24}{x}$ for y in the first equation
and solve for x.
$$x + \frac{24}{x} = 10$$
$$x\left(x + \frac{24}{x}\right) = x(10)$$
$$x^2 + 24 = 10x$$
$$x^2 - 10x + 24 = 0$$
$$(x - 6)(x - 4) = 0$$
Apply the zero product principle.
$$x - 6 = 0 \quad \text{or} \quad x - 4 = 0$$
$$x = 6 \qquad\qquad x = 4$$
Substitute 6 and 4 for x to find y.
$$x = 6 \qquad\qquad x = 4$$
$$y = \frac{24}{6} \quad \text{or} \quad y = \frac{24}{4}$$
$$y = 4 \qquad\qquad y = 6$$
The numbers are 4 and 6.

45. Let x = one of the numbers
Let y = the other number
$$x^2 - y^2 = 3$$
$$\underline{2x^2 + y^2 = 9}$$
$$3x^2 = 12$$
$$x^2 = 4$$
$$x = \pm 2$$
Substitute ± 2 for x to find y.

$$x = \pm 2$$
$$(\pm 2)^2 - y^2 = 3$$
$$4 - y^2 = 3$$
$$-y^2 = -1$$
$$y^2 = 1$$
$$y = \pm 1$$
The numbers are either 2 and –1, 2 and 1, –2 and –1, or –2 and 1.

47. $\quad 2x^2 + xy = 6$
$$x^2 + 2xy = 0$$
Multiply the first equation by –2 and add the two equations.
$$-4x^2 - 2xy = -12$$
$$\underline{x^2 + 2xy = 0}$$
$$-3x^2 = -12$$
$$x^2 = 4$$
$$x = \pm 2$$
Back-substitute these values for x in the second equation and solve for y.
For $x = -2$: $\ (-2)^2 + 2(-2)y = 0$
$$4 - 4y = 0$$
$$-4y = -4$$
$$y = 1$$
For $x = 2$: $\ (2)^2 + 2(2)y = 0$
$$4 + 4y = 0$$
$$4y = -4$$
$$y = -1$$
The solution set is $\{(-2,1),(2,-1)\}$.

48. $4x^2 + xy = 30$

$x^2 + 3xy = -9$

Multiply the first equation by -3 and add the equations.

$-12x^2 - 3xy = -90$

$\underline{x^2 + 3xy = -9}$

$-11x^2 = -99$

$x^2 = 9$

$x = \pm 3$

Back-substitute these values for x in the second equation and solve for y.

For $x = -3$: $(-3)^2 + 3(-3)\,y = -9$

$9 - 9y = -9$

$-9y = -18$

$y = 2$

For $x = 3$: $(3)^2 + 3(3)\,y = 9$

$9 + 9y = -9$

$9y = -18$

$y = -2$

The solution set is $\{(-3, 2), (3, -2)\}$.

49. $-4x + y = 12$

$y = x^3 + 3x^2$

Substitute $x^3 + 3x^2$ for y in the first equation and solve for x.

$-4x + \left(x^3 + 3x^2\right) = 12$

$x^3 + 3x^2 - 4x - 12 = 0$

$x^2(x + 3) - 4(x + 3) = 0$

$(x + 3)\left(x^2 - 4\right) = 0$

$(x + 3)(x - 2)(x + 2) = 0$

$x = -3$, $x = 2$, or $x = -2$

Substitute these values for x in the second equation and solve for y.

For $x = -3$: $y = (-3)^3 + 3(-3)^2$

$= -27 + 27$

$= 0$

For $x = 2$: $y = (2)^3 + 3(2)^2$

$= 8 + 12$

$= 20$

For $x = -2$: $y = (-2)^3 + 3(-2)^2$

$= -8 + 12$

$= 4$

The solution set is
$\{(-3, 0), (2, 20), (-2, 4)\}$.

50. $-9x + y = 45$

$y = x^3 + 5x^2$

Substitute $x^3 + 5x^2$ for y in the first equation and solve for x.

$-9x + \left(x^3 + 5x^2\right) = 45$

$x^3 + 5x^2 - 9x - 45 = 0$

$x^2(x + 5) - 9(x + 5) = 0$

$(x + 5)\left(x^2 - 9\right) = 0$

$(x + 5)(x - 3)(x + 3) = 0$

$x = -5$, $x = 3$, or $x = -3$

Substitute these values for x in the second equation and solve for y.

For $x = -5$: $y = (-5)^3 + 5(-5)^2$

$= -125 + 125 = 0$

For $x = 3$: $y = (3)^3 + 5(3)^2$

$= 27 + 45 = 72$

For $x = -3$: $y = (-3)^3 + 5(-3)^2$

$= -27 + 45 = 18$

The solution set
is $\{(-5, 0), (3, 72), (-3, 18)\}$.

51.

$$\frac{3}{x^2} + \frac{1}{y^2} = 7$$

$$\frac{5}{x^2} - \frac{2}{y^2} = -3$$

Multiply the first equation by 2 and add the equations.

$$\frac{6}{x^2} + \frac{2}{y^2} = 14$$

$$\frac{5}{x^2} - \frac{2}{y^2} = -3$$

$$\overline{\phantom{\frac{5}{x^2} - \frac{2}{y^2} = -3}}$$

$$\frac{11}{x^2} = 11$$

$$x^2 = 1$$

$$x = \pm 1$$

Back-substitute these values for x in the first equation and solve for y.

For $x = -1$:

$$\frac{3}{(-1)^2} + \frac{1}{y^2} = 7$$

$$3 + \frac{1}{y^2} = 7$$

$$\frac{1}{y^2} = 4$$

$$y^2 = \frac{1}{4}$$

$$y = \pm\frac{1}{2}$$

For $x = 1$:

$$\frac{3}{(1)^2} + \frac{1}{y^2} = 7$$

$$3 + \frac{1}{y^2} = 7$$

$$\frac{1}{y^2} = 4$$

$$y^2 = \frac{1}{4}$$

$$y = \pm\frac{1}{2}$$

The solution set is

$$\left\{\left(-1, -\frac{1}{2}\right), \left(-1, \frac{1}{2}\right), \left(1, -\frac{1}{2}\right), \left(1, \frac{1}{2}\right)\right\}.$$

52.

$$\frac{2}{x^2} + \frac{1}{y^2} = 11$$

$$\frac{4}{x^2} - \frac{2}{y^2} = -14$$

Multiply the first equation by 2 and add the two equations.

$$\frac{4}{x^2} + \frac{2}{y^2} = 22$$

$$\frac{4}{x^2} - \frac{2}{y^2} = -14$$

$$\overline{\phantom{\frac{4}{x^2} - \frac{2}{y^2} = -14}}$$

$$\frac{8}{x^2} = 8$$

$$x^2 = 1$$

$$x = \pm 1$$

Back-substitute these values for x in the first equation and solve for y.

For $x = -1$:

$$\frac{2}{(-1)^2} + \frac{1}{y^2} = 11$$

$$2 + \frac{1}{y^2} = 11$$

$$\frac{1}{y^2} = 9$$

$$y^2 = \frac{1}{9}$$

$$y = \pm\frac{1}{3}$$

For $x = 1$:

$$\frac{2}{(1)^2} + \frac{1}{y^2} = 11$$

$$2 + \frac{1}{y^2} = 11$$

$$\frac{1}{y^2} = 9$$

$$y^2 = \frac{1}{9}$$

$$y = \pm\frac{1}{3}$$

The solution set is $\left\{\left(-1, -\frac{1}{3}\right),\right.$

$\left.\left(-1, \frac{1}{3}\right), \left(1, -\frac{1}{3}\right), \left(1, \frac{1}{3}\right)\right\}$.

53. Answers will vary. One example:

Circle: $x^2 + y^2 = 9$

Ellipse: $\dfrac{x^2}{9} + \dfrac{y^2}{49} = 1$

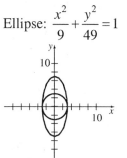

Solutions: $(-3, 0)$ and $(3, 0)$.

54. Answers will vary. One example
follows:

Line: $x - y = 2$

Parabola: $x = y^2$

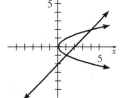

Solutions: $(1, -1)$ and $(4, 2)$

55. $16x^2 + 4y^2 = 64$

$$y = x^2 - 4$$

Solve the second equation for x^2.

$$y = x^2 - 4$$

$$y + 4 = x^2$$

Substitute $x^2 - 4$ for y in the first
equation and solve for x.

$$16(y + 4) + 4y^2 = 64$$

$$16y + 64 + 4y^2 = 64$$

$$16y + 4y^2 = 0$$

$$4y(4 + y) = 0$$

Apply the zero product principle.

$4y = 0$ or $4 + y = 0$

$\quad y = 0 \qquad\qquad y = -4$

Substitute 0 and 4 for y to find x.

$\quad y = 0 \qquad$ or $\qquad y = -4$

$\quad 0 = x^2 - 4 \qquad -4 = x^2 - 4$

$\quad 4 = x^2 \qquad\qquad 0 = x^2$

$\pm 2 = x \qquad\qquad 0 = x$

The comet intersects the planet's orbit
at the points $(2, 0), (-2, 0)$ and $(0, -4)$.

57. Let x = the length of the rectangle
Let y = the width of the rectangle
Perimeter: $2x + 2y = 36$

Area: $\qquad xy = 77$

Solve the second equation for y.
$xy = 77$

$$y = \frac{77}{x}$$

Substitute $\dfrac{77}{x}$ for y in the first equation
and solve for x.

$$2x + 2\left(\frac{77}{x}\right) = 36$$

$$2x + \frac{154}{x} = 36$$

$$x\left(2x + \frac{154}{x}\right) = x(36)$$

$$2x^2 + 154 = 36x$$

$$2x^2 - 36x + 154 = 0$$

$$x^2 - 18x + 77 = 0$$

$$(x - 7)(x - 11) = 0$$

Apply the zero product principle.
$x - 7 = 0 \quad$ or $\quad x - 11 = 0$

$\qquad x = 7 \qquad\qquad x = 11$

Substitute 7 and 11 for x to find y.
$x = 7 \quad$ or $\quad x = 11$

$$y = \frac{77}{7} \qquad\qquad y = \frac{77}{11}$$

$$y = 11 \qquad\qquad y = 7$$

The dimensions of the rectangle are 7 feet by 11 feet.

59. Let x = the length of the screen
Let y = the width of the screen
$x^2 + y^2 = 10^2$

$\qquad\qquad xy = 48$

Solve the second equation for y.
$xy = 48$

$$y = \frac{48}{x}$$

Substitute $\dfrac{48}{x}$ for y to find x.

$$x^2 + \left(\frac{48}{x}\right)^2 = 10^2$$

$$x^2 + \frac{2304}{x^2} = 100$$

$$x^2\left(x^2 + \frac{2304}{x^2}\right) = x^2(100)$$

$$x^4 + 2304 = 100x^2$$

$$x^4 - 100x^2 + 2304 = 0$$

$$(x^2 - 64)(x^2 - 36) = 0$$

$$(x + 8)(x - 8)(x + 6)(x - 6) = 0$$

Apply the zero product principle.
$x + 8 = 0 \qquad\qquad x - 8 = 0$

$\qquad x = -8 \qquad\qquad\qquad x = 8$

$x + 6 = 0 \qquad\qquad x + 6 = 0$

$\qquad x = -6 \qquad\qquad\qquad x = -6$

We disregard –8 and –6 because we cannot have a negative length.
Substitute 8 and 6 for x to find y.
$x = 8 \quad$ or $\quad x = 6$

$$y = \frac{48}{8} \qquad\qquad y = \frac{48}{6}$$

$$y = 6 \qquad\qquad y = 8$$

The dimensions of the screen are 8 inches by 6 inches.

61. $x^2 - y^2 = 21$

$4x + 2y = 24$

Solve for y in the second equation.

$4x + 2y = 24$

$$2y = 24 - 4x$$

$$y = 12 - 2x$$

Substitute $12 - 2x$ for y and solve for x.

$$x^2 - (12 - 2x)^2 = 21$$

$$x^2 - (144 - 48x + 4x^2) = 21$$

$$x^2 - 144 + 48x - 4x^2 = 21$$

$$-3x^2 + 48x - 144 = 21$$

$$-3x^2 + 48x - 165 = 0$$

$$x^2 - 16x + 55 = 0$$

$$(x - 5)(x - 11) = 0$$

Apply the zero product principle.

$x - 5 = 0$ or $x - 11 = 0$

$\quad x = 5 \qquad\qquad x = 11$

Substitute 5 and 11 for x to find y.

$x = 5$ or $x = 11$

$y = 12 - 2(5) \qquad y = 12 - 2(11)$

$y = 12 - 10 \qquad\quad y = 12 - 22$

$y = 2 \qquad\qquad\quad y = -10$

We disregard –10 because we can't have a negative length measurement. The larger square is 5 meters by 5 meters and the smaller square to be cut out is 2 meters by 2 meters.

63. Answers will vary.

65. Answers will vary.

67. Answers will vary. For example, consider Exercise 1.

$x + y = 2 \qquad\qquad y = x^2 - 4$

$y = -x + 2$

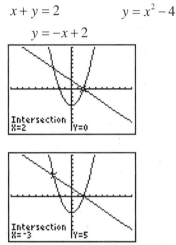

The solutions are $(2, 0)$ and $(-3, 5)$.

This is the same answer obtained in Exercise 1.

69. Statement **b.** is true. As shown in the graph below, a parabola and a circle can intersect in at most four points, and therefore, has at most four real solutions.

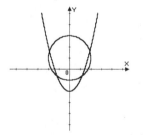

Statement **a.** is false. As shown in the graph below, a circle and a line can intersect in at most two points, and therefore has at most two real solutions.

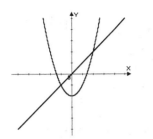

Statement **c.** is false. As shown in the graphs below, it is possible that a system of two equations in two variables whose graphs represent circles do not intersect, or intersect in a single point. This means that the system would have no solution, or a single solution, respectively.

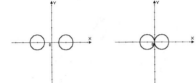

Statement **d.** is false. As shown in the graph below, a circle and a parabola can intersect in one point, and therefore have only one real solution.

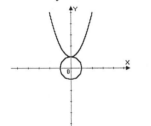

71.
$$\log_y x = 3$$
$$\log_y (4x) = 5$$
Rewrite the equations.
$$y^3 = x$$
$$y^5 = 4x$$
Substitute y^3 for x in the second equation and solve for y.
$$y^5 = 4y^3$$
$$y^5 - 4y^3 = 0$$
$$y^3 (y^2 - 4) = 0$$
$$y^3 (y + 2)(y - 2) = 0$$
Apply the zero product principle.
$$y^3 = 0 \qquad y + 2 = 0 \qquad y - 2 = 0$$
$$y = 0 \qquad\quad y = -2 \qquad\quad y = 2$$
We disregard 0 and -2 because the base of a logarithm must be greater than zero.
Substitute 2 for y to find x.
$$y^3 = x$$
$$2^3 = x$$
$$8 = x$$
The solution is $(8, 2)$ and the solution set is $\{(8, 2)\}$.

73. $3x - 2y \le 6$

First, find the intercepts to the equation $3x - 2y = 6$. Find the x–intercept by setting y equal to zero.
$$3x - 2\cancel{(0)} = 6$$
$$3x = 6$$
$$x = 2$$
Find the y–intercept by setting x equal to zero.
$$3\cancel{(0)} - 2y = 6$$
$$-2y = 6$$
$$y = -3$$

806

Next, use the origin as a test point.

$$3(0)-2(0)\le 6$$
$$0-0\le 6$$
$$0\le 6$$

This is a true statement. This means that the origin will fall in the shaded half-plane.

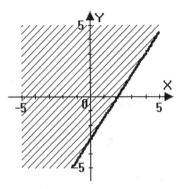

74.

$$m=\frac{y_2-y_1}{x_2-x_1}=\frac{5-(-3)}{1-(-2)}=\frac{5+3}{1+2}=\frac{8}{3}$$

The slope is $\frac{8}{3}$.

75.

$$(3x-2)(2x^2-4x+3)$$
$$=3x(2x^2-4x+3)-2(2x^2-4x+3)$$
$$=6x^3-12x^2+9x-4x^2+8x-6$$
$$=6x^3-16x^2+17x-6$$

Chapter 13 Review Exercises

1.

$$(x-0)^2+(y-0)^2=3^2$$
$$x^2+y^2=9$$

2.

$$(x-(-2))^2+(y-4)^2=6^2$$
$$(x+2)^2+(y-4)^2=36$$

3.

$$x^2+y^2=1$$
$$(x-0)^2+(y-0)^2=1^2$$

The center is $(0,0)$ and the radius is 1 units.

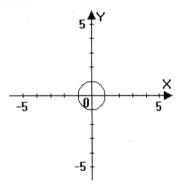

4.

$$(x+2)^2+(y-3)^2=9$$
$$(x-(-2))^2+(y-3)^2=3^2$$

The center is $(-2,3)$ and the radius is 3 units.

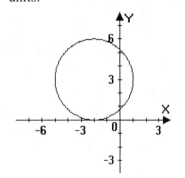

5.
$$x^2 + y^2 - 4x + 2y - 4 = 0$$
$$\left(x^2 - 4x \quad\right) + \left(y^2 + 2y \quad\right) = 4$$

Complete the squares.

$$\left(\frac{b}{2}\right)^2 = \left(\frac{-4}{2}\right)^2 = (-4)^2 = 4$$

$$\left(\frac{b}{2}\right)^2 = \left(\frac{2}{2}\right)^2 = 1^2 = 1$$

$$\left(x^2 - 4x + 4\right) + \left(y^2 + 2y + 1\right) = 4 + 4 + 1$$
$$\left(x - 2\right)^2 + \left(y + 1\right)^2 = 9$$
$$\left(x - 2\right)^2 + \left(y - (-1)\right)^2 = 3^2$$

The center is $(2, -1)$ and the radius is 3 units.

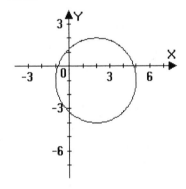

6.
$$x^2 + y^2 - 4y = 0$$
$$x^2 + \left(y^2 - 4y \quad\right) = 0$$

Complete the square.

$$\left(\frac{b}{2}\right)^2 = \left(\frac{-4}{2}\right)^2 = (-4)^2 = 4$$

$$x^2 + \left(y^2 - 4y + 4\right) = 0 + 4$$
$$\left(x - 0\right)^2 + \left(y - 2\right)^2 = 4$$
$$\left(x - 0\right)^2 + \left(y - 2\right)^2 = 2^2$$

The center is $(0, 2)$ and the radius is 2 units.

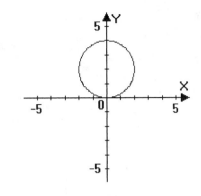

7.
$$\frac{x^2}{36} + \frac{y^2}{25} = 1$$

Because the denominator of the x^2 – term is greater than the denominator of the y^2 – term, the major axis is horizontal. Since $a^2 = 36$, $a = 6$ and the vertices are $(-6, 0)$ and $(6, 0)$. Since $b^2 = 25$, $b = 5$ and endpoints of the minor axis are $(0, -5)$ and $(0, 5)$.

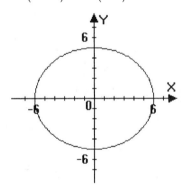

8.
$$\frac{x^2}{25} + \frac{y^2}{16} = 1$$

Because the denominator of the x^2 – term is greater than the denominator of the y^2 – term, the major axis is horizontal. Since $a^2 = 25$, $a = 5$ and the vertices are $(-5, 0)$ and $(5, 0)$. Since $b^2 = 16$,

$b = 4$ and endpoints of the minor axis are $(0, -4)$ and $(0, 4)$.

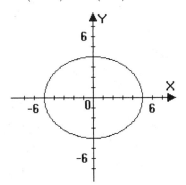

9. $4x^2 + y^2 = 16$

$$\frac{4x^2}{16} + \frac{y^2}{16} = \frac{16}{16}$$

$$\frac{x^2}{4} + \frac{y^2}{16} = 1$$

Because the denominator of the y^2 – term is greater than the denominator of the x^2 – term, the major axis is vertical. Since $a^2 = 16$, $a = 4$ and the vertices are $(0, -4)$ and $(0, 4)$. Since $b^2 = 4$, $b = 2$ and endpoints of the minor axis are $(-2, 0)$ and $(2, 0)$.

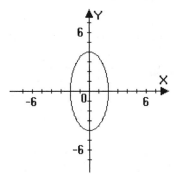

10. $4x^2 + 9y^2 = 36$

$$\frac{4x^2}{36} + \frac{9y^2}{36} = \frac{36}{36}$$

$$\frac{x^2}{9} + \frac{y^2}{4} = 1$$

Because the denominator of the x^2 – term is greater than the denominator of the y^2 – term, the major axis is horizontal. Since $a^2 = 9$, $a = 3$ and the vertices are $(-3, 0)$ and $(3, 0)$. Since $b^2 = 4$, $b = 2$ and endpoints of the minor axis are $(0, -2)$ and $(0, 2)$.

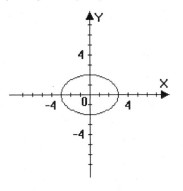

11. $\dfrac{(x-1)^2}{16} + \dfrac{(y+2)^2}{9} = 1$

The center of the ellipse is $(1, -2)$. Because the denominator of the x^2 – term is greater than the denominator of the y^2 – term, the major axis is horizontal. Since $a^2 = 16$, $a = 4$ and the vertices lie 4 units to the left and right of the center. Since $b^2 = 9$, $b = 3$ and endpoints of the minor axis lie 3 units above and below the center.

809

Center	Vertices	Endpoints of Minor Axis
$(1,-2)$	$(1-4,-2)$ $=(-3,-2)$	$(1,-2-3)$ $=(1,-5)$
	$(1+4,-2)$ $=(5,-2)$	$(1,-2+3)$ $=(1,1)$

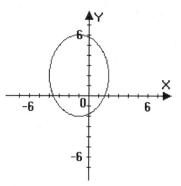

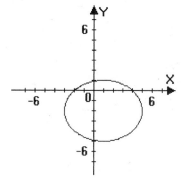

12. $\dfrac{(x+1)^2}{9}+\dfrac{(y-2)^2}{16}=1$

The center of the ellipse is $(-1,2)$.
Because the denominator of the
$y^2-\text{term}$ is greater than the
denominator of the $x^2-\text{term}$ the major
axis is vertical. Since $a^2=16$, $a=4$
and the vertices lie 4 units above and
below the center. Since $b^2=9$, $b=3$
and endpoints of the minor axis lie 3
units to the left and right of the center.

Center	Vertices	Endpoints of Minor Axis
$(-1,2)$	$(-1,2-4)$ $=(-1,-2)$	$(-1-3,2)$ $=(-4,2)$
	$(-1,2+4)$ $=(-1,6)$	$(-1+3,2)$ $=(2,2)$

13. From the figure, we see that the major
axis is horizontal with $a=25$, and
$b=15$.

$$\frac{x^2}{25^2}+\frac{y^2}{15^2}=1$$

$$\frac{x^2}{625}+\frac{y^2}{225}=1$$

Since the truck is 14 feet wide, we need
to determine the height of the archway
at 14 feet to the right of center.

$$\frac{14^2}{625}+\frac{y^2}{225}=1$$

$$\frac{196}{625}+\frac{y^2}{225}=1$$

$$5625\left(\frac{196}{625}+\frac{y^2}{225}\right)=5625(1)$$

$$9(196)+25y^2=5625$$

$$1764+25y^2=5625$$

$$25y^2=3861$$

$$y^2=\frac{3861}{25}$$

$$y=\sqrt{\frac{3861}{25}}\approx 12.43$$

The height of the archway 14 feet from
the center is approximately 12.43 feet.
Since the truck is 12 feet high, the truck
will clear the archway.

14. $\dfrac{x^2}{16} - y^2 = 1$

$\dfrac{x^2}{16} - \dfrac{y^2}{1} = 1$

The equation is in the form $\dfrac{x^2}{a^2} - \dfrac{y^2}{b^2} = 1$

with $a^2 = 16$, and $b^2 = 1$. We know the transverse axis lies on the x-axis and the vertices are $(-4, 0)$ and $(4, 0)$.

Because $a^2 = 16$ and $b^2 = 1$, $a = 4$ and $b = 1$. Construct a rectangle using -4 and 4 on the x–axis, and -1 and 1 on the y–axis. Draw extended diagonals to obtain the asymptotes. Graph the hyperbola.

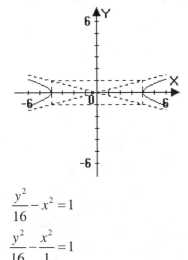

15. $\dfrac{y^2}{16} - x^2 = 1$

$\dfrac{y^2}{16} - \dfrac{x^2}{1} = 1$

The equation is in the form $\dfrac{y^2}{a^2} - \dfrac{x^2}{b^2} = 1$

with $a^2 = 16$, and $b^2 = 1$. We know the transverse axis lies on the y-axis and the vertices are $(0, -4)$ and $(0, 4)$.

Because $a^2 = 16$ and $b^2 = 1$, $a = 4$ and $b = 1$. Construct a rectangle using -1 and 1 on the x–axis, and -4 and 4 on the y–axis. Draw extended diagonals to obtain the asymptotes.

Graph the hyperbola.

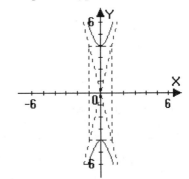

16. $9x^2 - 16y^2 = 144$

$\dfrac{9x^2}{144} - \dfrac{16y^2}{144} = \dfrac{144}{144}$

$\dfrac{x^2}{16} - \dfrac{y^2}{9} = 1$

The equation is in the form $\dfrac{x^2}{a^2} - \dfrac{y^2}{b^2} = 1$

with $a^2 = 16$, and $b^2 = 9$. We know the transverse axis lies on the x-axis and the vertices are $(-4, 0)$ and $(4, 0)$.

Because $a^2 = 16$ and $b^2 = 9$, $a = 4$ and $b = 3$. Construct a rectangle using -4 and 4 on the x–axis, and -3 and 3 on the y–axis. Draw extended diagonals to obtain the asymptotes. Graph the hyperbola.

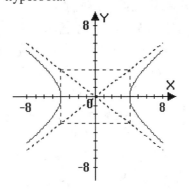

811

17. $4y^2 - x^2 = 16$

$$\frac{4y^2}{16} - \frac{x^2}{16} = \frac{16}{16}$$

$$\frac{y^2}{4} - \frac{x^2}{16} = 1$$

The equation is in the form $\dfrac{y^2}{a^2} - \dfrac{x^2}{b^2} = 1$

with $a^2 = 16$, and $b^2 = 4$. We know the transverse axis lies on the y-axis and the vertices are $(0, -4)$ and $(0, 4)$.

Because $a^2 = 16$ and $b^2 = 4$,

$a = 4$ and $b = 2$. Construct a rectangle using -2 and 2 on the x–axis, and -4 and 4 on the
y–axis. Draw extended diagonals to obtain the asymptotes. Graph the hyperbola.

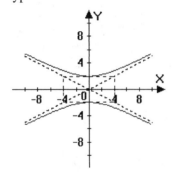

18. $x = (y - 3)^2 - 4$

This is a parabola of the form
$x = a(y - k)^2 + h$. Since $a = 1$ is
positive, the parabola opens to the right.
The vertex of the parabola is $(-4, 3)$.
The axis of symmetry is $y = 3$.
Replace y with 0 to find the x–intercept.
$x = (0 - 3)^2 - 4 = (-3)^2 - 4 = 9 - 4 = 5$
The x–intercept is 5. Replace x with 0
to find the y–intercepts.

$0 = (y - 3)^2 - 4$

$0 = y^2 - 6y + 9 - 4$

$0 = y^2 - 6y + 5$

$0 = (y - 5)(y - 1)$

Apply the zero product principle.

$y - 5 = 0$ and $y - 1 = 0$

$y = 5$ $\qquad\qquad y = 1$

The y–intercepts are 1 and 5.

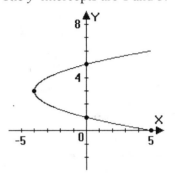

19. $x = -2(y + 3)^2 + 2$

This is a parabola of the form
$x = a(y - k)^2 + h$. Since $a = -2$ is
negative, the parabola opens to the left.
The vertex of the parabola is $(2, -3)$.
The axis of symmetry is $y = -3$.
Replace y with 0 to find the x–intercept.
$x = -2(0 + 3)^2 + 2 = -2(3)^2 + 2$

$\quad = -2(9) + 2 = -18 + 2 = -16$

The x–intercept is -16. Replace x with
0 to find the y–intercepts.

$0 = -2(y + 3)^2 + 2$

$0 = -2(y^2 + 6y + 9) + 2$

$0 = -2y^2 - 12y - 18 + 2$

$0 = -2y^2 - 12y - 16$

$0 = y^2 + 6y + 8$

$0 = (y + 4)(y + 2)$

Apply the zero product principle.

$y + 4 = 0$ and $y + 2 = 0$

$y = -4$ $\quad\quad$ $y = -2$

The y–intercepts are –4 and –2.

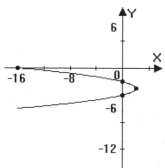

20. $x = y^2 - 8y + 12$

This is a parabola of the form $x = ay^2 + by + c$. Since $a = 1$ is positive, the parabola opens to the right. The y–coordinate of the vertex is

$$-\frac{b}{2a} = -\frac{-8}{2(1)} = -\frac{-8}{2} = 4.$$ The

x–coordinate of the vertex is

$x = 4^2 - 8(4) + 12 = 16 - 32 + 12$

$\quad = 16 - 32 + 12 = -4.$

The vertex of the parabola is $(-4, 4)$.

The axis of symmetry is $y = 4$.

Replace y with 0 to find the x–intercept.

$x = 0^2 - 8(0) + 12 = 12$

The x–intercept is 12. Replace x with 0 to find the y–intercepts.

$0 = y^2 - 8y + 12$

$0 = (y - 6)(y - 2)$

Apply the zero product principle.

$y - 6 = 0$ and $y - 2 = 0$

$\quad y = 6$ $\quad\quad$ $y = 2$

The y–intercepts are 2 and 6.

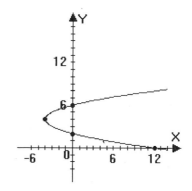

21. $x = -y^2 - 4y + 6$

This is a parabola of the form $x = ay^2 + by + c$. Since $a = -1$ is negative, the parabola opens to the left. The y–coordinate of the vertex is

$$-\frac{b}{2a} = -\frac{-4}{2(-1)} = -\frac{-4}{-2} = -2.$$ The

x–coordinate of the vertex is

$x = -(-2)^2 - 4(-2) + 6$

$\quad = -4 + 8 + 6 = 10.$

The vertex of the parabola is $(10, -2)$.

The axis of symmetry is $y = -2$.

Replace y with 0 to find the x–intercept.

$x = -0^2 - 4(0) + 6 = 0^2 - 0 + 6 = 6$

The x–intercept is 6. Replace x with 0 to find the y–intercepts.

$0 = -y^2 - 4y + 6$

Solve using the quadratic formula.

$$y = \frac{-b \pm \sqrt{b^2 - 4ac}}{2a}$$

$$= \frac{-(-4) \pm \sqrt{(-4)^2 - 4(-1)(6)}}{2(-1)}$$

$$= \frac{4 \pm \sqrt{16 + 24}}{-2} = \frac{4 \pm \sqrt{40}}{-2}$$

$$= \frac{4 \pm 2\sqrt{10}}{-2} = -2 \pm \sqrt{10}$$

The y–intercepts are $-2 \pm \sqrt{10}$.

813

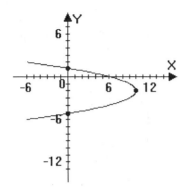

22. $x + 8y = y^2 + 10$

Since only one variable is squared, the graph of the equation is a parabola.

23.
$$16x^2 = 32 - y^2$$
$$16x^2 + y^2 = 32$$

Because x^2 and y^2 have different positive coefficients, the equation's graph is an ellipse.

24.
$$x^2 = 25 + 25y^2$$
$$x^2 - 25y^2 = 25$$

Because x^2 and y^2 have opposite signs, the equation's graph is a hyperbola.

25.
$$x^2 = 4 - y^2$$
$$x^2 + y^2 = 4$$

Because x^2 and y^2 have the same positive coefficient, the equation's graph is a circle.

26.
$$36y^2 = 576 + 16x^2$$
$$36y^2 - 16x^2 = 576$$

Because x^2 and y^2 have opposite signs, the equation's graph is a hyperbola.

27. $\dfrac{(x+3)^2}{9} + \dfrac{(y-4)^2}{25} = 1$

Because x^2 and y^2 have different positive coefficients, the equation's graph is an ellipse.

28. $y = x^2 + 6x + 9$

Since only one variable is squared, the graph of the equation is a parabola.

29. $5x^2 + 5y^2 = 180$

Because x^2 and y^2 have the same positive coefficient, the equation's graph is a circle.
Divide both sides of the equation by 5.
$$x^2 + y^2 = 36$$
The center is (0, 0) and the radius is 6 units.

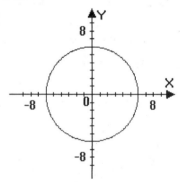

814

30. $4x^2 + 9y^2 = 36$

Because x^2 and y^2 have different positive coefficients, the equation's graph is an ellipse.

$$\frac{4x^2}{36} + \frac{9y^2}{36} = \frac{36}{36}$$

$$\frac{x^2}{9} + \frac{y^2}{4} = 1$$

Because the denominator of the $x^2 -$ term is greater than the denominator of the $y^2 -$ term, the major axis is horizontal. Since $a^2 = 9$, $a = 3$ and the vertices are $(-3,0)$ and $(3,0)$. Since $b^2 = 4$, $b = 2$ and endpoints of the minor axis are $(0,-2)$ and $(0,2)$.

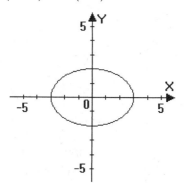

31. $4x^2 - 9y^2 = 36$

Because x^2 and y^2 have opposite signs, the equation's graph is a hyperbola.

$$\frac{4x^2}{36} - \frac{9y^2}{36} = \frac{36}{36}$$

$$\frac{x^2}{9} - \frac{y^2}{4} = 1$$

The equation is in the form $\frac{x^2}{a^2} - \frac{y^2}{b^2} = 1$

with $a^2 = 9$, and $b^2 = 4$.

We know the transverse axis lies on the x-axis and the vertices are $(-3,0)$ and $(3,0)$. Because $a^2 = 9$ and $b^2 = 4$, $a = 3$ and $b = 2$. Construct a rectangle using -3 and 3 on the x-axis, and -2 and 2 on the y-axis. Draw extended diagonals to obtain the asymptotes. Graph the hyperbola.

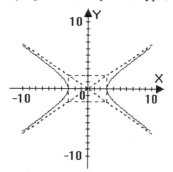

32. $\frac{x^2}{25} + \frac{y^2}{1} = 1$

Because x^2 and y^2 have different positive coefficients, the equation's graph is an ellipse.
Because the denominator of the $x^2 -$ term is greater than the denominator of the $y^2 -$ term, the major axis is horizontal. Since $a^2 = 25$, $a = 5$ and the vertices are $(-5,0)$ and $(5,0)$. Since $b^2 = 1$, $b = 1$ and endpoints of the minor axis are $(0,-1)$ and $(0,1)$.

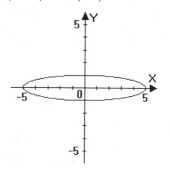

33. $x + 3 = -y^2 + 2y$

$\qquad x = -y^2 + 2y - 3$

Since only one variable is squared, the graph of the equation is a parabola. This is a parabola of the form $x = ay^2 + by + c$. Since $a = -1$ is negative, the parabola opens to the left. The y–coordinate of the vertex is

$-\dfrac{b}{2a} = -\dfrac{2}{2(-1)} = -\dfrac{2}{-2} = 1.$ The x–

coordinate of the vertex is

$x = -1^2 + 2(1) - 3 = -1 + 2 - 3 = -2.$

The vertex of the parabola is $(-2, 1)$.

Replace y with 0 to find the x–intercept.

$x = -0^2 + 2(0) - 3 = 0 + 0 - 3 = -3$

The x–intercept is –3. Replace x with 0 to find the y–intercepts.

$0 = -y^2 + 2y - 3$

Solve using the quadratic formula.

$y = \dfrac{-2 \pm \sqrt{2^2 - 4(-1)(-3)}}{2(-1)}$

$\quad = \dfrac{-2 \pm \sqrt{4 - 12}}{-2} = \dfrac{-2 \pm \sqrt{-8}}{-2}$

We do not need to simplify further. The solutions are complex and there are no y–intercepts.

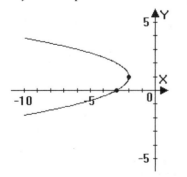

34. $y - 3 = x^2 - 2x$

$\qquad y = x^2 - 2x + 3$

Since only one variable is squared, the graph of the equation is a parabola. This is a parabola of the form $y = ax^2 + bx + c$. Since $a = 1$ is positive, the parabola opens to the right. The x–coordinate of the vertex is

$-\dfrac{b}{2a} = -\dfrac{-2}{2(1)} = -\dfrac{-2}{2} = 1.$ The y–

coordinate of the vertex is

$y = 1^2 - 2(1) + 3 = 1 - 2 + 3 = 2.$

The vertex of the parabola is $(1, 2)$.

Replace x with 0 to find the y–intercept.

$y = 0^2 - 2(0) + 3 = 0 - 0 + 3 = 3$

The y–intercept is 3. Replace y with 0 to find the x–intercepts.

$0 = x^2 - 2x + 3$

Solve using the quadratic formula.

$x = \dfrac{-2 \pm \sqrt{2^2 - 4(-1)(-3)}}{2(-1)}$

$\quad = \dfrac{-2 \pm \sqrt{4 - 12}}{-2} = \dfrac{-2 \pm \sqrt{-8}}{-2}$

We do not need to simplify further. The solutions are complex and there are no x–intercepts.

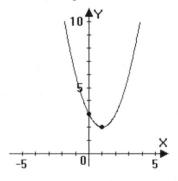

816

35. $\dfrac{(x+2)^2}{16}+\dfrac{(y-5)^2}{4}=1$

Because x^2 and y^2 have different positive coefficients, the equation's graph is an ellipse.

The center of the ellipse is $(-2,5)$.

Because the denominator of the $x^2-\text{term}$ is greater than the denominator of the $y^2-\text{term}$, the major axis is horizontal. Since $a^2=16$, $a=4$ and the vertices lie 4 units to the left and right of the center. Since $b^2=4$, $b=2$ and endpoints of the minor axis lie two units above and below the center.

Center	Vertices	Endpoints of Minor Axis
$(-2,5)$	$(-2-4,5)$ $=(-6,5)$	$(-2,5-2)$ $=(-2,3)$
	$(-2+4,5)$ $=(2,5)$	$(-2,5+2)$ $=(-2,7)$

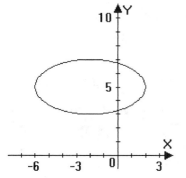

36. $(x-3)^2+(y+2)^2=4$

Because x^2 and y^2 have the same positive coefficient, the equation's graph is a circle.

$(x-3)^2+(y+2)^2=4$

The center is $(3,-2)$ and the radius is 2 units.

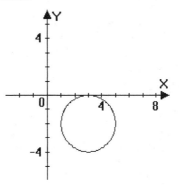

37. $x^2+y^2+6x-2y+6=0$

$\left(x^2+6x\quad\right)+\left(y^2-2y\quad\right)=-6$

Complete the squares.

$\left(\dfrac{b}{2}\right)^2=\left(\dfrac{6}{2}\right)^2=(3)^2=9$

$\left(\dfrac{b}{2}\right)^2=\left(\dfrac{-2}{2}\right)^2=(-1)^2=1$

$\left(x^2+6x+9\right)+\left(y^2-2y+1\right)=-6+9+1$

$(x+3)^2+(y-1)^2=4$

The center is $(-3,1)$ and the radius is 2 units.

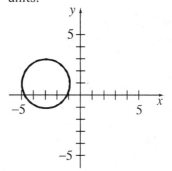

817

38. **a.** Using the point (6, 3), substitute for x and y to find a in $y = ax^2$.

$$3 = a(6)^2$$

$$3 = a(36)$$

$$a = \frac{3}{36} = \frac{1}{12}$$

The equation for the parabola is

$$y = \frac{1}{12}x^2.$$

b.
$$a = \frac{1}{4p}$$

$$\frac{1}{12} = \frac{1}{4p}$$

$$4p = 12$$

$$p = 3$$

The light source should be placed at the point (0, 3). This is the point 3 inches above the vertex.

39.
$$5y = x^2 - 1$$

$$x - y = 1$$

Solve the second equation for y.

$$x - y = 1$$

$$-y = -x + 1$$

$$y = x - 1$$

Substitute $x - 1$ for y in the first equation.

$$5(x-1) = x^2 - 1$$

$$5x - 5 = x^2 - 1$$

$$0 = x^2 - 5x + 4$$

$$0 = (x-4)(x-1)$$

Apply the zero product principle.

$$x - 4 = 0 \quad \text{and} \quad x - 1 = 0$$

$$x = 4 \qquad\qquad x = 1$$

Back-substitute 1 and 4 for x to find y.

$$x = 4 \qquad \text{and} \qquad x = 1$$

$$y = x - 1 \qquad\qquad y = x - 1$$

$$y = 4 - 1 \qquad\qquad y = 1 - 1$$

$$y = 3 \qquad\qquad y = 0$$

The solutions are $(1, 0)$ and $(4, 3)$ and the solution set is $\{(1,0),(4,3)\}$.

40.
$$y = x^2 + 2x + 1$$

$$x + y = 1$$

Solve the second equation for y.

$$x + y = 1$$

$$y = -x + 1$$

Substitute $-x + 1$ for y in the first equation.

$$-x + 1 = x^2 + 2x + 1$$

$$0 = x^2 + 3x$$

$$0 = x(x+3)$$

Apply the zero product principle.

$$x = 0 \quad \text{and} \quad x + 3 = 0$$

$$x = -3$$

Back-substitute -3 and 0 for x to find y.

$$x = 0 \qquad \text{and} \qquad x = -3$$

$$y = -x + 1 \qquad\qquad y = -x + 1$$

$$y = -0 + 1 \qquad\qquad y = -(-3) + 1$$

$$y = 1 \qquad\qquad y = 3 + 1$$

$$y = 4$$

The solutions are $(-3, 4)$ and $(0, 1)$ and the solution set is $\{(-3,4),(0,1)\}$.

41. $x^2 + y^2 = 2$

$x + y = 0$

Solve the second equation for y.

$x + y = 0$

$y = -x$

Substitute $-x$ for y in the first equation.

$x^2 + (-x)^2 = 2$

$x^2 + x^2 = 2$

$2x^2 = 2$

$x^2 = 1$

$x = \pm 1$

Back-substitute -1 and 1 for x to find y.

$x = -1$ and $x = 1$

$y = -x$ $\qquad y = -x\cdot$

$y = -(-1)$ $\qquad y = -1$

$y = 1$

The solution set is $\{(-1,1),\ (1,-1)\}$.

42. $2x^2 + y^2 = 24$

$x^2 + y^2 = 15$

Multiple the second equation by -1 and add to the first equation.

$2x^2 + y^2 = \ \ 24$

$\underline{-x^2 - y^2 = -15}$

$x^2 = 9$

$x = \pm 3$

Back-substitute -3 and 3 for x to find y.

$x = \pm 3$

$(\pm 3)^2 + y^2 = 15$

$9 + y^2 = 15$

$y^2 = 6$

$y = \pm\sqrt{6}$

The solution set is $\left\{\left(-3,-\sqrt{6}\right),\right.$

$\left.\left(-3,\sqrt{6}\right),\left(3,-\sqrt{6}\right),\left(3,\sqrt{6}\right)\right\}$.

43. $xy - 4 = 0$

$y - x = 0$

Solve the second equation for y.

$y - x = 0$

$y = x$

Substitute x for y in the first equation and solve for x.

$x(x) - 4 = 0$

$x^2 - 4 = 0$

$(x + 2)(x - 2) = 0$

Apply the zero product principle.

$x + 2 = 0$ and $x - 2 = 0$

$x = -2$ $\qquad x = 2$

Back-substitute -2 and 2 for x to find y.

$x = -2$ and $x = 2$

$y = x$ $\qquad y = x$

$y = -2$ $\qquad y = 2$

The solution set is $\{(-2,-2),\ (2,2)\}$.

44. $y^2 = 4x$

$x - 2y + 3 = 0$

Solve the second equation for x.

$x - 2y + 3 = 0$

$x = 2y - 3$

Substitute $2y - 3$ for x in the first equation and solve for y.

$y^2 = 4(2y - 3)$

$y^2 = 8y - 12$

$y^2 - 8y + 12 = 0$

$(y - 6)(y - 2) = 0$

Apply the zero product principle.

$y - 6 = 0$ and $y - 2 = 0$

$y = 6$ $\qquad y = 2$

Back-substitute 2 and 6 for y to find x.

$$y = 6 \quad \text{and} \quad y = 2$$
$$x = 2y - 3 \qquad\qquad x = 2y - 3$$
$$x = 2(6) - 3 \qquad\quad x = 2(2) - 3$$
$$x = 12 - 3 \qquad\qquad x = 4 - 3$$
$$x = 9 \qquad\qquad\quad x = 1$$

The solutions are $(1, 2)$ and $(9, 6)$ and the solution set is $\{(1, 2), (9, 6)\}$.

45. $x^2 + y^2 = 10$
$$y = x + 2$$

Substitute $x + 2$ for y in the first equation and solve for x.

$$x^2 + (x + 2)^2 = 10$$
$$x^2 + x^2 + 4x + 4 = 10$$
$$2x^2 + 4x + 4 = 10$$
$$2x^2 + 4x - 6 = 0$$
$$x^2 + 2x - 3 = 0$$
$$(x + 3)(x - 1) = 0$$

Apply the zero product principle.
$$x + 3 = 0 \quad \text{and} \quad x - 1 = 0$$
$$x = -3 \qquad\qquad x = 1$$

Back-substitute –3 and 1 for x to find y.

$$x = -3 \quad \text{and} \quad x = 1$$
$$y = x + 2 \qquad\qquad y = x + 2$$
$$y = -3 + 2 \qquad\quad y = 1 + 2$$
$$y = -1 \qquad\qquad\quad y = 3$$

The solutions are $(-3, -1)$ and $(1, 3)$ and the solution set is $\{(-3, -1),$ $(1, 3)\}$.

46. $xy = 1$
$$y = 2x + 1$$

Substitute $2x + 1$ for y in the first equation and solve for x.

$$x(2x + 1) = 1$$
$$2x^2 + x = 1$$
$$2x^2 + x - 1 = 0$$
$$(2x - 1)(x + 1) = 0$$

Apply the zero product principle.
$$2x - 1 = 0 \quad \text{and} \quad x + 1 = 0$$
$$2x = 1 \qquad\qquad\quad x = -1$$
$$x = \frac{1}{2}$$

Back-substitute -1 and $\dfrac{1}{2}$ for x to find y.

$$x = -1 \qquad \text{and} \qquad x = \frac{1}{2}$$
$$y = 2x + 1 \qquad\qquad y = 2x + 1$$
$$y = 2(-1) + 1 \qquad\quad y = 2\left(\frac{1}{2}\right) + 1$$
$$y = -2 + 1 \qquad\qquad y = 1 + 1$$
$$y = -1 \qquad\qquad\qquad y = 2$$

The solutions are $(-1, -1)$ and $\left(\dfrac{1}{2}, 2\right)$ and the solution set is

$$\left\{(-1, -1), \left(\frac{1}{2}, 2\right)\right\}.$$

47. $x + y + 1 = 0$
$$x^2 + y^2 + 6y - x = -5$$

Solve for y in the first equation.
$$x + y + 1 = 0$$
$$y = -x - 1$$

Substitute $-x - 1$ for y in the second equation and solve for x.

$$x^2 + (-x-1)^2 + 6(-x-1) - x = -5$$
$$x^2 + x^2 + 2x + 1 - 6x - 6 - x = -5$$
$$2x^2 - 5x - 5 = -5$$
$$2x^2 - 5x = 0$$
$$x(2x-5) = 0$$

Apply the zero product principle.
$$x = 0 \quad \text{and} \quad 2x - 5 = 0$$
$$2x = 5$$
$$x = \frac{5}{2}$$

Back-substitute 0 and $\frac{5}{2}$ for x to find y.

$$x = 0 \quad \text{and} \quad x = \frac{5}{2}$$

$$y = -x - 1 \qquad y = -x - 1$$
$$y = -0 - 1 \qquad y = -\frac{5}{2} - 1$$
$$y = -1 \qquad\qquad y = -\frac{7}{2}$$

The solutions are $(0, -1)$ and $\left(\frac{5}{2}, -\frac{7}{2}\right)$

and the solution set is

$$\left\{ (0, -1), \left(\frac{5}{2}, -\frac{7}{2}\right) \right\}.$$

48. $\quad x^2 + y^2 = 13$

$\qquad x^2 - y = 7$

Solve for x^2 in the second equation.
$$x^2 - y = 7$$
$$x^2 = y + 7$$

Substitute $y + 7$ for x^2 in the first equation and solve for y.
$$(y + 7) + y^2 = 13$$
$$y^2 + y + 7 = 13$$
$$y^2 + y - 6 = 0$$
$$(y + 3)(y - 2) = 0$$

Apply the zero product principle.
$$y + 3 = 0 \quad \text{and} \quad y - 2 = 0$$
$$y = -3 \qquad\qquad y = 2$$

Back-substitute -3 and 2 for y to find x.

$$y = -3 \quad \text{and} \quad y = 2$$
$$x^2 = y + 7 \qquad x^2 = y + 7$$
$$x^2 = -3 + 7 \qquad x^2 = 2 + 7$$
$$x^2 = 4 \qquad\qquad x^2 = 9$$
$$x = \pm 2 \qquad\qquad x = \pm 3$$

The solutions are $(-3, 2), (-2, -3)$,

$(2, -3)$ and $(3, 2)$ and the solution set is

$$\left\{ (-3, 2), (-2, -3), (2, -3), (3, 2) \right\}.$$

49. $\quad 2x^2 + 3y^2 = 21$

$\qquad 3x^2 - 4y^2 = 23$

Multiply the first equation by 4 and the second equation by 3.
$$8x^2 + 12y^2 = 84$$
$$\underline{9x^2 - 12y^2 = 69}$$
$$17x^2 = 153$$
$$x^2 = 9$$
$$x = \pm 3$$

Back-substitute ± 3 for x to find y.
$$x = \pm 3$$
$$2(\pm 3)^2 + 3y^2 = 21$$
$$2(9) + 3y^2 = 21$$
$$18 + 3y^2 = 21$$
$$3y^2 = 3$$
$$y^2 = 1$$
$$y = \pm 1$$

We have $x = \pm 3$ and $y = \pm 1$, the

solutions are $(-3, -1), (-3, 1), (3, -1)$

and $(3, 1)$ and the solution set is

$$\left\{ (-3, -1), (-3, 1), (3, -1), (3, 1) \right\}.$$

50. Let x = the length of the rectangle
Let y = the width of the rectangle
$$2x + 2y = 26$$
$$xy = 40$$
Solve the first equation for y.
$$2x + 2y = 26$$
$$x + y = 13$$
$$y = 13 - x$$
Substitute $13 - x$ for y in the second equation.
$$x(13 - x) = 40$$
$$13x - x^2 = 40$$
$$0 = x^2 - 13x + 40$$
$$0 = (x - 8)(x - 5)$$
Apply the zero product principle.
$$x - 8 = 0 \quad \text{and} \quad x - 5 = 0$$
$$x = 8 \qquad\qquad x = 5$$
Back-substitute 5 and 8 for x to find y.
$$x = 8 \qquad \text{and} \quad x = 5$$
$$y = 13 - 8 \qquad y = 13 - 5$$
$$y = 5 \qquad\qquad y = 8$$
The solutions are the same. The dimensions are 8 meters by 5 meters.

51. $$2x + y = 8$$
$$xy = 6$$
Solve the first equation for y.
$$2x + y = 8$$
$$y = -2x + 8$$
Substitute $-2x + 8$ for y in the second equation.
$$x(-2x + 8) = 6$$
$$-2x^2 + 8x = 6$$
$$-2x^2 + 8x - 6 = 0$$
$$x^2 - 4x + 3 = 0$$
$$(x - 3)(x - 1) = 0$$
Apply the zero product principle.

$$x - 3 = 0 \quad \text{and} \quad x - 1 = 0$$
$$x = 3 \qquad\qquad x = 1$$
Back-substitute 1 and 3 for x to find y.
$$x = 3 \qquad \text{and} \quad x = 1$$
$$y = -2x + 8 \qquad y = -2x + 8$$
$$y = -2(3) + 8 \qquad y = -2(1) + 8$$
$$y = -6 + 8 \qquad y = -2 + 8$$
$$y = 2 \qquad\qquad y = 6$$
The solutions are the points $(1, 6)$ and $(3, 2)$.

52. Using the formula for the area, we have $x^2 + y^2 = 2900$. Since there are 240 feet of fencing available, we have:
$$x + (x + y) + y + y + (x - y) + x = 240$$
$$x + x + y + y + y + x - y + x = 240$$
$$4x + 2y = 240.$$
The system of two variables in two equations is as follows.
$$x^2 + y^2 = 2900$$
$$4x + 2y = 240$$
Solve the second equation for y.
$$4x + 2y = 240$$
$$2y = -4x + 240$$
$$y = -2x + 120$$
Substitute $-2x + 120$ for y to find x.
$$x^2 + (-2x + 120)^2 = 2900$$
$$x^2 + 4x^2 - 480x + 14400 = 2900$$
$$5x^2 - 480x + 11500 = 0$$
$$x^2 - 96x + 2300 = 0$$
$$(x - 50)(x - 46) = 0$$
Apply the zero product principle.
$$x - 50 = 0 \quad \text{and} \quad x - 46 = 0$$
$$x = 50 \qquad\qquad x = 46$$
Back-substitute 46 and 50 for x to find y.

$x = 50$ $x = 46$

$y = -2x + 120$ $y = -2x + 120$

$y = -2(50) + 120$ $y = -2(46) + 120$

$y = -100 + 120$ $y = -92 + 120$

$y = 20$ $y = 28$

The solutions are $x = 50$ feet and $y = 20$ feet or $x = 46$ feet and $y = 28$ feet.

Chapter 13 Test

1. $(x-3)^2 + \left(y-(-2)\right)^2 = 5^2$

$(x-3)^2 + (y+2)^2 = 25$

2. $(x-5)^2 + (y+3)^2 = 49$

$(x-5)^2 + \left(y-(-3)\right)^2 = 7^2$

The center is $(5,-3)$ and the radius is 7 units.

3. $x^2 + y^2 + 4x - 6y - 3 = 0$

$\left(x^2 + 4x \quad\right) + \left(y^2 - 6y \quad\right) = 3$

Complete the squares.

$\left(\dfrac{b}{2}\right)^2 = \left(\dfrac{4}{2}\right)^2 = (2)^2 = 4$

$\left(\dfrac{b}{2}\right)^2 = \left(\dfrac{-6}{2}\right)^2 = (-3)^2 = 9$

$\left(x^2 + 4x + 4\right) + \left(y^2 - 6y + 9\right) = 3 + 4 + 9$

$(x+2)^2 + (y-3)^2 = 16$

$\left(x-(-2)\right)^2 + (y-3)^2 = 4^2$

The center is $(-2,3)$ and the radius is 4 units.

4. $x = -2(y+3)^2 + 7$

$x = -2\left(y-(-3)\right)^2 + 7$

The vertex of the parabola is $(7,-3)$.

5. $x = y^2 + 10y + 23$

The y–coordinate of the vertex is

$-\dfrac{b}{2a} = -\dfrac{10}{2(1)} = -\dfrac{10}{2} = -5.$

The x–coordinate of the vertex is

$x = (-5)^2 + 10(-5) + 23$

$= 25 - 50 + 23$

$= 25 - 50 + 23 = -2.$

The vertex of the parabola is $(-2,-5)$.

6. $\dfrac{x^2}{4} - \dfrac{y^2}{9} = 1$

Because x^2 and y^2 have opposite signs, the equation's graph is a hyperbola.

The equation is in the form $\dfrac{x^2}{a^2} - \dfrac{y^2}{b^2} = 1$

with $a^2 = 4$, and $b^2 = 9$. We know the transverse axis lies on the x-axis and the vertices are $(-2,0)$ and $(2,0)$.

Because $a^2 = 4$ and $b^2 = 9$, $a = 2$ and $b = 3$. Construct a rectangle using -2 and 2 on the x–axis, and -3 and 3 on the y–axis. Draw extended diagonals to obtain the asymptotes. Graph the hyperbola.

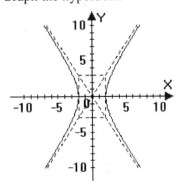

823

7. $4x^2 + 9y^2 = 36$

Because x^2 and y^2 have different positive coefficients, the equation's graph is an ellipse.

$$\frac{4x^2}{36} + \frac{9y^2}{36} = \frac{36}{36}$$

$$\frac{x^2}{9} + \frac{y^2}{4} = 1$$

Because the denominator of the $x^2 -$ term is greater than the denominator of the $y^2 -$ term, the major axis is horizontal. Since $a^2 = 9$, $a = 3$ and the vertices are $(-3,0)$ and $(3,0)$. Since $b^2 = 4$, $b = 2$ and endpoints of the minor axis are $(0,-2)$ and $(0,2)$.

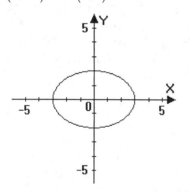

8. $x = (y+1)^2 - 4$

Since only one variable is squared, the graph of the equation is a parabola. This is a parabola of the form $x = a(y-k)^2 + h$. Since $a = 1$ is positive, the parabola opens to the right. The vertex of the parabola is $(4,-1)$.

Replace y with 0 to find the x–intercept.

$$x = (0+1)^2 - 4 = (1)^2 - 4 = 1 - 4 = -3.$$

The x–intercept is 0. Replace x with 0 to find the y–intercepts.

$$0 = (y+1)^2 - 4$$

$$0 = y^2 + 2y + 1 - 4$$

$$0 = y^2 + 2y - 3$$

$$0 = (y+3)(y-1)$$

Apply the zero product principle.

$y+3 = 0$ and $y+1 = 0$

$y = -3$ $\qquad\qquad$ $y = -1$

The y–intercepts are –3 and –1.

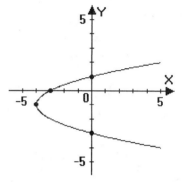

9. $16x^2 + y^2 = 16$

Because x^2 and y^2 have different positive coefficients, the equation's graph is an ellipse.

$$\frac{16x^2}{16} + \frac{y^2}{16} = \frac{16}{16}$$

$$\frac{x^2}{1} + \frac{y^2}{16} = 1$$

Because the denominator of the $y^2 -$ term is greater than the denominator of the $x^2 -$ term, the major axis is vertical. Since $a^2 = 16$, $a = 4$ and the vertices are $(0,-4)$ and $(0,4)$. Since $b^2 = 1$, $b = 1$ and endpoints of the minor axis are $(-1,0)$ and $(1,0)$.

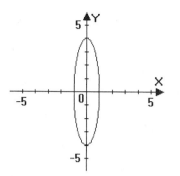

10.
$$25y^2 = 9x^2 + 225$$

$$25y^2 - 9x^2 = 225$$

Because x^2 and y^2 have opposite signs, the equation's graph is a hyperbola.

$$\frac{25y^2}{225} - \frac{9x^2}{225} = \frac{225}{225}$$

$$\frac{y^2}{9} - \frac{x^2}{25} = 1$$

The equation is in the form $\frac{y^2}{a^2} - \frac{x^2}{b^2} = 1$ with $a^2 = 9$, and $b^2 = 25$. We know the transverse axis lies on the y-axis and the vertices are $(0, -3)$ and $(0, 3)$.

Because $a^2 = 9$ and $b^2 = 25$, $a = 35$ and $b = 5$. Construct a rectangle using -5 and 5 on the x-axis, and -3 and 3 on the y-axis. Draw extended diagonals to obtain the asymptotes. Graph the hyperbola.

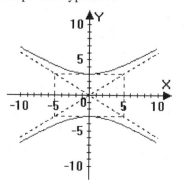

11. $x = -y^2 + 6y$

Since only one variable is squared, the graph of the equation is a parabola. This is a parabola of the form $x = ay^2 + by + c$. Since $a = 1$ is positive, the parabola opens to the right. The y-coordinate of the vertex is
$$-\frac{b}{2a} = -\frac{6}{2(-1)} = -\frac{6}{-2} = 3. \text{ The}$$
x-coordinate of the vertex is
$$x = -3^2 + 6(3) = -9 + 18 = 9.$$

The vertex of the parabola is $(9, 3)$.
Replace y with 0 to find the x-intercept.
$$x = -0^2 + 6(0) = 0 + 0 = 0$$

The x-intercept is 0. Replace x with 0 to find the y-intercepts.
$$0 = -y^2 + 6y$$
$$0 = -y(y - 6)$$

Apply the zero product principle.
$$-y = 0 \quad \text{and} \quad y - 6 = 0$$
$$y = 0 \qquad\qquad y = 6$$

The y-intercepts are 0 and 6.

825

12. $\dfrac{(x-2)^2}{16}+\dfrac{(y+3)^2}{9}=1$

Because x^2 and y^2 have different positive coefficients, the equation's graph is an ellipse.

The center of the ellipse is $(2,-3)$.

Because the denominator of the x^2 – term is greater than the denominator of the y^2 – term, the major axis is horizontal. Since $a^2=16$, $a=4$ and the vertices lie 4 units to the left and right of the center. Since $b^2=9$, $b=3$ and endpoints of the minor axis lie 3 units above and below the center.

Center	Vertices	Endpoints of Minor Axis
$(2,-3)$	$(2-4,-3)$ $=(-2,-3)$	$(2,-3-3)$ $=(2,-6)$
	$(2+4,-3)$ $=(6,-3)$	$(2,-3+3)$ $=(2,0)$

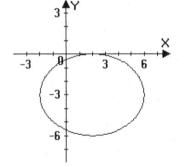

13. $(x+1)^2+(y+2)^2=9$

Because x^2 and y^2 have the same positive coefficient, the equation's graph is a circle.

The center of the circle is $(-1,-2)$ and the radius is 3.

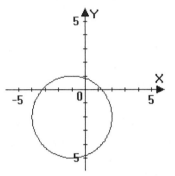

14. $\dfrac{x^2}{4}+\dfrac{y^2}{4}=1$

$4\left(\dfrac{x^2}{4}+\dfrac{y^2}{4}\right)=4(1)$

$x^2+y^2=4$

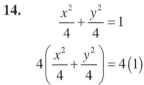

Because x^2 and y^2 have the same positive coefficient, the equation's graph is a circle.

The center of the circle is $(0,0)$ and the radius is 2.

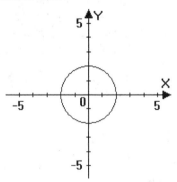

15. $x^2 + y^2 = 25$

$x + y = 1$

Solve the second equation for y.

$x + y = 1$

$y = -x + 1$

Substitute $-x + 1$ for y to find x.

$x^2 + (-x + 1)^2 = 25$

$x^2 + x^2 - 2x + 1 = 25$

$2x^2 - 2x + 1 = 25$

$2x^2 - 2x - 24 = 0$

$x^2 - x - 12 = 0$

$(x - 4)(x + 3) = 0$

Apply the zero product principle.

$x - 4 = 0$ and $x + 3 = 0$

$x = 4$ $x = -3$

Back-substitute -3 and 4 for x to find y.

$x = 4$ and $x = -3$

$y = -x + 1$ $y = -x + 1$

$y = -4 + 1$ $y = -(-3) + 1$

$y = -3$ $y = 3 + 1$

             $y = 4$

The solutions are $(-3, 4)$ and $(4, -3)$ and the solution set is $\{(-3, 4),$ $(4, -3)\}$.

16. $2x^2 - 5y^2 = -2$

$3x^2 + 2y^2 = 35$

Multiply the first equation by 2 and the second equation by 5.

$4x^2 - 10y^2 = -4$

$\underline{15x^2 + 10y^2 = 175}$

$19x^2 = 171$

$x^2 = 9$

$x = \pm 3$

In this case, we can back-substitute 9

for x^2 to find y.

$x^2 = 9$

$2x^2 - 5y^2 = -2$

$2(9) - 5y^2 = -2$

$18 - 5y^2 = -2$

$-5y^2 = -20$

$y^2 = 4$

$y = \pm 2$

We have $x = \pm 3$ and $y = \pm 2$, the solutions are $(-3, -2), (-3, 2), (3, -2)$ and $(3, 2)$ and the solution set is $\{(-3, -2), (-3, 2), (3, -2), (3, 2)\}$.

17. $2x + y = 39$

$xy = 180$

Solve the first equation for y.

$2x + y = 39$

$y = 39 - 2x$

Substitute $39 - 2x$ for y to find x.

$x(39 - 2x) = 180$

$39x - 2x^2 = 180$

$0 = 2x^2 - 39x + 180$

$0 = (2x - 15)(x - 12)$

Apply the zero product principle.

$2x - 15 = 0$ and $x - 12 = 0$

$2x = 15$ $x = 12$

$x = \dfrac{15}{2}$

Back-substitute $\dfrac{15}{2}$ and 12 for x to find y.

827

$$x = \frac{15}{2} \quad \text{and} \quad x = 12$$

$$y = 39 - 2x \qquad\qquad y = 39 - 2x$$

$$y = 39 - 2\left(\frac{15}{2}\right) \qquad y = 39 - 2(12) \text{ T}$$

$$y = 39 - 24$$

$$y = 39 - 15 \qquad\qquad y = 15$$

$$y = 24$$

he dimensions are 15 feet by 12 feet or

24 feet by $\frac{15}{2}$ or 7.5 feet.

18. Let x = the length of the rectangle
Let y = the width of the rectangle

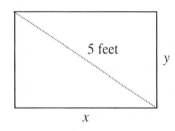

Using the Pythagorean Theorem, we
obtain $x^2 + y^2 = 5^2$. Since the perimeter
is 14 feet, we have $2x + 2y = 14$.
The system of two equations in two
variables is as follows.

$$x^2 + y^2 = 25$$

$$2x + 2y = 14$$

Solve the second equation for y.

$$2x + 2y = 14$$

$$2y = 14 - 2x$$

$$y = 7 - x$$

Substitute $7 - x$ for y to find x.

$$x^2 + (7 - x)^2 = 25$$

$$x^2 + 49 - 14x + x^2 = 25$$

$$2x^2 - 14x + 49 = 25$$

$$2x^2 - 14x + 24 = 0$$

$$x^2 - 7x + 12 = 0$$

$$(x - 4)(x - 3) = 0$$

Apply the zero product principle.

$$x - 4 = 0 \quad \text{and} \quad x - 3 = 0$$

$$x = 4 \qquad\qquad x = 3$$

Back-substitute 3 and 4 for x to find y.

$$x = 4 \quad \text{and} \quad x = 3$$

$$y = 7 - x \qquad\qquad y = 7 - x$$

$$y = 7 - 4 \qquad\qquad y = 7 - 3$$

$$y = 3 \qquad\qquad y = 4$$

The solutions are the same. The
dimensions are 4 feet by 3 feet.

**Cumulative Review Exercises
(Chapters 1-13)**

1. $3x + 7 > 4 \quad \text{or} \quad 6 - x < 1$

$$3x > -3 \qquad\qquad -x < -5$$

$$x > -1 \qquad\qquad x > 5$$

$$x > -1 \quad \text{or} \quad x > 5$$

The solution set is $\{x | x > -1\}$ or
$(-1, \infty)$.

2. $$x(2x - 7) = 4$$

$$2x^2 - 7x = 4$$

$$2x^2 - 7x - 4 = 0$$

$$(2x + 1)(x - 4) = 0$$

Apply the zero product principle.

$$2x + 1 = 0 \quad \text{and} \quad x - 4 = 0$$

$$2x = -1 \qquad\qquad x = 4$$

$$x = -\frac{1}{2}$$

The solutions are $-\frac{1}{2}$ and 4 and the

solution set is $\left\{-\frac{1}{2}, 4\right\}$.

828

3.
$$\frac{5}{x-3} = 1 + \frac{30}{x^2-9}$$
$$\frac{5}{x-3} = 1 + \frac{30}{(x+3)(x-3)}$$

Multiply both sides of the equation by the LCD, $(x+3)(x-3)$.

$$(x+3)(x-3)\left(\frac{5}{x-3}\right) = (x+3)(x-3)\left(1 + \frac{30}{(x+3)(x-3)}\right)$$
$$(x+3)(5) = (x+3)(x-3) + 30$$
$$5x+15 = x^2 - 9 + 30$$
$$15 = x^2 - 5x + 21$$
$$0 = x^2 - 5x + 6$$
$$0 = (x-3)(x-2)$$

Apply the zero product principle.
$$x-3=0 \quad \text{and} \quad x-2=0$$
$$x=3 \qquad\qquad x=2$$

We disregard 3 because it would make the denominator zero. The solution is 2 and the solution set is $\{2\}$.

4. $3x^2 + 8x + 5 < 0$
Solve the related quadratic equation.
$$3x^2 + 8x + 5 = 0$$
$$(3x+5)(x+1) = 0$$

Apply the zero product principle.
$$3x+5=0 \quad \text{or} \quad x+1=0$$
$$3x=-5 \qquad\qquad x=-1$$
$$x=-\frac{5}{3}$$

The boundary points are $-\frac{5}{3}$ and -1.

Test Interval	Test Number	Test	Conclusion
$\left(-\infty, -\dfrac{5}{3}\right)$	-2	$3(-2)^2 + 8(-2) + 5 < 0$ $1 < 0$, false	$\left(-\infty, -\dfrac{5}{3}\right)$ does not belong to the solution set.
$\left(-\dfrac{5}{3}, -1\right)$	$-\dfrac{4}{3}$	$3\left(-\dfrac{4}{3}\right)^2 + 8\left(-\dfrac{4}{3}\right) + 5 < 0$ $-11 < 0$, true	$\left(-\dfrac{5}{3}, -1\right)$ belongs to the solution set.
$(-1, \infty)$	0	$3(0)^2 + 8(0) + 5 < 0$ $5 < 0$, false	$(-1, \infty)$ does not belong to the solution set.

The solution set is $\left(-\dfrac{5}{3}, -1\right)$ or $\left\{ x \middle| -\dfrac{5}{3} < x < -1 \right\}$.

5. $3^{2x-1} = 81$

$3^{2x-1} = 3^4$

$2x - 1 = 4$

$2x = 5$

$x = \dfrac{5}{2}$

The solution is $\dfrac{5}{2}$ and the solution set

is $\left\{ \dfrac{5}{2} \right\}$.

6. $30e^{0.7x} = 240$

$e^{0.7x} = 80$

$\ln e^{0.7x} = \ln 8$

$0.7x = \ln 8$

$x = \dfrac{\ln 8}{0.7} = \dfrac{2.08}{0.7} \approx 2.97$

The solution is $\dfrac{2.08}{0.7} \approx 2.97$ and the

solution set is $\left\{ \dfrac{2.08}{0.7} \approx 2.97 \right\}$.

7. $3x^2 + 4y^2 = 39$

$5x^2 - 2y^2 = -13$

Multiply the second equation by 2 and add to the first equation.

$3x^2 + 4y^2 = 39$

$\underline{10x^2 - 4y^2 = -26}$

$13x^2 = 13$

$x^2 = 1$

$x = \pm 1$

In this case, we can back-substitute 9 for x^2 to find y.

$x^2 = 1$

$3x^2 + 4y^2 = 39$

$3(1) + 4y^2 = 39$

$3 + 4y^2 = 39$

$4y^2 = 36$

$y^2 = 9$

$y = \pm 3$

We have $x = \pm 1$ and $y = \pm 3$, the

solutions are $(-1, -3), (-1, 3), (1, -3)$

and $(1, 3)$ and the solution set is

$\left\{ (-1, -3), (-1, 3), (1, -3), (1, 3) \right\}$.

830

8.

$$f(x) = -\frac{2}{3}x + 4$$

$$y = -\frac{2}{3}x + 4$$

The y–intercept is 4 and the slope is $-\frac{2}{3}$. We can write the slope as

$$m = \frac{-2}{3} = \frac{\text{rise}}{\text{run}}$$ and use the intercept and the slope to graph the function.

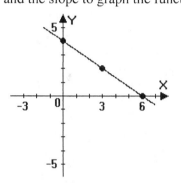

9. $3x - y > 6$

First, find the intercepts to the equation $3x - y = 6$.

Find the x–intercept by setting y equal to zero.

$$3x - 0 = 6$$
$$3x = 6$$
$$x = 2$$

Find the y–intercept by setting x equal to zero.

$$3(0) - y = 6$$
$$-y = 6$$
$$y = -6$$

Next, use the origin as a test point.

$$3(0) - 0 > 6$$
$$0 - 0 > 6$$
$$0 > 6$$

This is a false statement. This means that the origin will not fall in the shaded half-plane.

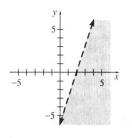

10. $x^2 + y^2 + 4x - 6y + 9 = 0$

Because x^2 and y^2 have the same positive coefficient, the equation's graph is a circle.

$$\left(x^2 + 4x \quad\right) + \left(y^2 - 6y \quad\right) = -9$$

Complete the squares.

$$\left(\frac{b}{2}\right)^2 = \left(\frac{4}{2}\right)^2 = (2)^2 = 4$$

$$\left(\frac{b}{2}\right)^2 = \left(\frac{-6}{2}\right)^2 = (-3)^2 = 9$$

$$\left(x^2 + 4x + 4\right) + \left(y^2 - 6y + 9 \quad\right) = -9 + 4 + 9$$

$$\left(x + 2\right)^2 + \left(y - 3\right)^2 = 4$$

The center of the circle is $(-2, 3)$ and the radius is 2.

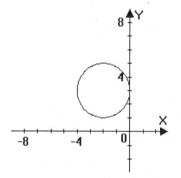

831

11. $9x^2 - 4y^2 = 36$

Because x^2 and y^2 have opposite signs, the equation's graph is a hyperbola.

$$\frac{9x^2}{36} - \frac{4y^2}{36} = \frac{36}{36}$$

$$\frac{x^2}{4} - \frac{y^2}{9} = 1$$

The equation is in the form

$$\frac{x^2}{a^2} - \frac{y^2}{b^2} = 1 \text{ with } a^2 = 4, \text{ and } b^2 = 9.$$

We know the transverse axis lies on the x-axis and the vertices are $(-2,0)$ and $(2,0)$. Because $a^2 = 4$ and $b^2 = 9$, $a = 2$ and $b = 3$.

Construct a rectangle using -2 and 2 on the x–axis, and -3 and 3 on the y–axis. Draw extended diagonals to obtain the asymptotes. Graph the hyperbola.

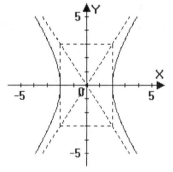

12. $-2(3^2 - 12)^3 - 45 \div 9 - 3$

$$= -2(9 - 12)^3 - 45 \div 9 - 3$$

$$= -2(-3)^3 - 45 \div 9 - 3$$

$$= -2(-27) - 45 \div 9 - 3$$

$$= 54 - 5 - 3 = 46$$

13. $(3x^3 - 19x^2 + 17x + 4) \div (3x - 4)$

Rewrite the polynomials in descending order and divide.

$$\begin{array}{r} x^2 - 5x - 1 \\ 3x - 4 \overline{) 3x^3 - 19x^2 + 17x + 4} \\ \underline{3x^3 - 4x^2} \\ -15x^2 + 17x \\ \underline{-15x^2 + 20x} \\ -3x + 4 \\ \underline{-3x + 4} \\ 0 \end{array}$$

$$\frac{3x^3 - 19x^2 + 17x + 4}{3x - 4} = x^2 - 5x - 1$$

14. $\sqrt[3]{4x^2 y^5} \cdot \sqrt[3]{4xy^2}$

$$= \sqrt[3]{4x^2 y^5 4xy^2} = \sqrt[3]{16x^3 y^7}$$

$$= \sqrt[3]{8 \cdot 2x^3 y^6 y} = 2xy^2 \sqrt[3]{2y}$$

15. $(2 + 3i)(4 - i)$

$$= 8 - 2i + 12i - 3i^2 = 8 + 10i - 3(-1)$$

$$= 8 + 10i + 3 = 11 + 10i$$

16. $12x^3 - 36x^2 + 27x = 3x(4x^2 - 12x + 9)$

$$= 3x(2x - 3)^2$$

17. $x^3 - 2x^2 - 9x + 18$

$$= x^2(x - 2) - 9(x - 2)$$

$$= (x - 2)(x^2 - 9)$$

$$= (x - 2)(x + 3)(x - 3)$$

18. Since the radicand must be positive, the domain will exclude all values of x which make the radicand less than zero.

$$6 - 3x \geq 0$$
$$-3x \geq -6$$
$$x \leq 2$$

The domain is $\{x | x \leq 2\}$ or $(-\infty, 2]$.

19.
$$\frac{1 - \sqrt{x}}{1 + \sqrt{x}} = \frac{1 - \sqrt{x}}{1 + \sqrt{x}} \cdot \frac{1 - \sqrt{x}}{1 - \sqrt{x}}$$

$$= \frac{\left(1 - \sqrt{x}\right)^2}{1^2 + \left(\sqrt{x}\right)^2}$$

$$= \frac{\left(1 - \sqrt{x}\right)^2}{1 + x} \text{ or } \frac{1 - 2\sqrt{x} + x}{1 + x}$$

20.
$$\frac{1}{3} \ln x + 7 \ln y = \ln x^{\frac{1}{3}} + \ln y^7 = \ln \left(x^{\frac{1}{3}} y^7 \right)$$

21. $\left(3x^3 - 5x^2 + 2x - 1\right) \div (x - 2)$

$$\underline{2|} \quad 3 \quad -5 \quad 2 \quad -1$$
$$\qquad \quad 6 \quad 2 \quad 8$$
$$\overline{\qquad 3 \quad 1 \quad 4 \quad 7}$$

$$\left(3x^3 - 5x^2 + 2x - 1\right) \div (x - 2)$$

$$= 3x^2 + x + 4 + \frac{7}{x - 2}$$

22. $x = -2\sqrt{3}$ and $x = 2\sqrt{3}$

$$x + 2\sqrt{3} = 0 \qquad x - 2\sqrt{3} = 0$$

Multiply the factors to obtain the polynomial.

$$\left(x + 2\sqrt{3}\right)\left(x - 2\sqrt{3}\right) = 0$$

$$x^2 - \left(2\sqrt{3}\right)^2 = 0$$

$$x^2 - 4 \cdot 3 = 0$$

$$x^2 - 12 = 0$$

23. Let x = the rate of the slower car

	r	$\bullet$ t	$= d$
Fast	$x + 10$	2	$2(x + 10)$
Slow	x	2	$2x$

$$2(x + 10) + 2x = 180$$
$$2x + 20 + 2x = 180$$
$$4x + 20 = 180$$
$$4x = 160$$
$$x = 40$$

The rate of the slower car is 40 miles per hour and the rate of the faster car is $40 + 10 = 50$ miles per hour.

24. Let x = the number of miles driven in a day

$$C_R = 39 + 0.16x$$
$$C_A = 25 + 0.24x$$

Set the costs equal.

$$39 + 0.16x = 25 + 0.24x$$
$$39 = 25 + 0.08x$$
$$14 = 0.08x$$
$$\frac{14}{0.08} = x$$
$$x = 175$$

The cost is the same when renting from either company when 175 miles are driven in a day.

$$C_R = 39 + 0.16(175) = 39 + 28 = 67$$

When 175 miles are driven, the cost is $67.

25. Let x = the number of apples
Let y = the number of bananas

$$3x + 2y = 354$$

$$2x + 3y = 381$$

Multiply the first equation by -3 and the second equation by 2 and solve by addition.

$$-9x - 6y = -1062$$

$$\underline{4x + 6y = \quad 762}$$

$$-5x = -300$$

$$x = 60$$

Back-substitute 60 for x to find y.

$$3(60) + 2y = 354$$

$$180 + 2y = 354$$

$$2y = 174$$

$$y = 87$$

There are 60 calories in an apple and 87 calories in a banana.

Chapter 14
Sequences, Series, and Probability

14.1 Exercise Set

1. $a_n = 3n + 2$

$a_1 = 3(1) + 2 = 3 + 2 = 5$

$a_2 = 3(2) + 2 = 6 + 2 = 8$

$a_3 = 3(3) + 2 = 9 + 2 = 11$

$a_4 = 3(4) + 2 = 12 + 2 = 14$

The first four terms are 5, 8, 11, 14.

3. $a_n = 3^n$

$a_1 = 3^1 = 3$

$a_2 = 3^2 = 9$

$a_3 = 3^3 = 27$

$a_4 = 3^4 = 81$

The first four terms are 3, 9, 27, 81.

5. $a_n = (-3)^n$

$a_1 = (-3)^1 = -3$

$a_2 = (-3)^2 = 9$

$a_3 = (-3)^3 = -27$

$a_4 = (-3)^4 = 81$

The first four terms are –3, 9, –27, 81.

7. $a_n = (-1)^n (n+3)$

$a_1 = (-1)^1 (1+3) = -1(4) = -4$

$a_2 = (-1)^2 (2+3) = 1(5) = 5$

$a_3 = (-1)^3 (3+3) = -1(6) = -6$

$a_4 = (-1)^4 (4+3) = 1(7) = 7$

The first four terms are –4, 5, –6, 7.

9. $a_n = \dfrac{2n}{n+4}$

$a_1 = \dfrac{2(1)}{1+4} = \dfrac{2}{5}$

$a_2 = \dfrac{2(2)}{2+4} = \dfrac{4}{6} = \dfrac{2}{3}$

$a_3 = \dfrac{2(3)}{3+4} = \dfrac{6}{7}$

$a_4 = \dfrac{2(4)}{4+4} = \dfrac{8}{8} = 1$

The first four terms are $\dfrac{2}{5}, \dfrac{2}{3}, \dfrac{6}{7}, 1$.

11. $a_n = \dfrac{(-1)^{n+1}}{2^n - 1}$

$a_1 = \dfrac{(-1)^{1+1}}{2^1 - 1} = \dfrac{(-1)^2}{2-1} = \dfrac{1}{1} = 1$

$a_2 = \dfrac{(-1)^{2+1}}{2^2 - 1} = \dfrac{(-1)^3}{4-1} = \dfrac{-1}{3} = -\dfrac{1}{3}$

$a_3 = \dfrac{(-1)^{3+1}}{2^3 - 1} = \dfrac{(-1)^4}{8-1} = \dfrac{1}{7}$

$a_4 = \dfrac{(-1)^{4+1}}{2^4 - 1} = \dfrac{(-1)^5}{16-1} = \dfrac{-1}{15} = -\dfrac{1}{15}$

The first four terms are $1, -\dfrac{1}{3}, \dfrac{1}{7}, -\dfrac{1}{15}$.

835

13.

$$a_n = \frac{n^2}{n!}$$

$$a_1 = \frac{1^2}{1!} = \frac{1}{1} = 1$$

$$a_2 = \frac{2^2}{2!} = \frac{4}{2 \cdot 1} = \frac{4}{2} = 2$$

$$a_3 = \frac{3^2}{3!} = \frac{9}{3 \cdot 2 \cdot 1} = \frac{3}{2}$$

$$a_4 = \frac{4^2}{4!} = \frac{16}{4 \cdot 3 \cdot 2 \cdot 1} = \frac{2}{3}$$

The first four terms are $1, 2, \dfrac{3}{2}, \dfrac{2}{3}$.

15.

$$a_n = 2(n+1)!$$

$$a_1 = 2(1+1)! = 2 \cdot 2! = 2 \cdot 2 \cdot 1 = 4$$

$$a_2 = 2(2+1)! = 2 \cdot 3! = 2 \cdot 3 \cdot 2 \cdot 1 = 12$$

$$a_3 = 2(3+1)! = 2 \cdot 4! = 2 \cdot 4 \cdot 3 \cdot 2 \cdot 1$$
$$= 48$$

$$a_4 = 2(4+1)! = 2 \cdot 5! = 2 \cdot 5 \cdot 4 \cdot 3 \cdot 2 \cdot 1$$
$$= 240$$

17.

$$\sum_{i=1}^{6} 5i = 5(1) + 5(2) + 5(3) + 5(4) + 5(5) + 5(6) = 5 + 10 + 15 + 20 + 25 + 30 = 105$$

19.

$$\sum_{i=1}^{4} 2i^2 = 2(1)^2 + 2(2)^2 + 2(3)^2 + 2(4)^2 = 2(1) + 2(4) + 2(9) + 2(16)$$
$$= 2 + 8 + 18 + 32 = 60$$

21.

$$\sum_{k=1}^{5} k(k+4) = 1(1+4) + 2(2+4) + 3(3+4) + 4(4+4) + 5(5+4)$$
$$= 1(5) + 2(6) + 3(7) + 4(8) + 5(9) = 5 + 12 + 21 + 32 + 45 = 115$$

23.

$$\sum_{i=1}^{4} \left(-\frac{1}{2}\right)^i = \left(-\frac{1}{2}\right)^1 + \left(-\frac{1}{2}\right)^2 + \left(-\frac{1}{2}\right)^3 + \left(-\frac{1}{2}\right)^4 = -\frac{1}{2} + \frac{1}{4} + \left(-\frac{1}{8}\right) + \frac{1}{16}$$

$$= -\frac{1}{2} \cdot \frac{8}{8} + \frac{1}{4} \cdot \frac{4}{4} + \left(-\frac{1}{8}\right)\frac{2}{2} + \frac{1}{16} = -\frac{8}{16} + \frac{4}{16} - \frac{2}{16} + \frac{1}{16}$$

$$= \frac{-8 + 4 - 2 + 1}{16} = -\frac{5}{16}$$

25.

$$\sum_{i=5}^{9} 11 = 11 + 11 + 11 + 11 + 11 = 55$$

27.
$$\sum_{i=0}^{4}\frac{(-1)^i}{i!} = \frac{(-1)^0}{0!} + \frac{(-1)^1}{1!} + \frac{(-1)^2}{2!} + \frac{(-1)^3}{3!} + \frac{(-1)^4}{4!} = \frac{1}{1} + \frac{-1}{1} + \frac{1}{2\cdot 1} + \frac{-1}{3\cdot 2\cdot 1} + \frac{1}{4\cdot 3\cdot 2\cdot 1}$$

$$= 1 - 1 + \frac{1}{2} - \frac{1}{6} + \frac{1}{24} = \frac{1}{2}\cdot\frac{12}{12} - \frac{1}{6}\cdot\frac{4}{4} + \frac{1}{24} = \frac{12}{24} - \frac{4}{24} + \frac{1}{24} = \frac{12-4+1}{24} = \frac{9}{24} = \frac{3}{8}$$

29.
$$\sum_{i=1}^{5}\frac{i!}{(i-1)!} = \frac{1!}{(1-1)!} + \frac{2!}{(2-1)!} + \frac{3!}{(3-1)!} + \frac{4!}{(4-1)!} + \frac{5!}{(5-1)!} = \frac{1!}{0!} + \frac{2!}{1!} + \frac{3!}{2!} + \frac{4!}{3!} + \frac{5!}{4!}$$

$$= \frac{1}{1} + \frac{2\cdot\cancel{1!}}{\cancel{1!}} + \frac{3\cdot\cancel{2!}}{\cancel{2!}} + \frac{4\cdot\cancel{3!}}{\cancel{3!}} + \frac{5\cdot\cancel{4!}}{\cancel{4!}} = 1 + 2 + 3 + 4 + 5 = 15$$

31.
$$1^2 + 2^2 + 3^2 + \ldots + 15^2 = \sum_{i=1}^{15} i^2$$

33.
$$2 + 2^2 + 2^3 + \ldots + 2^{11} = \sum_{i=1}^{11} 2^i$$

35.
$$1 + 2 + 3 + \ldots + 30 = \sum_{i=1}^{30} i$$

37.
$$\frac{1}{2} + \frac{2}{3} + \frac{3}{4} + \ldots + \frac{14}{14+1} = \sum_{i=1}^{14}\frac{i}{i+1}$$

39.
$$4 + \frac{4^2}{2} + \frac{4^3}{3} + \ldots + \frac{4^n}{n} = \sum_{i=1}^{n}\frac{4^i}{i}$$

41.
$$1 + 3 + 5 + \ldots + (2n-1) = \sum_{i=1}^{n}(2i-1)$$

43.
$$5 + 7 + 9 + 11 + \ldots + 31 = \sum_{k=2}^{15}(2k+1)\text{ or}$$

$$= \sum_{k=1}^{14}(2k+3)$$

45.
$$a + ar + ar^2 + \ldots + ar^{12} = \sum_{k=0}^{12} ar^k$$

47.
$$a + (a+d) + (a+2d) + \ldots + a(a+nd)$$

$$= \sum_{k=0}^{n}(a+kd)$$

49.
$$\sum_{i=1}^{5}(a_i^2 + 1) = \left((-4)^2 + 1\right) + \left((-2)^2 + 1\right) + \left((0)^2 + 1\right) + \left((2)^2 + 1\right) + \left((4)^2 + 1\right)$$

$$= 17 + 5 + 1 + 5 + 17$$

$$= 45$$

50.
$$\sum_{i=1}^{5}(b_i^2 - 1) = \left((4)^2 - 1\right) + \left((2)^2 - 1\right) + \left((0)^2 - 1\right) + \left((-2)^2 - 1\right) + \left((-4)^2 - 1\right)$$
$$= 15 + 3 + (-1) + 3 + 15$$
$$= 35$$

51.
$$\sum_{i=1}^{5}(2a_i + b_i) = \left(2(-4) + 4\right) + \left(2(-2) + 2\right) + \left(2(0) + 0\right) + \left(2(2) + (-2)\right) + \left(2(4) + (-4)\right)$$
$$= -4 + (-2) + 0 + 2 + 4 = 0$$

52.
$$\sum_{i=1}^{5}(a_i + 3b_i) = \left(-4 + 3(4)\right) + \left(-2 + 3(2)\right) + \left(0 + 3(0)\right) + \left(2 + 3(-2)\right) + \left(4 + 3(-4)\right)$$
$$= 8 + 4 + 0 - 4 - 8 = 0$$

53.
$$\sum_{i=4}^{5}\left(\frac{a_i}{b_i}\right)^2 = \left(\frac{2}{-2}\right)^2 + \left(\frac{4}{-4}\right)^2 = (-1)^2 + (-1)^2 = 1 + 1 = 2$$

54.
$$\sum_{i=4}^{5}\left(\frac{a_i}{b_i}\right)^3 = \left(\frac{2}{-2}\right)^3 + \left(\frac{4}{-4}\right)^3 = (-1)^3 + (-1)^3 = (-1) + (-1) = -2$$

55.
$$\sum_{i=1}^{5}a_i^2 + \sum_{i=1}^{5}b_i^2 = \left((-4)^2 + (-2)^2 + 0^2 + 2^2 + 4^2\right) + \left(4^2 + 2^2 + 0^2 + (-2)^2 + (-4)^2\right)$$
$$= (16 + 4 + 0 + 4 + 16) + (16 + 4 + 0 + 4 + 16) = 80$$

56.
$$\sum_{i=1}^{5}a_i^2 - \sum_{i=3}^{5}b_i^2 = \left((-4)^2 + (-2)^2 + 0^2 + 2^2 + 4^2\right) - \left(0^2 + (-2)^2 + (-4)^2\right)$$
$$= (16 + 4 + 0 + 4 + 16) - (0 + 4 + 16) = 40 - 20 = 20$$

57. a.
$$\sum_{i=1}^{7}a_i = 36.4 + 36.5 + 35.6 + 34.5 + 32.3 + 31.6 + 32.9 = 239.38$$

b.
$$\frac{\sum_{i=1}^{7}a_i}{7} = \frac{239.8}{7} = 34.3$$

From 1995 through 2001, the average number of people living below poverty level each year was approximately 34.3 million.

838

59.　a.

$$\frac{1}{8}\sum_{i=1}^{8}a_i = \frac{1}{8}(14.1+14.2+13.7+12.6+10.9+8.7+7.6+6.5) = \frac{1}{8}(88.3) = 11.0375$$

From 1993 through 2000, the average number of welfare recipients each year was 11.0375 million.

b.
$$a_1 = -1.23(1)+16.55 = 15.32 \qquad a_5 = -1.23(5)+16.55 = 10.4$$
$$a_2 = -1.23(2)+16.55 = 14.09 \qquad a_6 = -1.23(6)+16.55 = 9.17$$
$$a_3 = -1.23(3)+16.55 = 12.86 \qquad a_7 = -1.23(7)+16.55 = 7.94$$
$$a_4 = -1.23(4)+16.55 = 11.63 \qquad a_8 = -1.23(8)+16.55 = 6.71$$

$$\frac{1}{8}\sum_{i=1}^{8}a_i = \frac{1}{8}(15.32+14.09+12.86+11.63+10.4+9.17+7.94+6.71)$$

$$= \frac{1}{8}(88.12) = 11.015$$

This is a reasonable model.

61.
$$a_{20} = 6000\left(1+\frac{0.06}{4}\right)^{20} = 6000(1+0.015)^{20} = 6000(1.015)^{20} = 8081.13$$

The balance in the account after 5 years if $8081.13.

63. – 69. Answers will vary.

71. Answers will vary. For example, consider Exercise 17.

$$\sum_{i=1}^{6}5i$$

This is the same result obtained in Exercise 17.

73.
$$a_n = \frac{n}{n+1};$$

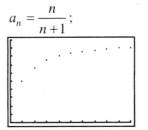

As n gets larger, the terms get closer to 1.

75.
$$a_n = \frac{2n^2+5n-7}{n^3}$$

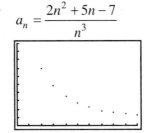

As n gets larger, the terms get closer to 0.

77. Statement **c.** is true. $\displaystyle\sum_{i=1}^{4} 3i + \sum_{i=1}^{4} 4i = \sum_{i=1}^{4} 7i$

$\displaystyle\sum_{i=1}^{4} 3i + \sum_{i=1}^{4} 4i = (3\cdot1+3\cdot2+3\cdot3+3\cdot4)+(4\cdot1+4\cdot2+4\cdot3+4\cdot4) = 3(1+2+3+4)+4(1+2+3+4)$

$\qquad = (1+2+3+4)(3+4) = (1+2+3+4)(7) = 7(1+2+3+4)$

$\displaystyle\sum_{i=1}^{4} 7i = 7\cdot1+7\cdot2+7\cdot3+7\cdot4 = 7(1+2+3+4)$

Statement **a.** is false. $\displaystyle\sum_{i=1}^{2}(-1)^i 2^i = (-1)^1 2^1 + (-1)^2 2^2 = -1(2)+1(4) = -2+4 = 2$

Statement **b.** is false. $\displaystyle\sum_{i=1}^{2} a_i b_i \neq \sum_{i=1}^{2} a_i \sum_{i=1}^{2} b_i$

$\displaystyle\sum_{i=1}^{2} a_i b_i = a_1 b_1 + a_2 b_2$

$\displaystyle\sum_{i=1}^{2} a_i \sum_{i=1}^{2} b_i = (a_1 + a_2)(b_1 + b_2) = a_1 b_1 + a_1 b_2 + a_2 b_1 + a_2 b_2$

Statement **d.** is false. $\displaystyle\sum_{i=0}^{6}(-1)^i (i+1)^2 \neq \sum_{j=1}^{7}(-1)^j j^2$

$\displaystyle\sum_{i=0}^{6}(-1)^i (i+1)^2$

$= (-1)^0 (0+1)^2 + (-1)^1 (1+1)^2 + (-1)^2 (2+1)^2 + (-1)^3 (3+1)^2 + (-1)^4 (4+1)^2 + (-1)^5 (5+1)^2 + (-1)^6 (6+1)^2$

$= 1(1)^2 - 1(2)^2 + 1(3)^2 - 1(4)^2 + 1(5)^2 - 1(6)^2 + 1(7)^2 = 1(1)-1(4)+1(9)-1(16)+1(25)-1(36)+1(49)$

$= 1-4+9-16+25-36+49 = 28$

$\displaystyle\sum_{j=1}^{7}(-1)^j j^2 = (-1)^1 1^2 + (-1)^2 2^2 + (-1)^3 3^2 + (-1)^4 4^2 + (-1)^5 5^2 + (-1)^6 6^2 + (-1)^7 7^2$

$= -1(1)+1(4)-1(9)+1(16)-1(25)+1(36)-1(49)$

$= -1+4-9+16-25+36-49 = -28$

79. $a_n = n^2$

81. $a_n = n(n+2)$

83. $a_n = 2n+3$

85. $a_n = (-2)^{n+1}$

87. $\dfrac{(n+4)!}{(n+2)!} == (n+3)(n+4) = n^2 + 7n + 12$

89. $\displaystyle\sum_{i=1}^{4} \log(2i)$

$= \log 2(1) + \log 2(2) + \log 2(3) + \log 2(4)$

$= \log 2 + \log 4 + \log 6 + \log 8 = \log 384$

91. $a_n = a_{n-1} + 5$

$a_1 = 7$

$a_2 = a_{2-1} + 5 = a_1 + 5 = 7 + 5 = 12$

$a_3 = a_{3-1} + 5 = a_2 + 5 = 12 + 5 = 17$

$a_4 = a_{4-1} + 5 = a_3 + 5 = 17 + 5 = 22$

The first four terms are 7, 12, 17, 22.

92. $\sqrt[3]{40x^4y^7} = \sqrt[3]{8 \cdot 5x^3xy^6y} = 2xy^2\sqrt[3]{5xy}$

93. $27x^3 - 8 = (3x-2)(9x^2+6x+4)$

94.
$$\frac{6}{x} + \frac{6}{x+2} = \frac{5}{2}$$
$$2x(x+2)\left(\frac{6}{x} + \frac{6}{x+2}\right) = 2x(x+2)\left(\frac{5}{2}\right)$$
$$2(x+2)(6) + 2x(6) = x(x+2)(5)$$
$$12(x+2) + 12x = 5x(x+2)$$
$$12x + 24 + 12x = 5x^2 + 10x$$
$$24x + 24 = 5x^2 + 10x$$
$$0 = 5x^2 - 14x - 24$$
$$0 = (5x+6)(x-4)$$

Apply the zero product principle.

$5x + 6 = 0 \quad$ or $\quad x - 4 = 0$

$\quad 5x = -6 \qquad\qquad x = 4$

$\quad\quad x = -\dfrac{6}{5}$

The solution set is $\left\{-\dfrac{6}{5}, 4\right\}$.

14.2 Exercise Set

1. Since $6 - 2 = 4$, $d = 4$.

3. Since $-2 - (-7) = 5$, $d = 5$.

5. Since $711 - 714 = -3$, $d = -3$.

7. $a_1 = 200$

$a_2 = 200 + 20 = 220$

$a_3 = 220 + 20 = 240$

$a_4 = 240 + 20 = 260$

$a_5 = 260 + 20 = 280$

$a_6 = 280 + 20 = 300$

The first six terms are 200, 220, 240, 260, 280, and 300.

9. $a_1 = -7$

$a_2 = -7 + 4 = -3$

$a_3 = -3 + 4 = 1$

$a_4 = 1 + 4 = 5$

$a_5 = 5 + 4 = 9$

$a_6 = 9 + 4 = 13$

The first six terms are -7, -3, 1, 5, 9, 13.

11. $a_1 = 300$

$a_2 = 300 - 90 = 210$

$a_3 = 210 - 90 = 120$

$a_4 = 120 - 90 = 30$

$a_5 = 30 - 90 = -60$

$a_6 = -60 - 90 = -150$

The first six terms are 300, 210, 120, 30, -60, -150.

13.
$a_1 = \dfrac{5}{2}$

$a_2 = \dfrac{5}{2} - \dfrac{1}{2} = \dfrac{4}{2} = 2$

$a_3 = \dfrac{4}{2} - \dfrac{1}{2} = \dfrac{3}{2}$

$a_4 = \dfrac{3}{2} - \dfrac{1}{2} = \dfrac{2}{2} = 1$

$a_5 = 1 - \dfrac{1}{2} = \dfrac{1}{2}$

$a_6 = \dfrac{1}{2} - \dfrac{1}{2} = 0$

The first six terms are $\dfrac{5}{2}, 2, \dfrac{3}{2}, 1, \dfrac{1}{2}, 0$.

15. $a_1 = -0.4$

$a_2 = -0.4 - 1.6 = -2$

$a_3 = -2 - 1.6 = -3.6$

$a_4 = -3.6 - 1.6 = -5.2$

$a_5 = -5.2 - 1.6 = -6.8$

$a_6 = -6.8 - 1.6 = -8.4$

The first six terms are $-0.4, -2, -3.6,$
$-5.2, -6.8, -8.4.$

17. $a_6 = 13 + (6-1)4 = 13 + (5)4$

$\qquad = 13 + 20 = 33$

19. $a_{50} = 7 + (50-1)5 = 7 + (49)5$

$\qquad = 7 + 245 = 252$

21. $a_{200} = -40 + (200-1)5 = -40 + (199)5$

$\qquad = -40 + 995 = 955$

23. $a_{60} = 35 + (60-1)(-3) = 35 + (59)(-3)$

$\qquad = 35 + (-177) = -142$

25. $a_n = a_1 + (n-1)d = 1 + (n-1)4$

$\qquad = 1 + 4n - 4 = 4n - 3$

$a_{20} = 4(20) - 3 = 80 - 3 = 77$

27. $a_n = a_1 + (n-1)d = 7 + (n-1)(-4)$

$\qquad = 7 - 4n + 4 = 11 - 4n$

$a_{20} = 11 - 4(20) = 11 - 80 = -69$

29. $a_n = a_1 + (n-1)d = -20 + (n-1)(-4)$

$\qquad = -20 - 4n + 4 = -4n - 16$

$a_{20} = -4(20) - 16 = -80 - 16 = -96$

31.
$$a_n = a_1 + (n-1)d = -\frac{1}{3} + (n-1)\left(\frac{1}{3}\right)$$

$$= -\frac{1}{3} + \frac{1}{3}n - \frac{1}{3} = \frac{1}{3}n - \frac{2}{3}$$

$$a_{20} = \frac{1}{3}(20) - \frac{2}{3} = \frac{20}{3} - \frac{2}{3} = \frac{18}{3} = 6$$

33. $a_n = a_1 + (n-1)d = 4 + (n-1)(-0.3)$

$\qquad = 4 - 0.3n + 0.3 = 4.3 - 0.3n$

$a_{20} = 4.3 - 0.3(20) = 4.3 - 6 = -1.7$

35. First find a_{20}.

$a_{20} = 4 + (20-1)6 = 4 + (19)6$

$\qquad = 4 + 114 = 118$

$S_{20} = \frac{20}{2}(4 + 118) = 10(122) = 1220$

37. First find a_{50}.

$a_{50} = -10 + (50-1)4 = -10 + (49)4$

$\qquad = -10 + 196 = 186$

$S_{50} = \frac{50}{2}(-10 + 186) = 25(176) = 4400$

39. First find a_{100}.

$a_{100} = 1 + (100-1)1 = 1 + (99)1$

$\qquad = 1 + 99 = 100$

$S_{100} = \frac{100}{2}(1 + 100) = 50(101) = 5050$

41. First find a_{60}.

$a_{60} = 2 + (60-1)2 = 2 + (59)2$

$\qquad = 2 + 118 = 120$

$S_{60} = \frac{60}{2}(2 + 120) = 30(122) = 3660$

43. Since there are 12 even integers between 21 and 45, find a_{12}.

$$a_{12} = 22 + (12 - 1)2 = 22 + (11)2 = 22 + 22 = 44$$

$$S_{12} = \frac{12}{2}(22 + 44) = 6(66) = 396$$

45.

$$\sum_{i=1}^{17}(5i + 3) = (5(1) + 3) + (5(2) + 3) + (5(3) + 3) + \ldots + (5(17) + 3)$$

$$= (5 + 3) + (10 + 3) + (15 + 3) + \ldots + (85 + 3) = 8 + 13 + 18 + \ldots + 88$$

$$S_{17} = \frac{17}{2}(8 + 88) = \frac{17}{2}(96) = 17(48) = 816$$

47.

$$\sum_{i=1}^{30}(-3i + 5) = (-3(1) + 5) + (-3(2) + 5) + (-3(3) + 5) + \ldots + (-3(30) + 5)$$

$$= (-3 + 5) + (-6 + 5) + (-9 + 5) + \ldots + (-90 + 5) = 2 + (-1) + (-4) + \ldots + (-85)$$

$$S_{30} = \frac{30}{2}(2 + (-85)) = 15(-83) = -1245$$

49.

$$\sum_{i=1}^{100}4i = 4(1) + 4(2) + 4(3) + \ldots + 4(100) = 4 + 8 + 12 + \ldots + 400$$

$$S_{100} = \frac{100}{2}(4 + 400) = 50(404) = 20,200$$

51. First find a_{14} and b_{12}:

$$a_{14} = a_1 + (n - 1)d$$
$$= 1 + (14 - 1)(-3 - 1) = -51$$
$$b_{12} = b_1 + (n - 1)d$$
$$= 3 + (12 - 1)(8 - 3) = 58$$

So, $a_{14} + b_{12} = -51 + 58 = 7$.

52. First find a_{16} and b_{18}:

$$a_{16} = a_1 + (n - 1)d$$
$$= 1 + (16 - 1)(-3 - 1) = -59$$
$$b_{18} = b_1 + (n - 1)d$$
$$= 3 + (18 - 1)(8 - 3) = 88$$

So, $a_{16} + b_{18} = -59 + 88 = 29$.

53.

$$a_n = a_1 + (n - 1)d$$
$$-83 = 1 + (n - 1)(-3 - 1)$$
$$-83 = 1 + -4(n - 1)$$
$$-84 = -4n + 4$$
$$-88 = -4n$$
$$n = 22$$

There are 22 terms.

54.

$$b_n = b_1 + (n - 1)d$$
$$93 = 3 + (n - 1)(8 - 3)$$
$$93 = 3 + 5(n - 1)$$
$$93 = 5n - 2$$
$$95 = 5n$$
$$n = 19$$

There are 19 terms.

55.
$$S_n = \frac{n}{2}(a_1 + a_n)$$
For $\{a_n\}$:
$$S_{14} = \frac{14}{2}(a_1 + a_{14}) = 7(1+(-51)) = -350$$
For $\{b_n\}$:
$$S_{14} = \frac{14}{2}(b_1 + b_{14}) = 7(3+68) = 497$$
So $\sum_{n=1}^{14} b_n - \sum_{n=1}^{14} a_n = 497 - (-350) = 847$

56. First find a_{15} and b_{15}:
$$a_{15} = a_1 + (n-1)d$$
$$= 1 + (15-1)(-3-1) = -55$$
$$b_{15} = b_1 + (n-1)d$$
$$= 3 + (15-1)(8-3) = 73$$
Using $S_n = \frac{n}{2}(a_1 + a_n)$ for $\{a_n\}$:
$$S_{15} = \frac{15}{2}(a_1 + a_{15}) = 7.5(1+(-55))$$
$$= -405$$
And then for $\{b_n\}$:
$$S_{15} = \frac{15}{2}(b_1 + b_{15}) = 7.5(3+73) = 570$$
So $\sum_{n=1}^{15} b_n - \sum_{n=1}^{15} a_n = 570 - (-405) = 975$

57. Two points on the graph are $(1, 1)$ and $(2, -3)$. Finding the slope of the line; $m = \dfrac{y_2 - y_1}{x_2 - x_2} = \dfrac{-3-1}{2-1} = \dfrac{-4}{1} = -4$

Using the point-slope form of an equation of a line;
$$y - y_2 = m(x - x_2)$$
$$y - 1 = -4(x-1)$$
$$y - 1 = -4x + 4$$
$$y = -4x + 5$$
Thus, $f(x) = -4x + 5$.

58. Two points on the graph are $(1, 3)$ and $(2, 8)$. Finding the slope of the line; $m = \dfrac{y_2 - y_1}{x_2 - x_2} = \dfrac{8-3}{2-1} = \dfrac{5}{1} = 5$

Using the point-slope form of an equation of a line;
$$y - y_2 = 5(x - x_2)$$
$$y - 3 = 5(x-1)$$
$$y - 3 = 5x - 5$$
$$y = 5x - 2$$
Thus, $g(x) = 5x - 2$.

59. Using $a_n = a_1 + (n-1)d$ and $a_2 = 4$:
$$a_2 = a_1 + (2-1)d$$
$$4 = a_1 + d$$
And since $a_6 = 16$:
$$a_6 = a_1 + (6-1)d$$
$$16 = a_1 + 5d$$
The system of equations is
$$4 = a_1 + d$$
$$16 = a_1 + 5d$$
Solving the first equation for a_1:
$$a_1 = 4 - d$$
Substituting the value into the second equation and solving for d:
$$16 = (4-d) + 5d$$
$$16 = 4 + 4d$$
$$12 = 4d$$
$$3 = d$$
Then $a_n = a_1 + (n-1)d$
$$a_n = 1 + (n-1)3$$
$$a_n = 1 + 3n - 3$$
$$a_n = 3n - 2$$

844

60. Using $a_n = a_1 + (n-1)d$ and $a_3 = 7$:

$a_3 = a_1 + (3-1)d$

$7 = a_1 + 2d$

And since $a_8 = 17$:

$a_8 = a_1 + (8-1)d$

$17 = a_1 + 7d$

The system of equations is

$7 = a_1 + 2d$

$17 = a_1 + 7d$

Solving the first equation for a_1:

$a_1 = 7 - 2d$

Substituting the value into the second equation and solving for d:

$17 = (7 - 2d) + 7d$

$17 = 7 + 5d$

$10 = 5d$

$2 = d$

So $a_1 = 7 - 2(2) = 7 - 4 = 3$.

Then $a_n = a_1 + (n-1)2$

$a_n = 3 + (n-1)2$

$a_n = 3 + 2n - 2$

$a_n = 2n + 1$

61. a. $a_n = a_1 + (n-1)d$

$a_n = 150 + (n-1)(1.7)$

$a_n = 150 + 1.7n - 1.7$

$a_n = 1.7n + 148.3$

b. $a_{40} = 1.7(40) + 148.3$

$= 68 + 148.3$

$= 216.3$ pounds

63. Answers will vary.

65. Company A

$a_n = 24000 + (n-1)1600$

$= 24000 + 1600n - 1600$

$= 1600n + 22400$

$a_{10} = 1600(10) + 22400$

$= 16000 + 22400 = 38400$

Company B

$a_n = 28000 + (n-1)1000$

$= 28000 + 1000n - 1000$

$= 1000n + 27000$

$a_{10} = 1000(10) + 27000$

$= 10000 + 27000 = 37000$

Company A will pay $1400 more in year 10.

67. a. Total cost:

$$\$7107 + \$7310 + \$7586 + \$8046$$
$$= \$30,049$$

b. $a_1 = 309(1) + 6739 = 7048$

$a_2 = 309(2) + 6739 = 7357$

$a_3 = 309(3) + 6739 = 7666$

$a_4 = 309(4) + 6739 = 7975$

Total cost:

$7048 + 7357 + 7666 + 7975$

$= \$30,046$

The model describes the actual sum very well.

69. Answers will vary.

845

71. Company A

$$a_n = 19000 + (n-1)2600$$

$$= 19000 + 2600n - 2600$$

$$= 2600n + 16400$$

$$a_{10} = 2600(10) + 16400$$

$$= 26000 + 16400 = 42400$$

$$S_n = \frac{n}{2}(a_1 + a_{10})$$

$$S_{10} = \frac{10}{2}(19000 + 42400)$$

$$= 5(61400) = \$307,000$$

Company B

$$a_n = 27000 + (n-1)1200$$

$$= 27000 + 1200n - 1200$$

$$= 1200n + 25800$$

$$a_{10} = 1200(10) + 25800$$

$$= 12000 + 25800$$

$$= 37800$$

$$S_n = \frac{n}{2}(a_1 + a_{10})$$

$$S_{10} = \frac{10}{2}(27000 + 37800)$$

$$= 5(64800) = \$324,000$$

Company B pays the greater total amount.

73.
$$a_{38} = a_1 + (n-1)d$$

$$= 20 + (38-1)(3)$$

$$= 20 + 37(3) = 131$$

$$S_{38} = \frac{n}{2}(a_1 + a_{38})$$

$$= \frac{38}{2}(20 + 131)$$

$$= 19(151)$$

$$= 2869$$

There are 2869 seats in this section of the stadium.

75. – 77. Answers will vary.

79. Answers will vary. For example, consider Exercise 45.

$$\sum_{i=1}^{17} (5i + 3)$$

```
sum(seq(5I+3,I,1
,17))
                816
```

This is the same result obtained in Exercise 45.

81. From the sequence, we see that $a_1 = 21700$ and $d = 23172 - 21700 = 1472$.

We know that $a_n = a_1 + (n-1)d$. We can substitute what we know to find n.

$$314628 = 21700 + (n-1)1472$$

$$292928 = (n-1)1472$$

$$\frac{292928}{1472} = \frac{(n-1)1472}{1472}$$

$$199 = n - 1$$

$$200 = n$$

314,628 is the 200th term of the sequence.

83.
$$1 + 3 + 5 + \ldots + (2n-1)$$

$$S_n = \frac{n}{2}(a_1 + a_n)$$

$$= \frac{n}{2}(1 + (2n-1))$$

$$= \frac{n}{2}(1 + 2n - 1)$$

$$= \frac{n}{2}(2n)$$

$$= n(n)$$

$$= n^2$$

846

84. $\log(x^2 - 25) - \log(x + 5) = 3$

$$\log\left(\frac{x^2 - 25}{x + 5}\right) = 3$$

$$\log\left(\frac{(x - 5)(\cancel{x + 5})}{\cancel{x + 5}}\right) = 3$$

$$\log(x - 5) = 3$$

$$x - 5 = 10^3$$

$$x - 5 = 1000$$

$$x = 1005$$

The solution set is $\{1005\}$.

85. $x^2 + 3x \leq 10$

Solve the related quadratic equation.

$$x^2 + 3x - 10 = 0$$

$$(x + 5)(x - 2) = 0$$

Apply the zero product principle.

$$x + 5 = 0 \quad \text{or} \quad x - 2 = 0$$

$$x = -5 \qquad\qquad x = 2$$

The boundary points are -5 and 2.

Test Interval	Test Number	Test	Conclusion
$(-\infty, -5]$	-6	$(-6)^2 + 3(-6) \leq 10$ $18 \leq 10$, false	$(-\infty, -5]$ does not belong to the solution set.
$[-5, 2]$	0	$0^2 + 3(0) \leq 10$ $0 \leq 10$, true	$[-5, 2]$ belongs to the solution set.
$[2, \infty)$	3	$3^2 + 3(3) \leq 10$ $18 \leq 10$, false	$[2, \infty)$ does not belong to the solution set.

The solution set is $[-5, 2]$ or $\{x \mid -5 \leq x \leq 2\}$.

86.
$$A = \frac{Pt}{P + t}$$

$$A(P + t) = Pt$$

$$AP + At = Pt$$

$$AP - Pt = -At$$

$$P(A - t) = -At$$

$$P = -\frac{At}{A - t} \quad \text{or} \quad \frac{At}{t - A}$$

847

14.3 Exercise Set

1. $r = \dfrac{a_2}{a_1} = \dfrac{15}{5} = 3$

3. $r = \dfrac{a_2}{a_1} = \dfrac{30}{-15} = -2$

5. $r = \dfrac{a_2}{a_1} = \dfrac{\frac{9}{2}}{3} = \dfrac{9}{2} \cdot \dfrac{1}{3} = \dfrac{3}{2}$

7. $r = \dfrac{a_2}{a_1} = \dfrac{0.04}{-0.4} = -0.1$

9. The first term is 2.
The second term is $2 \cdot 3 = 6$.
The third term is $6 \cdot 3 = 18$.
The fourth term is $18 \cdot 3 = 54$.
The fifth term is $54 \cdot 3 = 162$.

11. The first term is 20.

The second term is $20 \cdot \dfrac{1}{2} = 10$.

The third term is $10 \cdot \dfrac{1}{2} = 5$.

The fourth term is $5 \cdot \dfrac{1}{2} = \dfrac{5}{2}$.

The fifth term is $\dfrac{5}{2} \cdot \dfrac{1}{2} = \dfrac{5}{4}$.

13. The first term is –4.
The second term is $-4(-10) = 40$.
The third term is $40(-10) = -400$.
The fourth term is $-400(-10) = 4000$.
The fifth term is
$4000(-10) = -40,000$.

15. The first term is $-\dfrac{1}{4}$.

The second term is $-\dfrac{1}{4}(-2) = \dfrac{1}{2}$.

The third term is $\dfrac{1}{2}(-2) = -1$.

The fourth term is $-1(-2) = 2$.

The fifth term is $2(-2) = -4$.

17. $a_8 = 6(2)^{8-1} = 6(2)^7 = 6(128) = 768$

19. $a_{12} = 5(-2)^{12-1} = 5(-2)^{11}$
$\qquad = 5(-2048) = -10,240$

21. $a_6 = 6400\left(-\dfrac{1}{2}\right)^{6-1} = 6400\left(-\dfrac{1}{2}\right)^5$
$\qquad = -200$

23. $a_8 = 1,000,000(0.1)^{8-1}$
$\qquad = 1,000,000(0.1)^7$
$\qquad = 1,000,000(0.0000001) = 0.1$

25. $r = \dfrac{a_2}{a_1} = \dfrac{12}{3} = 4$
$a_n = a_1 r^{n-1} = 3(4)^{n-1}$
$a_7 = 3(4)^{7-1} = 3(4)^6$
$\qquad = 3(4096) = 12,288$

27. $r = \dfrac{a_2}{a_1} = \dfrac{6}{18} = \dfrac{1}{3}$

$a_n = a_1 r^{n-1} = 18\left(\dfrac{1}{3}\right)^{n-1}$

$a_7 = 18\left(\dfrac{1}{3}\right)^{7-1} = 18\left(\dfrac{1}{3}\right)^6$

$\qquad = 18\left(\dfrac{1}{729}\right) = \dfrac{18}{729} = \dfrac{2}{81}$

848

29.

$$r = \frac{a_2}{a_1} = \frac{-3}{1.5} = -2$$

$$a_n = a_1 r^{n-1} = 1.5(-2)^{n-1}$$

$$a_7 = 1.5(-2)^{7-1} = 1.5(-2)^6$$
$$= 1.5(64) = 96$$

31.

$$r = \frac{a_2}{a_1} = \frac{-0.004}{0.0004} = -10$$

$$a_n = a_1 r^{n-1} = 0.0004(-10)^{n-1}$$

$$a_7 = 0.0004(-10)^{7-1} = 0.0004(-10)^6$$
$$= 0.0004(1000000) = 400$$

33.

$$r = \frac{a_2}{a_1} = \frac{6}{2} = 3$$

$$S_{12} = \frac{2(1-3^{12})}{1-3} = \frac{2(1-531441)}{-2}$$

$$= \frac{2(-531440)}{-2} = \frac{-1,062,880}{-2}$$
$$= 531,440$$

35.

$$r = \frac{a_2}{a_1} = \frac{-6}{3} = -2$$

$$S_{11} = \frac{a_1(1-r^n)}{1-r} = \frac{3(1-(-2)^{11})}{1-(-2)}$$

$$= \frac{\cancel{3}(1-(-2048))}{\cancel{3}} = 2049$$

37.

$$r = \frac{a_2}{a_1} = \frac{3}{-\dfrac{3}{2}} = 3 \div \left(-\frac{3}{2}\right)$$

$$= 3 \cdot \left(-\frac{2}{3}\right) = -2$$

$$S_{14} = \frac{a_1(1-r^n)}{1-r} = \frac{-\dfrac{3}{2}\left(1-(-2)^{14}\right)}{1-(-2)}$$

$$= \frac{-\dfrac{3}{2}(1-(16384))}{3} = \frac{-\dfrac{3}{2}(-16385)}{3}$$

$$= -\frac{3}{2}(-16385) \div 3 = \frac{49155}{2} \cdot \frac{1}{3}$$

$$= \frac{16385}{2} = 8191.5$$

39.

$$\sum_{i=1}^{8} 3^i = \frac{3(1-3^8)}{1-3} = \frac{3(1-6561)}{-2}$$

$$= \frac{3(-6560)}{-2} = \frac{-19680}{-2} = 9840$$

41.

$$\sum_{i=1}^{10} 5 \cdot 2^i = \frac{10(1-2^{10})}{1-2} = \frac{10(1-1024)}{-1}$$

$$= \frac{10(-1023)}{-1} = 10,230$$

43.

$$\sum_{i=1}^{6}\left(\frac{1}{2}\right)^{i+1} = \frac{\dfrac{1}{4}\left(1-\left(\dfrac{1}{2}\right)^6\right)}{1-\dfrac{1}{2}} = \frac{\dfrac{1}{4}\left(1-\dfrac{1}{64}\right)}{\dfrac{1}{2}}$$

$$= \frac{\dfrac{1}{4}\left(\dfrac{64}{64}-\dfrac{1}{64}\right)}{\dfrac{1}{2}} = \frac{\dfrac{1}{4}\left(\dfrac{63}{64}\right)}{\dfrac{1}{2}}$$

$$= \frac{1}{4}\left(\frac{63}{64}\right) \div \frac{1}{2} = \frac{1}{4}\left(\frac{63}{64}\right) \cdot \frac{2}{1}$$

$$= \frac{63}{128}$$

45.

$$r = \frac{a_2}{a_1} = \frac{\frac{1}{3}}{1} = \frac{1}{3}$$

$$S = \frac{a_1}{1-r} = \frac{1}{1-\frac{1}{3}} = \frac{1}{\frac{2}{3}} = 1 \div \frac{2}{3} = 1 \cdot \frac{3}{2} = \frac{3}{2}$$

47.

$$r = \frac{a_2}{a_1} = \frac{\frac{3}{4}}{3} = \frac{3}{4} \div 3 = \frac{3}{4} \cdot \frac{1}{3} = \frac{1}{4}$$

$$S = \frac{a_1}{1-r} = \frac{3}{1-\frac{1}{4}} = \frac{3}{\frac{3}{4}} = 3 \div \frac{3}{4}$$

$$= 3 \cdot \frac{4}{3} = \frac{12}{3} = 4$$

49. $$r = \frac{a_2}{a_1} = \frac{-\frac{1}{2}}{1} = -\frac{1}{2}$$

$$S = \frac{a_1}{1-r} = \frac{1}{1-\left(-\frac{1}{2}\right)} = \frac{1}{\frac{3}{2}} = 1 \div \frac{3}{2}$$

$$= 1 \cdot \frac{2}{3} = \frac{2}{3}$$

51. $r = -0.3$

$$a_1 = 26(-0.3)^{1-1} = 26(-0.3)^0$$

$$= 26(1) = 26$$

$$S = \frac{26}{1-(-0.3)} = \frac{26}{1.3} = 20$$

53.

$$0.\overline{5} = \frac{a_1}{1-r} = \frac{\frac{5}{10}}{1-\frac{1}{10}} = \frac{\frac{5}{10}}{\frac{9}{10}} = \frac{5}{10} \div \frac{9}{10}$$

$$= \frac{5}{10} \cdot \frac{10}{9} = \frac{5}{9}$$

55.

$$0.\overline{47} = \frac{a_1}{1-r} = \frac{\frac{47}{100}}{1-\frac{1}{100}} = \frac{\frac{47}{100}}{\frac{99}{100}}$$

$$= \frac{47}{100} \div \frac{99}{100} = \frac{47}{100} \cdot \frac{100}{99} = \frac{47}{99}$$

57.

$$0.\overline{257} = \frac{a_1}{1-r} = \frac{\frac{257}{1000}}{1-\frac{1}{1000}} = \frac{\frac{257}{1000}}{\frac{999}{1000}}$$

$$= \frac{257}{1000} \div \frac{999}{1000} = \frac{257}{1000} \cdot \frac{1000}{999}$$

$$= \frac{257}{999}$$

59. The sequence is arithmetic with common difference $d = 1$.

61. The sequence is geometric with common ratio $r = 2$.

63. The sequence is neither arithmetic nor geometric.

65. First find a_{10} and b_{10}:

$$a_{10} = a_1 r^{n-1}$$

$$= (-5)\left(\frac{10}{-5}\right)^{10-1} = (-5)(-2)^9$$

$$= 2560$$

$$b_{10} = b_1 + (n-1)d$$

$$= 10 + (10-1)(-5-10)$$

$$= 10 + (9)(-15) = -125$$

So,

$$a_{10} + b_{10} = 2560 + (-125) = 2435.$$

66. First find a_{11} and b_{11}:

$$a_{11} = a_1 r^{n-1}$$

$$= (-5)\left(\frac{10}{-5}\right)^{11-1} = (-5)(-2)^{10}$$

$$= -5120$$

$$b_{11} = b_1 + (n-1)d$$

$$= 10 + (11-1)(-5-10)$$

$$= 10 + (10)(-15) = -140$$

So,

$$a_{11} + b_{11} = -5120 + (-140) = -5260.$$

67. From Exercise 65, $a_{10} = 2560$ and $b_{10} = -125$.

For $\{a_n\}$, $r = \dfrac{10}{-5} = -2$ and :

$$S_{10} = \frac{a_1(1-r^n)}{1-r} = \frac{(-5)\left(1-(-2)^{10}\right)}{1-(-2)}$$

$$= \frac{(-5)(-1023)}{3} = 1705$$

For $\{b_n\}$,

$$S_n = \frac{n}{2}(b_1 + b_n) = \frac{10}{2}(10 + (-125))$$

$$= 5(-115) = -575$$

So,

$$\sum_{n=1}^{10} a_n - \sum_{n=1}^{10} b_n = 1705 - (-575) = 2280$$

68. For $\{a_n\}$, $r = \dfrac{10}{-5} = -2$ and :

$$S_{11} = \frac{a_1(1-r^n)}{1-r} = \frac{(-5)\left(1-(-2)^{11}\right)}{1-(-2)}$$

$$= \frac{(-5)(2049)}{3} = -3415$$

For $\{b_n\}$,

$$b_{11} = b_1 + (n-1)d$$

$$= 10 + (11-1)(-5-10)$$

$$= 10 + (10)(-15) = -140$$

$$S_{11} = \frac{n}{2}(b_1 + b_n) = \frac{11}{2}(10 + (-140))$$

$$= 5.5(-130) = -715$$

So, $\displaystyle\sum_{n=1}^{11} a_n - \sum_{n=1}^{11} b_n = -3415 - (-715)$

$$= -2700$$

69. For $\{a_n\}$,

$$S_6 = \frac{a_1(1-r^n)}{1-r} = \frac{(-5)\left(1-(-2)^6\right)}{1-(-2)}$$

$$= \frac{(-5)(-63)}{3} = 105$$

For $\{c_n\}$,

$$S = \frac{a_1}{1-r} = \frac{-2}{1 - \dfrac{1}{-2}} = \frac{-2}{\dfrac{3}{2}} = -\frac{4}{3}$$

So, $S_6 \cdot S = 105\left(-\dfrac{4}{3}\right) = -140$

70. For $\{a_n\}$,

$$S_9 = \frac{a_1(1-r^n)}{1-r} = \frac{(-5)\left(1-(-2)^9\right)}{1-(-2)}$$

$$= \frac{(-5)(513)}{3} = -855$$

For $\{c_n\}$,

$$S = \frac{c_1}{1-r} = \frac{-2}{1 - \dfrac{1}{-2}} = \frac{-2}{\dfrac{3}{2}} = -\frac{4}{3}$$

So, $S_9 \cdot S = -855\left(-\dfrac{4}{3}\right) = 1140$

71. It is given that $a_4 = 27$. Using the formula $a_n = a_1 r^{n-1}$ when $n = 4$ we have:

$$27 = 8r^{4-1}$$

$$\frac{27}{8} = r^3$$

$$r = \sqrt[3]{\frac{27}{8}} = \frac{3}{2}$$

Then

$$a_n = a_1 r^{n-1}$$

$$a_2 = 8\left(\frac{3}{2}\right)^{2-1} = 8\left(\frac{3}{2}\right) = 12$$

$$a_3 = 8\left(\frac{3}{2}\right)^{3-1} = 8\left(\frac{3}{2}\right)^2 = 8\left(\frac{9}{4}\right) = 18$$

72. It is given that $a_4 = -54$. Using the formula $a_n = a_1 r^{n-1}$ when $n = 4$ we have:

$$-54 = 2r^{4-1}$$

$$-27 = r^3$$

$$r = \sqrt[3]{-27} = -3$$

Then

$$a_n = a_1 r^{n-1}$$

$$a_2 = 2(-3)^{2-1} = 2(-3) = -6$$

$$a_3 = 2(-3)^{3-1} = 2(-3)^2 = 2(9) = 18$$

73.

$$r = \frac{a_2}{a_1} = \frac{2}{1} = 2$$

$$a_{15} = 1(2)^{15-1} = (2)^{14} = 16384$$

On the fifteenth day, you will put aside $16,384 for savings.

75. $r = 1.04$

$$a_7 = 3,000,000(1.04)^{7-1}$$

$$= 3,000,000(1.04)^6$$

$$= 3,000,000(1.265319)$$

$$= 3,795,957$$

The athlete's salary for year 7 will be $3,795,957.

77. **a.**

$$r_{1990 \text{ to } 1991} = \frac{30.15}{29.76} \approx 1.013$$

$$r_{1991 \text{ to } 1992} = \frac{30.54}{30.15} \approx 1.013$$

$$r_{1992 \text{ to } 1993} = \frac{30.94}{30.54} \approx 1.013$$

$$r_{1993 \text{ to } 1994} = \frac{31.34}{30.94} \approx 1.013$$

$$r_{1994 \text{ to } 1995} = \frac{31.75}{31.34} \approx 1.013$$

$$r_{1995 \text{ to } 1996} = \frac{32.16}{31.75} \approx 1.013$$

$$r_{1996 \text{ to } 1997} = \frac{32.58}{32.16} \approx 1.013$$

Since the population of each year can be found by multiplying the preceding year by 1.013, the population is increasing geometrically.

b. $a_n = a_1 r^{n-1} = 29.76(1.013)^{n-1}$

c. Since year 2000 is the 11th term, find a_{11}.

$$a_{11} = 29.76(1.013)^{11-1}$$

$$= 29.76(1.013)^{10} \approx 33.86$$

The population of California will be approximately 33.86 million in 2000. The geometric sequence models the actual population of 33.87 million very well.

79.
$$r = \frac{a_2}{a_1} = \frac{2}{1} = 2$$

$$S_{15} = \frac{a_1\left(1 - r^n\right)}{1 - r} = \frac{1\left(1 - (2)^{15}\right)}{1 - 2}$$

$$= \frac{(1 - 32768)}{-1} = \frac{(-32767)}{-1} = 32767$$

Your savings will be \$32,767 over the 15 days.

81. $r = 1.05$

$$S_{20} = \frac{a_1\left(1 - r^n\right)}{1 - r} = \frac{24000\left(1 - (1.05)^{20}\right)}{1 - 1.05}$$

$$= \frac{24000(1 - 2.6533)}{-0.05}$$

$$= \frac{24000(-1.6533)}{-0.05} = 793583$$

The total lifetime salary over the 20 years is \$793,583.

83. $r = 0.9$

$$S_{10} = \frac{a_1\left(1 - r^n\right)}{1 - r} = \frac{20\left(1 - (0.9)^{10}\right)}{1 - 0.9}$$

$$= \frac{20(1 - 0.348678)}{0.1}$$

$$= \frac{20(0.651322)}{0.1} = 130.264$$

After 10 swings, the pendulum covers a distance of approximately 130.26 inches.

85.
$$A = P\frac{\left(1 + \dfrac{r}{n}\right)^{nt} - 1}{\dfrac{r}{n}}$$

$$= 2500\frac{\left(1 + \dfrac{0.09}{1}\right)^{1(40)} - 1}{\dfrac{0.09}{1}}$$

$$= 2500\frac{(1 + 0.09)^{40} - 1}{0.09}$$

$$= 2500\frac{(1.09)^{40} - 1}{0.09}$$

$$= 2500\frac{31.4094 - 1}{0.09}$$

$$= 2500\frac{30.4094}{0.09} = 844706$$

After 40 years, the value of the IRA will be \$844,706.

87.
$$A = P\frac{\left(1 + \dfrac{r}{n}\right)^{nt} - 1}{\dfrac{r}{n}}$$

$$= 600\frac{\left(1 + \dfrac{0.08}{4}\right)^{4(18)} - 1}{\dfrac{0.08}{4}}$$

$$= 600\frac{(1 + 0.02)^{72} - 1}{0.02}$$

$$= 600\frac{(1.02)^{72} - 1}{0.02}$$

$$= 600\frac{4.16114 - 1}{0.02} = 600\frac{3.16114}{0.02}$$

$$= 94834.2$$

The value of the TSA after 18 years will be \$94,834.20.

89. $r = 60\% = 0.6$

$a_1 = 6(.6) = 3.6$

$$S = \frac{3.6}{1 - 0.6} = \frac{3.6}{0.4} = 9$$

The total economic impact of the factory will be \$9 million per year.

91.

$$r = \frac{1}{4}$$

$$S = \frac{\frac{1}{4}}{1 - \frac{1}{4}} = \frac{\frac{1}{4}}{\frac{3}{4}} = \frac{1}{4} \div \frac{3}{4} = \frac{1}{4} \cdot \frac{4}{3} = \frac{1}{3}$$

Eventually $\frac{1}{3}$ of the largest square will be shaded.

93. – 99. Answers will vary.

101. Answers will vary. For example, consider Exercise 25.

$$a_n = 3(4)^{n-1}$$

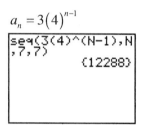

This matches the result obtained in Exercise 25.

103.

$$f(x) = \frac{2\left[1 - \left(\frac{1}{3}\right)^x\right]}{1 - \frac{1}{3}}$$

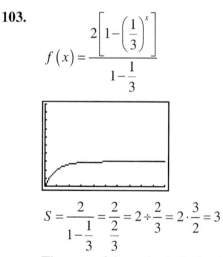

$$S = \frac{2}{1 - \frac{1}{3}} = \frac{2}{\frac{2}{3}} = 2 \div \frac{2}{3} = 2 \cdot \frac{3}{2} = 3$$

The sum of the series is 3; the horizontal asymptote is $y = 3$. Both are the same value 3.

105. Statement **d.** is true. The common ratio is $0.5 = \frac{1}{2}$.

Statement **a.** is false. The sequence is not geometric. The fourth term would have to be $24 \cdot 4 = 96$ for the sequence to be geometric.

Statement **b.** is false. We do not need to know the terms between $\frac{1}{8}$ and $\frac{1}{512}$, but we do need to know how many terms there are between $\frac{1}{8}$ and $\frac{1}{512}$.

Statement **c.** is false. The sum of the sequence is $\dfrac{10}{1 - \left(-\dfrac{1}{2}\right)}$.

107.

$$A = P \frac{\left(1 + \dfrac{r}{n}\right)^{nt} - 1}{\dfrac{r}{n}}$$

$$1,000,000 = P \frac{\left(1 + \dfrac{0.10}{12}\right)^{12(30)} - 1}{\dfrac{0.10}{12}}$$

$$1,000,000 = P \frac{\left(1 + \dfrac{1}{120}\right)^{360} - 1}{\dfrac{1}{120}}$$

$$1,000,000 = P \frac{\left(1\dfrac{1}{120}\right)^{360} - 1}{\dfrac{1}{120}}$$

$$1,000,000 = P \frac{19.8374 - 1}{\dfrac{1}{120}}$$

$$\frac{1}{120}(1{,}000{,}000) = \frac{1}{120}\left(P\frac{18.8374}{\frac{1}{120}}\right)$$

$$\frac{25000}{3} = 18.8374P$$

$$\frac{25000}{3(18.8374)} = P$$

$$442.382 = P$$

You should deposit approximately $442.38 per month.

108.
$$\sqrt{28} - 3\sqrt{7} + \sqrt{63}$$
$$= \sqrt{4\cdot 7} - 3\sqrt{7} + \sqrt{9\cdot 7}$$
$$= 2\sqrt{7} - 3\sqrt{7} + 3\sqrt{7}$$
$$= 2\sqrt{7}$$

109.
$$2x^2 = 4 - x$$
$$2x^2 + x - 4 = 0$$
$$a = 2 \quad b = 1 \quad c = -4$$

Solve using the quadratic formula.
$$x = \frac{-1 \pm \sqrt{1^2 - 4(2)(-4)}}{2(2)}$$
$$= \frac{-1 \pm \sqrt{1 + 32}}{4} = \frac{-1 \pm \sqrt{33}}{4}$$

The solution set is $\left\{\dfrac{-1 \pm \sqrt{33}}{4}\right\}$.

110.
$$\frac{6}{\sqrt{3} - \sqrt{5}} = \frac{6}{\sqrt{3} - \sqrt{5}} \cdot \frac{\sqrt{3} + \sqrt{5}}{\sqrt{3} + \sqrt{5}}$$
$$= \frac{6\left(\sqrt{3} + \sqrt{5}\right)}{3 - 5}$$
$$= \frac{6\left(\sqrt{3} + \sqrt{5}\right)}{-2}$$
$$= -3\left(\sqrt{3} + \sqrt{5}\right)$$

Mid-Chapter Check Point – Chapter 14

1.
$$a_n = (-1)^{n+1}\frac{n}{(n-1)!}$$
$$a_1 = (-1)^{1+1}\frac{1}{(1-1)!}$$
$$= (-1)^2\frac{1}{0!} = 1\cdot 1 = 1$$
$$a_2 = (-1)^{2+1}\frac{2}{(2-1)!}$$
$$= (-1)^3\frac{2}{1!} = (-1)(2) = -2$$
$$a_3 = (-1)^{3+1}\frac{3}{(3-1)!}$$
$$= (-1)^4\frac{3}{2!} = 1\cdot\frac{3}{2} = \frac{3}{2}$$
$$a_4 = (-1)^{4+1}\frac{4}{(4-1)!}$$
$$= (-1)^5\frac{4}{3!} = (-1)\frac{4}{6} = -\frac{2}{3}$$
$$a_5 = (-1)^{5+1}\frac{5}{(5-1)!}$$
$$= (-1)^6\frac{5}{4!} = 1\cdot\frac{5}{24} = \frac{5}{24}$$

2. Using $a_n = a_1 + (n-1)d$;
$$a_1 = 5$$
$$a_2 = 5 + (2-1)(-3)$$
$$= 5 + 1(-3) = 5 - 3 = 2$$
$$a_3 = 5 + (3-1)(-3)$$
$$= 5 + 2(-3) = 5 - 6 = -1$$
$$a_4 = 5 + (4-1)(-3)$$
$$= 5 + 3(-3) = 5 - 9 = -4$$
$$a_5 = 5 + (5-1)(-3)$$
$$= 5 + 4(-3) = 5 - 12 = -7$$

3. Using $a_n = a_1 r^{n-1}$;

$a_1 = 5$

$a_2 = 5(-3)^{2-1} = 5(-3)^1 = 5(-3) = -15$

$a_3 = 5(-3)^{3-1} = 5(-3)^2 = 5(9) = 45$

$a_4 = 5(-3)^{4-1} = 5(-3)^3 = 5(-27) = -135$

$a_5 = 5(-3)^{5-1} = 5(-3)^4 = 5(81) = 405$

4. $d = a_2 - a_1 = 6 - 2 = 4$

$\begin{aligned} a_n &= a_1 + (n-1)d \\ &= 2 + (n-1)4 \\ &= 2 + 4n - 4 \\ &= 4n - 2 \end{aligned}$

$a_{20} = 4(20) - 2 = 78$

5. $r = \dfrac{a_2}{a_1} = \dfrac{6}{3} = 2$

$\begin{aligned} a_n &= a_1 r^{n-1} \\ &= 3(2)^{n-1} \end{aligned}$

$\begin{aligned} a_{10} &= 3(2)^{10-1} \\ &= 3(2)^9 \\ &= 1536 \end{aligned}$

6. $d = a_2 - a_1 = 1 - \dfrac{3}{2} = -\dfrac{1}{2}$

$\begin{aligned} a_n &= a_1 + (n-1)d \\ &= \frac{3}{2} + (n-1)\left(-\frac{1}{2}\right) \\ &= \frac{3}{2} - \frac{1}{2}n + \frac{1}{2} \\ &= -\frac{1}{2}n + 2 \end{aligned}$

$\begin{aligned} a_{30} &= -\frac{1}{2}(30) + 2 \\ &= -15 + 2 \\ &= -13 \end{aligned}$

7. $S_n = \dfrac{a_1(1 - r^n)}{1 - r}; \quad r = \dfrac{a_2}{a_1} = \dfrac{10}{5} = 2$

$S_{10} = \dfrac{5(1 - 2^{10})}{1 - 2} = \dfrac{5(-1023)}{-1} = 5115$

8. First find a_{10};

$d = a_2 - a_1 = 0 - (-2) = 2$

$\begin{aligned} a_{50} &= a_1 + (n-1)d \\ &= -2 + (50-1)(2) \\ &= -2 + 49(2) = 96 \end{aligned}$

$\begin{aligned} S_{50} &= \frac{n}{2}(a_1 + a_n) \\ &= \frac{50}{2}(-2 + 96) \\ &= 25(94) = 2350 \end{aligned}$

9. First find a_{10};

$r = \dfrac{a_2}{a_1} = \dfrac{40}{-20} = -2$

$\begin{aligned} a_{10} &= a_1 r^{n-1} = -20(2)^{10-1} = -20(2)^9 \\ &= -20(512) = -10240 \end{aligned}$

$\begin{aligned} S_{10} &= \frac{a_1(1 - r^n)}{1 - r} = \frac{-20(-1 - (-2)^{10})}{1 - (-2)} \\ &= \frac{-20(-1023)}{3} = \frac{20460}{3} = 6820 \end{aligned}$

10. First find a_{100};

$d = a_2 - a_1 = -2 - 4 = -6$

$\begin{aligned} a_{100} &= a_1 + (n-1)d \\ &= 4 + (100-1)(-6) \\ &= 4 + 99(-6) = -590 \end{aligned}$

$\begin{aligned} S_{100} &= \frac{n}{2}(a_1 + a_n) = \frac{100}{2}(4 - 590) \\ &= 50(-586) = -29,300 \end{aligned}$

856

11.

$$\sum_{i=1}^{4}(i+4)(i-1) = (1+4)(1-1) + (2+4)(2-1) + (3+4)(3-1) + (4+4)(4-1)$$

$$= 5(0) + 6(1) + 7(2) + 8(3) = 0 + 6 + 14 + 24 = 44$$

12.

$$\sum_{i=1}^{50}(3i-2) = (3\cdot1-2) + (3\cdot2-2) + (3\cdot3-3) + \dots + (3\cdot50-2)$$

$$= (3-2) + (6-2) + (9-3) + \dots + (150-2)$$

$$= 1 + 4 + 6 + \dots + 148$$

The sum of this arithmetic sequence is given by $S_n = \dfrac{n}{2}(a_1 + a_n)$;

$$S_{50} = \dfrac{50}{2}(1+148) = 25(149) = 3725$$

13.

$$\sum_{i=1}^{6}\left(\dfrac{3}{2}\right)^i = \left(\dfrac{3}{2}\right)^1 + \left(\dfrac{3}{2}\right)^2 + \left(\dfrac{3}{2}\right)^3 + \left(\dfrac{3}{2}\right)^4 + \left(\dfrac{3}{2}\right)^5 + \left(\dfrac{3}{2}\right)^6$$

$$= \dfrac{3}{2} + \dfrac{9}{4} + \dfrac{27}{8} + \dfrac{81}{16} + \dfrac{243}{32} + \dfrac{729}{64} = \dfrac{1995}{64}$$

14.

$$\sum_{i=1}^{\infty}\left(-\dfrac{2}{5}\right)^{i-1} = \left(-\dfrac{2}{5}\right)^{1-1} + \left(-\dfrac{2}{5}\right)^{2-1} + \left(-\dfrac{2}{5}\right)^{3-1} + \dots$$

$$= \left(-\dfrac{2}{5}\right)^{0} + \left(-\dfrac{2}{5}\right)^{1} + \left(-\dfrac{2}{5}\right)^{2} + \dots$$

$$= 1 + \left(-\dfrac{2}{5}\right) + \dfrac{4}{25} + \dots$$

This is an infinite geometric sequence with $r = \dfrac{a_2}{a_1} = \dfrac{-\frac{2}{5}}{1} = -\dfrac{2}{5}$.

Using $S = \dfrac{a_1}{1-r} = \dfrac{1}{1-\left(-\frac{2}{5}\right)} = \dfrac{1}{\frac{7}{5}} = \dfrac{5}{7}$

15.

$$0.\overline{45} = \frac{a_1}{1-r} = \frac{\dfrac{45}{100}}{1-\dfrac{1}{100}}$$

$$= \frac{\dfrac{45}{100}}{\dfrac{99}{100}} = \frac{45}{100} \div \frac{99}{100}$$

$$= \frac{45}{100} \cdot \frac{100}{99} = \frac{45}{99} = \frac{5}{11}$$

16. Answers will vary. An example is

$$\sum_{i=1}^{18} \frac{i}{i+2}.$$

17 The arithmetic sequence is 16, 48, 80, 112, ….

First find a_{15} where

$$d = a_2 - a_1 = 48 - 16 = 32.$$

$$a_{15} = a_1 + (n-1)d$$

$$= 16 + (15-1)(32)$$

$$= 16 + 14(32) = 16 + 448 = 464$$

The distance the skydiver falls during the 15th second is 464 feet.

$$S_{15} = \frac{n}{2}(a_1 + a_n)$$

$$= \frac{15}{2}(16 + 464) = 7.5(480) = 3600$$

The total distance the skydiver falls in 15 seconds is 3600 feet.

18. $r = 0.10$

$$A = P(1+r)^t$$

$$= 120000(1+0.10)^{10} \approx 311249$$

The value of the house after 10 years is \$311,249.

11.4 Exercise Set

1. $\displaystyle \binom{8}{3} = \frac{8!}{3!(8-3)!}$

$$= \frac{8!}{3!5!} = \frac{8 \cdot 7 \cdot 6 \cdot 5!}{3 \cdot 2 \cdot 1 \cdot 5!}$$

$$= 56$$

3. $\displaystyle \binom{12}{1} = \frac{12!}{1!(12-1)!} = \frac{12 \cdot 11!}{1 \cdot 11!} = 12$

5. $\displaystyle \binom{6}{6} = \frac{6!}{6!(6-6)!} = \frac{1}{0!} = \frac{1}{1} = 1$

7. $\displaystyle \binom{100}{2} = \frac{100!}{2!(100-2)!} = \frac{100 \cdot 99 \cdot 98!}{2 \cdot 1 \cdot 98!}$

$$= 4950$$

9. Applying the Binomial Theorem to $(x+2)^3$, we have $a = x$, $b = 2$, and $n = 3$.

$$(x+2)^3$$

$$= \binom{3}{0}x^3 + \binom{3}{1}x^2(2) + \binom{3}{2}x(2)^2 + \binom{3}{3}2^3$$

$$= \frac{3!}{0!(3-0)!}x^3 + \frac{3!}{1!(3-1)!}2x^2$$

$$\qquad + \frac{3!}{2!(3-2)!}4x + \frac{3!}{3!(3-3)!}8$$

$$= \frac{3!}{1 \cdot 3!}x^3 + \frac{3 \cdot 2!}{1 \cdot 2!}2x^2 + \frac{3 \cdot 2!}{2!1!}4x + \frac{3!}{3!0!}8$$

$$= x^3 + 3(2x^2) + 3(4x) + 1(8)$$

$$= x^3 + 6x^2 + 12x + 8$$

858

11. Applying the Binomial Theorem to $(3x+y)^3$, we have $a=3x$, $b=y$, and $n=3$.

$$(3x+y)^3 = \binom{3}{0}(3x)^3 + \binom{3}{1}(3x)^2 y + \binom{3}{2}(3x) y^2 + \binom{3}{3} y^3$$

$$= \frac{3!}{0!(3-0)!}27x^3 + \frac{3!}{1!(3-1)!}9x^2 y + \frac{3!}{2!(3-2)!}3xy^2 + \frac{3!}{3!(3-3)!} y^3$$

$$= \frac{\cancel{3!}}{1\cdot\cancel{3!}}27x^3 + \frac{3\cdot\cancel{2!}}{1\cdot\cancel{2!}}9x^2 y + \frac{3\cdot\cancel{2!}}{\cancel{2!}1!}3xy^2 + \frac{\cancel{3!}}{\cancel{3!}0!} y^3 = 27x^3 + 3\left(9x^2 y\right) + 3\left(3xy^2\right) + 1\left(y^3\right)$$

$$= 27x^3 + 27x^2 y + 9xy^2 + y^3$$

13. Applying the Binomial Theorem to $(5x-1)^3$, we have $a=5x$, $b=-1$, and $n=3$.

$$(5x-1)^3 = \binom{3}{0}(5x)^3 + \binom{3}{1}(5x)^2(-1) + \binom{3}{2}(5x)(-1)^2 + \binom{3}{3}(-1)^3$$

$$= \frac{3!}{0!(3-0)!}125x^3 - \frac{3!}{1!(3-1)!}25x^2 + \frac{3!}{2!(3-2)!}5x(1) - \frac{3!}{3!(3-3)!}$$

$$= \frac{\cancel{3!}}{1\cdot\cancel{3!}}125x^3 - \frac{3\cdot\cancel{2!}}{1\cdot\cancel{2!}}25x^2 + \frac{3\cdot\cancel{2!}}{\cancel{2!}1!}5x - \frac{\cancel{3!}}{\cancel{3!}0!} = 125x^3 - 3\left(25x^2\right) + 3(5x) - 1$$

$$= 125x^3 - 75x^2 + 15x - 1$$

15. Applying the Binomial Theorem to $(2x+1)^4$, we have $a=2x$, $b=1$, and $n=4$.

$$(2x+1)^4 = \binom{4}{0}(2x)^4 + \binom{4}{1}(2x)^3 + \binom{4}{2}(2x)^2 + \binom{4}{3}2x + \binom{4}{4}$$

$$= \frac{4!}{0!(4-0)!}16x^4 + \frac{4!}{1!(4-1)!}8x^3 \cdot 1 + \frac{4!}{2!(4-2)!}4x^2 \cdot 1^2 + \frac{4!}{3!(4-3)!}2x \cdot 1^3 + \frac{4!}{4!(4-4)!}\cdot 1^4$$

$$= \frac{\cancel{4!}}{0!\cancel{4!}}16x^4 + \frac{4!}{1!3!}8x^3 \cdot 1 + \frac{4!}{2!2!}4x^2 \cdot 1 + \frac{4!}{3!1!}2x \cdot 1 + \frac{\cancel{4!}}{\cancel{4!}0!}\cdot 1$$

$$= 1\left(16x^4\right) + \frac{4\cdot\cancel{3!}}{1\cdot\cancel{3!}}8x^3 + \frac{4\cdot 3\cdot\cancel{2!}}{2\cdot 1\cdot\cancel{2!}}4x^2 + \frac{4\cdot\cancel{3!}}{\cancel{3!}\cdot 1}2x + 1 = 16x^4 + 4\left(8x^3\right) + 6\left(4x^2\right) + 4(2x) + 1$$

$$= 16x^4 + 32x^3 + 24x^2 + 8x + 1$$

17. Applying the Binomial Theorem to $\left(x^2 + 2y\right)^4$, we have $a = x^2$, $b = 2y$, and $n = 4$.

$$\left(x^2 + 2y\right)^4 = \binom{4}{0}\left(x^2\right)^4 + \binom{4}{1}\left(x^2\right)^3 (2y) + \binom{4}{2}\left(x^2\right)^2 (2y)^2 + \binom{4}{3}x^2 (2y)^3 + \binom{4}{4}(2y)^4$$

$$= \frac{4!}{0!(4-0)!}x^8 + \frac{4!}{1!(4-1)!}2x^6 y + \frac{4!}{2!(4-2)!}4x^4 y^2 + \frac{4!}{3!(4-3)!}8x^2 y^3 + \frac{4!}{4!(4-4)!}16y^4$$

$$= \frac{\cancel{4!}}{0!\cancel{4!}}x^8 + \frac{4!}{1!3!}2x^6 y + \frac{4!}{2!2!}4x^4 y^2 + \frac{4!}{3!1!}8x^2 y^3 + \frac{\cancel{4!}}{\cancel{4!}0!}16y^4$$

$$= 1\left(x^8\right) + \frac{4 \cdot \cancel{3!}}{1 \cdot \cancel{3!}}2x^6 y + \frac{4 \cdot 3 \cdot \cancel{2!}}{2 \cdot 1 \cdot \cancel{2!}}4x^4 y^2 + \frac{4 \cdot \cancel{3!}}{\cancel{3!} \cdot 1}8x^2 y^3 + 16y^4$$

$$= x^8 + 4\left(2x^6 y\right) + 6\left(4x^4 y^2\right) + 4\left(8x^2 y^3\right) + 16y^4 = x^8 + 8x^6 y + 24x^4 y^2 + 32x^2 y^3 + 16y^4$$

19. Applying the Binomial Theorem to $\left(y - 3\right)^4$, we have $a = y$, $b = -3$, and $n = 4$.

$$\left(y - 3\right)^4 = \binom{4}{0}y^4 + \binom{4}{1}y^3 (-3) + \binom{4}{2}y^2 (-3)^2 + \binom{4}{3}y(-3)^3 + \binom{4}{4}(-3)^4$$

$$= \frac{4!}{0!(4-0)!}y^4 - \frac{4!}{1!(4-1)!}3y^3 + \frac{4!}{2!(4-2)!}9y^2 - \frac{4!}{3!(4-3)!}27y + \frac{4!}{4!(4-4)!}81$$

$$= \frac{\cancel{4!}}{0!\cancel{4!}}y^4 - \frac{4!}{1!3!}3y^3 + \frac{4!}{2!2!}9y^2 - \frac{4!}{3!1!}27y + \frac{\cancel{4!}}{\cancel{4!}0!}81$$

$$= 1\left(y^4\right) - \frac{4 \cdot \cancel{3!}}{1 \cdot \cancel{3!}}3y^3 + \frac{4 \cdot 3 \cdot \cancel{2!}}{2 \cdot 1 \cdot \cancel{2!}}9y^2 - \frac{4 \cdot \cancel{3!}}{\cancel{3!} \cdot 1}27y + 81$$

$$= y^4 - 4\left(3y^3\right) + 6\left(9y^2\right) - 4\left(27y\right) + 81 = y^4 - 12y^3 + 54y^2 - 108y + 81$$

21. Applying the Binomial Theorem to $\left(2x^3 - 1\right)^4$, we have $a = 2x^3$, $b = -1$, and $n = 4$.

$$\left(2x^3 - 1\right)^4 = \binom{4}{0}\left(2x^3\right)^4 + \binom{4}{1}\left(2x^3\right)^3 (-1) + \binom{4}{2}\left(2x^3\right)^2 (-1)^2 + \binom{4}{3}\left(2x^3\right)(-1)^3 + \binom{4}{4}(-1)^4$$

$$= \frac{4!}{0!(4-0)!}16x^{12} - \frac{4!}{1!(4-1)!}8x^9 + \frac{4!}{2!(4-2)!}4x^6 - \frac{4!}{3!(4-3)!}2x^3 + \frac{4!}{4!(4-4)!}$$

$$= \frac{\cancel{4!}}{0!\cancel{4!}}16x^{12} - \frac{4!}{1!3!}8x^9 + \frac{4!}{2!2!}4x^6 - \frac{4!}{3!1!}2x^3 + \frac{\cancel{4!}}{\cancel{4!}0!}$$

$$= 1\left(16x^{12}\right) - \frac{4 \cdot \cancel{3!}}{1 \cdot \cancel{3!}}8x^9 + \frac{4 \cdot 3 \cdot \cancel{2!}}{2 \cdot 1 \cdot \cancel{2!}}4x^6 - \frac{4 \cdot \cancel{3!}}{\cancel{3!} \cdot 1}2x^3 + 1$$

$$= 16x^{12} - 4\left(8x^9\right) + 6\left(4x^6\right) - 4\left(2x^3\right) + 1 = 16x^{12} - 32x^9 + 24x^6 - 8x^3 + 1$$

23. Applying the Binomial Theorem to $(c+2)^5$, we have $a = c$, $b = 2$, and $n = 5$.

$$(c+2)^5 = \binom{5}{0}c^5 + \binom{5}{1}c^4(2) + \binom{5}{2}c^3(2)^2 + \binom{5}{3}c^2(2)^3 + \binom{5}{4}c(2)^4 + \binom{5}{5}2^5$$

$$= \frac{5!}{0!\,5!}c^5 + \frac{5!}{1!(5-1)!}2c^4 + \frac{5!}{2!(5-2)!}4c^3 + \frac{5!}{3!(5-3)!}8c^2 + \frac{5!}{4!(5-4)!}16c + \frac{5!}{5!(5-5)!}32$$

$$= 1c^5 + \frac{5 \cdot 4!}{1 \cdot 4!}2c^4 + \frac{5 \cdot 4 \cdot 3!}{2 \cdot 1 \cdot 3!}4c^3 + \frac{5 \cdot 4 \cdot 3!}{3!2 \cdot 1}8c^2 + \frac{5 \cdot 4!}{4! \cdot 1}16c + \frac{5!}{5!0!}32$$

$$= c^5 + 5(2c^4) + 10(4c^3) + 10(8c^2) + 5(16c) + 1(32) = c^5 + 10c^4 + 40c^3 + 80c^2 + 80c + 32$$

25. Applying the Binomial Theorem to $(x-1)^5$, we have $a = x$, $b = -1$, and $n = 5$.

$$(x-1)^5 = \binom{5}{0}x^5 + \binom{5}{1}x^4(-1) + \binom{5}{2}x^3(-1)^2 + \binom{5}{3}x^2(-1)^3 + \binom{5}{4}x(-1)^4 + \binom{5}{5}(-1)^5$$

$$= \frac{5!}{0!\,5!}x^5 - \frac{5!}{1!(5-1)!}x^4 + \frac{5!}{2!(5-2)!}x^3 - \frac{5!}{3!(5-3)!}x^2 + \frac{5!}{4!(5-4)!}x - \frac{5!}{5!(5-5)!}$$

$$= 1x^5 - \frac{5 \cdot 4!}{1 \cdot 4!}x^4 + \frac{5 \cdot 4 \cdot 3!}{2 \cdot 1 \cdot 3!}x^3 - \frac{5 \cdot 4 \cdot 3!}{3!2 \cdot 1}x^2 + \frac{5 \cdot 4!}{4! \cdot 1}x - \frac{5!}{5!0!}$$

$$= x^5 - 5x^4 + 10x^3 - 10x^2 + 5x - 1$$

27. Applying the Binomial Theorem to $(3x - y)^5$, we have $a = 3x$, $b = -y$, and $n = 5$.

$$(3x - y)^5$$

$$= \binom{5}{0}(3x)^5 + \binom{5}{1}(3x)^4(-y) + \binom{5}{2}(3x)^3(-y)^2 + \binom{5}{3}(3x)^2(-y)^3 + \binom{5}{4}3x(-y)^4 + \binom{5}{5}(-y)^5$$

$$= \frac{5!}{0!\,5!}243x^5 - \frac{5!}{1!(5-1)!}81x^4y + \frac{5!}{2!(5-2)!}27x^3y^2$$

$$- \frac{5!}{3!(5-3)!}9x^2y^3 + \frac{5!}{4!(5-4)!}3xy^4 - \frac{5!}{5!(5-5)!}y^5$$

$$= 243x^5 - \frac{5 \cdot 4!}{1 \cdot 4!}81x^4y + \frac{5 \cdot 4 \cdot 3!}{2 \cdot 1 \cdot 3!}27x^3y^2 - \frac{5 \cdot 4 \cdot 3!}{3!2 \cdot 1}9x^2y^3 + \frac{5 \cdot 4!}{4! \cdot 1}3xy^4 - \frac{5!}{5!0!}y^5$$

$$= 243x^5 - 5(81x^4y) + 10(27x^3y^2) - 10(9x^2y^3) + 5(3xy^4) - y^5$$

$$= 243x^5 - 405x^4y + 207x^3y^2 - 90x^2y^3 + 15xy^4 - y^5$$

29. Applying the Binomial Theorem to $(2a+b)^6$, we have $a = 2a$, $b = b$, and $n = 6$.

$(2a+b)^6$

$$= \binom{6}{0}(2a)^6 + \binom{6}{1}(2a)^5 b + \binom{6}{2}(2a)^4 b^2 + \binom{6}{3}(2a)^3 b^3 + \binom{6}{4}(2a)^2 b^4 + \binom{6}{5}2ab^5 + \binom{6}{6}b^6$$

$$= \frac{6!}{0!(6-0)!}64a^6 + \frac{6!}{1!(6-1)!}32a^5 b + \frac{6!}{2!(6-2)!}16a^4 b^2 + \frac{6!}{3!(6-3)!}8a^3 b^3$$

$$+ \frac{6!}{4!(6-4)!}4a^2 b^4 + \frac{6!}{5!(6-5)!}2ab^5 + \frac{6!}{6!(6-6)!}b^6$$

$$= \frac{\cancel{6!}}{1\cancel{6!}}64a^6 + \frac{6\cdot\cancel{5!}}{1\cdot\cancel{5!}}32a^5 b + \frac{6\cdot5\cdot\cancel{4!}}{2\cdot1\cdot\cancel{4!}}16a^4 b^2 + \frac{\cancel{6}\cdot5\cdot4\cdot\cancel{3!}}{3\cancel{\cdot}2\cdot1\cdot\cancel{3!}}8a^3 b^3$$

$$+ \frac{6\cdot5\cdot\cancel{4!}}{\cancel{4!}2\cdot1}4a^2 b^4 + \frac{6\cdot\cancel{5!}}{\cancel{5!}1}2ab^5 + \frac{\cancel{6!}}{\cancel{6!}\cdot1}b^6$$

$$= 64a^6 + 6(32a^5 b) + 15(16a^4 b^2) + 20(8a^3 b^3) + 15(4a^2 b^4) + 6(2ab^5) + 1b^6$$

$$= 64a^6 + 192a^5 b + 240a^4 b^2 + 160a^3 b^3 + 60a^2 b^4 + 12ab^5 + b^6$$

31. $(x+2)^8$

First Term $\quad \binom{n}{r-1}a^{n-r+1}b^{r-1} = \binom{8}{1-1}x^{8-1+1}2^{1-1} = \binom{8}{0}x^8 2^0$

$$= \frac{8!}{0!(8-0)!}x^8 \cdot 1 = \frac{\cancel{8!}}{0!\cancel{8!}}x^8 = x^8$$

Second Term $\quad \binom{n}{r-1}a^{n-r+1}b^{r-1} = \binom{8}{2-1}x^{8-2+1}2^{2-1} = \binom{8}{1}x^7 2^1 = \frac{8!}{1!(8-1)!}2x^7$

$$= \frac{8\cdot\cancel{7!}}{1\cdot\cancel{7!}}2x^7 = 8\cdot2x^7 = 16x^7$$

Third Term $\quad \binom{n}{r-1}a^{n-r+1}b^{r-1} = \binom{8}{3-1}x^{8-3+1}2^{3-1} = \binom{8}{2}x^6 2^2 = \frac{8!}{2!(8-2)!}4x^6$

$$= \frac{8\cdot7\cdot\cancel{6!}}{2\cdot1\cdot\cancel{6!}}4x^6 = 28\cdot4x^6 = 112x^6$$

33. $(x-2y)^{10}$

First Term $\quad \binom{n}{r-1} a^{n-r+1} b^{r-1} = \binom{10}{1-1} x^{10-1+1} (-2y)^{1-1} = \binom{10}{0} x^{10} (-2y)^0$

$$= \frac{10!}{0!(10-0)!} x^{10} \cdot 1 = \frac{10!}{0!\,10!} x^{10} = x^{10}$$

Second Term $\quad \binom{n}{r-1} a^{n-r+1} b^{r-1} = \binom{10}{2-1} x^{10-2+1} (-2y)^{2-1} = \binom{10}{1} x^9 (-2y)^1 = -\frac{10!}{1!(10-1)!} 2x^9 y$

$$= -\frac{10 \cdot 9!}{1 \cdot 9!} 2x^9 y = -10 \cdot 2x^9 y = -20x^9 y$$

Third Term $\quad \binom{n}{r-1} a^{n-r+1} b^{r-1} = \binom{10}{3-1} x^{10-3+1} (-2y)^{3-1} = \binom{10}{2} x^8 (-2y)^2 = \frac{10!}{2!(10-2)!} 4x^8 y^2$

$$= \frac{10 \cdot 9 \cdot 8!}{2 \cdot 1 \cdot 8!} 4x^8 y^2 = 45 \cdot 4x^8 y^2 = 180x^8 y^2$$

35. $(x^2+1)^{16}$

First Term $\quad \binom{n}{r-1} a^{n-r+1} b^{r-1} = \binom{16}{1-1} (x^2)^{16-1+1} (1)^{1-1} = \binom{16}{0} (x^2)^{16} 1^0$

$$= \frac{16!}{0!(16-0)!} x^{32} \cdot 1 = \frac{16!}{0!\,16!} x^{32} = x^{32}$$

Second Term $\quad \binom{n}{r-1} a^{n-r+1} b^{r-1} = \binom{16}{2-1} (x^2)^{16-2+1} (1)^{2-1} = \binom{16}{1} (x^2)^{15} 1^1$

$$= \frac{16!}{1!(16-1)!} x^{30} \cdot 1 = \frac{16 \cdot 15!}{1 \cdot 15!} x^{30} = 16x^{30}$$

Third Term $\quad \binom{n}{r-1} a^{n-r+1} b^{r-1} = \binom{16}{3-1} (x^2)^{16-3+1} (1)^{3-1} = \binom{16}{2} (x^2)^{14} 1^2$

$$= \frac{16!}{2!(16-2)!} x^{28} \cdot 1 = \frac{16 \cdot 15 \cdot 14!}{2 \cdot 1 \cdot 14!} x^{28} = 120x^{28}$$

37. $\left(y^3 - 1\right)^{20}$

First Term $\quad \binom{n}{r-1} a^{n-r+1} b^{r-1} = \binom{20}{1-1}\left(y^3\right)^{20-1+1}(-1)^{1-1} = \binom{20}{0}\left(y^3\right)^{20}(-1)^0$

$$= \frac{20!}{0!(20-0)!} y^{60} \cdot 1 = \frac{20!}{0! \, 20!} y^{60} = y^{60}$$

Second Term $\quad \binom{n}{r-1} a^{n-r+1} b^{r-1} = \binom{20}{2-1}\left(y^3\right)^{20-2+1}(-1)^{2-1} = \binom{20}{1}\left(y^3\right)^{19}(-1)^1$

$$= \frac{20!}{1!(20-1)!} y^{57} \cdot (-1) = -\frac{20 \cdot 19!}{1 \cdot 19!} y^{57} = -20 y^{57}$$

Third Term $\quad \binom{n}{r-1} a^{n-r+1} b^{r-1} = \binom{20}{3-1}\left(y^3\right)^{20-3+1}(-1)^{3-1} = \binom{20}{2}\left(y^3\right)^{18}(-1)^2$

$$= \frac{20!}{2!(20-2)!} y^{54} \cdot 1 = \frac{20 \cdot 19 \cdot 18!}{2 \cdot 1 \cdot 18!} y^{54} = 190 y^{54}$$

39. $\left(2x + y\right)^6$

Third Term $\quad \binom{n}{r-1} a^{n-r+1} b^{r-1} = \binom{6}{3-1}(2x)^{6-3+1} y^{3-1} = \binom{6}{2}(2x)^4 y^2 = \frac{6!}{2!(6-2)!} 16x^4 y^2$

$$= \frac{6 \cdot 5 \cdot 4!}{2 \cdot 1 \cdot 4!} 16x^4 y^2 = 15\left(16x^4 y^2\right) = 240x^4 y^2$$

41. $\left(x - 1\right)^9$

Fifth Term $\quad \binom{n}{r-1} a^{n-r+1} b^{r-1} = \binom{9}{5-1} x^{9-5+1}(-1)^{5-1} = \binom{9}{4} x^5 (-1)^4 = \frac{9!}{4!(9-4)!} x^5 \cdot 1$

$$= \frac{9 \cdot 8 \cdot 7 \cdot 6 \cdot 5!}{4 \cdot 3 \cdot 2 \cdot 1 \cdot 5!} x^5 = 126x^5$$

43. $\left(x^2 + y^3\right)^8$

Sixth Term $\quad \binom{n}{r-1} a^{n-r+1} b^{r-1} = \binom{8}{6-1}\left(x^2\right)^{8-6+1}\left(y^3\right)^{6-1} = \binom{8}{5}\left(x^2\right)^3\left(y^3\right)^5 = \frac{8!}{5!(8-5)!} x^6 y^{15}$

$$= \frac{8 \cdot 7 \cdot 6 \cdot 5!}{5! \cdot 3 \cdot 2 \cdot 1} x^6 y^{15} = 56x^6 y^{15}$$

45. $\left(x - \dfrac{1}{2}\right)^9$

Fourth Term $\dbinom{n}{r-1}a^{n-r+1}b^{r-1} = \dbinom{9}{4-1}x^{9-4+1}\left(-\dfrac{1}{2}\right)^{4-1} = \dbinom{9}{3}x^6\left(-\dfrac{1}{2}\right)^3 = -\dfrac{9!}{3!(9-3)!}\cdot\dfrac{1}{8}x^6$

$$= -\dfrac{9\cdot\cancel{8}\cdot7\cdot\cancel{6!}}{3\cdot2\cdot1\cdot\cancel{6!}}\cdot\dfrac{1}{\cancel{8}}x^6 = -\dfrac{21}{2}x^6$$

47. $\left(x^3 + x^{-2}\right)^4 = \dbinom{4}{0}\left(x^3\right)^4 + \dbinom{4}{1}\left(x^3\right)^3\left(x^{-2}\right) + \dbinom{4}{2}\left(x^3\right)^2\left(x^{-2}\right)^2 + \dbinom{4}{3}\left(x^3\right)^1\left(x^{-2}\right)^3 + \dbinom{4}{4}\left(x^{-2}\right)^4$

$$= \dfrac{4!}{0!(4-0)!}x^{12} + \dfrac{4!}{1!(4-1)!}x^9x^{-2} + \dfrac{4!}{2!(4-2)!}x^6x^{-4} + \dfrac{4!}{3!(4-3)!}x^3x^{-6} + \dfrac{4!}{4!(4-4)!}x^{-8}$$

$$= \dfrac{\cancel{4!}}{0!\cdot\cancel{4!}}x^{12} + \dfrac{4\cdot\cancel{3!}}{1!\cdot\cancel{3!}}x^7 + \dfrac{4\cdot3\cdot\cancel{2!}}{2\cdot1\cdot\cancel{2!}}x^2 + \dfrac{4\cdot\cancel{3!}}{\cancel{3!}\cdot1!}x^{-3} + \dfrac{\cancel{4!}}{\cancel{4!}\cdot0!}x^{-8}$$

$$= x^{12} + 4x^7 + 6x^2 + \dfrac{4}{x^3} + \dfrac{1}{x^8}$$

48. $\left(x^2 + x^{-3}\right)^4 = \dbinom{4}{0}\left(x^2\right)^4 + \dbinom{4}{1}\left(x^2\right)^3\left(x^{-3}\right) + \dbinom{4}{2}\left(x^2\right)^2\left(x^{-3}\right)^2 + \dbinom{4}{3}\left(x^2\right)^1\left(x^{-3}\right)^3 + \dbinom{4}{4}\left(x^{-3}\right)^4$

$$= \dfrac{4!}{0!(4-0)!}x^8 + \dfrac{4!}{1!(4-1)!}x^6x^{-3} + \dfrac{4!}{2!(4-2)!}x^4x^{-6} + \dfrac{4!}{3!(4-3)!}x^2x^{-9} + \dfrac{4!}{4!(4-4)!}x^{-12}$$

$$= \dfrac{\cancel{4!}}{0!\cdot\cancel{4!}}x^8 + \dfrac{4\cdot\cancel{3!}}{1!\cdot\cancel{3!}}x^3 + \dfrac{4\cdot3\cdot\cancel{2!}}{2\cdot1\cdot\cancel{2!}}x^{-2} + \dfrac{4\cdot\cancel{3!}}{\cancel{3!}\cdot1!}x^{-7} + \dfrac{\cancel{4!}}{\cancel{4!}\cdot0!}x^{-12}$$

$$= x^8 + 4x^3 + \dfrac{6}{x^2} + \dfrac{4}{x^7} + \dfrac{1}{x^{12}}$$

49. $\left(x^{\frac{1}{3}} - x^{-\frac{1}{3}}\right)^3 = \left(x^{\frac{1}{3}} + \left(-x^{-\frac{1}{3}}\right)\right)^3$

$$= \dbinom{3}{0}\left(x^{\frac{1}{3}}\right)^3 + \dbinom{3}{1}\left(x^{\frac{1}{3}}\right)^2\left(-x^{-\frac{1}{3}}\right) + \dbinom{3}{2}\left(x^{\frac{1}{3}}\right)^1\left(-x^{-\frac{1}{3}}\right)^2 + \dbinom{3}{3}\left(-x^{-\frac{1}{3}}\right)^3$$

$$= \dfrac{3!}{0!(3-0)!}x^1 + \dfrac{3!}{1!(3-1)!}x^{\frac{2}{3}}\cdot-x^{-\frac{1}{3}} + \dfrac{3!}{2!(3-2)!}x^{\frac{1}{3}}x^{-\frac{2}{3}} + \dfrac{3!}{3!(3-3)!}\cdot-x^{-1}$$

$$= \dfrac{\cancel{3!}}{0!\cdot\cancel{3!}}x + \dfrac{3\cdot\cancel{2!}}{1!\cdot\cancel{2!}}\cdot-x^{\frac{1}{3}} + \dfrac{\cdot3\cdot\cancel{2!}}{\cancel{2!}\cdot1!}x^{-\frac{1}{3}} + \dfrac{\cancel{3!}}{\cancel{3!}\cdot0!}\cdot-x^{-1}$$

$$= x - 3x^{\frac{1}{3}} + \dfrac{3}{x^{\frac{1}{3}}} - \dfrac{1}{x}$$

865

50.

$$\left(x^{\frac{2}{3}} - \frac{1}{\sqrt[3]{x}}\right)^3 = \left(x^{\frac{2}{3}} + \left(-\frac{1}{x^{\frac{1}{3}}}\right)\right)^3 = \left(x^{\frac{2}{3}} + \left(-x^{-\frac{1}{3}}\right)\right)^3$$

$$= \left(x^{\frac{2}{3}} + \left(-x^{-\frac{1}{3}}\right)\right)^3$$

$$= \binom{3}{0}\left(x^{\frac{2}{3}}\right)^3 + \binom{3}{1}\left(x^{\frac{2}{3}}\right)^2\left(-x^{-\frac{1}{3}}\right) + \binom{3}{2}\left(x^{\frac{2}{3}}\right)^1\left(-x^{-\frac{1}{3}}\right)^2 + \binom{3}{3}\left(-x^{-\frac{1}{3}}\right)^3$$

$$= \frac{3!}{0!(3-0)!}x^2 + \frac{3!}{1!(3-1)!}x^{\frac{4}{3}}\cdot -x^{-\frac{1}{3}} + \frac{3!}{2!(3-2)!}x^{\frac{2}{3}}x^{-\frac{2}{3}} + \frac{3!}{3!(3-3)!}\cdot -x^{-1}$$

$$= \frac{\cancel{3!}}{0!\,\cancel{3!}}x^2 + \frac{3\cdot\cancel{2!}}{1!\,\cancel{2!}}\cdot -x^1 + \frac{\cdot 3\cdot\cancel{2!}}{\cancel{2!}\cdot 1!}x^0 + \frac{\cancel{3!}}{\cancel{3!}\cdot 0!}\cdot -x^{-1}$$

$$= x^2 - 3x + 3 - \frac{1}{x}$$

51.

$$\left(-1+\sqrt{3}i\right)^3 = \binom{3}{0}(-1)^3 + \binom{3}{1}(-1)^2\left(\sqrt{3}i\right) + \binom{3}{2}(-1)^1\left(\sqrt{3}i\right)^2 + \binom{3}{3}\left(\sqrt{3}i\right)^3$$

$$= \frac{3!}{0!(3-0)!}\cdot -1 + \frac{3!}{1!(3-1)!}1\cdot\sqrt{3}i + \frac{3!}{2!(3-2)!}\cdot -1\cdot -3 + \frac{3!}{3!(3-3)!}\cdot -3\sqrt{3}i$$

$$= \frac{\cancel{3!}}{0!\,\cancel{3!}}(-1) + \frac{3\cdot\cancel{2!}}{1!\,\cancel{2!}}\sqrt{3}i + \frac{3\cdot\cancel{2!}}{\cancel{2!}1!}\cdot 3 + \frac{\cancel{3!}}{\cancel{3!}0!}\cdot -3\sqrt{3}i$$

$$= -1 + 3\sqrt{3}i + 9 - 3\sqrt{3}i = 8$$

52.

$$\left(-1-\sqrt{3}i\right)^3 = \binom{3}{0}(-1)^3 + \binom{3}{1}(-1)^2\left(-\sqrt{3}i\right) + \binom{3}{2}(-1)^1\left(-\sqrt{3}i\right)^2 + \binom{3}{3}\left(-\sqrt{3}i\right)^3$$

$$= \frac{3!}{0!(3-0)!}\cdot -1 + \frac{3!}{1!(3-1)!}1\cdot -\sqrt{3}i + \frac{3!}{2!(3-2)!}\cdot -1\cdot -3 + \frac{3!}{3!(3-3)!}\cdot 3\sqrt{3}i$$

$$= -\frac{\cancel{3!}}{0!\,\cancel{3!}} - \frac{3\cdot\cancel{2!}}{1!\,\cancel{2!}}\sqrt{3}i + \frac{3\cdot\cancel{2!}}{\cancel{2!}1!}\cdot 3 + \frac{\cancel{3!}}{\cancel{3!}0!}\cdot 3\sqrt{3}i$$

$$= -1 - 3\sqrt{3}i + 9 + 3\sqrt{3}i = 8$$

53. $f(x) = x^4 + 7$;

$$\frac{f(x+h) - f(x)}{h}$$

$$= \frac{(x+h)^4 + 7 - \left(x^4 + 7\right)}{h}$$

$$= \frac{\binom{4}{0}x^4 + \binom{4}{1}x^3h + \binom{4}{2}x^2h^2 + \binom{4}{3}xh^3 + \binom{4}{4}h^4 + 7 - x^4 - 7}{h}$$

$$= \frac{\dfrac{4!}{0!(4-0)!}x^4 + \dfrac{4!}{1!(4-1)!}x^3h + \dfrac{4!}{2!(4-2)!}x^2h^2 + \dfrac{4!}{3!(4-3)!}xh^3 + \dfrac{4!}{4!(4-4)!}h^4 - x^4}{h}$$

$$= \frac{\dfrac{\cancel{4!}}{0!\,\cancel{4!}}x^4 + \dfrac{4\cdot\cancel{3!}}{1!\,\cancel{3!}}x^3h + \dfrac{4\cdot 3\cdot\cancel{2!}}{\cancel{2!}\cdot 2\cdot 1}x^2h^2 + \dfrac{4\cdot\cancel{3!}}{\cancel{3!}\,1!}xh^3 + \dfrac{\cancel{4!}}{\cancel{4!}\,0!}h^4 - x^4}{h}$$

$$= \frac{\cancel{x^4} + 4x^3h + 6x^2h^2 + 4xh^3 + h^4 - \cancel{x^4}}{h}$$

$$= \frac{h(4x^3 + 6x^2h + 4xh^2 + h^3)}{h} = 4x^3 + 6x^2h + 4xh^2 + h^3$$

54. $f(x) = x^5 + 8$

$$\frac{f(x+h) - f(x)}{h}$$

$$= \frac{(x+h)^5 + 8 - (x^5 - 8)}{h}$$

$$= \frac{\binom{5}{0}x^5 + \binom{5}{1}x^4h + \binom{5}{2}x^3h^2 + \binom{5}{3}x^2h^3 + \binom{5}{4}xh^4 + \binom{5}{5}h^5 + 8 - x^5 - 8}{h}$$

$$= \frac{\dfrac{5!}{0!(5-0)!}x^5 + \dfrac{5!}{1!(5-1)!}x^4h + \dfrac{5!}{2!(5-2)!}x^3h^2 + \dfrac{5!}{3!(5-3)!}x^2h^3 + \dfrac{5!}{4!(5-4)!}xh^4 + \dfrac{5!}{5!(5-5)!}h^5 - x^5}{h}$$

$$= \frac{\dfrac{\cancel{5!}}{0!\,\cancel{5!}}x^5 + \dfrac{5\cdot\cancel{4!}}{1!\,\cancel{4!}}x^4h + \dfrac{5\cdot 4\cdot\cancel{3!}}{2!\,\cancel{3!}}x^3h^2 + \dfrac{5\cdot 4\cdot\cancel{3!}}{\cancel{3!}\,2!}x^2h^3 + \dfrac{5\cdot\cancel{4!}}{\cancel{4!}\,1!}xh^4 + \dfrac{\cancel{5!}}{\cancel{5!}\,0!}h^5 - x^5}{h}$$

$$= \frac{x^5 + 5x^4h + 10x^3h^2 + 10x^2h^3 + 5xh^4 + h^5 - x^5}{h} = \frac{5x^4h + 10x^3h^2 + 10x^2h^3 + 5xh^4 + h^5}{h}$$

$$= \frac{h(5x^4 + 10x^3h + 10x^2h^2 + 5xh^3 + h^4)}{h} = 5x^4 + 10x^3h + 10x^2h^2 + 5xh^3 + h^4$$

55. We want to find the $(5+1) = 6^{th}$ term.

$$\binom{n}{r}a^{n-r}b^r = \binom{10}{5}\left(\frac{3}{x}\right)^{10-5}\left(\frac{x}{3}\right)^5 = \frac{10!}{5!(10-5)!}\left(\frac{3}{x}\right)^5\left(\frac{x}{3}\right)^5$$

$$= \frac{10 \cdot 9 \cdot 8 \cdot 7 \cdot 6 \cdot 5!}{5! \cdot 5 \cdot 4 \cdot 3 \cdot 2 \cdot 1}\left(\frac{3}{x}\right)^5\left(\frac{x}{3}\right)^5 = 252 \cdot \frac{3^5}{x^5} \cdot \frac{x^5}{3^5} = 252$$

56. We want to find the $(6+1) = 7^{th}$ term.

$$\binom{n}{r}a^{n-r}b^r = \binom{12}{6}\left(\frac{1}{x}\right)^{12-6}\left(-x^2\right)^6 = \frac{12!}{6!(12-6)!}\left(\frac{1}{x}\right)^6\left(-x^2\right)^6$$

$$= \frac{12 \cdot 11 \cdot 10 \cdot 9 \cdot 8 \cdot 7 \cdot 6!}{6! \cdot 6 \cdot 5 \cdot 4 \cdot 3 \cdot 2 \cdot 1}\left(\frac{1}{x}\right)^6\left(-x^2\right)^6 = 924 \cdot \frac{1}{x^6} \cdot x^{12} = 924x^{12-6} = 924x^6$$

57. a. $g(x) = 0.12(x+3)^3 - (x+3)^2 + 3(x+3) + 15$

$$= 0.12\left[\binom{3}{0}x^3 + \binom{3}{1}x^2 \cdot 3 + \binom{3}{2}x \cdot 3^2 + \binom{3}{3} \cdot 3^3\right] - \left(x^2 + 6x + 9\right) + 3x + 9 + 15$$

$$= 0.12\left[\frac{3!}{0!(3-0)!}x^3 + \frac{3!}{1!(3-1)!}3x^2 + \frac{3!}{2!(3-2)!}9x + \frac{3!}{3!(3-3)!} \cdot 27\right]$$

$$- x^2 - 6x - 9 + 3x + 9 + 15$$

$$= 0.12\left(x^3 + 9x^2 + 27x + 27\right) - x^2 - 3x + 15$$

$$= 0.12x^3 + 1.08x^2 + 3.24x + 3.24 - x^2 - 3x + 15$$

$$= 0.12x^3 + 0.08x^2 + 0.24x + 18.24$$

b. $f(5) = 0.12(5)^3 - 5^2 + 3(5) + 15 = 20$

$g(2) = 0.12(2)^3 + 0.08(2)^2 + 0.24(2) + 18.24 = 20$

They give the exact value of the number shown.

59. – 67. Answers will vary.

69. $f_1(x) = (x+2)^3$

$f_2(x) = x^3$

$f_3(x) = x^3 + 6x^2$

$f_4(x) = x^3 + 6x^2 + 12x$

$f_5(x) = x^3 + 6x^2 + 12x + 8$

Graphs f_1 and f_5 are the same. This means that the functions are equivalent. Graphs f_2 through f_4 are increasingly similar to the graphs of f_1 and f_5.

71. Applying the Binomial Theorem to $(x-1)^3$, we have $a = x$, $b = -1$, and $n = 3$.

$$(x-1)^3 = \binom{3}{0}x^3 + \binom{3}{1}x^2(-1) + \binom{3}{2}x(-1)^2 + \binom{3}{3}(-1)^3$$

$$= \frac{3!}{0!(3-0)!}x^3 - \frac{3!}{1!(3-1)!}x^2 + \frac{3!}{2!(3-2)!}x(1) - \frac{3!}{3!(3-3)!}$$

$$= \frac{\cancel{3!}}{1 \cdot \cancel{3!}}x^3 - \frac{3 \cdot \cancel{2!}}{1 \cdot \cancel{2!}}x^2 + \frac{3 \cdot \cancel{2!}}{\cancel{2!}1!}x - \frac{\cancel{3!}}{\cancel{3!}0!} = x^3 - 3x^2 + 3x - 1$$

Graph using the method from Exercises 69 and 70.

$f_1(x) = (x-1)^3$ $\qquad\qquad$ $f_2(x) = x^3$

$f_3(x) = x^3 + 3x^2$ $\qquad\qquad$ $f_4(x) = x^3 + 3x^2 + 3x$

$f_5(x) = x^3 - 3x^2 + 3x - 1$

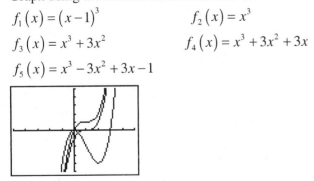

Graphs f_1 and f_5 are the same. This means that the functions are equivalent. Graphs f_2 through f_4 are increasingly similar to the graphs of f_1 and f_5.

73. Applying the Binomial Theorem to $(x+2)^6$, we have $a = x$, $b = 2$, and $n = 6$.

$$(x+2)^6 = \binom{6}{0}x^6 + \binom{6}{1}x^5 2 + \binom{6}{2}x^4 2^2 + \binom{6}{3}x^3 2^3 + \binom{6}{4}x^2 2^4 + \binom{6}{5}x 2^5 + \binom{6}{6}2^6$$

$$= \frac{6!}{0!(6-0)!}x^6 + \frac{6!}{1!(6-1)!}2x^5 + \frac{6!}{2!(6-2)!}4x^4 + \frac{6!}{3!(6-3)!}8x^3 + \frac{6!}{4!(6-4)!}16x^2$$
$$+ \frac{6!}{5!(6-5)!}32x + \frac{6!}{6!(6-6)!}64$$

$$= \frac{\cancel{6!}}{1\cancel{6!}}x^6 + \frac{6 \cdot \cancel{5!}}{1 \cdot \cancel{5!}}2x^5 + \frac{6 \cdot 5 \cdot \cancel{4!}}{2 \cdot 1 \cdot \cancel{4!}}4x^4 + \frac{\cancel{6} \cdot 5 \cdot 4 \cdot \cancel{3!}}{3 \cancel{2} \cdot 1 \cdot \cancel{3!}}8x^3 + \frac{6 \cdot 5 \cdot \cancel{4!}}{\cancel{4!}2 \cdot 1}16x^2 + \frac{6 \cdot \cancel{5!}}{\cancel{5!}1}32x + \frac{\cancel{6!}}{\cancel{6!} \cdot 1}64$$

$$= x^6 + 6(2x^5) + 15(4x^4) + 20(8x^3) + 15(16x^2) + 6(32x) + 1(64)$$

$$= x^6 + 12x^5 + 60x^4 + 160x^3 + 240x^2 + 192x + 64$$

Graph using the method from Exercises 69 and 70.

$$f_1(x) = (x+2)^6$$

$$f_2(x) = x^6$$

$$f_3(x) = x^6 + 12x^5$$

$$f_4(x) = x^6 + 12x^5 + 60x^4$$

$$f_5(x) = x^6 + 12x^5 + 60x^4 + 160x^3$$

$$f_6(x) = x^6 + 12x^5 + 60x^4 + 160x^3 + 240x^2$$

$$f_7(x) = x^6 + 12x^5 + 60x^4 + 160x^3 + 240x^2 + 192x$$

$$f_8(x) = x^6 + 12x^5 + 60x^4 + 160x^3 + 240x^2 + 192x + 64$$

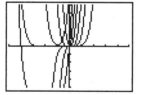

Graphs f_1 and f_8 are the same. This means that the functions are equivalent. Graphs f_2 through f_7 are increasingly similar to the graphs of f_1 and f_8.

75. Statement **b.** is true. The Binomial Theorem can be written in condensed

form as $(a+b)^n = \sum_{r=0}^{n} \binom{n}{r} a^{n-r} b^r$

Statement **a.** is false. The binomial expansion for $(a+b)^n$ contains $n+1$ terms.

Statement **c.** is false. The sum of the binomial coefficients in $(a+b)^n$ is 2^n.

Statement **d.** is false. There are values of a and b for which $(a+b)^4 = a^4 + b^4$. Consider $a = 0$ and $b = 1$.

$(0+1)^4 = 0^4 + 1^4$

$(1)^4 = 0+1$

$1 = 1$

77. In $(x^2 + y^2)^5$, the term containing x^4 is the term in which $a = x^2$ is squared. Applying the Binomial Theorem, the following pattern results. In the first term, x^2 is taken to the fifth power. In the second term, x^2 is taken to the fourth power. In the third term x^2 is taken to the third power. In the fourth term, x^2 is taken to the second power. This is the term we are looking for. Applying the Binomial Theorem to $(x^2 + y^2)^5$, we have $a = x^2$, $b = y^2$, and $n = 5$. We are looking for the rth term where $r = 4$.

$\binom{n}{r-1} a^{n-r+1} b^{r-1} = \binom{5}{4-1}(x^2)^{5-4+1}(y^2)^{4-1}$

$= \binom{5}{3}(x^2)^2(y^2)^3$

$= \dfrac{5!}{3!(5-3)!} x^4 y^6$

$= \dfrac{5!}{3!2!} x^4 y^6$

$= \dfrac{5 \cdot 4 \cdot \cancel{3!}}{\cancel{3!}2 \cdot 1} x^4 y^6$

$= 10x^4 y^6$

78. $f(a+1) = (a+1)^2 + 2(a+1) + 3$

$= a^2 + 2a + 1 + 2a + 2 + 3$

$= a^2 + 4a + 6$

79. $f(x) = x^2 + 5x \qquad g(x) = 2x - 3$

$f(g(x)) = f(2x-3)$

$= (2x-3)^2 + 5(2x-3)$

$= 4x^2 - 12x + 9 + 10x - 15$

$= 4x^2 - 2x - 6$

$g(f(x)) = g(x^2 + 5x)$

$= 2(x^2 + 5x) - 3$

$= 2x^2 + 10x - 3$

80.

$$\frac{x}{x+3} - \frac{x+1}{2x^2 - 2x - 24}$$

$$= \frac{x}{x+3} - \frac{x+1}{2(x^2 - x - 12)}$$

$$= \frac{x}{x+3} - \frac{x+1}{2(x-4)(x+3)}$$

$$= \frac{x}{x+3} \cdot \frac{2(x-4)}{2(x-4)} - \frac{x+1}{2(x-4)(x+3)}$$

$$= \frac{x}{x+3} \cdot \frac{2x-8}{2(x-4)} - \frac{x+1}{2(x-4)(x+3)}$$

$$= \frac{2x^2 - 8x}{2(x-4)(x+3)} - \frac{x+1}{2(x-4)(x+3)}$$

$$= \frac{2x^2 - 8x - (x+1)}{2(x-4)(x+3)}$$

$$= \frac{2x^2 - 8x - x - 1}{2(x-4)(x+3)}$$

$$= \frac{2x^2 - 9x - 1}{2(x-4)(x+3)}$$

14.5 Exercise Set

1.

$$_9P_4 = \frac{9!}{(9-4)!} = \frac{9!}{5!} = \frac{9 \cdot 8 \cdot 7 \cdot 6 \cdot \cancel{5!}}{\cancel{5!}}$$

$$= 9 \cdot 8 \cdot 7 \cdot 6 = 3024$$

3.

$$_8P_5 = \frac{8!}{(8-5)!} = \frac{8!}{3!} = \frac{8 \cdot 7 \cdot 6 \cdot 5 \cdot 4 \cdot \cancel{3!}}{\cancel{3!}}$$

$$= 8 \cdot 7 \cdot 6 \cdot 5 \cdot 4 = 6720$$

5.

$$_6P_6 = \frac{6!}{(6-6)!} = \frac{6!}{0!} = \frac{6 \cdot 5 \cdot 4 \cdot 3 \cdot 2 \cdot 1}{1}$$

$$= 720$$

7.

$$_8P_0 = \frac{8!}{(8-0)!} = \frac{8!}{8!} = 1$$

9.

$$_9C_5 = \frac{9!}{(9-5)!5!} = \frac{9!}{4!5!} = \frac{9 \cdot 8 \cdot 7 \cdot 6 \cdot \cancel{5!}}{4 \cdot 3 \cdot 2 \cdot 1 \cdot \cancel{5!}}$$

$$= 126$$

11.

$$_{11}C_4 = \frac{11!}{(11-4)!4!} = \frac{11!}{7!4!}$$

$$= \frac{11 \cdot 10 \cdot 9 \cdot 8 \cdot \cancel{7!}}{\cancel{7!} \cdot 4 \cdot 3 \cdot 2 \cdot 1} = 330$$

13.

$$_7C_7 = \frac{7!}{(7-7)!7!} = \frac{7!}{0!7!} = 1$$

15.

$$_5C_0 = \frac{5!}{(5-0)!0!} = \frac{5!}{5!0!} = 1$$

17. Combinations; the order in which the 6 people selected does not matter.

19. Permutations; the order in which the letters are selected does matter.

21.

$$\frac{_7P_3}{3!} - {_7C_3} = \frac{\dfrac{7!}{(7-3)!}}{3!} - \frac{7!}{(7-3)!3!}$$

$$= \frac{\dfrac{7!}{4!}}{3!} - \frac{7!}{4!3!}$$

$$= \frac{7!}{4!3!} - \frac{7!}{4!3!} = 0$$

23.

$$1 - \frac{_3P_2}{_4P_3} = 1 - \frac{\dfrac{3!}{(3-2)!}}{\dfrac{4!}{(4-3)!}} = 1 - \frac{\dfrac{3!}{1!}}{\dfrac{4!}{1!}} = 1 - \frac{3!}{4!}$$

$$= 1 - \frac{3!}{4 \cdot 3!} = 1 - \frac{1}{4} = \frac{3}{4}$$

25.

$$\frac{{}_7C_3}{{}_5C_4} - \frac{98!}{96!} = \frac{\dfrac{7!}{(7-3)!3!}}{\dfrac{5!}{(5-4)!4!}} - \frac{98 \cdot 97 \cdot \cancel{96!}}{\cancel{96!}}$$

$$= \frac{\dfrac{7!}{4!3!}}{\dfrac{5!}{1!4!}} - 95067$$

$$= \frac{\dfrac{7 \cdot 6 \cdot 5 \cdot \cancel{4!}}{\cancel{4!}3 \cdot 2 \cdot 1}}{\dfrac{5 \cdot \cancel{4!}}{1!\cancel{4!}}} - 9506$$

$$= \frac{35}{5} - 9506$$

$$= 7 - 9506 = -9499$$

27.

$$\frac{{}_4C_2 \cdot {}_6C_1}{{}_{18}C_3} = \frac{\dfrac{4!}{(4-2)!2!} \cdot \dfrac{6!}{(6-1)!1!}}{\dfrac{18!}{(18-3)!3!}}$$

$$= \frac{\dfrac{4!}{2!2!} \cdot \dfrac{6!}{5!1!}}{\dfrac{18!}{15!3!}}$$

$$= \frac{\dfrac{4 \cdot 3 \cdot \cancel{2!}}{\cancel{2!}2 \cdot 1} \cdot \dfrac{6 \cdot \cancel{5!}}{\cancel{5!}1!}}{\dfrac{18 \cdot 17 \cdot 16 \cdot \cancel{15!}}{\cancel{15!}3 \cdot 2 \cdot 1}}$$

$$= \frac{36}{816} = \frac{3}{68}$$

29. $9 \cdot 3 = 27$

There are 27 ways you can order the car.

31. $2 \cdot 4 \cdot 5 = 40$

There are 40 ways to order a drink.

33. $3 \cdot 3 \cdot 3 \cdot 3 \cdot 3 = 3^4 = 243$

There are 243 ways to answer the questions.

35. $8 \cdot 2 \cdot 9 = 144$

There are 144 area codes possible.

37. Find the number of ways the remaining five performers can by arranged:

$5 \cdot 4 \cdot 3 \cdot 2 \cdot 1 = 120$

There are 120 ways to schedule the appearances.

39. Find the number of arrangements for the remaining three paragraphs:

$3 \cdot 2 \cdot 1 = 6$

6 five-sentence paragraphs can be formed.

41. $${}_{10}P_3 = \frac{10!}{(10-3)!} = \frac{10!}{7!} = 720$$

There are 720 ways the offices can be filled.

43. $${}_{13}P_7 = \frac{13!}{(13-7)!} = \frac{13!}{6!} = 8648640$$

There are 8,648,640 ways to arrange the program for this segment.

45. $${}_6P_3 = \frac{6!}{(6-3)!} = \frac{6!}{3!} = 120$$

There are 120 ways the first three finishers can come in.

47. $${}_9P_5 = \frac{9!}{(9-5)!} = \frac{9!}{4!} = 15120$$

There are 15,120 lineups possible.

49. $${}_6C_2 = \frac{6!}{(6-2)!2!} = \frac{6!}{4!2!} = 20$$

There are 20 ways to select the three city commissioners.

51.
$$_{12}C_4 = \frac{12!}{(12-4)!4!} = \frac{12!}{8!4!} = 495$$

You can take 495 different collections of 4 books.

53.
$$_{17}C_8 = \frac{17!}{(17-8)!8!} = \frac{17!}{9!8!} = 24310$$

You can drive 24,310 different groups of 8 children.

55.
$$_{53}C_6 = \frac{53!}{(53-6)!6!} = \frac{53!}{47!6!} = 22957480$$

There are 22,957,480 selections possible.

57. $6 \cdot 5 \cdot 4 \cdot 3 = 360$

There are 360 ways the first four finishers can come in.

59.
$$_{13}C_6 = \frac{13!}{(13-6)!6!} = \frac{13!}{7!6!} = 1716$$

There are 1716 ways 6 people can be selected.

61.
$$_{20}C_3 = \frac{20!}{(20-3)!3!} = \frac{20!}{17!3!} = 1140$$

There are 1140 ways to select 3 members.

63.
$$_7P_4 = \frac{7!}{(7-4)!} = \frac{7!}{3!} = 840$$

840 four-letter passwords can be formed.

65.
$$_{15}P_3 = \frac{15!}{(15-3)!} = \frac{15!}{12!} = 2730$$

2730 cones can be created.

67. – 73. Answers will vary..

75. For example, consider Exercise 1.

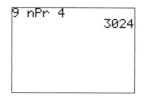

This matches the result obtained in Exercise 1.

77. Statement **c** is true.

$$3!_7C_3 = 3! \cdot \frac{7!}{(7-3)!3!} = \frac{7!}{(7-3)!} = {_7}P_3$$

Statement **a** is false. The number of ways to choose four questions out of ten questions is $_{10}C_4$.

Statement **b** is false. If $r > 1$, $_nP_r$ is greater than $_nC_r$.

Statement **d** is false. The number of ways to pick a winner and first runner-up is $_{20}C_2$

79. The first digit must be either 2 or 4. The second and third digits can be 2, 4, 6, 7, 8, or 9. The fourth digit must be either 7 or 9.
$2 \cdot 6 \cdot 6 \cdot 2 = 144$
There are 144 four-digit odd numbers less than 6000 that can be formed.

81.
$$\begin{aligned}
(f \circ g)(x) &= f(g(x)) = f(4x-1) \\
&= (4x-1)^2 + 2(4x-1) - 5 \\
&= 16x^2 - 8x + 1 + 8x - 2 - 5 \\
&= 16x^2 - 6
\end{aligned}$$

874

82. $|2x - 5| > 3$

$2x - 5 > 3 \quad \text{or} \quad 2x - 5 < -3$

$2x > 8 \qquad\qquad 2x < 2$

$x > 4 \qquad\qquad x < 1$

$\{x \mid x < 1 \text{ or } x > 4\}$ or $(-\infty, 1) \cup (4, \infty)$

83. $x^2 + y^2 - 2x + 4y - 4 = 0$

$x^2 - 2x \quad + y^2 + 4y \quad = 4$

$x^2 - 2x + 1 + y^2 + 4y + 4 = 4 + 1 + 4$

$(x - 1)^2 + (y + 2)^2 = 9$

$(x - 1)^2 + (y + 2)^2 = 3^2$

The center of the circle is $(1, -2)$, and the radius is 3.

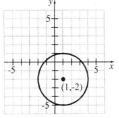

14.6 Exercise Set

1. $P(female) = \dfrac{23}{89}$

3. $P(in\ the\ Army) = \dfrac{36}{89}$

5. $P(a\ woman\ in\ the\ Air\ Force) = \dfrac{6}{89}$

7. $P(woman,\ among\ Air\ Force) = \dfrac{6}{18} = \dfrac{1}{3}$

9. $P(woman\ in\ Air\ Force) = \dfrac{6}{23}$

11. $P(4) = \dfrac{1}{6}$

13. $P(odd\ number) = \dfrac{3}{6} = \dfrac{1}{2}$

15. $P(greater\ than\ 4) = \dfrac{2}{6} = \dfrac{1}{3}$

17. $P(queen) = \dfrac{4}{52} = \dfrac{1}{13}$

19. $P(picture\ card) = \dfrac{12}{52} = \dfrac{3}{13}$

21. $P(two\ heads) = P(HH) = \dfrac{1}{4}$

23. $P(at\ least\ one\ male\ child) = \dfrac{7}{8}$

25. $P(sum\ is\ 4) = \dfrac{3}{36} = \dfrac{1}{12}$

27. First find the number of combinations of 6 out of 51 numbers:

$$_{51}C_6 = \frac{51!}{(51-6)!6!} = \frac{51!}{45!6!} = 18009460$$

The probability that a person with one combinations of six numbers will win is $\dfrac{1}{18,009,460} \approx 0.0000000555$.

If 100 different tickets are purchased, the probability of winning is

$$100 \cdot \frac{1}{18,009,460} = \frac{5}{900,473}$$

$$= 0.00000555$$

29. a.
$$_{52}C_5 = \frac{52!}{(52-5)!5!}$$
$$= \frac{52!}{47!5!} = 2,598,960$$

b.
$$_{12}C_5 = \frac{12!}{(12-5)!5!} = \frac{12!}{7!5!} = 1287$$

c.
$$P(\text{diamond flush}) = \frac{1287}{2,598,960}$$
$$\approx 0.000495$$

31.
$$P(\text{not completed 4 years of college})$$
$$= 1 - P(\text{completed 4 years of college})$$
$$= 1 - \frac{45}{174} = \frac{43}{58}$$

33.
$$P(\text{completed H.S. or}$$
$$\text{less than 4 yrs college})$$
$$= P(\text{completed H.S}) +$$
$$P(\text{less than 4 yrs college})$$
$$= \frac{56}{174} + \frac{44}{174} = \frac{100}{174} = \frac{50}{87}$$

35.
$$P(\text{completed 4 yrs H.S. or man})$$
$$= P(\text{completed 4 yrs H.S.}) + P(\text{man})$$
$$- P(\text{man who completed 4 yrs H.S})$$
$$= \frac{56}{174} + \frac{82}{174} - \frac{25}{174} = \frac{113}{174}$$

37. $P(\text{not king}) = 1 - P(\text{king})$
$$= 1 - \frac{4}{52} = 1 - \frac{1}{13} = \frac{12}{13}$$

39. $P(2 \text{ or } 3) = P(2) + P(3)$
$$= \frac{4}{52} + \frac{4}{52} = \frac{8}{52} = \frac{2}{13}$$

41. $P(7 \text{ or red card})$
$$= P(7) + P(\text{red card}) - P(7 \text{ and red})$$
$$= \frac{4}{52} + \frac{26}{52} - \frac{2}{52} = \frac{28}{52} = \frac{7}{13}$$

43. $P(\text{odd or less than 6})$
$$= P(\text{odd}) + P(\text{less than 6})$$
$$- P(\text{odd \# less than 6})$$
$$= \frac{4}{8} + \frac{5}{8} - \frac{3}{8} = \frac{6}{8} = \frac{3}{4}$$

45. $P(\text{professor or male}) = P(\text{professor}) \cdot$
$$= \frac{19}{40} + \frac{22}{40} - \frac{8}{40} = \frac{33}{40}$$

47.
$$P(2 \text{ and } 3) = P(2) \cdot P(3) = \frac{1}{6} \cdot \frac{1}{6} = \frac{1}{36}$$

49. $P(\text{even and greater than 2})$
$$= P(\text{even}) \cdot P(\text{greater than 2})$$
$$= \frac{3}{6} \cdot \frac{4}{6} = \frac{1}{3}$$

51.
$$P(\text{all heads}) = \frac{1}{2} \cdot \frac{1}{2} \cdot \frac{1}{2} \cdot \frac{1}{2} \cdot \frac{1}{2} \cdot \frac{1}{2}$$
$$= \left(\frac{1}{2}\right)^6 = \frac{1}{64}$$

53. a. $P(\text{hit 2 yrs in a row})$
$$= P(\text{hit in 1}^{st} \text{ year and 2}^{nd} \text{ year})$$
$$= P(\text{hit 1}^{st} \text{ year}) \cdot P(\text{hit 2}^{nd} \text{ year})$$
$$= \frac{1}{16} \cdot \frac{1}{16} = \frac{1}{256}$$

b.
$$P(\text{hit 3 yrs in a row}) = \frac{1}{16} \cdot \frac{1}{16} \cdot \frac{1}{16}$$
$$= \frac{1}{4096}$$

c. First find the probability that South Florida will not be hit by a major hurricane in a single year:

$$P(not\ hit) = 1 - \frac{1}{16} = \frac{15}{16}$$

$$P(not\ hit\ in\ next\ 10\ years) = \left(\frac{15}{16}\right)^{10} \approx 0.524$$

d.

$$P(hit\ at\ least\ once) = 1 - P(hit\ none) = 1 - \left(\frac{15}{16}\right)^{10} \approx 0.476$$

55. – 61. Answers will vary.

63. P(someone who tests positive for cocaine uses cocaine)

$$= \frac{\text{the number of employees who test positive and are cocaine users}}{\text{number of employees who test positive}}$$

$$= \frac{90\%\ \text{of}\ 1\%\ \text{of}\ 10{,}000}{\text{\# who test positive who actually use cocaine plus \# who test positive who do not use cocaine}}$$

$$= \frac{(.90)(0.01)(10{,}000)}{(0.90)(0.01)(10{,}000) + (0.10)(0.99)(10{,}000)}$$

$$= \frac{90}{90 + 990} = \frac{90}{1080} = \frac{1}{12};$$

Answers will vary.

65. Answers will vary.

67. a. P(Democrat who is not a business major)

$$= \frac{\text{\# of students who are Democrats but not business majors}}{\text{\# of students}}$$

$$= \frac{29 - 5}{50} = \frac{24}{50} = \frac{12}{25}$$

b. P(neither Democrat nor business major)

$$= 1 - P(\text{Democrat or business major})$$

$$= 1 - \left(P(\text{Democrat}) + P(\text{business major}) - P(\text{Democrat and business major})\right)$$

$$= 1 - \left(\frac{29}{50} + \frac{11}{50} - \frac{5}{50}\right) = 1 - \frac{35}{50} = \frac{15}{50} = \frac{3}{10}$$

877

69. $4x^2 + 25y^2 = 100$

$$\frac{4x^2 + 25y^2}{100} = \frac{100}{100}$$

$$\frac{x^2}{25} + \frac{y^2}{4} = 1$$

$$\frac{x^2}{5^2} + \frac{y^2}{2^2} = 1$$

The graph is an ellipse centered at the origin with x-intercepts ± 5 and y-intercepts ± 2.

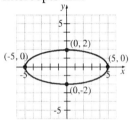

70. $\log_2(x+5) + \log_2(x-1) = 4$

$$\log_2(x+5)(x-1) = 4$$

$$\log_2\left(x^2 + 4x - 5\right) = 4$$

$$x^2 + 4x - 5 = 2^4$$

$$x^2 + 4x - 5 = 16$$

$$x^2 + 4x - 21 = 0$$

$$(x+7)(x-3) = 0$$

Using the zero product rule,
$x + 7 = 0$ or $x - 3 = 0$

$x = -7$ or $x = 3$

Omit $x = -7$ since
$\log_2(x+5) = \log_2(-7+5) = \log_2(-2)$
and we cannot take the log of a negative number. Thus, the solution set is $\{3\}$.

71. Using synthetic division:

$$\begin{array}{r|rrrr} -2 & 1 & 5 & 3 & -10 \\ & & -2 & -6 & 6 \\ \hline & 1 & 3 & -3 & -4 \end{array}$$

The quotient is $x^2 + 3x - 3x$ and the remainder is -4.

Then $\dfrac{x^3 + 5x^2 + 3x - 10}{x + 2}$

$$= x^2 + 3x - 3 - \frac{4}{x+2}$$

Chapter 14 Review Exercises

1. $a_n = 7n - 4$

$a_1 = 7(1) - 4 = 7 - 4 = 3$

$a_2 = 7(2) - 4 = 14 - 4 = 10$

$a_3 = 7(3) - 4 = 21 - 4 = 17$

$a_4 = 7(4) - 4 = 28 - 4 = 24$

The first four terms are 3, 10, 17, 24.

2. $a_n = (-1)^n \dfrac{n+2}{n+1}$

$a_1 = (-1)^1 \dfrac{1+2}{1+1} = -\dfrac{3}{2}$

$a_2 = (-1)^2 \dfrac{2+2}{2+1} = \dfrac{4}{3}$

$a_3 = (-1)^3 \dfrac{3+2}{3+1} = -\dfrac{5}{4}$

$a_4 = (-1)^4 \dfrac{4+2}{4+1} = \dfrac{6}{5}$

The first four terms are $-\dfrac{3}{2}, \dfrac{4}{3}, -\dfrac{5}{4}, \dfrac{6}{5}$.

3.

$$a_n = \frac{1}{(n-1)!}$$

$$a_1 = \frac{1}{(1-1)!} = \frac{1}{0!} = \frac{1}{1} = 1$$

$$a_2 = \frac{1}{(2-1)!} = \frac{1}{1!} = \frac{1}{1} = 1$$

$$a_3 = \frac{1}{(3-1)!} = \frac{1}{2!} = \frac{1}{2 \cdot 1} = \frac{1}{2}$$

$$a_4 = \frac{1}{(4-1)!} = \frac{1}{3!} = \frac{1}{3 \cdot 2 \cdot 1} = \frac{1}{6}$$

The first four terms are $1, 1, \frac{1}{2}, \frac{1}{6}$.

4.

$$a_n = \frac{(-1)^{n+1}}{2^n}$$

$$a_1 = \frac{(-1)^{1+1}}{2^1} = \frac{(-1)^2}{2} = \frac{1}{2}$$

$$a_2 = \frac{(-1)^{2+1}}{2^2} = \frac{(-1)^3}{4} = -\frac{1}{4}$$

$$a_3 = \frac{(-1)^{3+1}}{2^3} = \frac{(-1)^4}{8} = \frac{1}{8}$$

$$a_4 = \frac{(-1)^{4+1}}{2^4} = \frac{(-1)^5}{16} = -\frac{1}{16}$$

The first four terms are $\frac{1}{2}, -\frac{1}{4}, \frac{1}{8}, -\frac{1}{16}$.

5.

$$\sum_{i=1}^{5} \left(2i^2 - 3\right)$$

$$= \left(2(1)^2 - 3\right) + \left(2(2)^2 - 3\right) + \left(2(3)^2 - 3\right) + \left(2(4)^2 - 3\right) + \left(2(5)^2 - 3\right) + \left(2(6)^2 - 3\right)$$

$$= \left(2(1) - 3\right) + \left(2(4) - 3\right) + \left(2(9) - 3\right) + \left(2(16) - 3\right) + \left(2(25) - 3\right)$$

$$= (2-3) + (8-3) + (18-3) + (32-3) + (50-3) = -1 + 5 + 15 + 29 + 47 = 95$$

6.

$$\sum_{i=0}^{4} (-1)^{i+1} i! = (-1)^{0+1} 0! + (-1)^{1+1} 1! + (-1)^{2+1} 2! + (-1)^{3+1} 3! + (-1)^{4+1} 4!$$

$$= (-1)^1 1 + (-1)^2 1 + (-1)^3 2 \cdot 1 + (-1)^4 3 \cdot 2 \cdot 1 + (-1)^5 4 \cdot 3 \cdot 2 \cdot 1$$

$$= -1 + 1 - 2 + 6 - 24 = -20$$

7.

$$\frac{1}{3} + \frac{2}{4} + \frac{3}{5} + \dots + \frac{15}{17} = \sum_{i=1}^{15} \frac{i}{i+2}$$

8.

$$4^3 + 5^3 + 6^3 + \dots + 13^3 = \sum_{i=4}^{13} i^3$$

9.

$$a_1 = 7$$

$$a_2 = 7 + 4 = 11$$

$$a_3 = 11 + 4 = 15$$

$$a_4 = 15 + 4 = 19$$

$$a_5 = 19 + 4 = 23$$

$$a_6 = 23 + 4 = 27$$

The first six terms are
$7, 11, 15, 19, 23, 27$

10. $a_1 = -4$

$a_2 = -4 - 5 = -9$

$a_3 = -9 - 5 = -14$

$a_4 = -14 - 5 = -19$

$a_5 = -19 - 5 = -24$

$a_6 = -24 - 5 = -29$

The first six terms are
$-4, -9, -14, -19, -24, -29$.

11.

$a_1 = \dfrac{3}{2}$

$a_2 = \dfrac{3}{2} - \dfrac{1}{2} = \dfrac{2}{2} = 1$

$a_3 = 1 - \dfrac{1}{2} = \dfrac{1}{2}$

$a_4 = \dfrac{1}{2} - \dfrac{1}{2} = 0$

$a_5 = 0 - \dfrac{1}{2} = -\dfrac{1}{2}$

$a_6 = -\dfrac{1}{2} - \dfrac{1}{2} = -\dfrac{2}{2} = -1$

The first six terms are $\dfrac{3}{2}, 1, \dfrac{1}{2}, 0, -\dfrac{1}{2}, -1$.

12. $a_6 = 5 + (6-1)3 = 5 + (5)3 = 5 + 15 = 20$

13. $a_{12} = -8 + (12-1)(-2) = -8 + 11(-2)$

$= -8 + (-22) = -30$

14. $a_{14} = 14 + (14-1)(-4) = 14 + 13(-4)$

$= 14 + (-52) = -38$

15. $d = -3 - (-7) = 4$

$a_n = -7 + (n-1)4 = -7 + 4n - 4$

$= 4n - 11$

$a_{20} = 4(20) - 11 = 80 - 11 = 69$

16. $a_n = 200 + (n-1)(-20)$

$= 200 - 20n + 20$

$= 220 - 20n$

$a_{20} = 220 - 20(20) = 220 - 400 = -180$

17.

$a_n = -12 + (n-1)\left(-\dfrac{1}{2}\right)$

$= -12 - \dfrac{1}{2}n + \dfrac{1}{2}$

$= -\dfrac{24}{2} - \dfrac{1}{2}n + \dfrac{1}{2}$

$= -\dfrac{1}{2}n - \dfrac{23}{2}$

$a_{20} = -\dfrac{1}{2}(20) - \dfrac{23}{2} = -\dfrac{20}{2} - \dfrac{23}{2} = -\dfrac{43}{2}$

18. $d = 8 - 15 = -7$

$a_n = 15 + (n-1)(-7) = 15 - 7n + 7$

$= 22 - 7n$

$a_{20} = 22 - 7(20) = 22 - 140 = -118$

19. First, find d.

$d = 12 - 5 = 7$

Next, find a_{22}.

$a_{22} = 5 + (22-1)7 = 5 + (21)7$

$= 5 + 147 = 152$

Now, find the sum.

$S_{22} = \dfrac{22}{2}(5 + 152) = 11(157) = 1727$

20. First, find d.

$d = -3 - (-6) = 3$

Next, find a_{15}.

$a_{15} = -6 + (15-1)3 = -6 + (14)3$

$= -6 + 42 = 36$

Now, find the sum.

$S_{15} = \dfrac{15}{2}(-6 + 36) = \dfrac{15}{2}(30) = 225$

21. We are given that $a_1 = 300$.

$$S_{100} = \frac{100}{2}(3 + 300) = 50(303) = 15{,}150$$

22.

$$\sum_{i=1}^{16}(3i + 2) = (3(1) + 2) + (3(2) + 2) + (3(3) + 2) + \ldots + (3(16) + 2)$$

$$= (3 + 2) + (6 + 2) + (9 + 2) + \ldots + (48 + 2)$$

$$= 5 + 8 + 11 + \ldots + 50$$

$$S_{16} = \frac{16}{2}(5 + 50) = 8(55) = 440$$

23.

$$\sum_{i=1}^{25}(-2i + 6) = (-2(1) + 6) + (-2(2) + 6) + (-2(3) + 6) + \ldots + (-2(25) + 6)$$

$$= (-2 + 6) + (-4 + 6) + (-6 + 6) + \ldots + (-50 + 6)$$

$$= 4 + 2 + 0 + \ldots + (-44)$$

$$S_{25} = \frac{25}{2}(4 + (-44)) = \frac{25}{2}(-40) = -500$$

24.

$$\sum_{i=1}^{30}(-5i) = (-5(1)) + (-5(2)) + (-5(3)) + \ldots + (-5(30))$$

$$= -5 + (-10) + (-15) + \ldots + (-150)$$

$$S_{30} = \frac{30}{2}(-5 + (-150)) = 15(-155) = -2325$$

25. a. $a_n = 20 + (n - 1)(0.52)$

$$= 20 + 0.52n - 0.52$$

$$= 0.52n + 19.48$$

b. $a_n = 0.52(111) + 19.48$

$$= 57.72 + 19.48$$

$$= 77.2$$

The percentage of white-collar works in the labor force by the year 2010 is approximately 77.2%.

26. $a_{10} = 31500 + (10 - 1)2300$

$$= 31500 + (9)2300$$

$$= 31500 + 20700 = 52200$$

$$S_{10} = \frac{10}{2}(31500 + 52200)$$

$$= 5(83700) = 418500$$

The total salary over a ten-year period is $418,500.

881

27.
$$a_{35} = 25 + (35-1)1 = 25 + (34)1$$
$$= 25 + 34 = 59$$
$$S_{35} = \frac{35}{2}(25+59) = \frac{35}{2}(84) = 1470$$
There are 1470 seats in the theater.

28. The first term is 3.
The second term is $3 \cdot 2 = 6$.
The third term is $6 \cdot 2 = 12$.
The fourth term is $12 \cdot 2 = 24$.
The fifth term is $24 \cdot 2 = 48$.

29. The first term is $\frac{1}{2}$.

The second term is $\frac{1}{2} \cdot \frac{1}{2} = \frac{1}{4}$.

The third term is $\frac{1}{4} \cdot \frac{1}{2} = \frac{1}{8}$.

The fourth term is $\frac{1}{8} \cdot \frac{1}{2} = \frac{1}{16}$.

The fifth term is $\frac{1}{16} \cdot \frac{1}{2} = \frac{1}{32}$.

30. The first term is 16.

The second term is $16 \cdot -\frac{1}{4} = -4$.

The third term is $-4 \cdot -\frac{1}{4} = 1$.

The fourth term is $1 \cdot -\frac{1}{4} = -\frac{1}{4}$.

The fifth term is $-\frac{1}{4} \cdot -\frac{1}{4} = \frac{1}{16}$.

31. The first term is –5.
The second term is $-5 \cdot -1 = 5$.
The third term is $5 \cdot -1 = -5$.
The fourth term is $-5 \cdot -1 = 5$.
The fifth term is $5 \cdot -1 = -5$.

32. $a_7 = 2(3)^{7-1} = 2(3)^6 = 2(729) = 1458$

33. $a_6 = 16\left(\frac{1}{2}\right)^{6-1} = 16\left(\frac{1}{2}\right)^5 = 16\left(\frac{1}{32}\right) = \frac{1}{2}$

34. $a_5 = -3(2)^{5-1} = -3(2)^4 = -3(16) = -48$

35. $a_n = a_1 r^{n-1} = 1(2)^{n-1}$
$$a_8 = 1(2)^{8-1} = 1(2)^7 = 1(128) = 128$$

36. $a_n = a_1 r^{n-1} = 100\left(\frac{1}{10}\right)^{n-1}$
$$a_8 = 100\left(\frac{1}{10}\right)^{8-1} = 100\left(\frac{1}{10}\right)^7$$
$$= 100\left(\frac{1}{10,000,000}\right) = \frac{1}{100,000}$$

37. $d = \frac{-4}{12} = -\frac{1}{3}$
$$a_n = a_1 r^{n-1} = 12\left(-\frac{1}{3}\right)^{n-1}$$
$$a_8 = 12\left(-\frac{1}{3}\right)^{8-1} = 12\left(-\frac{1}{3}\right)^7$$
$$= 12\left(-\frac{1}{2187}\right) = -\frac{12}{2187} = -\frac{4}{729}$$

38. $r = \frac{a_2}{a_1} = \frac{-15}{5} = -3$
$$S_{15} = \frac{5\left(1-(-3)^{15}\right)}{1-(-3)}$$
$$= \frac{5\left(1-(-14348907)\right)}{4}$$
$$= \frac{5(14348908)}{4} = \frac{71744540}{4}$$
$$= 17,936,135$$

39. $r = \dfrac{a_2}{a_1} = \dfrac{4}{8} = \dfrac{1}{2}$

$S_7 = \dfrac{8\left(1-\left(\frac{1}{2}\right)^7\right)}{1-\frac{1}{2}} = \dfrac{8\left(1-\frac{1}{128}\right)}{\frac{1}{2}}$

$= \dfrac{8\left(\frac{128}{128}-\frac{1}{128}\right)}{\frac{1}{2}} = \dfrac{8\left(\frac{127}{128}\right)}{\frac{1}{2}}$

$= \dfrac{8}{1}\left(\dfrac{127}{128}\right) \div \dfrac{1}{2} = \dfrac{8}{1}\left(\dfrac{127}{128}\right)\cdot\dfrac{2}{1}$

$= \dfrac{2032}{128} = \dfrac{127}{8} = 15.875$

40. $\displaystyle\sum_{i=1}^{6} 5^i = \dfrac{5\left(1-5^6\right)}{1-5} = \dfrac{5\left(1-15625\right)}{-4}$

$= \dfrac{5(-15624)}{-4} = 5(3906)$

$= 19,530$

41. $\displaystyle\sum_{i=1}^{7} 3(-2)^i = \dfrac{-6\left(1-(-2)^7\right)}{1-(-2)}$

$= \dfrac{-6\left(1-(-128)\right)}{3}$

$= \dfrac{-6(129)}{3}$

$= -2(129) = -258$

42. $\displaystyle\sum_{i=1}^{5} 2\left(\dfrac{1}{4}\right)^{i-1} = \dfrac{2\left(1-\left(\frac{1}{4}\right)^5\right)}{1-\frac{1}{4}}$

$= \dfrac{2\left(1-\frac{1}{1024}\right)}{\frac{3}{4}} = \dfrac{2\left(\frac{1024}{1024}-\frac{1}{1024}\right)}{\frac{3}{4}}$

$= \dfrac{2\left(\frac{1023}{1024}\right)}{\frac{3}{4}} = \dfrac{\frac{2046}{1024}}{\frac{3}{4}} = \dfrac{2046}{1024} \div \dfrac{3}{4}$

$= \dfrac{2046}{1024}\cdot\dfrac{4}{3} = \dfrac{682}{256} = \dfrac{341}{128}$

43. $r = \dfrac{a_2}{a_1} = \dfrac{3}{9} = \dfrac{1}{3}$

$S = \dfrac{9}{1-\frac{1}{3}} = \dfrac{9}{\frac{2}{3}} = 9 \div \dfrac{2}{3} = 9\cdot\dfrac{3}{2} = \dfrac{27}{2}$

44. $r = \dfrac{a_2}{a_1} = \dfrac{-1}{2} = -\dfrac{1}{2}$

$S = \dfrac{2}{1-\left(-\frac{1}{2}\right)} = \dfrac{2}{\frac{3}{2}} = 2 \div \dfrac{3}{2} = 2\cdot\dfrac{2}{3} = \dfrac{4}{3}$

45. $r = \dfrac{a_2}{a_1} = \dfrac{4}{-6} = -\dfrac{2}{3}$

$S = \dfrac{-6}{1-\left(-\frac{2}{3}\right)} = \dfrac{-6}{\frac{5}{3}} = -6 \div \dfrac{5}{3}$

$= -6 \cdot \dfrac{3}{5} = -\dfrac{18}{5}$

46. $\displaystyle\sum_{i=1}^{\infty} 5(0.8)^i = \dfrac{4}{1-0.8} = \dfrac{4}{0.2} = 20$

883

47.

$$0.\overline{6} = \frac{a_1}{1-r} = \frac{\dfrac{6}{10}}{1-\dfrac{1}{10}} = \frac{\dfrac{6}{10}}{\dfrac{9}{10}} = \frac{6}{10} \div \frac{9}{10}$$

$$= \frac{6}{10} \cdot \frac{10}{9} = \frac{2}{3}$$

48.

$$0.\overline{47} = \frac{a_1}{1-r} = \frac{\dfrac{47}{100}}{1-\dfrac{1}{100}} = \frac{\dfrac{47}{100}}{\dfrac{99}{100}}$$

$$= \frac{47}{100} \div \frac{99}{100} = \frac{47}{100} \cdot \frac{100}{99} = \frac{47}{99}$$

49. a.

$$r_{1998-1999} = \frac{20.72}{19.96} \approx 1.038$$

$$r_{1999-2000} = \frac{21.51}{20.72} \approx 1.038$$

$$r_{2000-2001} = \frac{22.33}{21.51} \approx 1.038$$

The population is increasing geometrically since dividing the population for each year by the population for the preceding years gives approximately 1.038 for each division.

b. $a_n = a_1 r^{n-1} = 19.96(1.038)^{n-1}$

c. $a_{10} = 19.96(1.038)^{10-1} \approx 27.92$.
In 2008, the population will be approximately 27.92 million.

50. $r = 1.06$

$$a_n = a_1 r^{n-1} = 32000(1.06)^{n-1}$$

$$a_6 = 32000(1.06)^{6-1} = 32000(1.06)^5$$

$$= 32000(1.338226) = 42823.22$$

The salary in the sixth year is approximately $42,823.22.

$$S_6 = \frac{a_1(1-r^n)}{1-r} = \frac{32000\left(1-(1.06)^6\right)}{1-1.06}$$

$$= \frac{32000(1-1.418519)}{-0.06}$$

$$= \frac{32000(-0.418519)}{-0.06} = 223,210$$

The total salary over the six years is approximately $223,210.

51.

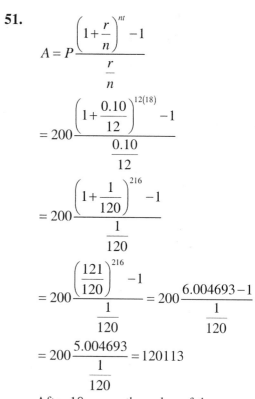

$$A = P\frac{\left(1+\dfrac{r}{n}\right)^{nt}-1}{\dfrac{r}{n}}$$

$$= 200\frac{\left(1+\dfrac{0.10}{12}\right)^{12(18)}-1}{\dfrac{0.10}{12}}$$

$$= 200\frac{\left(1+\dfrac{1}{120}\right)^{216}-1}{\dfrac{1}{120}}$$

$$= 200\frac{\left(\dfrac{121}{120}\right)^{216}-1}{\dfrac{1}{120}} = 200\frac{6.004693-1}{\dfrac{1}{120}}$$

$$= 200\frac{5.004693}{\dfrac{1}{120}} = 120113$$

After 18 years, the value of the account will be about $120,113.

52. $r = 70\% = 0.7$

$a_1 = 4(.7) = 2.8$

$S = \dfrac{2.8}{1 - 0.7} = \dfrac{2.8}{0.3} = 9.\overline{3}$

The total spending in the town will be
approximately $9.3 million each year.

53. $\dbinom{11}{8} = \dfrac{11!}{8!(11-8)!} = \dfrac{11 \cdot 10 \cdot 9 \cdot \cancel{8!}}{\cancel{8!} \cdot 3 \cdot 2 \cdot 1} = 165$

54. $\dbinom{90}{2} = \dfrac{90!}{2!(90-2)!} = \dfrac{90 \cdot 89 \cdot \cancel{88!}}{2 \cdot 1 \cdot \cancel{88!}} = 4005$

55. Applying the Binomial Theorem to $(2x+1)^3$, we have $a = 2x$, $b = 1$, and $n = 3$.

$(2x+1)^3 = \dbinom{3}{0}(2x)^3 + \dbinom{3}{1}(2x)^2 \cdot 1 + \dbinom{3}{2}(2x) \cdot 1^2 + \dbinom{3}{3}1^3$

$\quad = \dfrac{3!}{0!(3-0)!}8x^3 + \dfrac{3!}{1!(3-1)!}4x^2 \cdot 1 + \dfrac{3!}{2!(3-2)!}2x \cdot 1 + \dfrac{3!}{3!(3-3)!}1$

$\quad = \dfrac{\cancel{3!}}{1 \cdot \cancel{3!}}8x^3 + \dfrac{3 \cdot \cancel{2!}}{1 \cdot \cancel{2!}}4x^2 + \dfrac{3 \cdot \cancel{2!}}{\cancel{2!}1!}2x + \dfrac{\cancel{3!}}{\cancel{3!}0!}$

$\quad = 8x^3 + 3(4x^2) + 3(2x) + 1$

$\quad = 8x^3 + 12x^2 + 6x + 1$

56. Applying the Binomial Theorem to $(x^2 - 1)^4$, we have $a = x^2$, $b = -1$, and $n = 4$.

$(x^2 - 1)^4 = \dbinom{4}{0}(x^2)^4 + \dbinom{4}{1}(x^2)^3(-1) + \dbinom{4}{2}(x^2)^2(-1)^2 + \dbinom{4}{3}x^2(-1)^3 + \dbinom{4}{4}(-1)^4$

$\quad = \dfrac{4!}{0!(4-0)!}x^8 - \dfrac{4!}{1!(4-1)!}x^6 + \dfrac{4!}{2!(4-2)!}x^4 - \dfrac{4!}{3!(4-3)!}x^2 + \dfrac{4!}{4!(4-4)!}1$

$\quad = \dfrac{\cancel{4!}}{0!\cancel{4!}}x^8 - \dfrac{4!}{1!3!}x^6 + \dfrac{4!}{2!2!}x^4 - \dfrac{4!}{3!1!}x^2 + \dfrac{\cancel{4!}}{\cancel{4!}0!}$

$\quad = 1(x^8) - \dfrac{4 \cdot \cancel{3!}}{1 \cdot \cancel{3!}}x^6 + \dfrac{4 \cdot 3 \cdot \cancel{2!}}{2 \cdot 1 \cdot \cancel{2!}}x^4 - \dfrac{4 \cdot \cancel{3!}}{\cancel{3!} \cdot 1}x^2 + 1$

$\quad = x^8 - 4x^6 + 6x^4 - 4x^2 + 1$

57. Applying the Binomial Theorem to $(x+2y)^5$, we have $a=x$, $b=2y$, and $n=5$.

$$(x+2y)^5 = \binom{5}{0}x^5 + \binom{5}{1}x^4(2y) + \binom{5}{2}x^3(2y)^2 + \binom{5}{3}x^2(2y)^3 + \binom{5}{4}x(2y)^4 + \binom{5}{5}(2y)^5$$

$$= \frac{5!}{0!\,5!}x^5 + \frac{5!}{1!(5-1)!}2x^4y + \frac{5!}{2!(5-2)!}4x^3y^2 + \frac{5!}{3!(5-3)!}8x^2y^3$$

$$+ \frac{5!}{4!(5-4)!}16xy^4 + \frac{5!}{5!(5-5)!}32y^5$$

$$= 1x^5 + \frac{5\cdot4!}{1\cdot4!}2x^4y + \frac{5\cdot4\cdot3!}{2\cdot1\cdot3!}4x^3y^2 + \frac{5\cdot4\cdot3!}{3!2\cdot1}8x^2y^3 + \frac{5\cdot4!}{4!\cdot1}16xy^4 + \frac{5!}{5!0!}32y^5$$

$$= x^5 + 5(2x^4y) + 10(4x^3y^2) + 10(8x^2y^3) + 5(16xy^4) + 1(32y^5)$$

$$= x^5 + 10x^4y + 40x^3y^2 + 80x^2y^3 + 80xy^4 + 32y^5$$

58. Applying the Binomial Theorem to $(x-2)^6$, we have $a=x$, $b=-2$, and $n=6$.

$$(x-2)^6$$

$$= \binom{6}{0}x^6 + \binom{6}{1}x^5(-2) + \binom{6}{2}x^4(-2)^2 + \binom{6}{3}x^3(-2)^3 + \binom{6}{4}x^2(-2)^4 + \binom{6}{5}x(-2)^5 + \binom{6}{6}(-2)^6$$

$$= \frac{6!}{0!(6-0)!}x^6 + \frac{6!}{1!(6-1)!}x^5(-2) + \frac{6!}{2!(6-2)!}x^4(-2)^2 + \frac{6!}{3!(6-3)!}x^3(-2)^3$$

$$+ \frac{6!}{4!(6-4)!}x^2(-2)^4 + \frac{6!}{5!(6-5)!}x(-2)^5 + \frac{6!}{6!(6-6)!}(-2)^6$$

$$= \frac{6!}{1\,6!}x^6 - \frac{6\cdot5!}{1\cdot5!}2x^5 + \frac{6\cdot5\cdot4!}{2\cdot1\cdot4!}4x^4 - \frac{6\cdot5\cdot4\cdot3!}{3!2\cdot1\cdot3!}8x^3$$

$$+ \frac{6\cdot5\cdot4!}{4!2\cdot1}16x^2 - \frac{6\cdot5!}{5!1}32x + \frac{6!}{6!\cdot1}64$$

$$= x^6 - 6(2x^5) + 15(4x^4) - 20(8x^3) + 15(16x^2) - 6(32x) + 1\cdot64$$

$$= x^6 - 12x^5 + 60x^4 - 160x^3 + 240x^2 - 192x + 64$$

886

59. $\left(x^2+3\right)^8$

First Term $\quad\binom{n}{r-1}a^{n-r+1}b^{r-1}=\binom{8}{1-1}\left(x^2\right)^{8-1+1}3^{1-1}=\binom{8}{0}\left(x^2\right)^8 3^0$

$$=\frac{8!}{0!(8-0)!}x^{16}\cdot 1=\frac{\cancel{8!}}{0!\cancel{8!}}x^{16}=x^{16}$$

Second Term $\quad\binom{n}{r-1}a^{n-r+1}b^{r-1}=\binom{8}{2-1}\left(x^2\right)^{8-2+1}3^{2-1}=\binom{8}{1}\left(x^2\right)^7 3^1=\frac{8!}{1!(8-1)!}3x^{14}$

$$=\frac{8\cdot\cancel{7!}}{1\cdot\cancel{7!}}3x^{14}=8\cdot 3x^{14}=24x^{14}$$

Third Term $\quad\binom{n}{r-1}a^{n-r+1}b^{r-1}=\binom{8}{3-1}\left(x^2\right)^{8-3+1}3^{3-1}=\binom{8}{2}\left(x^2\right)^6 3^2=\frac{8!}{2!(8-2)!}9x^{12}$

$$=\frac{8\cdot 7\cdot\cancel{6!}}{2\cdot 1\cdot\cancel{6!}}9x^{12}=28\cdot 9x^{12}=252x^{12}$$

60. $\left(x-3\right)^9$

First Term $\quad\binom{n}{r-1}a^{n-r+1}b^{r-1}=\binom{9}{1-1}x^{9-1+1}(-3)^{1-1}=\binom{9}{0}x^9(-3)^0$

$$=\frac{9!}{0!(9-0)!}x^9\cdot 1=\frac{\cancel{9!}}{0!\cancel{9!}}x^9=x^9$$

Second Term $\quad\binom{n}{r-1}a^{n-r+1}b^{r-1}=\binom{9}{2-1}x^{9-2+1}(-3)^{2-1}=\binom{9}{1}x^8(-3)^1=-\frac{9!}{1!(9-1)!}3x^8$

$$=-\frac{9\cdot\cancel{8!}}{1\cdot\cancel{8!}}3x^8=-9\cdot 3x^8=-27x^8$$

Third Term $\quad\binom{n}{r-1}a^{n-r+1}b^{r-1}=\binom{9}{3-1}x^{9-3+1}(-3)^{3-1}=\binom{9}{2}x^7(-3)^2=\frac{9!}{2!(9-2)!}9x^7$

$$=\frac{9\cdot 8\cdot\cancel{7!}}{2\cdot 1\cdot\cancel{7!}}9x^7=36\cdot 9x^7=324x^7$$

SSM Chapter 14: Sequences, Series, and Probability

61. $(x+2)^5$

Fourth Term $\binom{n}{r-1}a^{n-r+1}b^{r-1} = \binom{5}{4-1}x^{5-4+1}(2)^{4-1} = \binom{5}{3}x^2(2)^3 = \dfrac{5!}{3!(5-3)!}8x^2$

$= \dfrac{5!}{3!2!}8x^2 = \dfrac{5\cdot4\cdot3!}{3!\cdot2\cdot1}8x^2 = (10)8x^2 = 80x^2$

62. $(2x-3)^6$

Fifth Term $\binom{n}{r-1}a^{n-r+1}b^{r-1} = \binom{6}{5-1}(2x)^{6-5+1}(-3)^{5-1} = \binom{6}{4}(2x)^2(-3)^4$

$= \dfrac{6!}{4!(6-4)!}4x^2(81) = \dfrac{6!}{4!2!}324x^2 = \dfrac{6\cdot5\cdot4!}{4!\cdot2\cdot1}324x^2$

$= (15)324x^2 = 4860x^2$

63. $_8P_3 = \dfrac{8!}{(8-3)!} = \dfrac{8\cdot7\cdot6\cdot5!}{5!} = 336$

64. $_9P_5 = \dfrac{9!}{(9-5)!} = \dfrac{9\cdot8\cdot7\cdot6\cdot5\cdot4!}{4!}15,120$

65. $_8C_3 = \dfrac{8!}{(8-3)!3!} = \dfrac{8\cdot7\cdot6\cdot5!}{5!3\cdot2\cdot1} = 56$

66. $_{13}C_{11} = \dfrac{13!}{(13-11)!11!} = \dfrac{13\cdot12\cdot11!}{2\cdot1\cdot11!} = 78$

67. $4\cdot5 = 20$
You have 20 choices with this brand of pens.

68. $3\cdot3\cdot3\cdot3\cdot3 = 3^5 = 243$
There are 243 possibilities.

69. $_{15}P_4 = \dfrac{15!}{(15-4)!} = \dfrac{15!}{11!} = 32760$
There are 32,760 ways to fill the offices.

70. $_{20}C_4 = \dfrac{20!}{(20-4)!4!} = \dfrac{20!}{16!4!} = 4845$
There are 4845 ways to select the 4 actors.

71. $_{20}C_3 = \dfrac{20!}{(20-3)!3!} = \dfrac{20!}{17!3!} = 1140$
You can take 1140 sets of 3 CDs.

72. $_{20}P_4 = \dfrac{20!}{(20-4)!} = \dfrac{20!}{16!} = 116280$
The director has 116,280 ways to select actors for the roles.

73. $5! = 120$
There are 120 ways to line up the five airplanes.

74. $P(liberal) = \dfrac{17}{100}$

75. $P(not\ conservative)$
$= 1 - P(conservative)$
$= 1 - \dfrac{33}{100} = \dfrac{67}{100}$

888

76. $P(\text{moderate or conservative})$

$= P(\text{moderate}) + P(\text{conservative})$

$= \dfrac{50}{100} + \dfrac{33}{100} = \dfrac{83}{100}$

77. $P(\text{conservative or attended college})$

$= P(\text{conservative}) + P(\text{attended college})$

$\quad - P(\text{conservative and attended college})$

$= \dfrac{33}{100} + \dfrac{45}{100} - \dfrac{20}{100} = \dfrac{58}{100} = \dfrac{29}{50}$

78. $P(\text{high school only}) = \dfrac{13}{33}$

79. $P(\text{liberal}) = \dfrac{10}{45} = \dfrac{2}{9}$

80. $P(\text{less than 5}) = P(\text{rolling a 1, 2, 3, 4})$

$= \dfrac{4}{6} = \dfrac{2}{3}$

81. $P(\text{less than 3 or greater than 4})$

$= P(\text{less than 3}) + P(\text{greater than 4})$

$= P(\text{rolling a 1, 2}) + P(\text{rolling a 5, 6})$

$= \dfrac{2}{6} + \dfrac{2}{6} = \dfrac{4}{6} = \dfrac{2}{3}$

82. $P(\text{ace or king}) = P(\text{ace}) + P(\text{king})$

$= \dfrac{4}{52} + \dfrac{4}{52} = \dfrac{8}{52} = \dfrac{2}{13}$

83. $P(\text{queen or red})$

$= P(\text{queen}) + P(\text{red}) - P(\text{red queen})$

$= \dfrac{4}{52} + \dfrac{26}{52} - \dfrac{2}{52} = \dfrac{28}{52} = \dfrac{7}{13}$

84. $P(\text{not yellow}) = \dfrac{5}{6}$

85. $P(\text{red or greater than 3})$

$= P(\text{red}) + P(\text{greater than 3})$

$\quad - P(\text{red and greater than 3})$

$= \dfrac{3}{6} + \dfrac{3}{6} - \dfrac{1}{6} = \dfrac{5}{6}$

86. $P(\text{green and less than 4})$

$= P(\text{green}) \cdot P(\text{less than 4})$

$= \dfrac{2}{6} \cdot \dfrac{3}{6} = \dfrac{1}{6}$

87. a. There are a total of $_{20}C_5 = 15{,}504$ combinations of 5 numbers from 1 to 20 that can be chosen.

$P(\text{winning}) = \dfrac{1}{15504} \approx 0.0000645$

b. $P(\text{winning}) = 100\left(\dfrac{1}{15504}\right)$

$= \dfrac{25}{3876} \approx 0.00645$

88.

$P(\text{five boys}) = \left(\dfrac{1}{2}\right)^5 = \dfrac{1}{32}$

89. a. $P(\text{flood 2 yrs in a row})$

$= (0.2)(0.2)$

$= 0.04$

The probability of a flood two years in a row is 0.04.

b. $P(\text{flood 3 yrs in a row})$

$= (0.2)(0.2)(0.2)$

$= 0.008$

The probability of a flood for three consecutive years is 0.008.

c. $P(\text{no flooding for 4 yrs}) = (0.8)^4$

$= 0.4096$

The probability of no flood for four consecutive years in 0.4096.

Chapter 14 Test

1.

$$a_n = \frac{(-1)^{n+1}}{n^2}$$

$$a_1 = \frac{(-1)^{1+1}}{1^2} = \frac{(-1)^2}{1} = \frac{1}{1} = 1$$

$$a_2 = \frac{(-1)^{2+1}}{2^2} = \frac{(-1)^3}{4} = \frac{-1}{4} = -\frac{1}{4}$$

$$a_3 = \frac{(-1)^{3+1}}{3^2} = \frac{(-1)^4}{9} = \frac{1}{9}$$

$$a_4 = \frac{(-1)^{4+1}}{4^2} = \frac{(-1)^5}{16} = \frac{-1}{16} = -\frac{1}{16}$$

$$a_5 = \frac{(-1)^{5+1}}{5^2} = \frac{(-1)^6}{25} = \frac{1}{25}$$

The first five terms are

$$1, -\frac{1}{4}, \frac{1}{9}, -\frac{1}{16}, \frac{1}{25}.$$

2.

$$\sum_{i=1}^{5}(i^2 + 10)$$

$$= (1^2 + 10) + (2^2 + 10) + (3^2 + 10)$$

$$\quad + (4^2 + 10) + (5^2 + 10)$$

$$= (1+10) + (4+10) + (9+10)$$

$$\quad + (16+10) + (25+10)$$

$$= 11 + 14 + 19 + 26 + 35 = 105$$

3.

$$\frac{2}{3} + \frac{3}{4} + \frac{4}{5} + \dots + \frac{21}{22} = \sum_{i=2}^{21} \frac{i}{i+1}$$

4.

$$d = 9 - 4 = 5$$

$$a_n = 4 + (n-1)5 = 4 + 5n - 5$$

$$\quad = 5n - 1$$

$$a_{12} = 5(12) - 1 = 60 - 1 = 59$$

5.

$$d = \frac{a_2}{a_1} = \frac{4}{16} = \frac{1}{4}$$

$$a_n = a_1 r^{n-1} = 16\left(\frac{1}{4}\right)^{n-1}$$

$$a_{12} = 16\left(\frac{1}{4}\right)^{12-1} = 16\left(\frac{1}{4}\right)^{11}$$

$$= 16\left(\frac{1}{4,194,304}\right) = \frac{16}{4,194,304}$$

$$= \frac{1}{262,144}$$

6.

$$d = -14 - (-7) = -7$$

$$a_{10} = -7 + (10-1)(-7)$$

$$\quad = -7 + (9)(-7) = -7 + (-63) = -70$$

$$S_{10} = \frac{10}{2}(-7 + (-70)) = 5(-77) = -385$$

7.

$$\sum_{i=1}^{20}(3i - 4)$$

$$= (3(1) - 4) + (3(2) - 4) + (3(3) - 4)$$

$$\quad + \dots + (3(20) - 4)$$

$$= (3 - 4) + (6 - 4) + (9 - 4)$$

$$\quad + \dots + (60 - 4)$$

$$= -1 + 2 + 5 + \dots + 56$$

$$S_{20} = \frac{20}{2}(-1 + 56) = 10(55) = 550$$

8.

$$r = \frac{a_2}{a_1} = \frac{-14}{7} = -2$$

$$S_{10} = \frac{7\left(1 - (-2)^{10}\right)}{1 - (-2)} = \frac{7(1 - 1024)}{3}$$

$$= \frac{7(-1023)}{3} = -2387$$

9.

$$\sum_{i=1}^{15}(-2)^i = \frac{-2\left(1-(-2)^{15}\right)}{1-(-2)}$$

$$= \frac{-2\left(1-(-32768)\right)}{3}$$

$$= \frac{-2(32769)}{3}$$

$$= -21,846$$

10.

$$r = \frac{1}{2}$$

$$S = \frac{4}{1-\frac{1}{2}} = \frac{4}{\frac{1}{2}} = 4 \div \frac{1}{2} = 4 \cdot \frac{2}{1} = 8$$

11.

$$0.\overline{73} = \frac{a_1}{1-r} = \frac{\frac{73}{100}}{1-\frac{1}{100}} = \frac{\frac{73}{100}}{\frac{99}{100}}$$

$$= \frac{73}{100} \div \frac{99}{100} = \frac{73}{100} \cdot \frac{100}{99} = \frac{73}{99}$$

12. $r = 1.04$

$$S_8 = \frac{a_1\left(1-r^n\right)}{1-r} = \frac{30000\left(1-(1.04)^8\right)}{1-1.04}$$

$$= \frac{30000\left(1-1.368569\right)}{-0.04}$$

$$= \frac{30000\left(-0.368569\right)}{-0.04}$$

$$= 276,426.75$$

The total salary over the eight years is approximately \$276,426.75

13.

$$\binom{9}{2} = \frac{9!}{2!(9-2)!}$$

$$= \frac{9!}{2!7!} = \frac{9 \cdot 8 \cdot 7!}{2 \cdot 1 \cdot 7!} = 36$$

14. Applying the Binomial Theorem to $\left(x^2-1\right)^5$, we have $a=x^2$, $b=-1$, and $n=5$.

$$\left(x^2-1\right)^5$$

$$= \binom{5}{0}\left(x^2\right)^5 + \binom{5}{1}\left(x^2\right)^4(-1) + \binom{5}{2}\left(x^2\right)^3(-1)^2 + \binom{5}{3}\left(x^2\right)^2(-1)^3 + \binom{5}{4}\left(x^2\right)(-1)^4 + \binom{5}{5}(-1)^5$$

$$= \frac{5!}{0!5!}x^{10} - \frac{5!}{1!(5-1)!}x^8 + \frac{5!}{2!(5-2)!}x^6 - \frac{5!}{3!(5-3)!}x^4 + \frac{5!}{4!(5-4)!}x^2 - \frac{5!}{5!(5-5)!}$$

$$= 1x^{10} - \frac{5 \cdot 4!}{1 \cdot 4!}x^8 + \frac{5 \cdot 4 \cdot 3!}{2 \cdot 1 \cdot 3!}x^6 - \frac{5 \cdot 4 \cdot 3!}{3!2 \cdot 1}x^4 + \frac{5 \cdot 4!}{4! \cdot 1}x^2 - \frac{5!}{5!0!}$$

$$= x^{10} - 5x^8 + 10x^6 - 10x^4 + 5x^2 - 1$$

891

15. First Term:

$$\binom{n}{r-1}a^{n-r+1}b^{r-1} = \binom{8}{1-1}x^{8-1+1}\left(y^2\right)^{1-1}$$

$$= \binom{8}{0}x^8\left(y^2\right)^0$$

$$= \frac{8!}{0!(8-0)!}x^8 \cdot 1$$

$$= \frac{\cancel{8!}}{0!\cancel{8!}}x^8$$

$$= x^8$$

Second Term:

$$\binom{n}{r-1}a^{n-r+1}b^{r-1} = \binom{8}{2-1}x^{8-2+1}\left(y^2\right)^{2-1}$$

$$= \binom{8}{1}x^7\left(y^2\right)^1$$

$$= \frac{8!}{1!(8-1)!}x^7y^2$$

$$= \frac{8 \cdot \cancel{7!}}{1 \cdot \cancel{7!}}x^7y^2$$

$$= 8x^7y^2$$

Third Term:

$$\binom{n}{r-1}a^{n-r+1}b^{r-1} = \binom{8}{3-1}x^{8-3+1}\left(y^2\right)^{3-1}$$

$$= \binom{8}{2}x^6\left(y^2\right)^2$$

$$= \frac{8!}{2!(8-2)!}x^6y^4$$

$$= \frac{8 \cdot 7 \cdot \cancel{6!}}{2 \cdot 1 \cdot \cancel{6!}}x^6y^4$$

$$= 28x^6y^4$$

16.

$$_{11}P_3 = \frac{11!}{(11-3)!} = \frac{11!}{8!} = 990$$

There are 990 ways to fill the three positions.

17.

$$_{10}C_4 = \frac{10!}{(10-4)!4!} = \frac{10!}{6!4!} = 210$$

You can take 210 different sets of four books.

18. $10 \cdot 10 \cdot 10 \cdot 10 = 10,000$

10,000 telephone numbers can be formed.

19. $P(\text{not brown eyes}) = 1 - P(\text{brown eyes})$

$$= 1 - \frac{40}{100}$$

$$= \frac{60}{100} = \frac{3}{5}$$

20. $P(\text{brown eyes or blue eyes})$

$$= P(\text{brown eyes}) + P(\text{blue eyes})$$

$$= \frac{40}{100} + \frac{38}{100} = \frac{78}{100} = \frac{39}{50}$$

21. $P(\text{female or green eyes})$

$$= P(\text{female}) + P(\text{green eyes})$$

$$- P(\text{female with green eyes})$$

$$= \frac{50}{100} + \frac{22}{100} - \frac{12}{100}$$

$$= \frac{60}{100} = \frac{3}{5}$$

22.

$$P(\text{male, given blue eyes}) = \frac{18}{38} = \frac{9}{19}$$

23. The number of ways to choose the six different numbers is

$$_{15}C_6 = \frac{15!}{(15-6)!6!} = \frac{15!}{9!6!} = 5005.$$

$$P(\text{winning}) = 50 \cdot \frac{1}{5005} = \frac{10}{1001}$$

24. $P(\text{black or picture})$

$$= P(\text{black}) + P(\text{picture})$$
$$\quad - P(\text{black picture card})$$
$$= \frac{26}{52} + \frac{12}{52} - \frac{6}{52} = \frac{32}{52} = \frac{8}{13}$$

25. $P(\text{freshman or female})$

$$= P(\text{fresh.}) + P(\text{female}) - P(\text{female fresh.})$$
$$= \frac{25}{50} + \frac{20}{50} - \frac{15}{50} = \frac{30}{50} = \frac{3}{5}$$

26.

$$P(\text{all questions correct}) = \left(\frac{1}{4}\right)^4 = \frac{1}{256}$$

27.

$$P(\text{red and blue}) = \frac{2}{8} \cdot \frac{2}{8} = \frac{4}{64} = \frac{1}{16}$$

Cumulative Review Exercises (Chapters 1 – 14)

1.
$$\sqrt{2x+5} - \sqrt{x+3} = 2$$
$$\sqrt{x+3} = 2 + \sqrt{2x+5}$$
$$x+3 = \left(2 + \sqrt{2x+5}\right)^2$$
$$x+3 = 4 + 4\sqrt{2x+5} + 2x+5$$
$$x+3 = 4\sqrt{2x+5} + 2x+9$$
$$-x-6 = 4\sqrt{2x+5}$$
$$(-x-6)^2 = 16(2x+5)$$
$$x^2 + 12x + 36 = 32x + 80$$
$$x^2 - 20x - 44 = 0$$
$$(x-22)(x+2) = 0$$
$$x = 22 \text{ or } x = -2$$

Check $x = 22$:
$$\sqrt{2(22)+5} - \sqrt{22+3} = 2$$
$$\sqrt{49} - \sqrt{25} = 2$$
$$7 - 5 = 2$$
$$2 = 2 \quad \text{True}$$

Check $x = -2$:
$$\sqrt{2(-2)+5} - \sqrt{-2+3} = 2$$
$$\sqrt{1} - \sqrt{1} = 2$$
$$1 - 1 = 2$$
$$0 = 2 \quad \text{False}$$

-2 is extraneous, so the only solution is 22. The solution set is $\{22\}$.

2.
$$(x-5)^2 = -49$$
$$x - 5 = \pm\sqrt{-49}$$
$$x = 5 \pm \sqrt{-49}$$
$$x = 5 \pm 7i$$

The solution set is $\{5 \pm 7i\}$.

3. $x^2 + x > 6$

Solve the related quadratic equation.

$$x^2 + x = 6$$

$$x^2 + x - 6 = 0$$

$$(x+3)(x-2) = 0$$

Apply the zero product principle.

$$x + 3 = 0 \quad \text{or} \quad x - 2 = 0$$

$$x = -3 \qquad\qquad x = 2$$

The boundary points are 3 and 2.

Test Interval	Test Number	Test	Conclusion
$(-\infty, -3)$	-4	$(-4)^2 + (-4) > 6$ $12 > 6$, true	$(-\infty, -3)$ does belong to the solution set.
$(-3, 2)$	0	$(0)^2 + 0 > 6$ $0 > 6$, false	$(-3, 2)$ does not belong to the solution set.
$(2, \infty)$	3	$(3)^2 + 3 > 6$ $12 > 6$, true	$(2, \infty)$ does not belong to the solution set.

The solution set is $(-\infty, -3) \cup (2, \infty)$ or $\{x \mid x < -3 \text{ or } x > 2\}$

4. $6x - 3(5x + 2) = 4(1 - x)$

$$6x - 15x - 6 = 4 - 4x$$

$$-9x - 6 = 4 - 4x$$

$$-5x = 10$$

$$x = -2$$

The solution set is $\{-2\}$.

5.

$$\frac{4}{x-3} - \frac{6}{x+3} = \frac{24}{x^2 - 9}$$

$$\frac{4}{x-3} - \frac{6}{x+3} = \frac{24}{(x-3)(x+3)}$$

$$(x-3)(x+3)\left(\frac{4}{x-3} - \frac{6}{x+3}\right) = (x-3)(x+3)\left(\frac{24}{(x-3)(x+3)}\right)$$

$$4(x+3) - 6(x-3) = 24$$

$$4x + 12 - 6x + 18 = 24$$

$$-2x + 30 = 24$$

$$-2x = -6$$

$$x = 3$$

Since 3 would make one or more of the denominators in the original equation zero, we disregard it and conclude that there is no solution. The solution set is $\varnothing$ or $\{\ \}$.

894

6. $3x + 2 < 4$ and $4 - x > 1$

$\quad\quad 3x < 2 \quad\quad\quad\quad -x > -3$

$\quad\quad x < \dfrac{2}{3} \quad\quad\quad\quad x < 3$

The solution set is $\left\{ x \middle| x < \dfrac{2}{3} \right\}$ or

$\left(-\infty, \dfrac{2}{3} \right)$.

7. $3x - 2y + z = 7$

$\quad 2x + 3y - z = 13$

$\quad x - y + 2z = -6$

Multiply the second equation by 2 and add to the third equation.

$\quad 4x + 6y - 2z = 26$

$\quad \underline{x - y + 2z = -6}$

$\quad\quad 5x + 5y = 20$

Add the first equation to the second equation.

$\quad 3x - 2y + z = 7$

$\quad \underline{2x + 3y - z = 13}$

$\quad\quad 5x + y = 20$

We now have a system of two equations in two variables.

$5x + 5y = 20$

$5x + y = 20$

Multiply the second equation by -1 and add to the first equation.

$\quad 5x + 5y = 20$

$\quad \underline{-5x - y = -20}$

$\quad\quad 4y = 0$

$\quad\quad y = 0$

Back-substitute 0 for y to find x.

$5x + y = 20$

$5x + 0 = 20$

$5x = 20$

$x = 4$

Back-substitute 4 for x and 0 for y to find z.

$\quad 3x - 2y + z = 7$

$\quad 3(4) - 2(0) + z = 7$

$\quad 12 - 0 + z = 7$

$\quad 12 + z = 7$

$\quad z = -5$

The solution set is $\{(4, 0, -5)\}$.

8. $\log_9 x + \log_9 (x - 8) = 1$

$\quad\quad \log_9 (x(x - 8)) = 1$

$\quad\quad\quad x(x - 8) = 9^1$

$\quad\quad\quad x^2 - 8x = 9$

$\quad\quad\quad x^2 - 8x - 9 = 0$

$\quad\quad\quad (x - 9)(x + 1) = 0$

Apply the zero product principle.

$x - 9 = 0$ or $x + 1 = 0$

$\quad x = 9 \quad\quad\quad\quad x = -1$

Since we cannot take a log of a negative number, we disregard -1 and conclude that the only viable solution is 9. The solution set is $\{9\}$.

9. $2x^2 - 3y^2 = 5$

$3x^2 - 4y^2 = 16$

Multiply the first equation by –3 and the second equation by 2 and solve by addition.

$-6x^2 + 9y^2 = -15$

$\underline{6x^2 + 8y^2 = \ \ 32}$

$17y^2 = 17$

$y^2 = 1$

$y = \pm 1$

Back-substitute ± 1 for y to find x.

$y = \pm 1$

$2x^2 - 3(\pm 1)^2 = 5$

$2x^2 - 3(1) = 5$

$2x^2 - 3 = 5$

$2x^2 = 8$

$x^2 = 4$

$x = \pm 2$

The solution set is

$\{(-2, -1), (-2, 1), (2, -1), (2, 1)\}$.

10. $2x^2 - y^2 = -8$

$x - y = 6$

Solve the second equation for x.

$x - y = 6$

$x = y + 6$

Substitute $y + 6$ for x.

$2(y + 6)^2 - y^2 = -8$

$2(y^2 + 12x + 36) - y^2 = -8$

$2y^2 + 24x + 72 - y^2 = -8$

$y^2 + 24x + 72 = -8$

$y^2 + 24x + 80 = 0$

$(y + 20)(y + 4) = 0$

Apply the zero product principle.

$y + 20 = 0$ or $y + 4 = 0$

$y = -20$ $\qquad$ $y = -4$

Back-substitute –4 and –20 for y to find x.

$y = -20$ or $y = -4$

$x = -20 + 6$ $\qquad$ $x = -4 + 6$

$x = -14$ $\qquad$ $x = 2$

The solution set is

$\{(-14, -20), (2, -4)\}$.

11. $f(x) = (x + 2)^2 - 4$

Graph $y = x^2$ and shift left 2 units and then down 4 units.

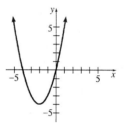

12. $y < -3x + 5$

Replace the > by = and graph the line $y = -3x + 5$ with a dashed line.

Choosing a test point of $(0, 0)$ on the left of the line:

$0 < -3(0) + 5$

$0 < 0 + 5$

$0 < 5$, true

Shade the half-plane containing the test point.

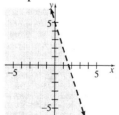

896

13. $f(x) = 3^{x-2}$

Graph $y = 3^x$ and shift right 2 units.

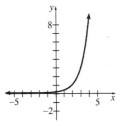

14. $\dfrac{x^2}{16} + \dfrac{y^2}{4} = 1$

Because x^2 and y^2 have different positive coefficients, the equation's graph is an ellipse. Since the denominator of the $x^2 -$ term is greater than the denominator of the $y^2 -$ term, the major axis is horizontal. Since $a^2 = 16$, $a = 4$ and the vertices are $(-4,0)$ and $(4,0)$. Since $b^2 = 4$, $b = 2$ and endpoints of the minor axis are $(0,-2)$ and $(0,2)$.

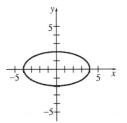

15. $x^2 - y^2 = 9$

$\dfrac{x^2}{9} - \dfrac{y^2}{9} = 1$

The equation is in the form

$\dfrac{x^2}{a^2} - \dfrac{y^2}{b^2} = 1$ with $a^2 = 9$, and $b^2 = 9$.

We know the transverse axis lies on the x-axis and the vertices are $(-3,0)$ and $(3,0)$. Because $a^2 = 3$ and $b^2 = 3$, $a = 3$ and $b = 3$. Construct a rectangle using -3 and 3 on the x–axis, and -3 and 3 on the y–axis. Draw extended diagonals to obtain the asymptotes. Graph the hyperbola.

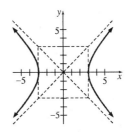

16. $\dfrac{2x+1}{x-5} - \dfrac{4}{x^2 - 3x - 10}$

$= \dfrac{2x+1}{x-5} - \dfrac{4}{(x-5)(x+2)}$

$= \dfrac{2x+1}{x-5} \cdot \dfrac{x+2}{x+2} - \dfrac{4}{(x-5)(x+2)}$

$= \dfrac{(2x+1)(x+2) - 4}{(x-5)(x+2)}$

$= \dfrac{2x^2 + 5x + 2 - 4}{(x-5)(x+2)}$

$= \dfrac{2x^2 + 5x - 2}{(x-5)(x+2)}$

17.
$$\frac{\dfrac{1}{x-1}+1}{\dfrac{1}{x+1}-1} = \frac{\dfrac{1}{x-1}+\dfrac{x-1}{x-1}}{\dfrac{1}{x+1}-\dfrac{x+1}{x+1}} = \frac{\dfrac{1+(x-1)}{x-1}}{\dfrac{1-(x+1)}{x+1}}$$

$$= \frac{\dfrac{x}{x-1}}{\dfrac{-x}{x+1}} = \frac{x}{x-1}\cdot\frac{x+1}{-x}$$

$$= -\frac{x+1}{x-1}$$

18.
$$\frac{6}{\sqrt{5}-\sqrt{2}}\cdot\frac{\sqrt{5}+\sqrt{2}}{\sqrt{5}+\sqrt{2}} = \frac{6\left(\sqrt{5}+\sqrt{2}\right)}{5-2}$$

$$= \frac{6\left(\sqrt{5}+\sqrt{2}\right)}{3}$$

$$= 2\left(\sqrt{5}+\sqrt{2}\right)$$

$$= 2\sqrt{5}+2\sqrt{2}$$

19. $8\sqrt{45}+2\sqrt{5}-7\sqrt{20}$

$$= 8\sqrt{9\cdot5}+2\sqrt{5}-7\sqrt{4\cdot5}$$

$$= 8\cdot3\sqrt{5}+2\sqrt{5}-7\cdot2\sqrt{5}$$

$$= 24\sqrt{5}+2\sqrt{5}-14\sqrt{5}$$

$$= 12\sqrt{5}$$

20.
$$\frac{5}{\sqrt[3]{2x^2y}} = \frac{5}{2^{\frac{1}{3}}x^{\frac{2}{3}}y^{\frac{1}{3}}}\cdot\frac{2^{\frac{2}{3}}x^{\frac{1}{3}}y^{\frac{2}{3}}}{2^{\frac{2}{3}}x^{\frac{1}{3}}y^{\frac{2}{3}}} = \frac{5\sqrt[3]{4xy^2}}{2xy}$$

21. $5ax+5ay-4bx-4by$

$$= 5a(x+y)-4b(x+y)$$

$$= (x+y)(5a-4b)$$

22.
$$5\log x-\frac{1}{2}\log y = \log x^5 - \log y^{\frac{1}{2}}$$

$$= \log\left(\frac{x^5}{y^{\frac{1}{2}}}\right)$$

$$= \log\left(\frac{x^5}{\sqrt{y}}\right)$$

23.
$$\frac{1}{p}+\frac{1}{q}=\frac{1}{f}$$

$$\frac{1}{p}=\frac{1}{f}-\frac{1}{q}$$

$$\frac{1}{p}=\frac{1}{f}\cdot\frac{q}{q}-\frac{1}{q}\cdot\frac{f}{f}$$

$$\frac{1}{p}=\frac{q}{qf}-\frac{f}{qf}$$

$$\frac{1}{p}=\frac{q-f}{qf}$$

$$p(q-f)=qf$$

$$p=\frac{qf}{q-f}$$

24.
$$d=\sqrt{\left(6-(-3)\right)^2+\left(-1-(-4)\right)^2}$$

$$=\sqrt{9^2+3^2}=\sqrt{81+9}=\sqrt{90}$$

$$=\sqrt{9\cdot10}=3\sqrt{10}\approx9.49$$

The distance is $3\sqrt{10}\approx9.49$ units.

25.
$$\sum_{i=2}^{5}\left(i^3-4\right)$$

$$=\left(2^3-4\right)+\left(3^3-4\right)+\left(4^3-4\right)+\left(5^3-4\right)$$

$$=(8-4)+(27-4)+(64-4)+(125-4)$$

$$=4+23+60+121=208$$

26. First, find d.

$d = 6 - 2 = 4$

Next, find a_{30}.

$a_{30} = 2 + (30-1)4 = 2 + (29)4$

$= 2 + 116 = 118$

Now, find the sum.

$S_{30} = \dfrac{30}{2}(2+118) = 15(120) = 1800$

27.

$0.\overline{3} = \dfrac{a_1}{1-r} = \dfrac{\dfrac{3}{10}}{1-\dfrac{1}{10}} = \dfrac{\dfrac{3}{10}}{\dfrac{9}{10}} = \dfrac{3}{10} \div \dfrac{9}{10}$

$= \dfrac{3}{10} \cdot \dfrac{10}{9} = \dfrac{1}{3}$

28. Applying the Binomial Theorem to $\left(2x - y^3\right)^4$, we have $a = 2x$, $b = -y^3$, and $n = 4$.

$\left(2x-y^3\right)^4 = \binom{4}{0}(2x)^4 + \binom{4}{1}(2x)^3\left(-y^3\right) + \binom{4}{2}(2x)^2\left(-y^3\right)^2 + \binom{4}{3}2x\left(-y^3\right)^3 + \binom{4}{4}\left(-y^3\right)^4$

$= \dfrac{4!}{0!(4-0)!}16x^4 - \dfrac{4!}{1!(4-1)!}8x^3y^3 + \dfrac{4!}{2!(4-2)!}4x^2y^6 - \dfrac{4!}{3!(4-3)!}2xy^9 + \dfrac{4!}{4!(4-4)!}y^{12}$

$= \dfrac{\cancel{4!}}{0!\,\cancel{4!}}16x^4 - \dfrac{4!}{1!3!}8x^3y^3 + \dfrac{4!}{2!2!}4x^2y^6 - \dfrac{4!}{3!1!}2xy^9 + \dfrac{\cancel{4!}}{\cancel{4!}0!}y^{12}$

$= 1\left(16x^4\right) - \dfrac{4\cdot\cancel{3!}}{1\cdot\cancel{3!}}8x^3y^3 + \dfrac{4\cdot3\cdot\cancel{2!}}{2\cdot1\cdot\cancel{2!}}4x^2y^6 - \dfrac{4\cdot\cancel{3!}}{\cancel{3!}\cdot1}2xy^9 + y^{12}$

$= 16x^4 - 4\left(8x^3y^3\right) + 6\left(4x^2y^6\right) - 4\left(2xy^9\right) + y^{12}$

$= 16x^4 - 32x^3y^3 + 24x^2y^6 - 8xy^9 + y^{12}$

29. $f(x) = \dfrac{2}{x^2 + 2x - 15}$

Set the denominator equal to 0 to find the domain:

$x^2 + 2x - 15 = 0$

$(x+5)(x-3) = 0$

$x = -5,\ x = 3$

So, $\{x \mid x$ is a real number

and $x \neq -5$ and $x \neq 3\}$

30. $f(x) = \sqrt{2x-6}$;

We can not take the square root of a negative number.

$2x - 6 \geq 0$

$2x \geq 6$

$x \geq 3$

So, $\{x \mid x \geq 3\}$ or $[3, \infty)$.

31. $f(x) = \ln(1-x)$

We can only take the ln of positive numbers.

$1 - x > 0$

$-x > -1$

$x < 1$

So, $\{x \mid x < 1\}$ or $(-\infty, 1)$.

32. Let $w =$ width of the rectangle. Then
$l = 2w + 2$.
The perimeter of a rectangle is given
by $P = 2w + 2l$.
Then $P = 2w + 2l$

$$22 = 2w + 2(2w + 2)$$
$$22 = 2w + 4w + 4$$
$$22 = 6w + 4$$
$$18 = 6w$$
$$w = 3$$

Then $l = 2w + 2 = 2(3) + 2 = 8$
The dimension of the rectangle is 8
feet by 3 feet.

33.
$$A = P(1 + r)^t$$
$$19610 = P(1 + 0.06)^1$$
$$19610 = 1.06P$$
$$P = 18500$$

Your salary before the raise is
$18,500.

34. $F(t) = 1 - k \ln(t + 1)$

$$\frac{1}{2} = 1 - k \ln(3 + 1)$$

$$\frac{1}{2} = 1 - k \ln 4$$

$$k \ln 4 = \frac{1}{2}$$

$$k = \frac{1}{2 \ln 4} \approx 0.3607$$

Then $F(t) \approx 1 - 0.3607 \ln(t + 1)$
$$F(6) \approx 1 - 0.3607 \ln(6 + 1)$$
$$\approx 1 - 0.3607 \ln(7)$$
$$\approx 1 - 0.7019$$
$$\approx 0.298 \text{ or } \frac{298}{100}$$

Appendix A
Matrix Solutions to Linear Systems

1. $x - 3y = 11$

$\quad y = -3$

Substitute -3 for y in the first equation.

$\quad x - 3y = 11$

$\quad x - 3(-3) = 11$

$\quad x + 9 = 11$

$\quad x = 2$

The solution set is $\{(2, -3)\}$.

3. $x - 3y = 1$

$\quad y = -1$

Substitute -1 for y in the first equation.

$\quad x - 3y = 1$

$\quad x - 3(-1) = 1$

$\quad x + 3 = 1$

$\quad x = -2$

The solution set is $\{(-2, -1)\}$.

5. $x \quad - 4z = 5$

$\quad y - 12z = 13$

$\quad\quad z = -\dfrac{1}{2}$

Substitute $-\dfrac{1}{2}$ for z in the second equation to find y.

$\quad y - 12z = 13$

$\quad y - 12\left(-\dfrac{1}{2}\right) = 13$

$\quad y + 6 = 13$

$\quad y = 7$

Substitute 7 for y in the first equation to find x.

$x - 4z = 5$

$x - 4\left(-\dfrac{1}{2}\right) = 5$

$x + 2 = 5$

$x = 3$

The solution set is $\left\{\left(3, 7, -\dfrac{1}{2}\right)\right\}$.

7. $x + \dfrac{1}{2}y + \quad z = \dfrac{11}{2}$

$\quad\quad y + \dfrac{3}{2}z = 7$

$\quad\quad\quad z = 4$

Substitute 4 for z in the second equation to find y.

$\quad y + \dfrac{3}{2}z = 7$

$\quad y + \dfrac{3}{2}(4) = 7$

$\quad y + 6 = 7$

$\quad y = 1$

Substitute 1 for y and 4 for z in the first equation to find x.

$x + \dfrac{1}{2}y + z = \dfrac{11}{2}$

$x + \dfrac{1}{2}(1) + 4 = \dfrac{11}{2}$

$x + \dfrac{9}{2} = \dfrac{11}{2}$

$x = \dfrac{2}{2} = 1$

The solution set is $\{(1, 1, 4)\}$.

9.
$$\begin{bmatrix} 2 & 2 & | & 5 \\ 1 & -\dfrac{3}{2} & | & 5 \end{bmatrix} R_1 \leftrightarrow R_2$$

$$= \begin{bmatrix} 1 & -\dfrac{3}{2} & | & 5 \\ 2 & 2 & | & 5 \end{bmatrix}$$

11.
$$\begin{bmatrix} -6 & 8 & | & -12 \\ 3 & 5 & | & -2 \end{bmatrix} -\dfrac{1}{6}R_1$$

$$= \begin{bmatrix} 1 & -\dfrac{4}{3} & | & 2 \\ 3 & 5 & | & -2 \end{bmatrix}$$

13.
$$\begin{bmatrix} 1 & -3 & | & 5 \\ 2 & 6 & | & 4 \end{bmatrix} -2R_1 + R_2$$

$$= \begin{bmatrix} 1 & -3 & | & 5 \\ 0 & 12 & | & -6 \end{bmatrix}$$

15.
$$\begin{bmatrix} 1 & -\dfrac{3}{2} & | & \dfrac{7}{2} \\ 3 & 4 & | & 2 \end{bmatrix} -3R_1 + R_2$$

$$= \begin{bmatrix} 1 & -\dfrac{3}{2} & | & \dfrac{7}{2} \\ 0 & \dfrac{17}{2} & | & -\dfrac{17}{2} \end{bmatrix}$$

17.
$$\begin{bmatrix} 2 & -6 & 4 & | & 10 \\ 1 & 5 & -5 & | & 0 \\ 3 & 0 & 4 & | & 7 \end{bmatrix} \dfrac{1}{2}R_1$$

$$= \begin{bmatrix} 1 & -3 & 2 & | & 5 \\ 1 & 5 & -5 & | & 0 \\ 3 & 0 & 4 & | & 7 \end{bmatrix}$$

19.
$$\begin{bmatrix} 1 & -3 & 2 & | & 0 \\ 3 & 1 & -1 & | & 7 \\ 2 & -2 & 1 & | & 3 \end{bmatrix} -3R_1 + R_2$$

$$= \begin{bmatrix} 1 & -3 & 2 & | & 0 \\ 0 & 10 & -7 & | & 7 \\ 2 & -2 & 1 & | & 3 \end{bmatrix}$$

21.
$$\begin{bmatrix} 1 & 1 & -1 & | & 6 \\ 2 & -1 & 1 & | & -3 \\ 3 & -1 & -1 & | & 4 \end{bmatrix} \begin{array}{l} -2R_1 + R_2 \\ \text{and} \\ -3R_1 + R_3 \end{array}$$

$$= \begin{bmatrix} 1 & 1 & -1 & | & 6 \\ 0 & -3 & 3 & | & -15 \\ 0 & -4 & 2 & | & -14 \end{bmatrix}$$

23.
$$\begin{bmatrix} 1 & 1 & | & 6 \\ 1 & -1 & | & 2 \end{bmatrix} -R_1 + R_2$$

$$= \begin{bmatrix} 1 & 1 & | & 6 \\ 0 & -2 & | & -4 \end{bmatrix} -\dfrac{1}{2}R_2$$

$$= \begin{bmatrix} 1 & 1 & | & 6 \\ 0 & 1 & | & 2 \end{bmatrix}$$

The resulting system is:
$$x + y = 6$$
$$y = 2$$

Back-substitute 2 for y in the first equation.
$$x + 2 = 6$$
$$x = 4$$
The solution set is $\{(4, 2)\}$.

25. $\begin{bmatrix} 2 & 1 & | & 3 \\ 1 & -3 & | & 12 \end{bmatrix} R_1 \leftrightarrow R_2$

$= \begin{bmatrix} 1 & -3 & | & 12 \\ 2 & 1 & | & 3 \end{bmatrix} -2R_1 + R_2$

$= \begin{bmatrix} 1 & -3 & | & 12 \\ 0 & 7 & | & -21 \end{bmatrix} \frac{1}{7}R_2$

$= \begin{bmatrix} 1 & -3 & | & 12 \\ 0 & 1 & | & -3 \end{bmatrix}$

The system is:

$x - 3y = 12$

$y = -3$

Back-substitute -3 for y in the first equation.

$x - 3y = 12$

$x - 3(-3) = 12$

$x + 9 = 12$

$x = 3$

The solution set is $\{(3, -3)\}$.

27. $\begin{bmatrix} 5 & 7 & | & -25 \\ 11 & 6 & | & -8 \end{bmatrix} \frac{1}{5}R_1$

$= \begin{bmatrix} 1 & \frac{7}{5} & | & -5 \\ 11 & 6 & | & -8 \end{bmatrix} -11R_1 + R_2$

$= \begin{bmatrix} 1 & \frac{7}{5} & | & -5 \\ 0 & -\frac{47}{5} & | & 47 \end{bmatrix} -\frac{5}{47}R_2$

$= \begin{bmatrix} 1 & \frac{7}{5} & | & -5 \\ 0 & 1 & | & -5 \end{bmatrix}$

The resulting system is:

$x + \frac{7}{5}y = -5$

$y = -5$

Back-substitute -5 for y in the first equation.

$x + \frac{7}{5}y = -5$

$x + \frac{7}{5}(-5) = -5$

$x - 7 = -5$

$x = 2$

The solution set is $\{(2, -5)\}$.

29. $\begin{bmatrix} 4 & -2 & | & 5 \\ -2 & 1 & | & 6 \end{bmatrix} \frac{1}{4}R_1$

$= \begin{bmatrix} 1 & -\frac{1}{2} & | & \frac{5}{2} \\ -2 & 1 & | & 6 \end{bmatrix} 2R_1 + R_2$

$= \begin{bmatrix} 1 & -\frac{1}{2} & | & \frac{5}{2} \\ 0 & 0 & | & \frac{17}{2} \end{bmatrix}$

The resulting system is:

$x - \frac{1}{2}y = \frac{5}{2}$

$0x + 0y = \frac{17}{2}$

This is a contradiction. The system is inconsistent. The solution set is $\varnothing$.

31. $\begin{bmatrix} 1 & -2 & | & 1 \\ -2 & 4 & | & -2 \end{bmatrix} 2R_1 + R_2$

$= \begin{bmatrix} 1 & -2 & | & 1 \\ 0 & 0 & | & 0 \end{bmatrix}$

The resulting system is:

$x - 2y = 1$

$0x + 0y = 0$

The system is dependent. There are infinitely many solutions.

33.
$$\begin{bmatrix} 1 & 1 & -1 & | & -2 \\ 2 & -1 & 1 & | & 5 \\ -1 & 2 & 2 & | & 1 \end{bmatrix} \quad -2R_1 + R_2$$

$$= \begin{bmatrix} 1 & 1 & -1 & | & -2 \\ 0 & -3 & 3 & | & 9 \\ -1 & 2 & 2 & | & 1 \end{bmatrix} \quad R_1 + R_3$$

$$= \begin{bmatrix} 1 & 1 & -1 & | & -2 \\ 0 & -3 & 3 & | & 9 \\ 0 & 3 & 1 & | & -1 \end{bmatrix} \quad R_2 + R_3$$

$$= \begin{bmatrix} 1 & 1 & -1 & | & -2 \\ 0 & -3 & 3 & | & 9 \\ 0 & 0 & 4 & | & 8 \end{bmatrix} \quad \frac{1}{4}R_3$$

$$= \begin{bmatrix} 1 & 1 & -1 & | & -2 \\ 0 & -3 & 3 & | & 9 \\ 0 & 0 & 1 & | & 2 \end{bmatrix}$$

The resulting system is:
$$x + y - z = -2$$
$$y - z = -3$$
$$z = 2$$
Back-substitute 2 for z to find y.
$$y - z = -3$$
$$y - 2 = -3$$
$$y = -1$$

Back-substitute 2 for z and -1 for y to find x.
$$x + y - z = -2$$
$$x - 1 - 2 = -2$$
$$x - 3 = -2$$
$$x = 1$$
The solution set is $\{(1, -1, 2)\}$.

35.
$$\begin{bmatrix} 1 & 3 & 0 & | & 0 \\ 1 & 1 & 1 & | & 1 \\ 3 & -1 & -1 & | & 11 \end{bmatrix} \quad -R_1 + R_2$$

$$= \begin{bmatrix} 1 & 3 & 0 & | & 0 \\ 0 & -2 & 1 & | & 1 \\ 3 & -1 & -1 & | & 11 \end{bmatrix} \quad -3R_1 + R_3$$

$$= \begin{bmatrix} 1 & 3 & 0 & | & 0 \\ 0 & -2 & 1 & | & 1 \\ 0 & -10 & -1 & | & 11 \end{bmatrix} \quad -\frac{1}{2}R_2$$

$$= \begin{bmatrix} 1 & 3 & 0 & | & 0 \\ 0 & 1 & -\frac{1}{2} & | & -\frac{1}{2} \\ 0 & -10 & -1 & | & 11 \end{bmatrix} \quad -\frac{1}{10}R_3$$

$$= \begin{bmatrix} 1 & 3 & 0 & | & 0 \\ 0 & 1 & -\frac{1}{2} & | & -\frac{1}{2} \\ 0 & 1 & \frac{1}{10} & | & -\frac{11}{10} \end{bmatrix} \quad -R_2 + R_3$$

$$= \begin{bmatrix} 1 & 3 & 0 & | & 0 \\ 0 & 1 & -\frac{1}{2} & | & -\frac{1}{2} \\ 0 & 0 & \frac{3}{5} & | & -\frac{3}{5} \end{bmatrix} \quad \frac{5}{3}R_3$$

$$= \begin{bmatrix} 1 & 3 & 0 & | & 0 \\ 0 & 1 & -\frac{1}{2} & | & -\frac{1}{2} \\ 0 & 0 & 1 & | & -1 \end{bmatrix}$$

The resulting system is:
$$x + 3y = 0$$
$$y - \frac{1}{2}z = -\frac{1}{2}$$
$$z = -1$$
Back-substitute -1 for z and solve for y.

904

$$y - \frac{1}{2}z = -\frac{1}{2}$$

$$y - \frac{1}{2}(-1) = -\frac{1}{2}$$

$$y + \frac{1}{2} = -\frac{1}{2}$$

$$y = -1$$

Back-substitute -1 for y to find x.

$$x + 3y = 0$$

$$x + 3(-1) = 0$$

$$x - 3 = 0$$

$$x = 3$$

The solution set is $\{(3, -1, -1)\}$.

37.
$$\begin{bmatrix} 2 & 2 & 7 & | & -1 \\ 2 & 1 & 2 & | & 2 \\ 4 & 6 & 1 & | & 15 \end{bmatrix} \quad \frac{1}{2}R_1$$

$$= \begin{bmatrix} 1 & 1 & \frac{7}{2} & | & -\frac{1}{2} \\ 2 & 1 & 2 & | & 2 \\ 4 & 6 & 1 & | & 15 \end{bmatrix} \quad -2R_1 + R_2$$

$$= \begin{bmatrix} 1 & 1 & \frac{7}{2} & | & -\frac{1}{2} \\ 0 & -1 & -5 & | & 3 \\ 4 & 6 & 1 & | & 15 \end{bmatrix} \quad -R_2$$

$$= \begin{bmatrix} 1 & 1 & \frac{7}{2} & | & -\frac{1}{2} \\ 0 & 1 & 5 & | & -3 \\ 4 & 6 & 1 & | & 15 \end{bmatrix} \quad -4R_1 + R_3$$

$$= \begin{bmatrix} 1 & 1 & \frac{7}{2} & | & -\frac{1}{2} \\ 0 & 1 & 5 & | & -3 \\ 0 & 2 & -13 & | & 17 \end{bmatrix} \quad -2R_2 + R_3$$

$$= \begin{bmatrix} 1 & 1 & \frac{7}{2} & | & -\frac{1}{2} \\ 0 & 1 & 5 & | & -3 \\ 0 & 0 & -23 & | & 23 \end{bmatrix} \quad -R_3$$

$$= \begin{bmatrix} 1 & 1 & \frac{7}{2} & | & -\frac{1}{2} \\ 0 & 1 & 5 & | & -3 \\ 0 & 0 & 1 & | & -1 \end{bmatrix}$$

The resulting system is:

$$x + y + \frac{7}{2}z = -\frac{1}{2}$$

$$y + 5z = -3$$

$$z = -1$$

Back-substitute -1 for z to find y.

$$y + 5z = -3$$

$$y + 5(-1) = -3$$

$$y - 5 = -3$$

$$y = 2$$

Back-substitute -1 for z and 2 for y to find x.

$$x + y + \frac{7}{2}z = -\frac{1}{2}$$

$$x + 2 + \frac{7}{2}(-1) = -\frac{1}{2}$$

$$x + 2 - \frac{7}{2} = -\frac{1}{2}$$

$$x - \frac{3}{2} = -\frac{1}{2}$$

$$x = 1$$

The solution set is $\{(1, 2, -1)\}$.

39.
$$\begin{bmatrix} 1 & 1 & 1 & | & 6 \\ 1 & 0 & -1 & | & -2 \\ 0 & 1 & 3 & | & 11 \end{bmatrix} R_2 \leftrightarrow R_3$$

$$= \begin{bmatrix} 1 & 1 & 1 & | & 6 \\ 0 & 1 & 3 & | & 11 \\ 1 & 0 & -1 & | & -2 \end{bmatrix} -R_1 + R_3$$

$$= \begin{bmatrix} 1 & 1 & 1 & | & 6 \\ 0 & 1 & 3 & | & 11 \\ 0 & -1 & -2 & | & -8 \end{bmatrix} R_2 + R_3$$

$$= \begin{bmatrix} 1 & 1 & 1 & | & 6 \\ 0 & 1 & 3 & | & 11 \\ 0 & 0 & 1 & | & 3 \end{bmatrix}$$

The resulting system is:
$$x + y + z = 6$$
$$y + 3z = 11$$
$$z = 3$$

Back-substitute 3 for z to find y.
$$y + 3z = 11$$
$$y + 3(3) = 11$$
$$y + 9 = 11$$
$$y = 2$$

Back-substitute 3 for z and 2 for y to find x.
$$x + y + z = 6$$
$$x + 2 + 3 = 6$$
$$x + 5 = 6$$
$$x = 1$$

The solution set is $\{(1, 2, 3)\}$.

41.
$$\begin{bmatrix} 1 & -1 & 3 & | & 4 \\ 2 & -2 & 6 & | & 7 \\ 3 & -1 & 5 & | & 14 \end{bmatrix} \begin{matrix} -2R_1 + R_2 \\ \text{and} \\ -3R_1 + R_3 \end{matrix}$$

$$= \begin{bmatrix} 1 & -1 & 3 & | & 4 \\ 0 & 0 & 0 & | & -1 \\ 0 & 2 & -4 & | & 2 \end{bmatrix}$$

The resulting system is:

$$x - y + 3z = 4$$
$$0x + 0y + 0z = -1$$
$$2y - 4z = 2$$

The second row is a contradiction, since $0x + 0y + 0z$ cannot equal -1. We conclude that the system is inconsistent. The solution set is $\varnothing$.

43.
$$\begin{bmatrix} 1 & -2 & 1 & | & 4 \\ 5 & -10 & 5 & | & 20 \\ -2 & 4 & -2 & | & -8 \end{bmatrix} \frac{1}{5}R_2$$

$$= \begin{bmatrix} 1 & -2 & 1 & | & 4 \\ 1 & -2 & 1 & | & 4 \\ -2 & 4 & -2 & | & -8 \end{bmatrix}$$

R_1 and R_2 are the same. The system is dependent and there are infinitely many solutions.

45.
$$\begin{bmatrix} 1 & 1 & 0 & | & 1 \\ 0 & 1 & 2 & | & -2 \\ 2 & 0 & -1 & | & 0 \end{bmatrix} -2R_1 + R_3$$

$$= \begin{bmatrix} 1 & 1 & 0 & | & 1 \\ 0 & 1 & 2 & | & -2 \\ 0 & -2 & -1 & | & -2 \end{bmatrix} 2R_2 + R_3$$

$$= \begin{bmatrix} 1 & 1 & 0 & | & 1 \\ 0 & 1 & 2 & | & -2 \\ 0 & 0 & 3 & | & -6 \end{bmatrix} \frac{1}{3}R_3$$

$$= \begin{bmatrix} 1 & 1 & 0 & | & 1 \\ 0 & 1 & 2 & | & -2 \\ 0 & 0 & 1 & | & -2 \end{bmatrix}$$

The resulting system is:
$$x + y = 1$$
$$y + 2z = -2$$
$$z = -2$$

Back-substitute -2 for z to find y.

$$y + 2z = -2$$
$$y + 2(-2) = -2$$
$$y - 4 = -2$$
$$y = 2$$

Back-substitute 2 for y to find x.
$$x + y = 1$$
$$x + 2 = 1$$
$$x = -1$$

The solution set is $\{(-1, 2, -2)\}$.

47. The system is
$$w - x + y + z = 3$$
$$x - 2y - z = 0$$
$$y + 6z = 17$$
$$z = 3$$

Back-substitute $z = 3$ to solve for y.
$$y + 6(3) = 17$$
$$y + 18 = 17$$
$$y = -1$$

Back-substitute $z = 3$ and $y = -1$ to solve for x.
$$x - 2(-1) - (3) = 0$$
$$x + 2 - 3 = 0$$
$$x = 1$$

Back-substitute $x = 1$, $y = -1$ and $z = 3$ to solve for w.
$$w - (1) + (-1) + (3) = 3$$
$$w - 1 - 1 + 3 = 3$$
$$w = 2$$

The solution set is $\{(2, 1, -1, 3)\}$.

48. The system is
$$w + 2x - y = 2$$
$$x + y - 2z = 0$$
$$2w + 3y + 4z = 11$$
$$y - z = -2$$
$$z = 3$$

Back-substitute $z = 3$ to solve for y.
$$y - (3) = -2$$
$$y = 1$$

Back-substitute $y = 1$ and $z = 3$ to solve for x.
$$x + (1) - 2(3) = -3$$
$$x + 1 - 6 = -3$$
$$x = 2$$

Back-substitute $x = 2$ and $y = 1$ to solve for w.
$$w + 2(2) - (1) = 2$$
$$w + 4 - 1 = 2$$
$$w = -1$$

The solution set is $\{(-1, 2, 1, 3)\}$.

49.
$$\begin{bmatrix} 1 & -1 & 1 & 1 & 3 \\ 0 & 1 & -2 & -1 & 0 \\ 2 & 0 & 3 & 4 & 11 \\ 5 & 1 & 2 & 4 & 6 \end{bmatrix} \begin{matrix} \\ \\ -2R_1 + R_3 \\ -5R_1 + R_4 \end{matrix}$$

$$= \begin{bmatrix} 1 & -1 & 1 & 1 & 3 \\ 0 & 1 & -2 & -1 & 0 \\ 0 & 2 & 1 & 2 & 5 \\ 0 & 6 & -3 & -1 & -9 \end{bmatrix}$$

50.
$$\begin{bmatrix} 1 & -5 & 2 & -2 & 4 \\ 0 & 1 & -3 & -1 & 0 \\ 3 & 0 & 2 & -1 & 6 \\ -4 & 1 & 4 & 2 & -3 \end{bmatrix} \begin{matrix} \\ \\ -3R_1 + R_3 \\ 4R_1 + R_4 \end{matrix}$$

$$= \begin{bmatrix} 1 & -5 & 2 & -2 & 4 \\ 0 & 1 & -3 & -1 & 0 \\ 0 & 15 & -4 & 5 & -6 \\ 0 & -19 & 12 & -6 & 13 \end{bmatrix}$$

907

51.
$$\left[\begin{array}{cccc|c} 1 & 1 & 1 & 1 & 4 \\ 2 & 1 & -2 & -1 & 0 \\ 1 & -2 & -1 & -2 & -2 \\ 3 & 2 & 1 & 3 & 4 \end{array}\right] \begin{array}{l} \\ -2R_1 + R_2 \\ -1R_1 + R_3 \\ -3R_1 + R_4 \end{array}$$

$$= \left[\begin{array}{cccc|c} 1 & 1 & 1 & 1 & 4 \\ 0 & -1 & -4 & -3 & -8 \\ 0 & -3 & -2 & -3 & -6 \\ 0 & -1 & -2 & 0 & -8 \end{array}\right] -1R_2$$

$$= \left[\begin{array}{cccc|c} 1 & 1 & 1 & 1 & 4 \\ 0 & 1 & 4 & 3 & 8 \\ 0 & -3 & -2 & -3 & -6 \\ 0 & -1 & -2 & 0 & -8 \end{array}\right] \begin{array}{l} \\ \\ 3R_2 + R_3 \\ R_2 + R_4 \end{array}$$

$$= \left[\begin{array}{cccc|c} 1 & 1 & 1 & 1 & 4 \\ 0 & 1 & 4 & 3 & 8 \\ 0 & 0 & 10 & 6 & 18 \\ 0 & 0 & 2 & 3 & 0 \end{array}\right] \begin{array}{l} \\ \\ \frac{1}{2}R_4 \\ R_3 \end{array}$$

$$= \left[\begin{array}{cccc|c} 1 & 1 & 1 & 1 & 4 \\ 0 & 1 & 4 & 3 & 8 \\ 0 & 0 & 1 & \frac{3}{2} & 0 \\ 0 & 0 & 10 & 6 & 18 \end{array}\right] \begin{array}{l} \\ \\ \\ -10R_3 + R_4 \end{array}$$

$$= \left[\begin{array}{cccc|c} 1 & 1 & 1 & 1 & 4 \\ 0 & 1 & 4 & 3 & 8 \\ 0 & 0 & 1 & \frac{3}{2} & 0 \\ 0 & 0 & 0 & -9 & 18 \end{array}\right] \begin{array}{l} \\ \\ \\ -\frac{1}{9}R_4 \end{array}$$

$$= \left[\begin{array}{cccc|c} 1 & 1 & 1 & 1 & 4 \\ 0 & 1 & 4 & 3 & 8 \\ 0 & 0 & 1 & \frac{3}{2} & 0 \\ 0 & 0 & 0 & 1 & -2 \end{array}\right]$$

The resulting system is

$w + x + y + z = 4$

$x + 4y + 3z = 8$

$y + \dfrac{3}{2}z = 0$

$z = -2$

Back-substitute $z = -2$ to solve for y.

$y + \dfrac{3}{2}(-2) = 0$

$y - 3 = 0$

$y = 3$

Back-substitute $y = 3$ and $z = -2$ to solve for x.

$x + 4(3) + 3(-2) = 8$

$x + 12 - 6 = 8$

$x = 2$

Back-substitute $x = 2$, $y = 3$, and $z = -2$ to solve for w.

$w + (2) + (3) + (-2) = 4$

$w + 5 - 2 = 4$

$w = 1$

The solution set is $\{(1, 2, 3, -2)\}$.

52.
$$\left[\begin{array}{cccc|c} 1 & 1 & 1 & 1 & 5 \\ 1 & 2 & -1 & -2 & -1 \\ 1 & -3 & -3 & -1 & -1 \\ 2 & -1 & 2 & -1 & -2 \end{array}\right] \begin{array}{l} \\ -1R_1 + R_2 \\ -1R_1 + R_3 \\ -2R_1 + R_4 \end{array}$$

$$= \left[\begin{array}{cccc|c} 1 & 1 & 1 & 1 & 5 \\ 0 & 1 & -2 & -3 & -6 \\ 0 & -4 & -4 & -2 & -6 \\ 0 & -3 & 0 & -3 & -12 \end{array}\right] \begin{array}{l} \\ \\ 4R_2 + R_3 \\ 3R_2 + R_4 \end{array}$$

$$= \left[\begin{array}{cccc|c} 1 & 1 & 1 & 1 & 5 \\ 0 & 1 & -2 & -3 & -6 \\ 0 & 0 & -12 & -14 & -30 \\ 0 & 0 & -6 & -12 & -30 \end{array}\right] \begin{array}{l} \\ \\ -\frac{1}{6}R_4 \\ R_3 \end{array}$$

$$= \left[\begin{array}{cccc|c} 1 & 1 & 1 & 1 & 5 \\ 0 & 1 & -2 & -3 & -6 \\ 0 & 0 & 1 & 2 & 5 \\ 0 & 0 & -12 & -14 & -30 \end{array}\right] 12R_3 + R_4$$

$$= \left[\begin{array}{cccc|c} 1 & 1 & 1 & 1 & 5 \\ 0 & 1 & -2 & -3 & -6 \\ 0 & 0 & 1 & 2 & 5 \\ 0 & 0 & 0 & 10 & 30 \end{array}\right] \frac{1}{10}R_4$$

$$= \left[\begin{array}{cccc|c} 1 & 1 & 1 & 1 & 5 \\ 0 & 1 & -2 & -3 & -6 \\ 0 & 0 & 1 & 2 & 5 \\ 0 & 0 & 0 & 1 & 3 \end{array}\right]$$

The resulting system is
$$w + x + y + z = 5$$
$$x - 2y - 3z = -6$$
$$y + 2z = 5$$
$$z = 3$$
Back-substitute $z = 3$ to solve for y.
$$y + 2(3) = 5$$
$$y + 6 = 5$$
$$y = -1$$
Back-substitute $y = -1$ and $z = 3$ to

solve for x.
$$x - 2(-1) - 3(3) = -6$$
$$x + 2 - 9 = -6$$
$$x = 1$$
Back-substitute $x = 1$, $y = -1$, and
$z = 3$ to solve for w.
$$w + (1) + (-1) + (3) = 5$$
$$w + 4 - 1 = 5$$
$$w = 2$$
The solution set is $\{(2, 1, -1, 3)\}$.

Appendix B
Determinants and Cramer's Rule

1.
$$\begin{vmatrix} 5 & 7 \\ 2 & 3 \end{vmatrix} = 5(3) - 2(7) = 15 - 14 = 1$$

3.
$$\begin{vmatrix} -4 & 1 \\ 5 & 6 \end{vmatrix} = -4(6) - 5(1) = -24 - 5 = -29$$

5.
$$\begin{vmatrix} -7 & 14 \\ 2 & -4 \end{vmatrix} = -7(-4) - 2(14) = 28 - 28 = 0$$

7.
$$\begin{vmatrix} -5 & -1 \\ -2 & -7 \end{vmatrix} = -5(-7) - (-2)(-1)$$
$$= 35 - 2 = 33$$

9.
$$\begin{vmatrix} \frac{1}{2} & \frac{1}{2} \\ \frac{1}{8} & -\frac{3}{4} \end{vmatrix} = \frac{1}{2}\left(-\frac{3}{4}\right) - \frac{1}{8}\left(\frac{1}{2}\right)$$
$$= -\frac{3}{8} - \frac{1}{16} = -\frac{6}{16} - \frac{1}{16} = -\frac{7}{16}$$

11.
$$D = \begin{vmatrix} 1 & 1 \\ 1 & -1 \end{vmatrix} = 1(-1) - 1(1)$$
$$= -1 - 1 = -2$$
$$D_x = \begin{vmatrix} 7 & 1 \\ 3 & -1 \end{vmatrix} = 7(-1) - 3(1)$$
$$= -7 - 3 = -10$$
$$D_y = \begin{vmatrix} 1 & 7 \\ 1 & 3 \end{vmatrix} = 1(3) - 1(7)$$
$$= 3 - 7 = -4$$
$$x = \frac{D_x}{D} = \frac{-10}{-2} = 5$$
$$y = \frac{D_y}{D} = \frac{-4}{-2} = 2$$
The solution set is $\{(5, 2)\}$.

13.
$$D = \begin{vmatrix} 12 & 3 \\ 2 & -3 \end{vmatrix} = 12(-3) - 2(3)$$
$$= -36 - 6 = -42$$
$$D_x = \begin{vmatrix} 15 & 3 \\ 13 & -3 \end{vmatrix} = 15(-3) - 13(3)$$
$$= -45 - 39 = -84$$
$$D_y = \begin{vmatrix} 12 & 15 \\ 2 & 13 \end{vmatrix} = 12(13) - 2(15)$$
$$= 156 - 30 = 126$$
$$x = \frac{D_x}{D} = \frac{-84}{-42} = 2$$
$$y = \frac{D_y}{D} = \frac{126}{-42} = -3$$
The solution set is $\{(2, -3)\}$.

15.
$$D = \begin{vmatrix} 4 & -5 \\ 2 & 3 \end{vmatrix} = 4(3) - 2(-5)$$
$$= 12 + 10 = 22$$
$$D_x = \begin{vmatrix} 17 & -5 \\ 3 & 3 \end{vmatrix} = 17(3) - 3(-5)$$
$$= 51 + 15 = 66$$
$$D_y = \begin{vmatrix} 4 & 17 \\ 2 & 3 \end{vmatrix} = 4(3) - 2(17)$$
$$= 12 - 34 = -22$$
$$x = \frac{D_x}{D} = \frac{66}{22} = 3$$
$$y = \frac{D_y}{D} = \frac{-22}{22} = -1$$
The solution set is $\{(3, -1)\}$.

17.

$$D = \begin{vmatrix} 1 & -3 \\ 3 & -4 \end{vmatrix} = 1(-4) - 3(-3)$$

$$= -4 + 9 = 5$$

$$D_x = \begin{vmatrix} 4 & -3 \\ 12 & -4 \end{vmatrix} = 4(-4) - 12(-3)$$

$$= -16 + 36 = 20$$

$$D_y = \begin{vmatrix} 1 & 4 \\ 3 & 12 \end{vmatrix} = 1(12) - 3(4)$$

$$= 12 - 12 = 0$$

$$x = \frac{D_x}{D} = \frac{20}{5} = 4$$

$$y = \frac{D_y}{D} = \frac{0}{5} = 0$$

The solution set is $\{(4, 0)\}$.

19.

$$D = \begin{vmatrix} 3 & -4 \\ 2 & 2 \end{vmatrix} = 3(2) - 2(-4)$$

$$= 6 + 8 = 14$$

$$D_x = \begin{vmatrix} 4 & -4 \\ 12 & 2 \end{vmatrix} = 4(2) - 12(-4)$$

$$= 8 + 48 = 56$$

$$D_y = \begin{vmatrix} 3 & 4 \\ 2 & 12 \end{vmatrix} = 3(12) - 2(4)$$

$$= 36 - 8 = 28$$

$$x = \frac{D_x}{D} = \frac{56}{14} = 4 \; ; \; y = \frac{D_y}{D} = \frac{28}{14} = 2$$

The solution set is $\{(4, 2)\}$.

21. First, rewrite the system in standard form.

$$2x - 3y = 2$$
$$5x + 4y = 51$$

$$D = \begin{vmatrix} 2 & -3 \\ 5 & 4 \end{vmatrix} = 2(4) - 5(-3) = 8 + 15 = 23$$

$$D_x = \begin{vmatrix} 2 & -3 \\ 51 & 4 \end{vmatrix} = 2(4) - 51(-3)$$

$$= 8 + 153 = 161$$

$$D_y = \begin{vmatrix} 2 & 2 \\ 5 & 51 \end{vmatrix} = 2(51) - 5(2)$$

$$= 102 - 10 = 92$$

$$x = \frac{D_x}{D} = \frac{161}{23} = 7 \; ; \; y = \frac{D_y}{D} = \frac{92}{23} = 4$$

The solution set is $\{(7, 4)\}$.

23.

$$3x + 3y = 2$$
$$2x + 2y = 3$$

First, rewrite the system in standard form.

$$D = \begin{vmatrix} 3 & 3 \\ 2 & 2 \end{vmatrix} = 3(2) - 2(3) = 6 - 6 = 0$$

$$D_x = \begin{vmatrix} 2 & 3 \\ 3 & 2 \end{vmatrix} = 2(2) - 3(3) = 4 - 9 = -5$$

$$D_y = \begin{vmatrix} 2 & 3 \\ 3 & 2 \end{vmatrix} = 2(2) - 3(3) = 4 - 9 = -5$$

Because $D = 0$ but neither D_x nor D_y is zero, Cramer's Rule cannot be used to solve the system. Instead, use matrices.

$$\begin{bmatrix} 3 & 3 & | & 2 \\ 2 & 2 & | & 3 \end{bmatrix} \quad \frac{1}{3} R_1$$

$$= \begin{bmatrix} 1 & 1 & | & 2/3 \\ 2 & 2 & | & 3 \end{bmatrix} \quad -2R_1 + R_2$$

$$= \begin{bmatrix} 1 & 1 & | & 2/3 \\ 0 & 0 & | & 5/3 \end{bmatrix}$$

This is a contradiction. There are no values for x and y for which $0 = \frac{5}{3}$.

The solution set is $\varnothing$ and the system is inconsistent.

25. Rewrite the system in standard form.

$$3x + 4y = 16$$

$$6x + 8y = 32$$

$$D = \begin{vmatrix} 3 & 4 \\ 6 & 8 \end{vmatrix} = 3(8) - 6(4) = 24 - 24 = 0$$

$$D_x = \begin{vmatrix} 16 & 4 \\ 32 & 8 \end{vmatrix} = 16(8) - 32(4) = 128 - 128 = 0$$

$$D_y = \begin{vmatrix} 3 & 16 \\ 6 & 32 \end{vmatrix} = 3(32) - 6(16) = 96 - 96 = 0$$

Since $D = 0$ and all determinants in the numerators are 0, the equations in the system are dependent and there are infinitely many solutions.

27.

$$\begin{vmatrix} 3 & 0 & 0 \\ 2 & 1 & -5 \\ 2 & 5 & -1 \end{vmatrix} = 3 \begin{vmatrix} 1 & -5 \\ 5 & -1 \end{vmatrix} - 2 \begin{vmatrix} 0 & 0 \\ 5 & -1 \end{vmatrix} + 2 \begin{vmatrix} 0 & 0 \\ 1 & -5 \end{vmatrix}$$

$$= 3(1(-1) - 5(-5)) - 2(0(-1) - 5(0)) + 2(0(-5) - 1(0))$$

$$= 3(-1 + 25) - 2(0 - 0) + 2(0 - 0)$$

$$= 3(24) - 2\cancel{(0)} + 2\cancel{(0)} = 72$$

29.

$$\begin{vmatrix} 3 & 1 & 0 \\ -3 & 4 & 0 \\ -1 & 3 & -5 \end{vmatrix} = 3 \begin{vmatrix} 4 & 0 \\ 3 & -5 \end{vmatrix} - (-3) \begin{vmatrix} 1 & 0 \\ 3 & -5 \end{vmatrix} + (-1) \begin{vmatrix} 1 & 0 \\ 4 & 0 \end{vmatrix}$$

$$= 3(4(-5) - 3(0)) + 3(1(-5) - 3(0)) - 1(1(0) - 4(0))$$

$$= 3(-20 - 0) + 3(-5 - 0) - 1(0 - 0)$$

$$= 3(-20) + 3(-5) - 1\cancel{(0)} = -60 - 15 = -75$$

31.

$$\begin{vmatrix} 1 & 1 & 1 \\ 2 & 2 & 2 \\ -3 & 4 & -5 \end{vmatrix} = 1 \begin{vmatrix} 2 & 2 \\ 4 & -5 \end{vmatrix} - 2 \begin{vmatrix} 1 & 1 \\ 4 & -5 \end{vmatrix} + (-3) \begin{vmatrix} 1 & 1 \\ 2 & 2 \end{vmatrix}$$

$$= 1(2(-5) - 4(2)) - 2(1(-5) - 4(1)) - 3(1(2) - 2(1))$$

$$= 1(-10 - 8) - 2(-5 - 4) - 3(2 - 2)$$

$$= 1(-18) - 2(-9) - 3\cancel{(0)} = -18 + 18 = 0$$

912

33.

$$x + y + z = 0$$
$$2x - y + z = -1$$
$$-x + 3y - z = -8$$

$$D = \begin{vmatrix} 1 & 1 & 1 \\ 2 & -1 & 1 \\ -1 & 3 & -1 \end{vmatrix} = 1\begin{vmatrix} -1 & 1 \\ 3 & -1 \end{vmatrix} - 2\begin{vmatrix} 1 & 1 \\ 3 & -1 \end{vmatrix} - 1\begin{vmatrix} 1 & 1 \\ -1 & 1 \end{vmatrix}$$

$$= 1\big(-1(-1) - 3(1)\big) - 2\big(1(-1) - 3(1)\big) - 1\big(1(1) - (-1)(1)\big)$$

$$= 1(1 - 3) - 2(-1 - 3) - 1(1 + 1)$$

$$= 1(-2) - 2(-4) - 1(2) = -2 + 8 - 2 = 4$$

$$D_x = \begin{vmatrix} 0 & 1 & 1 \\ -1 & -1 & 1 \\ -8 & 3 & -1 \end{vmatrix} = 0\begin{vmatrix} -1 & 1 \\ 3 & -1 \end{vmatrix} - (-1)\begin{vmatrix} 1 & 1 \\ 3 & -1 \end{vmatrix} - 8\begin{vmatrix} 1 & 1 \\ -1 & 1 \end{vmatrix}$$

$$= 1\big(1(-1) - 3(1)\big) - 8\big(1(1) - (-1)(1)\big)$$

$$= 1(-1 - 3) - 8(1 + 1)$$

$$= 1(-4) - 8(2) = -4 - 16 = -20$$

$$D_y = \begin{vmatrix} 1 & 0 & 1 \\ 2 & -1 & 1 \\ -1 & -8 & -1 \end{vmatrix} = 1\begin{vmatrix} -1 & 1 \\ -8 & -1 \end{vmatrix} - 2\begin{vmatrix} 0 & 1 \\ -8 & -1 \end{vmatrix} - 1\begin{vmatrix} 0 & 1 \\ -1 & 1 \end{vmatrix}$$

$$= 1\big(-1(-1) - (-8)1\big) - 2\big(0(-1) - (-8)1\big) - 1\big(0(1) - (-1)1\big)$$

$$= 1(1 + 8) - 2(0 + 8) - 1(0 + 1)$$

$$= 1(9) - 2(8) - 1(1) = 9 - 16 - 1 = -8$$

$$D_z = \begin{vmatrix} 1 & 1 & 0 \\ 2 & -1 & -1 \\ -1 & 3 & -8 \end{vmatrix} = 1\begin{vmatrix} -1 & -1 \\ 3 & -8 \end{vmatrix} - 2\begin{vmatrix} 1 & 0 \\ 3 & -8 \end{vmatrix} - 1\begin{vmatrix} 1 & 0 \\ -1 & -1 \end{vmatrix}$$

$$= 1\big(-1(-8) - 3(-1)\big) - 2\big(1(-8) - 3(0)\big) - 1\big(1(-1) - (-1)0\big)$$

$$= 1(8 + 3) - 2(-8 - 0) - 1(-1 + 0)$$

$$= 1(11) - 2(-8) - 1(-1) = 11 + 16 + 1 = 28$$

$$x = \frac{D_x}{D} = \frac{-20}{4} = -5 \qquad y = \frac{D_y}{D} = \frac{-8}{4} = -2 \qquad z = \frac{D_z}{D} = \frac{28}{4} = 7$$

The solution set is $\{(-5, -2, 7)\}$.

35. $4x - 5y - 6z = -1$

$\quad\quad x - 2y - 5z = -12$

$\quad\quad 2x - y \quad\quad = 7$

$$D = \begin{vmatrix} 4 & -5 & -6 \\ 1 & -2 & -5 \\ 2 & -1 & 0 \end{vmatrix} = 4\begin{vmatrix} -2 & -5 \\ -1 & 0 \end{vmatrix} - 1\begin{vmatrix} -5 & -6 \\ -1 & 0 \end{vmatrix} + 2\begin{vmatrix} -5 & -6 \\ -2 & -5 \end{vmatrix}$$

$\quad\quad = 4\left(-2(0) - (-1)(-5)\right) - 1\left(-5(0) - (-1)(-6)\right) + 2\left(-5(-5) - (-2)(-6)\right)$

$\quad\quad = 4(-5) - 1(-6) + 2(25 - 12)$

$\quad\quad = -20 + 6 + 2(13) = -20 + 6 + 26 = 12$

$$D_x = \begin{vmatrix} -1 & -5 & -6 \\ -12 & -2 & -5 \\ 7 & -1 & 0 \end{vmatrix} = -1\begin{vmatrix} -2 & -5 \\ -1 & 0 \end{vmatrix} - (-12)\begin{vmatrix} -5 & -6 \\ -1 & 0 \end{vmatrix} + 7\begin{vmatrix} -5 & -6 \\ -2 & -5 \end{vmatrix}$$

$\quad\quad = -1\left(-2(0) - (-1)(-5)\right) - (-12)\left(-5(0) - (-1)(-6)\right) + 7\left(-5(-5) - (-2)(-6)\right)$

$\quad\quad = -1(-5) - (-12)(-6) + 7(25 - 12)$

$\quad\quad = 5 - 72 + 7(13) = 5 - 72 + 91 = 24$

$$D_y = \begin{vmatrix} 4 & -1 & -6 \\ 1 & -12 & -5 \\ 2 & 7 & 0 \end{vmatrix} = 4\begin{vmatrix} -12 & -5 \\ 7 & 0 \end{vmatrix} - 1\begin{vmatrix} -1 & -6 \\ 7 & 0 \end{vmatrix} + 2\begin{vmatrix} -1 & -6 \\ -12 & -5 \end{vmatrix}$$

$\quad\quad = 4\left(-12(0) - 7(-5)\right) - 1\left(-1(0) - 7(-6)\right) + 2\left(-1(-5) - (-12)(-6)\right)$

$\quad\quad = 4(35) - 1(42) + 2(5 - 72)$

$\quad\quad = 140 - 42 + 2(-67) = 140 - 42 - 134 = -36$

$$D_z = \begin{vmatrix} 4 & -5 & -1 \\ 1 & -2 & -12 \\ 2 & -1 & 7 \end{vmatrix} = 4\begin{vmatrix} -2 & -12 \\ -1 & 7 \end{vmatrix} - 1\begin{vmatrix} -5 & -1 \\ -1 & 7 \end{vmatrix} + 2\begin{vmatrix} -5 & -1 \\ -2 & -12 \end{vmatrix}$$

$\quad\quad = 4\left(-2(7) - (-1)(-12)\right) - 1\left(-5(7) - (-1)(-1)\right) + 2\left(-5(-12) - (-2)(-1)\right)$

$\quad\quad = 4(-14 - 12) - 1(-35 - 1) + 2(60 - 2)$

$\quad\quad = 4(-26) - 1(-36) + 2(58) = -104 + 36 + 116 = 48$

$x = \dfrac{D_x}{D} = \dfrac{24}{12} = 2 \quad\quad y = \dfrac{D_y}{D} = \dfrac{-36}{12} = -3 \quad\quad z = \dfrac{D_z}{D} = \dfrac{48}{12} = 4$

The solution set is $\{(2, -3, 4)\}$.

37.

$$x+ y+ z = 4$$
$$x-2y+ z = 7$$
$$x+3y+2z = 4$$

$$D = \begin{vmatrix} 1 & 1 & 1 \\ 1 & -2 & 1 \\ 1 & 3 & 2 \end{vmatrix} = 1\begin{vmatrix} -2 & 1 \\ 3 & 2 \end{vmatrix} - 1\begin{vmatrix} 1 & 1 \\ 3 & 2 \end{vmatrix} + 1\begin{vmatrix} 1 & 1 \\ -2 & 1 \end{vmatrix}$$

$$= 1\big(-2(2)-3(1)\big) - 1\big(1(2)-3(1)\big) + 1\big(1(1)-(-2)1\big)$$
$$= 1(-4-3) - 1(2-3) + 1(1+2)$$
$$= 1(-7) - 1(-1) + 1(3) = -7+1+3 = -3$$

$$D_x = \begin{vmatrix} 4 & 1 & 1 \\ 7 & -2 & 1 \\ 4 & 3 & 2 \end{vmatrix} = 4\begin{vmatrix} -2 & 1 \\ 3 & 2 \end{vmatrix} - 7\begin{vmatrix} 1 & 1 \\ 3 & 2 \end{vmatrix} + 4\begin{vmatrix} 1 & 1 \\ -2 & 1 \end{vmatrix}$$

$$= 4\big(-2(2)-3(1)\big) - 7\big(1(2)-3(1)\big) + 4\big(1(1)-(-2)1\big)$$
$$= 4(-4-3) - 7(2-3) + 4(1+2)$$
$$= 4(-7) - 7(-1) + 4(3) = -28+7+12 = -9$$

$$D_y = \begin{vmatrix} 1 & 4 & 1 \\ 1 & 7 & 1 \\ 1 & 4 & 2 \end{vmatrix} = 1\begin{vmatrix} 7 & 1 \\ 4 & 2 \end{vmatrix} - 1\begin{vmatrix} 4 & 1 \\ 4 & 2 \end{vmatrix} + 1\begin{vmatrix} 4 & 1 \\ 7 & 1 \end{vmatrix}$$

$$= 1\big(7(2)-4(1)\big) - 1\big(4(2)-4(1)\big) + 1\big(4(1)-7(1)\big)$$
$$= 1(14-4) - 1(8-4) + 1(4-7)$$
$$= 1(10) - 1(4) + 1(-3) = 10-4-3 = 3$$

$$D_z = \begin{vmatrix} 1 & 1 & 4 \\ 1 & -2 & 7 \\ 1 & 3 & 4 \end{vmatrix} = 1\begin{vmatrix} -2 & 7 \\ 3 & 4 \end{vmatrix} - 1\begin{vmatrix} 1 & 4 \\ 3 & 4 \end{vmatrix} + 1\begin{vmatrix} 1 & 4 \\ -2 & 7 \end{vmatrix}$$

$$= 1\big(-2(4)-3(7)\big) - 1\big(1(4)-3(4)\big) + 1\big(1(7)-(-2)4\big)$$
$$= 1(-8-21) - 1(4-12) + 1(7+8)$$
$$= 1(-29) - 1(-8) + 1(15) = -29+8+15 = -6$$

$$x = \frac{D_x}{D} = \frac{-9}{-3} = 3 \qquad y = \frac{D_y}{D} = \frac{3}{-3} = -1 \qquad z = \frac{D_z}{D} = \frac{-6}{-3} = 2$$

The solution set is $\{(3,-1,2)\}$.

39.

$$x \qquad + 2z = 4$$
$$2y - z = 5$$
$$2x + 3y \qquad = 13$$

$$D = \begin{vmatrix} 1 & 0 & 2 \\ 0 & 2 & -1 \\ 2 & 3 & 0 \end{vmatrix} = 1\begin{vmatrix} 2 & -1 \\ 3 & 0 \end{vmatrix} - 0\begin{vmatrix} 0 & 2 \\ 3 & 0 \end{vmatrix} + 2\begin{vmatrix} 0 & 2 \\ 2 & -1 \end{vmatrix}$$

$$= 1\big(2(0) - 3(-1)\big) + 2\big(0(-1) - 2(2)\big)$$

$$= 1(3) + 2(-4) = 3 - 8 = -5$$

$$D_x = \begin{vmatrix} 4 & 0 & 2 \\ 5 & 2 & -1 \\ 13 & 3 & 0 \end{vmatrix} = 4\begin{vmatrix} 2 & -1 \\ 3 & 0 \end{vmatrix} - 5\begin{vmatrix} 0 & 2 \\ 3 & 0 \end{vmatrix} + 13\begin{vmatrix} 0 & 2 \\ 2 & -1 \end{vmatrix}$$

$$= 4\big(2(0) - 3(-1)\big) - 5\big(0(0) - 3(2)\big) + 13\big(0(-1) - 2(2)\big)$$

$$= 4(3) - 5(-6) + 13(-4) = 12 + 30 - 52 = -10$$

$$D_y = \begin{vmatrix} 1 & 4 & 2 \\ 0 & 5 & -1 \\ 2 & 13 & 0 \end{vmatrix} = 1\begin{vmatrix} 5 & -1 \\ 13 & 0 \end{vmatrix} - 0\begin{vmatrix} 4 & 2 \\ 13 & 0 \end{vmatrix} + 2\begin{vmatrix} 4 & 2 \\ 5 & -1 \end{vmatrix}$$

$$= 1\big(5(0) - 13(-1)\big) + 2\big(4(-1) - 5(2)\big)$$

$$= 1(13) + 2(-4 - 10)$$

$$= 1(13) + 2(-14) = 13 - 28 = -15$$

$$D_z = \begin{vmatrix} 1 & 0 & 4 \\ 0 & 2 & 5 \\ 2 & 3 & 13 \end{vmatrix} = 1\begin{vmatrix} 2 & 5 \\ 3 & 13 \end{vmatrix} - 0\begin{vmatrix} 0 & 4 \\ 3 & 13 \end{vmatrix} + 2\begin{vmatrix} 0 & 4 \\ 2 & 5 \end{vmatrix}$$

$$= 1\big(2(13) - 3(5)\big) + 2\big(0(5) - 2(4)\big)$$

$$= 1(26 - 15) + 2(-8)$$

$$= 1(11) - 16 = 11 - 16 = -5$$

$$x = \frac{D_x}{D} = \frac{-10}{-5} = 2 \qquad y = \frac{D_y}{D} = \frac{-15}{-5} = 3 \qquad z = \frac{D_z}{D} = \frac{-5}{-5} = 1$$

The solution set is $\{(2,3,1)\}$.

41.

$$\begin{Vmatrix} \begin{vmatrix} 3 & 1 \\ -2 & 3 \end{vmatrix} & \begin{vmatrix} 7 & 0 \\ 1 & 5 \end{vmatrix} \\ \begin{vmatrix} 3 & 0 \\ 0 & 7 \end{vmatrix} & \begin{vmatrix} 9 & -6 \\ 3 & 5 \end{vmatrix} \end{Vmatrix}$$

$$= \begin{vmatrix} 3(3)-(-2)(1) & 7(5)-1(0) \\ 3(7)-0(0) & 9(5)-3(-6) \end{vmatrix}$$

$$= \begin{vmatrix} 9+2 & 35-0 \\ 21-0 & 45+18 \end{vmatrix} = \begin{vmatrix} 11 & 35 \\ 21 & 63 \end{vmatrix}$$

$$= 11(63)-21(35)$$

$$= 693-735 = -42$$

42.

$$\begin{Vmatrix} \begin{vmatrix} 5 & 0 \\ 4 & -3 \end{vmatrix} & \begin{vmatrix} -1 & 0 \\ 0 & -1 \end{vmatrix} \\ \begin{vmatrix} 7 & -5 \\ 4 & 6 \end{vmatrix} & \begin{vmatrix} 4 & 1 \\ -3 & 5 \end{vmatrix} \end{Vmatrix}$$

$$= \begin{vmatrix} 5(-3)-4(0) & (-1)(-1)-0 \\ 7(6)-4(-5) & 4(5)-(-3)(1) \end{vmatrix}$$

$$= \begin{vmatrix} -15-0 & 1+0 \\ 42+20 & 20+3 \end{vmatrix} = \begin{vmatrix} -15 & 1 \\ 62 & 23 \end{vmatrix}$$

$$= (-15)(23)-62(1)$$

$$= -345-62 = -407$$

43.

From $D = \begin{vmatrix} 2 & -4 \\ 3 & 5 \end{vmatrix}$ we obtain the

coefficients of the variables in our
equations:

$$2x-4y=c_1$$

$$3x+5y=c_2$$

From $D_x = \begin{vmatrix} 8 & -4 \\ -10 & 5 \end{vmatrix}$ we obtain the

constant coefficients: 8 and -10

$$2x-4y=8$$

$$3x+5y=-10$$

44.

From $D = \begin{vmatrix} 2 & -3 \\ 5 & 6 \end{vmatrix}$ we obtain the

coefficients of the variables in our
equations:

$$2x-3y=c_1$$

$$5x+6y=c_2$$

From $D_x = \begin{vmatrix} 8 & -3 \\ 11 & 6 \end{vmatrix}$ we obtain the

constant coefficients: 8 and 11

$$2x-3y=8$$

$$5x+6y=11$$

45.

$$\begin{vmatrix} -2 & x \\ 4 & 6 \end{vmatrix} = 32$$

$$-2(6)-4(x)=32$$

$$-12-4x=32$$

$$-4x=44$$

$$x=-11$$

The solution is -11.

46.

$$\begin{vmatrix} x+3 & -6 \\ x-2 & -4 \end{vmatrix} = 28$$

$$(x+3)(-4)-(x-2)(-6)=28$$

$$-4x-12+6x-12=28$$

$$2x-24=28$$

$$2x=52$$

$$x=26$$

The solution is 26.

47.
$$\begin{vmatrix} 1 & x & -2 \\ 3 & 1 & 1 \\ 0 & -2 & 2 \end{vmatrix} = -8$$

$$0\begin{vmatrix} x & -2 \\ 1 & 1 \end{vmatrix} - (-2)\begin{vmatrix} 1 & -2 \\ 3 & 1 \end{vmatrix} + 2\begin{vmatrix} 1 & x \\ 3 & 1 \end{vmatrix} = -8$$

$$2\left[1(1) - 3(-2)\right] + 2\left[1(1) - 3(x)\right] = -8$$

$$2(1 + 6) + 2(1 - 3x) = -8$$

$$2(7) + 2(1 - 3x) = -8$$

$$14 + 2 - 6x = -8$$

$$-6x = -24$$

$$x = 4$$

The solution is 4.

48.
$$\begin{vmatrix} 2 & x & 1 \\ -3 & 1 & 0 \\ 2 & 1 & 4 \end{vmatrix} = 39$$

$$-(-3)\begin{vmatrix} x & 1 \\ 1 & 4 \end{vmatrix} + \begin{vmatrix} 2 & 1 \\ 2 & 4 \end{vmatrix} - 0\begin{vmatrix} 2 & x \\ 2 & 1 \end{vmatrix} = 39$$

$$3(4x - 1) + (8 - 2) = 39$$

$$12x - 3 + 6 = 39$$

$$12x = 36$$

$$x = 3$$

The solution is 3.

49.
$$\text{Area} = \pm\frac{1}{2}\begin{vmatrix} 3 & -5 & 1 \\ 2 & 6 & 1 \\ -3 & 5 & 1 \end{vmatrix} = \pm\frac{1}{2}\left[3\begin{vmatrix} 6 & 1 \\ 5 & 1 \end{vmatrix} - 2\begin{vmatrix} -5 & 1 \\ 5 & 1 \end{vmatrix} - 3\begin{vmatrix} -5 & 1 \\ 6 & 1 \end{vmatrix}\right]$$

$$= \pm\frac{1}{2}\left[3(6(1) - 5(1)) - 2(-5(1) - 5(1)) - 3(-5(1) - 6(1))\right]$$

$$= \pm\frac{1}{2}\left[3(6 - 5) - 2(-5 - 5) - 3(-5 - 6)\right]$$

$$= \pm\frac{1}{2}\left[3(1) - 2(-10) - 3(-11)\right]$$

$$= \pm\frac{1}{2}\left[3 + 20 + 33\right] = \pm\frac{1}{2}\left[56\right] = \pm 28$$

The area is 28 square units.

51.
$$\begin{vmatrix} 3 & -1 & 1 \\ 0 & -3 & 1 \\ 12 & 5 & 1 \end{vmatrix} = 3\begin{vmatrix} -3 & 1 \\ 5 & 1 \end{vmatrix} - 0\begin{vmatrix} -1 & 1 \\ 5 & 1 \end{vmatrix} + 12\begin{vmatrix} -1 & 1 \\ -3 & 1 \end{vmatrix}$$

$$= 3\left(-3(1) - 5(1)\right) + 12\left(-1(1) - (-3)1\right)$$

$$= 3(-3 - 5) + 12(-1 + 3)$$

$$= 3(-8) + 12(2) = -24 + 24 = 0$$

Because the determinant is equal to zero, the points are collinear.

53.

$$\begin{vmatrix} x & y & 1 \\ 3 & -5 & 1 \\ -2 & 6 & 1 \end{vmatrix} = x\begin{vmatrix} -5 & 1 \\ 6 & 1 \end{vmatrix} - 3\begin{vmatrix} y & 1 \\ 6 & 1 \end{vmatrix} - 2\begin{vmatrix} y & 1 \\ -5 & 1 \end{vmatrix}$$

$$= x\big(-5(1)-6(1)\big) - 3\big(y(1)-6(1)\big) - 2\big(y(1)-(-5)1\big)$$

$$= x(-5-6) - 3(y-6) - 2(y+5)$$

$$= x(-11) - 3y + 18 - 2y - 10 = -11x - 5y + 8$$

To find the equation of the line, set the determinant equal to zero.

$-11x - 5y + 8 = 0$

Solve for y to obtain slope-intercept form.

$-11x - 5y + 8 = 0$

$$-5y = 11x - 8$$

$$y = -\frac{11}{5}x + \frac{8}{5}$$

Appendix C
The Circle

1. $(x-h)^2 + (y-k)^2 = r^2$

$(x-0)^2 + (y-0)^2 = 7^2$

$x^2 + y^2 = 49$

3. $(x-h)^2 + (y-k)^2 = r^2$

$(x-3)^2 + (y-2)^2 = 5^2$

$(x-3)^2 + (y-2)^2 = 25$

5. $(x-h)^2 + (y-k)^2 = r^2$

$(x-(-1))^2 + (y-4)^2 = 2^2$

$(x+1)^2 + (y-4)^2 = 4$

7. $(x-h)^2 + (y-k)^2 = r^2$

$(x-(-3))^2 + (y-(-1))^2 = (\sqrt{3})^2$

$(x+3)^2 + (y+1)^2 = 3$

9. $(x-h)^2 + (y-k)^2 = r^2$

$(x-(-4))^2 + (y-0)^2 = 10^2$

$(x+4)^2 + y^2 = 100$

11. $x^2 + y^2 = 16$

$(x-0)^2 + (y-0)^2 = 4^2$

The center is $(0,0)$ and the radius is 4 units.

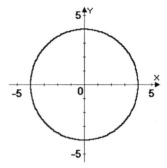

13. $(x-3)^2 + (y-1)^2 = 36$

$(x-3)^2 + (y-1)^2 = 6^2$

The center is $(3,1)$ and the radius is 6 units.

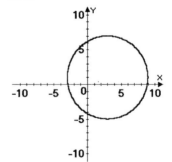

920

15.

$$(x+3)^2 + (y-2)^2 = 4$$

$$(x-(-3))^2 + (y-2)^2 = 2^2$$

The center is $(-3, 2)$ and the radius is 2 units.

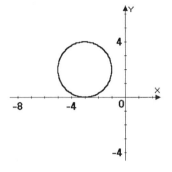

$$(x^2 + 6x + 9) + (y^2 + 2y + 1) = -6 + 9 + 1$$

$$(x+3)^2 + (y+1)^2 = 4$$

The center is $(-3, -1)$ and the radius is 2 units.

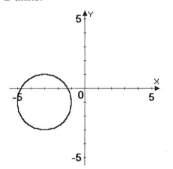

17.

$$(x+2)^2 + (y+2)^2 = 4$$

$$(x-(-2))^2 + (y-(-2))^2 = 2^2$$

The center is $(-2, -2)$ and the radius is 2 units.

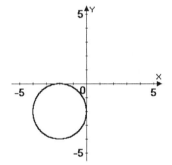

21.

$$x^2 + y^2 - 10x - 6y - 30 = 0$$

$$(x^2 - 10x \quad) + (y^2 - 6y \quad) = 30$$

Complete the squares.

$$\left(\frac{b}{2}\right)^2 = \left(\frac{-10}{2}\right)^2 = (-5)^2 = 25$$

$$\left(\frac{b}{2}\right)^2 = \left(\frac{-6}{2}\right)^2 = (-3)^2 = 9$$

$$(x^2 - 10x + 25) + (y^2 - 6y + 9) = 30 + 25 + 9$$

$$(x-5)^2 + (y-3)^2 = 64$$

The center is $(5, 3)$ and the radius is 8 units.

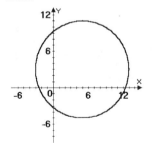

19.

$$x^2 + y^2 + 6x + 2y + 6 = 0$$

$$(x^2 + 6x \quad) + (y^2 + 2y \quad) = -6$$

Complete the squares.

$$\left(\frac{b}{2}\right)^2 = \left(\frac{6}{2}\right)^2 = (3)^2 = 9$$

$$\left(\frac{b}{2}\right)^2 = \left(\frac{2}{2}\right)^2 = (1)^2 = 1$$

23.
$$x^2 + y^2 + 8x - 2y - 8 = 0$$
$$\left(x^2 + 8x \quad\right) + \left(y^2 - 2y \quad\right) = 8$$
Complete the squares.
$$\left(\frac{b}{2}\right)^2 = \left(\frac{8}{2}\right)^2 = (4)^2 = 16$$
$$\left(\frac{b}{2}\right)^2 = \left(\frac{-2}{2}\right)^2 = (-1)^2 = 4$$
$$\left(x^2 + 8x + 16\right) + \left(y^2 - 2y + 1\right) = 8 + 16 + 1$$
$$\left(x + 4\right)^2 + \left(y - 1\right)^2 = 25$$
The center is $(-4, 1)$ and the radius is 5
units.

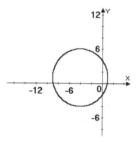

25.
$$x^2 - 2x + y^2 - 15 = 0$$
$$\left(x^2 - 2x \quad\right) + y^2 = 15$$
Complete the squares.
$$\left(\frac{b}{2}\right)^2 = \left(\frac{-2}{2}\right)^2 = (-1)^2 = 1$$
$$\left(x^2 - 2x + 1\right) + y^2 = 15 + 1$$
$$\left(x - 1\right)^2 + y^2 = 16$$
The center is $(1, 0)$ and the radius is 4
units.

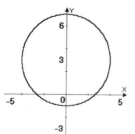

27.

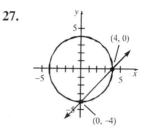

Intersection points: $(0, -4)$ and $(4, 0)$

Check $(0, -4)$:
$$0^2 + (-4)^2 = 16 \qquad 0 - (-4) = 4$$
$$16 = 16 \quad \text{true} \qquad 4 = 4 \quad \text{true}$$

Check $(4, 0)$:
$$4^2 + 0^2 = 16 \qquad 4 - 0 = 4$$
$$16 = 16 \quad \text{true} \qquad 4 = 4 \quad \text{true}$$

The solution set is $\left\{(0, -4), (4, 0)\right\}$.

28.

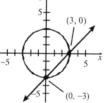

Intersection points: $(0, -3)$ and $(3, 0)$

Check $(0, -3)$:
$$0^2 + (-3)^2 = 9 \qquad 0 - (-3) = 3$$
$$9 = 9 \quad \text{true} \qquad 3 = 3 \quad \text{true}$$
Check $(3, 0)$:
$$3^2 + 0^2 = 9 \qquad 3 - 0 = 3$$
$$9 = 9 \quad \text{true} \qquad 3 = 3 \quad \text{true}$$

The solution set is $\left\{(0, -3), (3, 0)\right\}$.

29.

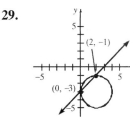

Intersection points: $(0,-3)$ and $(2,-1)$

Check $(0,-3)$:

$(0-2)^2 +(-3+3)^2 = 9 \qquad -3 = 0-3$

$\qquad (-2)^2 + 0^2 = 4 \qquad -3 = -3$ true

$\qquad\qquad 4 = 4$

$\qquad\qquad\qquad$ true

Check $(2,-1)$:

$(2-2)^2 +(-1+3)^2 = 4 \qquad -1 = 2-3$

$\qquad 0^2 + 2^2 = 4 \qquad -1 = -1$ true

$\qquad\qquad 4 = 4$

$\qquad\qquad\qquad$ true

The solution set is $\{(0,-3),(2,-1)\}$.

30.

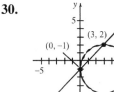

Intersection points: $(0,-1)$ and $(3,2)$

Check $(0,-1)$:

$(0-3)^2 +(-1+1)^2 = 9 \qquad -1 = 0-1$

$\qquad (-3)^2 + 0^2 = 9 \qquad -1 = -1$ true

$\qquad\qquad 9 = 9$

$\qquad\qquad\qquad$ true

Check $(3,2)$:

$(3-3)^2 +(2+1)^2 = 9 \qquad 2 = 3-1$

$\qquad\qquad 0^2 + 3^2 = 9 \qquad 2 = 2$ true

$\qquad\qquad\qquad 9 = 9$

$\qquad\qquad\qquad\qquad$ true

The solution set is $\{(0,-1),(3,2)\}$.

31. From the graph we can see that the center of the circle is at $(2,-1)$ and the radius is 2 units. Therefore, the equation is

$$(x-2)^2 +\left(y-(-1)\right)^2 = 2^2$$

$$(x-2)^2 +(y+1)^2 = 4$$

32. From the graph we can see that the center of the circle is at $(3,-1)$ and the radius is 3 units. Therefore, the equation is

$$(x-3)^2 +\left(y-(-1)\right)^2 = 3^2$$

$$(x-3)^2 +(y+1)^2 = 9$$

33. From the graph we can see that the center of the circle is at $(-3,-2)$ and the radius is 1 unit. Therefore, the equation is

$$\left(x-(-3)\right)^2 +\left(y-(-2)\right)^2 = 1^2$$

$$(x+3)^2 +(y+2)^2 = 1$$

34. From the graph we can see that the center of the circle is at $(-1,1)$ and the radius is 4 units. Therefore, the equation is

$$\left(x-(-1)\right)^2 +(y-1)^2 = 4^2$$

$$(x+1)^2 +(y-1)^2 = 16$$

35. a. Since the line segment passes through the center, the center is the midpoint of the segment.

$$M = \left(\frac{x_1 + x_2}{2}, \frac{y_1 + y_2}{2}\right)$$

$$= \left(\frac{3+7}{2}, \frac{9+11}{2}\right) = \left(\frac{10}{2}, \frac{20}{2}\right)$$

$$= (5,10)$$

The center is $(5,10)$.

b. The radius is the distance from the center to one of the points on the circle. Using the point $(3,9)$, we get:

$$d = \sqrt{(5-3)^2 + (10-9)^2}$$

$$= \sqrt{2^2 + 1^2} = \sqrt{4+1} = \sqrt{5}$$

The radius is $\sqrt{5}$ units.

c.
$$(x-5)^2 + (y-10)^2 = \left(\sqrt{5}\right)^2$$
$$(x-5)^2 + (y-10)^2 = 5$$

c.
$$(x-4)^2 + (y-5)^2 = \left(\sqrt{2}\right)^2$$
$$(x-4)^2 + (y-5)^2 = 2$$

36. a. Since the line segment passes through the center, the center is the midpoint of the segment.

$$M = \left(\frac{x_1 + x_2}{2}, \frac{y_1 + y_2}{2}\right)$$

$$= \left(\frac{3+5}{2}, \frac{6+4}{2}\right) = \left(\frac{8}{2}, \frac{10}{2}\right) = (4,5)$$

The center is $(4,5)$.

b. The radius is the distance from the center to one of the points on the circle. Using the point $(3,6)$, we get:

$$d = \sqrt{(4-3)^2 + (5-6)^2}$$

$$= \sqrt{1^2 + (-1)^2} = \sqrt{1+1} = \sqrt{2}$$

924

Appendix D
Summation Notation and the Binomial Theorem

1. $\displaystyle\sum_{i=1}^{6} 5i = 5(1) + 5(2) + 5(3) + 5(4) + 5(5) + 5(6) = 5 + 10 + 15 + 20 + 25 + 30 = 105$

3. $\displaystyle\sum_{i=1}^{4} 2i^2 = 2(1)^2 + 2(2)^2 + 2(3)^2 + 2(4)^2 = 2(1) + 2(4) + 2(9) + 2(16) = 2 + 8 + 18 + 32 = 60$

5. $\displaystyle\sum_{k=1}^{5} k(k+4) = 1(1+4) + 2(2+4) + 3(3+4) + 4(4+4) + 5(5+4)$

$\qquad = 1(5) + 2(6) + 3(7) + 4(8) + 5(9) = 5 + 12 + 21 + 32 + 45 = 115$

7. $\displaystyle\sum_{i=1}^{4} \left(-\frac{1}{2}\right)^i = \left(-\frac{1}{2}\right)^1 + \left(-\frac{1}{2}\right)^2 + \left(-\frac{1}{2}\right)^3 + \left(-\frac{1}{2}\right)^4 = -\frac{1}{2} + \frac{1}{4} + \left(-\frac{1}{8}\right) + \frac{1}{16}$

$\qquad = -\frac{1}{2}\cdot\frac{8}{8} + \frac{1}{4}\cdot\frac{4}{4} + \left(-\frac{1}{8}\right)\frac{2}{2} + \frac{1}{16} = -\frac{8}{16} + \frac{4}{16} - \frac{2}{16} + \frac{1}{16}$

$\qquad = \dfrac{-8+4-2+1}{16} = -\dfrac{5}{16}$

9. $\displaystyle\sum_{i=5}^{9} 11 = 11 + 11 + 11 + 11 + 11 = 55$

11. $\displaystyle\sum_{i=0}^{4} \frac{(-1)^i}{i!} = \frac{(-1)^0}{0!} + \frac{(-1)^1}{1!} + \frac{(-1)^2}{2!} + \frac{(-1)^3}{3!} + \frac{(-1)^4}{4!} = \frac{1}{1} + \frac{-1}{1} + \frac{1}{2\cdot 1} + \frac{-1}{3\cdot 2\cdot 1} + \frac{1}{4\cdot 3\cdot 2\cdot 1}$

$\qquad = 1 - 1 + \frac{1}{2} - \frac{1}{6} + \frac{1}{24} = \frac{1}{2}\cdot\frac{12}{12} - \frac{1}{6}\cdot\frac{4}{4} + \frac{1}{24} = \frac{12}{24} - \frac{4}{24} + \frac{1}{24} = \frac{12-4+1}{24} = \frac{9}{24} = \frac{3}{8}$

13. $\displaystyle\sum_{i=1}^{5} \frac{i!}{(i-1)!} = \frac{1!}{(1-1)!} + \frac{2!}{(2-1)!} + \frac{3!}{(3-1)!} + \frac{4!}{(4-1)!} + \frac{5!}{(5-1)!} = \frac{1!}{0!} + \frac{2!}{1!} + \frac{3!}{2!} + \frac{4!}{3!} + \frac{5!}{4!}$

$\qquad = \frac{1}{1} + \frac{2\cdot \cancel{1!}}{\cancel{1!}} + \frac{3\cdot \cancel{2!}}{\cancel{2!}} + \frac{4\cdot \cancel{3!}}{\cancel{3!}} + \frac{5\cdot \cancel{4!}}{\cancel{4!}} = 1 + 2 + 3 + 4 + 5 = 15$

15. $\displaystyle\binom{8}{3} = \frac{8!}{3!(8-3)!} = \frac{8!}{3!5!} = \frac{8\cdot 7\cdot \cancel{6}\cdot \cancel{5!}}{\cancel{3}\cancel{2}\cdot 1\cdot \cancel{5!}} = 56$

925

17. $\dbinom{12}{1} = \dfrac{12!}{1!(12-1)!} = \dfrac{12 \cdot \cancel{11!}}{1 \cdot \cancel{11!}} = 12$

19. $\dbinom{6}{6} = \dfrac{\cancel{6!}}{\cancel{6!}(6-6)!} = \dfrac{1}{0!} = \dfrac{1}{1} = 1$

21. $\dbinom{100}{2} = \dfrac{100!}{2!(100-2)!} = \dfrac{100 \cdot 99 \cdot \cancel{98!}}{2 \cdot 1 \cdot \cancel{98!}} = 4950$

23. $(x+2)^3 = \dbinom{3}{0}x^3 + \dbinom{3}{1}x^2(2) + \dbinom{3}{2}x(2)^2 + \dbinom{3}{3}2^3$

$= \dfrac{3!}{0!(3-0)!}x^3 + \dfrac{3!}{1!(3-1)!}2x^2 + \dfrac{3!}{2!(3-2)!}4x + \dfrac{3!}{3!(3-3)!}8$

$= \dfrac{\cancel{3!}}{1 \cdot \cancel{3!}}x^3 + \dfrac{3 \cdot \cancel{2!}}{1 \cdot \cancel{2!}}2x^2 + \dfrac{3 \cdot \cancel{2!}}{\cancel{2!}1!}4x + \dfrac{\cancel{3!}}{\cancel{3!}0!}8 = x^3 + 3(2x^2) + 3(4x) + 1(8)$

$= x^3 + 6x^2 + 12x + 8$

25. $(3x+y)^3 = \dbinom{3}{0}(3x)^3 + \dbinom{3}{1}(3x)^2 y + \dbinom{3}{2}(3x)y^2 + \dbinom{3}{3}y^3$

$= \dfrac{3!}{0!(3-0)!}27x^3 + \dfrac{3!}{1!(3-1)!}9x^2 y + \dfrac{3!}{2!(3-2)!}3xy^2 + \dfrac{3!}{3!(3-3)!}y^3$

$= \dfrac{\cancel{3!}}{1 \cdot \cancel{3!}}27x^3 + \dfrac{3 \cdot \cancel{2!}}{1 \cdot \cancel{2!}}9x^2 y + \dfrac{3 \cdot \cancel{2!}}{\cancel{2!}1!}3xy^2 + \dfrac{\cancel{3!}}{\cancel{3!}0!}y^3 = 27x^3 + 3(9x^2 y) + 3(3xy^2) + 1(y^3)$

$= 27x^3 + 27x^2 y + 9xy^2 + y^3$

27. $(5x-1)^3 = \dbinom{3}{0}(5x)^3 + \dbinom{3}{1}(5x)^2(-1) + \dbinom{3}{2}(5x)(-1)^2 + \dbinom{3}{3}(-1)^3$

$= \dfrac{3!}{0!(3-0)!}125x^3 - \dfrac{3!}{1!(3-1)!}25x^2 + \dfrac{3!}{2!(3-2)!}5x(1) - \dfrac{3!}{3!(3-3)!}$

$= \dfrac{\cancel{3!}}{1 \cdot \cancel{3!}}125x^3 - \dfrac{3 \cdot \cancel{2!}}{1 \cdot \cancel{2!}}25x^2 + \dfrac{3 \cdot \cancel{2!}}{\cancel{2!}1!}5x - \dfrac{\cancel{3!}}{\cancel{3!}0!} = 125x^3 - 3(25x^2) + 3(5x) - 1$

$= 125x^3 - 75x^2 + 15x - 1$

29.

$$(2x+1)^4 = \binom{4}{0}(2x)^4 + \binom{4}{1}(2x)^3 + \binom{4}{2}(2x)^2 + \binom{4}{3}2x + \binom{4}{4}$$

$$= \frac{4!}{0!(4-0)!}16x^4 + \frac{4!}{1!(4-1)!}8x^3 \cdot 1 + \frac{4!}{2!(4-2)!}4x^2 \cdot 1^2 + \frac{4!}{3!(4-3)!}2x \cdot 1^3 + \frac{4!}{4!(4-4)!} \cdot 1^4$$

$$= \frac{\cancel{4!}}{0!\,\cancel{4!}}16x^4 + \frac{4!}{1!3!}8x^3 \cdot 1 + \frac{4!}{2!2!}4x^2 \cdot 1 + \frac{4!}{3!1!}2x \cdot 1 + \frac{\cancel{4!}}{\cancel{4!}0!} \cdot 1$$

$$= 1(16x^4) + \frac{4 \cdot \cancel{3!}}{1 \cdot \cancel{3!}}8x^3 + \frac{4 \cdot 3 \cdot \cancel{2!}}{2 \cdot 1 \cdot \cancel{2!}}4x^2 + \frac{4 \cdot \cancel{3!}}{\cancel{3!} \cdot 1}2x + 1$$

$$= 16x^4 + 4(8x^3) + 6(4x^2) + 4(2x) + 1$$

$$= 16x^4 + 32x^3 + 24x^2 + 8x + 1$$

31.

$$(x^2+2y)^4 = \binom{4}{0}(x^2)^4 + \binom{4}{1}(x^2)^3(2y) + \binom{4}{2}(x^2)^2(2y)^2 + \binom{4}{3}x^2(2y)^3 + \binom{4}{4}(2y)^4$$

$$= \frac{4!}{0!(4-0)!}x^8 + \frac{4!}{1!(4-1)!}2x^6y + \frac{4!}{2!(4-2)!}4x^4y^2 + \frac{4!}{3!(4-3)!}8x^2y^3 + \frac{4!}{4!(4-4)!}16y^4$$

$$= \frac{\cancel{4!}}{0!\,\cancel{4!}}x^8 + \frac{4!}{1!3!}2x^6y + \frac{4!}{2!2!}4x^4y^2 + \frac{4!}{3!1!}8x^2y^3 + \frac{\cancel{4!}}{\cancel{4!}0!}16y^4$$

$$= 1(x^8) + \frac{4 \cdot \cancel{3!}}{1 \cdot \cancel{3!}}2x^6y + \frac{4 \cdot 3 \cdot \cancel{2!}}{2 \cdot 1 \cdot \cancel{2!}}4x^4y^2 + \frac{4 \cdot \cancel{3!}}{\cancel{3!} \cdot 1}8x^2y^3 + 16y^4$$

$$= x^8 + 4(2x^6y) + 6(4x^4y^2) + 4(8x^2y^3) + 16y^4$$

$$= x^8 + 8x^6y + 24x^4y^2 + 32x^2y^3 + 16y^4$$

33.

$$(y-3)^4 = \binom{4}{0}y^4 + \binom{4}{1}y^3(-3) + \binom{4}{2}y^2(-3)^2 + \binom{4}{3}y(-3)^3 + \binom{4}{4}(-3)^4$$

$$= \frac{4!}{0!(4-0)!}y^4 - \frac{4!}{1!(4-1)!}3y^3 + \frac{4!}{2!(4-2)!}9y^2 - \frac{4!}{3!(4-3)!}27y + \frac{4!}{4!(4-4)!}81$$

$$= \frac{\cancel{4!}}{0!\,\cancel{4!}}y^4 - \frac{4!}{1!3!}3y^3 + \frac{4!}{2!2!}9y^2 - \frac{4!}{3!1!}27y + \frac{\cancel{4!}}{\cancel{4!}0!}81$$

$$= 1(y^4) - \frac{4 \cdot \cancel{3!}}{1 \cdot \cancel{3!}}3y^3 + \frac{4 \cdot 3 \cdot \cancel{2!}}{2 \cdot 1 \cdot \cancel{2!}}9y^2 - \frac{4 \cdot \cancel{3!}}{\cancel{3!} \cdot 1}27y + 81$$

$$= y^4 - 4(3y^3) + 6(9y^2) - 4(27y) + 81$$

$$= y^4 - 12y^3 + 54y^2 - 108y + 81$$

927

35. $\left(2x^3 - 1\right)^4 = \binom{4}{0}\left(2x^3\right)^4 + \binom{4}{1}\left(2x^3\right)^3(-1) + \binom{4}{2}\left(2x^3\right)^2(-1)^2 + \binom{4}{3}\left(2x^3\right)(-1)^3 + \binom{4}{4}(-1)^4$

$$= \frac{4!}{0!(4-0)!}16x^{12} - \frac{4!}{1!(4-1)!}8x^9 + \frac{4!}{2!(4-2)!}4x^6 - \frac{4!}{3!(4-3)!}2x^3 + \frac{4!}{4!(4-4)!}$$

$$= \frac{\cancel{4!}}{0!\,\cancel{4!}}16x^{12} - \frac{4!}{1!3!}8x^9 + \frac{4!}{2!2!}4x^6 - \frac{4!}{3!1!}2x^3 + \frac{\cancel{4!}}{\cancel{4!}0!}$$

$$= 1\left(16x^{12}\right) - \frac{4\cdot\cancel{3!}}{1\cdot\cancel{3!}}8x^9 + \frac{4\cdot3\cdot\cancel{2!}}{2\cdot1\cdot\cancel{2!}}4x^6 - \frac{4\cdot\cancel{3!}}{\cancel{3!}\cdot1}2x^3 + 1$$

$$= 16x^{12} - 4\left(8x^9\right) + 6\left(4x^6\right) - 4\left(2x^3\right) + 1$$

$$= 16x^{12} - 32x^9 + 24x^6 - 8x^3 + 1$$

37. $(c + 2)^5 = \binom{5}{0}c^5 + \binom{5}{1}c^4(2) + \binom{5}{2}c^3(2)^2 + \binom{5}{3}c^2(2)^3 + \binom{5}{4}c(2)^4 + \binom{5}{5}2^5$

$$= \frac{\cancel{5!}}{0!\,\cancel{5!}}c^5 + \frac{5!}{1!(5-1)!}2c^4 + \frac{5!}{2!(5-2)!}4c^3 + \frac{5!}{3!(5-3)!}8c^2 + \frac{5!}{4!(5-4)!}16c + \frac{5!}{5!(5-5)!}32$$

$$= 1c^5 + \frac{5\cdot\cancel{4!}}{1\cdot\cancel{4!}}2c^4 + \frac{5\cdot4\cdot\cancel{3!}}{2\cdot1\cdot\cancel{3!}}4c^3 + \frac{5\cdot4\cdot\cancel{3!}}{\cancel{3!}2\cdot1}8c^2 + \frac{5\cdot\cancel{4!}}{\cancel{4!}\cdot1}16c + \frac{\cancel{5!}}{\cancel{5!}0!}32$$

$$= c^5 + 5\left(2c^4\right) + 10\left(4c^3\right) + 10\left(8c^2\right) + 5(16c) + 1(32)$$

$$= c^5 + 10c^4 + 40c^3 + 80c^2 + 80c + 32$$

39. $(x - 1)^5 = \binom{5}{0}x^5 + \binom{5}{1}x^4(-1) + \binom{5}{2}x^3(-1)^2 + \binom{5}{3}x^2(-1)^3 + \binom{5}{4}x(-1)^4 + \binom{5}{5}(-1)^5$

$$= \frac{\cancel{5!}}{0!\,\cancel{5!}}x^5 - \frac{5!}{1!(5-1)!}x^4 + \frac{5!}{2!(5-2)!}x^3 - \frac{5!}{3!(5-3)!}x^2 + \frac{5!}{4!(5-4)!}x - \frac{5!}{5!(5-5)!}$$

$$= 1x^5 - \frac{5\cdot\cancel{4!}}{1\cdot\cancel{4!}}x^4 + \frac{5\cdot4\cdot\cancel{3!}}{2\cdot1\cdot\cancel{3!}}x^3 - \frac{5\cdot4\cdot\cancel{3!}}{\cancel{3!}2\cdot1}x^2 + \frac{5\cdot\cancel{4!}}{\cancel{4!}\cdot1}x - \frac{\cancel{5!}}{\cancel{5!}0!}$$

$$= x^5 - 5x^4 + 10x^3 - 10x^2 + 5x - 1$$

928

41. $(3x-y)^5$

$$=\binom{5}{0}(3x)^5+\binom{5}{1}(3x)^4(-y)+\binom{5}{2}(3x)^3(-y)^2+\binom{5}{3}(3x)^2(-y)^3+\binom{5}{4}3x(-y)^4+\binom{5}{5}(-y)^5$$

$$=\frac{5!}{0!\,5!}243x^5-\frac{5!}{1!(5-1)!}81x^4y+\frac{5!}{2!(5-2)!}27x^3y^2$$

$$-\frac{5!}{3!(5-3)!}9x^2y^3+\frac{5!}{4!(5-4)!}3xy^4-\frac{5!}{5!(5-5)!}y^5$$

$$=243x^5-\frac{5\cdot4!}{1\cdot4!}81x^4y+\frac{5\cdot4\cdot3!}{2\cdot1\cdot3!}27x^3y^2-\frac{5\cdot4\cdot3!}{3!2\cdot1}9x^2y^3+\frac{5\cdot4!}{4!\cdot1}3xy^4-\frac{5!}{5!0!}y^5$$

$$=243x^5-5(81x^4y)+10(27x^3y^2)-10(9x^2y^3)+5(3xy^4)-y^5$$

$$=243x^5-405x^4y+207x^3y^2-90x^2y^3+15xy^4-y^5$$

43. $(2a+b)^6$

$$=\binom{6}{0}(2a)^6+\binom{6}{1}(2a)^5b+\binom{6}{2}(2a)^4b^2+\binom{6}{3}(2a)^3b^3+\binom{6}{4}(2a)^2b^4+\binom{6}{5}2ab^5+\binom{6}{6}b^6$$

$$=\frac{6!}{0!(6-0)!}64a^6+\frac{6!}{1!(6-1)!}32a^5b+\frac{6!}{2!(6-2)!}16a^4b^2+\frac{6!}{3!(6-3)!}8a^3b^3$$

$$+\frac{6!}{4!(6-4)!}4a^2b^4+\frac{6!}{5!(6-5)!}2ab^5+\frac{6!}{6!(6-6)!}b^6$$

$$=\frac{6!}{1\,6!}64a^6+\frac{6\cdot5!}{1\cdot5!}32a^5b+\frac{6\cdot5\cdot4!}{2\cdot1\cdot4!}16a^4b^2+\frac{6\cdot5\cdot4\cdot3!}{3\cdot2\cdot1\cdot3!}8a^3b^3$$

$$+\frac{6\cdot5\cdot4!}{4!2\cdot1}4a^2b^4+\frac{6\cdot5!}{5!1}2ab^5+\frac{6!}{6!\cdot1}b^6$$

$$=64a^6+6(32a^5b)+15(16a^4b^2)+20(8a^3b^3)+15(4a^2b^4)+6(2ab^5)+1b^6$$

$$=64a^6+192a^5b+240a^4b^2+160a^3b^3+60a^2b^4+12ab^5+b^6$$